D0459028

HUXFORD'S

OLD BOOK

VALUE GUIDE

25,000 Listings of Old Books
with Current Values

Twelfth Edition

COLLECTOR BOOKS

A Division of Schroeder Publishing Co., Inc.

The current values of this book should be used only as a guide. They are not intended to set prices, which vary from one section of the country to another. Auction prices as well as dealer prices vary and are affected by condition as well as demand. Neither the editor nor the publisher assumes responsibility for any losses that might be incurred as a result of consulting this guide.

On the Cover:

WALTON, Isaak and Charles Cotton. *The Complete Angler.* 1875. Piccadilly. Chatto & Windus. 5th Nicholas edition. brn cloth, gold decor, leather spine. one vol ed. reset from two vol set. 8vo. 60 illus. G/G. A8. $175.00.

VON BRAUN, Werner and Frederick Ordway III. *History of Rocketry and Space Travel.* 1966. Thomas Crowell. 1st. ltd. ed. decor mission leather. ils. Harry Lange. 4to. F/NF. A8. $125.00.

KAMAKAU, S. M. *Ruling Chiefs of Hawaii.* 1961. Kamehameha Schools Press. 1st. 8vo. 440 pp. gr cloth, gold spine title. illus. w/drawings & photos. NF/VG. A8. $100.00.

LEFFERTS, Charles M. *Uniforms of the American, British, French, and German Armies of the War of the American Revolution 1775 – 1783.* 1926. NY Historical Society. 1st ltd. ed. #43/500 copies. 50 tipped in color pl. tan & bl cloth cover. minor fading to spine, lt edge wear. F/VG. A8. $650.00.

LEFFERTS, Charles M. *Uniforms of the American, British, French, and German Armies of the War of the American Revolution 1775 – 1783.* WE, INC. reprint of orig. ltd. ed. 289p. pict. hc. 8vo. F/clear plastic dj. A8. $65.00.

ROHMER, Sax. *Fu Manchu Series.* ca. 1920. Collier. Orient ed. spider web emb. cover w/blk cloth, gold spine titles. 12mo. each vol approx. 300p. 8 vol set. F as issued, no printed dj. A8. $150.00.

Books featured on cover courtesy of AL-PAC, Lamar Kelley, 2625 E. Southern Ave., C-120, Tempe, AZ 85282
602-831-3121; fax 602-831-3193, alpac2625@aol.com

Editor: Lisa Stroup
Cover Design: Beth Summers
Book Design: Ben Faust

Searching for a Publisher?

We are always looking for knowledgeable people considered to be experts within their fields. If you feel there is a real need for a book on your collectible subject and have a large comprehensive collection, contact Collector Books.

COLLECTOR BOOKS
P.O. Box 3009
Paducah, KY 42002-3009

www.collectorbooks.com

Copyright © 2000 by Schroeder Publishing

Contents

Acknowledgments

Heartfelt thanks to the staff at Collector Books — Gail Ashburn, Ben Faust, Laurie Swick, Cherry Pyron, and Beth Summers. I'm indebted to these talented people who helped shape and develop this book from the jumble of digital files. Your talents impress me daily.

A special thank you goes to Bob & Sharon Huxford and Linda Holycross for their support and guidance.

Thanks to my good friends and family for their support. Much appreciation goes out to my new friends, Lamar Kelley, who so unselfishly loaned his books for use in our cover photo and Robert F. Lucas, who generously contibuted articles to this 12th edition.

Grateful thanks to both Bill Schroeder and Billy Schroeder for their never ending support and encouragement. My appreciation to all is much deeper than can ever be said here.

I would also like to take this opportunity to express our sincere gratitude and appreciation to each business who has contributed their time and knowledge to assist us in producing this new edition. We believe the credibility of our book is greatly enhanced through their efforts. Please see the codes in the Booksellers directory in the back of this book for their complete addresses and contact information. The Bookbuyers directory gives information concerning their specific genre interests.

A Tale of Two Sisters (A24)
A-Book-A-Brac Shop (A1)
Aard Books (A2)
Noreen Abbot Books (A3)
About Books (A4)
Ackley Books & Collectibles (A28)
Adelson Sports (A5)
AL-PAC, Lamar Kelley (A8)
American Botanist (A10)
An Uncommon Vision (A25)
Antiquarian Medical Books
   W. Bruce Frye (A13)
Aplan Antiques & Art (A19)
David Armstrong, Bookseller (A26)
Aslan Books (A27)
Authors of the West (A18)
Avonlea Books Search Service (A7)
Beasley Books (B2)
Bella Luna Books (B3)
Between the Covers (B4)
Bicentennial Book Shop
   Vaughn & Michael Baber (B5)
Book & Tackle Shop
   Bernard Gordon (B14)
Book Treasures (B15)
Books Now & Then
   Dennis Patrick (B29)
Books West Southwest
   W. David Laird (B19)
Bromer Booksellers
   David & Anne Bromer (B24)
Brooks Books (B26)
Chapel Hill Rare Books (C6)
Children's Book Adoption Agency (C8)
Steven Cieluch (C14)

Tom Davidson, Bookseller (D10)
Ursula Davidson (D1)
L. Clarice Davis (D2)
Dawson's Book Shop (D11)
Carol Docheff, Bookseller (D4)
Drusilla's Books (D6)
Eastside Books & Paper (E6)
Elder's Book Store (E4)
First Folio (F1)
Five Quail Books — West (F7)
Flo Silver Books (F3)
Fostoria Trading Post (F6)
John Gach Fine & Rare Books (G1)
Galerie De Boicourt
   Eva W. Boicourt (G2)
   Gloria Stobbes (G6)
Grave Matters (G8)
Henry F. Hain III (H1)
Ken Hebenstreit, Bookseller (H11)
Susan Heller, Pages for Sages (H4)
Heritage Book Shop, Inc. (H5)
Jordan Gallery (J2)
Kenneth Karimole (K1)
Knollwood Books
   Lee & Peggy Price (K5)
Ken Lopez, Bookseller (L3)
Melvin Marcher, Bookseller (M4)
Paul Melzer Fine & Rare Books (M9)
Meyer Boswell Books, Inc. (M11)
Mordida Books (M15)
My Bookhouse (M20)
Brian McMillan, Books (M21)
McGee's First Varieties (M23)
Monroe Stahr Books (M25)
Nerman's Books (N1)

Norris Books (N4)
Nutmeg Books (N2)
Oak Knoll Books (O10)
October Farm (O3)
David L. O'Neal
   Antiquarian Bookseller (O1)
Orpheus Books (O11)
K.C. & Jean C. Owings (O8)
Pacific Rim Books (P1)
Pandora's Books
   J. Grant Thiessen (P3)
R. Papinger, Baseball Books (P8)
Parmer Books (P4)
Parnassus Books (P5)
Quill & Brush
   Patricia & Allen Ahearn (Q1)
Kathleen Rais & Co. (R2)
Randall House, Pia Oliver (R3)
Jo Ann Reisler, Ltd. (R5)
Bill & Mimi Sachen (S1)
Stanley Schwartz (S3)
Second Harvest Books (S14)
Ellen Serxner (S13)
Snowy Egret Books (S15)
Thomas Books (T2)
Thorn Books (T10)
VERSEtility Books (V1)
Vintage Books
   Nancy & David Haines (V3)
Volume I Books (V4)
   Warren Gillespie Jr. (W2)
Yesterday's Books (Y1)

Listing of Standard Abbreviations

#d . . . . .numbered
12mo . . . . .about 7" tall
16mo . . . . .6" to 7" tall
1st thus . . . .not 1st edition, but rather the 1st published
   in this particular format
24mo . . . . .5" to 6" tall
32mo . . . . .4" to 5" tall
48mo . . . . .less than 4" tall
4to .between 11" to 13" tall
64mo . . . . .about 3" tall
8vo . . . . .8" to 9" tall
aeg . . . . .all edge gilt
aka . . . . .also known as
ALS . . . . .autographed letter, signed
Am . . . . .American
AN . . . . .as new
AP . . . . .proof, advance proof, advance uncorrected
   proof, or galley
APVA . . . . .Association for the Preservation of Virginia
   Antiquities
ARC . . . . advance reading or review copy
atlas folio . . . . .25"
b&w . . . . .black & white
BC,BCE . . . . .any book club edition
bdg . . . . .binding, bound
bds . . . . .boards
bfep . . . . .back free endpaper
bkplt . . . . .bookplate
bl . . . . .blue
blk . . . . .black
BOMC . . . . .Book of the Month Club
brd . . . . .boards
brn . . . . .brown, browning
bstp . . . . .blindstamp
c . . . . .copyright
ca . . . . .circa
cb . . . . .cardboard
cbdg . . . . .comb binding
chip . . . . .chipped
clip . . . . .clipped price
CMG . . . . .Coward McCann Geoghegan
dbl . . . . .double
decor . . . . .decoration, decorated
DIF . . . . .Donald I. Fine
dj . . . . .dust jacket
dk . . . . .dark
double elephant folio . . . . .larger than 25"
DSP . . . . .Duell Sloan Pearce
dtd . . . . .dated
E . . . . .east, eastern
ed . . . . .edition
edit . . . . .editor
elephant folio . . . . .23" or larger
emb . . . . .embossed, embossing
Eng . . . . .England, English

ep . . . . .end pages, endpapers
ERB .Edgar Rice Burroughs Inc.
ES . . . . .errata slip
ex lib . . . . .ex library copy
F . . . . .fine
facs . . . . .facsimile
fep . . . . .free endpaper
ffep .front free endpaper
fld . . . . .folding, folder
folio . . . . .13" or larger
fox . . . . .foxing, foxed
FSC . . . . .Farrar, Straus & Cudahy
FSG . . . . .Farrar, Straus & Giroux
FSY . . . . .Farrar, Straus & Young
ftspc . . . . .frontispiece
fwd . . . . .foreword
G . . . . .good
GPO . . . . .Government Printing Office
gr . . . . .green
gte . . . . .gilt top edge
HBJ . . . . .Harcourt Brace Jovanovich, Inc.
HBW . . . . .Harcourt Brace World
hc, hb . . . . .hard cover
hist . . . . .history
HRW . . . . .Holt Rinehart Winston
ils .illustrations, illustrated
imp . . . . .imprint, impression
inscr . . . . .inscribed
Inst . . . . .Institute
Internat . . . . .International
intl . . . . .initialed
intro . . . . .introduction
LEC . . . . .Limited Edition Club
lg . . . . .large
Lib . . . . .library
lt . . . . .light
ltd . . . . .limited
mc . . . . .multicolor
mfep . . . . .missing free endpaper
mini . . . . .miniature book
MIT . . . . .MA Institute of Technology
MOMA . . . . .Museum of Modern Art
mtd . . . . .mounted
MTI . . . . .movie tie-in
Mus . . . . .museum
N . . . . .north, northern
NAL . . . . .New American Library
Nat . . . . .national
nd . . . . .no date
ne . . . . .no edition given
NEL .New English Library
NF . . . . .near fine
NGS . . . . .National Geographic Society
np . . . . no place given, no publisher stated
NYGS . . . . .New York Graphic Society

obl	oblong
orig	original
OUP	Oxford University Press
o/w	otherwise
pb	paperback
pbo	paperback original
pc	piece
pict	pictorial
pl	plate, plates
poi	previous owner's inscription
p, pg	page, pages
Pr	press
pref	preface
pres	presentation
promo	promotion
prt	print, printing
ps	postscript
pub	publisher, publishing
rb	rebound
rem mk	remainder mark
repro	reproduction
rev	revised
rpl	replaced
rpr	repair
rpt	reprint
RS	review slip
rstr	restored
S	south, southern
S&S	Simon & Schuster
sans	none issued
sbdg	spiral binding
sc	softcover

SF	San Francisco, science fiction
sgn	signature, signed
slip	slip case or publisher's slip which is an inserted piece of paper — either promotional material or errata sheet
sltly	slightly
sm	small
sm 4to	about 10" tall, quarto
sm 8vo	7½" to 8" tall
soc.	society
sq	square
stp	stamp, stamped
supp	supplement
swrp	shrink wrap
TB	textbook
teg	top edge gilt
thus	see 1st thus
TLS	typed letter signed
trans	translated
TVTI	TV tie-in
U	University
unp	unpaged
UP	uncorrected proof
VG	very good
vol	volume
W	west, western
w/	with, indicates laid in material
wht	white
wrp	wrappers
xl	ex-library
yel	yellow

Introduction

Using This Guide

This book has been compiled to help both buyers and sellers. Two questions that we are asked most frequently are "Can you tell me the value of my books?" and "Where can I sell them?" *Huxford's Old Book Value Guide* can answer both of these questions. Not only does this book place secondary market retail values (values that an interested party would be willing to pay to obtain possession of the book) on more than 25,000 old books, it also lists scores of buyers along with the type of material each is interested in purchasing. These prices are taken from dealers' selling lists that have been issued within the past year. Every listing is coded (A1, S7, etc.) before the price. This coding refers to a specific dealer's listing for that book. When two or more dealers have listed the same book, their codes will be listed alphabetically in the description line. Please refer to the section in the back of this book titled "Booksellers" for codes.

If you were to sell your books to a dealer, you should expect to receive no more than 50% of the values listed in this book, unless the dealer has a specific buyer in mind for some of your material. In many cases, a dealer will pay less than 50% of retail for a book to stock.

Do not ask a dealer to evaluate your old books unless you intend to sell them to him. Most antiquarian book dealers will appraise your books and ephemera for a fee that ranges from a low of $10.00 per hour to $50.00 per hour (or more). If you have an extensive library of rare books, the $50.00-an-hour figure would be money well spent (assuming, of course, the appraiser to be qualified and honest).

Unlike other price guides on the market which focus on the rare and very valuable books that many collectors will rarely encounter, *Huxford's Old Book Value Guide* places values on the more common holdings that many seem to accumulate. You will notice that the majority of the books listed are in the $10.00 to $50.00 range.

The format is very simple: listings are alphabetized first by the name of the author, translator, editor, or illustrator; if more than one book is listed for a particular author, each title is listed alphabetically under his or her name. When pseudonyms are known, names have been cross-referenced. (Please also see the section titled "Pseudonyms" for additional information.) Dust jackets or wrappers are noted when present, and sizes (when given) are approximate. Condition is usually noted as well. (If condition is not stated, it is assumed to be very good.) Dates within parentheses indicate the copyright page dates while dates without parentheses are dates found on the title pages and/or are the actual publication dates.

Fine condition refers to books that are in perfect, as-issued condition with no defects. Books in near-fine condition are perfect, but not as crisp as those graded fine. Near-fine condition books show only a little wear from reading (such as very small marks on binding), but they still have no major defects. Books rated very good may show wear but must have no tears on pages, binding, or dust jacket (if issued). A rating of good applies to an average used book that has all of its pages and yet may have small tears and other defects. The term reading copy (some dealers also use "poor") describes a book having major defects; however, its text must be complete. Ex-library books are always indicated as such; they may be found in any condition. This rule also applies to any book club edition. Some of our booksellers indicate intermediate grades with a + or ++, or VG-EX. We have endeavored to use the grade that best corresponded to the description of condition as given in each dealer's listing. If you want to check further on the condition of a specific book, please consult the bookseller indicated. Please note that the condition stated in the description is often for the book and then the dust jacket. (Dust jackets on many modern first editions may account for up to 80% of their value.)

In the back of the book we have listed buyers of books and book-related material. When you correspond with these dealers, be sure to enclose a self-addressed, stamped envelope if you want a reply. Please do not send lists of books for an appraisal. If you wish to sell your books, quote the price that you want or negotiate price only on the items the buyer is interested in purchasing. When you list your books, do so by author, full title, publisher and place, date, and edition. Indicate condition, noting any defects on cover or contents.

When shipping your books, first wrap each book in paper such as brown kraft or a similar type of material. Never use newspaper for the inner wrap, since newsprint tends to rub off. (It may, however be used as a cushioning material within the outer carton.) Place your books in a sturdy corrugated box and use a good shipping tape to seal it. Tape reinforced with nylon string is preferable, as it will not tear. Books shipped by parcel post may be sent at a special fourth class book rate, which may be lower than regular parcel post zone rates.

The following essays were contributed by Robert F. Lucas of Lucas Books. The basic information is intended to give an overview of the field to those just beginning the exciting hobby of book collecting.

Starting a Collection

You may have already started collecting books, but if you haven't, we have a few suggestions about collecting and we will even provide a few interesting topics/areas for you to consider.

Here are a few "suggestions" for successful book collecting.

- Collect an author or a subject that you enjoy
- Collect an author or a subject which is challenging
- Avoid collecting the most popular authors or subjects (unless favorites of yours)
- Collect within your means — do not try to collect very expensive books if you are on a limited budget
- Spend time learning which references/bibliographies pertain to your collecting area
- Purchase the reference tools appropriate to your collection and use them
- Do not collect primarily for monetary gain
- Learn the cornerstone or key items for which you should be searching
- Pay close attention to the condition of items for your collection
- When collecting books, also consider collecting related ephemera
- Experience various methods of purchasing books available to you — mail order catalogs, online catalogs, local bookshops, flea markets, etc.
- Learn which booksellers, ephemera dealers, antique dealers et al specialize in buying and selling items in your collecting area(s)
- Develop expertise in your chosen collecting area(s)
- Share your collection and knowledge of the area with others with similar interests
- Be determined to form the best possible collection within your means
- Most important — enjoy your collecting pursuits

It is difficult, if not impossible, and perhaps a little presumptuous and pompous, to suggest collecting areas for new book collectors to consider, but ... here are a few possibilities!

Authors

Instead of collecting the first editions of your favorite author (which is a great idea), start a collection of books and autographs and ephemera that relate to the family, friends, and acquaintances of the author — this is probably best done relative to a deceased author rather than a living author! Such a collection would be biographical/historical relative to the life of the author, i.e. books about the author's friends will probably contain many references and anecdotes about the author. This type of collection actually is a good companion to the collection of the works of the author.

If the author you have chosen to collect is very popular and the value of many first editions are sky-high, you could collect early printings (second or third printings) of the books which are expensive in the first printing or you could (in many instances) collect the same author's first printings in periodicals. Usually most such printings are less expensive than first printings of books and also somewhat difficult and challenging to find.

You could make a list of authors you consider important for various reasons and then attempt to collect the first appearance in print of each of the authors. This would be a very challenging collecting area, because many authors appear first in print in obscure high school yearbooks, small town newspapers, college literary magazines, and other obscure publications.

Collecting Books in Established Lists or Catalogs

Some collectors like to have a relatively finite goal and an established list of books for which to search. You could choose this collecting route and attempt to find as many items in a particular catalog or bibliography as possible. Some suggested "lists" are:

Carter, John & Percy H. Muir (editors). Printing and the Mind of Man. A Descriptive Catalogue Illustrating the Impact of Print on the Evolution of Western Civilization during Five Centuries. (London, Cassell & Company, 1967). Begun as an exhibit at the IPEX Exhibition of 1963 (International Printing Machinery and Allied Trades Exhibition) this catalog presents 424 of the most important books & other printings in the history of Western Civilization. Many of these works are so rare as to be essentially unobtainable, but others are available — other collectors have attempted to find as many of these works as possible — it is a lofty challenge.

(Grolier Club) One Hundred Influential American Books Printed before 1900...Exhibition at The Grolier Club 1946. New York, The Grolier Club, 1947. Contains literary, political, historical, scientific, and other books considered to be influencial. Many titles are rare and desirable and somewhat difficult to obtain — another major challenge.

Parsons, Nicholas. The Book of Literary Lists. A Collection of Annotated Lists, Statistics, and Anecdotes Concerning Books. New York, Facts on File Publications (1987). Many lists from which to choose — although some are as short as six books — include "The hundred books that most influenced Henry Miller," "The most popular fiction in Britain 1578 –

1930," "U.S. bestsellers 1895 – 1975," "Fifty works of English and American Literature we could do without," "Famous Banned Authors," etc.

Books Shunned by Other Collectors

If you consider yourself to be a contrarian and wish to pursue a collecting area in that light, you could consider collecting in one of the following areas:

Book of the Month Club editions — These and many other book club editions are printed in large quantities, usually on inexpensive, poor quality paper and bound in inexpensive bindings. For these reasons most collectors avoid the BOMC editions. You should have no trouble (in the US) finding BOMC books. You could easily wait for fine copies with fine dust jackets rather than add good or very good copies to your collection. The books would be very inexpensive and many of them classics. The collection may never have a high value in a monetary sense, but who knows?

Textbooks — Even relatively early textbooks from the 1830s to the 1900s are usually in very worn, abused condition and relatively available, until you start looking for them. You could limit your collection to nineteenth century math texts or English texts or spelling books or history texts, etc. Most textbooks are available at very reasonable prices because of the lack of general demand.

Bibles — The Bible is probably the most common book in America. It certainly was during the nineteenth century; virtually every Christian family household had a Bible, even if there were no other books in the house. The supply should be there and the demand is relatively low, thus the prices are very reasonable for most common Bibles. You could make the collection very challenging by collecting the first Bible printed/published in each major city and town in your country or state or region.

Telephone directories — Few collectors look for telephone directories and since most old directories were disposed of when a newer directory was issued, this could be a challenging area. You could make it even more interesting by determining when the first public telephones were used in your state or country and collect telephone directories from the first decade of use; they are probably very scarce or rare.

If you have a lot of shelf space for your book collection, you could collect encyclopedia sets. In general, booksellers find that there is not much of a market for old encyclopedias unless they concern a narrow subject area such as medicine, aeronautics, etc. You should be able to gather a mass of encyclopedias in short order.

Collecting Imprints by Specific Printers & Publishers

There are many very good bibliographies available which provide details on books from specific publishers, books printed in specific cities or towns, and books printed by specific printers. If there were printers present in your home town and enough books and pamphlets were printed, you could collect imprints from your "old stomping grounds."

The first items printed in each of the fifty states in the U.S. — A reference has been published which would be an excellent guide for such a collection: Thienens, Roger J. Pioneer Imprints from Fifty States. Washington, Library of Congress, 1971. Most of these items would be difficult to obtain and many would be expensive, but they would make a great collection.

There are many very good bibliographies listing local imprints. You could pick an interesting town or city and attempt to collect as many items listed in the bibliography as possible. One such example is McKeon, Newton Felch and Katharine Conover Cowles. Amherst, Massachusetts, Imprints 1825 – 1876. Amherst, Amherst College, 1946. There were more than 700 books, pamphlets, etc. printed in Amherst during this time span.

Another possible collection could be developed by searching for books published by a specific publishing house. An example is the high quality productions from the 1890s by Copeland & Day; the bibliography is Kraus, Joe W. Messrs. Copeland & Day 69 Cornhill, Boston 1893 – 1899. Philadelphia, George S. MacManus Co., 1979. This bibliography describes 108 publications.

In summary, there are so many different subject areas in which to collect books, you should have no problem finding a niche to fit your interests. Collect books that interest you and enjoy the hunt or search for items to add to your collection. Don't forget the importance of references — read as much as you can about your chosen collecting area. And if you haven't started collecting yet — it is time to get your feet wet!

Condition and Its Importance

"Condition is important to book collectors" is probably an understatement! When considering the addition of a book to your collection — you must consider condition of the book. A good adage to follow would be to "always choose the best condition copy that you can afford" with two important "ifs": if the copy is reasonably priced and if you cannot expect to find a better copy, then you must decide whether to settle for a copy in lesser condition.

If you decide to settle for a volume in less than desirable condition, it is normally with the hopes of upgrading when you have the opportunity to purchase a better copy. This is a personal decision; some collectors would prefer to not have a book in their collection if the condition does not meet their standards, and other collectors prefer to have a copy of the book even in lesser condition because they believe that it may be a long time before they have an opportunity to locate a very good or fine copy.

What constitutes a very good copy or a fine copy? Defining catagories of condition is a subjective business and applying the categories to rate a specific book is even more subjective. Over the years there have been attempts to establish what one might call a "uniform code" of definitions of condition which would be acceptable to all. However, due to the subjective nature such categories or ratings have been applied with considerable variation by very new booksellers versus those in the business for decades, by collectors of modern first editions versus collectors of local histories and genealogies, by a knowledgeable collector offering duplicates for sale versus someone who found a carton of dusty books in the attic — it is possible to define categories of condition, but difficult and really impossible to enforce a standard application of the categories.

Probably the best avenue to follow when describing the condition of a book is to list all of the obvious problems, defects, and signs of wear, and also to provide your impression of the overall condition. When reading book descriptions one should pay attention to the listed details of condition and to regard an overall condition term such as "good," "very good," or "fine" as the general impression of the bookseller, which may or may not coincide with your general impression of the same volume.

Often you may find the volume to be in better condition than you expected, other times in lesser condition. Virtually all booksellers want you to be pleased with the book(s) you purchase and hope that you remain a customer and for that reason prefer that you return the book(s) for a refund if you are not happy with the condition.

Most of us have seen descriptions of book condition which read like "scattered foxing, rubbing at corners and extremities of spine, weak hinge, otherwise very good condition" or "dust jacket with minor chips, rear free endpaper lacking, signature on title page but really much better condition than it sounds." If you don't want a book with a weak hinge or a book with a missing endpaper, do not order the book. If the book is one for which you have been searching for ten years and this may be your only chance to purchase it, you probably should tolerate the damaged hinge or missing end paper. It is a personal decision.

Traditionally, book condition relates to the age of the book. A fine copy of a 1980 modern first edition is expected to be near perfect versus a fine copy of an 1840 traveler's guide to the western United States which will have very minor wear or perhaps very minor foxing or very minor soil or very minor rubbing on the covers — minor blemishes due to the expected handling of the book for approximately 160 years.

Some types of books are much more difficult to find in fine condition — those that normally receive considerable usage as opposed to being read once or a few times — cookbooks and children's books come to mind. If you collect eighteenth and nineteenth century cookbooks, you may have difficulty finding fine copies and may have to to settle for very good copies of the more common titles and good copies of the scarce or rare titles. And you will probably have to pay a premium should you have the opportunity to purchase a fine copy of a rare nineteenth century cookbook.

We will make an attempt to define some commonly used categories of condition for those of you who are new to book collecting to give you a general concept of what to expect when reading descriptions of condition. If you have been involved in book collecting or bookselling for some time, you will probably disagree with the definitions, having developed your own concepts over the years — we ask that you bear with us as we attempt these definitions.

Fine — If a twentieth century book, the condition should be almost like new with only very, very minor signs of use, no discernable wear or rubbing, no fading of the spine, no dogeared page corners, possibly lacking the fresh or crisp look of a brand new book and intact, nothing missing, no missing endpapers and if issued with a dust jacket, the dust jacket must be separately described. If an older book, nineteenth century or earlier, slightly more signs of usage are tolerated, but still a well-cared-for, fresh looking book with very minor rubbing , very minor fading of cloth or color of boards, but no cracked hinges, a few specks of foxing, nothing missing, no missing endpaper, half-title or spine labels. In both the twentieth century and the earlier book, there should not be any library markings (public or institutional), however there may be a bookplate from a private collector.

Very Good — A twentieth century book should show only minor rubbing at book extremities such as corners or spine, possibly very minor soil or very minor spots on covers, possibly a bumped corner, no fraying of spine extremities, no cracked hinges, no foxing, nothing missing, no missing endpapers, essentially just a little more evidence of use than a fine copy. If nineteenth century or earlier, minor rubbing of extremities is expected, no chipping (missing material) at top or bottom of spine, no signs of major fraying of cloth, no cracked hinges or cracked joints, possibly minor spots of soil or stain and occasional foxing is expected, nothing should be missing, no missing endpaper or half-title. A very good copy can be ex-library with library markings, but should be so described and with few exceptions the ex-library copy would not be a desirable book to add to your collection

Good — Either a twentieth century or an earlier book showing average use and wear, but not in need of a replacement binding, not all tattered and torn, not with moderate to heavy damp stain, basically still intact but worn, spine extremities can show minor chipping, corners can all be bumped, and (there is disagreement here) in the case of an earlier book a free endpaper, or other blank page such as a flyleaf, can be missing, a hinge can be cracked (the book should not be in need of recasing with the covers barely attached), there can be moderate to heavy foxing in earlier books, a good copy should be a book that has seen average/considerable use and is added to your collection because you care more about the content of the book than the condition or you hope someday to upgrade to a better copy of the same book

Fair — A book with much use and wear and multiple problems and/or defects and unless the book is very scarce or rare probably should not be added to your collection. A fair copy may exhibit moderate to heavy dampstain, excessive stain or foxing in the text, a very tattered cloth or very scuffed and rubbed leather binding with additional problems such as underlining in the text, lacking endpapers, both hinges cracked, heavy dogearring of page corners, in general only a step above a reading copy and not a desirable copy unless you value content much more than condition.

Binding copy — A copy in need of a replacement backstrip or spine or in need of recasing or reattachment of the original binding or recasing with a new binding; the book should be in very good condition otherwise, the cover's in very good condition in the case of need for new backstrip and the text portion of the book in clean, very good condition in both cases or the expense of rebinding is not warranted.

Reading copy — A copy in poor condition, practically synonymous with binding copy (when only the covers are excessively worn), but also used to describe a copy with excessive wear and/or abuse which does not warrant rebinding and is simply useful for the content it contains, sometimes referred to as a working copy.

Some booksellers choose to use intermediate categories such as "very good to fine" or "good to very good," when they believe that such categories are warranted. When a book is better than very good but not quite fine (in the case of a nineteenth century book perhaps a little too much rubbing on the cloth) we use the very good to fine designation. When a book is better than good condition, but is not quite very good (perhaps has moderate foxing or a small amount of very minor damp stain) we rate it as good to very good.

In summary, you should pay close attention to the listed details or specifics of wear and/or defects in a book description and you should realize that the overall rating of condition is the opinion of the bookseller or other individual writing the description. In most cases books are returnable for a refund when you believe they are not as described — and many booksellers allow the return of a book should you be dissatisfied with the condition for any reason. Read each bookseller's terms or policy statement prior to ordering to see if and when returns are allowed.

In general do not purchase books or pamphlets which are missing pages or portions of text, unless you have a personal reason for doing so — a book missing the top third of pages 102 – 103 will never have much value. And in general it is a poor idea to purchase odd volumes (not complete set) of a set, thinking that you will be able to find the missing volumes at a later date — it seldom happens.

As a beginning book collector, you should strive to collect books of very good or fine condition. There may be some bargains among the very worn books, but you should probably avoid the worn bargains unless you know the book is very scarce or rare.

Rarity and Scarcity

There are many rare books for which there is virtually no market, i.e., Arthur Deco's *Forty Years of My Poetry* which Art brought to a vanity publisher in 1965 and paid for the publication of 200 copies. Only Art's cousins are looking for a copy; even his local library has no interest in the book. To take this concept a step further, there are thousands of titles of older fiction, most of which went through only one printing and for which there is no interest, unless a scholar or bibliographer is studying that area of fiction. In general, there is a lack of demand for old textbooks, old Bibles, many self-help titles, long out-of-date technology handbooks, old encyclopedias, poetry by unknown poets, older fiction by unknown authors, and some local business histories; many of these books are either rare or scarce. In other words, not every rare book is valuable.

Another misconception is that every first edition is collectible and valuable. One has only to understand that every book has a first edition and only popular or successful titles have more than one printing to see that not every first edition is desirable. One could assemble an interesting (?) and fascinating (?) collection of esoteric, undesirable rare books for which there is little or no demand.

The concept of a rare book is easy to comprehend — it is a book which is seldom encountered and presumably exists in very small numbers. To define the term "rare book" is more difficult. I prefer to define it based on the frequency it is seen by the bibliographer, collector, or antiquarian bookseller who is searching for copies on a continual basis. A rare book is one encountered only occasionally by those working with and/or collecting books in the specifc genre. How frequently? That is the question that separates a rare book from a scarce book.

A book which is encountered about once every five years or less is a rare book (in the case of a specialized bookseller, in his/her stock, in the case of a collector, having a specific opportunity to purchase the book, in the case of a bibliographer, locating a "previously unrecorded" copy). A very scarce book might be encountered more frequently, but less often than once a year, perhaps once every two to four years. A scarce book is normally encountered approximately once a year by those actively seeking it. An uncommon book may be in the stock of a specialty bookseller four or five times a year, but is not always readily available as is a common book. Theoretically you should have no problem finding a fine copy of a common book at any time; an uncommon book may take a bit of searching.

These artificial standards provide you with at least some guide to understanding rarity and scarcity, but obviously are only a relative guide. A book you, as a collector, have the opportunity to purchase ten times per year obviously is neither rare nor is it scarce. When an antiquarian bookseller has five copies of a specific title for sale during any one year, it is neither a rare book nor is it scarce. There can be exceptions to the rule. We once had an opportunity to buy three copies at one time of a rare whaling narrative from a collector who had been fortunate to be able to locate that many copies during a decade. During more than 25 years of bookselling, we have only had one other copy of that same title.

The Internet with its speedy international communications will probably make scarce and even rare titles more accessible and the frequency of encounter will increase, thus a book which might have been available for purchase only once every five years might be encountered once every three years! Another factor that occasionally has an effect on the level of scarcity is the "sudden" appearance of an accumulation or quantity of a previously rare or scarce book. This seems to happen most often with pamphlets and broadsides. A carton full of a previously scarce bicycle catalog or a Civil War regimental history or a stack of 200 broadsides announcing the formation of a company of gold miners in 1849 may be found in an attic and soon after one starts to see clean, crisp, fine copies of these scarce or even rare items appearing on the market. This type of occurrence obviously changes the status of the item, and although it may still be uncommon and still desirable in your collection, it is no longer scarce or rare.

When a scarce or rare item is offered for sale in fine condition at a price which seems too good to be true, you might inquire whether a large quantity of the item has appeared on the market. Even if that is the case, you probably should still purchase the item if it fits well into your collection and you like the price. Accumulations like these often disappear into collections in fast order and the item almost as suddenly again becomes much more difficult to obtain.

When you are just starting as a book collector, you do not have the luxury of one or two decades of experience as a collector and you must rely on antiquarian book catalogs, bibliographies, annual compilations of auction records, and national bibliographic card catalogs such as the pre-1956 National Union Catalogue or the British Museum Catalogue to assist you in determining the relative scarcity of a book.

Many bibliographies list locations (libraries) which hold particular titles. Sometimes the bibliographer, rather than attempting to locate every known copy, limits the locations to a few as examples of where to find the item. Even when the bibliographer attempts to locate every known copy, there will usually be many unreported copies not listed. Be careful when using bibliographies as a guide to scarcity and read the preface and/or introduction to determine the bibliographer's intent.

One can use a reference such as Milton Drake's *Almanacs of the United States* as a relative guide to scarcity. Drake lists 20 or 30 or even more locations for reasonably common almanacs, but when he locates only one copy, the almanac is probably very scarce and possibly rare. When he locates only three or four copies the almanac is probably scarce. Use bibliographies such as Drake as a guide to relative scarcity.

Wright Howes's *U.S.iana (1650 – 1950) A Selective Bibliography* makes no attempt to provide library locations for books, but does provide a value symbol for each item listed. The values associated with each symbol are now out-of-date, but the value symbols do have value as a measure of relative scarcity.

a — mildly scarce, obtainable without much difficulty
aa — quite scarce, obtainable only with some difficulty
b — mildly rare, obtainable only with considerable difficulty
c — quite rare, obtainable only with much difficulty
d — very rare books, obtainable only with great difficulty
dd — superlatively rare books, almost unobtainable

Personally we do not regard most "a" rating books as scarce, we would categorize many of them as uncommon or common, but most "aa" books are scarce and books with a rating of "b" or higher are usually rare books which are not easy to obtain.

Another way of determining relative scarcity is to use the annual compilations of book auction records such as *American Book Prices Current*. Because such compilations usually exclude common items, one has to be cautious about making extrapolations. If you look through the last ten years of auction records and find no copy of a particular title listed, it is probably either very common or rare. One would be better off to find one copy listed in the last ten years rather than no copies.

When at least one copy of a title is listed in virtually every year of the auction records, one can assume that it is neither very scarce nor rare. When a copy is listed only once every five years, the item is probably at least very scarce and possibly rare. If you find a listing only once every ten years, the book should probably be considered rare. If multiple copies of a book are listed every year, the book can still be considered scarce and desirable and is probably very much in demand or it wouldn't be consigned to auction so frequently. One must remember that most auction houses are not interested in offering common books, thus most titles found in the auction records are at least uncommon and probably scarce.

We find the pre-1956 imprints National Union Catalogue (NUC) valuable in determining relative scarcity. The NUC with its huge number of volumes often takes up a whole wall of book shelving in many libraries and is a compilation of the holdings of all reporting libraries (hundreds, if not thousands of libraries in the United States). Most large college and university libraries and most major city libraries have the NUC.

In general, when there are only one or two or three locations given for a particular item, the assumption can be made that the item is rare. When there are a reasonable number of holdings listed, from three to ten, the item is probably scarce (very scarce might be represented by 4 or 5 locations). When there are quite a number of locations, 11 to 20 locations, the item may be considered uncommon in most cases. When there are 20 to 30 or more locations, the item is probably common. We find that with certain areas such as children's books and cookbooks, the generalizations may not apply due to fewer holdings in these areas in most libraries, i.e., a common cookbook may have only 10 locations listed. Please remember that we are making generalizations and that they are meant to be used only as a rough guide.

Antiquarian booksellers catalogs may also be used as a guide to scarcity, but be careful with your assumptions. Do not assume that because you did not find your favorite bird book listed in any of the ten ornithology catalogs you own, that the book is rare. In fact, the book may be so common or of so little demand that the natural history booksellers seldom catalog it.

Perhaps one of the best ways to use bookseller catalogs as a guide to scarcity is to rely on the expertise of the antiquarian bookseller and make note of items he or she lists as very scarce or rare. Obviously a decade or more in the business of selling antiquarian books provides the bookseller with the requisite experience for making knowledgeable judgements about scarcity (particularly in the specific speciality areas of that bookseller). Equally obvious would be that the experience found in catalog number 1 would not be the same as catalog number 20 from the same bookseller.

Robert F. Lucas
Lucas Books (L5)

Specializing in books by and about Emily Dickinson, Henry D. Thoreau,
Nineteenth century Americana and Manuscript Americana
http://lucasbooks.com

— A —

AADLAND, Florence. *Big Love.* 1986. Warner. 1st thus. F/wrp. C9. $60.00.

AAKER, David A. *Managing Brand Equity: Capitalizing on Value of Brand Name.* 1991. Macmillan. later prt. ils. F/dj. A2. $18.00.

AAMSDEN, Charles Avery. *Prehistoric Southwesterners from Basketmaker to Pueblo.* 1949. LA. Southwest Mus. photos/ils/maps. 163p. VG/wrp. F7. $95.00.

AARON, Henry. *Aaron, RF.* 1968. World. 1st. photos. F/dj. P8. $100.00.

AARON, Henry. *I Had a Hammer: The Hank Aaron Story.* 1991. Harper Collins. 1st. sgn. F/dj. S9. $75.00.

AARON, Jan & Georgine Sachs Salom. *Art of Mexican Cooking, The.* 1965. NY. Doubleday. 309p. VG/VG. A28. $7.50.

ABBATE, Francesco. *American Art.* 1972. London. Octopus. ils. 158p. VG/dj. M10. $7.50.

ABBATT, William. *Attack on Youngs' House (Or Four Corners).* 1926. Tarrytown. 1/250. sgn. ils/rear fld map. 21p. O1. $85.00.

ABBATT, William. *Battle of Pell Point (Or Pelham), October 18, 1776.* 1901. NY. self pub. 1st. 1/500. ils. G. M10. $50.00.

ABBE, Cleveland. *Account of Progress in Meteorology & Allied Subjects.* 1883. GPO. 121p. xl. F/wrp. B14. $125.00.

ABBEY, Edward. *Appalachian Wilderness.* (1970). NY. Dutton. 1st. photography by Eliot Porter. NF. some foxing/NF. minor edgewear. B3. $90.00.

ABBEY, Edward. *Back Roads of Arizona.* 1978. Northland. 1st. 168p. wrp. F7. $22.50.

ABBEY, Edward. *Beyond the Wall: Essays from the Outside.* 1984. NY. HRW. 1st. NF/clip. A14. $87.50.

ABBEY, Edward. *Cactus Country.* (1973). NY. Time-Life. 1st. photo-essay. F/issued w/o dj. B3. $50.00.

ABBEY, Edward. *Confessions of a Barbarian; Selections from the Journals of Ed Abbey, 1951 – 1989.* (1994). NY. Little, Brn. 1st. ed by/with David Peterson. sgn by Dave Peterson. F/F. B3. $35.00.

ABBEY, Edward. *Desert Images: American Landscape.* 1979. NY/London. HBJ. 1st. photos David Muench. NF/case. H4. $225.00.

ABBEY, Edward. *Desert Solitaire.* 1988. Tucson. AZ. 1st. 255p. F/F. B19. $25.00.

ABBEY, Edward. *Epitaph for a Desert Anarchist.* 1994. Atheneum. 1st. F/dj. T11. $25.00.

ABBEY, Edward. *Fool Progress.* 1988. NY. Henry Holt. 1st. F/F. D10. $50.00.

ABBEY, Edward. *Fool Progress: An Honest Novel.* 1988. NY. Holt. 1st. inscr/dtd 1988. NF/dj. S9. $300.00.

ABBEY, Edward. *Good News.* (1980). NY. Dutton. 1st. minor sunning to edges. lt soil to rear panel. NF/NF. B3. $125.00.

ABBEY, Edward. *Good News.* (1980). NY. Dutton. 1st. NF. minor sunning/NF. lt soiling to rear panel. B3. $125.00.

ABBEY, Edward. *Hayduke Lives.* (1990). Boston. Little, Brn. UP. prt yellow wrp. VG. moderate soiling. B3. $30.00.

ABBEY, Edward. *One Life at a Time, Please.* (1988). NY. Henry Holt. 1st. Abbey's last book of essays. VF/VF. B3. $100.00.

ABBEY, Edward. *Slumgullion Stew. An Edward Abbey Reader.* 1984. NY. Dutton. UP. VG in wrp. B2. $60.00.

ABBEY, Edward. *Sunset Canyon.* (1972). London. Talmy. Franklin. 1st UK ed of the Am title *Black Sun.* F/F. B3. $125.00.

ABBEY, Edward. *The Brave Cowboy.* (1993). Salt Lake City. Dream Garden Press. 1st. ltd to 500 copies. sgn by Kirk Douglas. many stills from the movie *Lonely Are the Brave.* VF/VF. B3. $150.00.

ABBEY, Edward. *The Fool Progress.* (1988). NY. Henry Holt. 1st. VF/F. B3. $40.00.

ABBEY, Edward. *The Fool Progress.* 1986. NY. Henry Holt. publicity copy. F/F. D10. $40.00.

ABBEY, Edward. *The Monkey Wrench Gang.* (1975). Philadelphia. JB Lippincott. 1st. NF. lt soiling/G. chip. soiling. B3. $75.00.

ABBEY, Edward. *Vox Lamantis in Desierto.* (1989). Santa Fe. Rydal Press. pub overrun. 1st. nonfiction. VF/in slipcase. B3. $150.00.

ABBEY, Edward and John Nichols. *In Praise of Mountain Lions.* (1984). Albuquerque. Sierra Club. small booklet. 1st. sgn by Abbey and Nichols. wrp. F. B3. $250.00.

ABBEY, Merrill. *Preaching to the Contemporary Mind.* 1963. Abingdon. 192p. VG/G. B29. $7.00.

ABBOT, Anthony. *About the Murder of Geraldine Foster.* 1930. NY. Covici Friede. 1st. VG/rpr. M15. $200.00.

ABBOT, Anthony. *The Shudders.* 1943. NY. Farrar & Rinehart. 1st. F/dj. M15. $150.00.

ABBOT, Charles G. *The Earth and the Stars.* 1925. NY. D. Van Nostrand. 8vo. 32 plates. 64 text figures. 264p. G/chipped. browned dj. pencil mks. lt foxing. K5. $25.00.

ABBOT, I. A. *Laau Hawaii: Traditional Hawaiian Uses of Plants.* 1992. Bishop Mus. 173 photos. 163p. F/wrp. B1. $36.00.

ABBOTT, Berenice. *World of Atget.* 1979. NY. Paragon. 1st thus. VG/glossy wrp. H4. $20.00.

ABBOTT, E. C. *We Pointed Them North.* 1991. Lakeside Classic. 1st thus. teg. brn cloth. F/sans. T11. $30.00.

ABBOTT, Jane. *Angels May Weep.* 1937. Lippincott. 1st. F/NF. B4. $85.00.

ABBOTT, John. *Scimitar.* 1992. NY. Crown. ARC/1st. F/ils wrp. A14. $21.00.

ABBOTT, Katharine M. *Old Paths & Legends of the New England Border.* 1907. NY. Putnam. 1st. ils. 408p. G. M10. $35.00.

ABBOTT, Katharine M. *Old Paths & Legends of the New England Border.* 1909 (1903). Putnam. rpt. 484p. gilt cloth. VG. O1. $30.00.

ABBOTT, Keene. *Wine O' the Winds.* 1920. Garden City. 336p. G. G11. $8.00.

ABBOTT, Lee K. *Strangers in Paradise.* 1987. Putnam. 1st. sgn/dtd 1994. NF/dj. R14. $50.00.

ABDULLAH, Achmed. *Bungalow on the Roof.* 1931. Mystery League. 1st. VG. G8. $15.00.

ABE, Kobo. *Friends.* 1969. NY. Grove. 1st. F in F dj. B2. $50.00.

ABE, Kobo. *The Little Elephant Is Dead.* 1979. Abe Kobo Studio. 1st. 12 p text. F in wrp. B2. $50.00.

ABEL, Drina Welch. *The Welch Airplane Story.* 1983. Terre Haute. Sunshine House. 1st. inscr by Alan Abel. 130p. VG+/chip dj. B18. $55.00.

ABEL, Kenneth. *Bait.* 1994. Delacorte. 1st. author's 1st book. F/F. H11. $30.00.

ABEL, Kenneth. *Bait.* 1994. NY. Delacorte. author's 1st book. VF/VF. H11. $35.00.

ABEL, Kenneth. *Bait.* 1994. NY. Delacorte. 1st. review copy. F/F. G8. $10.00.

ABEL, Robert. *Progress of a Fire.* 1985. S&S. 1st. 509p. VG/dj. R11. $15.00.

ABERNATHY, T. P. *Conspiracy.* 1954. NY. Oxford. 1st. 301p. VG/dj. M10. $20.00.

ABERNATHY, T. P. *From Frontier to Plantation in Tennessee: A Study.* NC U. 1st. 14 maps. 392p. F. M4. $110.00.

ABERNETHY, George L. *Pakistan: A Selected, Annotated Bibliography.* 1960. NY. Am Institute of Pacific Affairs. 2nd ed. revised. 4to. 39p. VG/VG. P1. $5.00.

ABISH, Walter. *Eclipse Fever.* (1993). NY. Knopf. 1st. F/F. B3. $20.00.

ABLOW, Keith. *Denial.* 1997. np. Pantheon. 1st. author's 1st novel. F/NF. R16. $35.00.

ABRAHAMS, Harold. *Extinct Medical Schools of Baltimore Maryland.* 1969. Baltimore. 1st. 332p. A13. $50.00.

ABRAHAMS, Peter. *Hard Rain.* 1988. NY. Dutton. 1st. F/F. H11. $25.00.

ABRAHAMS, Peter. *Lights Out.* (1994). London. Warner. UP. 1st UK ed. prt red wrp. VF. B3. $40.00.

ABRAHAMS, Peter. *The Fan.* 1995. Warner. 1st. F/dj. P8. $15.00.

ABRAHAMS, Peter. *The Fury of Rachel Monette.* 1980. NY. Macmillan. Canadian author's 1st book. NF/NF. H11. $35.00.

ABRAHAMS, Peter. *Tongues of Fire.* 1982. NY. Evans. 1st. NF/NF. H11. $20.00.

ABRAMSON, Harold A. *Use of LSD in Psychotherapy & Alcoholism.* 1967. Bobbs Merrill. 1st trade. NF. B2. $45.00.

ABRANSON, Erik. *Ships of the High Seas.* 1976. NY. Crescent. 4to. 124p. NF/dj. M10. $12.50.

ABS, Michael. *Physiology & Behavior of the Pigeon.* 1983. London. Academic. ils. 360p. laminated brd. G1. $65.00.

ABSE, Dannie. *Fire in Heaven.* 1956. London. Hutchinson. 1st. VG/dj. H4. $50.00.

ABSHIRE, Richard. *Dallas Deception.* 1992. NY. Morrow. 1st. F/F. H11. $20.00.

ABSHIRE, Richard. *Dallas Drop.* 1989. NY. Morrow. 1st. F/F. H11. $20.00.

ABSHIRE, Richard. *The Dallas Deception.* 1992. NY. Morrow. 1st. F/F. H11. $20.00.

ABSHIRE, Richard. *Turnaround Jack.* 1990. NY. Morrow. 1st. F/F. H11. $20.00.

ABUJABER, Raouf Sa'd. *Pioneers Over Jordan: Frontier of Settlement in Transjordan.* 1989. London. Tauris. 8 maps. 328p. cloth. F/dj. Q2. $40.00.

ACHEBE, Chinua. *Hopes and Impediments.* 1989. NY. Doubleday. 1st. F/F. M23. $30.00.

ACHTEMEIER, Paul J. *Harper Bible Dictionary.* 1985. Harper. 1178p. VG. B29. $17.00.

ACIER, Marcel, Ed. *From Spanish Trenches. Recent Letters from Spain.* 1937. NY. Modern Age. 2nd printing. wrps in dj. F/VG. B2. $25.00.

ACKER, Kathy. *Empire of the Senseless.* 1988. Grove. 1st. sgn. F/dj. O11. $30.00.

ACKER, Kathy. *In Memoriam to Identity.* 1990. Grove Weidenfeld. 1st. sgn. F/dj. O11. $30.00.

ACKER, Kathy. *Pussy, King of the Pirates.* (1996). NY. Grove Press. 1st. F/F. B3. $20.00.

ACKERLEY, J. R. *EM Forster: A Portrait.* 1970. London. 1st. F/self wrp. L3. $30.00.

ACKERMAN, Diane. *Natural History of the Senses.* 1990. Random. rem mk. 331p. VG/dj. A10. $25.00.

ACKERMAN, Diane. *Rarest of the Rare.* 1995. NY. Random House. 1st. sgn by author. F/F. O11. $25.00.

ACKERMAN, Diane. *Reverse Thunder: A Dramatic Poem.* 1988. NY. Lumen Books. PBO. 1st. sgn by author. F. O11. $15.00.

ACKERMAN, Diane. *The Moon by Whale Light: and Other Adventures Among Bats, Penguins, Crocodilians, and Whales.* 1991. NY. Random House. 1st. sgn by author. F/F. O11. $25.00.

ACKERMAN, Forrest J. & Jean Stine, Editors. *I, Vampire: Interviews with the Undead.* 1995. Stamford. Longmeadow Press. 1st. Ackerman sgn laid in. VF/VF. T2. $15.00.

ACKROYD, Peter. *Chatterton.* 1978. Hammish Hamilton. 1st. F/F. B3. $60.00.

ACKROYD, Peter. *First Light.* 1989. London. Hamish Hamilton. 1st. NF/VG. R14. $25.00.

ACKROYD, Peter. *First Light.* 1989. NY. Grove Weid. 1st. F/F. H11. $20.00.

ACKWORTH, Robert. *Dr Kildare: Assigned to Trouble.* 1963. Racine. TVTI. ils. VG. M20. $14.00.

ACKWORTH, Robert. *Mary Winters, Student Nurse.* 1966. Avalon. 191p. xl. VG/dj. B36. $12.50.

ACOSTA, Jorge & Javier Romero. *Exploraciones En Monte Negro, Oaxaca.* 1992. Mexico. 1st. ltd to 1000. 189p. G. wrp. F3. $25.00.

ACZEL, Amir D. *Fermat Last Theorem.* 1996. Four Walls Eight Windows. 1st. F/dj. M23. $40.00.

ADACHI, Choka. *Camellia: Its Appreciation and Artistic Arrangement.* 1960. Tokyo. np. 271 color photos. purple cloth w/color paste-on. 273p. VG in dj. B26. $54.00.

ADAM, Paul. *Saltmarsh Ecology.* 1990. Cambridge. England. np. ils. xii.461p. AN. dj. B26. $38.00.

ADAM, Paul. *Unholy Trinity.* 1999. London. Little, Brn. 1st. sgn. VF/VG. T2. $39.00.

ADAMIC, Louis. *Cradle of Life.* 1936. NY. Harper. 1st. inscr by author. VG/VG. B2. $25.00.

ADAMIC, Louis. *My Native Land.* 1943. NY. Harper. 1st. inscr by author. dj unfolds into poster. F/VG. B2. $75.00.

ADAMS, Adrienne. *Christmas Party.* 1978. Scribner. 1st. 32p. reinforced cloth. F/dj. D4. $45.00.

ADAMS, Alice. *Almost Perfect.* 1993. NY. Knopf. 1st. F/NF. H11. $20.00.

ADAMS, Alice. *Beautiful Girl.* (1978). NY. Knopf. 1st. sgn by author. short stories. F/NF two closed short tears. B3. $45.00.

ADAMS, Alice. *Beautiful Girl.* 1979. NY. Knopf. 1st. F/F. A24. $25.00.

ADAMS, Alice. *Families & Survivors.* 1974. Knopf. 1st. F/NF. M25. $45.00.

ADAMS, Alice. *Mexico. Some Travels and Some Travelers There.* 1990. NY. Prentice Hall. 1st. 216p. G. F3. $20.00.

ADAMS, Alice. *Rich Rewards.* 1980. NY. Knopf. 1st. F/F. A24. $25.00.

ADAMS, Alice. *Southern Exposure.* 1995. Knopf. 1st. sgn. AN/dj. B30. $30.00.

ADAMS, Alice. *Superior Women.* 1984. NY. Knopf. 1st. NF/F. A24. $15.00.

ADAMS, Alice. *The Last Lovely City.* 1999. Knopf. UP. F/wrp. M25. $45.00.

ADAMS, Ansel. *American Wilderness.* (1990). Boston/Toronto/London. Little, Brn. stated 1st. folio. 107 photos. AN/NF. H4. $120.00.

ADAMS, Ansel. *An Autobiography.* 1986. Boston. Little, Brn. later prt. quarto. bur-gungdy cloth lettered in silver on spine. pict dj. F. R3. $90.00.

ADAMS, Ansel. *Camera.* 1980. NYGS. 1st. F/dj. T10. $35.00.

ADAMS, Ansel. *Pageant of History in Northern California.* 1954. SF. Am Trust Co. cbdg/wrp. H4. $75.00.

ADAMS, Ansel. *This Is the American Earth.* (1971). SF. Sierra Club. 5th prt. sgn. folio. 89p. F/VG. H4. $100.00.

ADAMS, Ansel. *Yosemite & the Range of Light.* 1979. NYGS. VG/dj. S5. $125.00.

ADAMS, Ansel. *Yosemite & the Range of Light.* 1979. NYGS. obl folio. sgn pres/dtd 1979. 116 pl. maroon linen/bl cloth. dj. K1. $275.00.

ADAMS, Arthur. *Quimby.* 1988. St Martin. 1st. F/NF. R11. $15.00.

ADAMS, Ben. *Last Frontier: Short History of Alaska.* 1961. Hill Wang. 1st. VG/G. O1. $15.00.

ADAMS, Bronte. *Margin for Murder.* 1992. Carroll & Graf. 1st Am ed. NF/VG. G8. $12.50.

ADAMS, Carolyn. *Stars Over Texas.* 1969. Naylor. 1st. 122p. F/dj. D4. $30.00.

ADAMS, Charles Francis. *Antimomianism in the Colony of Massachusetts Bay 1636 – 1638.* 1894. Boston. Prince Soc. 1/250. 415+18p index. 3-quarter leather. H10. $125.00.

ADAMS, Charles Francis. *Columbus & the Spanish Discovery of America: A Study.* 1892. Cambridge. John Wilson. rpt. sgn pres. wrp. O1. $65.00.

ADAMS, Charles Francis. *Railroads: Their Origin & Problems.* 1878. Putnam. 1st. 12mo. inscr pres. 216p. O1. $115.00.

ADAMS, Charlotte. *Four Seasons Cookbook.* 1971. NY. Ridge. ils. F/clip. A16. $15.00.

ADAMS, Charlotte. *Singles' First Menu Cookbook.* 1975. Dodd Mead. G/dj. A16. $12.00.

ADAMS, Douglas. *Dirk Gently Holistic Detective Agency.* 1987. S&S. 1st. NF/dj. M20. $17.00.

ADAMS, Douglas. *Life, the Universe & Everything.* 1982. Harmony. 1st. NF/dj. M20. $27.00.

ADAMS, Douglas. *Mostly Harmless.* 1992. London. Heinemann. 1st. VG+/dj. A14. $21.00.

ADAMS, Douglas. *So Long, and Thanks for All the Fish.* 1984. London. Pan. 1st. NF/dj. A14. $28.00.

ADAMS, Douglas & John Lloyd. *The Deeper Meaning of Life.* 1993. NY. Harmony Books. 1st US ed. VF/VF. T2. $8.00.

ADAMS, Douglas & Mark Carwardine. *Last Chance to See.* (1991). NY. Harmony. UP. prt yellowing wrp. sgn by author. F. B3. $40.00.

ADAMS, E. Charles. *Origin & Development of Pueblo Katsina Cult.* 1991. Tucson, AZ. 1st. ils. 235p. NF/NF. B19. $35.00.

ADAMS, Eleanor. *A Bio-Bibliography of Franciscan Authors in Colonial Central America.* 1953. Washington, DC. Academy of American Franciscan History. 1st. Biographical Series Vol. 2. 97p. G/chipped dj. F3. $60.00.

ADAMS, Eustace L. *Air Combat Stories for Boys: Wings of the Navy (#6).* 1936. Grosset Dunlap. lists 7 titles. VG/dj. M20. $30.00.

ADAMS, Frank Dawson. *Birth & Development of Geological Sciences.* 1954. Dover. 1st thus. 506p. xl. VG. B14. $55.00.

ADAMS, Harold. *A Perfectly Proper Murder.* 1993. NY. Walker. 1st. VF/VF. T2. $20.00.

ADAMS, Harold. *A Way with the Widows.* 1994. NY. Walker. 1st. VF/VF. T2. $20.00.

ADAMS, Harold. *Barbed Wire Noose.* 1987. Mysterious. 1st. F/dj. T2. $25.00.

ADAMS, Harold. *The Barbed Wire Noose.* 1987. NY. Mysterious Press. 1st. VF/VF. T2. $25.00.

ADAMS, Harold. *The Ditched Blonde.* 1995. NY. Walker. 1st. sgn. VF/VF. T2. $25.00.

ADAMS, Harold. *The Fourth Widow.* 1986. NY. Mysterious Press. 1st. sgn. VF/VF. H11. $40.00.

ADAMS, Harold. *The Ice Pick Artist.* 1997. NY. Walker. 1st. sgn. VF/VF. T2. $25.00.

ADAMS, Harold. *The Man Who Met the Train.* 1988. NY. Mysterious Press. 1st. sgn. F/VF. H11. $25.00.

ADAMS, Harold. *The Man Who was Taller than God.* 1992. NY. Walker. 1st. sgn. VF/VF. T2. $25.00.

ADAMS, Harold. *The Naked Liar.* 1985. NY. Mysterious Press. 1st. sgn. VF/VF. H11. $40.00.

ADAMS, Henry. *Letters of Henry Adams 1858 – 1918.* (1930). Houghton Mifflin. 2 vol. MacDonald bdg. H4. $350.00.

ADAMS, Herbert. *Oddways.* 1929. Lippincott. 1st. VG. G8. $40.00.

ADAMS, I. William. *Kaiuolani, a Princess of Hawaii.* 1912. NY. The Mikilosch Press. 1st. red cloth & gilt. 296p. VG. B14. $75.00.

ADAMS, James Truslow. *Adams Family.* 1930. Little, Brn. 1st. ils. VG. H4. $15.00.

ADAMS, James Truslow. *Provincial Society...History of American Life Vol III.* 1927. NY. ils. 347p. VG. M4. $20.00.

ADAMS, Jane. *Bird.* 1997. London. Macmillan. 1st. sgn. VF/dj. M15. $50.00.

ADAMS, Jane. *Cast the First Stone.* 1996. London. Macmillan. 1st. sgn. VF/dj. M15. $65.00.

ADAMS, Jane. *Cast the First Stone.* 1996. London. Macmillan. 1st. F/F. A24. $45.00.

ADAMS, Jane. *The Greenway.* 1995. London. Macmillan. 1st. sgn. VF/dj. M15. $175.00.

ADAMS, Jane. *The Greenway.* 1995. London. Macmillan. 1st. author's 1st novel. VF/VF. T2. $125.00.

ADAMS, Jay. *Pulpit Speech.* 1981. Baker. pb ed. 169p. VG. B29. $6.00.

ADAMS, Jay. *The Biblical View of Self Esteem, Self Love, Self Image.* 1986. Harvest House. pb. 141p. VG/minor mks. B29. $5.50.

ADAMS, Jill. *Wild Flowers of the Northern Cape.* 1976. Cape Town. flexible covers. OP. ep map. 152p. F. B26. $29.00.

ADAMS, Joey. *On the Road for Uncle Sam.* 1963. np. Bernard Geis. 1st. photos/map ep. 311p. VG/torn. R11. $20.00.

ADAMS, John P. *Third Bottle Book.* 1972. Somersworth. New Hampshire Publishing Co. 1st. sm4to. b/w photos. Gift presentation on title page. 124p. G. H1. $37.50.

ADAMS, John Paul. *Milton Caniff: Rembrandt of the Comic Strips.* 1946. McKay. 1st. ils. VG. C9. $90.00.

ADAMS, John S. *5000 Musical Terms: A Complete Dictionary of Latin, Greek, Hebrew, Italian, French, German, Spanish, English....* (1851) Boston. Oliver Ditson & Co. 12mo. (168)p. printed bl brd. leather spine. probably later printing (circa 1860s?). Spine worn. esp. at top. G. L5. $25.00.

ADAMS, Joseph. *Salmon & Trout Angling: Its Theory & Practice.* 1923. NY. Dutton. 1st Am. ils. 288p. VG/dj. H10. $50.00.

ADAMS, Judith Porter. *Peacework: Oral Histories of Women Peace Activists.* 1990. Boston. Twayne. 1st. VG/G. V3. $12.00.

ADAMS, Laura. *Norman Mailer: A Comprehensive Bibliography.* (1979). Metuchen, NJ. slim 8vo. 131p. F. H4. $15.00.

ADAMS, Marcia. *Christmas in the Heartland.* 1992. NY. Clarkson Potter. 1st. NF/NF. A28. $14.95.

ADAMS, Mortimer J. *How to Read a Book: Art of Getting a Liberal Education.* (1972). S&S. 1st. 8vo. 426p. F/G. H4. $40.00.

ADAMS, Myron E. *History & Achievements of Ft Sheridan Officer's Training.* 1920. Ft Sheridan. 4to. 487p. gilt cloth. H4. $35.00.

ADAMS, Nancy M. *New Zealand Native Trees.* 1981. Wellington. np. 84p. spiral bd. VG. B26. $10.00.

ADAMS, Peter. *Wine Lover's Quiz Book: Challenging Questions and Answers for Wine Buffs and Bluffers.* 1987. Arizona. HP Books. trade sc. VG. A28. $9.95.

ADAMS, Richard. *Iron Wolf & Other Stories.* 1980. Allen Lane. 1st. ils Yvonne Gilbert/Jennifer Campbell. F/F. B3. $40.00.

ADAMS, Richard. *Maia.* 1984. Viking Penguin. 1st. NF/dj. A14. $42.00.

ADAMS, Richard. *Plague Dogs.* 1977. London. Allen Lane/Penguin. 1st. inscr by author. F/F. B2. $85.00.

ADAMS, Richard. *Prehistoric Mesoamerica.* (1977). Little, Brn. 370p. F3. $20.00.

ADAMS, Richard. *Shardik.* 1974. London. Allen Lane. 1st. inscr. author's 2nd novel. F/dj. B4. $350.00.

ADAMS, Richard. *The Plague Dogs.* 1977. London. Allen Lane. 1st. F/F. D10. $50.00.

ADAMS, Richard. *The Unbroken Web: Stories and Fables.* 1980. NY. Crown. 1st. VF/VF. T2. $25.00.

ADAMS, Richard. *Tyger Voyage.* 1976. Knopf. 1st Am. 8vo. 30p. NF/dj. D1. $45.00.

ADAMS, Richard. *Watership Down.* 1974. Macmillan. UP of Am ed. VG+ in yellow wrps. ltly soiled & bumped. short tear at foot of spine. M25. $100.00.

ADAMS, Richard. *Watership Down.* 1974. Macmillan. 1st Am ed. sgn & inscr. VG+/chipped dj. sunned on spine. M25. $100.00.

ADAMS, Richard. *Watership Down.* 1976. Harmonsworth. Penguin/Kestel. 1st ils ed. ils John Lawrence. decor slipcase. F/F. B2. $100.00.

ADAMS, Samuel Hopkins. *Harvey Girls.* 1946. World. Forum Motion Picture ed. 8vo. 327p. red cloth. G+. F7. $30.00.

ADAMS, Samuel Hopkins. *The Great American Fraud: Articles on the Nostrum Evil & Quackery.* 1912. Chicago. American Medical Association. 5th. 8vo A compilation of articles which first appear in *Collier's Magazine* during 1905 thru 1907. and again in 1912. Small abrasion on cover. 185p. VG. H1. $90.00.

ADAMS ROUND TABLE. *A Body Is Found.* 1990. NY. Wynwood Press. 1st. VF/VF. T2. $15.00.

ADAMS ROUND TABLE. *Missing in Manhattan.* 1992. Stamford. Longmeadow Press. 1st. VF/VF. T2. $15.00.

ADAMSON, David. *The Ruins of Time. Four and a Half Centuries of Conquest and Discovery Among the Maya.* 1975. NY. Praeger. 1st. 272p. G/chipped dj. F3. $30.00.

ADAMSON, R. S. *The Vegetation of South Africa.* 1938. London. np. ex lib. ils. xiii, 235p. corners bumped. B26. $42.50.

ADAY, Robert. *Locked Room Murders.* 1991. Minneapolis. Crossover Press. 1st. VF. M15. $45.00.

ADCOCK, Thomas. *Devil's Heaven.* 1995. NY. Pocket. 1st. F/F. H11. $15.00.

ADCOCK, Thomas. *Devil's Heaven.* 1995. NY. Pocket Books. 1st. sgn. VF/VF. T2. $25.00.

ADCOCK, Thomas. *Drown All the Dogs.* 1994. NY. Pocket. 1st. VF/VF. H11. $25.00.

ADCOCK, Thomas. *Precinct 19.* 1984. Garden City. Doubleday. 1st. author's 1st book. F/F. rem spray. H11. $45.00.

ADCOCK, Thomas. *Sea of Green.* 1989. NY. Mysterious Press. 1st. VF/VF. H11. $40.00.

ADCOCK, Thomas. *Sea of Green.* 1989. NY. Mysterious Press. 1st. VF/VF. T2. $55.00.

ADCOCK, Thomas. *Thrown Away Child.* 1996. NY. Pocket Books. 1st. sgn. VF/VF. T2. $25.00.

ADDAMS, Charles. *Dear Dead Days.* 1959. NY. Putnam. 1st. VG/G. L1. $55.00.

ADDAMS, Charles. *Homebodies.* 1954. S&S. 1st. VG/dj. L1. $45.00.

ADDAMS, Charles. *Homebodies.* 1954. NY. S&S. 1st. quarto. orig blk brds. lavender cloth spine. ils by author. pict dj. F/F. R3. $100.00.

ADDAMS, Jane. *Spirit of Youth & the City Streets.* 1909. Macmillan. 4th. xl. VG. A25. $15.00.

ADDAMS, Jane. *Twenty Years at Hull House.* 1910. NY. Macmillan. 1st. 8vo. 462p+3p index. VG+/acetate wrp. H4. $50.00.

ADKINS, Jan. *Cookie.* 1988. NY. Harper & Row. 1st. F/F. H11. $15.00.

ADLEMAN, Robert H. *Bloody Benders.* 1970. Stein Day. 1st. VG/dj. M20. $24.00.

ADLER, Bill. *Motherhood: A Celebration.* 1987. Carroll & Graf. 1st. F/F. H11. $20.00.

ADLER, Bill. *Murder Game.* 1991. Carroll & Graf. 1st. F/dj. N4. $22.50.

ADLER, Elmer. *Informal Talk by Elmer Adler at University of Kansas.* 1953. Plantin. sq 8vo. 46p. VG/dj. H4. $40.00.

ADLER, Irene. *I Remember Jimmy: Life & Times of Jimmy Durante.* 1980. NY. Arlington. 189p. VG/dj. C5. $15.00.

ADOFF, Arnold, editor. *It Is the Poem Singing Into Your Eyes.* 1971. NY. Harper & Row. 1st. NF in dj. M25. $25.00.

ADRIAN, Jack & Robert Adey, eds. *Murder Impossible.* 1990. Carroll & Graf. 1st Am ed. anthology. NF/NF. G8. $25.00.

AELLEN, Richard. *Redeye.* 1988. np. Donald Fine. 1st. author's 1st novel. VG+/VG. R16. $35.00.

AFFORD, Max. *Death's Mannikins.* 1937. NY. D. Appleton Century. 1st Am. dj has chipped spine ends. several closed tears along edges. F/VG. M15. $65.00.

AGAPIDA, Fra Antonio; See Irving, Washington.

AGASSIZ, Louis. *Bibliographia Zoologiae Et Geologiae.* 1968. NY. facs of 1848-54. 4 vol. A13. $150.00.

AGEE, Jon. *Ellsworth.* 1983. NY. Pantheon. 1st. ils. 31p. F. D4. $25.00.

AGEE, Jonis. *Strange Angels.* 1993. Ticknor Fields. 1st. sgn/dtd 1993. F/dj. R14. $35.00.

AGRAWALA, Vasudeva S. *Indian Art.* 1965. Varanasi. India. Prithiva Prakashan. 1st. 389p. maroon cloth. VG/poor. F1. $35.00.

AGUILAR, Grace. *Home Influence: A Tale for Mothers & Daughters.* 1858. Boston. Hickling Swan & Brewer. VG/dj. M20. $14.00.

AGUILAR, Mila D. *Comrade Is as Special as a Rice Seedling.* 1984. NY. Kitchin Table Women of Color. 1st. F/wrp. C6. $30.00.

AHEARN, Allen. *Book Collecting, A Comprehensive Guide.* (1989). NY. Putnam. 1st. reference. F/F. B3. $15.00.

AICKMAN, Robert. *Robert Aickman: The Collected Strange Stories.* 1999. East Sussex. Tartarus Press/Durtro Press. 1st. 2 volumes. 1/500 sets. VF/VF. T2. $140.00.

AICKMAN, Robert. *The Wine Dark Sea.* 1988. NY. Arbor House/Morrow. 1st. sgn by introducer Peter Straub. VF/VF. T2. $35.00.

AIKIN, Dr. & Mrs. Barbauld. *Evenings at Home, or the Juvenile Budget Opened....* 1845. London. Edward Lacey. 24mo. red cloth w/gilt. 556p. VG. D6. $95.00.

AIKIN, Dr. & Mrs. Barbauld. *Evenings at Home, or the Juvenile Budget Opened....* 1845. London. George Rutledge & Sons. corrected & revised ed. 24mo. gold cloth w/gilt & bl designs. 446p+26p adv. VG. D6. $70.00.

AIRD, Catherine. *Parting Breath.* 1977. Crime club. 1st Am. NF/NF. G8. $20.00.

AIRTH, Rennie. *River of Darkness.* 1999. London. Macmillan. 1st. VF/dj. M15. $125.00.

AIYAR, S.P. *Politics of Mass Violence in India.* 1967. Bombay. Manaktalas. 1st. VG/dj. N2. $15.00.

AKERS, Dwight. *Drivers Up: Story of American Harness Racing.* 1938. Putnam. 1st. VG/fair. O3. $48.00.

AKIN, Emma E. *Negro Boys & Girls.* 1938. OK City. Harlow Pub. 1st. G. B2. $65.00.

AKST, Daniel. *St. Burl's Obituary.* (1996). Denver. MacMurry & Becker. 1st. author's 1st book. F/F. B3. $30.00.

ALBA, Victor. *The Horizon Concise History of Mexico.* 1973. NY. American heritage pub. 1st. 224p. G/chipped. F3. $30.00.

ALBAUGH, William A. *Confederate Arms.* 1957. Stackpole. VG. A19. $50.00.

ALBERT, Arthur Lemuel. *Fundamentals of Telephony.* 1943. London. 1st/3rd prt. ils. 374p. H6. $38.00.

ALBERT, James W. *Through the Country of the Comanche Indians.* 1970. John Howell. 1st thus. 1/5000. 77p. beige cloth. F/VG. C6. $125.00.

ALBERT, Neil. *Appointment in May.* 1996. Walker. 1st. AN/dj. N4. $25.00.

ALBERT, Neil. *Burning March.* 1994. Dutton. 1st. F/F. H11. $40.00.

ALBERT, Neil. *Burning March.* 1994. NY. Dutton. 1st. F/F w/promo. B2. $45.00.

ALBERT, Neil. *Cruel April.* 1995. NY. Dutton. 1st. sgn. VF/VF. H11. $45.00.

ALBERT, Neil. *The February Trouble.* 1992. NY. Walker. 1st. faded dj. F/F. H11. $80.00.

ALBERT, Neil. *The January Corpse.* 1991. NY. Walker. 1st. author's 1st book. sgn. F/VF. H11. $190.00.

ALBERT, Susan Wittig. *Hangman's Root.* 1994. NY. Scribner's. 1st. NF/NF. G8. $20.00.

ALBERT, Susan Wittig. *Witches' Bane.* 1993. NY. Scribner's. 1st. H11. $25.00.

ALBERTS, Don E. *Rebels on the Rio Grande: Civil War Journal.* 1993. Albuquerque. 1st. ils. 187p. F/stiff wrp. $25.00.

ALBERTSON, Bessie. *Bessie.* 1972. NY. Stein & Day. 1st. F/NF. B2. $35.00.

ALBRAND, Martha. *Hunted Woman.* 1952. NY. Random House. 1st. NF/VG. G8. $10.00.

ALBRIGHT, John G. *Physical Meteorology.* 1939. NY. Prentice Hall. 246 photos & diagrams. 8vo. 392p. G in scuffed cloth; pencil notes. K5. $20.00.

ALCINA FRANCH, Jose. *Pre Columbian Art.* 1983. NY. Abrams. 1st. 1000+ ils. charts. maps. 614p. G/G. F3. $125.00.

ALCOSSER, Sandra. *Except by Nature.* 1998. Graywolf Press. 1st. F/F. V1. $10.00.

ALCOTT, Louisa May. *An Old Fashioned Girl.* 1912. NY. A.L. Burt. G. A16. $10.00.

ALCOTT, Louisa May. *An Old Fashioned Girl.* 1947. NY. World Publishing co. hc. G. A28. $6.50.

ALCOTT, Louisa May. *Jack & Jill.* 1903. Little, Brn. 12mo. gilt brn cloth. VG. M7. $30.00.

ALCOTT, Louisa May. *Jo's Boys.* 1925. NY. Grosset & Dunlap. G. A16. $12.00.

ALCOTT, Louisa May. *Life, Letters & Journals.* 1889. Roberts. 1st/1st issue. edit Ed Cheney. VG+. M5. $110.00.

ALCOTT, Louisa May. *Little Men.* 1947. NY. Grosset & Dunlap. Ill Junior Library. G. A28. $6.50.

ALCOTT, Louisa May. *Louisa's Wonder Book.* 1975. Central MI U. 1st thus. sm 4to. 126p. brn cloth. NF/dj. T5. $25.00.

ALCOTT, Louisa May. *Rose in Bloom.* 1933. Chicago. John C. Winston. G. A16. $22.50.

ALCOTT, Louisa May. *Under the Lilacs.* 1934. Little, Brn. cloth/pict label. VG/dj. M20. $22.00.

ALDEN, John Eliot. *Rhode Island Imprints.* 1949. NY. Bowker. 1st. 665p. gilt bl cloth. F. F1. $95.00.

ALDEN, John Richard. *General Gage in America.* 1948. LSG. 1st. 8vo. 313p. brn cloth. F/clip. C6. $50.00.

ALDEN, Paulette Bates. *Feeding the Eagles.* 1988. St Paul. Graywolf. 1st. author's 1st book. F/dj. R14. $25.00.

ALDERSON, John. *Some Useful Observations & Advices.* 1765. London. Luke Hinde. 1st. 12mo. 23p. unsewn pamphlet. V3. $75.00.

ALDIN, Cecil. *Farm Yard Puppies.* 1911. London. Henry Frowde/Hodder Stoughton. 4to. 12 pl. R5. $350.00.

ALDINGTON, Richard. *Dream in the Luxembourg.* 1930. London. 1/308. sgn. T9. $50.00.

ALDISS, Brian. *A Romance of the Equator.* 1990. NY. Atheneum. 1st US ed. F. bumped corner/VF. T2. $9.00.

ALDISS, Brian. *Billion Year Spree — The History of Science Fiction.* 1973. np. Weidenfeld & Nicolson. 1st Eng ed. prev own. inscr. F/VG dj. M19. $35.00.

ALDISS, Brian. *Bury My Heart at W. H. Smith's.* 1990. London. Hodder & Stoughton. 1st. F/F. M23. $30.00.

ALDISS, Brian. *Last Orders.* 1989. NY. Carroll & Graf. 1st US ed. VF/VF. T2. $9.00.

ALDISS, Brian. *Man in His Time.* 1989. NY. Atheneum. 1st US ed. VF/VF. T2. $10.00.

ALDISS, Brian. *The Twinkling of an Eye, Or My Life as an Englishman.* 1999. NY. St. Martin. AP. wrps. F. B2. $25.00.

ALDISS, Brian W. *And the Lurid Glare of the Comet.* 1986. Seattle. Serconia. 1st. sgn. F/NF. G10. $40.00.

ALDISS, Brian W. *Barefoot in the Head.* 1970. Doubleday. 1st Am. rem mk. F/dj. M25. $25.00.

ALDRICH, Ann; See Meaker, Marijane.

ALDRICH, T.B. *Still Water Tragedy.* 1880. Houghton Mifflin. 1st. VG. M20. $34.00.

ALDRIDGE, Alan. *Gnole.* 1991. Heinemann. 1st. inscr. ils Miller/Willock. F/dj. T10. $50.00.

ALDRIDGE, Janet. *Eight Rings on His Tail.* 1956. Viking. 1st. sgn. ils Kurt Wiese. VG/dj. M20. $30.00.

ALDRIN, Col. Edwin E. Buzz Jr. *Return to Earth.* 1973. NY. Random House. BCE. b/w photos. 8vo. 338p. VG/chipped. clipped dj. K5. $12.00.

ALEXANDER, Bruce. *Watery Grave.* 1996. NY. Putnam. 1st. NF/NF. G8. $20.00.

ALEXANDER, Bruce (Bruce Cook). *Death of a Colonial.* 1999. NY. Putnam. 1st. sgn. VF/VF. T2. $25.00.

ALEXANDER, Bruce (Bruce Cook). *Person or Persons Unknown.* 1997. NY. Putnam. 1st. sgn. VF/VF. T2. $26.00.

ALEXANDER, Charles C. *The Ku Klux Klan in the Southwest.* 1966. Lexington. Univ of KY Press. 1st pb ed. wrps. NF. B2. $25.00.

ALEXANDER, David. *A Sound of Horses. The World of Racing from Eclipse to Kelso.* 1966. Indianapolis. Bobbs Merrill. 1st. VG/G. O3. $45.00.

ALEXANDER, Frank and Heidi Siegmund Cuda. *Got Your Back Up.* 1998. NY. St. Martin. UP. wrp. F. B2. $25.00.

ALEXANDER, Gary. *Unfunny Money.* 1989. NY. Walker. 1st. VF/VF. T2. $8.00.

ALEXANDER, Kent. *Count Down to Glory.* 1989. Los Angeles. Price Stern Sloan. 1st. ils. 185p. VG/dj. K5. $25.00.

ALEXANDER, Kent. *Heroes of the Wild West.* 1992. NY. Mallard. 1st. NF/VG+. R16. $50.00.

ALEXANDER, L.M. *Candy.* 1954. Dodd Mead. 1st. ils Rockwell Kent. red/wht cloth. VG. B27. $150.00.

ALEXANDER, Lloyd. *First Two Lives of Lukas-Kasha.* 1978. Dutton. 1st (stated). sgn. 213p. rust cloth. NF/dj. T5. $45.00.

ALEXANDER, Lloyd. *Illyrian Adventure.* 1986. Dutton. 1st. 132p. F/dj. D4. $40.00.

ALEXANDER, Lloyd. *Kestrel.* 1982. Dutton. 1st. 8vo. 244p. gr brd. VG/dj. T5. $25.00.

ALEXANDER, Lloyd. *Marvelous Misadventures of Sebastian.* 1970. Dutton. 1st. 8vo. 204p. F/VG. T5. $30.00.

ALEXANDER, Lynne. *Safe Houses.* 1985. Atheneum. 1st. F/F. H11. $20.00.

ALEXANDER, Mary. *Life on the Astral.* 1976. Vantage. 153p. VG/VG. B29. $3.50.

ALEXANDER, Michael. *Discovering the New World.* (1976). NY. Harper. 1st Am. lg 4to. 224p. cloth. F3. $25.00.

ALEXANDER, Sidney. *The Celluloid Asylum.* 1951. Bobbs Merrill. 1st. dj missing a large chunk at the top of the spine. NF/NF. chipped. M25. $45.00.

ALEXANDER, Sue. *Lila on the Landing.* 1987. Clarion. 1st. ils Ellen Eagle. NF/VG. B36. $13.00.

ALEXIE, Sherman. *First Indian on the Moon.* 1993. NY. Hanging Loose Press. pbo simultaneous w/hc. sgn on title page. F in pict wrp. D10. $35.00.

ALEXIE, Sherman. *Old Shirts and New Skins.* (1993). Los Angeles. UCLA. pb orig. ed/ils by Elizabeth Woody. author's 3rd book of poetry. pict wrp. sgn by author. F. B3. $100.00.

ALEXIE, Sherman. *Reservation Blues.* 1995. NY. Atlantic Monthly Press. review copy. sgn. author's 2nd novel. F/F. D10. $45.00.

ALEXIE, Sherman. *The Lone Ranger and Tonto Fistfight in Heaven.* 1993. NY. Atlantic Monthly. 1st. F/F. M23. $45.00.

ALEXIE, Sherman. *The Summer of Black Widows.* (1996). NY. Hanging Loose Press. 1st. issued simultaneously w/pb ed. sgn by author. F/F. B3. $50.00.

ALEXIE, Sherman. *Water Flowing Home.* 1996. Boise. ID. Limberlost Press. 1st trade ed. 1/400 copies in wrp. sgn by author. F. O11. $65.00.

ALGER, Horatio. *Shifting for Himself.* nd. NY. Hurst & Co. G. A16. $10.00.

ALGER, Horatio. *Tattered Tom; or, Story of a Street Arab.* 1871. Boston. Loring. brn cloth. M20. $25.00.

ALGER, Horatio Jr. *A Boy's Fortune.* John C. Winston Co. 12mo impressed pictorial cover in red & blue against tan. 1909 presentation on endpaper. 325p. G. H1. $15.00.

ALGREN, Nelson. *Man with the Golden Arm.* 1956. NY. Cardinal/Pocket. MTI. 2nd. VG/wrp. C9. $20.00.

ALGREN, Nelson. *Never Come Morning.* 1942. NY. Harper. 1st author's 2nd novel. VG+. B2. $45.00.

ALGREN, Nelson. *The Last Carousel.* 1973. NY. Putnam. 1st. F/NF. D10. $45.00.

ALGREN, Nelson. *Who Lost an American?* 1963. NY. Macmillan. 1st. F/F. B2. $45.00.

ALKEN, Henry. *National Sports of Great Britian.* 1903. London. Metheun. 12mo. 50 pl. VG. O3. $38.00.

ALLABY, Michael (ed). *The Concise Oxford Dictionary of Botany.* 1992. Oxford. np. sc. 5000+entries. 442p. F. B26. $12.00.

ALLAIN, Marcel. *Juve in the Dock.* 1926. David McKay. 1st. VG. G8. $25.00.

ALLAIN, Marcel. *Silent Executioner.* nd. NY. Morrow. 1st thus. F/F. G8. $12.50.

ALLAN, John B.; See Westlake, Donald E.

ALLAN, Mea. *Darwin and His Flowers. The Key to Natural Selection.* 1977. NY. np. 19 color photos. 82 b&w photos & line drawings. 318p. VG+ in dj. B26. $34.00.

ALLAN, Stella. *A Mortal Affair.* 1979. NY. Scribner's. 1st. author's 2nd book. F/F. H11. $15.00.

ALLARD, William Albert. *Vanishing Breed: Photographs of the Cowboy & the West.* 1982. Little, Brn. photos. 144p. AN. J2. $135.00.

ALLARTON, G. *Mysteries of Medical Life; Or, Doctors & Their Doings.* 1856. London. 141p. VG. E6. $75.00.

ALLBEURY, Ted. *A Choice of Enemies.* 1973. London. Peter Davies. 1st English ed. author's 1st novel. VF/dj. M15. $175.00.

ALLBEURY, Ted. *Alpha List.* 1979. Metheun. 1st Am ed. NF/NF. G8. $10.00.

ALLBEURY, Ted. *Choice of Enemies.* 1972. St. Martin. 1st. author's 1st novel. F/NF. M15. $100.00.

ALLBEURY, Ted. *Where all the Girls Are Sweeter.* 1975. London. Peter Davies. 1st. F/dj. M15. $150.00.

ALLEGRETTO, Michael. *Blood Relative.* 1992. NY. Scribner's. 1st. F/F. G8. $17.50.

ALLEGRETTO, Michael. *Blood Stone.* 1988. NY. Scribner's. 1st. sgn. F in F dj. D10. $45.00.

ALLEGRETTO, Michael. *Shadow House.* (1994). NY. Carroll & Graf. 1st. sgn & dated in the month of pub. F/F. B3. $40.00.

ALLEN, Betsy; Connie Blair & Serial pen name for; See Cavana, Betty.

ALLEN, Captain Quincy. *Outdoor Chums on a Houseboat.* 1913. NY. Grosset & Dunlap. G+. A16. $7.50.

ALLEN, Charlotte Vale. *Intimate Friends.* 1983. McClelland Stewart. 1st. sgn. NF/clip. A14. $21.00.

ALLEN, David A. *Infrared; The New Astronomy.* 1975. NY. Falstead Press. 8vo. ils w/photos & diagrams. bkplt removed from ffep. 228p. VG/VG. K5. $15.00.

ALLEN, Francis H. *A Bibliography of Henry David Thoreau.* 1908. Boston and NY. Houghton Mifflin Co. 1908. 8vo. 201p. ftspc & folding facs. red cloth & paper spine label. lst ed. #478/530 copies. Mostly unopened. minor rubbing. VG to F. L5. $250.00.

ALLEN, Garrison. *Royal Cat.* 1995. London. Kensington. 1st. F/F. G8. $12.50.

ALLEN, Hervey. *Action at Aquila.* 1938. NY. Farrar & Rinehart. 1st. 369p. NF. M8. $45.00.

ALLEN, Hervey. *Isrefel: The Life and Times of Edgar Allan Poe.* 1934. np. Farrar & Rinehart. 1st issue in 1 volume. many ils. spine darkening. 748p. VG. B15. $60.00.

ALLEN, Hervey. *Toward the Morning.* 1948. Farrar Rinehart. 1st. sgn/dtd 1945. NF/VG. T11. $40.00.

ALLEN, Irene. *Quaker Testimony.* 1996. NY. St. Martin. 1st. F/F. G8. $20.00.

ALLEN, Isabel. *Circling Africa.* 1929. Boston. Marshall Jones. 1st. F/G. B11. $45.00.

ALLEN, Lois. *Bear for Alice.* 1970. Hawthorn. 1st. ils Lois Allen. VG/dj. P2. $12.50.

ALLEN, Raymond. *Medical Education & the Changing Order.* 1946. NY. 1st. 142p. dj. A13. $20.00.

ALLEN, Thomas B. *Blue & the Gray.* 1992. NGS. photos Sam Abell. VG/dj. M17. $17.50.

ALLEN, W. E. D. *Russian Embassies to the Georgian Kings (1589 – 1605).* 1970. Cambridge. Hakluyt Society. Second Series. blue cloth 8vo. gilt spine titles and cover decorations. 640p. NF. lightly worn dj. P4. $65.00.

ALLEN, Walter. *Ulysses S. Grant.* 1901. NY/Boston. Houghton Mifflin. 1st. orig cloth. 151p. VG. some stains. M8. $45.00.

ALLENDE, Isabel. *Eva Luna.* 1988. NY. Knopf. 1st. winner of 1989 American Book Award. VF/F. H11. $40.00.

ALLENDE, Isabel. *Of Love and Shadows.* 1987. NY. Knopf. 1st. NF/NF dj. M19. $25.00.

ALLENDE, Isabel. *Paula.* (1995). NY. Harper Collins. 1st. sgn by author. F/F. B3. $35.00.

ALLENDE, Isabel. *The House of Spirits.* (1985). NY. Knopf. 1st. author's 1st novel. sgn by author. F/F. B3. $125.00.

ALLENDE, Isabel. *The House of Spirits.* 1985. NY. Knopf. 1st. author's 1st book. shadow on front brd. NF/F. H11. $85.00.

ALLENDE, Isabel. *The Infinite Plan.* 1993. NY. Harper Collins. 1st. F/F. H11. $20.00.

ALLINGHAM, Margery. *Allingham Case-Book.* 1969. Morrow. 1st Am. G+/dj. G8. $20.00.

ALLINGHAM, Margery. *Coroner's Pidgin.* 1945. London. Heinemann. 1st. dj has small chips at spine ends. several short closed tears and light wear along edges. VF/dj. M15. $125.00.

ALLINGHAM, Margery. *Flowers For The Judge.* 1946. NY. Avon. pb ed. Mystery Monthly No. 35. F/wrp. M15. $50.00.

ALLINGHAM, Margery. *Tether's End.* 1958. Doubleday. 1st. VG/dj. P3. $30.00.

ALLINGHAM, Margery. *The Black Dudley Murder.* 1929. Garden City. Doubleday Crime Club. 1st Am ed. NF/dj. M15. $65.00.

ALLIS, Oswald T. *Prophecy & the Church.* 1972. 339p. VG/wrp. B29. $8.00.

ALLISON, Clyde; See Knowles, William.

ALLISON, Dorothy. *Bastard Out of Carolina.* (1992). NY. Dutton. 1st. F/F. B3. $140.00.

ALLISON, Dorothy. *Cavedweller.* (1998). NY. Dutton. 1st. F/F. B3. $30.00.

ALLISON, Dorothy. *Two or Three Things I Know for Sure.* 1995. NY. Dutton. 1st. sgn. F in F dj. D10. $45.00.

ALLYN, Doug. *All Creatures Dark and Dangerous.* 1999. Norfolk. Crippen & Landru. 1st. 1/200 numbered copies. sgn. VF/VF. T2. $40.00.

ALLYN, Doug. *Black Water.* 1996. NY. St. Martin. 1st. dj. minor rubbing at spines. F/F. H11. $15.00.

ALLYN, Doug. *Motown Underground.* 1993. NY. St. Martin. 1st. F/F. H11. $30.00.

ALLYN, Doug. *The Cheerio Killings.* 1989. NY. St. Martin. 1st. author's 1st book. VF/VF. H11. $80.00.

ALMANZAR, Alcedo & Brian Stickney. *The Coins and Paper Money of El Salvador.* 1973. Texas. Almanzar's Coins. 1st. 86p. G/wrp. F3. $10.00.

ALMEIDA, Manuel Lopes De. *Noticias Historicas De Portugal E Brasil.* 1961. Coimbra. 361p. uncut. slightly soiled wht cover. contents VG. F3. $30.00.

ALMOND, Linda Stevens. *When Peter Rabbit Went A-Fishing.* 1923. Altemus. 1st? ils Margaret Campbell Hoopees. VG/dj. M5. $85.00.

ALOE, Alfred. *Twelfth US Infantry 1798 – 1919: Its Story by Its Men.* 1919. US Infantry. NY. 1st. ils/rosters. 425p. VG. S16. $65.00.

ALOTTA, Robert I. *Civil War Justice: Union Army Executions Under Lincoln.* 1989. Wht Mane Pub. 1st. F/dj. A14. $21.00.

ALOTTA, Robert Ignatius. *Stop the Evil, A Civil War History of Desertion and Murder.* 1978. San Rafael. CA. Presidio Press. 1st. orig cloth. ils. 202p. NF/NF. M8. $35.00.

ALPERIN, Morton & George P. Sutton, editors. *Advanced Propulsion Systems.* 1959. NY. Pergamon. sm 4to. poi stamped on page edges. text figures. 237p. VG/chipped dj. K5. $65.00.

ALSBERG, Henry G. (ed.) *New Mexico, A Guide to the Colorful State.* 1953. NY. Hastings House. lt edgewear. front map ep. ils & maps. 471p. VG in torn dj. B18. $25.00.

ALSBERG, John & Rodolfo Petschek. *Ancient Sculpture from Western Mexico.* 1969. Berkeley. Nicole Gallery. 2nd printing. portfolio. 135p. F/G chipped. F3. $85.00.

ALSON, Peter. *Confessions of an Ivy League Bookie.* 1996. NY. Crown. 1st. author's 1st book. VF/VF. H11. $30.00.

ALTHER, Lisa. *Bedrock.* 1990. Knopf. 1st. F/NF. T12. $35.00.

ALTHER, Lisa. *Original Sins.* 1981. Knopf. 1st. F/NF. H11. $20.00.

ALTMAN, Stuart A. *Social Communication Among Primates.* 1974. Chicago. 3rd. 293p. VG. S15. $15.00.

ALTROCCHI, Julia Cooley. *Wolves Against the Moon.* 1957. Pageant Book Co. 572p. F/dj. A17. $25.00.

ALTSCHULE, Mark. *Essays on Rise & Decline of Bedside Medicine.* 1989. Phil. 1st. 458p. A13. $30.00.

ALVAREZ, Eugene. *Travel on the Southern Antebellum Railroads 1828 – 1860.* 1974. University, AL. Univ of Alabama Press. 1st. orig cloth. plates. ils. 221p. VG/VG. M8. $35.00.

ALVAREZ, Julia. *How the Garcia Girls Lost Their Accents.* 1991. Chapel Hill. Algonquin. 1st. author's 1st book. F/VF. H11. $95.00.

ALVAREZ, Julia. *The Other Side, El Otro Lado.* (1995). NY. Dutton. 1st. sgn & dated by author. promo postcard laid in. F/F. B3. $40.00.

ALVAREZ, Julia. *Yo!* 1997. Chapel Hill. Algonquin Books. 1st. sgn. F in F dj. D10. $40.00.

AMBLER, Eric. *Dirty Story.* 1967. London. head. 1st. Jacket has tiny wear at corners. F/dj. M15. $60.00.

AMBLER, Eric. *Doctor Frigo.* 1974. Atheneum. 1st Am ed. VG/VG. G8. $15.00.

AMBLER, Eric. *Kind of Anger.* 1964. Atheneum. 1st Am ed. VG+/VG. G8. $25.00.

AMBLER, Eric. *Light of Day.* 1963. Knopf. 1st Am. F/VG. G8. $25.00.

AMBLER, Eric. *The Care of Time.* 1981. NY. Farrar. 1st. UPC in wrappers. F. M15. $75.00.

AMBLER, Eric. *The Siege of the Villa Lipp.* 1977. NY. Random House. 1st ed. 2nd printing. 275p. NF/NF. D4. $20.00.

AMBLER, Eric. *The Story So Far: Memories and Other Fictions.* 1993. London. Weidenfeld & Nicolson. 1st. VF/dj. M15. $35.00.

AMBROSE, Stephen E. *Crazy Horse & Custer.* 1975. Doubleday. 1st. quarter bl cloth. F/NF. T11. $100.00.

AMBROSE, Stephen E. *Undaunted Courage.* 1996. NY. S&S. sgn 1st ed. dated. F/F. M23. $400.00.

AMES, Delano. *Death of a Fellow Traveller.* 1950. NY. Rinehart. 1st Am ed. VG/VG. G8. $20.00.

AMIS, Kingsley. *Crime of the Century.* 1987. Mysterious. 1st Am. NF/dj. G8. $15.00.

AMIS, Kingsley. *The James Bond Dossier.* 1965. NY. New American Library. BCE. F/F. T2. $4.00.

AMIS, Martin. *Einstein's Monsters.* 1987. NY. Harmony. 1st Am. sgn. rem mk. F/F. D10. $50.00.

AMIS, Martin. *Einstein's Monsters.* 1987. NY. Harmony Books. 1st. sgn. rem mk. F in F dj. D10. $50.00.

AMIS, Martin. *Information.* 1995. London. Cape. 1st. sgn. F/dj. O11. $35.00.

AMIS, Martin. *London Fields.* 1989. NY. Harmony. 1st Am. sgn. F/F. D10. $50.00.

AMIS, Martin. *Night Train.* 1998. NY. Harmony Books. 1st Am ed. sgn by author. F/F. O11. $35.00.

AMIS, Martin. *Other People: A Mystery Story.* 1981. NY. Viking. 1st Am. NF/VG+. G8. $15.00.

AMIS, Martin. *The Information.* (1995). London. Flamingo. 1st British ed. true first. F/F. B3. $40.00.

AMIS, Martin. *The Rachel Papers.* 1974. NY. Knopf. 1st. author's 1st book. sgn on title pg. book Is slanted. slight soiling. dj chipped. NF/NF. H11. $260.00.

AMIS, Martin. *Time's Arrow.* 1991. London. Cape. 1st. sgn. F/F. D10. $45.00.

AMIS, Martin. *Time's Arrow.* 1991. NY. Harmony/Crown. 1st. sgn. F/dj. O11. $35.00.

AMOS, James. *The Memorial.* 1989. NY. Crown. 1st. F in F dj. B2. $35.00.

AMUNDSEN, Roald & Lincoln Ellsworth. *First Crossing of the Polar Sea.* 1928. NY. later ed. 324p. G/some wear. B18. $45.00.

ANASTASSIADES, Michael, editor. *Solar Eclipses and the Ionosphere.* 1970. NY. Plenum Press. text figures. 4to. 309p. VG/cloth. K5. $30.00.

ANATOLE, Ray; See Weiss, Joe.

ANAYA, Rudolfo. *Albuquerque.* 1992. Albuquerque. Univ of New Mexico Press. 1st. sgn. VF/VF. T2. $35.00.

ANAYA, Rudolfo. *Jalamanta.* (1996). NY. Warner. ARC. pict wrp. sgn by author. F. B3. $40.00.

ANCKARSVARD, Karin. *Mysterious Schoolmaster.* 1959. Harcourt Brace. 1st Am. 8vo. 190p. G+/dj. T5. $25.00.

ANDERSEN, Hans Christian. *Snow Queen.* 1979. NY. 1st Am. adapted Naomi Lewis. ils Errol Le Cain. VG/dj. M17. $17.50.

ANDERSEN, Hans Christian. *The Little Match Girl.* 1944. NY. Grosset & Dunlap. ils by Gustaf Tenggren. sm 4to. color pict bds. dj ditto. incsr. 26p. NF/VG. D6. $50.00.

ANDERSEN, Hemming. *Historic Scientific Instruments in Denmark.* 1995. Copenhagen. Royal Danish Academy Sci & Letters. 446p. wrp. K5. $75.00.

ANDERSEN, Kurt. *Turn of the Century.* 1998. Random House. ARC. F/WRP. M25. $45.00.

ANDERSON, A.W. *Coming of the Flowers.* nd. FSY. 1st Am? 12mo. VG/dj. A2. $16.00.

ANDERSON, Alston. *All God's Children.* 1965. Bobbs Merrill. 1st. Lightly rubbed jacket that has a dime-size chip missing head of the spine. F/dj. M25. $60.00.

ANDERSON, Anne. *Aucassin and Nicolette, Translated and Edited with an Introduction by Harold Child.* 1911. London. Adam and Charles Black. 1st. sm 4to. white cloth w/gilt. floral design. 6 color plates. teg. 132p. NF. D6. $125.00.

ANDERSON, Bernhard. *Understanding the Old Testament.* 1957. Prentice Hall. 551p. G/worn dj. B29. $18.00.

ANDERSON, Bette Roda. *Weather in the West; from the Midcontinent to the Pacific.* 1975. Palo Alto, Ca. American West Publishing. 1st. ils w/photos. many color & diagrams. 4to. 223p. VG in quarter vinyl & cloth covered bds in slipcase. K5. $20.00.

ANDERSON, Frank J. *Illustrated History of the Herbals.* 1977. NY. Columbia. ils/biblio/index. 270p. F. H10. $35.00.

ANDERSON, Frank J. *Illustrated Treasury of Cultivated Flowers.* 1979. Crown. 50 full-p pl. AN/dj. A10. $40.00.

ANDERSON, Frank J. *Latin Jive.* 1984. Spartanburg. Kitemaug. mini. 1/100. red cloth/paper chemise. B24. $50.00.

ANDERSON, Gary Clayton. *Little Crow.* 1986. St. Paul, MN. MN Hist Soc. dj. A19. $25.00.

ANDERSON, Isabel. *The Great Sea Horse.* 1909. Boston. Little, Brn. 1st. 4to. red cloth w/gilt fish & merbaby designs. teg. 24 color plates. tissue guards. 251p. VG+. D6. $155.00.

ANDERSON, Jack. *Control.* 1988. NY. Zebra. F/F. H11. $25.00.

ANDERSON, James Douglas. *Making the American Thoroughbred.* 1916. Norwood, MA. Plimpton. 1st. VG. O3. $135.00.

ANDERSON, James H. *Life & Letters of Judge Thomas J. Anderson & His Wife.* 1904. np. 1st. ils. 535p. G. B18. $22.50.

ANDERSON, James L. *Cannibal: Photographic Audacity.* 1970. Sydney. Reed. VG/dj. S5. $25.00.

ANDERSON, Jim. *Billarooby.* 1988. NY. Ticknor. 1st. F/F. H11. $20.00.

ANDERSON, John and Hilary Hevenor. *Burning Down the House.* 1987. NY. Norton. 1st. F/NF. B2. $30.00.

ANDERSON, Kent. *Liquor, Guns & Ammo.* 1998. Tucson. Dennis McMillan. 1st. sgn. VF/VF. T2. $30.00.

ANDERSON, Kent. *Night Dogs.* 1998. Bantam. 1st thus. 1/1800. sgn. F/dj. R14. $50.00.

ANDERSON, Kent. *Night Dogs.* 1998. NY. Bantam. 1st. ARC. F. D10. $20.00.

ANDERSON, Kent. *Night Dogs.* 1996. Tucson. Dennis McMillan. 1st. sgn. VF/VF. T2. $150.00.

ANDERSON, Kent. *Night Dogs.* 1996. NY. Bantam. 1st trade ed. sgn. VF/VF. T2. $25.00.

ANDERSON, Kent. *Sympathy for the Devil.* 1987. Doubleday. ARC/1st. sgn. F/wrp. L3. $350.00.

ANDERSON, Kent. *Sympathy for the Devil.* 1987. Garden City. Doubleday. 1st. author's 1st novel. sgn. VF/VF. T2. $150.00.

ANDERSON, Murphy, & Burgess, eds. *Justification by Faith; Lutherans and Catholics in Dialogue VII.* 1985. Ausburg. pb. 381p. VG. B29. $5.00.

ANDERSON, Poul. *Infinite Voyage: Man's Future in Space.* 1969. NY. Crowell-Collier. ils. 160p. VG/dj. K5. $18.00.

ANDERSON, Poul. *Operation Chaos.* 1971. Doubleday. 1st. F/NF. M23. $35.00.

ANDERSON, Poul. *Three Hearts and Three Lions.* 1961. NY. Doubleday. 1st. Edward Gorey dj cover. VG/VG. M19. $125.00.

ANDERSON, Scott. *Triage.* 1998. NY. Scribner. 1st. author's 1st novel. sgn. VF/VF. T2. $25.00.

ANDREAE, Christine. *Grizzly.* 1994. NY. St. Martin. 1st. VF/VF. T2. $20.00.

ANDREWS, Roy Chapman. *Nature's Ways: How Nature Takes Care of Its Own.* 1951. NY. 206p. VG. A17. $15.00.

ANDREWS, Roy Chapman. *On the Trail of Ancient Man.* 1926. Putnam. 58 photos/index. 376p. teg. gr cloth. K1. $85.00.

ANDREWS, Sarah. *A Fall in Denver.* (1995). NY. Scribner. 1st. author's 2nd book. F/F. B3. $20.00.

ANDREWS, Sarah. *A Fall in Denver.* 1995. NY. Scribner. 1st. sgn. VF/VF. T2. $25.00.

ANDREWS, Sarah. *A Fall in Denver.* 1995. NY. Scribner. 1st. review copy. NF/NF. G8. $20.00.

ANDREWS, Sarah. *Only Flesh & Bones.* (1998). NY. St. Martin. 1st. F/F. B3. $15.00.

ANDREWS, Sarah. *Tensleep.* (1994). NY. Otto Penzler. 1st. author's 1st book. F/F. B3. $50.00.

ANDREWS, Val. *Sherlock Holmes and the Man Who Lost Himself.* 1997. London. Breese Books. 1st. VF/pict wrp. T2. $11.00.

ANDRIANCE, Guy W. & Fred R. Brison. *Propagation of Horticultural Plants.* 1955 (1939). NY. 2nd. ils in text. 298p. corners bumped. o/w F. B26. $22.50.

ANDRUS, Jeff. *Tracer, Inc.* 1994. NY. Scribner's. 1st. author's 1st book. VF/F. H11. $30.00.

ANGELL, Roger. *Five Seasons: A Baseball Companion.* 1977. S&S. 1st. poi on ffep. author's 2nd collection of essays. NF/clip dj. M25. $35.00.

ANGELL, Roger. *Late Innings: A Baseball Companion.* 1982. NY. S&S. 1st. VG+/NF. R16. $35.00.

ANGELOU, Maya. *Gather Together in My Name.* 1974. NY. Random House. 1st. sgn. NF/NF dj sunned at spine. M25. $100.00.

ANGELOU, Maya. *I Know Why the Caged Bird Sings.* 1969. Random House. 1st. top stained red. author's 1st book. NF/NF. dj slightly sunned at spine. M25. $250.00.

ANGELOU, Maya. *I Wouldn't Take Nothing for My Journey Now.* 1993. NY. Random House. 1st. F in F dj. B2. $25.00.

ANGELOU, Maya. *My Painted House My Friendly Chicken and Me.* 1994. NY. Clarkson Potter. 1st. hc. VG/NF. A28. $19.95.

ANGELOU, Maya. *Oh Pray My Wings Are Gonna Fit Me Well.* 1975. Random House. 1st. sgn. F/dj. M25. $125.00.

ANGELOU, Maya. *Shaker, Why Don't You Sing; More Poems.* (1983). NY. Random House. 1st. F/NF lt soiling. crease on inside front flap. B3. $75.00.

ANGELOU, Maya. *The Heart of a Woman.* 1981. NY. Random House. 1st. F/F. M25. $45.00.

ANGLE, Barbara. *Those That Mattered.* 1994. NY. Crown. 1st. author's 1st book. F/VF. H11. $25.00.

ANGLE, Paul M. (ed). *Created Equal? The Complete Lincoln Douglas Debates of 1858.* 1958. Chicago. later issue. 2nd printing. 422p. VG in torn dj. B18. $17.50.

ANGLUND, Joan Walsh. *Spring Is a New Beginning.* 1963. NY. Harcourt Brace & World. VG in dj. A16. $6.00.

ANNA, Timothy. *The Fall of the Royal Government in Peru.* 1979. Lincoln. Univ of Nebraska Press. 1st. 291p. G/chipped. F3. $20.00.

ANNEQUIN, Guy. *Civilization of the Maya.* (1978). Geneva. Ferni. 1st Eng. photos/ils. 234p. F3. $20.00.

ANONYMOUS. *A Treatise of the Faith of the Freewill Baptists: With an Apendix, Containing a Summary of Their Usages in Church Government.* Dover, The Trustees of The Freewill Baptist Connection. William Burr, Printer. 1841. 24mo (aprox. 5 inches tall). 160p. full calf. third ed. 2 tiny holes in spine. rubbed. minor foxing & stain. G to VG. L5. $45.00.

ANONYMOUS. *Book of Intertype Faces Shown in Series with One-Line Examples.* NY. Intertype Corporation. (1927). 4to. 226p. printed gr paper-covered brd. 1st ed (?) title on front brd Is *Book of Intertype Faces 1928.* small nick on edge of brd. NF. L5. $50.00.

ANONYMOUS. *Lives and Exploits of the Most Noted Highwaymen, Robbers and Murderers, of All Nations, Drawn from the Most Authentic Sources and Brought Down to the Present Time.* 1854. Hartford. Silas Andrus & Son. 1854. 12mo. 287p. ils. blk cloth with gilt decorated spine. later printing. small spine label. top of spine sltly chiped/torn. G to VG. L5. $50.00.

ANONYMOUS. *The Children's Carnival, Including Stories of Travel, Stories of Adventure, Stories of Hunting, Stories of All Kinds for Boys and Girls...To Instruct, Please and Amuse Our Lads and Lasses.* (1891). (NY?). Juvenile Publishing Company. Tall. square 8vo. 178p. Chromolitho ftspc. b&w ils. chromolitho paper covered brd with red cloth spine. 1st ed (?). extremities sltly worn. G to VG. L5. $20.00.

ANSA, Tina McElroy. *The Hand I Fan With.* 1996. NY. Doubleday. ARC. wrps. NF. B2. $35.00.

ANSA, Tina McElroy. *Ugly Ways.* (1993). NY. Harcourt Brace. 1st. author's 2nd book. F/F. B3. $50.00.

ANSAY, A. Manette. *Midnight Champagne.* 1999. NY. Morrow. 1st. UP. F. D10. $10.00.

ANSCOMBE, Roderick. *The Secret Life of Laszio, Count Dracula.* 1994. NY. Hyperion. 1st. VF/VF. T2. $12.00.

ANSELL, Mary. *Happy Garden.* 1912. London. Cassell. 224p. decor cloth. VG. A10. $18.00.

ANSHAW, Carol. *Aquamarine.* 1992. Boston. Houghton Mifflin. 1st. author's 1st book. VF/VF. H11. $40.00.

ANSON, Jay. *The Amityville Horror.* 1977. Englewood Cliffs. Prentice Hall. 1st. F/F. T2. $25.00.

ANTHOLOGY. *Little Verses, Big Names with an Introduction by Woodrow Wilson.* 1915. NY. George Doran. 1st. sm 4to. red cloth w/gilt decor. asst illustrators. 305p. G+. D6. $48.00.

ANTHOLOGY, Childrens. *The Home Story Book.* 1857. Philadelphia. Lindsay & Blakiston. 8vo. gr cloth w/gilt decor. ils. period fonts. 183p. VG. D6. $60.00.

ANTHONY, Edgar Waterman. *History of Mosaics.* 1935. Boston. Porter Sargent. 80 b&w pl. 333p. gilt blk cloth. F1. $35.00.

ANTHONY, Edward. *Every Dog Has His Say.* 1947. Watson-Guptill. 1st. ils Morgan Dennis. NF/dj. A21. $95.00.

ANTHONY, Evelyn. *Cardinal & the Queen.* 1968. Coward McCann. 1st. F/NF. M19. $25.00.

ANTHONY, Evelyn. *Company of Saints.* 1984. NY. Putnam. 1st Am ed. VG/VG. G8. $10.00.

ANTHONY, Evelyn. *Doll's House.* 1992. NY. Harper. 1st. NF/NF. G8. $10.00.

ANTHONY, Evelyn. *Legend.* 1969. NY. Coward. 1st Am ed. VG/VG-. G8. $10.00.

ANTHONY, Evelyn. *Persian Price.* 1975. NY. Coward. 1st Am ed. VG+/VG. G8. $10.00.

ANTHONY, Gordon. *The Sleeping Princess. Camera Studies, with Text by Nada Benois, Arnold Haskell and Constant Lambert.* 1940. London. George Rutledge & Sons. folio. 50 p text + 62 mtd photographic plates. orig bl cloth. corners a bit bumped. K1. $100.00.

ANTHONY, Katharine. *Dolly Madison: Her Life & Times.* 1949. Doubleday. 1st. 426p. VG/clip. V3. $16.00.

ANTHONY, Katharine. *Susan B. Anthony: Her Personal History & Her Era.* 1954. Garden City. Doubleday. 1st. 521p. VG/torn. V3. $11.50.

ANTHONY, Patricia. *Cold Allies.* 1993. HBJ. 2nd. author's 1st novel. AN/dj. M21. $10.00.

ANTHONY, Piers. *Ghost.* 1986. NY. Tom Doherty. 1st. VG/dj. A23. $22.00.

ANTHONY, Piers. *Unicorn Point.* 1989. Ace Putnam. 1st. 303p. AN/dj. M21. $15.00.

ANTHONY, Piers & Roberto Fuentes. *Dead Morn.* 1990. Houston. Tafford. 1st. NF/VG. R16. $25.00.

ANTON, Ferdinand. *Ancient Mexican Art.* 1969. NY. Putnam. 1st Am ed. lg 4to. ils photos b/w & color. 309p. F/chipped. F3. $100.00.

ANTON, Ferdinand. *Art of the Maya.* 1978. London. Thames & Hudson. 1st. lg 4to. 344p. F/chipped. F3. $100.00.

ANTUNES, Antonio Lobo. *An Explanation of the Birds.* 1991. NY. Grove Weidenfeld. 1st. ARC. F. D10. $10.00.

ANYI, Wang. *Baotown.* 1989. NY. Norton. 1st. author's 1st book. trans Martha Avery. F/VF. H11. $15.00.

APFEL, Necia H. *The Moon and Its Exploration.* 1982. NY. Franklin Watts. ex lib in pict cloth. juvenile. photos. some color. and diagrams. 8vo. 72p. G. K5. $16.00.

APOSTOLOU, Anna. *Murder in Macedon.* 1997. NY. St. Martin. 1st. F/F. G8. $27.50.

APOSTOLOU, Anna. *Murder in Thebes.* 1998. NY. St. Martin. 1st. F/F. G8. $25.00.

APPEL, Allen. *Till the End of Time.* 1990. Doubleday. 1st. NF/dj. A14. $21.00.

APPIA, P.L. *Ambulance Surgeon; Or, Practical Observations.* 1862. Edinburgh. Blk. 266p. xl. G7. $395.00.

APPLEBY, John. *Bad Summer.* 1958. Ives Washburn. 1st. VG. P3. $10.00.

APPLEMAN, Roy. *Okinawa: Last Battle.* 1964. Rutland. 2nd. VG/dj. B5. $35.00.

APPLETON, Budd. *A Guide to Akro Agate Glass.* 1966. Kensington. self-published. oblong 8vo plastic comb bound wraps. Minor spotting on cover. 28p. NVG. H1. $37.50.

APPLETON, Budd. *Akro Agate.* 1972. self-published. 8vo glossy ils. wraps. 120 color plates. 37p. VG. H1. $22.50.

APPLETON, George. *The Oxford Book of Prayer.* 1988. Oxford. pb. 399p. VG. B29. $7.50.

APPLETON, Victor. *Tom Swift and His Diving Seacopter.* 1956. np. Grosset & Dunlap. 1st. prev owner sgn. pc. VG/VG dj. M19. $17.50.

APPLETON, Victor. *Tom Swift & His Motor Boat.* 1910. Grosset & Dunlap. sm8vo. Pictorial cover in standard design with red & black on tan. Owner's name on endpaper. 212p. VG. H1. $8.00.

APSLEY, Lady. *Bridleways Through History.* 1948. London. Hutchinson. 2nd/revised. VG/G. O3. $45.00.

APTHEKER, Herbert. *Mission to Hanoi.* 1966. NY. Internat. sgn. photos. 128p. VG/wrp. R11. $30.00.

AQUILA, Richard. *Wanted Dead or Alive: American West in Popular Culture.* 1996. U IL. 313p. AN. J2. $35.00.

ARCHAMBAULT, A. Margaretta (ed). *Guide Book of Art, Architecture, and Historic Interests in Pennsylvania.* 1924. Philadelphia. John C. Winston. 1st. gilt decor cloth. ils. maps. F in soiled box. B18. $45.00.

ARCHER, Gleason, Jr. *A Survey of Old Testament Introduction.* 1964. Moody. 507p. G. B29. $9.50.

ARCHER, Jeffery. *A Twist in the Tale.* 1988. NY. S&S. 1st. F/F. H11. $25.00.

ARCHER, Jeffery. *Shall We Tell the President?.* 1977. NY. Viking. 1st. F/F-. H11. $30.00.

ARCHER, Kevin M. *History of Santa Monica Fire Dept 1889 – 1989.* 1989. Visalia. self pub. 166p. silver stp fabricoid. D11. $35.00.

ARCHER, M. *Natural History Drawings in the India Office Library.* 1962. London. 4to. ils. 116p. F/VG+. M12. $75.00.

ARCHER, Margaret & Douglas. *Glass Candlesticks.* 1975. Paducah. Collector Books. 1st. 8vo glossy. illustrated wraps. owner's stamp & inked-out price on title page. 108p. VG. H1. $52.50.

ARCHER, Robert. *The Case of the Vanishing Women.* 1942. NY. Howell Soskin. 1st. Some page edges darkened. F/dj. M15. $150.00.

ARCHIBALD, Norman. *Heaven High, Hell Deep, 1917 – 1918.* 1935. NY. wear to paper spine label. 350p. VG. B18. $25.00.

ARDEN, William. *3 Investigators: Mystery of the Moaning Cave.* 1973. Random. lists to Mystery of Monster Mtns. decor brd. VG. P3. $20.00.

ARDIZZONE, Tony. *The Evening News.* 1986. Athens. Univ of GA. 1st. inscr & dated by author. F/F. H11. $25.00.

ARENSBERG, Ann. *Incubus.* 1999. NY. Knopf. 1st. ARC. F. D10. $10.00.

ARENSBERG, Ann. *Sister Wolf.* 1980. NY. Knopf. 1st. author's 1st novel. F in dj. D10. $45.00.

ARIAS, Friar Antonio. *Franciscan Report on the Indians of the Nayarit.* 1975. F3. $15.00.

ARIdjIS, Homero. *Lord of the Last Days. Visions of the Year 1000.* 1995. NY. Morrow. 1st Am ed. sgn. F in F dj. D10. $50.00.

ARJOUNI, Jakob. *One Death to Die.* 1997. Fromm. 1st Am ed. F/F. G8. $20.00.

ARMATAGE, George. *The Horseowner and Stableman's Companion.* 1892. London. Warner. 4th ed. 12mo. VG. O3. $25.00.

ARMER, Laura Adams. *Forest Pool.* 1938. NY. 1st. 40p. VG. B18. $37.50.

ARMER, Laura Adams. *Waterless Mountain.* 1981 (1931). McKay. rprt. 8vo. 212p. Newberry Award. bl cloth. NF/VG. T5. $20.00.

ARMES, Roy. *Patterns of Realism.* 1971. Cranbury. 1st. dj. T9. $18.00.

ARMES, Roy. *Third World Film Making & the West.* 1987. Berkeley. U CA. 381p. VG/wrp. C5. $12.50.

ARMISTEAD, John. *Homecoming For Murder.* 1995. Carroll & Graf. 1st. NF/NF. G8. $12.50.

ARMISTEAD, John. *Legacy of Vengeance.* 1994. NY. Carroll & Graf. 1st. author's 1st book. VF/VF. H11. $30.00.

ARMITAGE, Thomas. *History of the Baptist; Traced by Their Vital Principles and Practices, From the Time of Our Lord and Saviour Jesus Christ to the Present.* 1893. Bryan. Taylor & Co. 160 engravings. 605p. F/detached brds. gilded front cover. B29. $47.00.

ARMS, Dorothy Noyes. *Fishing Memories.* 1938. np. Macmillan. 1st. ils by William Shaldach. NF/VG. M19. $35.00.

ARMSTRONG, Charlotte. *Mischief.* 1950. NY. Coward-McCann. 1st. price clip. F/NF. T2. $30.00.

ARMSTRONG, Charlotte. *The Albatross.* 1957. NY. Coward-McCann. 1st. F/VG dj. M15. $65.00.

ARMSTRONG, Charlotte. *The Chocolate Cobweb.* 1948. Coward-McCann. 1st. lightly worn jacket that Is darkened at the spine. VG/dj. M25. $50.00.

ARMSTRONG, Leroy. *Pictorial Atlas Illustrating the Spanish-American War.* 1899. NY. Cram. ils/maps. 231p. pict cloth. G+. B18. $125.00.

ARMSTRONG, Louis. *Satchmo: My Life in New Orleans.* 1954. Prentice Hall. 1st. 8vo. 240p. F/NF. B20. $45.00.

ARMSTRONG, Margaret. *Murder in Stained Glass.* 1939. NY. Random House. 1st. VG. G8. $27.50.

ARMSTRONG, Neil, Michael Collins & Edwin E. Aldrin Jr. *First on the Moon.* 1970. Boston. Little, Brn. BCE. written w/Gene Farmer & Dora Jane Hamblin. 28 b/w photo ils. 8vo. 511p. VG/chipped. rubbed dj. K5. $16.00.

ARNALL, Franklin M. *The Padlock Collector.* 1988. Claremont. self-published. 5th. 8vo wraps. ils & prices of 1800 padlocks. a few small cover stains. 191p. VG. H1. $18.00.

ARNDT, W. *Bible Difficulties.* 1932. Concordia. 117p. G. B29. $6.50.

ARNOLD, Edwin. *Conversations with Erskine Caldwell.* 1988. U MS. 1st. Literary Conversations series. F/wrp. T11. $22.00.

ARNOLD, Edwin. *Light of Asia.* 1926. Dodd Mead/Bodley Head. 1st. 1/3000. ils Hamzeh Carr. 177p. NF. B20. $60.00.

ARNOLD, Eve. *Marilyn Monroe: An Appreciation.* 1987. Knopf. 1st. ils. F/dj. C9. $150.00.

ARNOLD, Harry L. *Poisonous Plants of Hawaii.* 1973 (1968). Rutland. VT. np. 71p w/24 plate. VG. decor cloth. B26. $26.00.

ARNOLD, Joseph. *Yearbook of the Dept of Agriculture.* 1908. GPO. 822p. brd. G+. A10. $28.00.

ARNOLD, Schuyler. *Wayside Marketing.* 1929. NY. DeLaMare. 123p. VG/dj. A10. $28.00.

ARNOLD, Thurman W. *Bottlenecks of Business.* 1940. Reynal Hitchcock. cloth. M11. $50.00.

ARNOLD, William Harris. *Ventures in Book Collecting.* 1923. NY. Scribner. 1st. ils. 356p. gilt blk cloth/gray brd. VG. F1. $25.00.

ARNOTE, Ralph. *Fast Lane.* 1998. NY. Tom Doherty Forge. AP. F in wrp. B2. $25.00.

ARNSTEIN, Flora J. *Legacy of Hours.* 1927. Grabhorn. 1/250. 12mo. 61p. B20. $35.00.

ARONSON, T. *King In Love: King Edward VII's Mistresses.* 1988. Harper Row. 1st. F/NF. T12. $20.00.

ARRIAGA OCHOA, Antonio. *Escenas Mexicanas Del Siglo XIX.* 1984. Mexico. Edamex. 1st. sm folio. chipped dj. F3. $35.00.

ARRIAZA, Bernardo. *Beyond Death. The Chinchorro Mummies of Ancient Chile.* 1995. DC. Smithsonian Institution Press. 1st. sm 4to. 176p. G/G. F3. $40.00.

ARRIOLA, Jorge Luis. *El Libro De Las Geonimias De Guatemala.* 1973. Guatemala. Seminario. No. 31. dictionary. 710. G/wrp. F3. $35.00.

ARTHUR, Ella Bentley. *My Husband Keeps Telling Me to Go to Hell.* 1954. Hanover. 1st. ils R Taylor. 79p. F/VG+. B20. $25.00.

ARTHUR, R. *End of a Revolution.* 1965. NY. 1st. ils/maps. G/fair. M4. $13.00.

ARTHUR, Robert. *Ghosts & More Ghosts.* 1963. Random. 1st/revised. VG/dj. B36. $10.00.

ARWAS, Victor. *Art Nouveau to Art Deco: The Art of Glass.* 1996. NY. Rizzoli. 1st Am. 4to blk cloth with gilt spine. 150 illustrations. 100 in color. 111p. F/F. H1. $40.00.

ASARO, Catherine. *Primary Inversion.* 1995. NY. TOR. sgn 1st ed. author's 1st novel. F/F. M23. $50.00.

ASBURY, Herbert. *Golden Flood: Informal History of America's First Oil Field.* 1942. Knopf. thick 8vo. 324p. VG/dj. B20. $40.00.

ASBURY, Herbert. *The Barbary Coast.* 1933. np. Garden City. 1st. G+. S19. $45.00.

ASCARRUNZ, Moises. *La Confraternidad Peru Boliviana En El Centario De Ayacucho.* 1925. Lima. Peru. editora la opinion nacional. 1st. b/w photo. orig wrp lacks cover. 319p. G. F3. $25.00.

ASCH, Moses & Alan Lomax. *The Leadbelly Songbook.* 1962. NY. Oak Publications. 1st. VG/lib bdg. M25. $25.00.

ASDELL, S.A. *Cattle Fertility & Sterility.* 1955. Little, Brn. 1st. 227p. VG/dj. N2. $10.00.

ASHBERY, John. *April Galleons.* 1987. NY. Viking. 1st. sgn. F/F. D10. $60.00.

ASHBERY, John. *Flow Chart.* 1991. Knopf. 1st. inscr/dtd 1996. F/dj. R14. $45.00.

ASHBURN, P.M. *History of the Medical Department of the US Army.* 1929. Boston. 1st. 448p. A13. $100.00.

ASHBY, Thomas Almond. *Life of Turner Ashby.* 1914. NY. Neale Pub Co. 1st. orig cloth. 275p. NF. M8. $450.00.

ASHE, Arthur. *Off the Court.* 1981. NAL. 1st. 8vo. 230p. F/NF. B20. $75.00.

ASHFORD, Jeffrey. *Guilt with Honor.* 1982. Walker. 1st Am ed. NF/NF. G8. $15.00.

ASHFORD, Jeffrey. *Illegal Solution.* 1991. NY. St. Martin. 1st Am ed. NF/NF. G8. $12.50.

ASHFORD, Jeffrey. *Recipe for Murder.* 1980. Walker. 1st Am ed. VG/VG. G8. $12.50.

ASHLEY, Clifford W. *The Ashley Book of Knots.* 1953. NY. Doubleday. 1st. ils. 4to. VG/dj clip. R16. $55.00.

ASIMOV, Isaac. *A Whiff of Death.* 1958. NY. Walker. 1st. F/dj. M15. $150.00.

ASIMOV, Isaac. *Asimov's Guide to Halley's Comet.* 1985. NY. Walker. reprint. F/F. T2. $5.00.

ASIMOV, Isaac. *Asimov's Sherlockian Limericks.* 1978. NY. Mysterious Press. 1st. VF/F. T2. $25.00.

ASIMOV, Isaac. *Casebook of the Black Widowers.* 1980. Garden City. Doubleday. 1st. jacket price clipped. F/dj. M15. $45.00.

ASIMOV, Isaac. *Change!* 1981. Houghton Mifflin. 1st. 8vo. 201p. F/dj. W2. $30.00.

ASIMOV, Isaac. *Familiar Poems, Annotated.* 1977. Doubleday. 1st. VG/G. B30. $20.00.

ASIMOV, Isaac. *Foundation's Edge.* 1982. Doubleday. 1st. VG+/clip. A14. $32.00.

ASIMOV, Isaac. *Gods Themselves.* 1977. Norwalk, CT. Easton. reissue 1972 Doubleday 1st. aeg. leather. NF. A14. $35.00.

ASIMOV, Isaac. *Gold.* 1995. Harper Prism. 1st. NF/dj. P3. $20.00.

ASIMOV, Isaac. *How Did We Find Out About Outer Space?* 1977. NY. Walker. juvenile. ex lib in dj. ffep removed. usual lib mks. drawings by David Wool. 8vo. 62p. VG. K5. $5.00.

ASIMOV, Isaac. *Satellites in Outer Space.* 1960. Random. 1st. F/NF. B4. $125.00.

ASIMOV, Isaac. *Sun Shines Bright.* 1981. Garden City. Doubleday. 1st. VG+/clip. A14. $17.50.

ASIMOV, Isaac. *The Union Club Murders.* 1983. Garden city. Doubleday. 1st. Jacket has light wear at corners. F/dj. M15. $50.00.

ASIMOV, Isaac. *Visions of the Universe.* 1981. Montrose, CA. Cosmos Store. intro Carl Sagan. ils Iwasaki. F/VG. B11. $35.00.

ASIMOV, Issac. *Fantastic Voyage II.* 1987. Doubleday. 1st. NF/VG+. S18. $10.00.

ASKEW, Alice & Claude. *Aylmer Vance: Ghost Seer.* 1998. Ashcroft. BC. Ash Tree Press. 1st. VF/VF. T2. $36.00.

ASPREY, Robert B. *War in the Shadows.* 1975. NY. 2 vol. 1475p. dj. E1. $40.00.

ASPRIN, Robert. *The Cold Cash War.* 1977. London. New English Library. 1st British ed. VF/VF. T2. $20.00.

ASPRIN, Robert l. *The Bug Wars.* 1979. NY. St. Martin. 1st. F/VG dj. M19. $17.50.

ASQUITH, Cynthia. *This Mortal Coil.* 1947. Arkham. 1st. VG/dj. B30. $50.00.

ASTASHENKOV, P. T. *Akademik S. P. Korolev.* 1969. Moscow. Izdatelstvo Mashinovtroenie. 8vo. b/w photo ils. Russian text. 208p. VG/torn & rubbed dj. K5. $30.00.

ASTRACHAN, Samuel. *Malaparte in Jassy.* 1989. Wayne State. VG/dj. M17. $15.00.

ASTURIAS, Montenegro. *Earthquake SOS.* 1976. np. Guatemala. b/w photo ils. map. 128p. G/wrp. F3. $10.00.

ATCHISON, Stewart. *Naturalist's Guide to Hiking the Grand Canyon.* 1985. Prentice Hall. ils. 172p. VG+. F7. $15.00.

ATCHISON, Stewart. *Wilderness Called Grand Canyon.* 1991. Voyageur. ils/biblio. 128p. NF/NF. B19. $20.00.

ATCHITY, Kenneth John. *Eterne in Mutabilitie: Unity of the Faerie Queene.* 1972. Archon. 1st. F/clip. N2. $10.00.

ATHAUS, J. *On Paralysis, Neuralgia & Other Affections.* 1864. 3rd. VG. E6. $60.00.

ATHEARN, Robert G. *Forts of the Upper Missouri.* 1967. Englewood Cliffs. 339p. F/dj. M4. $45.00.

ATHEARN, Robert G. *High Country Empire.* 1960. McGraw Hill. F/dj. A19. $35.00.

ATHEARN, Robert G. *Rebel of the Rockies: Denver & Rio Grande Western Railroad.* 1962. Yale. 1st. 8vo. 395p. F/NF. B20. $65.00.

ATHEARN, Robert G. *William Tecumseh Sherman & Settlement of the West.* 1956. Norman. OK. 1st. beige cloth. VG. A14. $14.00.

ATHELING, William; see Blish, James.

ATHERTON, Gertrude. *Rulers of Kings.* 1904. Harper. 1st. VG. M20. $18.00.

ATHERTON, John. *Fly & the Fish.* 1951. NY. Macmillan. 1st. 195p. G. H10. $100.00.

ATHERTON, Nancy. *Aunt Dimity and the Duke.* (1994). NY. Viking. 1st. author's 2nd mystery. sgn by author. F/F. B3. $40.00.

ATKINS, Ace. *Crossroad Blues.* 1998. NY. St. Martin. 1st. VF/dj. M15. $65.00.

ATKINS, Ace. *Crossroad Blues.* 1998. NY. St. Martin. 1st. F/F. M23. $50.00.

ATKINS, Charles. *Risk Factor.* 1999. NY. St. Martin. 1st. sgn. VF/VF. T2. $26.00.

ATKINS, Chet. *Country Gentleman.* 1974. Chicago. 1st. VG/dj. B5. $20.00.

ATKINS, Meg Elizabeth. *Samain.* 1977. London. Cassell. 1st. NF/dj. P3. $25.00.

ATKINSON, Brooks. *Cleo for Short.* 1940. Howell Saskin. sgn. 31p. VG/dj. A21. $30.00.

ATKINSON, Frank B. *Dynamic Dominion: Realignment & Rise.* (1992). Geo Mason U. 518p. VG/dj. B10. $22.50.

ATKINSON, James. *Epitome of the Whole Art of Navigation.* 1782. London. Mount & Page. tables/tangents/secants. 336p. full leather. M10. $125.00.

ATKINSON, Jennifer McCabe. *Eugene O'Neill, A Descriptive Bibliography.* 1974. Pittsburgh. 410p. gilt blk/bl cloth. F1. $60.00.

ATKINSON, Kate. *Behind the Scenes at the Museum.* 1996. St. Martin. 1st Am. NF/dj. M23. $20.00.

ATKINSON, Kate. *Human Crochet.* nd. NY. Picador USA. ARC. 1st Am ed. F/wrp. B2. $35.00.

ATKINSON, Richard C. *Stevens' Handbook of Experimental Psychology.* 1988 (1958). John Wiley. 2 vol. 2nd revised. prt maroon cloth. VG. G1. $125.00.

ATKINSON, Wilmer. *Autobiography.* 1920. Phil. Atkinson. 375p. cloth. A10. $22.00.

ATLEE, Philip; see Philips, James Atlee.

ATTANASIO, A. A. *Beastmarks.* 1984. Willimantic. Mark V. Ziesing. 1st. sgn. VF/VF. T2. $30.00.

ATTANASIO, A. A. *Kingdom of the Grail.* 1992. NY. Harper Collins. 1st. F/dj. T10. $35.00.

ATTANASIO, A. A. *Silent.* 1996. Tucson. Dennis McMillan. 1st. sgn. VF/VF. T2. $30.00.

ATTANASIO, A. A. *Soltis.* 1994. Harper Collins. 1st. F/dj. A23. $35.00.

ATTENBOROUGH, Charles L. *Law of Pawnbroking, With Pawnbrokers' Act.* 1897. London. 1st. brn cloth. M11. $125.00.

ATTENBOROUGH, David. *Bridge to the Past.* 1961. NY. photos. 160p. VG/dj. S15. $12.00.

ATTENBOROUGH, Richard. *In Search of Gandhi.* 1982. London. Bodley Head/Piscataw. 1st. inscr/dtd 1982. ils. F/dj. O11. $65.00.

ATTOE, David. *Lion at the Door.* 1989. Little, Brn. 1st. author's 1st novel. F/F. H11. $30.00.

ATWATER, Caleb. *History of the State of Ohio, Natural & Civil.* (1838). Cincinnati. 2nd. 407p. full leather. B18. $150.00.

ATWOOD, Mae. *In Rupert's Land.* 1970. Toronto. McClelland & Stewart. 1st. F/dj. A26. $25.00.

ATWOOD, Margaret. *Barbed Lyres: Canadian Venomous Verse.* 1990. Porter. 1st. F/dj. T12. $30.00.

ATWOOD, Margaret. *Bluebeard's Egg.* 1983. McClelland Stewart. 1st Canadian. NF/NF. B3. $40.00.

ATWOOD, Margaret. *Bodily Harm.* (1982). NY. S&S. 1st. F/NF. B3. $30.00.

ATWOOD, Margaret. *Bodily Harm.* 1981. Toronto. McClelland & Stewart. 1st. F/F. price clip. B2. $30.00.

ATWOOD, Margaret. *Cat's Eye.* (1989). London. Bloomsbury. 1st UK ed. F/F. B3. $35.00.

ATWOOD, Margaret. *Dancing Girls and Other Stories.* 1977. Toronto. McClelland & Stewart. 1st. F/F. B2. $35.00.

ATWOOD, Margaret. *Good Bones and Simple Murders.* 1994. NY. Doubleday. ARC. F/wrp. B2. $35.00.

ATWOOD, Margaret. *Lady Oracle.* 1976. McClelland & Stewart. 1st Canadian. F/NF. B3. $125.00.

ATWOOD, Margaret. *Lady Oracle.* 1976. NY. S&S. 1st. NF/F dj. M19. $17.50.

ATWOOD, Margaret. *Life Before Man.* 1980. NY. S&S. 1st Am. inscr. F/F. D10. $50.00.

ATWOOD, Margaret. *Life Before Man.* 1979. Toronto. McClelland & Stewart. 1st. F/F. B2. $35.00.

ATWOOD, Margaret. *The Robber Bride.* 1993. NY. Nan Talese. 1st Am trade. F/dj. A23. $25.00.

ATWOOD, Margaret. *Selected Poems II, 1976 – 1986.* (1987). Boston. Houghton Mifflin. UP. prt red wrp. F. B3. $30.00.

ATWOOD, Margaret. *Strange Things.* (1995). Oxford. Oxford U Press. 1st. NF/F sm abrasion on front brd. B3. $30.00.

ATWOOD, Margaret. *Surfacing.* 1972. Toronto. McClelland & Stewart. 1st. F/NF. B2. $100.00.

ATWOOD, Margaret. *The Canlit Foodbook.* 1987. Toronto. 1st trade ed. wrp. NF. A26. $45.00.

ATWOOD, Margaret. *The Handmaid's Tale.* 1986. Boston. Houghton Mifflin. 1st U.S. F/F. D10. $40.00.

ATWOOD, Margaret. *The Journals of Susanna Moore.* (1997). Boston. Houghton Mifflin. 1st hc ed. ils by Charles Pachter. was a pb orig. w/new intro by David Staines. orig ed was ltd to 120 copies. F/in cb slipcase. B3. $20.00.

ATWOOD, Margaret. *The Robber Bride.* (1993). NY. Doubleday. 1st. sgn by author. F/F. B3. $40.00.

ATWOOD, Margaret. *The Robber Bride.* 1993. Toronto. McClelland & Stewart. 1st. F/F. B2. $30.00.

ATWOOD, Margaret. *Wilderness Tips.* (1991). London. Bloomsbury. 1st British ed. short stories. F/F. B3. $35.00.

AUBERT, Roger. *Concilium: Vol 27, Progress & Decline In History.* 1967. NY. Paulist. 1st Am. 8vo. VG/G. A2. $16.00.

AUBERT, Rosemary. *Free Reign.* 1997. Bridgehampton. NY. Bridge Works. 1st. 1st Ellis Portal mystery novel. F/F. M23. $70.00.

AUBREY, Edmund. *Sherlock Holmes in Dallas.* 1980. NY. Dodd. Mead. 1st. F. few wrinkled pgs/F. T2. $20.00.

AUCHINCLOSS, Louis. *Pursuit of the Prodigal.* 1959. np. F/VG. M19. $35.00.

AUCHINCLOSS, Louis. *The Rector of Justin.* 1964. np. Houghton Mifflin. 1st. VG/chip. S19. $40.00.

AUDEN, W. H. *Dance of Death.* 1933. London. Faber. 1st. 1/1200. G/dj. L3. $175.00.

AUDEN, W. H. *Epistle to a Godson and Other Poems.* 1972. London. Faber. 1st. NF/NF. B2. $45.00.

AUDEN, W. H. *For the Time Being.* 1944. Random. 1st. NF/G. L3. $125.00.

AUDEN, W. H. *Some Poems.* 1940. London. Faber. 1st. NF/dj. B20. $100.00.

AUDEN, W. H. *Spain.* 1937. London. 1st. stapled wrp. T9. $50.00.

AUDEN, W. H. *Tell Me the Truth about Love.* 1994. NY. Vintage Books. sc. F. F6. $3.00.

AUDEN, W. H. and Chester Kallman. *The Magic Flute.* 1956. NY. Random House. 1st. F/NF. B2. $75.00.

AUDEN, W. H. *Nones.* 1952. London. 1st. dj. T9. $75.00.

AUDOT, L. *La Cuisinere De La Campagne Et De La Ville.* 1882 Paris. ils. 701p. G+. E6. $50.00.

AUDUBON, John James. *Audubon Game Animals.* 1968. Hammond. IN/Maplewood. NJ. sgn. G. A19. $25.00.

AUDUBON, John James. *Birds of America.* 1937. Macmillan. 1/2500. sm folio. gilt gr cloth/marbled brd. F/case. F1. $95.00.

AUEL, Jean M. *The Clan of the Cave Bear.* 1980. NY. Crown. 1st. F/dj. M19/S13/T11. $65.00.

AUEL, Jean M. *The Mammoth Hunters.* 1985. Crown. 1st. NF/dj. L4. $20.00.

AUEL, Jean M. *The Mammoth Hunters.* 1985. NY. Crown. 1st. F/F. H11. $30.00.

AUEL, Jean M. *The Plains of Passage.* 1990. NY. Crown. 1st. sgn. F/dj. Q1. $50.00.

AUEL, Jean M. *The Plains of Passage.* 1990. NY. Crown. 1st. F/F. name on ffep. H11. $15.00.

AUEL, Jean M. *Valley of Horses.* 1982. Crown. 1st. F/NF. M19. $15.00.

AUGSBURGER, David. *Caring Enough to Confront.* 1973. Regal. pb. 142p. VG. B29. $3.50.

AUSFRANC, Otto E. *Constructive Surgery of the Hip.* 1962. St. Louis. Mosby Co. 1st. ils in color and b&w. buckram. 4to. 226p. VG. B14. $75.00.

AUSTEN, John. *As You Like It by Shakespeare, Decorations by John Austen.* 1930. London. William Jackson. ltd ed. #54/115. sgn by Austen. 4to. bl linen. handmade paper. 46 color plates tipped in. 20 line drawings. 114p. G+. D6. $75.00.

AUSTER, Paul. *African Trio by Georges Simenon.* 1979. NY. HBJ. 1st. F/F. B3. $75.00.

AUSTER, Paul. *Disappearances: Selected Poems.* 1988. NY. Overlook Press. 1st. sgn by author. F/NF. tiny tear. slight wear. O11. $100.00.

AUSTER, Paul. *Facing the Music.* 1980. Barrytown. NY. Station Hill Press. 1st. ils wrp. 1/1000. sgn by author. F. crisp. tight copy. O11. $135.00.

AUSTER, Paul. *Ghosts.* 1986. Sun & Moon Press. 1st. F/NF. sm stain along bottom edge. M25. $60.00.

AUSTER, Paul. *Hand to Mouth.* 1997. Henry holt. ARC. F/decor wrps. M25. $45.00.

AUSTER, Paul. *In the Country of Last Things.* 1987. NY. Viking. 1st. sgn by author. F/F. O11. $65.00.

AUSTER, Paul. *Leviathan.* 1992. Viking. 1st. sgn. F/dj. R14. $45.00.

AUSTER, Paul. *Lulu on the Bridge.* 1998. NY. Owl Books. UP of orig screenplay. F in wrp. D10. $35.00.

AUSTER, Paul. *Paul Aster's New York.* (1997). NY. Holt. 1st. pict brd. F/issued w/o dj. B3. $30.00.

AUSTER, Paul. *Paul Auster's New York.* 1997. NY. Holt. promo issue. photos by Frieder Blickle. sm hc volume. 100p. F. B2. $75.00.

AUSTER, Paul. *Smoke & Blue in the Face.* 1995. NY. Hyperion/Miramax. 1st. pbo. sgn by author. 2 screenplays. F/F. O11. $60.00.

AUSTER, Paul. *The Art of Hunger. Essays. Prefaces. Interviews.* 1992. Los Angeles. Sun & Moon Press. ltd #42/300 sgn. expanded version of pbo 1st pub in 1982; thus the 1st Am and 1st hc ed. F/F. D10. $125.00.

AUSTER, Paul. *The Locked Room.* 1986. Los Angeles. Sun & Moon Press. 1st. sgn. 3rd. elusive book in his celebrated New York Trilogy. F/F. D10. $385.00.

AUSTER, Paul. *The Music of Chance.* 1990. NY. Viking. review copy. author's 6th novel. sgn. F/F. D10. $65.00.

AUSTER, Paul. *The Music of Chance.* 1990. NY. Viking. 1st. sgn by author. F/F. O11. $140.00.

AUSTER, Paul. *The Music of Chance.* 1991. London. Faber & Faber. 1st British ed. F/F. O11. $25.00.

AUSTER, Paul. *The New York Trilogy.* 1987. London. Faber & Faber. 1st. F/dj. M15. $85.00.

AUSTER, Paul. *The New York Trilogy.* 1994. Los Angeles. Sun & Moon Press. 1st. cloth ed 1st time in US. poi on ffep. F/F. D10. $75.00.

AUSTER, Paul. *Timbuktu.* 1999. NY. Henry Holt. 1st. sgn. F/F. O11. $35.00.

AUSTIN, A. B. *Angler's Anthology.* 1931. London. ils Norman Wilkinson. NF. M4. $50.00.

AUSTIN, Gabriel. *Four Oaks Library.* 1957. Somerville. NJ. 1st. 1/1250. H13. $85.00.

AUSTIN, Jean. *Mexico in Your Pocket.* 1937. NY. Doubleday. 1st. maps. color foldouts. 140p. F. F3. $10.00.

AUSTIN, Mary. *Land of Little Rain.* 1950. Houghton Mifflin. 1st thus. 132p. NF/dj. B20. $125.00.

AUSTIN, Mary. *One-Smoke Stories.* 1934. Houghton Mifflin. 1st. 8vo. red-lettered gray cloth. F. R3. $65.00.

AUTRY, James A. *Life and Work a Manager's Search for Meaning.* 1994. NY. Morrow. 1st. NF/NF. A28. $10.95.

AVERILL, Esther. *Voyages of Jacques Cartier.* 1937. NY. Domino. 1st. F/G. M5. $75.00.

AVERY, Catherine B. *New Century Handbook of Greek Art & Architecture.* 1972. Appleton Century. ils. 222p. cloth. VG/dj. D1. $15.00.

AVERY, G. *Behold the Child: American Children & Their Books 1621 – 1922.* London. 1st. ils. 226p. F/dj. M4. $25.00.

AVERY, Gillian. *Lost Railway.* 1980. London. Collins. 1st (stated). 8vo. 220p. VG/G. T5. $30.00.

AVERY, Thomas Eugene. *Natural Resources Measurement.* 1975. McGraw Hill. 2nd. ils. 339p. G. H10. $17.50.

AVILA, George C. *The Pairpoint Glass Story.* 1968. New Bedford. self-published. 1st. sm4to. blue cloth. sgn. 238p. VG. H1. $145.00.

AXTON, David; see Koontz, Dean R.

AXTON, David. *Prison of Ice.* 1976. Philadelphia. Lippincott. 1st. 1st book by Dean Koontz under this pseudonym. NF/VG+. mild rubbing at corners. A24. $300.00.

AYALA, Mitzi. *Farmer's Cookbook: A Collection of Favorite Recipes.* 1981. Harbor. VG/dj. A16. $16.00.

AYCLIFFE, Jonathan. *The Lost.* 1996. NY. Harper. 1st. F/VF. H11. $20.00.

AYE, Lillian. *Iran Caboose.* 1952. Hollywood. House-Waarven. 8vo. 190p. cloth. VG/torn. W1. $18.00.

AYER, Jacqueline. *Nadang & His Kite.* 1959. Harcourt Brace. 1st. ils Jacqueline Ayer. VG/dj. P2. $25.00.

AYMAR, Gordon C. *Bird Flight.* 1938. NY. deluxe ed. 234p. VG/dj. A19. $17.50.

AYMARD, Andre. *Le Premiers Rapports De Rome Et De Confederation Achaienne.* 1938. Paris. 8vo. 438p. cloth. VG. Q2. $46.50.

AYRES, Atlee B. *Mexican Architecture, Domestic, Civil & Ecclesiastical.* 1926. NY. Wm Helburn. folio. photos/ils/ftspc. gilt gr cloth. dj. K1. $200.00.

AYRES, E. C. *Eye of the Gator.* 1995. NY. St. Martin. 1st. VF/F. H11. $25.00.

AYRES, E. C. *Hour of the Manatee.* 1994. St Martin. 1st. NF/dj. G8. $25.00.

AYRES, E. C. *Night of the Panther.* 1997. NY. St. Martin. 1st. VG/VG. G8. $15.00.

AYRES, Noreen. *A World the Color of Salt.* 1992. NY. Morrow. 1st. author's 1st book. F/F. H11. $25.00.

AYRES, Noreen. *Carcass Trade.* 1994. NY. Morrow. 1st. F/F. H11. $20.00.

AYRTON, Michael. *British Drawings.* 1946. Collins. 1st. 8 color plates. F/F dj. M19. $17.50.

AZOY, A.C.M. *Paul Revere's Horse.* 1949. Doubleday. 1st. VG. N2. $10.00.

— B —

B, E. V.; see Boyle, E. V.

BAADE, Fritz. *Race to the Year 2000.* 1963. Cresset. VG/VG. P3. $15.00.

BAADE, Walter. *Evolution of Stars & Galaxies.* 1963. Cambridge. Harvard. 8vo. 321p. VG/dj. K5. $20.00.

BAARS, D. L. *Geology of the Canyons of the San Juan River.* 1981. 4 Corners Geological Soc. 2nd. 8vo. 94p. stiff wrp. F7. $17.50.

BAARS & STEVENSON. *San Juan Canyons: A River Runner's Guide & Natural Hist...* 1991. Canon Pub. revised. sbdg. VG. F7. $12.50.

BAAS, J. H. *Outlines of the History of Medicine & Medical Profession.* 1889. NY. Vail. 1st Eng-language. 1173p. cloth. G7. $295.00.

BAAS, Johann. *Outlines of History of Medicine & Medical Profession.* 1971. Huntington. NY. facs of 1889. 2 vol. 1st Eng trans. A13. $175.00.

BAASKIN, John. *In Praise of Practical Fertilizer: Thoughts.* 1982. NY/London. Norton. 1st. F/NF. H4. $15.00.

BAAY, Henry Van L. *Boats, Boat Yards & Yachtsmen.* 1961. Van Nostrand. 1st. ils. 211p. dj. T7. $20.00.

BABA, Mehar. *Listen, Humanity.* 1957. Dodd. Mead. 1st. lightly rubbed priced clipped jacket. F/dj. M25. $35.00.

BABB, T. A. *In the Bosom of the Comanches. A Thrilling Tale...* 1923. TA Babb. 2nd. 146p. VG. J2. $225.00.

BABBITT, Bruce. *Grand Canyon: An Anthology.* nd. Northland. 1st. 8vo. 258p. VG/dj. F7. $65.00.

BABBITT, George Jr. *Arizona Mosaic.* 1977. B&H Pub. 1st. sgn. 180p. F/NF. B19. $35.00.

BABBITT, Natalie. *Knee-Knock Rise.* 1978 (1970). FSG. 6th. sgn. Newbery Award. NF/NF. T5. $25.00.

BABCOCK, Ernest B. *Genus Crepis.* 1947. Berkeley. ils. 1030p. new cloth. B26. $87.50.

BABCOCK, George. *Yezad: Romance of the Unknown.* 1922. Cooperative. 1st. G+. M2. $35.00.

BABCOCK, Havilah. *Education of Pretty Boy.* 1960. Holt. 1st. inscr. ils Arthur Fuller. NF/VG+. C15. $150.00.

BABCOCK, Mary Kent Davey. *Christ Church, Salem Street, Boston: Old North Church.* (1940). self pub. ils. 271p. VG/G. M10. $15.00.

BABCOCK, Philip H. *Falling Leaves.* 1937. Derrydale. 1/950. ils Aiden Ripley. NF. H4. $75.00.

BABER, D. F. *Longest Rope.* 1940. Caxton. dj. A19. $75.00.

BABER, Lucy Harrison Miller. *Behind the Old Brick Wall: A Cemetery Story.* 1968. Lynchburg. Colonial Dames. Lynchburg Comm. 307p. VG/dj. B10. $45.00.

BABINGTON. *Records of Fife Foxhounds.* 1883. Edinburgh. Blackwood. 1st. 4to. G. O3. $95.00.

BABITZ, Eve. *Eve's Hollywood.* 1974. Delacorte. 1st. F/NF. M25. $45.00.

BABITZ, Eve. *Sex & Rage.* 1979. Knopf. 1st. F/F. H11. $25.00.

BABSON, Marian. *Death in Fashion.* 1985. London. Collins Crime Club. 1st. F/dj. M15. $45.00.

BABSON, Marian. *Fatal Fortune.* 1987. London. Collins Crime Club. 1st. F/dj. M15. $45.00.

BABSON, Marian. *Guilty Party.* 1988. London. Collins Crime Club. 1st. F/dj. M15. $45.00.

BABSON, Marian. *Past Regret.* (1991). NY. St. Martin. 1st Am ed. F/F. B3. $15.00.

BABSON, Marian. *Reel Murder.* 1986. St. Martin. 1st Am. 180p. F/dj. D4. $30.00.

BABSON, Marian. *Reel Murder.* 1986. London. Collins Crime Club. 1st. F/dj. M15. $45.00.

BABSON, Marian. *There Must Be Some Mistake.* nd. St. Martin. 1st. F/F. P3. $15.00.

BABSON, Marian. *Untimely Guest.* 1976. London. Collins Crime Club. 1st. F/dj. M15. $45.00.

BABULA, William. *According to St John.* 1989. Lyle Stuart. 1st. VG/VG. P3. $18.00.

BABUN, Edward. *Varieties of Man.* 1969. Crowell-Collier. 2nd. 88p. F. D4. $20.00.

BABYAK, Jolene. *Eyewitness of Alcatraz.* 1988. Berkeley. Ariel Vamp. 128p. VG/wrp. B11. $14.50.

BACA, Jimmy Santiago. *Working in the Dark.* (1992). Santa Fe. Red Crane. 1st. sgn by author. F/F. B3. $45.00.

BACALL, Lauren. *By Myself.* 1979. Knopf. 1st. 377p. VG/dj. P12. $15.00.

BACALL, Lauren. *Now.* 1994. Knopf. 1st. sgn. VG/VG. A23. $40.00.

BACH, Richard. *Bridge Across Forever.* 1984. Morrow. 1st. VG/VG. P3. $20.00.

BACH, Richard. *Illusions.* (1977). NY. Delacorte Press. 1st. NF. prev owner's name on ffep/NF. lt edgewear. B3. $20.00.

BACH, Richard. *One.* 1988. Morrow. 1st. AN/dj. H4. $20.00.

BACHELDER, Louise. *Dogs, Cats & Other Friends.* 1972. NY. Peter Pauper. ils Marian Morton. 62p. F/dj. D4. $20.00.

BACHELLER, Irving. *Candle in the Wilderness: Tale of Beginning of New England.* (1930). Bobbs Merrill. 1st. 8vo. gilt gr cloth. F/NC Wyeth dj. R3. $65.00.

BACHELLER, Irving. *Eben Holden's Last Day A-Fishing.* 1907. Harper. 1st. F/VG+. H7. $40.00.

BACHELLER, Irving. *Keeping Up with Lizzie.* 1911. Harper. 1st. 12 pl. VG/dj. B11. $18.00.

BACHELLER, Irving. *Keeping Up with Lizzie.* 1911. NY. Harper. 158p. G. $8.00.

BACHELLER, Irving. *Light in the Clearing.* 1917. Bobbs Merrill. ils Arthur I Keller. 415p. G. G11. $10.00.

BACHELLER, Irving. *Man for the Ages.* 1919. Bobbs Merrill. ils John Wolcott Adams. 416p. G. G11. $8.00.

BACHELLER, Irving. *Story of a Passion.* 1917. E Aurora. Roycrofters. slim 16mo. 21p. VG/wrp. B11. $35.00.

BACHELLER, Irving. *Vergilius.* 1904. NY. Harper. 279p. G. G11. $12.00.

BACHMAN, Richard; See King, Stephen.

BACKEBERG, Curt. *Cactus Lexicon.* 1977. Poole. 3rd. ils/18 maps. 838p. VG+/dj. B26. $135.00.

BACKEBERG, Curt. *Das Kakteenlexikon.* 1966. Jena. 1st. ils/18 full-p maps. 741p. VG/dj. B26. $55.00.

BACKEBERG, Curt. *Wunderwelt Kakteen.* 1961. Jena. 1st. ils. 242p. yel cloth. VG. B26. $125.00.

BACKES, Clarus. *Growing Up Western.* 1990. Knopf. 1st. rem mk. NF/F. T11. $25.00.

BACKHOUSE, James. *Life & Correspondence of Wm & Alice Ellis of Airton.* 1849. London. Chas Gilpin. 12mo. 298p. worn cloth. xl. V3. $24.00.

BACKHOUSE & BLAND. *Annals & Memoirs of the Court of Peking.* 1914. Houghton Mifflin. 1st. photos/index. 531p. VG. W3. $110.00.

BACKUS, Anna Jean. *Mountain Meadows Witness.* 1995. Clark. 1st. 302p. M. J2. $85.00.

BACON, Edwin M. *Rambles Around Old Boston.* 1914. Little, Brn. 1st. ils Lester G Hornby. 205p. VG. B18. $17.50.

BACON, Francis. *Essays of Bacon.* 1927. Cleveland. Fined Eds. 140p. leather spine/cloth brds. VG. A10. $30.00.

BACON, Francis. *Works Of....Lord Chancellor of England.* 1856. Phil. Parry McMillan. 4to. 455p. xl. K3. $40.00.

BACON, John. *Forging: A Practical Treatise on Hand Forging...* 1938. Chicago. Am Technical Soc. 116p. VG. O3. $40.00.

BACON, Josephine Daskam. *Medusa's Head.* 1926. NY. D. Appleton. 1st. F/dj. M15. $75.00.

BACON, Peggy. *Magic Touch.* 1968. Little, Brn. 1st. 112p. VG-/G+. P2. $35.00.

BADARACCO, Claire. *American Culture & The Marketplace: RR Donnelley...* 1992. Lib of Congress. 67p. 4to. stiff wrp. A17. $15.00.

BADASH, Lawrence. *Radioactivity In America.* 1976. Baltimore/London. 1st. 327p. VG. K3. $45.00.

BADE, William Frederic. *Life & Letters of John Muir.* 1923. Houghton Mifflin. 2 vol. 1st. gr cloth. F. B20. $325.00.

BADEN POWELL, Col. R. S. S. *The Matabele Campaign 1896.* 1897. London. 1st. ils. ex lib. rebound. 500p. G. B18. $75.00.

BADER. *Bibliography of British Book Illustrators 1860 – 1900.* 1978. 1/1000. 4to. ils. 197p. F/G. A4. $125.00.

BADER, Barbara. *American Picturebooks from Noah's Ark to the Beast Within.* 1976. 1st. 4to. 700 ils. 623p. F/F. A4. $135.00.

BADER, Barbara. *American Picture Books from Noah's Ark to the Beast Within.* 1976. Collier/Macmillan. 1st. 4to. 700 ils. 615p. F/NF. H4. $115.00.

BADGER, Curtis J. *Eastern Shore: Pictorial History.* (1983). Donning. photos. VG/dj. B10. $40.00.

BADSHA, Omar. *South Africa: Cordoned Heart: Essays.* 1986. Capetown. 1st. ils. 186p. NF/dj. W1. $20.00.

BAECK, Leo. *Judaism & Christianity.* 1958. PA. JPS. 292p. VG/G+. S3. $22.00.

BAECK, Leo. *Pharisees & Other Essays.* 1947. Schocken. 164p. VG. S3. $30.00.

BAEDEKER, Karl. *Baedeker's Touring Guide to Yugoslavia.* 1964. Stuttgart. Baedeker's. tall 8vo. tables/plans/maps/ils. VG/dj. W1. $16.00.

BAEDEKER, Karl. *Mediterranean Sea Port & Sea Routes Including Madeira...* 1911. Leipzig. Baedeker. 1st. 12mo. 38 maps/49 plans. 607p. VG. W1. $50.00.

BAEDEKER, Karl. *Western Norway.* nd. Leipsic. Private Prt. ils/fld maps/42p index. full leather. VG. M12. $30.00.

BAER, Dallas C. *Messages of the Prophets to Their Day & Ours.* 1940. Pulpit. 152p. VG. B29. $11.50.

BAER, Helene G. *Heart Is Like Heaven: Life of Lydia Maria Child.* 1964. PA U. 339p. cloth. NF/dj. M20. $28.00.

BAER, Ludwig. *History of the German Steel Helmet 1916 – 1945.* 1985. San Jose. 1st. mc pl/photos. 448p. VG. S16. $40.00.

BAER, Will Christopher. *Kiss Me, Judas.* 1998. NY. Viking. 1st. author's 1st novel. sgn. VF/VF. T2. $25.00.

BAGBY, George. *Cop Killer.* 1956. Crime Club. 1st. NF/dj. M25. $15.00.

BAGBY, George. *Dead Wrong.* 1957. Crime Club. 1st. G/G. P3. $12.00.

BAGBY, George. *Evil Genius.* 1961. Crime Club. 1st. VG/dj. G8. $15.00.

BAGBY, George. *Mysteriouser & Mysteriouser.* 1965. Crime Club. 1st. F/VG. M19. $17.50.

BAGG, Rufus Mather. *Pliocene & Pleistocene Foraminifera from Southern CA.* 1912. WA. Dept Interior. 28 pl. 153p. prt wrp. D11. $20.00.

BAGGLEY & MCDOUGALL. *Plants of Yellowstone National Park.* 1956. Yellowstone Lib/Mus. 2nd. 8vo. VG. A22. $20.00.

BAGLEY, Desmond. *Bahama Crisis.* 1980. Summit. 1st. VG/VG. P3. $18.00.

BAGLEY, Desmond. *Enemy.* 1978. Doubleday. 1st. VG/VG. P3. $18.00.

BAGLEY, Desmond. *Flyaway.* 1978. Collins. 1st. VG/VG. P3. $20.00.

BAGLEY, Desmond. *Spoilers.* 1970. Doubleday. 1st. VG/G. P3. $15.00.

BAGLEY, Desmond. *Windfall.* 1982. NY. Summit. 1st Am ed. F/NF. A24. $25.00.

BAGLEY, Desmond. *Windfall.* 1982. Collins. 1st. NF/VG. P3. $18.00.

BAGNELL, Kenneth. *Canadese: Portrait of Italian Canadians.* 1989. Macmillan. 1st. sgn. F/dj. T12. $12.00.

BAHR, Edith-Jane. *Nice Neighborhood.* 1973. Collins Crime Club. 1st. VG/G. P3. $15.00.

BAHR, Howard. *The Black Flower.* 1997. Baltimore. NAP. sgn 1st ed. F/NF. some rubbing. M23. $90.00.

BAIGELL, Matthew. *Charles Burchfield.* 1976. Watson Guptill. 46 mc pl/100+ b&w ils. 208p. cloth. dj. D2. $225.00.

BAILEY, Alfred M. and J. H. Sorensen. *Subantarctic Campbell Island.* 1962. Denver. Denver Museum of History. 1st. orig red cloth. many ils. 305p. NF. P4. $125.00.

BAILEY, Alice Cooper. *Kating Gander.* (1927). Joliet. Volland. 4th. ils MH Myers. 93p. pict brd. VG/box. T5. $65.00.

BAILEY, Alice Cooper. *Katrina & Jan.* 1923. Volland. probable 1st. tall 8vo. pict brd. G+/AN box. T5. $65.00.

BAILEY, Arthur Scott. *Tale of Billy Woodchuck.* 1916. 1st. ils L Brehm. NF. M19. $25.00.

BAILEY, Arthur Scott. *Tale of Henrietta Hen.* 1921. Grosset Dunlap. 12mo. ils Harry L Smith. VG+. C8. $35.00.

BAILEY, Bernadine. *Picture Book of California.* Chicago. Albert Whitman and Company. 1949. Oblong 8vo. (26)p. colored brd. probable 1st ed. Ils by Kurt Wiese. minor soil on rear cover. VG. L5. $10.00.

BAILEY, Carolyn. *Lil' Hannibal.* 1938. Platt Munk. ils. cloth/pict label. C8. $75.00.

BAILEY, Carolyn. *Tops & Whistles.* 1937. Viking. 1st. 193p. F/VG. P2. $45.00.

BAILEY, Carolyn Sherwin. *Little Rabbit Who Wanted Red Wings.* 1945. Platt Munk. ils Dorothy Grider. red cloth. VG+/dj. M20. $25.00.

BAILEY, Covert. *The New Fit or Fat.* 1991. NY. Hougton Mifflin. VG. A28. $6.50.

BAILEY, Covert and Lea Bishop. *Target Recipes.* 1985. NY. Houghton Mifflin. hb. VG/VG-. A28. $6.50.

BAILEY, David. *Naked Eye: Great Photographs of the Nude.* (1987). NY. Amphoto. 1st. photos. 191p. F/dj. H4. $60.00.

BAILEY, F. M. *Comprehensive Catalogue of Queensland Plants.* 1909. Brisbane. Cumming. 2nd. 879p. B1. $120.00.

BAILEY, Flora L. *Some Sex Beliefs & Practices in Navaho Community.* 1950. Harvard. 4to. 108p. F. F7. $35.00.

BAILEY, Geoffrey. *Conspirators.* 1960. NY. 1st. 306p. G/dj. E1. $25.00.

BAILEY, George W. *Private Chapter of the War (1861 – 65).* 1880. St Louis. GI Jones. 271p. G+. B10. $100.00.

BAILEY, H. C. *Case for Mr. Fortune.* 1932. Canada. Doubleday Doran. VG/VG. P3. $45.00.

BAILEY, H. C. *Dead Man's Effects.* 1945. London. MacDonald. 1st Eng. jacket has short closed tear. F/dj. M15. $125.00.

BAILEY, H. C. *Life Sentence.* 1946. Crime Club. 1st Am ed. G/VG. G8. $30.00.

BAILEY, H. C. *Mr. Clunk's Text.* 1939. NY. Doubleday. 1st Am. jacket has tiny wear at spine eds and some light stains on back panel. F/dj. M15. $85.00.

BAILEY, H. C. *Mr. Fortune Wonders.* 1933. Crime Club. 1st. VG. P3. $40.00.

BAILEY, H. C. *Slippery Ann.* 1944. London. Victor Gollancz. 1st. jacket Is lightly soiled. F/dj. M15. $135.00.

BAILEY, H. J. *Reminiscences of a Christian Life.* 1885. Portland, ME. Hoyt Fogg & Donham. 2nd. 419p. aeg. xl. V3. $16.00.

BAILEY, Hilary. *The Strange Adventures of Charlotte Holmes.* 1994. London. Constable. 1st. VF/VF. T2. $30.00.

BAILEY, Howard. *ABC's of Play Producing.* 1955. McKay. 1st. sgn VG/VG. B11. $18.00.

BAILEY, James H. *Pictures of the Past: Petersburg Seen by Simpsons 1819 – 95.* (1989). Ft Henry Branch. APVA. ils. 55p. VG. B10. $15.00.

BAILEY, Jo. *Bagged.* 1991. NY. St. Martin. 1st. NF/NF. G8. $12.50.

BAILEY, Kenneth P. *Ohio Company of Virginia…* 1939. Glendale. Arthur Clark. 1st. 5 maps. teg. G+. B18. $125.00.

BAILEY, L. H. *Cyclopedia of American Horticulture.* 1904. NY. Macmillan. 3rd. 4 vol. A10. $150.00.

BAILEY, L. H. *First Lessons With Plants.* 1898. Macmillan. 1st. 117p. xl. A10. $30.00.

BAILEY, L. H. *How to Make a Flower Garden.* 1905. Doubleday. 370p. VG. A10. $25.00.

BAILEY, L. H. *Manual of Cultivated Plants.* 1977. Macmillan. revised/16th prt. 1116p. NF. W2. $25.00.

BAILEY, L. H. *Nursery Manual.* 1944. Macmillan. 456p. dj. A10. $22.00.

BAILEY, L. H. *Outlook to Nature.* 1924 (1905). Macmillan. 195p. dj. A10. $40.00.

BAILEY, L. H. *Plant-Breeding.* 1902. NY. Macmillan. 354p. gr cloth. VG. B14. $45.00.

BAILEY, L. H. *Principles of Agriculture.* 1910. Macmillan. 16th. 336p. cloth. A10. $28.00.

BAILEY, L. H. *Principles of Vegetable Gardening.* 1919. Macmillan. 17th. 458p. A10. $30.00.

BAILEY, L. H. *Standard Cyclopedia of Horticulture.* 1917 (1914). NY. 2nd. 6 vol. ils. 3639p. B26. $200.00.

BAILEY, L. h. *The Standard Cyclopedia of Horticulture (3 Vols).* 1961. NY. corrected ed. 19th printing. 4to. gr cloth. 3639p. cloth slightly rubbed & faded. pulled at heads. B26. $149.00.

BAILEY, Lee. *Lee Bailey's Soup Meals: Main Event Soups…* 1989. NY. 1st. 4to. mc photos. VG/dj. A16. $17.50.

BAILEY, P. *Oxford Book of London.* 1995. OUP. 1st. dj. T9. $18.00.

BAILEY, Paul. *Grandpa Was a Polygamist.* 1960. LA. Westernlore. 1st. sgn. poi. slight slant. dj darkened spine. NF/F. H11. $70.00.

BAILEY, Pearce. *Accident & Injury: Their Relations to Diseases of Nervous...* 1898. NY. 1st. 430p. half leather. A13. $250.00.

BAILEY, Pearl. *Hurry Up, America, and Spit.* 1976. HBJ. 2nd. sgn. VG/NF. M20. $15.00.

BAILEY, Pearl. *Pearl's Kitchen.* 1973. HBJ. 1st. sgn. F/dj. D10/Q1. $50.00.

BAILEY, Pearl. *The Raw Pearl.* 1968. H B W. 1st. sgn. NF/NF sunned at spine. M25. $45.00.

BAILEY, Truman. *Polynesian Venture.* 1939. Doubleday Doran. 1st. VG. N2. $12.00.

BAILEY, William W. *Botanizing: A Guide to Field-Collecting & Herbarium Work.* 1899. Providence. Preston Rounds. 142p. cloth. A10. $45.00.

BAILEY & BAILEY. *Hortus Second.* 1959. Macmillan. 10th. 778p. VG. B1. $40.00.

BAILEY & BISHOFF. *Tin Woodman.* 1979. Doubleday. 1st. sgn. NF/dj. M2. $30.00.

BAILEY & CHALMERS. *Report on Surface Geology...New Brunswick.* 1898. Ottawa. photos/map. disbound. A17. $15.00.

BAILEY & CHILDERS. *Applied Mineral Exploration with Special Reference...* 1977. Boulder. Westview. 542p. NF/dj. D8. $45.00.

BAILEY & COOKE. *Birds of New Mexico.* 1928. np. ils/figures/60 maps. 807p. NF. M12. $195.00.

BAILLIE, D. M. *Out of Nazareth.* 1958. NY. Scribner. 211p. VG/G. B29. $8.00.

BAIN, Alexander. *John Stuart Mill, A Criticism: With Personal Recollections.* 1882. London. Longman Gr. 12mo. 201p. decor gr cloth. VG. G1. $125.00.

BAIN, Alexander. *Practical Essays.* 1884. Longman Gr. 12mo. 338p. VG. G1. $75.00.

BAIN, David Howard. *Aftershocks: Tale of Two Victims.* 1980. Methuen. 1st. 241p. VG/dj. R11. $16.00.

BAIN, F. W. *Digit of the Moon.* 1905. Putnam. 1st. G+. M2. $25.00.

BAIN & HARRIS. *Mickey Mouse: Fifty Happy Years.* 1977. Harmony. 1st. F/lg wrp. M2. $20.00.

BAINBRIDGE, Beryl. *Birthday Boys.* 1994. NY. Carroll Graf. 8vo. 189p. M/dj. P4. $18.95.

BAINBRIDGE, Beryl. *Bottle Factory Outing.* 1975. Braziller. 1st Am. NF/dj. A24. $30.00.

BAINBRIDGE, Beryl. *Injury Time.* (1977). NY. George Braziller. 1st. F/F. B3. $25.00.

BAINBRIDGE, Beryl. *Injury Time.* 1977. Braziller. 1st Am. F/F. A24. $30.00.

BAINBRIDGE, Beryl. *Young Adolf.* (1978). London. Duckworth. 1st British ed. manufacturing flaw caused creased leaves. NF/F. B3. $50.00.

BAINTON, Ronald H. *Behold the Christ.* 1974. Harper. 224p. VG/worn dj. B29. $10.00.

BAINUM, Peter M. *International Space Year in the Pacific Basin.* 1992. San Diego. Am Astronautical Soc. 4to. 782p. VG/wrp. K5. $40.00.

BAIRD, Joseph Armstrong. *California's Pictorial Letter Sheets 1849 – 1869.* 1967. SF. David Magee. 1/475 prt Grabhorn/Hoyem. folio. ils. wht dj. R3. $250.00.

BAIRD, Robert. *Transplanting Flowers; or, Memoirs of Mrs. Rumpff.* 1839. NY. John S. Taylor. 1st. inscr/dtd 1839. 159p. gr cloth. C6. $150.00.

BAIRD, W. D. *Quapa People: A History of the Downstream People.* 1980. OK U. ils/maps. F. M4. $18.00.

BAIREI. *Vogel Und Blumen.* 1952. Leipzig. Wunderlich. 1st. ils. pict brd/cloth spine. VG. W3. $110.00.

BAIRNSFATHER, Bruce. *From Mud to Mufti: With Old Bill on All Fronts.* 1919. NY/London. Putnam. ils/cartoons. VG. M17. $45.00.

BAKARICH, Sara Grace. *Gunsmoke: True Story of Old Tombstone.* 1962. Gateway. 196p. wrp. B19. $15.00.

BAKELESS, John. *Daniel Boone, Master of the Wilderness.* 1939. NY. 2nd. 480p. VG. B18. $19.50.

BAKELESS, John. *Eyes of Discovery: Pageant of North America.* 1950. Lippincott. 1st. ils. 439p. VG. M10. $15.00.

BAKER, Alison. *Loving Wanda Beaver.* (1995). San Francisco. Chronicle. 1st. sgn by author. F/F. B3. $40.00.

BAKER, Carroll. *Roman Tale.* 1986. DIF. 1st. NF/dj. M25. $25.00.

BAKER, Charles H. *Esquire Culinary Companion.* 1959. NY. Crown. VG/dj. A16. $13.00.

BAKER, D. B. *Explorers & Discoveries of the World.* 1993. Detroit. 4to. photos/maps. F. M4. $45.00.

BAKER, David. *History of Manned Space Flight.* 1982. NY. Crown. 1st. lg 4to. ils. 544p. VG/dj. K5. $75.00.

BAKER, Denys Val. *Face in the Mirror.* 1971. Arkham. 1st. F/F. M2. $40.00.

BAKER, Denys Val. *Family at Sea.* 1981. Wm Kimber. 1st. F/F. P3. $20.00.

BAKER, Denys Val. *Phantom Lovers.* 1984. Wm Kimber. 1st. VG/VG. P3. $20.00.

BAKER, Denys Val. *Waterwheel Turns.* 1982. Wm Kimber. 1st. VG/VG. P3. $20.00.

BAKER, Don. *Beyond Forgiveness: The Healing Touch of Church Discipline.* 1984. Multnomah. 102p. VG/VG. B29. $7.00.

BAKER, G. S. *Ship Design, Resistance & Screw-Propulsion Vol 1 & Vol 2.* 1948 & 1951. Liverpool. Journal of Commerce. 2nd. 2 vol. ils/tables. T7. $110.00.

BAKER, George. *Sad Sack.* 1944. S&S. 4th. 115 cartoons. VG/dj. C9. $42.00.

BAKER, J. G. *Handbook of the Irideae.* 1892. London. orig gilt emb gr cloth. ruled in blk. 247p. VG+. B26. $79.00.

BAKER, J. H. *Legal Profession & the Common Law. Historical Essays.* 1986. London. Hambledon. only collected ed. M11. $65.00.

BAKER, J. H. *Manual of Law French, Second Edition.* 1990. Aldershot. Scholar Pr. M11. $65.00.

BAKER, John. *Death Minus Zero.* 1996. London. Gollancz. 1st. VF/dj. M15. $65.00.

BAKER, John. *Poet in the Gutter.* 1996. NY. St. Martin. 1st. author's 1st book. F/F. H11. $30.00.

BAKER, John. *Poet in the Gutter.* 1996. NY. St. Martin. 1st. NF/NF. G8. $15.00.

BAKER, Josephine & Jo Bouillon. *Josephine.* 1977. Harper & Row. 1st Am. jacket with two small tears at the head of the spine. F/dj. M25. $25.00.

BAKER, Josephine and Papich, Stephen. *Remembering Josephine.* 1976. Bobbs-Merrill. 1st. jacket has a few short tears at the edges. F/dj. M25. $35.00.

BAKER, Kevin. *Sometimes You See It Coming.* 1993. NY. Crown. 1st. author's 1st novel. NF/NF. R16. $50.00.

BAKER, LaFayette. *United States Secret Service in the Late War.* 1889. 1st. 398p. O8. $18.50.

BAKER, Margaret J. *Hannibal & the Bears.* 1966. FSG. 1st Am. 8vo. 115p. VG/dj. T5. $20.00.

BAKER, Mark. *Women.* 1990. S&S. 1st. F/F. A20. $10.00.

BAKER, Michael. *Doyle Diary.* 1978. Paddington. VG/VG. P3. $20.00.

BAKER, Nicholson. *Room Temperature.* (1990). London. Granta. 1st British ed. F/F. B3. $20.00.

BAKER, Nicholson. *Room Temperature.* 1990. NY. Grove Weidenfeld. 1st. sgn. F/F. O11. $35.00.

BAKER, Nicholson. *The Fermata.* 1994. NY. Random House. 1st. F/F. H11. $30.00.

BAKER, Nicholson. *The Mezzanine.* 1988. NY. Weidenfeld. 1st. author's 1st book. VF/VF. H11. $120.00.

BAKER, Nicholson. *U and I.* 1991. NY. Random House. 1st. VF/VF. H11. $40.00.

BAKER, Nicholson. *U & I.* (1991). London. Granta. 1st British ed. F/F. B3. $25.00.

BAKER, Nicholson. *Vox.* 1992. NY. Random House. 1st. F/F dj. M19. $35.00.

BAKER, Pearl. *Trail on the Water.* nd (1970). Boulder. sgn. Ils/5 fld maps. 134p. VG/VG. F7. $60.00.

BAKER, R. Robin. *Evolutionary Ecology of Animal Migration.* 1978. NY. ils. 1012p. F/NF. S15. $35.00.

BAKER, Richard. *Ten Thousand Years: Methodism's First Century in China.* 1947. Methodist. pb. 173p. VG. B29. $3.00.

BAKER, Richard M. *Death Stops the Rehearsal.* 1937. Scribner. 1st. VG/G. P3. $35.00.

BAKER, Roger. *Marilyn Monroe.* 1990. Portland. VG/VG. P3. $25.00.

BAKER, Russell. *Good Times.* 1989. Morrow. 1st. sgn. F/F. W2. $35.00.

BAKER, Samuel W. *Wild Beasts & Their Ways.* 1988. Prescott. facsimile 1890 ed. 1/1000. leatherette. F. A17. $17.50.

BAKER, Samuel W. *Wild Beasts & Their Ways: Reminiscences of Europe, Asia.* 1988. Prescott, AZ. 455p. leatherette. F. A17. $17.50.

BAKER, Scott. *Night Child.* 1979. Berkley. 1st. author's 2nd novel. F/F. M21. $30.00.

BAKER, Susan. *My First Murder.* 1989. NY. 1st. author's 1st novel. F/F. H11. $25.00.

BAKER, Susanne Devonshire. *Artists of Alberta.* 1980. Edmonton. 1st Canadian. F/dj. T12. $40.00.

BAKER, Willard F. *Bob Dexter & The Beacon Beach Mystery (#2).* 1925. Cupples Leon. lists 3 titles. VG/dj. M20. $25.00.

BAKER, William J. *Jessie Owens: An American Life.* 1986. NY/London. photos. VG/dj. M17. $15.00.

BAKER, William King. *John T. Dorland.* 1898. London. Headley. G+. V3. $35.00.

BAKER & BAKER. *Doctor Who: Ultimate Foe.* 1988. WH Allen. hc. F/F. P3. $14.00.

BAKER & BAKER. *Reindeer's Shoe & Other Stories.* 1988. Austin. TX. 1st. 4to. 112p. NF/dj. C14. $18.00.

BAKER & BERTHOZ. *Control by Brain Stem Neurons.* 1977. Amsterdam. Elsevier/North-Holland Biomedical Pr. 8vo. red cloth. G1. $65.00.

BAKER & MURPHY. *Handbook of Marine Science.* 1981. Boca Raton. CRC Pr. 223p. F. B1. $65.00.

BAKIS, Kirsten. *Lives of the Monster Dogs.* 1997. NY. FSG. 1st. author's 1st novel. F/F. M23. $50.00.

BAKKER, Elna. *Great Southwest.* 1972. Palo Alto. AM West Pub. hc. dj. A19. $20.00.

BAKKER, R. T. *Dinosaur Heresies.* 1986. Morrow. 481p. cloth. F/dj. D8. $36.00.

BALABAN, John. *After Our War.* 1974. Pittsburgh. 1st. author's 1st book. F/F. B4. $85.00.

BALABAN, John. *Remembering Heaven's Face. A Moral Witness in Vietnam.* 1991. Poseidon. 1st. photos. F/F. R14. $30.00.

BALANCHINE, George. *Complete Stories of the Great Ballets.* 1954. Doubleday. 1st. sgn. 615p. F/dj. B20. $100.00.

BALCH, Glenn. *Indian Paint: Story of an Indian Pony.* 1942. Crowell. 1st. VG/G. O3. $25.00.

BALCH, Glenn. *Lost Horse.* 1950. Crowell. 1st. VG. O3. $18.00.

BALCH, Glenn. *Midnight Colt.* 1952. Crowell. 2nd. sgn. ils Pers Crowell. VG. O3. $20.00.

BALCHEN, Bernt. *Come North with Me. An Autobiography.* 1958. NY. E.P. Dutton. 1st. blue cloth 8vo. photo ils. 318p. VG. P4. $55.00.

BALCHIN, Nigel. *Seen Dimly Before Dawn.* 1964. Rpt Soc. VG/VG. P3. $8.00.

BALCOM, Mary G. *Ketchikan: Alaska's Totemland.* 1974. Chicago. Adams. 3rd. 8vo. 139p. P4. $25.00.

BALDACCI, David. *Absolute Power.* 1996. NY. Warner. 1st. author's 1st book. F/VF. H11. $30.00.

BALDACCI, David. *Saving Faith.* 1999. NY. Warner Books. 1st. sgn. VF/VF. T2. $28.00.

BALDACCI, David. *Total Control.* 1997. NY. Warner. 1st. NF/NF. G8. $10.00.

BALDACCI, David. *Total Control.* 1997. NY. Warner Books. 1st. ARC. pub promo letter. VF in pict wrp. T2. $15.00.

BALDICK, Cris. *Oxford Book of Gothic Tales.* 1991. Oxford. 1st. F/F. P3. $25.00.

BALDOCK, Lt. Col. T. S. *Cromwell as a Soldier.* 1899. London. Kegan Paul. 1st. decor cloth. 538p. spine faded. some spots. G+. B18. $95.00.

BALDWIN, Faith. *Hotel Hostess.* 1943. np. Triangle Books. G. S19. $25.00.

BALDWIN, Faith. *Private Duty.* 1943. Triangle. 9th. 338p. VG/dj. A25. $12.00.

BALDWIN, Faith. *Self-Made Woman.* 1932. Farrar Rhinehart. 1st. F/F. B4. $85.00.

BALDWIN, Gary & Lee Carno. *Artistry in Glass 1857 – 1938.* 1988. Antique Publications. 4to. gray cloth. 124p. F/dj. H1. $50.00.

BALDWIN, HANSON W. *Battles Lost & Won.* 1966. NY. 1st. 532p. F/VG. E1. $40.00.

BALDWIN, Hanson W. *Sea Fights & Shipwrecks. True Tales of the Seven Seas.* 1955. Garden City. Hanover. 8vo. 315p. VG/dj. P4. $30.00.

BALDWIN, James. *Another Country.* 1962. Dial Press. 1st. NF/ltly worn dj. M25. $150.00.

BALDWIN, James. *Blues for Mister Charlie.* 1964. Dial Press. 1st. Jacket lightly rubbed with a chip missing from the rear panel. F/dj. M25. $50.00.

BALDWIN, James. *Cesar: Compressions D'Or.* 1973. np. Hachette. 1st. photos. 93p. F/VG+. B4. $450.00.

BALDWIN, James. *Devil Finds Work.* 1976. Dial. 1st. F/F. H11. $55.00.

BALDWIN, James. *Evidence of Things Not Seen.* 1985. Holt Rinehart. 1st. sm 8vo. F/F. C8. $60.00.

BALDWIN, James. *Fire Next Time.* 1963. NY. Dial. 1st. VG/dj. S13. $16.00.

BALDWIN, James. *Giovanni's Room.* 1956. Dial Press. 1st. Jacket lightly chipped and browned at the spine. F/dj. M25. $200.00.

BALDWIN, James. *Go Tell It on the Mountain.* 1953. Knopf. 1st. author's 1st book. F/NF clip. B4. $1,800.00.

BALDWIN, James. *Going to Meet the Man.* 1965. NY. Dial. 1st. NF/F. minor wear. H11. $80.00.

BALDWIN, James. *If Beale Street Could Talk.* 1974. Dial Press. 1st. 1/250 sgn/numbered. F. M25. $250.00.

BALDWIN, James. *If Beale Street Could Talk.* 1974. Dial. 1st. F/F. H11. $70.00.

BALDWIN, James. *Just Above My Head.* 1979. Dial Press. 1st. NF in dj. no rem spray. M25. $45.00.

BALDWIN, James. *Nobody Knows My Name.* 1964. London. 1st. dj. T9. $45.00.

BALDWIN, James. *Notes of a Native Son.* 1955. Beacon Press. 1st. author's 2nd book and 1st work of nonfiction. NF/slightly worn & sunned dj. 1st issue dj w/excerpt. M25. $450.00.

BALDWIN, James. *One Day, When I Was Lost.* 1976. Dial Press. 1st. NF/NF. M25. $45.00.

BALDWIN, James. *Price of the Ticket.* 1985. St Martin/Marek. 1st. F/dj. Q1. $40.00.

BALDWIN, James. *Tell Me How Long the Train's Been Gone.* 1968. NY. Dial. 1st. F/NF. B2/M25. $35.00.

BALDWIN, James. *The Amen Corner.* 1968. NY. Dial. 1st. F/VG. reinforced dj. B2. $50.00.

BALDWIN, James. *The Devil Finds Work.* 1976. Dial Press. 1st. NF/NF. M25. $50.00.

BALDWIN, James. *The Evidence of Things Not Seen.* 1985. HRW. 1st. NF in dj. M25. $35.00.

BALDWIN, James. *The Evidence of Things Not Seen.* 1979. NY. Holt. 1st. F/F. H11. $40.00.

BALDWIN, James. *The Fire Next Time.* 1963. Dial Press. 1st. NF/dj has few short closed tears. M25. $60.00.

BALDWIN, James & Margaret Mead. *A Rap on Race.* 1971. Lippincott. 1st. NF/NF. M25. $35.00.

BALDWIN, James Mark. *Thought & Things: A Study of Development & Meaning.* 1975. NY. Arno. 4 vol in 2. cream cloth. G1. $125.00.

BALDWIN, Leland D. *Keelboat Age on Western Waters.* 1941. Pittsburgh. ils. 268p. dj. T7. $50.00.

BALDWIN, Leland D. *Pittsburgh: Story of a City.* 1937. Pittsburgh. 3rd. 387p. AN/dj. H1. $20.00.

BALDWIN, Leland D. *Pittsburgh the Story of a City.* 1937. Pittsburgh. U. of Pittsburgh Press. 3rd. sm4to. ils by Ward Hunter. maps. 387p. F/dj. H1. $20.00.

BALDWIN, Leland D. *The Keelboat Age on Western Waters.* 1941. Pittsburgh. 1st. map ep. ils. 268p. VG+/dj. B18. $50.00.

BALDWIN, Victor & Jeane. *Little Kitten, Big World.* 1956. Morrow. 1st. ils. G+/G+. P2. $25.00.

BALDWIN & CAZAC. *Little Man, Little Man.* 1976. Michael Joseph. correct 1st. F/NF. B2. $65.00.

BALET, Jan. *What Makes An Orchestra.* nd (1951). NY. OUP. 1st. sm 4to. 41p. VG+. C14. $14.00.

BALFOUR, Michael. *Royal Baby Book: For the Prince & Princess of Wales.* 1981. London. Pan. 1st Eng. F/dj. T12. $45.00.

BALFOUR, Michael. *Royal Baby Book: For the Prince & Princess of Wales.* 1981. London. Pan. 1st. T12. $45.00.

BALINT, Alice. *Early Years of Life: A Psychoanalytic Study.* 1954. Basic. 1st. 149p. VG/VG. A25. $15.00.

BALKOSKI, Joseph. *Beyond the Beachhead: 29th Infantry Division in Normandy.* 1989. Stackpole. 1st. 304p. VG/dj. M20. $10.00.

BALL, Alice E. *Year with the Birds.* 1916. Gibbs/Van Vleck. 1st. sgn. ils RB Horsfall. 191p. gr cloth. NF. B20. $125.00.

BALL, Berenice M. *Barns of Chester County Pennsylvania.* 1974. W Chester. Chester County Hospital. 1st/ltd. sgn. VG/VG. O3. $95.00.

BALL, Brian. *Death of a Low Handicap Man.* 1974. Walker. 1st Am. VG/G. G8. $20.00.

BALL, Brian N. *Baker Street Boys.* 1983. BC. 1st. VG/VG. P3. $20.00.

BALL, Eustace Hale. *Gaucho.* 1928. Grosset Dunlap. 1st photoplay. VG/dj. C9. $102.00.

BALL, J A. *Mexico.* nd. Mexico. National Lines of Mexico. 2nd ed. wrp. 56p. chipped wrp. F3. $30.00.

BALL, John. *Cop Cade.* 1978. Crime Club. 1st. VG/VG. P3. $15.00.

BALL, John. *In the Heat of the Night.* 1965. NY. Harper & Row. 1st. price clip. darkened spine. hard to find. F/F. H11. $475.00.

BALL, John. *Johnny Get Your Gun.* 1969. Little, Brn. 1st. F/NF. Q1. $75.00.

BALL, John. *Kiwi Target.* 1989. Carroll Graf. 1st. F/F. P3. $16.00.

BALL, John. *Singapore.* 1986. NY. Dodd. 1st. F/F. lt edgewear. H11. $20.00.

BALL, John. *Singapore.* nd. Dodd Mead. 2nd. VG/VG. P3. $15.00.

BALL, John. *The Cool Cottontail.* 1966. NY. Harper & Row. 1st. rubbed spine ends. bumped corners. F-/F. H11. $50.00.

BALL, Larry D. *United Marshals of NM & AZ Territories, 1846 – 1912.* (1978). Albuquerque. 1st. 315p. cloth. dj. D11. $60.00.

BALL, M. W. *Fascinating Oil Business.* 1940. Bobbs Merrill. 420p. F. D8. $20.00.

BALL, Murray. *Eucalyptus.* 1998. FSG. ARC. F/wrp. M25. $25.00.

BALL, Zachary. *Kep.* 1961. Holiday House. 1st. 207p. F/dj. D4. $30.00.

BALL & BREEN. *Murder California Style.* 1987. St Martin. 1st. F/F. P3. $18.00.

BALLANCE & EDMUNDS. *Treatise on Ligation of Great Arteries...* 1891. London. 1st. xl. rpr head/tail spine. A13. $550.00.

BALLANTINE, Betty. *American Celebration: Art of Charles Wysocki.* 1985. Greenwich. 1st. 192p. NF/NF. M20. $30.00.

BALLANTINE, Richard and Jim Dutcher. *The Sawtooth Wolves.* 1996. NY. Rufus Publications. 1st. 4to. photos. NF/NF. R16. $35.00.

BALLARD, Allen B. *Education of Black Folk: Afro-American Struggle...* 1973. Harper. 1st. 173p. F/F. B4. $75.00.

BALLARD, Colin Robert. *The Military Genius of Abraham Lincoln.* 1926. London. Oxford Univ Press. 1st. orig cloth. plates. maps. 246p. NF/VG. scarce dj. M8. $250.00.

BALLARD, Frank. *Christian Findings After Fifty Years.* 1927. Epworth. 246p. G/dj. B29. $6.00.

BALLARD, G. A. *Rulers of the Indian Ocean.* 1928. Houghton Mifflin. ils/map ep. F. O7. $75.00.

BALLARD, J. G. *Cocaine Nights.* 1998. Washington, DC. Counterpoint. 1st Am. VF/VF. T2. $20.00.

BALLARD, J. G. *Crash.* 1973. Farrar. 1st Am. F/dj. M2. $65.00.

BALLARD, J. G. *Day of Creation.* 1988. FSG. 1st Am. NF/dj. M21. $12.00.

BALLARD, J. G. *Drowned World.* 1981. Dragon's Dream. F/dj. M2. $30.00.

BALLARD, J. G. *Empire of the Sun.* 1984. S&S. 1st. F/F. M19. $25.00.

BALLARD, J. G. *Hello America.* 1988. Carroll & Graf. 1st. F/F. P3. $18.00.

BALLARD, J. G. *High Rise.* 1975. NY. HRW. 1st Am ed. F in F dj. D10. $75.00.

BALLARD, J. G. *Kindness of Women.* 1991. NY. FSG. 1st Am. F/dj. T12. $25.00.

BALLARD, J. G. *Memories of the Space Age.* 1988. Arkham. 1st. F/F. M2. $17.00.

BALLARD, J. G. *Running Wild.* 1988. London. Hutchinson. 1st. F/F. A24. $30.00.

BALLARD, J. G. *The Company of Women.* 1991. London. Harper Collins. 1st. F in F dj. D10. $40.00.

BALLARD, J. G. *The Day of Creation.* (1987). NY. FSG. 1st Am ed. F/F. B3. $15.00.

BALLARD, J. G. *Unlimited Dream Company.* 1979. HRW. 1st. VG/VG. P3. $25.00.

BALLARD, Mignon F. *Minerva Cries Murder.* 1993. Carroll & Graf. 1st. sgn. NF/VG. G8. $12.50.

BALLARD, Robert D. *Discovery of the Bismarck.* 1990. Warner. 1st. sgn. 232p. VG/VG. B11. $65.00.

BALLARD, Todhunter. *Sheriff of Tombstone.* 1977. Doubleday. 1st. 187p. NF/NF. B19. $7.50.

BALLARD, Todhunter. *Californian.* 1971. Doubleday. 1st. VG/VG. P3. $20.00.

BALLARD, W. T. *Murder Can't Stop.* 1946. McKay. 1st. VG. G8. $20.00.

BALLARD, W. T. *Say Yes to Murder.* 1942. Putnam. 1st. VG. M25. $50.00.

BALLARD, Willis Todhunter. *Chance Elson.* 1958. Pocket Books. 1st. spine cocked. cover creases. VG+. wrps. M25. $15.00.

BALLARD, Willis Todhunter. *Murder Las Vegas Style.* 1967. Tower. 1st. F. wrp. M25. $25.00.

BALLARD, Willis Todhunter. *Three for the Money.* 1963. Pocket Books. 1st. crease and sm tear on lower front cover. VG+. wrps. M25. $15.00.

BALLEM, John. *Judas Conspiracy.* 1976. Musson. VG/VG. P3. $13.00.

BALLEM, John. *Moon Pool.* 1978. McClelland Stewart. 1st. VG/VG. P3. $20.00.

BALLENTINE, G. *Autobiography of an English Soldier in the US Army.* 1986. Lakeside Classic. ils. 347p. F. M4. $35.00.

BALLIETT, Whitney. *Ecstacy at the Onion.* 1971. Indianapolis. Bobbs-Merrill. ARC w/slip. F/NF. B2. $65.00.

BALLIETT, Whitney. *Improvisations: Fifteen Jazz Musicians and Their Art.* 1977. NY. Oxford. AP. NF/wrp. B2. $35.00.

BALLIETT, Whitney. *Night Creature.* 1981. NY. Oxford. ARC w/slip. F/F. B2. $45.00.

BALLIETT, Whitney. *Such Sweet Thunder.* 1966. Indianapolis. Bobbs-Merrill. 1st. F/lightly used dj. B2. $45.00.

BALLIETT, Whitney. *Such Sweet Thunder.* 1968. London. MacDonald. 1st UK ed. F/F. B2. $40.00.

BALLINGER, Bill S. *The Chinese Mask.* 1965. NY. New American Library. 1st. pb orig. F/wrp. M15. $35.00.

BALLINGER, James K. & Andrea D. Rubinstein. *Visitors to Arizona, 1846 to 1980.* 1980. Phoenix. Phoenix Art Museum. ils. 206p. NF. B19. $20.00.

BALLINGER, John. *Williamsburg Forgeries.* 1989. St. Martin. 1st. sgn. 276p. M/dj. K3. $15.00.

BALLINGER, W. A. *Rebellion.* 1967. Howard Baker. 1st. F/F. P3. $15.00.

BALLOU, Maturin. *Equatorical America.* 1900 (1892). Houghton Mifflin. 371p. gilt bl cloth. xl. F3. $15.00.

BALLOU, Robert, Ed. *World Bible.* 1944. NY. Viking. 605p. VG/VG. B29. $7.50.

BALMER, Edwin. *Wild Goose Chase.* 1915. Duffield. 1st. F/NF. B4. $200.00.

BALMER, Edwin & Philip Wylie. *The Golden Hoard.* 1934. NY. Frederick A. Stokes. 1st. VG/G dj. M15. $40.00.

BALSAM, Louis Gay. *A. G. Warshawsky. Master Painter and Humanist.* 1954. Monterey, CA. presentation copy inscr by Warshawsky. Carmel Valley Art Gallery ed. 4to. ils. gray printed brds. plate mtd on front cover. 114p. traces of removed tape from covers and ep. K1. $85.00.

BALTHASAR, Juan Antonio. *Juan Antonio Balthasar: Padre Visitador...1744 – 45.* 1957. AZ Pioneers Hist Soc. 1/600. 122p+1 fld facs & 1 pocket map. cloth. dj. D11. $40.00.

BALZER, Richard. *Optical Amusements: Magic Lanterns & Other Transforming Images, A Catalog of Popular Entertainments.* 1987. self-published. 4to sgn. Many color & b/w photographic ils. glossy wraps. 81. F. H1. $36.00.

BAMBRA, Toni Cade. *My Love.* 1972. Random House. 1st. Jacket Is lightly browned at the spine and has a short wrinkle along the top edge of the front panel. NF/dj. M25. $60.00.

BAMONTE, Tony. *Sheriffs, 1911 – 1989. A History of Murders in the Wilderness.* 1991. Clark. 1st. ils. 251p. M. J2. $75.00.

BANARD & PEPPER. *Christian Barnard: One Life.* 1970. NY. 1st Am. 402p. dj. A13. $25.00.

BANBURY, Jen. *Like a Hole in the Head.* 1998. Boston/NY. Little, Brn. 1st. F/F. M23. $40.00.

BANBURY, Jen. *Like a Hole in the Head.* 1998. Boston. Little, Brn. 1st. VG/VG+. G8. $40.00.

BANCROFT, A. L. *Author's Carnival Album.* 1880. SF. ils/line drawings. dk gr cloth. VG. K7. $150.00.

BANCROFT, Edith. *Jane Allen.* Center. 1920. Cupples Leon. 1st. ils Thelma Gooch. 310p. VG+. A25. $30.00.

BANCROFT, Hubert Howe. *History of Central America 1501 – 1887.* 1883 – 1887. Bancroft. 2 vol. maps. M4. $55.00.

BANCROFT, Hubert Howe. *Native Races. Vol IV: Antiquities.* 1886. SF. History Co Pub. ils/fld map. 3-quarter calf. VG. K7. $25.00.

BAND, Max. *Themes from the Bible.* 1964. Los Angeles. Univ of Judaism Press. 4to. ils. many color. red cloth over emb red velvet. inscr. sgn Band. 80p. owner's stp on title pg. K1. $75.00.

BANDEL, Eugene. *Frontier Life in the Army 1854 – 61.* 1932. Arthur H. Clark. fld map. 33p. D11. $125.00.

BANDELIER, Adolf F. *Delight Makers.* 1890. Dodd Mead. 8vo. 490p. brn cloth. VG-. F7. $145.00.

BANDELIER, Adolf F. *Delight Makers.* 1942. Dodd Mead. rpt. VG/G. O4. $15.00.

BANDELIER & HEWETT. *Indians of the Rio Grande Valley.* 1937. Albuquerque. 1st. VG/fair. B5. $55.00.

BANFIELD, E. J. *My Tropic Isle.* 1913. London. 3rd. 315p. A17. $15.00.

BANGS, John Kendrick. *Bikey the Skicycle & Other Tales of Jimmieboy.* 1902. Riggs. 1st. ils Peter Newell. lacks ffep. VG. M5. $75.00.

BANGS, John Kendrick. *Bikey the Skicycle & Other Tales of Jimmieboy.* 1902. NY. Riggs Publishing Co. 1st. sm 8vo. bl cloth w/gilt title. wht design. top edges stained bl. 321p. G+. D6. $40.00.

BANGS, John Kendrick. *House-Boat on the Styx.* 1896. Harper. 1st. 12mo. 172p+4p ads. gr cloth. VG. C6. $65.00.

BANGS, John Kendrick. *Mr. Bonaparte of Corsica.* 1895. Harper. 1st. ils HW McVicakr. 265p. G. H1. $35.00.

BANGS, John Kendrick. *Over the Plum Pudding.* 1901. Harper. 1st. VG. M2. $50.00.

BANGS, John Kendrick. *R Holmes & Co.* 1906. Arthur F Bird. 1st. G. P3. $75.00.

BANGS, John Kendrick. *Sherlock Holmes Again: A Wonderful Achievement in Ferreting.* 1999. NY. Mysterious Bookshop. 1st separate ed. 1/221 copies. A chapbook. VF/pict wrp. T2. $10.00.

BANGS, John Kendrick. *The Mystery of Pinkham's Diamond Stud: A Sherlock Holmes Adventure Dreamed by Fulton Streete.* 1999. NY. Mysterious Bookshop. 1st separate ed. 1/221 copies. A chapbook. VF/pict wrp. T2. $10.00.

BANISTER, Judith. *English Silver.* 1969. London. Hamlyn. 1st. 12mo. 71 mc pl. AN/dj. H1. $16.00.

BANKO, W. E. *Trumpeter Swan.* 1980. Lincoln. NE. 214p. ils wrp. B1. $22.50.

BANKS, Carolyn. *Darkroom.* 1980. Viking. 1st. F/F. P3. $15.00.

BANKS, Charles Edward. *Planters of the Commonwealth.* 1930. Houghton Mifflin. 1/787. ils. F. O7. $225.00.

BANKS, Iain M. *Canal Dreams.* 1991. NY. Doubleday. 1st. F/F. O11. $20.00.

BANKS, Iain M. *Complicity.* 1995. NY. Nan A. Talese/Doubleday. UP. F. O11. $15.00.

BANKS, Iain M. *Complicity.* (1995). NY. Talese. ARC of 1st Am ed. pict wrp. F. B3. $30.00.

BANKS, Iain M. *Consider Phlebas.* 1988. St Martin. 1st Am. F/dj. A24. $25.00.

BANKS, Iain M. *Player of Games.* 1988. Macmillan. 1st. F/F. P3. $30.00.

BANKS, Iain M. *State of the Art.* 1989. Ziesing. 1st. F/F. P3. $25.00.

BANKS, Iain M. *The Wasp Factory.* 1984. Boston. Houghton Mifflin. 1st Am ed. author's 1st book. F/NF. slight edgewear. O11. $40.00.

BANKS, Iain M. *Walking on Glass.* 1986. Boston. Houghton Mifflin. 1st Am ed. Not For Resale stp on dj. F/F. O11. $20.00.

BANKS, Iain M. *Walking on Glass.* (1985). London. Macmillan. 1st British ed. F/F. B3. $60.00.

BANKS, Joanne Trautmann. *Literature & Medicine, Vol 5: Use & Abuse Literary Concepts.* 1986. Johns Hopkins. 8vo. 185p. brd. F. C14. $15.00.

BANKS, Louis Albert. *Story of the Hall of Fame.* 1902. NY. Christian Herald. A19. $25.00.

BANKS, Lynne Reid. *Airy Rebel.* 1985. NY. Doubleday. 1st. sgn. VG/VG. A23. $32.00.

BANKS, Lynne Reid. *House of Hope.* 1962. NY. S&S. 1st. NF/VG dj. M19. $25.00.

BANKS, Lynne Reid. *I, Houdini.* 1988. Doubleday. 1st. sgn. VG/VG. A23. $32.00.

BANKS, Lynne Reid. *Return of the Indian.* 1986. Doubleday. 1st. NF/dj. M25. $25.00.

BANKS, Roger. *Unrelenting Ice.* 1962. London. Constable. 8vo. 197p. VG/worn. P4. $45.00.

BANKS, Russell. *Affliction.* 1989. Harper Row. 1st. 8vo. 355p. F/dj. C6. $20.00.

BANKS, Russell. *Cloudsplitter.* 1998. NY. Harper Flamingo. 1st. ARC. F. D10. $20.00.

BANKS, Russell. *Continental Drift.* 1985. NY. Harper & Row. 1st. NF/NF+. H11. $20.00.

BANKS, Russell. *Hamilton Stark.* 1978. Boston. Houghton Mifflin. sgn 1st ed. F/NF. dj spine ls sunned. sm tear. M23. $100.00.

BANKS, Russell. *Relationship of My Imprisonment.* 1983. Sun Moon. 1st. F/F. R14. $40.00.

BANKS, Russell. *Rule of the Bone.* 1995. NY. Harper Collins. 1st. sgn. F/F. O11. $30.00.

BANKS, Russell. *Searching for Survivors.* 1975. NY. Fiction Collective. sgn 1st ed. author's 1st book. F/F. M23. $150.00.

BANKS, Russell. *Success Stories.* 1986. NY. Harper Row. 1st. F/dj. Q1. $25.00.

BANKS, Russell. *The Sweet Hereafter.* 1991. Harper Collins. 1st. sgn. F/F. M25. $35.00.

BANKS, Russell. *The Sweet Hereafter.* 1991. NY. Harper Collins. 1st. VF/F+. H11. $40.00.

BANKS & READ. *History of the San Francisco Disaster & Mt Vesuvius Horror.* nd. SF. self pub. ils. 8vo. VG. O4. $25.00.

BANN & HUBBARD. *Impressions: Short Sketches & Intimacies...Elbert Hubbard.* 1927 (1921). Roycrofters. 2nd. 12 tipped-in photos. teg. F/G. H3. $85.00.

BANNATYNE, Gilbert. *Rheumatoid Arthritis: Its Pathology.* Morbid Anatomy... 1896. Bristol. ils. 173p. A13. $300.00.

BANNERMAN, Helen. *Little Black Sambo.* 1948. NY. S&S. a Golden Book. pict brds. ils Gustaf Tenggren. lightly soiled w/edgewear. G+. B18. $35.00.

BANNERMAN, Helen. *Little Black Sambo.* 1932. Whitman. ils Nina Jordan. 16mo. pict brd. R5. $150.00.

BANNERMAN, Helen. *Little Black Sambo.* 1942. Saalfield. ils Ethel Hays. 16p. VG. M5. $125.00.

BANNERMAN, Helen. *Little Black Sambo Also the Gingerbread Man & Titty Mouse and Tatty Mouse.* (1928). Chicago. Rand McNally. 1934 ed. ils Margaret Evans Price. 16mo. 64p. VG+. D6. $85.00.

BANNERMAN, Helen. *Little Black Sambo.* ca 1920s. Chicago. Whitman. Just Right Books. enlarged prt ed. ils Shinn. 63p. D1. $400.00.

BANNERMAN, Helen. *Story of Little Black Mingo.* 1901. London. Nesbit. 2nd. 16mo. gray textured cloth. R5. $225.00.

BANNERMAN, Helen. *Story of Little Black Quibba.* 1903. NY. Stokes. 1st Am. 16mo. R5. $350.00.

BANNERMAN, Helen. *Story of Little Black Sambo.* 1919. Donohue. Peter Rabbit series. ils. 8vo. red brd/pict label. G. D1. $200.00.

BANNERMAN & NEILL. *Peter Rabbit & Black Sambo Painting Book.* 1908. Reilly Britton. sm 12mo. VG. C8. $35.00.

BANNING, G. H. *In Mexican Waters.* 1925. Boston. Lauriat. 8vo. ils/photos/map. cloth. VG. M12/O4. $65.00.

BANNING, Kendall. *Pirates! Or, Cruise of the Black Revenge, a Tale...* 1918 (1916). Chicago. Woodworth. rpt. ils Gustave Baumann. F/mailing envelope. D4. $95.00.

BANNING, William. *Heritage Years: Second Marine Division Commememorative...* 1988. Paducah. 1st. 1/1000. 191p. VG. S16. $50.00.

BANNING & HUGH. *Six Horses.* 1930. Century. VG. O3. $35.00.

BANNION, Della; See Sellers, Con.

BANNISTER, Jo. *No Birds Sing.* 1996. NY. St. Martin. 1st Am ed. NF/NF. G8. $15.00.

BANNISTER, Jo. *Primrose Convention.* 1998. NY. St. Martin. 1st Am ed. F/F. G8. $15.00.

BANNISTER, Jo. *Taste for Burning.* 1995. NY. St. Martin. 1st Am ed. NF/NF. G8. $20.00.

BANTA, R. E. *The Ohio.* 1949. NY. ils Edward Shenton. 592p. VG in dj. torn. B18. $35.00.

BANTOCK, Nick. *Egyptian Jukebox.* 1993. Viking. 1st. rem mk. F/dj. B17. $15.00.

BANTOCK, Nick. *Griffin & Sabine.* 1991. Chronicle. 1st prt. F/F. B3. $125.00.

BANTOCK, Nick. *Griffin & Sabine.* (1991). San Francisco. Chronicle. 1st. very rare. children's ils. F/NF price clip. B3. $75.00.

BANTOCK, Nick. *Runners, Sliders, Bouncers, Climbers.* 1992. Hyperion. 1st. obl 8vo. VG+. B17. $16.00.

BANTOCK, Nick. *Solomon Grundi.* 1992. Viking. probable 1st. sm 16mo. rem mk. F. B17. $6.00.

BANTOCK, Nick. *The Forgetting Room.* 1997. Harper Collins. special ARC. sgn bkplt on ffep. F/F. M25. $50.00.

BANTON, O.T. *Decatur, Illinois: A Pictorial History.* 1983. Macon Co Hist Soc. VG. B9. $15.00.

BANVILLE, John. *Athena.* 1995. London. Secker Warburg. 1st. NF/dj. A24. $35.00.

BANVILLE, John. *Book of Evidence.* 1990. Scribner. 1st Am. sgn. F/dj. D10. $40.00.

BANVILLE, John. *Book of Evidence.* 1989. London. 1st. dj. T9. $20.00.

BANVILLE, John. *Doctor Copernicus.* 1976. Norton. 1st Am ed. author's 3rd book. NF/chipped dj. short tear on front cover. M25. $60.00.

BANVILLE, John. *Ghosts.* 1993. London. Secker & Warburg. true 1st UK ed. author's 9th novel. NF/NF. D10. $40.00.

BANVILLE, John. *Kepler.* 1983. Boston. Godine. 1st Am ed. author's 5th novel. NF/NF. lt wear. D10. $55.00.

BANVILLE, John. *Long Lankin.* 1970. London. Secker Warburg. UP. sgn. NF/wrp. B4. $850.00.

BANVILLE, John. *Mefisto.* 1986. London. Secker & Warburg. 1st. F/F. D10. $50.00.

BANVILLE, John. *The Newton Letter.* 1987. Boston. Godine. 1st Am ed. sgn by author. F/F. D10. $50.00.

BAPTIST, R. Hernekin. *Cargo of Parrots.* 1937. Boston. Little, Brn. 1st. F/F. B4. $85.00.

BARAGA, Frederic. *Dictionary of the Ojibway Language.* 1992. MN Hist Soc. rpt 1878 ed. 736p. M/wrp. A17. $25.00.

BARAGWANATH, A.K. *Currier & Ives Favorites.* 1979. NY. Crown. 1st. 160p. F/dj. O10. $45.00.

BARAKA, Amiri. *Dikt for Viderekomne.* 1983. Oslo. 1st Norwegian. author's sgn copy. VG/wrp. B4. $125.00.

BARAKA, Amiri and Leroy Jones. *Selected Poetry of.* 1979. William Morrow. 1st. w/publicity sheet. F/F. V1. $75.00.

BARAKA, Imamu Amiri. *Afrikan Revolution.* 1973. Newark. Jihad. 1st. wrps. F. B2. $25.00.

BARBER, Charles William. *An Illustrated Outline of Weather Science.* 1943. NY. Pitman. 2nd printing. 118 b/w photos & diagrams. 8vo. 248p. VG/chipped dj. scattered pencil mks. K5. $15.00.

BARBER, Edwin A. *American Glassware.* 1900. McKay. 1st. 112p. VG. M20. $25.00.

BARBER, N. *Sinister Twilight: Fall of Singapore.* 1942. 1968. MA. map/index. 364p. VG/VG. S16. $20.00.

BARBER, Noel. *Sultans.* 1973. S&S. 1st. 8vo. ils/pl. 304p. cloth. VG/dj. W1. $18.00.

BARBER, Rowland. *The Night They Raided Minsky's.* 1960. np. 1st. dj. NF/NF. M19. $17.50.

BARBER, W. A. & R. F. Schabelitz. *Murder Enters the Picture.* 1942. Crime Club. 1st. G/VG. G8. $20.00.

BARBER, Wiletta Ann. *Drawback to Murder.* 1947. Scribner. 1st. G+. P3. $30.00.

BARBIER, Dominique. *Dressage for the New Age.* 1990. Prentice Hall. 1st. F/F. O3. $22.00.

BARBOT, Jean. *Barbot on Guinea. The Writings of Jean Barbot on West Africa. 1678 – 1712. 2 Volumes.* 1992. London. Hakluyt Society. 1st. 2nd series. vols. 175 & 176. ed by P.E.H. Hair, Adam Jones, Robin Law. blue cloth. 8vo. 916p. New in rubbed dj. P4. $100.00.

BARBOUR, John. *Footprints on the Moon.* 1969. Assoc Pr. 216p. lg 4to. dj. A17. $12.50.

BARCLAY, Bill; See Moorcock, Michael.

BARCLAY, Florence L. *Wall of Partition.* 1914. Putnam. 1st. 421p. VG. W2. $40.00.

BARCLAY, Glen St. John. *Anatomy of Horror: Masters of Occult Fiction.* 1978. St Martin. 1st. F/dj. M2. $25.00.

BARCLAY, John. *Apology for the True Christian Divinity…* 1789. Phil. Joseph James. 574p. leather/rpl leather spine. V3. $55.00.

BARCLAY, John. *Memoirs of the Rise. Progress & Persecutions…Quakers…* 1835. Phil. Nathan Kite. 354p. leather. V3. $32.00.

BARCLAY, John. *Selection from Letters & Papers Of.* 1847. Phil. Longstreth. 1st Am. 328p. xl. V3. $18.00.

BARCLAY, John. *Truth Triumphant Through the Spiritual Warfare.* 1831. Phil. BC Stanton. 3 vol. G. V3. $165.00.

BARCLAY, William. *Daily Study Bible: Revelation Vol 1 & 2.* 1975 – 76. Westminster. VG. B29. $8.00.

BARCLAY, William. *Ethics in a Permissive Society.* 1971. Harper. 223p. VG. B29. $7.50.

BARCLAY, William. *Letters to the Philippians, Colossians & Thessalonians.* 1959. Westminster. 253p. VG/dj. B29. $6.50.

BARCLAY, Wilson. *The Seventh Man.* 1935. NY. Dial. 1st Am ed. F/VG dj. M15. $45.00.

BARD, Samuel A. *Waikna; or, Adventures on the Mosquito Shore.* 1855. NY. Harper & Bros. 1st. orig blk cloth. rebacked. An artist's tour of Jamaica. w/60 ils & map. foxed. nice. B14. $125.00.

BARDACH, J. E. *Aquaculture: Farming & Husbandry of Fresh-Water & Marine…* 1972. NY. Wiley. photos/figures/tables. 868p. cloth. F. M12. $37.50.

BARDI, P.M. *Lasar Segall.* 1952. Sao Paulo. Museu De Sao Paulo. Italian text. sm 4to. ils. G/poor. F1. $40.00.

BARDIN, John Franklin. *Last of Philip Banter.* 1947. Dodd Mead. 1st. VG/clip. M15. $75.00.

BARDIN, John Franklin. *Purloining Tiny.* 1978. Harper Row. 1st. VG/VG. P3. $35.00.

BARDWELL, Harrison. *Girl Sky Pilot: Roberta's Flying Courage (#1).* 1930. Saalfield. 1st thus. ils. VG/dj. A25. $30.00.

BAREA, Arturo. *Forging of a Rebel.* 1972. London. trans I Barea. dj. T9. $25.00.

BARENHOLTZ, Edith F. *George Brown Toy Sketchbook.* 1971. Princeton. Pyne. 1st. ils Geo Brown. 60p. NF/case. D1. $125.00.

BARER, Burl. *Man Overboard: Counterfeit Resurrection of Phil Champagne.* 1994. Salt Lake City. 1st. F/dj. A23. $30.00.

BARER, Burl. *Maverick.* 1994. Boston. Tuttle. 1st. 222p. VG/wrp. C5. $12.50.

BARHLOTT, Wilhelm. *Cacti.* 1979. Cheltenham. 249p. F/dj. B26. $29.00.

BARICH, Bill. *Carson Valley.* 1997. Pantheon. ARC. F/decor wrps. M25. $25.00.

BARING-GOULD, Sabine. *A Book of Ghosts.* 1996. Penyffordd. Chester. Ash Tree Press. reissue. 1st thus. collects 23 ghost stories. VF/VF. T2. $50.00.

BARING-GOULD, Sabine. *Domitia.* 1898. Stokes. VG. P3. $25.00.

BARING-GOULD, William S. *Annotated Sherlock Holmes.* 1972. Clarkson Potter. 2nd/8th prt. 2 vol. 4to. F/VG case. H1. $60.00.

BARING-GOULD & BARING-GOULD. *The Annotated Mother Goose.* 1962. Clarkson Potter. 1st. 900 rhymes. cloth brd. F/dj. B24. $125.00.

BARIO, Joanne. *Fatal Dreams.* 1985. NY. Dial. 1st. author's 1st book. F/F. H11. $30.00.

BARJAVEL, Rene. *Immortals.* 1974. Morrow. 1st. VG/VG. P3. $20.00.

BARKER, A. J. *German Infantry Weapons of WWII.* 1969. NY. 1st. 76p. F/dj. E1. $25.00.

BARKER, A. J. Dunkirk. *Great Escape.* 1977. NY. 1st Am. 240p. VG/VG. S16. $22.50.

BARKER, B. U. *Houses of the Revolution in Hanover, Massachusetts.* 1976. Hanover. photos/fld map. 151p. M4. $20.00.

BARKER, Catherine. *Yesterday Today.* 1941. Caxton. 1st. ils. 263p. VG/dj. B5. $25.00.

BARKER, Cicely Mary. *Fairies of the Trees.* 1940. London. Blackie. 4 full-p pl. 16mo. tan pict brd/mc label. dj. R5. $125.00.

BARKER, Cicely Mary. *Flower Fairies of the Summer.* 1925. London. Blackie. 16mo. tan brd/pict label. dj. R5. $125.00.

BARKER, Cicely Mary. *Little Book of Old Rhymes.* 1976. London. Blackie. sm 4to. unp. NF/dj. C14. $10.00.

BARKER, Clive. *Books of Blood Volume 1.* 1991. MacDonald. F/F. P3. $25.00.

BARKER, Clive. *Books of Blood: Volume II.* 1991. London. MacDonald. reissue. NF/dj. A14. $21.00.

BARKER, Clive. *Cabal.* 1988. NY. Poseidon. 1st. F/F. rem mk. H11. $25.00.

BARKER, Clive. *Everville.* (1994). NY. Harper Collins. 1st. F/F. B3. $30.00.

BARKER, Clive. *Everville.* 1994. Harper Collins. 1st. inscr. F/F. M19. $25.00.

BARKER, Clive. *Great & Secret Show.* 1990. Harper Row. 1st. F/F. P3. $20.00.

BARKER, Clive. *Imajica.* (1991). NY. Harper Collins. 1st. F/F. B3. $40.00.

BARKER, Clive. *Imajica.* (1991). NY. Harper Collins. 1st. sgn by author. F/VG lt wear and soiling. B3. $50.00.

BARKER, Clive. *In the Flesh.* 1986. NY. Poseidon. 1st. F/F. rem mk. H11. $25.00.

BARKER, Clive. *In the Flesh.* 1986. Poseidon. 1st. sgn. F/F. B3. $75.00.

BARKER, Clive. *In the Flesh.* 1986. Poseidon. 1st. F/F. P3. $30.00.

BARKER, Clive. *Inhuman Condition.* 1986. NY. Poseidon. 1st U.S. sgn. F/F. D10. $85.00.

BARKER, Clive. *Inhuman Condition.* 1986. Poseidon. 1st Am. sgn. F/F. D10. $85.00.

BARKER, Clive. *The Damnation Game.* (1987). NY. Putnam. 1st. sgn by author. lt edgewear. F/NF. B3. $65.00.

BARKER, Clive. *The Damnation Game.* 1987. NY. Ace/Putnam. 1st Am ed. sgn. F/F. A24. $50.00.

BARKER, Clive. *The Damnation Game.* 1987. NY. Putnam. 1st. author's 1st novel. VF/VF. H11. $65.00.

BARKER, Clive. *The Great and Secret Show.* 1989. NY. Harper & Row. 1st. F/F-. H11. $20.00.

BARKER, Clive. *The Thief of Always.* (1992). NY. Harper Collins. 1st. sgn by author. F/F. B3. $55.00.

BARKER, Clive. *Weaveworld.* 1987. NY. Poseidon. 1st. F/F. H11. $25.00.

BARKER, Clive. *Weaveworld.* 1987. Collins. 1st. F/F. P3. $25.00.

BARKER, Eileen. *Of Gods and Men: New Religious Movements in the West.* 1983. Mercer. 347p. VG/VG. B29. $13.00.

BARKER, George C. *Pachuco: An American Spanish Argot and Its Social Functions in Tucson, Arizona.* 1958. Univ of Arizona Press. 46p. ex lib. B19. $3.50.

BARKER, Lady. *Station Amusements in New Zealand.* 1953. Christchurch, NZ. Whitcombe Tombs. 1st thus. ils/map. 236p. VG/dj. A25. $18.00.

BARKER, M. H. *Tough Yarns.* 1835. London. Effingham Wilson. ils George Cruikshank. 351p. older half calf. T7. $110.00.

BARKER, Pat. *The Ghost Road.* 1995. London. Viking. 1st. F in F dj. B2. $125.00.

BARKER, Pat. *The Ghost Road.* 1995. NY. Dutton. 1st Am ed. F/F. A24. $20.00.

BARKER, Pat. *Union Street.* 1983. NY. Putnam. 1st Am ed. author's 1st book. F/F. D10. $65.00.

BARKER, Ralph. *Small Fruits.* 1954. NY. Rinehart's Garden Lib. ils. photo brd. B26. $11.00.

BARKER, Shirley. *Liza Bowe.* 1956. Random. ARC. RS. F/F clip. B4. $50.00.

BARKER, Shirley. *Peace, My Daughters.* 1949. Crown. NF/dj. M2. $15.00.

BARKER, Shirley. *Swear By Apollo.* 1958. Random. 1st. VG/VG. P3. $35.00.

BARKER, Wayne. *Cryptanalysis of Single Columnar Transposition Cipher.* 1961. 1st. full leather. VG. E6. $25.00.

BARKER, William P. *Everyone in the Bible.* 1966. Revell. 370p. VG. B29. $9.00.

BARKWORTH, S. *Nijmegen Proof.* 1988. Phil. Holmes. 1st. 1/650. sgn. F/dj. K3. $40.00.

BARLAY, Stephen. *Tsunami.* 1986. Hamish Hamilton. 1st. NF/NF. P3. $22.00.

BARLOW, James. *The Patriots.* 1960. London. Hamish Hamilton. 1st. sgn. F/F. D10. $45.00.

BARLOW, James. *The Patriots.* 1960. London. Hamish Hamilton. true 1st UK ed. author's 4th novel. sgn in pencil on ffep. NF/NF. D10. $50.00.

BARLOW, Jean. *End of Elfintown.* 1894. London. Macmillan. 1st. 77p. aeg. G+. P2. $150.00.

BARLOW, Roger. *A Brief Summe of Geographie.* 1932. London. Haluyt Society. 1st. 2nd series. no. LXIX. blue cloth 8vo w/ gilt spine titles and cover vignette. 210p. VG. corners bumped in faded dj. P4. $150.00.

BARLOW, Roger. *Sandy Steele: Black Treasure (#1).* 1959. S&S. 1st. VG/G. P3. $10.00.

BARLOWE, Wayne-Douglas. *Star Wars: A Popup Book.* 1978. Random. 1st. VG. M2. $25.00.

BARMBY, Cuthbert. *James Cope.* 1899. NY. New Amsterdam. 1st. Label on front pastedown. Pictorial cloth covered boards. F. M15. $75.00.

BARMEY, Libeus. *Letters of the Pike's Peak Gold Rush.* 1959. San Jose, CA. Talisman. 1/975. red/gray bdg. M/F. K7. $85.00.

BARNAO, Jack. *Lockestep.* 1987. NY. Scribner's. 1st. NF/NF. G8. $20.00.

BARNAO, Jack. *Timelocke.* (1991). NY. Scribner's. 1st. F/F. B3. $15.00.

BARNARD, Christian. *Night Season.* 1978. Prentice Hall. 1st. VG/dj. M20. $14.00.

BARNARD, J. Edwin. *Practical Photo-Micrography.* 1911. London. Edward Arnold. ne. ils. orig cloth. 322p. extra nice. B14. $125.00.

BARNARD, Robert. *A City of Strangers.* 1990. NY. Scribners. 1st. sgn. VF/VF. T2. $25.00.

BARNARD, Robert. *A Hovering of Vultures.* 1993. London. Bantam Press. 1st. VF/VF. T2. $25.00.

BARNARD, Robert. *Black Brotherhood.* 1977. London. Collins Crime Club. 1st. inscr. F/dj. M15. $500.00.

BARNARD, Robert. *Bodies.* 1986. Scribner. 1st. VG/VG. P3. $14.00.

BARNARD, Robert. *Cherry Blossom Corpse.* 1987. Scribner. 1st. VG/VG. P3. $15.00.

BARNARD, Robert. *Corpse in a Gilded Cage.* 1984. NY. Scribners. 1st. F/F. H11. $35.00.

BARNARD, Robert. *Death and the Chaste Apprentice.* 1989. NY. Scribners. 1st. VF/F. H11. $30.00.

BARNARD, Robert. *Death by Sheer Torture.* 1982. NY. Scribners. 1st Am. sgn. F/F. D10. $50.00.

BARNARD, Robert. *Death in a Cold Climate.* 1980. London. Collins Crime Club. 1st. F/dj. M15. $200.00.

BARNARD, Robert. *Death of a Literary Widow.* 1980. NY. Scribners. 1st. F/F. H11. $40.00.

BARNARD, Robert. *Death of a Mystery Writer.* 1979. NY. Scribners. 1st. NF/F. H11. $30.00.

BARNARD, Robert. *Death of a Perfect Mother.* 1981. NY. Scribners. 1st. review copy. F/F. H11. $30.00.

BARNARD, Robert. *Death of a Princess.* 1982. NY. Scribners. 1st U. S. sgn. F/F. D10. $55.00.

BARNARD, Robert. *Death of an Old Goat.* 1974. London. Collins Crime Club. F/dj. M15. $200.00.

BARNARD, Robert. *Death on the High C's.* 1977. London. Collins Crime Club. 1st. sgn. clip. F/dj. M15. $350.00.

BARNARD, Robert. *Fete Fatal.* 1985. NY. Scribners. 1st. F+/F+. H11. $30.00.

BARNARD, Robert. *Political Suicide.* 1986. Scribner. 1st. VG/VG. P3. $14.00.

BARNARD, Robert. *School for Murder.* 1984. NY. Scribners. 1st. F+/VF. H11. $40.00.

BARNARD, Robert. *Touched by the Dead.* 1999. London. Harper Collins. 1st. sgn. VF/VF. T2. $38.00.

BARNES, Claude, Jr. *John F. Kennedy. Scrimshaw Collector.* 1969. Boston. Little, Brn & Co. 1st. blue cloth 4to. 129p. NF/VG dj. P4. $150.00.

BARNES, Djuna. *Ryder.* 1928. Horace Livveright. 1st. VG. B2. $50.00.

BARNES, F. A. *Canyon Country Geology for the Layman & Rockhound.* 1993. Wasatach. 8vo. 160p. VG. F7. $6.00.

BARNES, F. A. *Utah Canyon Country.* 1986. UT Geog series. obl 4to. 117p. wrp. F7. $17.00.

BARNES, Joanna. *Silverwood.* 1985. Linden. 1st. VG/VG. P3. $12.00.

BARNES, John. *Evita First Lady — A Biography of Eva Peron.* 1978. np. Grove Press. 1st. F/VG dj. M19. $25.00.

BARNES, John. *Kaleidoscope Century.* 1995. NY. TOR. 1st. errata list. VF/VF. T2. $45.00.

BARNES, John. *Man Who Pulled Down the Sky.* 1986. Cogdon Weed. 1st. VG/VG. P3. $20.00.

BARNES, Julian. *A History of the World in 10½ Chapters.* 1989. NY. Knopf. 1st. poi. F/F. clip. H11. $35.00.

BARNES, Julian. *Cross Channel.* 1996. NY. Knopf. 1st Am ed. review copy. sgn on title pg. F/F. D10. $45.00.

BARNES, Julian. *Duffy.* 1980. London. Jonathan Cape. 1st. Jacket price clipped. VF/dj. M15. $75.00.

BARNES, Julian. *England, England.* 1999. NY. Knopf. 1st Am. sgn. F in F dj. D10. $35.00.

BARNES, Julian. *Flaubert's Parrot.* 1985. NY. Knopf. 1st Am ed. author's 3rd book. NF/NF. D10. $75.00.

BARNES, Julian. *Flaubert's Parrot.* 1985. NY. Knopf. 1st Am ed. sgn. F/F. O11. $135.00.

BARNES, Julian. *Going to the Dogs.* 1987. London. Viking. 1st. F/dj. M25. $45.00.

BARNES, Julian. *Metroland.* 1980. London. Jonathan Cape. 1st British ed. NF/NF. dj Is clip w/sticker affixed to front flap. M23. $225.00.

BARNES, Julian. *Staring at the Sun.* 1986. London. Jonathan Cape. 1st ed. sgn. F/F. clip/pub price sticker. O11. $60.00.

BARNES, Julian. *Talking it Over.* 1991. NY. Knopf. 1st Am ed. sgn. F in F dj. B2. $45.00.

BARNES, Julian. *Talking it Over.* 1991. London. Cape. 1st. sgn. F/F. R14. $45.00.

BARNES, Julian. *The Porcupine.* 1992. London. Jonathan Cape. 1st ed. sgn. F/F. O11. $45.00.

BARNES, Julian. *The Porcupine.* 1992. NY. Knopf. UP. sgn. F. O11. $40.00.

BARNES, Kim. *In the Wilderness.* (1995). NY. Bantam. 1st. author's 1st book. sgn by author and dated. F/F. B3. $45.00.

BARNES, Linda. *A Trouble of Fools.* 1987. NY. St. Martin. 1st. F/F+. H11. $85.00.

BARNES, Linda. *Cities of the Dead.* 1985. NY. St. Martin. 1st. F/dj. M15. $80.00.

BARNES, Linda. *Coyote.* 1990. NY. Delacorte. 1st. F/dj. M15. $45.00.

BARNES, Linda. *Flashpoint.* 1999. NY. Hyperion. 1st. ARC. sgn. F in pict wrp. T2. $20.00.

BARNES, Linda. *Snake Tattoo.* 1989. St. Martin. 1st. VG/dj. N4. $25.00.

BARNES, Linda. *Snapshot.* 1993. NY. Delacorte. 1st. F/F. A24. $15.00.

BARNES, Linda. *Steel Guitar.* 1991. NY. Delacorte. 1st. inscr review copy. F/F. H11. $50.00.

BARNES, R. *Money, Soldiers of London: Imperial Services Lib Vol VI.* 1963. London. Seeley. ils. 376p. VG/dj. S16. $40.00.

BARNES, Simon. *Rogue Lion Safaris.* 1997. London. Harper Collins. 1st. author's 1st novel. VF/VF. T2. $25.00.

BARNES, Trevor. *A Midsummer Night's Killing.* 1989. NY. Morrow. 1st. author's 1st book. F/F. H11. $25.00.

BARNES, Trevor. *Pound of Flesh.* 1991. Morrow. 1st Am. F/F. M22. $10.00.

BARNETT, Albert E. *The New Testament: Its Making and Meaning.* 1946. Abingdon. 304p. VG. B29. $9.00.

BARNETT, Albert E. *The New Testament: Its Making and Meaning.* 1946. Abingdon. 304p. G/torn dj. B29. $5.00.

BARNETT, Correlli. *Desert Generals.* 1961. NY. ils/maps. 320p. VG/VG. S16. $25.00.

BARNETT, James. *Backfire Is Hostile!* 1979. NY. St. Martin. 1st. NF/NF. G8. $15.00.

BARNETT, Lincoln. *The Universe and Dr. Einstein.* 1948. NY. William Sloane. 3rd printing. 8vo. photos. diagrams. inscr on ffep. clip. 127p. G/torn dj. K5. $12.00.

BARNETT, Lincoln. *Treasure of Our Tongue.* 1964. Knopf. 1st. F/F. B35. $28.00.

BARNEY, Maginel Wright. *Valley of the God Almighty Joneses.* 1965. NY. 1st. VG/dj. B5. $40.00.

BARNHARDT, Wilton. *Gospel.* (1993). NY. St. Martin. 1st. inscr & dated by author. F/F. B3. $25.00.

BARNHART, John Hendley. *Bibliography of John Kunkel Small.* 1935. NY. 1st. 15p. VG/wrp. M8. $45.00.

BARNHOUSE, Donald G. *Invisible War.* 1965. Zondervan. 288p. VG/torn. B29. $9.00.

BARNSTONE, H. *Galveston That Was.* 1966. NY/Houston. 1st. photos HC Bresson. VG/VG. B5. $75.00.

BARNUM, H. L. *The American Farrier.* 1845. Philadelphia. Uriah Hunt & Son. (1st ed was 1832). Leather. G/edges scuffed. top of spine torn. inside tight and clean. O3. $45.00.

BARNUM, P. T. *Life of PT Barnum: Written By Himself.* 1855. NY. Redfield. 1st. author's 1st book. VG. Q1. $175.00.

BARNUM, P. T. *Struggles and Triumphs; or the Life of P. T. Barnum.* 1927. NY. Knopf. 2 vols. bstp cloth. some ils. 879p. F in soiled slipcase. B18. $95.00.

BARON, Randall. *Bridge Player's Dictionary.* nd. VG. S1. $12.00.

BARON, Virginia. *Sunset in the Spider Web.* 1974. HRW. 1st. 82p. F/F. D4. $30.00.

BARON & CARVER. *Bud Stewart: Michigan's Legendary Lure Maker.* 1990. Marceline, MO. 1st. 227p. w/price list. M. A17. $75.00.

BARONI, Aldo. *Yucatan.* 1937. Mexico. Ediciones Botas. 1st. 211p. G/wrp. F3. $20.00.

BARR, Donald. *Space Relations.* 1973. Charterhouse. 1st. F/dj. M2. $15.00.

BARR, George. *Upon the Winds of Yesterday.* 1976. Donald Grant. 1st. sgn. F/F. P3. $40.00.

BARR, Nevada. *A Superior Death.* 1994. NY. Putnam. 1st. F/F. H11. $70.00.

BARR, Nevada. *Bearing Secrets.* 1996. Walker. UP. sgn. sticker on cover. NF. orange wrp. M25. $45.00.

BARR, Nevada. *Blind Descent.* (1998). NY. Putnam. 1st. sgn by author on tipped in sheet. F/F. B3. $40.00.

BARR, Nevada. *Blind Descent.* 1998. NY. Putnam. ARC. F in wrp. B2. $35.00.

BARR, Nevada. *Endangered Species.* 1997. Putnam. ARC. NF. wrp. M25. $35.00.

BARR, Nevada. *Endangered Species.* 1997. NY. Putnam. 1st. F/VF. H11. $25.00.

BARR, Nevada. *Firestorm.* 1996. Putnam. ARC. NF. decor wrp. M25. $35.00.

BARR, Nevada. *Firestorm.* 1996. NY. Putnam. 1st. sgn. VF/VF. T2. $35.00.

BARR, Nevada. *Ill Wind.* 1995. NY. Putnam. 1st. VF/F. H11. $35.00.

BARR, Nevada. *Ill Wind.* 1995. Putnam. ARC. sgn. F/F. D10. $45.00.

BARR, Nevada. *Liberty Falling.* 1999. NY. Putnam. UP. sgn. F in wrp. D10. $40.00.

BARR, Nevada. *Liberty Falling.* 1999. NY. Putnam. 1st. F/F. G8. $25.00.

BARR, Nevada. *Liberty Falling.* 1999. NY. Putnam. 1st. sgn. VF/VF. T2. $25.00.

BARR, Nevada. *Superior Death.* 1994. Putnam. 1st. author's 2nd mystery. rem mk. F/F. B2. $85.00.

BARR, Nevada. *Track of the Cat.* 1993. NY. Putnam. 1st. VF/dj. M15. $250.00.

BARR, Roseanne. *My Life as a Woman.* 1989. Harper Row. 1st. F/F. A20. $15.00.

BARR, William and Glyndwr Williams. *Voyages in Search of a Northwest Passage, 1741 – 1747. Vol. 2. The Voyage of William Moor and Francis Smith 1746 – 1747.* 1995. London. Hakluyt Society. second series. no. 181. blue cloth 8vo with gilt spine titles. vignette on cover. 393p. NF/rubbed dj. P4. $65.00.

BARRAS DE ARAGON, Francisco. *Documentos Referentes A Mutis Y Su Tiempo.* 1933. Madrid. 35p. VG/wrp. F3. $20.00.

BARRATT, Glynn. *Southern & Eastern Polynesia.* 1988. Vancouver. 1st. 8vo. 302p. AN/dj. P4. $57.00.

BARRE, Richard. *Bearing Secrets.* 1996. NY. Walker. 1st. sgn. F/dj. T2. $35.00.

BARRE, Richard. *Blackheart Highway.* 1999. NY. Berkley. 1st. sgn. VF/VF. T2. $25.00.

BARRE, Richard. *Ghosts of Morning.* 1998. np. 1st. sgn. F/F. G8. $25.00.

BARRE, Richard. *The Innocents.* 1995. NY. Walker. 1st. sgn. author's 1st novel. VF/dj. M15. $65.00.

BARRE, Richard. *The Innocents.* 1995. NY. Walker. 1st. F/F. M23. $45.00.

BARRET, Richard Carter. *A Collectors Handbook of American Art Glass.* 1971. Manchester, VT. Foward's Color Productions. 1st. 8vo 20 color plates with opposing text. Glossy. illustrated wraps with plastic comb binding. Owner's stamp on ffep. VG. H1. $45.00.

BARRET, Richard Carter. *Bennington Pottery & Porcelain.* 1958. Bonanza. ils/index/457 pl. 342p. dk gr cloth. F/dj. H1. $45.00.

BARRET, Richard Carter. *Popular American Ruby-Stained Pattern Glass.* 1968. Manchester, VT. Foward's Color Productions. 1st. unpaginated. text & 14 color plates + color plates on covers. stiff, glossy paper. sbdg. 28p. F. H1. $26.00.

BARRET, William. *Irrational Man.* 1958. NY. Doubleday. 8vo. Some underlining in pencil. upper right corner bumped. Some edge chips & light soil. 278p. VG. H1. $6.50.

BARRETO, Jose Maria. *El Problema Peruano Chileno.* 1912. Lima. np. 274p. G/bds worn. front hinge split. rear cover w/paper rubbed off. F3. $35.00.

BARRETT, Andrea. *Lucid Stars.* 1989. London. S&S. 1st hc of author's 1st book. was PBO in US. F/VF. H11. $95.00.

BARRETT, Andrea. *Lucid Stars.* 1988. Delta Fiction. ARC/author's 1st book. VG/wrp. Q1. $50.00.

BARRETT, Andrea. *Secret Harmonies.* (1989). NY. Delacorte. proof. prt yellow wrp. NF+. very minor soiling. very tight. B3. $40.00.

BARRETT, Andrea. *Ship Fever and Other Stories.* 1996. NY. Norton. 1st. F/F. H11. $65.00.

BARRETT, Andrea. *The Forms of Water.* 1993. NY. Pocket Books. ARC. sgn. F in F dj. D10. $65.00.

BARRETT, Andrea. *The Forms of Water.* 1993. NY. Pocket. 1st. sgn. F/F. H11. $60.00.

BARRETT, Andrea. *The Middle Kingdom.* 1991. NY. Pocket Books. 1st. F in F clip dj. B2. $40.00.

BARRETT, Andrea. *The Middle Kingdom.* (1991). NY. Pocket. 1st. author's third book. sgn by author. F/F. B3. $75.00.

BARRETT, Dean. *Hangman's Point: A Novel of Hong Kong.* 1999. NY. Village East Books. 1st. sgn. VF/VF. T2. $25.00.

BARRETT, Lindsey. *Songs for Mumu.* 1974. Washington. Howard U. 1st. inscr to Walter Mosley. F/NF. D10. $50.00.

BARRETT, Michael. *Antarctic Secret.* 1966. NY. Roy Pub. 2nd. 170p. VG/dj. P4. $25.00.

BARRETT, N. S. *The Picture World of Astronauts.* 1990. NY. Franklin Watts. juvenile. 4to. color photo ils. 30p. F/laminated pict bds. K5. $11.00.

BARRETT, Neal, Jr. *Dead Dog Blues.* 1994. NY. St. Martin. 1st. sgn. VF/VF. H11. $50.00.

BARRETT, Neal Jr. *Hereafter Gang.* 1991. Zeising. 1st. sgn. F/dj. A24. $50.00.

BARRETT, Neal, Jr. *Pink Vodka Blues.* 1992. NY. St. Martin. 1st. inscr. F/F. H11. $110.00.

BARRETT, Neal, Jr. *Skinny Annie Blues.* 1996. NY. Kensington. 1st. sgn. VF/VF. H11. $45.00.

BARRIE, J. M. *Peter and Wendy.* 1911. NY. Scribners. 1st. 8vo. ils by F.D. Bedford. olive gr cloth w/elaborate gilt decor. 267p. NF. D6. $225.00.

BARRIE, J. M. *The Little White Bird or Adventures in Kensington Gardens.* 1902. NY. Scribners. 1st. sm 8vo. ils by H.J. Ford. gr cloth w/gilt. contains first mention of Peter Pan. 349p. VG. D6. $100.00.

BARRIE, James M. *Admirable Crichton.* 1914. Hodder Stoughton. 1st trade. pres. 20 mtd pl. F/case. B20. $600.00.

BARRIE, James M. *Courage: Rectorial Address Delivered St Andrews U.* 1923 (1905). NY. Scribner. 16mo. 49p. VG+/G. C14. $7.00.

BARRIE, James M. *Farewell Miss Julie Logan.* 1932. Scribner. 1st. VG. P3. $20.00.

BARRIE, James M. *Jess.* 1898. Dana Estes. 1st. NF. M19. $45.00.

BARRIE, James M. *Peter Pan.* 1957. Random. ils Marjorie Torrey. 4to. F. M5. $45.00.

BARRIE, James M. *Peter Pan in Kensington Gardens.* 1906. London. Hodder Stoughton. ils Rackham/50 tipped-in pl. G+. B5. $450.00.

BARRIE, James M. *Peter Pan & Wendy.* 1921. Scribner. 1st thus. ils ML Attwell. 4to. olive cloth. M5. $275.00.

BARRIE, James M. *Peter Pan & Wendy.* 1927 (1921). Scribner. ils Mabel L Attwell. VG. B15. $115.00.

BARRIE, James M. *When a Man's Single: Tale of Literary Life.* 1888. Hodder Stoughton. 1st. gilt navy cloth. VG+. S13. $40.00.

BARRINGTON, E. J. W. *Hormones & Evolution.* 1964. Krieger. 154p. cloth. A10. $10.00.

BARRIS, Alex. *Hollywood's Other Men.* 1975. NY. AS Barnes. 223p. VG/dj. C5. $12.50.

BARRIS, Anna Andrews. *Red Tassels for Huki in Peru.* 1939. Chicago. Albert Whitman & Co. ils Iris Beatty Johnson. VG. no dj. A28. $45.95.

BARRON, George L. *Genera of Hyphomycetes from Soil.* 1968. NY. Mershon. 12mo. 221p. gilt bl cloth. VG. A22. $16.00.

BARRON, Stephanie. *Jane and the Genius of the Place.* 1999. NY. Bantam. 1st. sgn. F/F. G8. $22.50.

BARRON, Stephanie. *Jane and the Man of the Cloth.* 1997. NY. Bantam. 1st. sgn. F/F. G8. $22.50.

BARRON, Stephanie. *Jane and the Unpleasantness at Scargrave Manor.* 1996. NY. Bantam. 1st. F/F. M23. $40.00.

BARRON, Stephanie. *Jane and the Wandering Eye.* 1998. NY. Bantam. 1st. sgn. F/F. G8. $20.00.

BARROW, A. H. *Fifty Years in Western Africa: Being a Record of Work…* 1969 (1900). NY. Negro U. rpt. 8vo. map/ils. 157p. cloth. VG. W1. $25.00.

BARROW, Frances Elizabeth. *Bird Stories by Aunt Laura.* 1863. Buffalo. Breed & Butler. 47x37mm. aeg. gilt gr pub cloth. F. B24. $165.00.

BARROW, Frances Elizabeth. *Carl's Visit to the Child Island by Aunt Laura.* 1863. Buffalo. Breed & Butler. 47x36mm. 61p. aeg. gilt pub cloth. B24. $140.00.

BARROW, Frances Elizabeth. *Doll's Surprise by Aunt Laura.* 1863. Buffalo. Breed & Butler. 47x36mm. 64p. aeg. gilt pub cloth. F. B24. $200.00.

BARROW, Frances Elizabeth. *Morsels of History by Aunt Laura.* 1863. Buffalo. Breed & Butler. mini. 64p. aeg. gilt pub cloth. B24. $135.00.

BARROW, Frances Elizabeth. *New Testament Stories by Aunt Laura.* 1862. Buffalo. Breed & Butler. 53x40mm. 64p. aeg. gilt cloth. B24. $135.00.

BARROW, Joe Louis Jr. *Joe Louis: 50 Years an American Hero.* 1988. McGraw Hill. lg 8vo. F/F. C8. $30.00.

BARROW, Terence. *Illustrated Guide to Maori Art.* 1984. New Zealand. Methuen. 104p. VG+/prt wrp. P4. $25.00.

BARROWS, Walter Bradford. *Michigan Bird Life.* 1912. MI Agric College. 822p. lg 8vo. wrp. A17. $50.00.

BARRY, J. *Strange Story of Harper's Ferry with Legends.* 1969. Shepherdstown. 200p. NF. M4. $15.00.

BARRY, James P. *Fate of the Lakes: Portrait of the Great Lakes.* 1972. Grand Rapids. Baker. ils. 192p. dj. T7. $28.00.

BARRY, Jerome. *Fall Guy.* 1960. Crime Club. 1st. VG/G. P3. $18.00.

BARRY, Jerome. *Murder With Your Malted.* 1941. Doubleday Crime Club. 1st. F/clip. M15. $90.00.

BARRY, Patrick. *Barry's Fruit Garden.* 1872. Orange Judd. 491p. cloth. A10. $22.00.

BARRY & LIBBY. *Confessions of a Basketball Gypsy.* 1972. Prentice Hall. photos. VG+/dj. P8. $25.00.

BARRYMORE, Ethel. *Memories.* 1956. London. Hulton. 1st Eng. photos. VG/dj. C9. $24.00.

BARRYMORE, John. *Confessions of an Actor.* 1926. Bobbs Merrill. 1st. VG. C9. $90.00.

BARSLEY, M. *Orient Express.* 1967. NY. 1st. 204p. VG/dj. B5. $30.00.

BARTH, John. *Chimera.* 1972. NY. Random House. 1st. clip. F/F. H11. $30.00.

BARTH, John. *Floating Opera.* 1956. Appleton Century Crofts. 1st. author's 1st book. NF/NF. L3. $450.00.

BARTH, John. *Friday Book.* 1984. Putnam. 1st. NF/VG. B3. $30.00.

BARTH, John. *Giles Goat-Boy.* 1967. Secker Warburg. 1st. VG/VG. P3. $20.00.

BARTH, John. *Last Voyage of Somebody the Sailor.* 1991. Little, Brn. 1st. sgn. F/F. A23. $32.00.

BARTH, John. *Letters.* 1979. NY. Putnam. 1st. issued in 2 dj; silver on blk or gold on blk. no priority in value. F in F dj. B2. $35.00.

BARTH, John. *Sabbatical.* (1982). NY. Putnam. 1st. NF. lt edgewear/NF. lt scratches. B3. $20.00.

BARTH, John. *The Friday Book.* (1984). NY. Putnam. 1st. NF. lt sunning to edges/VG. edgewear. B3. $30.00.

BARTH, Karl. *Church Dogmatics: Doctrine of Creation Vol III.* Part 4. 1985. T&T Clark. 740p. VG. B29. $21.00.

BARTH, Karl. *Ethics.* 1981. NY. Seabury. 534p. VG/G. H10. $35.00.

BARTHEL, Joan. *A Death in California.* 1981. NY. Congdon. 1st. F/F. H11. $15.00.

BARTHELME, Donald. *Amateurs.* 1976. NY. FS6. 1st. F/F. D10. $50.00.

BARTHELME, Donald. *Amateurs.* 1976. FSG. 1st. F/F. B35. $30.00.

BARTHELME, Donald. *Come Back, Dr. Caligari.* 1964. Boston. Little, Brn. 1st. F/NF. B2. $150.00.

BARTHELME, Donald. *Great Days.* 1979. FSG. 1st. F/F. B35. $25.00.

BARTHELME, Donald. *King.* 1990. Harper Row. 1st. NF/NF. A20. $20.00.

BARTHELME, Donald. *Overnight to Many Distant Cities.* 1983. NY. Putnam. 1st. F/NF. D10. $40.00.

BARTHELME, Donald. *Sixty Stories.* 1981. NY. Putnam. UP. NF. M19. $35.00.

BARTHELME, Donald. *Snow White.* 1967. Atheneum. 1st. F/dj. Q1. $100.00.

BARTHELME, Frederick. *Brothers.* 1993. Viking. ARC. F/wrp. B30. $30.00.

BARTHLEME, Donald. *Amateurs.* 1976. NY. FSG. 1st. F/F. clip. O11. $20.00.

BARTHOLOMEW, Ed. *Western Hard-Cases; or, Gunfighers Named Smith.* 1960. Ruidoso. Frontier Book Co. sgn. 191p. cloth. dj. D11. $50.00.

BARTHOLOMEW, Ed. *Wyatt Earp, the Man & the Myth.* 1964. Frontier Book. 1st. photos. 335p. VG/VG. J2. $195.00.

BARTHOLOMEW, Mel. *Square Foot Gardening.* 1981. Emmaus. Rodale. 347p. VG/dj. A10. $18.00.

BARTLETT, Charles H. & Richard H. Lyon. *La Salle in the Valley of the St. Joseph.* 1899. South Bend, IN. Tribune Printing Co. 1st. ils. photos. map. 119p. lt wear to cover edges. G+. B18. $35.00.

BARTLETT, Dana W. *Bush Aflame.* 1923. Grafton Pub. 1st. VG/sans. O4. $25.00.

BARTLETT, David Vandewater G. *Life & Public Services of Hon Abraham Lincoln…* 1860. NY. Derby Jackson. 1st. 354p. cloth. NF. M8. $250.00.

BARTLETT, Frederick Orin. *Web of the Spider.* 1909. Sm Maynard. 1st. VG. M2. $35.00.

BARTLETT, J. Henry. *John H Dillingham 1839 – 1910. Teacher, Minister, Editor.* 1911. Knickerbocker. 190p. VG. V3. $14.00.

BARTLETT, James y. *Death Is a Two Stroke Penalty.* 1991. NY. St. Martin. 1st. VG+/VG+. G8. $12.50.

BARTLETT, John Russell. *Personal Narrative of Explorations & Incidents in Texico, NM.* 1965. Rio Grande Pr. 2 vol. ils/maps. F/sans. B19. $95.00.

BARTLETT, Mary. *Gentians.* 1975. Poole. Dorset. 1st. color plates. photos. line drawings. 160p. F in dj. B26. $21.00.

BARTLETT, Nancy W. *Then Pity, Then Embrace.* 1967. NY. Macmillan. 1st. author's 1st book. F-/F. H11. $35.00.

BARTLETT, Paul. *Haciendas of Mexico.* 1990. Niwot. Univ Press of Colorado. 1st. oblong 4to. 126p. G/G. F3. $30.00.

BARTLETT, W. H. *Forty Days in the Desert.* ca 1850. London. Arthur Hall. 4th. 8vo. 206p. aeg. full red morocco. C6. $125.00.

BARTLETT, W. H. *Walks About the City & Environs of Jerusalem.* Ca 1850. London. Hall Virtue. 2nd. 8vo. 24 hand-colored steel engravings. teg. F. B24. $500.00.

BARTLEY, Whitman S. Lt. Col. *Iwo Jima: Amphibious Epic.* 1954. Washington. GPO. paper covered brds. ils from official photos. 256p+folding maps. G. B18. $50.00.

BARTLEY, William. *Iwo Jima: Amphibious Epic.* 1954. WA. fld maps/photos/index. 253p. VG. S16. $85.00.

BARTON, Benjamin Smith. *Collections for an Essay Towards Materia Medical of US.* 1810. Phil. 3rd. 2 parts. contemporary tree sheep. B14. $150.00.

BARTON, Bruce. *Boy Nobody Knows & the Man Nobody Knows.* 1925 & 1926. Indianapolis. 1st. sgn pres. VG/dj/G box. B5. $40.00.

BARTON, Frank Townsend. *Horses, Their Points and Management in Health and Disease.* nd (1906). London. Everett. 1st. 4to. G. O3. $45.00.

BARTON, Fredrick. *With Extreme Prejudice.* 1993. NY. Villard books. 1st. VF/VF. T2. $20.00.

BARTON, George. *Adventures of World's Greatest Detectives.* 1909. Phil. Winston. 1st. VG/dj. M15. $45.00.

BARTON, George A. *Archaeology and the Bible.* 1952. American. 745p. VG/worn dj. B29. $8.50.

BARTON, George A. *Miscellaneous Babylonian Inscriptions. Part I. Sumarian...* 1918. New Haven/Yale. 1st. 61 pl. half cloth. VG. W1. $55.00.

BARTON, May Hollis. *Barton Books for Girls: Kate Martin's Problem (#10).* 1929. Cupples Leon. lists 15 titles. VG/dj. M20. $40.00.

BARTON, Ralph. *Science in Rhyme without Reason.* 1924. Putnam. 1st. 147p. VG. D4. $25.00.

BARTON, Rebecca Chalmers. *Witnesses for Freedom.* 1948. Harper. 1st. 294p. VG+/VG. B4. $85.00.

BARTON, William Eleazar. *The Lincolns in Their Old Kentucky Home an Address Delivered Before the Filson Club Louisville, Ky Dec. 4, 1922.* 1923. Berea, KY. Berea College Press. 1st. # 23 of ltd 300 copies. orig printed wrp. quarto. 24p. NF. M8. $85.00.

BARTRAM, George. *Job Abroad.* 1975. Macmillan. 1st. VG/VG. P3. $20.00.

BARTRAM, John. *Travels in Pennsylvania & Canada.* 1966. Ann Arbor. Micro. 94p. F. A10. $45.00.

BARTRUM, Douglas. *Growing Cacti & Succulents.* 1973. NY. 12 mc pl. F/dj. B26. $12.50.

BARTRUM, Douglas. *Rhododendrons & Magnolias.* 1957. London. Garden BC. 176p. dj. A10. $28.00.

BARTSCH & NICHOLS. *Fishes & Shells of the Pacific World.* 1945. NY. Macmillan. 1st. 201p. bl cloth. P4. $22.50.

BARUCH, Dorothy W. *In and Out with Betty Anne, More Small Stories for Small People.* 1928. NY. Harper. 1st. 8vo. ils by Winifred Broomhall. 145p. NF. D6. $30.00.

BARUCH & MONTGOMERY. *Sally Does It.* 1940. Appleton. 13th. ils Robb Beebe. 73p. cloth. VG. M20. $125.00.

BARUK, Henri. *Tsedek.* 1972. Swan House. 291p. VG/G+. S3. $21.00.

BARZUN, Jacques. *Catalogue of Crime.* 1971. Harper Row. 1st. xl. VG+/dj. N4. $30.00.

BARZUN, Jacques. *Delights of Detection.* 1961. Criterion. 1st. VG. M2. $10.00.

BARZUN, Jacques & Wendell Hertig Taylor. *A Catalogue of Crime.* 1971. NY. Harper & Row. 1st. Jacket has a closed tear and a couple of scrapes. F/dj. M15. $75.00.

BASCOM, John. *Problems in Philosophy.* 1885. Putnam. 1st. 222p. purple silk-type cloth. VG. B22. $9.50.

BASCULE. *Royal Spades Auction Bridge with Laws...1909.* 1913. London. 180p. VG. S1. $20.00.

BASHO. *Back Roads to Far Towns.* 1968. NY. Bilingual ed. trans Corman/Susumu. VG+/wrp. W3. $15.00.

BASIE, Count. *Count Basie's Piano Styles.* 1940. NY. Bregman. Vocco & Conn. 1st. F/wrp. B2. $40.00.

BASINGER, J. Martin. *Artistry in Silver & Steel. The Adolph Bayers Legend.* 1st. ils Ben Miller. J2. $85.00.

BASINGER, Jeanine. *Woman's View: How Hollywood Spoke to Women 1930 – 1960.* 1993. Knopf. 1st. F/F. V4. $17.50.

BASKERVILLE, Peter. *Bank of Upper Canada. A Collection of Documents.* 1987. Toronto. Champlain Soc. 400p. gilt red cloth. F. P4. $95.00.

BASKIN, Leonard. *Hosie's Alphabet.* 1972. Viking. 1st. 4to. VG/G. P2. $65.00.

BASKIN, Leonard. *Imps, Demons, Hobgoblins, Witches, Fairies & Elves.* 1984. Pantheon. 1st. F/dj. M2. $10.00.

BASS, Charlotta A. *Forty Years: Memoirs from the Pages of a Newspaper.* 1960. Los Angeles. self pub. 1st. inscr/dtd 1960. ils. VG. B4. $175.00.

BASS, Rick. *Deer Pasture.* 1985. TX A&M. 1st. author's 1st book. F/NF. D10. $125.00.

BASS, Rick. *Fathers and Sons.* (1992). NY. Grove Weidenfeld. 1st. ed by David Seybold. other authors included are Kittredge, Gerber, Olmstead, Chatham. sgn by Bass at his contribution. F/F. B3. $75.00.

BASS, Rick. *Fathers & Sons.* 1992. Grove Weidenfeld. 1st. sgn. F/F. B3. $60.00.

BASS, Rick. *Fiber.* (1998). Athens, GA. U of Georgia. 1st. sgn by author. cover ils by Russell Chatham. Ils by Elizabeth Hughes Bass. F/F. B3. $40.00.

BASS, Rick. *In the Loyal Mountains.* 1995. Boston. Houghton Mifflin. 1st. sgn. F/F. D10. $45.00.

BASS, Rick. *In the Loyal Mountains.* (1995). NY. Houghton Mifflin. 1st. sgn by author. F/F. B3. $45.00.

BASS, Rick. *Ninemile Wolves.* 1992. Livingston. Clark City. 1st. sgn. F/F. B3. $75.00.

BASS, Rick. *Oil Notes.* 1989. Boston. Houghton Mifflin. 1st. F/F. M19. $25.00.

BASS, Rick. *Oil Notes.* (1989). Boston. Houghton Mifflin. 1st. ils Elizabeth Hughes (Bass). sgn by author. VF/F. B3. $75.00.

BASS, Rick. *Platte River.* 1994. Boston. Houghton Mifflin. 1st. sgn. F/F. D10. $50.00.

BASS, Rick. *The Book of Yaak.* (1996). NY. Houghton Mifflin. 1st. sgn by author. F/F. B3. $45.00.

BASS, Rick. *The Lost Grizzlies.* (1995). Boston. Houghton Mifflin. ARC. pict wrp. sgn by author. F. B3. $80.00.

BASS, Rick. *The Lost Grizzlies.* (1995). Boston. Houghton Mifflin. ARC. pict wrp. sgn by author. NF. shows lt use. B3. $50.00.

BASS, Rick. *Watch.* 1989. Norton. 1st. author's 3rd book. F/F. T11. $50.00.

BASS, Rick. *Where the Sea Used to Be.* 1998. Houghton Mifflin. UP. NF/printed wrps. M25. $75.00.

BASS, Rick. *Where the Sea Used to Be.* (1998). Boston. Houghton Mifflin. 1st. author's 1st novel. sgn by author. F/F. B3. $40.00.

BASS, Rick. *Wild to the Heart.* 1987. Stackpole. 1st. author's 2nd book. F/F. D10. $85.00.

BASS, Rick. *Wild to the Heart.* 1987. Stackpole. 1st. sgn. author's 2nd book. VG/VG. L1. $150.00.

BASS, Rick. *Winter.* (1991). Boston. Houghton Mifflin. 1st. ils by Elizabeth Hughes (Bass). sgn by author & ils. VF/VF. B3. $75.00.

BASS, T.J. *Godwhale.* 1975. Methuen. 1st. NF/NF. P3. $40.00.

BASSANI, Giorgio. *Garden of the Finzi-Continis.* 1965. Atheneum. 1st Am. NF/clip. D10. $125.00.

BASSANI, Giorgio. *The Garden of Finzi-Continis.* 1965. NY. Atheneum. 1st Am ed. review copy. author's 4th novel. F/F. 2 nicks on slightly darkened spine. D10. $75.00.

BASSET, A. B. *A Treatise on Physical Optics.* 1892. Cambridge. Deighton Bell. 1st. text figures. 8vo. 411p. G/cloth. worn. frayed. hinges neatly reinforced. K5. $60.00.

BASSETT, Lucinda. *From Panic to Power.* 1995. NY. Harper Collins. 1st. bl brds. wht spine. VG/VG. A28. $11.95.

BASSETT, Marnie. *Realms and Islands. The World Voyage of Rose De Freycinet in the Corvette Uranie, 1817 – 1820.* 1962. London. Oxford U Press. 1st. poi on ffep. blue/gray cloth 8vo. map ep. 275p. VG/worn dj. P4. $100.00.

BASSIE-SWEET, Karen. *From the Mouth of the Dark Cave.* 1991. Norman. Univ of Oklahoma Press. 1st. 4to. 287p. F/F. F3. $30.00.

BASSIN, Moshe. *American Yiddish Poetry.* Anthology. 1940. NY. sm 4to. Yiddish text. 601p. VG. S3. $40.00.

BASSO, Hamilton. *Beauregard the Great Creole.* 1933. NY. 1st. VG/VG. B5. $65.00.

BASTABLE, Bernard; See Barnard, Robert.

BATCHELDER, Robert C. *Irreversible Decision 1939 – 1950.* 1962. Boston. Houghton Mifflin. 1st. inscr. NF. K3. $35.00.

BATCHELOR, John Calvin. *American Falls.* 1985. NY. Norton. 1st. F/F. H11. $35.00.

BATCHELOR, John Calvin. *Birth of the People's Republic of Antarctica.* 1985. NY. Dial. 1st. 1/6000. author's 2nd novel. F/F. D10. $65.00.

BATCHELOR, John Calvin. *Father's Day.* 1994. NY. Holt. 1st. F/F. H11. $20.00.

BATCHELOR, John Calvin. *Gordon Liddy Is My Muse.* 1990. NY. Linden Press. 1st. sgn. F/F. D10. $40.00.

BATEMAN, Colin. *Divorcing Jack.* 1995. NY. Arcade. 1st Am ed. VF/VF. T2. $20.00.

BATEMAN, Donald. *Berkeley Moynihan. Surgeon.* 1940. NY. 1st. 354p. A13. $20.00.

BATEMAN, James. *Trapping: A Practical Guide.* 1979. Harrisburg, PA. Stackpole. 1st. NF/VG+. R16. $25.00.

BATEMAN, Robert. *When the Whites Went.* 1963. Walker. 1st. F/NF. B2. $25.00.

BATES, Edward. *Diary of Edward Bates 1859 – 1866.* Edited by Howard K Beale. 1933. GPO. 1st. 685p. cloth. NF. M8. $65.00.

BATES, Frank. *How to Make Old Orchards Profitable.* 1912. Boston. Ball. 123p. VG. A10. $30.00.

BATES, Henry W. *The Naturalist on the River Amazons.* 1915. London. Popular Ed. 40 woodcut ils. 394p. spine faded. inner hinges rpr. red cloth soiled. wrinkled. ep foxed. B26. $19.00.

BATES, Joseph D. *Atlantic Salmon Flies & Fishing.* 1970. Stackpole. 1st. 362p. VG/dj. M20. $80.00.

BATES, Joseph D. *Streamer Fly Tying & Fishing.* 1966. Stackpole. 1st. 368p+8 mc pl. NF/dj. A17. $60.00.

BATES, Katherine Lee. *Fairy Gold, Poems By.* 1916. NY. Dutton. 1st. author of poem America the Beautiful. 223p. G+. D6. $45.00.

BATES, M. Searle. *Religious Liberty: An Inquiry.* 1945. Harper. 604p. G/torn. B29. $7.00.

BATES, Marston. *Land & Wildlife of South America.* (1968). NY. Time. 4to. 200p. pict brd. F3. $10.00.

BATES, Nancy Bell. *East of the Andes and West of Nowhere. A Naturalist's Wife in Columbia.* 1947. NY. 1st. 72 photos. 237p. G. B26. $17.50.

BATES, Tom. *Rads. The 1971 Bombing…At the University of Wisconsin.* 1992. NY. Harper Collins. ARC. F/wrps. B2. $25.00.

BATTAN, Louis J. *The Unclean Sky; A Meteorologist Looks At Air Pollution.* 1966. Garden City. NY. Anchor Books. ex lib in cloth. usual lib mks. ils by author & DC Perceny. 141p. G. K5. $6.00.

BATTEN, Jack. *Crang Plays the Ace.* 1987. Canada. Macmillan. 1st. F/F. P3. $20.00.

BATTEN, Jack. *Straight No Chaser.* 1989. Canada. Macmillan. 1st. F/F. P3. $20.00.

BAUDEZ, Claude. *Maya Sculpture of Copan.* 1994. Norman. Univ of Oklahoma Press. 1st. 4to. 300p. F/F. F3. $60.00.

BAUDOUIN, Frans. *PP Rubens.* 1989. ils. VG/VG. M17. $40.00.

BAUER, C. Max. *Yellowstone: Its Underworld.* 1953. NM U. ils/photos/maps. 122p. VG/wrp. J2. $45.00.

BAUER, Douglas. *The Very Air.* 1993. NY. William Morrow. 1st. ARC. F. D10. $10.00.

BAUER, K. Jack. *Mexican War, 1846 – 1848.* 1974. Macmillan. 1st. ils. 454p. dj. $11.00.

BAUER, Steven. *Satyrday.* 1980. Berkley Putnam. 1st. NF/NF. P3. $15.00.

BAUGHER, Ruby Dell. *Listening Hills.* 1947. NY. Hobson Book Press. 1st. lt wear to cover. VG. B18. $22.50.

BAUGHMAN, Harry. *Jeremiah for Today.* 1947. Muhlenberg. 221p. G/G. B29. $5.00.

BAUGHMAN, T.H. *Before the Heroes Came. Antarctica in the 1890s.* 1994. Lincoln/London. 8vo. 160p. dk bl cloth. M/dj. P4. $22.95.

BAUM, L. Frank. *Annotated Wizard of Oz.* 1973. 1st. ils Denslow. biblio MP Hearn. VG/VG. M17. $50.00.

BAUM, L. Frank. *Glinda of Oz.* pre 1935. Reilly Lee. ils JR Neill/12 mc pl. brick cloth/pict label. G+. D1. $175.00.

BAUM, L. Frank. *Journeys Through Oz.* 1982. Galley Pr. VG/VG. P3. $12.00.

BAUM, L. Frank. *Junior Edition Oz Books.* 1939. Chicago. Rand McNally. Jr ed/complete set of 9 vol. lg 16mo. VG. C8. $350.00.

BAUM, L. Frank. *Land of Oz.* nd. Reilly Lee. Popular ed. VG. M2. $40.00.

BAUM, L. Frank. *Master Key.* 1974 (1901). Hyperion. rpt. F. M2. $30.00.

BAUM, L. Frank. *Mother Goose in Prose.* 1974 reprint. NY. Bounty Books. G. A16. $9.00.

BAUM, L. Frank. *Patchwork Girl of Oz.* 1913. Reilly Britton. 1st/later state. ils JR Neill. olive gr cloth. R5. $685.00.

BAUM, L. Frank. *Queen Zixi of Ix.* 1905. NY. Century. 1st/2nd state. ils Richardson. gr cloth. R5. $400.00.

BAUM, L. Frank. *Road to Oz.* 1941. Reilly Lee. NF/NF. P3. $100.00.

BAUM, L. Frank. *Wizard of Oz.* 1939 (1903). Bobbs Merrill. photoplay ed w/all 1st issue points. F/VG+. B4. $550.00.

BAUM, L. Frank. *Wonderful Wizard of Oz/Marvelous Land of Oz.* 1966. Dover. 2 vol. ils WW Denslow. half cloth/brd. G+/case. B18. $35.00.

BAUM, Richard. *Planets: Some Myths & Realities.* 1973. Halsted. 8vo. 200p. VG/dj. K5. $25.00.

BAUM, Vicki. *Grand Opera.* 1947 (1942). London. Bles. F/G. T12. $10.00.

BAUM, Vicki. *Hotel Berlin '43.* 1944. Doubleday Doran. 1st. VG/dj. M20. $15.00.

BAUMAN, Janina. *Winter in the Morning: Young Girl's Life in Warsaw Ghetto.* 1986. NY. Free Pr. 195p. VG/dj. S3. $25.00.

BAUMAN, Louis S. *Light from the Bible.* 1940. Revell. 169p. VG. B29. $5.50.

BAUMAN, Louis S. *Russian Events in Light of Bible Prophecy.* 1942. Revell. 191p. VG. B29. $6.00.

BAUMER, William. *Sports as Taught & Played at West Point.* 1939. Military Service Pub. 1st. ils/photos. G+. P8. $20.00.

BAUMGARTEN, E. Lee. *Price Guide for Children's & Illustrated Books for the Years 1880 – 1945.* 1991. self-published. 4to unpaginated. wraps. VG. H1. $27.50.

BAURGEAU, Art. *Seduction.* 1988. Fine. 1st. sgn. NF/NF. G8. $15.00.

BAURNE, Hester. *In the Event of My Death.* 1964. Crime Club. 1st Am ed. VG/VG. G8. $10.00.

BAUSANI, Alessandro. *Persians from the Earliest Days to 20th Century.* 1975. London. Elek. ils/maps. 204p. cloth. F/dj. Q2. $20.00.

BAUSCH, Edwin. *Manipulation of the Microscope.* 1891. Rochester. Bausch Lomb. 12mo. 127p. cloth. K3. $20.00.

BAUSCH, Richard. *Take Me Back.* 1981. NY. Dial. 1st. sgn. rem mk. F/F. R14. $75.00.

BAUSCH, Richard. *Violence.* 1992. Houghton Mifflin. 1st. sgn. F/dj. M23. $25.00.

BAUSCH, Richard. *Violence.* 1992. Houghton Mifflin. 1st. F/F. M22. $25.00.

BAWDEN, F. C. *Plant Viruses and Virus Diseases.* 1956 (1940). Waltham, MA. Chronica Botanica Vol 23. 3rd rev ed. 2nd printing. text figures. indexes. 335p. G. bl cloth. B26. $40.00.

BAXENDALE, Walter. *Dictionary of Illustrations for Pulpit & Platform.* 1955. Moody. 690p. VG/dj. B29. $13.00.

BAXT, George. *A Queer Kind of Umbrella.* 1995. NY. S&S. 1st. VF/VF. T2. $20.00.

BAXT, George. *Marlene Dietrich Murder Case.* 1993. St Martin. 1st. sgn. NF/VG. G8. $30.00.

BAXT, George. *Parade of Cockeyed Creatures.* 1967. Random. 1st. VG/G+. G8. $25.00.

BAXT, George. *The Neon Graveyard.* 1979. NY. St. Martin. 1st. F/F dj. M19. $25.00.

BAXT, George. *The Noel Coward Murder Case.* (1992). NY. St. Martin. 1st. F/F. B3. $15.00.

BAXTER, Charles. *First Light.* 1987. NY. Viking. 1st. sgn. F/dj. R14. $90.00.

BAXTER, Charles. *First Light.* 1987. NY. Viking. 1st. author's 5th book overall. F/NF. L3. $50.00.

BAXTER, Charles. *Relative Stranger.* 1990. Norton. 1st. F/F. B4. $50.00.

BAXTER, Charles. *Shadow Play.* 1993. NY. Norton. ARC. F/wrp. M23. $30.00.

BAXTER, Charles. *Shadow Play.* 1993. NY. Norton. 1st. F/F. M23. $60.00.

BAXTER, Charles. *Through the Safety Net.* 1985. NY. Viking. 1st. sgn by author in 1993. F/F. B2. $60.00.

BAXTER, Doreen. *Woodland Frolics.* 1952. Leicester. Brockhampton. 1st. 4to. gr lettered wheat cloth. R5. $200.00.

BAXTER, E.M. *California Cactus.* 1935. Los Angeles. 1/1000. ils/photos. blk cloth. VG. B26. $75.00.

BAXTER, Gregory. *Calamity Comes of Age.* 1935. NY. Macaulay. 1st. VG/G dj. M15. $50.00.

BAXTER, J.P. *Introduction of the Ironclad Warship.* 1968 (1933). NY. rpt. ils. 398p. F. M4. $30.00.

BAXTER, John & Thomas Atkins. *The Fire Came By; The Riddle of the Great Siberian Explosion.* 1976. Garden City. Doubleday. ex lib. 8vo. 28 b/w photos. rear fep removed. lib mks. 165p. G/dj. K5. $10.00.

BAXTER, L. *Housekeeper's Handy Book.* 1931. 1st. photos. VG. E6. $30.00.

BAXTER, Lorna. *Eggchild.* 1979. Dutton. 1st. VG/VG. P3. $18.00.

BAXTER, Richard. *The Saints Everlasting Rest; or, A Treatise of the Blessed State of the Saints, in Their Enjoyment of God in Glory. Extracted from the Works of Richard Baxter by John Wesley.* 1794. Philadelphia. printed by Henry Tuckniss. 12mo. contemporary plain calf. 400p. worn. spine extremities chipped. title soiled. K1. $75.00.

BAXTER, Walter. *Look Down in Mercy.* 1952. Putnam. 1st Am. NF/VG. B4. $85.00.

BAYARD, Samuel J. *Sketch of Life of Com Robert F Stockton.* 1856. NY. Derby Jackson. VG. T7. $185.00.

BAYER, William. *Blind Side.* 1989. NY. Villard. 1st. VF/F. H11. $35.00.

BAYER, William. *Pattern Crimes.* 1987. NY. Villard. 1st. VF/VF. H11. $35.00.

BAYER, William. *Peregrine.* 1981. NY. Congdon & Lattes. 1st. F/dj. M15. $50.00.

BAYER, William. *Punish Me with Kisses.* 1980. NY. Congdon. 1st. VF/F. H11. $50.00.

BAYER, William. *Switch.* 1984. NY. S&S. 1st. VF/F. H11. $75.00.

BAYER, William. *Tangier.* 1978. NY. Dutton. 1st. F/F. H11. $60.00.

BAYER, William. *Blind Side.* 1989. Villard. 1st. VG/VG. P3. $20.00.

BAYER, William. *Mirror Maze.* 1994. Villard. 1st. NF/VG+. G8. $15.00.

BAYLEY, Barrington. *Garments of Caean.* 1976. Doubleday. 1st. F/dj. M2. $10.00.

BAYLEY, Nicola. *As I was Going Up & Down & Other Nonsense Rhymes.* 1986. Macmillan. 1st Am. 24p. VG+/F. D4. $35.00.

BAYLEY & DAVIS, Less-Than-Perfect Rider. *1994.* NY. Howell. 1st. VG/VG. O3. $20.00.

BAYLOR, Byrd. *When Clay Sings.* 1972. Scribner. 1st. 4to. NF/VG+. P2. $95.00.

BAYLOR, Byrd. *Yes Is Better than No.* 1977. Scribner. 1st. F/NF. M25. $45.00.

BAYLOR, Don. *Don Baylor.* 1989. St Martin. 1st. inscr. F/dj. P8. $45.00.

BAYLOR, Frances Courtenay. *Juan & Juanita.* 1926. Houghton Mifflin. ils Gustaf Tenggren. VG+/G. M5. $40.00.

BAYNTON-WILLIAMS, *Investing in Maps.* 1969. London. 4to. ils. 160p. VG/VG. A4. $65.00.

BAZELON, Irwin. *Knowing the Score: Notes on Film Music.* 1975. NY. 1st. 352p. xl. F/F. A17. $15.00.

BAZIN, Germain. *Paradeisos: Art of the Garden.* 1990. Boston. 1st Am. ils/photos/glossary/index. F/dj. B26. $32.00.

BEACH, Charles Amory. *Air Service Boys Flying for France.* 1919. World Syndicate. VG/dj. M20. $15.00.

BEACH, Edward L. *Cold Is the Sea.* 1978. Holt. 1st. F/F. H11. $20.00.

BEACH, Edward L. *Cold Is the Sea.* 1978. NY. Holt. 1st. F/F. H11. $20.00.

BEACH, Edward L. *Dust on the Sea.* 1972. HRW. 3rd. 8vo. NF/dj. M7. $12.00.

BEACH, Edward L. *Dust on the Sea.* 1972. NY. Holt. 1st. F/F-. H11. $30.00.

BEACH, S. A. *Apples of New York.* 1905. Albany. Lyon. 2 vol. 1st. ils/index. VG. H10. $200.00.

BEACH, Sylvia. *Shakespeare & Company.* 1959. Harcourt. 1st. 230p. VG/dj. A17. $25.00.

BEACH & NIEBUHR, eds. *Christian Ethics: Sources of the Living Tradition.* 1955. Ronald Press. 496p. VG/minor wear to dj. B29. $12.00.

BEADLE, J.H. *Brigham's Destroying Angel, Being the Life, Confession.* 1904. Shepard. 1st. 221p. VG. J2. $285.00.

BEADLE, J.H. *Life In Utah; or, Mysteries & Crimes of Mormonism.* 1870. National Pub. 1st. ils/fld map/rear ads. 540p. VG. J2. $135.00.

BEAGLE, Peter S. *A Fine and Private Place.* 1960. NY. Viking. 1st. 8vo. gr cloth. author's 1st book. reveals life in a cemetery. 272p. VG/G. D6. $150.00.

BEAGLE, Peter S. *Fantasy Worlds of.* 1978. Viking. 1st. F/dj. M2. $25.00.

BEAGLE, Peter S. *Folk of the Air.* 1986. Ballantine. 1st. F/NF. M21. $14.00.

BEAGLE, Peter S. *Folk of the Air.* 1986. London. Headline. 1st ed. F/F. B3. $40.00.

BEAGLE, Peter S. *Last Unicorn.* 1968. Viking. 1st. F/NF/custom box. M21. $150.00.

BEAGLE, Peter S. *The Rhinoceros Who Quoted Nietzsche and Other Odd Acquaintances.* 1997. San Francisco. Tachyon Publications. 1st. 1/100 # copies. sgn. VF/VF. T2. $50.00.

BEAGLE, Peter S., Ed. *Immortal Unicorn.* (1995). NY. Harper Prism. 1st. collection of stories. F/NF. lt soiling and wear. B3. $20.00.

BEAGLEHOLE, J.C. *Exploration of the Pacific.* 1975. London. Blk. 3rd. 346p. VG/clip. P4. $75.00.

BEAGLEHOLE, J. C. *The Life of Captain James Cook.* 1974. Stanford. Stanford U. 1st. blue cloth. gilt titles. thick 8vo. color ftspc. 760p. VG in dj. P4. $95.00.

BEAHM, George. *Stephen King Story.* 1991. Andrews McMeel. 1st. F/F. P3. $20.00.

BEAL, Fred E. *Proletarian Journey: Fugitive in Two Worlds.* 1937. Hillman Curl. 1st. VG/dj. V4. $35.00.

BEAL, Merrill D. *Grand Canyon: Story Behind the Scenery.* 1967. Flagstaff. KC Pub. 1st. 4to. 38p. mc wrp. F7. $10.00.

BEALE, Joseph Henry. *Bibliography of Early English Law Books.* 1926. Cambridge. maroon cloth. M11. $150.00.

BEALL, Banks & Smith. *Old Testament Parsing Guide: Job to Malachi.* 1990. Moody. 299p. VG/VG. B29. $24.00.

BEALS, Carleton. *Banana Gold.* 1932. Philadelphia. Lippincott. 1st. gilt lettering & spine decor. 367p. F. F3. $30.00.

BEALS, Carleton. *Dawn Over the Amazon.* 1943. DSP. NF. P3. $13.00.

BEAR, Fred. *Field Notes.* 1993. Derrydale. photos. 288p. aeg. gilt leather. F. A17. $35.00.

BEAR, Greg. *Early Harvest.* 1988. Cambridge. NESFA Press. 1st. 1/225 # copies. sgn by Bear & artist Mattingly. VF/VF dj & slipcase. T2. $125.00.

BEAR, Greg. *Eon.* 1985. Bluejay. 1st. F/dj. M2. $85.00.

BEAR, Greg. *Eternity.* 1988. Warner. 1st. AN/dj. M21. $15.00.

BEAR, Greg. *Eternity.* 1988. NY. Warner books. 1st. sgn. VF/VF. T2. $35.00.

BEAR, Greg. *Heads.* 1991. St. Martin. 1st Am. sgn. F/dj. O11. $30.00.

BEAR, Greg. *Heads.* 1990. London. century/Legend. 1st. 1/300 # copies. sgn. VF/VF w/o dj in slipcase as issued. T2. $50.00.

BEAR, Greg. *Heads.* 1991. St. Martin. 1st. NF/NF. P3. $15.00.

BEAR, Greg. *Moving Mars.* 1993. NY. Tor. ARC. inscr by author. NF. O11. $25.00.

BEAR, Greg. *Moving Mars.* 1993. NY. Tor. 1st. sgn by author. F/F. O11. $35.00.

BEAR, Greg. *Tangents.* 1989. NY. Warner books. 1st. sgn. VF/VF. T2. $35.00.

BEAR, Greg. *The Forge of God.* 1987. NY. Tor. 1st. sgn. VF/VF. T2. $45.00.

BEAR, Greg. *Forge of God.* 1987. Tor. 1st. VG/VG. P3. $18.00.

BEAR, Greg. *Wind from a Burning Woman.* 1983. Arkham. 1st. F/dj. M2. $125.00.

BEARD, Charles A. *Century of Progress.* 1933. Harper. 1st. gilt red brd. G. A28. $7.50.

BEARD, Charles Austin. *Office of Justice of Peace in England. In Its Origin…* nd. NY. Burt Franklin. orig cloth. xl. M11. $65.00.

BEARD, D.C. *American Boy's Handy Book.* 1909. Scribner. expanded. 441p. G. H7. $20.00.

BEARD, J.S. *Natural Vegetation of Trinidad.* 1946. London. ils/fld map. 152p. B26. $40.00.

BEARD, James. *American Cookery.* 1972. Boston. Little, Brn. 1st. VG/dj. A16. $37.50.

BEARD, James. *Great Cooks Cookbook.* 1974. NY. Ferguson/Doubleday. VG/dj. A16. $20.00.

BEARD, James. *New James Beard.* 1981. Knopf. 1st. VG+/dj. A16. $22.50.

BEARD, James. *Theory & Practice of Good Cooking.* 1977. Knopf. 5th. VG/dj. A16. $12.00.

BEARD, James. *Treasury of Outdoor Cooking.* 1960. Ridge. 282p. G+/fair. B10. $15.00.

BEARD, John S. *Proteas of Tropical Africa.* 1992. Kenthurst. Australia. ils/maps/photos. 112p. AN. B26. $65.00.

BEARD, Patten. *The Jolly Book of Boxcraft.* 1918. London. George G. Harrap & Co. ils by Margaret Tarrant. 8vo. bl cloth. hobby book. 208p. VG. D6. $40.00.

BEARD, Tyler. *100 Years of Western Wear.* 1993. Salt Lake. Gobbs-Smith. photos by Jim Arndt. 4to. 160p. F/F. O3. $22.00.

BEARDSLEY, Aubrey. *Under the Hill and Other Essays in Prose and Verse.* 1904. London. John Lane/Bodley Head. 1st. sm 4to. ils by author. royal bl cloth w/elaborate gilt. issued after Beardsley's death. contains list of his works. 90p. G. some water damage. spine pierced. D6. $150.00.

BEARE, George. *Snake on the Grave.* 1974. Houghton Mifflin. 1st. VG/VG. P3. $15.00.

BEART, Charles A. *President Roosevelt & the Coming of the War 1941.* 1948. Yale. 1st. 614p. VG. M19. $18.00.

BEASLEY, Conger. *Hidalgo's Beard.* 1979. Andrews McMeel. 1st. VG/VG. P3. $20.00.

BEASLEY, Norman. *Freighters of Fortune.* 1930. NY. 1st. ils. 311p. G. B18. $45.00.

BEASLEY-MURRAY, G.R. *Jesus & the Kingdom of God.* 1986. Eerdmans. 446p. VG/dj. B29. $17.50.

BEATER, Jack. *Tales of South Florida & the Ten Thousand Islands.* 1965. Ft Myers. self pub. 192p. VG/VG. B11. $45.00.

BEATH, Robert B. *Grand Army Blue-Book Containing Rules & Regulations.* 1884. Phil. 168P. gilt bl brd. H6. $42.00.

BEATIE, R. H. *Road to Manassas: Growth of Union Command…* 1961. Cooper Square. 1st. 285p. VG/dj. S16. $35.00.

BEATON, Cecil. *Far East.* 1945. London. Batsford. 1st. photos. VG/dj. A25. $45.00.

BEATON, Cecil. *The Face of the World: An International Scrapbook of People & Places.* 1957. John Day Co. 1st Am. 4to. 240p. VG. H1. $20.00.

BEATON, M. C. *Death of a Hussy.* 1990. NY. 1st. F/NF. H11. $20.00.

BEATON, M. C. *Death of a Prankster.* 1992. NY. St. Martin. 1st. VF/F+. H11. $20.00.

BEATON, M. C. *Death of a Scriptwriter.* 1998. Mysterious Press. 1st. F/F. G8. $15.00.

BEATTIE, Ann. *Alex Katz.* 1987. Abrams. 1st. sgn. F/F. R14. $40.00.

BEATTIE, Ann. *Chilly Scenes of Winter.* 1976. Doubleday. 1st. author's 1st novel. F/NF. L3. $150.00.

BEATTIE, Ann. *Distortions.* 1976. Doubleday. 1st. sgn. F/F. B35. $125.00.

BEATTIE, Ann. *Falling in Place.* 1980. NY. Random House. 1st. F/NF. A24. $25.00.

BEATTIE, Ann. *Love Always.* 1985. NY. Random House. 1st. sgn. F/F. D10. $50.00.

BEATTIE, Ann. *Picturing Will.* 1989. Random. 1st. sgn. F/F. R13. $35.00.

BEATTIE, Ann. *Secrets & Surprises.* 1978. Random. 1st. author's 3rd book. F/F. D10. $40.00.

BEATTIE, Ann. *The Burning House.* 1982. NY. Random House. 1st. sgn. F/VG+. A24. $25.00.

BEATTIE, Ann. *What was Mine.* 1991. NY. Random House. 1st. F/F. A24. $15.00.

BEATTIE, Ann. *Where You'll Find Me.* 1986. S&S. 1st. inscr. F/F. R13. $45.00.

BEATTIE, Geoffrey. *The Corner Boys.* 1998. London. Gollancz. 1st. author's 1st novel. VF/VF. T2. $32.00.

BEATTIE, Jessie L. *Strength for the Bridge.* 1966. Toronto. McClelland & Stewart. 1st. G/VG dj. A26. $6.00.

BEATTIE, William. *Switzerland.* Vol II. 1839. London. fld map. half leather. B18. $195.00.

BEATTY, Bessie. *Red Heart of Russia.* 1918. NY. Century. 1st. photos. 480p. VG+. A25. $40.00.

BEATTY, Jerome. *Matthew Loony & the Space Pirates.* 1972. Addison. 1st. ils Gahan Wilson. VG/dj. S18. $11.00.

BEATTY, Jerome Jr. *Clambake Mutiny.* 1964. Young Scott Books. 1st. 66p. VG/dj. M20. $20.00.

BEATTY, John. *Acolhuans: A Narrative of Sojourn & Adventure…* 1902. Columbus. 1st. ils. 423p. G. B18. $75.00.

BEATTY, Robert. *Sapo.* 1996. Corvallis. Ecopress. 1st. sgn. clip. VF/VF. H11. $45.00.

BEATY, John O. *Swords in the Dawn: Story of First Englishman.* 1937. Longman Gr. 1st Am. 12mo. 212p. NF. C14. $12.00.

BEAUCHAMP, Loren; see Silverberg, Robert.

BEAUCLERK, Helen. *Green Lacquer Pavilion.* 1926. Doran. 1st Am. F/NF. B4. $150.00.

BEAUDRY, Evien C. *Puppy Stories.* 1934. Saalfield. ils Diana Thorne. VG. A21. $45.00.

BEAUMONT, Charles. *Selected Stories.* 1988. Dark Harvest. 1st. F/dj. M2. $45.00.

BEAUMONT, William. *Experiments & Observations on the Gastric Juice.* 1833. Plattsburgh. 1st. recent half leather/marbled brd. F. A13. $2.500.00.

BEAUMONT, William. *Physiology of Digestion.* 1847. Burlington, VT. Goodrich. 2nd. sm 8vo. 303p. VG. $1.00.

BEBEL, August. *Bebel's Reminiscences. Part 1.* 1911. NY. Socialist Literature Co. 1st. NF. B2. $35.00.

BECHDOLT, Jack. *Torch.* 1948. Prime. 1st. F/dj. M2. $15.00.

BECHERVAISE, John. *Blizzard & Fire: Year at Mawson.* Antarctica. 1963. Sydney. Angus Robertson. 1st. 252p. VG/dj. P4. $125.00.

BECHERVAISE, John. *Far South.* 1961. Sydney. Angus Robertson. 1st. 8vo. 103p. map ep. VG/dj. $4.00.

BECHET, Sidney. *Treat it Gentle.* 1960. Hill and Wang. 1st. VG/lt soiled orange cloth bds. missing dj. M25. $25.00.

BECHSTEIN, Ludwig. *Rabbit Catcher & Other Fairy Tales.* 1962. Macmillan. probable 1st. folio. VG. B17. $15.00.

BECHTEREV, Vladimir M. *General Principles of Human Reflexology: An Introduction.* 1928 (1917). NY. Internat Pub. 1st Eng-language/Am issue. 467p. blk cloth. G1. $85.00.

BECK, Henry Houghton. *History of South Africa & the British-Boer War.* 1900. Phil. 493p+2p fld map. gilt leather. G. A17. $20.00.

BECK, James Reed. *The Dover-New Philadelphia, Ohio Area....* 1942. Chicago. wrp. some wear. 23 maps and plates in rear pocket. dissertation submitted to Univ of Chicago. dept of geography. 103p. G. B18. $95.00.

BECK, K. K. *Amateur Night.* 1993. Mysterious Press. 1st. F/F. G8. $10.00.

BECK, K. K. *Electric City.* 1994. Mysterious Press. 1st. F/F. G8. $15.00.

BECK, K. K. *Murder in a Mummy Case.* 1986. NY. Walker. 1st. F/F. O11. $20.00.

BECK, K. K. *The Revenge of Kali Ra.* 1999. NY. Mysterious Press. 1st. sgn. VF/VF. T2. $25.00.

BECK, K. K. *Unwanted Attentions.* 1989. Mysterious Press. 1st. NF/NF. G8. $15.00.

BECK, K. K. *We Interrupt this Broadcast.* 1997. Mysterious Press. 1st. VG+/VG+. G8. $15.00.

BECK, L. Adams. *Garden of Vision.* 1929. Cosmopolitan. 1st. VG. M2. $10.00.

BECK, Melissa. *Typographic Bookplates of Ward Ritchie.* 1990. Karamole. 1st. fwd/sgn Ward Ritchie. 96p. F. B19. $40.00.

BECK, Phineas. *Clementine in the Kitchen.* 1943. NY. Hastings. G/dj. A16. $10.00.

BECKDOLT, Jack. *Mystery at Hurricane Hill.* 1951. Dutton. 1st. VG/dj. M20. $15.00.

BECKE, Louis. *Rodiman the Boatsteerer.* 1898. Lippincott. 1st. VG. M2. $15.00.

BECKER, Bob. *Devil Bird.* 1933. Reilly Lee. 1st. VG. M2. $35.00.

BECKER, Charlotte. *Three Little Steps.* 1947. Scribner. 1st/A. 8vo. VG/dj. M5. $38.00.

BECKER, Charlotte. *Unlike Twins.* 1943. Scribner. lg 12mo. VG/dj. M5. $22.00.

BECKER, Ernest. *Escape from Evil.* 1975. Free Press. 1st. top stain evident on front paste-down & ffep. VG/rubbed dj. M25. $35.00.

BECKER, Ethel. *Treasury of Alaskana: The Alaska Story.* 1977. NY. Bonanza. 1st. 4to. photos. VG/VG. R16. $30.00.

BECKER, John. *New Feathers for the Old Goose.* 1956. Pantheon. 1st. 63p. cloth. F/NF. D4. $25.00.

BECKER, Robert H. *Thomas Christy's Road Across the Plains.* 1969. Sacramento. Old West Pub. 1st. F/F. O4. $35.00.

BECKER, Stephen. *Blue Eyed Shan.* 1982. Random. 1st. F/G. T12. $20.00.

BECKER, Stephen. *Chinese Bandit.* 1975. Random. 1st. VG/VG. P3. $25.00.

BECKER, Stephen. *Dog Tags.* 1973. NY. Random. 1st. F/VF. H11. $40.00.

BECKER, Stephen. *Last Mandarin.* 1979. Random. 1st. VG/VG. P3. $25.00.

BECKETT, Elspeth. *Wild Flowers of Majorca. Minorca & Ibiza.* 1988. Rotterdam. Balkema. ils. 221p. M. B26. $60.00.

BECKETT, Samuel. *Cascando.* 1970. Grove. 1st. F/F. M19. $35.00.

BECKETT, Samuel. *How It Is.* 1964. np. Grove Press. 1st. NF/VG. M19. $65.00.

BECKETT, Samuel. *Lessness.* 1970. London. Calder Boyars. 1st. 1/100. sgn. trans from French. F/case. L3. $500.00.

BECKETT, Samuel. *Poems in English.* 1961. London. John Calder. 1st. F/dj. Q1. $200.00.

BECKETT, Samuel. *Rockaby & Other Short Pieces.* 1981. Grove. 1st. F/F. B35. $22.00.

BECKETT, Samuel. *Three Novels. Malloy/ Malone Dies/The Unnamable.* 1959. Grove. 1st. trans Patrick Bowles. F/F. D10. $150.00.

BECKFORD, Peter. *Thoughts on Hunting.* 1926. Methuen. 6th. ils. G. A21. $45.00.

BECKFORD, Peter. *Thoughts Upon Hare & Fox Hunting in a Series of Letters.* 1932. NY. Cape/Ballou. 16 mc engravings. 327p. VG. H10. $50.00.

BECKFORD, William. *Recollections of Late Wm Beckford of Fonthill...* nd. Bath. Facs. 1/750. H13. $65.00.

BECKFORD, William. *Vathek.* 1928. John Day. 1st Am. 229p. NF/dj/case. M20. $65.00.

BECKFORD, William. *William Beckford of Fonthill: Writer.* Traveller. 1960. Yale. F. H13. $65.00.

BECKWITH, Henry. *Lovecraft's Providence & Adjacent Parts.* 1986. Donald Grant. 2nd revised. F/dj. M2. $15.00.

BECKWITH, John. *Art of Constantinople: An Introduction to Byzantine Art.* 1961. London. Phaidon. 8vo. ils. 184p. cloth. G+/torn. Q2. $25.00.

BECKWITH, Lillian. *Hills Is Lonely.* 1962. London. Hutchinson. 10th. ils. VG+/G+. H7. $15.00.

BECQUERL, Henri Et Deslandres. *Contribution A L'Edude Du Phenomene De Zeeman.* 1898. Paris. Gauthier-Villars et Fils. xl. K3. $45.00.

BECQUERL, Henri Et Deslandres. *Sur Le Rayonnement De L'Uranium.* 1900. Paris. Gauthier-Villars et Fils. xl. K3. $50.00.

BECVAR, Antonin. *Atlas of the Heavens II.* 1964. Cambridge, MA. Sky. 4th. VG. K5. $25.00.

BEDDIE, M. K. *Bibliography of Captain James Cook.* 1970. Sydney. Mitchell Library. 2nd. thick blue cloth 8vo. over 4000 entries. 894p. Near new in lightly rubbed & soiled dj. P4. $80.00.

BEDDOME, R.H. *Handbook to the Ferns of British India.* 1892. Calcutta. Thacker Spink. 1st ed thus. 300 pl. NF. A22. $85.00.

BEDELL, L. Frank. *Quaker Heritage: Friends Coming Into Heartland of America.* 1966. Cono. 306p. VG. V3. $22.00.

BEDELL, Mary Crehore. *Modern Gypsies: Story of 12,000-Mile Motor Camping Trip.* 1924. Brentano. ils. VG. K3. $20.00.

BEDFORD, Annie North. *Susie's New Stove.* 1950. Little Golden. 1st. VG. M5. $55.00.

BEDFORD, Denton R. *Foxes & the Lumwoods.* 1977. Vantage. 1st. F/VG. L3. $125.00.

BEDFORD, Francis D. *Book of Nursery Rhymes.* 1897. London. Methuen. 8vo. all edges red. R5. $250.00.

BEDFORD, Gunning S. *Principles & Practice of Obstetrics.* 1862. NY. Wood. 100 wood engravings. 731p. cloth/rb spine. G7. $115.00.

BEDFORD, Martyn. *Acts of Revision.* 1996. London. Bantam. 1st. VF/dj. M15. $65.00.

BEDFORD, Sybille. *Aldous Huxley Vol I: 1894 – 1939.* 1973. Chatto Windus. VG/VG. P3. $25.00.

BEDFORD-JONES, H. *Years Between.* 1928. Longman. 2 vol. F/dj/case. M2. $60.00.

BEDICHEK, Roy. *Adventures with a Texas Naturalist.* 1961. Austin. TX. VG/dj. A19. $25.00.

BEDIER, J. *Romance of Tristan & Iseult.* 1960. LEC. 1/1500. ils Serge Ivanoff. quarter morocco/paper brd. F/case. T10. $130.00.

BEDINGFIELD, James. *Compendium of Medical Practice Ils.* 1823. Greenfield, MA. 1st Am from last London ed. 192p. sheep/marbled brd. B14. $175.00.

BEDNAR, Kamil. *Puppets & Fairy Tales.* 1958. Prague. 52p. dj. A17. $20.00.

BEE, Clair. *Chip Hilton: A Pass & a Prayer.* (1951). Grosset Dunlap. not 1st. 216p. F/dj. H1. $15.00.

BEE, Clair. *Chip Hilton: Backcourt Ace (#19).* 1961. Grosset Dunlap. 182p. lists to #20. VG. M20. $45.00.

BEE, Clair. *Chip Hilton: Blackboard Fever (#10).* 1953. Grosset Dunlap. 210p. lists to #20. VG. M20. $16.00.

BEE, Clair. *Chip Hilton: Buzzer Basket (#20).* 1962. Grosset Dunlap. 1st. 175p. VG+/dj (last title listed). M20. $95.00.

BEE, Clair. *Chip Hilton: Hardcourt Upset (#15).* 1957. Grosset Dunlap. lists 18 titles. 181p. cloth. VG/dj. M20. $25.00.

BEE, Clair. *Chip Hilton: Home Run Feud (#22).* 1964. Grosset Dunlap. 1st. 176p. lists to #21. VG+. M20. $200.00.

BEE, Clair. *Chip Hilton: Hungry Hurler (#23).* 1966. Grosset Dunlap. 1st. 184p. last title in series. pict brd. M20. $625.00.

BEE, Robert L. *Crosscurrents Along the Colorado. Impact of Government.* 1981. Tucson. 184p. pict wrp. F7. $15.00.

BEEBE, B.F. *American Wolves, Coyotes & Foxes.* 1967. McKay. ils JR Johnson. 151p. cloth. F/VG. M12. $20.00.

BEEBE, Lucius. *American West.* 1955. Bonanza. dj. A19. $35.00.

BEEBE, Lucius. *Mixed Train Daily: Book of Short-Line Railroads.* 1947. Dutton. 2nd. 365p. cloth. VG/dj. M20. $45.00.

BEEBE, Lucius. *When Beauty Rode the Rails.* 1962. Garden City. 1st. VG/VG. B5. $45.00.

BEEBE, Lucius & Charles Clegg. *U. S. West, The Saga of Wells Fargo.* 1949. NY. Dutton. 2nd printing. sgn by both authors. ils & photos. ils ep. VG in torn dj. B18. $27.50.

BEEBE, W. *Nonesuch: Land of Water.* 1932. NY. Brewer Warren. ils/photos. 259p. F/VG. M12. $30.00.

BEEBE, William. *Arcturus Adventure.* 1926. Putnam. ils/maps. 439p. T7. $60.00.

BEEBE, William. *Half Mile Down.* 1934. NY. 1st. ils. 344p. F. B14. $35.00.

BEEBE, William. *Half Mile Down.* 1934. Harcourt Brace. 1st. 8vo. 344p. VG/dj. K3. $45.00.

BEEBE & CLEGG. *Hear the Train Blow.* 1952. EP Dutton. 1st. 414p. pict buckram. VG/torn. B18. $27.50.

BEEBE & CLEGG. *San Francisco's Golden Era.* 1960. Howell North. 1st. 255p. VG+. B18. $35.00.

BEEBEE, Chris. *Hub.* 1987. MacDonald. F/F. P3. $22.00.

BEECHER, Elizabeth. *Roy Rogers on the Double-R Ranch.* 1951. S&S. VG. P3. $15.00.

BEECHEY, Alan. *An Embarrassment of Corpses.* 1997. NY. St. Martin. sgn 1st ed. F/F. M23. $50.00.

BEECHEY, Alan. *Murdering Ministers.* 1999. NY. St. Martin. 1st. sgn. VF/VF. T2. $26.00.

BEECHEY, Frederick W. *Narrative of Voyage to the Pacific & Bering Strait.* 1832. Phil. Carey Lea. 1st Am. 8vo. 493p. linen cloth. xl. $7.00.

BEECKMAN, Ross. *Last Woman.* 1909. NY. Watts. ils HC Christie. VG. M20. $15.00.

BEECROFT, John. *Rocco Came In.* 1959. Dodd Mead. 1st. ils Kurt Wiese. 4to. VG/VG. P2. $50.00.

BEEDING, Francis. *Death Walks in Eastrepps.* 1931. Mystery League. 1st. VG. N4. $27.50.

BEEDING, Francis. *The Secret Weapon.* 1940. NY. Harper & Bros. 1st Am ed. F/VG dj. M15. $45.00.

BEEDING, Francis. *The Ten Holy Terrors.* 1939. London. Hodder & Stoughton. 1st. F/dj. M15. $350.00.

BEEDING, Francis. *Three Fishers.* 1931. Little, Brn. 1st Am ed. G-VG. G8. $15.00.

BEEHLER, B.M. *Birds of New Guinea.* 1986. Princeton. 8vo. ils Zimmerman/Coe. 21 maps. 293p. VG+/stiff wrp. M12. $30.00.

BEEMAN, Major Howard N. *Veterinary Obstetrics and Zoo Technics.* 1932. Washington. American Remount Assoc. 131p. VG. O3. $45.00.

BEER, George Louis. *African Questions at the Paris Peace Conference.* 1969 (1923). NY. Negro Universities. rpt. 8vo. fld map. 628p. VG. $1.00.

BEERBOHM, Max. *Christmas Garland.* 1912. London. Heinemann. 198p. gilt bl cloth. VG. B14. $45.00.

BEERBOHM, Max. *Fifty Caricatures by Max Beerbohm.* NY. E. P. Dutton & Company. 1913. 8vo. (4)p & 50 plates. gr cloth. 1st Am ed. All but the last two plates are tipped in on brn paper. Final two plates printed directly on wht text paper. Cloth worn with a small gouge on spine. 1st plate with scribble. foxing. mostly confined to wht text pages. G. L5. $90.00.

BEERBOHM, Max. *Happy Hypocrite.* 1915. NY. John Lane. 1st. ils Sheringham. VG. M19. $50.00.

BEERBOHM, Max. *Mainly on the Air.* 1958. Knopf. 1st Am. F. B14. $45.00.

BEERBOHM, Max. *Rossetti and His Circle.* 1922. London. William Heinemann. ne. color repros of 21 caricatures. w/ text. orig blue cloth. bdg rubbed & stained. B14. $125.00.

BEERBOHM, Max. *Zuleika Dobson; or, An Oxford Love Story,* 1960. LEC. 1st thus. 1/1500. ils/sgn George Him. F/case. Q1. $100.00.

BEERY, Jesse. *Saddle-Horse Instructions: Horse Training...Breeding.* 1940s. Pleasant Hill. 23 pamphlets+ephemera. orig case. A17. $22.50.

BEESTON, Diane. *Of Wind, Fog & Sail.* 1972. SF. Chronicle. obl 4to. ils. dj. T7. $36.00.

BEETLE, Alan A. *Distribution of the Native Grasses of California.* 1947. Berkeley. 184 distribution maps. VG. B26. $24.00.

BEETLE, David H. *Up Old Forge Way: Central Adirondack Story.* 1948. Utica Observer-Dispatch. 1st. 183p. VG/G. H7. $25.00.

BEETLE, David H. *West Canada Creek.* 1946. Utica Observer-Dispatch. 1st. 159p. VG. H7. $20.00.

BEETLES, Chris. *Mabel Lucie Atwell.* 1988. Eng. Pavilion Books. 1st thus. 4to. 120p. F/heavy bl wrp. T5. $45.00.

BEEVOR, Anthony. *Faustian Pact.* 1983. London. Cape. 1st. VG/VG. P3. $20.00.

BEEZLEY, William. *Insurgent Governor.* 1973. Lincoln. Univ of Nebraska Press. 1st. 195p. F/chipped dj. F3. $15.00.

BEGAY, Shonto. *Ma'Ii & Cousin Horned Toad.* 1992. Scholastic Inc. 1st. inscr. thin 4to. F/dj. T10. $50.00.

BEGIEBING, Robert J. *Strange Death of Mistress Coffin.* 1991. Algonquin. 1st. NF/dj. M20. $15.00.

BEGLEY, Louis. *About Schmidt.* 1996. NY. Knopf. 1st. review copy w/pub material. F/F. O11. $35.00.

BEGLEY, Louis. *Wartime Lies.* (1993). NY. Knopf. 1st. author's 1st book. F/F. B3. $150.00.

BEHERNDS, A. J. F. *Socialism and Christianity.* 1886. NY. Baker & Taylor. 1st. VG. sm tear. B2. $30.00.

BEHME, R. L. *Bonsai, Saikei & Bonkei: Japanese Dwarf Trees.* 1969. Morrow. ils. 255p. F. W3. $42.00.

BEHN, Noel. *Shadowboxer.* 1969. S&S. 1st. VG. P3. $12.00.

BEHRENS, Helen Kindler. *Diplomatic Dining.* 1974. NY Times. G/dj. A16. $12.50.

BEILENSON, Peter. *Little Treasury of Haiku.* 1980. NY. Avenel. 96p. F/NF. W3. $12.00.

BEILHARZ, Peter. *Trostky, Troskyism & Transition to Socialism.* 1987. Barnes Noble. 1st. AN/dj. V4. $20.00.

BEIM, Lorraine. *Carol's Side of the Street.* 1951. World. ils Malman. VG/clip. B36. $6.50.

BEIMLER, Rosalind. *The Days of the Dead.* 1991. San Francisco. Harper Collins. 1st. 4to. wrp. 113p. G. F3. $20.00.

BEINHART, Larry. *American Hero.* 1993. NY. Pantheon. 1st. F. H11. $15.00.

BEINHART, Larry. *No One Rides for Free.* 1986. NY. Morrow. 1st. F/dj. M15. $60.00.

BEINHART, Larry. *You Get What You Pay For.* 1988. NY. Morrow. 1st. F/VF. H11. $20.00.

BEISER, Arthur. *Proper Yacht.* 1970. London. 2nd. 307p. F/dj. A17. $20.00.

BEITO, Gretchen Umes. *Coya Come Home: A Congresswoman's Journey.* 1990. Pomegranate. 1st. 334p. VG/dj. A25. $15.00.

BEKESSY, Emery. *Barabbas.* 1946. NY. Prentice. 1st. bookplate on front pastedown. F/F. H11. $50.00.

BELAYEV, Alexander. *Amphibian.* nd. Moscow. Foreign Languages Pub House. 12mo. tan cloth. VG/worn. F1. $30.00.

BELDEN, Bauman L. *Indian Peace Medals Issued in the United States.* 1966. Milford. CT. rpt of 1927. 1/350. 46p. VG/dj. B18. $65.00.

BELFORD, Barbara. *Violet.* 1990. NY. 1st. dj. T9. $12.00.

BELFORT, Sophie. *Lace Curtain Murders.* 1986. Atheneum. 1st. NF/NF. G8. $17.50.

BELIAEV, Alexander. *Professor Dowell's Head.* 1980. Macmillan. 1st. VG/VG. P3. $15.00.

BELKNAP, Buzz. *Powell Centennial Grand Canyon River Guide.* 1973. Westwater Book. waterpoof ed. 8vo. VG/bl wrp. F7. $15.00.

BELKNAP, Charles Eugene. *History of the Michigan Organizations at Chickamauga.* 1899. Lansing. MI. Robert Smith. 2nd. 374p. cloth (bookplate removed). M8. $65.00.

BELKNAP, George. *Letters of Captain George Hamilton Perkins.* USN. 1970 (1886). 533p. O8. $18.50.

BELL, Anne Oliver. *Diary of Virginia Wolff.* 1984. HBJ. 1st. Am. NF/NF. W2. $30.00.

BELL, Bob. *Hunting the Long-Tailed Bird.* 1975. Freshnet. 212p. M/dj. A17. $15.00.

BELL, Charles. *Engravings of the Brain & Nerves.* 1982. Birmingham. facsimile of 3 eds/1st collected. 4to. full leather. A13. $150.00.

BELL, Charles. *Essays on Anatomy of Expression in Painting.* 1806. London. Longman Hurst. 1st. lg 4to. 186p. contemporary bdg. M1. $850.00.

BELL, Charles. *Essays on Anatomy of Expression in Painting.* 1984. Birmingham. facsimile 1806 London. 4to. 186p. full leather. A13. $100.00.

BELL, Charles. *Nervous System of the Human Body.* 1988 (1830). Birmingham. Classics of Neurology/Neurosurgery Lib. facsimile. G1. $85.00.

BELL, Charles. *System of Dissections. Explaining Anatomy.* 1814. Baltimore. Samuel Jefferis. 1st Am. 18mo. contemporary bdg. M1. $325.00.

BELL, Christine. *Perez Family.* 1990. Norton. 1st. F/dj. A24. $25.00.

BELL, Christine. *Saint.* 1985. Englewood. Pineapple. 1st. author's 1st book. F/F. H11. $110.00.

BELL, Edward I. *Political Shame of Mexico.* 1914. McBride. 1st. VG. V4. $30.00.

BELL, Eric. *Seeds of Life.* 1951. Fantasy. 1st. 255p. brn cloth. NF/fair. B22. $12.50.

BELL, Gordon B. *Golden Troubadour.* 1980. McGraw Hill. F/F. P3. $13.00.

BELL, Isaac. *Foxiana.* 1929. Country Life. 1st. VG. O3. $40.00.

BELL, Jean K. *Tucky the Tiny Clown by Jean B Kell.* 1951. Asbury Park, NJ. Schuyler Pr. 14p. pict brd. R5. $250.00.

BELL, Josephine. *Catalyst.* 1966. Macmillan. 1st Am. NF/dj. G8. $10.00.

BELL, Josephine. *Double Doom.* 1957. NY. Macmillan. 1st Am ed. VG/VG. G8. $15.00.

BELL, Josephine. *Easy Prey.* 1959. H & S. 1st British ed. VG/VG. G8. $30.00.

BELL, Josephine. *Fennister Affair.* 1969. NY. H & S. 1st Am ed. VG/VG. G8. $12.50.

BELL, Josephine. *No Escape.* 1966. Macmillan. 1st. VG/G. P3. $13.00.

BELL, Katie. *Legend of Kohl's Ranch.* 1985. Central AZ Pub. 1st. sgn. ils/maps/bibliography. NF. B19. $25.00.

BELL, Madison Smartt. *All Soul's Rising.* 1995. Pantheon. ltd. sgn tipped-in leaf. F/dj. R14. $35.00.

BELL, Madison Smartt. *All Soul's Rising.* (1995). NY. Pantheon. ARC. pict wrp. F. B3. $50.00.

BELL, Madison Smartt. *Barking Man & Other Stories.* 1990. NY. Ticknor. 1st. F/F. H11. $30.00.

BELL, Madison Smartt. *Doctor Sleep.* (1992). London. Bloomsbury. 1st British ed. sgn by author. F/F. B3. $45.00.

BELL, Madison Smartt. *Doctor Sleep.* (1991). NY. HBJ. 1st. sgn by author. F/F. B3. $55.00.

BELL, Madison Smartt. *Straight Cut.* 1986. NY. Ticknor. 1st. F/F. H11. $35.00.

BELL, Madison Smartt. *Waiting for the End of the World.* 1985. NY. Ticknor. 1st. jacket has two small closed tears and wear to spine ends. F/NF. H11. $60.00.

BELL, Madison Smartt. *Waiting for the End of the World.* 1985. NY. Ticknor & Fields. 1st. VNF/F. D10. $85.00.

BELL, Madison Smartt. *Washington Square Ensemble.* 1983. London. Deutsch. 1st. F/NF. R14. $100.00.

BELL, Madison Smartt. *Washington Square Ensemble.* 1983. Viking. 1st. sgn/dtd. F/dj. M25. $150.00.

BELL, Madison Smartt. *Zero DB & Other Stories.* 1987. Ticknor Fields. 1st. sgn. F/F. B3. $50.00.

BELL, Marty. *Legend of Dr. J: Story of Julius Erving.* 1975. NY. CMG. 1st. VG+/VG+. R16. $25.00.

BELL, Ramsey. *Dragon Under Ground.* 1937. London. Hodder & Stoughton. 1st. G/dj. M15. $145.00.

BELL, Syndey. *Wives of the Prophet.* 1935. NY. Macaulay. 1st. F/VG+. B4. $125.00.

BELL, Thelma Harnington. *Pawnee.* 1950. Viking. 1st. 63p. VG/G+. P2. $25.00.

BELL, Vereen M. *Achievement of Cormac McCarthy.* 1988. Baton Rouge. LSU. 1st. F/F. R13. $45.00.

BELL, William Dixon. *Moon Colony.* 1937. Goldsmith. VG. P3. $10.00.

BELLAIRS, George. *Intruder in the Dark.* 1966. John Gifford. 1st. VG/G. P3. $20.00.

BELLAMY, Edward. *Equality.* 1897. Appleton. NF. M22. $35.00.

BELLAMY, J.G. *Crime & Public Order in England & the Later Middle Ages.* 1973. London. Kegan Paul. M11. $50.00.

BELLAMY, J.G. *Criminal Law & Society in Late Medieval & Tudor England.* 1984. Gloucester. M11. $65.00.

BELLI, Melvin. *Blood Money.* 1956. NY. 1st. author's 1st book. F/dj. A17. $15.00.

BELLOC, Hilaire. *Cautionary Tales for Children.* nd. London. Duckworth. 8vo. ils. 79p. gray brd. G+. $5.00.

BELLOC, Hilaire. *Emerald of Catherine the Great.* 1926. London. Arrowsmith. 1st. NF/dj. M15. $250.00.

BELLOC, Hilaire. *Joan of Arc.* 1929. London. 1st. VG/dj. T9. $60.00.

BELLOC, Hilaire. *Matilda Who Told Lies & Was Burned to Death.* 1970. Dial. 1st thus. 32p. cloth. F/F. D4. $40.00.

BELLONI, Gian Guido. *Prehistoric to Classical Painting.* 1962. London. Hamlyn. 1st. folio. 24 mc pl. VG. W1. $10.00.

BELLOW, Saul. *Dean's December.* 1982. Harper Row. 1st. F/VG. B3. $25.00.

BELLOW, Saul. *Henderson the Rain King.* 1959. NY. Viking. 1st. F/F. sm chip. B2. $65.00.

BELLOW, Saul. *Humboldt's Gift.* 1975. NY. Viking. 1st. F/F. H11. $60.00.

BELLOW, Saul. *More Die of Heartbreak.* 1987. Morrow. 1st. F/F. B3. $20.00.

BELLOW, Saul. *Mosby's Memoirs & Other Stories.* 1968. Viking. 1st. F/F. B2. $45.00.

BELLOW, Saul. *Mr. Sammler's Planet.* 1970. NY. Viking. 1st. F/F. D10. $50.00.

BELLOW, Saul. *Something to Remember Me By.* 1991. Signet. UP. NF/tan wrps. M25. $45.00.

BELLOW, Saul. *The Dean's December.* 1982. NY. Harper & Row. 1st. F/F. H11. $35.00.

BELLOW, Saul. *Victim.* 1948. London. Lehmann. 1st Eng. author's 2nd book. F/F. B4. $300.00.

BELLOWS, Henry Whitney. *Speech of the Rev. Dr. Bellows, President of the United States Sanitary Commission Made at the Academy of Music, Philadelphia.* 1863. Philadelphia. C. Sherman, Son & Co. 1st. orig printed wrp. VG. M8. $85.00.

BELLROSE, Frank C. *Ducks, Geese & Swans of North America.* 1980. ils. VG/VG. M17. $20.00.

BELLWOOD, Peter. *Man's Conquest of the Pacific.* 1979. NY. Oxford. 1st Am. 4to. 462p. VG/dj. P4. $85.00.

BELMONT, Bob; See Reynolds, Mack.

BELOFF, Max. *Foreign Policy & the Democratic Process.* 1955. Johns Hopkins. 1st. sm 8vo. xl. VG/dj. W1. $8.00.

BELOTE, T.T. *American & European Sword in Collection of US National Mus.* 1932. WA. photos. 163p. VG. M4. $35.00.

BELOUS & WEINSTEIN, *Will Soule: Indian Photographer at Ft Sill, OK 1869 – 1874.* 1969. Ward Ritchie. 120p. cloth. dj. D11. $150.00.

BEMELMANS, Ludwig. *Blue Danube.* 1945. Viking. 1st. F/dj. B35. $60.00.

BEMELMANS, Ludwig. *Eye of God.* 1949. Viking. 1st. F/VG+. B4. $65.00.

BEMELMANS, Ludwig. *High World.* 1954. Harper. 1st. ils. 8vo. 113p. VG/VG. D1. $40.00.

BEMELMANS, Ludwig. *Hotel Splendide.* 1941. Viking. 1st. F/NF. M19. $45.00.

BEMELMANS, Ludwig. *Madeline's Christmas.* 1956. McCall's. 1st. 12mo. sc. M5. $75.00.

BEMELMANS, Ludwig. *Sunshine.* 1950. S&S. 1st. ils. 42p. NF/NF. D1. $200.00.

BEMELMANS, Ludwig. *The Donkey Inside.* 1947. London. Hamish Hamilton. 1st ed. 4 double page color plates. 155p. VG/no dj. ep foxed. F3. $15.00.

BEMIS, Samuel Flagg. *John Quincy Adams & Foundations of American Policy.* 1949. Knopf. 1st. 588p. F/dj. H1. $28.00.

BEMMANN, Hans. *Stone & the Flute.* 1986. Viking. 1st. VG/VG. P3. $20.00.

BEN-GURION, David. *Jews in Their Land.* 1974. Doubleday. 1st revised. ils. 351p. VG/dj. B5. $25.00.

BEN-ZVI, Itzhak. *Exile & the Redeemed.* 1958. London. 1st. photos/notes/index. 334p. F. W3. $38.00.

BENAGH, Jim. *Terry Bradshaw: Superarm of Pro Football.* 1976. Putnam. 1st. VG. P8. $20.00.

BENARD, Cheryl. *Moghul Buffet.* 1998. NY. FSG. 1st. author's 1st novel. sgn. VF/VF. T2. $30.00.

BENARY-ISBERT, Margot. *Wicked Enchantment.* 1955. Harcourt Brace. 1st. 181p. VG/G. P2. $35.00.

BENCHLEY, Nathaniel. *Monument.* 1966. McGraw Hill. 1st. VG/VG. P3. $20.00.

BENCHLEY, Nathaniel. *Visitors.* 1965. McGraw Hill. 1st. VG/VG. P3. $25.00.

BENCHLEY, Peter. *Deep.* 1976. Andre Deutsch. 1st. F/F. P3. $20.00.

BENCHLEY, Peter. *Girl of the Sea of Cortez.* 1982. Andre Deutsch. 1st. VG/VG. P3. $20.00.

BENCHLEY, Peter. *Q Clearance.* 1986. NY. Random House. 1st ed. 2nd printing. 340p. NF/NF. D4. $20.00.

BENCHLEY, Peter. *Rummies.* 1989. NY. Random House. 1st. VF/VF. T2. $8.00.

BENDER, Lauretta. *Visual Motor Gestalt Test & Its Clinical Use.* (1938). Am Orthopsychiatric Assn. tall 8vo. 176p. prt blk cloth. G1. $22.50.

BENDER, Morris B. *Oculomotor System.* (1964). Hoeber Medical Division. 8vo. 556p. gr cloth. VG/dj. G1. $50.00.

BENDER, Texas Bix. *Don't Squat With Yer Spurs On!* 1992. Gibbs Smith. A19. $8.00.

BENDER & TAYLOR. *Uniforms, Organization & History of the Waffen SS.* 5 vol. S16. $85.00.

BENEDICT, Elizabeth. *The Beginner's Book of Dreams.* 1988. NY. Knopf. 1st. F+/VG. H11. $20.00.

BENEDICT, Pickney. *Town Smokes.* 1987. Princeton. Ontario review. 1st. F/wrp. B2. $75.00.

BENEDICT, Pinckney. *Dogs of God.* 1994. NY. Doubleday. 1st. VF/VF. H11. $30.00.

BENEDICT, Pinckney. *The Wrecking Yard.* 1992. NY. Doubleday. 1st. F/F. D10. $35.00.

BENEDICT, Pinckney. *The Wrecking Yard and Other Stories.* 1992. NY. Doubleday. 1st. 1/500 copies sgn on limitation pg. author's 2nd book. F/F. D10. $45.00.

BENEDICT, Pinckney. *Town Smokes.* 1987. Princeton. Ontario review Press. pbo. author's 1st book. no comparable hc. F in pict wrp. tiny nick at spine. D10. $50.00.

BENEDICT, Ruth. *In Henry's Backyard.* 1948. 1st. VG/clip. S13. $25.00.

BENEDICTUS, David. *Fourth of June.* 1962. London. 1st. dj. T9. $40.00.

BENEDIKT, Elliot T., editor. *Weightlessness — Physical Phenomena and Biological Effects.* 1961. NY. Plenum Press. 1st. ex lib in cloth; usual lib mks. 170p. G. K5. $20.00.

BENEDITTI, Mario. *Unstill Life, An Intro to Spanish Poetry of Latin America.* 1969. HBW. 1st. 127p. cloth. F/NF. D4. $45.00.

BENES, MAREK & TUREK. *Fossils of the World.* 1989. Arch Cape. 4to. 495p. F/F. B1. $65.00.

BENET, Laura. *Hidden Valley.* 1940 (1938). Dodd Mead. 8vo. 207p. VG. T5. $20.00.

BENET & BENET. *Book of Americans.* 1933. Farrar Rhinehart. 1st. 115p. cloth. VG+. D4. $25.00.

BENETAR, Judith. *Admissions: Notes from a Woman Psychiatrist.* 1974. NY. Charterhouse. 1st. inscr. 219p. VG/VG. A25. $20.00.

BENFORD, Gregory. *Artifact.* 1985. Tor. 1st. F/F. P3. $17.00.

BENFORD, Gregory. *At the Double Solstice.* 1986. New Castle, VA. Cheap Street. 1st. sgn. F. T2. $65.00.

BENFORD, Gregory. *Centigrade 233.* 1990. New Castle. Cheap Street. 1st. 1/126 # copies. a chapbook. sgn by Benford & publishers. VF. T2. $60.00.

BENFORD, Gregory. *Centigrade 233.* 1990. New Castle, VA. Cheap Street. 1st. sgn. pub/sgn O'Nale. F. $2.00.

BENFORD, Gregory. *Great Sky River.* 1987. Bantam. hc. F/F. P3. $18.00.

BENFORD, Gregory. *In Alien Flesh.* 1986. Tor. 1st. F/F. M2. $20.00.

BENFORD, Gregory. *Of Space/Time and the River.* 1985. New Castle. Cheap Street. 1st. 1/121 # copies. a chapbook. sgn by Benford & artist Judy King-Rieniets. VF/VF dj & slipcase. T2. $125.00.

BENFORD, Gregory. *Stars in Shroud.* 1978. Berkley Putnam. 1st. F/dj. M2/T2. $25.00.

BENFORD, Gregory. *Tides of Light.* 1989. Bantam. 1st. F/F. P3. $18.00.

BENGTSSON, F.G. *Long Ships: Saga of Viking Age.* 1954. Knopf. 2 maps. 503p. T7. $22.00.

BENHAM, F. & H. A. Holley. *A Short Introduction to the Economy of Latin America.* 1964. London. Oxford Univ Press. 1st. 169p. F/G. chipped. F3. $20.00.

BENITEZ, Conrado. *History of the Philippines.* 1940. Ginn. VG. P3. $20.00.

BENITEZ, Fernando. *In the Footsteps of Cortez.* 1952. NY. Pantheon Books. 1st. color drawings by Alberto Beltran. 256p. F. F3. $15.00.

BENITEZ, Sandra. *Bitter Grounds.* (1997). NY. Hyperion. 1st. author's 2nd novel. inscr by author. F/F. B3. $35.00.

BENJAMIN, Carol Lea. *This Dog for Hire.* 1996. NY. Walker. 1st. F/F. M23. $45.00.

BENJAMIN, David. *Idol.* 1979. Putnam. 1st. F/clip. M25. $25.00.

BENJAMIN, Paul; see Auster, Paul.

BENKOVITZ, Miriam J. *Rolfe: A Biography.* 1977. NY. 1st. VG. T9. $20.00.

BENNER, Samuel. *Benner's Prophecies of Future Ups & Downs in Prices.* 1888. Cincinnati. Clarke. 181p. VG. A10. $35.00.

BENNET, Robert Ames. *Bowl of Baal.* 1973. Donald Grant. VG/VG. P3. $20.00.

BENNETT, Arnold. *Imperial Palace.* 1931. Doubleday Doran. 769p. VG/dj. H1. $12.00.

BENNETT, Arnold. *Loot of Cities.* 1972. Oswald Train. 1st Am. F/dj. M2. $10.00.

BENNETT, Edgar B. *The Bennett Family 1628 – 1910.* East Berlin, CT. E. B. Bennett, Publisher. 1910. 12mo. 50p. ils. with pages for record keeping at rear of volume. red cloth. 1st ed. minor spots on cloth. VG. L5. $35.00.

BENNETT, Geoffrey. *Death in the Dog Watches.* 1974. Wht Lion. VG/VG. P3. $15.00.

BENNETT, H. E. *Gold Robbers. A Story of Australia.* 1863. Boston. Elliott Thomes Talbot. 8vo. pink prt wrp. R12. $75.00.

BENNETT, Hall. *Wilderness of Vines.* 1966. Doubleday. 1st. author's 1st book. F/F. B4. $250.00.

BENNETT, Jack. *Gallipoli.* 1981. NY. St. Martin. 1st. Book has number in corner of front ffep and owner name and date on rear ffep. F-/F. H11. $30.00.

BENNETT, James. *Overland to California: Journal of James Bennett.* 1987. Ye Galleon. 1st thus. ils/index. 91p. F/sans. A18. $17.50.

BENNETT, Jill. *Teeny Tiny.* 1986. Putnam. 1st Am. F/NF. P2. $35.00.

BENNETT, John. *Doctor to the Dead.* 1946. Rinehart. 1st. VG/dj. M2. $22.00.

BENNETT, John. *Master Skylark.* 1922. Century. 1st. thick 4to. F/VG. M5. $65.00.

BENNETT, John. *Pigtails of Ah Lee Ben Loo.* 1928. Longman Gr. 1st. ils J Bennett. 8vo. 298p. orange cloth. VG. $1.00.

BENNETT, Kay. *Kaibah: Recollection of a Navajo Girlhood.* 1964. Los Angeles. Westernlore. 1st. ils. F/NF. L3. $65.00.

BENNETT, Lerone. *Black Power USA.* 1967. Chicago. Johnson. 1st. F/NF. B4. $85.00.

BENNETT, Lerone. *Challenge of Blackness.* 1972. Chicago. Johnson. 1st. inscr. 312p. F/NF. B4. $200.00.

BENNETT, Logan J. *Blue-Winged Teal.* 1966 (1938). Ames. rpt. ils. 144p. VG. S15. $24.00.

BENNETT, Ralph. *Ultra in the West: Normandy Campaign of 1944 – 45.* 1980. NY. BC. 336p. F/dj. J2. $10.00.

BENNETT, Rowena. *Animal ABC.* 1935. Merrill. ils Milo Winter. pict paper wrp. R5. $75.00.

BENNETT, Whitman. *Practical Guide to American 19th-C Color Plate Books.* 1949. NY. Bennett. 8vo. 132p. red cloth. NF. B24. $100.00.

BENSON, Ann. *The Burning Road.* 1999. NY. Delacorte. 1st. sgn. VF/VF. T2. $25.00.

BENSON, Ann. *The Plague Tales.* 1997. NY. Delacorte. 1st. sgn. author's 1st novel. VF/VF. T2. $35.00.

BENSON, Ben. *Ninth Hour.* 1956. MS Mill. VG/G. P3. $25.00.

BENSON, Donald. *And Having Writ.* 1978. Bobbs Merrill. 1st. F/dj. M2. $12.00.

BENSON, E.F. *Angel of Pain.* nd. Lippincott. VG. P3. $40.00.

BENSON, E.F. *Secret Lives.* 1932. Hodder Stoughton. xl. VG. P3. $20.00.

BENSON, E. F. *The Passenger: Collected Spook Stories.* 1999. Ashcroft. BC. Ash Tree Press. 1st. Jack Adrian, editor. VF/VF. T2. $40.00.

BENSON, E. F. *The Terror by Night: Collected Spook Stories.* 1998. Ashcroft. BC. Ash Tree Press. 1st. Jack Adrian, editor. VF/VF. T2. $40.00.

BENSON, E.F. *Visible & Invisible.* 1924. Doran. 1st Am. F/NF. B4. $250.00.

BENSON, Elizabeth & Beatriz De La Fuente, editors. *Olmec Art of Ancient Mexico.* 1996. NY. Abrams. 1st. 4to. color & b/w photos. drawings. 288p. G/G. F3. $80.00.

BENSON, Irene Eliott. *Campfire Girls in the Forest; Or, Lost Trail Found.* 1918. Chicago. Donohue. 1st. ils. 149p. VG+. $25.00.

BENSON, Lyman. *Cacti of Arizona.* 1950. Tucson. 2nd. ils/39 pl. F. B26. $22.50.

BENSON, Lyman. *Native Cacti of California.* 1969. Stanford. 16 mc pl/distribution maps. 243p. VG+/dj. B26. $29.00.

BENSON, Lyman. *Plant Classification.* 1957. Boston. ils/photos/drawings. 688p. B26. $37.50.

BENSON, Robert H. *Necromancers.* 1910. Tauchnitz. VG. M2. $50.00.

BENSON, Stella. *Kwan-Yin.* 1922. SF. Grabhorn. 1/100. 8vo. inscr Benson/ Grabhorn. F. T10. $100.00.

BENT, Arthur Cleveland. *Life Histories of North American Gallinaceous Birds.* 1932. Smithsonian. ils/pl. 490p. VG. S15. $25.00.

BENT, Arthur Cleveland. *Life Histories of North American Wood Warblers.* 1953. Smithsonian. 83 pl. 734p. VG. S15. $27.00.

BENT, Newell. *American Polo.* 1929. NY. 1st. 8vo. 407p. gilt gr cloth. F. H3. $90.00.

BENTLEY, E.C. *Trent's Last Case.* 1946. Tower. VG/VG. P3. $13.00.

BENTLEY, James. *Secrets of Mt Sinai.* 1986. Garden City. 1st Am. ils. VG/dj. K3. $20.00.

BENTLEY, John. *Great American Automobiles…Their Achievements.* 1957. Englewood Cliffs. 374p. dj. A17. $17.50.

BENTLEY, John. *It Was Murder, They Said.* 1948. Hutchinson. 1st British ed. VG+/G+. G8. $10.00.

BENTLEY, John. *The Eyes of Death.* 1934. Garden City. Doubleday Crime Club. 1st Am ed. VG/dj. M15. $50.00.

BENTLEY, KHOSLA & SECKLER. *Agroforestry in South Asia.* 1993. Internat'l Sci Pub. 367p. dj. B1. $35.00.

BENTLEY, Nicolas. *Floating Dutchman.* 1951. DSP. 1st. VG/G. P3. $25.00.

BENTON, Arthur Lester. *Right-Left Discrimination & Finger Localization.* 1979. NY. Hoeber-Harper. 185p. prt bl cloth. G1. $50.00.

BENTON, Kenneth. *Level.* 1970. Dodd Mead. VG/VG. P3. $13.00.

BENTON, Kenneth. *Sole Agent.* 1974. Walker. 1st. NF/NF. H11. $15.00.

BENTON, Kenneth. *Spy in Chancery.* 1972. Collins Crime Club. 1st. VG/VG. P3. $20.00.

BENTZ, D.O. *Tuners' Handbook & Manual.* 1908. Lima. OH. 74p. 12mo. A17. $15.00.

BENWELL, H.A. *History of the Yankee Division.* 1919. photos. VG. M17. $25.00.

BERBER, Thomas. *Reinhart in Love.* 1962. Scribner. 1st. author's 2nd book. F/dj. M25. $75.00.

BERCKMAN, Evelyn. *She Asked for It.* 1969. Doubleday. 1st. VG/VG. P3. $20.00.

BERDOE, E. *Origin & Growth of the Healing Art.* 1893. London. 1st. 509p. A13. $90.00.

BERE, R. *World of Animals: The African Elephant.* 1966. London. Barker. ils/photos/distribution maps. 94p. NF/VG. M12. $12.50.

BERENDA, Ruth W. *Influence of the Group on the Judgements of Children.* 1950. King's Crown. tall 8vo. 186p. VG. H1. $17.50.

BERENDT, John. *Midnight in the Garden of Good and Evil.* 1994. NY. Random House. 1st. VF/dj. M15. $250.00.

BERENDT, John. *Midnight in the Garden of Good and Evil.* 1994. NY. Random House. 1st. sgn by author. F/F. B2. $175.00.

BERENDT, John. *Midnight in the Garden of Good & Evil.* 1994. Random. 1st. author's 1st book. F/F. M19. $125.00.

BERENDZEN, Richard, Richard Hart & Daniel Seeley. *Man Discovers the Galaxies.* 1976. NY. Science History Publications. 4to. b/w photos. 228p. VG/VG clip. K5. $25.00.

BERESFORD, Elisabeth. *Wombles at Work.* 1974 (1973). London. Ernest Benn. 2nd. 8vo. 191p. gr brd. VG/G+. $5.00.

BERG, A. Scott. *Lindbergh.* 1998. NY. Putnam. 1st. orig cloth. plates. 628p. F/F. M8. $30.00.

BERG, Elizabeth. *Durable Goods.* 1993. Random. 1st. sgn. F/F. B3. $75.00.

BERG, Stephen. *Nothing in the Word.* 1972. Grossman. 1st. assn copy. F/wrp/ dj. V1. $20.00.

BERG, Steven. *With Akhmatova at the Black Gates.* 1981. Univ of Illinois. 1st. F/NF. V1. $35.00.

BERGAUST, Erik. *Colonizing the Planets.* 1975. NY. Putnam. ex lib in pict cloth lib bdg. usual lib mks. b/w photo ils. 8vo. 93p. G. K5. $10.00.

BERGAUST, Erik. *Planet for Conquest.* 1967. Putnam. 8vo. 95p. VG/dj. K5. $20.00.

BERGAUST, Erik & Seabrook Hull. *Rocket to the Moon.* 1958. Princeton. NJ. D. Van Nostrand. 8vo. b/w photo ils. 270p. VG/chipped & torn dj. K5. $30.00.

BERGENDOFF, Conrad. *The Church of Lutheranism.* 1967. Concordia. 339p. VG/VG. ex lib. B29. $12.00.

BERGER, J. *Wild Horses of the Great Basin: Social Competition.* 1986. Chicago. 8vo. ils/photos/figures. 326p. cloth. F/VG. M12. $22.50.

BERGER, John. *A Painter of Our Time.* 1959. NY. S&S. 1st Am ed. author's 1st book. F. owner's name. browning pgs/lightly used dj. B2. $40.00.

BERGER, Thomas. *Changing the Past.* 1989. Little, Brn. 1st. F/F. H11. $30.00.

BERGER, Thomas. *Crazy in Berlin.* 1958. Scribner. 1st. author's 1st book. F/NF. B2. $250.00.

BERGER, Thomas. *Meeting Evil.* 1992. Little, Brn. 1st. F/F. A20. $15.00.

BERGER, Thomas. *Neighbors.* 1980. Delacorte. 3rd. NF/NF. P3. $13.00.

BERGER, Thomas. *Orrie's Story.* (1990). Boston. Little, Brn. 1st. F/F. B3. $15.00.

BERGER, Thomas. *Reinhart's Women.* 1981. Delacorte. 1st. NF/F. A20. $30.00.

BERGER, Thomas. *The Houseguest.* 1988. Boston. Little, Brn. 1st. F/F. H11. $25.00.

BERGERHOFF, Walther. *Atlas of Normal Radiographs of the Skull.* 1961. Berlin. 1st. folio. 57p. A13. $30.00.

BERGGRAV, Eivind. *Man and State.* 1951. Muhlenberg. 319p. VG/worn dj. B29. $10.50.

BERGLAND, Martha. *Farm Under a Lake.* 1989. Graywolf. 1st. F/dj. R13. $20.00.

BERGMAN, Andrew. *Big Kiss-Off of 1944.* 1974. HRW. 1st. VG/VG. P3. $25.00.

BERGMAN, Andrew. *Hollywood & Levine.* 1975. Holt. 1st. NF/dj. M25. $35.00.

BERGMAN, Andrew. *James Cagney.* 1981. NY. Galahad. 156p. VG. C5. $12.50.

BERGMAN, Deborah. *Southern Cross.* 1990. Putnam. 1st. F/dj. T12. $15.00.

BERGMAN, Peter G. *Riddle of Gravitation.* 1968. Scribner. 1st. VG/dj. O4. $15.00.

BERGMAN, Peter M. *The Chronological History of the Negro in America.* 1969. Harper & Row. 1st. NF/darkened dj. M25. $35.00.

BERGMAN, Ray. *Fresh-Water Bass.* 1942. Penn. 1st. 436p+10 mc pl. A17. $30.00.

BERKELEY, Anthony. *Poisoned Chocolate Case.* 1929. Crime Club. G. P3. $18.00.

BERKELEY, Anthony. *Silk Stocking Murders.* nd. Canada. Doubleday Doran. VG. P3. $35.00.

BERKELEY, Henry J. *Treatise on Mental Disease Based on Lecture Course.* 1900. Appleton. 8vo. 15 pl. panelled gr buckram. xl. G1. $65.00.

BERKHOF, L. *Principles of Biblical Interpretation.* 1966. Baker. 169p. VG. B29. $9.00.

BERKLEY, James D. *Preaching to Convict.* 1986. Word. 169p. G/G. B29. $6.00.

BERKOUWER, G. C. *Studies in Dogmatics; Man; The Image of God.* 1978. Eerdmans. 375p. VG/VG. B29. $18.00.

BERKOW, Ira. *Pitchers Do Get Lonely.* 1988. Atheneum. 1st. F/F. P8. $15.00.

BERLE, A.A. *World Significance of a Jewish State.* 1981. Mitchell Kennerley. 47p. VG+. S3. $25.00.

BERLITZ, Charles. *Atlantis: The Lost Continent Revealed.* 1984. Macmillan. 1st. VG. P3. $15.00.

BERLITZ, Charles. *Bermuda Triangle.* 1974. Doubleday. 1st. ils. 203p. NF. S14. $12.00.

BERLITZ, Charles. *Lost Ship of Noah.* 1987. Putnam. VG/dj. A19. $25.00.

BERMAN, Arthur I. *The Physical Principles of Astronautics; Fundamentals of Dynamical Astronomy and Space Flight.* 1961. NY. John Wiley & Sons. 127 text figures. 8vo. 350p. VG/chipped dj; pencil notes on ep. K5. $45.00.

BERMANT, Chaim. *Jews.* 1977. NY. Times Books. 278p. VG/dj. S3. $23.00.

BERNADOTTE, Folke. *Curtain Falls. Eyewitness Account of Last Days Third Reich.* 1945. 1st. F/VG. E6. $25.00.

BERNAL, Ignacio. *100 Great Masterpieces of the Mexican Museum of Anthropology.* 1969. NY. Abrams. 1st. folio. color & b/w photo ils. 162p. G/G. F3. $75.00.

BERNAL, Ignacio. *A History of Mexican Archaeology. The Vanished Civilizations of Middle America.* 1980. NY. Thames. 1st. wrp. b/w photos ils. 208p. G. F3. $15.00.

BERNARD, April. *Pirate Jenny.* 1990. NY. Norton. 1st. VF/VF. H11. $30.00.

BERNARD, Desire. *De L'Aphasie Et De Ses Diverses Formes.* 1889. Paris. 2nd. ils. contemporary brd. xl. VG. G1. $125.00.

BERNARD, Raymond. *Hollow Earth.* 1979. Bell. VG/VG. P3. $12.00.

BERNAU, George. *Black Phoenix.* 1994. NY. Warner. 1st. VF/VF. H11. $25.00.

BERNHARD, Ruth. *Gift of the Commonplace.* 1996. Carmel, CA. Woodrose Pub/Center for Photographic Art. 1st. sgn by Bernhard. F w/o dj as issued. O11. $125.00.

BERNHARDT, P. *Wily Violets & Underground Orchids.* 1989. NY. Morrow. 1st. 255p. F/F. B1. $19.00.

BERNIER, Francois. *Voyages...Contenant La Description Des Etats Du Grand Mogul.* 1699. Amsterdam. Marret. 2 vol. 8vo. 13 engraved pl/maps. vellum. R12. $750.00.

BERNIER, O. *Lafayette: Hero of Two Worlds.* 1983. NY. 1st. ils. F/rpr. M4. $15.00.

BERNINGER, Ernst. *Otto Hahn: Ein Bild-Dokumentation.* 1969. Munchen. 137 ils. NF. K3. $45.00.

BERNSTEIN, Jeremy. *Experiencing Science.* 1978. NY. 1st. 275p. A13. $17.50.

BERNSTEIN, Leonard. *Young People's Concerts.* 1962. ils. w/records. VG/VG cases. M17. $20.00.

BERRIAULT, Gina. *Conference of Victims.* 1962. NY. Atheneum. 1st. Jacket has slightly darkened spine and light wear along bottom of spine and rear panel. F/NF. H11. $60.00.

BERRIAULT, Gina. *Descent.* 1960. Atheneum. 1st. VG/dj. M2. $13.00.

BERRIAULT, Gina. *Lights of Earth.* 1984. San Francisco. North Point Press. 1st. F/F. minor shelfwear. D10. $45.00.

BERRIAULT, Gina. *Women In Their Beds.* (1996). Washington. Counterpoint. 1st. F/NF very minor edgewear. B3. $40.00.

BERRIDGE, Jesse. *Tudor Rose.* 1925. London. 1st. VG. M2. $12.00.

BERRIE, BERRIE & EZE. *Tropical Plant Science.* 1987. Longman. 410p. F. B1. $25.00.

BERRIGAN, Daniel. *Time Without Number.* Selected Poems. 1957. Macmillan. 1st. F/NF. R13. $25.00.

BERRIGAN, Daniel. *World for Wedding Ring.* 1962. 1st. VG/VG. M19. $25.00.

BERROW, Norman. *Ghost House.* 1979. St Martin. 1st Am. F/dj. M2. $15.00.

BERROW, Norman. *Words Have Wings.* 1946. Ward Lock. 1st. F/clip. M15. $100.00.

BERRY, Barbara. *Look of Eagles.* 1973. BC. G. O3. $10.00.

BERRY, Carole. *Year of the Monkey.* 1988. St Martin. 1st. F/F. P3. $17.00.

BERRY, Don. *Moontrap.* 1962. Viking. 1st. F/VG+. A18. $40.00.

BERRY, Don. *Trask.* 1961. Viking. 1st. F/VG. A18. $50.00.

BERRY, Erick. *Girls in Africa.* 1928. Macmillan. 1st. ils. 128p. VG/VG. D1. $65.00.

BERRY, Mike; see Malzberg, Barry.

BERRY, R.J.A. *Stoke Park Monographs on Mental Deficiency & Other Problems.* 1933. London. Macmillan. 29 half-tones. 249p. gr cloth. G1. $50.00.

BERRY, Rose V.S. *Dream City: Its Art in Story & Symbolism.* 1915. self pub. 8vo. ils/drawings. 335p. brn cloth. NF. K7. $30.00.

BERRY, Wendell. *A World Lost.* 1996. Washington. Counterpoint Press. 1st. sgn. F in F dj. D10. $45.00.

BERRY, Wendell. *Clearing.* (1977). NY. HBJ. 1st. F/F. B3. $65.00.

BERRY, Wendell. *Collected Poems 1957 – 1982.* 1985. Northpoint. 1st. F/F. D10. $35.00.

BERRY, Wendell. *Continuous Harmony.* 1972. HBJ. 1st. F/F. D10. $45.00.

BERRY, Wendell. *Entries.* (1994). NY. Pantheon. review copy. F/F. B3. $35.00.

BERRY, Wendell. *Riverdure.* 1974. np. U CO. 1/100. sgn. F/Japanese-stitched wrp. B4. $350.00.

BERRY, Wendell. *Sabbaths.* 1987. SF. Northpoint. 1st. sgn. F/F. R14. $50.00.

BERRY, Wendell. *Sayings & Doings.* 1975. Lexington. Gnomon. 1st. F/sans. L3. $45.00.

BERRY, Wendell. *The Gift of Good Land.* (1981). San Francisco. North Point Press. 1st. sgn by author. F/F. B3. $50.00.

BERRY, Wendell. *The Selected Poems Of.* 1998. Washington DC. Counterpoint. 1st. F/F. V1. $10.00.

BERRY, Wendell. *The Wild Birds.* (1986). San Francisco. North Point Press. 1st. sgn by author. F/F. B3. $45.00.

BERRY, Wendell. *Two More Stories of the Port William Membership.* (1997). Frankfort. KY. Gnomon. 1st. sgn by author. F/F. B3. $30.00.

BERRY, Wendell. *Wild Birds.* 1986. Northpoint. 1st. pres. pub slip. F/F. D10. $35.00.

BERRYMAN, John. *Homage to Mistress Bradstreet.* 1956. FSC. 1st. 61p. F/F. D4. $145.00.

BERRYMAN, John. *Recovery.* 1973. FSG. 1st. VG+/dj. A20. $20.00.

BERTHOLLET, C.L. *Researches into Laws of Chemical Affinity.* 1809. Baltimore. Nicklin. 1st. 12mo. 212p. contemporary calf. M1. $225.00.

BERTIN, Jack. *Interplanetary Adventures.* 1970. Lenox Hill. VG. P3. $10.00.

BERTO, Giusseppe. *Sky Is Red.* 1948. New Directions. 1st. NF/dj. B35. $20.00.

BERTON, Pierre. *The Dionne Years: A Thirties Melodrama.* 1977. Toronto. McClelland & Stewart. 1st. F/dj. A26. $20.00.

BERTRAND, A. *Succulent Plants.* 1959. (1953). London. 2nd. ils/photos. VG/dj. B26. $20.00.

BERVEILER, David. *Strategic Solitaire.* 1984. NC. 142p. VG. S1. $8.00.

BESANT, Walter. *Beyond the Dreams of Avarice.* 1895. London. Chatto & Windus. 1st. cloth covered boards. NF. M15. $125.00.

BESHOAR, Barron B. *Hippocrates in a Red Vest.* 1973. Palo Alto, CA. Am West Pub. G/dj. A19. $35.00.

BESHOAR, Barron B. *Out of the Depths. The Story of John R. Lawson.* nd. Denver. Golden Bell Press. non-1st?. F/VG. B2. $30.00.

BESKOW, Elsa. *Children of the Forest.* (1969). Delacorte. 1st Am. ils. VG/dj. D1. $65.00.

BESKOW, Elsa. *Hanschen Im Blaubeerenwald.* nd. (1903). Stuttgart. Ferdinand Carl. obl 4to. red bdg. VG. M5. $115.00.

BESKOW, Katja. *Astonishing Adventures of Patrick the Mouse.* 1965. Delacorte. 1st Am. 84p. cloth. VG/dj. M20. $25.00.

BESSIE, Alvah. *One for My Baby.* 1980. HRW. 1st. NF/VG+. A24. $20.00.

BESSIE, Alvah. *Symbol.* 1966. Random. 1st. M25/V4. $25.00.

BESSIE, Alvah. *Un-Americans.* 1957. Cameron Assoc. 1st. VG/dj. M25. $35.00.

BEST, Marc. *Those Endearing Young Charms.* 1971. AS Barnes. 278p. VG/dj. M20. $16.00.

BESTER, Alfred. *Computer Connection.* 1975. Berkley. 1st. F/NF. M2. $15.00.

BESTER, Alfred. *Demolished Man.* 1953. Shasta. 1st. sgn subscriber copy. F/dj. M2. $450.00.

BESTER, Alfred. *Golem 100.* 1980. S&S. 1st. F/dj. M2. $15.00.

BESTER, Alfred. *Light Fantastic.* 1976. Berkley Putnam. 1st. VG/VG. P3. $20.00.

BESTER, Alfred. *Light Fantastic.* 1977. Gollancz. VG/VG. P3. $25.00.

BESTER, Alfred. *The Life and Death of a Satellite; A Biography of the Men and Machines at War.* 1966. Boston. Little, Brn. 1st ed. b/w photo ils. 8vo. 239p. VG/chipped dj. K5. $22.00.

BESTON, Henry. *Songs of Kai: Story of the Indian Told.* 1926. Macmillan. 1st. ils. 55p. VG+. B19. $45.00.

BETETA, Ramon. *Jarano.* 1970. Austin. Univ of Texas. 1st. 163p. G/G chipped. F3. $20.00.

BETTER HOMES AND GARDENS. *Favorite American Wines and How to Enjoy Them.* 1979. IA. Meredith Corporation. 1st. 4to. hc. VG. A28. $6.95.

BETTER HOMES AND GARDENS. *Golden Treasury of Cooking.* 1973. IA. Meredith Corporation. hc folio. G. A28. $18.95.

BETTER HOMES AND GARDENS. *Junior Cookbook.* 1963 (1955). Des Moines, IA. Meredith Press. rev 3rd printing. sm4to. 78p. VG+. S14. $10.00.

BETTER HOMES AND GARDENS. *Quick and Easy Diet Recipes.* 1989. IA. Meredith Corporation. hc folio. VG-. A28. $6.95.

BEVIS, H. U. *Alien Abductors.* 1971. Lenox Hill. G/G. P3. $10.00.

BEWER, Julius. *The Literature of the Old Testament.* 1945. Columbia. 464p. G. B29. $9.00.

BEWICK, John. *Proverbs Exemplified & Ils by Pictures from Real Life…* 1790. London. Rev J Trusler. 1st. 16mo. 196p. rebound/leather spine. R5. $400.00.

BEWICK, Thomas. *General History of Quadrupeds.* 1790. Newcastle-Upon-Tyne. Hodgson Beilly Bewick. 1st. tall 8vo. 456p. recent bdg. H13. $895.00.

BEWICK, Thomas. *Poetical Works of Robert Burns; With His Life.* 1808. Wm Davison. 1st thus. 2 vol. 8vo. full-p pl. later 19th-C morocco. F. $24.00.

BEWS, J. W. *Plant Forms and Their Evolution in South Africa.* 1925. London. gilt & bstp gr cloth. 199p. ep tanned. VG. B26. $45.00.

BEYER, Harold. *History of Norwegian Literature.* 1956. NYU. 1st ed. 370p. F/dj. A17. $15.00.

BEYER, William Gray. *Minions of the Moon.* 1950. Gnome. 1st. F/VG. P3. $35.00.

BIANCHI, Leonardo. *Mechanism of the Brain & Function of the Frontal Lobes.* 1922. Edinburgh. Livingston. 1st Eng-language. 348p. purple cloth. xl. G1. $200.00.

BIANCO, Margery. *House that Grew Smaller.* 1931. Macmillan. 1st. 8vo. gr cloth. dj. R5. $100.00.

BIANCO, Margery. *Hurdy-Gurdy Man.* 1933. Oxford. 1st. sq 8vo. VG+. P2. $75.00.

BIANCO, Pamela. *Beginning With A.* 1947. Oxford. 1st. bl cloth. F/dj. R5. $150.00.

BIANCO, Pamela. *Doll in the Window.* 1953. Oxford. 1st. sq 8vo. VG/VG-. P2. $75.00.

BIANCO, Pamela. *Paradise Square.* 1950. Oxford. 1st. 96p. VG+/G+. P2. $60.00.

BIANCO, Pamela. *Starlit Journey.* 1933. Macmillan. 1st. pres. 12mo. bl cloth. dj. R5. $200.00.

BIART, Lucien. *Aztecs: Their History, Manner & Customs.* 1887. Chicago. ils/fld map. 343p. B18. $45.00.

BIBB, Henry. *Puttin' on Ole Massa: Slave Narratives of Henry Bibb.* 1969. 1st. edit Osofsky. VG/VG. M17. $25.00.

BIBBY, Geoffrey. *Looking for Dilum.* 1969. Knopf. ils/maps. 383p. xl. NF/dj. W1. $22.00.

BIBLE. *Children's King James Bible: New Testament.* 1960. Evansville, IN. Modern Bible Translations. ils Manning Lee. 688p. VG+/G. S14. $9.00.

BIBLE. *Personal Reference, King James.* 1983 (1977). MI. Zondervan. 7th printing. maps. 8vo. name emb on front cover. rubbed. 1494p. VG. S14. $10.00.

BIBLE. *Bible Atlas Containing Nine Maps with Explanations.* 1827. Phil. Am Sunday School. 1st. sq 18mo. orig engraved yel wrp. M1. $275.00.

BIBLE. *Bible in Miniature; or, Concise Hist of Old/New Testaments.* 1780. London. Newbery. 1st/3rd state. 45x30mm. brn leather. F. B24. $550.00.

BIBLE. *Biblia.* Nuremberg: Anton Koberger. Apr 14. 1478. folio. 468 leaves. 16th-C stp leather/wood brd. C6. $10,500.00.

BIBLE. *Book of Ecclesiastes.* 1968. NY. LEC. RKJ. Hebrew/Eng text. ils/sgn Edgar Miller. leather. S3. $65.00.

BIBLE. *Book of Ruth.* 1947. LEC. 1/1950. ils/sgn Arthur Szyk. VG/case. D1. $225.00.

BIBLE. *Child's Bible.* 1834. Phil. Fisher & Brother. 57x48mm. full-p pl. 192p. gilt lavender cloth. NF. B24. $85.00.

BIBLE. *Daily Devotional Bible.* nd. Nelson. KJV. arranged for daily devotion for 1 year. swrp. B29. $10.50.

BIBLE. *Dakota Wowapi Woken Sioux Holy Bible.* 1919. NY. Am Bible Soc. A19. $250.00.

BIBLE. *God's Victorious Army Bible.* nd. Morris Cerullo. KJV. F. B29. $6.50.

BIBLE. *Gospel According to Saint Luke. Translated into Seneca.* 1829. NY. Am Bible Soc. 1st. trans TS Harris. 16mo. 149p. contemporary bdg. $1.00.

BIBLE. *History of the Bible.* 1850. New London. Bolles. 54x45mm. 24 woodcuts. 192p. full calf. B24. $185.00.

BIBLE. *History of the Bible.* 1954. LA. Dudie Studio. facsimile. 56x40mm. 231p. gilt full brn leather. B24. $100.00.

BIBLE. *Holy Bible.* 1972. Nelson. RSV. reference/concordance/maps. leatherette. VG. B29. $12.00.

BIBLE. *Holy Bible.* 1975. Falwell Ministries. Am Bicentennial Ed. ils. wht w/Liberty Bell bdg. VG. B29. $10.50.

BIBLE. *Holy Bible.* 1976. Regency. KJV. Giant Prt. red letter/reference. 1855p. VG. B29. $10.50.

BIBLE. *Holy Bible, Containing the Old & New Testaments.* 1919. NY. Oxford/Am Branch. 44x30mm. aeg. limp maroon leather. w/magnifying glass. B24. $225.00.

BIBLE. *Layman's Parallel Bible.* 1980. Zondervan. KJV/MLB/LB/RSV. 3037p. VG/dj. B29. $17.00.

BIBLE. *Le Nouveau Testament De Notre Seigneur Jesus-Christ.* 1810. Boston. Buckingham. 1st. thick 8vo. 2-toned brd. uncut. M1. $375.00.

BIBLE. *New Open Bible.* 1982. Nelson. KJV. Lg Prt ed. references/trans/indexes. leather. G. B29. $15.50.

BIBLE. *One Year Bible.* 1986. Tyndale. NIV. arranged in 365 daily readings. VG/dj. B29. $10.50.

BIBLE. *Pentateuch With Haftaroth & Five Megiloth.* 1928. Hebrew Pub. Eng trans revised by Alexander Harkavy. G. B29. $13.00.

BIBLE. Reader's Digest Bible. 1982. Reader's Digest. RSV. 799p. VG/torn. B29. $7.00.

BICKEL, Lennard. *Deadly Element.* 1979. Stein Day. 1st. ils. 312p. VG/dj. K3. $20.00.

BICKEL, Walter. *Hering's Dictionary of Classical & Modern Cookery.* nd. London. Virtue. 7th Eng. VG. A16. $30.00.

BICKERMAN, Elias. *Maccabees.* 1947. Schocken. 125p. VG/G. S3. $23.00.

BICKERSTETH, M. Cyril. *Unity & Holiness.* 1914. Mawbray. 272p. VG/VG. B29. $4.50.

BICKHAM, Jack M. *Dropshot.* 1990. NY. tor. 1st. F/NF. T2. $7.00.

BICKHAM, Jack M. *Tiebreaker.* 1989. NY. tor. 1st. F/F. T2. $8.00.

BIDDLE, Shelia. *Bolingbroke & Harley.* 1974. Knopf. 1st. 307p. VG+/clip. M20. $12.00.

BIDLOO, Govert. *Anatomia Humani Corporis. Centum et Quinque Tabulis…* 1685. Amsterdam. 1st. lg folio. ftspc/pl. contemporary vellum. xl.

BIDWELL, John. *First Emigrant Train to California.* 1966. Menlo Park. Penlitho. 1/500. ils Remington. 52p. whit buckram. F. $7.00.

BIDWELL, John. *Life in California Before the Gold Discovery.* 1966. Palo Alto. Lewis Osborne. 1/1950. gilt sage cloth. M. K7. $45.00.

BIERCE, Ambrose. *Enlarged Devil's Dictionary.* 1967. Doubleday. 1st. F/dj. M2. $25.00.

BIERCE, Ambrose. *Tales of Soldiers & Civilians.* 1891. SF. ELG Steele. 1st. 12mo. 300p. gr cloth. M1. $1,500.00.

BIERCE, Ambrose. *Vision of Doom.* 1980. Donald Grant. 1st. F/dj. M2. $12.00.

BIERCE, L.V. *Historical Reminiscences of Summit County.* 1854. Akron. 1st. 157p. G. B18. $225.00.

BIERDS, Linda. *Flights of the Harvest-Mare.* 1985. Boise. Ahsahta. 1st. sgn. F. O11. $30.00.

BIERHORST, John. *The Hungry Woman. Myths and Legends of the Aztecs.* 1993. NY. Morrow. 1st. 148p. G/wrp. F3. $10.00.

BIERMAN, John. *Dark Safari: Life Behind Legend of Henry Morton Stanley.* 1990. NY. 1st. ils/maps. 401p. F/dj. M4. $20.00.

BIERMAN, John. *Odyssey.* 1984. S&S. 255p. F/VG. S3. $25.00.

BIERNE, F.F. *War of 1812.* 1949. NY. 1st. 11 maps. F/G. M4. $25.00.

BIERSTADT, Edward Hale. *Dunsany the Dramatist.* 1917. Little, Brn. 1st. NF. R10. $25.00.

BIESTERVELD, Betty. *Peter's Wagon.* 1968. Racine. Whitman. lg 32mo. ils Nagel. AN. C8. $20.00.

BIGELOW, Henry J. *Memoir of Henry Jacob Bigelow.* 1900. Boston. 1st. 297p. A13. $75.00.

BIGELOW, Jacob. *Florula Bostoniensis: A Collection of Boston and Its Vicinity.* 1824 (1814). Boston. 2nd ed. greatly enlarged. modern ¼ cloth. 424p. lightly browned. foxed throughout. B26. $69.00.

BIGELOW, John. *Life of Benjamin Franklin Written by Himself.* 1879. Lippincott. 2nd/revised/corrected. 2 vol. bl cloth. VG. T10. $45.00.

BIGELOW, John. *Memoir of the Life & Public Services of John Chas Fremont.* 1856. NY. 1st. 480p. O8. $32.50.

BIGELOW, John. *Supreme Court & the Electoral Commission: An Open Letter…* 1903. NY. Knickerbocker. pres. prt sewn wrp. M11. $75.00.

BIGELOW, John Mason. *Death Is an Early Riser.* 1940. NY. Charles Scribner's Sons. 1st. F/dj. M15. $45.00.

BIGELOW, Poultney. *Borderland of Czar & Kaiser.* 1895. NY. Harper. 1st. ils Remington. 343p. tan cloth. NF. $7.00.

BIGELOW, S. Tupper. *An Irregular Anglo-American Glossary of More or Less Unfamiliar Words, Terms and Phrases in the Sherlock Holmes Saga.* 1998. Shelburne. Ontario. Battered silicon dispatch box. revised ed. 1st thus. VF/VF. T2. $24.00.

BIGELOW, Wilfred Abram. *Forceps.* Fin & Feather. (1969). Altona, Manitoba. DW Friesen. 1st. 116p. NF/VG+. $7.00.

BIGGER, Ruby Vaughan. *My Miss Nancy: Nancy Astor's Virginia Mammy…* 1924. Macon. JW Burke. inscr. 45p. G. B10. $275.00.

BIGGERS, Earl Der. *The House Without a Key.* 1925. NY. Grosset & Dunlap. Reprint. Top of page edges foxed. Jacket has internal tape repair and darkened spine. NF/dj. M15. $75.00.

BIGGERS, Earl Derr. *Agony Column.* 1916. Bobbs Merrill. 194p. G. G11. $20.00.

BIGGERS, Earl Derr. *Black Camel.* 1929. Bobbs Merrill. VG. M22. $15.00.

BIGGERS, Earl Derr. *Celebrated Cases of Charlie Chan.* 1985. New Orchard. MTI. VG/VG. P3. $20.00.

BIGGERS, Earl Derr. *Charlie Chan Carries On.* 1930. Indianapolis. Bobbs-Merrill. 1st. VG/G dj. M15. $450.00.

BIGGERS, Earl Derr. *Earl Derr Biggers Tells Ten Stories.* 1933. Bobbs Merrill. 1st. VG. G8. $25.00.

BIGGERS, Earl Derr. *House Without a Key.* 1925. Bobbs Merrill. VG. M2. $15.00.

BIGGERS, Earl Derr. *Keeper of the Keys.* 1932. McClelland Stewart. 1st. VG. P3. $35.00.

BIGGLE, Jacob. *Biggle Berry Book.* 1913. Atkinson. 144p. cloth. A10. $32.00.

BIGGLE, Jacob. *Biggle Horse Book.* 1907. Phil. Atkinson. 136p. VG. A10. $30.00.

BIGGLE, Lloyd. *Light that Never Was.* 1974. London. 1st. F/dj. M2. $12.00.

BIGGLE, Lloyd. *Metallic Muse.* 1972. Doubleday. 1st. xl. VG/VG. P3. $8.00.

BIGGLE, Lloyd. *Monument.* 1974. Doubleday. 1st. F/F. M2. $20.00.

BIGGLE, Lloyd Jr. *The Quallsford Inheritance: A Memoir of Sherlock Holmes from the Papers of Edward Porter Jones His Late Assistant.* 1986. NY. St. Martin. 1st. F/F. lt wear. T2. $25.00.

BILENKIN, Dmitri. *Uncertainty Principle.* 1978. Macmillan. F/F. P3. $15.00.

BILEZIKIAN, Gilbert. *Christianity 101: Your Guide to Eight Basic Christian…* 1993. Zondervan. 287p. F/dj. M4. $6.50.

BILLIAS, George Athan. *George Washington's Opponents.* 1969. Morrow. 1st. 362p. VG/dj. M20. $20.00.

BILLINGS, Charlene W. *Space Station; Bold New Step Beyond Earth.* 1986. NY. Dodd. Mead. ex lib in dj. usual lib mks. 8vo. many photos. some color. 63p. G. K5. $10.00.

BILLINGS, John S. *Description of Johns Hopkins Hospital.* 1890. Baltimore. 1st. 56 pl. 116p. quarter leather/marbled brd. A13. $1.500.00.

BILLINGS, John S. *National Medical Dictionary: Including English.* French. 1890. Edinburgh. 2 vol. 1st. A13. $200.00.

BILLINGS, M.P. *Structural Geology.* 1972. Englewood Cliffs. 3rd. NF. D8. $16.00.

BILLINGTON, C. *Shrubs of Michigan.* 1977. Bloomfield Hills. Cranbrook. 2nd/3rd prt. 339p. F/NF. B1. $27.50.

BILOFSKY, Frank. *Lion Country: Inside Penn State Football.* 1982. West Point, NY. Leisure Press. 1st. photos. NF/dj clip. R16. $30.00.

BILROTH, Theodor. *General Surgical Pathology & Therapeutics.* 1871. NY. 1st Eng trans. 676p. A13. $250.00.

BILYEU, Richard. *Tanelorn Archives.* 1981. Pandora. 1/250. sgn. ils Steve Leialoha. F/sans. P3. $25.00.

BIMBA, Anthony. *History of the American Working Class.* 1927. Internat Pub. 1st. VG/dj. V4. $40.00.

BIMBA, Anthony. *Molly Maguires: True Story of Labor's Martyred Pioneers...* 1932. NY. Internat Pub. VG/fair. V4. $15.00.

BIMSON, Walter. *West & Walter Bimson.* 1971. AZ. 1st. 223p. F/dj. E1. $65.00.

BINDER, Eando. *Enslaved Brains.* 1965. Avalon. 1st. F/dj. M2. $25.00.

BINDER, Eando. *Lords of Creation.* 1949. Prime. 1st. F/VG. P3. $80.00.

BINDER, Otto O. *Victory in Space.* 1962. Walker. 8vo. 211p. G/dj. K5. $25.00.

BINDING, Tim. *A Perfect Execution.* 1996. London. Picador. 1st. VF/VF. T2. $35.00.

BINDING, Tim. *A Perfect Execution.* 1996. NY. Doubleday. 1st Am ed. VF/VF. T2. $25.00.

BINET, Alfred. *The Psychic Life of Micro-Organisms: A Study in Experimental Psychology, Translated from French by Thomas McCormack.* 1889. Chicago. Open Court Pub Co. 1st. xxii. addenda + 4pp adv. gilt on green cloth. ils. 120p. VG. B14. $150.00.

BINGHAM, Hiram. *Across South America.* (1911). Houghton Mifflin. ils/maps. 405p. gilt gr cloth. F3. $45.00.

BINGHAM, Hiram. *Lost City of the Incas.* 1962. NY. VG/VG. B5. $30.00.

BINGHAM, Millicent Todd. *Emily Dickinson. A Revelation.* NY. Harper and Brothers Publishers. (1954). 8vo. 109p. ils. blk cloth spine & printed bl boards. dj. lst ed. VG/torn dj. L5. $45.00.

BINGHAM, Sallie. *Upstate.* 1993. Sag Harbor. Permanent Press. 1st. sgn. VF/VF. T2. $25.00.

BINNIE, G.M. *Early Victorian Water Engineers.* 1981. ils. VG/VG. M17. $35.00.

BINNS, Archie. *Northwest Gateway: Story of Port of Seattle.* 1941. Doubleday. ils. 313p. dj. T7. $30.00.

BINNS, Archie. *Roaring Land.* 1942. McBride. 1st. sgn. 284p. VG/VG. B11. $40.00.

BINNS, Henry Bryan. *Life of Abraham Lincoln.* 1927. 1st. 379p. O8. $9.50.

BINYON, Lawrence. *Engraved Designs of William Blake.* 1926. London. Ernest Benn. 140p. teg. NF. B24. $250.00.

BIRCHLEY, W. *British Birds for Cages, Aviaries & Exhibition.* 1909. London. Sherratt Hughes. 2 vol. royal 8vo. ils/pl. xl. VG. M12. $60.00.

BIRD, Larry. *Drive.* 1989. Doubleday. 1st. photos. fwd Magic Johnson. F/F. P8. $80.00.

BIRD, Sarah. *The Boyfriend School.* (1989). NY. Doubleday. 1st. author's 3rd book. F/F. B3. $60.00.

BIRD, Sarah. *The Mommy Club.* (1991). NY. Doubleday. 1st. F/F. B3. $45.00.

BIRDWELL, Cleo (Don DeLillo). *Amazons.* 1980. NY. Holt. 1st. book has three nicks on board edges. NF/F. H11. $55.00.

BIRKENHEAD, Earl. *World In 2030.* 1930. Brewer Warren. 1st Am. VG. M2. $40.00.

BIRKENHEAD, J. *Ferns & Fern Culture.* 1897 (1892). Manchester. 2nd. 128p. gilt cloth. B26. $24.00.

BIRKLEY, Dolan. *Unloved.* 1965. Crime Club. 1st. VG/VG. P3. $18.00.

BIRNEY, Hoffman. *Zealots of Zion.* 1931. Phil. 1st. ils. 317p. VG/dj. B5. $50.00.

BIRRELL, Anne. *Popular Songs & Ballads of Han China.* 1988. London. Unwin Hayman. 1st. 226p. F/dj. W3. $46.00.

BISCHOF, Werner. *Japan.* 1954. NY. 1st/1st prt. photos. NF. W3. $55.00.

BISHER, Furman. *Stolen Faces.* 1977. Harper Row. 1st. F/F. P3. $15.00.

BISHER, Furman. *Strange But True Baseball Stories.* 1976. Harper Row. 1st. F/F. P3. $15.00.

BISHOP, Charles. *The Journal and Letters of Captain Charles Bishop.* 1967. Cambridge. Hakluyt Society. 1st. blue cloth 8vo. gilt titles and decoration. folding map. frontis and 5 addl maps. 341p. VG in faded dj. P4. $60.00.

BISHOP, Claire Huchet. *Pancakes-Paris.* 1947. Viking. 1st. ils Georges Schreiber. 62p. VG. T5. $30.00.

BISHOP, Elizabeth. *Ballad of the Burglar of Babylon.* 1968. NY. 1st. ils Ann Grifalconi. unp. VG. B18. $75.00.

BISHOP, Elizabeth. *Diary of Helena Morley.* 1957. FSC. 1st. VG/VG. R14. $35.00.

BISHOP, Elizabeth. *Questions of Travel.* 1965. NY. FSG. 1st. F/F. O11. $150.00.

BISHOP, M.S. *Subsurface Mapping.* 1960. John Wiley. 198p. cloth. F/G. D8. $22.50.

BISHOP, Michael. *A Funeral for the Eyes of Fire.* 1989. Worcester Park. Surrey. Kerosina Books. 1st hc ed. author's 1st novel. VF/VF. T2. $30.00.

BISHOP, Michael. *And Strange at Ecbatan the Trees.* 1976. Harper. 1st. sgn. F/F. M2. $30.00.

BISHOP, Michael. *Apartheid, Superstrings, and Mordecai Thubana.* 1989. Eugene. Axolotl Press/ Pulphouse Publishing. 1st. 1/500 perfectbound copies. sgn by Bishop & introducer Lewis Shiner. VF/pict wrp. T2. $15.00.

BISHOP, Michael. *Blooded on Arachine.* 1982. Arkham. 1st. F/dj. M2. $14.00.

BISHOP, Michael. *Brittle Innings.* 1994. NY. Bantam. 1st. VF/F. H11. $20.00.

BISHOP, Michael. *Count Geiger's Blues.* 1992. NY. Tor. 1st. F/NF. H11. $20.00.

BISHOP, Michael. *Little Knowledge.* 1977. Berkeley. 1st. F/NF. M2. $20.00.

BISHOP, Michael. *One Winter in Eden.* 1983. Arkham. 1st. F/dj. M2. $25.00.

BISHOP, Michael. *Stolen Faces.* 1977. Harper. 1st. F/dj. M2. $20.00.

BISHOP, Michael. *The Secret Ascension: Philip K. Dick Is Dead, Alas.* 1987. NY. Tor. 1st. F/VF. T2. $40.00.

BISHOP, Paul. *Chapel of Ravens.* 1991. NY. Tor. 1st. sgn. VF/VF. T2. $20.00.

BISHOP, Paul. *Citadel Run.* 1988. NY. Tor. 1st. VF/F. H11. $25.00.

BISHOP, Zealia. *Curse of Yig.* 1953. Arkham. 1st. F/dj. M2. $200.00.

BISMAN, Ron. *Cardigan Bay.* 1972. S. Brunswick. Barnes. 1st ed. VG/F. O3. $25.00.

BISSETT, Clark Prescott. *Abraham Lincoln: A Universal Man.* 1923. Grabhorn. 1/125. sgn/#d. O8. $75.00.

BISSON, Terry. *Talking Man.* 1986. NY. Arbor House. 1st. NF/F. M23. $30.00.

BITTMAN, S. *Seeds.* 1989. NY. Bantam. 243p. F/F. B1. $40.00.

BIXBY-SMITH, Sarah. *Adobe Days: Being the Truthful Narrative of Events.* 1931. LA. Jake Zeitlin. 3rd. inscr Zeitlin. photos. 148p. w/prospectus. $11.00.

BIZONY, M. T., editor. *The Space Encyclopaedia; A Guide to Astronomy and Space Research.* 1960. NY. Dutton. revised ed. ex lib in dj. rear fep removed. usual lib mks. 320 ils. lg 8vo. 288p. G. K5. $12.00.

BJERRE, Jens. *Kalahari.* 1960. Hill Wang. 8vo. ils. 227p. NF/dj. W1. $18.00.

BJORN, Thyra Ferre. *Home as a Heart.* 1968. NY. HRW. 1st. sgn. F/VG. B11. $25.00.

BLACK, Campbell. *Brainfire.* 1979. Morrow. 1st. VG/G. P3. $15.00.

BLACK, Gavin. *Bitter Tea.* 1971. Harper Row. 1st. xl. VG/VG. P3. $6.00.

BLACK, Gavin. *Dragon for Christmas.* 1963. NY. Harper. 1st Am ed. VG/VG. G8. $15.00.

BLACK, Henry Campbell. *Black's Law Dictionary.* 1968. St Paul. W Pub Co. gilt gr buckram. M11. $75.00.

BLACK, Hugh. *Work.* 1903. Revell. 1st. VG. V4. $25.00.

BLACK, John J. *Cultivation of the Peach & the Pear.* 1887 (1886). NY. ils. 397p. B26. $55.00.

BLACK, Lionel. *Breakaway.* 1970. Collins Crime Club. VG/VG. P3. $15.00.

BLACK, Lionel. *Flood.* 1971. Stein Day. VG/VG. P3. $13.00.

BLACK, Lionel. *Life & Death of Peter Wade.* 1974. Stein Day. 1st. VG/VG. P3. $13.00.

BLACK, Mary Martin. *Summerfield Farm.* 1951. Viking. 1st. ils Wesley Dennis. 143p. VG+/dj. M20. $30.00.

BLACK, Matthew. *An Aramaic Approach to the Gospels and Acts.* 1967. Oxford. 359p. VG/torn dj. B29. $19.00.

BLACK, Veronica. *Vow of Devotion.* 1995. NY. St. Martin. 1st Am ed. VG/VG. G8. $15.00.

BLACKBURN, Benjamin. *Trees & Shrubs in Eastern North America.* 1952. NY. 358p. map ep. VG. B26. $20.00.

BLACKBURN, John. *Bury Him Darkly.* 1970. Putnam. 1st. VG/VG. P3. $45.00.

BLACKBURN, Julia. *Emperor's Last Island: Journey to St Helena.* 1991. NY. 1st. VG/dj. M17. $15.00.

BLACKBURN, Paul. *In, on, or about the Premises.* 1968. London. Cape Goliard. 1/750 (7750 total). F/dj. L3. $55.00.

BLACKBURN, Susan Stone. *Robertson Davies, Playwright: A Search for the Self on the Canadian Stage.* (1985). Vancouver. U of British Columbia Press. 1st. F/F. B3. $25.00.

BLACKBURN, William. *Under Twenty-Five: Duke Narrative & Verse. 1945 – 1962.* 1963. Durham. Duke. 1st. intro William Styron. F/dj. B4. $175.00.

BLACKER, Irwin. *Search and Destroy.* 1966. NY. Random. 1st. Book has slight slant. lightly sunned top edges. one bumped corner. Jacket Is price clipped. NF+/F. H11. $70.00.

BLACKFORD, Mansel G. & K. Austen Kerr. *B F Goodrich, Tradition and Transformation, 1870 – 1995.* 1996. Columbus. Ohio State Univ Press. 1st. ils. 507p. New. B18. $30.00.

BLACKFORD, Mrs. *Arthur Monteith: A Moral Tale & The Young West Indian.* 1832. NY. William Burgess. F. A16. $15.00.

BLACKLEDGE, S. D. *Open Book on Hidden Mysteries.* 1925. Elkton. MD. self pub. 1st. 123p. stiff cloth brd. VG/sans. $4.00.

BLACKMAN, E. C. *Biblical Interpretation.* 1957. Westminster. 212p. VG/VG. B29. $9.00.

BLACKMON, Anita. *Murder A La Richelieu.* 1937. Crime Club. 1st. VG. P3. $30.00.

BLACKMORE, Howard L. *Guns & Rifles of the World.* 1965. Viking. 1st. 134p. cloth. VG+/dj. M20. $50.00.

BLACKMORE, Jane. *Perilous Waters.* 1957. Collins. VG/VG. P3. $15.00.

BLACKMORE, R. D. *Perlycross.* 1894. Harper. 1st. VG. M19. $25.00.

BLACKSTOCK, Charity. *Briar Patch.* 1973. Hodder Stoughton. G/VG. P3. $10.00.

BLACKSTOCK, Charity Lee. *Ghost Town.* 1976. Coward. 1st Am ed. VG/VG+. G8. $15.00.

BLACKSTOCK, Lee. *All Men Are Murderers.* 1958. Collins Crime Club. 1st. VG/VG. P3. $15.00.

BLACKWOOD, Algernon. *Best Supernatural Tales of Blackwood.* 1973. Causeway. VG/VG. P3. $30.00.

BLACKWOOD, Algernon. *John Silence.* 1962. London. VG. M2. $17.00.

BLACKWOOD, Algernon. *Promise of Air.* 1918. Dutton. 1st. VG/dj. M2. $175.00.

BLACKWOOD, Algernon. *Tales of the Mysterious & Macabre.* 1967. Spring Books. 1st. VG. P3. $15.00.

BLACKWOOD, Andrew. *Preparations of Sermons.* 1948. Abingdon-Cokesbury. 272p. G/torn. B29. $6.50.

BLADES, John. *Small Game.* 1992. np. Henry Holt. 1st. author's 1st book. NF/NF. R16. $40.00.

BLADES, William F. *Fishing Flies & Fly Tying: American Insects...* 1962. Stackpole. enlarged 2nd. ils. 319p. VG. A17. $45.00.

BLAGOWIDOW, George. *Last Train from Berlin.* 1977. Doubleday. 1st. VG/VG. P3. $13.00.

BLAIKLOCK, E. M. *Cities of the New Testament.* 1965. Revell. 128p. VG. B29. $9.00.

BLAINE, John. *Rick Brant: Rocket's Shadow.* 1947. Grosset Dunlap. 1st. F/F. M2. $40.00.

BLAINE, John. *Rick Brant: Veiled Raiders (#20).* 1965. Grosset Dunlap. 1st. 178p. lists to this title. VG+. M20. $85.00.

BLAINE, Marge. *Terrible Thing that Happened at Our House.* 1975. Parent's Magazine. 1st. ils JC Wallner. unp. VG/dj. M20. $18.00.

BLAIR, Clay. *Atomic Submarine & Admiral Rickover.* 1954. NY. xl. K3. $15.00.

BLAIR, Henry. *Biological Effects of External Radiation.* 1954. NY. 1st. 508p. A13. $100.00.

BLAIR, John M. *Control of Oil.* 1976. Pantheon. 1st. charts/tables. 441p. NF/dj. W1. $25.00.

BLAIR, Millard F. *Practical Tree Surgery.* 1937. Boston. ils. 297p. B26. $65.00.

BLAIR, Sam. *Dallas Cowboys Pro or Con?* 1970. Doubleday. later prt. 418p. VG+/G. P8. $30.00.

BLAIR, Sam. *Earl Campbell: Driving Force.* 1980. World. 1st. F/VG. P8. $20.00.

BLAKE, Forrester. *Johnny Christmas.* 1948. Morrow. 1st. map ep. F/VG. A18. $50.00.

BLAKE, James Carlos. *In the Rogue Blood.* (1997). NY. Avon. 1st. F/F. B3. $15.00.

BLAKE, James Vila. *An Anchor of the Soul: A Study of the Nature of Faith.* Chicago. Charles H. Kerr & Company. 1894. 12mo. 146p. gr cloth. spine title label. 1st ed. Presentation inscr sgn and dated by Blake; with a cabinet photo (circa 1890) of Blake identified on verso in his handwriting. VG. L5. $75.00.

BLAKE, Mary E. *On the Wing. Rambling Notes of a Trip to the Pacific.* 1883. Boston. Lee and Shepard. 12mo. (8). 236p+4p ads. orig brown & gilt stp decor orange cloth. K1. $100.00.

BLAKE, Michael. *Airman Mortensen.* 1991. Los Angeles. Seven Wolves. 1st. Scratch on rear panel. F/NF. H11. $30.00.

BLAKE, Michael. *Marching to Valhalla.* 1996. NY. Villard. 1st. UP. F. D10. $10.00.

BLAKE, Nelson. *William Mahone of Virginia.* 1935. Richmond. 1st. VG. B5. $50.00.

BLAKE, Nicholas. *Morning After Death.* 1966. NY. Harper. 1st Am ed. VG/VG. G8. $20.00.

BLAKE, Pamela. *Peep Show.* 1973. Macmillan. 1st Am. 32p. F/F. D4. $25.00.

BLAKE, Sterling. *Chiller.* 1993. NY. Bantam. 1st. VF/VF. H11. $25.00.

BLAKE, William. *Land of Dreams.* 1928. Macmillan. 1st. ils Pamela Bianco. VG. D4. $35.00.

BLAKE, William. *Land of Dreams.* 1928. Macmillan. 1st. 42p. VG/G+. P2. $75.00.

BLAKEMORE, Colin. *Mechanics of the Mind.* 1977. Cambridge. tall 8vo. 208p. VG/dj. G1. $40.00.

BLAKENEY, John. *Heroes: US Marine Corps, 1861–1955.* 1957. WA. 1st. ils. 621p. VG/dj. B5. $45.00.

BLAKEY, E. S. *Tulsa Spirit.* 1979. Tulsa. ils. 192p. F/NF/case. M4. $20.00.

BLAKEY, George C. *Gambler's Companion.* 1979. Paddington. 1st. NF/NF. P3. $20.00.

BLANC, Suzanne. *Rose Window.* 1968. Cassell. VG/VG. P3. $15.00.

BLANCHARD, Arlene. *Bear & Henry.* 1987. Barrons. 1st. 4to. ils Jean Claverie. F/dj. M5. $20.00.

BLANCHARD, Amy E. *My Own Dolly.* ca 1900. Dutton. ils Ida Waugh. 64p. VG. D1. $160.00.

BLANCHARD, Charles. *With Heaps O'Love.* 1925. Des Moines. Nichols Book & Travel. inscr. 12mo. 288p. gilt cloth. B11. $25.00.

BLANCHARD, Dr. Charles. *Getting Things from God.* 1953. Sword of the Lord. 270p. G/G. B29. $5.00.

BLANCHARD, Frank N. *Revision of the King Snakes: Genus Lampropeltis.* 1921. Smithsonian. 260p. S15. $22.00.

BLANCHET, Francois Norbert. *Notices & Voyages of Famed Quebec Mission to Pacific.* 1961. Portland, OR Hist Soc. 1/1000. ils/lg fld map. F. O7. $65.00.

BLAND, Eleanor Taylor. *Keep Still.* 1996. NY. St. Martin. 1st. sgn. F/F. G8. $25.00.

BLAND, Eleanor Taylor. *See No Evil.* 1998. NY. St. Martin. 1st. sgn. F/F. G8. $25.00.

BLANDING, Don. *Songs of the Seven Senses.* 1931. Dodd Mead. 1st. sgn. 12mo. VG. B11. $35.00.

BLANK, Clair. *Beverly Gray at the World's Fair.* 1934. NY. AL Burt. 1st. ils. 250p. G. A25. $8.00.

BLANK, Clair. *Beverly Gray's Assignment (#17).* 1947. Grosset Dunlap. 1st. 212p. lists to #16. VG/dj. M20. $20.00.

BLANK, Howard E. *A Long Way from the Creek.* 1998. Baltimore. Pilesville Press. 1st. sgn. author's 1st novel. VF/VF. T2. $25.00.

BLANKENSHIP, W. D. *Leavenworth Irregulars.* 1974. Bobbs Merrill. stated 1st. 264p. dj. R11. $60.00.

BLANKSTEN, George. *Ecuador: Constitutions and Caudillos.* 1951. Berkeley. Univ of California Press. Vol 3. No. 1. 196p. G. F3. $20.00.

BLANSHARD, Paul. *Democracy & Empire in the Caribbean.* 1947. NY. Macmillan. 1st. 379p. G/chipped dj. F3. $25.00.

BLASSINGAME, W. *Live from the Devil.* 1949. Garden City. 1st. VG/VG. B5. $20.00.

BLATCHFORD, Robert. *Merrie England, A Plain Expostition of Socialism.* 1895. NY. Commonwealth. early ed. not 1st. wrp. VG. B2. $35.00.

BLATH, MIDDLETON & MURRY. *Origin of Sedimentary Rocks.* 1980. Englewood Cliffs. 2nd. 782p. NF. D8. $30.00.

BLATT, Sidney J. *Continuity & Change in Art: Development Modes...* 1984. Lawrence Erlbaum. pres. ils. 411p. VG/dj. G1. $50.00.

BLATTER, Ethelbert. *Beautiful Flowers of Kashmir (2 Vols).* 1984 (1927/30). Dehra Dun. reprint. New in djs. B26. $15.00.

BLATTY, William Peter. *Exorcist.* 1971. Harper Row. 1st. F/F. H11. $130.00.

BLATTY, William Peter. *Legion.* 1983. S&S. 1st. VG/VG. P3. $15.00.

BLAUNER, Peter. *Casino Moon.* 1994. NY. S&S. 1st. F/F. H11. $30.00.

BLAUNER, Peter. *Slow Motion Riot.* 1991. np. Morrow. 1st. author's 1st novel. VG+/VG. R16. $45.00.

BLAUNER, Peter. *The Intruder.* 1996. NY. S&S. 1st. F/F. H11. $25.00.

BLAYLOCK, James P. *Homunculus.* 1988. Morrigan. 1st. F/F. P3. $30.00.

BLAYLOCK, James P. *Last Coin.* 1988. Ace. 1st trade. F/NF. M21. $10.00.

BLAYLOCK, James P. *Magic Spectacles.* 1991. Morrigan. 1st. F/F. P3. $30.00.

BLAYLOCK, James P. *The Old Curiosity Shop.* 1999. Royal Oak/ Missin Viejo. ASAP publishing. 1st. 1/150# copies. sgn by author, artist, and authors of front matter. VF w/o dj as issued. T2. $50.00.

BLAZER, Don. *Natural Western Riding.* 1979. Boston. Houghton Mifflin. VG/VG. O3. $20.00.

BLECH, Gustavus. *Clinical Electrosurgery.* 1938. London. 1st. 389p. A13. $150.00.

BLEECK, Oliver; See Thomas, Ross.

BLEEDING, Francis. *Hidden Kingdom.* 1927. Little, Brn. 1st. VG. M2. $22.00.

BLEILER, E.F. *Year's Best Science Fiction Novels 1954.* 1954. Fell. 1st. F/dj. M2. $40.00.

BLESH, Rudi. *Shining Trumpets.* 1946. NY. Knopf. 1st. F/lightly used dj. B2. $50.00.

BLESH, Rudi. *Shining Trumpets.* 1946. Knopf. 1st. VG/VG. B2. $40.00.

BLEVINS, Winfred. *Dictionary of the American West.* 1993. Facts on File. 400p. F/dj. A17. $15.00.

BLEVINS, Winfred. *Misadventures of Silk & Shakespeare.* 1985. Ottawa. Jameson Books. 1st. sgn. F. R14. $35.00.

BLICHFELDT, E. H. *A Mexican Journey.* 1919. NY. Chautauqua Press. b/w plates. index. 280p. VG/lt shelf wear. F3. $20.00.

BLIER, Bertrand. *Going Places.* 1974. Lippincott. 1st Am. F/F clip. B4. $125.00.

BLISH, James. *A Torrent of Faces.* 1968. London. Faber & Faber. 1st British ed. Norman L. Knight co-author. F/F clip. T2. $25.00.

BLISH, James. *Anywhen.* 1970. Doubleday. 1st. NF/dj. M2. $30.00.

BLISH, James. *Frozen Year.* 1957. Ballantine. 1st. VG. M2. $50.00.

BLISH, James. *Jack of Eagles.* 1952. Greenberg. 1st. VG/VG. P3. $85.00.

BLISH, James. *Midsummer Century.* 1973. London. Faber & Faber. 1st British ed. VF/VF clip. T2. $20.00.

BLISH, James. *Tale That Wags the God.* 1987. Advent. 1st. F/dj. M2. $17.00.

BLISH, James. *The Quincunx of Time.* 1975. London. Faber. 1st hc. F/NF. T2. $20.00.

BLISH, James. *The Quincunx of Time.* 1975. London. Faber & Faber. 1st hc ed. F/F lt wear to extremeties. T2. $20.00.

BLISHEN, Edward. *Oxford Book of Poetry for Children.* 1963. London. Oxford. 1st. 168p. NF/NF. D4. $65.00.

BLIVEN, Bruce Jr. *American Revolution (Landmark Book No 83).* 1960. Random. 1st. 8vo. NF/VG+. C8. $20.00.

BLIXEN, B. *African Letters.* 1988. St Martin. ils/photos. 197p. F/NF. M12. $30.00.

BLKER, J. F. *The ABC of English Salt-Glaze Stoneware from Dwight to Doulton.* London. Stanley Paul & Co. 1922. 8vo. 243p. well-ils (more than 50 ils). pict. coarse linen-like cloth. 1st ed. Some scattered lt foxing. VG. L5. $75.00.

BLOCH, Eugene B. *Fabric of Guilt.* 1968. Doubleday. 1st. VG/VG. P3. $20.00.

BLOCH, Robert. *American Gothic.* 1974. NY. S&S. 2nd. 8vo beige cloth. 222p. F/VG. H1. $12.00.

BLOCH, Robert. *Blood Runs Cold.* 1961. NY. S&S. 1st. NF in VG dj. B2. $75.00.

BLOCH, Robert. *Cold Chills.* 1977. Doubleday. 1st. RS. F/F. P3. $45.00.

BLOCH, Robert. *Dead Beat.* 1960. S&S. 1st. VG/dj. M2. $80.00.

BLOCH, Robert. *Dragons & Nightmares.* 1968. Mirage. 1st. 1/1000. F/dj. M2. $75.00.

BLOCH, Robert. *The Jekyll Legacy.* 1990. NY. Tor. 1st. VF/VF. T2. $9.00.

BLOCH, Robert. *Last Rites.* 1987. Underwood Miller. 1st. NF. P3. $40.00.

BLOCH, Robert. *Midnight Pleasures.* 1987. Garden City. Doubleday. 1st. VF/VF. closed tear. lt wear. T2. $45.00.

BLOCH, Robert. *Night of the Ripper.* 1984. Doubleday. 1st. F/dj. M2. $25.00.

BLOCH, Robert. *Night-World.* 1972. S&S. 1st. VG/VG. P3. $30.00.

BLOCH, Robert. *Pleasant Dreams.* 1960. Arkham. 1st. sgn. F/dj. M2. $175.00.

BLOCH, Robert. *Psycho.* 1959. S&S. 1st. F/F. B4. $950.00.

BLOCH, Robert. *Psycho 2.* 1982. Binghamton. Whispers Press. 1st. 1/750 # copies. sgn by Bloch & publisher Stuart Schiff. VF/VF dj & slipcase. T2. $50.00.

BLOCH, Robert. *Psycho II.* 1982. Whispers. 1st. F/F. N4. $40.00.

BLOCH, Robert. *Strange Eons.* 1979. Whispers. 1st. F/dj. M2/P3. $30.00.

BLOCH, Robert. *The Early Years.* 1994. Minneapolis. Fedogan & Bremer. 1st. sgn laid in. VF/VF. T2. $35.00.

BLOCH, Robert. *The Lost Bloch, Volume One: The Devil With You!* 1999. Burton. Subterranean Press. 1st. 1/724 # copies. sgn by editor Schow & author of foreword Dziemianowicz. Bloch's sgn laid in. VF/VF. T2. $45.00.

BLOCH, Robert. *Todd Dossier.* 1969. Delacorte. 1st. xl. F/dj. M2. $75.00.

BLOCH, Robert. *Unholy Trinity: Three Novels of Suspense.* 1986. Santa Cruz. Scream. 1st combined. sgn bookplate. F/dj. T2. $50.00.

BLOCK, Eugene B. *Great Stagecoach Robbers of the West.* 1962. Garden City. Doubleday. 1st. VG/VG. O3. $35.00.

BLOCK, Lawrence. *A Long Line of Dead Men.* 1994. NY. Morrow. 1st. sgn. F/F. D10. $40.00.

BLOCK, Lawrence. *A Ticket to the Boneyard.* 1990. NY. Morrow. 1st. F/F. H11. $30.00.

BLOCK, Lawrence. *A Walk Among the Tombstones.* 1992. NY. Morrow. 1st. sgn. F/F. A24. $35.00.

BLOCK, Lawrence. *After Hours: Conversations with Lawrence Block.* 1995. Albuquerque. Univ of New Mexico Press. 1st. sgn by Block & interviewer Ernie Bulow. VF/VF. T2. $30.00.

BLOCK, Lawrence. *Ariel.* 1996. Delavan. G & G Books. ltd ed. 1/500 # copies. sgn. VF/VF. T2. $35.00.

BLOCK, Lawrence. *Hit Man.* (1998). NY. Morrow. 1st. F/F. B3. $15.00.

BLOCK, Lawrence. *Into the Night.* 1987. NY. Mysterious Press. 1st. sgn. F/F. T2. $25.00.

BLOCK, Lawrence. *Like a Lamb to Slaughter.* 1984. NY. Arbor. 1st. F/dj. M15. $75.00.

BLOCK, Lawrence. *Random Walk.* 1988. Tor. 1st. F/dj. M2. $22.00.

BLOCK, Lawrence. *Some Days You Get the Bear.* 1993. NY. Morrow. 1st. F/F. H11. $20.00.

BLOCK, Lawrence. *Sometimes They Bite.* 1983. Arbor. 1st. F/VG. M19. $45.00.

BLOCK, Lawrence. *Spider, Spin Me a Web.* 1988. Cincinnati. Writer's Digest. 1st. F/dj. M15. $65.00.

BLOCK, Lawrence. *The Burglar in the Library.* 1997. Harpenden. Herts. No Exit Press. 1st. sgn. VF/VF. T2. $65.00.

BLOCK, Lawrence. *The Burglar Who Studied Spinoza.* 1980. NY. Random House. 1st. F/ faded dj. M15. $100.00.

BLOCK, Lawrence. *The Burglar Who Traded Ted Williams.* 1994. NY. Dutton. 1st. sgn. VF/dj. M15. $40.00.

BLOCK, Lawrence. *The Canceled Czech.* 1994. NY. Armchair Detective Library. 1st hc ed. sgn. VF/VF. T2. $25.00.

BLOCK, Lawrence. *The Devil Knows You're Dead.* 1993. NY. Morrow. 1st. F/F. H11. $20.00.

BLOCK, Lawrence. *The Specialists.* 1996. Aliso Viejo. James Cahill Pub. 1st hc ed. sgn. VF/VF. T2. $25.00.

BLOCK, Libbie. *Hills of Beverly.* 1957. Doubleday. 1st. NF/dj. M25. $20.00.

BLOCK, Thomas H. *Airship Nine.* 1984. Putnam. 1st. VG/VG. P3. $17.00.

BLOCK, Valerie. *Was It Something I Said?* 1998. NY. Soho. 1st. F/VF. H11. $30.00.

BLOCKSON, Charles L. *Pennsylvania's Black History.* 1975. Phil. Portfolio Assoc. 1/5000. inscr/#d. F/NF. B4. $100.00.

BLODGET, Lorin. *Climatology of the United States and of the Temperate Latitudes of the North Am Continent.* Philadelphia. J. B. Lipincott and Co. 1857. 4to. 536p. dark gr cloth. folding charts. 1st ed. minor wear. scattered foxing. VG. L5. $150.00.

BLODGETT, Mabel Fuller. *Giant's Ruby.* 1903. 1st. ils Katherine Pyle. NF. M19. $75.00.

BLOETSCHER, Virginia Chase. *Indians of the Cuyahoga Valley.* 1987. Akron. 2nd. 111p. VG/wrp. B18. $17.50.

BLOFELD, John. *I Ching: Book of Change.* 1968. Dutton. trans of ancient text. 228p. F/dj. W3. $32.00.

BLOM, K. *Arne. Moment of Truth.* 1977. Harper Row. 1st Am. 147p. VG/dj. M20. $10.00.

BLOMBERY, A. M. *Native Australian Plants. Their Propagation and Cultivation.* 1955. Sydney. VG in slightly worn dj. B26. $25.00.

BLOND, Georges. *Elephants.* 1962. London. trans from French. photos. 180p. VG/worn. S15. $12.00.

BLONDELL, Joan. *Center Door Fantasy.* 1972. Delacorte. 1st. NF/dj. M25. $35.00.

BLOODSTONE, John; See Byrne, Stuart.

BLOOM, Amy. *Come to Me.* 1993. NY. Harper Collins. 1st. author's 1st book. sgn. F/F. A24. $60.00.

BLOOM, Amy. *Love Invents Us.* 1997. NY. Random House. 1st. sgn. F/F. A24. $35.00.

BLOOMFIELD, Robert. *From This Death Forward.* 1952. Crime Club. 1st. VG/VG-. G8. $12.50.

BLOOMFIELD, Robert. *Vengeance Street.* 1952. Crime Club. 1st. VG/VG-. G8. $15.00.

BLOOR, Ella Reeve. *We Are Many.* 1940. NY. International. 1st. inscr by author. F in VG dj. B2. $150.00.

BLOUNT, Roy Jr. *About Three Bricks Shy of a Load.* 1974. Little, Brn. 1st. inscr. photos. VG/dj. P8. $25.00.

BLOUNT, T.P. *Essays on Several Subjects.* 1697. London. 3rd imp. G. A15. $30.00.

BLUDEN, Edmund. *Shepherd & Other Poems of Peace & War.* 1922. Knopf. 1st thus. 86p. decor brd/cloth spine. VG. B22. $18.00.

BLUE, Allan G. *B-24 Liberator.* ca 1975. NY. 1st Am. 223p. VG/VG. B18. $25.00.

BLUE, Ron. *Master Your Money: Step-By-Step Plan For Financial Freedom.* 1986. Nelson. 236p. Vg/dj. B29. $7.50.

BLUM, Daniel. *Pictorial History of the American Theatre 1900 – 1956.* 1956. NY. 320p. dj. A17. $22.50.

BLUM, Daniel. *Pictorial Treasury of Opera in America.* 1954. NY. 320p. lg 4to. A17. $17.50.

BLUME, Judy. *Starring Sally J. Freedman as Herself.* 1986. NY. Dell Publishing. A Yearling Book. pb. G. A28. $1.95.

BLUME, Judy. *Superfudge.* 1980. Dutton. 1st. 8vo. VG/dj. B17. $25.00.

BLUMENTHAL, Walter Hart. *Book Gluttons & Book Gourmets.* 1962. Chicago. Blk Cat. mini. 1/300. 84p. aeg. gilt gr leather. F. B24. $135.00.

BLUMENTHAL, Walter Hart. *Women Camp Followers of the American Revolution.* 1952. Philadelphia. MacManus. 1st. ltd to 300 copies. VG in dj. B18. $125.00.

BLUMLEIN, Michael. *Movement of Mountains.* 1987. St Martin. 1st. author's 1st book. F/F. M21. $25.00.

BLUNDELL, Michael. *Wild Flowers of Kenya.* 1982. London. 160p. F/NF. B26. $42.50.

BLUNDELL, Nigel. *World's Greatest Crooks & Conmen.* 1982. Octopus. 1st. F. P3. $13.00.

BLUNT, Joseph. *Shipmaster's Assistant & Commercial Digest.* 1970s. NY/London. facsimile of 1837 ed. 672p. T7. $50.00.

BLUNT, Wilfrid. *Cockerell.* 1965 (1964). Knopf. 1st Am. 385p. VG/clip. M20. $30.00.

BLUNT, Wilfrid. *My Diaries: Part Two 1900 – 1914.* 1922. Knopf. 2nd. 484p. G. A17. $17.50.

BLY, Robert. *Crooked Hearts.* 1987. Knopf. 1st. sgn. F/F. R14. $60.00.

BLY, Robert. *Iron John — A Book About Men.* 1990. np. Addison Wesley. 1st. F/F dj. M19. $25.00.

BLY, Robert. *Loving a Woman in Two Worlds.* 1985. Dial. 1st. NF/dj. B2. $30.00.

BLY, Robert. *Loving a Woman in Two Worlds.* 1985. Dial. 1st. sgn. F/NF. V1. $35.00.

BLY, Robert. *Man in the Black Coat Turns.* 1981. Dial. 1st. sgn. F/F. R14. $45.00.

BLY, Robert. *This Tree Will Be Here for a Thousand Years.* 1979. Harper Row. UP. sgn. NF/wrp. R14. $90.00.

BLYTH, R.H. *Senryu: Japanese Satirical Verses.* 1949. Tokyo. 1st. 230p. VG/dj. W3. $86.00.

BLYTON, Enid. *Five Go Down to the Sea.* 1961. Reilly Lee. 1st Am. 8vo. VG/dj. M5. $35.00.

BLYTON, Enid. *Ship of Adventure.* 1950. Macmillan. stated 1st. 8vo. VG/dj. M5. $65.00.

BLYTON, Enid. *Shock for the Secret Seven.* 1961. Brockhampton. 1st. sm 8vo. NF/VG. M5. $45.00.

BLYTON, Enid. *Tales After Tea.* 1963. Collins. VG. P3. $10.00.

BLYTON, Enid. *Valley of Adventure.* 1955 (1947). Macmillan. 2nd. ils Stuart Tresilian. NF/dj. M5. $48.00.

BOADT, Lawrence. *Reading the Old Testament: An Introduction.* 1984. Paulist. 571p. F. B29. $8.50.

BOARDER, Arthur. *Starting With Cacti.* 1968. London. 1st. ils/pl/drawings. 96p. VG/dj. B26. $22.50.

BOARDMAN, Elizabeth Jelinek. *Phoenix Trip: Notes on a Quaker Mission to Haiphong.* 1985. Burnsville, NC. Celo. 174p. VG. V3. $12.00.

BOARDMAN, Tom. *Science Fiction Stories.* 1979. Octopus. 1st. VG/VG. P3. $15.00.

BOAS, I. *Diseases of the Intestines.* 1901. NY. 1st Eng trans. 562p. A13. $75.00.

BOATRIGHT, Mody C. *From Hell to Breakfast.* 1944. TX Folk-Lore Soc. inscr. VG. A19. $45.00.

BOBA, Antonio. *Hypothermia for the Neurosurgical Patient.* 1960. Springfield. 1st. 124p. A13. $20.00.

BOBKER, Lee R. *Flight of a Dragon.* 1981. NY. Morrow. 1st. F/F. H11. $15.00.

BOCCACCIO, Giovanni. *Decameron.* 1982. Berkeley. U CA. 3 vol. 1st thus. trans John Payne. F/case. F1. $65.00.

BOCHER, T.W. *Gronlands Flora.* 1966 (1957). Copenhagen. 2nd. Danish text. ils/map. 307p. decor cloth. dj. $26.00.

BODARD, Lucien. *Green Hell.* 1971. NY. Dutton. 1st. glossary. map. b/w photo ils. 291p. G/chipped dj. F3. $15.00.

BODDY, Frederick A. *Foliage Plants.* 1974 (1972). London. GBC ed. 215p w/32 b&w photos. VG in dj. B26. $12.50.

BODE, William. *Lights & Shadows of Chinatown.* 1896. np. HS Crocker. 1st. 32 mtd ils on tissue. F. R3. $500.00.

BODECKER, N.M. *Hurry, Hurry Mary Dear & Other Nonsense Poems.* 1976. Atheneum. 1st. 118p. cloth. F/dj. D4. $45.00.

BODELSEN, Anders. *Straus.* 1974. Harper Row. F/F. P3. $13.00.

BODENHEIM, Maxwell. *My Life & Loves in Greenwich Village.* 1954. 1st. VG/clip. S13. $45.00.

BODENHEIM, Maxwell. *Replenishing Jessica.* 1925. Boni Liveright. 1st. NF/dj. Q1. $150.00.

BODETT, Tom. *As Far as You Can Go Without a Passport.* 1985. Reading. Addison. 1st. VF/VF. H11. $30.00.

BODIN, Alvin. *Influence of Matthew Baillie's Morbid Anatomy.* 1973. Springfield. 1st. 293p. A13. $150.00.

BOETTNER, Loraine. *Immortality.* 1957. Eerdmans. 159p. G. B29. $5.00.

BOETTNER, Loraine. *Roman Catholicism.* 1968. Presb & Reformed. 466p. G/worn dj. B29. $4.50.

BOGART, Stephen Humphrey. *Play It Again.* 1995. NY. Forge. 1st. VF/F. H11. $55.00.

BOGDANOVICH, Peter. *Killing of the Unicorn.* 1984. Morrow. 1st. NF/VG. A20. $15.00.

BOGEL, GOLDMAN & MARKS. *Birds & Flowers.* 1988. Braziller. 1st. 192p+91 full-p mc pl. F/dj. A17. $45.00.

BOHM, David. *Quantum Theory.* 1951. Prentice Hall. 1st. xl. K3. $40.00.

BOHMONT, D. W. & H. P. Alley. *Weeds of Wyoming.* 1961. Laramie. 171p w/160 full pg line drawings. stiff wrp. VG. B26. $15.00.

BOHNE, P. W. *Highlights in History of American Whaling.* 1968. Rosemead, CA. Bookhaven. mini. 1/500. ils. gray mottled brd/gilt leather. F. B24. $95.00.

BOHR, Niels. *Atomic Physics and Human Knowledge.* 1958. NY. John Wiley & Sons. Inc. 1st. ils w/8 text figures. viii. (2) 102p. wht & blk stp blue cloth. dj. K1. $75.00.

BOICE, James. *Christ of the Empty Tombs.* 1985. Moody. 126p. VG/dj. B29. $7.00.

BOICE, James Montgomery. *Christ's Call to Discipleship.* 1986. Grason. 170p. VG/VG. B29. $7.50.

BOISGILBERT, Edmund. *Caesar's Column.* nd. Ward Lock. decor brd. G. P3. $40.00.

BOK, Edward W. *Man from Maine.* 1923. Scribner. 1st. ils. 278p. VG. S14. $17.50.

BOKER, Ben Zion. *From the World of the Cabbalah: Philosophy of Rabbi Loew.* 1954. Philosophical Lib. 210p. VG/dj. S3. $23.00.

BOLAND, Eavan. *The Lost Land.* 1998. NY. Norton. 1st. F/F. V1. $10.00.

BOLAND, John C. *Rich Man's Blood.* 1993. NY. St. Martin. 1st. VG/G. G8. $10.00.

BOLDEN, Vernie L. *Lyrical Poetry and Philosophical Expressions.* nd. Quill Publications. sc. G. F6. $2,00.

BOLESLAVSKY, Richard. *Acting the First Lessons.* 1949. NY. Theatre Arts Books. 134p. VG/dj. C5. $12.50.

BOLITHO, Hector. *Batsford Century: A Record of a Hundred Years.* 1943. London. Batsford. 1st. ils. VG/dj. K3. $18.00.

BOLITHO, Janie. *Ripe for Revenge.* 1995. NY. St. Martin. 1st Am ed. NF/NF. G8. $12.50.

BOLL, Heinrich. *Safety Net.* 1982. Knopf. 1st trade. VG/dj. B35. $16.00.

BOLL, Heinrich. *Women in a River Landscape.* 1988. Knopf. 1st. NF/dj. B35. $18.00.

BOLLAND, William Craddock. *Manual of Year Book Studies.* 1925. Cambridge. M11. $85.00.

BOLLES, John. *Las Monjas. A Major Pre Mexican Architectural Complex At Chichen Itza.* 1977. Norman. Univ of Oklahoma Press. 1st. oblong 4to. b/w photo ils. drawings. 304p. G/chipped dj. F3. $95.00.

BOLLINGER, E. *Rails that Climb: Story of the Moffat Road.* 1950. Santa Fe. 2nd. sgn. ils. 402p. VG/G. B5. $50.00.

BOLT, Robert. *Flowering Cherry: A Play in Two Acts.* 1958. London. Heinemann. 1st. NF/dj. Q1. $60.00.

BOLTON, Herbert E. *Pageant in the Wilderness. Story of Escalante Expedition...* 1951. Salt Lake City. ils/rear pocket map. maroon fabrikoid. VG+. F7. $75.00.

BOLTON, Herbert Eugene. *Anza's California Expeditions.* 1930. Berkeley. 1st. 5 vol. 8vo. ils/maps. bl cloth. F. $3.00.

BOLTON, Herbert Eugene. *Padre on Horseback.* 1963. Loyola. 1st. 91p. F/NF. B19. $25.00.

BOLTON, Herbert Eugene. *Plate of Brass: Evidence of Visit of Francis Drake...1579.* 1953. CA Hist Soc. 2 vol. 4to. ils. gilt brn cloth. F. R3. $40.00.

BOLUS, Harry. *The Orchids of the Cape Peninsula.* 1918 (1888). Cape Town. 2nd ed. ils color plates. gilt gr cloth. lt shelfwear. 142p + plates. ep tanned. else VG. B26. $385.00.

BOMBACK, R.H. *Basic Leica Technique.* 1954. London. Fountain. dj. A19. $20.00.

BON APPETIT. *Cooking With Bon Appetit: Recipe Yearbook 1991.* 1991. CA. Knapp Press. 1st. corners bumped. VG. A28. $7.95.

BON APPETIT. *Too Busy to Cook? Time Saving Recipes and Easy Menus from Bon Appetit.* 1981. CA. Knapp Press. gr brds. VG/VG. A28. $10.50.

BONANNO, Joseph. *Man of Honor: Autobiography of Joseph Bonanno.* 1983. S&S. 1st. ils/index. F/NF. B19. $35.00.

BONAR, Horatio. *The Desert of Sinai: Notes of a Spring – Journey From Cairo to Beersheba.* NY. Robert Carter & Brothers. 1857. 12mo. 408p. ftspc. original gr cloth. 1st Am ed. ex-lib. cloth dust soiled. top of spine chiped. G to VG. L5. $90.00.

BOND, Carrie Jacobs. *Perfect Day & Other Poems.* (1926). Chicago. Volland. unp. F/F box. D4. $50.00.

BOND, Francis. *Gothic Architecture in England.* 1906. Batsford/Scribner. 1st. 792p. G+. H1. $55.00.

BOND, Geoffrey. *Lakonia.* 1966. London. Oldbourne. ils. 199p. dj. T7. $28.00.

BOND, Gladys Baker. *Buffy Finds a Star.* 1970. Whitman. TVTI. VG. P3. $8.00.

BOND, Julian. *A Time to Speak, a Time to Act.* 1972. S&S. 1st. sgn & inscr. F/sunned dj. M25. $150.00.

BOND, Larry. *Cauldron.* 1993. NY. Warner. 1st. VF/F. H11. $15.00.

BOND, Larry. *Red Phoenix.* 1989. NY. Warner. 1st. F/F. H11. $30.00.

BOND, Marcelle. *The Beauty of Albany Glass.* 1972. Albany, IN. self-published. 8vo sgn. Owner's name written twice on cover. some written notes on title page. some check marks & pattern name notes throughout. 125p. G. H1. $45.00.

BOND, Mary Wickham. *How 007 Got His Name.* 1966. London. Collins. 1st. Price clipped jacket with tiny wear at corners. F/dj. M15. $125.00.

BOND, Michael. *Monsieur Pamplemousse on the Spot.* 1986. Beaufort. 1st Am ed. F/F. G8. $17.50.

BOND, Michael. *Thursday in Paris.* 1971. Harrap. 1st. ils Leslie Wood. 128p. NF/VG. P2. $25.00.

BOND, Nelson. *Lancelot Biggs: Spaceman.* 1950. Doubleday. 1st. NF/VG. P3. $85.00.

BOND, Nelson. *Mr Mergenthwirker's Lobblies.* 1946. Coward McCann. 1st. VG/dj. M2. $50.00.

BOND, Nelson. *Thirty-First of February.* 1949. Gnome. 1st. F/rpr. M2. $13.00.

BONDY, Louis W. *Miniature Books: Their History from the Beginnings…* 1981. London. Shepard. 1st. ils. gilt red cloth. F/dj. F1. $75.00.

BONDY, Ruth. *Israelis: Profile of a People.* 1969. Sabra Books/Funk Wagnall. 1st. inscr. 8vo. 320p. VG/dj. T10. $50.00.

BONES, Jim Jr. *Texas West of the Pecos.* 1981. TX A&M. 1st. ils. 136p. F/F. B19. $25.00.

BONETT, John & Emery. *Better Off Dead.* 1964. Garden City. Doubleday Crime Club. 1st Am ed. F/dj. M15. $35.00.

BONFIGLIOLI, Kyril. *After You with the Pistol.* 1979. Secker Warburg. 1st. F/F. P3. $20.00.

BONHAM, Frank. *Lost Stage Valley.* 1948. NY. Essandess Westerns (S&S). 1st. NF/VG dj. M19. $35.00.

BONHOEFFER, Dietrich. *Cost of Discipleship.* 1961. Macmillan. 285p. VG/dj. B29. $6.50.

BONHOEFFER, Dietrich. *Theology of Dietrich Bonhoeffer.* 1960. Westminster. 299p. VG. B29. $14.00.

BONICA, John J. *Advances in Pain Research & Therapy Vol 1.* 1976. NY. Raven. heavy 8vo. 1012p. blk cloth. VG/dj. G1. $85.00.

BONNARD, Abel. *In China 1920 – 1921.* 1926. Routledge. 361p. VG. W3. $46.00.

BONNER, Cindy. *Lily.* 1995. Chapel Hill. Algonquin. 1st. F/F. M23. $40.00.

BONNER, Willard Hallam. *Pirate Laureate: Life & Legends of Captain Kidd.* 1947. New Brunswick. 1st. 239p. gr cloth. VG/worn. P4. $45.00.

BONNET, Theodore. *Dutch.* 1955. Doubleday. 1st. VG/VG. P3. $20.00.

BONNET, Theodore. *The Mudlark.* 1949. NY. Doubleday. 1st. 8vo. 305p. G. H1. $5.00.

BONNEY, Joseph L. *Murder Without Clues.* 1940. NY. Carrick & Evans. 1st. inscr. VG/dj soiled. M15. $45.00.

BONNEY, T.G. *Story of Our Planet.* 1902 (1893). London. Cassell. 8vo. ils. 592p. cloth. K5. $30.00.

BONSTELLE, Jessie and Marian De Forest. *Little Women; Letters from the House of Alcott.* 1914. Boston. Little, Brn. and Co. 1914. 12mo. 197p. illustrations. gr cloth. pictorial front cover. 1st ed. Very minor wear. spine dull. G to VG. L5. $60.00.

BONTEMPS, Arna. *American Negro Poetry: An Anthology.* 1974. Hill and Wang. pb ed of this revised ed. NF/orange wrps. sunned at spine. M25. $25.00.

BONTEMPS, Arna. *Famous Negro Athletes.* 1964. NY. Dodd Mead. 1st. F/NF lt wear & rubbing. B2. $75.00.

BONTLY, Thomas. *Celestial Chess.* 1979. Harper Row. 1st. VG/VG. P3. $18.00.

BONWICK, James. *Egyptian Belief & Modern Thought.* 1956. Indian Hills. Falcon's Wing. VG. D2. $20.00.

BOOL, S.W. *Soil Genesis & Classification.* 1973. Ames, IA. 360p. VG. A10. $20.00.

BOOM, B. K. & H. Kleijn. *The Glory of the Tree.* 1966. Garden City. Doubleday. 4to. 128p w/194 color photos. VG in torn dj. B26. $29.00.

BOONE, Bob, ed. *Exploring Barns of Medina County.* 1987. Medina, OH. Historical Projects of Medina Co. ES. ils. lt wear & rubbing to cover. 244p. VG. B18. $25.00.

BOONE, Elizabeth. *The Aztec World.* 1994. DC. Smithsonian Books. 1st. sq 4to. pict bds. 160p. G. F3. $20.00.

BOORMAN, John. *Emerald Forest Diary.* 1985. FSG. 1st. F/F. P3. $15.00.

BOOTH, Christopher B. *House of Rogues.* 1923. Chelsea. 1st. VG. G8. $20.00.

BOOTH, George. *Rehearsal's Off!* 1976. Dodd Mead. 1st. F/clip. M25. $45.00.

BOOTH, Martin. *Winters Night: Knotting.* 1979. Sceptre. 1/50. sgn. hand-tied wrp. F. V1. $35.00.

BOOTH, Nicholas. *Space; The Next 100 Years.* 1990. NY. Orion. color photos & drawings. 4to. 128p. VG/VG. K5. $23.00.

BOOTH, Russell H., Jr. *The Tuscarawas Valley In Indian Days 1750 – 1797.* 1994. Cambridge, OH. Gomber House Press. sgn 1st ed. brds. ils. 329p. VG in dj. B18. $27.50.

BOOTHBY, Guy. *My Indian Queen.* nd. Ward Lock. VG. P3. $35.00.

BOOTHBY, Guy. *Sherah McLeod.* 1897. London. 1st. VG. M2. $75.00.

BORAH, Woodrow. *Justice by Insurance.* 1983. Berkeley. Univ of California Press. 1st. 479p. G/G. F3. $20.00.

BORCHERT, Wolfgang. *Sad Geraniums.* 1973. Ecco. 1st. F/F. B35. $10.00.

BORDEAUX, Henry. *Pathway to Heaven.* 1952. Pellegrini Cudahy. 1st Am. F/NF. Q1. $100.00.

BORDEN, Spencer. *The Arab Horse.* 1906. NY. Doubleday. Page. 1st. VG. O3. $125.00.

BORDEN, W. *Use of the Rontgen Ray by the Medical Dept of US Army...* 1900. GPO. 1st. 4to. 98p. VG. E6. $350.00.

BOREIN, Edward. *Borein's West.* 1952. Santa Barbara, CA. Schauer Prt Studio. ils. F. A19. $125.00.

BOREL, Antoine Jr. *San Francisco Is No More.* 1963. Menlo Park. 1/200. prt paper brd/bl cloth spine. F. K7. $75.00.

BORER, Eva Maria. *Tante Heidi's Swiss Kitchen.* 1965. Gramercy. VG/dj. A16. $10.00.

BORG, Bjorn. *Bjorn Borg Story.* 1975. Henry Regency. 1st Am. photos. F/F. P8. $30.00.

BORGENICHT, Miriam. *Bad Medicine.* 1984. Macmillan. 1st. F/F. P3. $15.00.

BORGENICHT, Miriam. *False Colors.* 1985. St Martin. 1st. VG/VG. P3. $15.00.

BORGENICHT, Miriam. *Roadblock.* 1973. Bobbs Merrill. 1st. VG/VG. P3. $18.00.

BORGES, Jorge Luis. *Book of Sand.* 1979. Allen Lane. 1st. VG/VG. P3. $20.00.

BORN, Max. *La Constitution De La Matiere.* 1922. Paris. Blanchard. ils. 8vo. 84p. prt wrp. K3. $45.00.

BORNEMAN, Henry. *Pennsylvania Greman Illuminated Manuscripts.* 1927. Norristown, PA German Soc. 1st. obl folio. VG. C6. $175.00.

BORNKAMM, Gunther. *Jesus of Nazareth.* 1975. Harper. pb. 239p. VG. B29. $8.50.

BORNKAMM, Gunther. *Paul.* 1970. Harper. 359p. VG/VG. B29. $7.00.

BORODINI, George. *Spurious Sun.* 1948. London. 1st. F/dj. M2. $20.00.

BOROWITZ, Albert. *Innocence & Arsenic: Studies in Crime & Literature.* 1977. Harper Row. 1st. 170p. F/dj. O10. $25.00.

BOROWITZ, Eugene B. *How Can a Jew Speak of Faith Today?* 1969. Westminster. 221p. VG/dj. S3. $21.00.

BORREAL, Roger. *Texan Revolution of 1836, A Concise Historical Perspective Based on Original Sources.* 1989. La Villita. ils. index. 158p. NF. B19. $7.50.

BORST, Raymond R. *Henry David Thoreau A Descriptive Bibliography.* 1982. (Pittsburgh). Univ of Pittsburgh Press. 8vo. 232p. facsimiles of many title p.s. bl cloth. 1st ed. F. L5. $75.00.

BORST, Ronald V. *Graven Images.* 1992. Grove. 1st. VG/dj. L1. $50.00.

BORSTEIN, Larry. *Len Dawson: Superbowl Quarterback.* 1970. Grosset Dunlap. 1st. photos. F/VG. P8. $20.00.

BORTHWICK, J.D. *Three Years in California.* 1857. Edinburgh/London. Blackwood. 1st. 8vo. 8 tinted ils. gilt red cloth. case. $3.00.

BORTHWICK, J.D. *Three Years in California.* 1948. Biobooks. 1/1000. lg 8vo. 318p. NF. K7. $55.00.

BORTHWICK, J. S. *Bodies of Water.* 1990. NY. St. Martin. 1st. NF/VG. G8. $20.00.

BORTHWICK, J. S. *Bridled Groom.* 1994. NY. St. Martin. 1st. F/VG-. G8. $20.00.

BORTON, Helen. *Jungle.* 1968. HBW. stated 1st. sm 4to. unp. F/G+. C14. $10.00.

BORTSTEIN, Larry. *Superjoe: The Joe Namath Story.* 1969. Grosset Dunlap. 1st. VG/dj. P8. $30.00.

BORUP, George. *Tenderfoot With Peary.* 1911. NY. Stokes. 8vo. 317p. pict cloth. worn. P4. $40.00.

BORWN, EDGERTON & MCCORKLE. *Algonquin Sampler.* 1990. Algonquin. 1st. F. B3. $30.00.

BORYCZKA, Raymond. *No Strength Without Union: Ils History of Ohio Workers.* 1982. OH Hist Soc. 1st. VG/dj. V4. $45.00.

BOSLEY, Harold A. *The Deeds of Christ.* 1969. Abingdon. 176p. VG/VG. B29. $6.00.

BOSNAN, Richard. *Captivity Narrative of Hannah Duston.* 1987. Arion. 1/425. sgn. folio. 56p. hand-made paper brd/backed cloth. M. $24.00.

BOSTWICK, Arthur E. *Librarian's Open Shelf.* 1920. NY. Wilson. 1st. 8vo. 344p. VG. K3. $15.00.

BOSWELL, Hazel. *French Canada.* 1938. Viking. 1st. ils. NF/NF. D1. $75.00.

BOSWELL, James. *Journal of Tour to Hebrides with Samuel Johnson.* LLD. (1852). London. Nat Ils Lib. 8vo. 361p. Seton Mackenzie bdg. F. $13.00.

BOSWELL, James. *Life of Johnson.* 1924. London. 3 vol. ils. w/facsimile letter. VG. M17. $50.00.

BOSWELL, James. *Life of Samuel Johnson.* 1897. London. Dent. Temple Classics. 6 vol. NF. A24. $125.00.

BOSWELL, Robert. *Crooked Hearts.* 1987. NY. Knopf. 1st. Sgn. F/F. H11. $60.00.

BOSWELL, Robert. *Dancing at the Movies.* 1986. Iowa City. Univ of Iowa Press. 1st printing of only 1500 hc copies. author's 1st book. F/F. D10. $150.00.

BOSWELL, Thomas. *Heart of the Order.* 1989. NY. Doubleday. 1st. VG/VG+. R16. $25.00.

BOSWELL, Tom. *Strokes of Genius.* 1987. Doubleday. 1st. inscr. F/F. P8. $45.00.

BOTKIN, B.A. *Treasury of Southern Folklore.* 1949. NY. 1st. sgn. VG/dj. B5. $25.00.

BOTTOME, Phyllis. *Murder in the Bud.* 1939. London. Faber & Faber. 1st. covers lightly soiled; page edges and ep spotted. Jacket has several short closed tears and chipping at spine ends and at corners. VG/dj. M15. $90.00.

BOUCHARD, Charles Jaques. *Study of Some Points in Pathology of Cerebral.* 1990. Birmingham. Classics Neurology/Neurosurgery Lib. facsimile. G1. $65.00.

BOUCHARD, Dave. *If Sarah Will Take Me.* 1997. Victoria, BC. Orca Book Publishers. ARC. stp. label. VG/VG. A28. $9.95.

BOUCHARILAT, J.L. *Elements De Mecanique.* 1861. Paris. Mallet-Bachelier. 4th. 8vo. 364p. xl. K3. $75.00.

BOUCHER, Anthony. *Best Detective Stories.* 1964. Dutton. 1st. VG/VG. P3. $25.00.

BOUCHER, Anthony. *Case of the Baker Street Irregulars.* 1942. Tower. VG. P3. $25.00.

BOUCHER, Anthony. *Exeunt Murderers: The Best Mystery Stories of Anthony Boucher.* 1983. Carbondale. Southern Illinois University. 1st. VF/dj. M15. $45.00.

BOUCHER, Anthony. *Great American Detective Stories*. 1945. World. 1st. G+. N4. $25.00.

BOUCSEIN, Wolfram. *Electrodermal Activity*. Plenum Series. 1992. NY. Plenum. 442p. prt blk cloth. G1. $40.00.

BOULDING, Kenneth E. *Sonnets from Later Life. 1981 – 1993*. 1994. Wallingford, PA. Pendle Hill. 179p. VG. V3. $10.00.

BOULLE, Pierre. *Good Leviathan*. 1978. Vanguard. 1st. F/dj. M2. $15.00.

BOULLEMIER, Leo. *A Plantsman's Guide to Fuchsias*. 1989. London. color photos & line drawings. new in dj. B26. $14.00.

BOULTON, Rudyerd. *Traveling with the Birds; A Book on Migration*. 1933. M. A. Donohue. 1st. ils by Walter Weber; bookplate. dj. NF/G dj. M19. $17.50.

BOUNDS, Sydney J. *Dimension of Horror*. 1953. Hamilton Panther. VG/G. P3. $35.00.

BOUQUET, A.G.B. *Cauliflower & Broccoli Culture*. 1929. Orange Judd. 125p. dj. A10. $40.00.

BOURGUIGNON, Georges. *La Chronaxie Chez L'Homme*. 1923. Paris. Masson et Cie. ils/192 tables. 417p. prt stiff brn wrp. G1. $65.00.

BOURJAILY, Vance. *Great Fake Book*. 1986. Franklin Lib. 1st/ltd. sgn. full leather. Q1. $35.00.

BOURKE-WHITE, Margaret; see White, Margaret Bourke.

BOURNE, Eulalia. *Nine Months Is a Year at Baboquivari School*. 1968. AZ U. 1st. ils/maps/notes. NF/NF. B19. $30.00.

BOURNE, Gwen. *Wonder World Fairy Tale Book*. 1931. London. Cecil Palmer. 1st. 4to. pict cloth. dj. R5. $375.00.

BOURNE, Peter. *Flames of Empire*. 1949. Putnam. 1st. VG/G. P3. $18.00.

BOURNE, Peter. *Twilight of the Dragon*. 1954. Putnam. 1st. VG/VG. P3. $20.00.

BOURNE, William. *Regiment for the Sea & Other Writings on Navigation...* 1963. Cambridge. Hakluyt Soc. ils/fld map. 464p. pict bl cloth. dj. K1. $45.00.

BOUSFIELD, E.L. *Shallow-Water Gammaridean Amphipoda of New England*. 1973. Ithaca. 312p. F. S15. $22.50.

BOUSSARD, Leon. *Le Secret Du Colonel Lawrence*. 1941. Paris. Mont-Louis Clermont Ferrand. 1st. 124p. G/VG. M7. $60.00.

BOUSSEL, Patrice. *Leonardo Da Vinci*. nd. Chartwell. F/F. P3. $75.00.

BOUTON, Jim. *Ball Four*. 1993. Barnes Noble. 1st thus. sgn. F/dj. C15. $18.00.

BOUTON, Jim. *Ball Four: My Life & Hard Times Throwing the Knuckleball*. 1970. NY. World. 1st. F/F. B4. $150.00.

BOUTON, Jim. *Ball Four Plus Five*. 1981. Stein Day. 1st. sgn. F/F. B11. $50.00.

BOUTON, Jim & Eliot Asinof. *Strike Zone*. (1994). NY. Viking. 1st. sgn by Bouton. F/F. B3. $20.00.

BOUTON, John. *Enchanted*. 1891. Cassell. 1st. VG. M2. $50.00.

BOUVIER, E.L. *Psychic Life of Insects*. 1922. NY. Century. 1st Eng-language. 12mo. trans LO Howard. 377p. G1. $45.00.

BOVA, Ben. *Aliens*. 1977. St Martin. 1st. F/dj. M2. $20.00.

BOVA, Ben. *Cyberbooks*. 1989. Tor. 1st. F/F. M2/P3. $20.00.

BOVA, Ben. *Dueling Machine*. 1971. Faber. 1st. sgn. F/F. P3. $35.00.

BOVA, Ben. *End of Exile*. 1975. Dutton. 1st. RS. F/F. P3. $35.00.

BOVA, Ben. *Kinsman*. 1979. NY. Dial Press. 1st. sgn inscr. VF/F. T2. $35.00.

BOVA, Ben. *Millenium*. 1976. Random. 1st. NF/NF. P3. $30.00.

BOVA, Ben. *Multiple Man*. 1976. Bobbs Merrill. 1st. NF/NF. P3. $25.00.

BOVA, Ben. *Peacekeepers*. 1988. Tor. 1st. F/F. P3. $18.00.

BOVA, Ben. *Privateers*. 1985. NY. Tor. 1st. sgn inscr. VF/VF. T2. $25.00.

BOVA, Ben. *Starflight and Other Improbabilities*. 1973. Philadelphia. Westminster. BCE. ex lib in dj. ffep removed. usual lib mks. b/w photos. 126p. G. K5. $13.00.

BOVA, Ben. *The High Road*. 1981. Boston. Houghton Mifflin. 1st printing. 8vo. foreword by Harrison Schmitt, Apollo 17 astronaut. 289p. VG/VG. K5. $20.00.

BOVA, Ben. *Vengeance of Orion*. 1988. Tor. 1st. F/F. P3. $18.00.

BOVA, Ben. *Viewpoint*. 1977. Cambridge. Nesfa Press. 1st. sgn. 1/800 # copies. VF/VF. T2. $25.00.

BOVILL, E.W. *Missions to the Niger*. 1964-1966. Hakluyt Soc. 4 vol. 26 maps/33 pl/fld Pocket map. NF. O7. $150.00.

BOWAN, Gail. *A Colder Kind of Death*. 1994. Toronto. McClelland & Stewart. 1st. sgn. F. A26. $35.00.

BOWDEN, Charles. *Blood Orchid*. (1995). NY. Random House. 1st sgn & dated. F/F. B3. $40.00.

BOWDEN, Charles. *Blue Desert*. (1986). Tucson. U of Arizona. 1st. F/F. B3. $125.00.

BOWDEN, Charles. *Killing the Hidden Waters*. 1977. Austin. TX U. 1st. author's 1st book. F/VG. L3. $350.00.

BOWDEN, Charles. *Mezcal*. 1988. Univ of Arizona. 1st. sgn. F/M. M25. $75.00.

BOWDEN, Charles and Michael Binstein. *Trust Me, Charles Keating and the Great American Bank Robbery*. (1993). NY. Random House. 1st. F/F. B3. $35.00.

BOWDITCH, Nathaniel. *Discourse on the Life & Character of Hon Nathaniel Bowditch*. 1838. Boston. Little, Brn. 1st. 8vo. 119p. xl. K3. $35.00.

BOWE, Richard J. *Historical Album of Colorado*. 1959. Denver. ils sgn. G. A19. $30.00.

BOWEN, Abel. *Naval Monument: Containing Official & Other Accounts...* ca 1816. Boston. Phillips Sampson. 23 engravings. full calf. T7. $325.00.

BOWEN, B.V. *Faster than Thought*. 1963. London. Pitman. 18 pl. 416p. VG. K3. $30.00.

BOWEN, Barbara. *Strange Scriptures that Perplex the Western Mind*. 1947. Eerdmans. 121p. G. B29. $11.00.

BOWEN, Elizabeth. *Eva Trout or Changing Scenes*. 1968. NY. Knopf. 1st. Jacket has small abrasion on rear panel and nick at top of front panel. F+/F. H11. $35.00.

BOWEN, Elizabeth. *House in Paris*. 1936. Knopf. 1st. VG/VG. P3. $20.00.

BOWEN, Elizabeth. *Ivy Gripped the Steps*. 1946. Knopf. 1st Am. VG. M2. $32.00.

BOWEN, Marjorie. *Twilight and Other Supernatural Romances.* 1998. Ashcroft, BC. Ash Tree Press. 1st. Jessica Amanda Salmonson, editor. VF/VF. T2. $45.00.

BOWEN, Michael. *Badger Game.* 1989. NY. St. Martin. 1st. F/F. G8. $20.00.

BOWEN, Michael. *Faithfully Executed.* 1992. NY. St. Martin. 1st. VF/VF. T2. $25.00.

BOWEN, Peter. *Coyote Wind.* 1994. NY. St. Martin. 1st. VF/VF. T2. $45.00.

BOWEN, Peter. *Wolf, No Wolf.* (1996). NY. St. Martin. 1st. F/F. B3. $25.00.

BOWEN, Peter. *Yellowstone Kelly.* 1987. Ottawa, IL. Jameson Books. 1st. NF. corner bumped/NF sunned spine. M23. $35.00.

BOWEN, R. Sidney. *Dave Dawson in Libya.* nd. Saalfield. VG/VG. P3. $15.00.

BOWEN, R. Sidney. *Hawaii Five-O Top Secret,* 1969. Whitman. TVTI. VG. P3. $10.00.

BOWEN, R. Sidney. *Red Randall on Active Duty* (#2). 1944. Grosset Dunlap. 211p. VG/dj. M20. $16.00.

BOWEN, R.H. *Frenchman in Lincoln's America.* 1974. Lakeside Classic. 2 vol. ils/map. F. M4. $25.00.

BOWER, B.M. *Dark Horse.* 1943. Triangle. VG. P3. $12.00.

BOWER, B.M. *Her Prairie Knight.* 1907. Dillingham. A19. $10.00.

BOWER, F.O. *Plants & Man.* 1925. London. Macmillan. 365p. cloth. A10. $45.00.

BOWER, F.O. *Sixty Years of Botany in Britain (1875 – 1935).* 1938. London. Macmillan. 112p. dj. A10. $75.00.

BOWER, F. O. *Size and Form in Plants With Special Reference to the Primary Conducting Tracts.* 1930. London. 232p w/72 text figures & 25 tables. VG. chipped dj. B26. $37.50.

BOWER, F. O. *The Origin of a Land Flora. A Theory Based Upon the Facts of Alteration.* 1908. London. some flecking. VG. chip dj. B26. $47.50.

BOWERS, Alfred W. *Mandan Social & Ceremonial Organization.* 1950. Chicago U. Social Anthropological series. 407p. NF/dj. K7. $95.00.

BOWERS, Elisabeth. *No Forwarding Address.* 1991. Seal. F/F. P3. $20.00.

BOWERS, Janice Emily. *Mountains Next Door.* 1991. AZ U. 1st. inscr. 147p. F/F. B19. $35.00.

BOWES, Anne LaBastille. *Bird Kingdom of the Mayas.* 1967. Van Nostrand. 1st. 90p. dj. F3. $15.00.

BOWIE, Walter Russell. *Story of the Bible.* 1962. Abingdon. 557p. VG/dj. B29. $7.50.

BOWKER, Gordon. *Through the Dark Labyrinth.* 1997. NY. St. Martin. ARC. F/wrps. B2. $25.00.

BOWKER, Richard. *Marlborough Street.* 1987. Doubleday. 1st. RS. F/F. P3. $18.00.

BOWLBY, John. *Charles Darwin: A New Life.* 1990. NY. ils. VG/dj. M17. $15.00.

BOWLES, E.A. *Handbook of Crocus & Colchicum.* 1952. Van Nostrand. 222p. xl. A10. $25.00.

BOWLES, E.A. *My Garden In Spring.* ca 1914. Dodge Pub. 8vo. 24 halftone/16 mc pl. teg. VG. A22. $65.00.

BOWLES, Jane. *Collected Works of Jane Bowles.* 1966. Farrar. 1st ed. F/F. B2. $40.00.

BOWLES, Paul. *Days Tangier Journal: 1987 – 1989.* 1991. Ecco. 1st. F/dj. A24. $25.00.

BOWLES, Paul. *Their Heads are Green & Their Hands are Blue.* 1963. Random. 1st. F/F. B4. $225.00.

BOWMAN, David. *Bunny Modern.* 1998. Boston. Little, Brn. 1st. Sgn. F/F. D10. $35.00.

BOWMAN, David. *Let the Dog Drive.* 1992. NY. New York University. 1st. VF/dj. M15. $165.00.

BOWMAN, Gerald. *From Scott to Fuchs.* 1958. London. Evans Bros. 1st. 8vo. 191p. VG/dj. P4. $40.00.

BOWMAN, Heath & Stirling Dickinson. *Death Is Incidental. A Story of Revolution.* 1937. Chicago. Willett. 1st. 111p. G/chipped dj. F3. $20.00.

BOWMAN, Isaiah. *Pioneer Fringe.* 1931. NY. 1st ed. 361p. A17. $25.00.

BOWMAN, P.B. *Little Brown Bowl with Other Tales & Verse.* 1928. NY. Nelson. sgn. 311p. G. B11. $100.00.

BOWMAN, Sheridan. *Radiocarbon Dating.* 1990. Berkeley. ils. 64p. M/wrp. K3. $18.00.

BOWMAN & LA MARCA. *Pleasures of the Porch: Ideas for Gracious Outdoor Living.* 1997. Rizoli. folio. photos. F/dj. A28. $16.00.

BOWREY, Thomas. *Papers of Thomas Bowrey 1669 – 1713 Discovered in 1913.* 1927. London. Hakluyt Soc. 1st. 8vo. 398p. bl cloth. P4. $95.00.

BOX, Edgar; see Vidal, Luther.

BOXER, C.R. *Dutch in Brazil. 1624 – 1654.* 1957. Clarendon. 4 maps+ftspc portrait. F/rpr. O7. $100.00.

BOXER, C.R. *Portuguese Embassy to Japan (1644 – 1647).* 1928. London. Kegan Paul. 8vo. 2 ils. prt brd/cloth spine. O7. $350.00.

BOYCE, Chris. *Catchworld.* 1977. Doubleday. F/F. P3. $15.00.

BOYD, Andrew. *Chinese Architecture.* 1962. 1st Am. 144 pl/84 drawings. 166p. VG/G. A8. $75.00.

BOYD, Frank; see Kane, Frank.

BOYD, James. *Drums.* 1956. NY. Scribner. ils by N.C. Wyeth. as Is. A16. $20.00.

BOYD, John. *The Girl with the Jade Green Eyes.* 1978. NY. Viking. 1st. F/F. T2. $6.00.

BOYD, Malcolm. *Runner.* 1974. Waco. Word. 1st. sgn. 8vo. 203p. F/VG. $11.00.

BOYD, Thomas. *Through the Wheat.* 1923. Scribner. 1st. NF. B2. $35.00.

BOYD, William. *Good Man in Africa.* 1982. Morrow. 1st Am. sgn. F/F. B4. $175.00.

BOYD, William. *Ice-Cream War.* 1983. Morrow. 1st Am. F/F. B4. $100.00.

BOYD, William. *New Confessions.* 1988. Morrow. 1st. F/dj. Q1. $40.00.

BOYD, William. *On the Yankee Station.* 1984. Morrow. 1st Am. sgn. F/F. B4. $125.00.

BOYD, William. *School Ties.* 1985. Morrow. 1st Am. NF/NF. R14. $40.00.

BOYD, William. *Stars and Bars.* 1985. NY. Morrow. 1st Am ed. F/F. D10. $45.00.

BOYDEN, Polly. *The Pink Egg.* 1942. Truro, MA. Pamet Press. 1st. radical novel in which all characters are birds. NF in VG dj. B2. $75.00.

BOYER, Dwight. *True Tales of the Great Lakes.* 1971. Dodd Mead. 1st. 340p. VG/clip. M20. $20.00.

BOYER, Glenn. *Illustrated Life of Doc Holliday.* 1966. Reminder Pub. 1st. ils. wrp. B19. $40.00.

BOYER, Richard. *Giant Rat of Sumatra.* 1991. Mysterious. 1st. F/F. M2. $25.00.

BOYER, Richard O. *Legend of John Brown.* 1973. Knopf. 1st. 627p. F/dj. H1. $28.00.

BOYER, Rick. *Billingsgate Shoal.* 1982. Boston. Houghton Mifflin. 1st. F/dj. M15. $85.00.

BOYER, Rick. *Moscow Metal.* 1987. Boston. 1st. NF/sans. T12. $20.00.

BOYER, Rick. *The Penny Ferry.* 1984. Boston. Houghton Mifflin. 1st. VF/dj. M15. $35.00.

BOYER, Rick. *The Whale's Footprints.* 1988. Boston. Houghton Mifflin. 1st. VF/dj. M15. $35.00.

BOYLAN, Clare. *Last Resorts.* 1986. Summit. 1st. F/dj. A23. $32.00.

BOYLAN, Eleanor. *Working Murder.* 1989. NY. Henry Holt. 1st. F/NF. crease. M23. $20.00.

BOYLE, E.V. *Beauty & the Beast.* 1875. Sampson Low. 1st. 4to. aeg. deluxe bdg. R5. $675.00.

BOYLE, Kay. *My Next Bride.* 1934. HBJ. 1st. 327p. VG. A25. $10.00.

BOYLE, Louis M. *Out West Growing Cymbidium Orchids.* 1952. LA. self pub. 8vo. ils/photos. 526p. F/VG. A22. $35.00.

BOYLE, Martin. *Yanks Don't Cry: A Marine's-Eye View of 4 Heroic Years.* 1963. NY. 1st. 250p. VG/VG. S16. $35.00.

BOYLE, T. Coraghessan. *East Is East.* 1990. NY. Viking. 1st. Sgn. F/F. D10. $50.00.

BOYLE, T. Coraghessan. *Greasy Lake and Other Stories.* 1985. NY. Viking. 1st. sgn. F in F dj. D10. $65.00.

BOYLE, T. Coraghessan. *If the River Was Whiskey.* 1989. NY. Viking. 1st. sgn. F in F dj. D10. $50.00.

BOYLE, T. Coraghessan. *The Road to Wellville.* 1993. NY. Viking. 1st. sgn. F/F. D10. $45.00.

BOYLE, T. Coraghessan. *The Tortilla Curtain.* 1995. Viking. UP. F/golden wrps. M25. $60.00.

BOYLE, T. Coraghessan. *The Tortilla Curtain.* 1995. NY. Viking. AP. F. slightly bumped corner/wrp. B2. $30.00.

BOYLE, T. Coraghessan. *Water Music.* 1981. Boston. Little, Brn. 1st. sgn. F in NF dj. D10. $85.00.

BOYLE, T. Coraghessan. *World's End.* (1987). NY. Viking. 1st. sgn by author. F/F. D3. $60.00.

BOYLSTON, Helen Dore. *Sue Barton, Senior Nurse (#2).* 1952 (1937). Little, Brn. 220p. VG/dj. M20. $30.00.

BOYLSTON, Helen Dore. *Sue Barton, Superintendent of Nurses (#5).* 1952 (1940). Little, Brn. 239p. VG/dj. M20. $22.00.

BOYNTON, Henry Van Ness. *The Annual Address Delivered at the 23rd Reunion of the Society of the Army of the Cumberland Held at Chickamauga.* 1892. Cincinnati. Robert Clark & Co. 1st. orig printed wrp. VG. M8. $150.00.

BRACE, G. *Farm Shop Work.* 1915. 1st. xl. G+. E6. $22.00.

BRACE, Timothy. *Murder Goes Fishing.* 1936. Dutton. 1st. VG. N4. $20.00.

BRACKETT, Leigh. *Long Tomorrow.* 1955. Doubleday. 1st. F/NF. P3. $125.00.

BRACKETT, Leigh. *No Good from a Corpse.* 1999. Tucson. Dennis McMillan. 1st. VF/dj. M15. $35.00.

BRACKETT, Leigh. *Starmen.* 1952. Gnome. 1st. F/dj. M2. $125.00.

BRACKETT, Leigh. *Stranger at Home.* 1946. NY. S&S. 1st. G/dj. M15. $45.00.

BRACKMAN, Arnold C. *Search for the Gold of Tutankhamen.* 1976. NY. Mason Charter. 1st. 8vo. VG/dj. W1. $18.00.

BRADBERRY, James. *Ruins of Civility.* 1996. NY. St. Martin. 1st. sgn. VF/VF. T2. $25.00.

BRADBURN, John. *Breeding & Developing the Trotter.* 1905. Boston. 1st. VG. O3. $58.00.

BRADBURY, Edward P.; See Moorcock, Michael.

BRADBURY, Ray. *A Graveyard for Lunatics.* 1990. NY. Knopf. 1st. F/F. H11. $30.00.

BRADBURY, Ray. *A Graveyard for Lunatics.* 1990. Knopf. 1st. F/dj. M2. $20.00.

BRADBURY, Ray. *Death Is a Lonely Business.* 1985. NY. Knopf. 1st. F/F. H11. $30.00.

BRADBURY, Ray. *Golden Apples of the Sun.* 1953. Doubleday. 1st. NF/VG. M2. $185.00.

BRADBURY, Ray. *Halloween Tree.* 1972. Knopf. 1st. F/dj. M2. $75.00.

BRADBURY, Ray. *I Sing the Body Electric.* 1969. Knopf. 1st. F/dj. M2. $85.00.

BRADBURY, Ray. *Martian Chronicles.* 1950. Doubleday. 1st. VG/dj. M2. $325.00.

BRADBURY, Ray. *Quicker Than the Eye.* (1996). NY. Avon. 1st. sgn by author. F/F. B3. $50.00.

BRADBURY, Ray. *S Is for Space.* 1966. Doubleday. 1st. F/dj. M2. $75.00.

BRADBURY, Ray. *Something Wicked This Way Comes.* 1999. Springfield. Gauntlet Press. 1st. Ltd Ed. 1/500 # copies. sgn by Bradbury and Joe Lansdale. Peter Crowther. VF/VF. T2. $65.00.

BRADBURY, Ray. *The Haunter Computer and the Android Pope.* 1981. NY. Knopf. 1st. F/F. D10. $45.00.

BRADBURY, Ray. *The October Country: The 40th Anniversary Edition.* 1997. Springfield. Gauntlet Press. 1st. ltd ed. 1/500 # copies. sgn by Bradbury. introducer Dennis Etchison & author of afterword Robert R. McCammon. VF/VF dj & slipcase. T2. $65.00.

BRADBURY, Ray. *Toynbee Convector.* 1992. Atlanta. Turner. 1st thus. inscr. F. A23. $45.00.

BRADBURY, Ray. *Where Robot Mice & Robot Men Run Round in Robot Towns.* 1977. Knopf. 1st. sgn. F/F. A23. $60.00.

BRADBURY, Will. *Into the Unknown.* 1981. Reader's Digest. P3. $15.00.

BRADBY, Violet. *Matthew and the Miller.* nd. NY. Dodge Publishing. fat 12mo. gray cloth. ils by H.R. Millar. 100p. NF/VG. D6. $45.00.

BRADDON, George. *Microbe's Kiss.* 1940. Faber. 1st. G/G. P3. $30.00.

BRADDON, Russell. *When the Enemy Is Tired.* 1969. Viking. ne. 251p. NF/VG. W2. $15.00.

BRADEN, Charles. *The World's Religions; A Short History.* 1939. Abingdon Cokesbury. 256p. VG/VG. B29. $8.50.

BRADEN, James A. *Centennial History of Akron 1825 – 1925.* 1925. Akron. 666p. half leather. B18. $47.50.

BRADFORD, Barbara Taylor. *Remember.* 1991. Random. 1st. sgn. F/F. A23. $36.00.

BRADFORD, Richard. *Red Sky at Morning.* 1968. Phil. 1st. VG/VG. B5. $45.00.

BRADFORD, Roark. *Ol' Man Adam An' His Chillun.* 1928. Harper. early prt. 12mo. NF/NF. C8. $75.00.

BRADFORD, Sarah H. *Harriet Tubman, The Moses of Her People.* 1981. Gloucester, MA. Peter Smith. 2nd. 8vo red cloth. Owner's stamp on front ep. lower right corner of cover bumped. 149p. VG. H1. $15.00.

BRADFORD, William. *Of Plymouth Plantation 1620 – 1647.* 1952. NY. 1st. VG/G. M17. $30.00.

BRADLEY, Alice; See Sheldon, Alice Bradley.

BRADLEY, Bill. *Life on the Run.* 1976. Quadrangle. 1st. VG/VG. P8. $25.00.

BRADLEY, Bill. *Time Present, Time Past.* 1996. NY. Knopf. 1st. sgn. F/F. O11. $50.00.

BRADLEY, Bill. *Values of the Game.* 1998. NY. Artisan. 1st. sgn by Bradley. fwd by Phil Jackson. F/F. O11. $65.00.

BRADLEY, David. *No Place to Hide.* 1948. BOMC. VG/dj. K3. $10.00.

BRADLEY, David. *The Chaneysville Incident.* 1981. NY. Harper & Row. ARC. NF in wrp. D10. $50.00.

BRADLEY, Marion Zimmer. *Best of Marion Zimmer Bradley.* 1985. Chicago. F/F. P3. $17.00.

BRADLEY, Marion Zimmer. *Catch Trap.* 1979. Ballantine. 1st. NF/VG. P3. $23.00.

BRADLEY, Marion Zimmer. *Firebrand.* 1987. S&S. 1st. F/F. N4. $25.00.

BRADLEY, Marion Zimmer. *Heirs of Hammerfell.* 1989. DAW. 1st. F/dj. M2. $30.00.

BRADLEY, Marion Zimmer. *Mists of Avalon.* 1982. Knopf. 1st. F/dj. M2. $75.00.

BRADLEY, Mary Hastings. *On the Gorilla Trail.* 1922. NY/London. Appleton. 8vo. 47 pl/map ep. cloth. VG. W1. $20.00.

BRADLEY, Muriel. *Murder Twice Removed.* 1951. Crime Club. 1st. VG/VG. G8. $25.00.

BRADLEY, Omar. *Soldier's Story.* 1951. NY. sgn. maps/photos/index. VG. S16. $125.00.

BRADLEY, Will. *Bradley His Book. Vol. 1, No. 1.* Springfield. (The Wayside Press). May, 1896. tall narrow 8vo. (28)p. ils. ils wrps. 1st printing. Sewn as-issued. F. L5. $300.00.

BRADLEY, Will. *The Book of Ruth and the Book of Esther.* 1897. NY. R. K. Russell. 8vo. cream paper brds w/title label on spine. deckle edge pages. printed in red & black calligraphic type. inscr & sgn by Bradley. 99p. VG. D6. $150.00.

BRADNER, Enos. *Northwest Angling.* 1950. NY. 239p. dj. A17. $20.00.

BRADNEY, Gail, ed. *Best Wines! Gold Medal Winners from the Leading Competitions Worldwide.* nd. The Print Project. sc. F. A28. $8.95.

BRADSHAW, Gilliam. *Beyond the North Wind.* 1993. NY. Greenwillow Books. 1st. NF/NF. A28. $7.95.

BRADSHAW, Gillian. *Hawk of May.* 1980. S&S. 1st. F/dj. M2. $30.00.

BRADSHAW, Gillian. *Kingdom Summer.* 1981. S&S. 1st. F/F. M2. $25.00.

BRADSHAW, Marion J. *Maine Land: A Portfolio of Views.* 1941. Bangor, ME. 1/1000. 2nd prt. sgn. ils. 176p. $7.00.

BRADSHAW, Marion J. *Nature of Maine.* 1945. Bangor, ME. self pub. 1/1000. sgn. gilt blk cloth. B11. $65.00.

BRADSHAW, Percy V. *Brother Savages & Guests.* 1958. London. inscr. 162p. G/dj. B18. $27.50.

BRADY, Cyrus Townsend. *Indian Fights & Fighters.* Dec 1904. McClure Phillips. hc. A19. $65.00.

BRADY, Cyrus Townsend. *Recollections of a Missionary in Great West.* 1901. NY. 200p. VG. B5. $30.00.

BRADY, Cyrus Townsend. *Sir Henry Morgan, Buccaneer.* 1903. Dillingham. 1st. VG. M2. $35.00.

BRADY, Judge Paul L. *A Certain Blindness. A Black Family's Quest for the Promise of America.* 1990. Atlanta. ALP. 1st. inscr by author. F in lightly chip dj. B2. $35.00.

BRADY, Leo. *Edge of Doom.* 1949. Dutton. 1st. VG/G. P3. $13.00.

BRADY, Nyle C. *The Nature and Properties of Soils.* 1984. NY. 9th ed. agriculture textbook. 750p. numerous figures. VG. B26. $21.00.

BRADY, Ryder. *Instar.* 1976. Doubleday F/F. P3. $13.00.

BRADY, Virginia. *Kittens & Cat Book.* 1960. McGraw Hill. 1st. ils Nitsa Savramis. sbdg. VG. M5. $55.00.

BRAGADIN, Marc. *Italian Navy World War II.* 1957. Annapolis. 1st. maps/photos/index. 380p. VG/VG. S16. $30.00.

BRAGDON, Elspeth. *New Adventures of Peter Rabbit.* ca 1950. Cincinnati. Artcraft. ils LV Schmeing/5 3-D popups. 8vo. pict brd. R5. $125.00.

BRAGG, Bill. *Campbell Country, the Slumbering Giant.* 1978. Gilette, WY. 1st. inscr. ils/photos. 20p.

BRAGG, Lawrence. *Crystalline State: A General Survey.* 1949. London. Bell. rpt. ils. xl. VG. K3. $35.00.

BRAGG, Lawrence. *Determination of Crystal Structures.* 1957. London. Bell. 2nd. 8vo. VG/dj. K3. $35.00.

BRAGG, Melvyn. *Richard Burton: A Life.* 1989. Little, Brn. 1st Am. NF. W2. $25.00.

BRAIN, Russell. *Nature of Experience: Riddell Memorial Lectures.* 1959. London. Oxford. 12mo. 73p. bl cloth. VG/clip. G1. $35.00.

BRAINE, John. *Life at the Top.* 1962. Houghton Mifflin. 1st Am. author's 3rd book. F/NF. D10. $50.00.

BRAINE, Sheila. *To Tell the King the Sky Is Falling.* ca 1898. Scribner. ils Alice Woodward. 171p. aeg. VG. P2. $50.00.

BRAINERD, George. *The Maya Civilization.* 1963. LA. Southwest Museum. 1st. foldout maps. b/w photo ils. 93p. F. F3. $15.00.

BRAKHAGE, Stan. *Metaphors on Vision.* 1976. Film Culture. 2nd. intro/edit PA Sitney. NF/stiff cb wrp. C9. $35.00.

BRAKHAGE, Stan. *The Brakhage Lectures.* 1972. Chicago. Good Lion. 1st. stiffcard wrps in dj. F/VG. B2. $45.00.

BRAM, Christopher. *Father of Frankenstein.* 1995. Dutton. 1st. F/dj. C9. $36.00.

BRAMAH, Ernest. *Kai Lung's Golden Hours.* 1923. Doran. 1st. VG. M2. $60.00.

BRAMAH, Ernest. *Mirror of Kong Ho.* 1930. Doubleday. 1st. VG/dj. M2. $150.00.

BRAMBLE, Forbes. *Strange Case of Deacon Brodie.* 1975. Hamish Hamilton. 1st. F/F. P3. $20.00.

BRAMHALL, Marion. *Tragedy in Blue.* 1945. Crime Club. 1st. VG. P3. $18.00.

BRAMWELL, Byron. *Diseases of the Spinal Cord.* 1985 (1885). Birmingham. Classics Neurology/Neurosurgery Lib. facsimile. F. G1. $75.00.

BRANCH, Hettye Wallace. *Story of 80 John: Biography of Respected Negro Ranchmen…* 1960. Greenwich. VG/dj. J2. $95.00.

BRAND, Christianna. *Death in High Heels.* 1954. Scribner. 1st. VG/G. P3. $30.00.

BRAND, Christianna. *Heaven Knows Who.* 1960. Michael Joseph. 1st. VG/VG. P3. $35.00.

BRAND, Christianna. *Suddenly at His Residence.* 1947. London. Bodley Head. 1st. jacket has darkened spine and small chips at spine ends. VG/dj. M15. $200.00.

BRAND, Christianna. *The Rose in Darkness.* 1979. London. Michael Joseph. 1st. Jacket has some spotting on inner flaps. F/dj. M15. $75.00.

BRAND, Christianna. *Three Cornered Halo.* 1957. NY. Scribner's. 1st Am ed. mfep. VG/VG. G8. $40.00.

BRAND, Eirck D. *Band Instrument Repairing Manual.* 1946. self pub. 198p. VG. S5. $15.00.

BRAND, John. *Observations on Popular Antiquities…* 1810. London. Baynes. 424p. 3-quarter leather. VG. M10. $175.00.

BRAND, Max. *Murder Me!* 1995. NY. St. Martin. 1st. VF/dj. M15. $35.00.

BRAND, Max; See Faust, Fredrick S.

BRANDAO, Ambrosis Fernandes. *Dialogues of the Great Things of Brazil.* 1987. Albuquerque. Univ of New Mexico Press. 1st. 385p. G/G. F3. $25.00.

BRANDEIS, Madeline. *Little Rose of the Mesa.* 1935. Grosset Dunlap. 8vo. 155p. dj. F7. $35.00.

BRANDNER, Gary. *Doomstalker.* 1990. UK. Severn. 1st hc ed. NF/dj. M21. $20.00.

BRANDO, Anna. *Brando for Breakfast.* 1979. Crown. 1st. F/NF. A20. $20.00.

BRANDON, Jay. *Fade the Heat.* 1990. Pocket. 1st. F/NF. P3. $19.00.

BRANDON, Jay. *Predator's Waltz.* 1989. NY. St. Martin. 1st. VF/VF. T2. $8.00.

BRANDON, Jay. *Rules of Evidence.* 1992. NY. Pocket Books. 1st. VF/VF. T2. $9.00.

BRANDON, John G. *The Joy Ride.* 1927. NY. Dial. 1st Am. Jacket has darkened spine. chips at corners and several closed tears. VG/dj. M15. $45.00.

BRANDON, R. *Life & Many Deaths of Harry Houdini.* 1993. NY. 1st. photos. 355p. F/dj. M4. $25.00.

BRANDON, William. *Last Americans: Indian in American Culture.* 1974. McGraw Hill. VG/dj. A19. $30.00.

BRANDT, Herbert. *Arizona & Its Bird Life.* 1951. Bird Research Found. 1st. ils/index/map ep. 724p. NF. B19. $175.00.

BRANDT, Johanna. *Grape Cure.* 1950. Harmony Centre. 191p. VG/dj. A10. $26.00.

BRANDT, John C. & Stephen P. Maran, Editors. *New Horizons in Astronomy.* 1972. San Francisco. W. H. Freeman. sm 4to. 11 color plates. b/w photos. diagrams. 496p. ex lib in cloth lib bdg. margins soiled. o/w G. K5. $8.00.

BRANDT, Karl. *Management of Agriculture & Food in German-Occupied…* 1953. Stanford. 707p. VG/dj. A10. $45.00.

BRANDT, Tom; see Dewey, Thomas B.

BRANLEY, Franklyn. *Lodestar Rocket Ship to Mars.* 1951. Crowell. 1st. VG/VG. P3. $18.00.

BRANLEY, Franklyn M. *Columbia and Beyond; The Story of the Space Shuttle.* 1979. NY. Collin. ex lib in dj. ffep removed. usual lib mks. photos. some in color. 88p. G. K5. $8.00.

BRANLEY, Franklyn M. *Exploration of the Moon; An Account of Man's Dramatic Quest For the Moon.* 1965. London. T. Nelson & Sons. 8vo. 8 b/w plates. text figures. 125p. G/chipped & torn dj. K5. $12.00.

BRANNER, Robert. *Gothic Architecture.* 1961. Brazillier. 1st. 125p. VG/VG. A8. $12.00.

BRANSON, H. C. *Pricking Thumb.* 1942. NY. S&S. 1st. VG. G8. $15.00.

BRANSTON, Frank. *Sergeant Ritchie's Conscience.* 1978. NY. St. Martin. 1st Am. VG/VG. G8. $15.00.

BRANT, Beth. *Mohawk Trail.* 1985. Ithaca. Firebrand Books. 1st. author's 1st book. F/wrp. L3. $45.00.

BRANTLEY, Rabun Lee. *Georgia Journalism of the Civil War Period.* 1929. Nashville. George Peabody College for Teachers. 1st. pres. NF/wrp. M8. $250.00.

BRAQUE, Gerorges. *Georges Braque: His Graphic Work.* 1961. NY. Abrams. 1st. intro by Werner Hoffmann. F. O11. $35.00.

BRASHEAR, John A. *Man Who Loved the Stars.* 1988 (1924). Cambridge. 8vo. 190p. VG. K5. $10.00.

BRASHER, Rex. *Birds & Trees of North America.* 1961. NY. Rowan Littlefield. 4 vol. folio. 875 mc pl. quarter leatherette/cloth. F. $24.00.

BRASHLER, William. *Josh Gibson: Life in the Negro Leagues.* 1978. Harper Row. 1st. F/dj. M25. $60.00.

BRASHLER, William. *The Bingo Long Traveling All Stars and Motor Kings.* 1973. NY. Harper & Row. 1st. author's 1st book. slightly cocked in lightly used dj. B2. $75.00.

BRASHLER, William. *The Chosen Prey.* 1982. NY. Harper & Row. 1st. VF/VF. H11. $45.00.

BRAUDY, Susan. *Who Killed Sal Mineo?* 1982. Wyndham. 1st. F/dj. M25. $25.00.

BRAUN, Ernest. *Grand Canyon of the Living Colorado.* 1970. Ballantine. 8vo. 144p. VG+. F7. $25.00.

BRAUN, Lillian Jackson. *Cat Who Came to Breakfast.* 1994. NY. Putnam. 1st. F/NF. G8. $10.00.

BRAUN, Lillian Jackson. *Cat Who Moved a Mountain.* 1992. NY. Putnam. 1st. NF/F. G8. $15.00.

BRAUTIGAN, Richard. *Dreaming of Babylon.* (1971). NY. Delacorte. 1st. price clip. lt wear. F/NF. B3. $50.00.

BRAUTIGAN, Richard. *Hawkline Monster: A Gothic Western.* 1974. S&S. 1st. F/F. P3. $25.00.

BRAUTIGAN, Richard. *So the Wind Won't Blow it All Away.* 1982. NY. Delacorte. 1st. Light remainder spray. F/F. H11. $40.00.

BRAUTIGAN, Richard. *Sombrero Fallout.* 1976. S&S. 1st. F/F. H11. $50.00.

BRAUTIGAN, Richard. *The Hawkline Monster. A Gothic Western.* 1974. NY. S&S. 1st. rem mk. NF in dj. D10. $40.00.

BRAUTIGAN, Richard. *The Tokyo Montana Express.* 1980. np. Delacorte. 3rd prt. VG/G. S19. $25.00.

BRAVERMAN, Kate. *Lithium for Medea.* 1979. Harper. 1st. F/NF. M19. $25.00.

BRAVO UGARTE, Jose. *Cuestiones Historicas Guadalupanas.* 1966. Mexico. editorial jus. 2nd ed. b/w photo ils. 118p. G/wrp. F3. $10.00.

BRAYMER, Marjorie. *Atlantis: Biography of a Legend.* 1983. Atheneum. 1st. VG/VG. P3. $20.00.

BRAZELTON, T. Berry. *Toddlers and Parents: A Declaration of Independence.* 1989. Delacorte Press. NY. revised ed. VG hc. A28. $5.95.

BRAZIER, Mary A.B. *Electrical Activity of the Nervous System.* 1977. Turnbridge Wells. Kent. Pitman Medical. 4th. 248p. prt laminated brd. G1. $65.00.

BREAKENRIDGE, William M. *Helldorado: Bringing the Law to the Mesquite.* 1982. RR Donnelley. Lakeside Classics #80. ils/ notes/index. 454p. F. B19. $25.00.

BREAN, Herbert. *Traces of Merrilee.* 1966. Morrow. 1st. VG-/G. G8. $12.50.

BREARLEY, Harry C. *Time Telling Through the Ages.* 1919. Doubleday Page. 1st. ils. 8vo. 294p. K3. $40.00.

BRECHT, Bertolt. *Seven Plays.* 1961. NY. Grove. 1st. F/NF. B2. $30.00.

BRECKINRIDGE, S.P. *New Homes for Old.* 1921. Harper. 1st. photos. xl. VG. A25. $25.00.

BREDES, Don. *Muldoon.* 1982. Holt. 1st. F/F. M25. $15.00.

BREEN, Jon L. *Touch of the Past.* 1988. NY. Walker. 1st. sgn. NF/NF. G8. $20.00.

BREEN, Quirinus. *Christianity and Humanism.* 1968. Eerdmans. 283p. VG/VG. B29. $10.50.

BREEN, Richard. *Made for TV.* 1982. NY. Beaufort. 1st. F/F. H11. $20.00.

BREMSER, Ray. *Angel.* 1967. NY. Thompkins Square Press. 1st. NF soiled rear wrp. B2. $35.00.

BRENDEL, Frederick. *Flora Peoriana.* 1887. Peoria. Franks. 89p. cloth. A10. $100.00.

BRENNAN, Carol. *Full Commission.* 1993. Carroll & Graf. 1st. VG+/VG. G8. $12.50.

BRENNAN, Carol. *In the Dark.* 1994. Putnam. 1st. F/NF. G8. $15.00.

BRENNAN, Joseph P. *Chronicles of Lucius Leffing.* 1977. Donald Grant. 1st. F/F. M2. $30.00.

BRENNAN, Joseph P. *Nightmare Need.* 1964. Arkham. 1st. F/NF. M2. $250.00.

BRENNAN, Joseph P. *Stories of Darkness & Dread.* 1973. Arkham. 1st. F/dj. M2. $40.00.

BRENNAN, Joseph Payne & Donald M. Grant. *Act of Providence.* 1979. West Kingston. Donald M. Grant. 1st. VF/VF. T2. $30.00.

BRENNAN, Noel-Anne. *Winter Reckoning.* 1986. Donald Grant. 1st. 1/650. sgn. F/dj. M2. $30.00.

BRENNER, Anita. *Timid Ghost.* 1966. Wm Scott. 1st. inscr w/original drawing Jean Chalot. G+/G. P2. $65.00.

BRENNER, Anita. *Wind That Swept Mexico.* (1971). Austin. TX. new ed. 310p. dj. F3. $30.00.

BRENNER, Gary. *Naked Grape.* 1975. Bobbs Merrill. VG/dj. A16. $8.00.

BRENNERT, Alan. *Her Pilgrim Soul & Other Stories.* 1990. Tor. 1st. VG/VG. P3. $18.00.

BRENT, Madeleine; see O'Donnell, Peter.

BRENT, P. *Charles Darwin: Man of Enlarged Curiosity.* 1981. Harper Row. 1st. 536p. F/dj. D8. $22.00.

BRERETON, F.S. *Great Aeroplane.* nd. Blackie & Son. decor brd. VG. P3. $35.00.

BRESKIN, Adelyn. *Graphic Art of Mary Cassatt.* 1967. 1st. ils. NF/VG+. S13. $40.00.

BRESLER, Fenton. *The Mystery of Georges Simenon: A Biography.* 1983. NY. Beaufort Books. 1st. F/F. T2. $15.00.

BRESLIN, Howard. *Silver Oar.* 1954. Crowell. 1st. VG/VG. P3. $15.00.

BRESLIN, Jimmy. *Sunny Jim: Life of America's Most Beloved Horseman.* 1962. Garden City. Doubleday. 1st. VG/VG. O3. $45.00.

BRESSCIANNI, Loretta. *Original Prints III: New Writings From Scottish Women.* 1989. Edinburgh. Polygon. 1st. 125p. sc. VG+. A25. $15.00.

BRETNOR, Reginald. *Modern Science Fiction.* 1953. Coward McCann. 1st. VG/dj. M2. $15.00.

BRETON, Andre. *Ode to Charles Fourier.* 1970. Cape Goliard/Grossman. 1st. F/NF. B2. $45.00.

BRETT, Bill. *Stolen Steers.* 1977. TX A&M 3rd. sgn. VG/G. A23. $30.00.

BRETT, Leo. *Alien Ones.* 1969. Arcadia. VG/VG. P3. $10.00.

BRETT, Simon. *A Comedian Dies.* (1979). NY. Scribner's. 1st Am ed. F/F. B3. $20.00.

BRETT, Simon. *A Series of Murders.* 1989. NY. Scribners. 1st. F/VF. H11. $25.00.

BRETT, Simon. *Amateur Corpse.* 1978. Scribner. 1st. VG/VG. P3. $20.00.

BRETT, Simon. *An Amateur Corpse.* 1978. NY. Scribners. 1st. Jacket has minor edge wear. F/NF. H11. $30.00.

BRETT, Simon. *Box of Tricks.* 1985. Gollancz. 1st. F/F. P3. $25.00.

BRETT, Simon. *Cast, in Order of Disappearance.* 1975. Scribner. 1st Am ed. sgn. NF/VG+. G8. $35.00.

BRETT, Simon. *Corporate Bodies.* 1992. NY. Scribners. 1st. F/F. H11. $20.00.

BRETT, Simon. *Dead Romantic.* (1986). NY. Scribner's. 1st Am ed. F/F. B3. $20.00.

BRETT, Simon. *Mrs. Pargeter's Package.* 1991. NY. Scribners. 1st. VF/VF. T2. $8.00.

BRETT, Simon. *Not Dead, Only Resting.* (1984). NY. Scribner's. 1st Am ed. F/F. B3. $15.00.

BRETT, Simon. *Singled Out.* (1995). NY. Scribner's. 1st Am ed. F/F. B3. $15.00.

BRETT, Simon. *Situation Tragedy.* (1981). NY. Scribner's. 1st Am ed. F/F. B3. $20.00.

BRETT, Simon. *So Much Blood.* 1976. Scribner. 1st Am. VG/G+. N4. $17.50.

BRETT, Simon. *What Bloody Man Is That.* (1987). NY. Scribner's. 1st Am ed. F/F. B3. $15.00.

BRETT, Simon. *What Bloody Man Is That?* 1987. London. Gollancz. 1st. sgn. F/F. M15. $65.00.

BREUER, W. *Operation Torch: Allied Gamble to Invade North Africa.* 1983. NY. 1st. ils. 272p. VG/VG. S16. $20.00.

BREWER, James D. *No Remorse.* 1997. Walker. 1st. VG/VG. G8. $15.00.

BREWER, Jeutonne. *Anthony Burgess: A Bibliography.* 1980. Metuchen. Scarecrow Press. 1st. foreword by Burgess. VF w/o dj as issued. T2. $20.00.

BREWER, Reginald. *Delightful Diversion.* 1934. Macmillan. rpt. ils. VG/dj. K3. $20.00.

BREWER, Stella. *Chimps of Mt Asserik.* 1978. NY. ils. 302p. VG/VG. S15. $10.00.

BREWINGTON, M.V. *Chesapeake Bay: Pictorial Maritime History.* 1953. Cambridge, MD. Cornell Maritime. 1st. ils. 229p. dj. $7.00.

BREWSTER, David. *Treatise on Optics.* 1931. London. Longman Gr. new ed. 383p. G. K5. $90.00.

BREYTENBACH, Breyten. *The True Confessions of an Albino Terrorist.* 1984. London. Faber. 1st. F/clip dj. old price sticker on flap. B2. $25.00.

BRIAN, Denis. *Einstein; A Life.* 1996. NY. John Wiley & Sons. 1st pb ed. 8vo. b/w photos. 509p. VG/wrp. K5. $20.00.

BRIANS, Paul. *Nuclear Holocausts: Atomic War in Fiction 1895 – 1984.* 1987. Kent Sate. 1st. F/dj. M2. $30.00.

BRICE, Marshall M. *Stonewall Brigade Band.* 1967. McClure. 213p. VG. B10. $40.00.

BRICK, John. *Raid.* 1960. DSP. 184p. xl. VG. B36. $7.00.

BRICKDALE, Eleanor Fortescue. *Sweet & Touching Tale of Fleur & Blanchefleur.* 1922. London. 1st thus. 4to. VG. M5. $65.00.

BRICKHILL, Paul. *Dam Busters.* 1951. London. Evans. 1st. F/F clip. B4. $175.00.

BRICKMAN, Richard P. *Bringing Down the House.* 1972. Scribner. 1st. F/NF. H11. $25.00.

BRIDGE, Ann. *Numbered Account.* 1960. NY. McGraw Hill. 1st. G/G. G8. $10.00.

BRIDGEMAN, P.H. *Tree Surgery.* 1979. Pomfret. VT. photos/diagrams. 144p. VG/dj. B26. $22.50.

BRIDGES, Ann. *Alphonse Mucha: Complete Graphic Works.* 1980. 1st. 4to. 163 pl. 192p. F/NF. A4. $85.00.

BRIDGES, Robert. *Testament of Beauty.* 1930. 1st Am. NF. M19. $25.00.

BRIDGMAN, L. J. *Guess.* 1901. Caldwell. ils Bridgman. 4to. G+. P2. $125.00.

BRIDGMAN, L. J. *Mother Wild Goose and Her Wild Beast Show, Verse and Pictures by….* 1904. Boston. H. M. Caldwell Co. 1st. sm 4to. ils by author. 106p. G+. D6. $175.00.

BRIGGS, Asa. *Haut-Brion: An Illustrious Lineage.* 1994. London. Faber. 1st sc ed. front wrp creased. VG. A28. $7.95.

BRIGGS, Barbara. *Licorice.* 1949. Aladdin. NY. pre ISBN ed. sm 4to. pict brd. C8. $20.00.

BRIGGS, Charles A. *The Study of the Holy Scriptures.* 1970. Baker. 688p. VG. B29. $14.00.

BRIGGS, Joe Bob. *Cosmic Wisdom of Joe Bob Briggs.* 1990. Random. 1st. F/F. H11. $25.00.

BRIGGS, Kenneth A. *Holy Siege: Year That Shook Catholic America.* 1992. Harper Collins. 1st. photos. F/dj. A2. $13.00.

BRIGGS, Peter. *200,000,000 Years Beneath The Sea.* 1972. HRW. 2nd. 8vo. 227p. gr cloth. P4. $25.00.

BRIGGS, Philip. *Escape from Gravity.* 1955. Lutterworth. 1st. VG/VG. P3. $15.00.

BRIGGS, Raymond. *Father Christmas.* 1973. CMG. 1st Am. sq 4to. F/NF. P2. $40.00.

BRIGGS, Raymond. *Father Christmas.* 1973. London. Hamish Hamilton. 1st. F/F. C8. $55.00.

BRIGHT, Robert. *Georgie's Halloween.* (1958). Doubleday. 10th. unp. pict brd. VG/dj. T5. $40.00.

BRIGHT-HOLMES, John. *Lords & Commons.* 1988. Deutsch. 1st. F/F. P8. $15.00.

BRILL, Toni. *Date With a Dead Doctor.* 1991. St Martin. 1st Am. NF/VG. G8. $12.50.

BRIN, David. *Glory Season.* 1993. NY. Bantam. 1st. sgn. VF/VF. T2. $35.00.

BRIN, David. *The Postman.* 1985. NY. Bantam. 1st. sgn. F/NF. O11. $30.00.

BRINE, Mary D. *Happy Little People.* 1898. Lee Shepard. ils Paul King. 4to. VG. M5. $120.00.

BRINK, Andre. *Act of Terror.* 1991. Summit. 1st. F/F. P3. $25.00.

BRINK, Carol. *Andy Buckram's Tin Men.* 1966. Viking. 1st. 8vo. 192p. xl. G. T5. $20.00.

BRINK, Carol. *Lad With a Whistle.* 1941. Macmillan. 1st. ils Robert Ball. 235p. VG+/VG. P2. $40.00.

BRINKLEY, Frank. *Japan & China.* 1901-1902. Boston. Author's ed. 12 vol. 1/1000. tall 8vo. ils. teg.

BRINKLEY, William. *Ninety & Nine.* 1966. Doubleday. 1st. VG/dj. T11. $20.00.

BRINTON, Henry. *Apprentice to Fear.* 1959. NY. Macmillan. 1st Am ed. VG/VG. G8. $10.00.

BRINTON, Henry. *Coppers and Gold.* 1957. NY. Macmillan. 1st. VG/G. G8. $12.50.

BRION, Patrick. *Tex Avery.* 1986. Schuler. Herrsching. German text. ils/fld drawing. NF/dj. C9. $150.00.

BRISCO, Paula. *Asthma Questions You Have, Answers You Need.* 1994. People's Medical Society. 1st prt. sc. F. F6. $3.00.

BRISCOE, Connie. *A Long Way from Home.* 1999. NY. Harper Collins. ARC. wrps. F in presentation slipcase w/photos printed on inside front cover. B2. $40.00.

BRISCOE, Connie. *Sisters & Lovers.* 1994. NY. Harper Collins. ARC. F. M19. $25.00.

BRISCOE, D. Stuart. *Taking God Seriously; Major Lessons from the Minor Prophets.* 1986. word. 190p. VG. B29. $5.50.

BRISTER, Bob. *Shotgunning: The Art & the Science.* 1977. Winchester. 3rd. 321p. F/dj. A17. $15.00.

BRISTOL, Margaret Cochran. *Handbook of Social Case Recording.* 1937. Chicago. 2nd. 219p. VG. A25. $15.00.

BRISTOL, Roger P. *Supplement to Charles Evans' American Bibliography.* 1970. Charlottesville. 1st. AN. F1. $50.00.

BRISTOW, Gwen. *Tomorrow Is Forever.* 1944. Consolidated Book Pub. BC. NF/dj. M25. $45.00.

BRISTOWE, John. *Diseases of the Intestines & Peritoneum.* 1879. NY. 1st Am. 243p. A13. $25.00.

BRITE, Poppy Z. *Lost Souls.* 1992. Delacorte. 1st. author's 1st novel. F/F. M21. $30.00.

BRITE, Poppy Z. *The Seed of Lost Souls.* 1999. Burton. Subterranean Press. 1st. sgn. 1/500 # copies. VF/pict wrp. T2. $15.00.

BRITO, Silvester J. *Man of a Rainbow.* 1983. Marvin. Bl Cloud Quarterly. F/wrp. L3. $45.00.

BRNLOW, W. G. *Sketches of the Rise, Progress, and Decline of Secession; With a Narrative of Personal Adventures Among the Rebels.* Philadelphia. George W. Childs. 1862. 12mo. 458p. & ads. frontis. ils. gr cloth. 1st ed. scattered lt foxing. VG. L5. $25.00.

BROAD, Robin. *Unequal Alliance.* 1988. Berkeley. Univ of California Press. 1st prt. tables. charts. 352p. F/F. P1. $15.00.

BROADFOOT, Barry. *Ten Lost Years 1929 – 1939: Memories of Canadians Who Survived the Depression.* 1973. Toronto. Doubleday. 1st. owner's stamp on title p. F/VG dj. A26. $17.00.

BROADUS, John A. *On the Preparation & Delivery of Sermons.* 1944. Harper. new/revised by Weatherspoon. 392p. VG. B29. $8.00.

BROCK, Darryl. *If I Never Get Back.* 1990. NY. Crown. 1st. F/F. H11. $25.00.

BROCK, Edwin. *Invisibility Is the Art of Survival.* 1972. New Directions. 1st. F/NF. V1. $15.00.

BROCK, Emma L. *Plug-Horse Derby.* 1955. Knopf. 1st. VG/G. O3. $20.00.

BROCK, H. I. *Colonial Churches in Virginia.* 1972. Port Washington. 4to. 39 photos. 95p. NF. M4. $25.00.

BROCK, Rose; see Hansen, Joseph.

BROCK, Stuart. *Just Around the Coroner.* 1948. Mill. 1st. VG/VG. G8. $25.00.

BROCKETT, I. P. *Men of Our Day.* 1972. ils. VG. M17. $35.00.

BROCKLESBY, John. *Elements of Meteorology.* 1849. NY. Pratt Woodford. revised/stereotyped ed. ils. 8vo. 240p. K3. $65.00.

BRODEUR, Paul. *The Stunt Man.* 1970. NY. Atheneum. 1st. F/NF. H11. $35.00.

BRODIE, F. M. *Devil Drives: Life of Sir Richard Burton.* 1967. NY. photos/maps. VG/fair. M4. $25.00.

BRODIE, Fawn M. *Richard Nixon: The Shaping of His Character.* 1981. Norton. 1st. 574p. VG/dj. V3. $12.50.

BRODIE, Fawn M. *Thomas Jefferson An Intimate History.* 1981. NY. Bantam. 9th prt. sc. VG. F6. $2.00.

BRODSKY, Joseph. *Less Than One.* Selected Essays. 1986. FSG. 1st. F/F. D10. $45.00.

BRODSKY & WEISS. *Cleopatra Papers: A Private Correspondence.* 1963. S&S. 1st. VG/dj. C9. $25.00.

BRODY, J. J. *Anasazi & Pueblo Painting.* 1991. NM U. 1st. 191p. F/dj. A17. $25.00.

BROGAN, James; See Hodder-Williams, C.

BROHL, Ted. *In a Fine Frenzy Rolling.* 1992. Vantage. 1st. sgn. F/F. P3. $20.00.

BROKERING & BAINTON. *A Pilgrimage to Luther's Germany.* 1983. Winston. 75p. VG/torn dj. B29. $9.50.

BROMFIELD, Louis. *Few Brass Tacks.* 1946. Harper. 1st. 303p. VG/dj. M20. $25.00.

BROMFIELD, Louis. *Strange Case of Miss Annie Spragg.* 1928. Stokes. 1st. G. P3. $25.00.

BROMFIELD, Louis. *Twenty-Four Hours.* 1930. Grosset Dunlap. 5th prt. inscr. NF. T12. $20.00.

BROMMEL, Bernard. *Eugene V Debs: Spokesman for Labor & Socialism.* 1978. Chicago. Kerr. 1st. sgn. F/F. B2. $35.00.

BRONK, William. *Life Supports.* 1981. Northpoint. 1st. F/dj. V1. $40.00.

BRONTE, Charlotte. *Jane Eyre.* 1922. NY. Dutton. 1st ed thus. ils by Edmund Dulac. 8vo. gr cloth w/ gilt. 457p. VG. spine ends bent but not chipped. D6. $45.00.

BRONTE, Charlotte. *Shirley in 2 Volumes.* 1905. NY. Dutton. 1st ed thus. ils by Edmund Dulac. 363p/352p. NF/NF. D6. $100.00.

BRONTE, Charlotte. *Villette in 2 Volumes.* 1905. NY. Dutton. 1st ed thus. ils by Edmund Dulac. 327p/322p. VG/VG. D6. $100.00.

BRONTE, Emily. *Wuthering Heights.* 1905. NY. Dutton. 1st ed thus. ils by Edmund Dulac. 371p. G+. D6. $100.00.

BROOKE, L. Leslie. *The Golden Goose and Other Favorites.* nd. NY. Avenel Books. F in F dj. A16. $12.00.

BROOKES, Owen. *Deadly Communion.* 1984. NY. HRW. 1st. F/F. T2. $5.00.

BROOKNER, Anita. *The Misalliance.* 1986. NY. Pantheon. 1st. F/F. H11. $40.00.

BROOKS, Amy. *Randy's Good Times (#5).* 1904. Lee Shepard. 265p. VG. M20. $25.00.

BROOKS, Charles H. *Official History of the First African Baptist Church.* 1922. Phil. self pub. 1st. photos. 167p. VG. B4. $350.00.

BROOKS, Elisha. *Pioneer Mother in California: Written for His Grandchildren.* 1922. SF. Harr Wagner. 2nd. 8vo. gr buckram. VG. R3. $60.00.

BROOKS, Gwendolyn. *Street in Bronzville.* 1945. Harper. 1st. F/F. B4. $550.00.

BROOKS, Gwendolyn. *The World of Gwendolyn Brooks.* 1971. Harper & Row. 1st. 5 vols. Jacket Is browned at the spine. F/dj. M25. $50.00.

BROOKS, John. *Small Garden.* 1978. Macmillan. 1st Am. 256p. dj. A10. $28.00.

BROOKS, Juanita. *Mountain Meadows Massacre.* 1962 (1950). Norman. rpt. 318p. VG. F7. $35.00.

BROOKS, Patricia. *Meals That Can Wait.* 1970. Gramercy. G/dj. A16. $10.00.

BROOKS, Richard. *Brick Foxhole.* 1946. NY. 238p. VG. S16. $30.00.

BROOKS, Terry. *Hook.* 1992. NY. Fawcett. 1st. F/F. H11. $25.00.

BROOKS, Terry. *Wizard at Large.* 1988. Ballantine. 1st. sgn. F/NF. B3. $35.00.

BROOKS, Walter R. *Freddy Goes to the North Pole.* 1951 (1930). Knopf. 8th. lg 12mo. NF/VG+. C8. $100.00.

BROOKS, Walter R. *Freddy the Cowboy.* 1952 (1950). Knopf. 2nd. 12mo. xl. G. C8. $35.00.

BROOKS, Walter R. *Wiggins for President.* 1939. Knopf. 1st. ils Kurt Weise. VG+/dj. D8. $150.00.

BROOM, Winston. *Gone the Sun.* 1988. Doubleday. 1st. F/F. M19. $25.00.

BROOMALL, Wick. *Biblical Criticism.* 1957. Zondervan. 320p. G/G. B29. $10.00.

BROOME, Errol. *Tangles.* 1994. NY. Knopf. Borzoi Book. 1st Am ed. ils Ann James. NF/NF. A28. $6.95.

BROPHY, Brigid. *Flesh.* 1963. Cleveland. World. 1st Am ed. F/very lightly used dj. B2. $25.00.

BROSNAN, Jim. *Long Season.* 1960. Harper. 1st. F/G. B4. $75.00.

BROSNAN, John. *The Sky Lords.* 1988. London. Gollancz. 1st. VF/VF. T2. $30.00.

BROSNAN, John. *War of the Sky Lords.* 1989. Gollancz. 1st. NF/NF. P3. $20.00.

BROUGHTON, James. *A Long Undressing: Collected Poems 1949 – 1969.* 1971. NY. The Jargon Society. 1st. inscr by author. NF w/some darkening to spine. O11. $45.00.

BROUMAS, Olga. *Soie Sauvage.* 1979. Port Townsend. Copper Canyon. 1st. inscr by author. F in wrp. B2. $40.00.

BROUN, Heywood. *It Seems to Me: 1925 – 1935.* 1935. NY. Harcourt. 1st. 335p. F/partial dj. B14. $45.00.

BROWER, Brock. *Late Great Creature.* 1972. Atheneum. 1st. VG/dj. M2. $25.00.

BROWER, Kenneth. *Starship & the Canoe.* 1978. HRW. 1st. 8vo. 270p. VG/dj. K3. $15.00.

BROWN, Alan. *Audrey Hepburn's Neck.* 1996. NY. Pocket. 1st. F/VF. H11. $30.00.

BROWN, Alec. *Angelo's Moon.* 1955. London. 1st. F/dj. M2. $22.00.

BROWN, Arthur. *Footprints of God.* 1943. Fundamental Truth. 246p. VG. B29. $8.00.

BROWN, Beth. *Universal Station.* 1944. Regent. 1st. NF/dj. M2. $27.00.

BROWN, CAROTHERS & JOHNSON. *Grand Canyon Birds.* 1987. Tucson. 8vo. 302p. orange cloth. F/dj. F7. $22.00.

BROWN, Carrie. *Lamb in Love.* 1999. Chapel Hill. Algonquin. sgn. 1st ed. F/F. M23. $25.00.

BROWN, Clair A. *Louisiana Trees and Shrubs.* 1945. Baton Rouge. 262p w/147 figures. wrp. B26. $20.00.

BROWN, Claude. *Manchild in the Promised Land.* 1965. Macmillan. later printing. NF/dj sunned at spine. M25. $25.00.

BROWN, Dale. *Flight of the Old Dog.* 1987. np. 1st. author's 1st novel. F/F. N4. $40.00.

BROWN, Dale. *Hammerheads.* 1990. 1st. NF/F. N4. $25.00.

BROWN, Dee. *Bury My Heart at Wounded Knee.* 1970. Barrie Jenkins. 1st. map/photos. VG/dj. J2. $125.00.

BROWN, Dee. *Conspiracy of Knaves.* 1987. Holt. 1st. F/F. B3. $20.00.

BROWN, Dee. *Fetterman Massacre.* 1972. Barrie Jenkins. 1st. F/F. P3. $20.00.

BROWN, Dee. *Killdeer Mountain.* (1983). NY. HRW. 1st. minor bump to one corner. corresponding crease. F/F. B3. $15.00.

BROWN, Douglas; See Gibson, Walter B.

BROWN, Douglas Summers. *Historical & Biographical Sketches of Greensville...* 1968. Riparian Woman's Club. 2nd. ils. 439p. VG/dj. B10. $50.00.

BROWN, Eric. *The Time Lapsed Man and Other Stories.* 1990. Birmingham, England. Drunken Dragon Press. 1st hc ed. author's 1st book. VF/VF. T2. $30.00.

BROWN, Ernest W. *Theory of the Motion of the Moon.* 1908. London. Royal Astronomical Society. 4to. spine browned. lt foxing to fore edge. 103p. G in wrp. K5. $90.00.

BROWN, F. Martin. *America's Yesterday.* 1937. Philadelphia. Lippincott. 1st. 319p. G. F3. $15.00.

BROWN, Frank E. *Roman Architecuture.* 1961. Brazillier. 1st. 125p. VG/VG. A8. $12.00.

BROWN, Frederic. *And the Gods Laughed.* 1987. West Bloomfield. Phantasia. 1st. 1/475 sgn. VF/dj w/slipcase. M15. $165.00.

BROWN, Fredric. *Compliments of a Friend.* 1950. Dutton. 1st. NF/VG. Q1. $250.00.

BROWN, Fredric. *Dead Ringer.* 1948. Dutton. 1st. VG/poor. H11. $135.00.

BROWN, Fredric. *Rogue in Space.* 1957. Dutton. 1st. F/dj. M2. $400.00.

BROWN, Fredric. *Space on My Hands.* 1951. Shasta. 1st. VG/dj. M2. $100.00.

BROWN, Fredric. *The Screaming Mimi.* 1949. Dutton. 1st. 12mo. yel prt brd. dj. T10. $275.00.

BROWN, Frederic. *The Screaming Mimi.* 1949. NY. Dutton. 1st. F/dj. M15. $400.00.

BROWN, Fredric. *What Mad Universe.* 1978. Pennyfarthing. 1st thus. F/dj. M2. $30.00.

BROWN, Geoff. *I Want What I Want.* 1967. Putnam. 1st Am. F/F. B4. $85.00.

BROWN, George T. *Fragments of Life.* 1946. Batavia. Clarmont. 1st. gilt ribbed cloth. F. B4. $275.00.

BROWN, Gerald A. *Hazard.* 1973. Arbor. VG/VG. P3. $13.00.

BROWN, J.R. *Unusual Plants: 110 Spectacular Photographs of Succulents.* 1954. Pasadena. 110 full-p photos. 230p. decor cloth. VG. B26. $40.00.

BROWN, Jimmy. *Off My Chest.* 1964. Garden City. 1st. sgn pres. VG/VG. A4. $50.00.

BROWN, John K. *Baldwin Locomotive Works.* 1995. Johns Hopkins. 1st. 8vo. 328p. F/dj. T10. $45.00.

BROWN, Joseph Epes. *Sacred Pipe.* 1953. Norman. OK. 1st. F/VG. L3. $450.00.

BROWN, Kay. *Willy's Summer Dream.* 1989. NY. H B J. Gulliver Books. 1st. NF/NF. A28. $7.95.

BROWN, Larry. *Big Bad Love.* (1989). Chapel Hill. Algonquin. 1st. VF/VF. B3. $30.00.

BROWN, Larry. *Dirty Work.* (1989). Chapel Hill. Algonquin. 1st. author's 1st novel. sgn by author. VF/VF. B3. $35.00.

BROWN, Larry. *Father and Son.* 1996. Chapel Hill. Algonquin Books. 1st. VF/VF. T2. $20.00.

BROWN, Larry. *Joe.* (1991). Chapel Hill. Algonquin. 1st. VF/VF. B3. $40.00.

BROWN, Lloyd A. *The Story of Maps.* 1949. Boston. Little, Brn. 1st. green pict cloth. 397p. VG. B14. $125.00.

BROWN, M.L. *Firearms in Colonial America: Impact on History...1492 – 1792.* 1980. WA. 1st. ils. 448p. F/dj. M4. $40.00.

BROWN, M.L.T. *Gems for the Taking.* 1971. Macmillan. 193p. VG/dj. D8. $12.00.

BROWN, Marcia. *Felice.* 1958. Scribner. 1st. 4to. NF/G+. P2. $65.00.

BROWN, Margaret Wise. *Big Dog Little Dog.* 1943. Doubleday Doran. early prt. sq 4to. VG/G-. P2. $40.00.

BROWN, Margaret Wise. *Golden Egg Book.* 1975. NY. Golden. rpt. ils Leonard Weisgard. glazed brd. C14. $14.00.

BROWN, Margaret Wise. *Nibble Nibble: Poems for Children.* 1959. Young Scott. 1st. ils Leonard Weisgard. F. M5. $70.00.

BROWN, Margaret Wise. *Red Light Green Light.* 1944. Doubleday Doran. 1st thus. ils Leonard Weisgard. F/G. P2. $110.00.

BROWN, Margaret Wise. *The Little Cowboy.* 1948. NY. William R. Scott. sm 4to. ils by Esphyr Slobodkina. color ils brds. 36p. VG/VG+. D6. $50.00.

BROWN, Mark. *Yellowfin.* 1992. Ox bow. 1st. F/F. G8. $10.00.

BROWN, Mary. *The Unlikely Ones.* 1986. NY. McGraw. 1st. F/F. H11. $20.00.

BROWN, Michael. *Santa Mouse.* 1968. NY. ils Elfrieda DeWitt. VG. M5. $15.00.

BROWN, Michael. *Tsewa's Gift. Magic and Meaning in an Amazonian Society.* 1985. DC. Smithsonian Institution Press. 1st. 220p. G/G. F3. $25.00.

BROWN, Milton W. *Story of the Armory Show.* 1963. NY. Joseph Hirschhorn Found. 1st. F/clip. Q1. $75.00.

BROWN, Norman O. *Love's Body.* 1966. Random. 1st. F/F. B4. $85.00.

BROWN, Palmer. *Hickory.* 1978. Harper Row. 1st. 42p. VG/VG. P2. $40.00.

BROWN, Paul. *Insignia of the Services.* 1941. Scribner. 1st Am. G. O3. $40.00.

BROWN, Philip. *Return of the Osprey.* 1962. London. 223p. VG. S15. $15.00.

BROWN, Riley. *Men, Wind & Sea.* 1939. NY. Carlyle. 1st. ils. 266p. T7. $35.00.

BROWN, Rita Mae. *Bingo.* 1988. Bantam. 1st. sgn. F/F. B3. $35.00.

BROWN, Rita Mae. *Murder at Monticello.* 1994. NY. Bantam. 1st. F/F. A24. $15.00.

BROWN, Rita Mae. *Rest in Pieces.* 1992. NY. Bantam. 1st. NF/NF. A24. $20.00.

BROWN, Rita Mae. *Six of One.* (1978). NY. Harper & Row. 1st. F/NF lt edgewear. closed tear near front panel. B3. $75.00.

BROWN, Rita Mae. *Sudden Death.* 1983. NY. Bantam. 1st. F/NF. price clip. minor wear. A24. $25.00.

BROWN, Rita Mae. *Wish You Were Here.* 1990. NY. Bantam. 1st. F/F. A24. $30.00.

BROWN, Rosellen. *Autobiography of My Mother.* 1976. Doubleday. 1st. F/NF. M25. $35.00.

BROWN, Rosellen. *Before and After.* 1992. NY. F S G. 1st. F/F. H11. $25.00.

BROWN, Rosellen. *Cora Fry.* 1977. Norton. 1st. F/F. M19. $25.00.

BROWN, Sterling, ed. *The Negro Caravan.* nd. NY. Citadel. reprint of the Dryden Press ed. F. B2. $60.00.

BROWN, William A. *Christian Hope.* 1912. Scribner. 216p. VG. B29. $8.50.

BROWN, William Moseley. *Freemasonry in Winchester.* VA. 1949. McClure. sgn. 284p. B11. $50.00.

BROWN, William Robinson. *Last Crusade: A Negotiator's Middle East Handbook.* 1980. Chicago. Nelson Hall. 399p. VG/wrp. W1. $10.00.

BROWN, William Robinson. *Horse of the Desert.* 1967. Springville. J Shuler. Deluxe/ltd. ils/photos/maps. 295p. VG+. M12. $95.00.

BROWN, William Robinson. *The Horse of the Desert.* 1929. NY. Derrydale Press. 4to. VG. O3. $325.00.

BROWN, William W. *Narrative Of... A Fugitive Slave. Written by Himself.* 1847. Boston. Anti-Slavery Office. 1st. 12mo. 110p.

BROWN & MIERS, Gettysburg. *1948.* New Brunswick. ils/maps. 308p. G+/dj. B18. $17.50.

BROWNE, Arline M. *In the Wake of the Topinabee.* 1967. Hubbard Map Service. sgn. 139p. VG+/dj. M20. $22.00.

BROWNE, Belmore. *Frozen Barrier: Story Of...Behring Sea.* 1921. NY. Putnam. 5th imp. 267p. bl cloth. VG/worn. P4. $40.00.

BROWNE, Borden P. *Introduction to Psychological Theory.* 1886. NY. Harper. 329p. gilt bl cloth. F. B14. $75.00.

BROWNE, Gerald A. *19 Purchase Street.* 1982. NY. Arbor House. 1st. F/F. H11. $15.00.

BROWNE, Harold. *Return of Tharn.* 1956. Donald Grant. 1st. sgn. F/VG. M2. $150.00.

BROWNE, Howard. *Incredible Ink.* 1997. Tucson. Dennis McMillan. 1st. sgn 1/350. VF/dj w/slipcase. M15. $85.00.

BROWNE, Howard. *Murder Wears a Halo.* 1997. Brooklyn. Gryphon books. 1st. 1/100 # copies. sgn by author. artist Ron Turner. introducer Robert Barrett. VF in pict wrp & dj. T2. $40.00.

BROWNE, Howard. *Scotch on the Rocks.* 1991. NY. St. Martin. 1st. sgn. VF/dj. M15. $60.00.

BROWNE, Howard. *Warrior of the Dawn.* 1943. Reilly Lee. 1st. NF/dj. M2. $125.00.

BROWNE, Lewis. *The Wisdom of Israel.* 1945. Modern Library. 748p. VG/VG. B29. $13.50.

BROWNE, Thomas. *Religio Medici.* 1939. Eugene. LEC. 1/1500. sgn/#d. 113p. B11. $65.00.

BROWNELL, Charles De Wolf. *Indian Races of North & South America.* 1853. Boston. Horace Westworth. 40 hand-colored pl. 640p. gilt rebacked calf. K7. $295.00.

BROWNELL, Henry H. *War-Lyrics & Other Poems.* 1866 (1865). Boston. 243p. VG. E6. $25.00.

BROWNING, Elizabeth Barrett. *Essays on the Greek Christian Poets & the English Poets.* 1863. James Miller. 1st Am. VG. M19. $35.00.

BROWNING, Robert. *Letters of Robert Browning to Miss Isa Blagden. Arrranged for Publication by A. Joseph Armstrong.* Waco, TX. Printed in a ltd ed for private distribution at the Baylor University Press. (1923). 8vo. 208p. dark red cloth with gilt lettering on spine. 1st ed (limited). many pages unopened. a sgn or other writing removed from previously blank ffep by cliping. VG. L5. $85.00.

BROWNING, Robert. *Pied Piper of Hamelin.* 1910. Rand McNally. 1st thus. ils Hope Dunlap. tall 4to. VG. M5. $85.00.

BROXON, Mildred Downey. *Too Long a Sacrifice.* 1984. Bluejay. 1/350. sgn/#d. F/case. M2. $75.00.

BROYLES, Frank. *Hogwild.* 1979. Memphis. 1st. sgn. F/G. A23. $40.00.

BRUCCOLI, Matthew J. *James Gould Cozzens. A Descriptive Bibliography.* 1981. Pittsburgh. U of Pittsburgh Press. 1st. bl cloth 8vo. silver gilt spine and cover titles. 193p. VF. P4. $60.00.

BRUCCOLI, Matthew J. *Raymond Chandler: A Checklist.* 1968. Kent State. 1st. 35p. cloth. A17. $15.00.

BRUCE, F.F. *In Retrospect: Remembrance of Things Past.* 1993. Baker. 336p. VG. B29. $10.00.

BRUCE, Jean. *Deep Freeze.* 1963. Cassell. 1st. VG. P3. $12.00.

BRUCE, Lenny. *How to Talk Dirty & Influence People.* 1965. Chicago. Playboy. 1st. VG/dj. B5. $25.00.

BRUCE, Leo. *Case for Sergeant Beef.* 1980. Chicago. Academy Chicago. 1st Am. F/dj. M15. $45.00.

BRUCE, Leo. *Death in Albert Park.* 1979. NY. Scribners. 1st Am. Jacket has slight spine fading. F/dj. M15. $45.00.

BRUCE, Leo. *Our Jubilee Is Death.* 1959. London. Peter Davies. 1st. page edges foxed. Jacket has wear along edges and several short closed tears and nicks at top of spine. VG/dj. M15. $65.00.

BRUCHAC, Joseph. *Ancestry.* 1980. Ft Kent. Great Raven. 1st. sgn. F/stapled vinyl wrp. L3. $65.00.

BRUNDAGE, Burr. *Empire of the Inca.* (1969). Norman. OK. 2nd. 396p. dj. F3. $20.00.

BRUNDAGE, Burr. *Lords of Cuzco.* (1967). Norman. OK. 1st. 458p. dj. F3. $30.00.

BRUNDAGE, Frances. *What Happened to Tommy.* 1921. Rochester, NY. Stecher Lithographic. 4to. mc pict paper wrp. R5. $85.00.

BRUNHOUSE, Robert. *Frans Blom, Maya Explorer.* 1976. Albuquerque. Univ of New Mexico Press. 1st. 291p. G/G. chipped. F3. $30.00.

BRUNHOUSE, Robert. *In Search of the Maya. The First Archaelologists.* 1973. Albuquerque. Univ of New Mexico Press. 1st. 243p. G/G. chipped. F3. $30.00.

BRUNHOUSE, Robert. *Sylvanus G. Morley & the World of the Ancient Maya.* 1971. Norman. Univ of Oklahoma Press. 1st. 353p. VG/wrp. fading. F3. $20.00.

BRUNNER, Emil. *Our Faith.* 1949. Scribners. 244p. VG/VG. B29. $10.00.

BRUNNER, Emil. *The Christian Doctrine of Creation and Redemption.* 1974. Westminster. 386p. VG/VG. ex lib. B29. $14.50.

BRUNNER, John. *Long Result.* 1965. Faber. 1st. VG/VG. P3. $30.00.

BRUNNER, John. *Quicksand.* 1967. Doubleday. 1st. xl. VG/VG. P3. $8.00.

BRUNNER, John. *Times Without Number.* 1974. Elmfield. VG/VG. P3. $20.00.

BRUNNER, John. *Timescoop.* 1972. London. Sidgwick Jackson. 1st hc. F/clip. T2. $35.00.

BRUNNER, John. *Total Eclipse.* 1974. Doubleday. 1st. F/F. M2. $15.00.

BRUNNER, John. *Whole Man.* 1964. Walker. 1st. F/F. P3. $20.00.

BRUNNER, Robert K. *Shocking Tales.* 1946. Wynn. 1st. VG. M2. $20.00.

BRUNO, Anthony. *Bad Apple.* 1994. NY. Delacorte. 1st. sgn. F/NF. G8. $30.00.

BRUNO, Anthony. *Bad Business.* 1991. NY. Delacorte. 1st. F/F. H11. $25.00.

BRUNO, Anthony. *Bad Moon.* 1992. NY. Delacorte. 1st. sgn. NF/NF. G8. $20.00.

BRUNO, Anthony. *Devil's Food.* 1997. NY. Delacorte. 1st. F/NF. G8. $15.00.

BRUNTON, Paul. *Hidden Teaching Beyond Yoga.* 1946. Dutton. revised. 431p. VG/dj. W3. $42.00.

BRUNTON, Paul. *Quest of the Overself.* 1953. NY. 304p. F/dj. W3. $40.00.

BRUNTON, Paul. *Search in Secret Egypt.* 1953. Dutton. 5th. 287p. VG. W3. $42.00.

BRUSH, D.H. *Growing Up in Southern Illinois 1820 to 1861.* 1944. Lakeside Classic. 265p. F. M4. $10.00.

BRUSH, Peter. *The Hunter Chaser.* 1948. London. Hutchinson. G. O3. $15.00.

BRUST, Stephen. *To Reign in Hell.* 1984. Steeldragon. 1/1000. sgn/#d. F/dj. M2. $25.00.

BRUTON, Eric. *Dictionary of Clocks & Watches.* 1963. Archer. ils. 201p. VG/dj. K3. $22.00.

BRYAN, C.D.B. *PS Wilkinson.* 1965. Harper Row. 1st. sgn. NF/VG. R14. $60.00.

BRYAN, Christopher. *Night of the Wolf.* 1983. Harper Row. 1st. VG/VG. P3. $15.00.

BRYAN, Kirk. *Routes to Desert Watering Places in the Papago Country.* 1922. GPO 1st ed. glossary. notes. folding maps. ils. 126p. spine Is tape reinforced else. NF. B19. $75.00.

BRYAN, William Jennings. *The Prince of Peace.* 1914. np. Funk & Wagnalls. 1st. prev owner stp. NF. M19. $45.00.

BRYANT, Anita. *Bless This Food: The Anita Bryant Family Cookbook.* 1975. Doubleday. 1st. dj. A16. $15.00.

BRYANT, Edward. *Among the Dead.* 1973. Macmillan. 1st. F/dj. M2. $27.00.

BRYANT, Edward. *Neon Twilight, Author's Choice Monthly Issue 7.* (1990). Eugene. Pulphouse. 1st. sgn by author. F/F. B3. $60.00.

BRYANT, Marguerite. *Heights.* 1924. Duffield. F. P3. $8.00.

BRYANT, Sara Cone. *Epaminodas & His Auntie.* 1938 (1907). ils Inez Hogan. F/NF. C8. $150.00.

BRYANT, Will. *Escape from Sonora.* 1973. NY. Random. 1st. Book has light shelf wear and a minor binding flaw on rear paste-down. F/F. H11. $30.00.

BRYANT, William Cullen. *Odyssey of Homer.* 1873. Boston. 2 vol. 12mo. half brn leather/marbled brd. VG. H3. $75.00.

BUBER, Martin. *Tales of Rabbi Nachman.* 1956. Horizon. 214p. VG/G. S3. $23.00.

BUCHAN, James. *Golden Plough.* 1995. FSG. 1st Am. F/F. B4. $45.00.

BUCHAN, John. *Far Islands.* 1984. Donald Grant. 1st. F/dj. M2. $17.00.

BUCHAN, John. *John Buchan by His Wife & Friends.* 1947. Hodder Stoughton. 1st. VG/G. P3. $30.00.

BUCHAN, John. *Memory Hold the Door.* 1940. Musson. 1st. VG. P3. $30.00.

BUCHAN, John. *Sick Heart River.* 1941. Musson. 1st. VG. P3. $20.00.

BUCHANAN, Edna. *Miami, It's Murder.* 1994. NY. Hyperion. 1st. VF/VF. T2. $11.00.

BUCHANAN, Edna. *Nobody Lives Forever.* 1990. Random. 1st. VG/VG. P3. $18.00.

BUCHANAN, Edna. *The Corpse Had a Familiar Face.* 1987. NY. Random. 1st. Inscribed on front fep. F/F. H11. $45.00.

BUCHANAN, Hayle. *Living Color.* 1979 (1974). Bryce Canyon, UT. 2nd. ils/125 mc photos. 65p. wrp. B26. $14.00.

BUCHANAN, Marie. *Morgana.* 1977. Doubleday. 1st. VG/VG. P3. $15.00.

BUCHER, Elmer E. *Practical Wireless Telegraphy.* 1918 (1917). NY. Wireless Pr. revised. 8vo. 336p. G. K5. $45.00.

BUCHHEIM, Lothar-Gunther. *The Boat.* 1975. NY. Knopf. 1st. F/NF. H11. $50.00.

BUCHNER, Alexander. *Mechanical Musical Instruments.* nd. London. Batchworth. 174p of pl. VG/dj. K3. $90.00.

BUCHSBAUM, Tony. *Total Eclipse.* 1988. NY. Doubleday. 1st. F/F. H11. $25.00.

BUCK, Margaret Waring. *Where They Go in Winter.* 1968. ils. VG/VG. M17. $17.50.

BUCK, Pearl S. *All Men are Brothers.* 1957. Grove. corrected/amended ed. 2 vol. 1279p. F/NF/box. W3. $65.00.

BUCK, Pearl S. *All Under Heaven.* 1973. John Day. 1/1000 special bdg. facsimile sgn. VG/dj. W3. $42.00.

BUCK, Pearl S. *East Wind, West Wind.* 1944. Cleveland/NY. World. 277p. dj. W3. $20.00.

BUCK, Pearl S. *Letter from Peking.* 1957. John Day. 1st. NF/VG. M19. $25.00.

BUCK, Pearl S. *Patriot.* 1939. NY. 1st. 372p. VG/dj. W3. $36.00.

BUCK, William J. *History of the Indian Walk.* 1886. Phil. 1st. 1/210. xl. B18. $125.00.

BUCKINGHAM, Bruce. *Boiled Alive.* 1957. Michael Joseph. 1st. VG/VG. P3. $30.00.

BUCKINGHAM, Nash. *Blood Lines: Tales of Shooting & Fishing.* (1947). Putnam. 1st trade. 192p. VG. H7. $35.00.

BUCKINGHAM, Nash. *Ole Miss.* (1946). Putnam. 1st trade. 178p. VG/damaged. H7. $45.00.

BUCKLEY, Arabella B. *Fairy-Land of Science.* ca 1900. NY. AL Burt. 1st thus. ils. 298p. VG. A25. $20.00.

BUCKLEY, Christopher. *Sycamore Canyon Nocturne.* nd. Greenhouse Review Press. ltd 1/90. F. V1. $55.00.

BUCKLEY, Cornelius M. *Nicolas Point...Life & Northwest Indian Chronicles.* 1989. Loyola. 520p. F/dj. A17. $22.50.

BUCKLEY, Fiona. *To Shield the Queen.* 1997. NY. Scribner. 1st. F/F. G8. $25.00.

BUCKLEY, William F. *Saving the Queen.* 1976. Doubleday. 1st. VG/VG. P3. $13.00.

BUCKLEY, William F. *Stained Glass.* 1978. Doubleday. 1st. F/dj. T10. $45.00.

BUCKLEY, William F. *Who's on First.* 1980. Doubleday. 1st. VG/VG. P3. $20.00.

BUCKMASTER, Henrietta. *Women Who Shaped History.* 1966. Collier. 1st thus. 152p. VG/VG. V3. $10.00.

BUCKSTAFF, Kathryn. *No One Dies in Branson.* 1994. St. Martin. 1st. NF/VG. G8. $12.50.

BUDAY, G. *History of the Christmas Card.* 1965. London. ils. 304p. VG. M4. $30.00.

BUDD, Elaine. *13 Mistresses of Murder.* 1986. NY. ungar. 1st. F/F+. H11. $30.00.

BUDNITZ, Judy. *If I Told You Once.* 1999. NY. Picador USA. ARC. F/wrp. B2. $25.00.

BUDRYS, Algis. *Iron Thorn.* 1969. British SF BC. VG/VG. P3. $12.00.

BUECHER, Thomas S. *Norman Rockwell: Artist & Illustrator.* 1970. Abrams. 328p. cloth. VG+/dj. M20. $125.00.

BUECHNER, Frederick. *A Long Day's Dying.* 1949. NY. Knopf. 1st. NF/NF. D10. $55.00.

BUECHNER, Frederick. *Open Heart.* 1972. Atheneum. ARC. RS. F/dj. R13. $40.00.

BUECHNER, Frederick. *Season's Difference.* 1952. Knopf. ARC. F/dj. R13. $85.00.

BUECHNER, Helmut. *Bighorn Sheep in the United States.* 1960. Wildlife Monographs 4. 1974. VG. S15. $15.00.

BUELL, John. *Playground.* 1976. FSG. 1st. VG/VG. P3. $20.00.

BUELL, John. *Shrewsdale Exit.* 1972. FSG. 1st. VG/VG. P3. $23.00.

BUFALINO, Gesualdo. *Lies of the Night.* 1991. NY. Atheneum. 1st. F/VF. H11. $15.00.

BUFF, Mary Marsh. *Dancing Cloud.* 1945. Viking. 3rd prt. ils Conrad Buff. VG/tattered. D1. $32.00.

BUFFA, D.W. *The Defense.* 1997. NY. Holt. 1st. VF/VF. H11. $20.00.

BUFFETT, Jimmy. *Tales from Margaritaville.* 1989. Harcourt Brace. 1st. F/F. B35. $22.00.

BUHLER, W.K. *Gauss: A Biographical Study.* 1987 (1981). Berlin. Springer. corrected 2nd. 8vo. 208p. F. K5. $45.00.

BUIE, Louis. *Practical Proctology.* 1938. Phil. 1st. 512p. A13. $50.00.

BUIST, Robert. *American Flower Garden Directory.* 1845. Phil. Carey Hart. 3rd. 345p. VG. A10. $85.00.

BUIST, Robert. *Family Kitchen Gardener.* 1867 (1847). ils. VG. E6. $50.00.

BUJOLD, Lois McMaster. *Mirror Dance.* 1994. NY. Baen. sgn 1st ed. Hugo award winner. F/F. M23. $60.00.

BUKOWSKI, Charles. *War All the Time.* 1984. Santa Barbara. Blk Sparrow. 1st trade. 1/500. 8vo. F/acetate dj. T10. $100.00.

BUKOWSKI, Charles. *War All the Time. Poems 1981 – 1984.* 1984. Blk Sparrow. 1/400. sgn/#d. F/F. B2. $200.00.

BULFINCH, Thomas. *Age of Fables; Or, Stories of Gods & Heroes.* 1958. LEC. 1st thus. 1/1500. ils/sgn Joe Mugnaini. F/glassine/case. Q1. $100.00.

BULGAKOV, Mikhail. *Master & Margarita.* 1967. Harper Row. 1st. VG/VG. P3. $30.00.

BULKLEY, R.J. *At Close Quarters.* 1962. DC. ils/maps. 573p. VG. S16. $35.00.

BULL, Emma & Will Shetterly. *Double Feature.* 1994. Framingham. NESFA Press. 1st. 1/815 # copies. sgn by both authors. VF/VF. T2. $30.00.

BULLA, Clyde R. *Viking Adventure.* 1963. ils. VG/VG. M17. $15.00.

BULLARD, Arthur. *The Russian Pendulum. Autocracy, Democracy, Bolshivism* (Sic). 1919. NY. Macmillan. NF. B2. $45.00.

BULLEN, K.E. *Introduction to Theory of Seismology.* 1965. Cambridge. 3rd. cloth. F/torn. D8. $22.00.

BULLEN & PROUT. *Yachting: How to Sail & Manage a Small Modern Yacht.* 1930. Glasgow. 2nd. ils. VG. M17. $25.00.

BULLER, Michael. *Winemaker's Year, The: Four Seasons in Bordeaux.* 1991. NY. Thames and Hudson. hb. AN. A28. $21.50.

BULLINS, Ed. *The Reluctant Rapist.* 1973. Harper & Row. 1st. F/dj. M25. $45.00.

BULLOCK, C. Hassell. *An Introduction to the Old Testament Poetic Books.* 1988. Moody. 271p. VG/torn dj. B29. $11.50.

BULLY, PRATT & SMITH. *Yours in Struggle: 3 Feminist Perspectives.* 1984. Brooklyn. Long Haul. 1st. 233p. sc. VG+. A25. $15.00.

BULOW, Ernie. *Sleight of Hand: Conversations with Walter Satterthwait.* 1993. Albuquerque. Univ of Mexico Press. 1st. sgn by Bulow and Satterthwait. VF/VF. T2. $35.00.

BULWER-LYTTON, Edward. *Coming Race.* 1873. Hinton. VG. M2. $30.00.

BULWER-LYTTON, Edward. *New Timon.* 1847. Carey Hart. 2nd Am. spine missing o/w VG. M2. $100.00.

BUNKER, Edward. *Dog Eat Dog.* 1996. NY. St. Martin. 1st. sgn. VF/VF. T2. $35.00.

BUNN, Alfred. *Old England and New England, in a Series of Views Taken on the Spot.* London. Richard Bentley. 1853. 2 volumes. 12mo. 313p. color lithographic frontis. & folding table. 328p. gilt stamped blue cloth. 1st ed. Extremities worn. G to VG. L5. $50.00.

BUNN, Thomas. *Closing Costs.* 1990. Holt. 1st. F/F. P3. $10.00.

BUNTING, Eve. *Yesterday's Island.* 1983. NY. Frederick Warne & Co. ils Stephan Gammell. rem mk. G. no dj. A28. $5.95.

BUPP, Walter; See Garrett, Randall.

BURANELLI, Vincent. *King & the Quaker: Study of William Penn & James II.* 1962. Phil. U PA. 1st. 241p. xl. dj. V3. $11.00.

BURANELLI, Vincent & Nan. *SPY/Counterspy: An Encyclopedia of Espionage.* 1982. NY. McGraw Hill. 1st. Tiny spot on fore edge. F/dj. M15. $50.00.

BURCHAM, L. T. *Observations on the Grass Flora of Certain Pacific Islands.* 1948. Washington. DC. wrp darkened. B26. $9.00.

BURCHARD, Peter. *River Queen.* 1957. Macmillan. 1st. 4op. VG+/G+. C14. $14.00.

BURCK, Jacob. *Hunger & Revolt: Cartoons by Burck.* nd. Daily Worker. 2nd. VG. V4. $75.00.

BURCKHARDT, Jacob. *Civilization of the Renaissance in Italy.* 1944. London. Phaidon. 1st thus. ils. 12mo. 462p. F/dj. $1.00.

BURDEKIN, Kay. *Burning Ring.* 1929. Morrow. 1st Am. VG. M2. $30.00.

BURDETTE, Robert Jones. *Drums of the 47th.* 1914. Bobbs Merrill. 1st. 212p. cloth. NF. M8. $125.00.

BURDITT, Joyce. *Buck Naked.* 1996. NY. Ballantine. 1st. UP. sgn. F/pict wrp. T2. $6.00.

BURFORD, E.J. *In the Clink.* 1977. London. NEL. VG/dj. M11. $65.00.

BURGESS, Alan. *Small Woman.* 1957. Dutton. 1st. photos/2 maps. 256p. VG/dj. W3. $32.00.

BURGESS, Anthony. *Any Old Iron.* 1989. Random. 1st. F/F. B35/P3. $20.00.

BURGESS, Anthony. *Devil's Mode.* 1989. Random. 1st. F/F. B35. $30.00.

BURGESS, Anthony. *Earthly Powers.* 1980. S&S. 1st. F/F. B35. $25.00.

BURGESS, Anthony. *Kingdom of the Wicked.* 1985. Arbor. 1st. NF/NF. W2. $30.00.

BURGESS, Anthony. *Little Wilson & Big God.* 1986. Weidenfeld Nicolson. 1st. VG. P3. $25.00.

BURGESS, Anthony. *Long Trip to Teatime.* 1976. Dempsey & Squires. F/dj. P3. $15.00.

BURGESS, Anthony. *Moses.* 1976. np. Stonehill. 1st. F/F. M19. $17.50.

BURGESS, Anthony. *Pianoplayers.* 1986. Hutchinson. 1st. F/F. P3. $18.00.

BURGESS, Anthony. *Shakespeare.* 1970. np. Knopf. 1st. F/VG dj. M19. $25.00.

BURGESS, Eric. *Outpost on Apollo's Moon.* 1993. NY. Columbia Univ Press. 1st printing. b/w photos & diagrams. 4to. 274p. F/F. K5. $35.00.

BURGESS, Gelett. *Purple Cow & Other Poems.* 1968. Pasadena. Castle. facsimile. 4to. 14p. NF. C14. $10.00.

BURGESS, J. *Rock-Temples of Elephanta or Gharapuri.* 1871. Bombay. DH Skykes. pres. ils/plans. 4to. 80p. K3. $75.00.

BURGESS, Thornton W. *Adventures of Chatterer the Red Squirrel.* 1934. Little, Brn. ils Harrison Cady. sm 8vo. stp gray cloth. F/dj. M5. $40.00.

BURGESS, Thornton W. *Adventures of Peter Cottontail.* 1958. London. MacDonald. ils Phoebe Erickson. 4to. dj. R5. $85.00.

BURGESS, Thornton W. *Adventures of Poor Mrs Quack.* 1917. Little, Brn. 1st. ils Harrison Cady. 12mo. pict cloth. R5. $100.00.

BURGESS, Thornton W. *At the Smiling Pool.* 1945. Little, Brn. stated 1st. ils Harrison Cady. VG/dj. M5. $65.00.

BURGESS, Thornton W. *Aunt Sally's Friends in Fur.* 1955. Little, Brn. stated 1st. F/dj. M5. $65.00.

BURGESS, Thornton W. *Mother West Wind When Stories.* 1937. Little, Brn. ils Harrison Cady. tan cloth. VG. M5. $45.00.

BURGESS, Thornton W. *Tales From the Story Teller's House.* 1937. Little, Brn. ils Lemuel Palmer. 195p. beige cloth. VG. D1. $65.00.

BURGESS, Thornton W. *While the Story-Log Burns.* 1938. Little, Brn. stated 1st. ils Lemuel Palmer. lg 8vo. VG+. M5. $75.00.

BURGIN, Richard. *Conversations With Jorge Luis Borges.* 1969. NY. Holt. 1st. F in NF dj. B2. $40.00.

BURKE, James Lee. *A Morning for Flamingos.* 1990. Boston. Little, Brn. 1st. VF/dj. M15. $135.00.

BURKE, James Lee. *A Stained White Radiance.* 1992. NY. Hyperion. 1st. F/F. H11. $40.00.

BURKE, James Lee. *Black Cherry Blues.* 1989. Boston. Little, Brn. 1st. VF/dj. M15. $145.00.

BURKE, James Lee. *Burning Angel.* 1995. Hyperion. 1st. F/F. G8. $15.00.

BURKE, James Lee. *Cadillac Jukebox.* 1996. NY. Hyperion. 1st. VF/VF. T2. $20.00.

BURKE, James Lee. *Cimarron Rose.* 1997. NY. Hyperion. 1st. VF/VF. H11. $25.00.

BURKE, James Lee. *Cimarron Rose.* 1997. London. Orion. 1st. precedes Am ed. VF/dj. M15. $85.00.

BURKE, James Lee. *Dixie City Jam.* 1994. NY. Hyperion. 1st. VF/VF. H11. $35.00.

BURKE, James Lee. *Heartwood.* 1999. NY. Doubleday. 1st. sgn. VF/VF. T2. $27.00.

BURKE, James Lee. *Heaven's Prisoners.* 1988. NY. Holt. 1st. F/F. H11. $135.00.

BURKE, James Lee. *In the Electric Mist With Confederate Dead.* 1993. NY. Hyperion. 1st. F/VF. H11. $40.00.

BURKE, James Lee. *Lay Down My Sword and Shield.* 1971. NY. Crowell. 1st. sgn. clip. VF/dj. M15. $1.350.00.

BURKE, James Lee. *Present for Santa.* 1986. NY. St. Martin. 1st. VG+/VG+. G8. $12.50.

BURKE, James Lee. *Sunset Limited.* 1998. NY. Doubleday. 1st. F/F+. H11. $20.00.

BURKE, James Lee. *The Neon Rain.* 1987. NY. Henry Holt. 1st. sgn. VF/dj. M15. $350.00.

BURKE, James Lee. *Two for Texas.* (1982). NY. Pocket Books. pb orig. pict wrp. #4 written in ink on ffep. VG. lt wear and creasing to extremities. B3. $75.00.

BURKE, Jan. *Bones.* 1999. NY. S&S. 1st. UP. F. D10. $10.00.

BURKE, Jan. *Dear Irene.* 1995. NY. S&S. 1st. sgn. F/F. G8. $30.00.

BURKE, Jan. *Goodnight, Irene.* 1993. NY. S&S. 1st. sgn. F/F. G8. $40.00.

BURKE, Jonathan. *Pursuit Through Time.* 1956. Ward Lock. 1st. VG/VG. P3. $30.00.

BURKE, Ken. *Trees.* 1982. Mt Vernon, VA. ils. 144p. F. B26. $15.00.

BURKE, Kenneth. *Permanence and Change.* 1935. NY. New Republic Books. 1st. VG w/bookplate. B2. $35.00.

BURKE, Martyn. *Laughing War.* 1980. Garden City. Doubleday. 1st. rem mk. F in NF dj. B2. $50.00.

BURKE, Thomas. *East of Mansion House.* 1926. Doran. 1st. F/NF. M2. $50.00.

BURKERT, Nancy Ekholm. *Valentine & Orson.* 1989. FSG. 1st. F/VG. M5. $40.00.

BURKETT, Larry. *Coming Economic Earthquake.* 1991. Moody. 230p. F/dj. B29. $8.00.

BURKHARD, Oscar. *German Poems.* 1917. NY. Henry Holt. b&w photos. poi. NF/no dj. F6. $6.00.

BURKHARDT, V. *Chinese Creeds & Customs, 1959 & 1972.* Hong Kong. 3 vol. ils. F/dj. W3. $92.00.

BURKHOLDER, Mark & D. S. Chandler. *From Impotence to Authority.* 1977. Columbia. Univ of Missouri Press. 1st. 253p. G/G. chipped. F3. $25.00.

BURKS, Arthur J. *Black Medicine.* 1966. Arkham. 1st. F/dj. M2. $60.00.

BURLAND, Cottie. *Eskimo Art.* 1973. London. Hamlyn. 100 ils. 96p. map ep. VG/VG. P4. $65.00.

BURLEY, Andrew S. *Uncle Sam's Army Boys.* 1919. Donohue. A19. $10.00.

BURLEY, W.J. *Charles & Elizabeth.* 1981. Walker. 1st. NF/NF. P3. $13.00.

BURLINGAME, Roger. *Of Making Many Books.* 1946. Scribner. 1st. 8vo. 347p. gilt beige cloth. NF. T10. $35.00.

BURMAN, Ben Lucien. *Steamboat Round the Bend.* 1933. Farrar Rhinehart. 1st. F/VG+ clip. B4. $150.00.

BURMAN, L. & A. Bean. *Hottentotos Holland to Hermanus. South African Wild Flower Guide 5.* 1985. Claremont. RSA. sc. 375 color photos. 224p. VG. B26. $24.00.

BURMEISTER, Eugene. *Golden Empire: Kern County, California.* 1977. Beverly Hills. Autograph Pr. photos. 168p. D11. $25.00.

BURNARD, Bonnie. *Casino & Other Stories.* 1994. NY. Harper & Row. 1st. VF/VF. H11. $40.00.

BURNETT, Frances Hodgson. *A Little Princess.* 1905. NY. Scribner. ils by Ethel Franklin Betts. F. A16. $45.00.

BURNETT, Frances Hodgson. *Land of the Blue Flower.* 1913. Moffat Yard. G+. M2. $20.00.

BURNETT, Frances Hodgson. *Little Lord Fauntlerory.* 1911. London. Scribners. 1st ed thus. sm 4to. ils by Reginald B. Birch. 246p. NF. D6. $125.00.

BURNETT, Frances Hodgson. *Louisiana/Pretty Sister of Jose.* 1914. Scribner. VG. P3. $15.00.

BURNETT, Frances Hodgson. *Secret Garden.* 1911. Stokes. 1st. teg. G. M5. $95.00.

BURNETT, Hallie. *Brain Pickers.* 1957. Messner. 1st. VG+/VG. B4. $85.00.

BURNETT, Jim. *High Lonesome: Tales of Bisbee & Southern Arizona.* 1990. private prt. 1st. ils. 278p. F/F. B19. $30.00.

BURNETT, Virgil. *Towers at the Edge of a World.* 1980. St Martin. 1st. F/F. P3. $15.00.

BURNETT, W.R. *Iron Man.* 1930. Lincoln Mac Veagh/Dial. NF/G. M22. $30.00.

BURNETT, W.R. *Little Caesar.* 1929. Dial. VG. M22. $45.00.

BURNETT, W.R. *Mi Amigo.* 1959. Knopf. 1st. NF/VG clip. B4. $125.00.

BURNETT, W.R. *Pale Moon.* 1956. Knopf. 1st. F/VG+. B4. $150.00.

BURNETT, W.R. *Romelle.* 1946. NY. Knopf. 1st. F/NF. M15. $85.00.

BURNETT, W.R. *Romelle.* 1946. Knopf. 1st. VG+/dj. M25. $25.00.

BURNETT, W.R. *Underdog.* 1957. Knopf. 1st. VG/VG. P3. $30.00.

BURNEY, Joseph John. *Familiar Letters to Henry Clay of Kentucky.* 1840. NY. Mahlon Day. gilt bdg. xl. VG. O7. $75.00.

BURNFORD, Sheila. *Incredible Journey: Tale of Three Animals.* 1961. Atlantic Monthly. stated 1st. 8vo. F/VG. M5. $125.00.

BURNHAM, Eleanor Waring. *Justin Morgan Founder of His Race. The Romantic History of a Horse.* 1911. NY. The Shakespeare Press. 12mo. 160p. ils. tan wrp (softbound). 1st ed. small nick at base of wrp spine. VG to F. $40.00.

BURNS, John. *Burns's Obstetrical Works.* 1809. NY. 3 vol in 1. contemporary sheep. B14. $275.00.

BURNS, Margery. *Nottingham System of Contact Bridge.* 1969. London. 3rd. VG. S1. $10.00.

BURNS, Olive Ann. *Cold Sassy Tree.* 1984. NY. Ticknor & Fields. 1st. F/NF lt wear. D10. $75.00.

BURNS, Rex. *The Farnsworth Score.* 1977. NY. Harper & Row. 1st. Jacket spine ends wrinkled. F/F. H11. $35.00.

BURNS, Tex; See L'Amour, Louis.

BURNS, Walter Noble. *Year With a Whaler.* 1913. NY. Outing. 1st. ils. 250p. T7. $65.00.

BURNSHAW, Stanley. *Caged in an Animal's Mind.* 1963. HRW. 1st. inscr. F/NF. B4. $125.00.

BURR, Anna R. *West of the Moon.* 1926. Duffield. 1st. VG/dj. M2. $25.00.

BURR, G.L. *Narratives of the Witchcraft Cases 1648 – 1706.* 1914. VG. M17. $50.00.

BURR, Harold Saxton. *Neural Basis of Behavior.* 1960. Springfield. 262p. gr cloth. VG/dj. G1. $28.50.

BURRELL, Maurice. *Wide of the Truth; Mormons, What They Believe.* 1972. Marshall. Morgan & Scott. 148p. VG/VG. ex lib. B29. $6.50.

BURRIS, Marcus L. *Chips & Whetstones.* 1913. NY. Every Where Pub. sgn. gr cloth. G. B11. $18.00.

BURROUGHS, Alan. *Art Criticism from a Laboratory.* 1936. Little, Brn. 1st. ils. 277p. VG/dj. K3. $30.00.

BURROUGHS, Edgar Rice. *Apache Devil.* nd. Grosset Dunlap. NF. P3. $30.00.

BURROUGHS, Edgar Rice. *Beasts of Tarzan.* 1917. AL Burt. VG. P3. $35.00.

BURROUGHS, Edgar Rice. *Cave Girl.* 1926. Grosset Dunlap. VG. P3. $35.00.

BURROUGHS, Edgar Rice. *Fighting Man of Mars.* 1932. Grosset Dunlap. 1st. 319p. blk lettered red cloth. VG/dj. H1. $45.00.

BURROUGHS, Edgar Rice. *Jungle Tales of Tarzan.* 1919. McClurg. 3rd. VG. P3. $150.00.

BURROUGHS, Edgar Rice. *Lad & the Lion.* 1964. Canaveral. F/dj. M2. $95.00.

BURROUGHS, Edgar Rice. *Llana of Gathol.* 1948. ERB. 1st. F/dj. M2. $145.00.

BURROUGHS, Edgar Rice. *Lost on Venus.* 1935. ERB. 1st. ils St John. VG. S13. $85.00.

BURROUGHS, Edgar Rice. *Mastermind of Mars.* 1929. Grosset Dunlap. 1st. 8vo. 312p. blk lettered red cloth. VG/dj. H1. $65.00.

BURROUGHS, Edgar Rice. *Moon Maid.* 1927. Grosset Dunlap. G. P3. $25.00.

BURROUGHS, Edgar Rice. *Moon Men.* 1962. Canaveral. NF/NF. P3. $50.00.

BURROUGHS, Edgar Rice. *Princess of Mars.* 1952. Methuen. 13th. VG. P3. $20.00.

BURROUGHS, Edgar Rice. *Son of Tarzan.* 1917. Chicago. McClurg. 1st. VG. T12. $125.00.

BURROUGHS, Edgar Rice. *Tarzan and the Foreign Legion.* 1947. Tarzana. ERB. 1st. F/VG. T2. $45.00.

BURROUGHS, Edgar Rice. *Tarzan & the Foreign Legion.* 1948. ERB. 1st. VG/dj. M2. $80.00.

BURROUGHS, Edgar Rice. *Tarzan & the Golden Lion.* 1923. McClurg. 1st. VG/mc Canon dj. M2. $75.00.

BURROUGHS, Edgar Rice. *Tarzan & the Jewels of Opar.* 1912. McClurg. 2nd. VG. P3. $90.00.

BURROUGHS, Edgar Rice. *Tarzan & the Lost Empire.* 1931. Grosset Dunlap. VG/fair. P3. $30.00.

BURROUGHS, Edgar Rice. *Tarzan & the Lost Safari.* 1966. Whitman. decor brd. G. P3. $10.00.

BURROUGHS, Edgar Rice. *Tarzan the Untamed.* 1920. McClurg. 1st. G+/mc Canon dj. M2. $50.00.

BURROUGHS, Edgar Rice. *War Chief.* 1928. Grosset Dunlap. VG. P3. $40.00.

BURROUGHS, Edgar Rice. *Warlord of Mars.* 1919. McClurg. 1st. G. P3. $75.00.

BURROUGHS, John. *Camping & Tramping With Roosevelt.* 1907. Houghton Mifflin. 1st. 111p. VG. J2. $75.00.

BURROUGHS, Polly. *Great Ice Ship Bear: 89 Years in Polar Seas.* 1970. NY. Van Nostrand. 1st. 104p. VG/dj. P4. $45.00.

BURROUGHS, William S. *Cities of the Red Night.* 1981. HRW. 1st. sgn. F/F. R14. $90.00.

BURROUGHS, William S. *Exterminator!* 1973. Viking, 1st, xl. VG/VG. P3. $20.00.

BURROUGHS, William S. *Nova Express.* 1964. Grove. 1st Am ed. F/F. M25. $100.00.

BURROUGHS, William S. *Nova Express.* 1964. Grove. 1st. NF/dj. M2. $50.00.

BURROUGHS, William S. *The Adding Machine.* (1986). NY. Seaver. 1st. F/F. B3. $40.00.

BURROUGHS, William S. *The Cat Inside.* 1992. Viking. ARC. F/decor wrps. M25. $75.00.

BURROUGHS, William S. *The Last Words of Dutch Schultz.* 1975. NY. Viking. 1st. F/F. H11. $75.00.

BURROUGHS, William S. *Western Lands.* 1987. Viking. 1st. inscr/sgn/dtd 1996. F/F. R14. $90.00.

BURROWS, George Man. *On Disorders of Cerebral Circulation.* 1994 (1846). NY. Classics Neurology/Neurosurgery Lib. facsimile. G1. $65.00.

BURROWS, Larry. *Larry Burrows: Compassionate Photographer.* 1972. Time-Life. 156p. cloth. cb case. D11. $150.00.

BURROWS, Millar. *An Outline of Biblical Theology.* 1946. Westminster. 380p. G/worn dj. B29. $9.50.

BURROWS, Millar. *The Dead Sea Scrolls.* 1961. Viking. 435p. VG/worn dj. B29. $9.50.

BURSEY, Jack. *Antarctic Night.* 1957. NY. Rand McNally. 1st prt. photos/map. 256p. dj. P4. $40.00.

BURTON, Jack. *Blue Book of Hollywood Musicals.* 1953. Century House. photos. cloth. NF. C9. $50.00.

BURTON, Jean. *Sir Richard Burton's Wife.* 1941. Knopf. 1st. 12 pl. VG/dj. W1. $55.00.

BURTON, Richard. *Christmas Story.* 1964. Morrow. 2nd. VG/VG. P3. $10.00.

BURTON, Richard. *City of the Saints & Across the Rocky Mountains to CA.* 1963. Knopf. 1st. 654p. VG/VG. J2. $65.00.

BURTON, Robert A. *Cellmates.* 1997. San Francisco. Russian. 1st. VF/VF. H11. $15.00.

BUSBY, F.M. *Long View.* 1976. Berkley Putnam. 1st. F/dj. M2. $20.00.

BUSCAGLIA, Leo. *Love.* 1972. Thorofare. NJ. Chas B Slack. 1st. NF/VG+. B4. $150.00.

BUSCH, Frederick. *Breathing Trouble & Other Stories.* 1973. London. Calder Boyars. 1st. sgn. F/F. R14. $75.00.

BUSCH, Frederick. *Girls.* 1997. Crown. 1st. AN/dj. S18. $17.00.

BUSCH, Frederick. *Hardwater Country.* 1979. Knopf. 1st. NF/dj. A24. $20.00.

BUSCH, Frederick. *I Wanted a Year Without Fall.* 1971. London. Calder Boyars. 1st. author's 1st book. F/clip. L3. $125.00.

BUSCH, Frederick. *Too Late American Boyhood Blues.* 1984. Boston. Godine. 1st. F/dj. A24. $20.00.

BUSH, Barbara. *A Memoir.* 1994. Scribner. 1st. sgn. F/F. A23. $55.00.

BUSH, Christopher. *Case of the Triple Twist.* 1958. Macmillan. 1st. F/VG. T12. $20.00.

BUSH, F. A. *Trees and Shrubs.* 1965. NY. color and b&w ils. 224p. blk cloth. VG+ in dj. B26. $19.00.

BUSH, Vannevar. *Pieces of the Action.* 1970. Morrow. 1st. VG/dj. K3. $15.00.

BUSIA, Akosua. *The Seasons of Beento Blackbird.* 1996. Boston. Little, Brn. wrp. ARC. F. B2. $25.00.

BUTCHART, Harvey. *Grand Canyon Treks.* 1970. La Siesta. 72p. VG/stiff wrp. F7. $12.50.

BUTENKO, R.G. *Plant Cell Culture.* 1985. Moscow. MIR Pub. 207p. VG/wrp. B1. $21.00.

BUTLER, C. *American Gentleman.* 1839. G+. M17. $20.00.

BUTLER, Gwendoline. *Coffin in Fashion.* 1987. St Martin. 1st. VG/VG. P3. $15.00.

BUTLER, Jack. *Living in Little Rock With Miss Little Rock.* 1993. NY. Knopf. 1st. VF/VF. T2. $25.00.

BUTLER, Jack. *Nightshade*. 1989. NY. Atlantic Monthly Press. 1st. VF/VF. T2. $25.00.

BUTLER, M. *Valley of the Ohio*. 1971. KY Hist Soc. 302p. F/dj. M4. $30.00.

BUTLER, Octavia E. *Blood Child and Other Stories*. 1985. NY. Four Walls Eight Windows. 1st. sgn. F/F. O11. $30.00.

BUTLER, Octavia E. *Dawn*. 1987. NY. Warner. 1st. sgn. F/F. O11. $35.00.

BUTLER, Octavia E. *Wild Seed*. 1980. Garden City. NY. Doubleday. 1st. F/F. M23. $110.00.

BUTLER, Robert Olen. *Alleys of Eden*. 1981. Horizon. 1st. F/NF. B4. $85.00.

BUTLER, Robert Olen. *Countrymen of Bones*. 1983. Horizon. 1st. sgn. F/NF. Q1. $125.00.

BUTLER, Robert Olen. *Good Scent From a Strange Mountain*. 1992. Holt. 1st. sgn. F/F. A23. $50.00.

BUTLER, Robert Olen. *On Distant Ground*. 1985. NY. Knopf. 1st. F/VNF. D10. $45.00.

BUTLER, Robert Olen. *Sun Dogs*. (1982). NY. Horizon. 1st. author's 2nd book. sgn by author. F/F. B3. $150.00.

BUTLER, Robert Olen. *Tabloid Dreams*. 1996. np. 1st. sgn. F/F dj M19. $25.00.

BUTLER, Robert Olen. *The Alleys of Eden*. 1981. NY. Horizon. 1st. F/F. H11. $175.00.

BUTLER, Robert Olen. *Wabash: A Novel*. 1987. Knopf. 1st. F/F. H11. $35.00.

BUTT, Archie. *Taft & Roosevelt: The Intimate Letters of Archie Butt*. 1930. Garden City. 2 vol. 1st. VG/G. B5. $45.00.

BUTTERFIELD, H. *Origins of Modern Science 1300 – 1800*. 1956. Macmillan. 187p. VG/dj. B14. $30.00.

BUTTERWORTH, Michael. *Festival*. 1976. Collins Crime Club. 1st. VG/G. P3. $15.00.

BUXTON, J. *Redstart*. 1950. London. Collins. 8vo. ils/20 maps. 180p. cloth. VG $12.00.

BUZZATI, Dino. *Bears Famous Invasion of Sicily*. 1947. Pantheon. 1st Am. 16 full-p mc ils. VG/poor. P2. $90.00.

BYATT, A.S. *Possession*. 1990. Random. 1st Am. sgn. F/dj. D10. $60.00.

BYATT, A. S. *Still Life*. 1985. NY. Scribner's. 1st Am ed. author's 4th novel. F/F w/trace of rubbing on rear panel. D10. $50.00.

BYE, John O. *At the End of the Rainbow*. 1959. Seattle. 1st inscr. 474p. VG. B11. $100.00.

BYERS, Michael. *The Coast of Good Intentions*. 1998. Boston. Houghton Mifflin/Mariner Books. 1st. PBO. sgn. F/F. O11. $30.00.

BYFIELD, Bruce. *Witches of the Mind: A Critical Study of Fritz Leiber*. 1991. West Warwick. Necronomicon Press. 1st. VF/pict wrp. T2. $12.00.

BYI, Charlot. *Christmas on Stage*. 1950. Polygraphic Company Am. obl 4to. stiff paper wrp/sbdg. R5. $75.00.

BYINGTON, Eloise. *Pancake Brownies*. 1928. Chicago. Whitman. 8vo. bl cloth. R5. $100.00.

BYINGTON, Eloise. *Wishbone Children*. 1934. Whitman. 1st. ils. VG+/dj. M5. $35.00.

BYRD, Martha. *Chennault: Giving Wings to the Tiger*. 1987. Tuscaloosa. ils/photos/biblio/index. 451p. VG/VG. S16. $24.00.

BYRD, Richard E. *Big Aviation Book for Boys*. 1929. Springfield. MA. 285p. F/dj. A17. $25.00.

BYRD, Richard E. *Little America*. 1930. NY. 1st. sgn. 422p. dj. A17. $35.00.

BYRD, Richard E. *Skyward*. 1928. Putnam. 1st. 8vo. map ep. bl cloth. VG. P4. $45.00.

BYRNES, Gene. *Complete Guide to Professional Cartooning*. 1950. Drexel Hill. 1st. 255p. VG. A17. $25.00.

BYRON, May. *Little Yellow Duckling*. 1928. Nelson. 1st. ils Rudge. NF. M5. $95.00.

— C —

CABELL, James Branch. *Letter Of*. 1975. OK U. 1st. NF/dj. M2. $25.00.

CABELL, James Branch. *Silver Stallion*. 1926. McBride. 1st. G. P3. $30.00.

CABELL, James Branch. *Silver Stallion*. 1926. McBride. 1st. 358p. cloth. VG. M20. $45.00.

CABEZA DE VACA, Alvar Nunez. *Narrative of*. 1972. Barre, MA. Imp Soc. ils Michael McCurdy. AN/case. O7. $75.00.

CABLE, George Washington. *The Cavalier*. 1901. NY. Scribners. 1st. orig cloth. plates. 311p. VG. M8. $25.00.

CABLE, Mary. *The Blizzard of '88*. 1988. NY. Atheneum. 8vo. b/w photos. 197p. VG/VG. K5. $25.00.

CADBURY, Henry J. *George Fox's Book of Miracles*. 1948. Cambridge. 162p. VG/dj. V3. $60.00.

CADIGAN, Pat. *Mindplayers*. 1988. London. 1st. F/dj. M2. $25.00.

CADIGAN, Pat. *Patterns*. 1989. Kansas City. Ursus Imprints. 1st. VF/VF. T2. $20.00.

CADOGAN, Mary. *Women With Wings*. 1992. London. 1st. 280p. F/dj. B18. $25.00.

CADY, Edwin H. *John Woolman: Mind of the Quaker Saint*. 1966. NY. WA Square Pr. 182p. G. V3. $15.00.

CADY, Jack. *The Well*. 1980. NY. Arbor House. 1st. author's 1st novel. VF/VF. T2. $50.00.

CADY, John H. *Arizona's Yesterday*. 1916. private prt. 1st. sgn. ils. 120p. F. B19. $40.00.

CADZOW, Donald A. *Achaeological Studies of Susquehannock Indians of P.A.* 1936. Harrisburg. 1st. 8vo. ils/pl/maps. VG. H1. $40.00.

CAGNEY, Peter. *Grave for Madam*. 1961. Herbert Jenkins. 1st. VG/G. P3. $18.00.

CAHILL, Holger. *The Shadow of My Hand*. 1956. Harcourt Brace & Co. 1st. VG/chip. S19. $35.00.

CAHILL, Tim. *Road Fever*. 1991. Random. 1st. sgn. F/F. B3. $45.00.

CAIANELLO, E.R. *Physics of Cognitive Processes*. 1987. NY. World Scientific. 463p. prt gr laminated brd. G1. $75.00.

CAIDIN, Martin. *Destination Mars*. 1972. Doubleday. 1st. VG/VG. P3. $22.00.

CAIDIN, Martin. *Devil Take All*. 1966. Dutton. 1st. NF/VG. N4. $15.00.

CAIE, Norman MacLeod. *Night Scenes of Scripture*. 1923. Doran. 199p. VG/ex lib. B29. $8.50.

CAILLOU, Alan. *Alien Virus*. 1957. Davies. 1st British ed. VG/G. G8. $17.50.

CAIN, James M. *Butterfly*. 1947. Knopf. 1st. VG/G. M19. $35.00.

CAIN, James M. *Cloud Nine.* 1984. Mysterious. 1st. VG/VG. P3. $18.00.

CAIN, James M. *Postman Always Rings Twice.* 1934. Knopf. 3rd. NF. M22. $15.00.

CAIN, James M. *Serenade.* 1937. Knopf. 1st. VG. P3. $35.00.

CAIN, Paul. *Fast One.* 1978. Carbondale. Southern Illinois University. 1st. afterword by Irvin Faust. reprint ed. F/dj. M15. $75.00.

CAIRNS, Bob. *Pen Men: Baseball's Greatest Bullpen Stories.* 1992. St Martin. 1st. F/F. T12. $25.00.

CAIRNS, Earle. *Christianity Through the Centuries.* 1967. Zondervan. 511p. VG/VG. B29. $6.00.

CALAHAN, H.A. *Ship's Husband: Guide to Yachtsmen in Care of Their Craft.* 1937. NY. 1st. 323p. VG. A17. $15.00.

CALDECOTT, Andrew. *Fires Burn Blue.* 1948. London. 1st. VG/dj. M2. $35.00.

CALDECOTT, Randolph. *The House that Jack Built.* nd. NY. Avenel. F in F dj. A16. $12.00.

CALDER, Alexander. *Animal Sketching.* 1926. London. The Bodley Head Ltd. 1st. ils. Calder's 1st book. 62p. orig tan cloth. K1. $150.00.

CALDER, Richard. *Dead Girls.* 1992. London. Harper Collins. 1st. author's 1st novel. VF/VF. T2. $20.00.

CALDERON DE LA BARCA, Frances. *Life in Mexico.* 1982. London. Century. intro by Sir Nicolas Cheetham. 542p. G/wrp. F3. $15.00.

CALDWELL, E. *Fairy Ship.* ca 1890. London. Marcus Ward. ltd. sq 12mo. pict wrp. R5. $75.00.

CALDWELL, Erskine. *Sure Hand of God.* 1947. DSP. 1st. F/NF. D10. $40.00.

CALDWELL, Taylor. *Pillar of Iron.* 1965. Doubleday. 1st. 649p. VG/G. W2. $40.00.

CALDWELL, Taylor. *There Was a Time.* 1947. Scribner. 1st. VG/VG. P3. $25.00.

CALHOUN, Alfred R. *Lost in the Canyon.* 1888. NY. AL Burt. 8vo. 267p. gr cloth. G+. F7. $30.00.

CALHOUN, Frances Boyd. *Miss Minerva & William Green Hill.* 1911 (1909). Reilly Britton. 212p. pict cloth. VG. M20. $20.00.

CALISHER, Hortense. *Journal from Ellipsia.* 1963. Boston. Little, Brn. 1st. VNF/VNF. D10. $40.00.

CALISHER, Hortense. *Tale for the Mirror.* 1962. Little, Brn. 1st. NF/dj. B35. $18.00.

CALKINS, Christopher Miles. *36 Hours Before Appomattox....* 1980. Farmville, VA. Farmville Herald Press. 1st. orig printed wrp. ils. maps. portfolio. 80p. VG. M8. $27.50.

CALLAGHAN, Morley. *A Passion in Rome.* 1961. Coward-McCann. 1st Am ed. NF/worn dj. M25. $45.00.

CALLAHAN, North. *Henry Knox: General Washington's General.* 1958. NY. Rinehart. 1st. sgn. 404p. VG/G. B11. $25.00.

CALLAWAY, Lew L. *Montana's Righteous Hangmen: Vigilantes in Action.* 1973. Norman. 1st. inscr edit. F/NF. T11. $65.00.

CALLISON, Brian. *Trapp's Peace.* 1980. NY. Dutton. 1st. Page edges are very lightly foxed. F-/F. H11. $25.00.

CALLOWAY, Cab. *Of Minnie the Moocher & Me.* 1976. Crowell. 1st. F/NF. B2. $35.00.

CALVERT, George H. *Charlotte Von Stein: A Memoir.* 1877. Boston. Lee Shepard. 1st. ils. 280p. teg. VG+. $25.00.

CALVERTON, V.F. *Man Inside.* 1936. Scribner. 1st. Vg/dj. M2. $35.00.

CALVIN, Jack. *Sitka.* 1936. Arrowhead. 1st. 40p+photos. G/wrp. A17. $25.00.

CALVIN, William H. *How the Shaman Stole the Moon.* 1991. NY. Bantam. 1st. 223p. M/wrp. K3. $13.00.

CAM, Helen. *Selected Historical Essays of FW Maitland.* 1957. Cambridge. G/dj. M11. $85.00.

CAMERON, Carey. *Daddy Boy.* 1989. Chapel Hill. Algonquin. 1st. VF/VF. H11. $40.00.

CAMERON, Eleanor. *Spell Is Cast.* 1964. Atlantic Monthly. 1st. 271p. VG/G. P2. $35.00.

CAMERON, John. *Seven Stabs.* 1929. Crime club. 1st. G/VG. G8. $35.00.

CAMERON, L. *The Music of Light.* 1998. NY. Free Press. ARC. wrps. F. B2. $25.00.

CAMERON, Owen. *Butcher's Wife.* 1954. S&S. 1st. VG/G. P3. $20.00.

CAMERON, Owen. *Catch a Tiger.* 1952. NY. S&S. 1st. Jacket has chipping at top of spine and several closed tears. all tape reinforced. F/NF. H11. $25.00.

CAMERON, Sarah. *Natural Enemies.* (1993). Atlanta. Turner. 1st. sgn by author. VF/VF. B3. $30.00.

CAMERON, Thomas W.M. *Internal Parasites of Domestic Animals.* 1934. London. Blk. 1st. VG. O3. $35.00.

CAMP, Charles L. & Francis P. Farquahar. *Essays for Henry R. Wagner.* 1947. San Francisco. Grabhorn Press. 1/260 copies. quarto. decor brds. F. R3. $60.00.

CAMP, John. *The Fool's Run.* 1989. NY. Holt. 1st. F/F. H11. $55.00.

CAMP, John; See Sandford, John.

CAMP, Samuel G. *Art of Fishing.* 1911. NY. Outing. 1st. 177p. VG. H7. $25.00.

CAMP, William Martin. *San Francisco.* 1947. Doubleday. 1st. VG/G. O4. $15.00.

CAMPANELLA, Roy. *It's Good to be Alive.* 1959. Boston. 1st. VG/dj. B5. $20.00.

CAMPBELL, A.B. *When I Was in Patagonia.* (1953). London. Christopher Johnson. 1st. 202p. F3. $15.00.

CAMPBELL, Alice. *Click of the Gate.* 1931. Farrar Rhinehart. 1st. F/dj. M15. $75.00.

CAMPBELL, Bebe Moore. *Brothers and Sisters.* (1994). NY. Putnam. 1st. F/F. B3. $30.00.

CAMPBELL, Bruce. *Ken Holt: Mystery of Sultan's Scimitar (#18).* 1963. Grosset Dunlap. 1st. 177p. last title in series. VG. M20. $350.00.

CAMPBELL, Craig S. *Water in Landscape Architecture.* 1978. NY. ils. 128p. F/dj. B26. $17.50.

CAMPBELL, H.J. *Beyond the Visible.* 1952. Hamish Hamilton. 1st. VG/VG. P3. $25.00.

CAMPBELL, Harlan. *Monkey on a Chain.* 1993. np. Doubleday. 1st. author's 1st book. NF/NF. R16. $40.00.

CAMPBELL, Harriette R. *Moor Fires Mystery.* 1939. NY. Harper. 1st. G-VG. G8. $12.50.

CAMPBELL, J. *Mythic Image.* 1974. Princeton. ils. 552p. F/rpr. M4. $45.00.

CAMPBELL, John W. *Black Star Passes.* 1953. Fantasy. 1st. F/dj. M2. $125.00.

CAMPBELL, John W. *Incredible Planet.* 1949. Fantasy. 1st. F/dj. M2. $100.00.

CAMPBELL, John W. *Moon Is Hell.* 1951. Fantasy. 1st. sgn/#d. F/NF. P3. $200.00.

CAMPBELL, Karen. *Wheel of Fortune.* 1973. Bobbs Merrill. 1st. VG/VG. P3. $15.00.

CAMPBELL, Maria. *Halfbreed.* 1973. Saturday review. 1st. F/NF. L3. $45.00.

CAMPBELL, Patrick. *Shades of Sherlock.* 1997. Shelburne. Ontario. Battered Silicon Dispatch Box. 1st. sgn. VF/F. T2. $25.00.

CAMPBELL, R. Wright. *Honor.* 1987. NY. Tor. 1st. VG/NF. G8. $10.00.

CAMPBELL, Ramsey. *Ancient Images.* 1989. NY. Scribners. 1st. VF/VF. T2. $9.00.

CAMPBELL, Ramsey. *Doll Who Ate His Mother.* 1976. Bobbs Merrill. 1st. author's 1st novel. F/F. P3. $125.00.

CAMPBELL, Ramsey. *Fantasy Readers Guide to Ramsey Campbell.* 1980. Cosmos/Borgo. 62p. NF/sans. R10. $15.00.

CAMPBELL, Ramsey. *Incarnate.* 1983. Macmillan. 1st. F/NF. N4. $40.00.

CAMPBELL, Ramsey. *Midnight Sun.* 1991. NY. Tor. 1st. VF/VF. T2. $9.00.

CAMPBELL, Ramsey. *Parasite.* 1980. Macmillan. 1st. VG/G. L1. $50.00.

CAMPBELL, Ramsey. *Scared Stiff: Tales of Sex & Death.* 1987. LA. Scream/Press. 1st. sgn by artist J.K. Potter. VF/VF. T2. $40.00.

CAMPBELL, Robert. *Alice in La-La Land.* 1987. Poseidon. 1st. VG/VG. P3. $17.00.

CAMPBELL, Robert. *Juice.* 1988. NY. Poseidon Press. 1st. F/F. T2. $8.00.

CAMPBELL, Robert. *Nibbled to Death by Ducks.* 1989. Pocket. 1st. F/F. P3. $18.00.

CAMPBELL, Sam. *Beloved Rascals.* 1957. Bobbs Merrill. 1st. sgn. VG. B11. $25.00.

CAMPBELL, Scott. *Touched.* 1996. NY. Bantam. 1st. author's 1st book. VF/VF. H11. $20.00.

CAMPBELL, Thomas. *Gertrude of Wyoming.* 1809. London. Longman. 1st. wide folio. 134p. uncut. orig pub brd.

CAMPBELL, Thomas. *Life of Mrs Siddons.* 1972. NY. Blom. 378p. wrp. A17. $12.50.

CAMPBELL, Thomas J. *Jesuits 1534 – 1921.* 1921. Encyclopedia Pr. 937p. gilt cloth. A17. $25.00.

CAMPIOIN, Jane & Kate Pullinger. *The Piano.* 1994. NY. Miramax. 1st. Book has small dampstain at bottom of rear board. F-/F. H11. $20.00.

CAMPION, Lynn. *Training & Showing the Cutting Horse.* 1990. Prentice Hall. 1st. F/F. O3. $19.00.

CAMPOLO, Tony. *How to be Pentecostal Withouth Speaking in Tongues.* 1991. Word. 176p. F/F. B29. $9.50.

CAMPOLO, Tony. *How to Rescue the Earth Without Worshiping Nature.* 1992. Nelson. 1st. sgn. VG/dj. B29. $8.50.

CAMUS, Albert. *Exile & The Kingdom.* 1958. Knopf. 1st. F/NF. B35. $40.00.

CAMUS, Albert. *Outsider.* 1946. London. Hamish Hamilton. 1st Eng trans. author's 1st book. F/dj. Q1. $400.00.

CANADY, John. *The Lives of the Painters.* 1969. London. Thames and Hudson. 4 vols. quarto. gr cloth. gilt on covers. F. R3. $60.00.

CANCIAN, Frank. *Change & Uncertainty in Peasant Economy.* 1972. Stanford. 1st. 208p. dj. F3. $20.00.

CANDY, Edward. *Words for Murder Perhaps.* nd. Crime Club. 1st Am ed. VG+/VG+. G8. $15.00.

CANFIELD, Cook. *Lucky Terrell: Springboard to Tokyo (#5).* 1943. Grosset Dunlap. 210p. VG/dj (lists to #6). M20. $20.00.

CANIFF, W. *History of the Province of Ontario.* 1872. Toronto. 672p. new cloth. NF. M4. $30.00.

CANIN, Ethan. *Blue River.* 1991. Boston. Houghton Mifflin. 1st. sgn. F in F dj. B2. $45.00.

CANIN, Ethan. *Emperor of the Air.* 1988. Houghton Mifflin. 1st. author's 1st book. F/dj. A24. $75.00.

CANIN, Ethan. *The Palace Thief.* (1994). NY. Random House. 1st. inscr & dated by author. F/F. B3. $30.00.

CANNELL, Stephen J. *The Plan.* 1995. np. Morrow. 1st. author's 1st book. NF/NF. R16. $40.00.

CANNING, John. *50 Great Horror Stories.* 1971. Bell. 1st. F/dj. M2. $18.00.

CANNING, Victor. *Dragon Tree.* 1958. Sloane. 1st. NF/NF. P3. $45.00.

CANNING, Victor. *Rainbird Pattern.* 1972. Morrow. 1st Am. NF/VG. M22. $15.00.

CANNON, Curt; See Hunter, Evan.

CANNON, Peter H. *Tales of Lovecraftian Horror and Humor: The Early Cannon Volume Two.* 1997. West Hills. Tsathoggua Press. 1st. VF/pict wrp. T2. $7.00.

CANNON, Taffy. *Pocketful of Karma.* 1993. Carroll & Graf. 1st. sgn. NF/NF. G8. $20.00.

CANNON, Taffy. *Tangled Roots.* 1995. Carroll & Graf. 1st. sgn. F/F. G8. $15.00.

CANSLER, Charles W. *Three Generations: Story of a Colored Family in East Tennessee.* 1939. private prt. 1st. NF. B4. $300.00.

CANTINE, Marguerite. *Beggar T Bear.* 1981. Cantine Kilpatrick. photos. 62p. F/wrp. H1. $17.50.

CANTOR, Jay. *The Death of Che Guevara.* 1983. NY. Knopf. 1st. author's first novel. F/F. H11. $25.00.

CANTWELL, R. *Alexander Wilson: Naturalist & Pioneer.* 1961. 1st. VG/VG. M17. $35.00.

CANTY, Kevin. *A Stranger in this World.* 1994. NY. Doubleday. 1st. author's 1st book. F/VF. H11. $45.00.

CANTY, Kevin. *Into the Great Wide Open.* 1996. NY. Doubleday. 1st. VF/VF. H11. $25.00.

CANTY, Kevin. *Nine Below Zero.* 1999. NY. Doubleday. 1st. sgn on title pg. AN. D10. $35.00.

CANTY, Thomas. *Monster at Christmas.* 1985. Donald Grant. 1st. 1/1050. sgn. F/dj. M2. $30.00.

CAPE, Bernard. *The Black Reaper.* 1998. Ashcroft, BC. Ash Tree Press. expanded ed. Hugh Lamb. editor. VF/VF. T2. $40.00.

CAPEK, Abe. *Chinese Stone Pictures.* 1962. London. Spring. ils. gilt cloth. F/F/case. W3. $65.00.

CAPEK, Karel. *Absolute at Large.* 1974 (1927). Hyperion. rpt. F. M2. $25.00.

CAPON, Edward. *Chinese Painting*. 1979. NY. Phaidon/Dutton. ils. F/wrp. W3. $32.00.

CAPOTE, Truman. *Answered Prayers: Unfinished Novel*. 1987. Random. 1st. NF. T12. $15.00.

CAPOTE, Truman. *Dogs Bark*. 1973. Random. 1st. F/dj. Q1. $60.00.

CAPOTE, Truman. *Grove Day*. 1969. NY. 1st. fwd James Michener. VG/VG. B5. $40.00.

CAPOTE, Truman. *In Cold Blood*. 1965. NY. Random House. 1st. sgn. VG+/VG. A24. $500.00.

CAPOTE, Truman. *In Cold Blood*. 1965. Random. 1st. F/F. Q1. $75.00.

CAPOTE, Truman. *One Christmas*. (1983). NY. Random House. 1st. boxed. F. B3. $30.00.

CAPOTE, Truman. *One Christmas*. 1983. Random. 1st. 1/500. sgn. F/sans/case. Q1. $350.00.

CAPOTE, Truman. *Thanksgiving Visitor*. 1967. NY. 1st. F/box. B5. $35.00.

CAPOTE, Truman. *The Muses are Heard*. 1956. NY. Random House. 1st. VG/VG. A24. $35.00.

CAPPON, Lester J. *History of Expedition Under Command of Capts Lewis & Clark*. 1970. NY. Columbia. AN/stiff wrp. O7. $25.00.

CAPPS, Benjamin. *Indians*. 1975. Time Life. A19. $20.00.

CAPPS, Benjamin. *Woman of the People*. 1966. DSP. 1st. F/VG+. B4. $25.00.

CAPUTO, Philip. *Horn of Africa*. 1980. Holt. 1st. F/F. H11. $45.00.

CAPUTO, Philip. *Horn of Africa*. 1980. HRW. 1/250. sgn. F/acetate dj/case. R14. $100.00.

CARAS, Roger A. *North American Mammals*. 1967. NY. ils/pl. 577p. VG. S15. $12.00.

CARAS, Roger A. *Panther*. 1969. Little, Brn. 1st. sgn. VG/VG. B11. $40.00.

CARD, Orson Scott. *Abyss*. 1989. London. Legend/Century. 1st hc. F/F. M21. $35.00.

CARD, Orson Scott. *Lost Boys*. 1992. Harper Collins. 1st. F/F. N4. $30.00.

CARD, Orson Scott. *Red Prophet*. 1988. NY. TOR. sgn 1st ed. F/F. M23. $50.00.

CARD, Orson Scott. *Seventh Son*. 1987. NY. Tor. 1st. sgn. F/F. M23. $55.00.

CARD, Orson Scott. *Ships of Earth*. 1994. NY. Tom Doherty. VG/dj. B9. $15.00.

CARD, Orson Scott. *Speaker for the Dead*. 1986. NY. Tor. 1st. sgn. xl. VG/NF. M23. $75.00.

CARD, Orson Scott. *The Memory of Earth*. 1992. NY. Tor. 1st. sgn. VF/VF. T2. $30.00.

CARD, Orson Scott. *The Short Fiction of Orson Scott Card*. (1990). NY. Tor. 1st. inscr by author. F/F. B3. $40.00.

CARD, Orson Scott. *Xenocide*. 1991. NY. Tor. 1st. F/F. H11. $25.00.

CARDENAS, Lazaro. *Messages to the Mexican Nation on the Oil Question*. 1938. DAPP. Mexico. 21p. G/wrp. F3. $15.00.

CARELL, Paul. *Scorched Earth*. 1966. Boston. 1st. VG/VG. B5. $75.00.

CAREY, Arthur A. *Memoirs of a Murder Man*. 1930. Doubleday Doran. 1st. VG. P3. $20.00.

CAREY, Peter. *Illywhacker*. 1985. Harper Row. 1st. F/F. M19. $25.00.

CAREY, Peter. *Jack Maggs*. 1998. NY. Knopf. 1st. sgn. F/F. D10. $40.00.

CAREY, Peter. *The Tax Inspector*. (1992). NY. Knopf. 1st sgn by author. F/F. B3. $25.00.

CARFAX, Catherine. *Silence With Voices*. 1969. Macmillan. 1st. VG/VG. P3. $20.00.

CARGILL, Morris. *Ian Fleming Introduces Jamaica*. 1965. Andre Deutsch. 1st. VG/G. P3. $30.00.

CARKEET, David. *Greatest Slump of All Time*. 1984. Harper Row. 1st. F/F. M25. $35.00.

CARLETON, Mark A. *Small Grains*. 1920. Macmillan. 699p. VG. A10. $28.00.

CARLEY, K. *Minnesota in the Civil War*. 1961. Minneapolis. 1st. ils/maps. 168p. F/dj. M4. $20.00.

CARLING, John R. *The Weird Picture*. 1905. London. Ward Lock. 1st. NF. M15. $150.00.

CARLSON, Ed. *Look Back Once in Awhile*. 1981. Phoenix, AZ. self pub. sgn. A19. $20.00.

CARLSON, John Roy. *Plotters*. 1946. Dutton. 1st. F/VG. B2. $30.00.

CARLSON, Raymond. *Flowering Cactus*. 1954. NY. ils/photos. 96p. VG/dj. B26. $20.00.

CARLSON, Ron. *News of the World*. 1987. Norton. 1st. F/F. H11. $45.00.

CARLSON, Ron. *Plan B for the Middle Class*. 1992. NY. Norton. 1st. F/F. H11. $35.00.

CARLSON, William. *Sunrise West*. 1981. Doubleday. 1st. F/dj. M2. $12.00.

CARMER, Carl. *Susquehanna*. 1955. Rinehart. 2nd. sm 8vo. 493p. F/G. H1. $22.50.

CARMICHAEL, Harry; See Creasey, John.

CARMICHAEL, Hoagey. *The Stardust Road*. 1946. NY. Rinehart. 1st. F in worn. trimmed dj. B2. $50.00.

CARNAC, Carol. *Upstairs and Downstairs*. 1950. Crime Club. 1st Am ed. G/G. stained. G8. $25.00.

CARNEGIE, Andrew. *American Four-In-Hand in Britain*. 1884. NY. ils. 338p. G. B18. $35.00.

CARNEGIE, D. *Among the Matabele*. 1970 (1894). Negro U. rpt. 128p. VG. W1. $25.00.

CARNELL, John. *New Writings in Science Fiction 15*. 1969. Dennis Dobson. 1st. VG/VG. P3. $30.00.

CARPENTER, Edward. *Angel's Wings: Series of Essays on Art...Relation to Life*. 1908. Swan Sonnenschein. 1st. VG. w/letter. V4. $75.00.

CARPENTER, F.B. *Six Months at the White House*. 1866. NY. 1st. F. O8. $32.50.

CARPENTER, Frances. *Holiday in Washington*. 1958. Knopf. 1st. sgn. 207p. VG/dj. M20. $20.00.

CARPENTER, Humphrey. *The Letters of J. R. R. Tolkien*. 1981. Boston. Houghton Mifflin. 1st. VF/VF. T2. $25.00.

CARPENTER, Iris. *No Woman's World*. 1946. Houghton Mifflin. 1st. 378p. VG. A25. $28.00.

CARPENTIER, Alejo. *Kingdom of this World*. 1957. Knopf. 1st. NF/dj. M25. $150.00.

CARR, Archie. *Handbook of Turtles*. 1983 (1952). Cornell. 9th. 542p. F. S15. $40.00.

CARR, Caleb. *The Alienist.* (1994). NY. Random House. 1st. F/F. B3. $75.00.

CARR, Caleb. *The Angel of Darkness.* 1997. NY. Random. 1st. F/VF. H11. $25.00.

CARR, Charles. *Colonists of Space.* 1954. Ward Lock. VG/VG. P3. $20.00.

CARR, Frank G.G. *Sailing Barges.* 1931. London. Hodder Stoughton. 1st. 68 pl. 328p. T7. $85.00.

CARR, Jayge. *Treasure in the Heart of the Maze.* 1985. Doubleday. 1st. F/dj. M2. $15.00.

CARR, John Dickson. *Bride of Newgate.* 1950. Harper. 1st. VG/G. P3. $25.00.

CARR, John Dickson. *He Wouldn't Kill Patience.* 1944. Morrow. 1st. NF/dj. M15. $250.00.

CARR, John Dickson. *Papa La-Bas.* 1968. NY. Harper & Row. 1st. F/dj. M15. $50.00.

CARR, John Dickson. *Scandal at High Chimneys.* 1959. Hamish Hamilton. 1st. NF/NF. P3. $35.00.

CARR, John Dickson. *The Demoniacs.* 1962. NY. Harper & Row. 1st. VF/dj. M15. $75.00.

CARR, Jolyon (Edith Parger). *Murder in the Dispensary.* 1999. Hassocks. Sussex. Post Mortem Books. Ltd Ed. 1/350 # copies. VF/no dj as issued. T2. $45.00.

CARR, Philippa; see Hibbert, Eleanor Alice.

CARR, Robyn. *Mind Tryst.* 1992. NY. St. Martin. 1st. VF/VF. T2. $8.00.

CARR, SAUNDERS & STOM. *Geology of The Terrestrial Planets.* 1984. NASA SP-469. 317p. G. D8. $25.00.

CARR, Terry. *Fellowship of the Stars.* 1974. S&S. 1st. F/NF. M2. $25.00.

CARR, Terry. *Infinite Arena.* 1977. Thomas Nelson. 1st. VG/VG. P3. $18.00.

CARR, William H. *Desert Parade.* 1947. NY. 1st. ils. map ep. VG/rpr. B26. $15.00.

CARRASCO, David. *To Change Place.* 1991. Niwot. CO U. 1st. 254p. dj. F3. $30.00.

CARREL, Alexis. *Voyage to Lourdes.* 1950. NY. 1st. 52p. cloth. G. B5. $25.00.

CARRIER, Jim. *Down the Colorado.* 1989. Rinehart. 8vo. 141p. stiff wrp. F7. $17.50.

CARRIGHAR, Sally. *Wild Heritage.* 1965. Houghton Mifflin. dj. A19. $20.00.

CARRILLO, Leo. *California I Love.* 1961. Englewood Cliffs. Prentice Hall. 1st. 8vo. 280p. half cloth. F/VG. $10.00.

CARRINGTON, Grant. *Time's Fool.* 1981. Doubleday. 1st. F/F. P3. $13.00.

CARROLL, Alice. *Complete Guide to Modern Knitting & Crocheting.* 1943. NY. Wise. 1st. ils/photos. 310p. VG+. A25. $18.00.

CARROLL, James. *Supply of Heroes.* 1986. Dutton. ne. F/F. W2. $20.00.

CARROLL, John. *Black Experience in the American West.* 1971. Liveright. 1st. ils. 591p. VG/VG. J2. $325.00.

CARROLL, John. *Two Battles of the Little Big Horn.* 1974. Liveright. 1/1000. sgn. 214p. w/fld painting by Bjorklund. AN/case. J2. $275.00.

CARROLL, Jonathan. *After Silence.* 1992. London. MacDonald. 1st. VF/VF. T2. $30.00.

CARROLL, Jonathan. *Land of Laughs.* 1980. 1st. author's 1st book. F/NF. M19. $45.00.

CARROLL, Jonathan. *Outside the Dog Museum.* 1991. London. MacDonald. 1st. VF/VF. T2. $25.00.

CARROLL, Kay. *Han Solo's Rescue.* 1983. Random Pop-Up Book. F. P3. $10.00.

CARROLL, Lewis. *Alice in Wonderland.* ca 1915. London. Blackie. ils Frank Adams. 12mo. top edge gr. gr cloth. R5. $100.00.

CARROLL, Lewis. *Alice in Wonderland.* 1921. London. Raphael Tuck. 1st thus. ils AL Bowley. gr cloth/pict label. R5. $125.00.

CARROLL, Lewis. *Alice in Wonderland.* 1934. Rand McNally. ils. VG. P3. $20.00.

CARROLL, Lewis. *Alice's Adventures in Wonderland.* 1946. NY. Random House. G. A16. $7.50.

CARROLL, Lewis. *Alice's Adventures in Wonderland & Through Looking Glass.* 1957 (1954). London. Dent. ils Tennell/Stanley. VG+/G+. N1. $7.50.

CARROLL, Lewis. *Hunting of the Snark.* 1970. NY. Watts. 1st Am. 48p. NF/dj. D4. $55.00.

CARROLL, Lewis. *Pig-Tale.* 1975. Little, Brn. 1st thus. 30p. VG+/dj. M20. $25.00.

CARROLL, Lewis. *Walt Disney's Alice in Wonderland.* 1951. London. Dean. 1st Eng thus. 4to. pict brd. R5. $275.00.

CARROLL, Paul. *Poem in Its Skin.* 1968. Follett. 1st. F/NF. V1. $25.00.

CARRUTH, Hayden. *For You — Poems.* 1970. New Directions. 1st. sgn. F/F. R14. $60.00.

CARRUTH, Vance. *Teton Sketches of Summer.* 1969. Johnson Pub. 1st. sgn. 30p. VG/torn. J2. $35.00.

CARSE, Robert. *Blockade the Civil War at Sea.* 1958. NY. Rinehart & Co. 1st. orig cloth. 279p. NF/VG. M8. $35.00.

CARSON, Gerald. *Social History of Bourbon.* 1963. NY. 1st. ils. 280p. VG/dj. B18. $17.50.

CARSON, James. *Saddle Boys in the Grand Canyon.* 1913. Cupples Leon. 12mo. VG. F7. $37.50.

CARSON, John F. *Boys Who Vanished.* 1959. DSP. 1st. 212p. cloth. VG/dj. M20. $15.00.

CARSON, Mina. *Settlement Folk.* 1990. Chicago. 1st. AN/dj. V4. $20.00.

CARSON, Rachel. *Silent Spring.* 1962. Houghton Mifflin. 1st. F/NF. Q1. $150.00.

CARSON, Robin. *Dawn of Time.* 1957. Holt. 1st. VG/worn. M2. $18.00.

CARTER, Angela. *Fireworks.* 1981. Harper Row. 1st Am. F/NF. A24. $25.00.

CARTER, Angela. *Nights at the Circus.* 1985. Viking. 1st. F/NF. A24. $25.00.

CARTER, Charlotte. *Coq Au Vin.* 1999. NY. Mysterious Press. 1st. sgn. VF/VF. T2. $25.00.

CARTER, G.S. *General Zoology of the Invertebrates.* 1948. London. Sidgwick Jackson. 3rd. 13 pl. clip dj. B1. $35.00.

CARTER, Henry. *Methodist Heritage.* 1951. Abingdon-Cokesbury. 246p. VG/dj. B29. $9.00.

CARTER, Herbert R. *Spinning & Twisting of Long Vegetable Fibres.* 1919. London. Griffin. 434p. cloth. A10. $45.00.

CARTER, Howard. *Tomb of Tutankhamen.* 1972. NY. Excalibur. 1st Am. 238p. NF/dj. W1. $22.00.

CARTER, Jared. *Work For the Night Is Coming.* 1981. NY. Macmillan. 1st. F/NF. V1. $20.00.

CARTER, Jimmy. *Always a Reckoning.* 1995. Times Books. 1st. sgn. F/F. S13. $55.00.

CARTER, Jimmy. *Blood of Abraham: Insights to the Middle East.* 1985. Houghton Mifflin. 1st. sgn. VG/VG. A23. $75.00.

CARTER, Jimmy. *Living Faith.* 1996. Times Books. 1st. sgn. F/F. A23. $75.00.

CARTER, Jimmy. *Outdoor Journal.* 1988. Bantam. 1st. VG/VG. A23. $75.00.

CARTER, Lin. *Dreams from R'Lyeh.* 1975. Arkham. 1st. F/dj. T2. $35.00.

CARTER, Lin. *Man Who Loved Mars.* 1973. Wht Lion. hc. VG/G. P3. $17.00.

CARTER, Lin. *Valley Where Time Stood Still.* 1974. Doubleday. 1st. NF/NF. P3. $20.00.

CARTER, M. *Isabella Stewart Gardner & Fenway Court.* 1972. photos. VG/VG. M17. $20.00.

CARTER, Nick; see Avallone, Mike.

CARTER, Paul. *Road to Botany Bay.* 1988. NY. Knopf. 1st Am. 384p. half cloth. AN/dj. P4. $23.00.

CARTER, Samuel. *Final Fortress.* 1980. 354p. O8. $12.50.

CARTER, William Harding. *Horses of the World.* 1923. NGS. ils. VG. O3. $45.00.

CARTER, Youngman. *Mr. Campion's Quarry.* 1971. Morrow. 1st. VG/VG. P3. $18.00.

CARTIER, Ed. *Known & the Unknown.* 1977. De La Ree. NF/NF. P3. $35.00.

CARTIER, John O. *Getting the Most Out of Modern Wildfowling.* 1974. NY. 396p. dj. A17. $15.00.

CARTIN, Hazel. *Elijah.* 1980. St Martin. 1st. inscr. F/NF clip. L3. $75.00.

CARTLEDGE, Samuel. *A Conservative Introduction to the New Testament.* 1951. Zondervan. 238p. VG. B29. $5.00.

CARUS, Titus Lucretius. *Of the Nature of Things.* 1957. LEC. 1st thus. 1/1500. ils/sgn Paul Landacre. F/remnant glassine/case. Q1. $125.00.

CARUTHERS, William. *Loafing Along Death Valley Trails.* 1951. Death Valley Pub. 1st. VG/sans. O4. $15.00.

CARVEL, John L. *Stephen of Linthouse.* 1950. Glasgow. Stephen & Sons. ils. 311p. torn dj. T7. $50.00.

CARVER, Jeffrey A. *Rapture Effect.* 1987. Tor. 1st. RS. F/F. P3. $20.00.

CARVER, Norman. *Silent Cities of Mexico & the Maya.* 1988. MI. np. 2nd printing. sq 4to. photo ils. site plans. 216p. G/G wrp. F3. $30.00.

CARVER, Raymond. *Carver Country: World of Raymond Carver.* 1990. Scribner. 1st. F/torn. A18. $35.00.

CARVER, Raymond. *My Crow.* 1984. Ewert. 1/150. ils Thomas Berwick. F/wrp. V1. $30.00.

CARVER, Raymond. *No Heroics, Please.* 1992. NY. Vintage Contemporaries. pbo. F/wrps. B2. $25.00.

CARVER, Raymond. *Ultramarine.* 1986. Random. 1st. sgn. F/F. D10. $175.00.

CARVER, Raymond. *What We Talk About When We Talk About Love.* 1981. NY. Knopf. 1st. NF in NF dj; sunned edges. B2. $150.00.

CARVER, Raymond. *Where I'm Calling From.* 1988. NY. Atlantic Monthly. 1st. F/F. B2. $40.00.

CARVER, Raymond. *Where Water Comes Together With Other Water.* 1985. Random. 1st. NF/dj. D10. $75.00.

CARVIC, Heron. *Miss Seeton Sings.* 1973. Harper Row. VG. P3. $22.00.

CARY, Diana Serra. *Hollywood Posse: Story of a Gallant Band of Horsemen.* 1975. Houghton Mifflin. 1st. 268p. VG/VG. J2. $75.00.

CARY, James. *Tanks & Armor in Modern Warfare.* 1966. NY. 1st. ils. VG/dj. B18. $22.50.

CARY, Joyce. *Prisoner of Grace.* 1952. Michael Joseph. 1st. 398p. VG+/dj. M20. $38.00.

CARY, Lorene. *The Price of a Child.* 1995. NY. Knopf. 1st. F/F. H11. $30.00.

CASE, David. *Third Grave.* 1981. Arkham. 1st. F/dj. M2. $25.00.

CASEWIT, Curtis. *Peacemakers.* 1960. Avalon. 1st. F/dj. M2. $15.00.

CASEY, Bernie. *Look at the People.* 1969. Doubleday. 1st. F/dj chipped. M25. $25.00.

CASEY, John. *Spartina.* 1989. Knopf. 1st. F/dj. M25. $60.00.

CASEY, John. *Testimony & Demeanor.* 1979. Knopf. 1st. F/F. B3. $75.00.

CASEY, Robert J. *Black Hills.* 1949. Bobbs Merrill. map. VG. A19. $55.00.

CASEY, Robert J. *Hot Ice.* 1933. Greenberg. 1st. VG. G8. $20.00.

CASEY, Robert J. *Torpedo Junction: With the Pacific Fleet from Pearl Harbor.* 1942. Indianapolis. 1st. photos/map. 423p. VG/G. S16. $27.50.

CASHMAN, A. W. *Vice-Regal Cowboy.* 1957. Edmonton. 1st prt. inscr. 199p. P4. $35.00.

CASO, Alfonso. *Thirteen Masterpieces of Mexican Archaeology.* 1938. Mexico. np. 1st. wrp. 4to. 131p. lt shelf wear. VG. F3. $45.00.

CASPARY, Vera. *Weeping & the Laughter.* 1950. Little, Brn. 1st. VG/VG. P3. $35.00.

CASSANDRA, Knye; See Disch, Thomas.

CASSERLY, Gordon. *Elephant God.* 1921. Putnam. 1st. VG. M2. $15.00.

CASSERLY, Langmead. *The Retreat from Christianity.* 1953. Longman. 178p. VG. ex lib. B29. $12.50.

CASSIDY, Joseph. *Mexico, Land of Mary's Wonder.* 1958. NY. St. Anthony Guild Press. 1st. 192p. G/G chipped dj. F3. $25.00.

CASSIRER, Ernst. *Substance & Function & Einstein's Theory of Relativity.* 1923. Open Court. 8vo. 465p. G/tattered. K5. $25.00.

CASSON, Lionel. *Ancient Egypt.* 1978. NY. Time. 11th. 191p. VG. W1. $10.00.

CASTANEDA, Carlos. *Fire from Within.* 1984. S&S. 1st. F/dj. B4. $45.00.

CASTANEDA, Pedro. *Journey of Coronado.* 1966. Readex Microprint. rpt. 8vo. F. F7. $30.00.

CASTIGLIONI, Arturo. *History of Medicine.* 1941. NY. 1st. 1013p. A13. $175.00.

CASTILLO, Ana. *Massacre of the Dreamers, Essays in Xicanisma.* (1994). Albuquerque. U of NM. 1st. F/F. B3. $30.00.

CASTILLO, Ana. *So Far from God.* (1995). NY. Norton. 1st. F/F. B3. $45.00.

CASTLE, Lewis. *Cactaceous Plants: Their History & Culture.* 1974 (1884). Annapolis. ils. 94p. B26. $15.00.

CASTLEMAN & SUTTON. *Massachusetts General Hospital 1955 – 1980.* 1983. Boston. 1st. 410p. A13. $30.00.

CASTRO, Michael. *Interpreting the Indian.* 1983. Albuquerque. NM U. 1st. F/dj. L3. $50.00.

CATANZARO, Angela. *Italian Desserts & Antipasto.* 1958. NY. Liveright. VG/dj. A16. $15.00.

CATENA, Teobaldo. *Manuel Del Coleccionista De Monedas.* 1988. MN. Latin Am Press. 1st. 114p. G. wrp. F3. $10.00.

CATHER, Willa. *Death Comes for the Archbishop.* 1927. Knopf. 1st. F/dj. Q1. $350.00.

CATHER, Willa. *Lucy Gayheart.* 1935. NY. Knopf. 1st. owner's stp. NF/VG dj. M19. $85.00.

CATHER, Willa. *Sapphira & the Slave Girl.* 1940. Knopf. ARC. F/F. D10. $175.00.

CATHER, Willa. *Shadows on the Rock.* 1931. Knopf. 1st. NF/VG. M23. $75.00.

CATLIN, George. *Catlin's North American Indian Portfolio.* 1970. Chicago. Sage. 1/1000. facsimile 1844 London. stiff portfolio. B24. $500.00.

CATTELL, Ann. *Mind Juggler & Other Ghost Stories.* 1966. Exposition. 1st. VG/VG. P3. $15.00.

CATTERMOLE, Peter. *Venus; The Geological Story.* 1994. Baltimore. Johns Hopkins Univ Press. 4to. 11 color plates. b/w photos. diagrams & maps. 250p. F/F. K5. $30.00.

CATTON, Bruce. *Glory Road: Bloody Route from Fredericksburg to Gettysburg.* 1952. Doubleday. 1st. 416p. cloth. NF/dj. M8. $35.00.

CATTON, Bruce. *Grant Takes Command.* 1969. Boston. Little, Brn. BCE. orig cloth. 556p. NF/VG. M8. $15.00.

CATTON, Bruce. *Reflections on the Civil War.* 1981. NY. 1st. ils John Geyser. F/dj. M4. $30.00.

CATTON, Bruce. *Waiting for the Morning Train: An American Boyhood.* 1972. Doubleday. 1/250. sgn/#d. F/sans/case. Q1. $75.00.

CAUFFIEL, Lowell. *Marker.* 1997. NY. St. Martin. 1st. review copy. author's 1st novel. F/VF. T2. $9.00.

CAUNITZ, William J. *Black Sand.* 1989. Crown. 1st. NF/NF. G8. $10.00.

CAUNITZ, William J. *Exceptional Clearance.* 1991. Crown. 1st. F/F. N4. $20.00.

CAUNITZ, William J. *Suspects.* 1986. NY. Crown. 1st. VF/VF. T2. $25.00.

CAVANNA, Betty. *Accent on April.* (1960). Morrow. BC. 8vo. 188p. bl brd. G+/dj. T5. $14.00.

CAVANNA, Betty. *Boy Next Door.* 1956. Morrow. 1st. 253p. VG/dj. M20. $30.00.

CAVANNA, Betty. *Passport to Romance.* 1955. Morrow. 1st. 249p. VG/dj. M20. $15.00.

CAVE, Emma. *Blood Bond.* 1979. Harper Row. 1st. F/F. P3. $25.00.

CAVE, Hugh B. *Death Stalks the Night.* 1995. Minneapolis. Fedogan & Bremer. 1st. VF/VF. T2. $29.00.

CAVE, Hugh B. *Isle of Whisperers.* 1999. Nottingham. Pumpkin books. 1st. sgn laid in. VF/VF. T2. $30.00.

CAVERLY, Carol. *All the Old Lions.* 1994. Aurora, CO. Write Way. 1st. sgn. F/F. B3. $35.00.

CAVERO ALVAREZ, Jesus. *El Mercado De Trabajo.* 1984. Mexico. Universidad De Valladolid. 1st. 319p. G/G wrp. F3. $20.00.

CAWEIN, Madison. *Myth & Romance.* 1899. NY. /London. 1st. 12mo. cloth. M1. $200.00.

CAZALET-KEIR, Thelma. *Homage to PG Wodehouse.* 1973. Barrie Jenkins. 1st. VG/VG. P3. $25.00.

CECIL, David. *Two Quiet Lives.* 1948. London. 1st. VG/dj. T9. $20.00.

CECIL, Henry. *Brief to Counsel.* 1958. Michael Joseph. 1st. VG. P3. $20.00.

CECIL, Henry. *Settled Out of Court.* 1959. NY. Harper. 1st Am ed. VG/G+. G8. $15.00.

CEDAR, Hughes. *Mastering the Pastoral Role.* 1991. Multnomah. 150p. VG/VG. B29. $7.00.

CELY, Michael. *Canada Calling.* nd. Frederick Warne. 240p. VG/ragged. M20. $17.50.

CENDRARS, Blaise. *Shadow.* 1982. Scribner. 1st. 4to. VG+/NF. P2. $95.00.

CENDRARS, Blaise & Leger, F. *Paris Ma Ville.* 1987. France. Bibliotheque de Arts. 1st. F in NF slipcase. M19. $75.00.

CERAM, C.W. *First American: Story of North American Archaeology.* 1971. HBJ. 1st. VG/dj. R11. $27.00.

CERF, Bennett. *Favorite One Act Plays.* 1958. Doubleday. dj. A19. $20.00.

CERF, Leon. *Letters of Napoleon to Josephine.* (1928). Paris. 12mo. French text. ils. 188p. three-quarter leather. H3. $50.00.

CERISE, Laurent-Alexis-P. *Des Fonctions Et Des Maladies Nerveuses.* 1870 (1842). Paris. Victor Masson. 2nd. 508p. prt gr wrp. G1. $100.00.

CERWIN, Herbert. *These are the Mexicans.* 1947. NY. Reynal & Hitchcock. 384p. G/G chipped dj. F3. $15.00.

CH'ANG, Lo-Huang. *Ming-Hsien Mo-Chi.* 1971. Shanghai. Commercial Pr. 2 vol. VG/bl wrp. W3. $65.00.

CHABER, M.E. *Acid Nightmare.* 1967. HRW. 1st. VG/VG. P3. $22.00.

CHABER, M. E. *Green Grow the Graves.* 1970. NY. Holt. 1st. F+/F+. H11. $25.00.

CHABER, M.E. *Wanted: Dead Men.* 1965. HRW. 1st. VG/VG. P3. $18.00.

CHABON, Michael. *A Model World and Other Stories.* 1991. NY. Morrow. 1st. F/F. H11. $30.00.

CHABON, Michael. *Mysteries of Pittsburgh.* 1988. Morrow. 1st. NF/dj. A20. $30.00.

CHABON, Michael. *Wonder Boys.* (1994). NY. Villard. ARC. pict wrp. sgn by author. F. B3. $60.00.

CHABOT, Ernest. *How to Grow Rare Greenhouse Plants. 260 Flowering Varieties for Amateur and Florist.* 1952. NY. 1st. color and b&w ils/photos. 182p. VG in spine faded dj. B26. $15.00.

CHADWICK, Douglas. *Fate of the Elephant.* 1993. Viking. 1st. 492p. F. S15. $10.00.

CHAFER, Lewis Sperry. *Kingdom in History & Prophecy.* 1943. Dunham. 167p. VG/torn. B29. $6.50.

CHAFER, Lewis Sperry. *True Evangelism or Winning Souls by Prayer.* 1944. Moody. 143p. G. B29. $5.00.

CHAFETS, Zev. *Inherit the Mob.* 1991. Random House. 1st. VG+/VG+. G8. $15.00.

CHAGALL, Marc. *The Jerusalem Windows.* 1967. Braziller. VG/torn dj. B29. $18.00.

CHAHINIAN, B. *Juan.* Sansevieria Trifasciata Varieties. 1986. Reseda, CA. photos. 109p. F/dj. B26. $17.50.

CHAILLEY, Jacques. *40,000 Years of Music: Man in Search of Music.* 1964. FSG. 1st Am. 229p. VG/dj. M20. $22.00.

CHAIS, Pamela. *Final Cut.* 1981. S&S. 1st. F/dj. M25. $25.00.

CHALFONT, Lord. *Waterloo.* 1979. Knopf. 1st Am. 239p. VG/dj. M20. $30.00.

CHALK, Douglas. *Hebes and Parahebes.* 1988. Portland. now OP. ils. 152p. New in dj. B26. $29.00.

CHALK, Ocania. *Black College Sport.* 1976. Dodd Mead. 1st. photos. F/VG. P8. $30.00.

CHALKER, Jack L. *Demons at Rainbow Bridge.* 1989. Ace. 1st. F/F. P3. $18.00.

CHALMERS, Audrey. *Fancy be Good.* 1941. Viking. 1st. 8vo. VG+/dj. M5. $20.00.

CHALMERS, Stephen. *Affair of the Gallows Tree.* 1930. Crime Club. 1st. VG. G8. $15.00.

CHAMALES, Tom. *Never So Few.* 1957. NY. 1st. VG/VG. B5. $35.00.

CHAMBERLAIN, Allen. *Beacon Hill: Its Ancient Pastures & Early Mansions.* 1925. photos. VG. M17. $30.00.

CHAMBERLAIN, George Agnew. *In Defense of Mrs. Maxon.* 1938. Bobbs Merrill. 1st. VG+. G8. $20.00.

CHAMBERLAIN, George Agnew. *Scudda A-Hoo! Scudda-Hay!* 1946. Bobbs Merrill. 1st. VG/VG. O3. $48.00.

CHAMBERLAIN, Hope Summerell. *Old Days in Chapel Hill Being Life & Letters CP Spencer.* 1926. Chapel Hill. 1st. 325p. cloth. NF. M8. $45.00.

CHAMBERLAIN, Joseph W. *Physics of the Aurora & Airglow.* 1961. Academic. 8vo. 704p. VG/dj. K5. $60.00.

CHAMBERLAIN, Samuel. *Bouquet De France.* 1960. NY. Gourmet. G+. A16. $20.00.

CHAMBERLAIN, Samuel. *British Bouquet.* 1973. Gourmet. G+. A16. $25.00.

CHAMBERLAIN, Sarah. *Frog He Would A-Wooing Go.* 1981. Chamberlain. 1/125. sgn. 7 full-p wood engravings. Oriental-style bdg. F. B24. $300.00.

CHAMBERLIN, Charles. *Methods in Plant Histology.* 1928. Chicago. 4th. 349p. dj. A10. $28.00.

CHAMBERLIN, F. *Private Character of Queen Elizabeth.* 1922. NY. ils. VG. M17. $17.50.

CHAMBERS, Anne. *Practical Guide to Marbling Paper.* 1986. Thames Hudson. 1st. ils. 88p. cloth. F/dj. O10. $35.00.

CHAMBERS, Dana. *Death Against Venus.* 1946. Dial. VG/VG. P3. $23.00.

CHAMBERS, G.F. *Story of the Solar System.* 1905 (1895). NY. Appleton. ils. 188p. cloth. G. K5. $12.00.

CHAMBERS, Oswald. *My Utmost for His Highest.* 1935. Dodd. Mead & Co. 375p. VG/worn dj. B29. $9.50.

CHAMBERS, Peter; See Phillips, Dennis.

CHAMBERS, Robert E.S. *John Tom Alligator & Others.* 1937. Dutton. 1st. VG/dj. M2. $12.00.

CHAMBERS, Robert W. *In Search of the Unknown.* 1974 (1904). Hyperion. rpt. F. M2. $30.00.

CHAMBERS, Robert W. *Mountain Land.* 1906. NY. D. Appleton & Co. 1st. ils by Frederick Richardson. 123p. VG. D6. $75.00.

CHAMBERS, Robert W. *Out of the Dark, Volume One: Origins.* 1998. Ashcroft, BC. Ash Tree Press. 1st. Hugh Lamb editor. VF/VF. T2. $50.00.

CHAMBERS, Robert W. *Slayer of Souls.* 1920. Doran. 1st. VG/facsimile Mc Canon dj. M2. $45.00.

CHAMBERS, Whitman. *Invasion!* 1943. Dutton. 1st. VG. P3. $20.00.

CHAMPOMIER, P. A. *Statement of the Sugar Crop Made in Louisiana in 1851 – 52.* 1852. New Orleans. Cook Young. 1st. 16mo. 52p. prt wrp. M1. $400.00.

CHAN, Stella. *Stella Chan's Secrets in the Art of Chinese Cooking.* 1974. CA. Academic Cultural Co. hc. ils Au Ho-nien. VG/VG. A28. $14.95.

CHANDLER, Ann C. *Pan the Piper & Other Marvelous Tales.* 1923. Harper. 1st. ils. 234p. gilt bl cloth. VG. D1. $40.00.

CHANDLER, Edna Walker. *Cowboy Sam & Big Bill.* 1960. Chicago. Benefic. ils Jack Merryweather. xl. VG. C8. $15.00.

CHANDLER, Edna Walker. *Cowboy Sam & the Rodeo.* 1959. Chicago. Benefic. 8vo. VG. C8. $15.00.

CHANDLER, John Greene. *Remarkable History of Chicken Little.* 1979. Boston. Bromer/Hyder. 1/150. 59x50mm. ils Janet Hobbs. marbled brd. F. $24.00.

CHANDLER, Raymond. *Farewell My Lovely.* 1940. NY. Alfred A. Knopf. 1st. slight stains/wear on pg edges. otherwise. F/VG dj. M15. $3.500.00.

CHANDLER, Raymond. *Killer in the Rain.* 1964. London. Hamish Hamilton. 1st. precedes Am ed. F/dj. M15. $400.00.

CHANDLER, Raymond. *Midnight Raymond Chandler.* 1971. Houghton Mifflin. 1st. VG. M22. $15.00.

CHANDLER, Raymond. *Playback.* 1958. Boston. Houghton Mifflin. 1st. NF in dj. D10. $125.00.

CHANDLER, Raymond. *Playback.* 1958. Thriller BC. VG/G. P3. $15.00.

CHANDLER, Raymond. *Red Wind.* 1946. World. 1st. VG. M22. $15.00.

CHANDLER, Raymond. *Spanish Blood.* 1946. World. 1st. VG. M22. $15.00.

CHANDLER, Raymond. *The Big Sleep.* 1989. San Francisco. North Point Press. reissue. ils w/photos by Lou Stouman. VF/VF. T2. $20.00.

CHANDLER & PARKER. *Poodle Springs.* 1989. Putnam. 1st. F/F. M22. $15.00.

CHANEY, Jack. *Foolish Questions.* Yellowstone Best. 1924. Woodruff. 3rd. 104p. VG/wrp. J2. $165.00.

CHANG, Kwang-Chih. *Archeology of Ancient China.* 1963. Yale. 1st. 346p. F/VG. W3. $75.00.

CHANG, Kwang-Chih. *Shang Civilization.* 1980. Yale. 1st. ils/charts/tables. 417p. F. W3. $68.00.

CHANNING, Steven. *Crisis of Fear.* 1972. 315p. O8. $7.50.

CHANSLOR, Roy. *Ballad of Cat Ballou.* 1956. Little, Brn. 1st. F/F. B4. $175.00.

CHANSLOR, Roy. *Johnny Guitar.* 1953. NY. S&S. 1st. F/F. B4. $200.00.

CHANTER, Charlotte. *Ferny Combes.* 1856. London. Lovell Reeve. 2nd. 16mo. A22. $85.00.

CHAO, Yuen-Ren. *Aspects of Chinese Socio-Linguistics.* 1976. Stanford. 1st. F/F. W3. $52.00.

CHAPEL, Charles Edward. *Art of Shooting.* 1960. Barnes. 409p. dj. A17. $15.00.

CHAPELLE, Howard I. *History of American Sailing Ships.* (1935). NY. Norton. later prt. 400p. VG/worn. P4. $35.00.

CHAPELLE, Howard I. *History of the American Sailing Navy: Ships & Developement.* (1949). Bonanza. later prt. 558p. VG/worn. P4. $40.00.

CHAPIN, Anna Alice. *The Everyday Fairy Book.* 1915. NY. Dodd. Mead & Co. 1st & only ed. ils by Jessie Wilcox Smith. 4to. gr cloth. 160p. VG. D6. $250.00.

CHAPIN, Howard Millar. *Tartar: Armed Sloop of the Colony of Rhode Island.* 1922. Providence. Soc of Colonial Wars. 7 pl. 67p. T7. $50.00.

CHAPIN, James Henry. *From Japan to Granada.* 1889. Putnam. 1st. inscr. 12mo. gr cloth. G. B11. $25.00.

CHAPIN, Rev. E. H. *Humanity in the City.* 1854. NY. De Witt & Davenport. 1st. VG. B2. $40.00.

CHAPLIN, Charles. *My Autobiography.* 1966. London. 545p. F/dj. A17. $25.00.

CHAPLIN, Gordon. *Joyride.* 1982. NY. Coward. 1st. author's 1st book. Jacket has wear at extremities. crease on front flap and small scrape on rear panel. F/NF. H11. $40.00.

CHAPLIN, Ralph. *Somewhat Barbaric.* 1944. Seattle. McCaffrey Dogwood. 1st. inscr. F/NF. B2. $125.00.

CHAPMAN, Allen. *Radio Boys with the Iceberg Patrol (#7).* 1924. Grosset Dunlap. 218p. cloth. VG/dj (lists to #11). M20. $45.00.

CHAPMAN, Clark R. *Planets of Rock & Ice: From Mercury to Moons of Saturn.* 1982. Scribner. 1st. F/dj. M2. $15.00.

CHAPMAN, Frank. *Life in an Air Castle.* 1938. NY. Appleton. 1st. 250p. xl. F3. $20.00.

CHAPMAN, Frank M. *Handbook of Birds of Eastern North America.* 1966. NY. rpt (2nd). ils. 581p. VG. S15. $15.00.

CHAPMAN, Hames B. *The Terminology of Holiness.* 1947. Beacon Hill. 112p. VG. B29. $8.00.

CHAPMAN, John Jay. *Treason & Death of Benedict Arnold.* 1910. Moffat Yard. 1st. 76p. brd/paper label. M1. $75.00.

CHAPMAN, John Jay. *Two Greek Plays.* 1928. Houghton Mifflin. 1st. 12mo. 118p. salmon brd. dj. M1. $85.00.

CHAPMAN, Kenneth M. *Pottery of the Santo Domingo Pueblo.* 1936. Santa Fe. NM. Laboratory of Anthropology. 191p. VG. K7. $225.00.

CHAPMAN, Lee; see Bradley, Marion Zimmer.

CHAPMAN, Paul H. *Spirit Runestones: A Study of Linguistics.* 1994. SF. Epigraphic Soc. 60p. F/prt wrp. P4. $22.50.

CHAPMAN, Sally. *Cyberkiss.* 1996. NY. St. Martin. 1st. review copy w/pub promo letter. VF/VF. T2. $15.00.

CHAPMAN, Sally. *Love Bytes.* 1994. NY. St. Martin. ARC. wrp. F. B2. $30.00.

CHAPPELL, Fred. *Farewell, I'm Bound to Leave You.* (1996). NY. Picador. 1st. sgn by author. F/F. B3. $40.00.

CHAPPELL, Fred. *Inkling.* 1965. HBW. 1st. author's 2nd book. F/NF. B3. $100.00.

CHAPUT, Don. *Virgil Earp, Western Peace Officer.* 1994. Affiliated Writers of Am. 1st. photos/maps. 255p. AN. J2. $39.00.

CHAPUT, W.J. *Dead in the Water.* 1991. St Martin. 1st. VG/VG. P3. $16.00.

CHARBONNEAU, Louis. *Way Out.* 1966. Barrie Rockliff. 1st. VG/VG. P3. $25.00.

CHARGAFF, Erwin. *Heraclitean Fire.* 1978. Rockefeller U. 1st. 252p. xl. VG. K3. $15.00.

CHARLES, Kate. *A Drink of Deadly Wine.* 1992. NY. Mysterious Press. 1st Am ed. VF/VF. T2. $15.00.

CHARLES, R.H. *Apocrypha & Pseudepigrapha of Old Testament in English.* 1963. Oxford. 2 vol. NF/dj. W3. $625.00.

CHARLES, Robert H. *Roundabout Turn.* 1930. London. Warne. unp. cloth. G+/VG+. D4. $35.00.

CHARLES, V.K. *Introduction to Mushroom Hunting.* 1974. Dover. 48p. VG/stiff wrp. B1. $12.50.

CHARLESWORTH, J.K. *Historical Geology of Ireland.* 1963. London. Oliver Boyd Ltd. 565p. VG/dj. D8. $30.00.

CHARLOT, Jean. *Charlot Murals in Georgia.* 1945. Athens. 1st. VG/VG. B5. $65.00.

CHARON, Mural K. *Ludwig (Ludvik) Moser King of Glass.* 1984. Charon/Ferguson. 4to sgn. 111p. NF. H1. $87.50.

CHARRIERE, Henri. *Papillon.* 1970. Morrow. 1st Am. NF/NF. M22. $15.00.

CHARTERIS, Leslie. *Enter the Saint.* nd. Detective Story Club. NF/G. P3. $30.00.

CHARTERIS, Leslie. *Saint on the Spanish Main.* 1955. Doubleday Crime Club. 1st. NF/rpr. M15. $65.00.

CHARTERIS, Leslie. *The First Saint Omnibus.* 1939. London. Hodder & Stoughton. 1st. some wear. F w/VG dj. M15. $350.00.

CHARTERIS, Leslie. *The Last Hero.* 1930. NY. Doubleday Crime Club. 1st. 1st Am ed. F w/o dj. M15. $75.00.

CHARTERIS, Leslie. *The White Rider.* 1930. NY. Doubleday Crime Club. 1st. 1st Am ed. NF w/o dj. M15. $75.00.

CHARTERIS, Leslie. *Vendetta for the Saint.* 1964. Crime Club. 1st. F/NF. M19. $25.00.

CHARTERS, Ann. *Kerouac.* 1973. Straight Arrow. 1st. VG/VG. P3. $40.00.

CHARTERS, Ann. *Nobody: The Story of Bert Williams.* 1970. Macmillan. 1st. NF/NF. one short tear to rear panel of dj. M25. $45.00.

CHARTERS, Samuel. *Robert Johnson.* 1973. NY. Oak. 1st. sm 4to. 88p. F/wrp. B2. $40.00.

CHARTERS, Samuel B. *The Country Blues.* 1959. NY. Rinehart. 1st. F/NF. B2. $50.00.

CHARYN, Jerome. *Darlin' Bill.* 1980. Arbor. 1st. F/F. T11. $30.00.

CHARYN, Jerome. *Good Policeman.* 1990. Mysterious. 1st. VG+/NF. G8. $15.00.

CHARYN, Jerome. *Isaac Quartet.* 1984. Zomba. 1st. F/F. P3. $30.00.

CHARYN, Jerome. *Pinocchio Nose.* 1983. Arbor. 1st. F/NF. T12. $20.00.

CHASE, Glen; see Fox, Gardner F.

CHASE, James Hadley. *Figure it Out for Yourself.* nd. Robert Hale. VG/G. P3. $20.00.

CHASE, James Hadley. *Safer Dead.* 1954. Hale. 1st. VG. G8. $10.00.

CHASE, James Hadley. *Twelve Chinks & a Woman.* nd. Jarrolds. VG. P3. $25.00.

CHASE, Mary Ellen. *The Prophets for the Common Reader.* 1963. Norton. 1st. 183p. VG. 29. $9.50.

CHASE, Pearl. *Cacti & Other Succulents.* 1930. Santa Barbara. 107p. sc. B26. $21.00.

CHASE, Richard. *Old Songs & Singing Games.* 1938. Chapel Hill. 42p. VG+/wrp. O4. $35.00.

CHASE, Robert. *Atlas of Hand Surgery.* 1973. Phil. 1st. 438p. A13. $150.00.

CHASE, W.H. *Pioneers of Alaska.* 1951. KS City. sgn. ils/photos. 203p. F. M4. $30.00.

CHASTAIN, Thomas. *Pandora's Box.* 1974. Mason Lipscomb. 1st. VG/VG. P3. $20.00.

CHATHAM, Russell. *Angler's Coast.* 1976. Doubleday. 1st. author's 1st book. F/VG clip. B3. $100.00.

CHATTERTON, Fenimore C. *Yesterday's Wyoming.* 1957. Powder River. dj. A19. $100.00.

CHATWIN, Bruce. *In Patagonia.* 1978. Summit. 1st Am. author's 1st book. F/F. O10. $125.00.

CHATWIN, Bruce. *On the Black Hill.* 1983. NY. Viking. 1st Am ed. F in F dj. D10. $50.00.

CHATWIN, Bruce. *Songlines.* 1987. Viking. 1st. F/dj. A24. $35.00.

CHATWIN, Bruce. *The Viceroy of Quidah.* 1980. London. Jonathan Cape. 1st. printing of only 5,500 copies. NF/NF. A24. $155.00.

CHATWIN, Bruce. *Utz.* 1988. NY. Viking. 1st. F/VF. H11. $35.00.

CHAUCER, Geoffrey. *Canterbury Tales.* 1934. Covici Friede. 1st trade. ils. tan cloth. VG. B27. $100.00.

CHAYEFSKY, Paddy. *Altered States.* 1978. Harper Row. 1st. NF/NF. M22. $20.00.

CHEESMAN, Evelyn. *Islands Near the Sun: Off the Beaten Track.* 1927. London. Witherby. 1st. ils. 304p. VG/VG. S25. $50.00.

CHEETHAM, Anthony. *Science Against Man.* 1971. MacDonald. 1st. VG/VG. P3. $28.00.

CHEETHAM, Sir Nicholas. *Mexico. A Short History.* 1971. NY. Crowell. 1st Am ed. b/w photos. map. index. 302p. G/G. chipped dj. F3. $15.00.

CHEEVER, John. *Wapshot Chronicle.* 1957. NY. Harper. 1st. author's 3rd book. F/NF. L3. $200.00.

CHEEVER, John. *Way Some People Live.* 1943. Random. 1st. author's 1st book. F/dj. B24. $950.00.

CHENAK, Susan. *Smithereens.* 1995. Doubleday. 1st. sgn. F/F. A23. $34.00.

CHENAULT, John Cabell. *Old Cane Springs.* 1937. Louisville, KY. 2nd. 257p. G. B18. $45.00.

CHENEVIX-TRENCH, Charles. *History of Horsemanship.* 1970. Doubleday. 1st Am. VG/VG. O3. $45.00.

CHENEY, Margaret. *Tesla: Man Out of Time.* 1981. Dorset. 320p. F/dj. K3. $15.00.

CHENG, Chu-Yuan. *Scientific & Engineering Manpower in Communist China.* 1965. National Science Found. 588p. VG/stiff wrp. W3. $95.00.

CHER, Ming. *Spider Boys.* 1995. NY. Morrow. 1st. author's 1st book. VF/F. H11. $20.00.

CHERFAS, Jeremy. *Man Made Life.* 1982. NY. Pantheon Books. 1st. VG/VG. A28. $8.50.

CHERIKOFF, V. & J Issacs. *The Bush Food Handbook. How to Gather, Grow, Process & Cook Australian Wild Foods.* nd (circa 1990). Balmain. NSW. sc. 4to. upper edge faded. else VG in dj. B26. $39.00.

CHERNIN, Kim. *Obsession.* 1981. Harper Row. 1st. author's 1st book. F/NF. M19. $25.00.

CHERRY-GARRARD, Apsley. *Worst Journey in the World.* 1994. London. Picador. 4 maps. 607p. NF/dj. P4. $40.00.

CHERRYH, C. J. *Cyteen.* 1988. Warner. 1st. F/F. M21. $60.00.

CHERRYH, C. J. *Kif Strike Back.* 1985. Phantasia. 1st. F/F. P3. $25.00.

CHERRYH, C. J. *Rimrunners.* 1989. Warner. 1st. F/F. W2. $20.00.

CHESBRO, George C. *Bone.* 1989. NY. Mysterious. 1st. F/F. H11. $15.00.

CHESBRO, George C. *Jungle of Steel & Stone.* 1988. NY. Mysterious. 1st. F/F. H11. $20.00.

CHESBRO, George C. *Shadow of a Broken Man.* 1977. S&S. 1st. VG/VG. P3. $30.00.

CHESBRO, George C. *The Fear in Yesterday's Rings.* 1991. NY. Mysterious Press. 1st. sgn. VF/VF. T2. $25.00.

CHESBRO, George C. *Two Songs This Archangel Sings.* 1986. NY. Atheneum. 1st. F/F. H11. $35.00.

CHESELDEN, William. *Anatomy of the Human Body.* 1806. Boston. 2nd Am. 352p. half leather. A13. $400.00.

CHESHIRE, Giff. *Stronghold.* 1963. Doubleday. 1st. F/NF clip. B4. $65.00.

CHESNEY, Charles Cornwallis. *Essays in Military Biography.* 1874. NY. Henry Holt. 1st. orig cloth. expertly rebacked. 398p. VG. M8. $350.00.

CHESNUTT, Charles W. *Conjure Tales.* 1975. London. Collins. 1st thus. 1st. ils Ross/ Romano. 8vo. NF/VG. $8.00.

CHESSON, W. H. *George Cruikshank.* London. Duckworth & Co. nd (circa 1890). 16mo. 282p. ils. brnbrd. 1st ed. More than 50 ils. 30p biblio index (annotated). minor dust soiling. VG. L5. $40.00.

CHESTER, Peter; see Phillips, Dennis.

CHESTERTON, G. K. *Annotated Innocence of Father Brown.* 1987. Oxford. 1st. F. M2. $20.00.

CHESTERTON, G. K. *Collected Poems of GK Chesterton.* 1927. Great Britain. Cecil Palmer. 1st. G+. M23. $25.00.

CHESTERTON, G. K. *Common Man.* 1950. Sheed Ward. 1st. VG/VG. P3. $30.00.

CHESTERTON, G. K. *Father Brown of the Church of Rome: Selected Mystery Stories.* 1996. San Francisco. Ignatius Press. 1st. VF/VF. T2. $20.00.

CHESTERTON, G. K. *Gloria in Profundis.* nd. 1/350. ils Eric Gill. yel brd. VG+. S13. $20.00.

CHESTERTON, G. K. *Man Who Was Thursday.* 1908. Bristol/London. 1st. G-. M23. $50.00.

CHETWODE, Penelope. *Two Middle-Aged Ladies in Adalusia.* 1963. London. John Murray. 3rd. photos. VG/VG. A25. $18.00.

CHETWYND-HAYES, R. *Quiver of Ghosts.* 1984. Wm Kimber. 1st. F/F. P3. $25.00.

CHEUNG, D. *Isle Full of Noises.* 1987. Columbia. 1st. 257p. F. W3. $38.00.

CHEUSE, Alan. *Grandmother's Club.* 1986. Peregrine Smith. 1st. F/F. A20. $20.00.

CHEVALIER, Haakon. *Last Voyage of the Schooner Rosamond.* 1970. London. Deutsch. 248p. dj. T7. $35.00.

CHEVALIER, Maurice. *Mome a Cheveux Blancs.* 1969. Paris. inscr. 280p. F/dj. B14. $60.00.

CHEW, Peter. *Kentucky Derby: The First 100 Years.* 1974. Houghton Mifflin. 1st. 4to. VG. O3. $45.00.

CHEWYND-HAYES, Ronald. *Ghosts from the Mist of Time.* 1985. London. William Kimber. 1st. sgn. VF/VF. T2. $40.00.

CHEWYND-HAYES, Ronald. *Kepple.* 1992. London. Robert Hale. 1st. sgn. VF/VF. T2. $30.00.

CHEWYND-HAYES, Ronald. *The Curse of the Snake God.* 1991. London. Inner Circle. 1st. sgn. VF/VF. T2. $30.00.

CHEWYND-HAYES, Ronald. *The House of Dracula.* 1987. London. William Kimber. 1st. VF/VF. T2. $30.00.

CHEYNEY, Peter. *Curiosity of Etienne MacGregor.* 1952. 1st Eng. NF/VG. M19. $25.00.

CHEYNEY, Peter. *Dark Bahama.* 1950. Collins. VG/VG. P3. $15.00.

CHEYNEY, Peter. *Uneasy Terms.* 1947. Dodd Mead. 1st. VG/G. P3. $25.00.

CHIANG, Yee. *Chinese Calligraphy: an Introduction.* 1955. Harvard. 230p. VG/dj. W3. $52.00.

CHICKERING, Carol. *Flowers of Guatemala.* 1973. Norman. OK. 128p. VG. A10. $25.00.

CHIDAMIAN, Claude. *Book of Cacti & Other Succulents.* 1958. Garden City, BC. 243p. VG/dj. B26. $12.50.

CHIDSEY, Donald Barr. *Captain Adam.* 1953. Crown. 1st. VG/VG. P3. $20.00.

CHILD, Frank. *Colonial Witch.* 1897. Baker Taylor. VG. M2. $75.00.

CHILD, Georgie Boynton. *Efficient Kitchen.* 1914. McBride Nast. G. A16. $25.00.

CHILD, Harold. *Aucassin and Nicolette, Translated and Edited with an Introduction by.* 1911. London. Adam and Charles Black. 1st. sm 4to. white cloth w/gilt. floral design. 6 color plates. teg. ils Anne Anderson. 132p. NF. D6. $125.00.

CHILD, Julia. *Cooking with Master Chefs.* 1993. NY. Knopf. 1st. sgn. F/F. O11. $70.00.

CHILD, Julia. *Julia Child & Company.* 1978. Knopf. 1st. 243p. B10. $10.00.

CHILD, Julia. *Mastering the Art of French Cooking.* 1950. Knopf. BC. ils. 622p. VG/fair. B10. $15.00.

CHILD, Lee. *Die Trying.* 1998. NY. Putnam. 1st Am ed. sgn. VF/VF. T2. $25.00.

CHILD, Lee. *Killing Floor.* 1997. NY. Putnam. 1st. sgn. author's 1st novel. VF/VF. T2. $35.00.

CHILD, Lee. *Tripwire.* 1999. London. Bantam Press. 1st. sgn. VF/VF. T2. $30.00.

CHILD, Lincoln. *Riptide.* 1998. NY. Warner. 1st. F-/VF. H11. $15.00.

CHILD, Theodore. *Spanish-American Republics.* 1891. Harper. 1st. 444p. xl. F3. $25.00.

CHILDRESS, Mark. *A World Made of Fire.* 1984. NY. Knopf. 1st. review copy. author's 1st book. F/F. D10. $75.00.

CHILDRESS, Mark. *Crazy in Alabama.* 1993. NY. Putnam. 1st. F/F. H11. $25.00.

CHILDRESS, Mark. *Tender.* 1990. NY. Harmony Books. 1st. sgn. F/F. O11. $20.00.

CHILL, Abraham. *Mizvot: Commandments & Their Rationale.* 1974. Jerusalem. Keter. 508p. VG/dj. S3. $34.00.

CHIN, Ann-Ping. *Children of China: Voices from Recent Years.* 1988. Knopf. 1st. F/dj. W3. $42.00.

CHIN, Art. *Anything Anytime, Anywhere: Legacy of Flying Tiger Line.* 1993. Seattle. 293p. 4to. wrp. A17. $17.50.

CHIN, S. S. *Missile Configuration Design.* 1961. McGraw Hill. 8vo. 279p. VG/dj. K5. $45.00.

CHINIQUY, Charles. *Fifty Years in the Church of Rome.* 1960. Baker. 597p. G. B29. $20.00.

CHIPAULT, Antoine Maxime. *Travaux De Neurologie Chirugicle.* 1896. Paris. Vigot Freres. 352p+208 woodcuts. contemporary bdg. xl. G1. $100.00.

CHIPENDALE, Captain Harry Allen. *Sails and Whales.* (1951). Boston. Houghton Mifflin Company. 8vo. 232p. gr cloth. torn dj. 1st ed. Not much left of dj. large pieces missing. book VG. L5. $10.00.

CHIPMAN, Jack & Judy Stangler. *The Complete Collectors Guide to Bauer Pottery.* 1982. Culver City, California Spectrum. 8vo sgn. 124p. VG. H1. $48.00.

CHISHOLM, Shirley. *The Good Fight.* 1973. Harper & Row. 1st. Jacket is lightly sunned at the spine. NF/dj. M25. $25.00.

CHITTENDEN, Alfred K. *Red Gum.* 1905. WA. DC. ils/fld map. 56p. tan wrp. B26. $15.00.

CHITTENDEN, H.M. *History of Early Steamboat Navigation on Missouri River.* 1962 (1903). Minneapolis. 2 vol in 1. 1/1500. F/dj. M4. $55.00.

CHITTENDEN, H.M. *History of the American Fur Trade of the Far West.* 1954. Academic. 2 vol. VG/dj. J2. $195.00.

CHITTENDEN, L.E. *Personal Reminiscences 1840 – 1890.* 1893. NY. 434p. O8. $12.50.

CHIU, Hong Yee & Amador Muriel, editors. *Stellar Evolution.* 1972. MIT Press. Cambridge, MA. sm 4to. text figures. 812p. VG/chipped. torn dj. K5. $60.00.

CHIZMAR, Richard T. *Midnight Promises.* 1996. Springfield. Gauntlet Press. 1st. 1/500 # copies. sgn by Chizmar, Gorman, Garton. author's 1st collection. VF/VF. T2. $35.00.

CHIZMAR, Richard T. *The Best of Cemetery Dance.* 1998. Baltimore. C D Publications. 1st. VF/VF. T2. $35.00.

CHIZMAR, Richard T., editor. *Thrillers.* 1993. Baltimore. C D Publications. 1st. 1/500 # copies. sgn by all of 18 contributors + editors. VF/VF dj & slipcase. T2. $60.00.

CHOI, Susan. *The Foreign Student.* 1998. NY. Harper Flamingo. sgn 1st ed. F/F. M23. $35.00.

CHOMSKY, William. *Hebrew: Eternal Language.* 1957. JPS. ils. 321p. VG/dj. S3. $22.00.

CHOPPING, Richard. *Fly.* 1965. FSG. 1st. author's 1st book. NF/F. H11. $40.00.

CHORAO, Kay. *Lester's Overnight.* 1977. Dutton. 1st. lg 8vo. unp. F/VG. C14. $17.00.

CHOURAQUI, Andre. *Between East & West: Brief History of Jews in North America.* 1968. Phil. Jewish Pub Soc. 1st. 376p. NF. W3. $46.00.

CHRISMAN, Miriam Usher. *Bibliography of Strasbourg Imprints, 1480 – 1599.* 1982. New Haven. Yale. 1st. 8vo. gilt purple cloth. F/sans. $10.00.

CHRISTENSEN, Edwin O. *Index of American Design.* 1950. Macmillan. 1st. 229p. VG. A8. $26.50.

CHRISTIAN, Purnell. *Modern Physics and Other Tales.* 1991. Wichita. Watermark Press. 1st. sgn. author's 1st book. VF/VF. T2. $30.00.

CHRISTIAN, Purnell. *Rude Awakening.* 1996. Tucson. Dennis Mcmillan. 1st. 1 or 10 author copies from ltd ed 30 hc copies. sgn by author, artist, and publisher. VF/VF. T2. $200.00.

CHRISTIANSEN, Harry. *Northern Ohio's Interurbans and Rapid Transit Railways.* 1965. Cleveland. 1st. ils. wrp. 176p. G. lt soiling. B18. $37.50.

CHRISTIANSON, Gale E. *Edwin Hubble; Mariner of the Nebulae.* 1995. NY. FSG. 8vo. 8p b/w photo ils. 420p. VG/VG. K5. $17.00.

CHRISTIE, Agatha. *A Caribbean Mystery.* 1964. London. Collins Crime Club. 1st. lt edge spotting. F/dj. M15. $50.00.

CHRISTIE, Agatha. *Agatha Christie: First Lady of Crime.* 1977. London. Weidenfeld & Nicolson. 1st. VF/dj. M15. $65.00.

CHRISTIE, Agatha. *And Then There Were None.* 1945. Grosset Dunlap. photoplay ed. VG/VG. M22. $30.00.

CHRISTIE, Agatha. *By the Pricking of My Thumbs.* 1968. Dodd Mead. 1st. VG/G. P3. $25.00.

CHRISTIE, Agatha. *Come Tell Me How You Live.* 1946. London. Collins. 1st. Jacket has nicks and minor wear at spine ends and wear along folds. F/VG. M15. $250.00.

CHRISTIE, Agatha. *Elephants Can Remember.* 1972. Collins. 1st. F/NF. M25. $25.00.

CHRISTIE, Agatha. *Endless Night.* 1967. London. Collins Crime Club. 1st. F/F. B2. $35.00.

CHRISTIE, Agatha. *Murder of Roger Ackroyd.* Oct 1926. Dodd Mead. 5th. VG. M22. $25.00.

CHRISTIE, Agatha. *Nemesis.* 1971. Collins Crime Club. 1st. VG/fair. P3. $18.00.

CHRISTIE, Agatha. *Passenger to Frankfurt.* 1970. London. Collins Crime Club. 1st. F/dj. Q1. $75.00.

CHRISTIE, Agatha. *Postern of Fate.* 1973. Dodd Mead. 1st. VG/VG. P3. $25.00.

CHRISTIE, Agatha. *Taken at the Flood.* 1948. London. Collins Crime Club. 1st. VG/dj. M15. $45.00.

CHRISTIE, Agatha. *The Man in the Brown Suit.* 1924. London. John Lane (Bodley Head). 1st. short crease at corner of spine head; lt foxing to ep. some fading. VG w/o dj. A24. $750.00.

CHRISTIE, Agatha. *The Mirror Crack'd from Side to Side.* 1962. London. Collins Crime Club. 1st. F/dj clip. M15. $65.00.

CHRISTIE, Agatha. *The Pale Horse.* 1961. London. Collins Crime Club. 1st. F/dj. M15. $85.00.

CHRISTIE, Agatha. *The Unexpected Guest.* 1999. NY. St. Martin. 1st. play adapted by Charles Osborne. sgn. VF/VF. T2. $26.00.

CHRISTIE, Agatha. *Third Girl.* 1967. Dodd Mead. 1st. VG/VG. P3. $20.00.

CHRISTIE, Agatha. *Triple Threat.* 1943. Dodd Mead. omnibus ed. F/NF. M15. $150.00.

CHRISTOPHER, John. *Little People.* 1966. S&S. 1st. VG/dj. M2. $15.00.

CHRISTOPHER, John. *Pendulum.* 1968. S&S. 1st. VG/VG. P3. $15.00.

CHRISTOPHER, John. *Scent of White Poppies.* 1959. 1st. NF/VG. M19. $25.00.

CHRISTY, Howard Chandler. *Our Girls.* 1907. NY. 1st. VG. B5. $95.00

CHUBIN, Barry. *Feet of a Snake.* 1984. Arbor. 1st. VG/VG. P3. $18.00.

CHUKOVSKY, Kornei. *Telephone.* 1977. Delacorte. 1st Am. 48p. F/F. D4. $45.00.

CHUNG, Wa Nan. *Art of Chinese Gardens.* 1982. Hong Kong U. sm obl 4to. 251p. F. S15. $20.00.

CHURCH, Archibald. *Diseases of the Nervous System.* 1908. NY. Appleton. 1st Eng-language. 8vo. 1205p. rebound. G1. $65.00.

CHURCH, Thomas. *Your Private World. A Study of Intimate Gardens.* 1969. San Francisco. 4to. 202p. VG in dj. B26. $95.00.

CHURCHILL, Fleetwood. *On the Theory & Practice of Midwifery.* 1946. Phil. 2nd Am. 525p. full leather. A13. $200.00.

CHURCHILL, Luana. *Grinning Ghoul.* 1974. Lenox Hill. 1st. VG/G. G8. $10.00.

CHURCHILL, Winston S. *London to Ladysmith Via Pretoria.* 1900. NY. 1st Am. VG. M17. $250.00.

CHURCHILL, Winston S. *Secret Session Speeches.* 1946. London. Cassell. 1st. ils. octavo. bl cloth. F/F. R3. $65.00.

CHURCHILL, Winston S. *The Dawn of Liberation.* 1945. NY. 1st Am ed. corners slightly bumped. 417p. VG/G. B18. $25.00.

CHUTE, Carolyn. *Beans.* 1985. Chatto Windus/Hogarth. 1st Eng. rem mk. F/F. R14. $35.00.

CHUTE, Carolyn. *Letourneau's Used Auto Parts.* 1988. Ticknor Fields. 1st. sgn. F/F. B3. $45.00.

CHUTE, Carolyn. *Snow Man.* 1999. Harcourt Brace. UP. F/wrp. M25. $50.00.

CIARDI, John. *You Know Who.* 1964. Lippincott. 1st. 63p. VG/dj. M20. $50.00.

CIMENT, Jill. *Small Claims.* 1986. NY. 1st. author's 1st book. NF/dj. R13. $25.00.

CIMENT, Michael. *Kubrick.* 1983. NY. HRW. 1st Am ed. trans Gilbert Adair. F/NF. O11. $150.00.

CINTRON, Lola. *Goddess of the Bullring, Story of Conchita Cintron.* (1960). Bobbs Merrill. 1st. 349p. dj. F3. $25.00.

CIORAN, E. M. *History and Utopia.* 1987. NY. Seaver Books. 1st. F/F. B2. $25.00.

CISNEROS, Sandra. *La Casa En Mango Street.* (1994). NY. Vintage Espanol. UP. prt green wrp. sgn by author. F. B3. $50.00.

CISNEROS, Sandra. *The House on Mango Street.* (1994). NY. Knopf. 1st hc UK ed. F/NF. faint creasing. B3. $35.00.

CISNEROS, Sandra. *Woman Hollering Creek.* 1991. NY. Random House. 1st. F/F. D10. $40.00.

CIST, Henry M. *Army of the Cumberland.* 1882. NY. 1st. 289p. F. O8. $21.50.

CLAGETT, Marshall. *Critical Problems in History of Science.* 1959. Madison, WI. 8vo. 547p. wrp. K3. $10.00.

CLAIR, Maxine. *Coping with Gravity.* 1988. DC. Washington Writers' Publishing House. 1st. author's 1st book. F in decor bl wrp. A24. $75.00.

CLAIR, Maxine. *Rattlebone.* 1994. NY. FSG. 1st. author's 1st novel. F/F. A24. $30.00.

CLAIRON, Claire Hyppolite. *Memoires Et Reflections Sur L'Art Dramatique.* 1799. Paris. Buisson. An VII. 8vo. calf/brd. R12. $250.00.

CLAMPITT, Amy. *The Kingfisher.* 1983. NY. Knopf. 1st. F/F w/sm tear. D10. $95.00.

CLAMPITT, John W. *Echoes from the Rocky Mountains.* 1889. ils. 671p. O8. $55.00.

CLANCY, Tom. *Cardinal of the Kremlin.* 1988. Putnam. 1st. F/F. H11. $35.00.

CLANCY, Tom. *Clear & Present Danger.* 1989. Putnam. 1st. NF/NF. P3. $40.00.

CLANCY, Tom. *Debt of Honor.* 1994. NY. Putnam. ARC. NF/ printed white wrp. M25. $45.00.

CLANCY, Tom. *Hunt for Red October.* 1984. Taiwan. piracy ed. 8vo. author's 1st book. VG/NF. S9. $125.00.

CLANCY, Tom. *Hunt for Red October.* 1985. Annapolis. Naval Inst. 1st. author's 1st book. F/NF. L3. $650.00.

CLANCY, Tom. *Patriot Games.* 1987. NY. Putnam. 1st. F/F. H11. $50.00.

CLANCY, Tom. *Red Storm Rising.* 1986. NY. Putnam. 1st. F/F. H11. $65.00.

CLANCY, Tom. *Sum of All Fears.* 1991. Putnam. 1st. NF/NF. P3. $25.00.

CLANCY, Tom. *Without Remorse.* 1993. NY. Putnam. 1st. NF/NF. H11. $20.00.

CLAPESATTLE, Helen. *Doctors Mayo.* 1941. Minneapolis. 1st. 822p. A13. $30.00.

CLAPHAM, A R, etal. *Flora of the British Isles.* 1962 (1952). Cambridge, England. 2nd ed. gr cloth. 1269p. VG in dj. B26. $24.00.

CLAPP, Edward Latimer. *Andersonville, Six Months a Prisoner of War…* 1865. Milwaukee. Daily Wisconsin Steam Printing House. 1st. orig printed wrp. backstrip tape repr. minor edge chipping. VG. M8. $150.00.

CLARE, Alys. *Fortune Like the Moon: A Hawkenlye Mystery.* 1999. London. Hodder & Stoughton. 1st. VF/VF. T2. $29.00.

CLARE, John. *Dwellers in the Wood.* 1967. Macmillan. ARC/1st. 43p. F/F. D4. $35.00.

CLARK, Alice M. *Begonia Portraits.* 1984 (1880). Dehra Dun. ltd 1000 copies. sm 4to. 159p. F. B26. $44.00.

CLARK, Ann Nolan. *Bear Cub.* 1965. Viking. 1st. 62p. F/F. D4. $45.00.

CLARK, Ann Nolan. *Blue Canyon Horse.* 1954. Viking. 1st. tall 8vo. F/VG. M5. $85.00.

CLARK, Ann Nolan. *Magic Money.* 1950. Viking. 1st. 121p. VG/VG. P2. $80.00.

CLARK, Ann Nolan. *Secret of the Andes.* 1953 (1952). Viking. 3rd. 8vo. 130p. VG/G+. T5. $25.00.

CLARK, Ann Nolan. *Tia Maria's Garden.* 1966 (1963). NY. Viking. 3rd. ils Ezra Jack Keats. xl. VG/NF. C8. $15.00.

CLARK, Anna Morris. *Sylvia of the Hills.* 1936. Custer, SD. Chronicle Shop. box. A19. $45.00.

CLARK, Arthur. *History of Yachting 1600 – 1815.* 1904. NY. Putnam. ils. 249p. teg. rebound. T7. $210.00.

CLARK, B.F. *How Many Miles from St Jo?* 1929. SF. Private Prt. sm 8vo. marbled brd/maroon cloth. VG. O4. $45.00.

CLARK, B.L. *Fauna of the San Pablo Group of Middle California.* 1915. Berkeley. CA U. pres. ils/pl. VG+/wrp. M12. $37.50.

CLARK, Badger. *Sun & Saddle Leather.* 1920. Boston. Gorham. A19. $35.00.

CLARK, Carol. *Thomas Moran: Watercolors of the American West.* 1980. Austin. 4to. cream cloth. F/NF. F7. $60.00.

CLARK, Carol Higgins. *Decked.* 1992. NY. Warner. 1st. author's 1st book. VF/VF. H11. $35.00.

CLARK, Carol Higgins. *Snagged.* 1993. NY. Warner. 1st. VF/VF. H11. $15.00.

CLARK, Curt; See Westlake, Donald E.

CLARK, Dorothy. *Little Joe.* 1940. Lee Shepard. 1st. ils Leonard Weisgard. VG+/G. P2. $50.00.

CLARK, Douglas. *Big Grouse.* 1986. Gollancz. 1st. NF/NF. P3. $25.00.

CLARK, Douglas. *Sick to Death.* 1971. Stein Day. 1st. VG/VG. P3. $20.00.

CLARK, E.E. *Poetry: An Interpretation of Life.* 1935. Farrar Rhinehart. 1st. 584p. VG. W2. $30.00.

CLARK, Eleanor. *Oysters of Locmariaquer.* 1964. Pantheon. 1st. 203p. F/VG. H1. $25.00.

CLARK, Emma Chickester. *Story of Horrible Hilda & Henry.* 1988. Little, Brn. 1st. glossy pict brd. VG/dj. M20. $18.00.

CLARK, Francis E. *In Christ's Own Country.* 1914. Grosset Dunlap. 1st. 8vo. 25 pl. VG. W1. $12.00.

CLARK, H.H. *Lost in Pompeii.* 1883. Lothrop Lee Shepard. 1st. VG. M2. $30.00.

CLARK, James. *Shoeing and Balancing the Light Harness Horse.* 1916. Buffalo. The Horse World Co. 1st. Scarce. VG. O3. $185.00.

CLARK, John Willis. *Liber Memorandorum Ecclesie De Bernewelle.* 1907. Cambridge. M11. $150.00.

CLARK, Kate. *Maori Tales & Legends.* 1896. London. Nutt. 1st. 18 woodcuts. 186p. VG. W3. $86.00.

CLARK, Leonard. *Flutes & Cymbals.* 1969. Crowell. ARC/1st. ils Shirley Hughes. 104p. F/F. D4. $35.00.

CLARK, Margery. *The Poppy Seed Cakes.* 1926. Doubleday. ils Maud & Miska Petersham. VG. B15. $85.00.

CLARK, Mary Higgins. *A Stranger Is Watching.* 1977. NY. S&S. 1st. F/dj. M15. $50.00.

CLARK, Mary Higgins. *All Around Town.* 1992. S&S. 1st. sgn. F/F. A23. $25.00.

CLARK, Mary Higgins. *I'll be Seeing You.* (1993). NY. S&S. 1st. F/F. B3. $20.00.

CLARK, Mary Higgins. *Loves Music, Loves to Dance.* (1991). NY. S&S. 1st. F/F. B3. $20.00.

CLARK, Mary Higgins. *While My Pretty One Sleeps.* 1989. NY. S&S. 1st. VG/VG. R16. $25.00.

CLARK, Robert. *In the Deep Midwinter.* (1997). NY. Picador. 1st. author's first novel. F/F. B3. $35.00.

CLARK, Robert. *Mr. White's Confession.* 1998. NY. Picador. 1st. sgn. F/F. O11. $55.00.

CLARK, Roland. *Gunner's Dawn, Ils with Colour Plates and Drawings by the Author.* 1937. NY. The Derrydale Press. tall 8vo. 125p. red cloth. 1st ed. #857 of 950 copies. Top of spine with minor bump. gilt decorations "tarnished" or worn in places. VG. L5. $245.00.

CLARK, Ronald W. *JBS: The Life & Work of JBS Haldane.* 1969. Coward McCann. 1st Am. ils. 326p. VG/dj. K3. $15.00.

CLARK, Thomas Curtis, ed. *Poems of Justice.* 1929. Chicago. Willet, Clark & Colby. 1st. 306p. NF. B2. $60.00.

CLARK, Walter H. *The Psychology of Religion.* 1963. Macmillan. 485p. G. B29. $8.50.

CLARK, Walter Van Tilborg. *Grove Day.* 1969. NY. 1st. VG/VG. B5. $45.00.

CLARK, William. *Field Notes of Captain William Clark.* 1964. Yale. sgn. 335p. NF/dj. O7. $275.00.

CLARKE, Anna. *Last Voyage.* 1976. NY. St. Martin. 1st. VG+/VG. G8. $10.00.

CLARKE, Anna. *Legacy of Evil.* 1976. Collins Crime Club. 1st. VG/VG. P3. $20.00.

CLARKE, Arthur C. *2010: Odyssey Two.* 1982. Del Rey. 1st. NF/dj. P3. $30.00.

CLARKE, Arthur C. *Deep Range.* 1957. Harcourt. 1st. F/dj. M2. $200.00.

CLARKE, Arthur C. *Expedition to Earth.* 1955. London. 1st. F/dj. M2. $100.00.

CLARKE, Arthur C. *Imperial Earth.* 1976. Harcourt Brace. 1st. NF/dj. M2. $37.00.

CLARKE, Arthur C. *Other Side of the Sky.* 1957. Harcourt Brace. 1st. VG/dj. M2. $100.00.

CLARKE, Arthur C. *Promise of Space.* 1968. Harper. sgn. F/dj. M2. $40.00.

CLARKE, Arthur C. *Songs of Distant Earth.* 1986. Del Rey. 1/500. sgn/#d. F/case. M2. $85.00.

CLARKE, Arthur C. *Songs of Distant Earth.* 1986. Del Rey. 1st. NF/VG+. N4. $20.00.

CLARKE, Covington. *For Valor.* 1928. Chicago. 264p. VG. B18. $25.00.

CLARKE, Covington. *Mystery Flight of the Q2.* 1932. Reilly Lee. 270p. cloth. VG/dj. M20. $25.00.

CLARKE, Donald Henderson. *That Mrs. Renney.* 1937. Vanguard. 1st. F/NF. M19. $25.00.

CLARKE, Edward H. *Visions: Study of False Sight.* 1878. Boston. Houghton Osgood. 1st. 12mo. cloth. xl. M1. $125.00.

CLARKE, John Henrik. *Harlem.* USA. 1964. Seven Seas. ne. VG/wrp. M25. $45.00.

CLARKE, L. Lane. *Objects for the Microscope...* 1887. London. Groombridge & Sons. 7th ed. sm 8vo. 8 color plates. 230p. G/ils cloth. aeg. K5. $70.00.

CLARKE, Sara. *Lord Will Love Thee.* 1959. 1st. ils Tasha Tudor. VG+. S13. $25.00.

CLARKE, T.E.B. *Murder at Buckingham Palace.* 1981. Hale. 1st. VG/VG. P3. $20.00.

CLARKE, William M. *Secret Life of Wilkie Collins.* 1991. Chicago. Ivan R Dee. 1st. 8vo. 239p. F/dj. T10. $50.00.

CLARKSON, Henry E. *Yachtsman's A – Z.* 1979. Arco. 1st. 160p. F/F. W2. $20.00.

CLARKSON, Rosetta E. *Magic Gardens.* 1939. Macmillan. 1st. 8vo. cloth. VG. A22. $30.00.

CLARKSON, Roy B. *Tumult on the Mountains, Lumbering in West Virginia 1770 – 1920.* 1964. Parsons, McClain. 1st. ils. drawings by William A. Lunk. 410p. VG+/torn dj. B18. $37.50.

CLARKSON, Stephen. *The Canonical Compendium.* 1999. Ashcroft. Calabash Press. 1st. VF/pict brds. T2. $45.00.

CLARKSON, Thomas. *Memoirs of the Private & Public Life of William Penn.* 1813. London. Longman. 2 vol. 1st. thick 8vo. modern bdg. F. $13.00.

CLAUDE, Blair. *Pistols of the World.* 1968. Viking. 205p. cloth. VG+/dj. M20. $50.00.

CLAUDE, Henri. *Maladies Du Cervelet Et De L'Isthme De L'Encephale.* 1922. Paris. JB Bailliere et Fils. pres. 439p. VG. G1. $75.00.

CLAUSEN, Jens. *Stages in the Evolution of Plant Species.* 1951. Ithaca. Cornell. 206p. VG. A10. $24.00.

CLAVELL, James. *Shogun.* 1983. Delacorte. 1st. NF/F. H11. $45.00.

CLAVELL, James. *Tai-Pan.* 1966. NY. Atheneum. 1st. author's 2nd novel. NF/NF. D10. $135.00.

CLAVELL, James. *Whirlwind.* 1986. Morrow. 1st. NF/NF. P3/T12. $35.00.

CLAVER, Scott. *Under the Lash.* 1954. London. 1st. ils. 288p. G. B18. $15.00.

CLAY, Catherine Lee. *Season of Love.* 1968. Atheneum. 1st. inscr. F/dj. T10. $45.00.

CLAY, Steven and Rodney Phillips. *A Secret Location on the Lower East Side. Adventures in Writing, 1960 – 1980.* 1998. NY. NYPL/Granary Books. 1st. heavily ils. 344p. F. B2. $28.00.

CLAYMORE, Tod. *Appointment in New Orleans.* 1950. Cassell. 1st. VG/G. P3. $30.00.

CLAYTON, Edward T. *Negro Politician: His Success & Failure.* 1964. Chicago. Johnson. 1st. F/NF. B4. $85.00.

CLEARY, Beverly. *Dr Mr Henshaw.* 1983. Morrow. 1st. ils/sgn Zelinsky. 1983 Newberry Honor. 134p. NF/dj. T5. $55.00.

CLEARY, Beverly. *Ramona and Her Mother.* 1988. NY. Dell. in wrps. pb. G. A28. $2.50.

CLEARY, Jon. *Liberators.* 1971. Morrow. 1st. VG/VG. P3. $25.00.

CLEARY, Jon. *Man's Estate.* 1972. Collins. 1st. VG/VG. P3. $20.00.

CLEARY, Jon. *Very Private War.* 1980. Collins. 1st. NF/NF. P3. $25.00.

CLEBSH, Betsy. *A Book of Salvias. Sages for Every Garden.* 1997. Portland. 87 color photos. 9 color plates. line drawings. 250p. New in dj. B26. $30.00.

CLEEVE, Brian. *Death of a Painted Lady.* 1962. Hammond Hammond. 1st. VG/VG. P3. $25.00.

CLEGG, Anthony & Ray Corley. *Canadian National Steam Power.* 1969. Montreal. Trains & Trolleys. oblong 8vo. 128p. VG/torn dj. B18. $35.00.

CLELAND, Hugh. *George Washington in the Ohio Valley.* 1955. Pittsburgh. 1st. 405p. AN/dj. H1. $32.00.

CLELAND, Robert Glass. *Cattle on a Thousand Hills.* 1941. Huntington Lib. 1st. VG. O4. $40.00.

CLELAND, Robert Glass. *Irvine Ranch.* 1966. San Marino. 2nd. NF/VG. O4. $15.00.

CLELAND, Robert Glass. *Irvine Ranch of Orange Country.* 1952. San Marino. Huntington Lib. 1st. VG/sans. O4. $25.00.

CLEMENS, Samuel L. *American Claimant.* 1892. NY. 1st. ils. 227p. xl on rear ep only. VG. B18. $95.00.

CLEMENS, Samuel L. *Christian Science.* 1907. Harper. 1st. VG. M19. $35.00.

CLEMENS, Samuel L. *Extracts from Adam's Diary.* 1904. Harper. 1st. ils. 89p. pict cloth. G+. B18. $35.00.

CLEMENS, Samuel L. *Prince & the Pauper.* 1937. Winston. 1st thus. ils Lawson. gilt red cloth. VG. M5. $45.00.

CLEMENT, Hal. *Cycle of Fire.* 1957. Ballantine. 1st. F/NF. M2. $750.00.

CLEMENT, Hal. *Intuit.* 1987. Cambridge. NESFA Press. 1st. Intro by Paul Anderson. Foreword by author. VF/VF. T2. $35.00.

CLEMENT, Hal. *Mission of Gravity.* 1954. Doubleday. 1st. F/F. P3. $225.00.

CLEMENT, Hal. *Needle.* 1950. Doubleday. 1st. VG/VG. P3. $60.00.

CLEMENTS, F. E. *Minnesota Plant Studies I – III.* 1909 – 10. tall 8vo. VG/wrp. A22. $50.00.

CLEMENTS, F. E. *Plant Succession & Indicators.* 1928. Wilson. ils/pl/figures. 453p. cloth. VG. A22. $65.00.

CLERKE, Agnes M. *Familiar Studies in Homer.* 1892. London. Longman Gr. 8vo. 302p. xl. K5. $45.00.

CLERKE, Agnes M. *Problems in Astrophysics.* 1903. London. Adam & Charles black. 8vo. 31 plates. 50 text figures. 567p. VG/lightly scuffed & spotted cloth. K5. $100.00.

CLEVE, John; See Offutt, Andrew.

CLEVELAND, Anne. *It's Better with Your Shoes Off.* 1958. Rutland. Tuttle. 4th. ils. 94p. VG+. A25. $15.00.

CLIFFORD, A.G. *Conquest of North Africa.* 1943. MA. 1st. 450p. VG. S16. $25.00.

CLIFFORD, Derek. *Pelargoniums Including the Popular Geranium.* 1970 (1958). London. rev 2nd ed. 350p. VG in dj. B26. $37.50.

CLIFFORD, Francis. *Act of Mercy.* 1960. NY. Coward. 1st. F/F. H11. $45.00.

CLIFFORD, Francis. *Amigo, Amigo.* 1973. NY. Coward. 1st. F/NF. H11. $25.00.

CLIFFORD, Francis. *The Blind Side.* 1971. NY. Coward. 1st. F/F. H11. $30.00.

CLIFFORD, Francis. *Wild Justice.* 1972. CMG. 1st. VG/VG. P3. $25.00.

CLIFFORD, Hugh. *Further Side of Silence.* 1916. Doubleday. 1st. F. M2. $50.00.

CLIFFORD, James L. *Dictionary Johnson: The Middle Years.* 1979. McGraw Hill. 1st. F/dj. H13. $85.00.

CLIFTON, Bud; See Stacton, David.

CLIFTON, Lucille. *Everett Anderson's Christmas Coming.* 1971. Holt Rinehart. 1st. sm 4to. F/F. C8. $25.00.

CLIFTON, Lucille. *My Friend Jacob.* 1980. Dutton. 1st. F/F. C8. $35.00.

CLIFTON, Mark. *Eight Keys to Eden.* 1960. Doubleday. 1st. VG/VG. P3. $40.00.

CLIFTON, V. *Book of Talbot.* 1933. NY. 1st. ils/fld maps. 439p. VG/dj. B5. $45.00.

CLINE, Isaac Monroe. *Storms, Floods, and Sunshine; A Book of Memoirs.* 1945. New Orleans. Pelican. 2nd ed. inscr & sgn on ffep. b/w photo ils. 8vo. 293p. VG/torn & chipped dj. K5. $40.00.

CLINE, John. *Forever Beat.* 1990. Dutton. 1st. VG/VG. P3. $20.00.

CLINE, Platt. *They Came to the Mountain.* 1976. N AZ U. 1st. ils/index. 364p. NF/NF. B19. $35.00.

CLINEBELL, Howard. *Mental Health Through Christian Community.* 1965. Abingdon. 300p. VG/VG. B29. $18.00.

CLINTON, Catherine. *Plantation Mistress.* 1982. Pantheon. 1st. 331p. VG/dj. M20. $22.00.

CLINTON-BADDELEY, V. C. *Only a Matter of Time.* 1969. London. Victor Gollancz. 1st. Jacket has slightly darkened spine. F/dj. M15. $45.00.

CLISE, Michele Durkson. *Ophelia's World. Memoirs of Parisian Shop Girl.* 1984. Clarkson Potter. 1st. sgn. F/clip. A23. $40.00.

CLIVE, William. *Tune That They Play.* 1973. Macmillan. 1st. VG/VG. P3. $15.00.

CLOSE, Robin. *The Boheme Combination.* 1974. NY. Walker. 1st. clipped. F/F. H11. $40.00.

CLUTE, John. *Science Fiction — The Illustrated Encyclopedia.* 1995. NY. Dorling Kindersley. 1st. winner of 1996 Hugo award for best nonfiction book. F/F. M23. $40.00.

CLUTE, Nelson. *Our Ferns in Their Haunts.* 1901. Stokes. 332p. VG. A10. $48.00.

CLUTESI, George. *Potlatch.* 1969. Sydney. BC. Gray's. 1st. ils. F/NF. L3. $85.00.

CLYNE, Densey. *Australian Ground Orchids.* 1970. Melbourne. ils/photos. 112p. sc. VG. B26. $27.50.

CLYNE, Douglas. *Anchorage on the Costa Brava.* 1957. Christopher Douglas. 1st. VG/dj. P2. $10.00.

CLYNES, Michael. *White Rose Murders.* 1991. St. Martin. 1st Am ed. F/F. G8. $30.00.

CLYNES, Michael/ Paul Doherty. *A Brood of Vipers.* 1996. NY. St. Martin. 1st US ed. VF/VF. T2. $20.00.

COADY, Chantal. *Chocolate. The Food of the Gods.* 1993. San Francisco. Chronicle Books. 1st. 120p. G/G. F3. $15.00.

COATES, R.M. *Outlaw Years: History of Land Pirates of Natchez Trace.* 1930. Literary Guild. ils. VG. M17. $20.00.

COATS, Alice. *Plant Hunters.* 1969. McGraw Hill. 400p. VG/dj. A10. $48.00.

COATS, Peter. *Flowers in History.* 1970. NY. ils. 264p. VG in dj. B26. $37.50.

COATSWORTH, Elizabeth. *Children Come Running.* 1960. Golden Pr/Western Pub. 1st. 8vo. VG+/VG+. C8. $15.00.

COATSWORTH, Elizabeth. *Door to the North.* (1950). Winston. Land of the Free series. 1st. brn bdg. F/VG+. N1. $10.00.

COATSWORTH, Elizabeth. *Down Half the World.* 1968. Macmillan. 1st. 98p. F/F. D4. $35.00.

COATSWORTH, Elizabeth. *Princess & the Lion.* 1963. Pantheon. 1st. 78p. NF/VG. P3. $35.00.

COBB, Belton. *With Intent to Kill.* 1958. W. H. Allen. 1st British ed. G-VG. G8. $20.00.

COBB, Humphrey. *Paths of Glory.* 1935. NY. Viking. 1st. NF/NF. D10. $65.00.

COBB, Irvin S. *Roughing it Deluxe.* 1914. NY. Doran. 1st. 12mo. 219p. gray cloth. VG. $7.00.

COBB, James H. *West on 66.* 1999. NY. St. Martin. 1st. sgn. VF/VF. T2. $25.00.

COBBETT, William. *American Gardener.* ca 1830s. Claremont. NH. 16mo. 230p. A22. $125.00.

COBEN, Harlan. *Deal Breaker.* 1995. NY. Dell. 1st. pb orig. VF/wrp. M15. $35.00.

OBLEIGH, Rolfe. *Handy Farm Devices & ow to Make Them.* 1912. Orange Judd. 288p. G. A10. $50.00.

OBLENTZ, Stanton A. *After 12,000 Years.* 950. Fantasy. 1st. F/dj. M2. $20.00.

OBLENTZ, Stanton A. *Decline of Man.* 925. Minton Balch. 1st. VG. M2. $35.00.

OBLENTZ, Stanton A. *When the Birds Fly outh.* 1945. Wings. 1st. F/NF. M2. $50.00.

OBLENTZ, Stanton A. *Winds of Chaos.* 942. Wings. 1st. inscr. NF/G. M19. $25.00.

OBO, Father Bernabe. *Inca Religion & ustoms.* 1990. Austin. Univ of Texas. 1st. 79p. G/wrp. F3. $20.00.

OBURN, Andrew. *Sweetheart.* 1985. Secker Warburg. 1st. VG/VG. P3. $20.00.

OBURN, Walt. *Barbwire.* 1931. Chicago. L Burt. dj. A19. $30.00.

OCHISE, Ciye Nino. *First Hundred Years f Nino Cochise: Untold Story…* 1971. Abelard chuman. ils/map ep. 346p. VG/NF. B19. 45.00.

OCHRAN, Johnnie. *Journey to Justice.* 996. Ballantine. 1st. sgn bookplate. F/F. 23. $50.00.

OCHRAN, Mike. *And Deliver Us from Evil.* 989. TX Monthly. 1st. 213p. F/F. W2. 20.00.

OCKAYNE, L. *New Zealand Plants and heir Story.* 1967. Wellington. 4th ed. ils loth. 269p. lib stp. bumped. else VG. B26. 27.50.

OCKBURN, J. S. *Crime in England 1550 – 800.* 1977. London. Methuen. 11 essays. 111. $45.00.

OCKCROFT, G. L. *Index to the Weird iction Magazines.* 1975. Arno. 1st hc. VG. 12. $50.00.

OCKERELL, Sidney. *Psalter & Hours.* 905. London. Chiswick. 1st/only. obl folio. 5 full-p gravure pl. w/ALS. H13. $285.00.

OCKRILL, Pauline. *Ultimate Teddy Bear ook.* 1991. NY. Kindersley. 1st Am. 128p. /dj. H1. $22.50.

ODDINGTON, Edwin. *Gettysburg ampaign.* 1968. NY. 1st. VG/dj. B5. $50.00.

ODMAN, C. R. *Drive.* 1957. MA. 1st. ils. 35p. VG/VG. S16. $30.00.

CODRESCU, Andrei. *Craving for Swan.* 1986. Columbus. OH State. 1st. sgn. NF/NF. B4. $85.00.

CODRESCU, Andrei. *Messiah.* (1999). NY. S&S. 1st sgn by author. F/F. B3. $35.00.

CODY, Liza. *Backhand.* 1992. NY. Doubleday. 1st. F/F. H11. $20.00.

CODY, Liza. *Stalker.* 1984. London. Collins Crime Club. 1st. F/dj. M15. $125.00.

COE, David B. *The Children of Amarid.* 1997. NY. Tor. sgn 1st ed. author's 1st book. F/F. M23. $60.00.

COE, David B. *The Outlanders.* 1998. NY. Tor. sgn 1st ed. F/F. M23. $55.00.

COE, Michael & Elizabeth Benson. *Three Maya Relief Panels at Dumbarton Oaks.* 1966. np. Washington. foldout b/w photo ils. 31p. G/wrp. F3. $15.00.

COE, Tucker. *Don't Lie to Me.* 1972. Random. 1st. 181p. NF/NF. W2. $10.00.

COEL, Margaret. *Dead End.* 1997. Mission Viejo. ASAP. 1st. 1/150. sgns. F/sans. M15. $50.00.

COEL, Margaret. *Ghost Walker.* 1996. Berkley. 1st. NF/F. G8. $20.00.

COEL, Margaret. *Lost Bird.* 1999. Berkeley. 1st. sgn. F/F. G8. $25.00.

COEL, Margaret. *The Eagle Catcher.* 1995. Niwot. Univ Press of Colorado. 1st. author's 1st novel. sgn. VF/VF. T2. $175.00.

COELHO, Paul. *Valkyries: An Encounter with Angels.* 1992. Harper Collins. 1st. F/F. B3. $25.00.

COETZEE, J. M. *From the Heart of the Country.* 1977. Harper & Row. 1st Am ed. NF/lightly rubbed dj. M25. $45.00.

COETZEE, J. M. *The Master of Petersburg.* 1994. Viking. 1st Am ed. sgn bkplt on ffep. NF/NF. M25. $60.00.

COFFEEN, J. A. *Seismic Exploration Fundamentals.* 1978. Tulsa, OK. Petroleum Pub. 277p. VG/dj. D8. $30.00.

COFFEY, Barbara. *Beauty Begins At 40.* 1984. NY. HRW. VG/VG. A28. $7.95.

COFFEY, Brian; See Koontz, Dean R.

COFFEY, Timothy. *History & Folklore of North American Wildflowers.* nd. Facts on File. 356p. dj. A10. $32.00.

COFFIN, Charles Carleton. *Our New Way Round the World.* 1869. Boston. Osgood. 524p. VG. W1. $35.00.

COFFIN, Geoffrey; see Mason, Van Wyck.

COFFIN, Henry Sloane. *Religion Yesterday and Today.* 1940. Cokesbury. 183p. G/minor mks. B29. $4.00.

COFFIN, Margaret. *American Country Tinware 1700 – 1900.* 1968. photos. NF/VG. S13. $18.00.

COGGESHALL, George. *History of American Privateers.* 1861 (1856). aeg. half leather/raised bands. VG. E6. $175.00.

COGNIAT, Raymond. *XXth Century Drawings & Watercolors.* nd. NY. Crown. trans from French by Anne Ross. ils/list of artists. dj. D2. $75.00.

COGSWELL, H.L. *Water Birds of California.* 1977. Berkeley. 399p. F/F. B1. $30.00.

COHAN, George. *Broadway Jones.* 1913. Dillingham. 1st. F/NF. B4. $350.00.

COHANE, Tim. *Great College Football Coaches of the Twenties & Thirties.* 1973. Arlington. 1st. photos. VG/dj. P8. $20.00.

COHEN, Bernard. *Sensing & Controlling Motion: Vestibular & Sensorimotor.* 1992. NY. Academy of Sciences. 1st. thick 8vo. 989p. F/wrp. G1. $65.00.

COHEN, Herman. *History of the English Bar & Attornatus to 1450.* 1967. London. Wildy & Sons Ltd. facsimile. cloth. M11. $125.00.

COHEN, Julius Henry. *An American Labor Policy.* 1919. NY. Macmillan. 1st. F. B2. $35.00.

COHEN, Norm. *Folk Song America. A 20th Century Revival.* 1990. Washington, DC. Smithsonian. 1st. wrp. heavily ils booklet designed to accompany a set of CDs. 106p. NF. B2. $25.00.

COHEN, Octavius Roy. *Bullet for My Love.* 1950. Macmillan. 1st. VG/dj. M25. $45.00.

COHEN, Octavius Roy. *Eric Peters.* Pullman Porter. 1930. Appleton. 1st. 12mo. VG+/G. C8. $75.00.

COHEN, Octavus Roy. *My Love Wears Black.* 1948. Macmillan. 1st. Chipped and torn jacket. VG/dj. M25. $60.00.

COHEN, Peter Zachary. *Bee.* 1975. Atheneum. 1st. VG/VG. O3. $18.00.

COHEN, Robert. *Organ Builder.* 1988. Harper. 1st. F/NF. R13. $35.00.

COHEN, S. *Images of the Spanish-American War.* April – August, 1898. Missoula. ils/photos. 293p. F. M4. $40.00.

COHEN, Sam. *Truth About the Neutron Bomb.* 1983. NY. 1st. F/dj. K3. $10.00.

COHEN, Stan. *Homestead & Warm Springs Valley of Virginia: Pict Heritage.* (1984). Pict Histories Pub. 4th. ils/maps. 96p. VG. B10. $6.00.

COHEN, Stanley. *Man in the Crowd.* 1981. Random. 1st. VG+/dj. P8. $10.00.

COHEN, Stanley. *Park.* 1977. Putnam. 1st. F/F. P3. $15.00.

COHEN, Stephen Paul. *Heartless.* 1986. NY. Morrow. 1st. author's 1st book. F/VF. H11. $20.00.

COHN, Isadore. *Rudolph Matas: Biography of One Great Pioneers in Surgery.* 1960. Garden City. 1st. 431p. A13. $30.00.

COHN, Norma. *Little People in a Big Country.* 1945. Oxford. 1st. sm 12mo. F/VG. M5. $45.00.

COHN, Roy. *How to Fight for Your Rights & Win.* 1981. S&S. 1st. F/F. A20. $30.00.

COHON, Samuel S. *Essays in Jewish Theology.* 1987. HUC Pr. 366p. VG/dj. S3. $25.00.

COKE, Edward. *First Part of the Institutes of Laws of England.* 1703. London. contemporary calf/rebacked. M11. $650.00.

COKER, Elizabeth Boatwright. *Bees.* 1968. Dutton. 1st. sgn. VG/VG. B11. $40.00.

COKER, ELizabeth Boatwright. *India Allan.* 1953. Dutton. 1st. VG/G. P3. $15.00.

COLACELLO, Bob. *Holy Terror: Andy Warhol Close Up.* 1990. Harper Collins. 1st. F/F. P3. $23.00.

COLBERG, Nancy. *Wallace Stegner: Descriptive Bibliography.* 1990. Confluence. 1st. M/sans. A18. $50.00.

COLBERT, E.H. *Age of Reptiles.* 1965. Norton. ils/drawings. 228p. F/NF. D8. $25.00.

COLBERT, E.H. *Fosssil Hunter's Notebook.* 1980. Dutton. dj. A19. $25.00.

COLBY, C.B. *Moon Exploration.* 1970. Coward McCann. 4to. 48p. xl. K5. $10.00.

COLCHIE, Thomas. *Hammock Beneath the Mangoes.* 1991. Dutton. 1st. F/dj. M2. $30.00.

COLE, Adrian. *Place Among the Fallen.* 1987. Arbor. 1st. NF/NF. P3. $20.00.

COLE, Burt. *Quick.* 1989. Morrow. 1st. NF/NF. P3. $20.00.

COLE, Diane. *Murder at the White Tulip.* 1960. Arcadia. 1st. VG/VG. G8. $10.00.

COLE, Duane. *Vagabond Club.* 1967. Ken Cook Pub. 1st. sgn pres. 183p. VG/dj. B5. $30.00.

COLE, G.D.H. *Last Will & Testament.* 1985. Collins Crime Club. VG/VG. P3. $15.00.

COLE, H. *Heraldry: Decoration & Floral Forms.* 1988. ils. VG/VG. M17. $15.00.

COLE, Maria. *Nat King Cole: An Intimate Biography.* 1971. Morrow. 1st. F/F. M25. $35.00.

COLE, S.W. *American Fruit Book.* 1849. Boston. John P Jewett. 288p. leather. VG. M20. $50.00.

COLE, S.W. *American Fruit Book.* 1866. Orange Judd. 276p. cloth. VG. A10. $30.00.

COLE, S.W. *Soil Management for Conservation & Production.* 1962. NY. Wiley. 527p. dj. A10. $20.00.

COLE, W.R. *Checklist of Science Fiction Anthologies.* 1964. Cole. 1st. F/F. P3. $100.00.

COLE, William. *Book of Animal Poems.* 1973. Viking. ARC/1st. 288p. F/F. D4. $35.00.

COLE, William. *Book of Nature Poems.* 1969. Viking. 1st. ils RA Parker. F/NF. D4. $35.00.

COLE, William. *Poems from Ireland.* 1972. Crowell. 1st. ils Wm Stobbs. 237p. F/F. D4. $30.00.

COLEGATE, Isabel. *The Shooting Party.* 1981. NY. Viking. 1st. VF/V. H11. $35.00.

COLEMAN, E.L. *New England Captives Carried to Canada Between 1677.* 1925. Portland. 2 vol. gilt maroon cloth. VG. M4. $60.00.

COLEMAN, J. Winston Jr. *A Bibliography of the Writings of J. Winston Coleman, Jr.* 1953. Lexington, KY. Winburn Press. 1st. orig printed wrp. VG. chipped. M8. $75.00.

COLEMAN, Ken. *So You Want to be a Sportscaster.* 1973. Hawthorn. 1st. photos. VG+/dj. P8. $25.00.

COLEMAN, McAlister. *Eugene V Debs: Man Unafraid.* 1930. Greenberg. 1st. VG/VG. V4. $50.00.

COLEMAN, Satis N. *Book of Bells.* 1938. NY. 177p. xl. A17. $45.00.

COLERIDGE, Anthony. *Chippendal Furniture: Work of Thomas Chippendale.* 1968. Clarkson Potter. 1st Am. 229p. cloth. VG/dj. M20. $60.00.

COLERIDGE, S.T. *Phantasmion.* 1874. Roberts Bros. G. M2. $150.00.

COLES, Manning. *All That Glitters.* 1954. Doubleday/Crime Club. 1st. VG+/dj. M20. $35.00.

COLES, Manning. *Drink to Yesterday.* 1944. Canada. Musson. VG/VG. P3. $30.00.

COLES, Manning. *Without Lawfu Authority.* 1944. Canada. Musson. 1st. VG/G+. P3. $20.00.

COLETTA, Paolo. *Annotated Bibliography o US Marine Corps History.* 1986. Lanham. 1st. 417p. VG. S16. $45.00.

COLETTE, Chats. *1945.* Lausanne. 1st. photos. natural linen. F/VG+. A11. $135.00.

COLLENS, J. H. *A Guide to Trinidad.* 1888. np. London. 2nd ed. ex lib. 278p. fair. part of bdg missing. some tears. hinges broken. F3 $30.00.

COLLETT, Marjorie. *Elizabeth in Toyland.* 1925. Harrap. 1st. ils Tarrant. 12mo. beige brd. pict dj. R5. $150.00.

COLLIDGE, Mary Roberts. *Chinese Immigration: American Public Problems.* 1909. NY. Holt. thick 8vo. gilt bl cloth. F. R3. $125.00.

COLLIER, James Lincoln. *Winchesters, The.* 1988. NY. Macmillan. VG/VG. A28. $6.50.

COLLIER, John. *Defy the Foul Fiend.* 1934. London. Macmillan. 1st. F/dj. M15. $500.00.

COLLIER, John. *Fancies & Goodnights.* 1951. Doubleday. 1st. F/dj. M2. $100.00.

COLLIER, John. *Green Thoughts.* 1932. London. 1/550. sgn/#d. VG. M2. $125.00.

COLLIER, John. *His Monkey Wife.* 1931. Appleton. 1st. VG. P3. $35.00.

COLLIER, Peter. *Kennedys: An American Drama.* 1984. Summit. 1st. sgn. VG/VG. A23. $32.00.

COLLIER, Richard. *House Called Memory.* 1961. Dutton. 1st. VG/VG. P3. $15.00.

COLLIER, V.W.F. *Dogs of China & Japan in Nature & Art.* 1921. London. Heinemann. ils. 107p. remnant rear xl Pocket. VG. W3. $95.00.

COLLIER & EATON. *The Warrior.* (1934). Harcourt Brace. ils Frank Schoonover. G+. B15. $45.00.

COLLIGNON, Jeff. *Her Monster.* 1992. NY. Soho. 1st. F/F. H11. $40.00.

COLLING, Susan. *Frogmorton.* 1956. Knopf. 1st Am. 148p. gr cloth/red spine. VG/torn. T5. $30.00.

COLLINGWOOD, W.G. *Life & Works of John Ruskin.* 1893. Houghton Mifflin. 2 vol. 1st. 8vo. aeg. dk red ribbed cloth. H13. $95.00.

COLLINS, Erroll. *Mariners of Space.* 1949. London. VG. M2. $15.00.

COLLINS, Freda. *Shrove-Tide Fair.* 1960. Faith Pr. 1st. F/F. N1. $4.00.

COLLINS, G.B. *Wildcats & Shamrocks.* 1977. Mennonite Pr. 2nd. inscr. VG/dj. D8. $12.00.

COLLINS, Gary R. *The Magnificent Mind.* 1985. Word. 262p. VG/VG. B29. $8.00.

COLLINS, Gilbert. *Valley of Eyes Unseen.* 1924. McBride. 1st Am. VG. M2. $37.00.

COLLINS, Hunt; see Hunter, Evan.

COLLINS, Jackie. *Lady Boss.* 1990. S&S. 1st. NF/F. T12. $20.00.

COLLINS, Jackie. *Thrill.* 1998. S&S. 1st. F/chip dj. S19. $30.00.

COLLINS, Larry. *Maze.* 1989. S&S. 1st. VG/VG. P3. $20.00.

COLLINS, Mary. *Sister of Cain.* 1943. Scribner. 1st. VG. P3. $20.00.

COLLINS, Max Allan. *A Shroud for Aquarius.* (1985). NY. Walker. 1st. sgn by author. F/F. B3. $30.00.

COLLINS, Max Allan. *Murder by the Numbers.* 1993. NY. St. Martin. 1st. sgn. VF/VF. T2. $20.00.

COLLINS, Michael. *Emerald Underground.* 1998. London. Phoenix House. 1st. VF/VF. T2. $38.00.

COLLINS, Michael. *Liftoff; The Story of America's Adventure into Space.* 1988. NY. Grove Press. 1st printing. ils by James Dean. 4to. 288p. VG in quarter cloth & paper covered bds. bkplt. K5. $20.00.

COLLINS, Nancy. *Midnight Blue: Sonia Blue Collection.* 1995. Stone Mtn. 1st collection. VG+/dj. M21. $20.00.

COLLINS, Paul. *Alien Worlds.* 1979. Void Pub. 1st. NF/NF. P3. $30.00.

COLLINS, Randall. *The Case of the Philosopher's Ring.* 1978. NY. Crown. 1st. VF/VF. T2. $30.00.

COLLINS, Richard L. *Thunderstorms & Airplanes.* 1982. Delacorte. 1st. 8vo. 280p. VG/dj. K5. $15.00.

COLLINS, Wilkie. *Man and Wife.* 1870. NY. Harper & Bros. 1st Am ed. VG/sc. M15. $100.00.

COLLINS, Wilkie. *The Moonstone.* 1868. NY. Harper & Bros. 1st Am ed. VG/soiled cloth covered brd. M15. $500.00.

COLLIS, LOUISE. *Soldier in Paradise: Life of Capt John Stedman 1744 – 97.* (1966). Harcourt Brace. 1st Am. 231p. F3. $20.00.

COLLIS, Maurice. *Grand Peregrination.* 1959. London. Faber. 2nd. cloth. VG/dj. M20. $20.00.

COLLODI, Carlo. *Pinocchio.* 1904. Ginn. Once Upon a Time series. 12mo. gilt gr cloth. M5. $55.00.

COLMONT, Marie. *Le Roi Chat.* 1944. Flammarion. 1st. ils Andre Paul. sq 12mo. VG+. M5. $65.00.

COLNETT, James. *Voyage to the South Atlantic & Round Cape Horn.* 1968. Amsterdam. rpt. fld maps/charts. 179p. P4. $110.00.

COLOMBO, John Robert. *Not to be Taken at Night.* 1981. Lester Denys. F/NF. P3. $20.00.

COLSON, Charles. *Loving God.* 1983. Zondervan. 255p. VG/VG. B29. $9.50.

COLTMAN, Paul. *Witch Watch.* 1989. FSG. 1st. unp. VG/dj. M20. $20.00.

COLTON, James; See Hansen, Joseph.

COLTON, Walter. *Three Years in California.* 1850. NY. Barnes. 456p. red cloth. VG. K7. $175.00.

COLUM, Mary & Padraic. *Our Friend James Joyce.* 1958. Garden City. Doubleday. 1st. F/NF. B2. $25.00.

COLUM, Padraic. *Collected Poems.* 1953. NY. Devin-Adair. 1st thus. sgn. F/VG. B4. $85.00.

COLUM, Padraic. *Six Who Were Left in a Shoe.* 1923. Chicago. Volland. ils Dugald Stewart Walker. 40p. NF. A4. $65.00.

COLVILLE, Jessie. *Kentucky Woman's Handy Cookbook.* 1912. self pub. VG. E6. $45.00.

COLVIN, Fred H. *The Aircraft Mechanics Handbook...* 1918. NY. np. 5th prt. photo ils. drawings. 402p. edgewear. G. B18. $45.00.

COLVIN, Verna Rae. *Garden & How it Grew: Eden 1881 – 1981.* nd (1981). private prt. 1st. 1/200. ils. 206p. F/sans. B19. $95.00.

COLWIN, Laurie. *Passion & Affect.* 1974. NY. Viking. 1st. author's 1st book. NF/VG. L3. $50.00.

COMAN, Carolyn. *Losing Things at Mr. Mudd's.* 1992. NY. F & G. 1st. gr brds. wht cloth spine. AN. A28. $7.95.

COMBS, Sarah V. *South African Plants for American Gardens.* 1936. NY. 364p. VG. B26. $35.00.

COMENIUS, Joannes Amos. *Orbis Sensualium Pictus.* 1777. London. Leacroft. 12th. 150 woodcuts. rebound/rpl ep/marbled brd/label. R5. $285.00.

COMFORT, Alex. *The Joy of Sex: A Gourmet Guide to Love Making.* 1972. Crown. 1st. Very lightly worn jacket. F/dj. M25. $45.00.

COMMAGER, Henry Steele. *Blue & the Gray.* 1950. Indianapolis. 2 vol. 1st. VG/dj. B5. $125.00.

COMPERTZ, M. *Corn from Egypt: Beginning of Agriculture.* 1928. 87p. xl. VG. E6. $15.00.

COMPTON, Arthur Holly. *Cosmos of Arthur Holly Compton.* 1967. Knopf. 1st. VG/dj. K3. $20.00.

COMPTON, D. G. *Ascendancies.* 1980. NY. Berkley/Putnam. 1st Am ed. F. lt wear/F. T2. $15.00.

COMPTON, D. G. *Justice City.* 1994. London. Gollancz. 1st. VF/VF. T2. $25.00.

COMPTON, D. G. *Windows.* 1979. Berkley Putnam. 1st. VG/VG. P3. $13.00.

COMPTON, R. R. *Manual of Field Geology.* 1962. John Wiley. 378p. G. D8. $12.00.

COMPTON-BURNETT, I. *First & the Last.* 1971. Knopf. 1st Am. F/NF. B4. $50.00.

COMSTOCK, J. L. *Elements of Chemistry.* 1850. Pratt Woodford. 32nd ed from the 54th. 422p. full leather. G+. H1. $35.00.

COMSTOCK, Sarah. *Moon Is Made of Green Cheese.* 1929. Doubleday. 1st. VG. M2. $12.00.

CON, J. *American Orders & Societies & Their Decorations.* 1917. Phil. ils. VG. E6. $125.00.

CONANT, Charles A. *History of Modern Banks of Issue.* 1896. Putnam. 1st. 8vo. 595p. teg. gilt brn cloth. VG. $10.00.

CONANT, Paul. *Dr. Gatskill's Blue Shoes.* 1952. Wyn. 1st. VG/G-VG. G8. $15.00.

CONCHA, Joseph L. *Lonely Deer.* 1969. Taos Pueblo Council. 1st. sgn. NF/wrp. L3. $250.00.

CONDON, Eddie and Thomas Sugrue. *We Called it Music.* 1947. NY. Holt. 1st. F. no dj. B2. $25.00.

CONDON, Richard. *An Infinity of Mirrors.* 1967. NY. Dial. 1st. F/F. H11. $40.00.

CONDON, Richard. *Ecstasy Business.* 1967. Dial. 1st. VG/VG. M22. $20.00.

CONDON, Richard. *Prizzi's Family.* 1986. Putnam. 1st. F/F. H11. $20.00.

CONDON, Richard. *Prizzi's Honor.* 1982. Coward. 1st. F/NF. H11. $35.00.

CONDON, Richard. *Trembling Upon Rome.* 1983. Michael Joseph. 1st. F/F. P3. $25.00.

CONDON, Richard. *Vertical Smile.* 1971. Dial. 1st. VG/VG. P3. $25.00.

CONEY, Michael G. *Celestial Steam Locomotive.* 1983. Houghton Mifflin. 1st. F/dj. M2. $15.00.

CONEY, Michael G. *Fang the Gnome.* 1988. NAL. 1st/1st prt. 8vo. 345p. F/F. T10. $75.00.

CONEY, Michael G. *Gods of the Greataway.* 1984. Houghton Mifflin. 1st. VG/VG. P3. $16.00.

CONGREVE, William. *Way of the World: Comedy in Five Acts.* 1959. LEC. 1st thus. 1/1500. ils/sgn TM Cleland. F/glassine/case. Q1. $75.00.

CONKLIN, E. *Picturesque Arizona: Being Result of Travels & Observations.* 1878. Mining Record Prt Establishment. 1st. 390p. B19. $200.00.

CONKLIN, Groff. *Science Fiction in Mutation.* 1955. Vanguard. 1st. VG/dj. P3. $35.00.

CONLEY, Robert J. *Back to Malachi.* 1986. Doubleday. 1st. inscr. F/F. L3. $125.00.

CONLEY, Robert J. *Saga of Henry Starr.* 1989. Doubleday. 1st. F/NF. L3. $65.00.

CONNELL, Evan S. *Mrs. Bridge.* 1960. London. Heinemann. 1st Eng. F/VG+ clip. B4. $225.00.

CONNELL, Will. *In Pictures: A Hollywood Satire.* 1937. NY. TJ Maloney. 106p. wrp/sbdg/cb case. D11. $500.00.

CONNELLEY, William E. *Collections of the Kansas State Historical Society.* 1918. Topeka, KS. 896p. F/case. E1. $150.00.

CONNELLY, Michael. *Angels Flight.* 1998. Boston. Little, Brn. 1st. sgn. VF/VF. T2. $25.00.

CONNELLY, Michael. *Angels Flight.* 1999. London. Orion. 1st UK ed. sgn. VF/VF. T2. $35.00.

CONNELLY, Michael. *Bloodwork.* 1997. Boston. Little, Brn. 1st. sgn. VF/dj. M15. $50.00.

CONNELLY, Michael. *Michael Connelly Sampler.* 1996. NY. St. Martin. 1st. sgn. VF/VF. T2. $5.00.

CONNELLY, Michael. *The Black Echo.* 1992. Boston. Little, Brn. 1st. sgn. VF/dj. M15. $80.00.

CONNELLY, Michael. *The Black Ice.* 1993. Boston. Little, Brn. 1st. sgn. VF/dj. M15. $75.00.

CONNELLY, Michael. *The Concrete Blonde.* 1994. Boston. Little, Brn. 1st. F/F. H11. $40.00.

CONNELLY, Michael. *The Last Coyote.* 1995. Boston. Little, Brn. 1st. sgn. VF/VF. T2. $30.00.

CONNELLY, Michael. *The Poet.* 1996. Boston. Little, Brn. 1st. VF/dj. M15. $60.00.

CONNELLY, Michael. *Trunk Music.* (1997). Boston. Little, Brn. 1st. sgn by author. F/F. B3. $40.00.

CONNELLY, Michael. *Void Moon.* 1999. Boston. Little, Brn. 1st. sgn. VF/VF. T2. $25.00.

CONNELLY, Michael. *Void Moon.* 1999. Tucson. Dennis McMillan. 1st. copie. signed. VF/dj. M15. $1,500.00.

CONNER, Howard. *Spearhead: World War I History of the 5th Marine Division.* 1950. Washington, DC. 1st. photos/maps/casualty lists. VG. S16. $125.00.

CONNER, J. Patrick. *Blood Moon.* 1987. NY. Doubleday. 1st. author's 1st book. F/F. H11. $30.00.

CONNINGTON, J. J. *Death at Swaythling Court.* 1926. Boston. Little, Brn. 1st Am ed. VG+. G8. $20.00.

CONNINGTON, J. J. *No Past Is Dead.* 1942. Little, Brn. 1st Am. VG/dj. M15. $50.00.

CONNOLLY, Cyril. *Condemned Playground.* Essays. 1945. London. 1st. VG. T9. $20.00.

CONNOLLY, John. *Every Dead Thing.* 1999. London. Hodder & Stoughton. 1st. VF/dj. M15. $85.00.

CONNOR, Beverly. *A Rumor of Bones.* 1996. Nashville. Cumberland House. 1st. sgn. author's 1st novel. VF/VF. T2. $30.00.

CONNOR, Beverly. *Skeleton Crew.* 1999. Nashville. Cumberland House. 1st. sgn. VF/VF. T2. $25.00.

CONNOR, D. Russell and Warren W. Hicks. *B G on the Record. A Biodiscography of Benny Goodman.* 1969. New Rochelle. Arlington House. 1st. NF/lightly used. chip dj. B2. $45.00.

CONNOR, Ralph. *Foreigner: A Tale of Saskatchewan.* 1909. Hodder Stoughton. dj. A19. $20.00.

CONRAD, Barnaby. *How to Fight a Bull.* 1968. Doubleday. 1st. 224p. dj. F3. $20.00.

CONRAD, Earl. *Invention of the Negro.* 1966. NY. Ericksson. 1st. NF/VG. B4. $45.00.

CONRAD, Henry S. *How to Know the Mosses & Liverworts.* 1956. Dubuque. revised 2nd. Picture-Keyed Nature series. F. B26. $17.50.

CONRAD, Joseph. *Conrad Argosy.* 1942. Doubleday Doran. 4to. 713p. T7. $40.00.

CONRAD, Joseph. *Secret Agent.* 1907. Harper. 1st Am. 372p. gilt bl bdg. G+. H1. $40.00.

CONRAD, Joseph. *Suspense: A Napoleonic Novel*. 1925. Doubleday. 1st. 1/377. gilt cream brd/bl trim. inner & outer dj/case. 24. $250.00.

CONRAD, Joseph. *Tremolino*. 1942. NY. Muschnes. 1st separate. ils/sgn EA Wilson. /case. B24. $150.00.

CONRAD, Joseph. *Victory*. 1921. Modern lib. ne. G. W2. $250.00.

CONRAD, L. J. *Bibliography of Antarctic Exploration: Expedition Accounts from 1768 to 1960*. 1999. Washougal. L.J. Conrad. 1st. dk blue cloth hc. gilt spine & cover titles. 424p. F. issued w/o dj. P4. $100.00.

CONRAN, Shirley. *Savages*. 1987. S&S. 1st. F/F. T12. $25.00.

CONRAN, Terence. *Vegetable Book*. 1976. Crescent. VG/dj. A16. $6.00.

CONRNSWEET, Tom N. *Visual Perception*. 1970. Academic. 3rd. tall 8vo. 475p. blk cloth. G1. $65.00.

CONROY, Albert; see Albert, Marvin H.

CONROY, Frank. *Midair*. 1985. Dutton. 1st. NF/F. H11. $25.00.

CONROY, Frank. *Stop-Time*. 1967. Viking. 1st. F/F. B4. $150.00.

CONROY, Pat. *Beach Music*. (1995). NY. Bantam. 1st. sgn & dated by author. F/F. B3. $60.00.

CONROY, Pat. *Great Santini*. 1976. Houghton Mifflin. 1st. G/G. M19. $65.00.

CONROY, Pat. *The Prince of Tides*. 1986. Boston. Houghton Mifflin. 1st. F/F. A24. $40.00.

CONSIDINE, Shaun. *Barbra Streisand: Woman, Myth, Music*. 1985. Delacorte. 1st. photos. 335p. VG/G. $25.00.

CONSTANTINE, K. C. *Cranks and Shadows*. 1995. Warner. 1st. NF/NF. G8. $15.00.

CONSTANTINE, K. C. *Family Values*. 1997. Mysterious. 1st. F/F. G8. $15.00.

CONSTANTINE, K. C. *Man Who Liked Slow Tomatoes*. 1982. Godine. 1st. NF/NF. M22. $75.00.

CONSTANTINE, K. C. *Upon Some Midnight's Clear*. 1985. Godine. 1st. NF/NF. M22. $25.00.

CONTE, Christine. *Maya Culture & Costume*. 1984. Colorado. Taylor Museum. 1st. wrp. sm 4to. 120p. G. F3. $25.00.

CONWAY, Tom (A Few); see Avallone, Mike.

CONWELL, Russell H. *Magnolia Journey: A Union Veteran Revisits...* 1974. AL U. 1st. 190p. cloth. VG/dj. M20. $25.00.

COOK, A.H. *Physics of the Earth & Planets*. 1973. Wiley. 8vo. 316p. VG/VG. K5. $20.00.

COOK, Allyn Austin. *Diseases of Tropical & Subtropical Fruits & Nuts*. 1975. Hafner. 8vo. 317p. xl. A22. $22.00.

COOK, Bruce. *Sidewalk Hilton*. 1994. NY. St. Martin. 1st. F/F. G8. $17.50.

COOK, Canfield. *Lucky Terrell: Springboard to Tokyo (#5)*. 1943. Grosset Dunlap. 210p. cloth. VG/rpr. M20. $20.00.

COOK, Frederick A. *Return from the Pole*. 1951. NY. Pellegrini & Cudahy. 1st. Ed by Frederick J. Pohlbl cloth 8vo. gilt spine titles. 335p. VG in slightly worn dj. P4. $65.00.

COOK, Harold J. *Tales of the 04 Ranch*. 1968. U NE. 1st. 221p. VG/VG. J2. $90.00.

COOK, J. Gordon. *Our Astonishing Atmosphere*. 1955. London. Scientific Book Club. BCE. b/w photo ils. 8vo. 200p. VG/chipped dj. K5. $8.00.

COOK, James. *Explorations of Capt James Cook in the Pacific*. nd (1955). Heritage. 292p. gilt bdg. VG/poor case. P4. $45.00.

COOK, James. *James Cook. Gifts and Treasures from the South Seas*. 1998. Munich/NY. Prestel. 1st. bl cloth. 350p. New in dj. P4. $65.00.

COOK, Marc. *Wilderness Cure*. 1881. NY. 153p. pict cloth. VG. B14. $95.00.

COOK, Robin. *Brain*. 1981. Putnam. 1st. VG/VG. P3. $25.00.

COOK, Robin. *Coma*. 1977. Little, Brn. 1st. NF/NF. M19. $45.00.

COOK, Robin. *Fever*. 1982. Putnam. 1st. sgn. NF/NF. M19. $25.00.

COOK, Robin. *Mindbend*. 1985. Putnam. 1st. VG/VG. P3. $15.00.

COOK, Robin. *Outbreak*. 1987. NY. Putnam. 1st. F/VF. T2. $8.00.

COOK, Robin. *Private Parts in Public Places*. 1969. Atheneum. 1st. VG/VG. P3. $40.00.

COOK, Robin. *Sphinx*. 1979. NY. Putnam. 1st. F/F. T2. $12.00.

COOK, Thomas H. *Night Secrets*. 1990. Putnam. 1st. F/F. P3. $20.00.

COOK, Thomas H. *Orchids*. 1982. Houghton Mifflin. 1st. F/F. T2. $45.00.

COOK, Thomas H. *Streets of Fire*. 1989. NY. Putnam. 1st. VF/VF. T2. $10.00.

COOK, Thomas H. *The Chatham School Affair*. 1996. NY. Bantam. 1st. sgn. VF/dj. M15. $55.00.

COOK, Thomas H. *The City When it Rains*. 1991. NY. Putnam. 1st. VF/VF. T2. $8.00.

COOK, Warren L. *Flood Tide of Empire: Spain & Pacific Northwest 1543 – 1819*. 1973. New Haven. Yale. Yale W Am series 24. 4to. 620p. F. O7. $35.00.

COOK-LYNN, Elizabeth. *Badger Said This*. 1977. NY. Vantage. 1st. author's 1st book. NF/VG. L3. $350.00.

COOK-LYNN, Elizabeth. *Power of Horses & Other Stories*. 1990. NY. Arcade/Little, Brn. AP. wrp. R13. $30.00.

COOKBOOK. *America's Best Recipes, A 1996 Hometown Collection*. 1996. AL. Oxmoor House. spiral bd. NF. A28. $7.95.

COOKBOOK. *Best of Gourmet, The 1988 Edition*. 1988. NY. Conde Nast. 1st. hc. decor brds. VG+/VG+. A28. $9.95.

COOKBOOK. *Complete Microwave Cookbook*. nd. JC Penney. sm4to. 160p. VG. S14. $6.00.

COOKBOOK. *Successful Housekeeper, Manual of Universal Application, Especially Adapted to the Every Day Wants of American Housewives*. 1882. Detroit. M. W. Ellsworth. pict cloth. ils. some wear to edges. 608p. VG. B18. $27.50.

COOKE, Alistair. *Americans: Fifty Letters from America*. 1979. London. 1st. VG/dj. T9. $20.00.

COOKE, Alistair. *Patient Has the Floor*. 1986. Franklin Lib. 1st/ltd. sgn. full leather. F. Q1. $35.00.

COOKE, Alistair. *Patient Has the Floor*. 1986. Knopf. 1st trade. F/F. B35. $16.00.

COOKE, Catherine, editor. *Collecting Sherlockiana: John Bennett Shaw's Basic Holmesian Library*. 1998. Cambridge. Rupert Books. reissue. 1st thus. VF/printed wrp. T2. $18.00.

COOKE, D.E. *Firebird.* 1939. Winston. 1st. ils. red cloth. VG. M5. $45.00.

COOKE, David C. *Best Detective Stories of the Year 1950.* 1950. Dutton. 1st. VG/G+. P3. $20.00.

COOKE, Donald. *For Conspicuous Gallantry: Winners of Medal of Honor.* 1966. Maplewood. ils/roster/index. 93p. VG/VG. S16. $15.00.

COOKE, George Willis, ed. *Early Letters of George Wm. Curtis to John S. Dwight, Brook Farm and Concord.* NY and London. Harper & Brothers. 1898. 12mo. teg. brn cloth. 1st ed. minor scattered foxing. most apparent on title p. extremities sltly worn. VG. L5. $50.00.

COOKE, Michael. *The Ancient Curse of the Baskervilles.* 1984. Bloomington. Gaslight Publications. reissue. 1st thus. repro of 1885 1st ed. VF/no dj as issued. T2. $12.00.

COOLIDGE, Louis Arthur. *Ulysses S. Grant.* 1917. Boston & NY. Houghton Mifflin. 1st. orig cloth. 596p. VG. M8. $45.00.

COOLIDGE, Olivia. *George Bernard Shaw.* 1968. Houghton Mifflin. 1st. VG/dj. V4. $20.00.

COOLIDGE, Susan. *What Katy Did.* (1936). Little, Brn. ils Ralph Pallen Coleman. 271p. VG/dj. T5. $17.00.

COOMBS, Charles. *Maverick.* 1959. Whitman. TVTI. VG. P3. $15.00.

COOMBS, Patricia. *Molly Mullett.* 1975. Lee Shepard. 1st. sm 4to. unp. brn cloth. F/NF. T5. $25.00.

COON, Carleton S. *Living Races of Man.* 1965. Knopf. 1st. NF/VG. A20. $15.00.

COONEY, Barbara. *Chanticleer & the Fox.* 1958. Crowell. 1st. Caldecott Medal. VG+/VG. P2. $125.00.

COONTS, Stephen. *Final Flight.* 1988. NY. Doubleday. 1st. F/F. H11. $30.00.

COONTS, Stephen. *Flight of the Intruder.* 1986. Naval Inst. 1st. author's 1st book. F/F. N4. $35.00.

COONTS, Stephen. *Under Siege.* 1990. NY. Pocket Books. 1st. VG/VG. R16. $20.00.

COOPER, Basil. *Great White Space.* 1975. St Martin. 1st Am. F/dj. M2. $85.00.

COOPER, Dennis. *Closer.* 1989. NY. Grove. 1st. F/F. H11. $25.00.

COOPER, Dennis. *Wrong.* 1980. Knopf. 1st. F/F. B35. $15.00.

COOPER, Douglas. *Amnesia.* 1994. NY. Hyperion. ARC. F/wrps. B2. $30.00.

COOPER, Douglas. *Great Private Collections.* 1961. 1st. lg 4to. ils. NF/VG. S13. $18.00.

COOPER, Edmund. *Prisoner of Fire.* 1974. Walker. 1st. F/dj. M2. $12.00.

COOPER, J. California. *Family.* 1991. NY. Doubleday. 1st. sgn. F/F. A24. $45.00.

COOPER, J. California. *Some Soul to Keep.* 1987. NY. St. Martin. 1st. sgn. F/NF. A24. $45.00.

COOPER, James Fenimore. *Last of the Mohicans.* 1919. Scribner. 1st. ils NC Wyeth. VG. M17. $85.00.

COOPER, James Fenimore. *Last of the Mohicans.* 1977. Franklin Lib. ils NC Wyeth. aeg. F. A18. $50.00.

COOPER, Jefferson; See Fox, Gardner F.

COOPER, John R. *Mel Martin: Mystery at the Ball Park (#1).* 1947. Cupples Leon. 1st. 208p. VG/dj. M20. $35.00.

COOPER, Lenna Frances. *New Cookery.* 1924. Battle Creek. Modern Medicine. G. A16. $25.00.

COOPER, Lettice. *Gunpowder, Treason and Plot.* 1970. Abelard-Schuman, Ltd. ils. VG/chip dj. S19. $25.00.

COOPER, Merian C. *Grass.* 1925. Putnam. 2nd. inscr. VG/dj. B4. $450.00.

COOPER, Natasha. *A Common Death.* 1990. NY. Crown. 1st Am ed. F/F. T2. $8.00.

COOPER, Natasha. *Bitter Herbs.* 1994. S&S. 1st Am ed. NF/NF. G8. $17.50.

COOPER, Ph.D. Robert K. and Leslie. *Low Fat Living.* 1996. PA. Rodale Press. VG. A28. $7.95.

COOPER, Susan Rogers. *Funny as a Dead Comic.* 1993. NY. St. Martin. 1st. F/NF. T2. $15.00.

COOPER, Susan Rogers. *Gray King.* 1975. NY. Atheneum. 1st. ils Michael Heslop. gray-gr cloth. VG/VG. R5. $110.00.

COOPER, Susan Rogers. *Gray King.* 1975. Atheneum. 1st. Newberry Medal. ils Michael Heslop. 208p. NF/VG+. P2. $145.00.

COOPER, Susan Rogers. *Houston in the Rear View Mirror.* 1990. St Martin. 1st. sgn author's 2nd book. NF/F. A24. $90.00.

COOPER, Susan Rogers. *One, Two, What Did Daddy Do?* 1992. NY. St. Martin. 1st. sgn F/F. A24. $45.00.

COOPER, Susan Rogers. *Seaward.* 1983 Atheneum. 1st. 167p. NF/NF. P2. $35.00.

COOPER, Will. *Death Has a Thousand Doors.* 1976. Bobbs Merrill. 1st. VG/VG. P3. $15.00.

COOVER, Robert. *Pricksongs & Descants.* 1969. Dutton. 1st. author's 3rd book. F/NF D10. $70.00.

COOVER, Robert. *Public Burning.* 1977. Viking. 1st. F/F. A20. $25.00.

COPE, Myron. *Broken Cigars.* 1968. Prentice Hall. 1st. VG/G+. P8. $25.00.

COPE, Zachary. *Clinical Researches in Acute Abdominal Disease.* 1925. London. 1st. 148p. A13. $150.00.

COPELAND, Bonnie. *Lady of Moray.* 1979. Atheneum. 1st. 313p. F/NF. W2. $25.00.

COPELAND, Richard. *No Face in a Mirror.* 1980. Macmillan. 1st. VG/VG. P3. $15.00.

COPP, DeWitt S. *Forged in Fire.* 1982. Garden City. NY. 1st. 521p. quarter cloth. VG/dj. B18. $19.50.

COPPARD, A.E. *Collected Tales Of.* 1951. Knopf. VG/dj. M2. $30.00.

COPPARD, A.E. *Nixey's Harlequin.* 1932. Knopf. 1st Am. VG. M2. $25.00.

COPPEE, Henry. *Grant & His Campaigns.* 1866. NY. ils/maps. G. M17. $20.00.

COPPEL, Alfred. *Dragon.* 1977. HBJ. 1st. VG/VG. P3. $15.00.

COPPER, Basil. *From Evil's Pillow.* 1973. Arkham. 1st. F/dj. M2/M19. $25.00.

COPPER, Basil. *Necropolis.* 1980. Arkham. 1st. F/dj. M2. $100.00.

COPPER, Basil. *The Black Death.* 1991. Minneapolis. Fedogan & Bremer. 1st. VF/VF. T2. $32.00.

COPPER, Basil. *The Exploits of Solar Pons.* 1993. Minneapolis. Fedogan & Bremer. 1st. VF/VF. T2. $24.00.

COPPER, Basil. *The Recollections of Solar Pons.* 1995. Minneapolis. Fedogan & Bremer. 1st. VF/VF. T2. $25.00.

COPPER, Edmund. *All Fools' Day.* 1966. Hodder Stoughton. 1st. VG/VG. P3. $20.00.

COPPER, Edmund. *Transit.* 1964. Faber. 1st. VG/VG. P3. $30.00.

COQUIA, Jorge R. *Legal Status of the Church of the Philippines.* 1950. WA. Catholic U of Am Pr. 224p. F. P1. $20.00.

CORBETT, Bertha L. *Sun-Bonnet Babies.* 1900. Minneapolis. 1st. sq 8vo. pale gr pict brd. R5. $200.00.

CORBETT, Helen. *Helen Corbett Cooks for Company.* 1974. Houghton Mifflin. 1t. dj. A16. $10.00.

CORBETT, James. *Death Pool.* 1936. Herbert Jenkins. 1st. VG/VG. P3. $75.00.

CORBETT, James. *Roar of the Crowd.* 1925. Garden City. VG/VG. B5. $40.00.

CORBETT, Scott. *Hairy Horror Trick.* 1969. Little, Brn. 1st. 8vo. F/VG+. C8. $17.50.

CORBITT, Helen. *Cooks for Looks: An Adventure in Low Calorie Eating.* 1967. Boston. Houghton Mifflin. VG/VG. A28. $9.95.

CORCORAN, Tom. *Gumbo Limbo.* 1999. NY. St. Martin. 1st. sgn. VF/VF. T2. $25.00.

CORCORAN, Tom. *The Mango Opera.* 1998. NY. St. Martin. 1st. sgn. author's 1st novel. VF/VF. T2. $35.00.

CORDELL, Alexander. *Fire People.* 1972. Hodder Stoughton. 1st. VG/VG. P3. $15.00.

CORDELL, Alexander. *Rape of the Fair Country.* 1959. Doubleday. VG/VG. P3. $10.00.

CORDELL, L. S. *Prehistory of the Southwest.* 1984. Orlando. Academic. 50 maps/photos/drawings. 490p. VG/wrp. M12. $30.00.

CORDER, Eric. *Murder, My Love.* 1973. Playboy. 1st. VG/G+. P3. $12.00.

CORE, Sue. *Maid In Panama.* 1938. NY. Clermont Pub. 1st. ils by Anne Cordts McKeown. decor ep. pict cloth. 195p. G/chipped dj. F3. $25.00.

CORELLI, Marie. *Secret Power.* 1961. London. VG/dj. M2. $15.00.

CORELLI, Marie. *Young Diana.* 1918. Doran. 1st. F/NF. M2. $50.00.

COREVON, Henry. *Fleurs Des Champ Et Des Bois Des Haies Et Des Murs.* 1911. Geneva. Albert Kundig. 8vo. VG. A22. $65.00.

COREY, Deborah Joy. *Losing Eddie.* (1994). Chapel Hill. Algonquin. 1st. author's 1st novel. F/F. B3. $20.00.

CORK, Barry. *Dead Ball.* 1989. Scribner. 1st. F/F. P8. $12.50.

CORK, Barry. *Laid Dead.* 1991. NY. Scribner's. 1st Am ed. F/F. G8. $17.50.

CORLE, Edwin. *Listen, Bright Angel.* 1946. DSP. 1st. 8vo. 312p. brn cloth. VG/VG. $7.00.

CORLE, Edwin. *Story of the Grand Canyon.* nd. London. Sampson Low. 8vo. 312p. VG+/G+. F7. $35.00.

CORLISS, Philip G. *Hemerocallis.* 1951. SF. self pub. 1/1000. 8vo. red cloth. NF. A22. $35.00.

CORLISS, William R. *Moon & the Planets.* 1985. Glen Arm. MD. Sourcebook Project. 4to. 377p. VG. K5. $30.00.

CORLISS, William R. *Radioisotopic Power Generation.* 1964. Englewood Cliffs. 8vo. 304p. VG/dj. K5. $60.00.

CORMAN, Cid. *Words for Each Other.* 1967. London. Rapp & Carroll. 1st Eng ed. F/VG. sm tears. some edgewear. V1. $25.00.

CORMAN, H.E. *Phrenological Analysis of Harry Crouse.* 1914. Coburn, PA. 10p. B18. $125.00.

CORMIER, Robert. *Fade.* 1988. NY. Delacorte Press. 1st. NF. minor wear. bumps/F. mild wear. tear. M23. $20.00.

CORNELIUS, Mrs. *Young Housekeeper's Friend.* Brn Taggard Chase. facsimile 1859 revised ed. 254p. B10. $12.00.

CORNELL, John J. *Essays on the View of Friends...* 1884. Friends Book Assn. 2nd. 95p. V3. $12.00.

CORNELL, Ralph D. *Conspicuous California Plants.* 1938. Pasadena. 1st. 1/1500. inscr. 192p. VG. B26. $65.00.

CORNER, George. *Anatomy.* 1930. NY. 1st. 82p. A13. $60.00.

CORNING, Howard McKinley. *This Earth & Another Country: New & Selected Poems.* (1969). Portland. Tall Pine Imp. 1st. wrp. A18. $10.00.

CORNING, James Leonard. *Treatise on Headache & Neuralgia.* 1894. NY. EB Treat. 3rd enlarged. 12mo. pebbled mauve cloth. G. G1. $50.00.

CORNWELL, Bernard. *Crackdown.* 1990. NY. Harper Collins. 1st. F/F. T2. $8.00.

CORNWELL, Bernard. *Excalibur. A Novel of Arthur.* 1998. NY. St. Martin. ARC. wrps. F. B2. $30.00.

CORNWELL, Bernard. *Rebel.* 1993. NY. Harper Collins. 1st. ARC. F. D10. $10.00.

CORNWELL, Bernard. *Sharpe's Devil.* 1992. Harper Collins. 1st. sgn. F/dj. Q1. $60.00.

CORNWELL, Bernard. *Sharpe's Eagle.* 1981. NY. Viking. 1st Am. F/F. M23. $50.00.

CORNWELL, Bernard. *Sharpe's Rifles.* 1982. NY. Viking. 1st. F/VNF. D10. $85.00.

CORNWELL, Bernard. *Stormchild.* 1991. NY. Harper Collins. 1st. VF/VF. T2. $8.00.

CORNWELL, Bernard. *Wildtrack.* 1988. Putnam. 1st. NF/F. T12. $30.00.

CORNWELL, Patricia D. *All That Remains.* 1992. NY. Scribners. 1st. VF/VF. T2. $35.00.

CORNWELL, Patricia D. *All That Remains.* 1992. London. Little, Brn. 1st. precedes Am ed. VF/dj. M15. $125.00.

CORNWELL, Patricia D. *Body of Evidence.* 1990. NY. Scribners. 1st. ARC. F/pict wrp. T2. $45.00.

CORNWELL, Patricia D. *Body of Evidence.* 1991. Scribner. 1st. F/NF. A20. $85.00.

CORNWELL, Patricia D. *Cruel & Unusual.* 1993. NY. Scribners. 1st. VF/VF. T2. $30.00.

CORNWELL, Patricia D. *The Body Farm.* 1994. NY. Scribners. 1st. VF/VF. T2. $25.00.

CORNWELL, Patricia D. *The Body Farm.* 1994. NY. Scribners. 1st. ARC. sgn. VF/pict wrp. T2. $35.00.

CORPI, Lucha. *Eulogy for a Brown Angel.* 1992. Houston. Arte Publico Press. 1st. author's 1st mystery novel. sgn. VF/VF. T2. $25.00.

CORPUZ, O. D. *The Philippines.* 1965. NJ. Prentice Hall. sm8vo. 149p. VG. P1. $6.00.

CORRAL, Jesus C. *Caro Amigo: Autobiography of Jesus C Corral.* 1984. Westernlore. 1st. sgn. 238p. F/VG+. B19. $50.00.

CORREDOR-MATHEOS, Jose. *Miro's Posters.* 1987. Barcelona. Poligrafa. 119 pl. 269p. dj. D2. $150.00.

CORRELL, D.S. *Potato & Its Wild Relatives.* 1962. TX Research Found. 606p. cloth. dj. B1. $45.00.

CORREVON, Henry. *Rock Gardens & Alpine Plants.* 1930. NY. ils/pl. 544p. VG. B26. $25.00.

CORRIGAN, J.D. *Working with the Microscope.* 1971. McGraw Hill. 418p. F. D8. $15.00.

CORRO VINA, J. Manuel. *Sucesion O Reeleccion Del Presidente Cardenas.* 1939. np. Mexico. 119p. G/chipped spine. F3. $25.00.

CORROTHERS, James D. *Black Cat Club.* 1902. NY. ils JK Bryans. 264p. pict cloth. B18. $45.00.

CORTAZAR, Julio. *A Manual for Manuel.* 1978. NY. Pantheon. 1st. F/F. H11. $40.00.

CORTES DE FIGUEROA, Leslie. *Tasco. The Enchanted City.* 1950. Mexico. Editorial Fischgrund. 1st. 127p. G. F3. $20.00.

CORTWRIGHT, Edgar. *Exploring Space with a Camera.* 1968. NASA. F. M2. $15.00.

CORVO, Baron. *Without Prejudice.* 1963. London. Allen Lane. 1st. 1/600. F/salmon dj. Q1. $250.00.

CORY, Charles B. *Birds of Illinois & Wisconsin.* 1909. Field Mus Natural Hist. ils. 764p. VG. S15. $55.00.

CORY, David. *Little Jack Rabbit & The Big Brown Bear.* 1921. Grosset Dunlap. 128p. cloth. VG/dj. M20. $12.50.

CORY, Desmond. *Bennett.* 1977. Crime Club. 1st. VG/VG. P3. $15.00.

CORY, H.T. *Imperial Valley & The Salton Sink.* 1915. SF. John J Newgegin. ils/fld maps/plans. gilt stp cloth. D11. $150.00.

COSBY, Bill. *Fatherhood.* 1986. Doubleday. 1st. F/F. W2. $30.00.

COSE, Ellis. *The Best Defense.* 1998. NY. Harper Collins. 1st. author's 1st novel. VF/VF. T2. $15.00.

COSELL, Howard. *Cosell.* 1973. Playboy. 1st. sgn. VG/G. B11. $18.00.

COSSE, Laurence. *A Corner of the Veil.* 1999. NY. Scribner. 1st. F/F. M23. $30.00.

COSTAIN, Thomas B. *Below the Salt.* 1957. Doubleday. 1st. VG/VG. P3. $35.00.

COSTAIN, Thomas B. *Silver Chalice.* 1952. Doubleday. 1st. inscr. VG. T12. $18.00.

COTE, Phyllis. *Rabbit-Go-Lucky.* 1944. Doubleday Doran. 1st. 175p. VG/dj. M20. $15.00.

COTTER, Clay. *Mystery & Adventure Stories: Hidden Peril (#8).* 1939. Cupples Leon. 204p. cloth. VG+/dj. M20. $10.00.

COTTON, Charles. *Poetical Works.* 1734. London. 34d. half leather/brd. A15. $25.00.

COTTRELL, Edwin A. *Pasadena Social Agencies Survey.* 1940. Pasadena. 378p+4p ES. wrp/cloth spine (as issued). D11. $40.00.

COTTRILL, GREENBERG & WAUGH. *Science Fiction & Fantasy Series & Sequels.* 1986. Garland. 1st. F. P3. $45.00.

COUGHLIN, William J. *Death Penalty.* 1992. NY. Harper. 1st. F/F. G8. $12.50.

COUGHLIN, William J. *Heart of Justice.* 1995. NY. St. Martin. 1st. VG/NF. G8. $10.00.

COUGHLIN, William J. *In the Presence of Enemies.* 1993. NY. St. Martin. 1st Am ed. VF/VF. T2. $7.00.

COUGHLIN, William J. *Judgment.* 1997. NY. St. Martin. 1st. VG/NF. G8. $12.50.

COUGHLIN, William J. *Shadow of a Doubt.* 1991. NY. St. Martin. 1st. VF/VF. T2. $8.00.

COUNSELMAN, Mary Elizabeth. *Half in Shadow.* 1978. Arkham. 1st. F/dj. Q1. $30.00.

COUPER, Greta Elena. *American Sculptor on Grand Tour. William Couper.* 1988. LA. TreCavalli. ils/photos/footnotes. 157p. dj. D2. $45.00.

COUPPEY, Madeleine. *Rumor of the Forest.* 1947. Scribner. 1st. VG/VG. A4. $15.00.

COURANT, Maurice. *Bibliographie Coreene, 1894 – 1896.* NY. Burt Franklin. 4 vol in 3. ils/charts/tables. French/Chinese text. F. W3. $525.00.

COURET, Pierre. *Joyas De Las Orquideas Venezolanas.* 1977. Caracas. ils/photos. 104p. VG+/dj. B26. $52.50.

COURT, Arnold, editor. *Eclectic Climatology; Selected Essays Written in Memory of David Il Blumenstock 1913 – 1963.* 1968. Corvallis. Oregon State Univ Press. text figures. 8vo. 184p. VG/cloth. K5. $18.00.

COURTIER, S. H. *Murder's Burning.* 1967. NY. Random House. 1st Am ed. NF/VG+. G8. $10.00.

COURTNEY, W. *Farmers' & Mechanics Manual.* 1868. revised. ils. 505p. G+. E6 $95.00.

COURTRIGHT, G. *Tropicals.* 1988. Timber 155p. B1. $38.00.

COUSINS, Geoffrey. *Golfers at Law.* 1959 Knopf. 1st. VG/VG. P8. $30.00.

COUSTEAU, Jacques Yves & Mose Richards. *Jacques Cousteau's Amazon Journey* 1984. NY. Abrams. 1st. lg 4to. all color photos. 235p. G/G. F3. $35.00.

COUTANT, F. *ABC of Goat-Keeping.* 1946 photos. sc. G+. E6. $12.00.

COUTEAU, Paul. *Observing Visual Double Stars.* 1981. MIT Press. Cambridge, MA. translated by Alan H. Batten. 8vo. text ils. 257p. VG/slightly chipped dj. K5. $25.00.

COUTINHO, Gago. *Nautica Dos Descubrimentos Maritimos Vistos Por Navegador.* 1969. Lisboa. Agencia-Geral Ultramar. lg 4to. 14 maps/50 ils. F/wrp. O7. $75.00.

COVARRUBIAS, M. *Indian Art of Mexico & Central America.* 1957. NY. 1st. VG/G. B5. $65.00.

COVARRUBIAS, Miguel. *Mexico South. The Isthmus of Tehuantepec.* nd. London. plates all b/w. 427p. G/wrp. F3. $20.00.

COVENTRY, George. *Critical Inquiry Regarding the Real Authorship of Letters.* 1825. London. Wm Philips/G Woodfall. 1st. tall 8vo. 382p. H13. $195.00.

COVINGTON, Dennis. *Salvation on Sand Mountain.* 1994. Reading, PA. Addison Wesley. sgn 1st ed. Natl Book Award finalist. F/F. M23. $40.00.

COVINGTON, Vicki. *Bird of Paradise.* 1990. S&S. 1st. sgn. F/F. B3. $45.00.

COVINGTON, Vicki. *Gathering Home.* 1988. S&S. 1st. author's 1st book. F/F. B3. $60.00.

COVINGTON, Vicki. *Night Ride Home.* 1992. NY. S&S. sgn 1st ed. F/F. M23. $30.00.

COWAN, James. *Maori Folk-Tales of Port Hills.* 1923. Auckland. Whitcombe Tombes. 73p. gray wrp. P4. $50.00.

COWAN, L. *Wit of the Jews.* 1970. VG/VG. E6. $8.00.

COWAN, May. *Inverewe: Garden in the NW Highlands.* 1964. London. ils/photos/ map/plan. 152p. VG/dj. B26. $15.00.

COWAN, Paul. *Orphan in History: Retrieving Jewish Legacy.* 1982. Doubleday. 246p. VG/dj. S3. $24.00.

COWAN, Robert Ernest. *Bibliographical Notes on Early California.* 1905. GPO. sgn Holliday. prt wrp. D11. $30.00.

COWAN, Robert G. *Ranchos of California.* 1977. Los Angeles. rpt. VG. H1. $20.00.

COWAN, Sam. *Sergeant York.* 1928. NY. 1st. sgn Alvin York. VG/torn. S16. $450.00.

COWARD, Noel. *Play Parade.* 1933. NY. 1st. VG. T9. $20.00.

COWARD, Noel. *Pretty Polly & Other Stories.* 1965. Doubleday. 1st Am. 8vo. NF/clip. T10. $40.00.

COWELL, John. *Institvtiones Ivris Anglicani.* 1630. Frankfurt. Fitzer. 8vo. vellum. R12. $475.00.

COWEN, D. V. *Flowering Trees and Shrubs in India.* 1950. Bombay. 1st. 4to. upper corners bumped. minor spotting on fore edge. else VG. B26. $42.50.

COWLES, Frederick. *The Night Wind Howls: Complete Supernatural Stories.* 1999. Ashcroft, BC. Ash Tree Press. 1st combined ed. collects 61 stories from 3 collections. VF/VF. T2. $55.00.

COWLEY, Cecil. *Schiwikkard of Natal & Old Transvaal.* 1974. Cape Town. Struik. 1st. 8vo. ils Paul Wiles. VG/dj. W1. $12.00.

COWLEY, Stewart. *Spacewreck: Ghostships & Derelicts.* 1979. Exeter. 1st. F/dj. M2. $15.00.

COWMAN, Mrs. Charles E. *Streams in the Desert.* 1976. Zondervan. 376p. VG/VG. B29. $6.00.

COWPER, Richard. *Breakthrough.* 1967. London. Dennis Dobson. 1st. F/F. T2. $30.00.

COWPER, Richard. *Clone.* 1972. London. Gollancz. 1st. F/F. T2. $45.00.

COWPER, Richard. *Dream of Kinship.* 1981. London. Gollancz. 1st. F/F. T2. $25.00.

COWPER, Richard. *Kuldesak.* 1972. Doubleday. 1st Am. F/NF. T2. $20.00.

COWPER, Richard. *Profundis.* 1979. London. Gollancz. 1st. F/F. T2. $40.00.

COWPER, Richard. *Shades of Darkness.* 1986. Salisbury. Wilts. Kerosina Books. 1st. F/F. T2. $25.00.

COWPER, Richard. *Tapestry of Time.* 1982. London. Gollancz. 1st. F/F. T2. $25.00.

COWPER, Richard. *Tithonian Factor.* 1984. Gollancz. 1st. F/F. P3. $25.00.

COWPER, Richard. *Web of the Magi.* 1980. London. 1st. F/dj. M2/T2. $40.00.

COWPER, William. *Task.* 1856. NY. Robert Carter. ils Birket Foster. 263p. aeg. bl cloth. NF. $24.00.

COX, A.E. *Potato: A Practical & Scientific Guide.* 1967. London. Collingridge. 176p. dj. A10. $38.00.

COX, C.B. *Biogeography: Ecological & Evolutionary Approach.* 1977. Oxford. Blackwell Scientific. 2nd/2nd prt. 194p. wrp. B1. $18.50.

COX, E.H. *Plant Hunting in China.* 1945. London. 1st. ils/maps. 230p. VG/dj. W3. $95.00.

COX, Erle. *Missing Angel.* 1947. Australia. 1st. VG. M2. $35.00.

COX, Isaac. *Annals of Trinity County.* 1940. Eugene, OR. Nash. 1/350. 4to. 265p. NF/NF. $10.00.

COX, Jacob D. *Atlanta.* 1882. NY. 274p. O8. $21.50.

COX, Jacob D. *Franklin & Nashville: The March to the Sea.* 1882. NY. 1st. 265p. O8. $23.50.

COX, James. *Biblical Preaching: An Expositor's Treasury.* 1983. Westminster. 372p. VG/G. B29. $11.50.

COX, James. *My Native Land.* 1903. ils. 400p. O8. $18.50.

COX, Michael. *A Study in Celluloid: A Producer's Account of Jeremy Brett as Sherlock Holmes.* 1999. Cambridge. Rupert Books. 1st. VF/VF. T2. $35.00.

COX, Michael & R. Dixon Smith. *Remembering Jeremy Brett.* 1997. Cambridge, UK. Rupert Books. 1st. sgn by Smith. VF/printed wrp. T2. $18.00.

COX, Palmer. *Another Brownie Book.* 1890. Century. 1st. pict brd. R5. $275.00.

COX, Palmer. *Brownies and Other Stories.* nd. Chicago. M. A. Donohue & Co. told in prose by E. Veale. G. A16. $40.00.

COX, Palmer. *Brownies at Home.* 1893. NY. Century. 1st. 4to. 144p. pict brd. R5. $250.00.

COX, Palmer. *Brownies & Prince Florimel.* 1918. Century. 1st. ils. 8vo. gray cloth/mc pl. VG. M5. $110.00.

COX, Palmer. *Queer Stories About Queer Animals Told in Rhymes & Jingles.* 1905. Phil. unp. decor cloth. G+. B18. $65.00.

COX, R. *Columbia River or Scenes & Adventures During a Residence.* 1957. OK U. 1st. ils/maps. 396p. F/dj. M4. $45.00.

COX, Thomas R. *Park Builders: History of State Parks in Pacific Northwest.* 1988. WA U. 248p. F/F. S15. $15.00.

COX, Wally. *Mr Peepers: A Sort of Novel.* 1955. S&S. 1st. NF/VG. B4. $85.00.

COX-MCCORMACK, Nancy. *Peeps: The Really Truly Sunshine Fairy.* 1918. Volland. 1st. ils Katharine Sturges Dodge. 8vo. pict brd. R5. $75.00.

COXE, George Harmon. *Dangerous Legacy.* 1946. NY. Knopf. 1st. F/dj. M15. $45.00.

COXE, George Harmon. *Groom Lay Dead.* 1944. Knopf. 1st. VG/VG. G8. $15.00.

COXE, George Harmon. *Man on a Rope.* 1956. Knopf. 1st. VG/G+. G8. $20.00.

COXE, George Harmon. *One Way Out.* 1959. Knopf. 1st. VG/G. G8. $10.00.

COXE, George Harmon. *Ring of Truth.* 1966. Knopf. 1st. 176p. VG/dj. M20. $15.00.

COXE, George Harmon. *Silent Witness.* 1973. Knopf. 1st. VG/VG. P3. $20.00.

COXE, George Harmon. *The Man Who Died Twice.* 1951. NY. Knopf. 1st. F/dj. M15. $45.00.

COXE, George Harmon. *With Intent to Kill.* 1964. Knopf. 1st. G/G. G8. $10.00.

COYLE, Harold. *Code of Honor.* 1994. NY. S&S. 1st. NF/VG+. R16. $25.00.

COYLE, William. *Firestorm.* 1988. NY. Morror. 1st. VF/VF. H11. $15.00.

COYNE, John. *Hobgoblin.* 1981. Putnam. 1st. F/dj. M2. $25.00.

COYNE, John. *Piercing.* 1979. Putnam. 1st. inscr. F/dj. M2. $40.00.

COZZENS, James Gould. *Morning Noon and Night.* 1968. NY. Harcourt Brace. 1st. VG+/VG. A24. $25.00.

COZZENS, James Gould. *SS San Pedro.* 1931. NY. Harcourt Brace. 1st. VG+/G+. A24. $35.00.

CRACE, Jim. *Continent.* 1987. NY. Harper & Row. 1st. author's 1st book. F/F. M23. $20.00.

CRACE, Jim. *Continent.* 1986. Harper Row. 1st. NF/F. M11. $25.00.

CRACE, Jim. *Quarantine.* 1997. NY. FSG. ARC in pict wrp. F. tiny tear. M23. $25.00.

CRADDOCK, Fred. *Luke.* 1990. John Knox. 298p. VG/VG. B29. $12.50.

CRADDOCK, Harry. *Savoy Cocktail Book.* 1934. S&S. 287p. B10. $35.00.

CRADDOCK, Patricia B. *Edward Gibbon: A Reference Guide.* 1987. 525p. F. A4. $55.00.

CRAIG, Alisa. *Wrong Rite.* 1992. NY. Morrow. 1st. NF/NF. G8. $10.00.

CRAIG, David. *Albion Case.* 1975. Macmillan. 1st. VG/VG. P3. $20.00.

CRAIG, Gordon. *Henry Irving.* 1930. ils. VG. M17. $15.00.

CRAIG, Helen. *Angelena on Stage.* 1986. Clarkson Potter. 1st. ils Katherine Holabird. F. C8. $25.00.

CRAIG, John A. *Judging Livestock.* 1906. Austin. self pub. 193p. photos. cloth. NF. A10. $10.00.

CRAIG, Kit. *Gone.* 1992. Boston. Little, Brn. 1st. VF/VF. T2. $7.00.

CRAIG, Philip A. *Death on a Vineyard Beach.* 1996. NY. Scribners. 1st. sgn. VF/VF. T2. $25.00.

CRAIG, Robert T. *Mammillaria Handbook With Descriptions.* 1945. Pasadena. 1st. 390p. VG+. B26. $75.00.

CRAIG, William N. *Lilies and Their Culture in North America.* 1928. Chicago. gilt emb gr cloth. VG. B26. $24.00.

CRAINE, Eric R. *A Handbook of Quasistellar and Bl Lacertae Objects.* 1977. Tucson. Pachart. ils w/charts. 283p. VG in pb. K5. $25.00.

CRAIS, Robert. *Free Fall.* 1993. NY. Bantam. 1st. VF/dj. M15. $55.00.

CRAIS, Robert. *Indigo Slam.* 1997. NY. Hyperion. 1st. sgn. F/F. O11. $35.00.

CRAIS, Robert. *Stalking the Angel.* 1989. NY. Bantam. 1st. F/F. M23. $45.00.

CRAIS, Robert. *Sunset Express.* 1996. NY. Hyperion. 1st. sgn. F/F. O11. $35.00.

CRAIS, Robert. *Voodoo River.* 1995. NY. Hyperion. 1st. VF/dj. M15. $45.00.

CRAM, Mildred. *Promise.* 1949. Knopf. 1st. VG/VG. P3. $30.00.

CRAM, Ralph Adams. *Impressions of Japanese Architecture & Allied Arts.* 1905. NY. Baker Taylor. 1st. 227p. NF. W3. $165.00.

CRAMER, C. H. *Case Western Reserve.* 1976. Boston. Little, Brn. 1st. ils. 401p. F/VG. B18. $22.50.

CRAMER, Kathryn, editor. *Walls of Fear.* 1990. NY. Morrow. 1st. 16 horror tales. sgn by one contributor. Edward Bryant. VF/VF. T2. $20.00.

CRAMER, Maurice. *Phoenix in East Hadley.* 1941. Houghton Mifflin. 1st. NF/dj. M2. $30.00.

CRAMOND, Mike. *Killing Bears.* 1982. Outdoor Life. 2nd. 312p. VG/VG. S15. $15.00.

CRAMP, Arthur J. *Nostrums & Quackery.* Vol 2. 1921. Chicago. AMA. 8vo. 832p. gilt dk gr cloth. H1. $37.50.

CRAMPTON, J. *Falling Stars.* nd (ca 1866). London. Macintosh. xl. K5. $35.00.

CRAN, Marion. *Garden of Experience.* ca 1920s. Herbert Jenkins. 6th. 8vo. 316p. VG. A22. $25.00.

CRAN, Marion. *Gardens of Character.* 1939. Herbert Jenkins. 1st. 8vo. 284p. G. A22. $30.00.

CRAN, Marion. *Story of My Ruin.* 1924. London. Herbert Jenkins. 1st. 8vo. 320p. G. A22. $25.00.

CRANE, Aimee. *Marines At War.* 1943. NY. ils. 182p. S16. $28.50.

CRANE, Clinton H. *Clinton Crane's Yachting Memories.* 1952. Van Nostrand. ils. 216p. T7. $35.00.

CRANE, Frances. *The Shocking Pink Hat.* 1946. NY. Random House. 1st. F/dj. M15. $50.00.

CRANE, Hamilton. *Sold to Miss Seeton.* 1995. Berkley. 1st. review copy. NF/NF. G8. $20.00.

CRANE, J. *Fiddler Crabs of the World.* 1975. Princeton. 50 pl. cloth. dj. B1. $75.00.

CRANE, Joan. *Willa Cather: A Bibliography.* 1982. NE U. 440p. F/F. A4. $45.00.

CRANE, Laura Dent. *Automobile Girls at Chicago (#4).* 1912. Altemus. lists 6 titles. VG/ragged. M20. $20.00.

CRANE, Leo. *Indians of the Enchanted Desert.* 1925. Little, Brn. 1st. 8vo. 32 pl/fld map. pict bl cloth. VG. T10. $75.00.

CRANE, Paul. *Korean Patterns.* 1967. Seoul. Hollyn. 1st. Royal Asiatic Soc Handbook series. VG/dj. W3. $38.00.

CRANE, Stephen. *Red Badge of Courage.* 1896. NY. Appleton. 2nd. decor tan cloth. VG. T11. $145.00.

CRANE, T. *Architectural Construction: Choice of Structural Design.* 1947. NY. Wiley. 1st. ils/index. 414p. VG/dj. B5. $20.00.

CRANE, Teresa. *The Hawthorne Heritage.* 1988. St. Martin Press. 1st. VG/G. S19. $20.00.

CRANE, Walter. *Beatrice Crane: Her Book.* 1983. Toronto. Osborne Collection. facsimile. 12mo. gilt blk cloth. VG. D1. $45.00.

CRANE, Walter. *Best Loved Fairy Tales of Walter Crane.* nd. NY. Avenel Books. F in F dj. A16. $12.00.

CRANE, Walter. *Sing a Song of Sixpence.* ca 1900. John Lane. reissue. 8 pl. VG. M5. $65.00.

CRANSTON, Edwin. *Izumi Shikibu Diary: Romance of the Heian Court.* 1969. Harvard. 1st. notes/bibliography. 332p. NF/NF. W3. $67.00.

CRASE, Douglas. *Revisionist.* 1981. Little, Brn. 1st. assn copy. F/F. V1. $15.00.

CRAVEN, Avery O. *Soil Exhaustion as a Factor in Agricultural History.* 1965. Gloucester. Smith. rpt. 179p. VG. A10. $25.00.

CRAVEN, J.H. *Chiropractic Orthopedy.* 1922. Davenport. 2nd. ils. 399p. VG. B5. $45.00.

CRAVEN, Roy. *Ceremonial Centers of the Maya.* 1974. Gainesville. Univ of Florida Press. 1st. 4to. 152p. G/G. chipped. F3. $45.00.

CRAVEN, Thomas. *Treasury of American Prints.* 1939. S&S. 100 b&w pl. sbdg. D2. $65.00.

CRAVEN, Tunis. *Naval Campaign in the Californias 1846 – 1849: Journal Of.* 1973. SF. BC of CA. 1/400. edit/inscr/sgn Kemble. AN/plain dj. O7/R3. $125.00.

CRAVENS, Gwyneth. *Speed of Light.* 1979. S&S. 1st. F/dj. M2. $17.00.

CRAWFORD, F. Marion. *Lady of Rome.* 1906. Macmillan. 1st. VG. M2. $25.00.

CRAWFORD, Hubert. *Crawford's Encyclopedia of Comic Books.* 1978. David. 1st. F/dj. M2. $40.00.

CRAWFORD, Isabel. *Kiowa.* 1915. NY. Revell. G. A19. $75.00.

CRAWFORD, Lewis F. *Medora-Deadwood Stage Line.* 1925. Capital Book. 1st. sgn. 17p. VG/wrp. J2. $55.00.

CRAWFORD, M.H. *Methods & Theories of Anthropoligical Genetics.* (1973). Albuquerque. 1st. 509p. dj. F3. $15.00.

CRAWFORD, Samuel. *Kansas in the Sixties.* 1911. McClurg. 1st. 438p. VG. J2. $285.00.

CRAWLEY, Rayburn. *Chattering Gods.* 1931. Harper. 1st. G. M2. $17.00.

CREAMER, Robert. *Stengel: His Life and Times.* 1984. NY. S&S. 1st. VG+/VG. R16. $35.00.

CREASEY, John. *Alibi.* 1971. Scribner. 1st. VG/VG. P3. $15.00.

CREASEY, John. *As Merry as Hell.* 1973. Hodder Stoughton. 1st. VG/VG. P3. $18.00.

CREASEY, John. *Baron & the Chinese Puzzle.* 1966. Scribner. 1st. VG/VG. P3. $20.00.

CREASEY, John. *Gallows are Waiting.* 1973. David McKay. 1st. VG/VG. P3. $20.00.

CREASEY, John. *Gideon's Staff.* 1959. Harper. 1st. VG/NF. M19. $25.00.

CREASEY, John. *Hang the Little Man.* 1963. Hodder Stoughton. 1st. NF/NF. P3. $25.00.

CREASEY, John. *Inspector West Alone.* 1975. Scribner. 1st. VG/VG. P3. $15.00.

CREASEY, John. *Life for a Death.* 1973. HRW. 1st. NF/NF. P3. $15.00.

CREASEY, John. *Sly as a Serpent.* 1967. Macmillan. 1st. 183p. cloth. VG/dj. M20. $12.00.

CREASEY, John. *So Young to Burn.* 1968. Scribner. 1st. VG/VG. P3. $15.00.

CREASEY, John. *Theft of Magna Carta.* 1973. Scribner. 1st. VG/VG. P3. $15.00.

CREASEY, John. *Toff Proceeds.* 1968. Walker. 1st. F/F. P3. $15.00.

CREASY, R. *Complete Book of Edible Landscaping.* 1983. Sierra Club. 3rd. 379p. dj. A10. $30.00.

CREDLE, Ellis. *Flop-Eared Hound.* 1938. Oxford. 3rd. ils Chas Townsend. VG/VG. P2. $75.00.

CREEL, H.G. *Studies in Early Chinese Culture.* 1938. Baltimore. 1st. 266p. F. W3. $125.00.

CREELEY, Robert. *A Day Book.* 1972. NY. Scribner's. 1st. sgn. wht printed cloth designed by Robert Indiana. F/NF mylar dj. O11. $65.00.

CREELEY, Robert. *Hello: A Journal February 19/May 3, 1976.* 1978. NY. New Directions. 1st. sgn. F/F. O11. $75.00.

CREELEY, Robert. *Presences: A Text for Marisol.* 1976. NY. Scribner's. 1st. sgn. F/F. O11. $35.00.

CREIGHTON, Helen. *Maritime Folk Songs.* 1979. np. Breakwater. Canada's Atlantic Folklore Series 5. 210p. dj. T7. $25.00.

CREMER, Jan. *I Jan Cremer.* 1965. 1st. VG/VG. S13. $35.00.

CRESPELLE, Jean-Paul. *Fauves.* 1962. NY. GS. 100 b&w pl. 351p. dj. D2. $150.00.

CRESSWELL, Helen. *Bagthorpes Abroad.* 1984. London. Faber. 1st. ils Jill Bennett. 186p. xl. VG. $5.00.

CREWS, Donald. *Light.* 1981. Bodley Head. 1st. sm 4to. NF. C8. $25.00.

CREWS, Donald. *Ten Black Dots Redesigned & Revised.* 1986. Greewnwillow. 1st. ils. F/NF. C8. $25.00.

CREWS, Harry. *All We Need of Hell.* 1987. Harper Row. 1st. F/M. M23. $50.00.

CREWS, Harry. *Blood and Grits.* 1979. NY. Harper & Row. 1st. F/F. H11. $90.00.

CREWS, Harry. *Childhood: The Biography of a Place.* 1978. Harper Row. 1st. F/dj. Q1. $150.00.

CREWS, Harry. *Karate Is a Thing of the Spirit.* 1971. NY. Morrow. 1st. F/F. O11. $275.00.

CREWS, Harry. *Naked in Garden Hills.* 1969. Morrow. 1st. 1st issue dj. red star on ffep. NF/yellowed white dj. M25. $200.00.

CREWS, Harry. *Scarlover.* 1992. Poseidon. 1st. sgn. F/F. B11/R13. $55.00.

CREWS, Harry. *The Knockout Artist.* 1988. NY. Harper & Row. 1st. F/F. H11. $45.00.

CRIBB, Phillip. *The Forgotten Orchids of Alexandre Brun.* 1992. NY. folio. 159p. F in dj. B26. $39.00.

CRICHTON, Michael. *Andromeda Strain.* 1969. Knopf. 1st. F/F. D10. $200.00.

CRICHTON, Michael. *Congo.* 1980. NY. Alfred A. Knopf. 1st trade ed. F/dj. M15. $45.00.

CRICHTON, Michael. *Disclosure.* 1994. NY. Knopf. 1st. VF/VF. T2. $15.00.

CRICHTON, Michael. *Eaters of the Dead.* 1976. NY. Viking. 1st. author's 4th novel. F/clip. D10. $50.00.

CRICHTON, Michael. *Electronic Life.* 1983. Knopf. 1st. NF/NF. T11. $40.00.

CRICHTON, Michael. *Jurassic Park.* 1990. NY. Knopf. 1st. NF/NF. M19. $17.50.

CRICHTON, Michael. *Lost World.* 1995. NY. Knopf. 1st trade. NF/NF. R16. $25.00.

CRICHTON, Michael. *Sphere.* 1987. NY. Knopf. 1st. F/F. D10. $45.00.

CRICHTON, Michael. *The Great Train Robbery.* 1975. NY. Knopf. 1st. F/F. H11. $60.00.

CRICHTON, Michael. *The Terminal Man.* (1972). NY. Knopf. 1st. F/NF. one closed tear at front gutter. B3. $50.00.

CRICHTON, Michael. *Travels.* 1988. Knopf. 1st. F/F. B35. $35.00.

CRICK, Francis. *What Mad Pursuit.* 1988. Basic Books. 8vo. ils. NF/dj. K3. $10.00.

CRIDER, Bill. *Booked for a Hanging.* 1992. NY. St. Martin. 1st. sgn. VF/VF. T2. $25.00.

CRIDER, Bill. *Galveston Gunman.* 1988. Evans. 1st. VG/VG. P3. $15.00.

CRIDER, Bill. *Medicine Show.* 1990. NY. M. Evans. 1st. sgn. VF/VF. T2. $25.00.

CRIDER, Bill. *Shotgun Saturday Night.* 1987. NY. Walker. 1st. sgn. F/F. A24. $20.00.

CRILE, George. *Anoci-Association.* 1914. Phil. 1st/1st prt. 259p. A13. $200.00.

CRILE, George. *Hemorrhage & Transfusion: Experimental & Clinical Research.* 1909. NY. 1st. sgn. 560p. xl. A13. $350.00.

CRIPPEN, David. *Two Sides of the River.* 1976. Nashville. Abingdon. 1st probable. obl sm 4to. AN/dj. C8. $25.00.

CRIPPEN, T. G. *Christmas & Christmas Lore.* 1923. London. Blackie. ils. 221p. G-. B18. $30.00.

CRISLER, Lois. *Arctic Wild.* 1958. Harper. 1st. 301p. VG/G. W2. $30.00.

CRISP, Frank. *Medieval Gardens.* 1924. London. Lane. 2 vol. A10. $150.00.

CRISP, N. J. *Brink.* 1982. Viking. 1st. F/F. P3. $15.00.

CRISP, N. J. *Gotland Deal.* 1976. NY. Viking. 1st Am ed. VG/VG. G8. $10.00.

CRISP, N. J. *London Deal.* 1978. St. Martin. 1st. VG/VG. P3. $18.00.

CRISP, William. *Compleat Agent.* 1984. Macmillan. 1st. F/F. P3. $15.00.

CRISPIN, Edmund. *Best of Science Fiction Three.* 1958. London. F/dj. M2. $20.00.

CRISPIN, Edmund. *The Glimpses of the Moon.* 1977. London. Victor Gollancz. 1st. NF/dj. M15. $70.00.

CRISPIN, William Frost. *Bibliographical & Historical Sketch of Capt Wm Crispin...* 1901. Akron. ils. 144p. fair. B18. $22.50.

CRISWELL, D. R., ed. *Interactions of the Interplanetary Plasma with the Modern and Ancient Moon.* 1975. Dordrecht. Holland. D. Reidel. lg 8vo. VG in wrp. K5. $12.00.

CROCKER, Betty; see Betty Crocker.

CROCKER, William. *The Canela.* 1990. DC. Smithsonian Institution Press. 1st. 4to. 487p. G/wrp. F3. $30.00.

CROCKETT, Lucy Herndon. *Kings without Castles.* 1957. Rand McNally. 1st. sgn. VG/VG. B11. $18.00.

CROCKETT, S.R. *Adventurer in Spain.* 1903. Isibster. VG. P3. $20.00.

CROCKETT, S.R. *Black Douglas.* 1899. Doubleday. 1st Am. VG. M2. $35.00.

CROCKETT, S.R. *Flower O'the Corn.* 1902. London. 1st. VG. M2. $20.00.

CROFT, Terrell. *Library of Practical Electricity.* 1924. NY. 8 vol. 4th. limp cloth. A17. $30.00.

CROFT-COOKE, Rupert. *Exotic Food.* 1971. NY. Herder. G/dj. A16. $20.00.

CROFTON, Algernon. *Goat's Hoof.* 1928. Covici Friede. 1st. F. w/pub brochure. M2. $25.00.

CROFTS, Freeman Wills. *Many a Slip.* 1955. London. Hodder & Stoughton. 1st. F/dj. M15. $300.00.

CROFTS, Freeman Wills. *The Four Gospels in One Story.* 1949. London. Longmans Green. 1st. NF/dj clip. M15. $100.00.

CROFTS, Freeman Wills. *Tragedy in the Hollow.* 1939. Dodd Mead. 1st. VG. P3. $35.00.

CROFUT, William. *Moon on the One Hand.* 1975. Atheneum. 1st. 80p. F/NF. D4. $45.00.

CROLY, George. *Salathiel.* nd. Funk Wagnall. NF. M2. $25.00.

CROMARTIE, Countess. *Temple of the Winds.* 1925. London. 1st. VG. M2. $15.00.

CROMBIE, Deborah. *All Shall be Well.* 1994. NY. Scribners. 1st. F/VF. H11. $30.00.

CROMBIE, Deborah. *Mourn Not Your Dead.* 1996. NY. Scribners. 1st. sgn. VF/VF. T2. $30.00.

CROMIE, Robert. *From the Cliffs of Croaghaun.* 1904. Saalfield. 1st. VG. M2. $27.00.

CRONIN, A. J. *The Spanish Gardener.* 1950. Boston. Little, Brn. 1st. F/NF dj. M19. $25.00.

CRONIN, Michael. *Night of the Party.* 1958. Ives Washburn. 1st. VG/VG. P3. $13.00.

CRONKITE, Walter. *Reporter's Life.* 1996. Knopf. 1st sgn bookplate. F/F. A23. $46.00.

CRONLEY, Jay. *Quick Change.* 1981. Doubleday. 1st. VG/VG. M22. $35.00.

CRONQUIST, Arthur. *Evolution & Classification of Flowering Plants.* 1968. Boston. ils. 396p. B26. $30.00.

CRONQUIST, Arthur. *Intermountain Flora.* 1986. NY. Botanical Garden. rpt. 270p. B1. $37.50.

CROOK, H. Clifford. *Campanulas: Their Cultivation & Classification.* 1977 (1951). Sakonnet, RI. reprint. scarce. 256p. VG in slightly edgeworn dj. B26. $65.00.

CROOKES, Marguerite. *New Zealand Ferns.* 1963. Whitcombe Tombs. 6th. 8vo. cloth. VG/dj. A22. $40.00.

CROSBY, Alexander. *Steamboat Up the Colorado... 1857 – 1858.* 1965. Little, Brn. 1st. ils Bjorklund. VG/dj. F7. $32.50.

CROSBY, Bing. *Call Me Lucky.* 1953. S&S. 1st. VG/clip. A20. $40.00.

CROSBY, Edward. *Radiana.* 1906. Ivy. 1st. VG. M2. $40.00.

CROSBY, Fanny. *Fanny Crosby's Life-Story.* 1903. NY. Every Where Publishing Company. 12mo. 160p. frontis. bl cloth. 1st ed. With intro & poem by Will Carleton and a poem by Margaret Sangster. ep foxed. VG. L5. $45.00.

CROSBY, John. *Company of Friends.* 1977. Stein Day. 1st. VG/VG. P3. $13.00.

CROSBY, Percy. *Skippy.* 1929. Grosset Dunlap. ils. VG/dj. A21. $50.00.

CROSLAND, Margaret. *Colette: Difficulty of Loving.* 1973. Bobbs Merrill. 1st Am. photos. VG/dj. A25. $18.00.

CROSS, Amanda. *Death in a Tenured Postion.* 1981. NY. Doubleday. 1st. VG+/VG. G8. $20.00.

CROSS, Amanda. *No Word from Winifred.* 1986. Dutton. 1st. NF/NF. G8. $15.00.

CROSS, Amanda. *Trap for Fools.* 1989. NY. Dutton. 1st. VG+/VG. G8. $15.00.

CROSS, Amanda; see Heilbrun, Carolyn G.

CROSS, Helen Reid. *Simple Simon.* 1908. London. Chatto Windus. Dumpy Books. 24 full-p pl. 95p. brn cloth. R5. $200.00.

CROSS, John Kier. *Angry Planet.* 1946. Coward McCann. NF/dj. M2. $25.00.

CROSS, John Kier. *Best Black Magic Stories.* 1960. London. 1st. F/dj. M2. $30.00.

CROSS, Melinda. *Bloomsbury Needlepoint: From Tapestries at Charleston.* 1992. ils. VG/VG. M17. $25.00.

CROSSEN, Kendell Foster. *Adventures in Tomorrow.* 1950. Greenberg. VG/VG. P3. $40.00.

CROSSEN, Kendell Foster. *Future Tense.* 1952. Greenberg. 1st. NF/VG. P3. $45.00.

CROTHER, Ruth. *Manly Manners.* 1946. Encee Pub. ils Ethel Hays. 115p. VG+/G. P2. $35.00.

CROTHERS, Samuel McChord. *The Children of Dickens.* 1947. NY. Scribner. G. A16. $25.00.

CROUCH, D.E. *Carl Rungius: Complete Prints.* 1989. Missoula. ils/figures. 203p. F/dj. M4. $55.00.

CROUCH, Tom D. *Eagle Aloft: Two Centuries of the Balloon in America.* 1983. Smithsonian. thick 8vo. 770p. F/dj. T10. $60.00.

CROW, John. *Mexico Today.* 1957. NY. Harper. b/w photo ils. ep maps. index. 336p. G/G. chipped dj. F3. $10.00.

CROW, John. *The Epic of Latin America.* 1946. NY. Doubleday. 756p. G/chipped dj. F3. $15.00.

CROWDER, Herbert. *Ambush at Osirak.* 1988. Presidio. 1st. F/NF. W2. $25.00.

CROWDER, William. *Naturalist at the Seashore.* 1928. NY. 384p. VG. S15. $25.00.

CROWE, Earle. *Men of El Tejon: Empire in the Tehachapis.* 1957. Ward Ritchie. 1st. NF/VG. O4. $25.00.

CROWE, Jack. *Hopalong Cassidy Lends a Helping Hand.* 1950. John Martin's House. Bonnie Book. pict brd. VG+. M20. $40.00.

CROWE, John; see Lynds, Dennis.

CROWE, Philip. *The Empty Ark.* 1967. NY. Scribners. 1st. 301p. G/G chipped dj. F3. $20.00.

CROWE, Samuel. *Halsted of Johns Hopkins: Man & His Men.* 1957. Springfield. 1st. 247p. A13. $75.00.

CROWELL, Ann. *Hogan for the Bluebird.* 1969. NY. Scribner. 1st/Weekly Reader BC. VG. L3. $30.00.

CROWELL, Benedict. *America's Munitions 1917 – 1918.* 1919. Washington. 592p. G. edgewear. cover spotted. B18. $45.00.

CROWELL, Pers. *First Horseman.* 1948. Whittlesey. 1st. obl 4to. VG/fair. O3. $30.00.

CROWL, Philip. *Campaign in the Marianas: US Army in WWII. War in Pacific.* 1985. WA. fld mc maps/photos/index. 505p. VG. S16. $35.00.

CROWLEY, John. *Engine Summer.* 1979. Doubleday. 1st. F/F. M2. $125.00.

CROWLEY, John. *Love & Sleep.* 1994. Bantam. 1st. F/F clip. B4. $45.00.

CROWNINSHIELD, Ethel. *For You: Stories. Songs, Rhythm & Dramatization.* nd (1956). Boston, MA. Boston Music Co. 8vo. 35p.

CROWTHER, Charles. *Steamboat Bill.* nd. London. pre WWII ed. ils Chas Crowther. NF. C8. $95.00.

CROWTHER, Samuel. *Romance & Rise of the American Tropics.* 1929. Doubleday. 1st. 390p. F3. $15.00.

CRUM, H. *Focus on Peatlands & Peat Mosses.* 1988. Ann Arbor. 306p. F. B1. $50.00.

CRUMBO, Kim. *River Runner's Guide to the History of the Grand Canyon.* 1988. Boulder, CO. 3rd. sm 8vo. 61p. VG/pict wrp. F7. $12.00.

CRUMLEY, James. *Bordersnakes.* 1996. NY. Mysterious Press. 1st trade ed. ARC. sgn. VF/pict wrp. T2. $25.00.

CRUMLEY, James. *Bordersnakes.* 1996. NY. Mysterious Press. 1st trade ed. sgn. VF/VF. T2. $25.00.

CRUMLEY, James. *Dancing Bear.* 1983. NY. Random House. 1st. F/dj. M15. $135.00.

CRUMLEY, James. *The Last Good Kiss.* (1978). NY. Random House. 1st. author's 3rd book. sgn by author. F/F. B3. $100.00.

CRUMLEY, James. *The Mexican Pig Bandit.* 1998. Mission Viejo. A.S.A.P. 1st. One of 300 numbered copies signed. VF/. M15. $60.00.

CRUMLEY, James. *The Mexican tree Duck.* 1993. London. Picador. 1st. 1st English ed. F/dj. M15. $45.00.

CRUMLEY, James. *The Mexican Tree Duck.* 1993. NY. Mysterious Press. 1st. sgn by author. F/F. B2. $60.00.

CRUMLEY, James. *The Muddy Fork.* 1984. Northridge. Lord John Press. 1st. 1/350 sgn. VF. M15. $150.00.

CRUMLEY, James. *Wrong Case.* 1975. Random. 1st. author's 1st mystery. G/VG. M22. $250.00.

CRUMMELL, Alex. *Relations & Duties of Free Colored Men in America.* 1861. Hartford. 1st. 8vo. 54p. prt wrp. M1. $450.00.

CRUMP, Irving. *Boy's Book of Airmen.* 1927. Dodd Mead. 278p. VG+/dj. M20. $35.00.

CRUMP, Irving. *Boy's Book of Mounted Police.* 1917. Dodd Mead. sgn/dtd 1917. 297p. cloth. VG. M20. $75.00.

CRUMRINE, N. Ross. *The Power of Symbols. Masks & Masquerade in the Americas.* 1983. Vancouver. Univ of British Columbia Press. 1st. 244p. G/G. F3. $30.00.

CRUSO, Solomon. *Last of the Jews & the Japs.* 1933. Lefkowitz. 1st. VG. M2. $75.00.

CRUSO, Solomon. *Messiah on the Horizon.* 1940. Audobon. 1st. F/dj. M2. $45.00.

CSONKA, Larry. *Always on the Run.* 1973. Random. 1st. VG/dj. P8. $15.00.

CUBITT, G. *Portraits of the African Wild.* 1986. Chartwell. ils/200+ mc photos. 208p. brd. VG. M12. $25.00.

CUEVAS, P. Mariano. *El Libertador.* 1947. np. Mexico. sm folio. color & b/w photo ils. 480p. G/chipped wrp. F3. $45.00.

CULBERT, T. Patrick. *Maya Civilization.* 1993. DC. Smithsonian Books. 1st. sq 4to. pict bds. 160p. G. F3. $25.00.

CULLEN, Countee. *Color.* 1925. Harper. 1st. author's 1st book. 3-pc cover. VG. M25. $200.00.

CULLEN, Countee. *One Way to Heaven.* 1932. Harper. 1st. cloth. VG. M25. $75.00.

CULLEN, Countee. *The Black Christ.* 1929. Harper & Bros. 1st. ffep removed. G/rubbed 3 pc bds. lacking dj. M25. $50.00.

CULLEN, Joseph P. *The Peninsula Campaign 1862 Mc Clellan & Lee Struggle For Richmond.* 1973. NY. Bonanza Books. 1st. thus. orig cloth. 192p. NF/NF. M8. $35.00.

CULLEN, Thomas S. *Early Medicine in Maryland.* 1927. Baltimore. ils. 15p. brd. K3. $15.00.

CULLMANN, Oscar. *Christology of the New Testament.* 1963. Westminster. revised. 331p. VG/dj. B29. $13.00.

CULPAN, Maurice. *Minister of Injustice.* 1966. Walker. 1st. VG/VG. P3. $10.00.

CULPEPPER, R. Alan. *Anatomy of the Fourth Gospel: A Study in Literary Design.* 1983. Fortress. 266p. VG/VG. B29. $12.00.

CULVER, Francis Barnum. *Blooded Horses of Colonial Days.* 1922. Baltimore. self pub. 1st. VG. O3. $65.00.

CULVER, Henry B. *Book of Old Ships.* 1974. NY. Bonanza Books. hc. VG/VG. A28. $19.95.

CULVER, Timothy; see Westlake, Donald E.

CUMBERLAND, Charles. *Mexican Revolution.* 1972. Austin, TX. 1st. 449p. dj. F3. $20.00.

CUMMING, Primrose. *Ben: Story of a Cart Horse.* 1940. Dutton. 1st Am. VG. O3. $25.00.

CUMMING, W.P. *Exploration of North America 1630 – 1776.* 1974. NY. 400 pl/5 maps. 272p. VG+/dj. B26. $75.00.

CUMMINGS, Abbott Lowell. *The Alfred Kelley House.* 1953. Columbus. Franklin Co. Historical Society. gilt decor cloth. ils. 51p. VG. B18. $22.50.

CUMMINGS, Ray. *Insect Invasion.* 1967. Avalon. 1st. RS. F/dj. M2. $40.00.

CUNEY-HARE, Maud. *Negro Musicians and Their Music.* 1936. Washington. Assoc. Pub. 1st. scarce work by black author. F. B2. $275.00.

CUNNINGHAM, E. V. *Case of Kidnapped Angel.* 1982. Delacorte. 1st. F/NF. M25. $25.00.

CUNNINGHAM, E. V. *Millie.* 1973. Morrow. 1st. VG/NF. G8. $15.00.

CUNNINGHAM, E. V. *The Assassin Who Gave Up His Gun.* 1969. NY. Morrow. 1st. F in F dj. B2. $45.00.

CUNNINGHAM, J. Morgan; see Westlake. Donald E.

CUNNINGHAM, Jere. *The Abyss.* 1981. NY. Wyndham. 1st. F/NF. H11. $30.00.

CUNNINGHAM, Michael. *A Home at the End of the World.* (1990). NY. FSG. 1st. NF. lt shelfwear/NF. closed tear top front gutter. B3. $35.00.

CUNNINGHAM, Michael. *Flesh & Blood.* 1995. FSG. 1st. author's 2nd novel. F/F. B3. $25.00.

CUNNINGHAM, Michael. *Golden States.* 1984. Crown. 1st. author's 1st book. F/dj. M25. $60.00.

CUNNINGHAM, Michael. *The Hours.* 1998. NY. FSG. 1st. winner of Pulitzer Prize for fiction. F/F. M23. $40.00.

CUNNINGHAM, W. *Christianity & Social Questions.* 1910. Scribner. 232p. VG. B29. $7.50.

CUNY, Hilaire. *Man & His Theories (Einstein).* 1965. NY. Erikson. 1st Am. ils. VG/dj. K3. $15.00.

CURIE, Eve. *Journey Among the Warriors.* 1943. NY. sgn/dtd 1943. 501p. VG. S16. $25.00.

CURIE, Marie. *Pierre Curie.* 1926. Macmillan. 2nd. ils. VG-. K3. $35.00.

CURRAN, Bob. *Violence Game.* 1966. Macmillan. 1st. photos. F/VG+. P8. $35.00.

CURRAN, Terrie. *All Booked Up.* 1987. Dodd Mead. 1st. NF/NF. P3. $16.00.

CURREY, L.W. *Science Fiction & Fantasy Authors.* 1979. GK Hall. VG/sans. P3. $75.00.

CURREY, Richard. *Fatal Light.* 1988. NY. Dutton/Seymour Lawrence. 1st. author's 1st book. F/F. O11. $35.00.

CURREY, Richard. *The Wars of Heaven.* 1990. Boston. Houghton Mifflin. 1st. F/F. O11. $20.00.

CURRIE, Barton. *Fishers of Books.* 1931. 1st. VG/G. K3. $20.00.

CURRIE, Ellen. *Available Light.* 1986. Summit. 1st. F/NF. M23. $40.00.

CURRINGTON, O.J. *Breath-Out.* 1978. Andre Deutsch. 1st. VG/VG. P3. $18.00.

CURRY, Jane Louise. *The Change-Child.* 1969. NY. H B W. 1st. Rear board has faint stain. Jacket has light wear at spine ends. NF+/F. H11. $45.00.

CURRY, Jane Louise. *The Sleepers.* 1968. NY. H B W. 1st. has minor wear at extremities and very slightly faded spine. VF/NF+. H11. $50.00.

CURRY, Larry. *American West: Painters From Catlin to Russell.* 1972. Viking. 1st. 132 pl. F/clip. A14. $40.00.

CURTIES, Henry. *Out of the Shadows.* 1911. Greening. decor brd. VG. P3. $35.00.

CURTIS, Anna L. *Stories of the Underground Railroad.* 1941. Island Workshop Pr Co-op. 1st. sgn. F/NF. B4. $85.00.

CURTIS, Carlton C. *A Guide to the Trees.* (1937). Garden City, NY. Garden City Publishing Company. 12mo. 208p. ils. gr cloth. dj. Later ed. Newscliping taped to free endpaper. G. L5. $10.00.

CURTIS, Charles. *Orchids: Their Description & Cultivation.* 1950. London. Putnam. 1st. 274p. dj. A10. $125.00.

CURTIS, George William. *Equal Rights for All.* 1967. Rochester. 8vo. stitched. R12. $60.00.

CURTIS, Jack. *Crow's Parliament.* 1987. NY. Dutton. 1st. F/VF. H11. $20.00.

CURTIS, Jack. *Glory.* 1988. Dutton. 1st. VG/VG. P3. $25.00.

CURTIS, M.M. *Book of Snuff & Snuff Boxes With 119 Rare & Unusual.* 1935. NY. 1st. 119 photos. 137p. F. M4. $35.00.

CURTIS, Mary. *Stories in Trees.* 1925. Chicago. Lyons. 224p. VG. A10. $25.00.

CURTIS, Olin Alfred. *The Christian Faith: A System of Doctrine.* 1956. Kregel. 541p. G/G. B29. $8.00.

CURTIS, Wardon. *Strange Adventures of Mr. Middleton.* 1903. Stone. 1st. G+. M2. $30.00.

CURTISS, Ursula. *Noonday Devil.* 1953. Eyre Spottiswoode. 1st. VG/VG. P3. $25.00.

CURWOOD, James O. *Country Beyond.* 1922. Cosmopolitan. 1st. ils Walt Louderback. VG+/dj. A18. $50.00.

CURZON, Claire. *Close Quarters.* 1997. NY. St. Martin. 1st Am ed. F/F. G8. $12.50.

CURZON, Claire. *Death Prone.* 1994. NY. St. Martin. 1st Am ed. VG/VG. G8. $17.50.

CURZON, Clare. *Cat's Cradle.* 1992. St. Martin. 1st Am ed. NF/NF. G8. $20.00.

CURZON, Clare. *Three-Core Lead.* 1988. Collins Crime Club. 1st. F/F. P3. $20.00.

CUSHING, Harvey. *Consecratio Medici & Other Papers.* 1928. Boston. 1st/1st prt. 276p. A13. $150.00.

CUSHING, Harvey. *Medical Career & Other Papers.* 1940. Boston. 1st. 302p. A13. $100.00.

CUSHION, John P. *Animals in Pottery & Porcelain.* 1974. Crown. 1st. VG/G. O3. $35.00.

CUSHMAN, Dan. *Brothers in Kickapoo.* 1962. McGraw Hill. 1st. F/NF. M25. $35.00.

CUSHMAN, J. A. *Foraminifera.* 1948. Harvard. 4th. 478p. VG. D8. $30.00.

CUSSLER, Clive. *Atlantis Found.* 1999. NY. Putnam. 1st. sgn. VF/VF. T2. $28.00.

CUSSLER, Clive. *Dragon.* 1990. NY. S&S. 1st. F/F. H11. $25.00.

CUSSLER, Clive. *Dragon.* 1990. Pocket. 1st. VG/VG. G8. $10.00.

CUSSLER, Clive. *Flood Tide.* 1997. NY. S&S. 1st. sgn. NF/NF. R16. $50.00.

CUSSLER, Clive. *Inca Gold.* 1997. NY. S&S. 1st. F/F. H11. $25.00.

CUSSLER, Clive. *Night Probe!* 1981. NY. Bantam. 1st. F/dj. M15. $90.00.

CUSSLER, Clive. *Raise the Titanic!* 1976. NY. Viking. 1st. F/dj. M15. $100.00.

CUSSLER, Clive. *Raise the Titanic.* (1976). NY. Viking. 1st. author's third book. NF. very slight spine slant/F. B3. $75.00.

CUSSLER, Clive. *Sahara.* 1992. NY. S&S. 1st. F/VF. H11. $30.00.

CUSSLER, Clive. *Shock Wave.* 1995. NY. S&S. 1st. F/F. G8. $12.50.

CUSSLER, Clive. *Treasure.* 1988. S&S. 1st. F/F. H11/T2. $25.00.

CUSSLER, Clive. *Vixen 03.* (1978). NY. Viking. 1st. F/NF. very lt edgewear. B3. $30.00.

CUSSLER, Clive & Craig Dirgo. *The Sea Hunters.* 1996. NY. S&S. 1st. sgn by Cussler. VF/VF. T2. $30.00.

CUSTER, Elizabeth. *Boots & Saddles.* 1885. 1st. 312p. O8. $37.50.

CUTAK, Ladislaus. *Cactus Guide.* 1956. Princeton. ils. VG/dj. B26. $15.00.

CUTLER, Carl C. *Queens of Western Ocean: Story of America's Mail Lines.* 1961. ils. VG/VG. M17. $25.00.

CUTLER, Stan. *Best Performance by a Patsy.* 1991. NY. Dutton. 1st. author's 1st book. VF/F+. H11. $40.00.

CUTLER, Stan. *The Face on the Cutting Room Floor.* 1991. NY. Dutton. 1st. F/F. H11. $30.00.

CUTLER, Thomas. *Surgeon's Practical Guide In Dressing...* 1838. Phil. Barrington Haswell. 1st Am. 16mo. 208p. cloth. M1. $250.00.

— D —

D'AGUIAR, Fred. *The Longest Memory.* 1995. NY. Poseidon. 1st. F/F. A24. $35.00.

D'AMATO, Barbara. *Hard Bargain.* 1997. NY. Scribner's. 1st. sgn. F/F. G8. $20.00.

D'AMATO, Barbara. *Hard Case.* 1994. NY. Scribner's. 1st. sgn. F/F. G8. $20.00.

D'AMATO, Barbara. *Hard Luck.* 1992. NY. Dutton. 1st. VF/VF. H11. $25.00.

D'AMATO, Barbara. *Hard Tack.* 1991. NY. Scribners. 1st. VF/dj. M15. $35.00.

D'AMATO, Barbara. *Hardball.* 1990. NY. Scribners. 1st. VF/dj. M15. $35.00.

D'AMATO, Brian. *Beauty.* 1992. NY. Delacort. 1st. F/F. H11. $25.00.

D'AMBROSIO, Charles. *The Point.* 1995. Boston. Little, Brn. 1st. sgn. F/F. O11. $40.00.

D'IGNAZIO, Fred. *Katie and the Computer.* 1979. Morris Plains, NJ. Creative Computing. 5th ed. ils by Stan Gilliam. oblong 4to. 35p. VG. D6. $25.00.

D'IGNAZIO, Fred. *The Computer Parade.* 1983. Morris Plains, NJ. Creative Computing. 1st. ils by Stan Gilliam. oblong 4to. 39p. VG-. D6. $25.00.

DAHL, Roald. *Ah, Sweet Mystery of Life.* (1990). NY. Knopf. 1st. ils by John Lawrence. F/F. B3. $25.00.

DAHL, Roald. *Fantastic Mr. Fox.* 1970. NY. Knopf. 1st. ils by Donald Chaffin. G/VG dj. M19. $25.00.

DAHL, Roald. *James and the Giant Peach.* (1995). NY. Viking. ils ed. ils by Quentin Blake. 1st thus. F/F. B3. $45.00.

DAHL, Roald. *My Uncle Oswald.* 1979. London. Michael Joseph. 1st. F/F. D10. $50.00.

DAILEY, Janet. *Heiress.* 1987. Little, Brn. 2nd prt. F/F. S19. $35.00.

DAKIN, Susanna Bryant. *The Perennial Adventure. A Tribute To Alice Eastwood 1859 – 1953.* 1954. San Francisco. ltd to 2,000 copies. 48p. VG. B26. $29.00.

DALE, Celia. *Helping with Inquiries.* 1979. Macmillan. 1st British ed. VG+/VG. G8. $25.00.

DALESSANDRO, James. *Bohemian Heart.* 1993. NY. St. Martin. 1st. sgn. author's 1st novel. VF/VF. T2. $25.00.

DALEY, Brian. *Han Solo at Star's End.* 1979. NY. Ballantine. 1st. F/NF. M23. $20.00.

DALEY, Conor. *Outside Agency.* 1997. Kensington. 1st. F/F. G8. $17.50.

DALEY, Robert. *A Faint Cold Fear.* 1990. Boston. Little, Brn. 1st. F/VF. H11. $25.00.

DALEY, Robert. *Treasure.* 1977. NY. Random House. 1st. 341p. G/chipped dj. F3. $15.00.

DALI, Salvador. *Les Diners De Gala.* 1973. NY. Felicie, Inc. Dali's famous ils cookbook. tall 4to. 322.(2)p. ils cloth. dj minor tear. K1. $150.00.

DALLAS, Sandra. *Buster Midnight's Cafe.* 1990. NY. Random. 1st. F/F. H11. $35.00.

DALY, Conor. *Local Knowledge.* 1995. Kensington. 1st. F/F. G8. $35.00.

DALY, Conor. *Local Knowledge.* 1995. NY. Kensington. 1st. VF/dj. M15. $45.00.

DAME, Lawrence. *Yucatan.* 1941. NY. Random House. 1st. 374p. G. F3. $25.00.

DAMS, Jeanne M. *The Body in the Transept.* 1995. NY. Walker. 1st. F/M. M23. $50.00.

DAMS, Jeanne M. *The Victim in Victoria Station.* 1999. NY. Walker. 1st. sgn. VF/VF. T2. $25.00.

DANA, Richard H. *Two Years Before the Mast.* 1947. NY. Ltd Editions Club. ils & sgn by H.A. Mueller. white cloth. spine label. NF. slightly soiled slipcase. P4. $150.00.

DANBY, J. M. A. *Fundamentals of Celestial Mechanics.* 1964. NY. Macmillan. 2nd printing. text figures. 8vo. 348p. VG in cloth. K5. $50.00.

DANCER, Rex. *Postcard from Hell.* 1995. S&S. 1st. VG+/NF. G8. $12.50.

DANIEL, Mark. *The Bold Thing.* 1990. Boston. Little, Brn. 1st Am ed. VF/VF. T2. $8.00.

DANIEL, Mark. *The Devil to Pay.* 1992. Boston. Little, Brn. 1st Am ed. VF/VF. T2. $7.00.

DANIEL, Mark. *Unbridled.* 1990. NY. Ticknor & Fields. 1st Am ed. VF/VF. T2. $20.00.

DANK, Gloria. *Misfortunes of Others.* 1993. Doubleday. 1st. F/NF. G8. $15.00.

DANTICAT, Edwidge. *Breath, Eyes, Memory.* 1994. NY. Soho Press. 1st. sgn. F in F dj. D10. $90.00.

DANTICAT, Edwidge. *Krik? Krak?* (1995). NY. Soho. 1st. short stories. F/F. B3. $40.00.

DANTICAT, Edwidge. *The Farming of Bones.* 1998. NY. Soho Press. 1st. sgn. F in F dj. D10. $40.00.

DARING-GOULD, William S. *The Annotated Sherlock Holmes.* 1972. Clarkson N. Potter. Inc. 2nd. 4to. 688p. VG. H1. $60.00.

DARNTON, John. *Neanderthal.* 1996. NY. Random House. 1st. author's 1st book. NF/NF. R16. $45.00.

DARTON, Eric. *Free City.* 1998. NY. Norton. 1st. sgn. F/. D10. $35.00.

DARTT, Robert L. *G. A. Henty: A Bibliography.* 1971. 201p. F/NF. A4. $150.00.

DARWIN, Bernard. *Golf Between Two Wars.* 1985. Chatto Windus. Classics of Golf series. 8vo. 227p. NF. H4. $35.00.

DARWIN, Charles Robert. *The Different Forms of Flowers on Plants of the Same Species.* 1896. NY. 15 woodcuts. 38 tables. 352p. half leather. backstrip darkened. B26. $75.00.

DARWIN, Charles Robert. *Expression of Emotions in Man & Animals.* 1872. London. John Murray. 7 heliotype pl/21 text ils. 374p. emb gr cloth. G1. $575.00.

DARWIN, Charles Robert. *Geological Observations on the Volcanic Islands & Parts of South America Visited During the Voyage of H. M. S. Beagle.* 1915. D. Appleton & Co. 1st. 12mo Spine a little worn. endpapers lightly foxed. weaking hinge. 648p. G. H1. $25.00.

DARWIN, Charles Robert. *Insectivorous Plants.* 1895 (1875). NY. 30 text woodcuts. 462p. red leather/marbled brd. B26. $75.00.

DARWIN, George Howard. *Tides & Kindred Phenomena in Solar System.* 1898. NY. gr cloth. VG. B14. $75.00.

DARY, David A. *Buffalo Book.* 1974. Chicago. 1st. ils. 374p. VG/NF. S15. $30.00.

DATER, Judy. *Imogen Cunningham: Portrait.* 1979. NYGS. 1st. sgn. NF/clip. S9. $125.00.

DAUGHERTY, James. *Bold Dragoon & Other Ghostly Tales.* 1942. Knopf. 5th. sgn pres. 8vo. orange cloth. pict dj. R5. $75.00.

DAUGHERTY, James. *Lincoln's Gettysburg Address.* 1947. Whitman. 1st. lg 4to. 16 full-p ils. bl textured cloth. pict dj. R5. $100.00.

DAVENPORT, Basil, Ed. *13 Ways to Kill a Man.* 1965. NY. Dodd. 1st. F/lightly used. clip dj. marker code on rear panel. B2. $25.00.

DAVENPORT, Cyril. *Beautiful Books.* (1929). London. Metheun. 1st. sq 8vo. 110p. H4. $22.00.

DAVENPORT, Guy. *Ecologues: Eight Stories.* 1981. SF. ils Roy Behrens. VG/dj. M17. $20.00.

DAVENPORT, L. *Bride's Cookbook.* 1908. 1st. 12 tabs on title. E6. $95.00.

DAVENPORT, Marcia. *Mozart.* 1932. Scribner. 1st Am. NF/VG. W2. $125.00.

DAVENPORT, Steward. *Carribbean Cavalier.* 1957. Dutton. 1st. VG/dj. L1. $15.00.

DAVENPORT, W. A. *Art of the Gawain: Poet.* 1978. London. 1st. gr cloth. F/dj. T10. $45.00.

DAVENTRY, Leonard. *Man of Double Deed.* 1965. Doubleday. VG/dj. P3. $20.00.

DAVID, Catherine. *Simone Signoret.* 1993. Woodstock. Overlook. 213p. VG/dj. C5. $15.00.

DAVID, Peter. *Star Trek: Next Generation: Imzadi.* 1992. S&S. 1st. F/dj. T12. $20.00.

DAVID-NEEL, Alexandra. *Magic and Mystery in Tibet.* 1958. Univ Books. 1st. NF/darkened dj. M25. $45.00.

DAVIDS, Arlette. *Flowers: Rock Plants. Drawn by Arlette Davids.* (1939). London/Paris/NY. Hyperion. 1st. Folio. $40.00.

DAVIDSON, Avram. *The Investigations of Avram Davidson.* 1999. NY. St. Martin. ARC. F wrp. B2. $30.00.

DAVIDSON, Avram. *The Phoenix and the Mirror.* 1969. Garden City. Doubleday. 1st. F/F. lt wear. T2. $65.00.

DAVIDSON, Avram. *Vergil in Averno.* 1987. Garden City. Doubleday. 1st. VF/VF. T2. $45.00.

DAVIDSON, Christine. *Staying Home Instead, How to Quit the Working Mom Rat Race and Survive Financially.* 1986. MA. Lexington Books. VG/G+. A28. $7.95.

DAVIDSON, Diane Mott. *Grilling Season.* 1997. Bantam. 1st. sgn. F/dj. A23. $38.00.

DAVIDSON, Diane Mott. *Killer Pancake.* (1995). NY. Bantam. 1st. sgn by author. F/F. B3. $35.00.

DAVIDSON, Diane Mott. *Main Corpse.* 1996. NY. Bantam. 1st. F/dj. A23. $36.00.

DAVIDSON, Diane Mott. *The Cereal Murders.* 1993. NY. Bantam. 1st. F/F. H11. $35.00.

DAVIDSON, Donald. *Outland Paper.* 1924. Houghton Mifflin. 1st. F. L3. $250.00.

DAVIDSON, Donald. *Tennessee: New River: Civil War to TVA.* 1948. Rinehart. 1st. 8vo. 377p. NF/dj. B20. $65.00.

DAVIDSON, Edgar Stanton. *Before the Memory Fades 1795 – 1950.* 1975. Ohio. Wellsville Historical Society. photo ils. 72p. VG in dj. B18. $35.00.

DAVIDSON, George. *Identification of Sir Francis Drake's Anchorage.* 1890. CA Hist Soc. inscr to WH Davis. 13 fld maps. 58p. prt wrp. $11.00.

DAVIDSON, James West and John Rugge. *Great Heart. The History of A Labrador Adventure.* 1988. NY. Viking. half cloth 8vo. map ep. b&w photos. 385p. VG in slightly worn dj. P4. $60.00.

DAVIDSON, Lionel. *A Long Way to Shiloh.* 1966. London. Victor Gollancz. 1st. F/dj clip. M15. $75.00.

DAVIDSON, Lionel. *Kolymsky Heights.* 1994. NY. St. Martin. 1st Am ed. F/F. T2. $8.00.

DAVIDSON, Lionel. *Kolymsky Heights.* 1994. London. Heinemann. 1st. F/dj. M15. $50.00.

DAVIDSON, Orlando. *Deadeyes: Story of the 96th Infantry Division.* 1974. WA. 1st. 310p. VG. S16. $75.00.

DAVIDSON, Robert. *The Bible Speaks.* 1959. Crowell. 258p. VG/VG. ex lib. B29. $4.50.

DAVIDSON, Stephen. *Soft Songs.* 1976. Creative Living Enterprises. 1st prt stated. sc. G. F6. $3.00.

DAVIE, M. *Titanic: Life & Death of a Legend.* 1987. NY. 1st. VG/dj. B5. $40.00.

DAVIES, David Stuart. *Sherlock Holmes: The Last Act!* 1999. Ashcroft. Calabash Press. 1st. VF/pict wrp. T2. $15.00.

DAVIES, David Stuart. *The Scroll of the Dead: A Sherlock Holmes Adventure.* 1998. Ashcroft. Calabash Press. 1st. VF/VF. T2. $35.00.

DAVIES, David Stuart. *The Shadow of the Rat: A Sherlock Holmes Adventure.* 1999. Ashcroft. Calabash Press. 1st. VF/VF. T2. $30.00.

DAVIES, Hunter. *The Beatles: The Authorized Biography.* 1968. McGraw Hill. 1st. NF/NF. M25. $45.00.

DAVIES, Jennifer. *Victorian Kitchen.* 1889. London. 1st. 4to. mc woodcuts. F/F. E6. $25.00.

DAVIES, John. *Legend of Hoby Baker.* 1966. Boston. 1st. ils. B14. $75.00.

DAVIES, L. P. *The Reluctant Medium.* 1967. Garden City. Doubleday. 1st Am. Jacket has minor wear at spine ends. F/dj. M15. $45.00.

DAVIES, L. P. *Who Is Lewis Pinder?* 1966. Garden City. Doubleday Crime Club. 1st Am ed. F/dj some wear. M15. $45.00.

DAVIES, Linda. *Wilderness of Mirrors.* (1996). London. Orion. 1st UK ed. true 1st. author's 2nd book. F/F. B3. $30.00.

DAVIES, Nigel. *The Toltec Heritage.* 1980. Norman. Univ of Oklahoma Press. 1st. b/w photo ils. 401p. G/G. F3. $30.00.

DAVIES, Randall. *English Society of the 18th Century in Contemporary Art.* 1907. London. Seeley. 4to. ils. xl. VG. H13. $35.00.

DAVIES, Rhys. *Stars, World & the Women.* 1930. London. 1/550. sgn. VG+. A15. $60.00.

DAVIES, Robertson. *A Mixture of Frailties.* 1958. Toronto. Macmillan. true 1st. Canadian ed. NF/VG sm chips. lt wear. D10. $95.00.

DAVIES, Robertson. *Cunning Man.* 1995. Viking. 1st Am ed. NF/NF. G8. $12.50.

DAVIES, Robertson. *Fifth Business.* 1970. NY. Viking. 1st Am ed. F/F. D10. $85.00.

DAVIES, Robertson. *Lyre of Orpheus.* 1989. Viking. 1st. VG/F. B30. $25.00.

DAVIES, Robertson. *Murther & Walking Spirits.* 1991. NY. 1st. VG/dj. M17. $15.00.

DAVIES, Robertson. *One Half of Robertson Davies.* 1978. NY. Viking. 1st. G/VNF. D10. $40.00.

DAVIES, Robertson. *Rebel Angels.* 1981. Toronto. Canada. Macmillan. 1st. VG/VG. M21. $45.00.

DAVIES, Robertson. *The Rebel Angels.* 1981. Toronto. Macmillan. 1st. F/lightly used dj. B2. $40.00.

DAVIES, Robertson. *What's Bred in the Bone.* 1985. Viking. 1st. NF/NF. G8. $25.00.

DAVIES, Russell. *Ronald Searle: A Biography.* 1990. London. 4to. 192p. F/F. A4. $85.00.

DAVIES, Valentine. *Miracle on 34th Street.* 1947. Harcourt Brace. 1st. sm 8vo. 120p. stp red cloth. F/clip. H5. $300.00.

DAVIES, W. D. *Jewish and Pauline Studies.* 1984. Fortress. 419p. VG/VG. B29. $25.50.

DAVINE, David. *Hadrian's Wall: Study of the NW Frontier of Rome.* 1969. Boston. 1st Am. 244p. VG/dj. B18. $22. 50.

DAVIS, Albert Belisle. *Marquis at Bay.* 1992. Baton Rouge. 1st. F/dj. A23. $34.00.

DAVIS, Alec. *Package & Print: Development of a Container & Label Design.* 1968. Clarkson Potter. 1st Am. 4to. ils. 112p. cloth. F/dj. $10.00.

DAVIS, Archie K. *Boy Colonel of the Confederacy: the Life and Times of Henry King Burgwyn, Jr.* 1985. Chapel Hill. Univ of North Carolina Press. 1st. orig cloth. plates. maps. 406p. VG. M8. $25.00.

DAVIS, Ben. *Strange Angel.* 1991. San Antonio. Corona. 1st. F/dj. A23. $30.00.

DAVIS, Bertram. *Johnson Before Boswell.* 1960. Yale. 1st. dj. H13. $65.00.

DAVIS, Bertram. *Proof of Eminence: Life of Sir John Hawkins.* 1973. Bloomington. IN. IU. 1st. dj. H13. $65.00.

DAVIS, Burke. *Cowpens-Guilford Courthouse Campaign.* 1962. Lippincott. 1st. 208p. F/dj. H1. $17. 50.

DAVIS, Charles. *Marine & Fresh-Water Plankton.* 1955. MI State. VG. S15. $12.00.

DAVIS, Charles G. *Ship Model Builder's Assistant.* 1977 (1926). Edward Sweetman. VG. M20. $15.00.

DAVIS, Christopher. *Philadelphia.* 1993. NY. Bantam. 1st. F/dj. A23. $35.00.

DAVIS, Clyde. *Eyes of Boyhood.* 1953. Lippincott. 1st. 323p. F/dj. D4. $35.00.

DAVIS, Daphne. *Stars!* 1983. NY. Stewart Tabori Chang. 277p. VG/dj. C5. $25.00.

DAVIS, Deering. *American Cow Pony.* 1962. Van Nostrand. 1st. NF/dj. A21. $45.00.

DAVIS, Dorothy Salisbury. *Lullaby of Murder.* 1984. Scribners. 1st. review copy. sgn. F/F. G8. $20.00.

DAVIS, Dorothy Salisbury. *Old Sinners Never Die.* 1959. Scribners. 1st. VG/VG. G8. $15.00.

DAVIS, Dorothy Salisbury. *Scarlet Night.* 1980. Scribners. 1st. inscr. NF/NF. G8. $20.00.

DAVIS, Duke. *Flashlights from Mountain & Plain.* 1911. Pentecostal Union. 1st. 266p. gilt red cloth. VG+. B20. $65.00.

DAVIS, Frank Marshall. *47th Street.* 1948. Prairie City. Decker. 1st. VG/dj. B2. $275.00.

DAVIS, Frederick C. *Night Drop.* 1955. Garden City. Doubleday. 1st. F/dj. M15. $45.00.

DAVIS, Harriet Eager. *Elmira: Girl Who Loved Edgar Allan Poe.* 1966. Houghton Mifflin. 1st. 137p. VG/dj. M21. $20.00.

DAVIS, Howard Charles. *Murder Starts From Fishguard.* 1966. London. John Long. 1st. NF/dj. M15. $45.00.

DAVIS, Howell. *South American Handbook.* 1939. London. 694p. gilt red cloth. F3. $10.00.

DAVIS, J. Madison. *Bloody Marko.* 1991. NY. Walker. 1st. F/VF. H11. $25.00.

DAVIS, Jefferson. *Short History of the Confederate States of America.* 1890. Belford Co. 1 vol complete. ils. 505p. gray cloth. G. S17. $27.00.

DAVIS, Joel. *Journey to the Center of Our Galaxy; a Voyage in Space and Time.* 1991. Chicago. Contemporary Books. 8vo. 24p photo ils. most in color. 335p. VG/VG. K5. $20.00.

DAVIS, John J. *Evangelical Ethics: Issues Facing the Church Today.* 1985. Presb/Reford. 299p. VG/dj. B29. $11. 50.

DAVIS, John P. *Let Us Build a National Negro Congress.* 1935. WA. Sponsor Nat Negro Congress. NF/wrp. B2. $25.00.

DAVIS, Lindsey. *A Dying Light in Corduba.* 1996. London. Century. 1st. VF/dj. M15. $60.00.

DAVIS, Lindsey. *Iron Hand of Mars.* 1993. NY. Crown. 1st Am. sgn. F/dj. T2. $35.00.

DAVIS, Lindsey. *Last Act in Palmyra.* 1996. Mysterious. 1st Am. VG/dj. M17. $15.00.

DAVIS, Lindsey. *Silver Pigs.* 1989. London. Sidgwick Jackson. 1st. F/NF. M15. $600.00.

DAVIS, Lindsey. *Silver Pigs.* 1989. NY. Crown. 1st Am. sgn. author's 1st novel. F/dj. T2. $65.00.

DAVIS, Lindsey. *Three Hands in the Fountain.* 1997. London. Century. 1st. sgn. F/dj. M15. $55.00.

DAVIS, Lindsey. *Time to Depart.* 1995. London. Century. 1st. F/dj. M15. $60.00.

DAVIS, Lindsey. *Venus in Copper.* 1991. London. Fawcett. 1st. VF/dj. M15. $150.00.

DAVIS, Matthew L. *Memoirs of Aaron Burr.* 1858. Harper. 696p. G. B18. $35.00.

DAVIS, Norma. *Trade Winds Cookery: Tropical Recipes for all America.* 1956. Richmond. self pub. sbdg. VG. E6. $25.00.

DAVIS, Patti. *Way I See It.* 1992. Putnam. 1st. F/dj. P12. $8.00.

DAVIS, Paxton. *Battle of New Market.* (1963). Little, Brn. 1st. 145p. F/F. B10. $25.00.

DAVIS, Richard C. (ed.). *Lobsticks and Stone Cairns: Human Landmarks in the Arctic.* 1996. Calgary, Alberta. Univ of Calvary. 1st. gr paper over brd w/ photo ils dj. 326p. New in dj. P4. $89.00.

DAVIS, Richard Harding. *Captain Macklin.* 1902. NY. Scribner. 1st. 329p. G. G11. $10.00.

DAVIS, Richard Harding. *Notes of a War Correspondent.* (1912). NY. later prt. 263p. VG. E1. $25.00.

DAVIS, Richard Harding. *Once Upon a Time.* 1910. NY. Scribner. 1st. 280p. G+. G11. $15.00.

DAVIS, Richard Harding. *Ranson's Folly.* 1902. NY. Scribner. 1st. 345p. VG. G1. $8.00.

DAVIS, Robert. *Historical Dictionary of Colombia.* 1993. NJ. Scarecrow Press. 2nd ed. 600p. G. F3. $35.00.

DAVIS, Skeeter. *Bus Fare to Kentucky.* 1993. NY. Birch Lane. 338p. G/dj. C5. $12. 50.

DAVIS, Thulani. *1959.* 1992. NY. Grove Weid. 1st. Author's first novel. F/F. H11. $35.00.

DAVIS, Val. *Track of the Scorpion.* 1996. St Martin. 1st. F/dj. M23. $40.00.

DAVIS, Wade. *Serpent & the Rainbow.* 1985. S&S. 1st. F/VG. L4. $25.00.

DAVIS, William. *Janus.* 1965. San Francisco. Auerhahn. 1/750 printed by Andrew Hoyem. F in wrp. B2. $25.00.

DAVIS, William C. *Battle at Bull Run: A History.* 1977. Garden City. 1st. 298p. VG/clip. B18. $15.00.

DAVIS, William C. *Touched by Fire: Photographic Portrait of Civil War I & II.* 1986. Boston. 2 vol. 1st. F/dj. E1. $95.00.

DAVIS & MIDDLEMAS. *Colored Glass.* London. Hamlyn Pub. 2nd. 4to. NF/dj. M21. $35.00.

DAVISON, Grace L. *Gates of Memory.* 1955. Santa Ynez. 1st. inscr. VG/dj. O4. $20.00.

DAVISON, Peter. *Walking the Boundaries.* 1974. Atheneum. 1st. inscr. F/NF. L3. $45.00.

DAWN, Marva J. *Reaching Out Without Dumbing Down: A Theology.* 1995. Eerdmans. 316p. F/wrp. B29. $9.00.

DAWSON, Carol. *Body of Knowledge.* (1994). Chapel Hill. np. 1st. sgn by author. F/F. B3. $40.00.

DAWSON, Carol. *Meeting the Minotaur.* (1997). Chapel Hill. Algonquin. 1st. author's 3rd book. sgn & dated by author. F/F. B3. $40.00.

DAWSON, Carol. *Waking Spell.* 1992. Algonquin. 1st. author's 1st book. F/dj. O11. $35.00.

DAWSON, Christopher. *Mongol Mission: Narratives & Letters.* 1955. NY. Sheed Ward. ils/tables. 246p. VG/torn. $2.00.

DAWSON, Elmer. *Buck's Winning Hit.* 1930. Grosset Dunlap. 1st. G. P8. $12.50.

DAWSON, Emma Frances. *Gracious Visitation.* 1921. BC of CA. 1/300. 8vo. gilt red cloth. NF. R3. $50.00.

DAWSON, Fielding. *Great Day for a Ballgame.* 1973. Bobbs Merrill. 1st. F/VG. P8. $45.00.

DAWSON, Fielding. *Virginia Dare: Stories 1976 – 1981.* 1985. Blk Sparrow. 1st. VG. B9. $15.00.

DAWSON, George Francis. *Life & Services of Gen. John A. Logan, Soldier & Statesman.* 1884. National Tribune. 467p. B19. $95.00.

DAWSON, George Francis. *Life & Services of General John A. Logan, Soldier & Statesman.* 1884. Chicago. National Tribune. 1st. 467p. G/G. B18. $95.00.

DAWSON, Grace. *California.* 1939. Macmillan. 1st. VG/G. P2. $15.00.

DAWSON, Janet. *Don't Turn Your Back on the Ocean.* (1994). NY. Fawcett. 1st. inscr by author. F/F. B3. $35.00.

DAWSON, Janet. *Kindred Crimes.* 1990. NY. St. Martin. 1st. author's 1st book. NF/NF. A24. $35.00.

DAWSON, Jill (ed). *Kisses on Paper: Love Letters by Women from the Thirteenth Century to the Present.* 1995. NY. Faber. VG/VG. A28. $10.50.

DAY, Alexandra. *Carl's Christmas Day.* 1996. FSG. 4th. VG. B36. $10.00.

DAY, Barry. *Sherlock Holmes and the Shakespeare Globe Murders.* 1997. London. Oberon Books. 1st. VF/pict wrp. T2. $11.00.

DAY, Clarence. *Crow's Nest.* 1921. Knopf. 1st. author's 2nd book. F/NF. B20. $150.00.

DAY, Clarence. *God & My Father.* 1932. Knopf. 1st. photos. NF/dj. S13. $20.00.

DAY, Deforest. *August Ice.* 1990. NY. St. Martin. 1st. author's 1st book. F/F. H11. $30.00.

DAY, Deforest. *Cold Killing.* 1990. NY. Carroll Graf. 1st. F/F. H11. $20.00.

DAY, Dianne. *Fire & Fog.* 1996. Doubleday. 1st. F/dj. G8/T2. $25.00.

DAY, Dianne. *The Bohemian Murders.* 1997. NY. Doubleday. 1st. F/F. H11. $25.00.

DAY, James. *Six Flags of Texas.* 1968. Waco. 1st. mc pl. 138p. VG/dj. S16. $45.00.

DAY, Richard. *Summer Landmark.* 1947. Macmillan. 1st. 106p. F/dj. D4. $35.00.

DAY, Susan De Forest. *The Cruise of the Scythian in the West Indies.* 1899. NY. F. Tennyson Neely. 1st. inscr. b/w photo ils. pict cloth cover. 297p. G. F3. $75.00.

DAY, Thomas. *History of Sandford & Merton.* 1845. New Haven. Babcock. 222p. emb cloth. VG. F1. $45.00.

DAY-LEWIS, Sean. *Bullied Last Giant of Steam.* 1964. London. 1st. 300p. VG/dj. B5. $25.00.

DAYTON, Dorothy. *Epic of Alexandra.* 1979. Winston-Salem. JF Blair. ARC/1st. ils Virginia Ingram. VG/dj. M20. $40.00.

DE ALARCON, Pedron. *Three-Cornered Hat.* 1959. LA. LEC. 1st thus. 1/1500. ils/sgn Roger Duvoisin. F/glassine/F case. Q1. $75.00.

DE ANDREA, William L. *Five O'Clock Lightning.* 1982. St Martin. BC. F/VG. P8. $10.00.

DE ANGELI, Marguerite. *Prayers & Graces for Small Children.* 1941. Grosset Dunlap. early. 8vo. VG/dj. B17. $30.00.

DE ANGELI, Marguerite. *Ted & Nina Have a Happy Rainy Day.* 1936. Doubleday Doran. possible 1st. obl 24mo. gray buckram. reading copy. T5. $45.00.

DE BAETS, Maurice. *Apostle of Alaska: Life of Most Reverend Chas John Seghers.* 1943. St Anthony Guild. 8vo. 282p. gilt gr cloth. VG/dj. P4. $45.00.

DE BEAUMONT, Edouard. *Sword & Womankind: Being Informative History.* 1929. NY. Panurge. 1/1000. VG. M20. $18.00.

DE BEAUMONT, Marguerite. *Way of the Horse.* 1953. London. Hurst Blackett. 1st. VG/G. O3. $25.00.

DE BEAUVOIR, Simone. *Prime of Life.* 1962. Cleveland. World. VG/dj. M20. $15.00.

DE BEER, Gavin. *Sciences Were Never at War.* 1960. London. 1st. 279p. A13. $30.00.

DE BERARDINIS, Olivia. *Let Them Eat Cheesecake: Art of Olivia.* 1993. Ozone Productions. ils. VG/dj. M17. $25.00.

DE BERNIERES, Louis. *Corelli's Mandolin.* 1994. NY. Pantheon. 1st Am ed. F in F clip dj. B2. $40.00.

DE BERNIERES, Louis. *Senor Vivo and the Coca Lord.* 1991. NY. Morrow. 1st Am ed. sgn. F/F. O11. $55.00.

DE BERNIERES, Louis. *The Troublesome Offspring of Cardinal Guzman.* 1994. NY. Morrow. 1st Am ed. sgn. FF. O11. $55.00.

DE BESAULT, L. *President Trujillo.* 1941. Dominican Republic. Santiago. ils. 509p. VG/G. B5. $17. $50.00.

DE BLASIS, Celeste. *Graveyard Peaches.* 1991. St Martin. 1st. F/NF. P3. $18.00.

DE BOLD, Joseph W. *Happening Worlds of John Brunner.* 1975. Kennikat. 1st. F/dj. P3. $20.00.

DE BOSSCHERE, Jean. *Peacocks and Other Mysteries. Translated from the French by Frederick S. Hoppin.* (1941). NY. Ed Byrne Hackett. The Brick Row Book Shop. ne. floral decor cloth. gilt leather label. dj. 157p. AN. B14. $75.00.

DE BRAY, Emile Frederic. *A Frenchman in Search of Franklin. Debay's Arctic Journal 1852 – 1854.* 1992. Toronto. U of Toronto Press. 1st. 8vo. xxii. trans & ed by William Barr. 339p. F in dj. P4. $65.00.

DE BRAY, Lys. *Art of Botanical Illustration.* 1997 (1989). Bromley. Kent. ils. 192p. sc. B26. $26.00.

DE BRUNHOFF, Jean. *Babar & Father Christmas.* 1940. NY. Random. 1st Am. sm folio. mc pict dj. R5. $400.00.

DE BRUNHOFF, Jean. *Babar and Zephir.* 1965. NY. Random House. F. A16. $15.00.

DE CALLATAY, Vincent. *Atlas of the Sky.* 1958. London. Macmillan. trans Harold Spences Jones. 157p. G. K5. $35.00.

DE CAMP, L. Sprague. *Heroes and Hobgoblins.* 1981. West Kingston. Donald I. Grant. 1st. sgn by De Camp & artist Tim Kirk. VF/VF clip corner. T2. $30.00.

DE CAMP, L. Sprague. *The Glory that Was.* 1960. NY. Avalon Books. 1st. F/F. lt wear. T2. $50.00.

DE CAMP, L. Sprague. *The Great Fetish.* 1978. Garden City. Doubleday. 1st. F/F. corners bumped. T2. $15.00.

DE CAMP, L. Sprague. *The Purple Pterodactyls.* 1979. Huntington Woods. Phantasia Press. 1st. 1/200 # copies. sgn. F/F. lt wear. T2. $45.00.

DE CAMP, L. Sprague. *The Search For Zei.* 1962. NY. Avalon Books. 1st. F/F. T2. $50.00.

DE CAMP, L. Sprague. *Time & Chance: An Autobiography.* 1996. Hampton Falls. Donald M. Grant. 1st. VF/VF. T2. $35.00.

DE CARLO, Yvonne. *Yvonne.* 1987. St Martin. 1st. VG/dj. C9. $30.00.

DE CASTRO, V. A. *Second NY Infantry at the Mexican Border.* 1916. Schenetady. G+. E6. $45.00.

DE CERVANTES SAAVEDRA, Miguel. *Adventures of Don Quixote.* 1928. Houghton Mifflin. 1st. ils Herman Bacharach. VG. M19. $25.00.

DE CHASTELLUX, Marquis. *Travels in North America in Years 1780, 1781 & 1782.* 1963. Inst Early Am Hist. 2 vol. ils. VG. M17. $45.00.

DE CLEYRE, Voltairine. *Anarchism and American Traditions.* 1932. Chicago. Free Society Group. 1st. wrp. NF. B2. $50.00.

DE CONDILLAC, Etienne Bonnot. *Condillac's Treatise on Sensations.* 1930. London. Favil. 1st Eng-language/British issue. 250p. NF. G1. $75.00.

DE CRESPIGNY, Rose Champion. *Norton Vyse Psychic.* 1999. Ashcroft, BC. Ash Tree Press. 1st. VF/VF. T2. $35.00.

DE DIENES, Andre. *Marilyn Mon Amour: Private Album of Andre DeDienes.* 1985. St Martin. VG/dj. S5. $75.00.

DE DIENES, Andre. *Nude Pattern.* 1958. Bodley Head. 1st. photos. NF/dj. S9. $150.00.

DE FIERRO BLANCO, Antonio. *Journey of the Flame.* 1933. Houghton Mifflin. 1st. gilt blk cloth. VG/dj. T10. $75.00.

DE FOE, Daniel. *Life & Strange Surprising Adventures of Robinson Crusoe.* nd. Dutton. ils JA Symington. teg. pict gray cloth. F1. $30.00.

DE FOE, Daniel. *Robinson Crusoe.* 1920. Cosmopolitan. 1st thus. ils NC Wyeth. red cloth/pict pl. VG+. M5. $155.00.

DE FRANCA, Isabella. *Journal of a Visit to Maderia & Portugal (1853 – 1854).* 1970. Portugal. Junta Geral. 4to. 270p. VG/dj. B11. $75.00.

DE GAURY, Gerald. *Arabia Phoenix.* 1947 (1946). London. Harrap. ils/map ep. cloth. G+. Q2. $26. $50.00.

DE GREGORIO, George. *Joe DiMaggio.* 1983. Scarborough. 1st. VG/dj. P8. $35.00.

DE GROOT, Roy A. *Feasts for All Seasons.* 1966. Knopf. VG/dj. A16. $12.00.

DE GROOT, Roy A. *Revolutionizing French Cooking.* 1976. McGraw Hill. 1st. NF. W2. $30.00.

DE HALSALLE, Henry. *Romance of Modern First Editions.* 1931. Lippincott. 192p. gilt rose cloth. VG. F1. $15.00.

DE HARTOG, Jan. *Children: A Personal Record for the Use of Adoptive Parents.* 1969. Atheneum. 1st. 265p. VG/G. V3. $15.00.

DE HARTOG, Jan. *Distant Shore.* 1952. Harper. 1st. author's 2nd book. NF/VG. H11. $25.00.

DE HAURAANE, Ernest Duv. *Frenchman in Lincoln's America.* Vol I. 1974. Lakeside Classic. 1st thus. teg. dk bl cloth. F/sans. T11. $35.00.

DE HAVEN, Tom. *Jersey Luck.* 1980. Harper Row. 1st. sgn/dtd 1987. NF/dj. R14. $45.00.

DE KRUIF, Paul. *Hunger Fighters.* 1928. NY. Harcourt Brace. 1st. ils Zadig. VG+/dj. B20. $20.00.

DE KRUIF, Paul. *Kaiser Wakes the Doctors.* 1943. NY. 1st. 158p. A13. $25.00.

DE LA MARE, Walter. *Listeners & Other Poems.* 1927. London. Constable. 1st ils. 80p. F/dj. B20. $85.00.

DE LA MARE, Walter. *Motley & Other Poems.* 1927. London. Constable. 1st ils. 70p. F/dj. B20. $85.00.

DE LA MARE, Walter. *Penny a Day.* 1960. Knopf. 1st thus. ils Paul Kennedy. 209p. NF/VG. T5. $25.00.

DE LA METTRIE, Julien Ofray. *Man a Machine.* 1993. NY. Classics of Psychiatry & Behavioral Sciences Lib. 216p. G1. $65.00.

DE LA ROCHE, Mazo. *Portrait of a Dog.* 1930. Little, Brn. 1st. ils Morgan Dennis. VG. A21. $45.00.

DE LEEUW, H. *Woman, the Dominant Sex: From Bloomers to Bikinis.* 1957. London. Arco Pub. 1st printing stated. VG. B15. $75.00.

DE LEEUW, Henrik. *Crossroads of the Java Sea.* (1931). Garden City. Garden City Publ. ils Alexander King in b&w. VG. B15. $65.00.

DE LEON, Josefina V. *Mexican Cook Book Devoted to American Homes.* 1977. Spanish/Eng text. VG/wrp. A16. $25.00.

DE LILLO, Don. *Day Room.* 1987. Knopf. 1st. F/dj. A24. $50.00.

DE LILLO, Don. *Libra.* 1988. NY. Viking. 1st. F/F. H11. $40.00.

DE LILLO, Don. *Players.* 1977. Knopf. 1st. NF/VG. B3. $90.00.

DE LILLO, Don. *The Names.* 1982. NY. Knopf. 1st. F/F. H11. $80.00.

DE LILLO, Don. *Underworld.* 1997. NY. Scribners. 1st. VF/VF. H11. $65.00.

DE LINT, Charles. *The Little Country.* 1991. NY. Morrow. 1st. F/F. crease on front flap. M23. $25.00.

DE LOACH, Nora. *Mama Stalks the Past.* 1997. NY. Bantam. 1st. F/VF. H11. $25.00.

DE MARCO, Angelus A. *Rome & the Vernacular.* 1961. Westminster, MD. Newman. 8vo. Vg/dj. A2. $20.00.

DE MARIA, Robert. *Johnson's Dictionary & Language of Learning.* 1986. Oxford. Clarendon. 1st. F/dj. H13. $65.00.

DE MARIA, Robert. *Life of Samuel Johnson.* 1993. Oxford. Blackwell. 1st. F/dj. H13. $75.00.

DE MARIA, Robert. *To Be a King: Novel About Christopher Marlowe.* 1976. Bobbs Merrill. 1st. NF/dj. A14. $25.00.

DE MARINIS, Rick. *Lovely Monster: Adventures of Claude Raines & Dr Tellenbeck.* 1975. S&S. 1st. F/NF. R14. $50.00.

DE MEDICI, Lorenza. *Italy: The Beautiful Cookbook.* 1988. Intercontinental Pub. 1st. folio. 256p. F/dj. W2. $60.00.

DE MEDINA Y ORMAECHEA, A. A. *La Legislacion Penal De Los Pueblos Latinos.* 1899. Mexico. Tipofraffa Oficina Timbre. 54 dbl-fld leaves. 40p. F3. $125.00.

DE MEJO, Oscar. *There's a Hand in the Sky.* 1983. Pantheon. 1st. VG/dj. B9. $20.00.

DE MERE, Antoine Gombaud. *Les Oeuvres.* 1692. Amsterdam. Mortier. 2 vol in 1. 1st collected ed. 8vo. ils. vellum. $12.00.

DE MEYER, Adolph. *Singular Elegance: Photographs of Baron Adolpf DeMeyer.* 1994. Chronicle. folio. photos. brn cloth. NF/dj. A28. $45.00.

DE MILLE, Agnes. *Dance to the Piper.* 1952. Little, Brn. 1st. VG/dj. C9. $36.00.

DE MILLE, Nelson. *By the Rivers of Babylon.* 1978. NY. Harcourt. 1st. F/dj. M15. $100.00.

DE MILLE, Nelson. *The General's Daughter.* 1992. NY. Warner. 1st. VF/F. H11. $40.00.

DE MILLE, Richard. *My Secret Mother: Lorna Moon.* 1998. FSG. UP. NF/tan wrps. M25. $45.00.

DE MONTAIGNE, Michel. *Essays.* nd. NY. trans Chas Cotton. 3-quarter brn leather. VG. M17. $40.00.

DE MONTAIGNE, Michel. *Montaigne's Essays.* 1931. London. Nonesuch. 2 vol. 1/1375. teg. Riviere bdg. F. $5.00.

DE NADAILLAC, Marquis. *Pre-Historic America.* 1893 (1884). NY. Putnam. 219 ils/index. 566p. teg. gilt pict bdg. F3. $75.00.

DE NOLHAC, Pierre. *Marie Antoinette.* 1905. London. 3-quarter bl leather/bl cloth brd. VG M17. $50.00.

DE PEYSTER, John Watts. *Winter Campaigns: The Test of Generalship.* 1862. NY. Charles G. Stone. 1st. orig printed wrp. VG. M8. $45.00.

DE PORTE, Michael V. *Nightmares & Hobbyhorses.* 1974. Huntington Lib. 1st. F/NF clip. O4. $15.00.

DE PROFT, Melanie. *American Family Cookbook.* 1971. Doubleday. 1st. 800p. VG. S14. $20.00.

DE QUINCEY, Thomas. *Diary of Thomas De Quincey.* 1803. 1927. Payson Clarke. 1/1500. 252p. gilt brn buckram. VG/G. F1. $50.00.

DE REAUMUR, R. A. F. *Natural History of Ants.* 1926. Knopf. 8vo. ils. 280p. F/VG. $12.00.

DE REGNIERS, Beatrice Schenk. *Week in the Life of Best Friends & Other Poems.* 1986. Atheneum. 1st. 47p. lavender cloth. F/NF. $5.00.

DE RELY, Jehan. *L'Ordre Tenv Et Garde En L'Assemblee Des Trois Estats.* 1558. Paris. Galliot de Pre. 8vo. prt device at end. vellum. $12.00.

DE ROCOLES, Jean Baptiste. *Les Imposteurs Insignes.* 1683. Amsterdam. thick 12mo. 16 full-p portraits. calf. R12. $575.00.

DE ROSIER, Arthur H. *Removal of the Choctaw Indians.* 1970. U TN. ARC. 208p. RS. F/NF. B20. $45.00.

DE ROUGEMONT, Denis. *Devil's Share.* 1945. Pantheon. 221p. VG. B29. $15.00.

DE SAINT-EXUPERY, Antoine. *Night Flight.* 1932. NY. Century. 1st Am. sm 8vo. trans Stuart Gilbert. gilt bl cloth. NF/dj. $5.00.

DE SANTILLANA, Giogio. *The Crime of Galileo.* 1955. Chicago. Univ of Chicago Press. 8vo. photo ils. 339p. VG/chipped. faded dj. clip. K5. $30.00.

DE SARIO, Joseph P. *Sanctuary.* 1989. NY. Doubleday. 1st. F/VF. H11. $15.00.

DE SEGUR, Madame. *Happy Surprises.* 1929. Whitman. 1st. 8vo. ils. VG. M5. $20.00.

DE SIRCA, Vittorio. *Bicycle Thief.* 1968. S&S. 1st. F/wrp. C9. $36.00.

DE SITTER, W. *Kosmos.* 1932. Cambridge. Ma. Harvard Univ Press. ex lib in cloth. lib mks. yellowed. 138p. VG. K5. $50.00.

DE SOUZA, Baretto. *Advanced Equitation.* 1926. Dutton. G. O3. $20.00.

DE TOLEDANO, Ralph. *Frontiers of Jazz.* 1947. NY. Oliver Durrel. 1st. F/VG. B2. $40.00.

DE TREVINO, Elizabeth. *Casilda of the Rising Moon: A Tale of Magic & Faith.* 1967. SG. 1st. 8vo. xl. G+. $5.00.

DE VAUCOULEURS, Gerard. *Discovery of the Universe.* 1957. NY. Macmillan. 1st printing. 8vo. 328p. VG/chipped. clipped dj. K5. $30.00.

DE VERA, Jose Maria. *Educational Television in Japan.* 1967. Sophia U/Chas Tuttle. 1st. 140p. VG/clip. N2. $12.50.

DE VILAMIL, R. *Resistance of Air.* 1917. London. 1st. ils. 192p. xl. B18. $35.00.

DE VOLTAIRE, Francois Maria; See Voltaire.

DE VOS, Miriam P. *The Genus Romulea in South Africa.* 1972. Newlands. C.P. Journal of South African Botany. Sup. Vol. No. 9. 307p. VG. B26. $39.00.

DE VOTO, Bernard. *Across the Wide Missouri.* 1947. Houghton Mifflin. G/rpr. A19. $35.00.

DE VOTO, Bernard. *Year of Decision.* 1846. nd (1943). Houghton Mifflin. rpt. NF/VG. A14. $21.00.

DE VRIES, Peter. *Reuben, Reuben.* 1964. Little, Brn. 1st. 8vo. 435p. NM/VG. H1. $28.00.

DE VRIES, Peter. *Sauce for the Goose.* 1981. Little, Brn. 1st. rem mk. NF/dj. R14. $25.00.

DE WAAL, Ronald Burt. *The World Bibliography of Sherlock Holmes & Dr. Watson.* 1974. Boston. New York Graphic Society. 1st. F/. M15. $150.00.

DE WALL, Frans. *Chimpanzee Politics: Power & Sex Among Apes.* 1982. Harper Row. 1st Am. VG/dj. N2. $10.00.

DE WEERD, Harvey. *President Wilson Fights His War.* 1968. NY. 1st. 457p. E1. $40.00.

DE WINTER, B. etal. *Sixty-Six Transvaal Trees.* 1966. Pretoria. double pg color plates. 175p. VG. B26. $32.50.

DE ZEMBLER, Charles. *Once Over Lightly.* 1939. NY. 1st. ils. NF/dj. S13. $18.00.

DE ZOUCHE, Dorothy E. *Rodean School 1885 – 1955.* 1955. private prt. 1st. photos/fld ils. 225p. VG. H7. $10.00.

DE ZUMARRAGA, Juan. *Colleccion De Documentos Ineditos Relativos.* 1884. Madrid. Hernandez. 556p. modern tree sheep/red & olive calf labels. K1. $100.00.

DEACHMAN, T. *Auto Bio Chemic Treatment.* 1922. self pub. 1st. VG. E6. $65.00.

DEAN, Abner. *Come As You Are.* 1952. S&S. 1st. 4to. VG/dj. N2. $8.50.

DEAN, Amber. *Dead Man's Float.* 1944. Crime Club. F/dj. P3. $15.00.

DEAN, Amber. *Wrap It Up.* nd. Collins. VG. P3. $15.00.

DEAN, Blanche E. *Ferns of Alabama.* 1969. np. rev ed. sc. 222p. B26. $22.50.

DEAN, Elizabeth Lippincott. *Dolly Madison: Nation's Hostess.* 1928. Lee Shepard. 250p. pict label. V3. $14.00.

DEAN, Graham M. *Herb Kent: West Point Cadet.* 1936. Goldsmith. 250p. red bdg. VG. B36. $8.00.

DEANDREA, William l. *Five O'Clock Lightning.* 1982. NY. St. Martin. 1st. sgn. NF/NF. G8. $27.50.

DEANDREA, William L. *Killed on the Rocks.* 1990. NY. Mysterious. 1st. F/F. G8. $12.50.

DEANDREA, William L. *Snark.* 1985. NY. Mysterious. 1st. NF/NF. G8. $17.50.

DEANDREA, William L. *Written in Fire.* 1995. NY. Walker. 1st. VF/VF. T2. $15.00.

DEANE, Norman; See Creasey, John.

DEANE, Seamus. *Reading in the Dark.* 1996. London. 1st. dj. T9. $65.00.

DEAR, Ian. *America's Cup: Informal History.* 1980. NY. Dodd Mead. 1st. VG/dj. P4. $30.00.

DEARDEN, Seton. *Arabian Knight: Study of Sir Richard Burton.* 1953. London. Barker. revised. 8vo. ils/map ep. 256p. cloth.

DEARMENT, Bob. *Alias Frank Canton.* ils/index. 402p. dj. E1. $30.00.

DEAS, Michael J. *Portraits & Daguerreotypes of Edgar Allan Poe.* 1989. VA U. 1st. 198p. VG. B10. $15.00.

DEAVER, Jeffery. *Maidens Grave.* 1994. Viking. 1st. sgn. An/dj. S18. $35.00.

DEAVER, Jeffery. *Praying for Sleep.* 1993. Viking. 1st. sgn. F/F. S18. $45.00.

DEAVER, Jeffery Wilds. *Bone Collector.* 1997. Viking. 1st. NF/F. G8. $20.00.

DEBIN, David. *Nice Guys Finish Dead.* 1992. NY. Turtle Bay Books. 1st. author's 1st novel. VF/VF. T2. $30.00.

DECARAVA, Roy & Langston Hughes. *The Sweet Flypaper of Life.* 1967. Hill and Wang. later printing of reprint. NF/decor wrps. M25. $35.00.

DECHANCIE, John. *Magicnet.* 1993. Baltimore. Borderlands Press. 1st. 1/350 # copies. sgn. VF/VF. T2. $25.00.

DEDERA, Don. *A Mile in His Moccasins.* 1960. Phoenix. McGrew. 1st. sgn. VG+/F. A24. $25.00.

DEDERA, Don. *Little War of Our Own: Pleasant Valley Feud Revisited.* 1988. Northland. ils/notes/index. 308p. F/wrp. B19. $20.00.

DEDMON, Emmett. *Fabulous Chicago.* 1981. NY. Atheneum. enlarged ed. 1 of 250 numbered. sgn bound ed. F in F dj w/slipcase. B2. $75.00.

DEE, Ed. *14 Peck Slip.* 1994. NY. Warner. 1st. author's 1st book. F/F. H11. $40.00.

DEE, Jonathan. *Lover of History.* 1990. Ticknor Fields. 1st. author's 1st book. F/dj. A24. $25.00.

DEERING, Freemont B. *Border Boys on the Trail (#1).* 1911. AL Burt. VG/dj. M20. $30.00.

DEFERRARI, Gabriella. *A Cloud on Sand.* 1990. MY. Knopf. 1st. ARC. F. D10. $10.00.

DEFERRARI, Gabriella. *Gringa Latina.* 1995. Boston. Houghton Mifflin. 1st. UP. F. D10. $10.00.

DEFORD, Frank. *Casey on the Loose.* 1989. Viking. 1st. F/dj. P8. $10.00.

DEFORD, Frank. *Cut 'N' Run.* 1973. Viking. 1st. author's 1st novel. NF/F. H11. $20.00.

DEFOREST, J. A. *Volunteer's Adventure: Union Captain's Record of Civil War.* 1946. Yale. 2nd. F/VG. E6. $20.00.

DEGENER, Otto. *Ferns and Flowering Plants of Hawaii National Park with Descriptions of Ancient Hawaiian Customs...* 1930. Honolulu. ep maps. color ftspc. scarce in orig cloth. 312p. VG. B26. $44.00.

DEGENER, Otto. *Plants of Hawaii National Parks.* 1945 (1930). Ann Arbor. ils/pl. 312p. sc. B26. $16.00.

DEGENHARDT, William G.; Charles W. Painter; Andrew H. Price. *Amphibians and Reptiles of New Mexico.* 1996. Albuquerque. U of New Mexico Press. 1st. lt gr cloth. copper spine titles. maps & color plates. 431p. NF in dj. P4. $65.00.

DEIDER, Antonio. *Dissertatio Medica De Morbis Venereis.* 1742. London. Palmer. 129p. contemporary calf/rb. G7. $150.00.

DEIGHTON, Barbara. *Little Learning.* 1988. Quartet. 1st British ed. NF/NF. G8. $10.00.

DEIGHTON, Len. *Battle of Britain.* 1980. London. Cape. 1st. 224p. bl cloth. F/dj. M7. $45.00.

DEIGHTON, Len. *Berlin Game.* 1983. Hutchinson. 1st. F/NF. B3. $30.00.

DEIGHTON, Len. *Berlin Game.* 1984. NY. Knopf. 1st. F/F. H11. $30.00.

DEIGHTON, Len. *Billion Dollar Brain.* 1966. London. Jonathan Cape. 1st. F/VG+. minor wear. A24. $65.00.

DEIGHTON, Len. *Close-Up.* 1972. Atheneum. 1st. F/F. H11. $30.00.

DEIGHTON, Len. *Funeral in Berlin.* 1965. NY. Putnam. 1st. F/NF. H11. $50.00.

DEIGHTON, Len. *Goodbye Mickey Mouse.* 1982. London. Hutchinson. 1st. F/NF clip. B3. $40.00.

DEIGHTON, Len. *London Match.* 1985. London. Hutchinson. 1st. F/F. B3. $40.00.

DEIGHTON, Len. *London Match.* 1985. NY. Knopf. 1st. F/NF. H11. $20.00.

DEIGHTON, Len. *Spy Sinker.* 1990. NY. Harper Collins. ARC. F/dj. A23. $30.00.

DEIGHTON, Len. *Spy Story.* 1974. NY. HBJ. UP. F. M19. $45.00.

DEIGHTON, Len. *Twinkle, Twinkle, Little Spy.* 1976. London. Cape. 1st. NF/F. H11. $60.00.

DEIGHTON, Len. *Yesterday's Spy.* 1975. London. Cape. 1st. NF/F. B3. $75.00.

DEISSMANN, Adolf. *Bible Studies.* 1979. Alpha. rpt (1923 T&T Clark). 384p. VG. B29. $28.00.

DEISSMANN, Adolf. *Light from the Ancient East.* 1980. Baker. 535p. VG/wrp. B29. $14.50.

DEJONG, Meindert. *Horse Came Running.* 1970. Macmillan. 1st. ils Paul Sagsoorian. xl. B36. $10.00.

DEKEL, Efraim. *Shai: Exploits of Hagana Intelligence.* 1959. Yoseloff. 1st. 8vo. 369p. VG. W1. $20.00.

DEKNATEL, Frederick B. *Edvard Munch.* 1950. NY. Moma. 8vo. ils. 120p. G/dj. F1. $20.00.

DEKOBRA, Maurice. *Wings of Desire.* 1925. MaCaulay. 1st. pict cloth. VG. N2. $10.00.

DEL GAUDIO, Sybil. *Dressing the Part: Sternberg.* Dietrich & Costume. 1993. London. Fairleigh Dickinson. 95p. VG/dj. C5. $12.50.

DEL GIUDICE. *Takeoff.* (1996). NY. Harcourt Brace. 1st. F/F. B3. $30.00.

DEL PLAINE, Carlos. *Son of Orizaba: Memoirs of Childhood in Mexico.* 1954. NY. Exposition. 1st. 62p. dj. F3. $15.00.

DEL REY, Lester. *Early Del Rey.* 1975. Doubleday. 1st. F/VG. M19. $17.50.

DEL VECCHIO, John M. *13th Valley.* 1982. Toronto. Bantam. 1st Canadian. F/F. B3. $75.00.

DEL VECCHIO, John M. *For the Sake of All Living Things.* 1990. Bantam. 1st. NF/dj. R11/R14. $25.00.

DELAHAYE, G. *Pamela Learns to Ride.* 1968. Hart. 1st. ils Marcel Marlier. F/VG. M5. $30.00.

DELAND, Margaret. *Dr Lavendar's People.* 1903. NY. Harper. 1st. 370p. G. G11. $8.00.

DELAND, Margaret. *New Friends in Old Chester.* (1924). NY/London. Harper. 1st. 12mo. 272p. gilt red cloth. VG/dj. $3.00.

DELANY, Samuel R. *Bridge of Lost Desire.* 1987. Arbor. 1st. F/dj. M25. $15.00.

DELANY, Samuel R. *They Fly at Ciron.* 1995. NY. Tor. 1st thus. sgn. F/dj. C9. $48.00.

DELAPLANE, Stanton & Robert De Roos. *Delaplane in Mexico.* 1960. NY. Coward McCann. 1st. drawings. 250p. G/chipped dj. F3. $15.00.

DELAPORTE, Francois. *History of Yellow Fever: An Essay.* 1991. Cambridge. 1st. 181p. A13. $35.00.

DELAUNEY, Charles. *Jazz Parody.* 1948. London. ils/photos. 110p. VG/dj. B5. $35.00.

DELDERFIELD, R. F. *Seven Men of Gascony.* 1973. S&S. 1st. F/NF clip. T11. $25.00.

DELDERFIELD, R. F. *Too Few Drums.* 1964. S&S. 1st. NF/VG. T11. $20.00.

DELGADILLO, Daniel. *Atlas Geographico De La Republica Mexicana.* Atlas General. May 22 1910. Mexico City. Edicion Centenario. 31 full-p pl. 76p. ES. VG. $14.00.

DELILLO, Don. *Great Jones Street.* 1973. Boston. Houghton Mifflin. 1st. author's 3rd novel. inscr by author. F/NF. lt fading on spine. D10. $165.00.

DELILLO, Don. *Running Dog.* 1978. NY. Knopf. 1st. rem mk. NF in dj. D10. $75.00.

DELILLO, Don. *The Names.* 1982. NY. Knopf. 1st. F/F dj. M19. $35.00.

DELILLO, Don. *Underworld.* 1998. NY. Scribner. 1st. F/F. D10. $75.00.

DELILLO, Don. *Underworld.* 1998. London. Picador. 1st British ed. VF/VF. T2. $30.00.

DELINSKY, Barbara. *For My Daughters.* 1994. NY. Harper Collins. 1st. F/dj. T12. $35.00.

DELITZSCH, Franz Julius. *System Der Biblischen Psychologie.* 1861 (1855). Dorffling Franke. 2nd revised/enlarged. German text. 500p. VG. G1. $100.00.

DELL, Anthony. *Llama Land: East & West of the Andreas in Peru.* 1927. NY. Doran. 8vo. 248p. red cloth. NF. O1. $75.00.

DELL'ISOLA, Frank. *Thomas Merton. A Bibliography.* 1956. NY. Farrar. 1st. owner's name/bookplate. F in G dj. B2. $25.00.

DELLACHIESA, Carolyn. *Pinocchio Under the Sea.* 1913. Macmillan. 1st. ils Florence Wilde. VG. B5. $40.00.

DELLENBAUGH, Frederick S. *Breaking the Wilderness.* 1905. Putnam. 1st. 360p. pict cloth. D11. $100.00.

DELLENBAUGH, Frederick S. *Canyon Voyage: Narrative of the 2nd Powell Expedition.* 1926. Yale. gilt bl cloth. VG. F7. $75.00.

DELLENBAUGH, Frederick S. *Romance of the Colorado River.* 1902. Putnam. 8vo. 213p. VG. F7. $110.00.

DELORIA, Ella. *Speaking of Indians.* (1944). Friendship. 163p. VG/wrp. B18. $45.00.

DELORIA, Vine Jr. *Custer Died for Your Sins.* 1969. Macmillan. 1st. VG/dj. R8. $45.00.

DELORIA, Vine Jr. *Red Earth, White Lies: Native Americans and the Myth of Scientific Fact.* (1995). NY. Scribner's. 1st. sgn by author. F/F. B3. $35.00.

DELPIERRE, G. R. & N. M. Du Plessis. *The Winter Growing Gladioli of South Africa. A Pictorial Record with Descriptions.* 1974. Cape Town. 71p w/120 color photos. ep maps. F in dj. B26. $37.50.

DELVING, Michael. *Shadow of Himself.* 1972. NY. Scribner. 1st. sgn. VG/G. G8. $12.50.

DELYSER, Femmy. *Jane Fonda's New Pregnancy Workout and Total Birth Program.* 1989. NY. S&S. 1st. VG/G+. A28. $10.95.

DEMARINIS, Rick. *The Mortician's Apprentice.* (1994). NY. Norton. 1st. F/F. B3. $15.00.

DEMARINIS, Rick. *The Year of the Zinc Penny.* (1989). NY. WW Norton. 1st. F/F. B3. $15.00.

DEMBNER, S. *Arthur & William E Massee: Modern Circulation Methods.* 1968. McGraw Hill. 1st. 4to. cloth. F/dj. O10. $15.00.

DEMIJOHN, Thomas; See Disch, Thomas.

DEMILLE, Nelson. *Cathedral.* 1981. Delacorte. 1st. NF/lightly worn dj. rem spray on bottom of text block. M25. $45.00.

DEMING, Richard. *American Spies: Real Life Stories of Undercover Agents.* 1960. Whitman. ils Leonard Vosburgh. 210p. NF. B36. $10.00.

DEMOOR, Jean. *Die Anormalen Kinder Und Ihre Behandlung In Haus Und Schule.* 1901. Altenburg. Druck/Oskar Bonde. German text. 292p. modern line. G1. $100.00.

DENHARDT. *Quarter Horses. A Story of Two Centuries.* 1969. Norman. U of OK Press & AQHA. VG/VG. O3. $25.00.

DENHARDT, Robert M. *Foundation Sires of the American Quarter Horse.* 1977. OK U. 2nd. NF/dj. A21. $45.00.

DENHART, Jeffrey. *Just Bones.* 1996. Aurora. Write Way publishing. 1st. author's 1st novel. sgn. VF/VF. T2. $35.00.

DENIS, Michaela. *Leopard on My Lap.* 1955. Messner. 1st. 8vo. 254p. F/NF. B20. $30.00.

DENISE, Christopher. *Fool of the World & the Flying Ship.* 1994. Philomel. 1st. F/dj. B17. $12. 50.

DENISON, George Burlingame. *Record of the Descendants of Samuel Denison.* 1884. Muscatine, IA. 72p. G. S5. $35.00.

DENLINGER, Milo. *Complete Dachshund.* 1947. Denlinger. 1st. Ils Edwin McGargee. NF. A21. $45.00.

DENNEY, James. *The Death of Christ.* 1952. London. Tyndale. R V G Tasker. 207p. VG. B29. $7.00.

DENNIE, Charles. *History of Syphilis.* 1962. Springfield. 1st. 137p. A13. $50.00.

DENNIE, James. *Remarks on Judge Thacher's Sentence in Case.* 1841. Boston. Dutton Wentworth. orig stabbed wrp. M11. $75.00.

DENNIS, Ian. *The Prince of Stars in the Cavern of Time.* 1989. Woodstock. Overlook Press. 1st Am ed. author's 1st novel. VF/VF. T2. $35.00.

DENNIS, Jerry. *Place on the Water: An Angler's Reflections on Home.* 1993. NY. 2nd. ils Glenn Wolf. 224p. F/dj. A17. $15.00.

DENNIS, Morgan. *Morgan Dennis Dog Book.* 1946. Viking. 1st. ils. NF/dj. A21. $75.00.

DENNIS, Morgan. *Purebreds.* 1954. Winston. 1st. VG. A21. $45.00.

DENNY, Arthur H. *Pioneer Days on Puget Sound.* 1965. Fairfield. Ye Galleon. 8vo. 83p. B20. $50.00.

DENNY, George H. *Dread Fishwish & Other Tales.* 1975. Freshet. 222p. F/dj. A17. $15.00.

DENON, Vivant. *Travels in Lower & Upper Egypt During Campaigns Bonaparte.* 1804. London. R Taylor. 2 vol in 1. rb modern gr calf/gr cloth. K1. $250.00.

DENONN, Lester E. *Wit & Wisdom of Oliver Wendell Holmes: Father & Son.* 1953. Boston. Beacon. 1st. 116p. gr cloth. F/dj. B14. $25.00.

DENSMORE, Frances. *Music of Santo Domingo Pueblo.* New Mexico. 1938. SW Mus. 1st. ils. 186p. NF. B19. $50.00.

DENSMORE, Frances. *Yuman & Yaqui Music.* 1932. GPO. 1st. ils/nots. 216p. wrp. B19. $45.00.

DENT, Lester. *Hades & Hocus Pocus.* 1979. Chicago. Pulp Press. 1st. Jacket has soiled back panel. F/dj. M15. $65.00.

DENTINGER, Jane. *Death Mask.* 1988. NY. Scribner's. 1st. F/NF. G8. $12.50.

DENTINGER, Jane. *Who Dropped Peter Pan.* 1995. Viking. 1st. F/F. G8. $15.00.

DENTON, Bradley. *Buddy Holly Is Alive & Well on Ganymede.* 1991. Morrow. 1st. author's 2nd book. NF/dj. R14. $25.00.

DENTON, Wallace. *The Role of the Minister's Wife.* 1962. Westminster. 175p. VG. B29. $6.00.

DEPEW, Albert N. *Gunner Depew.* 1918. Chicago. Reilly Britton. 1st? sm 8vo. 312p. gilt bl cloth. VG+. M7. $35.00.

DERBYSHIRE, John. *Seeing Calvin Coolidge in a Dream.* 1996. NY. St. Martin. 1st. author's 1st novel. F/F. M23. $45.00.

DERLETH, August. *Boy's Way.* 1947. Stanton Lee. 1st. 8vo. 109p. bl cloth. NF/dj. J3. $250.00.

DERLETH, August. *Countryman's Journal.* 1963. DSP. 1st. NF/VG. P3. $25.00.

DERLETH, August. *Fire & Sleet & Candlelight.* 1961. Arkham. 1st. VG/dj. B30. $125.00.

DERLETH, August. *Harrigan's File.* 1975. Sauk City. 1st. F/dj. T10. $40.00.

DERLETH, August. *Mr. Fairlie's Final Journey.* 1968. Sauk City. Mycroft & Moran. 1st. F/dj. M15. $45.00.

DERLETH, August. *Night Side.* 1947. Rinehart. 1st. NF/VG. M19. $35.00.

DERLETH, August. *The Chronicles of Solar Pons.* 1973. Arkham. 1st. collects 10 stories. F/dj. T2. $25.00.

DERLETH, August. *The Chronicles of Solar Pons.* 1973. Sauk City. Mycroft & Moran. 1st. 4176 copies printed. VF/VF. T2. $25.00.

DERLETH, August. *The Memoirs of Solar Pons.* 1951. Sauk City. Mycroft & Moran. 1st. F/dj. M15. $200.00.

DERLETH, August. *Village Daybook: A Sac Prairie Journal.* 1947. Pellegrini Cudahy. 1st. VG. P3. $20.00.

DEROCHES, Catherine F. *La Puce De Mme Desroches.* 1872. Paris. Librairie des Bibliophiles. sm 8vo. B20. $275.00.

DERR, Mark. *Frontiersman.* 1993. Morrow. 1st. gilt bdg. F/dj. T11. $15.00.

DESCALZI, Ricardo. *La Real Audiencia De Quito Claustro En Los Andes.* 1978. Quito. Ecuador. 1st. 4to. 396p. G/chipped dj. F3. $35.00.

DESCAMPS, Emilio. *Nomenclator De Guatemala.* 1937. NP. Guatemala. 1st. oblong 8vo. several tiny worm holes. 598p. G. F3. $45.00.

DESCHIN, Jacob. *Canon Photography: A Working Manual.* 1957. Camera Craft. 1st. VG/dj. S5. $10.00.

DESMOND, Alice Curtis. *George Washington's Mother.* 1961. Dodd Mead. 1st. VG/dj. w/TLS. T11. $30.00.

DESMOND, Lawrence & Phyllis Messenger. *A Dream of Maya.* 1983. Albuquerque. Univ of New Mexico Press. 1st. 4to. 147p. spine faded dj over wrp. F3. $30.00.

DESROCHES-NOBLECOURT, C. *Life & Death of a Pharaoh: Tutankhamen.* 1963. NYGS. photos FL Kenett. 312p. cloth. dj. D2. $25.00.

DEUEL, Leo. *Conquistadors without Swords.* 1967. St Martin. 1st. 647p. dj. F3. $25.00.

DEUTCH, Yvonne (ed). *Cooking for Two.* 1978. London. Marshall Cavendish Books. VG/VG. A28. $10.95.

DEUTSCH, Felix. *Psychosomatic Concept in Psychoanalysis.* 1953. Internat U Pr. 1st. 8vo. 182p. xl. NF. C14. $15.00.

DEVAMBEZ, Pierre. *Greek Sculpture.* 1961. NY. Tudor. photos Robert Deschames. unp. cloth. dj. D2. $20.00.

DEVERDUN, Alfred. *True Mexico: Mexico-Tenochtitlan.* 1938. Menasha, WI. Geo Banta. 1st. sgn. 304p. tattered dj. $3.00.

DEVINE, Dominic. *Devil at Your Elbow.* 1966. London. Collins Crime Club. 1st. F/NF. M15. $65.00.

DEVINE, Dominic. *His Own Appointed Day.* 1965. Walker. 1st Am ed. VG/VG. G8. $20.00.

DEVINE, Dominic. *This Is Your Death.* 1982. St. Martin. 1st Am ed. NF/NF. G8. $17.50.

DEVINE, Laurie. *Nile.* 1983. London. Andre Deutsch. 1st. NF/clip. A14. $25.00.

DEVIVIER, W. *Christian Apologetics: A Rational Exposition.* 1924. NY. Wagner. 2 vol. index. xl. G. H10. $37.50.

DEVON, Gary. *Bad Desire.* 1990. NY. Random House. 1st. VF/VF. T2. $8.00.

DEVON, Gary. *Lost.* 1986. NY. Knopf. 1st. author's 1st novel. VF/VF. T2. $10.00.

DEWAR, Lindsay. *An Outline of New Testament Ethics.* 1959. Westminster. 280p. VG. B29. $7.00.

DEWEES, W. *Treatise on Diseases of Females.* 1847 (1827). 12 pl. full leather. E6. $125.00.

DEWEY, Thomas B. *Sad Song Singing.* 1963. S&S. 1st. VG/VG. G8. $15.00.

DEWHURST, Eileen. *Dear Mr. Right.* 1990. NY. Doubleday. 1st. VF/VF. H11. $15.00.

DEWSBURY, Donald A. *Comparative Psychology in 20th Century.* 1984. Stroudsburg, PA. Hutchinson Ross. 411p. pebbled prt gr fabricoid. G1. $65.00.

DEWSBURY, Donald A. *Mammalian Sexual Behavior.* 1981. Hutchinson Ross. 382p. F. S15. $36.00.

DEXTER, Colin. *As Good as Gold.* 1994. London. Kodak. 1st appearance. F/wrp. M15. $45.00.

DEXTER, Colin. *Death Is Now My Neighbour.* 1996. London. Macmillan. 1st. sgn. F/dj. M15. $65.00.

DEXTER, Colin. *Last Seen Wearing.* 1976. St Martin. 1st Am. F/NF. M15. $500.00.

DEXTER, Colin. *Neighbourhood Watch.* 1993. Richmond. Moorhouse Sorenson. 1st. sgn. F. M15. $250.00.

DEXTER, Colin. *The Daughters of Cain.* 1994. London. Macmillan. 1st. VF/dj. M15. $7575.00.

DEXTER, Colin. *The Jewel that was Ours.* 1991. London. Macmillan. 1st. VF/dj. M15. $75.00.

DEXTER, Colin. *The Riddle of the Third Mile.* 1983. London. Macmillan. 1st. F/dj clip. M15. $350.00.

DEXTER, Colin. *The Third Inspector Morse Omnibus.* 1993. London. Macmillan. 1st Omnibus. VF/dj. M15. $85.00.

DEXTER, Dave, Jr. *Jazz Cavalcade.* 1946. NY. Criterion. 1st. F in G dj. B2. $50.00.

DEXTER, Dave, Jr. *The Jazz Story.* 1964. Englewood Cliffs. Prentice-Hall. 1st. owner's inscr. uncommon in cloth. F/used dj. B2. $30.00.

DEXTER, Pete. *Brotherly Love.* 1991. NY. Random. 1st. sgn. F/F. H11. $45.00.

DEXTER, Pete. *Deadwood.* 1986. Random. 1st. inscr/dtd 1989. NF/F. R14. $50.00.

DEXTER, Pete. *Paris Trout.* 1988. NY. Random. 1st. VF/F. H11. $50.00.

DEXTER, Pete. *The Paperboy.* 1995. NY. Random House. 1st. F/F. O11. $50.00.

DI FILIPPO, Paul. *Ribofunk.* 1996. Four Walls Eight Windows. 1st. F/NF. M23. $25.00.

DI FILIPPO, Paul. *Steampunk Trilogy.* 1995. Four Walls Eight Windows. 1st. F/F. H11. $30.00.

DI FUSCO, John. *Tracers.* 1986. Hill Wang. 1st. F/dj. R11. $50.00.

DI MAGGIO, Joe. *Lucky to be a Yankee.* 1946. Field. 1st. photos. VG/dj. P8. $200.00.

DI MONA, Joseph. *Last Man at Arlington.* 1973. NY. Fields. 1st. NF/F. H11. $20.00.

DI PRIMA, Diane. *Earthsong.* 1968. NY. Poets Press. 1st. F/wrp. M25. $45.00.

DIAL, Harry. *All This Jazz About Jazz.* 1984. Chigwell. Storyville. 1st. issued w/o dj. F. B2. $60.00.

DIAMANT, L. *Chaining the Hudson: Fight for the River in Am Revolution.* 1989. NY. ils/map. F/dj. M4. $25.00.

DIAMOND, Solomon. *Roots of Psychology: Sourcebook in History of Ideas.* 1977. NY. Basic. thick 8vo. 781p. russet cloth. VG/dj. G1. $65.00.

DIAZ, Junot. *Drown.* 1996. Riverhead. 1st. author's 1st book. F/dj. R14. $25.00.

DIAZ CINTORA, Salvador. *Xochiquetzal.* 1990. UNAM. Mexico. 1st. 91p. G in wrp. $25.00.

DIAZ DEL CASTILLO, Bernal. *Memoirs of The Conquistador Bernal Diaz Del Castillo.* 1844. London. Hatchard. 2 vol. trans JI Lockhart. stp cloth. $11.00.

DIBDIN, Michael. *A Rich Full Death.* 1986. London. Faber & Faber. 1st. F/dj. M15. $250.00.

DIBDIN, Michael. *Blood Rain.* 1999. London. Faber & Faber. 1st. sgn. VF/VF. T2. $40.00.

DIBDIN, Michael. *Cabal.* 1993. NY. Doubleday Crime. 1st Am. sgn. F/dj. O11. $30.00.

DIBDIN, Michael. *Cosi Fan Tutti.* 1997. Pantheon. 1st Am ed. F/F. G8. $15.00.

DIBDIN, Michael. *Dark Specter*. 1995. Pantheon. 1st Am ed. NF/VG+. G8. $15.00.

DIBDIN, Michael. *Ratking*. 1988. London. Faber & Faber. 1st. F/dj. M15. $250.00.

DIBDIN, Michael. *The Dying of the Light*. 1993. London. Faber & Faber. 1st. sgn. F/F. T2. $30.00.

DIBDIN, Michael. *The Tryst*. 1989. London. Faber & Faber. 1st. F/dj. M15. $100.00.

DIBDIN, Michael. *Vendetta*. 1991. Doubleday. 1st Am. F/dj. N4. $25.00.

DIBNER, Martin. *Admiral*. 1967. Doubleday. BC. NF/VG. T11. $10.00.

DICK, Erma Biesel. *Old House: Holiday & Party Cookbook*. (1969). Cowles. 1st. ils. VG/dj. A16. $25.00.

DICK, Philip K. *Beyond Lies the Wub: Volume One of Collected Stories Of*. 1988. London. Gollancz. 1st Eng. 25 stories. F/dj. $2.00.

DICK, Philip K. *Man in the High Castle*. nd. BC. VG/dj. P3. $10.00.

DICK, Philip K. *Our Friends from Frolix 8*. 1989. Middlesex. Kinnell. 1st Eng hc. F/dj. T2. $30.00.

DICK, Philip K. *Scanner Darkly*. 1977. Doubleday. 2nd. rem mk. F/dj. P3. $25.00.

DICK, Philip K. *The Broken Bubble*. 1989. London. Gollancz. 1st British ed. VF/VF. T2. $30.00.

DICK, Philip K. *The Crack in Space*. 1989. London. Severn House. 1st separate hc ed. VF/VF. T2. $35.00.

DICKASON, Christie. *Indochine: Epic Novel of Vietnam*. 1987. Villard/Random. Special Readers ed of 1st Am. NF/ils wrp. A14. $14.00.

DICKASON, David Howard. *Daring Young Men: Story of American Pre-Raphaelites*. 1970. NY. Benj Blom. ils/notes/index. NF. D2. $25.00.

DICKASON, Olive Patricia. *Indian Arts in Canada*. 1972. Ottawa. Dept Indian Affairs & Northern Development. 138p. P4. $85.00.

DICKENS, Charles. *Christmas Carol*. 1995. Harcourt Brace. lg 8vo. F. B36. $22.00.

DICKENS, Charles. *David Copperfield*. 1980. Franklin Lib. ils Paul Degen. 803p. VG. B36. $20.00.

DICKENS, Charles. *Dicken's Stories About Children*. 1929. Winston. 8vo. 274p. VG. W2. $30.00.

DICKENS, Charles. *Doctor Marigold's Perscriptions*. 1865. London. Chapman Hall. 1st. VG/bl prt wrp. w/ad of Our Mutual Friend. M24. $85.00.

DICKENS, Charles. *Great Expectations*. 1861. Phil. TB Peterson. 1st ils ed. 16mo. 523p. gilt blk cloth. M24. $250.00.

DICKENS, Charles. *Life of Our Lord*. 1934. St Martin. 1st Am. F/VG. M19. $35.00.

DICKENS, Charles. *Little Dorritt*. 1857. Phil. TB Peterson. 1st Am. gilt blk cloth. NF. M24. $450.00.

DICKENS, Charles. *Mystery of Edwin Drood*. 1870. London. 1st (from parts. bdg w/covers+ads). 3-quarter leather. M17. $300.00.

DICKENS, Charles. *No Thoroughfare*. 1867. London. 1st. F/bl prt wrp. M24. $165.00.

DICKENS, Charles. *Posthumous Papers of The Pickwick Club*. 1844. Dodd Mead. ils. 687p. 3-quarter morocco. F. F1. $125.00.

DICKENS, Homer. *Films of Marlene Dietrich*. 1968. Citadel. 1st. ils. VG/dj. C9. $48.00.

DICKENS, Monica. *Great Escape*. 1971. London. Kaye Ward. 1st. Early Bird series. F/dj. D4. $20.00.

DICKERSON, Albert Inskip. *Selected Writings*. 1974. Dartmouth. 1st. 8vo. F/dj. A2. $15.00.

DICKEY, Christopher. *With the Contras: A Reporter in Wilds of Nicaragua*. 1985. S&S. 1st. 327p. dj. F3. $10.00.

DICKEY, Herbert. *Misadventures of a Tropical Medico*. 1929. Dodd Mead. 1st. 304p. F3. $20.00.

DICKEY, James. *Puella*. 1982. Doubleday. 1st. sgn. F/dj. B30. $55.00.

DICKEY, James. *Sorties, Journals and New Essays*. 1971. NY. Doubleday. 1st. F/dj. D10. $40.00.

DICKEY, James. *To the White Sea*. 1993. Houghton Mifflin. 1st. inscr. NF/dj. R14. $60.00.

DICKEY, James. *Tucky the Hunter*. 1978. Crown. 1st. NF. C14. $16.00.

DICKEY, James. *Zodiac*. 1976. Doubleday. 1st. NF/dj. w/inscr card. J3. $40.00.

DICKEY, Page. *Breaking Ground: Portraits of Ten Garden Designers*. 1997. NY. Artisan. 1st. folio. ils/index. 207p. F/dj. $10.00.

DICKEY, R. P. *Acting Immortal*. 1970. Univ of Missouri. 1st. author sgn/inscr to fellow poet. vinyl covered hc. F/F. V1. $25.00.

DICKEY & VAN ROSSEM. *Birds of El Salavdor*. 1938. Chicago. Field Nat Hist Mus. lg 8vo. ils/photos. 609p. VG/wrp. C12. $130.00.

DICKIE, Edgar Primrose. *God Is Light*. 1954. Scribner. 261p. VG/torn. B29. $13.00.

DICKINSON, Charles. *With or Without*. 1987. Knopf. 1st. NF/F. R14. $30.00.

DICKINSON, Emily. *Further Poems of Emily Dickinson*. 1929. Little, Brn. 1st. 8vo. 208p. teg. dk gr cloth. NF/dj. $5.00.

DICKINSON, Peter. *Death of a Unicorn*. 1984. NY. Pantheon. 1st Am ed. NF/NF. G8. $10.00.

DICKINSON, Peter. *Healer*. 1983. NY. Delacorte. 1st Am. 184p. F/dj. D4. $40.00.

DICKINSON, Peter. *Hindsight*. 1983. Pantheon. 1st Am ed. VG+/VG+. G8. $15.00.

DICKINSON, Peter. *Lively Dead*. 1975. NY. H & S. 1st British ed. VG+/VG. G8. $20.00.

DICKINSON, Peter. *Merlin Dreams*. 1988. Delacorte. 1st. ils Alan Lee. F/dj. B17. $25.00.

DICKINSON, Peter. *Perfect Gallows*. 1988. Pantheon. F/G+. L4. $12.00.

DICKINSON, Peter. *Play Dead*. 1992. Mysterious. 1st Am. rem mk. F/dj. N4. $15.00.

DICKINSON, Terence & Jack Newton. *Splendors of the Universe*. 1997. Buffalo, NY. Firefly Books. ils color photos. 4to. 144p. VG in laminated pict bds. K5. $40.00.

DICKSON, Carter; See Carr, John Dickson.

DICKSON, Gordon R. *Star Road*. 1975. Robert Hale. 1st. VG/dj. P3. $15.00.

DICTIONARY. *Brewer's Dictionary of Phrase and Fable*. nd. London. Cassell. rev reprint ed. edgewear. bookplate ffep. creasing & soiling. 977p. G. S14. $9.50.

DICTIONARY. *Webster's Home Medical Dictionary*. 1995. Kappa Books. Inc. pb. NF. F6. $1.50.

DIDIER, Eugene Lemoine. *The Life & Letters of Madame Bonaparte.* 1879. NY. Scribners. 1st. sm8vo. some edges bumped. light soil. 276p. G. H1. $37.50.

DIDION, Joan. *Miami.* 1987. S&S. 1st. inscr/dtd 1994. rem mk. F/dj. R14. $45.00.

DIDION, Joan. *Play it as it Lays.* 1970. FSG. 1st. VG/dj. C9. $36.00.

DIDION, Joan. *Slouching Towards Bethlehem.* 1968. FSG. 1st. author's 2nd book. F/sbdg wrp. L3. $750.00.

DIEHL, Charles. *Byzantium: Greatness and Decline.* 1957. Rutgers. 366p. VG. B29. $10.50.

DIEHL, Edith. *Bookbinding: Its Background & Technique.* 1946. Rinehart. 2 vol. 1st. 8vo. cloth. VG. P2. $90.00.

DIEHL, Gaston. *Fauves.* 1975. NY. Abrams. ils. 4to. tan cloth. F/dj. F1. $75.00.

DIEHL, William. *Chameleon.* 1981. Random. 1st. author's 2nd novel. NF/dj. S18. $30.00.

DIEHL, William. *Hooligans.* 1984. Villard. 1st. F/F. H11. $25.00.

DIEHL, William. *Sharky's Machine.* 1978. NY. Delacorte. 1st. F/F. D10. $65.00.

DIEHL, William. *Thai Horse.* 1987. NY. Villard. 1st. F/F. H11. $25.00.

DIETRICH, William. *Final Forest.* 1992. S&S. 1st. sm 4to. 303p. F/dj. W2. $30.00.

DIETZ, Howard. *Dancing in the Dark.* 1974. Quadrangle/NY Times. 1st. inscr. 370p. NF/dj. B20. $150.00.

DIGBY, Kenelm. *Discours Fait En Une Celebre Assemblee.* 1669. Paris. Thos Jolly. 12mo. 91+4p. contemporary calf. G7. $650.00.

DIKTY, Alan S. *Boy's Book Collector.* nd. Starmount. F. P3. $75.00.

DILENSCHNEIDER, Robert L. *Power & Influence.* 1990. Prentice Hall. 1st. 8vo. 258p. F/dj. W2. $30.00.

DILLARD, Annie. *American Childhood.* 1987. Harper Row. 1st. F/NF. M23. $25.00.

DILLARD, Annie. *Encounters with Chinese Writers.* 1984. Wesleyan U. 1st. F/VG. B30. $20.00.

DILLARD, Annie. *Holy the Firm.* 1977. NY. Harper & Row. 1st. sgn. F. D10. $75.00.

DILLARD, Annie. *Living.* 1992. Harper Collins. F/dj. V4. $15.00.

DILLARD, Annie. *Pilgrim at Tinker Creek.* (1974). NY. Harper's Magazine Press. true 1st ed. author's 1st work of prose. F/NF. lt edgewear/NF. lt creasing to top corners. B3. $175.00.

DILLARD, Annie. *Teaching a Stone to Talk.* 1982. NY. Harper & Row. 1st. sgn. F in dj. D10. $60.00.

DILLARD, Annie. *The Writing Life.* 1989. NY. Harper & Row. 1st. F/F. M23. $20.00.

DILLARD, R. H. W. *The Day I Stopped Dreaming about Barbara Steele.* 1966. Univ of North Carolina. 1st. sgn/inscr to fellow poet. wrp. NF. V1. $22.00.

DILLE, John. *Americans in Space.* 1965. NY. American Heritage. 2nd printing. ex lib in pict cloth. usual lib mks. photos. many in color. 4to. 153p. G. K5. $12.00.

DILLEN, Frederick G. *Hero.* 1994. Steerforth. 1st. author's 1st novel. F/dj. R14. $35.00.

DILLENBERGER, John. *Protestant Thought and Natural Science.* 1960. Doubleday. 310p. VG. B29. $10.50.

DILLING, Elizabeth. *The Red Network.* 1934. Kenilworth & Chicago. self pub. 1st printing. VG. B2. $35.00.

DILLISTONE, F. W. *Jesus Christ and His Cross.* 1952. Westminster. 143p. G. B29. $4.00.

DILLON, Brian. *Salinas De Los Nueve Cerros.* Guatemala. 1977. NY. Ballena. 1st. 94p. wrp. F3. $20.00.

DILLON, Helen. *Garden Artistry: Secrets of Planting & Designing.* 1995. Macmillan. 1st. ils/biblio. 190p. F/VG. $10.00.

DILLON, Julia L. *Blossom Circle of the Year in Southern Gardens.* 1922. NY. photos. 201p. VG/dj. B26. $25.00.

DILLON, Richard. *Burnt-Out Fires.* 1973. Englewood Cliffs. Prentice Hall. F/dj. A19. $25.00.

DILTS, James D. *The Great Road, the Building of the Baltimore and Ohio....* 1993. Stanford. Stanford Univ Press. 1st. photo ils. maps. 472p. F/dj. B18. $35.00.

DIMBLEBY, Jonathan. *Palestinians.* 1979. London/Melbourne/NY. Quartet. 1st. ils. 256p. VG/dj. W1. $25.00.

DIMITRI, Ivan. *Flight to Everywhere.* 1944. NY. Whittlesey. 4to. ils. 240p. VG/fair. B11. $20.00.

DIMITROFF, George Z. & James G. Baker. *Telescopes and Accessories.* 1948. Philadelphia. Blakiston. 8vo. 149 text ils. 309p. G in cloth. spine faded. spots. lt foxing. K5. $25.00.

DINE, Jim. *Apocalypse: Revelation of Saint John the Divine.* 1982. SF. Arion. 1/150. sgns Dine/prt Andrew Hoyem. oak brd/pigskin. AN. B24. $4.00.

DINESEN, Isak. *Anecdotes of Destiny.* 1958. Random. 1st. NF/dj. B30. $50.00.

DINESEN, Isak. *Shadow on the Grass.* 1960. Michael Joseph. 1st Eng. F/NF. M19. $45.00.

DINGWALL, Eric J. *Some Human Oddities: Studies in the Queer.* 1962. Hyde Park, NY. University Books. 1st. 198p. F/VG. B20. $25.00.

DIRVIN, Joseph I. *Louise De Marillac: of the Ladies & Daughters of Charity.* 1970. NY. 1st. VG/dj. M17. $20.00.

DISCH, Thomas M. *Businessman.* 1984. Harper Row. 1st. F/NF. M21. $30.00.

DISCH, Thomas M. *Fun with your New Head.* 1971. Doubleday. 1st Am. rem mk. F/dj. B2. $25.00.

DISCH, Thomas M. *On Wings of Song.* 1979. London. Gollancz. 1st. VF/VF. T2. $40.00.

DISCH, Thomas M. *Priest.* 1994. Knopf. 1st. F. S18. $7.00.

DISCH, Thomas M. *The Businessman.* 1984. NY. Harper & Row. 1st. F/F. H11. $40.00.

DISNEY, Doris Miles. *Chandler Policy.* 1971. Putnam. 1st. VG/VG. G8. $20.00.

DISNEY, Doris Miles. *Last Straw.* 1954. Crime Club. 1st. VG/VG. G8. $30.00.

DISNEY STUDIOS. *Baby Weems.* 1941. Doubleday Doran. 1st. 4to. lg bl cloth. mc pict dj. R5. $485.00.

DISNEY STUDIOS. *Cold Blooded Penguin.* 1946. Little Golden Book D2. 24p. red mk on cover. K2. $20.00.

DISNEY STUDIOS. *Donald Duck.* Abbeville. 1st. 1975. sm folio. 195p. NF. B20. $85.00.

DISNEY STUDIOS. *Elmer Elephant.* 1936. Australia. Photogravures Ltd. 12p booklet. G. C9. $60.00.

DISNEY STUDIOS. *Snow White & the Seven Dwarfs.* 1937. NY. Harper. 1st. lg 4to. mc ils. 0p. mc dj. R5. $250.00.

DISNEY STUDIOS, Thumper. *Little Golden Book D119.* A ed. K2. $20.00.

DISSTON, Harry. *Beginning Polo.* 1973. S Brunswick. Barnes. 1st. VG/G. O3. $35.00.

DITKA, Mike. *Ditka.* 1986. Bonus Books. 1st. 8vo. 271p. F/dj. W2. $25.00.

DITMARS, Raymond L. *Reptile Book.* 1908. Doubleday Page. ils. 472p. VG. M7. $25.00.

DITMARS, Raymond L. *Reptiles of the World.* 1941. NY. revised. 321p. VG. A17. $15.00.

DITMARS, Raymond L. *Thrills of a Naturalist's Quest.* 1932. NY. ils. 268p. VG. 515. $10.00.

DITZEL, Paul C. *Fire Engines & Firefighters.* 1976. Crown. 1st. ils. 256p. F/clip. T11. $36.00.

DIVAKARUNI, Chitra Banerjee. *Sister of My Heart.* 1999. NY. Doubleday. ARC. F in wrp. B2. $35.00.

DIX, Morgan. *Lectures on the First Prayer Book of King Edward VI.* 1881. NY. Young. 1st. 103p. G/wrp. H10. $45.00.

DIXON, Edward H. *Scenes in the Practice of a New York Surgeon.* 1855. De Witt/Davenport. 1st. thick 8vo. 407p. bl cloth. G+. B20. $75.00.

DIXON, Franklin. *Hardy Boys, The Secret of the Old Mill #3.* 1962. NY. Grosset & Dunlap. hc. some bumping of corners. G. A28. $5.95.

DIXON, Franklin W. *South of the Border.* nd. Grosset Dunlap. VG/dj. P3. $15.00.

DIXON, Hepworth. *John Howard & the Prison: World of Europe.* 1852. Webster, MA. 442. gilt cloth. VG. B14. $75.00.

DIXON, Roger. *Noah II.* 1975. Harwood-Smart. F/VG clip. P3. $15.00.

DIXON, Stephen. *14 Stories.* 1980. Baltimore. Johns Hopkins U. Press. 1st. sgn. F in NF dj. D10. $50.00.

DIXON, Stephen. *Fall & Rise.* 1985. San Francisco. North Point Press. 1st sgn by author. F/F. D10. $50.00.

DIXON, Stephen. *Love and Will.* 1989. NY. Paris Review. 1st. sgn by author. F/F. D10. $45.00.

DIXON, Stephen. *Work.* 1977. Ann Arbor. Street Fiction Press. pb orig. F in wrp. D10. $75.00.

DIXON, Thomas. *Birth of a Nation.* 1915. Grosset Dunlap. MTI. VG/dj. C9. $180.00.

DIXON, Thomas. *Life Worth Living: a Personal Experience.* 1910 (1905). Doubleday Page. rpt. 140p. lt gr ils cloth. B20. $25.00.

DIXON, William Hepworth. *Personal History of Lord Bacon.* 1861. Leipzig. Tauchnitz. 3-quarter brn leather/marbled brd. M17. $20.00.

DIXON, Winifred Hawkridge. *Westward Hoboes: Ups & Downs of Frontier Motoring.* 1922. Scribner. ils/map ep. 377p. VG. F7. $50.00.

DOANE, A. Sidney. *Surgery Illustrated. Compiled from the Works of Cutler, Hind, Velpeau, and Blasius.* 1837. NY. Harper & Bros. 2nd. 52 pl. orig cloth. rebacked. foxed. some minor staining. 200p. G. B14. $275.00.

DOANE, Michael. *Bullet Heart.* 1994. NY. Knopf. 1st. F/F. H11. $15.00.

DOANE, Michael. *City of Light.* 1992. NY. Knopf. 1st. F/F. H11. $20.00.

DOBELL, Clifford. *Antony Van Leeuwenhoek & His Little Animals.* 1958. NY. Russell. 435p. VG/dj. A10. $25.00.

DOBKIN, Alix. *Alix Dobkin's Adventures in Women's Music.* 1979. NY. Tomato. 1st. ils/photos. 70p. AN. A25. $25.00.

DOBKIN, Marjorie Housepian. *Making of a Feminist: Early Journals & Letters of MC Thomas.* 1979. Kent State. 314p. wrp. V3. $11.00.

DOBLHOFER, Ernst. *Voices in Stone: Decipherment of Ancient Scripts & Writings.* 1961. Viking. 1st. 8vo. 327p. NF/dj. W1. $12.00.

DOBSON, Austin. *Miscellanies.* 1898. Dodd Mead. sm 8vo. H13. $45.00.

DOBSON, James. *Love Must be Tough: New Hope for Families in Crisis.* 1984. Word. 212p. VG/VG. B29. $4.50.

DOBSON, James C. *Straight Talk.* 1991. World. 1st. sm 4to. 237p. F/dj. W2. $30.00.

DOBSON, Joanne. *Quieter than Sleep.* 1997. NY. Doubleday. 1st. sgn. F/NF. G8. $15.00.

DOBSON, Joanne. *The Raven and the Nightingale: A Modern Mystery of Edgar Allan Poe.* 1999. NY. Doubleday. 1st. sgn by Dobson. VF/VF. T2. $25.00.

DOBYNS, Stephen. *Cold Dog Soup.* 1985. Viking. 1st. NF/NF. H11. $30.00.

DOBYNS, Stephen. *Dancer with One Leg.* 1983. NY. Dutton. 1st. sgn. NF/VG. R14. $40.00.

DOBYNS, Stephen. *Saratoga Backtalk.* 1994. NY. W.W. Norton. 1st prt. VG/G. O3. $20.00.

DOBYNS, Stephen. *Saratoga Headhunter.* 1985. NY. Viking. 1st. F in dj. M25. $35.00.

DOBYNS, Stephen. *Saratoga Snapper.* 1986. Viking Penguin. 1st. NF/dj. A14. $28.00.

DOBYNS, Stephen. *The Church of Dead Girls.* 1997. Metropolitan. ARC. F in decor wrp. M25. $25.00.

DOCKSTADER, Frederick J. *American Indian in Graduate Studies.* 1973. NY. 2nd. 362p. VG. M8. $45.00.

DOCTOROW, E. L. *Billy Bathgate.* 1989. NY. Random House. 1st trade. VG+/VG. R16. $25.00.

DOCTOROW, E. L. *Lives of the Poets.* 1984. NY. Random House. 1st. sgn. F/F. D10. $60.00.

DOCTOROW, E. L. *Loon Lake.* 1980. NY. Random House. sgn by author on tipped in leaf. F in F dj. B2. $75.00.

DOCTOROW, E. L. *Ragtime.* 1974. Random House. ltd ed. 1 of 150 sgn & # copies. F in slipcase. M25. $200.00.

DOCTOROW, E. L. *Ragtime.* 1974. NY. Random House. 1st. NF/VG+. A24. $50.00.

DOCTOROW, E. L. *Waterworks.* 1994. Random House. 1st. sgn. VF/VF. M25. $100.00.

DOCTOROW, E. L. *World's Fair.* 1985. NY. Random House. 1st. VG/VG. R16. $30.00.

DODD, C. H. *The Interpretation of the Fourth Gospel.* 1954. Cambridge. 478p. VG. B29. $16.00.

DODD, C. H. *The Moffatt Commentary: Romans.* nd. Harper. 246p. VG/VG. ex lib. B29. $13.00.

DODDS, Baby, and Larry Gara. *The Baby Dodds Story.* 1959. Los Angeles. Contemporary. 1st. wrps. NF. B2. $40.00.

DODGE, Bertha S. *It Started in Eden. How the Plant Hunters & Plants They Found Changed the Course of History.* 1979. NY. 288p. NF in dj w/closed tear. B26. $26.00.

DODGE, Bertha S. *Plants that Changed the World.* 1959. Boston. 1st ed. 183p w/ils at chapter heads. VG in dj. B26. $24.00.

DODGE, Bertha S. *Potatoes & People.* 1970. Boston. 1st. 190p. VG/dj. B26. $15.00.

DODGE, David. *The Crazy Glasspecker.* 1949. NY. Random House. 1st. F/NF dj. M19. $25.00.

DODGE, David. *Troubleshooter.* 1971. NY. Macmillan. 1st. F/dj. M15. $45.00.

DODGE, Ernest. *New England & the South Seas.* 1965. Cambridge. 1st. 216p. gr cloth. F/dj. P4. $40.00.

DODGE, Jim. *Fup.* 1984. NY. S&S. 1st. F/F. D10. $45.00.

DODGE, Jim. *Stone Junction.* 1990. NY. Atlantic Monthly. 1st. F. D10. $10.00.

DODGE, Mary A. *Gail Hamilton's Life in Letters.* 1901. Lee Shepard. 2 vol. 1st. 8vo. VG. A2. $50.00.

DODGE, Mary Mapes. *Hans Brinker; or, The Silver Skates.* 1917. Phil. McKay. 1st thus. ils Maginel Wright Enright. 345p. gray cloth. $0.00.

DODGE, Richard Irving. *Our Wild Indians: 33 Years' Personal Experience.* 1885. Hartford. 653p. G+. B18. $95.00.

DODGE & DODGE. *Making Miniatures in ¹⁄₁₂ Scale.* UK. 1991. photos/diagrams. VG/dj. M17. $15.00.

DODGE & RATNER. *Baking with Jim Dodge.* S&S. 1991. 1st. F/dj. V4. $25.00.

DODGSON, Campbell. *Old French Colour Prints.* 1924. London. Halton Truscott. 1/1250. NF. B20. $85.00.

DODSLEY, Robert. *Collection of Poems by Several Hands.* 1775. London. Dodsley. 6 vol. sm 8vo. full polished mottled calf. H13. $295.00.

DODSLEY, Robert. *Toy-Shop: A Dramatick Satire.* 1735. London. Prt for Lawton Gulliver at Homer's Head. 5th. 46p. B14. $95.00.

DODSON, Kenneth. *Away All Boats.* 1954. np. Little, Brn. 1st. VG/G dj. M19. $25.00.

DOERFLINGER, Thomas M. *Vigorous Spirit of Enterprise: Merchants & Economic.* 1986. Norton. VG. M10. $12.50.

DOERR, Harriet. *Consider This, Senora.* 1993. NY. Harcourt. 1st. sgn. Jacket Is price clipped. F/F. H11. $55.00.

DOERR, Harriet. *Stones for Ibarra.* 1984. Viking. 1st. author's 1st novel. F/dj. B4. $85.00.

DOERR, Harriet. *Stones for Ibarra.* (1985). London. Andre Deutsch. 1st British ed. author's 1st book. F/F. B3. $50.00.

DOERR, Harriet. *Tiger in the Grass.* 1995. Viking. ARC. sgn/dtd 1997. F/dj. R14. $65.00.

DOESTOEVKSKY, Fyodor. *Notebooks for Crime & Punishment.* 1967. Chicago. hc. VG/dj. B9. $15.00.

DOHERTY, Hugh. *False Association and its Remedy; or, A Critical Introduction to the Late Charles Fourier's Theory of Attractive Industry, and the Moral Harmony of the Passions, to Which Is Prefixed a Memoir of Fourier.* 1841. London. Published at the Office of the London Phalanx. 8vo. 167. (1)p. gr cloth. 1st. some lt contemporary pencil underlining on a few p in an early chapter. VG. L5. $475.00.

DOHERTY, P. C. *A Tapestry of Murder.* 1996. NY. St. Martin. 1st Am ed. VF/VF. T2. $20.00.

DOHERTY, P. C. *An Ancient Evil.* 1995. NY. St. Martin. 1st Am ed. VF/VF. T2. $20.00.

DOHERTY, P. C. *Satan's Fire.* 1996. NY. St. Martin. 1st Am ed. VF/VF. T2. $20.00.

DOHERTY, P. C. *The Serpent Amongst the Lilies.* 1990. NY. St. Martin. 1st Am ed. NF. bumping to extremities/F. B3. $15.00.

DOHERTY, P. C. *The Song of a Dark Angel.* 1995. NY. St. Martin. 1st Am ed. VF/VF. T2. $20.00.

DOHERTY, Paul. *The Demon Archer.* 1999. London. Headline. 1st. sgn. VF/VF. T2. $40.00.

DOHERTY, Paul. *The Field of Blood.* 1999. London. Headline. 1st. sgn. VF/VF. T2. $38.00.

DOHERTY, Paul. *The Horus Killings.* 1999. London. Headline. 1st. sgn. VF/VF. T2. $40.00.

DOHERTY, Paul. *The Soul Slayer.* 1998. London. Headline. 1st. sgn. VF/VF. T2. $38.00.

DOHERTY, Robert W. *Hicksite Separation: Sociological Analysis.* 1967. Rutgers. 157p. VG/G. V3. $25.00.

DOHERTY, Terence. *The Anatomical Works of George Stubbs.* 1975. Boston. Godine. 1s Am ed. folio. color ils. 345p. VG. O3. $95.00

DOIG, Ivan. *Bucking the Sun.* 1996. S&S. 1st F/dj. O11/R14. $25.00.

DOIG, Ivan. *Bucking the Sun.* 1996. S&S. ARC. VF/decor wrps. M25. $35.00.

DOIG, Ivan. *Dancing at the Rascal Fair.* 1987. NY. Atheneum. 1st. inscr & sgn. F/clip dj M25. $50.00.

DOIG, Ivan. *English Creek.* 1984. Atheneum. 1st. sgn. F/NF. O11. $55.00.

DOIG, Ivan. *English Creek.* (1984). NY. Atheneum. 1st. F/F. B3. $75.00.

DOIG, Ivan. *Heart Earth.* 1993. NY. Atheneum. 1st. sgn. F/F. M25. $45.00.

DOIG, Ivan. *This House of Sky.* 1978. Harcourt Brace. 1st. inscr. 314p. F/NF. B20. $225.00.

DOIG, Ivan. *This House of Sky.* 1978. Harcourt. 1st. poi on ffep. NF/chipped. torn dj. lightly sunned on spine. M25. $60.00.

DOIG, Ivan. *Winter Brothers.* 1980. HBJ. 1st. NF/clip dj. M25. $75.00.

DOIG, Ivan. *Winter Brothers. A Season at the Edge of America.* 1980. NY. HBJ. 1st. author's 2nd book. F/F. D10. $95.00.

DOLCI, Danilo. *Man Who Plays Alone.* 1968. Pantheon. 1st Am. 8vo. VG/dj. A2. $12.50.

DOLD, Gaylord. *The Devil to Pay.* 1999. NY. St. Martin. 1st. sgn. VF/VF. T2. $25.00.

DOLD, Gaylord. *World Beat.* 1993. St. Martin. 1st. NF/NF. G8. $12.50.

DOLE, Charles. *The Burden of Poverty.* 1912. NY. Huebsch. 1st. inscr "compliments of the author." VG. B2. $40.00.

DOLINGER, Glenna Louise. *Dr. Thomas Walker, Father of Kentucky.* 1950. private prt. fld map. VG. B10. $35.00.

DOLLARD, John. *Caste & Class in a Southern Town.* 1937. OUP. 502p. blk cloth. VG. G1. $75.00.

DOLLARD, John. *Victory Over Fear.* 1942. Reynal Hitchcock. thick 12mo. inscr. 213p+3p. gray cloth. G1. $75.00.

DOLMAN, D. H. *Simple Talks on the Tabernacle.* 1954. Zondervan. 223p. VG. B29. $8.00.

DOLNICK, Amy. *Between Deep Valley & the Great World: Maud Hart Lovelace.* 1993. Twin Cities. Betsy-Tacy Soc. 1st. 38p. S14. $8.00.

DOLPH, Jack. *Hot Tip.* 1951. Doubleday Crime Club. 1st. VG/dj. M15. $35.00.

DOLPH, Jack. *Murder Is Mutual.* 1948. NY. Morrow. 1st. F/VG. M15. $40.00.

DOLSON, H. *Great Oildorado: Gaudy & Turbulent Years of 1st Oil Rush.* 1959. NY. ils/maps. 406p. NF. M4. $23.00.

DOMES, Jurgen. *China After the Cultural Revolution.* 1977 (1975). Berkeley. 1st Am. 8vo. F/dj. A2. $25.00.

DOMINICK, Mabel A. *Bible & Historical Design: A Perspective.* 1961 (1936). Plimpton. 9th. ils. F/VG. A2. $12.00.

DONAHEY, Mary Dickerson. *Down Spider Web Lane.* 1909. Barse Hopkins. 1st. 130p. bl cloth/paper label. NF. B20. $75.00.

DONAHEY, William. *Teenie Weenie Neighbors.* (1945). Whittlesey House. 1st. 8vo. mc pict brd. R5. $175.00.

DONALD, Anabel. *In at the Deep End.* 1994. NY. St. Martin. 1st. NF/VG. G8. $10.00.

DONALD, David. *Charles Sumner & the Rights of Man.* 1970. Knopf. 1st. NF/VG. A14. $28.00.

DONALDSON, Alfred L. *History of the Adirondacks.* Vol 1. 1977. Harrison. Harbor Hill. maps/photos. 383p. F/dj. A17. $25.00.

DONALDSON, D. J. *No Mardi Gras for the Dead.* 1992. St. Martin. 1st. F/F. G8. $30.00.

DONALDSON, Henry Herbert. *Growth of the Brain.* 1895. London. Walter Scott Ltd/ Scribner. 1st. 12mo. 374p. cloth. Xl. $1.00.

DONALDSON, J. *Real Pretend.* 1992. Checkerboard. 1st. obl 8vo. F/dj. B17. $45.00.

DONALDSON, Norman. *In Search of Dr. Thorndyke: The Story of R. Austin Freeman's Great Scientific Investigator and His Creator.* 1998. Shelburne. Ontario. battered silicon dispatch box. revised ed. 1st thus. VF/VF. T2. $28.00.

DONALDSON, Stephen R. *Gap Into Conflict: The Real Story.* 1991. NY. Bantam. 1st Am trade. sgn. F/NF. G10. $27.00.

DONALDSON, Stephen R. *Gilden-Fire.* 1983. London. Collins. 1st thus. ils Peter Goodfellow. VG+/dj. A14. $17.50.

DONALDSON, Stephen R. *Mirror of Her Dreams.* 1986. Ballantine/Del Rey. 1st. sm 4to. 642p. F. H11/W2. $25.00.

DONALDSON, Stephen R. *One Tree.* 1982. Del Rey/Ballantine. 1st. Chronicles of Thomas Covenant #2. VG+/dj. A14. $21.00.

DONALDSON, Stephen R. *The One Tree.* 1982. NY. Ballantine/Del Rey. 1st. sgn. VF/VF. T2. $25.00.

DONALDSON, Thomas. *George Catlin Indian Gallery in the US National Museum.* 1887. GPO. thick 8vo. 144 #d maps/pl. 939p. cloth. O1. $300.00.

DONALDSON & ROYCE. *Affair to Remember: My Life with Cary Grant.* Putnam. 1989. 1st. F/dj. T12. $20.00.

DONASO, Jose. *The Obscene Bird of Night.* 1973. NY. Knopf. 1st Am ed. NF. D10. $75.00.

DONAT, Peter C. & Barney Gould. *Sherlock Holmes and the Shakespeare Solution: A Play in Two Acts.* 1997. Shelburne, Ontario. battered silicon dispatch box. 1st. VF/VF. T2. $24.00.

DONIA & FINE. *Bosnia & Hercegovina: Tradition Betrayed.* Columbia. 2nd. ils. F/dj. A2. $18.00.

DONLEAVY, J. P. *The Saddest Summer of Samuel S.* 1966. np. np. 1st. F/VG dj. M19. $25.00.

DONLEAVY, J. P. *Wrong Information Is Being Given Out at Princeton.* 1998. NY. St. Martin. ARC. wrps. F. B2. $35.00.

DONNELLY, Elfie. *Offbeat Friends.* 1982. Crown. 1st Am. 119p. NF/clip. C14. $14.00.

DONNELLY, Liza. *Dinosaurs' Halloween.* 1987. Scholastic. 1st. sq 8vo. unp. NF/NF. T5. $30.00.

DONNELLY, Ralph W. *Biographical Sketches of the Commissioned Officers of the Confederate States Marine Corps.* 1973. Washington, DC. by author. 1st. ltd ed of 300 copies. orig stiff printed wrp. VG. M8. $150.00.

DONNELLY, Ralph W. *Confederate States Marine Corps: Rebel Leathernecks.* 1989. Wht Mane Pub. 1st. NF/dj. A14. $21.00.

DONOGHUE, Denis. *Lover of Strange Souls.* 1995. NY. 1st. dj. T9. $15.00.

DONOHUE, Phil. *Donohue: My Own Story.* 1979. S&S. 1st. sgn. NF/VG. W2. $30.00.

DONOSO, Jose. *House in the Country.* 1984. London. Allen Lane. 1st. NF/dj. A14. $21.00.

DONOSO, Jose. *The Garden Next Door.* 1992. NY. Grove Press. 1st English language ed. F/F. A24. $20.00.

DONOVAN, Dick. *Chronicles of Michael Danevitch.* 1897. London. Chatto Windus. 1st. silvered bl cloth. NF. M15. $100.00.

DONOVAN, Dick. *In the Face of Night.* 1908. London. John Long. 1st. dk bl pict cloth. VG. M15. $100.00.

DONOVAN, Frank. *Unlucky Hero.* 1963. NY. 1st. 179p. VG/dj. E1. $25.00.

DONOVAN, Professor. *US Army Physical Exercises Revised.* (1902). Street Smith. sm 8vo. 130p. VG. H1. $12.00.

DONOVAN, Robert J. *Tumultuous Years.* 1982. Norton. 1st. sm 4to. 444p. VG/F. W2. $25.00.

DOODY, Margaret. *Aristotle Detective.* 1978. London. Bodley Head. 1st. F/dj. M15. $65.00.

DOOLIN, William. *Wayfarers in Medicine.* 1949. London. 1st. 284p. A13. $30.00.

DOOLING, Richard. *White Man's Grave.* 1994. FSG. 1st. F/dj. M23. $25.00.

DOOLITTLE, Jerome. *Body Scissors.* 1990. Pocket. 1st. F/NF. H11. $20.00.

DOOLITTLE, Jerome. *Bombing Officer.* 1982. Dutton. 1st. F/dj. R11. $25.00.

DOOLITTLE, Jerome. *Half Nelson.* 1994. NY. Pocket. 1st. VF/VF. H11. $25.00.

DOOLITTLE, Jerome. *Head Lock.* 1993. NY. Pocket. 1st. Remainder mark. F/F. H11. $20.00.

DOOLITTLE, Jerome. *Strangle Hold.* 1991. Pocket. 1st. F/F. H11. $25.00.

DOOLY, William G. *Great Weapons of World War II.* 1969. Bonanza. rpt. ils. VG. E1. $35.00.

DOPAGNE, Jacques. *Dali.* 1974. Leon Amiel. 1st. VG/dj. P3. $15.00.

DORAN, Dave. *Highway of Hunger: Story of America's Homeless Youth.* 1933. Workers Lib/Young Worker. 1st. VG/wrp. B2. $30.00.

DORESS, Paula Brown. *Ourselves, Growing Older.* 1987. NY. S&S. 1st pb ed. VG. A28. $9.50.

DORF, Philip. *Liberty Hyde Bailey.* 1956. Ithaca. 1st. ils. AN/dj. B26. $22.50.

DORFLES, Gillo. *Kitsch: World of Bad Taste.* 1973. Bell. photos. VG/dj. C9. $60.00.

DORIAN, Edith. *Ask Dr. Christmas.* 1951. Whittlesey. 1st. ils Nora Unwin. VG/dj. M5. $28.00.

DORIN, Patrick C. *The Grand Trunk Western Railroad, A Canadian National Railway.* 1977. Seattle. Superior. 1st. brds. ils. VG in dj w/lt edgewear. B18. $35.00.

DORN, Edward. *Geography.* (1968). London. Fulcrum. 1st Eng. F/VG. A18. $35.00.

DORN, Edward. *North Atlantic Turbine.* (1967). London. Fulcrum. 1st Eng. map ep. F/VG. A18. $35.00.

DORN, William S. *The Parlour Games of Sherlock Holmes: Exercises in Logic.* 1996. Shelburne. Ontario. Battered Silicon Dispatch Box. 1st. VF/pict wrp. T2. $8.00.

DORNBUSCH, Charles E. *Military Bibliography of the Civil War, 1961 – 72.* NY Public Lib. 3 vol in 9. 1st. VG. M8. $250.00.

DORNBUSCH, Charles E. *Military Bibliography of the Civil War, Volume 2.* 1967. NY. 1st. VG/prt wrp. M8. $45.00.

DORR, Frank I. *Hayseed & Sawdust.* 1934. Boston. Wormsted Smith. 8vo. ils. 228p. red brd. VG. $11.00.

DORRIE, Doris. *Love, Pain, and the Whole Damn Thing.* 1989. NY. Knopf. 1st Am ed. F/F. A24. $20.00.

DORRIS, Michael. *A Yellow Raft in Blue Water.* (1987). NY. Henry Holt. 1st. sgn by author. author's 1st novel. F/F. B3. $100.00.

DORRIS, Michael. *Broken Cord.* 1989. Harper Row. 1st. F/F. B3. $40.00.

DORRIS, Michael. *Broken Cord.* 1989. Harper Row. 1st. sgn. NF/NF. R14. $75.00.

DORRIS, Michael. *Morning Girl.* 1992. NY. Hyperion. 1st. author's 1st children's book. sgn. F/F. O11. $45.00.

DORRIS, Michael. *Sees Behind Trees.* 1996. NY. Hyperion. 1st. sgn. F/F. O11. $35.00.

DORRIS, Michael. *Working Men.* (1993). NY. Henry Holt. 1st. sgn by author. VF/VF. B3. $35.00.

DORRIS, Michael. *Yellow Raft in Blue Water.* 1987. Holt. 1st. inscr/sgn. author's 1st book. F/dj. B4. $150.00.

DORRIS & ERDRICH. *Crown of Columbus.* Harper Collins. 1991. 1st. sgn. F/F. B3. $60.00.

DORSEY, F. *Master of the Mississippi.* 1941. Boston. 1st. VG/G. B5. $45.00.

DORSHEIMER, William. *Life & Public Services of Hon Grover Cleveland.* 1884. Russell Henderson. 8vo. 575p. bl cloth. G. $17.00.

DORSON, Richard. *America Begins.* 1950. Pantheon. 438p. AN/dj. A10. $18.00.

DORST, Jean. *Before Nature Dies.* 1970. Houghton Mifflin. 1st. ils. 352p. xl. VG. S14. $8.00.

DORST, Jean. *South America and Central America: A Natural History.* 1967. Random. 1st. 298p. VG/dj. M12. $30.00.

DOS PASSOS, John. *A Pushcart at the Curb.* 1922. Doran. 1st. 1/1313. VG. D10. $75.00.

DOS PASSOS, John. *A Pushcart at the Curb.* 1922. NY. Doran. 1st. NF. D10. $65.00.

DOS PASSOS, John. *Garbage Man: A Parade with Shouting.* 1926. Harper. 1st. 1/1000. 1st state bdg. NF/dj. Q1. $200.00.

DOS PASSOS, John. *Grand Design.* 1949. Houghton Mifflin. 1st. VG/VG. H11. $40.00.

DOS PASSOS, John. *Midcentury.* 1961. Andre Deutsch. VG/G. M19. $17.50.

DOS PASSOS, John. *Number One.* 1943. Houghton Mifflin. 1st. NF/VG. A24. $60.00.

DOS PASSOS, John. *State of the Nation.* 1944. Houghton Mifflin. 1st. inscr. NF/dj. L3. $550.00.

DOSKOW, Ambrose. *Historic Opinions of the United States Supreme Court.* 1935. NY. Vanguard. blk cloth. M11. $250.00.

DOSS, James D. *The Night Visitor.* 1999. NY. Avon Books. 1st. sgn. VF/VF. T2. $25.00.

DOSS, James D. *The Shaman Laughs.* (1995). NY. St. Martin. 1st. author's 2nd book. sgn by author. F/F. B3. $35.00.

DOSS, James D. *The Shaman's Bones.* (1997). NY. St. Martin. 1st. sgn by author. F/F. B3. $20.00.

DOTY, Robert. *Photography in America.* 1974. Random. 1st. 4to. 255p. VG/NF. B20. $35.00.

DOUGHERTY, James. *Secret Happiness of Marilyn Monroe.* 1976. Playboy. 1st thus. photos. VG/wrp. C9. $90.00.

DOUGHERTY, Raymond Philip. *Records From Erech: Time of Nabonidus.* 1920. OUP/Yale. ils/84 pl. 47p. cloth. VG+. Q2. $20.00.

DOUGHTY, Paul. *Huaylas. An Andean District in Search of Progress.* 1968. Ithaca. Cornell Univ Press. 1st. 284p. G/chipped dj. F3. $15.00.

DOUGHTY, Robert A. *Breaking Point: Sedan & the Fall of France.* 1940. 1990. Hamden, CT. 1st. maps. F/dj. A2. $25.00.

DOUGLAS, Amanda M. *Kathie's Aunt Ruth.* 1912. Lee Shepard. ils C Howard. 257p. VG. P12. $25.00.

DOUGLAS, Amanda M. *Red House Children's Vacation.* 1914. Lee Shepard. 1st. 8vo. VG. M5. $10.00.

DOUGLAS, Bruce. *New Bible Dictionary.* 1982. Tyndale. 1326p. G/G. B29. $17.50.

DOUGLAS, Byrd. *Steamboatin' on the Cumberland.* 1961. Nashville. TN Book Co. ils. 407p. gray cloth. F1. $25.00.

DOUGLAS, Carole Nelson. *Cat in a Flamingo Fedora.* 1997. Forge. 1st. sgn. F/F. G8. $20.00.

DOUGLAS, Carole Nelson. *Cat with an Emerald Eye.* 1996. Forge. 1st. sgn. F/NF. G8. $22.50.

DOUGLAS, Carole Nelson. *Catnap.* 1992. NY. Tor. 1st. sgn. F/F. A24. $30.00.

DOUGLAS, Carole Nelson. *Irene at Large.* 1992. NY. Tor. 1st. sgn. F/VG+. A24. $25.00.

DOUGLAS, Carole Nelson. *Pussyfoot.* 1993. NY. Tor. 1st. sgn. F/F. A24. $25.00.

DOUGLAS, Drake. *Horrors!* 1989. Woodstock, NY. Overlook. 1st. 418p. F/NF. M21. $20.00.

DOUGLAS, Henry Kyd. *I Rode with Stonewall: War Experiences.* nd. Chapel Hill. 1st/12th imp. NF/clip. A14. $28.00.

DOUGLAS, Kirk. *The Gift.* 1992. Warner Books. ne. inscr. F/chip dj. S19. $30.00.

DOUGLAS, Lloyd C. *Big Fisherman.* 1959. Random. unp. VG. C5. $12.50.

DOUGLAS, Lloyd C. *Magnificent Obsession.* 1929. Grosset Dunlap. ne. 330p. VG. W2. $25.00.

DOUGLAS, Marjory Stoneman. *Hurricane.* 1976. Atlanta. Mockingbird. revised ed. photo ils. 8vo. 119p. G in wrp. K5. $8.00.

DOUGLAS, Roy. *Who Is Nemo?* 1937. Philadelphia. JB Lippencott. 1st Am ed. VG/dj some wear. M15. $75.00.

DOUGLAS, Stephen Arnold. *Admission of Kansas Under Wyandott Constitution.* 1860. WA. Lemuel Towers. 1st. dbl-column text. $8.00.

DOUGLAS, William O. *Democracy's Manifesto: Counter Plan for Free Society.* 1962. Doubleday. 1st. VG/dj. B9. $15.00.

DOUGLAS, William O. *My Wilderness: The Pacific West.* 1960. Doubleday. sgn Frances Lee Jaques. 206p. VG. J2. $40.00.

DOUGLAS, William O. *Russian Journey.* 1956. Doubleday. 1st. ils. 255p. G/dj. S14. $5.00.

DOUGLASS, Barbara. *Good as New.* 1982. Lee Shepard. 1st Am. sm 4to. wht pict brd. VG/G+. T5. $30.00.

DOUGLASS, Donald Mcnutt. *Rebecca's Pride.* 1956. NY. Harper & Brothers. 1st. Jacket has wear along edges. at corners and at spine ends. F/VG. M15. $65.00.

DOURNOVO, Lydia A. *Armenian Miniatures.* 1961. Abrams. 1st. thick 4to. 181+7p. F/NF. O10. $115.00.

DOVE, Rita. *On the Bus with Rosa Parks.* 1999. NY. Norton. 1st. sgn. F in F dj. D10. $35.00.

DOVE, Rita. *Through the Ivory Gate.* 1992. NY. Pantheon. author's 1st novel. sgn. F in dj. D10. $50.00.

DOW, George Francis. *Slave Ships & Slaving.* 1927. Salem. 1st. 349p. G. B5. $100.00.

DOW, Lorenzo. *History of Cosmopolite; or 4 Vols of Lorenzo Dow's Journal.* 1848. VA. Joshua Martin. 720p. G+. B18. $75.00.

DOWD, James Patrick. *Custer Lives.* 1982. Ye Galleon. F/dj. A19. $35.00.

DOWDEY, Clifford. *Death of a Nation: Story of Lee & His Men at Gettysburg.* (1958). Knopf. 1st. 383p. VG/dj. B10. $35.00.

DOWELL, Coleman. *Silver Swanne.* 1983. NY. Grenfell. 1/115. sgn. Claudia Cohen bdg. F. F1. $175.00.

DOWLING, Gregory. *Nice Steady Job.* 1994. St. Martin. 1st. NF/VF. G8. $12.50.

DOWLING, Noel T. *Cases on Constitutional Law.* 1950. Foundation Pr. M11. $25.00.

DOWLING, William C. *Language & Logos in Boswell's Life of Johnson.* 1981. Princeton. 1st. dj. H13. $45.00.

DOWMAN, Keith. *Masters of Enchantment: Lives & Legends of Mahasiddhas.* 1988. Rochester, VT. ils Robert Beers. VG/dj. M17. $25.00.

DOWNER, Jane. *Happy Dieter.* 1974. Regional Ent. G. A16. $10.00.

DOWNES, Stephen. *New Compleat Angler.* 1984. London. Orbis. 4to. ils. NF/dj. M10. $16.50.

DOWNEY, F. *Texas & The War With Mexico.* 1961. Am Heritage Jr Lib. 1st. ils. 153p. NF. M4. $20.00.

DOWNEY, Fairfax. *Dog of War.* 1943. NY. Dodd Mead. 1st. ils by Paul Brown. VG/G. O3. $38.00.

DOWNEY, Fairfax. *Dog of War.* 1943. NY. Dodd Mead. 1st. ils by Paul Brown. VG/cover stained. O3. $25.00.

DOWNEY, John F. *The New Revelation through the Spectroscope and the Telescope.* 1914. NY. Abingdon. 8vo. 87p. VG in cloth. K5. $30.00.

DOWNING, Elliot R. *Naturalist in the Great Lakes Region.* 1922. Chicago. 2nd. 328p. VG. A17. $20.00.

DOWNING, G. *Massage Book.* 1972. Esalen Inst. 4to. VG/G. E6. $15.00.

DOWNING, Todd. *The Mexican Earth.* 1940. NY. Doubleday. 1st. ils by Howard Willard. ep maps. 337p. G. F3. $15.00.

DOYLE, A. Conan. *A Duet with an Occasional Chorus.* 1990. Bloomington. Gaslight Publications. reissue. 1st thus. VF/no dj as issued. T2. $15.00.

DOYLE, A. Conan. *Beyond the City: The Idyll of a Suburb.* 1982. Bloomington. Gaslight Publications. reissue. 1st thus. VF/no dj as issued. T2. $15.00.

DOYLE, A. Conan. *The Doings of Raffles Haw.* 1981. Bloomington. Gaslight Publications. reissue. 1st thus. VF/no dj as issued. T2. $15.00.

DOYLE, A. Conan. *The Stark Munro Letters.* 1982. Bloomington. Gaslight Publications. reissue. 1st thus. VF/no dj as issued. T2. $15.00.

DOYLE, Arthur Conan. *Adventures of Sherlock Holmes.* 1892. NY. 1st/later prt. VG. M17. $40.00.

DOYLE, Arthur Conan. *Conan Doyle Stories.* (1960). Platt Munk. 8vo. 494p. gilt cloth. VG/dj. M7. $20.00.

DOYLE, Arthur Conan. *Croxley Master.* (1925). NY. Doran. 1st Am. VG/dj. M15. $125.00.

DOYLE, Arthur Conan. *Great Boer War.* nd. London. Thos Nelson. 575p. gilt bl cloth. VG. M7. $35.00.

DOYLE, Arthur Conan. *Hound of the Baskervilles.* 1902. McClure Phillips. 1st Am. G. P3. $100.00.

DOYLE, Arthur Conan. *Rodney Stone.* 1896. NY. Appleton. gilt decor brd. G. V4. $25.00.

DOYLE, Arthur Conan. *Stories For Boys.* ca 1938. Cupples Leon. 1st. ils. VG+. S18. $15.00.

DOYLE, Arthur Conan. *Study in Scarlet.* 1985. Peerage. VG/dj. P3. $20.00.

DOYLE, Arthur Conan. *Tragedy of the Korosko.* 1898. London. Smith Elder. 1st. 8vo. 326p. gilt maroon cloth. VG+. $20.00.

DOYLE, Roddy. *The Commitments.* 1989. NY. Vintage Contemporaries. 1st Am ed. PBO. author's 1st book. poi. F in pict wrp. D10. $55.00.

DOYLE, Roddy. *The Woman Who Walked into Doors.* 1996. London. Jonathan Cape. 1st. F in f dj. D10. $45.00.

DOYLE, Roddy. *Van.* 1992. Viking Penguin. 1st Am. sgn. F/dj. O11. $75.00.

DOYLE, William B. *Centennial History of Summit County.* Ohio. 1908. Chicago. 1st. 1115p. aeg. rb buckram. VG. $18.00.

DOZOIS, Gardner. *Geodesic Dreams: The Best Short Fiction of Gardner Dozois.* 1992. NY. St. Martin. 1st. VF/VF. T2. $9.00.

DR, A; see Asimov, Isaac.

DR. SEUSS; see Geisel, Theodore Seuss.

DRACHMAN, Virginia. *Hospital with a Heart: Women Doctors & Paradox.* 1984. Ithaca. 1st. 258p. A13. $40.00.

DRACO, F. *Devil's Church.* 1951. NY. Rinehart. 1st. VG/VG. G8. $20.00.

DRAGOO, Don W. *Mounds for the Dead: An Analysis of the Adena Culture.* 1963. Pittsburgh. Annals of Carnegie Museum. photos. lt soiling. ep foxed. 315p. VG. B18. $45.00.

DRAKE, Benjamin. *Great Indian Chief of the West; or, Life and Adventures of Black Hawk.* 1854. Cincinnati. later ed. ils. cover spotted w/ some fading. sprung sgn. foxing. 288p. G. B18. $75.00.

DRAKE, Benjamin. *Life of Tecumseh & His Brother the Prophet.* 1852. Cincinnati. 235p. G. B18. $65.00.

DRAKE, Charles D. *Labour Law, Third Edition.* 1981. London. Sweet Maxwell. 278p. prt sewn wrp. M11. $15.00.

DRAKE, Daniel. *Pioneer Life in Kentucky.* 1948. NY. 1st. 257p. A13. $50.00.

DRAKE, David. *Fortress.* 1987. NY. Tor. 1st. F/VF. T2. $8.00.

DRAKE, Samuel Adams. *Old Landmarks and Historic Personages of Boston.* 1900. Boston. Little, Brn. gilt & pict cloth. ils. lt wear to cover. 484p. G+. B18. $25.00.

DRAPER, Lyman C. *King's Mountain and Its Heroes: History of the Battle of King's Mountain, Oct 7th, 1780.* 1954. Mariella, GA. later printing. gilt decor cloth. ils. pub letter. F. pict bdg. B18. $125.00.

DRAPER, Robert. *Hadrian's Walls.* 1999. NY. Knopf. 1st. author's 1st novel. sgn. VF/VF. T2. $25.00.

DREADSTONE, Carl; See Campbell, Ramsey.

DREIKURS, Rudolf. *Children: The Challenge.* 1964. Hawthorn. 335p. VG/G. B29. $5.50.

DREISER, Theodore. *Dreiser Looks at Russia.* 1928. NY. Horace Liveright. 1st. octavo. blk cloth stp in red & gilt. NF/faded. R3. $40.00.

DREISER, Theodore. *Hand of the Potter.* 1918. NY. Boni Liveright. 1st. F. B2. $100.00.

DREISER, Theodore. *Notes on Life.* 1974. Univ of Alabama. Univ Press. octavo. blk cloth. gilt stp spine. dj. F. R3. $25.00.

DREISER, Theodore. *The Bulwark.* 1946. Doubleday & Co. 1st. G. S19. $35.00.

DREW, Thomas. *John Brown Invasion: An Authentic History of Harper's Ferry.* 1860. Boston. James Campbell. 1st. M24. $450.00.

DREYER, Eileen. *Man to Die For.* nd. Severn House. 1st British ed. VG/VG. G8. $10.00.

DREYER, Peter. *Gardner Touched with Genius: Life of Luther Burbank.* 1975. CMG. 1st. ils/biblio/index. 322p. VG. H10. $20.00.

DRIGGS & LEWINE. *Black Beauty, White Heat.* 1982. Morrow. 1st. 4to. F/dj. B2. $200.00.

DRIMMER, Frederick. *Very Special People.* 1973. Amjon. 1st. NF/VG. S18. $20.00.

DRINKARD, Michael. *Green Bananas.* 1989. NY. Knopf. 1st. author's 1st novel. F/F. A24. $32.00.

DRINKLE, Ruth Wolfley. *Heritage of Architecture & Arts.* (1994). Fairfield Heritage Assn. 2nd/revised. 186p. pict brd. VG/dj. B18. $25.00.

DRINKWATER, John. *Life & Adventures of Carl Laemmle.* 1931. London. Heinemann. 1st. photos. VG/dj. C9. $150.00.

DRINKWATER, John. *Lincoln the World Emancipator.* 1920. Boston/NY. Houghton Mifflin Co. 1st. 4th printing. orig paper covered bds. 118p. NF/VG. M8. $45.00.

DROSCHER, Vitus B. *They Love & Kill.* 1976. NY. ils. VG/dj. M17. $20.00.

DRUCKER, Mary J. *Rubber Industry in Ohio.* 1937. Occupational Study 1. 1st. 76p. prt wrp. B18. $25.00.

DRUCKER, Philip. *Native Brotherhoods: Modern International Organizations.* 1958. GPO. BAE Bulletin #168. 8vo. 194p. olive cloth. NF. P4. $45.00.

DRUETT, Joan. *She Was a Sister Sailor: Whaling Journals of Mary Brewster.* 1992. Mystic Seaport Mus. 1st. 449p. AN/dj. P4. $40.00.

DRUMMOND, Henry. *Natural Law in the Spiritual World.* nd. Altemus. 371p. VG/case. B29. $20.00.

DRUMMOND, Henry. *Tropical Africa.* 1888. NY. Humboldt. woodcuts. 68p. VG. H7. $12. $50.00.

DRUMMOND, Ivor. *Frog in the Moonflower.* 1972. St. Martin. 1st Am ed. VG/G. G8. $10.00.

DRUMMOND, June. *I Saw Him Die.* 1979. Gollancz. 1st British ed. NF/NF. G8. $12.50.

DRUMMOND, June. *Patriots.* 1979. Gollancz. 1st British ed. NF/NF. G8. $12.50.

DRUMMOND, Walter; See Silverberg, Robert.

DRURY, Allen. *Decision.* 1983. Doubleday. VG/dj. P3. $15.00.

DRURY, Allen. *Decision.* 1983. Franklin Lib. ltd 1st. sgn. gr leather. F. A24. $40.00.

DRURY, Allen. *Preserve & Protect.* 1968. Doubleday. 1st. G/dj. A28. $10.00.

DRURY, Heber. *Useful Plants of India.* 1985 (1873). Dehra Dun. 2nd/rpt. 512p. dj. B26. $15.00.

DRURY, Tom. *End of Vandalism.* 1994. Houghton Mifflin. 1st. F/dj. A24. $40.00.

DRUSE, Ken. *Collector's Garden: Designing with Extraordinary Plants.* 1996. NY. Clarkson Potter. ils/index. 248p. VG/dj. H10. $25.00.

DRUSE, Ken. *Natural Shade Garden.* 1992. NY. Clarkson Potter. 4to. 238p. VG/dj. H10. $22.50.

DRYDENK, James. *Poultry Breeding & Management.* 1928. Orange Judd. 402p. cloth. VG. A10. $20.00.

DRYSDALE, Don. *Once a Bum, Always a Dodger.* 1990. NY. St. Martin. 1st. NF/VG. R16. $20.00.

DTLENSCHNEIDER, Robert L. *Power & Influence.* 1990. Prentice Hall. 1st. 8vo. 258p. F/dj. W2. $30.00.

DU BOIS, William Pene. *Gentleman Bear.* 1985. FSG. 1st. F/NF. T11. $30.00.

DU BOIS, William Pene. *Giant.* 1954. NY. Viking. 1st. 8vo. mc dj. R5. $85.00.

DU BOIS, William Pene. *Twenty-One Balloons.* 1947. Viking. 1st. ils. 180p. VG. D1. $35.00.

DU BOSE, Heyward. *Mamba's Daughters: A Novel of Charleston.* 1929. NY. Literary Guild. 311p. deckle edged/ils ep. H6. $34.00.

DU CHAILLU, Paul. *Explorations & Adventures in Equatorial Africa.* 1861. NY. Harper. 1st Am. ils. 531p. 3-quarter leather. H7. $100.00.

U CHAILLU, Paul. *My Apingi Kingdom: with Life in the Great Sahara.* 1871. NY. Harper. 2nd. 8vo. ils. xl. W1. $30.00.

U MAURIER, Daphne. *Don't Look Now.* 1971. Doubleday. 1st. VG/dj. B30. $75.00.

U MAURIER, Daphne. *Echoes from the Macabre.* 1976 (1952). Doubleday. 1st m/revised. VG/dj. G8. $20.00.

U MAURIER, Daphne. *Hungry Hill.* 1943. Doubledy. 1st. VG+. S18. $8.00.

U MAURIER, Daphne. *Kiss Me Again, Stranger.* 1952. Doubleday. 1st. ils. VG+. S18. $5.00.

U MAURIER, Daphne. *Rock Cried Out.* 1979. HBJ. 1st. sgn. F/dj. B30. $30.00.

U MONT, John S. *Custer Battle Guns.* 1974. Ft Collins, CO. Old Army. F/dj. A19. $75.00.

UANE, Diane. *High Wizardry.* 1990. NY. Delacorte Press. hc. VG/G. A28. $7.50.

UBIE, Norman. *The City of the Olesha Fruit.* 1979. NY. Doubleday. 1st. F/NF. V1. $30.00.

UBOIS, Brendan. *Resurrection Day.* 1999. NY. Putnam. 1st. sgn. VF/VF. T2. $25.00.

UBOIS, Jules. *Danger of Panama.* 1964. Indianapolis. Bobbs Merrill. 1st. 409p. G/chipped dj. F3. $10.00.

UBUS, Andre. *Broken Vessels.* 1991. Boston. Godine. 1st. sgn. F/dj. R14. $60.00.

UBUS, Andre. *Dancing After Hours.* 1996. Knopf. 1st. sgn. 14 stories. F/dj. R14/S9. $50.00.

UBUS, Andre. *Finding a Girl in America.* 1980. Boston. Godine. 1st. sgn. 8vo. NF/dj. 9. $125.00.

UBUS, Andre. *Selected Stories.* (1988). Boston. David R. Godine. 1st. VF/F. B3. $25.00.

UBUS, Andre. *The Lieutenant.* 1967. NY. Dial. 1st. chip. old price stickers on rear panel. F in worn dj. B2. $125.00.

UBUS, Andre. *Voices from the Moon.* 1984. Boston. Godine. 1st. F/F. B3. $35.00.

UCASSE, Isadore. *Maldoror (Les Chants De Maldoror).* 1943. np. New Directions. 8vo. /case. B2. $85.00.

DUCHENE, Commandant. *Flight without Formulae.* 1918. London. Longmans. Green. trans John H. Ledeboer. ils. 211p. VG. B18. $25.00.

DUCKWORTH, Paul. *Experimental & Trick Photography.* 1964. Universal Photo Books. 2nd. VG. C9. $30.00.

DUDEN, Gottfired. *Report on Journey to Western States of North America.* 1980. Columbia, MO. rpt. 372p. VG/dj. B5. $30.00.

DUDLEY & WILLIAMS. *Mr Popper's Penguins.* Little, Brn. 1st. 4to. popups. VG. B17. $14.00.

DUE, Tananarive. *Between.* 1995. Harper Collins. 1st. author's 1st book. F/F. H11. $25.00.

DUERRENMATT, Friedrich. *Quarry.* 1962. Greenwich, CT. 1st Am. VG/dj. B4. $85.00.

DUFF, Annis. *Bequest of Wings: A Family's Pleasures with Books.* 1944. NY. Viking. 1st. 207p. cloth. F/dj. O10. $12.00.

DUFFIELD, Mrs. William. *The Art of Flower Painting.* 1856. London. 12mo. sc. damaged backstrip. lt fox not affecting plates. B26. $66.00.

DUFFY, Brian. *Head Count.* 1991. NY. Putnam. 1st. author's 1st novel. F/F. H11. $15.00.

DUFFY, John. *Tulane University Medical Center: 150 Years of Medicine.* 1984. Baton Rouge. 1st. 253p. A13. $27.50.

DUFFY, Margaret. *Dressed to Kill.* 1994. St. Martin. 1st Am ed. F/F. G8. $15.00.

DUFFY, Steve. *The Night Comes On.* 1998. Ashcroft, BC. Ash Tree Press. 1st. VF/VF. T2. $42.00.

DUFRESNE, John. *Louisiana Power & Light.* (1994). NY. Norton. 1st. author's highly acclaimed 1st novel. F/F. B3. $75.00.

DUFRESNE, John. *Love Warps the Mind a Little.* 1997. Norton. 1st. sgn. F/dj. R14. $45.00.

DUFRESNE, John. *Way That Water Enters Stone.* 1991. Norton. 1st. 1/5000. sgn. F/dj. R14. $150.00.

DUGGAN, Alfred. *Little Emperors.* 1953. Coward McCann. 1st. F/dj. T10. $35.00.

DUGGER, Ronnie. *On Reagan: The Man & His Presidency.* 1983. McGraw Hill. 1st. sm 4to. NF/F. W2. $30.00.

DUGUID, Julian. *Green Hell. Adventures in the Mysterious Jungles of Eastern Bolivia.* 1936 (1931). NY. Appleton. b/w photo ils. ep maps. 339p. G/hinges starting. lt shelf wear. F3. $15.00.

DUHEME, Jacqueline. *Birthdays.* 1966. Determined. ils. 16p. brd. F/NF. D4. $35.00.

DUKE, Alton. *When the Colorado River Quit the Ocean.* 1974. Yuma. Southwest Prt. 1st. 122p. gr paper over brd. VG/dj. F7. $50.00.

DUKE, Donald. *Water Trails West.* 1978. Doubleday. 1st. VG/dj. P3. $20.00.

DUKE, Marc. *DuPonts.* 1976. Dutton. 1st. F/NF. W2. $40.00.

DUKTHAS, Ann. *Time for the Death of a King.* 1994. St. Martin. 1st Am ed. NF/VG+. G8. $20.00.

DULAC, Edmund. *Stories from the Arabian Nights.* 1920s. Doran. rpt. 16 mc pl. VG. B17. $85.00.

DULANY, Harris. *One Kiss Led to Another.* 1994. NY. Harper Collins. 1st. author's 1st novel. sgn. VF/VF. T2. $25.00.

DULL, P. *Battle History of Imperial Japanese Navy 1941 – 45.* 1982 (1978). lg 8vo. F/F. E6. $15.00.

DUMAS, Alexandre. *Love & Liberty.* nd. London. Stanley Paul. 1st Eng. trans RS Garnett. NF/G. O4. $25.00.

DUMAS, Henry. *Ark of Bones and Other Stories.* 1974. NY. Random House. 1st. rem mk. F/NF dj. M19. $25.00.

DUMAUIER, Daphne. *Echoes from the Macabre.* 1952 – 76. NY. Doubleday. 1st Am ed/rev. VG/VG. G8. $15.00.

DUMBARTON, Oaks. *Death & Afterlife in Pre-Columbian America.* 1975. DC. 1st. 196p. F3. $45.00.

DUMBARTON, Oaks. *Emblem & State in the Classic Maya Lowlands.* 1976. DC. 1st. photos. 204p. F3. $45.00.

DUMBARTON, Oaks. *Highland Lowland Interaction in Mesoamerica; Interdisciplinary Approaches.* 1983. np. Washington. 1st. biblio. 263p. G. F3. $30.00.

DUMMELOW, J. R. *The One Volume Bible Commentary.* 1974. Macmillan. 36th printing. 1092p. VG. ex lib. B29. $18.50.

DUMOND, Don E. *The Eskimos and Aleuts.* 1977. London. Thames & Hudson. 1st. 119 ils. 180p. VG/VG. P4. $50.00.

DUMONT, Frank. *The Witmark Amateur Minstrel Guide and Burnt Clock Encyclopedia.* 1899. Chicago. Witmark & Sons. pict cloth. ils. edgewear. G+. B18. $50.00.

DUN, John. *No New Frontiers: 11 Stories Inspired by Arizona Sunshine.* 1938. Roycrofters. 1st. 175p. VG/sans. B19. $20.00.

DUNANT, Sarah. *Snowstorms in a Hot Climate.* 1988. NY. Random House. 1st Am ed. author's 1st novel. F/F. T2. $25.00.

DUNAWAY, David King. *Aldous Huxley Recollected, an Oral History.* 1995. NY. 1st. dj. T9. $10.00.

DUNBAR, Anthony P. *Against the Grain: Southern Radicals & Prophets 1929 – 1959.* 1982. Charlottesville, VA. 2nd. AN/dj. V4. $30.00.

DUNBAR, Harris T. *The Wept of Wish Ton Wish, An Indian Romance.* East Aurora. Roycrofters. ¼ suede leather. ils. 60p. VG. spine faded. B18. $37.50.

DUNBAR, Paul Laurance. *Love of Landry.* 1900. NY. Dodd Mead. 1st. G. G11. $50.00.

DUNBAR, Robert L. *China Dawn.* 1988. NY. Delacorte. 1st. library sale mark on bottom edges. F/F. H11. $20.00.

DUNBAR, Sophie. *Behind Eclaire's Doors.* 1993. NY. St. Martin. 1st. author's 1st book. F/F. H11. $25.00.

DUNBAR, Tom. *City of Beads.* 1995. NY. Putnam. 1st. VF/VF. H11. $20.00.

DUNBAR, Tom. *Crooked Man.* 1994. NY. Putnam. 1st. Author's first novel. VF/VF. H11. $40.00.

DUNCAN, David Douglas. *Goodbye Picasso.* nd (1974). NY. Grosset Dunlap. 4to. thick-grained cloth. NF/VG. F1. $50.00.

DUNCAN, David Douglas. *Self-Portrait: USA.* 1969. Abrams. VG/dj. S5. $37.00.

DUNCAN, David Douglas. *The Silent Studio.* 1976. NY. Norton. 1st Am ed. photo essay. b&w. F in NF dj. D10. $45.00.

DUNCAN, David James. *River Teeth.* (1995). NY. Doubleday. 1st. sgn by author. F/F. B3. $35.00.

DUNCAN, Dayton. *Out West.* 1987. NY. Viking. 1st. F/F. H11. $25.00.

DUNCAN, Frederic Chandler. *The Sea Alphabet.* 1991. Marquette, MI. Avery Color Studios. wrp. VG. A16. $7.00.

DUNCAN, Robert. *Serpent's Mask.* 1989. St Martin. 1st. F/dj. S18. $24.00.

DUNCAN, Robert L. *Fire Storm.* 1978. NY. Morrow. 1st. NF/F. H11. $15.00.

DUNDES, Alan. *Study of Folklore.* (1965). Berkeley. ils. VG. M17. $20.00.

DUNGLISON, Robley. *History of Medicine from Earliest Ages.* 1872. Phil. 1st. 287p. A13. $50.00.

DUNHAM, Sam C. *Goldsmith of Nome & Other Verse.* 1901. Washington, DC. Neale. 1st. 80p. H7. $20.00.

DUNHAM, T. Richard. *Unveiling the Future: Twelve Prophetic Messages.* 1934. Fundamental Truth. 165p. VG. B29. $5.00.

DUNHAM, Wayland A. *It's a Date.* 1948. San Marino, CA. 159p w/18 full pg photos. VG. B26. $26.00.

DUNLAP, Knight. *Religion: Its Functions in Human Life.* 1946. McGraw Hill. 362p. emb red cloth. G1. $50.00.

DUNLAP, Susan. *Death & Taxes.* 1992. Delacorte. 1st. sgn. NF/dj. G8. $25.00.

DUNLAP, Susan. *Time Expired.* 1993. NY. Delacorte. 1st. sgn. F/VF. T2. $20.00.

DUNLAP, Thomas R. *Saving America's Wildlife.* 1988. Princeton. 222p. NF/dj. S15. $12.00.

DUNLOP, Ian. *Degas.* 1979. NY. Harper. 1st Am. 240p. VG/dj. B11. $30.00.

DUNLOP, Richard. *Doctors of the American Frontier.* 1965. NY. 1st. 228p. dj. A13. $40.00.

DUNN, Arthur Wallace. *Gridiron Nights.* 1915. NY. 1st. 371p. VG. B5. $45.00.

DUNN, Dorothy. *Plains Indian Sketch Books of Zo-Tom & Howling Wolf.* 1969. Northland. 1st. ils. NF/VG+. B19. $75.00.

DUNN, James Taylor. *St Croix.* 1965. NY. 1st. Rivers of Am series. ils Gerald Hazzard. 309p. VG. B18. $22.00.

DUNN, Katherine. *Geek Love.* 1989. Knopf. 1st. sgn. F/dj. M19. $65.00.

DUNN, Katherine. *Truck.* 1971. Harper Row. 1st. NF/dj. B3. $150.00.

DUNN, Stephen. *University & College Poetry Prizes 1967 – 1972.* 1974. The Academy of American Poets. 48 poets. wrp. 94p. F. V1. $25.00.

DUNN & TROXELL. *By the Roadside.* 1928. Evanston. Row Peterson. 4th. ils Nell Hukle. 256p. VG+. A25. $12.00.

DUNNE, Dominick. *Inconvenient Woman.* 1990. Crown. 1st. NF/NF. G8. $10.00.

DUNNE, John Gregory. *Dutch Shea, Jr.* 1982. S&S. 1st. F/clip. Q1. $25.00.

DUNNE, John Gregory. *Harp.* 1989. S&S. 1st. F/G. S19. $40.00.

DUNNE, John Gregory. *True Confessions.* 1977. NY. Dutton. 1st. sgn by author. F/NF. B2. $40.00.

DUNNE, John Gregory. *Vegas.* 1974. NY. Random. 1st. F/F. H11. $40.00.

DUNNETT, Alastair M. *Alistair Maclean Introduces Scotland.* 1972. Andre Deutsch. 1st. NF/dj. P3. $30.00.

DUNNETT, Dorothy. *Niccolo Rising: House of Niccolo Book One.* 1986. London. Michael Joseph. 1st. NF/dj. A14. $22.00.

DUNNETT, Dorothy. *Ringed Castle: Lymond Chronicles, Volume Five.* 1971. London. Cassell. 1st. VG+/VG. A14. $140.00.

DUNNING, John. *Booked to Die.* 1992. Scribner. 1st. F/dj. B2. $600.00.

DUNNING, John. *Booked to Die.* 1993. London. Allison Busby. 1st/pbo. sgn. F. B3. $50.00.

DUNNING, John. *Bookman's Wake.* 1995. Scribner. 1st. F/F. H11. $45.00.

DUNNING, John. *On the Air: The Encyclopedia of Old Time Radio.* 1998. NY. Oxford Univ Press. 1st. sgn. VF/VF. T2. $65.00.

DUNNING, John. *The Torch Passes.* (1995). Huntington Beach. Cahill. 1st. sgn & dated by author. prt wrp. F. B3. $125.00.

DUNNING, John. *Tune in Yesterday Ultimate Encyclopedia.* 1976. Prentice Hall. 1st. author's 1st book. F/VG. B2. $100.00.

DUNSANY, Lord. *The Sword of Welleran and Other Stories.* 1908. London. George Allen & Sons. sm 8vo. dk gr cloth w/gilt decor. early fantasy writer. 243p. NF. D6. $95.00.

DUPIN, Jacques. *Miro.* (1962). Abrams. ils/46 pl. 596p. blk cloth. NF/dj. F1. $175.00.

DUPUIS, Robert. *Bunny Berrigan. Elusive Legend of Jazz.* 1993. Baton Rouge. LSU Press. 1st. F/F. B2. $25.00.

DUPUY, Trevor N. *Military Life of Genghis, Kahn of Khans.* 1969. NY. 1st. ils. 131p. VG/VG. B18. $15.00.

DUPUY, William Atherton. *Baron of the Colorados.* 1940. Naylor. 1st. 177p. VG/VG. 319. $30.00.

DURAN, P. *Bibliografica Juridica Boliviana.* 1957. Oruro. Bolivia. 370p. G. F3. $35.00.

DURAND, Loup. *Jaquar.* 1990. NY. Villard. 1st. F/F. H11. $25.00.

DURANT, John. *Dodgers.* 1948. Hastings. 1st. ils. VG. P8. $50.00.

DURANT & RICE. *Come Out Fighting: Pictorial History of the Ring.* 1946. NY. Essential/DSP. 1st. 4to. F/VG+. B4. $150.00.

DURBRIDGE, Francis. *My Friend Charles.* 1963. Hodder. 1st British ed. VG. G8. $15.00.

DURDEN, Charles. *Fifth Law of Hawkins.* 1990. NY. St Martin. 1st. F/dj. R11. $15.00.

DURHAM, Philip. *Down These Mean Streets a Man Must Go.* (1963). Chapel Hill. 1st. 8vo. gilt gray cloth. F/dj. R3. $60.00.

DURHAM, Victor G. *The Submarine Boys and the Middies.* 1909. Akron. Saalfield. very yellowed paper. G in chip dj. A16. $6.00.

DUROCHER, Leo & Ed Linn. *Nice Guys Finish Last.* 1975. NY. S&S. 1st. 8vo. 448p. AN/dj. H1. $15.00.

DURRANT, MEACOCK & WHITWORTH. *Machine Printing.* 1973. NY. Hastings. 1st Am. 8vo. 245p. cloth. F/dj. $10.00.

DURRANT, Tom. *Camellia Story.* 1982. Auckland. special ed. inscr. photos/ils. F/case. B26. $50.00.

DURRELL, Alexis. *Crockery Cooking.* 1975. Weathervane. G/dj. A16. $8.00.

DURRELL, Lawrence. *Blue Thirst.* 1975. Santa Barbara. Capra. 1st. 56p. F/wrp. M7. $30.00.

DURRELL, Lawrence. *Clea.* 1960. London. Faber. 1st. VG/VG. T9. $60.00.

DURRELL, Lawrence. *Justine.* 1957. Dutton. 1st Am. 8vo. 253p. red/blk cloth. VG/dj. J3. $75.00.

DURRELL, Lawrence. *Nunquam.* 1970. London. Faber. 1st. NF/dj. A14. $35.00.

DUSTIN, F. *Custer Tragedy: Events Leading Up to & Following.* 1987 (1939). El Segundo. rpt. 1/200. 3 fld maps/photos. F. $4.00.

DUTTON, Bertha. *Sun Father's Way: Kiva Murals of Kuaua.* 1963. U NM. 100+ photos. 237p. VG/dj. J2. $95.00.

DUTTON, Charles J. *The Shadow of Evil.* 1930. NY. Dodd Mead. 1st. pl on front. F/ dj clip/mend. M15. $175.00.

DUVAL, Mathias. *Artistic Anatomy.* 1886. London. 2nd. 324p. A13. $90.00.

DUVOISIN, Roger. *A for the Ark.* 1952. Lee Shepard. 1st. 4to. mc pict brd. R5. $150.00.

DWIGGINS, Don. *On Silent Wings, Adventures in Motorless Flight.* 1970. NY. Grosset & Dunlap. b&w ils. 151p. VG in clip dj. worn. B18. $12.50.

DWIGGINS, W. A. *Layout in Advertising.* 1928. Harper. 1st. 8vo. 200p. cloth. VG/dj. $20.00.

DWIGHT, T. *Frozen Sections of a Child.* 1881. 1st. 4to. 15 pl. 66p. VG. E6. $125.00.

DWYER, Deanna; see Koontz, Dean R.

DWYER, K. R.; see Koontz, Dean R.

DWYER-JOYCE, Alice. *The Storm of Wrath.* 1978. NY. St. Mark Press. 1st. VF/VF. H11. $30.00.

DYBEK, Stuart. *Childhood & Other Neighborhoods.* 1980. NY. Viking. 1st. sgn. author's 1st book. F/NF clip. O11. $20.00.

DYE, Eva Emery. *The Conquest, The True Story of Lewis and Clark.* 1902. Chicago. McClurg. 1st. pict cloth. frontis. paper browning. 443p. VG. B18. $22.50.

DYER, Mary M. *Portraiture of Shakerism.* 1822. New Hampshire. full leather. G. B30. $50.00.

DYER & FRASER. *Rocking Chair: An American Institution.* 1928. NY. Century. 1st. 8vo. 124p. brn cloth. NF. B20. $65.00.

DYJA, Tom. *Play for a Kingdom.* (1997). NY. HBJ. 1st. author's 1st book. F/F. B3. $40.00.

DYKSTRA, C. *Colorado River Development & Related Problems.* 1930. Am Academy Political/Social Sci. 8vo. red brd. F7. $30.00.

DYNES. *Encyclopedia of Homosexuality.* St James. 1990. 2 vol. 4to. F. A4. $95.00.

— E —

EAGER, Harriet Ide. *Tommy Tiptoe.* 1924. NY. Knopf. 2nd printing. ils by Edna Cooke. 8vo. gray cloth w/bl lettering. 76p. VG. D6. $45.00.

EAGLE, D. Chief. *Winter Count.* 1967. Boulder. Johnson Pub. 1st. sgn by author. F/F. B2. $35.00.

EAGLEMAN, Joe R. *Severe and Unusual Weather.* 1983. NY. Van Nostrand Reinhold. 8vo. b/w photos & diagrams. 372p. VG/VG. K5. $30.00.

EAMES, Jane Anthony. *Another Budget; or Things Which I Saw in the East.* 1855. Boston. Ticknor & Fields. 2nd. orig blk cloth. 481p. VG. B14. $95.00.

EARLE, Peter. *Prophet in the Wilderness.* 1971. Austin. Univ of Texas Press. 1st. 254p. G/G. F3. $20.00.

EARLEY, Tony. *Here We Are in Paradise.* (1994). Boston. Little, Brn. 1st. author's 1st book. F/F. B3. $50.00.

EARLY, Joe. *The Pitch.* 1968. np. 1st. ils by Fielding Dawson and others. 1 of 500 copies. F. B2. $25.00.

EASTON, W. Burnet, Jr. *Thinking Christianly.* 1948. Macmillan. 136p. VG/VG minor mks. B29. $4.00.

EATON, Kenneth Oxner. *Men Who Talked with God.* 1964. Abingdon. 95p. VG/G torn. B29. $4.00.

EAVENSON, Howard N. *Map Maker & Indian Traders, An Account of John Patten Trader, Arctic Explorer, and Map Maker....* 1949. Univ of Pittsburgh. #213 of 300 copies. foldout maps. 275p. VG+. ep discolored. B18. $125.00.

EAVEY, C. B. *History of Christian Education.* 1978. Moody. 430p. VG/VG. B29. $10.00.

EBERHARD, Frederick G. *Skeleton Talks.* 1933. Macaulay. 1st. VG. G8. $20.00.

EBERHART, Mignon G. *Alpine Condo Crossfire.* 1984. Random House. 1st. F/VG. G8. $15.00.

EBERHART, Mignon G. *Cup, the Blade, or the Gun.* 1961. Random House. 1st. VG/G+. G8. $20.00.

EBERHART, Mignon G. *El Rancho Rio.* 1970. Random House. 1st. NF/VG. G8. $15.00.

EBERHART, Mignon G. *Family Affair.* 1981. NY. Random. 1st. F/F. H11. $20.00.

EBERHART, Mignon G. *Hunt with the Hounds.* 1950. Random House. 1st. VG. G8. $15.00.

EBERHART, Mignon G. *Unidentified Woman.* 1943. Random House. 1st. G-VG/G+. G8. $17.50.

ECCLES, Marjorie. *Company She Kept.* 1996. NY. St. Martin. 1st Am ed. F/F. G8. $17.50.

ECKMAN, Fern Marja. *The Furious Passage of James Baldwin.* 1966. Evans. 1st. NF/worn. sunned dj. M25. $25.00.

ECKSTEIN, Rabbi Yechiel. *What Christians Should Know About Jews and Judaism.* 1984. Word. 336p. VG/VG. B29. $11.00.

ECO, Umberto. *Postscript to the Name of the Rose.* 1984. NY. HBJ. 1st English language ed. dk bl cloth. 84p. F/F. A24. $40.00.

EDBERG, Stephen J. *International Halley Watch Amateur Observers' Manual for Scientific Comet Studies.* 1983. Hillside, NJ: Enslow. Cambridge: Sky Publishing. 4to. ils. 165p. VG in wrp. glue residue inside front cover. K5. $12.00.

EDDINGS, David. *Guardians of the West.* 1987. NY. Ballantine. 1st. NF. bumps/NF. some scratches & mild wear. M23. $30.00.

EDDY, Mary Baker Glover. *Science & Health with Key to the Scriptures.* 1887. Boston. author published. 29th. 8vo. 590p. G+. H1. $85.00.

EDEL, Abraham. *The Theory and Practice of Philosophy.* 1946. Harcourt Brace & Co. 475p. G. B29. $6.00.

EDERSHEIM, Alfred. *History of the Jewish Nation.* nd. Baker. 553p. G. B29. $21.00.

EDGERTON, Clyde. *Floatplane Notebooks.* (1988). London. Viking. review copy w/slips laid in. F/F. B3. $15.00.

EDGERTON, Clyde. *In Memory of Junior.* (1992). Chapel Hill. Algonquin. 1st. F/F. B3. $30.00.

EDGERTON, Clyde. *The Floatplane Notebooks.* 1988. Chapel Hill. Algonquin. 1st. sgn. F/F. D10. $45.00.

EDGERTON, Clyde. *Walking Across Egypt.* 1987. Chapel Hill. Algonquin. 1st. F/VF. H11. $60.00.

EDGLEY, Leslie. *False Face.* 1947. S&S. 1st. Jacket chipped and sunned at the spine. VG/dj. M25. $45.00.

EDLIN, H. L. *British Woodland Trees.* 1949 (1944). London. rev 3rd ed. VG in dj. B26. $21.00.

EDLIN, Herbert L. *Trees and Man.* 1976. NY. 269p w/28p of plates. 23 line drawings. VG in dj. B26. $29.00.

EDSON, Lee. *Worlds Around the Sun; The Emerging Portrait of the Solar System.* 1969. NY. American Heritage. for Smithsonian Institution. 4to. ils. 159p. VG in rubbed dj. clip. K5. $15.00.

EDWARDS, Amelia B. *The Phantom Coach: Collected Ghost Stories.* 1999. Ashcroft, BC. Ash Tree Press. 1st. VF/VF. T2. $43.00.

EDWARDS, Anne. *The Hesitant Heart.* NY. Random House. (1974). 8vo. 247p. red cloth. dj. 1st ed. 2nd prt. F/F. L5. $35.00.

EDWARDS, Louis N. *A Romantic Mystery.* 1997. NY. Dutton. 1st. F/F. G8. $10.00.

EDWARDS, Ruth Dudley. *Matricide at St. Martha's.* 1995. NY. St. Martin. 1st Am ed. VF/VF. T2. $8.00.

EDWARDS, Ruth Dudley. *Saint Valentine's Day Murders.* 1984. quartet. 1st British ed. F/F. G8. $20.00.

EFFINGER, George Alec. *Relatives.* 1973. NY. Harper & Row. 1st. F/F. lt wear. T2. $20.00.

EFFINGER, George Alec. *When Gravity Fails.* 1987. NY. Arbor House. 1st. VF/VF. T2. $20.00.

EGAN, Lesley. *In the Death of a Man.* 1970. Harper. 1st. VG/VG+. G8. $17.50.

EGGERS, Paul. *Saviors.* 1998. Harcourt Brace. UP. F/wrp. M25. $35.00.

EGGLESTON, George Cary. *Recollections of a Varied Life.* 1910. NY. Henry Holt. 1st. orig cloth. 354p. VG. M8. $85.00.

EGUIGUREN, Luis. *Gerra Separatista Del Peru, 1812.* 1913. Lima. np. G/old leather bds w/worm holes. front hinge broken. 200p. F3. $25.00.

EHRLICH, Gretel. *A Match to the Heart.* 1994. NY. Pantheon. 1st. F/F. H11. $25.00.

EHRLICH, Gretel. *Heart Mountain.* (1988). NY. Viking. 1st. F/F. B3. $60.00.

EHRLICH, Gretel, Ed. *Life in the Saddle, Writings and Photographs.* (1995). San Diego. HBJ. 1st. oversize pict wrp. photo-essay. w/an orig essay and intro by Ehrlich. F. B3. $30.00.

EHRLICH, Max. *The Reincarnation of Peter Proud.* 1974. Indianapolis. Bobbs Merrill. 1st. F/F. T2. $5.00.

EIDSON, Bill. *Dangerous Waters.* 1991. Holt. 1st. inscr. NF/NF. G8. $17.50.

EIDUS, Janice. *Urban Bliss.* 1994. NY. Fromm. 1st. VF/VF. H11. $15.00.

EINSTEIN, Charles. *Willie's Time: Willie May's Story.* 1979. NY. Lippincott. 1st. VG/VG clip. R16. $35.00.

EISELEY, Loren. *How Flowers Changed the World.* (1996). San Francisco. Sierra Club. 1st. photography by Gerald Ackerman. F/F. B3. $15.00.

EISELEY, Loren. *The Innocent Assassins.* (1973). NY. Scribner's. 1st. ils by Laszlo Kubinyi. dj Is bright and whole. better than it sounds. NF. lt sunning to edges/NF. one 2" closed tear and several sm ones. B3. $35.00.

EISELEY, Loren. *The Unexpected Universe.* 1969. np. Harcourt Brace. 1st. bookplate. NF/VG dj. M19. $25.00.

EISEMAN, Fred & Margaret. *Flowers of Bali.* 1988. np. colorful photo brds. 60p. B26. $9.00.

EISENBERG, Deborah. *Transactions in a Foreign Currency.* 1986. NY. Knopf. 1st. F/F. D10. $45.00.

EISENSTADT, Jill. *From Rockaway.* 1987. NY. Knopf. 1st. author's 1st book. F/F. H11. $30.00.

EISNER, Lotte. *L'Ecran Demoniaque.* 1965. Paris. Losfeld/ Le Terrain Vague. 1st. photos. 288p. F. B2. $25.00.

EISSFELDT, Otto. *The Old Testament; An Introduction.* 1966. Basil Blackwell. 861p. VG. B29. $31.00.

EKLUND, Gordon. *The Grayspace Beast.* 1976. Garden City. Doubleday. 1st. F. rem specking on bottom of text block/F. T2. $5.00.

ELFLANDSSON, Galad. *The Black Wolf.* 1979. West Kingston. Donald I. Grant. 1st. sgn. author's 1st book. VF/VF. T2. $40.00.

ELGUERA, Cesar. *Memoria Que El Ministro De Relaciones Exteriores.* 1926. Lima. np. 225p. G/cover chipped. old water mk. F3. $25.00.

ELIOT, T. S. *Murder in the Cathedral.* 1935. NY. Harcourt Brace. 1st. NF/G dj. M19. $150.00.

ELIOT, T. S. *The Confidential Clerk.* 1954. Harcourt Brace. 1st Am ed. NF/sunned dj. M25. $45.00.

LKINS, Aaron J. *A Deceptive Clarity*. 1987. Y. Walker. 1st. VF/dj. M15. $100.00.

LKINS, Aaron J. *Glancing Light*. 1991. cribners. 1st. sgn. F/F. G8. $25.00.

LKINS, Aaron J. *Icy Clutches*. 1990. Mysterious. 1st. sgn. review copy. NF/NF. 8. $35.00.

LKINS, Aaron J. *Murder in the Queen's* rmies. 1985. Collins Crime Club. 1st British d. sgn. NF/VG+. G8. $50.00.

LKINS, Aaron J. *Murder in the Queen's* rmies. 1985. NY. Walker. 1st. F/dj. M15. 200.00.

LKINS, Aaron J. *Old Bones*. 1987. NY. Mysterious. 1st. VF/dj. M15. $95.00.

LKINS, Aaron J. *Old Scores*. 1993. NY. cribner's. 1st. sgn. F/F. G8. $17.50.

LKINS, Aaron J. *The Dark Place*. 1983. NY. Walker. 1st. author's 2nd mystery. F/dj. M15. $600.00.

LKINS, Charlotte & Aaron J. *Nasty Breaks*. 997. Mysterious. 1st. sgn. F/F. G8. $25.00.

LKINS, Charlotte & Aaron J. *Wicked Slice*. 989. St. Martin. 1st. sgn. NF/VG+. G8. 30.00.

LLIN, Stanley. *Dark Fantastic*. 1983. Mysterious. 1st. NF/VG. G8. $20.00.

LLIN, Stanley. *Luxembourg Run*. 1977. NY. Random House. 1st. VG/VG. G8. $10.00.

LLIN, Stanley. *Valentine Estate*. 1968. NY. Random House. 1st. VG/G+. G8. $15.00.

ELLINGTON, Duke. *Boogie Woogie Piano* Transcriptions. 1944. NY. Robbins. 1st. wrp. 28p. VG. B2. $40.00.

ELLINGTON, Duke. *Music Is My Mistress*. 1973. Garden City. Doubleday. 1st. F in G dj. B2. $50.00.

ELLIOT, George Fielding. *Caleb Pettengill, U S N*. 1956. NY. Julian Messner. inc 1st. orig cloth. historical novel. 284p. VG. M8. $15.00.

ELLIOTT, James. *Cold Cold Heart*. 1994. NY. Delacorte. 1st. VF/VF. H11. $30.00.

ELLIOTT, L. E. *Chile: Today and Tomorrow*. 1922. NY. Macmillan. 1st. 345p. G/pict cover. hinges starting. lt shelf wear. F3. $20.00.

ELLIS, Amanda. *Elizabeth the Woman*. 1951. np. Dutton. 1st. sgn by author. NF/VG. M19. $35.00.

ELLIS, Bret Easton. *American Psycho*. 1998. London. Picador. 1st. sgn. author's 2nd novel. VF/VF. T2. $45.00.

ELLIS, Kate. *The Armada Boy*. 1999. London. Piatkus. 1st. VF/VF. T2. $38.00.

ELLIS, O. O. And E. B. Garey. *The Plattsburg Manual. A Handbook for Federal Training Camps*. NY. The Century Co. 1917. 8vo. 303p. ils. tan cloth. 1st ed. Both inner hinges cracked. spine sltly darkened. G to VG. L5. $20.00.

ELLIS, Peter Berresford. *The Last Adventurer: The Life of Talbot Mundy 1879 – 1940*. 1984. West Kingston. Donald M. Grant. 1st. VF/VF. T2. $30.00.

ELLIS, Ron. *Ears of the City*. 1998. London. Headline. 1st. author's 1st novel. VF/VF. T2. $35.00.

ELLIS, Ron. *Mean Streets*. 1998. London. Headline. 1st. VF/VF. T2. $30.00.

ELLISON, Harlan. *Mefisto in Onyx*. 1993. Shingletown. Mark V. Ziesing. 1st. sgn. VF/VF. T2. $50.00.

ELLISON, Harlan. *The Essential Ellison: A 35 Year Retrospective*. 1987. Omaha. Nemo Press. 1st. 1/1200 # copies. edited by Terry Dowling w/Richard Delap. Gil Lamont. 1000+ pg collection. sgn by Ellison. VF/VF dj & slipcase. T2. $100.00.

ELLROY, James. *American Tabloid*. 1995. NY. Knopf. 1st. F/VF. H11. $20.00.

ELLROY, James. *Brown's Requiem*. 1994. NY. Penzler. 1st. VF/VF. H11. $35.00.

ELLROY, James. *Hollywood Nocturnes*. 1994. Otto Penzler. UP. F in gray wrp. M25. $45.00.

ELLROY, James. *L. A. Confidential*. 1990. NY. Mysterious. 1st. Jacket has crease on spine. F/dj. M15. $85.00.

ELLROY, James. *My Dark Places*. (1996). NY. Knopf. 1st. sgn on a tipped in pg. F/F. B3. $30.00.

ELLROY, James. *The Big Nowhere*. 1988. NY. Mysterious. 1st. F/VF. H11. $50.00.

ELLROY, James. *White Jazz*. (1992). NY. Knopf. 1st. sgn by author. F/F. B3. $40.00.

ELLWANGER, George H. *The Sphere of Thoreau. In Idyllists of the Country Side: Being Six Commentaries Concerning Some of Those Who Have Apostrophized the Joys of the Open Air*. NY. Dodd, Mead and Co. 1896. 1st. 12mo. 263p. pictorial gr cloth lending library bookplate (no spine markings and no library cards or pocket). minor soiling on cloth. G to VG. L5. $40.00.

ELON, Amos. *Herzl*. 1975. Rinehart & Winston. 1st. tall 8vo. 448p. NM/VG. H1. $20.00.

ELTON, Ben. *Popcorn*. 1996. London. S&S. 1st. VF/dj. M15. $100.00.

ELWOOD, Roger, editor. *Crisis: Ten Original Stories of Science Fiction*. 1974. Nashville. Thomas Nelson. 1st. F. lt shelf wear/NF. wear. T2. $10.00.

ELY, Richard T. *An Introduction to Political Economy*. 1889. NY. Chautauqua. 1st. NF. B2. $50.00.

EMERSON, Earl. *Morons and Madmen*. (1993). NY. Morrow. 1st. F/F. B3. $15.00.

EMERSON, Earl. *The Dead Horse Paint Company*. (1997). NY. Morrow. 1st. sgn by author. F/NF. sm closed tear on rear gutter. B3. $25.00.

EMERSON, Earl. *Yellow Dog Party*. (1991). NY. Morrow. 1st. sgn & dated by author. F/F. B3. $40.00.

EMERSON, Earl W. *Going Crazy in Public*. 1996. NY. Morrow. 1st. review copy. NF/NF. G8. $17.50.

EMERSON, Kathy L. *Face Down Among the Winchester Geese*. 1999. NY. St. Martin. 1st. sgn. F/F. G8. $25.00.

EMERSON, Ralph Waldo. *The Complete Writings of Ralph Waldo Emerson*. 1929. Wm. H. Wise & Co. tal 8vo some light fading spots on cover. 1435p. VG. H1. $30.00.

ENARI, Leonid. *Plants of the Pacific Northwest*. 1956. Portland. 315p w/185 line drawings. VG in chip dj. B26. $15.00.

ENCISO, Jorge. *Designs from Pre-Columbian Mexico*. 1971. NY. Dover. 1st. wrp. 105p. F. F3. $15.00.

ENDE, Michael. *The Neverending Story*. 1983. Garden City. Doubleday. 1st. bottom corners are bumped. clipped. F/F. H11. $80.00.

ENGEL, Howard. *The Suicide Murders*. 1980. St. Martin. 1st Am ed. VF/dj. M25. $35.00.

ENGEL, Marian. *Bear.* 1976. Toronto. McClelland & Stewart. 1st. NF/dj. A26. $30.00.

ENGLANDER, Nathan. *For the Relief of Unbearable Urges.* 1999. NY. Knopf. 1st. F/F. M23. $45.00.

ENGLE, Paul. *Images of China.* 1981. Beijing. New World Press. 1st. author inscr to fellow poet. F/VG+. V1. $30.00.

ENNIS, George Pearse. *Making a Watercolour.* 1933. np. The Studio Limited. 1st. many tipped in plates. VG. M19. $25.00.

ENROTH, Ronald. *Churches That Abuse.* 1992. Zondervan. 231p. VG/VG. B29. $8.00.

EPHRON, Nora. *Heartburn.* (1983). NY. Knopf. 1st. author's 1st novel. F/NF. very lt edgewear. B3. $25.00.

EPPERSON, S. K. *Dumford Blood.* 1991. NY. St. Martin. 1st. F/F. H11. $25.00.

EPPS, Archie, editor. *The Speeches of Malcolm X.* 1969. Morrow. later printing. NF/lightly rubbed dj. M25. $35.00.

EPSTEIN, Carole. *Perilous Friends.* 1996. Walker. 1st. VG/VG. G8. $17.50.

ERDMAN, Charles. *The First Epistle of Paul to the Corinthians.* 1929. Westminster. 158p. G. B29. $4.50.

ERDMAN, Charles. *The Gospel of Matthew.* 1948. Westminster. 224p. G. B29. $4.50.

ERDRICH, Louise. *The Bingo Palace.* (1994). NY. Harper Collins. 1st. sgn by author. F/F. B3. $35.00.

ERDRICH, Louise. *Tracks.* 198. np. Holt. ARC. owner's inscr. F. M19. $17.50.

ERICKSON, Steve. *American Nomad.* 1997. NY. Henry Holt. 1st. sgn. F/F. O11. $30.00.

ERICKSON, Steve. *Days Between Stations.* 1985. NY. Poseidon. AP. F/wrps. B2. $45.00.

ERICKSON, Steve. *Tours of the Black Clock.* 1989. London. S&S. 1st British ed. sgn. F/F. O11. $40.00.

ERICSON, Jonathon. *Peopling of the New World.* 1982. California. Ballena Press. 1st. 4to. 364p. G/wrp. F3. $25.00.

ERICSON, Sibyl. *The Curate's Crime.* 1946. NY. Mystery House. 1st Am ed. F/dj. M15. $75.00.

ERNSBERGER, George. *The Mountain King.* 1978. NY. Morrow. 1st. F/F. H11. $45.00.

ERNST, Jim. *Coincidence.* 1991. NY. Vantage. 1st. author's 1st book. VF/F. H11. $30.00.

ERSKINE, Dorothy. *Dr. Smith and the Antic Assembly.* 1959. NY. Putnam. 1st. VF/F. H11. $40.00.

ESBACH, Lloyd Arthur. *Tyant of Time.* 1955. Reading. Fantasy Press. 1st. VF/VF. T2. $20.00.

ESHBACH, Lloyd Arthur. *Over My Shoulder: Reflections on a Science Fiction Era.* 1983. Philadelphia. Oswald Train. 1st. VF/VF. T2. $25.00.

ESQUIVEL, Laura. *Like Water for Chocolate.* 1992. NY. Doubleday. 1st. F/F. D10. $85.00.

ESTELMAN, Loren. *Gun Man.* 1985. Garden City. Doubleday. 1st. F/dj. M15. $50.00.

ESTELMAN, Loren. *Mister St. John.* 1983. Garden City. Doubleday. 1st. F/dj. M15. $80.00.

ESTELMAN, Loren. *Sudden Country.* 1991. NY. Doubleday. 1st. VF/dj. M15. $45.00.

ESTEP, Maggie. *Diary of an Emotional Idiot.* 1997. NY. Harmony. 1st. Author's 1st book. F/F. H11. $40.00.

ESTERLINE, John H and Mae H. *How the Dominoes Fell: Southeast Asia in Perspective.* 1990. Lanham, MD. Univ Press of America. 2nd ed. 428p. VG. P1. $6.00.

ESTES, Clarissa Pinkola. *The Faithful Gardener.* (1995). San Francisco. Harper. 1st. sgn by author. F/F. B3. $25.00.

ESTLEMAN, Loren. *Roses are Dead.* 1985. np. Mysterious Press. 1st. F/F dj. M19. $25.00.

ESTLEMAN, Loren D. *Downriver.* 1988. Boston. Houghton Mifflin. 1st. sgn. VF/VF. T2. $30.00.

ESTLEMAN, Loren D. *Edsel.* 1995. NY. Mysterious Press. 1st. ARC. sgn. VF/pict wrp. T2. $20.00.

ESTLEMAN, Loren D. *Every Brilliant Eye.* 1986. Boston. Houghton Mifflin. 1st. sgn. VF/VF. T2. $30.00.

ESTLEMAN, Loren D. *Kill Zone.* 1984. NY. Mysterious Press. 1st. sgn. VF/VF. T2. $30.00.

ESTLEMAN, Loren D. *King of the Corner* 1992. NY. Bantam. 1st. sgn. VF/VF. T2 $25.00.

ESTLEMAN, Loren D. *Sherlock Holmes vs Dracula; or, The Adventure of the Sanguinary Count.* 1978. Garden City. Doubleday. 1st sgn by Estleman. F/F. T2. $50.00.

ESTLEMAN, Loren D. *Silent Thunder* (1989). Boston. Houghton Mifflin. 1st. F/F B3. $25.00.

ESTRELLA, Conrado F. *The Democratic Answer to the Philippine Agrarian Problem* 1969. Manila. Solidaridad Pub House. 142p. VG. P1. $10.00.

EUGENIDES, Jeffrey. *The Virgin Suicides* 1993. NY. FSG. 1st. F/F. D10. $50.00.

EUSTACE, Grant. *Absolute Discretion.* 1997 Ashcroft. Calabash Press. 1st. VF/pict wrp T2. $20.00.

EVANOVICH, Janet. *High Five.* 1999. NY St. Martin. 1st. ARC. F. D10. $10.00.

EVANOVICH, Janet. *One for the Money* (1994). NY. Scribner's. 1st. sgn by author F/F. B3. $85.00.

EVANOVICH, Janet. *Two for the Dough* 1996. NY. Scribners. 1st. VF/VF. H11 $40.00.

EVANS, Col. Albert S. *Our Sister Republic* 1870. Hartford. Columbian Book Co. 1st. 518p. VG. F3. $85.00.

EVANS, David. *Big Road Blues.* 1982. Berkeley. Univ of CA Press. 1st. F/F. B2 $65.00.

EVANS, David S. & J. Derral Mulholland *Big and Bright; A History of the McDonald Observatory.* 1986. Austin. Univ of Texas Press. 8vo. b/w photo ils. 186p. VG in pb. K5. $12.00.

EVANS, Donald P. *Hanover: The Greatest Name in Harness Racing.* 1976. S. Brunswick. Barnes. VG/G. O3. $35.00.

EVANS, Geraldine. *Dead Before Morning.* 1993. St. Martin. 1st Am ed. F/F. G8. $15.00.

EVANS, Geraldine. *Down Among the Dead Men.* 1994. Macmillan. 1st British ed. NF/NF. G8. $25.00.

EVANS, John. *If You Have Tears.* 1947. Mystery House. 1st. VG/VG. G8. $25.00.

EVANS, L. T. (ed). *The Induction of Flowering: Some Case Histories.* 1969. Ithaca. NY. numerous text figures. 488p. VG. B26. $42.50.

EVANS, Max. *Bluefeather Fellini.* (1993). Niwot. University Press of Colorado. 1st. F/F. B3. $30.00.

EVANS, Mike. *The Return.* 1986. Thomas Nelson Pub. 1st. F/F. S19. $30.00.

EVANS, Nicholas. *The Horse Whisperer.* 1995. NY. Delacorte. 1st. F/F. H11. $45.00.

EVANS, Richard Paul. *The Christmas Box.* 1993. NY. S&S. 1st. author's 1st book. VF/F. H11. $35.00.

EVANS, Robert. *A Jew in the Plan of God.* 1950. Loizeaux. 196p. VG. B29. $9.00.

EVANS, William. *Personal Soul Winner: A Guide to Effective Methods.* 1978. Moody. 160p. G/G. B29. $5.00.

EVANS-PRITCHARD, Ambrose. *The Secret Life of Bill Clinton; the Unreported Stories.* 1997. Washinton, DC. Regnery Publishing. inc. 1st. orig cloth. 460p. F/F. M8. $25.00.

EVERETT, Marshall, ed. *Wreck and Sinking of the Titanic the Ocean's Greatest Disaster. A Graphic and Thrilling Account....* 1912. np. official ed. orig red cloth w/photo paste-down. slight foxing. rubbed edge spine. 320p. G. B14. $150.00.

EVERETT-GREEN, E. *The Mystery of Alton Grange.* nd. London. Thomas Nelson. G. A16. $35.00.

EVERS, Crabbe. *Fear in Fenway.* 1993. NY. Morrow. 1st. VF/F. H11. $20.00.

EVERSON, William. *Earth Poetry.* 1971. Oyez. VG/NF. V1. $30.00.

EVERSZ, Robert M. *Shooting Elvis.* 1996. NY. Grove Press. 1st. VF/VF. T2. $20.00.

EVERTON, Francis. *Dalehouse Murder.* 1927. Bobbs Merrill. 1st Am ed. G+. G8. $10.00.

EVERTON, Macduff. *The Modern Maya.* 1991. Albuquerque. Univ of New Mexico Press. 1st. lg 4to. 260p. G/wrp. F3. $30.00.

EVRE, S. R. *Vegetation and Soils: A World Picture.* 1971 (1968). London. 2nd ed. VG in dj. B26. $19.00.

EWART, Ron. *Fuchsia Lexicon.* 1988 (1983). London. rev 2nd ed. 362p w/200 color photos. dj. B26. $35.00.

EWART, Ron. *The Fuchsia Grower's Handbook.* 1989. London. 120p w/20 color photos. VG in dj. B26. $21.00.

EXELL, Joseph. *The Biblical Illustrator.* 1955. Baker. 688p. G. B29. $9.00.

EYLES, Desmond. *The Doulton Lambeth Wares.* 1975. London. Hutchinson & Co. 1st. 4to corners bumped. 179p. VG. H1. $120.00.

— F —

FACKLER, Elizabeth. *Arson.* 1984. NY. Dodd, Mead. 1st. author's 1st novel. F/F. T2. $20.00.

FACKLER, Elizabeth. *Barbed Wire.* 1986. NY. St. Martin. 1st. F/F. T2. $15.00.

FADIMAN, Anne. *Ex Libris.* 1998. NY. FSG. 1st. F/F. M23. $30.00.

FAGIN, N. Bryllion. *The Histrionic Mr. Poe.* Baltimore. The Johns Hopkins Press. 1949. 8vo. 289p. ftspc. red cloth. dj. 1sted. dj w/some small tears and knicks. book VG. L5. $35.00.

FAHERTY, Terence. *Kill Me Again.* 1996. NY. S&S. 1st. sgn. VF/VF. T2. $25.00.

FAHERTY, Terence. *Live to Regret.* 1992. NY. St. Martin. 1st. VF/VF. T2. $25.00.

FAHERTY, Terence. *Orion Rising.* 1999. NY. St. Martin. 1st. sgn. F/F. G8. $25.00.

FAHERTY, Terence. *The Ordained.* 1997. NY. St. Martin. 1st. sgn. VF/VF. T2. $25.00.

FAIDLEY, Warren. *Storm Chaser; In Pursuit of Untamed Skies.* 1996. Atlanta. The Weather Channel. 1st. color photos by author. 4to. 182p. VG in glossy wrp. K5. $22.00.

FAIR, James R. *The Louisiana and Arkansas Railway, the Story of a Regional Line.* 1997. Dekalb. Northern Illinois Univ Press. 1st. photos. 158p. VG+/VG+. B18. $25.00.

FAIRCHILD, David. *The World Was My Garden. Travels of a Plant Explorer.* 1939. NY. lg 8vo. 494p. 128 photo plates. ep tanned. else VG. B26. $29.00.

FAIRCHILD, Rev. T. B. *History of the Town of Cuyahoga Falls, Summit County, Ohio.* 1876. Cleveland. 1st. inscr. ex lib. new wrps. 39p and 8p of ads. VG in protective case. B18. $125.00.

FAIRLIE, Gerard. *Deadline for Macall.* 1956. Mill. 1st Am ed. VG/G+. G8. $20.00.

FAIRSTEIN, Linda. *Cold Hit.* 1999. NY. Scribners. 1st. sgn. VF/VF. T2. $25.00.

FAIRSTEIN, Linda. *Final Jeopardy.* 1996. NY. Scribners. 1st. sgn. author's 1st mystery. VF/VF. T2. $25.00.

FAIRWEATHER, Lori. *Blood & Water.* 1999. NY. Morrow. 1st. UP. author's 1st novel. sgn. VF/pict wrp. T2. $20.00.

FALKNER, David. *The Short Season.* 1986. NY. Times. 1st. NF/NF. R16. $45.00.

FALOR, William A. (ed). *Pictorial of Akron and Summit County of Yesteryear.* nd. Akron. ltd ed. sgn by author. oblong. B18. $47.50.

FALWELL, Jerry. *If I Should Die Before I Wake....* 1986. Nelson. 219p. VG/VG. B29. $5.00.

FAMOL, Jeffery. *Honourable Mr. Tawnish.* 1913. 1921. Boston. Little, Brn. 1st Am ed. VG. G8. $17.50.

FARINA, Richard. *Been Down So Long it Looks Like Up to Me.* 1966. NY. Random House. 1st. author's 1st and only book pub before his death. F/F. D10. $225.00.

FARMER, Nell R. (ed). *Early Days of Lakewood.* 1936. np. Daughters of Am Revolution. Lakewood Chapter. ils. mark on rear cover. 111p. G. B18. $27.50.

FARMER, Philip Jose. *Dayworld.* 1985. NY. Putnam. 1st. F/F. T2. $8.00.

FARMER, Philip Jose. *Dayworld Rebel.* 1987. NY. Putnam. 1st. F/F. H11. $20.00.

FARRELL, Gillian B. *Alibi for an Actress.* 1992. NY. Pocket. 1st. author's 1st book. VF/F. H11. $30.00.

FARRIS, Jack. *A Man to Ride with.* 1957. Philadelphia. Lippincott. 1st. F/F. H11. $195.00.

FARRIS, John. *Scare Tactics.* 1988. NY. Tor. 1st. VF/VF. T2. $9.00.

FASH, William. *Scribes, Warriors & Kings.* 1991. NY. Thames & Hudson. 1st. 4to. 192p. G/G. F3. $45.00.

FASSETT, Norman C. *Grasses of Wisconsin.* 1951. Madison. 173p. 182 maps. 356 text figures. VG. B26. $17.50.

FAST, Julius. *Street of Fear.* 1958. NY. Rinehart. 1st. VG/VG. G8. $10.00.

FAULKINER, Suzanne. *Room to Move: An Anthology of Australian Women's Short Stories.* 1986. NY. Watts. 1st. VF/F. H11. $30.00.

FAULKNER, William. *A Fable.* (1954). NY. Random House. 1st printing stated. slight tears. VG+/G. B15. $75.00.

FAULKNER, William. *Intruder in the Dust.* 1948. NY. Random House. 1st. F/F. price clip; superior copy. D10. $300.00.

FAULKNER, William. *Knight's Gambit.* 1951. London. Chatto & Windus. 1st British ed. VG+/VG. minor wear and spotting. A24. $125.00.

FAULKNER, William. *New Orleans Sketches.* 1958. Brunswick, NJ. Rutgers Univ Press. 1st thus. intro by Carvel Collins. includes all 16 sketches. sgn & dated on ffep. VG. some fading/VG. minor wear. A24. $75.00.

FAULKNER, William. *Requiem for a Nun.* 1951. NY. Random House. 1st. pc. dj. F/VG. M19. $125.00.

FAULKNER, William. *The Mansion.* 1959. NY. Random House. 1st. F/lightly used dj. B2. $65.00.

FAULKS, Sevastian. *Charlotte Gray.* (1998). NY. Random House. 1st Am ed. sgn by author. F/F. B3. $40.00.

FAUST, Miklos. *Physiology of Temperate Zone Fruit Trees.* 1989. NY. F in dj. B26. $42.50.

FAUST, Ron. *In the Forest of the Night.* 1993. NY. Tor. 1st. F/F. H11. $15.00.

FAWCETT, Quinn. *Against the Brotherhood.* 1997. Forge. 1st. F/F. G8. $20.00.

FEATHER, Leonard. *From Satchmo to Miles.* 1972. NY. Stein and Day. ARC w/slip. F/NF. B2. $45.00.

FEATHER, Leonard. *Jazz.* nd. Los Angeles. Trend Books. 1st. wrp. ils. 80p. NF. B2. $40.00.

FEATHER, Leonard. *The Book of Jazz. A Guide to the Entire Field.* 1957. NY. Horizon. 1st. creased pgs. soiling. G+/VG. sunned. worn. B2. $25.00.

FEATHER, Leonard. *The Encyclopedia Yearbook of Jazz.* 1956. NY. Horizon. 1st. F/VG w/tears. B2. $50.00.

FEATHER, Leonard; and Jack Tracy. *Laughter from the Hip. The Lighter Side of Jazz.* 1963. NY. Horizon. 1st. F/lightly soiled dj. B2. $35.00.

FEHL, Noah Edward. *Science and Culture.* 1966. Hong Kong. Chinese Univ. 417p. G/some marginal notes. B29. $32.00.

FEIED, Frederick. *No Pie in the Sky.* 1964. NY. Citadel. 1st. NF. owner's name/wrps. B2. $30.00.

FEIFFER, Jules. *Passionella and Other Stories.* 1959. NY. McGraw-Hill. 1st. sgn by author. VG+/wrps. owner's name upper edge front cover. B2. $50.00.

FEIKEMA, Feike; See Manfred, Frederick.

FEIST, Raymond E. *Faerie Tale.* 1988. NY. Doubleday. 1st. F/VF. H11. $35.00.

FELTON, Harold W. *John Henry and His Hammer.* 1950. NY. Knopf. 1st. Gilbraltar Lib bdg. F. B2. $25.00.

FENNELLY, Tony. *Glory Hole Murders.* 1985. Carroll & Graf. 1st. VG+/VG+. G8. $25.00.

FENNO, Jack. *Small Bang — A Literary Mystery.* 1992. Random House. 1st. NF/NF. G8. $15.00.

FENWICK, E. P. *Two Named for Death.* 1945. NY. Farrar & Rinehart. 1st. F/dj lt wear. M15. $45.00.

FERBER, Edna. *Giant.* 1952. Garden City. Doubleday. 1st. F/NF. H11. $50.00.

FERBER, Edna. *Great Son.* 1945. Doubleday. Doran & Co. G+. S19. $25.00.

FERGUSON, Don. *Lion King.* 1994. Walt Disney. 94p. VG. C5. $12.50.

FERGUSSON, Bruce Chandler. *The Piper's Sons.* 1999. NY. Dutton. 1st. author's 1st novel. sgn. VF/VF. T2. $25.00.

FERGUSSON, Erna. *Dancing Gods.* 1957. Albuquerque. rpt. G/dj. A19. $45.00.

FERGUSSON, Erna. *Venezuela.* 1939. Knopf. 1st. 346p. VG. F3. $10.00.

FERM, Vergilius. *Classics of Protestantism.* 1959. Philosophical Library. 587p. VG. B29. $7.50.

FERM, Vergilius. *The Protestant Credo.* 1953. Philosophical Library. 241p. VG. B29. $10.00.

FERNETT, Gene. *A Thousand Golden Horns.* 1966. Midland. Pendell. 1st. glossy paper. 2nd state dj. F. B2. $60.00.

FERRARS, E. X. *Pretty Pink Shroud.* 1977. Collins Crime Club. 1st British ed. VG/VG. G8. $22.50.

FERRE, Nels. *Christian Faith and Higher Education.* 1954. Harper. 251p. VG. B29. $4.50.

FERRE, Nels. *Retrun to Christianity.* 1943. Harper. 76p. VG/VG. B29. $4.50.

FERRIGNO, Robert. *Dead Man's Dance.* 1995. NY. Putnam. 1st. F/F. T2. $8.00.

FERRIGNO, Robert. *The Cheshire Moon.* 1993. NY. William Morrow & Co. 1st. sgn. F/F. O11. $30.00.

FERRIGNO, Robert. *The Horse Latitudes.* 1990. NY. Morrow. 1st. inscr by author. author's 1st book. F/F. B2. $40.00.

FERRIMAN, Z. Duckett. *Turkey and the Turks.* 1911. NY. James Pott. pict cloth. photos. lt edgewear. rear cover spotted. 334p. VG. B18. $75.00.

FERRIS, Timothy. *The Mind's Sky; Human Intelligence in Cosmic Context.* 1992. London. Bantam. 8vo. 281p. VG/VG. K5. $16.00.

FERRIS, Timothy, editor. *The World Treasury of Physics, Astronomy, and Mathematics.* 1991. Boston. Little, Brn. lg 8vo. bkplt. 859p. VG/cloth. K5. $25.00.

FERRIS, William, Jr. *Blues from the Delta.* 1970. London. Studio Vista. 1st. wrp. F except tape on spine. B2. $45.00.

FESPERMAN, Dan. *Lie in the Dark.* 1999. NY. Soho Press. 1st. author's 1st novel. sgn. VF/VF. T2. $28.00.

FETTA, Emma Lou. *Murder on the Face of It.* 1940. Crime Club. 1st. G-VG. G8. $15.00.

FEUER, Leon I. *Jewish Literature Since the Bible.* 1957. Am Hebrew Cong. Book One. 297p. VG. B29. $8.50.

FICHTER, Joseph. *America's Forgotten Priests: What They are Saying.* 1968. Harper. 254p. VG/G. B29. $10.50.

FIELD, Edward. *Revolutionary Defences in Rhode Island.* 1896. Providence. Preston & Rounds. 1st. fold out maps. ils. gilt decor cloth. 161p. VG. B18. $95.00.

FIELD, Edward. *Variety Photoplays.* 1967. NY. Grove Press. pbo. wrp. inscr by author. NF. B2. $40.00.

FIELD, Eugene. *Auto-Analysis.* 1901. NY. HM Caldwell. 37p. lacks ffep. G11. $10.00.

FIELD, Eugene. *Poems of Childhood.* 1904. NY. Scribners. 1st. ils by Maxfield Parrish. sm 4to. black cloth. 199p. VF. some wear. D6. $165.00.

FIELD, Michael. *Michael Field's Cooking School.* 1965. NY. M. Barrows and Co. BCE/BOMC. ils Roderick Wells. G/G. A28. $7.95.

FIELD, Rachel. *Hitty: Her First Hundred Years.* 1931 (1920). Macmillan. ils Dorothy Lathrop. VG. B15. $100.00.

FIELDING, A. *Cluny Problem.* 1929. NY. Knopf. 1st Am ed. VG. G8. $17.50.

FIELDING, Helen. *Bridget Jones' Diary.* 1998. NY. Viking. 1st. F/F. M23. $40.00.

FIELDING, Howard. *Straight Crooks.* 1927. Chelsea House. 1st. VG. G8. $10.00.

FIELDING, Joy. *See Jane Run.* 1991. NY. Morrow. 1st. ARC. VF/pict wpr. T2. $5.00.

FIELDING, Joy. *Tell Me No Secrets.* 1993. NY. Morrow. 1st. VF/VF. T2. $8.00.

FIELDING, Mantle. *Dictionary of American Painters, Sculptors, and Engravers.* 1974. Green Farms. Modern Books & Crafts. enlarged from 1926 ed. F in rubbed dj. B2. $25.00.

FIGUEROA, Brigadier General Jose. *Manifesto to the Mexican Republic.* 1978. Berkeley. Univ of Ca Press. 1st. facsimile of 1835 document. 156p. G/G. F3. $20.00.

FILBY, F. A. *Creation Revealed; A Study of Genesis Chapter One in the Light of Science.* 1965. Revell. 160p. VG/VG. B29. $8.50.

FILLER, Louis. *Randolph Bourne.* 1943. Washington, DC. Am Council Public Affairs. 1st. 158p. VG/wrp. B2. $25.00.

FINCH, Phillip. *F 2 F.* 1996. NY. Bantam. 1st. NF/VG+. R16. $25.00.

FINDER, Joseph. *High Crimes.* 1998. NY. Morrow. 1st. ARC. sgn. F/pict wrp. T2. $20.00.

FINE, Donald I. *Rasputin's Revenge: The Further Startling Adventures of Auguste Lupa, Son of Holmes.* 1987. NY. 1st. F/F. T2. $20.00.

FINGER, Charles J. *Tales From Silver Lands.* 1924. NY. Doubleday. VG in dj. A16. $8.00.

FINK, Joseph J. *Joe Fink Tells Tall Sherlockian Tales.* 1998. Shelburne, Ontario. battered silcon dispatch box. 1st. VF/VF. T2. $22.00.

FINKELSTEIN, Sidney. *Jazz. A People's Music.* 1948. NY. Citadel. 1st state dj. blue; binding. blk & yellow. F. chipped dj. B2. $35.00.

FINLAY, Ian. *Scottish Gold and Silver Work.* 1956. London. Chatto & Windus. 1st. lg 8vo. bl gilt cloth in ils dj. 178p + 96 plate of ils. K1. $75.00.

FINLAY, Virgil. *Third Book of Virgil Finlay.* 1979. de la Ree. 1st. NF/dj. P3. $65.00.

FINNEY, Ben. *Feet First.* 1971. NY. Crown. 1st. Inscribed on half-title page. Book has slight slant. F-/F. H11. $50.00.

FINNEY, Charles G. *The Magician Out of Manchuria.* 1989. Hampton Falls. Donald M. Grant. 1st hc ed. 1/600 # copies. sgn by artist Richard Salvucci. VF/VF. T2. $25.00.

FINNEY, Humphrey S. *A Stud Farm Diary.* 1949. Berryville. Blue Ridge. 1st. 12mo. flexible leather bdg. VG. O3. $38.00.

FINNEY, Jack. *Forgotten News.* 1983. NY. Doubleday. 1st. F/VNF. D10. $50.00.

FINNEY, Jack. *From Time to Time.* 1995. NY. S&S. 1st. VF/VF. H11. $20.00.

FINNEY, Patricia. *Unicorn's Blood.* 1998. London. Orion. 1st. VF/dj. M15. $55.00.

FINNIE, David H. *Pioneers East: The Early American Experience in the Middle East.* 1967. Harvard U. Press. 1st. 8vo owner's name on title page. light soil with wear at spine extremes. 333p. VG. H1. $22.50.

FIRSOFF, V. A. *The Moon.* 1966/1964. NY. New American Library. 24 b/w plates. text figures. 127p. G in pb. K5. $6.00.

FISCHER, Bruno. *The Hornet's Nest.* 1944. NY. Morrow. 1st. dj has tiny wear at spine ends. NF/dj. M15. $65.00.

FISCHER, Erwin. *The Berlin Indictment.* 1971. Cleveland. World. 1st. F/F. H11. $35.00.

FISCHER, Paul. *Variegated Foliage Plants.* 1960. London. color. b&w photos. F in dj. B26. $24.00.

FISCHER, Tibor. *The Collector.* (1997). NY. Holt. 1st. F/F. B3. $30.00.

FISH, Robert L. *Schlock Holmes: The Complete Bagel Street Saga.* 1990. Bloomington. Gaslight Publications. 1st. VF/VF. T2. $20.00.

FISH, Robert L. *The Gold of Troy.* 1980. Garden City. Doubleday. 1st. inscr. VF/dj. M15. $45.00.

FISH, Robert L. *The Memoirs of Schlock Holmes.* 1974. Indianapolis. Bobbs Merrill. 1st. F/F. T2. $35.00.

FISH, Robert L. *The Murder League.* 1968. NY. S&S. 1st. book has faint stain on spine and bookplate. Remainder stripe. F/F. H11. $25.00.

FISHEL, Wesley R. *Vietnam: Anatomy of A Conflict.* 1968. FE Peacock Pub. 879p. F/VG. R11. $40.00.

FISHER, David. *Wrong Man.* 1993. NY. Random House. 1st. VG/VG+. G8. $10.00.

FISHER, David E. *The Scariest Place on Earth; Eye to Eye with Hurricanes.* 1994. NY. Random House. 2nd printing. text ils. 8vo. 250p. F/F. K5. $15.00.

FISHER, Douglas A. *Steel Serves the Nation 1901 – 1951.* 1956. NY. ils ep. 227p. VG. B18. $15.00.

FISHER, George P. *Out of the Woods: Romance of Camp Life.* 1896. Chicago. McClurg. 1st. 12mo. 270p. gr cloth. NF/dj. J3. $75.00.

FISHER, John. *Reform & Insurrection in Bourbon. New Granada & Peru.* 1990. LSU. 1st. 356p. dj. F3. $20.00.

FISHER, Leonard Everett. *Printers: Colonial American Craftsmen.* 1965. NY. Franklin Watts. 1st. ils. cloth. F/NF. O10. $25.00.

FISHER, M. E., E. Satchell & J. M. Watkins. *Gardening with New Zealand Plants, Shrubs, and Trees.* 1975 (1970). Auckland. rev & enlarged ed. VG in dj. B26. $37.50.

FISHER, M. F. K. *Dubious Honors.* (1988). San Francisco. Northpoint. 1st. F/F. B3. $35.00.

FISHER, M. F. K. *Sister Age.* (1983). NY. Knopf. 1st. F/F. B3. $40.00.

FISHER, M. F. K. *Stay Me, Oh Comfort Me.* (1993). NY. Pantheon. 1st. F/F. B3. $30.00.

FISHER, M. F. K. *To Begin Again, Stories and Memories 1908 – 1929.* (1992). NY. Pantheon. 1st. F/F. B3. $25.00.

FISHER, M. L. *Albatross of Midway Island.* 1974 (1970). Carbondale, IL. photos/maps. 156p. cloth. F/dj. C12. $15.00.

FISHER, Raymond. *Bering's Voyages. Wither and Why.* ca 1977. Seattle & Washington. U of Washington. 8vo. map ep. 31 maps in text. 217p. VG+ in lightly worn dj. P4. $75.00.

FISHER, Richard Swainson. *The Progress of the United States of America. From the Earliest Periods. Geographical, Statistical, and Historical.* 1854. NY. J. H. Colton & Co. lg 8vo. ils woodcut plates of official state seals. 432p. elaborate blindstamp. pict blk calf. sm gouge on lower spine. K1. $125.00.

FISHER, Robert Moore. *How About the Weather?* 1951. NY. Harper. 16 maps. 16 plates. 8vo. line drawings. 186p. VG/chipped dj. pgs yellowed. K5. $10.00.

FISHER & JONES. *Wheats of Commerce: Commercial Wheat Classes.* 1937. London. 55p. VG/wrp. A10. $26.00.

FISK, Wilbur. *Hard Marching Every Day: Civil War Letters Of...1861 – 65.* 1992. U KS. edit Rosenblatt. fwd Reid Mitchell. VG/dj. M17. $20.00.

FISKE, John. *American Revolution.* 1898. Houghton Mifflin. 8vo. ils/maps. 403p. cloth. F. O1. $35.00.

FISKE, John. *Darwinism & Other Essays.* 1896. Boston. 2nd. 374p. A13. $35.00.

FISKE, Willard. *Chess Tales & Chess Miscellanies.* 1912. Longman Gr. 1st. 8vo. 427p. gilt maroon cloth. VG+. B20. $75.00.

FITCH, C. G. *The Handling and General Management of the Thoroughbred Stallion.* nd (1947). London. Hutchinson. 1st. VG/G. O3. $25.00.

FITCH, Henry. *The Perfect Calendar for Every Year of the Christian Era....* 1928. NY. Funk & Wagnalls. 8vo. 47p. G/soiled cloth. ink stain. K5. $15.00.

FITZ & ODLUM. *Lady Sourdough.* 1941. NY. 1st. VG/VG. B5. $25.00.

FITZGERALD, Edward. *Rubaiyat of Omar Khayyam.* 1943. Jamaica. mini. 24 full-p ils. 112p. gilt gr vinyl cloth/box. B24. $250.00.

FITZGERALD, Emily McCorkle. *Army Doctor's Wife on the Frontier: Letters...1874 – 1878.* 1962. Pittsburgh. 1st. 8vo. photos. 352p. bl cloth. P4. $55.00.

FITZGERALD, F. Scott. *Dear Scott/Dear Max: Fitzgerald-Perkins Correspondence.* 1971. Scribner. 8vo. 282p. VG/dj. P4. $25.00.

FITZGERALD, F. Scott. *Golden Moment: Novels Of...* 1970. U IL. VG/dj. M17. $15.00.

FITZGERALD, F. Scott. *Love in the Night.* 1994. NY. Clarkson Potter. 1st separate Am. bl pict brd/ribbon ties. F/sans. Q1. $35.00.

FITZGERALD, Ken. *Weathervanes & Whirligigs.* 1967. Clarkson Potter. 1st. VG/dj. O3. $35.00.

FITZGERALD, Penelope. *Knox Brothers.* 1977. NY. 1st. photos. VG/dj. M17. $20.00.

FITZGERALD, Percy. *Boswell's Autobiography.* 1912. London. Chatto Windus. 1st. VG. H13. $45.00.

FITZGERALD, Zelda. *Collected Writings.* 1991. Scribner. 1st. thick 8vo. 480p. F/dj. J3. $35.00.

FITZHUGH, Bill. *The Organ Grinders.* 1998. NY. Avon Books. 1st. UP. sgn. VF/pict wrp. T2. $20.00.

FITZHUGH, Percy Keese. *Roy Blakeley's Tangled Trail.* 1924. NY. Grosset & Dunlap. spine edges frayed. G. A16. $10.00.

FITZPATRICK, T. J. *Rafinesque, a Sketch of His Life....* 1911. Des Moines, IA. Historical Dept. of Iowa. 1st. 32 plates. ils. brds. 239p. VG. lt wear to corners. unopened pgs. B18. $75.00.

FITZWYGRAM, Lt Gen. Sir F. *Horses and Stables.* 1894. London. Longmans Green. 4th ed. VG. O3. $45.00.

FLAGG, Fannie. *Coming Attractions.* 1981. Morrow. 1st. sgn & dated. 1st novel. F/worn dj. M25. $75.00.

FLAGG, Fannie. *Fried Green Tomatoes at the Whistle Stop Cafe.* (1987). NY. Random House. 1st. author's 2nd book. NF. very minor wear/F. B3. $75.00.

FLAGG, John H. *Lyrics of New England & Other Poems.* 1909. Cedar Rapids. Torch. sgn. thin 8vo. 3-quarter tan leather/gr cloth. VG. S17. $25.00.

FLAMMARION, Camile. *Popular Astronomy; A General Description of the Heavens.* 1897. London. Chatto & Windus. translated by J. Ellard Gore. 3 plates. 288 text ils. 8vo. 686p. G in cloth. library # painted on spine. K5. $90.00.

FLANAGAN, Thomas. *End of the Hunt.* 1994. Dutton. 1st. VG/dj. M17. $15.00.

FLAVELL, A. J. *T. E. Lawrence: Legend & Man.* 1988. Oxford. Bodleian Lib. 113p. AN. M7. $25.00.

FLAVELL, George F. *Log of the Panthon: Account of 1896 River Voyage...* 1987. Boulder. Pruett. 8vo. 107p. VG+. F7. $15.00.

FLAVELL, M. Kay. *George Grosz: A Biography.* 1988. Yale. ils. VG/dj. M17. $30.00.

FLAVELL, Ray & Claude Smale. *Studio Glassmaking.* 1974. Van Nostrand Reinhold Co. 1st. Square 8vo. 108p. VG/VG. H1. $62.50.

FLAWN, Louis. *Gardening with Cloches.* 1957. London. Gifford. 202p. VG/dj. A10. $28.00.

FLEET, Betsy. *Green Mount After the War: Correspondence Of...* (1978). U VA. photos. VG/fair. B10. $15.00.

FLEET, H. *Concise Natural History of New Zealand.* 1986. Auckland. Heinemann. ils/photos/map. 275p. VG. M12. $22.50.

FLEITMANN, Lida L. *Comments on Hacks and Hunters.* 1921. NY. Scribner. 1st ed. G. O3. $45.00.

FLEMING, Beatrice J. and Marion J. Pryde. *Distinguished Negroes Abroad.* 1946. Washington, DC. Associated Publishers. VF in brownish bds. M25. $75.00.

FLEMING, Ian. *Gilt-Edged Bonds.* 1961. Macmillan. 1st thus. VG/dj. B11. $45.00.

FLEMING, Ian. *Octopussy and the Living Daylights.* 1966. London. Jonathan Cape. 1st. VF/dj. M15. $65.00.

FLEMING, Ian. *On Her Majesty's Secret Service.* 1963. London. Jonathan Cape. 1st. some staining. F/dj. M15. $275.00.

FLEMING, Ian. *The Man with the Golden Gun.* 1965. NAL. 1st. F/NF clip. B3. $25.00.

FLEMING, Ian. *The Man with the Golden Gun.* 1965. NY. New American Library. 1st. F/F. T2. $30.00.

FLEMING, Ian. *Thunderball.* 1993. NY. M J F books. reissue. 1st ed thus. VF/VF. T2. $5.00.

FLEMING, Ian. *Thunderball.* 1961. London. Jonathan Cape. 1st. F/dj. M15. $400.00.

FLEMING, Ian. *You Only Live Twice.* 1964. NY. NAL. 1st Am ed. F except owner's name in G dj. B2. $35.00.

FLEMING, Peter. *Brazilian Adventure.* 1934. np. New York. 412p. G/chipped dj. F3. $25.00.

FLEMING, Theodore H. *Short-Tailed Fruit Bat.* 1988. U Chicago. 365p. F/dj. S15. $30.00.

FLEMING, Walter Lynnwood. *The Sequel to Appomattox. A Chronicle of the Reunion of the States.* 1919. New Haven. Yale Univ Press. 1st. orig cloth. wear to spine. 322p. VG. M8. $45.00.

FLETCHER, Chrys Paul. *Cry for a Shadow.* 1968. NY. Putnam. 1st Am ed of UK novel. F/F. B2. $25.00.

FLETCHER, Inglis. *Roanoke Hundred.* 1948. Bobbs Merrill. 1st. sgn. VG. B11. $50.00.

FLETCHER, J. M. *Proceedings of Dorset Natural History...Vols 52 & 54.* 1931 & 1933. Dorchester. private prt. 2 vol. ils/fld map. NF. M12. $30.00.

FLETCHER, J. S. *Murder of the Ninth Baronet.* 1932. NY. Knopf. 1st Am. Price clipped jacket with some internal tape mends. F/dj. M15. $65.00.

FLETCHER, N. H. *The Physics of Rain Clouds.* 1962. Cambridge. Cambridge Univ Press. 1st. photos & text figures. 8vo. 386p. VG/rubbed dj. K5. $40.00.

FLETCHER, Stevenson Whitcomb. *Pennsylvania Agriculture & Country Life 1640 – 1840.* 1950. Historical & Museum Commission. 8vo. 605p. VG/AN. H1. $25.00.

FLOOD, John. *Bag Men.* 1997. NY. Norton. 1st. author's 1st book. Book has one bumped corner. F-/F. H11. $25.00.

FLOOD, Richard. *Fighting Southpaw.* 1949. Houghton Mifflin. probable 1st. VG. P8. $35.00.

FLOOK, Maria. *Family Night.* 1993. NY. Pantheon. 1st. review copy. F/F. H11. $40.00.

FLORA, Fletcher. *Irrepressible Peccadillo.* 1962. NY. Macmillan. 1st. VG/VG. G8. $15.00.

FLORA, Snowden D. *Hailstorms of the United States.* 1956. Norman. Univ of Oklahoma Press. 8vo. b/w photo ils. 201p. VG/VG. K5. $20.00.

FLORESCU, Radu. *In Search of Frankenstein.* 1975. NYGS. 1st. rem mk. VG/G+. L1. $75.00.

FLORESCU & MCNALLY. *Essential Dracula.* 1978. NY. Mayflower. VG/G clip. L1. $55.00.

FLORY, Jane. *Mr Snitzel's Cookies.* 1950. Rand McNally. 1st. 16mo. VG. M5. $12.00.

FLOYD, Grace C. *The Six Swans.* nd. NY. Raphael Tuck & Sons. color ils. Poor. A16. $15.00.

FLOYD, Samuel, Jr.; Martha J. Reisser. *Black Music Biography. An Annotated Bibliography.* 1987. White Plains. Kraus. 1st. 302p. F. issued w/o dj. B2. $40.00.

FLYNN, Carol Houlihan. *Washed in the Blood.* 1983. NY. Seaview. 1st. F/F. H11. $25.00.

FLYNN, Don. *Murder in a Flat.* 1988. Walker. 1st Am ed. VG/NF. G8. $10.00.

FLYNN, Robert. *The Last Klick.* 1994. Dallas. Baskerville. 1st. F/F. H11. $25.00.

FLYNN, Vince. *Term Limits.* 1998. np. Pocket Books. 1st. author's 1st novel. NF/NF. R16. $25.00.

FODEN, Giles. *The Last King of Scotland.* 1998. NY. Knopf. ARC. wrps. F. B2. $25.00.

FODER & GARRETT. *Psychology of Language: Introduction to Psycholinguistics...* 1974. McGraw Hill. 537p. prt blk cloth. G1. $65.00.

FODOR, Laszlo. *Argentina.* 1941. Hastings. 1st. 23p. dj. F3. $15.00.

FOEHL & HARGREAVES. *Story of Logging: The White Pine in Saginaw Valley.* 1964. Bay City. Red Key. ils/reading list/photos. 70p. A17. $30.00.

FOGG, Lawrence Daniel. *Shady Sinners of the Styx: A Posthumous Adventure of Sherlock Holmes.* 1999. NY. Mysterious Bookshop. 1st separate ed. 1/221 copies. A chapbook. VF/printed wrp. T2. $10.00.

FOGLIA, Leonard & David Richards. *1 Ragged Ridge Road.* 1997. Pocket. 1st. NF/F. G8. $15.00.

FOLEY, Daniel J. *Ground Covers For Easier Gardening.* 1961. Philadelphia. extensively ils. photos. drawings. 4p of color. 224p. VG in dj. B26. $12.50.

FOLEY, Daniel J. *The Complete Book of Garden Ornaments, Complements, and Accessories.* 1972. NY. VG+ in dj. B26. $25.00.

FOLLETT, Helen. *Islands on Guard.* 1943. NY. photos. VG. M17. $15.00.

FOLLETT, Ken. *A Dangerous Fortune.* 1993. NY. Delacorte. 1st. F/F. H11. $25.00.

FOLLETT, Ken. *Night Over Water.* 1991. NY. Morrow. 1st. F/F. H11. $35.00.

FOLLETT, Ken. *Night Over Water.* 1991. London. Macmillan. 1st. F/dj. M15. $45.00.

FOLLETT, Ken. *The Bear Raid.* 1976. London. Harwood-Smart. 1st. F/dj. M15. $150.00.

FOLLETT, Ken. *The Hammer of Eden.* 1998. NY. Crown. 1st. F/F. H11. $15.00.

FOLLETT, Ken. *The Key to Rebecca.* 1980. NY. Morrow. 1st. F/F. H11. $40.00.

FOLLETT, Ken. *The Third Twin.* 1996. NY. Crown. 1st. F/F. H11. $15.00.

FOLLETT, Ken & Rene Louis Maurice. *The Gentlemen of 16 July.* 1978. NY. Arbor. 1st. F/F. H11. $35.00.

FOLSOM, Allan. *The Day After Tomorrow.* 1994. Boston. Little, Brn. 1st. VF/VF. T2. $10.00.

FOLSOM, Merrill. *More Great American Mansions & Their Stories.* 1962. Hastings. photos. VG/dj. M17. $17.50.

FOLTZ, Charles Steinman. *Surgeon of the Seas: Adventurous Life of Jonathan Foltz...* 1931. Bobbs Merrill. 1st. 351p. cloth. VG. M8. $65.00.

FONDILLER, Harvey. *Best of Popular Photography.* 1979. Ziff-Davis. 1st. ils. 392p. VG/dj. S14. $20.00.

FONER, Philip. *The Fur and Leather Workers Union.* 1950. Newark. Norden Press. 1st. NF/NF. B2. $35.00.

FONER & MAHONEY. *House Divided: America in the Age of Lincoln.* 1990. Chicago Hist Soc. 1st. ils. 179p. NF/dj. M10. $32.50.

FONES, Alfred C. *Mouth Hygiene: A Text-Book for Dental Hygienists.* 1934. Lea Febiger. 4th. 372p. NF. C14. $20.00.

FONTAINE, Andre. *History of the Cold War from Korean War to Present.* 1969. NY. Pantheon. 1st. VG/dj. N2. $10.00.

FONTAINE, Joan. *No Bed of Roses, an Autobiography.* 1978. NY. Morrow. 2nd. inscr. photos. VG/dj. C9. $90.00.

FONTANE, Theodor. *Entanglements.* 1986. Three Rivers Books. 1st. An Everyday Berlin Story translated by Derek Bowman. F/F. S19. $40.00.

FOOS, Laurie. *Ex Utero.* (1995). Minneapolis. Coffee House Press. 1st. author's 1st book. F/F. B3. $25.00.

FOOTE, Horton. *Cousins and the Death of Papa.* 1989. NY. Grove Press. 1st. final 2 plays of the Orphans' Home Cycle. intro by Samuel G. Freedman. sgn by Foote. F/F. A24. $35.00.

FOOTE, Shelby. *View of History.* 1981. Palaemon. 1st. 1/140. sgn. F/as issued. B30. $200.00.

FOOTMAN, Robert. *China Spy.* 1987. NY. Dodd. 1st. F/F. H11. $20.00.

FOOTNER, Hulbert. *Murder of a Bad Man.* 1936. NY. Harper. 1st Am. VG/dj. M15. $60.00.

FOOTNER, Hulbert. *Rivers of the Eastern Shore, Seventeen Maryland Rivers.* 1944. Farrar & Rinehart. 4th. sm8vo. owner's stamp on ep. 375p. F/G. H1. $16.00.

FORBES, Allan. *Our Garden Friends the Bugs.* 1962. NY. Exposition. 1st. 190p. VG/dj. A10. $15.00.

FORBES, Allan. *Towns of New England & Old England.* Ireland & Scotland. 1921. Putnam. 2 vol. teg. gilt cloth. VG. B18. $65.00.

FORBES, Esther. *Johnny Tremain.* (1943). Houghton Mifflin. 27th. gr cloth. F/VG. T11. $30.00.

FORBES, Leslie. *Bombay Ice.* 1998. London. Phoenix House. 1st. VF/dj. M15. $250.00.

FORBES, Leslie. *Bombay Ice.* 1998. NY. Farrar. ARC. wrp. F. B2. $30.00.

FORBES, R. J. & D. R. O' Beirne. *This Technical Development of the Royal Dutch/ Shell 1890 – 1940.* 1957. Leyden. E.J. Brill. 4to. profusely ils w/photos, drawings, charts, maps. (10). 670p. bl cloth. K1. $75.00.

FORD, G. M. *Cast in Stone.* 1996. NY. Walker. 1st. sgn. VF/VF. T2. $35.00.

FORD, G. M. *Slow Burn.* (1998). NY. Avon. 1st. F/F. B3. $20.00.

FORD, G. M. *The Bum's Rush.* 1997. NY. Walker. 1st. sgn. VF/VF. T2. $30.00.

FORD, G. M. *Who in Hell Is Wanda Fuca?* 1995. NY. Walker. 1st. sgn. author's 1st book. F/F. A24. $95.00.

FORD, Gerald R. *A Time to Heal.* 1979. np. np. inscr 1st. F/VG dj. M19. $100.00.

FORD, James A. *Judge of Men.* 1968. Hodder Stoughton. NF/dj. P3. $7.00.

FORD, Jesse Hill. *Feast of St Barnabas.* 1969. Atlantic/Little, Brn. 1st. VG/dj. B30. $25.00.

FORD, Jesse Hill. *Raider.* 1975. Atlantic/ Little, Brn. 1st. sgn. G/dj. B30. $55.00.

FORD, Leslie. *Bahamas Murder Case.* 1952. Scribners. 1st. G-VG. G8. $12.50.

FORD, Leslie. *Honolulu Murders.* 1946. Scribners. 1st. VG/VG. G8. $45.00.

FORD, Leslie. *Sound of Footsteps.* 1931. Crime Club. 1st Am ed. G-VG. G8. $25.00.

FORD, Leslie. *Trial by Ambush.* 1962. Scribners. 1st. VG/G-VG. G8. $22.50.

FORD, Leslie. *Woman in Black.* 1947. Scribner. 1st. VG/G. N4. $20.00.

FORD, Paul Leicester. *A Checked Love Affair.* 1903. np. Dodd Mead. 1st. ils by Harrison Fisher & George Wharton Edwards; bookplate. F. M19. $65.00.

FORD, Richard. *A Piece of My Heart.* (1976). NY. Harper & Row. 1st. author's 1st book. NF. lt shelfwear to spine. lt foxing/NF. price clip. lt wear to top & bottom of spine. B3. $400.00.

FORD, Richard. *Independence Day.* 1995. NY. Knopf. 1st. sgn. F/F. D10. $85.00.

FORD, Richard. *The Ultimate Good Luck.* (1989). London. Collins Harvill. 1st British ed. F/F. B3. $75.00.

FORD, Richard. *Wildlife.* 1990. NY. Atlantic. 1st. F/F. H11. $25.00.

FORD, Thomas. *History of Illinois.* 1945. Lakeside Classic. 1st thus. edit Quaife. teg. red cloth. NF/sans. T11. $25.00.

FORESTER, C. S. *Barbary Pirates.* 1953. Random. VG/dj. B36. $8.50.

FORESTER, C. S. *Captain from Connecticut.* 1941. Little, Brn. 1st. NF/VG. T11. $65.00.

FORESTER, C. S. *Commodore Hornblower.* 1945. London. 1st. VG/dj. T9. $50.00.

FORESTER, C. S. *Hornblower Companion.* 1964. Boston. 1st. dj. T9. $30.00.

FORESTER, C. S. *Naval War of 1812.* 1957. London. Michael Joseph. 1st. 1/7500. dk bl cloth. F/NF. T11. $130.00.

FORESTER, C. S. *Nightmare.* 1954. Little, Brn. 1st. gray cloth. F/NF. T11. $60.00.

FORESTER, C. S. *Payment Deferred.* 1942. Boston. Little, Brn. 1st Am ed. VF/dj. M15. $250.00.

FORESTER, Thomas. *Norway and Its Scenery, Comprising the Journal of a Tour by Edward Price, Esq. with Considerable Additions and a Road-Book for Tourists, with Hints to Anglers and Sportsmen.* 1853. London. Henry G Bohn. 12mo. 470p. contemp marbled brd. with taped spine. 1st ed. ex-lib. spine taped. lacking 5 plates. reading copy. L5. $30.00.

FORLINES, Charles Edward. *Finding God Through Christ.* 1947. Abingdon. 207p. VG. B29. $4.50.

FORREST, Anthony. *Captain Justice.* 1981 Penguin Books Ltd. 1st. F/G. S19. $35.00.

FORREST, Earle R. *Missions & Pueblos of the Old Southwest.* 1929. Arthur H Clark. 1st. photos. 386p. teg. bl cloth. NF. P4. $215.00.

FORREST, Richard. *Child's Garden of Death* 1975. Bobbs Merrill. 1st. F/NF. G8. $17.50.

FORRESTER, Victoria. *Latch Against the Wind.* 1985. Atheneum. 1st. 48p. F/dj. D4. $25.00.

FORSYTH, Cecil. *Orchestration.* 1947. Macmillan. 2nd. 530p. G. S5. $15.00.

FORSYTH, Frederick. *No Comebacks.* 1982. London. Hutchinson. 1st. F/dj. M15. $65.00.

FORSYTH, Frederick. *The Biafra Story: The Making of an African Legend.* 1983. London. Severn House. 1st. F/dj. M15. $200.00.

FORSYTH, Frederick. *The Day of the Jackal.* 1971. London. Hutchinson. 1st. F/dj. M15. $300.00.

FORSYTH, Frederick. *The Dogs of War.* 1974. NY. Viking. 1st. F/F. lt wear. T2. $20.00.

FORSYTH, Frederick. *The Fist of God.* 1994. NY. Bantam. 1st. VF/VF. H11. $25.00.

FORSYTH, Frederick. *The Fourth Protocol.* 1984. London. Hutchinson. 1st. F/F. A24. $25.00.

FORSYTH, P. T. *Postive Preaching and Modern Mind.* nd. Hodder & Stoughton. 374p. VG/marks. B29. $7.00.

FOSDICK, Charles Austin. *Frank on the Lower Mississippi by Harry Castelmon (Pseud).* 1868. Philadelphia. Henry T. Coates. 1st. The Gun Boat Series. orig decor cloth. historical novel. 236p. VG. M8. $17.50.

FOSTER, Elon. *6000 Sermon Illustrations.* 1953. Baker. 704p. G. B29. $11.00.

FOSTER, George. *Sierra Popoluca Folklore & Beliefs.* 1945. Berkeley. Univ of Ca Press. vol 42. no 2. G. F3. $25.00.

FOSTER, H. Lincoln. *Rock Gardening. A Guide to Growing Alpines & Other Wildflowers in the American Garden.* 1968. NY. VG in dj. B26. $15.00.

FOSTER, Harry. *A Tropical Tramp with the Tourists.* 1925. NY. Dodd, Mead. 1st. 335p. G. F3. $20.00.

FOSTER, Jeannette H. *Sex Variant Women in Literature.* 1975. Baltimore. Diana Press. 2nd. Afterword by Barbara Grier. wrp in dj. F. B2. $25.00.

FOSTER, Jeannette H. *Sex Variant Women in Literature.* 1956. NY. Vantage. 1st. F. owner's name/NF. B2. $35.00.

FOSTER, Richard. *Prayer: Finding the Heart's True Home.* 1992. Harper. notes/index. AN/dj. A27. $15.00.

FOSTER, W. Bert. *In Alaskan Waters.* 1910. Phil, PA. 363p. lt bl cloth. P4. $30.00.

FOSTER, William H. *New England Grouse Shooting.* 1970 (1941). NY. rpt. ils. fwd Bruette. F/dj. A17. $60.00.

FOSTER-HARRIS. *The Look of the Old West.* 1955. NY. Viking. 4to. ils b&w drawings. 316p. VG. O3. $35.00.

FOUCAULT, Michel. *I, Pierre Riviere, Having Slaughtered My Mother, My Sister & My Brother...A Case of Parricide in the 19th Century.* 1975. np. np. 1st. NF/G dj. M19. $17.50.

FOURNIER, Keith. *Evangelical Catholics.* 1990. Nelson. 223p. VG/VG. B29. $6.00.

FOWLER. *Sarah Canary.* 1991. NY. Holt. 1st. F/F. H11. $35.00.

FOWLER, Christopher. *Rune.* 1990. London. Century. 1st. VF/VF. T2. $30.00.

FOWLER, Christopher. *The Bureau of Lost Souls.* 1989. London. Century. 1st. VF/VF clip. T2. $20.00.

FOWLER, Connie May. *River of Hidden Dreams.* 1994. Putnam. 1st. F/G. S19. $30.00.

FOWLER, Connie May. *Sugar Cage.* (1992). NY. Putnam. 1st. author's 1st novel. F/F. B3. $50.00.

FOWLER, Don D. *Western Photographs of John K Hillers: Myself in the Water.* 1989. Smithsonian. VG/dj. J2. $75.00.

FOWLER, Earlene. *Dove in the Window.* 1998. Berkley. 1st. sgn. F/F. G8. $25.00.

FOWLER, Earlene. *Kansas Troubles.* 1996. Berkley. 1st. sgn. F/F. G8. $30.00.

FOWLER, Gene. *A Solo in Tom Toms.* 1946. np. np. sgn 1st ed. F/VG dj. M19. $45.00.

FOWLER, Guy. *Dawn Patrol.* 1930. Grosset Dunlap. MTI/true 1st. F/VG+. B4. $350.00.

FOWLER, H. W. *Dictionary of Modern English Usage.* 1926. London. Humphrey Milford. 1st. VG. Q1. $250.00.

FOWLER, Henry T. *The History and Literature of the New Testament.* 1934. Macmillan. 443p. VG/VG. B29. $8.50.

FOWLER, Karen Joy. *The Sweetheart Season.* 1996. Henry Holt. 1st. sgn. VG/VG. M25. $45.00.

FOWLER, W. M. *Baron of Beacon Hill: Biography of John Hancock.* 1980. Boston. 1st. ils. 366p. F/dj. M4. $30.00.

FOWLES, John. *A Maggot.* 1985. Boston. Little, Brn. 1st. VF/F. H11. $30.00.

FOWLES, John. *Aristos: Self-Portrait in Ideas.* 1964. Little, Brn. 1st. author's 2nd book. NF/VG. J3. $150.00.

FOWLES, John. *Maggot.* 1985. Boston. Little, Brn. 1st. F/NF. H11. $20.00.

FOWLKES, Martha. *Behind Every Successful Man: Wives of Medicine & Academe.* 1980. NY. 1st. 223p. A13. $40.00.

FOX, George. *Warlord's Hill.* 1982. Times Books. 1st. VG/dj. N4. $17.50.

FOX, Helen M. *Years in My Herb Garden.* 1953. BC. photos/plans. VG/dj. B26. $11.00.

FOX, James M. *A Shroud for Mr. Bundy.* 1952. Little, Brn. 1st. F/dj. M25. $45.00.

FOX, James M. *Code Three.* 1953. Little, Brn. 1st. Lightly rubbed jacket; sgn; insc. F/dj. M25. $60.00.

FOX, James M. *The Gentle Hangman.* 1950. Little, Brn. 1st. Rubbed jacket has a few short tears. VG/dj. M25. $45.00.

FOX, John Jr. *Trail of the Lonesome Pine.* 1908. Scribner. 1st. 422p. G. G11. $15.00.

FOX, Michael W. *Supercat: Raising the Perfect Feline Companion.* 1990. NY. Howell. VG/dj. O3. $6.00.

FOX, Roy. *Hollywood, Mayfair and all That Jazz.* 1975. London. Leslie Frewin. 1st. 30 photos. F/NF. sticker removal tear. B2. $30.00.

FOX, Sally. *Medieval Woman: Illustrated Book of Days.* 1985. Toronto. 1st Canadian. F/sans. T12. $15.00.

FOX, Selina F. *A Chain of Prayer Across the Ages: 40 Centuries of Prayer.* 1936. John Murray. 308p. G. B29. $7.00.

FOX, Ted. *Showtime at the Apollo.* 1983. HRW. 1st. F/F. M25. $25.00.

FOXX, Jack; See Pronzini, Bill.

FRALEY, Tobin. *Great American Carousel: A Century of Master Craftmanship.* 1994. SF. Chronicle. 1st. ils. 132p. F/dj. O3. $18.00.

FRANCATELLI, C. *Modern Cook: Practical Guide to Culinary Art.* 1880 (1846). lg 8vo. 560p. VG. E6. $75.00.

FRANCIS, Daniel. *Discovery of the North: Exploration of Canada's Arctic.* 1986. Edmonton. Hurtig Pub Ltd. 224p. F/dj. P4. $35.00.

FRANCIS, Dick. *10 Lb Penalty.* 1997. NY. Putnam. 1st. VF/VF. H11. $15.00.

FRANCIS, Dick. *Banker.* 1982. London. Michael Joseph. 1st. F/dj. M15. $65.00.

FRANCIS, Dick. *Bolt.* 1986. London. Michael Joseph. 1st. sgn. F/dj. M15. $85.00.

FRANCIS, Dick. *Break In.* 1986. NY. Putnam. 1st. F/F. H11. $15.00.

FRANCIS, Dick. *Come to Grief.* 1995. NY. Putnam. 1st. VF/VF. H11. $15.00.

FRANCIS, Dick. *Decider.* 1993. NY. Putnam. 1st Am ed. UP. F/pict wrp. T2. $15.00.

FRANCIS, Dick. *Field of 13.* 1998. London. Michael Joseph. 1st. author's 1st collection. VF/VF. T2. $35.00.

FRANCIS, Dick. *High Stakes.* 1975. London. Michael Joseph. 1st. F/dj. M15. $125.00.

FRANCIS, Dick. *Hot Money.* 1988. NY. Putnam. 1st. F/F. H11. $15.00.

FRANCIS, Dick. *In the Frame.* 1976. London. Michael Joseph. 1st. F/dj. M15. $125.00.

FRANCIS, Dick. *Lester.* 1986. London. Michael Joseph. 1st. F/dj. M15. $65.00.

FRANCIS, Dick. *Proof.* 1984. London. Michael Joseph. 1st. F/dj. M15. $50.00.

FRANCIS, Dick. *Rat Race.* 1971. Harper. 1st Am ed. F/clip dj. M25. $75.00.

FRANCIS, Dick. *Reflex.* 1981. NY. Putnam. 1st. NF/NF. H11. $30.00.

FRANCIS, Dick. *Risk.* 1977. NY. Harper & Row. 1st. NF/VG+. A24. $25.00.

FRANCIS, Dick. *Straight.* 1989. London. Michael Joseph. 1st. F/dj. M15. $50.00.

FRANCIS, Dick. *The Edge.* 1988. London. Michael Joseph. 1st. F/dj. M15. $50.00.

FRANCIS, Dick. *To the Hilt.* 1996. Blakeney. Scorpion Press. 1st. VF/dj. M15. $55.00.

FRANCIS, Dick. *Twice Shy.* 1981. London. Michael Joseph. 1st. F/dj. M15. $65.00.

FRANCISCO, Clyde T. *Introducing the Old Testament.* 1977. Broadman. revised ed. 301p. VG/VG. B29. $11.00.

FRANCL, Joseph. *Overland Journey of Joseph Francl.* 1968. SF. Wm Wreden. 1/540. ils Patricia Oberhaus. 55p. F. P4. $95.00.

FRANCOME, John. *Outsider.* 1993. London. Headline. 1st. VF/VF. T2. $35.00.

FRANCOME, John. *Rough Ride.* 1992. London. Headline. 1st. VF/F. T2. $30.00.

FRANCOME, John & James MacGregor. *Declared Dead.* 1988. London. Headline. 1st. F/VF. T2. $40.00.

FRANCOME, John & James MacGregor. *Riding High.* 1987. London. MacDonald. 1st. VF/VF. T2. $45.00.

FRANK, Joseph. *Hobbled Pegasus. A Descriptive Bibliography of Minor English Poetry 1641 – 1660.* Albuquerque. University of New Mexico Press. (1968). 8vo. 482p. bl cloth. dj. 1st ed. Blank corner of flyleaf cliped off. very minor wear. dj with few minor nicks. VG. book NF. L5. $30.00.

FRANK, Suzanne. *Shadows on the Aegean.* 1998. NY. Warner Books. 1st. sgn. VF/VF. T2. $25.00.

FRANKLIN, Benjamin. *Benjamin Franklin: Biography in His Own Words.* 1972. NY. ils. 416p. F/dj. M4. $27.00.

FRANKLIN, Benjamin. *The Autobiography of Benjamin Franklin.* 1944. NY. Random House. 12mo. 264p. F. H1. $10.00.

FRANKLIN, Colin. *Private Presses.* 1969. Chester Springs, PA. Dudour. gilt ochre cloth. F/VG+. F1. $60.00.

FRANKLIN, Eugene. *Bold House Murders.* 1973. Stein Day. 1st. sm 8vo. cloth. F/dj. O10. $25.00.

FRANKLIN, Jay. *Rat Race.* 1940. FPCI. 1st. VG/dj. P3. $35.00.

FRANKLIN, John Hope. *Militant South, 1800 – 1861.* 1956. Cambridge. 1st. 317p. VG/dj. B18. $37.50.

FRANKLIN, Tom. *Poachers.* 1999. NY. Morrow. 1st. UP. VF/printed wrp. T2. $25.00.

FRANTZ, Joe B. *Driskill Hotel.* 1973. Austin. Encino. 1st. F/clear acetate as issued. A24. $40.00.

FRANZEN, Jonathan. *Strong Motion.* 1992. NY. Farrar. 1st. F/F. H11. $35.00.

FRASE, H. Michael. *The Last Goodbye.* 1998. NY. Carroll & Graf. 1st. VF/VF. T2. $15.00.

FRASER, Anthea. *Island in Waiting.* 1979. St. Martin. 1st Am ed. NF/NF. G8. $20.00.

FRASER, C. Lovat. *Pirates.* 1922. NY. Robert M. McBride & Co. 1st Am ed. 1/4 cloth. ils. cover soiled. browning. G. B18. $27.50.

FRASER, George MacDonald. *Black Ajax.* (1997). London. Collins. 1st British ed. F/F. B3. $35.00.

FRASER, George MacDonald. *Flashman and the Dragon.* 1985. London. Collins Harvill. 1st. VF/dj. M15. $90.00.

FRASER, George MacDonald. *Flashman and the Mountain of Light.* 1990. London. Collins Harvill. 1st. F/dj. M15. $75.00.

FRASER, George MacDonald. *Flashman and the Redskins.* 1982. Knopf. 1st Am. F/dj. M25. $60.00.

FRASER, George MacDonald. *Flashman in the Great Game.* 1975. NY. Knopf. 1st Am ed. F/NF. B2. $60.00.

FRASER, J. & A. Hemsley. *Johnson's Gardener's Dictionary and Cultural Instructor.* 1985 (1917). Dehra Dun. reprint. 923p. B26. $19.00.

FRAZER, Robert W. *Forts of the West.* (1965). Norman, OK. 1st. 246p. F/VG. E1. $60.00.

FRAZER, Robert W. *Forts & Supplies: Role of the Army in Economy of SW...* 1983. NM U. 1st. 253p. F/F. B19. $30.00.

FRAZIER, Charles. *Cold Mountain.* 1997. NY. Atlantic. 1st. Author's 1st book. VF/VF. H11. $230.00.

FRAZIER, Ian. *Dating Your Mom.* 1986. NY. FSG. 1st. author's 1st book. sgn. F/F dj. D10. $50.00.

FRAZIER, Robert Caine; See Creasey, John.

FREDE, Richard. *Secret Circus.* 1967. Random. 1st. F/F. H11. $25.00.

FREDERICK, J. V. *Ben Holladay: Stagecoach King.* 1940. Glendale, CA. Arthur H Clark. F/dj. A19. $250.00.

FREDERICK, William. *100 Great Garden Plants.* 1975. Knopf. 214p. VG/dj. A10. $18.00.

FREEBORN, Peter. *Stark Truth.* 1989. Boston. Houghton Mifflin. 1st. NF/NF. G8. $12.50.

FREEBORN, Peter. *Stark Truth.* 1989. Boston. Houghton Mifflin. 1st. NF/NF. G8. $12.50.

FREEDMAN, J. F. *Against the Wind.* 1991. NY. Viking. 1st. author's 1st book. F/F. H11. $25.00.

FREEDMAN, J. F. *House of Smoke.* 1996. NY. Viking. 1st. F/F. H11. $15.00.

FREELING, Nicholas. *Those in Peril.* 1990. Mysterious. 1st Am ed. NF/NF. G8. $10.00.

FREELING, Nicolas. *Not as Far as Velma.* 1989. NY. Mysterious Press. 1st Am ed. NF/VG+. G8. $12.50.

FREELING, Nicolas. *Valparaiso.* 1964. NY. Harper. 1st. F. lib stp/NF. B2. $40.00.

FREEMAN, Douglas Southall. *George Washington, a Biography. 1948 – 1954.* NY. Scribners. 6 volumes. 1st eds. orig cloth NF/orig pub slipcases. M8. $350.00.

FREEMAN, Joseph. *The Long Pursuit.* 1947. NY. Rinehart. 1st. NF/lightly used dj. B2. $40.00.

FREEMAN, Judith. *A Desert of Pure Feeling.* 1996. Pantheon. ARC. F/decor wrps. M25. $35.00.

FREEMAN, Mae & Ira. *Fun with Astronomy, Entertainment and Instruction for Young People.* 1953. NY. Random House. 4to. lt shelf wear. 58p. VG/chipped dj. K5. $11.00.

FREEMAN, Mary Eleanor Wilkins. *Yates Pride: A Romance.* 1912. NY/London. Harper. 1st. 16mo. 65p. brn cloth. F/dj. J3. $125.00.

FREEMAN, R. B. *The Works of Charles Darwin. An Annotated Bibliographical Handlist.* 1965. London. F in spine faded dj. B26. $45.00.

FREEMAN, Roland L. *Southern Roads/City Pavements. Photographs of Black Americans.* 1981. Washington, DC. pub by the author. 1st. wrp. oblong 8vo. F. B2. $35.00.

FREEMANTLE, Brian. *Charlie Muffin.* 1977. London. Jonathan Cape. 1st. F/dj. M15. $100.00.

FREMONT, Jessie Benton. *Year of American Travel.* 1960. SF. Plantin/BC of CA. 1/450. 121p. half cloth/decor brd. P4. $95.00.

FREMONT, John Charles. *Narratives of Exploration & Adventure.* 1957. NY. Longman Gr. rpt. 532p. dk bl cloth. P4. $40.00.

FRENCH, Albert. *Billy.* (1993). NY. Viking. 1st. author's first novel. F/F. B3. $75.00.

FRENCH, George. *Printing in Relation to Graphic Art.* Cleveland. The Imperial Press. 1903. 12mo. 118p. beige spine cloth & marbled brd. 1st ed. no. 90 of 935 #d copies. Unopened pages. F. L5. $75.00.

FRENCH, L. H. *Nome Nuggets. Some of the Experiences of a Party of Gold...* 1901. NY. Montross Clarke Emmons. 1st. 8vo. cloth. P4. $125.00.

FRENCH, Nicci. *Killing Me Softly.* 1999. London. Michael Joseph. 1st. VF/dj. M15. $90.00.

FRENCH, Nicci. *The Memory Game.* 1997. London. Heinemann. 1st. VF/dj. M15. $85.00.

FRENCH, Patrick. *Younghusband: Last Great Imperial Adventurer.* 1994. NY. ils. VG/dj. M17. $15.00.

FRENCH, Peter. *Philosophers in Wonderland.* 1975. Llewellyn. 1st. ils. fair/dj. B27. $25.00.

FRENCH, Thomas E. *The Missionary Whaleship.* 1961. NY. Vantage Press. 1st; review copy. 134p. VG in spine faded dj. pages yellowed. P4. $50.00.

FREUD, Sigmund. *Collected Papers.* 1950. London. Institute of Psycho-analysis. 6th. 8vo Complete in 5 vol. All have darkened spines & minor edge tears. F/dj. H1. $125.00.

FREUD, Sigmund. *Origins of Psychoanalysis: Letters to Wilhelm Fliess...* 1954. Basic Books. 1st. 8vo. 486p. VG/G. C14. $25.00.

FREY, Ruby Frazier. *Red Morning.* 1946. Putnam & Sons. 1st. yellowing. G-. S19. $20.00.

FREY, Stephen J. *The Takeover.* 1993. np. Dutton. 1st. author's 1st novel. NF/VG+. R16. $35.00.

FREYRE, Gilberto. *The Masters and the Slaves.* 1971. NY. Knopf. 2nd English ed. revised. 537p. G/chipped dj. F3. $15.00.

FRIDAY, Nancy. *Jealousy.* 1985. NY. Morrow. VG/VG. A28. $10.50.

FRIEDAN, Betty. *The Fountain of Age.* 1993. NY. S&S. 1st. rem mk. VG/G+. A28. $12.50.

FRIEDLANDER & ROSENBERG. *Paintings of Lucas Cranach.* 1978. Secaucus. Wellfleet. 162p+434 monochrome pl. gilt blk cloth. F/dj. F1. $65.00.

FRIEDMAN, Bruce Jay. *Tokyo Woes.* 1985. NY. Fine. 1st. inscr. VF/VF. H11. $35.00.

FRIEDMAN, Hal. *Over The Edge.* 1998. NY. Harper Collins. 1st. VF/VF. T2. $15.00.

FRIEDMAN, Jake. *Common Sense Candy Teacher.* 1915 (1911). VG. E6. $60.00.

FRIEDMAN, Kinky. *Armadillos & Old Lace.* 1994. NY. S&S. 1st. VF/VF. H11. $20.00.

FRIEDMAN, Kinky. *Blast from the Past.* 1998. S&S. 1st. F/NF. G8. $15.00.

FRIEDMAN, Kinky. *Frequent Flyer.* 1989. NY. Morrow. 1st. F/F. H11. $30.00.

FRIEDMAN, Kinky. *Musical Chairs.* 1991. NY. Morrow. 1st. F/VF. H11. $115.00.

FRIEDMAN, Kinky. *When the Cat's Away.* 1988. NY. Beech Tree. 1st. F/F. H11. $35.00.

FRIEDMAN, Mickey. *Paper Phoenix.* 1986. Dutton. 1st. VG+/VG+. G8. $17.50.

FRIEDRICH, Carl Joachim. *Philosophy of Law in Historical Perspective.* 1958. Chicago U. VG/dj. M11. $45.00.

FRIEDWALD, Will. *Jazz Singing: America's Great Voices from Bessie Smith...* 1990. NY. 1st. VG/dj. M17. $25.00.

FRIENDLY, Alfred. *Beaufort of the Admiralty: Life of Sir Frances Beaufort...* 1977. NY. 1st. ils. VG/dj. M17. $27.50.

FRIES & WEST. *Chemical Warfare.* 1921. NY. 445p. A13. $100.00.

FRITZ, Samuel. *Journal of the Travels & Labours of Father Samuel Fritz.* 1922. London. Hakluyt. 2nd Series #LI. 8vo. 164p. bl cloth. P4. $135.00.

FROESCHELS, Emil. *Selected Papers of Emil Froeschels. 1940 – 1964.* 1964. Amsterdam. North-Holland Pub. pres. 232p. stiff gray wrp. G1. $45.00.

FROILAND, S. G. *Natural History of the Black Hills.* 1982. Sioux Falls. Center West Studies. ils/fld map. 175p. VG+. M12. $17.50.

FROME, David. *Homicide House.* 1950. NY. Rinehart. 1st. VG/clip dj. M15. $45.00.

FROMMER, Sara Hoskinson. *Murder & Sullivan.* 1997. NY. St. Martin. 1st. sgn. F/F. G8. $12.50.

FRONTINUS, Sextus Julius. *Water Supply of the City of Rome.* 1973. New Eng Water Works Assn. photos. trans Clemens Herschel. VG. M17. $40.00.

FROSCHER, Jon. *Woodstock Murders; or, Happiness Is a Naked Policeman.* 1998. Overlook. 1st. F/F. G8. $12.50.

FROST, David. *I Gave Them a Sword: Behind the Scenes of Nixon Interviews.* 1978. Morrow. 1st. sm 4to. 320p. NF/G. W2. $20.00.

FROST, Edwin Brant. *Astronomer's Life.* 1933. Houghton Mifflin. 8vo. 300p. G/dj. K5. $50.00.

FROST, John. *Indian Wars of the United States...* 1859. NY. CM Saxton. ils. 300p. bstp cloth. G+. B18. $45.00.

FROST, Mark. *Six Messiahs.* 1995. NY. Morrow. 1st. F/F. G8. $20.00.

FROST, Mark. *The List of 7.* 1993. NY. Morrow. 1st. VF/VF. T2. $20.00.

FROST, Robert. *A Witness Tree.* 1942. np. Henry Holt. 1st trade ed. F/NF dj. M19. $65.00.

FRUCHT, Abby. *Are You Mine?* 1993. NY. Grove Press. 1st. sgn & dated. F/F. A24. $30.00.

FRUCHT, Abby. *Licorice.* 1990. St Paul. Graywolf. 1st. VF/F. H11. $25.00.

FRYE, Northrop. *Words with Power.* 1990. 1st. VG/dj. M17. $15.00.

FRYER, Jane Eayre. *Mary Frances Cookbook.* 1912. John Winston. ils Hays/Boyer. 175p. bl cloth/paper label. VG. D1. $160.00.

FUENTES, Carlos. *The Crystal Frontier.* 1997. FSG. UP of Am ed. F/blue wrps. M25. $35.00.

FUGUET, Alberto. *Bad Vibes.* 1997. NY. St. Martin. ARC. F/wrp. B2. $25.00.

FUHRMAN, Chris. *The Dangerous Lives of Altar Boys.* 1994. np. Univ of GA Press. 1st. author's 1st and only novel. F/F. A24. $40.00.

FUJIKAWA, Gyo. *Mother Goose.* 1968. NY. Grosset & Dunlap. 1st ed deluxe. ils by author. orange cloth w/gilt decor. 125p. AN/NF. D6. $75.00.

FULGHUM, Robert. *Maybe (Maybe Not).* 1993. Villard Books. 1st. F/F. S19. $20.00.

FULLER, Jack. *Fragments.* 1984. Morrow. 1st. F/dj. R11. $30.00.

FULLER, Roger; see Tracy, Don.

FULLERTON, Alexander. *Publisher.* 1971. NY. Putnam. 1st Am. 254p. F/dj. O10. $30.00.

FULLERTON, Hugh. *Jimmy Kirkland of the Shasta Boys Team.* 1915. Winston. later prt. 1st of series. VG/G. P8. $75.00.

FULTON, James. *Peach Culture.* 1870. Orange Judd. 190p. beveled brd. VG. A10. $35.00.

FUNK, Benjamin (ed). *Life and Labors of Elder John Kline the Martyr Missionary.* 1900. Elgin, IL. Brethren Pub. 1st. lt wear & spotting to cover/ browning to paper. 780p. G. B18. $25.00.

FURNEAUX, Patrick. *Arts of the Eskimo: Prints.* 1974. Signum Oxford. NF/VG. P3. $75.00.

FURNEAUX, R. *Krakatoa.* 1964. Englewood Cliffs. photos/map. 224p. NF. M4. $18.00.

FURST, Alan. *Shadow Trade.* 1983. Delacorte. 1st. NF/NF. H11. $15.00.

FURTANI, Dale. *The Toyotomi Blades.* 1997. St. Martin. UP. NF in red wrp. M25. $35.00.

FYFE, H. Hamilton. *The Real Mexico. A Study on the Spot.* nd. NY. McBride. rear foldout map. 247p. G. F3. $20.00.

FYFE, Thomas Alexander. *Who's Who in Dickens.* 1971. Haskell. VG. P3. $75.00.

FYNN, A. J. *American Indian as Product of Environment.* 1907. Boston. Little, Brn. 1st. ils. 275p. VG. B5. $65.00.

— G —

GABLE, Kathleen. *Clark Gable, a Personal Portrait.* 1961. Prentice Hall. 1st. VG/dj. C9. $36.00.

GABORIAU, Emile. *Count's Millions.* 1913. NY. Scribner. 391p. G+. G11. $10.00.

GACHET, Jacqueline. *Ladybug.* 1970. McCall. 1st. pict cloth. VG/dj. M20. $15.00.

GADD, L. *Deadly Beautiful: World's Most Poisonous Animals & Plants.* 1980. Macmillan. ils/photos. 208p. cloth/brd. VG+/NF. M12. $25.00.

GADDIS, William. *A Frolic of His Own.* 1994. NY. Poseidon. 1st. VF/F. H11. $40.00.

GADDIS, William. *Carpenter's Gothic.* 1985. NY. Viking. 1st. VF/F. H11. $40.00.

GADER, June Rose. *LA Live: Profiles of a City.* 1980. St. Martin. ARC. F/NF. O4. $15.00.

GADOL, Peter. *The Long Rain.* 1997. NY. Picador. 1st. sgn. VF/VF. T2. $35.00.

GADOL, Peter. *The Mystery Roast.* 1993. NY. Crown. 1st. author's second novel. F/F. M23. $25.00.

GAEBELEIN, Frank E. *A Varied Harvest; Out of a Teacher's Life and Thought.* 1967. Eerdmans. 198p. VG/VG. B29. $8.00.

GAEDDERT, Lou Ann. *Split-Level Cookbook: Family Meals to Cook.* 1967. NY. TY Crowell. 1st. 228p. VG/dj. A25. $15.00.

GAER, Joseph. *Bibliography of California Literature.* 1970. Burt Franklin. rpt. F. O4. $25.00.

GAG, Flavia. *Sing a Song of Seasons.* 1936. Coward McCann. 1st. 4to. 30p. pict brd. VG. T5. $55.00.

GAG, Wanda. *Millions of Cats.* 1928. Coward McCann. 1st. obl 8vo. VG. M5. $175.00.

GAGE, Jack R. *Tensleep & No Rest.* 1958. Prairie Pub. 1st. sgn. map/pl/facsimiles. 222p. VG/dj. J2. $145.00.

GAGE, Rev. William. *Trinitarian Sermons Preached to a Unitarian Congregation, with an Introduction on the Unitarian Failure.* 1859. Boston. John P. Jewett and Company. 16mo. 153p. blk cloth. 1st ed. very minor wear. VG. L5. $15.00.

GAGER, John G. *Moses in Greco Roman Paganism.* 1972. Abingdon. 173p. VG/VG. B29. $19.50.

GAGER, Leroy. *Handbook for Soul Winners.* 1956. Zondervan. 190p. VG/G. B29. $5.00.

GAGNON, Maurice. *Inner Ring.* 1985. Collins Crime Club. 1st. VG/VG. P3. $18.00.

GAILHARD, Jean. *Present State of the Republick of Venice.* 1669. London. 12mo. pub list at end. calf. R12. $385.00.

GAINES, Ernest J. *A Lesson Before Dying.* 1993. NY. Knopf. 1st. F/F. D10. $60.00.

GAINES, Ernest J. *Autobiography of Miss Jane Pittman.* 1973. Michael Joseph. 1st. NF/NF clip. B3. $75.00.

GAINES, Ernest J. *In My Father's House.* 1978. Knopf. 1st. NF/dj. D10. $55.00.

GAINHAM, Sarah. *Appointment in Vienna.* 1958. Dutton. 1st. VG/dj. P3. $15.00.

GAINHAM, Sarah. *Cold Dark Night.* 1961. Walker. VG/dj. P3. $15.00.

GAITHER, Frances. *Double Muscadine.* 1949. Toronto. Macmillan. 1st. VG. T12. $20.00.

GAITO, John. *Macromolecules & Behavior.* 1966. Appleton Century. 197p. bl cloth. VG/dj. G1. $27.50.

GAITSKILL, Mary. *Bad Behavior.* 1988. Poseidon. 1st. F/dj. D10. $45.00.

GALBRAITH, Den. *Turbulent Taos.* 1970. Taos, NM. Pr Territorian. 1st. ils. 1/1500 copies. 48p. NF. B19. $15.00.

GALBRAITH, Jean. *Wildflowers of Victoria.* nd. Melbourne. 2nd ed. intro by J. H. Willis. silver emb bl cloth. B26. $17.50.

GALBRAITH, John K. *Affluent Society.* 1958. Houghton Mifflin. 1st. author's 6th book. tan cloth. dj. M24. $45.00.

GALBRAITH, Lettice. *The Blue Room and Other Ghost Stories.* 1999. Wales. Sarob Press. 1st. 1/250 # copies. VF/VF. T2. $35.00.

GALDONE, Paul. *Frog Prince.* (1975). McGraw Hill. rpt. ils Galdone. VG. C8. $15.00.

GALDSTON, Iago. *Behind the Sulfa Drugs: A Short History of Chemotherapy.* 1943. NY. 1st. 174p. A13. $40.00.

GALE, Oliver Marble. *Carnack: Lifebringer.* 1928. Wise. 1st. NF/dj. M2. $35.00.

GALE, Zona. *Preface to a Life.* 1926. Appleton. 1st. 346p. VG+. A25. $10.00.

GALEANO, Eduardo. *The Book of Embraces.* 1991. NY. Norton. 1st Am ed. author's 6th book. ils by author. inscr. F/F. D10. $45.00.

GALET, Pierre. *Grapevine Identification.* 1979. Cornell. 1st. VG/dj. W2. $35.00.

GALINDO, Sergio. *Precipice (El Bordo).* 1969. Austin/London. 8vo. 185p. gray cloth. P4. $15.00.

GALLAGHER, C.H. *Nutritional Factors & Enzymological Disturbances...* 1964. Phil. Lippincott. 181p. F. B1. $28.50.

GALLAGHER, Elaine. *Candidly Caine.* 1992. NY. Robson Books. 318p. VG/dj. C5. $12.50.

GALLAGHER, Stephen. *Down River.* 1989. London. New English Library. 1st. sgn. VF/VF. T2. $25.00.

GALLAGHER, Stephen. *Down River.* 1989. NEL. 1st. F/F. P3. $25.00.

GALLAGHER, Stephen. *Oktober.* 1988. London. New English Library. 1st. sgn. VF/VF. T2. $50.00.

GALLAGHER, Tess. *Lover of Horses.* 1986. NY. Harper Row. 1st. F/F. D10. $40.00.

GALLANCE, George. *In Her Birthday Dress.* 1977. Paisley. Scotland. Gleniffer. 1/150. 51x52mm. prt/sgn Ian MacDonald. box. $24.00.

GALLANT, Mavis. *The Other Paris.* 1956. Boston. Houghton Mifflin. 1st ed of author's 1st book. F in dj. B2. $100.00.

GALLANT, Roy A. *Exploring the Planets.* 1967/1958. Garden City. Doubleday. revised ed. 4to. ils by John Polgreen. 119p. VG/chipped & rubbed dj. K5. $15.00.

GALLANT, Roy A. *Man's Reach into Space.* 1959. Garden City. 4to. 152p. G. K5. $12.00.

GALLICO, Paul. *Abandoned.* 1950. Knopf. 1st. VG/dj. M2. $20.00.

GALLICO, Paul. *Hand of Mary Constable.* 1964. Doubleday. 1st. VG/VG. P3. $25.00.

GALLICO, Paul. *Lonely.* 1949. Knopf. 1st. NF/NF. M19. $25.00.

GALLICO, Paul. *Poseidon Adventure.* 1969. Coward. 1st. F/NF clip. H11. $40.00.

GALLISON, Kate. *Death Tape.* 1987. Little, Brn. 1st. VG/VG. P3. $15.00.

GALLISON, Kate. *Jersey Monkey.* 1992. NY. St. Martin. 1st. F/F. G8. $15.00.

GALLOWAY, Janice. *Blood.* 1991. Random. ARC. author's 1st story collection. F/F. w/promo material. R13. $35.00.

GALLUP, Donald. *TS Eliot: A Bibliography.* 1952. London. Faber. 1st. gilt gray cloth. F/VG. M24. $65.00.

GALLUP, George. *Adventures in Immortality: A Look Beyond Threshold of Death.* 1982. McGraw. 226p. VG. B29. $8.00.

GALSWORTHY, John. *Arthur & Critic.* 1933. NY. House of Books Ltd. 1/300. F. A17. $30.00.

GALSWORTHY, John. *Modern Comedy.* 1929. Heinemann. 1st Eng. NF/G. M19. $25.00.

GALSWORTHY, John. *Modern Comedy.* 1929. Scribner. 1st. VG. P3. $30.00.

GALSWORTHY, John. *White Monkey.* nd (1924). London. Heinemann. 1st. sgn. VG+. B4. $125.00.

GALT, Katherine Keene. *The Girl Scout's Triumph of Rosanna's Sacrifice.* nd. np. A16. $5.00.

GALTON, Francis. *Fingerprint Directories.* 1895. London. Macmillan & Co. ne. orig cloth. 9 pl. 127p. slight chip & rubbing. B14. $200.00.

GALVEZ. *Instructions for Governing the Interior Provinces New Spain.* 1951. Quivira. 1/500. NF. A4. $275.00.

GAMMON, John K. *Overcoming Obstacles in Environmental Policymaking.* 1994. SUNY. 250p. NF/wrp. S15. $5.00.

GAMMONS, Peter. *Beyond the Sixth Game.* 1985. Houghton Mifflin. 1st. F/VG. P8. $25.00.

GAMOW, George. *Creation of the Universe.* 1952. Viking. 1st. VG/torn. K5. $12.00.

GAMOW, George. *My World Line: An Informal Autobiography.* 1970. Viking. 1st. VG/dj. K3. $15.00.

GAMOW, George. *Planet Called Earth.* 1963. Viking. 8vo. 257p. Vg/dj. K5. $15.00.

GANACHILLY, Alfred. *Whispering Dead.* 1920. Knopf. 1st. VG. M2. $15.00.

GANN, Ernest K. *Gentlemen of Adventure.* 1984. NY. Arbor. 1st. NF/F. H11. $25.00.

GANN, Ernest K. *In the Company of Eagles.* 1966. S&S. 1st. F/NF. H11. $35.00.

GANN, Ernest K. *Trouble with Lazy Ethel.* 1958. Sloane. 1st. NF/VG. M19. $25.00.

GANN, Thomas. *Discoveries & Adventures in Central America.* 1929. Scribner. 1st. xl. reading copy. F3. $20.00.

GANN, W.D. *Tunnel Thru the Air.* 1927. Financial Guardian. 1st. VG. P3. $40.00.

GANT, Roland. *World in a Jug.* 1961. NY. Vanguard. 1st. F/lightly used dj. B2. $40.00.

GANZEL, Dewey. *Fortune & Men's Eyes.* 1982. Oxford. ils. 8vo. F/dj. K3. $40.00.

GARBER, Joseph R. *Vertical Run.* 1995. Bantam. 1st. FF. G8. $25.00.

GARCES, Francisco. *Record of Travels in Arizona & California 1775 – 1776.* 1965. SF. John Howell. 1/1250. 4to. ils/maps. 113p. VG+. F7. $75.00.

GARCIA, Andrew. *Tough Trip Through Paradise 1878 – 1879.* 1967. Houghton Mifflin. 1st. 446p. map ep. VG/dj. J2. $265.00.

GARCIA, Christina. *Dreaming in Cuban.* 1992. NY. Knopf. 1st. F/F. D10. $75.00.

GARCIA, Elise. *Guatemala in Six Tours.* 1976. np. Guatemala. 1st. 12mo. biblio. maps. b/w photos. 102p. G/wrp. F3. $10.00.

GARCIA LORCA, Federico. *Five Plays: Comedies & Tragicomedies.* 1963. New Directions. 1st Am. F/dj. Q1. $60.00.

GARCIA MARQUEZ, Gabriel. *Bloody Shame.* 1997. NY. Putnam. 1st. VF/VF. H11. $20.00.

GARCIA MARQUEZ, Gabriel. *Chronicle of a Death Foretold.* 1983. NY. Knopf. 1st Am ed. F/F. D10. $50.00.

GARCIA MARQUEZ, Gabriel. *Love in the Time of Cholera.* (1988). NY. Knopf. 1st Am ed. NF+. very lt use/NF. creasing to spine. B3. $30.00.

GARCIA MARQUEZ, Gabriel. *Strange Pilgrims.* 1993. NY. Knopf. 1st. F/F. H11. $40.00.

GARCIA MOLL, Roberto. *The Maya World.* 1991. Mexico. Inverlat. 1st. sm folio. color photo ils. 238p. G/G. F3. $75.00.

GARCIA-AGUILERA, Carolina. *A Miracle in Paradise.* 1999. NY. Avon Books. 1st. sgn. VF/VF. T2. $25.00.

GARCIA-AGUILERA, Carolina. *Bloody Secrets.* 1998. NY. Putnam. 1st. sgn. VF/VF. T2. $25.00.

GARD, R. Max. *End of the Morgan Raid.* 1963. Lisbon, OH. ils. 22p. wrp. B18. $12.50.

GARD, Robert. *Horse Named Joe.* 1956. Little, Brn. 1st. ils CW Anderson. 237p. VG/VG-. P2. $30.00.

GARD, Wayne. *Frontier Justice.* 1949. Norman, OK. 1st. map. ils. 324p. VG in dj. B18. $45.00.

GARD, Wayne. *Great Buffalo Hunt.* 1959. Knopf. VG. A19. $35.00.

GARD, Wayne. *Retracing the Chisholm Trail.* 1956. TX State Hist Assn. 24p. VG. J2. $45.00.

GARDAM, Jane. *Bilgewater.* 1976. London. Hamish Hamilton. NF/NF. B3. $75.00.

GARDEN, J.F. *Bugaboos.* 1987. Revelstoke. 1st. 156p. F/dj. A17. $25.00.

GARDENIER, Andrew A. *Hand-Book of Ready Reference.* 1897. Springfield. King-Richardson Pub. 1st. VG. O3. $65.00.

GARDINER, Dorothy. *Great Betrayal.* 1949. Doubleday. 1st. VG/VG. P3. $20.00.

GARDINER, Howard C. *In Pursuit of the Golden Dream.* 1970. Stoughton, MA. Western Hemisphere. 390p. gilt red cloth. AN. K7. $50.00.

GARDNER, Alan. *Six Day Week.* 1966. Coward McCann. 1st Am. VG/dj. P3. $15.00.

GARDNER, Alexander. *Gardner's Photographic Sketch Book of the Civil War.* 1959. Dover. 8vo. 100+ pl. cloth. F/G. H1. $60.00.

GARDNER, C.A. *Flora of Western Australia.* Vol I. Part I. 1952. Gramineae. ils/pl/diagrams. 400p. red cloth. F. $26.00.

GARDNER, E.S. *Desert Is Yours: Spirited Account of Adventure in Present.* 1963. NY. Morrow. ils/photos. 256p. cloth. VG+/VG+. M12. $30.00.

GARDNER, E.S. *Hunting Lost Mines by Helicopter.* 1965. Morrow. photos. 387p. VG/G. M12. $30.00.

GARDNER, Erle Stanley. *Beware the Curves.* 1956. Morrow. 1st. NF/dj. M25. $25.00.

GARDNER, Erle Stanley. *Count of Nine.* 1958. Morrow. 1st. G+/torn. M25. $15.00.

GARDNER, Erle Stanley. *Dead Men's Letters.* 1990. NY. Carroll & Graf. 1st. F/F. H11. $20.00.

GARDNER, Erle Stanley. *Off the Beaten Track in Baja.* 1967. Morrow. 1st. ils. F/F. O4. $25.00.

GARDNER, Erle Stanley. *The Case of the Beautiful Beggar.* 1965. NY. Morrow. 1st. Name on front fep. F/F. H11. $50.00.

GARDNER, Erle Stanley. *The Case of the Borrowed Brunette.* 1946. NY. Morrow. 1st. Owner inscription. Light chipping. F/NF. H11. $65.00.

GARDNER, Erle Stanley. *The Case of the Fenced in Woman.* 1972. NY. Morrow. 1st. F/F. B2. $25.00.

GARDNER, Erle Stanley. *The Case of the Lucky Loser.* 1957. NY. Morrow. 1st. VG/VG. H11. $20.00.

GARDNER, Erle Stanley. *The Case of the Screaming Woman.* 1957. Morrow. 1st. NF/worn dj. sunned at spine. M25. $25.00.

GARDNER, Erle Stanley. *Up for Grabs.* 1964. Morrow. 1st. inscr. F/F. M15. $175.00.

GARDNER, Ethel. *Soarings.* 1990. Cherokee. 1st. sgn. 120p. F/wrp. B11. $18.00.

GARDNER, John. *Amber Nine.* 1966. Viking. 1st. F/NF. H11. $35.00.

GARDNER, John. *Brokenclaw.* 1990. NY. Putnam. 1st Am ed. NF/NF. G8. $10.00.

GARDNER, John. *Cornermen.* 1976. Doubleday. 1st. F/F. M19/P3. $35.00.

GARDNER, John. *Death Is Forever.* 1992. NY. Putnam. 1st Am ed. NF/NF. G8. $10.00.

GARDNER, John. *Icebreaker.* 1983. NY. Putnam. 1st. NF/F. H11. $20.00.

GARDNER, John. *In the Suicide Mountains.* 1977. Knopf. 1st. F/dj. Q1. $60.00.

GARDNER, John. *Maestro.* 1993. NY. Otto Penzler books. 1st. sgn. VF/VF. T2. $25.00.

GARDNER, John. *Nickel Mountain.* 1973. Knopf. 1st. VG/dj. P3. $30.00.

GARDNER, John. *Nickel Mountain.* 1973. NY. Knopf. 1st. F/VG+. very lt wear. A24. $40.00.

GARDNER, John. *Nobody Lives Forever.* 1986. NY. Putnam. 1st Am ed. NF/VG+. G8. $10.00.

GARDNER, John. *Role of Honour.* 1984. Jonathan Cape. 1st. VG/dj. P3. $25.00.

GARDNER, John. *Secret Families.* 1989. Putnam. 1st Am. NF/dj. A24. $25.00.

GARDNER, John. *The Art of Living and Other Stories.* 1981. NY. Knopf. 1st. rem mk. F/F. D10. $50.00.

GARDNER, John. *The Liquidator.* 1964. NY. Viking. 1st. VF/VF. T2. $25.00.

GARDNER, John. *The Man from Barbarossa.* 1991. NY. Putnam. 1st. sgn. VF/VF. T2. $10.00.

GARDNER, John. *The Secret Generations.* 1985. NY. Putnam. 1st Am ed. sgn & inscr by author. F/F. minor shelfwear. A24. $35.00.

GARDNER, John. *The Secret Houses.* 1987. NY. Putnam. 1st Am ed. sgn & inscr by author. F/F. minor shelfwear. A24. $35.00.

GARDNER, John. *Understrike.* 1965. Viking. 1st. F/NF clip. H11. $25.00.

GARDNER, John. *Werewolf Trace.* nd. NY. Doubleday. 1st Am ed. VG/VG. G8. $10.00.

GARDNER, Martin. *Annotated Snark.* 1962. S&S. 1st. 111p. VG/worn. M20. $35.00.

GARDNER, Mary. *Boat People.* 1995. Norton. 1st. sgn. F/F. A23. $40.00.

GARDNER, Miriam; see Bradley, Marion Zimmer.

GARDNER, Paul V. *Glass of Frederick Carder.* 1971. Crown. 4th. 400 photos. 373p. VG. H1. $350.00.

GARDNER, Richard A. *Objective Diagnosis of Minimal Brain Dysfunction.* 1979. Cresskill. NJ. Creative Therapeutics. 452p. gray cloth. VG/dj. G1. $22.50.

GARDNER, Will. *The Clock that Talks and What it Tells.* 1954. Nantucket Island, MA. Whaling Museum Publications. 8vo. ils photo. 143p. VG in cloth. K5. $75.00.

GARFIELD, Brian. *Death Sentence.* 1975. NY. Evans. 1st. F/F. M15. $45.00.

GARFIELD, Brian. *Line of Succession.* 1972. Delacorte. 1st. VG/dj. P3. $23.00.

GARFIELD, Brian. *Paladin.* 1980. Macmillan. 1st. NF/dj. P3. $20.00.

GARFIELD, Brian. *Recoil.* 1977. Morrow. 1st. VG/dj. P3. $40.00.

GARFIELD, Brian. *Romanov Succession.* 1974. Evans. 1st. VG/dj. P3. $25.00.

GARFINKLE, Richard. *Celestial Matters.* 1986. Tor. 1st. F/dj. P3. $25.00.

GARIS, Cleo F. *Arden Blake: Orchard Secret (#1).* 1934. AL Burt. 250p. VG/dj. M20. $35.00.

GARIS, Howard R. *Uncle Wiggily & Alice in Wonderland.* 1918. Donohue. ils Edward Bloomfield. 8vo. dk bl cloth/label. R5. $150.00.

GARIS, Howard R. *Uncle Wiggily & His Flying Rug.* 1940. Racine. NF/NF. C8. $45.00.

GARIS, Howard R. *Uncle Wiggily on Roller Skates.* (1940). Racine. Whitman. ils. NF/NF. C8. $45.00.

GARIS, Howard R. *Uncle Wiggily Stories.* 1977 (1965). Grosset Dunlap. ils Art Seiden. NF. C8. $15.00.

GARLAND, Alex. *The Tesseract.* (1999). NY. Riverhead. 1st. F/F. B3. $20.00.

GARLAND, Hamlin. *Book of the American Indian.* 1923. NY/London. Harper. 1st thus. 274p. NF. K7. $200.00.

GARLAND, Hamlin. *Boy's Life on the Prairie.* 1899. Macmillan. 1st. F. A18. $75.00.

GARLAND, Joseph E. *Great Pattillo.* 1966. Little, Brn. 1st. 342p. cloth. VG/dj. M20. $25.00.

GARNER, Alan. *Elidor.* 1966. London. VG/dj. M2. $20.00.

GARNER, Alan. *Red Shift.* 1973. Macmillan. 1st. VG/fair. P3. $13.00.

GARNER, Bess. *Mexico.* 1937. Houghton Mifflin. 1st. ils. 164p. F3. $15.00.

GARNER, Harry. *Chinese & Japanese Cloisonne Enamels.* 1977. London/Boston. Faber. 2nd revised. ils. F/NF. W3. $65.00.

GARNER, R. J. *The Grafter's Handbook.* 1947. London. 1st. gr cloth. VG. B26. $19.00.

GARNETT, Bill. *Down Bound Train.* 1973. Doubleday. 1st. F/dj. M2. $12.00.

GARNETT, David. *Letters of T. E. Lawrence.* 1939. Doubleday Doran. 1st Am. ils/maps. 896p. VG. K3. $40.00.

GARNETT, Garet. *Blue Wound.* 1921. Putnam. 1st. VG. M2. $20.00.

GARNETT, Louise A. *Muffin Shop.* 1908. Rand McNally. 1st. ils Hope Dunlap. 80p. VG. D1. $150.00.

GARNETT, Louise Ayres. *Creature Songs.* nd. Boston. Oliver Ditson Co. F. A16. $35.00.

GARRARD, J. & H. W. Hannau. *Fairchild Tropical Garden.* 1980. Miami. rev ed. photo ords. 32p full color. F. B26. $10.00.

GARRARD, Jeanne. *Growing Orchids for Pleasure.* 1966. NY. ils. 302p. VG in dj. B26. $14.00.

GARRETT, Annette. *Counseling Methods for Personnel Workers.* 1945. NY. Family Welfare Assn. 1st. 187p. xl. VG. A25. $16.00.

GARRETT, George. *Death of the Fox.* 1971. Doubleday. 1st. sgn. F/F. D10. $65.00.

GARRETT, George. *Entered from the Sun.* 1990. Doubleday. 1st. sgn. F/F. D10. $40.00.

GARRETT, George. *Succession.* 1983. Doubleday. 1st. F/NF. D10. $40.00.

GARRICK, David. *Private Correspondence Of...* 1831. London. 2 vol. 4to. A15. $40.00.

GARRISON, Jim. *Heritage of Stone.* 1970. NY. VG/G. B5. $45.00.

GARRISON, Jim. *Star Spangled Contract.* 1976. McGraw Hill. 1st. F/dj. P3. $18.00.

GARRISON, Omar. *Balboa: Conquistador.* 1971. NY. Lyle Stuart. 1st. 256p. G/chipped dj. F3. $25.00.

GARRISON, R.E. *Dolomites of the Monterey Formation...* 1984. Los Angeles. 215p. F/stiff wrp. B1. $18.50.

GARRISON, Webb B. *Sermon Seeds from the Gospels.* 1958. Revell. 126p. VG. B29. $5.00.

GARSIDE, E. *Cranberry Red.* 1938. Boston. 1st. VG/VG. B5. $35.00.

GARST, Shannon. *Cowboy-Artist: Charles M. Russell.* 1966. Messner. A19. $20.00.

GARSTIN, Crosbie. *Samuel Kelly: An Eighteenth-Century Seaman.* 1925. NY. Stokes. 1st. 320p. gilt cloth. P4. $60.00.

GARTHWAITE, Jimmy. *Puddin' an' Pie.* 1929. Harper. 1st. 93p. cloth. VG. D4. $30.00.

GARTON, Ray. *Crucifax Autumn.* 1988. Arlington Heights. Dark Harvest. 1st. VF/VF. T2. $40.00.

GARTON, Ray. *Methods of Madness.* 1990. Arlington Heights. Dark Harvest. 1st. VF/VF. T2. $20.00.

GARTON, Ray. *Website.* 1997. Burton. Subterranean Press. 1st. 1/250 # copies. sgn. VF/pict wrp. T2. $25.00.

GARVE, Andrew. *Case of Robert Quarry.* 1972. Collins Crime Club. 1st British ed. VG/VG. G8. $20.00.

GARVE, Andrew. *Counterstroke.* 1978. Crowell. 1st Am ed. NF/NF. G8. $17.50.

GARVE, Andrew. *Hide and Go Seek.* 1966. Harper. 1st Am ed. VG/VG. G8. $20.00.

GARVE, Andrew. *Late Bill Smith.* 1971. Harper. 1st Am ed. VG/VG. G8. $10.00.

GARVEY & WICK. *Arts of the French Book 1900 – 1965.* 1967. Dallas. S Methodist U. ils. 120p. stiff wrp. F1. $40.00.

GARVIN, Richard & Edmon G. Addeo. *The Midnight Special, The Legend of Leadbelly.* 1971. NY. Geis. ARC w/slip. F/F. B2. $45.00.

GARY, Romain. *King Solomon.* 1983. NY. Harper & Row. 1st. VF/VF. H11. $25.00.

GASH, Jonathan. *Gondola Scam.* 1984. St Martin. 1st. F/VG. M19. $45.00.

GASH, Jonathan. *Grail Tree.* 1979. Harper. 1st Am. VG/VG. M22. $20.00.

GASH, Jonathan. *Great California Game.* 1991. St Martin. 1st. F/F. M19. $25.00.

GASH, Jonathan. *Jade Woman.* 1988. London. Collins. 1st. sgn. F in dj. M25. $100.00.

GASH, Jonathan. *Possessions of a Lady.* 1996. NY. Viking. 1st Am ed. NF/NF. G8. $15.00.

GASH, Jonathan. *Spend Game.* 1981. Ticknor Fields. 1st. VG/dj. P3. $40.00.

GASH, Jonathan. *The Sleepers of Erin.* 1983. Dutton. 1st Am ed. F in dj. M25. $45.00.

GASH, Jonathan. *Very Last Gambado.* 1990. St Martin. 1st. sgn. NF/dj. B3. $25.00.

GASK, Arthur. *Silent Dead.* 1950. Herbert Jenkins. 1st. VG. P3. $25.00.

GASKELL, E.C. *Life of Charlotte Bronte.* 1857. Appleton. 2 vol. 1st. rear ep removed o/w VG. M20. $125.00.

GASKELL, Jane. *Strange Evil.* 1958. Dutton. 1st Am. VG. M2. $20.00.

GASS, William H. *Fiction & Figures on Life.* 1970. Knopf. 1st. sgn. NF/NF. R14. $65.00.

GASS, William H. *Tunnel.* 1995. Knopf. 1st. sgn. F/F. B2. $50.00.

GASSER, M. *Self-Portraits.* 1963. ils. VG/VG. M17. $25.00.

GATENBY, Rosemary. *Fugitive Affair.* 1976. Dodd Mead. 1st. VG/dj. P3. $15.00.

GATES, Doris. *Sensible Kate.* 1943. Viking. 1st. 189p. F/G+. P2. $35.00.

GATES, Henry Louis. *Loose Canons.* 1992. NY. Oxford. 1st. sgn. F/F. R13. $35.00.

GATEWOOD, Charles. *Photographs.* 1993. SF. Flash. 1/2000. sgn. F/F. B4. $85.00.

GATHORNE-HARDY, Robert. *Traveler's Trio.* 1963. London. slight chipping to dj. B26. $37.50.

GATLAND, Kenneth. *Ils Encyclopedia of Space Technology.* 1984. NY. Harmony. revised. 4to. 301p. K5. $35.00.

GATLAND, Kenneth. *Manned Spacecraft.* 1967. Macmillan. 256p. VG/VG. K5. $12.00.

GATS, HUBER & SALISBURY. *Ted & Sally.* 1952. Macmillan. 2nd. 8vo. 144p. red cloth. T5. $30.00.

GATT, G. *Oskar Kokoschka.* 1970. ils. Italian text. VG/VG. M17. $12.50.

GAUL, Albro. *Wonderful World of Insects.* 1953. Rinehart. 219p. dj. A10. $18.00.

GAULKNER, Georgene. *Little Peachling & Other Tales from Old Japan.* 1928. Volland. 1st. ils Frederick Richardson. 8vo. cloth. pict box. R5. $250.00.

GAULT, William Campbell. *Cat & Mouse.* 1988. St Martin. 1st. F/F. M25. $25.00.

GAULT, William Campbell. *Come Die with Me.* 1959. Random. 1st. VG. P3. $20.00.

GAULT, William Campbell. *Death in Donegal Bay.* 1984. Walker. 1st. NF/dj. P3. $15.00.

GAUS, P. L. *Blood of the Prodigal.* 1999. Athens. Ohio Univ Press. 1st. first printing of 1000 copies. F/F. M23. $50.00.

GAUSTAD, Edwin S. *A Religious History of America.* 1966. Harper. 1st ed. 421p. VG/VG. B29. $15.00.

GAVIN, J. *War & Peace in the Space Age.* 1959. 1st. F/VG. E6. $18.00.

GAVRON, Jeremy. *King Leopold's Dream.* 1993. NY. 288p. F/F. S15. $10.00.

GAWRON, Jean Mark. *Apology for Rain.* 1974. Doubleday. 1st. F/dj. M2/P3. $17.00.

GAY, Zhenya. *Bits & Pieces.* 1958. Viking. 1st. VG. M5. $22.00.

GAYLIN, Willard. *In the Service of Their Country: War Registers in Prison.* 1970. Viking. 1st. 344p. dj. V3. $10.00.

GAYTON, Bertram. *Gland Stealers.* 1922. Herbert Jenkins. 1st. G. P3. $25.00.

GAZARIAN GAUTIER, Marie Lise. *Interviews with Latin American Writers.* 1992. IL. Dalkey Archive Press. 1st. 363p. G/wrp. F3. $15.00.

GAZE, Harold. *Goblin's Glen.* 1924. Little, Brn. 1st. 6 full-p pl. 8vo. dk bl cloth. R5. $125.00.

GAZZANIGA, Michael S. *Handbook of Cognitive Neuroscience.* 1984. NY. Plenum. 416p. prt brn cloth. F. G1. $50.00.

GEAR, Kathleen O' Neal & W. Michael Gear. *The Visitant.* 1999. NY. Forge. 1st. sgn. VF/VF. T2. $25.00.

GEARE, Michael & Michael Corby. *Dracula's Diary.* 1982. NY. Beaufort Books. 1st. F/F. T2. $15.00.

GEARINO, G. D. *Blue Hole.* 1999. NY. S&S. 1st. sgn. VF/VF. T2. $25.00.

GEDGE, Pauline. *Stargate.* 1982. NY. Dial Press. 1st. F/F. T2. $7.00.

GEER, John James. *Beyond the Lines; Or, A Yankee Prisoner Loose in Dixie.* 1864 (1863). VG. E6. $75.00.

GEHLEN, Reinhard. *Service: Memoirs of General Reinhard Gehlen.* 1972. NY. 1st. photos/glossary. 386p. VG/VG. S16. $25.00.

GEIGER, Kenneth. *Further Insights into Holiness.* 1963. Beacon Hill. 349p. G. B29. $7.00.

GEIGER, Thelma. *Alliance Centennial Souvenir Book.* 1950. np. ils. wrp. VG. B18. $25.00.

GEIKIE, A. *Landscape in History.* 1905. NY/Glasgow. Macmillan. 352p. G. D8. $12.00.

GEIOGAMAH, Hanay. *New Native American Drama: Three Plays.* 1980. Norman, OK. 1st. F/NF. L3. $85.00.

GEIS, Darlene, ed. *A Colorslide Tour of Mexico.* 1961. NY. Columbia Record Co. 4to. laminated bds. unpaged (45p). G. F3. $10.00.

GEISEL, Theodore Seuss. *And to Think that I Saw It on Mulberry Street.* 1937. NY. Vanguard Press. 1st. ils by author. inscr Christmas 1937. sm 4to. color ils pict bds. Dr. Seuss's 1st book. G. D6. $250.00.

GEISEL, Theodore Seuss. *Cat's Quizzer.* 1976. Random. 1st. 4to. 62p. VG/sans. P2. $125.00.

GEISEL, Theodore Seuss. *Dr Seuss's Sleep Book.* 1962. Random. 1st. 4to. VG/VG. D1. $60.00.

GEISEL, Theodore Seuss. *Horton Hears a Who!* 1954. Random. 1st. 4to. pict brd. F. B4. $650.00.

GEISEL, Theodore Seuss. *I Had Trouble in Getting to Solla Sollew.* 1965. Random. 1st. 4to. VG/G+. P2. $450.00.

GEISEL, Theodore Seuss. *If I Ran the Zoo.* (1950). Random. early ed. VG/$2.50 dj. D1. $250.00.

GEISEL, Theodore Seuss. *One Fish Two Fish Red Fish Blue Fish.* (1960). Random. 1st. sm 4to. 63p. VG/VG. D1. $500.00.

GEISEL, Theodore Seuss. *The Cat in the Hat Comes Back!* 1958. NY. Beginner Books/ Random House. 1st ed as stated. ils by author. sm 4to. color ils pict bds. same dj. color ils. 62p. VG/G. spine ends chipped. D6. $400.00.

GEIST, Valerus. *Mule Deer Country.* 1990. North Word. photos Michael Francis. 176p. F/F. S15. $20.00.

GELATT, R. *Fabulous Phonograph.* 1955. Phil. 1st. VG/dj. B5. $45.00.

GELB, Ignace J. *Hittite Hieroglyphs.* 1931. Chicago. 3 parts. 1st. VG/wrp. W1. $65.00.

GELLER, Stephen. *Gad.* 1979. Harper Row. 1st. NF/dj. P3. $20.00.

GELLERT, Hugo. *Comrade Gulliver.* 1935. Putnam. 1st. VG. B2. $50.00.

GEMMELL, David. *Last Guardian.* 1989. Legend. 1st. F/dj. P3. $25.00.

GENDERS, Roy. *Bedding Plants.* 1956. London. 192p. 21 b&w photos. dj heavily chip. B26. $16.00.

GENDERS, Roy. *Collecting Hardy Plants for Interest & Profit.* 1959. London. Stanley. 1st. 191p. dj. A10. $22.00.

GENDERS, Roy. *Pansies, Violas, and Violets.* 1958. London. GBC. VG in chip dj. B26. $17.50.

GENDZIER, Irene L. *Frantz Fanon: A Critical Study.* 1973. Pantheon. 300p. xl. VG/dj. W1. $12.00.

GENET, Jean. *Miracle of the Rose.* 1966. Grove. 1st Am. F/F. M19. $25.00.

GENT, Peter. *North Dallas Forty.* 1973. Morrow. 1st. VG+/VG+. P8. $25.00.

GENTHE, Arnold. *Old China Town.* 1913. NY. Mitchell Kennerly. G+. B5. $75.00.

GENTLE, Mary. *Rats & Gargoyles.* 1990. Bantam (British). 1st. F/dj. P3. $30.00.

NTRY, A. H. *Field Guide to the Families & nera of Woody Plants.* 1993. WA. nservation Internat'l. 895p. F/wrp. B1. 8.00.

NTRY, Curt. *Madams of San Francisco.* 64. Doubleday. 1st. VG/VG. O4. $15.00.

NTRY, Howard S. *Agaves of Baja lifornia.* 1978. SF. ils/figures/tables/pl. wrp. B26. $30.00.

EORGE, Don. *Sweet Man. The Real Duke ington.* 1981. NY. Putnam. 1st. F/NF. B2. 0.00.

EORGE, Elizabeth. *A Great Deliverance.* 88. NY. Bantam. 1st. F/VF. H11. $70.00.

EORGE, Elizabeth. *A Suitable Vengeance.* 91. NY. Bantam. 1st. VF/VF. H11. $25.00.

EORGE, Peter. *Commander 1.* 1965. elacorte. 1st. VG+/VG. G8. $20.00.

EORGE, R. D. *Minerals & Rocks: Their ature, Occurrence & Uses.* 1943. Appleton ntury. 1st. 595p. G. D8. $20.00.

EORGE, Theodore. *Murders on the Square.* 71. Dodd. Mead. 1st. VG/VG. G8. $10.00.

ERARD, Francis. *Secret Sceptre.* 1971. Tom acey. VG/VG. P3. $15.00.

ERARD, Louise. *Golden Centipede.* 1927. utton. 1st. VG. M2. $15.00.

ERBER, Dan. *A Last Bridge Home.* (1995). vingston. Clark City Press. 1st. ils Russell natham. F/F. B3. $25.00.

ERHARD, Peter. *The Southeast Frontier of ew Spain.* 1993. Norman. Univ of klahoma Press. revised ed. 1st thus. 4to. 9p. G. F3. $40.00.

ERLACH, Don R. *Philip Schuyler & the merican Revolution.* 1964. NE U. 1st. 358p. N/dj. H1. $40.00.

ERLACH, Rex. *Fly Fishing for Rainbows.* 988. Stackpole. 1st. sgn. M/dj. A17. $30.00.

ERNSHEIM, Helmut. *Incunabula of British otographic Literature.* 1984. 4to. 180 ils. 61 entries. 159p. F/F. A4. $95.00.

ERRITSEN, Tess. *Bloodstream.* 1998. ocket. 1st. sgn. NF/NF. G8. $20.00.

ERRITSEN, Tess. *Life Support.* 1997. ocket. 1st. sgn. F/F. G8. $20.00.

ERROLD, David. *Chess with a Dragon.* 987. NY. Walker. 1st. VF/VF. T2. $16.00.

GERROLD, David. *The Man Who Folded Himself.* 1973. NY. Random House. 1st. sgn. F/F. T2. $30.00.

GERROLD, David. *Yesterday's Children.* 1974. London. Faber. 1st hc. sgn. F/F. T2. $40.00.

GERSI, Douchan. *Explorer.* 1987. Tarcher. 1st. 285p. F/F. W2. $30.00.

GERSON, Noel B. *Neptune.* 1976. Dodd Mead. 1st. VG/dj. P3. $18.00.

GERSTER, Arpad. *Rules of Aseptic & Antiseptic Surgery.* 1888. NY. 2nd. 332p. leather. A13. $125.00.

GERT ZUR HEIDE, Karl. *Deep South Piano. The Story of Little Brother Montgomery.* 1970. London. Studio Vista. 1st. wrps. F. B2. $30.00.

GESSLER, Clifford. *Pattern of Mexico.* 1941. NY. Appleton. 1st. ils by E. H. Suydam. 442p. G/chipped dj. F3. $20.00.

GETTY, J. P. *My Life & Fortunes.* 1963. DSP. 1st. 300p. F/clip. D8. $18.00.

GHENT, W. J. *Socialism and Success. Some Uninvited Messages.* 1910. NY. John Lane. 1st. inscr w/owner's name. NF. B2. $40.00.

GHITELMAN, David. *Space Telescope.* 1987. Mitchell. 1st. F/F. T12. $60.00.

GIACOMINI, Carlo. *Guida Allo Studio Delle Circonvoluzioni Cerebrali...* 1884. Torino. Ermanno Loescher. 2nd revised. 47 wood-cuts. G. G1. $150.00.

GIANOLI, Luigi. *Horses & Horsemanship Through the Ages.* 1969. NY. Crown. 1st Am. VG/VG. O3. $48.00.

GIBB, H.A.R. *Arabic Literature: An Introduction.* 1926. London. Oxford. 1st. 12mo. 128p. cloth. VG. $1.00.

GIBBENS, Byrd. *This Is a Strange Country: Letters of Westering Family...* 1988. Albuquerque. 1st. 8vo. 438p. brn cloth. AN/dj. P4. $30.00.

GIBBINGS, Robert. *Blue Angels & Whales: Record of Personal Experiences...* 1946. Dutton. 1st. offset from laid-in review. VG/worn. P4. $35.00.

GIBBINGS, Robert. *Charm of Birds.* 1927. NY. Stokes. 1st Am. 8vo. 286p. F/NF. T10. $50.00.

GIBBINGS, Robert. *Over the Reefs & Far Away.* 1948. Dutton. 1st. 240p. burgundy cloth. P4. $65.00.

GIBBINGS, Robert. *Wood Engravings Of.* 1959. Chicago. Quadrangel. 1st Am. edit Patience Empson. gilt cloth. M/Lucite dj. B24. $125.00.

GIBBON, David. *Old South.* 1979. Crescent. 1st Am. VG/VG clip. A8. $10.00.

GIBBON, J. M. *Romantic History of the Canadian Pacific.* 1937. NY. photos/fld map. 423p. F. M4. $25.00.

GIBBONS, Kaye. *A Cure for Dreams.* 1991. Chapel Hill. Algonquin. 1st. F+/F+. H11. $25.00.

GIBBONS, Kaye. *Ellen Foster.* 1987. Algonquin. 1st. author's 1st book. F/F. B3/L1. $175.00.

GIBBONS, Kaye. *Sights Unseen.* 1995. Putnam. 1st. sgn. F/F. A23. $40.00.

GIBBONS, Kaye. *Virtuous Woman.* 1989. Algonquin. 1st. sgn. author's 2nd book. VG/VG. L1. $100.00.

GIBBONS, Stella. *Cold Comfort Farm.* 1957 (1932). Longman Gr. 17th. 307p. VG/dj. A25. $12.00.

GIBBS, James W. *Buckeye Horology, a Review of Ohio Clock and Watch Makers.* 1971. Columbia, PA. 1st. ils. 128p. VG/VG. B18. $75.00.

GIBBS, Joe. *Fourth & One.* 1991. Nashville. Nelson. 1st. sgn. VG/VG. A23. $40.00.

GIBBS, May. *Gum-Blossom Babies.* 1916. Sydney. Angus Robertson. 1st. 8vo. brn paper wrp/label. R5. $400.00.

GIBBS, May. *Scotty in Gumnut Land.* 1950 (1941). Sydney. Angus Robertson. VG/G. M5. $60.00.

GIBBS, Philip. *Out of the Ruins.* 1928. Doubleday. 1st Am. VG. M2. $20.00.

GIBBS, Tony. *Capitol Offense.* 1995. Warner. 1st. NF/NF. G8. $12.50.

GIBBS, Tony. *Landfall.* 1992. NY. Morrow. 1st. VF/VF. T2. $8.00.

GIBRAN, Kahil. *Mirrors of the Soul.* 1965. Philosophical Library. 101p. VG/VG. B29. $4.50.

GIBRAN, Kahil. *The Prophet.* 1970. Knopf. 96p. VG/torn dj. B29. $5.00.

GIBRAN, Kahlil. *Tears & Laughter.* 1947. Phil Lib. 1st. F/VG. M19. $25.00.

GIBSON, A.M. *Kickapoos: Lords of the Middle Border.* 1963. OK U. ils. 391p. cloth. dj. D11. $35.00.

GIBSON, Arrell Morgan. *America's Exiles: Indian Colonization of Oklahoma.* 1976. OK Hist Soc. ils. 155p. F. M4. $15.00.

GIBSON, Charles. *Spain in America.* 1966. Harper Row. 25 ils/4 maps. F/rpr. O7. $35.00.

GIBSON, Charles. *The Aztecs Under Spanish Rule.* 1964. CA. Stanford Univ Press. 1st. 657p. VG/chipped dj. poi stamped on edges. F3. $35.00.

GIBSON, Edward. *Reach.* 1989. Doubleday. 1st. F/dj. M2. $10.00.

GIBSON, Eva Katharine. *Zauberlinda the Witch.* 1901. Robert Smith. 255p. VG. P2. $75.00.

GIBSON, Robert. *Theory & Practice of Surveying.* 1828. Harper. 14 fld pl/ils/frontis. T7. $120.00.

GIBSON, Walter. *Magic with Science.* 1974. Collins. 3rd. NF. P3. $18.00.

GIBSON, Walter Murray. *Diaries of Walter Murray Gibson 1886.* 1887. 1973. HI U. 1st. tall 8vo. 199p. P4. $30.00.

GIBSON, William. *All Tomorrow's Parties.* 1999. NY. Putnam. 1st. sgn. VF/VF. T2. $27.00.

GIBSON, William. *Burning Chrome.* 1986. NY. Arbor House. 1st. F/F. B2. $35.00.

GIBSON, William. *Count Zero.* 1986. NY. Arbor House. 1st. F/F. soil spot on bottom edge. B2. $65.00.

GIBSON, William. *Mona Lisa Overdrive.* 1988. London. Gollancz. 1st. sgn. VF/VF. T2. $65.00.

GIBSON, William. *Virtural Light.* 1993. London. Viking. 1st. VF/VF. T2. $40.00.

GIBSON, William Hamilton. *Our Native Orchids.* 1905. Doubleday. 158p. VG. A10. $85.00.

GIDDINGS, J. L. *Kobuck River People.* 1961. College. Studies of Northern Peoples #1. 159p. F. P4. $38.50.

GIDDINS, Gary. *Riding on a Blue Note. Jazz and American Pop.* 1981. NY. Oxford. 1st. F/F. B2. $25.00.

GIDE, Andre. *Amyntas.* 1958. London. 1/1500. trans V David. VG/dj. T9. $30.00.

GIDE, Andre. *Corydon.* 1950. Farrar. 1st Am. F/NF. M19. $25.00.

GIDE, Andre. *Counterfeiters.* 1928. London. 1st. trans D. Bussy. fair/dj. T9. $45.00.

GIDE, Charles. *Communist & Co-Operative Societies.* nd. Crowell. 1st. G. V4. $15.00.

GIELGUD, Val. *And Died So?* 1961. Collins Crime Club. 1st British ed. ex lib. VG. G8. $10.00.

GIERACH, John. *Another Lousy Day in Paradise.* (1996). NY. S&S. 1st. sgn by author. nonfiction. F/F. B3. $30.00.

GIERACH, John. *Even Brook Trout Get the Blues.* (1992). NY. S&S. 1st. nonfiction. F/F. B3. $75.00.

GIERACH, John. *Where Trout are as Long as Your Leg.* (1991). NY. Lynn & Burford. 1st. nonfiction. F/F. B3. $75.00.

GIERKE, Otto. *Natural Law & Theory of Society 1500 to 1800.* 1957. Boston. Beacon. 423p. prt wrp. M11. $50.00.

GIERKE, Otto. *Political Theories of the Middle Ages.* 1938. Cambridge. G/dj. M11. $85.00.

GIESY, J.U. *Mystery Woman.* 1929. Whitman. 1st. VG/dj. P3. $60.00.

GIEURE, Maurice. *G. Braque.* 1956. NY. Universe Books. Inc. 1st. F/NF. O11. $150.00.

GIFFORD, Barry. *A Good Man to Know.* (1992). Livingston. Clark City. 1st. F/F. B3. $15.00.

GIFFORD, Barry. *Landscape with Traveler.* (1980). NY. Dutton. 1st. author's first novel. F/NF. very minor creasing to top of spine. B3. $45.00.

GIFFORD, Barry. *Night People.* 1992. Grove. 1st. NF/NF. B3. $20.00.

GIFFORD, Thomas. *Man from Lisbon.* 1977. McGraw Hill. 1st. VG/dj. P3. $25.00.

GIFFORD, Thomas. *Wind Chill Factor.* 1975. NY. Putnam. 1st. author's 1st novel. F/clip. M15. $65.00.

GIKES, Lillian. *Cora Crane: Biography of Mrs Stephen Crane.* 1960. IN U. 1st. cloth. VG/dj. M20. $25.00.

GILB, Dagaberto. *The Last Known Residence of Mickey Acuna.* 1994. NY. Grove. 1st. F/F. D10. $40.00.

GILB, Dagoberto. *The Magic of Blood.* (1993 Albuquerque. Univ of NM. 1st. ils by Lu Jimenez. F/F. B3. $50.00.

GILBERT, Anthony. *After the Verdict.* 196 Random House. 1st Am ed. VG/VG. G $15.00.

GILBERT, Anthony. *By Hook or by Croo* 1947. AS Barnes. 1st. 186p. cloth. VG/d M20. $15.00.

GILBERT, Anthony. *Murder Anonymou* 1968. Random. 1st. VG/dj. P3. $20.00.

GILBERT, Anthony. *Murder's a Waitin Game.* 1972. Random House. 1st Am ed VG+/VG+. G8. $12.50.

GILBERT, Arthur. *Jew in Christian America* 1966. Sheed Ward. 235p. VG+/VG. S3 $17.00.

GILBERT, Dale L. *Black Star Murders.* 198 St. Martin. 1st. NF/NF. G8. $15.00.

GILBERT, George. *Bucking with Bar C.* 192 Chelsea House. A19. $15.00.

GILBERT, George. *Quick Draw Kid.* 1927 Chelsea. VG/dj. M2. $20.00.

GILBERT, Harriet. *Hotels with Empt Rooms.* 1973. NY. Harper. 1st Am ed VG/VG. G8. $15.00.

GILBERT, J. *Warren. Blue & Gray.* 1922. np A19. $40.00.

GILBERT, Jack. *Monolihos Poems 1962 & 1982.* 1982. Knopf. 1st. assn copy. F/dj. V1 $55.00.

GILBERT, MARTIN & SAVAGE. *Avia* *Osteology.* 1985. Flagstaff. 2nd. 252p. B1 $25.00.

GILBERT, Michael. *After the Fine Weather* 1963. Hodder Stoughton. 1st Eng. VG/G G8. $40.00.

GILBERT, Michael. *Body of a Girl.* 1972 Harper Row. 1st. VG/VG. P3. $13.00.

GILBERT, Michael. *Flash Point.* 1974 Harper Row. 1st. VG/VG. P3. $18.00.

GILBERT, Michael. *Stay of Execution.* 1971 London. Hodder & Stoughton. 1st. F/dj M15. $65.00.

GILBERT, Paul. *Bertram & His Funny Animals.* 1937. Chicago. Rand McNally. VG/G. B5. $45.00.

ILBERT, Sarah. *Dixie Riggs*. 1991. NY. arner. 1st. small red dot on top edges. 'F. H11. $15.00.

ILBERT, Sarah. *Hairdo*. 1990. NY. Warner. t. author's 1st book. F/F. H11. $25.00.

ILBERT, W.S. *Complete Plays of Gilbert & ullivan*. 1938. Garden City. tall 8vo. 711p. G+/dj. H1. $20.00.

ILBRETH, Frank. *Cheaper by the Dozen*. 48. Crowell. 1st. F/NF clip. B4. $275.00.

ILCHRIST, Ellen. *Anabasis*. 1994. Jackson. niv Press of Mississippi. 1st. sgn. F/F. lt ear. A24. $40.00.

ILCHRIST, Ellen. *Drunk with Love*. 1986. ttle, Brn. 1st. inscr. VG/VG. A23. $50.00.

ILCHRIST, Ellen. *Net of Jewels*. 1992. oston. Little, Brn. 1st. sgn. F/F. A24. $40.00.

ILCHRIST, Ellen. *The Age of Miracles*. 95. Boston. Little, Brn. 1st. F/F. A24. 8.00.

ILCHRIST, Ellen. *Victory Over Japan*. 84. Little, Brn. 1st. VG+/VG. A20. $20.00.

ILCHRIST, Harry L. & Philip B. Matz. he Residual Effects of Warfare Gases*. 1933. ashington. inscr. 93p. faded. owned/VG. B18. $45.00.

ILDER, George. *Men & Marriage*. 1986. elican. 219p. F/dj. B29. $6.00.

ILES, H. *GI Journal of Sgt Giles*. 1965. MA. s. 399p. VG/VG. S16. $27.50.

ILES, Herbert. *Glossary of eference...Connected with Far East*. 1974. ondon. Curzon. 328p. F. W3. $56.00.

ILES, Herbert A. *Chinese Poetry in English erse*. 1898. Shanghai. Kelly Walsh. 1st. 8vo. 12p. contemporary calf. M1. $125.00.

ILES, Jeff. *Back in the Blue House*. 1992. Y. Ticknor. 1st. author's 1st book. VF/F. 11. $15.00.

ILES, Kenneth. *Death Among the Stars*. 969. Walker. 1st. F/dj. P3. $10.00.

ILES, Molly. *Rough Translations*. 1985. thens, GA. 1st. author's 1st book. F/F. R13. 35.00.

ILFILLAN, Archer B. *Goat's Eye-View of ue Black Hills*. 1953. Rapid City, SD. Dean. 19. $20.00.

GILKEY, Helen M. *Handbook of Northwest Flowering Plants*. 1951. Portland. 2nd. 412p. B26. $12.50.

GILL, B.M.; see Trimble, Barbara Margaret.

GILL, Bartholomew. *Death of a Busker King*. 1997. London. Severn House. 1st. VF/VF. T2. $38.00.

GILL, Bartholomew. *McGarr and the Method of Descartes*. 1984. NY. Viking. 1st. F/F. H11. $35.00.

GILL, Brendan. *Here at the New Yorker*. 1975. Random. 1st. inscr/dtd 1975. VG/NF. B4. $200.00.

GILL, Eric. *Social Justice & the Stations of the Cross*. 1939. London. James Clarke. 1st. 12mo. 21p. F. B24. $125.00.

GILL, Patrick; see Creasey, John.

GILLELAN, Howard G. *Complete Book of the Bow & Arrow*. 1994. Derrydale. 1/1250. gilt leather. F. A17. $22.00.

GILLESPIE, Dizzy and Al Fraser. *To Be or Not to Bop*. 1979. Garden City. Doubleday. 1st. F/F. B2. $50.00.

GILLESPIE, Dizzy and Al Fraser. *To Be or Not to Bop*. 1979. Garden City. Doubleday. later printing. NF/NF. B2. $25.00.

GILLESPIE, Emer. *Five Dead Men*. 1999. London. Headline. 1st. sgn. VF/VF. T2. $38.00.

GILLESPIE, Noel. *Endotrachael Anesthesia*. 1941. Madison. 1st. 187p. A13. $125.00.

GILLESPIE, W.M. *Treatise on Land-Surveying*. 1855. Appleton. 6th. 424p+84p tables. G. A17. $45.00.

GILLET, Louis. *Claybook for James Joyce*. 1958. London & NY. Abelard/Schuman. UK price clip. US price stp on flap. F/lightly used dj. B2. $25.00.

GILLETT, Eric. *Film Fairyland*. nd. London. lg 8vo. ils. cloth. G. C8. $15.00.

GILLIAM, Harold. *San Francisco Bay*. 1957. Doubleday. 1st. sgn. 8vo. 336p. bl cloth. M/VG. $7.00.

GILLIES, Ed. *My Own Sea Kingdom*. 1994. Chicago. Aspen. as issued. P4. $20.00.

GILLIGAN, Edmund. *Gaunt Woman*. 1943. Scribner. 1st. VG/VG. P3. $20.00.

GILLIS, Charles. *Yellowstone Park & Alaska*. 1893. np. sgn. 76p. VG. J2. $175.00.

GILLIS, J.M. *US Naval Astonomical Expedition to the Southern Hemisphere*. 1855. WA. Vol 2 only. ils. 300p. VG. B5. $150.00.

GILLIS, Leon. *Amputations*. 1954. London. 1st. 423p. A13. $100.00.

GILLSTATER, S. *Wave After Wave*. 1964. London. ils/maps. brd. F/NF. M12. $20.00.

GILMAN, A. *Practical Bee Breeding*. 1929. NY. 1st. 264p. VG/VG. B5. $17.50.

GILMAN, Dorothy. *Caravan*. nd. Doubleday. 1st. sgn plate. NF/NF. G8. $15.00.

GILMAN, Dorothy. *Mrs. Polifax & the Golden Triangle*. 1988. Doubleday. 1st. VG/dj. P3. $16.00.

GILMAN, Dorothy. *Tightrope Walker*. 1979. Doubleday. 1st. 186p. cloth. VG/clip. M20. $12.00.

GILMAN, Edgar Dow (ed). *The Mess Kit, Fifth Corps Area, Camp Knox KY*. 1924. Chicago. Military Training Camps Assoc. vol. 3. photos. 228p. VG. B18. $45.00.

GILMAN, Kay Iselin. *Inside the Pressure Cooker*. 1973. Berkley. 1st. VG/G+. P8. $20.00.

GILMAN, Laselle. *Red Gate*. 1953. Ballantine. 1st. VG/dj. P3. $30.00.

GILPATRICK, Noreen. *Shadow of Death*. 1995. Mysterious. 1st. F/F. G8. $20.00.

GILPATRICK, Noreen. *The Piano Man*. 1991. NY. St. Martin. 1st. F+/VF. H11. $225.00.

GILPIN, Laura. *Enduring Navaho*. 1968. Austin. TX U. 1st. photos. F/F. L3. $65.00.

GILSSANT, Edouard. *Faulkner, Mississippi*. 1999. FSG. UP. F/wrp. M25. $35.00.

GILSTRAP, John. *At All Costs*. 1998. NY. Warner. 1st. F/F. H11. $15.00.

GILSTRAP, John. *Nathan's Run*. 1996. NY. Harper Collins. 1st. author's 1st novel. VF/VF. T2. $20.00.

GILSVIK, Bob. *Modern Trapline*. 1980. Radnor, PA. Chilton. dj. A19. $20.00.

GINSBERG, Allen. *Empty Mirror*. 1961. NY. Cornith/Totem. 1st. sgn/dtd 1963. NF/wrp. B4. $350.00.

GINSBERG, Allen. *Kaddish & Other Poems 1958 – 1960*. 1961. SF. City Lights. 1st prt. NF/wrp. B4. $250.00.

GINSBERG, H.L. *Book of Isaiah: A New Translation*. 1972 – 73. JPS. 1st. sm 4to. 116p. VG+/G. S3. $23.00.

GINSBERG, Louis. *Photographers in Virginia 1839 – 1900: A Checklist*. 1986. Petersburg, VA. self pub. 1st. 1/200. pres. 64p.

GINSBURG, Art. *Mr. Food Cooks Pasta*. 1993. NY. Morrow. 1st. NF/NF. A28. $7.95.

GINSBURG, Isaac. *Western Atlantic Scorpion Fishes*. 1953. Smithsonian. 103p. NF. S15. $10.00.

GINSBURG, Mirra. *Last Door to Aiya*. 1968. SG Phillips. 1st. F/dj. P3. $23.00.

GINSBURG, Mirra. *Ultimate Threshold*. 1970. Holt. 1st. VG/dj. M2. $10.00.

GINZBERG, Louis. *On Jewish Law & Lore*. 1955. JPS. 262p. VG/G+. S3. $22.00.

GIOVANNI, Nikki. *Sacred Cows and Other Edibles*. 1988. Morrow. 1st. VG/dj. M25. $25.00.

GIOVINAZZO, Buddy. *Life Is Hot in Cracktown*. 1993. NY. Thunder. 1st. author's 1st book. F/F. H11. $30.00.

GIPSON, Morrell. *Mr. Bear Squash-You-All-Flat*. 1950. Wonder. ils Angela. VG. M5. $145.00.

GIPSON, Morrell. *Surprise Doll*. 1949. Wonder. 1st. ils Steffie Lerch. VG. M5. $35.00.

GIRARDI, Robert. *Madeline's Ghost*. (1995). NY. Delacorte. 1st. author's 1st book. F/F. B3. $45.00.

GIRARDI, Robert. *The Pirate's Daughter*. (1997). NY. Delacorte. 1st. author's 2nd book. F/F. B3. $30.00.

GIRAUDOUX, Jean. *Ondine*. 1954. NY. Random House. 1st. a Random House Play. adapted by Maurice Valency. NF/VG+. A24. $30.00.

GIRLING, Richard. *Forest on the Hill*. 1982. Viking. 1st. F/F. M2. $15.00.

GIROUARD, Mark. *Cities & People: A Social Architectural History*. 1986. ils. VG/VG. M17. $22.50.

GIROUX, E. X. *Death for a Double*. 1990. St. Martin. 1st. VG/VG. G8. $12.50.

GIRZONE, Joseph F. *Joshua in the Holy Land*. 1992. Macmillan. 205p. F/F. B29. $7.00.

GISH, Franklin. *First Horses*. 1993. Reno. NV U. 1st. F/F. L3. $35.00.

GITLER, Ira. *Blood on the Ice*. 1974. Regenry. 1st. photos. F/VG. P8. $25.00.

GITLOW, Benjamin. *The Whole of Their Lives*. 1948. NY. Scribner's. 1st. NF/used dj. B2. $35.00.

GITTINGER, Roy. *Formation of the State of Oklahoma, 1803 – 1906*. 1917. Berkeley. 256p. gilt cloth. D11. $50.00.

GITTINGS, Robert. *Peach Blossom Forest & Other Chinese*. 1951. Oxford. 1st. VG/dj. P3. $20.00.

GIVEN, James Buchanan. *Society & Homicide in 13th-Century England*. 1977. Stanford. ES. dj. M11. $50.00.

GIVENS, Charles J. *Financial Self-Defense*. 1990. S&S. 1st. 488p. F/F. W2. $25.00.

GLADSTONE, Bernard. *Complete Book of Garden & Outdoor Lighting*. 1956. NY. photos/drawings. 120p. VG/dj. B26. $14.00.

GLADSTONE, William E. *Female Suffrage*. 1892. np. Am Women Remonstrants. 8vo. stitched. R12. $75.00.

GLADSTONE, William E. *Might of Right*. 1898. Boston. Lee Shepard. New ed/1st thus. 302p. gray cloth. B22. $8.50.

GLADWIN, Thomas. *East Is a Big Bird*. 1970. Cambridge. Harvard. photos/9 maps/diagrams. 241p. dj. T7. $45.00.

GLANCY, Diane. *Firesticks*. 1993. Norman. OK. 1st. F/F. L3. $45.00.

GLANCY, Diane. *Trigger Dance*. 1990. Boulder. Fiction Collective Two. 1st hc. F/F. L3. $75.00.

GLANTZ, David M. *When Titans Clashed: How the Red Army Stopped Hitler*. 1995. Kansas City. 1st. F/F. V4. $17.50.

GLASBY, John S. *Boundaries of the Universe*. 1971. Cambridge, MA. Harvard Univ Press. 8vo. text figures. 18 b/w plates. 296p. VG/chipped & clipped dj. K5. $25.00.

GLASPELL, Susan. *A Jury of Her Peers*. 1927. London. Ernest Benn. 1st. 1/250 sgn. VF/sc. M15. $350.00.

GLASS, C. *Family Album: Cactus Succulent Journal 1966 Yearbook*. 196 Reseda. photos. 296p. VG. B26. $35.00.

GLASS, David C. *Neurophysiology Emotion*. 1967. Rockefeller. 234p. gr/gr cloth. VG. G1. $25.00.

GLASS, INNES & SCHNECK. *Identifyi Cacti*. 1996. Edison, NJ. 80 mc photos. M/ B26. $8.00.

GLASS, Leslie. *Judging Time*. 1998. N Dutton. 1st. sgn. F/F. G8. $20.00.

GLASS, Leslie. *Loving Time*. 1996. N Bantam. 1st. sgn. F/F. G8. $20.00.

GLASS-GRAY, Charles. *Off at Sunris Overland Journal of Charles Glass-Gray*. 197 San Marino. Huntington Lib. 1st. F/F. O $25.00.

GLASSER, Otto. *Physical Foundations Radiology*. 1944. NY. 1st. 426p. A13. $20.00

GLASSMAN, Judith. *Year in Music*. 197 NY. Columbia. 184p. G/dj. C5. $12.50.

GLATZER, Nahum. *Dynamics Emancipation: Jew in the Modern Age*. 196 Beacon. 70 essays. 320p. VG/dj. S3. $23.00

GLATZER, Nahum. *In Time & Eternity: Jewish Reader*. 1946. Schocken. 255p. VG. S $22.00.

GLAZIER, Willard. *Heroes of Three War* 1884. Phil. ils. gilt cloth. VG. B18. $25.00.

GLEASON, Duncan. *Islands of Californi* 1951. Sea Pub. 1st. inscr. NF/G. O4. $30.00

GLEASON, Henry Allan. *Vegetation History of the Middle West*. 1923. NY. offprin tall 8vo. wrp. A22. $25.00.

GLEASON, Ralph, ed. *Jam Session. A Anthology of Jazz*. 1958. NY. Putnam. 1s F/lightly chip dj. B2. $35.00.

GLEASON, Ralph J. *Celebrating the Duk* 1975. Boston. Atlantic Monthly. 1st. F/F. B: $30.00.

GLEITER, Jan. *A House by the Side of th Road*. 1998. NY. St. Martin. 1st. sgn. VF/VI T2. $25.00.

GLEITER, Jan. *Lie Down with Dogs*. 199 NY. St. Martin. 1st. sgn. author's 1st nove VF/VF. T2. $35.00.

GLEN, Alison. *Showcase*. 1992. S&S. 1s sgn. NF/NF. G8. $15.00.

GLEN, Alison. *Trunk Show.* 1995. S&S. 1st. sgn. F/F. G8. $15.00.

GLENN, Lois. *Charles W. S. Williams: A Checklist.* 1975. Kent State. 128p. cloth. A17. $12.50.

GLESSING, Robert J. *Underground Press in America.* 1970. Bloomington. 1st. F/F. B4. $125.00.

GLEYE, Paul. *Behind the Wall: American in East Germany 1988 – 1989.* 1991. S IL U. 1st. AN/dj. V4. $12.50.

GLICK, Allen. *Winters Coming.* 1984. NY. Pinnacle. 1st. Author's first book. F/F. H11. $30.00.

GLICK, Thomas F. (ed). *The Comparative Reception of Darwinism.* 1972. Austin. sm 4to. VG in torn dj. B26. $32.50.

GLOAG, Julian. *Only Yesterday.* 1986. Holt. 1st. F/F. A20. $10.00.

GLOSTER, Hugh Morris. *Negro Voices in American Fiction.* 1948. Chapel Hill. 1st. F/VG. B2. $85.00.

GLOVER, Richard. *Leonidas, a Poem.* 1737. London. Dodsley. 1st. tall wide 4to. 335p. ES. $13.00.

GLOVER, Robert H. *The Progress of the World Wide Missions.* 1960. Harper. 502p. VG/VG. B29. $4.00.

GLUBB, John Bagot. *Short History of the Arab Peoples.* 1969. Hodder Stoughton. 43 maps/14 tables. 318p. cloth. VG/dj. Q2. $20.00.

GLUCK, Louise. *Firstborn.* 1969. Anvil. 1st Eng. assn copy. NF/dj. V1. $40.00.

GLUCK, Sinclair. *Dragon in Harness.* 1932. Dodd Mead. 1st. VG. M2. $15.00.

GLYN, Elinor. *Three Weeks.* 1924. Macaulay. 1st thus. F/F. B4. $85.00.

GOBLE, Neil. *Asimov Analyzed.* 1972. Mirage. 1st. VG/dj. P3. $45.00.

GOBLE, Warwick. *Folk Tales of Bengal.* 1912. Macmillan. 1st. 32 mtd pl. 274p. VG. P2. $300.00.

GODDARD, Anthea. *Aztec Skull.* 1977. Walker. 1st. F/dj. M2. $15.00.

GODDARD, Donald. *Joey (Gallo).* 1974. Harper Row. 1st. F/NF. A20. $25.00.

GODDARD, Ken. *Prey.* 1992. NY. Tor. 1st. VF/VF. T2. $9.00.

GODDARD, Kenneth. *Balefire.* 1983. Bantam. 1st. F/VG. N4. $20.00.

GODDARD, Robert. *Beyond Recall.* 1998. Holt. 1st. F/F. G8. $20.00.

GODDARD, Robert. *In Pale Battalions.* 1988. NY. Poseidon Press. 1st British hc ed. VF/VF. T2. $25.00.

GODDARD, Robert. *Out of the Sun.* 1997. NY. Henry Holt. 1st Am ed. sgn. VF/VF. T2. $30.00.

GODDEN, Geoffrey A. *Illustrated Encyclopedia of British Pottery & Porcelain.* 1966. Crown. 1st Am. 390p. gilt bl cloth. F/VG. H1. $40.00.

GODDEN, Rumer. *A House with Four Rooms.* 1989. NY. Morrow. 1st. Tall 8vo. 319p. F/F. H1. $28.50.

GODDEN, Rumer. *A Kindle of Kittens.* 1978. NY. Viking Press. 1st Am ed. ils by Lynne Byrnes. F in dj. A16. $25.00.

GODDEN, Rumer. *China Court.* 1961. Viking. 1st. F/NF. M19. $25.00.

GODDEN, Rumer. *River.* 1946. Little, Brn. 1st. F/VG. M19. $35.00.

GODDEN, Rumer. *St Jerome & the Lion.* 1961. Viking. 1st. 32p. F/F. D4. $30.00.

GODET, F. *Commentary on Romans.* 1956. Zondervan. Classic Commentary Library. 530p. G. B29. $12.00.

GODEY, John. *Nella.* 1981. Delacorte. 1st. G+/dj. N4. $17.50.

GODEY, John. *Never Put Off Till Tomorrow What You Can Kill Today.* 1970. Random. 1st. VG/dj. P3. $25.00.

GODEY, John. *Talisman.* 1976. Putnam. 1st. VG/dj. P3. $20.00.

GODFREY, Henry. *Your Yucatan Guide.* 1967. Funk Wagnalls. 1st. 196p. dj. F3. $15.00.

GODFREY & WOOTEN. *Aquatic & Wetland Plants of Southeastern United States.* 1979. Athens. Monocotyledons. 712p. F. B26. $46.00.

GODFROY, Chief Clarence. *Miami Indian Stories.* 1961. Winona Lake. Light/Life Pr. 1st. VG. L3. $150.00.

GODOLPHIN, Mary. *Robinson Crusoe, in Words of One Syllable.* nd. London. Shoe Lane. sm 4to. ils John Harris. VG. C8. $22.50.

GODWIN, Gail. *Finishing School.* 1985. London. Heinemann. 1st Eng. NF/dj. R13. $25.00.

GODWIN, Gail. *Violet Clay.* 1978. Knopf. 1st. F/dj. Q1. $50.00.

GODWIN, Joan. *Baffling World.* 1968. Hart. 1st. NF/dj. M2. $17.00.

GODWIN, Parke. *Firelord.* 1979. Doubleday. 1st. F/dj. M2. $25.00.

GODWIN, Parke. *Waiting for the Galactic Bus.* 1988. Doubleday. 1st. F/dj. P3. $20.00.

GOEDICKE, Patricia. *Wind of Our Going.* 1985. Copper Canyon. inscr. assn copy. NF/wrp. V1. $15.00.

GOELDNER, Christian. *The Thoroughbred Hunter.* 1977. S. Brunswick. Barnes. 1st. VG/G. O3. $20.00.

GOEMER, Fred. *Search for Amelia Earhart.* 1966. London. Bodley Head. 1st Eng. photos. 286p. VG/clip. A25. $18.00.

GOETCHIUS, Eugene Van Ness. *The Language of the New Testament.* 1965. Scribner's. 449p. G. some loose pages. B29. $13.00.

GOETHE; see Von Goethe.

GOETZMANN & WILLIAMS. *Atlas of North American Exploration…* 1992. 4to. 90 portraits/100 mc maps. 224p. F/F. A4. $35.00.

GOFF, Frederick. *John Dunlap Broadside: First Printing of Declaration.* 1976. Lib Congress. 4to. ils/tipped-in portrait. F/F case. A4. $45.00.

GOFF, John S. *George W. P. Hunt & His Arizona.* 1972. Socio Technical Pub. 1st. ils/notes/index. 286p. NF/NF. B19. $45.00.

GOFF, John S. *Governors 1863 – 1912: Arizona Territorial Officials II.* 1978. Blk Mtn Pr. 1st. 212p. F/sans. B19. $30.00.

GOLAY, Frank H. (ed). *The United States and the Philippines.* 1966. NJ. Prentice Hall. 1st ed. 10th prt. sm8vo. 179p. VG. P1. $5.00.

GOLB, Norman. *Who Wrote the Dead Sea Scrolls?* 1995. Scribner. 1st. 446p. NF/dj. W1. $20.00.

GOLD, H.L. *Fifth Galaxy Reader.* 1961. BC. VG/VG. P3. $30.00.

GOLD, H.L. *Mind Partner & 8 Other Novelettes From Galaxy.* 1961. Doubleday. 1st. F/dj. M2. $25.00.

GOLD, H.L. *Old Die Rich.* 1955. Crown. 1st. VG/dj. M2. $50.00.

GOLD, Herbert. *Biafra Goodbye.* 1970. np. Two Winds. 1st. inscr. wrp. NF. M19. $25.00.

GOLD, M. *Jews Without Money.* 1941 (1930). ils Howard Simon. G+. E6. $22.00.

GOLD, Robert S. *A Jazz Lexicon.* 1964. NY. Knopf. 1st. F/NF. some wear. B2. $35.00.

GOLDBERG, Elkhonon. *Contemporary Neuropsychology & Legacy of Luria.* 1990. Hillsdale. NJ. Lawrence Erlbaum Assoc. 287p. prt bl cloth. F. G1. $50.00.

GOLDBERG, Lee. *Television Series Revivals.* 1993. McFarland. 196p. VG. C5. $12.50.

GOLDBERG, Stanley. *Understanding Relativity; Origin and Impact of a Scientific Revolution.* 1984. Boston. Birkhauser. lg 8vo. photos & diagrams. 494p. G/VG. K5. $20.00.

GOLDBLATT, Peter. *The Woody Iridaceae: Nivenia, Klattia, and Witsenia.* 1993. Portland. new in dj. B26. $30.00.

GOLDEN, Arthur. *Memoirs of a Geisha.* 1997. Knopf. 1st. F/dj. M25. $100.00.

GOLDEN, Arthur. *Memoirs of a Geisha.* 1997. NY. Knopf. 1st. first state. author's 1st novel. NF/F. M23. $70.00.

GOLDEN, Christopher, editor. *Cut! Horror Writers on Horror Film.* 1992. Baltimore. Borderlands Press. 1st. 1/500 # copies. sgn by most all contributors. VF/VF in dj & slipcase. T2. $65.00.

GOLDEN, Marita. *Long Distance Life.* 1989. Doubleday. 1st. F/F. B4. $45.00.

GOLDFARB, Clifford S. *The Great Shadow: Arthur Conan Doyle, Brigadier Gerard, and Napoleon.* 1997. Ashcroft. Calabash Press. 1st. 1/150 # copies. sgn. VF/VF. T2. $45.00.

GOLDFLUSS, Howard E. *The Judgment.* 1986. NY. Fine. 1st. author's 1st book. F/F. H11. $40.00.

GOLDIN, Hayman E. *Jewish Woman & Her Home.* 1941. Hebrew Pub. ils Nota Koslowsky. 354p. VG/dj. S3. $22.00.

GOLDIN, Stephen. *A World Called Solitude.* 1981. Garden City. Doubleday. 1st. VF/VF. T2. $6.00.

GOLDING, Harry. *Wonder Book of Nature.* 1934 (1934). London. Ward. 5th. inscr. NF. T12. $50.00.

GOLDING, Harry. *Zoo Days.* 1919. Ward Lock. 1st. 8vo. red cloth. R5. $175.00.

GOLDING, Louis. *Jewish Problem.* 1939. Penguin. 5th. 213p. sc. VG. S3. $19.00.

GOLDING, William. *Brass Butterfly: A Play in Three Acts.* 1958. London. Faber. 1st. F/dj. Q1. $150.00.

GOLDING, William. *Darkness Visible.* 1979. FSG. 1st. F/F. B35. $18.00.

GOLDING, William. *Lord of the Flies.* 1955. Coward McCann. 1st Am. author's 1st book. NF/VG. L3. $650.00.

GOLDING, William. *Paper Men.* 1984. FSG. 1st. F/dj. P3. $15.00.

GOLDING, William. *Spire.* 1964. Harcourt. 1st Am. F/dj. M2. $25.00.

GOLDMAN, Albert. *Lives of John Lennon.* 1988. Morrow. 1st. F/F. A20. $15.00.

GOLDMAN, Alex J. *Giants of Faith: Great American Rabbis.* 1964. NY. Citadel. 349p. VG/G+. S3. $24.00.

GOLDMAN, Emma. *Living My Life.* 1931. Knopf. 2 vol. 993p. S3. $45.00.

GOLDMAN, Emma. *Marriage and Love.* 1914. NY. Mother Earth Pub. 2nd. wrp. G to VG. some wear, repair. B2. $25.00.

GOLDMAN, Emma. *Syndicalism.* 1913. Mother Earth. 1st. VG/wrp. B2. $60.00.

GOLDMAN, Emma. *The Place of the Individual in Society.* nd. Chicago. Free Society. 1st. wrp. lightly soiled. VG+. B2. $45.00.

GOLDMAN, Francesco. *The Ordinary Seaman.* (1997). NY. Atlantic Monthly Press. 1st. F/F. B3. $25.00.

GOLDMAN, Francisco. *Long Night of White Chickens.* 1992. Atlantic Monthly. 1st. author's 1st novel. F/NF. D10. $45.00.

GOLDMAN, Laurel. *Sounding the Territory.* 1982. Knopf. 1st. F/dj. M25. $15.00.

GOLDMAN, William. *Brothers.* 1987. NY. Warner. 1st. VF/VF. H11. $30.00.

GOLDMAN, William. *Color of Light.* 1984. Granada. 1st. VG/dj. P3. $23.00.

GOLDMAN, William. *Control.* 1982. Delacorte. 1st. VG/dj. P3. $25.00.

GOLDMAN, William. *Heat.* 1985. NY. Warner Books. 1st. VF/VF. T2. $7.00.

GOLDMAN, William. *Heat.* 1985. Warner. 1st. F/F. A20. $20.00.

GOLDMAN, William. *Marathon Man.* 1974. Delacorte. 1st. sgn. F/VG. A23. $40.00.

GOLDMAN, William. *Princess Bride.* nd. BC. F/dj. M2. $15.00.

GOLDMAN, William. *Temple of Gold.* 1957. NY. 1st. sgn. NF/NF. A11. $125.00.

GOLDMARK, Josephine. *Fatigue & Efficiency: A Study in Industry.* 1912. Charities Pub Comm of Russell Sage Foundation. 3rd. sgn. H1. $30.00.

GOLDOWSKY, Seebert. *Yankee Surgeon: Life & Times of Usher Parsons.* 1988. Canton, MA. 1st. 450p. dj. A13. $30.00.

GOLDSBOROUGH, Robert. *Death on Deadline.* 1987. NY. Bantam. 1st. VF/VF. H11. $40.00.

GOLDSBOROUGH, Robert. *Last Coincidence.* nd. Bantam. 1st. NF/NF. G8. $12.50.

GOLDSBOROUGH, Robert. *Murder in E Minor.* 1986. Bantam. 1st. F/dj. P3. $15.00.

GOLDSCHEIDER, Ludwig. *Sculptures of Michelangelo.* 1950. London. Phaidon. 2nd. ils/pl/footnotes/bibliography. cloth. dj. D2. $60.00.

GOLDSCHMIDT, Sidney G. *Eye for a Horse: A Guide to Buying & Judging.* 1933. Scribner. 1st Am. VG/fair. O3. $35.00.

GOLDSCHMIDT, Walter. *Sebei Law.* 1967. Berkeley. M11. $35.00.

GOLDSMITH, Barbara. *Johnson Versus Johnson.* 1987. Knopf. 1st. 285p. VG/dj. P12. $10.00.

GOLDSMITH, Donald. *The Hunt for Life on Mars.* 1997. NY. Dutton. 1st printing. 8vo. b/w photo ils. 267p. F/F. K5. $24.00.

GOLDSMITH, Donald. *Worlds Unnumbered; The Search for Extrasolar Planets.* 1997. Sausalito, CA. Univ Science Books. 2nd printing. 8vo. 24 color plates. 237p. F/F. K5. $25.00.

GOLDSMITH, Margaret. *Christina of Sweden: A Psychological Biography.* 1935. Doubleday Doran. 1st. 308p. VG+. A25. $15.00.

GOLDSMITH, Oliver. *Deserted Village.* 1857. NY. Appleton. 8vo. 46p. aeg. gilt gr morocco. B24. $100.00.

GOLDSMITH, Oliver. *Miscellaneous Works Oliver Goldsmith*. 1850 (1837). Putnam. rpt. vol. G. H1. $85.00.

GOLDSMITH, Oliver. *She Stoops to Conquer; or, The Mistakes of a Night*. Illus by Hugh Thomson. nd (circa 1912). London. Hodder & Stoughton. numerous drawings, 25 tipped in color plates. ils title in gr & blk. ornate gilt stp gr cloth. spine a bit darkned. lightly rubbed. free ep show offset browning. K1. $125.00.

GOLDSMITH, Oliver. *Vicar of Wakefield*. nd. Phil. McKay. 1st Am. ils Rackham/12 c pl. 231p. NF/dj. M20. $175.00.

GOLDSTEIN, Joseph. *Government of British Trade Unions: A Study*. 1952. Allen Unwin. G/VG. V4. $25.00.

GOLDSTEIN, Lisa. *Dream Years*. 1985. Bantam. 1st. F/dj. P3. $15.00.

GOLDSTEIN, Milton. *Magnificent West: Grand Canyon*. 1980. NY. Bonanza. 4to. ils. 201p. gr brd. dj. $7.00.

GOLDSTEIN & ZORNOW. *Screen Image of Youth: Movies About Children & Adolescents*. 1980. Scarecrow. 1st. sgn Goldstein. F. C9. $30.00.

GOLDSTONE, Lawrence and Nancy. *Slightly Chipped. Footnotes in Booklore*. 1999. NY. St. Martin. ARC. wrps. F. B2. $25.00.

GOLDSTONE, Lawrence & Nancy. *Slightly Chipped*. 1999. NY. St. Martin. 1st. F/F. M23. $35.00.

GOLDSTONE, Lawrence & Nancy. *Used and Rare*. 1997. NY. St. Martin. 1st. F/F. M23. $40.00.

GOLDTHWAITE, Eaton K. *Cat & Mouse*. 1946. DSP. 1st. VG/dj. P3. $25.00.

GOLDWASSER, Janet. *Huan-Ying: Workers' China*. 1975. Monthly Review. 1st. VG/dj. V4. $25.00.

GOLDWATER, Barry. *Goldwater*. 1988. Doubleday. 1st. sgn. F/F. A23. $50.00.

GOLDWATER, Barry M. *Delightful Journey Down the Green & Colorado Rivers*. 1970. AZ Hist Found. 1/100. deluxe ed. sgn. rust cloth/leather spine. case/photo. F7. $295.00.

GOLDWORTH, Bella. *Across the Border: Short Stories*. 1971. Yiddisher Kultur. 269p. VG/G+. S3. $29.00.

GOLLANCZ, Victor. *Devil's Repertoire or Nuclear Bombing & the Life of Man*. 1959. VG/dj. K3. $10.00.

GOLLER, Nicholas. *Tomorrow's Silence*. 1979. Macmillan. 1st. VG/VG. P3. $15.00.

GOLLIN, James. *Broken Consort*. 1989. NY. St. Martin. 1st. NF/NF. G8. $10.00.

GOLOVANOV, Yaroslav. *Our Gagarin*. 1978. Moscow. Progress. lg 4to. 317p. VG. K5. $100.00.

GOLOVIN, Pavel N. *End of Russian America: Capt P. N. Golovin's Last Report 1862*. 1979. Portland. OR Hist Soc. 4to. 8 maps. AN/dj. O7. $35.00.

GOMBROWICZ, Witold. *Ferdydurke*. 1961. HRW. 1st Am. F/NF clip. B4. $200.00.

GOMEZ ARISTIZABAL, Horacio. *Dicionario De La Historica De Colombia*. 1985. np. Bogata. 3rd ed. 269p. G. F3. $30.00.

GONNE, Captian C. M. *Hints on Horses: How to Judge Them, Buy Them, Ride Them, Drive Them, and Depict Them*. 1905. NY. Dutton. 1st Am prt from 2nd London prt. obl sm 4to. G. O3. $35.00.

GONZALES, Ambrose. *With Aesop Along the Black Border*. 1924. Columbia, SC. The State Co. 1st. NF. owner's inscr. dulled spine. B2. $50.00.

GONZALES, Babs. *I Paid My Dues*. 1967. East Orange. Expubidence. wrp. pb orig. NF. B2. $50.00.

GONZALES DAVILA, Francisco. *Ancient Cultures of Mexico*. (1968). Mexico. INAH. ils. 80p. wrp. F3. $10.00.

GONZALES PENA, Carlos. *Historia De La Literature Mexicana*. 1940. Mexico. Tercera edicion. 2nd ed. 327p. VG/wrp. F3. $25.00.

GONZALES-GERTH, Miguel. *Ruben Dario Centennial Studies*. 1972. Austin, TX. 120p. dj. F3. $10.00.

GONZALEZ, Ray. *The Heat of Arrivals*. (1996). Brockport, NY, BOA Editions. UP. prt yellow wrp. F. B3. $25.00.

GOOCH, Fanny Chambers. *Face to Face with the Mexicans: The Domestic Life, Educations, Social and Business...As Seen and Studied by an Am Woman During Seven Years of Intercourse with Them*. (1887). NY. Fords, Howard & Hulbert. 8vo. 584. (4)p. illus. (some color plates). pict brn cloth. 1st ed. Front inner hinge weak. bookplate removed and library number removed from spine. minor wear and fw spots on spine. G to VG. L5. $85.00.

GOOD, Gregory. *Earth, the Heavens & the Carnegie Institute of Washington*. 1994. Am Geophysical Union. 4to. 252p. K5. $42.00.

GOOD, John Mason. *Book of Nature*. 1831. NY. from London ed. 467p. full calf. A17. $20.00.

GOOD, John Mason. *Book of Nature*. 1831. NY. 467p. full calf. A17. $20.00.

GOOD, Kenneth. *Into the Heart. One Man's Pursuit of Love & Knowledge Among the Yanomama*. 1991. NY. S&S. 1st. 349p. G/G. F3. $20.00.

GOODALL, A. *Wandering Gorillas*. 1979. London. Collins. ils/photos. F/F. M12. $27.50.

GOODALL, Jane. *Chimpanzees of Gombe*. 1986. Harvard. ils. F/NF. S15. $35.00.

GOODALL, John. *Sleeping Beauty*. 1979. London. Macmillan. 1st. ils. 20p. F. P2. $20.00.

GOODALL, John S. *Edwardian Christmas*. 1978. Atheneum. 1st Am. obl 8vo. VG/dj. B17. $30.00.

GOODCHILD, George. *Splendid Crime*. 1930. Houghton Mifflin. 1st Am. F/dj. M15. $60.00.

GOODE, G. B. *Origins of Natural Science in America*. 1991. WA. ils. F/dj. M4. $35.00.

GOODERS, J. *Birds of Canada*. 1984. Limps. Dragons World. ils Pledger/Boyer. 159p. brd. NF/NF. M12. $37.50.

GOODING, G. & C. E. Hall. *Flowers of the Islands of the Sun. Bermuda, Barbados, Bahamas, Caribbean Islands, Hawaii*. 1966. NY. sq 4to. chip dj. B26. $19.00.

GOODING, James Henry. *On the Altar of Freedom: A Black Solder's Civil War Letters*. 1991. Amherst. 1st. edit VM Adams. 139p. F/F. B4. $50.00.

GOODIS, David. *Of Missing Persons*. 1950. Morrow. 1st. NF/NF. B4. $650.00.

GOODIS, David. *Retreat from Oblivion*. 1939. Dutton. 1st F/VG+. B4. $2.000.00.

GOODKIND, Terry. *Blood of the Fold*. 1996. NY. Tor. 1st. F/VF. H11. $30.00.

GOODKIND, Terry. *Temple of the Winds*. 1997. NY. Tor. 1st. F/F. H11. $25.00.

GOODLANDER, C. W. *Memoirs & Recollections of CW Goodlander of Early Ft. Scott*. 1900. Monitor Prt. 1st. ils. 147p. NF. B19. $50.00.

GOODMAN, A. J. *Jurassic & Carboniferous of Western Canada.* 1958. Tulsa. AAGA John Andrew Allan Memorial Vol. 514p. xl. D8. $15.00.

GOODMAN, Allegra. *Kaaterskill Falls.* 1998. NY. Dial Press. 1st. F/F. M23. $40.00.

GOODMAN, Allegra. *The Family Markowitz.* 1996. NY. FSG. 1st. F in F dj. D10. $85.00.

GOODMAN, Benny. *Kingdom of Swing.* 1939. Stackpole. 1st. sgn by 13 members of Goodman's band. NF/G+. B4. $350.00.

GOODMAN, David Michael. *Western Panorama 1849 – 1875: Travels, Writings.* 1966. Clark. 1st. ils/notes/index. 326p. NF/brn wrp. B19. $45.00.

GOODMAN, Edward J. *Exploration of South America: Annotated Bibliography.* 1983. NY. Garland. 174p. F. O7. $35.00.

GOODMAN, Paul. *Growing Up Absurd.* 1960. NY. 1st. VG/VG. T9. $32.00.

GOODRICH, A. J. *Goodrich's Analytical Harmony: Theory Musical Composition.* nd (1893). Cincinnati. John Church. 1st. 404p. purple buckram. F. B22. $7.00.

GOODRICH, Frank B. *Women of Beauty & Heroism.* 1861. NY. HW Derby. engravings. 400p. teg. VG+. A25. $100.00.

GOODRICH, Lloyd. *Thomas Eakins.* 1970. Whitney Mus. ils. VG/VG. M17. $20.00.

GOODRICH, S. G. *Johnson's Natural History.* 1874. NY. 2 vol. ils. 3-quarter leather. VG. M17. $60.00.

GOODRICH, Ward L. *Modern Clock: A Study of Time Keeping Mechanism.* 1905. Chicago. Hazlitt Walker. 1st. ils. 502p. VG. K3. $55.00.

GOODRUM, Charles A. *Best Cellar.* 1987. St Martin. 1st. VG/VG. P3. $15.00.

GOODRUM, Charles A. *Dewey Decimated.* 1977. NY. Crown. 1st. F/F. T2. $35.00.

GOODSPEED, Charles E. *Nathaniel Hawthorne & Museum of Salem East India Marine Soc.* 1946. Peabody Mus. ils. 32p. wrp. T7. $24.00.

GOODSPEED, Charles E. *Yankee Bookseller.* 1937. Houghton Mifflin. 1st. ils. G+. K3. $35.00.

GOODSPEED, Thomas H. *Genus Nicotiana.* 1954. Waltham, MA. ils/50 tables. 536p. VG/dj. B26. $62.50.

GOODSTONE, Tony. *Pulps.* 1970. Chelsea House. 1st. VG/dj. P3. $35.00.

GOODWIN, Brian. *How the Leopard Changed its Spots...* 1994. NY. ils. VG/dj. M17. $15.00.

GOODWIN, Doris Kearns. *Wait Till Next Year.* (1977). NY. S&S. 1st. sgn & dated by author. F/F. B3. $50.00.

GOODWIN, Harold Leland. *The Science Book of Space Travel.* 1955. NY. Pocket Books. 1st pb ed. ils by Jack Coggins. 213p. G/wrp. spine chip. K5. $7.00.

GOODWIN, John. *Idols & the Prey: A Novel of Haiti.* 1953. NY. Harper. 1st. F/NF. B4. $85.00.

GOODWIN, John C. *The Zig Zag Man.* 1925. London. Hutchinson. 1st. lt spotting. F/dj. M15. $200.00.

GOODWIN, Tim. *Blood of the Forest.* 1999. London. Constable. 1st. sgn. VF/VF. T2. $38.00.

GOODWYN, Frank. *Poems About the West.* 1976. Pioneer Am Soc. ils. VG. J2. $25.00.

GOOLD-ADAMS, Richard. *Middle East Journey.* 1947. London. Murray. 8vo. ils/pl/dbl-p map. 195p. cloth. VG. Q2. $20.00.

GOOSE, Phillip Henry. *Evenings at the Microscope.* 1860. Appleton. VG. K3. $60.00.

GOOSMAN, Bessie. *History of Old Northfield Township.* 1973. Northfield, OH. 169p. VG. B18. $15.00.

GORD, G. M. *Cast in Stone.* 1996. NY. Walker. 1st. sgn GM Ford. F/dj. T2. $35.00.

GORDEEVA, Ekaterina. *My Sergi.* 1996. Warner. 1st. sgn. F/dj. T11. $60.00.

GORDIMER, Nadine. *Burger's Daughter.* 1979. Viking. 1st. F/F. M19. $25.00.

GORDIMER, Nadine. *Conservationist.* 1975. Viking. 1st. F/F. M19. $35.00.

GORDIMER, Nadine. *Lying Days.* 1953. London. Gollancz. 1st. sgn. NF/VG. B3. $150.00.

GORDIMER, Nadine. *Soft Voice of the Serpent & Other Stories.* 1952. S&S. 1st Am. author's 1st book. NF/dj. D10/L3. $200.00.

GORDIMER, Nadine. *Sport of Nature.* 1987. London. Cape. 1st. F/F. R13. $25.00.

GORDINIER, H. C. *Gross & Minute Anatomy of Central Nervous System.* 1899. Phil. Blakiston. 8vo. 48 full-p pl/213 text ils. VG. G1. $85.00.

GORDON, Alison. *Dead Pull Hitter.* 1988. St. Martin. 1st Am ed. VG/VG. G8. $12.50.

GORDON, Barbara. *Jennifer Fever: Older Men Younger Women.* 1988. NY. Harper & Row. NF/VG+. A28. $9.50.

GORDON, Caroline. *Malefactors.* 1956. Harcourt Brace. 1st. inscr. NF. B4. $300.00.

GORDON, Dixie. *How Sweet It Is: Story of Dixie Crystals & Savannah Foods.* 1992. Savannah Foods. 109p. H6. $30.00.

GORDON, Elizabeth. *Buddy Jim.* 1922. Volland. 1st. ils John Rae. pict brd. VG. M20. $22.00.

GORDON, Elizabeth. *Four Footed Folk or the Children of the Farm & Forest.* 1914. Whitman. 1st. 8vo. pict cloth. R5. $125.00.

GORDON, Elizabeth. *Mother Earth's Children.* 1914. Volland. 2nd. ils MT Ross. 8vo. pict brd. R5. $100.00.

GORDON, Elizabeth. *Watermelon Pete & Others.* 1914. Rand McNally. 1st. ils Clara Powers Wilson. red cloth. VG. M5. $250.00.

GORDON, Frederick. *Fairview Boys at Camp Mystery (#4).* 1914. Chas E. Graham. 126p. cloth. VG. M20. $10.00.

GORDON, G. B. *Notes on the Western Eskimo.* 1906. Phil. Dept Archaeology. 18 pl. F. P4. $45.00.

GORDON, Howard. *African in Me.* 1993. Brazille. 1st. sgn. F/F. B4. $45.00.

GORDON, John. *Borzoi.* 1974. Arco. VG/dj. A21. $20.00.

GORDON, John B. *Reminiscences of the Civil War.* 1903. NY. 1st. VG. B5. $125.00.

GORDON, John B. *Reminiscences of the Civil War.* 1981. Time-Life. rpt. 474p. aeg. gilt bl leather. F. M4. $30.00.

GORDON, John Brown. *Reminiscences of the Civil War.* 1981. Dayton. Morningside Bookshop. Memorial ed. scarce reprint of 1904 ed. No. 28 in ltd ed of 300 # copies. orig cloth. plates. 474p. NF. M8. $75.00.

GORDON, John Steele. *Scarlet Woman of Wall Street.* 1988. Weidenfeld. 1st. F/F. W2. $40.00.

GORDON, Lesley. *Green Magic. Flowers, Plants & Herbs in Lore & Legend.* 1977. NY. sq 8vo. 200p. VG in dj. B26. $29.00.

GORDON, Mary. *Final Payments.* 1978. Random. 1st. sgn. F/NF. R14. $75.00.

GORDON, Mary. *Temporary Shelter.* 1987. Random. 1st. sgn. NF/F. R14. $60.00.

GORDON, Neil. *Sacrifice of Isaac.* 1995. NY. Random House. 1st. ARC. VF/pict wrp. T2. $10.00.

GORDON, Nikki. *Gemini: An Extended Autobiographical Statement.* 1972. Bobbs Merrill. 1st. F/dj. M25. $45.00.

GORDON, Patricia. *Not-Mrs Murphy.* 1942. Viking. 1st. ils Ralph Boyer. 122p. F/VG. P2. $30.00.

GORDON, Pearl Scott. *Simply Elegant.* sgn. VG/G. A16. $14.00.

GORDON, Ralph. *The Gordon Collection of Coins of the West Indies & the American Colonies.* 1996. London. Baldwin's Auctions ltd. lg 4to. G. F3. $30.00.

GORDON, Ralph. *West Indies Countermarked Gold Coins.* 1987. np. Eric Press. 480/500. 122p. G. F3. $40.00.

GORDON, Richard. *Doctor at Large.* 1955. Michael Joseph. 1st. VG/dj. P3. $30.00.

GORDON, Richard. *Doctor in the Swim.* 1962. Michael Joseph. 1st. VG/dj. P3. $20.00.

GORDON, Roxy. *Breeds.* 1984. Austin. Place of Herons. 1st hc issue. F. L3. $125.00.

GORDON, Ruth. *Myself Among Others.* 1971. Atheneum. 1st. sgn; inscr. F/dj. M25. $50.00.

GORDON, Stuart. *Suane & the Crow God.* 1975. NEL. 1st. F/dj. M2. $17.00.

GORDON, Stuart. *Two-Eyes.* 1975. Sidgwick Jackson. 1st. VG/dj. P3. $20.00.

GORDON & MEDARIS. *Countdown for Decision.* 1960. NY. 1st. inscr Medaris. 303p. F/dj. B18. $35.00.

GORDONS, The. *Power Play.* 1965. NY. Doubleday. 1st. VG/VG. G8. $10.00.

GORDONS, The. *Tiger on My Back.* 1960. Crime Club. 1st. VG/VG. G8. $10.00.

GORE, Al. *Earth in the Balance.* (1995). Boston. Houghton Mifflin. 1st. F/F. B3. $40.00.

GOREN, Arthur. *New York Jews & Quest for Community: Kehillah Experiment.* 1970. Columbia. 361p. VG/G+. S3. $24.00.

GOREN, Charles H. *Contract Bridge in a Nutshell.* 1946. Doubleday. 1st. 128p. VG. H1. $18.00.

GOREN, Charles H. *Goren's Easy Steps to Winning Bridge: Programmed Textbook.* 1963. NY. 1st. 287p. dj. S1. $10.00.

GORENSTEIN, Shirley. *Not Forever on Earth.* 1975. Scribner. 1st. ils/index. 153p. dj. F3. $15.00.

GORES, Joe. *Cases.* 1999. NY. Mysterious Press. 1st. sgn. VF/VF. T2. $25.00.

GORES, Joe. *Come Morning.* 1986. NY. Mysterious Press. 1st. sgn. VF/VF. T2. $35.00.

GORES, Joe. *Dead Man.* 1993. NY. Mysterious Press. 1st. sgn. VF/VF. T2. $30.00.

GORES, Joe. *Final Notice.* 1973. NY. Random House. 1st. F/dj. M15. $75.00.

GORES, Joe. *Menaced Assassin.* 1994. NY. Mysterious Press. 1st. VF/VF. T2. $30.00.

GOREY, Edward. *Amphigorey.* 1972. Putnam. 1st. VG. M2. $20.00.

GOREY, Edward. *Broken Spoke.* 1976. Dodd Mead. 1st. F/F. A11. $80.00.

GOREY, Edward. *Dwindling Party: A Pop-Up Book.* 1982. Random. 1st. glossy ils brd. F. A11. $125.00.

GOREY, Edward. *Fletcher & Zenobia.* 1967. Meredith. stated 1st. ils Victoria Chess. VG. M5. $25.00.

GOREY, Edward. *Gilded Bat.* 1966. S&S. 1st stated. VG. D1. $60.00.

GOREY, Edward. *The Gashlycrumb Tinies; or, After the Outing.* 1997. NY. Harcourt Brace. reissue. 1st thus. VF no dj as issued. T2. $10.00.

GOREY, Edward. *Utter Zoo.* 1967. Meredith. 1st. unp. VG/dj. M20. $95.00.

GOREY, Edward. *Willowdale Handcar.* 1979. Dodd Mead. 1st. ils Gorey. F/F. D1. $25.00.

GORKY, Maxim. *Life of a Useless Man.* 1972. Andre Deutsch. 1st. NF/dj. P3. $25.00.

GORMAN, Ed. *Modern Treasury of Great Detective.* 1984. Carroll Graf. 1st. sgn. F/dj. P3. $27.00.

GORMAN, Ed. *Murder Straight Up.* 1986. NY. 1st. F/F. H11. $30.00.

GORMAN, Ed. *Out There in the Darkness.* 1995. Burton. Subterranean Press. 1st. 1/500# copies. sgn. VF/pict wrp. T2. $12.00.

GORMAN, Ed. *The Poker Club.* 1999. Baltimore. Cemetery Dance Publications. 1st. sgn. VF/VF. T2. $40.00.

GORMAN, Ed & M. H. Greenberg, editors. *Invitation to Murder — 18 Stories by Today's Top Mystery Writers.* 1991. Dark Harvest. 1st. sgn. NF. G8. $10.00.

GORMAN, Ed & Richard T. Chizmar. *Dirty Coppers.* 1997. Springfield. Gauntlet Publications. 1st. 1/350 # copies. sgn by both authors. VF/VF. T2. $35.00.

GORNICK, Vivian. *In Search of Ali Mahmould, an American Woman in Egypt.* 1973. Dutton. 1st. 8vo. 343p. VG. W1. $10.00.

GORZALKA, Ann. *Saddlemakers of Sheridan, Wyoming.* 1984. Pruett. 1st. photos. 91p. VG. J2. $295.00.

GOSLING, Paula. *A Few Dying Words.* (1994). NY. Mysterious Press. 1st. F/F. B3. $15.00.

GOSLING, Paula. *Body in Backwater Bay.* 1992. Mysterious. 1st. NF/NF. G8. $20.00.

GOSLING, Paula. *Death Penalties.* 1991. Mysterious. 1st. NF/NF. G8. $20.00.

GOSLING, Paula. *Fair Game.* 1978. CMG. 1st. author's 1st novel. F/F. M23. $45.00.

GOSLINGA, Cornelis C. *Dutch in the Caribbean & on the Wild Coast 1580 – 1680.* 1971. Gainesville. thick 8vo. 12 fld maps/map ep. F/dj. O7. $55.00.

GOSNER, Kenneth. *Working Decoys of the Jersey Coast & Delaware Valley.* 1985. Phil. 184p+16p mc pl. M/dj. A17. $27.50.

GOSS, John. *Mapping of North America.* 1990. Secaucus. Wellfleet. 85 maps. 184p. NF/dj. P4. $75.00.

GOSSE, Philip. *History of Piracy.* 1976. Detroit. Gale. rpt. 4 maps. F. O7. $35.00.

GOSWAMI, Amil. *Cosmic Dancers.* 1983. Harper. 1st. F/dj. M2. $18.00.

GOTHEIN, Marie Luise. *History of Garden Art.* 1928. London. Dent. 2 vol. A10. $350.00.

GOTLIEB, Judy. *Wife of...: An Irreverent Account of Life in Washington.* 1985. Toronto. Macmillan. 1st. F/F. T12. $20.00.

GOTLIEB, Phyllis. *O Master Caliban!* 1976. Harper Row. 1st. F/dj. P3. $20.00.

GOTSHALL, D. W. *Marine Animals of Baja California.* 1982. Los Osos. Sea Challengers. 112p. NF/wrp. B1. $18.50.

GOTTEHRER, Barry. *Giants of New York.* 1963. Putnam. 1st. photos/records/stats. VG/G+. P8. $30.00.

GOTTLIEB, Hinko. *Key to the Great Gate.* 1947. S&S. 1st. F/dj. M2. $10.00.

GOTTLIEB, Phyllis. *Heart of Red Iron.* 1989. St Martin. 1st. F/dj. M2. $17.00.

GOTTLIEB, Samuel Hirsch. *Overbooked in Arizona.* 1994. Scottsdale. Camelback Gallery. 1st ed. trade pb orig. sgn. VF/pict wrp. T2. $15.00.

GOUDEY, Alice E. *Here Come the Elephants!* 1955. Scribner. 1st. ils MacKenzie. VG/G+. C8. $15.00.

GOUDGE, Eileen. *Trail of Secrets.* 1996. Viking. 1st. F/F. S19. $25.00.

GOUDGE, Elizabeth. *Castle on the Hill.* 1949 (1942). London. Duckworth. sm 8vo. 296p. VG/dj. T5. $30.00.

GOUDGE, Elizabeth. *Little White Horse.* 1946. London. 1st. sm 8vo. VG. M5. $120.00.

GOUGH, J. W. *Fundamental Law in English Constitutional History.* 1955. Clarendon. M11. $85.00.

GOUGH, Laurence. *Goldfish Bowl.* 1987. NY. St. Martin. 1st Am ed. NF/VG+. G8. $15.00.

GOUGH, Laurence. *Hot Shots.* 1989. Gollancz. 1st. NF/NF. P3. $22.00.

GOULART, Ron. *Broke Down Engine.* 1971. Macmillan. 1st. VG/VG. P3. $30.00.

GOULART, Ron. *Cowboy Heaven.* 1979. Doubleday. 1st. F/dj. M2. $20.00.

GOULART, Ron. *Even the Butler was Poor.* 1990. Walker. 1st. F/F. G8. $15.00.

GOULART, Ron. *Land of Terror.* 1933. Street Smith. 1st. F. M2. $175.00.

GOULART, Ron. *Murder In 221B: Sherlock Holmes Solves the Murder of Professor Moriarty.* 1999. NY. Mysterious Bookshop. 1st. 1/221 copies. A chapbook. VF/pict wrp. T2. $10.00.

GOULART, Ron. *Odd Job #101.* 1975. Scribner. 1st. F/dj. P3. $20.00.

GOULART, Ron. *Odd Job #101 and Other Future Crimes and Intrigues.* 1975. NY. Scribners. 1st. F/F. T2. $15.00.

GOULD, C. N. *Covered Wagon Geologist.* 1959. Norman. 282p. VG. D8. $25.00.

GOULD, Ed. *Ralph Edwards of Lonesome Lake.* 1979. Saanichton. BC. Hancock. 1st. AN/dj. A26. $30.00.

GOULD, Elizabeth Lincoln. *The Admiral's Granddaughter.* 1926. Philadelphia. Penn Publishing. G in F dj. A16. $8.00.

GOULD, George. *Borderland Studies: Miscellaneous Addresses & Essays...* 1896. Phil. 1st. inscr. 24 essays. 384p. A13. $50.00.

GOULD, George Milbry. *Righthandedness & Lefthandedness...Writing Posture...* 1908. Lippincott. 12mo. 210p. gr cloth. G1. $65.00.

GOULD, J. *Hummingbirds.* 1990. Secaucus, NJ. Wellfleet. 2 vol. facs. folio. ils. 76p. F. C12. $100.00.

GOULD, John. *Monstrous Depravity.* 1963. Morrow. G/dj. A16. $10.00.

GOULD, Laurence McKinley. *Cold: Record of Antarctic Sledge Journey.* 1984. Carleton College. ltd. 213p. NF/dj. P4. $75.00.

GOULD, Mary Earle. *Early American Wooden Ware.* 1962. Charles E. Tuttle Co. Tall 8vo. 243p. F/F. H1. $37.50.

GOULD, Nat. *Fast as the Wind.* 1918. AL Burt. 265p. cloth. VG/ragged. M20. $15.00.

GOULD, Philip and Barry Jean Ancelet. *Cajun Music and Zydeco.* 1992. Baton Rouge. LSU Press. 1st. 4to. superb portfolio of color photos. F in F dj. B2. $40.00.

GOULD, Rupert T. *Oddities: A Book of Unexplained Facts.* 1965. University Books. 1st. 228p. cloth. VG/clip. M20. $22.00.

GOULD, S. J. *Bully for Brontasaurus Reflections in Natural History.* 1991. Norton. 1st. 540p. F/dj. D8. $22.00.

GOULD, Stephen J. *Wonderful Life.* 1989. NY. 347p. F/NF. S15. $13.00.

GOULD & PYLE. *Anomalies & Curiosities of Medicine...* 1901. Phil. Saunders. 295 ils/12 pl. 968p. xl. G7. $125.00.

GOULD & PYLE. *Anomalies & Curiousities of Medicine.* 1962. NY. ils/index. 968p. VG/G. B5. $30.00.

GOULDEN, Shirley. *Royal Book of Ballet.* 1962. Follett. 2nd. folio. F/VG. M5. $20.00.

GOULDING, E. J. *Fuchsias. A Guide to Cultivation and Identification.* 1973. NY. red cloth. 128p. 38 color photos & other ils. VG. B26. $15.00.

GOULDING, M. *Fishes & the Forest.* 1980. Berkeley. 379p. dj. B1. $20.00.

GOULDSBURY, G. E. *Tiger Slayer by Order.* 1916. London. Chapman Hall. 2nd. tall 8vo. 240p. gilt bl cloth. VG. $7.00.

GOURARD, Aimee. *Moon-Madness.* 1928. Broadway. VG. M2. $25.00.

GOURSE, Leslie. *Madame Jazz: Comtemporary Women Instrumentalists.* 1996. NY. Oxford Univ Press. 1st pb ed. NF. A28. $7.95.

GOURSE, Leslie. *Unforgettable. The Life and Mystique of Nat King Cole.* 1991. NY. St. Martin. 1st. inscr by author. F/F. B2. $40.00.

GOVER, Robert. *Here Goes Kitten.* 1964. Grove. 1st. sgn. F/F. B11. $65.00.

GOVER, Robert. *The Maniac Responsible.* 1963. NY. Grove. 1st. Jacket has minor wear along top edge. F/F. H11. $40.00.

GOVIER, Katherine. *Angel Walk.* 1966. Toronto. Little, Brn. UP. sgn. F. A26. $60.00.

GOVIER, Katherine. *Random Descent.* 1979. Toronto. Macmillan. 1st. author's 1st book. NF/NF dj. A26. $40.00.

GOVINDA, Lama Anagarika. *Foundations of Tibetan Mysticism.* 1960. Dutton. 1st Am ed. NF/bumped dj. M25. $60.00.

GOWAN, Donald E. *Reclaiming the Old Testament for the Christian Pulpit.* 1980. John Knox. 163p. VG/water stained dj. B29. $8.50.

GOWAN, Donald E. *The Triumph of Faith in Havakkuk.* 1976. John Knox. 94p. VG/VG. B29. $8.00.

GOWDY, Barbara. *The White Bone.* 1998. NY. Metropolitan. ARC. wrp. F. B2. $25.00.

GOWER, Charlotte. *Northern & Southern Afflictions on Antillean Culture.* 1927. Menasha, WI. Am Anthrop Assn Memoirs 35. 4to. 60p. wrp. F3. $30.00.

GOWERS, William R. *Lectures on Diagnosis of Diseases of Brain.* 1887. Phil. Blakiston. 2nd revised/1st Am prt. 254p. olive cloth. NF. G1. $175.00.

GOWING, Margaret. *Britain & Atomic Energy 1939 – 1945.* 1965. London. Macmillan. 2nd. ils. 464p. VG/dj. K3. $45.00.

GOYEN, William. *Arcadio.* 1983. Potter. 1st. F/NF. A24. $25.00.

GOYNE, Richard. *Overnight.* 1953. London. Stanley Paul. 1st. F/F. M15. $45.00.

GOYTISOLO, Juan. *Landscapes After the Battle.* 1987. NY. Seaver Books. 1st Am ed. review copy. trans by Helen Lane. sgn on ffep. F/NF. D10. $95.00.

GRAAF, Peter. *Sapphire Conference.* 1959. Washburn. 1st Am ed. VG/VG. G8. $17.50.

GRACE, C. L. *Eye of God.* 1994. STMS. 1st. F/F. G8. $30.00.

GRACE, C. L. *Shrine of Murders.* 1993. St. Martin. 1st Am ed. VG/VG. G8. $20.00.

GRACE, Peter. *Polo.* 1991. NY. 1st Am. VG/VG. O3. $40.00.

GRACE, Tom. *Spyder Web.* 1999. np. Warner. 1st. author's 1st novel. NF/NF. R16. $30.00.

GRACQ, Julien. *Balcony in the Forest.* 1959. Braziller. 1st. F/NF. B2. $30.00.

GRADY, James. *Rivers of Darkness.* 1991. NY. Warner. 1st. F/F. H11. $25.00.

GRADY, James. *Six Days of the Condor.* 1974. Norton. 1st. VG/NF. M22. $40.00.

GRADY, James. *Steeltown.* 1989. Bantam. 1st. VG/VG. P3. $20.00.

GRAEBNER, Theodore. *The Pastor as Student and Literary Worker.* 1925. St. Louis. Concordia. 147p. VG. B29. $8.00.

GRAFTON, C. W. *My Name Is Christopher Nagel.* 1947. Rinehart. 1st. F/VG. B4. $200.00.

GRAFTON, Sue. *A Is for Alibi.* 1982. HRW. 1st. sgn. author's 3rd book. F/F. D10. $1.250.00.

GRAFTON, Sue. *C Is for Corpse.* 1986. NY. Holt. ARC. F/wht glossy wrp. D10. $275.00.

GRAFTON, Sue. *E Is for Evidence.* 1988. NY. Henry Holt. 1st. F/F. D10. $165.00.

GRAFTON, Sue. *F Is for Fugitive.* 1989. Holt. ARC. sgn/dtd 1989. NF/wrp. B3. $100.00.

GRAFTON, Sue. *F Is for Fugitive.* 1989. Holt. 1st. NF/F. B2. $50.00.

GRAFTON, Sue. *G Is for Gumshoe.* 1990. NY. Henry Holt. 1st. F/F. D10. $50.00.

GRAFTON, Sue. *G Is for Gumshoe.* (1990). NY. Henry Holt. 1st. F/F. B3. $60.00.

GRAFTON, Sue. *H Is for Homicide.* 1991. HRW. 1st. sgn. F/F. A23/A24. $50.00.

GRAFTON, Sue. *I Is for Innocent.* 1992. NY. Henry Holt. 1st. sgn. VF/VF. T2. $35.00.

GRAFTON, Sue. *K Is for Killer.* 1994. NY. Henry Holt. 1st. sgn. VF/VF. T2. $25.00.

GRAFTON, Sue. *Keziah Dane.* 1967. Macmillan. 1st. author's 1st book. F/F. H11. $750.00.

GRAHAM, Alan (ed). *Vegetation and Vegetational History of Northern Latin America.* 1973. Amsterdam. 393p. VG/torn dj. B26. $55.00.

GRAHAM, Anthony. *Death Business.* 1967. Boardman. 1st. VG/VG. P3. $25.00.

GRAHAM, Billy. *Hope for the Troubled Heart.* 1991. Word. 230p. F/dj. B29. $7.50.

GRAHAM, Caroline. *A Place of Safety.* 1999. London. Headline. 1st. sgn. VF/VF. T2. $35.00.

GRAHAM, Caroline. *Written in Blood.* 1995. Morrow. 1st Am ed. NF/NF. G8. $20.00.

GRAHAM, David. *Down to the Sunless Sea.* 1981. S&S. 1st. F/dj. M2. $12.00.

GRAHAM, Don. *No Name on the Bullet.* 1989. NY. 1st. VG/VG. B5. $42.50.

GRAHAM, Duff. *How Peter Rabbit Went to Sea.* 1935 (1917). Platt Munk. lg 24mo. F/VG+. C8. $75.00.

GRAHAM, Ethel. *Creative Wok Cooking.* 1976. Weathervane. VG/dj. A16. $15.00.

GRAHAM, James; See Patterson, Henry.

GRAHAM, John Alexander. *Babe Ruth Caught in a Snowstorm.* 1973. Houghton Mifflin. 1st. F/VG. P8. $75.00.

GRAHAM, Jorie. *The End of Beauty.* 1987. Ecco Press. 1st. F/F. V1. $40.00.

GRAHAM, Lawrence Otis. *Our Kind of People.* 1998. NY. Harper Collins. sgn 1st ed. F/F. M23. $50.00.

GRAHAM, Otto. *Otto Graham: T Quarterback.* 1963. Prentice Hall. 1st. photos. VG. P8. $25.00.

GRAHAM, R. B. *Cunninghame. North American Sketches of RB Cunninghame.* 1986. U AL. 8vo. 145p. gr cloth. P4. $20.00.

GRAHAM, Robert; See Haldeman, Joe.

GRAHAM, Sheilah. *Garden of Allah.* 1970. Crown. 1st. F/NF. H11. $40.00.

GRAHAM, Shirley. *There Was Once a Slave.* 1947. Messner. 1st. NF/remnant. M25. $15.00.

GRAHAM, Tim. *Royal Review.* 1984. Michael Joseph. 1st. F/F. T12. $40.00.

GRAHAM, Victor. *Growing Succulent Plants.* 1987. Newton Abbot. Devon. 200p. VG/dj. B26. $35.00.

GRAHAM, W. A. *Custer Myth.* 1953. Bonanza/Crown. B rpt. ils. VG/dj. A2. $16.00.

GRAHAM, W.A. *Custer Myth.* 1953. Stackpole. dj. A19. $40.00.

GRAHAM, W. A. *Story of the Little Big Horn.* 1926. Century. 1st. 174p. VG/VG. J2. $265.00.

GRAHAM, Whidden. *Crimson Hairs: An Erotic Mystery.* 1970. Grove. 1st. F/dj. P3. $20.00.

GRAHAM, Winston. *Black Moon: Novel of Cornwall 1794 – 1795.* 1973. London. Collins. 1st. VG+/NF clip. A14. $32.00.

GRAHAM, Winston. *Merciless Ladies.* 1979. Bodley Head. 1st. VG/dj. P3. $20.00.

GRAHAM, Winston. *Woman in the Mirror.* 1975. Bodley Head. 1st. VG/VG. P3. $18.00.

GRAHAME, Kenneth. *Bertie's Escapade.* 1949. Lippincott. 1st thus. ils Ernest Shepard. VG+/VG. P2. $65.00.

GRAHAME, Kenneth. *Bertie's Escapade.* 1949. Methuen. 1st. ils EH Shepard. 12mo. pink pict brd. dj. R5. $150.00.

GRAHAME, Kenneth. *Wind in the Willows.* 1913. Scribner. 1st thus. 8vo. ils Paul Bransom. teg. bl ribbed cloth. R5. $300.00.

GRAHAME, Kenneth. *Wind in the Willows.* (1929). London. 12mo. heavy gilt tooled full red leather. F. H3. $55.00.

GRAHAME, Kenneth. *Wind in the Willows.* 1940. Heritage. 1st thus. ils Rackham/12 full-p mc pl. dj/case. R5. $150.00.

GRAHAME, Kenneth. *Wind in the Willows.* 1940. Heritage. 1st thus. ils Rackham. VG+/G. P2. $65.00.

GRAN, Trggve. *Norwegian with Scott.* 1984. London. Nat Maritime Mus. 1st Eng. 8vo. 258p. F/dj. T10. $35.00.

GRANBERG, Wilber. *People of the Maguey. The Otomi Indians of Mexico.* 1970. NY. Praeger. 1st. 160p. G/chipped dj. F3. $15.00.

GRAND, Gordon. *Colonel Weatherford & His Friends.* 1991. Derrydale. 1/1450. gilt leather. F. A17. $25.00.

GRAND, Gordon. *Millbeck Hounds.* 1947. Scribner. 1st. VG. O3. $40.00.

GRAND, Gordon. *Old Man & Other Colonel Weatherford Stories.* 1991. Derrydale. 1/2500. aeg. gilt bdg. F. A17. $25.00.

GRAND, Gordon. *Silver Horn.* 1932. Derrydale. 1st. 1/950. VG. O3. $275.00.

GRAND, P. M. *Prehistoric Art: Paleolithic Painting & Sculpture.* 1967. NYGS. ils/maps/pl. 103p. cloth. VG/dj. D2. $25.00.

GRANDES, Almudena. *The Ages of Lulu.* 1994. NY. Grove. 1st. UP. F. D10. $10.00.

GRANGER, Bill. *British Cross.* 1983. Crown. 1st. F/F. A20. $20.00.

GRANGER, Bill. *Hemingway's Notebook.* 1986. NY. Crown. 1st. F/F. H11. $20.00.

GRANGER, Bill. *Infant of Prague.* 1987. Warner. 1st. VG/dj. P3. $17.00.

GRANGER, Bill. *Man Who Heard Too Much.* 1989. Warner. 1st. F/F. N4. $25.00.

GRANGER, Bill. *There Are No Spies.* 1986. Warner. 1st. NF/NF. G8. $12.50.

GRANGER, Bill. *Zurich Numbers.* 1984. Crown. 1st. F/NF. N4. $25.00.

GRANGER, Byrd H. *Grand Canyon Place Names.* 1960. Tucson. 1st. 8vo. stiff magenta wrp. F7. $10.00.

GRANICH, Louis. *Guide to Retaining.* 1947. NY. Gurne Stratton. 108p. prt bl-gray cloth. xl. G1. $20.00.

GRANOVSKY, Abraham. *Land Policy in Palestine.* 1940. NY. Bloch. 208p. VG/dj. S3. $24.00.

GRANT, Anne. *Memoirs of an American Lady: With Sketches of Manners.* 1808. London. 2 vol. 1st. 12mo. teg. 3-quarter leather/raised bands. F. $3.00.

GRANT, Bruce. *Cowboy Encyclopedia.* 1951. ils. VG. M17. $17.50.

GRANT, Bruce. *Trip in Space.* 1968. Rand McNally. 8vo. 20p. G. K5. $8.00.

GRANT, Charles L. *Fire Mask.* 1991. NY. Bantam. 1st. VF/VF. T2. $5.00.

GRANT, Charles L. *Nightmare Seasons.* 1982. Doubleday. 1st. F/dj. P3. $50.00.

GRANT, Charles L. *Raven.* 1993. NY. Tor. 1st. VF/VF. T2. $7.00.

GRANT, Charles L. *Ravens of the Moon.* 1978. Doubleday. 1st. VG/dj. P3. $20.00.

GRANT, Charles L. *Shadows 2.* 1979. Doubleday. 1st. NF/dj. P3. $25.00.

GRANT, Charles L. *Sound of Midnight.* 1978. Doubleday. 1st. F/dj. P3. $30.00.

GRANT, Charles L. *The Dark Cry of the Moon.* 1985. West Kingston. Donald M. Grant. 1st. sgn. VF/VF. T2. $50.00.

GRANT, Charles L. *The Pet.* 1986. NY. Tor. 1st. sgn. F/F. T2. $35.00.

GRANT, Charles L. *The Soft Whisper of the Dead.* 1982. West Kingston. Donald M. Grant. 1st. sgn. VF/VF. T2. $35.00.

GRANT, Donald. *Talbot Mundy: Messenger of Destiny.* 1983. West Kingston. Donald M. Grant. 1st. VF/VF. T2. $25.00.

GRANT, G. M. *Between the Testaments.* nd. Revell. 146p. G. B29. $7.50.

GRANT, Hugh Duncan. *Cloud and Weather Atlas.* 1944. NY. Coward McCann. 4to. 100+ b/w photos. 294p. G/chipped. faded dj. ep browned. K5. $75.00.

GRANT, Hugh Duncan. *Cloud & Weather Atlas.* 1944. Coward McCann. 4to. 294p. G/dj. K5. $65.00.

GRANT, Joan. *Lord of the Horizon.* 1948. London. F/dj. M2. $15.00.

GRANT, Joan. *Winged Pharoah.* 1938. Harper. 1st. VG. M2. $20.00.

GRANT, John W. *Watt & the Steam Age.* 1917. London. St Bride. sgn. K3. $25.00.

GRANT, Linda. *Blind Trust.* 1990. NY. Scribners. 1st. VF/VF. H11. $30.00.

GRANT, Linda. *Lethal Genes.* 1996. NY. Scribner. 1st. sgn. VF/VF. T2. $25.00.

GRANT, Linda. *Woman's Place.* 1994. NY. Scribner's. 1st. NF/NF. G8. $15.00.

GRANT, Maxwell. *Norgil the Magician.* 1977. NY. Mysterious. 1st. F/dj. M15. $45.00.

GRANT, Michael. *Founders of the Western World.* 1991. Scribner. 1st. F/dj. P3. $28.00.

GRANT, Michael. *Line of Duty.* 1991. NY. Doubleday. 1st. VF/VF. H11. $30.00.

GRANT, P. J. *Gulls: A Guide to Identification.* 1982. Vermillion. photos. 280p. xl. VG. S15. $20.00.

GRANT, Peter. *Surgical Arena.* 1993. Newmark Pub. 1st. NF/dj. A28. $12.00.

GRANT, Rob. *Backwards.* 1996. London. Viking. 1st. VF/VF. T2. $10.00.

GRANT, Robert. *History of Physical Astronomy.* nd (1852). London. Henry Bohn. inscr/dtd 1869. 637p. gilt full leather. VG. K5. $150.00.

GRANT, Robert M. *Historical Introduction to the New Testament.* 1963. Harper Row. 448p. VG/dj. H10. $22.50.

GRANT, Roderick. *Private Vendetta.* 1978. Scribner. 1st. F/dj. P3. $15.00.

GRANT, Ulysses S. *Personal Memoirs of US Grant. Edited with Notes…EB Long.* 1952. NY. World. 1st thus. 608p. cloth. NF/VG. $8.00.

GRANT, Verne. *Plant Speciation.* 1971. NY. ils/figures. 435p. dj. B26. $37.50.

GRANT-ANDERSON, Lesley. *Face of Death.* 1985. Scribners. 1st Am ed. NF/NF. G8. $15.00.

GRANT-ANDERSON, Lesley. *Face of Death.* 1985. Scribners. 1st Am ed. NF/NF. G8. $15.00.

GRANT-ANDERSON, Lesley. *Too Many Questions.* 1991. St. Martin. 1st Am ed. F/F. G8. $15.00.

GRANVILLE, A.B. *Spas of England/Principal Sea-Bathing Places.* 1971 (1841). Bath. Adams Dart. 2 vol. facsimile. 8vo. F/djs. H13. $185.00.

RASS, Gunther. *Cat & Mouse*. 1963. HBW. t Am. 189p. VG/dj. M20. $30.00.

RASS, Gunther. *Dog Years*. 1963. HBW. t. NF/NF. B35. $25.00.

RASS, Gunther. *Flounder*. 1977. HBJ. 1st. F/dj. B35. $20.00.

RASSI, Joseph S. *Grassi Block Substitution st for Measuring Organic*. 1953. Springfield, .. Chas Thomas. sm 8vo. flexible blk cloth. 5p. G1. $17.50.

RATACAP, L. P. *Benjamin the Jew*. 1913. Y. ils Thomas Benton. 492p. VG. S3. 25.00.

RATTAN-SMITH, T. E. *Cave of a housand Columns*. 1938. London. 1st. VG. 12. $25.00.

RAU, Shirley Ann. *House on Coliseum treet*. 1961. Knopf. 1st. author's 2nd novel. F/dj. D10. $65.00.

RAU, Shirley Ann. *Keepers of the House*. 964. Knopf. 1st. NF/NF. M23. $50.00.

RAU, Shirley Ann. *Wind Shifting West*. 973. Knopf. 1st. NF/dj. Q1. $35.00.

RAUMONT, Raoul. *Encyclopedia of Knots Fancy Rope Work*. 1970. Cambridge, MD. ornell Maritime. A19. $45.00.

RAVER, Elizabeth. *Have You Seen Me?* 991. Pittsburgh. 1st. author's 1st book. /NF. R13. $25.00.

RAVES, Charles Burr. *Catalogue of the lowering Plants & Ferns of Connecticut*. 1910. lartford. 1st. 8vo. 567p. xl. A22. $40.00.

RAVES, Henry S. *Principles of Handling Voodlands*. 1911. NY. 1st. 1/1000. ils. 325p. l. B26. $35.00.

RAVES, J. A. *California Memories 1857 – 930*. 1930. Times-Mirror. 1st. VG. O4. 20.00.

RAVES, J. A. *My Seventy Years in alifornia 1857 – 1927*. 1927. Los Angeles. imes-Mirror. 1st. VG. O4. $20.00.

RAVES, J. A. *Out of Doors in California & regon*. 1912. Los Angeles. inscr. 122p. O8. 21.50.

RAVES, John. *Last Running*. 1974. Austin. ncino Pr. ils John Groth. 47p. brd/cloth pine. D11. $50.00.

RAVES, Robert. *Ann at Highwood Hall, oems for Children*. 1964. London. Cassell. st. gilt bl brd. F. M24. $75.00.

GRAVES, Robert. *Claudius the God*. 1935. Smith Haas. 1st. G+. P3. $25.00.

GRAVES, Robert. *Collected Poems*. 1961. Doubleday. 1st. F/F. B35. $32.00.

GRAVES, Robert. *Lawrence & the Arabian Adventure*. 1928. Doubleday Doran. ils/23 pl/map ep. 400p. cloth. VG. Q2. $33.00.

GRAVES, Robert. *More Poems*. 1961. London. Cassell. 1st. 1/3913. gilt red cloth. F/NF. M24. $45.00.

GRAVES, Robert. *No More Ghosts*. 1940. London. Faber. 1st. 1/2000. tan prt brd. F/dj. M24. $100.00.

GRAVES, Robert. *Sergeant Lamb of the Ninth*. 1940. London. Methuen. 1st. 1/10,000. wht lettered red cloth. F. M24. $45.00.

GRAVES, Robert. *Wife to Mr. Milton*. 1944. Creative Age. 1st Am. F/NF. B2. $35.00.

GRAVES, Robert J. *I, Claudius*. 1934. NY. Random House. 12mo. 427p. F/F. H1. $10.00.

GRAVES, Valerie; see Bradley, Marion Zimmer.

GRAVESON, S. *History of Life of Thomas Ellwood*. 1906. London. Headley Bros. 372p. V3. $28.00.

GRAY, A. W. *Bino's Blues*. 1995. S&S. 1st. NF/NF. G8. $15.00.

GRAY, A. W. *Killings*. 1993. NY. Dutton. 1st. VF/F. H11. $25.00.

GRAY, Charles Wright. *Sporting Spirit: An Anthology*. 1925. NY. 1st. 319p. gilt cloth. A17. $30.00.

GRAY, Elizabeth Janet. *Adam of the Road*. 1942. Viking. 1st. ils Marguerite DeAngeli. 317p. NF/VG. P2. $125.00.

GRAY, Elizabeth Janet. *Cheerful Heart*. 1959. Viking. 1st. 176p. xl. dj. V3. $8.50.

GRAY, Elizabeth Janet. *I Will Adventure*. 1962. Viking. 1st. 208p. VG/G. V3. $15.00.

GRAY, Henry. *Anatomy of the Human Body. 26th Edition…* 1955. Phil. Lea Febiger. 1202 ils. 1480p. cloth. G7. $295.00.

GRAY, Henry. *Gray's Anatomy*. 1977. Bounty. Classic Collector. 1257p. F/NF. W2. $250.00.

GRAY, James. *Intro to Arithmetic*. 1827. Edinburgh. 26th. 108p. 16mo. full leather. G. A17. $20.00.

GRAY, James Kendricks; see Fox, Gardener F.

GRAY, Joseph. *Navajo Sunrise*. 1976. Corte Madera, CA. Omega. sgn. 166p. VG. K7. $15.00.

GRAY, Millicent Ethelreda. *Treasure Book of Children's Verse*. nd. Doran. 20 mtd mc pl. F. M5. $95.00.

GRAY, P. N. *From the Peace to the Fraser: Newly Discovered…* 1994. Boone & Crockett. 1st. photos/maps. 400p. F/dj. M4. $60.00.

GRAY & OSBORNE. *Elvis Altas: Journey Through Elvis Presley's America*. 1996. NY. Holt. F/dj. B9. $17.50.

GRAYSMITH, Robert. *Sleeping Lady*. 1990. Dutton. 1st. VG/VG. P3. $20.00.

GRAYSON, Charles. *Venus Rising*. 1954. Holt. 1st. chipped and torn jacket. VG/dj. M25. $50.00.

GRAYSON, Richard. *Death Off Stage*. 1992. St. Martin. 1st Am ed. NF/NF. G8. $15.00.

GRAZIANO, Rocky. *Somebody Down Here Likes Me Too*. 1981. Stein Day. 1st. photos. F/VG+. P8. $20.00.

GRAZULIS, Thomas P. *Significant Tornadoes, 1880 – 1989*. 1991. St Johnsbury. VT. Environmental Films. 4to. 526p. VG/wrp. K5. $100.00.

GREAVES, Griselda. *Burning Thorn*. 1971. Macmillan. ARC/1st. 201p. cloth. F/NF. D4. $35.00.

GREBANIER, Bernard. *Great Shakespeare Forgery*. 1965. Norton. ils. 8vo. 308p. xl. dj. K3. $20.00.

GREELEY, Andrew W. *Irish Whiskey*. 1998. Forge Books. 1st. F/F. S19. $35.00.

GREELEY, Andrew W. *Lord of the Dance*. 1984. Warner Books. 1st. G+. S19. $25.00.

GREELEY, Horace. *American Conflict: History of Great Rebellion in USA*. 1869. Hartford. OD Case. 1st. 2 vol. cloth. NF. M8. $125.00.

GREELEY, Horace. *Essays Designed to Educate the Science of Political Economy*. Boston. Fields, Osgood & Co. 1870. 12mo. 384p. gr cloth. small sheet describing a Farmer's Club Library tipped in on ffep. minor wear. G. L5. $45.00.

GREELY, Adolphus W. *Report on Proceedings US Expedition to Lady Franklin Bay.* 1888. GPO. 2 vol. 4to. blk cloth. P4. $500.00.

GREEN, A. H. *The Birth and Growth of Worlds.* 1890. London. Society for Promoting Christian Knowledge. sm 8vo. text figures. G in ils cloth. K5. $13.00.

GREEN, Anna Katharine. *Circular Study.* 1902. Ward Lock. 1st. decor brd. VG. P3. $60.00.

GREEN, Anna Katharine. *Filigree Ball.* 1902. Bobbs Merrill. 1st. NF. P3. $60.00.

GREEN, Archie. *Only a Miner. Studies in Recorded Coal Mining Songs.* 1972. Urbana. U of Illinois Press. 1st. F/NF dj. B2. $60.00.

GREEN, Arthur. *Tormented Master: Life of Rabbi Nahman of Bratslav.* 1979. AL U. 395p. S3. $26.00.

GREEN, Ben K. *Horse Conformation.* 1982. Northland. VG/VG. O3. $25.00.

GREEN, Ben K. *The Village Horse Doctor, West of the Pecos.* 1980. NY. Knopf. ils by Lorance Bjorklund. VG/VG. O3. $30.00.

GREEN, C. E. *Plant Tissue & Cell Culture.* 1987. NY. ils/index. F. B26. $36.00.

GREEN, F. H. & J. W. Congdon. *Analytical Class Book of Botany, Designed for Academies & Private Students. In Two Parts.* 1857 (1854). gr cloth faded. worn at tips & spine ends. 228p. 29 plates. 50 text figures. dampstains at inner columns. head & foot. B26. $36.00.

GREEN, Garrett. *Imagining God: Theology & the Religious Imagination.* 1980s. Harper. 1st. 179p. VG/dj. B29. $11.50.

GREEN, Gate. *Night Angel.* 1989. Delacorte. 1st. F/NF. N4. $17.50.

GREEN, George Dawes. *The Caveman's Valentine.* 1994. NY. Warner. 1st. VF/VF. H11. $55.00.

GREEN, George Dawes. *The Juror.* 1995. NY. Warner Books. 1st. VF/VF. T2. $20.00.

GREEN, Gerald. *Last Angry Man.* 1956. 1st. author's 1st book. VG/VG. S13. $25.00.

GREEN, Gilbert G. *Cacti & Succulents.* 1953. London. 17 mc pl/166 photos/ils. 240p. B26. $25.00.

GREEN, Hannah. *In the City of Paris.* 1980. Doubleday. 1st. sm 4to. F/VG+. C8. $45.00.

GREEN, Henry. *Back.* 1946. London. 1st. author's 6th novel. VG+/VG. A11. $125.00.

GREEN, J. *Sasquatch: Apes Among Us.* 1978. Seattle. Hancock. ils/map/photo. 492p. F/F. M12. $37.50.

GREEN, Joseph. *Conscience Interplanetary.* 1973. Doubleday. 1st. F/dj. P3. $15.00.

GREEN, Judith. *Laughing Souls.* 1969. San Diego Mus of Man. 1st. 4to. 27p. wrp. F3. $10.00.

GREEN, N. W. *Mormonism Rise Progress.* 1870. Hartford. 1st. 472p. 3-quarter leather. B5. $50.00.

GREEN, Paul. *This Body the Earth.* 1935. NY. Harper. ex lib. VG dj. B2. $35.00.

GREEN, Peter. *Kenneth Grahame.* 1959. World. 1st. 400p. VG/VG. D1. $45.00.

GREEN, Richard Lancelyn. *The Mystery of the Spot Ball: An Unrecorded 1893 Sherlock Holmes Parody from the Edinburgh Student.* 1997. Cambridge, UK. Rupert Books. reissue. 1st thus. sgn by Green. VF/printed wrp. T2. $18.00.

GREEN, Richard Lancelyn, ed. *Ten Tales of Deception.* 1967. Dent. 1st British ed. young adult. VG+/VG+. G8. $12.50.

GREEN, Roger Lancelyn. *Andrew Lang; Critical Biography with Short Title Biblio.* 1946. Leicester, England. ils. 276p. NF/VG. A4. $65.00.

GREEN, S. G. *Pictures from Bible Lands.* 1879. ils Edward Whymper/others. VG. M17. $25.00.

GREEN, Thomas. *John Woolman: A Study for Young Men.* 1885. Manchester. Brook Chrystal. 126p. VG. V3. $14.00.

GREEN, Thomas J. *Flowered Box.* 1980. Beaufort. 1st. VG/dj. P3. $15.00.

GREEN, William M. *Salisbury Manuscript.* 1973. Bobbs Merrill. 1st. F/dj. P3. $15.00.

GREENAWAY, Kate. *A Mother Goose Treasury.* nd. NY. Avenel Books. F/F. A16. $12.00.

GREENAWAY, Kate. *Almanack for 1884.* nd. London. Routledge. 1st. 12mo. professionally rpr spine. G+. P2. $90.00.

GREENAWAY, Kate. *Language of Flowers.* nd. Routledge. 1st. 12mo. VG. M5. $95.00.

GREENAWAY, Kate. *Under Willow.* nd. NY. Avenel Books. F/F. A16. $12.00.

GREENBERG, Eric Rolfe. *Celebrant.* 1983. Everest. 1st. F/F. B4. $250.00.

GREENBERG, Julie T. *Duplicate Decisions. A Club Director's Guide for Ruling.* 1982. 1st. VG/wrp. S1. $8.00.

GREENBERG, Martin H. *Dawn of Time.* 1979. Elsevier/Nelson. 1st. F/dj. M2. $15.00.

GREENE, Annie. *Bright River Trilogy.* 1984. NY. S&S. 1st. 256p. F/F. D4. $20.00.

GREENE, Brian. *The Elegant Universe.* 1999. NY. Norton. 1st. F/F. M23. $55.00.

GREENE, Edward Lee. *Carolus Linnaeus.* 1912. Philadelphia. intro by Barton W Evermann. orig gilt decor cloth. VG. B26. $55.00.

GREENE, F. V. *Mississippi.* 1882. np. 1st. fld maps. O8. $21.50.

GREENE, Graham. *19 Stories.* 1949. Viking 1st Am. Worn jacket. NF/dj. M25. $60.00.

GREENE, Graham. *A Burnt Out Case.* 1961. London. Heinemann. 1st. VG/VG. A24. $50.00.

GREENE, Graham. *Captain & the Enemy.* 1988. Toronto. Dennys. 1st. F/NF. A24. $25.00.

GREENE, Graham. *Collected Essays.* 1969. London. Bodley Head. 1st. NF/VG+. A24. $70.00.

GREENE, Graham. *Comedians.* 1966. Viking. 1st. VG. P3. $15.00.

GREENE, Graham. *End of the Affair.* 1951. Viking. 1st. NF/NF. P3. $100.00.

GREENE, Graham. *Getting to Know the General.* 1984. Canada. Dennys. reported true 1st ed. F/F. A24. $32.00.

GREENE, Graham. *Heart of the Matter.* 1948. Canada. Viking. 1st. VG. P3. $50.00.

GREENE, Graham. *Human Factor.* 1978. Bodley Head/Clarke Irwin. 1st. VG/dj. P3. $25.00.

GREENE, Graham. *May We Borrow Your Husband? & Other Comedies of the Sexual Life.* 1967. NY. Viking. 1st Am ed. NF/VG+. A24. $38.00.

GREENE, Graham. *Monsignor Quixote.* 1982. Lester/Orpen Denys. 1st. G+/dj. P3. $15.00.

GREENE, Graham. *Our Man in Havana.* 1958. London. Heinemann. 1st. F/NF. A24. $100.00.

GREENE, Graham. *Our Man in Havana.* 1958. Viking. 1st Am. F/VG. M22. $75.00.

GREENE, Graham. *Tenth Man.* 1985. S&S. 1st. F/dj. P3. $20.00.

GREENE, Graham. *The Last Word.* 1990. Toronto. Lester & Orpen Dennys. 1st Canadian ed. F/F. A24. $20.00.

GREENE, Graham. *The Tenth Man.* 1985. NY. S&S. 1st Am ed. NF/NF. A24. $25.00.

GREENE, Graham. *Travels with My Aunt.* 1969. London. Bodley Head. 1st. F/dj. Q1. $75.00.

GREENE, Graham. *Ways of Escape.* 1980. London. Bodley Head. 1st British ed. NF/NF. A24. $40.00.

GREENE, Graham. *Ways of Escape.* 1980. NY. S&S. 1st Am ed. NF/NF. A24. $30.00.

GREENE, Hugh. *American Rivals of Sherlock Holmes.* 1976. Bodley Head. 1st. VG/dj. P3. $30.00.

GREENE, Hugh. *Cosmopolitan Crimes: Foreign Rivals of Sherlock Holmes.* 1973. NY. Pantheon Books. 1st Am ed. F/NF. T2. $25.00.

GREENE, Jacob W. *Greene Brothers' Clinical Course in Dental Prosthesis.* 1910. self pub. 1st. 210p. G+. H1. $45.00.

GREENE, Julia. *Flash Back.* 1983. Severn. VG/dj. P3. $20.00.

GREENE, Oliver B. *The Epistle of Paul to the Colossians.* 1970. Gospel Hour. 235p. F. B29. $9.00.

GREENE, Oliver B. *The Epistle of Paul to the Hebrews.* 1969. Gospel Hour. 602p. VG. B29. $9.50.

GREENE, Oliver B. *The Epistle of Paul to the Romans.* 1971. Gospel Hour. 334p. VG. B29. $9.00.

GREENE, Oliver B. *The Second Coming of Jesus.* 1974. Gospel Hour. 380p. G. B29. $5.00.

GREENEWALT, Crawford H. *Hummingbirds.* 1960. NY. Doubleday. 4to. NF. T10. $100.00.

GREENEWOOD, Edwin. *Deadly Dowager.* 1937. Doubleday. VG/dj. M2. $25.00.

GREENFIELD, Arthur II. *Anatomy of a Bullfight.* 1961. Longman Gr. 1st. ils. VG. P8. $20.00.

GREENFIELD, Eloise. *She Came Bringing Me that Little Baby Girl.* (1974). Lippincott. 8vo. unp. mauve cloth. rem mk. VG+/dj. T5. $20.00.

GREENLEAF, Stephen. *Death Bed.* 1980. NY. Dial Press. 1st. author's 2nd novel. VF/NVF closed tear top of front panel. T2. $35.00.

GREENLEAF, Stephen. *False Conception.* 1994. NY. Otto Penzler Books. 1st. sgn. VF/VF. T2. $25.00.

GREENLEAF, Stephen. *Fatal Obsession.* 1983. Dial. 1st. F/F. M15. $45.00.

GREENLEAF, Stephen. *Southern Cross.* 1993. NY. Morrow. 1st. NF/NF. G8. $15.00.

GREENLEAF, Stephen. *Toll Call.* 1987. Villard. 1st. F/F. M15. $45.00.

GREENMAN, J. *Diary of a Common Soldier in the American Revolution.* 1978. N IL U. ils. 333p. F/dj. M4. $30.00.

GREENSBERG, Martin. *Robot & the Man.* 1953. Gnome. 1st. VG. P3. $25.00.

GREENSITE, Arthur L. *Analysis and Design of Space Vehicle Flight Control Systems.* 1970. NY. Spartan Bbooks. lg 8vo. text figures. 732p. VG/chipped. worn dj. K5. $75.00.

GREENSPAN, Dorie. *Cooking with Jullia.* 1996. NY. Morrow. 1st. sgn by Julia Child & Baker Leslie Mackie. F/F. O11. $85.00.

GREENSTED, Richard. *Parting Shot.* 1997. London. Headline. 1st. sgn. VF/VF. T2. $30.00.

GREENSTONE, Julius. *The Messiah Idea in Jewish History.* 1906. Jewish Pub Society. 347p. VG. B29. $15.00.

GREENWOOD, Edwin. *French Farce.* 1936. NY. Doubleday. 1st. VG. G8. $20.00.

GREENWOOD, John. *Mists Over Mosley.* 1986. Walker. 1st. F/NF. P3. $18.00.

GREENWOOD, L. B. *Sherlock Holmes and the Case of Sabina Hall.* 1988. S&S. 1st. NF/NF. G8. $25.00.

GREENWOOD, L. B. *Sherlock Holmes and the Thistle of Scotland.* nd. S&S. 1st. NF/NF. G8. $25.00.

GREENWOOD, Marianne. *Tattooed Heart of Livingston.* 1965. Stein Day. 1st. 187p. dj. F3. $20.00.

GREENWOOD, Robert. *California Imprints 1833 – 1862: A Bibliography.* 1961. Los Gatos. Talisman. 1/750. facsimile ils. red cloth. NF. R3. $100.00.

GREER, Germaine. *Female Eunuch.* 1971. McGraw Hill. 1st Am. NF/VG. R14. $35.00.

GREER, H.E. *Greer's Guide Book to Available Rhododendrons.* 1982. Eugene. Offshoot. 152p. G/pict wrp. $28.00.

GREER, Robert. *The Devil's Red Nickel.* 1997. NY. Mysterious Press. 1st. sgn by author. F/F. D10. $35.00.

GREER, Robert O. *Devil's Backbone.* 1998. Mysterious. 1st. sgn. F/F. G8. $20.00.

GREER, Robert O. *The Devil's Hatband.* 1996. NY. Mysterious Press. 1st. sgn. author's 1st novel. VF/VF. T2. $30.00.

GREGG, Andy. *Drums of Yesterday.* 1968. Santa Fe. 1st. 40p. F/stiff wrp. E1. $30.00.

GREGG, Joshia. *Commerce of the Prairies.* 1968. Citadel. rpt. VG/G. O3. $45.00.

GREGG, Linda. *Sacraments of Desire.* 1991. Graywolf. 1st. sgn. F/dj. V1. $30.00.

GREGOIRE, Henri-Baptiste. *Historie Du Mariage Des Pretres En France…1789.* 1826. Paris. Baudouin. 1st. 8vo. cloth. R12. $485.00.

GREGOIRE, Henri-Baptiste. *Rapport Sur La Bibliographie.* 1794. Paris. Quiber-Pallissaux. 8vo. stitched. R12. $375.00.

GREGOIRE, Henri-Baptiste. *Rapport Sur Les Encouragemens.* Recompenses et Pensions… 1795. Paris. Imprimerie Nationale. 8vo. wrp. R12. $200.00.

GREGOR, A. James. *Crisis in the Philippines. A Threat to United States Interests.* 1984. Washington. Ethics and Public Policy Center. 110p. AN. P1. $5.00.

GREGORY, Dick. *Dick Gregory's Political Primer.* 1972. Harper Row. 1st. NF/dj. M25. $35.00.

GREGORY, Dick. *From the Back of the Bus.* 1962. NY. Dutton. 1st. author's 1st book. VG. pb ed. M25. $35.00.

GREGORY, Dick. *No More Lies: Myth & Reality of American History.* 1971. Harper Row. 1st. NF/dj. M25. $35.00.

GREGORY, Jackson. *Border Line.* 1942. Grosset & Dunlap. 1st. yellowing. G. S19. $15.00.

GREGORY, Jackson. *Case for Mr. Paul Savoy.* 1933. Scribners. 1st. VG. G8. $25.00.

GREGORY, Lady. *Spreading the News, a Play in One Act.* 1904. NY. John Quinn. 1st. 1/50. sgn. F/wrp. $24.00.

GREGORY, Susanna. *Unholy Alliance.* 1996. NY. St. Martin. 1st Am ed. F/F. G8. $17.50.

GREGSON, J. M. *Dead on Course.* 1991. London. Collins Crime Club. 1st. F/dj. M15. $45.00.

GREGSON, J. M. *Malice Aforethought.* 1999. London. Severn House. 1st. VF/dj. M15. $50.00.

GREIDER, Walter. *Pierrot & His Friends in the Circus.* 1967. np. Delacorte Press. 1st. prev owner inscr. NF/VG dj. M19. $25.00.

GRENDON, Stephen; see Derleth, August.

GRENNAN, Eamon. *As if it Matters.* 1991. Dublin, Ireland. Gallery Books. 1st pb ed. sgn. F. V1. $15.00.

GRENNAN, Eamon. *What Light There Is.* 1987. Dublin, Ireland. Gallery Books. 1st pb ed. sgn. F. V1. $20.00.

GRENNAN, Eamon. *Wildlly of Days.* 1983. Dublin, Ireland. Gallery Books. 1st pb ed. author sgn. F. V1. $30.00.

GRENZ, Stanley J. *The Moral Quest: Foundations of Christian Ethics.* 1997. LVP. 379p. F/F. B29. $9.50.

GRESHAM, Matilda McGrain. *Life of Walter Quintin Gresham, 1832 – 1895.* 1919. Rand McNally. 2 vol. 1st. ils. xl. cloth. M8. $150.00.

GRESHAM, William Lindsay. *Nightmare Alley.* 1946. Rinehart. 1st. VG. M2. $17.00.

GREUB, Suzanne. *Art of Northwest New Guinea.* 1992. NY. Rizzoli. 1st. half cloth 4to. ils in b&w/color. 224p. NF in dj. P4. $75.00.

GREY, Harry. *Hoods.* 1952. Crown. 1st. F/VG+. B4. $250.00.

GREY, Zane. *Black Mesa.* 1955. Harper. 1st. NF/dj. P3. $25.00.

GREY, Zane. *Fighting Caravans.* 1929. Toronto. Musson. 1st. inscr/dtd 1931. G. T12. $100.00.

GREY, Zane. *Light of Western Stars.* 1914. Grosset Dunlap. A19. $15.00.

GREY, Zane. *Nevada.* 1928. Harper. 1st. VG. P3. $40.00.

GREY, Zane. *Reef Girl.* 1977. NY. 1st. VG/VG. B5. $35.00.

GREY, Zane. *Roping Lions in the Grand Canyon.* (1922). Grosset Dunlap. 1st. NF. T12. $100.00.

GREY, Zane. *Tales of Southern Rivers.* 1924. Grosset Dunlap. 249p. VG+/rpr. M20. $95.00.

GREY, Zane. *Thundering Herd.* 1925. Grosset Dunlap. VG+. M2. $40.00.

GREY, Zane. *Vanishing American.* 1925. Canada. Musson. 1st. VG/fair. P3. $35.00.

GREY, Zane. *Wanderer of the Wasteland.* 1923. Harper. 1st. VG. M2. $35.00.

GREY-WILSON, C. *Impatiens of Africa. Morphology, Pollination & Pollinators, Ecology, Phytogeography, Hybridisation, Keys….* 1980. Rotterdam. maps. figures. color. 4to. F in dj. B26. $69.00.

GREYER, Siegfried. *Battleships & Battle Cruisers, 1905 – 1970.* 1974. Doubleday. sm 4to. ils. 480p. F/VG. H1. $24.00.

GRIBBIN, William. *The Chruches Militant: The War of 1812 and American Religion.* 1973. Yale. 210p. VG/VG. B29. $19.50.

GRIBBLE, Leonard. *Strip Tease Macabre.* 1967. H. Jenkins. 1st British ed. VG. G8. $20.00.

GRIERSON, H. J. C. *William Blake's Designs For Gray's Poems Reproduced.* 1922. Oxford. 1st. 1/650. folio. 122 pl. rust cloth. VG. $6.00.

GRIESBACH, Marc. *Combat History of the 8th Infantry Division in WWII.* 1946. Baton Rouge. 98p. sc. VG. S16. $85.00.

GRIESS, Thomas. *Atlas for the Second World War: Asia & The Pacific.* 1985. Wayne. 53p. sbdg. VG. S16. $22.00.

GRIFFIN, George Butler. *California Coast: Documents from Sutro Collection.* 1969 (1891). Norman, OK. Bilingual ed. maps. AN/dj. O7. $50.00.

GRIFFIN, John Howard. *Devil Rides Outside.* 1953. London. Collins. 1st. VG/VG. B4. $100.00.

GRIFFIN, Marjorie. *How to Cook.* 1944. Hall. 223p. B10. $12.00.

GRIFFIN, Susan. *Let Them Be Said.* 1973. Oakland. Mama's Press. 1st. sgn. wrp. F. B2. $60.00.

GRIFFIN, Susan. *Sink.* 1974. San Lorenzo. Shameless Hussy. 1st. ils. 48p. VG+. A25. $20.00.

GRIFFIN, W. E. B. *Battleground.* 1991. NY. Putnam. 1st. F/F. H11. $20.00.

GRIFFIN, W. E. B. *Murderers.* 1995. NY. Putnam. 1st. F/F. G8. $10.00.

GRIFFIN, William. *The Fleetwood Correspondence; A Devilish Tale of Temptation.* 1989. NY. Doubleday. 1st. 166p. F/F. D4. $25.00.

GRIFFIS, William E. *Verbeck of Japan.* 1900. NY. Fleming Revell. 1st. photos/index. 376p. VG. W3. $245.00.

GRIFFITH, Corinne. *Eggs I Have Known.* 1955. 1st. VG/G+. E6. $20.00.

GRIFFITH, Corinne. *Papa's Delicate Condition.* 1952. Houghton Mifflin. 1st. inscr. F/VG. B4. $175.00.

GRIFFITH, George. *Angel of the Revolution.* 1974 (1894). Hyperion. rpt. F. M2. $35.00.

GRIFFITH, J. W. *Elementary Text-Book of the Microscope.* 1864. London. Van Voorst. 1st. 12mo. 192p. cloth. VG. $10.00.

GRIFFITH, Patricia Browning. *Tennessee Blue.* 1981. NY. Potter. 1st. VF/VF. H11. $25.00.

GRIFFITH, Samuel. *Battle For Guadalcanal.* 1979. Baltimore. maps/notes/index. 282p. VG. S16. $22.50.

GRIFFITHS, A. B. *Treatise on Manures; Or, Philosophy of Manuring.* 1889. London. Whittaker. 399p. cloth. VG. A10. $40.00.

GRIFFITHS, Ella. *Murder on Page Three.* 1984. Quartet Crime. NF/dj. P3. $18.00.

GRIFFITHS, Julia. *Autographs for Freedom.* 1854. Auburn/Rochester. Alden Beardsley. 1st. gilt brn cloth. M24. $165.00.

GRIGGS, Edward Howard. *The Poetry and Philosophy of Browning. A Handbook of Eight Lectures.* 1905. NY. B.W. Huebsch. hc. G/no dj. F6. $4.25.

GRIGSON, Geoffrey. *Cherry Tree.* 1959. Pantheon. 1st. 517p. cloth. F/NF. D4. $35.00.

GRIMEK, H. C. B. *Grimek's Animal Life Encyclopedia.* Vol 3. 1972. Van Nostrand. 541p. F/F. B1. $60.00.

RIMES, Martha. *Dirty Duck*. 1984. Little, n. 1st. NF/dj. M25. $35.00.

RIMES, Martha. *End of the Pier*. 1992. hopf. 1st. sgn. F/F clip. A23. $35.00.

RIMES, Martha. *Five Bells & Bladebone*. '87. Little, Brn. 1st. VG/dj. P3. $16.00.

RIMES, Martha. *Hotel Paradise*. 1996. NY. hopf. 1st. sgn. VF/VF. T2. $25.00.

RIMES, Martha. *Old Contemptibles*. 1991. ttle, Brn. 1st. F/F. A23/T12. $35.00.

RIMES, Martha. *Old Fox Deceiv'd*. 1982. ondon. Michael O'Mara. 1st Eng. F/dj. Q1. 50.00.

RIMES, Martha. *Old Silent*. 1989. Little, n. 1st. sgn. F/F. A23. $35.00.

RIMES, Martha. *Rainbow's End*. 1995. NY. hopf. 1st. sgn. VF/VF. T2. $25.00.

RIMES, Martha. *Send Bygraves*. 1989. utnam. 1st. decor brd. VG. P3. $15.00.

RIMES, Martha. *The Case Altered*. (1997). Y. Holt. 1st. sgn by author. F/F. B3. $35.00.

RIMES, Martha. *The Lamorna Wink*. 1999. Y. Viking. 1st. sgn. VF/VF. T2. $25.00.

RIMM, The Brothers. *Hansel and Gretel d Other Stories*. (1925). NY. George H. oran Co. 1st. ils by Kay Nielsen. 4to. red oth w/gilt. 310p. rare title in very eplorable condition; plates all present. D6. 95.00.

RIMM, The Brothers. *Household Tales*. 946. London. Eyre & Spottiswoode. 1st ed hus. ils by Mervyn Peake. 8vo. yellow cloth. ecor. 303p. VG. D6. $100.00.

RIMM, William C. *Home Guide to Trees, hrubs, and Wildflowers*. 1970. Harrisburg. 20p. VG+ in dj. B26. $15.00.

RIMMILL, W. N. *Salem Witch Trials*. 1924. hicago. 1st. ils. 240p. VG. B5. $32.50.

RIMSHAW, Beatrice. *Sorcerer's Stone*. 914. Winston. 1st. VG. M2. $15.00.

RIMSHAW, William Robinson. *rimshaw's Narrative*. 1964. Sacramento ook Collectors Club. tall 8vo. AN. K7. 45.00.

RIMSLEY, Jim. *Dream Boy*. (1995). Chapel ill. Algonquin. 1st. sgn & dated by author. /F. B3. $45.00.

RIMWOOD, Ken. *Into the Deep*. 1995. NY. Morrow. 1st. F/F. H11. $25.00.

GRIMWOOD, Ken. *Replay*. 1986. NY. Arbor. 1st. F/F. H11. $45.00.

GRINDAL, E. W. *Everyday Gardening in India*. 1963. Bombay. 17th prt. VG in dj. B26. $14.00.

GRINDAL, Richard. *Over the Sea to Die*. 1989. Macmillan. 1st British ed. VG/VG+. G8. $20.00.

GRINDON, Leo H. *Phenomena of Plant Life*. 1866. Boston. 93p. gilt emb cloth/beveled brd. VG+. B26. $22.50.

GRINKO, G. T. *5-Year Plan of the Soviet Union: A Political Interpretation*. 1930. Internat Pub. 1st. G. V4. $22.50.

GRINNELL, David; see Wollheim, Don.

GRINNELL, George Bird. *American Duck Shooting*. 1918 (1901). NY. Forest/Stream. 2nd. ils. 627p. VG. H7. $75.00.

GRINNELL, George Bird. *American Game Bird Shooting*. 1910. Forest/Stream. 1st. ils. 558p. VG. H7. $75.00.

GRINNELL, George Bird. *Fighting the Cheyennes*. 1995 (1915). np rpt. map. 431p. F/dj. M4. $20.00.

GRINNELL, Joseph. *Distributional Summation of the Ornithology of Lower CA*. 1928. Berkeley, CA U Pub Zoology Vol 32 #1. 300p. VG. S15. $22.00.

GRINSPOON, Lester. *Cocaine: Drug & Its Social Evolution*. 1976. NY. 1st. 308p. A13. $25.00.

GRIPPANDO, James. *Found Money*. 1999. NY. Harper Collins. 1st. VF/VF. T2. $12.00.

GRIPPANDO, James. *Pardon*. 1994. Harper Collins. 1st. F/F. H11. $20.00.

GRIS, Henry. *New Soviet Psychic Discoveries*. 1979. Souvenir. 1st. F/NF. P3. $20.00.

GRISANTI, Mary Lee. *Art of the Vatican*. 1983. Excalibur. 1st Am. 4to. 70 mc pl. 143p. F/dj. T10. $20.00.

GRISET, Ernest. *Funny Picture-Book*. 1874. London. Wm Nimmon. 4to. gilt emb pict brn cloth. R5. $400.00.

GRISHAM, John. *The Chamber*. 1994. NY. Doubleday. 1st. VF/VF. T2. $25.00.

GRISHAM, John. *The Firm*. 1991. NY. Doubleday. 1st. F/dj. M15. $250.00.

GRISHAM, John. *The Partner*. 1997. Doubleday. 1st. F/F. S19. $50.00.

GRISHAM, John. *The Pelican Brief*. 1992. NY. Doubleday. 1st. VF/VF. T2. $40.00.

GRISMER, Raymond. *A Reference Index to Twelve Thousand Spanish American Authors*. 1970. NY. Burt Franklin. ex lib. 150p. G. F3. $15.00.

GRISWOLD, John. *Fuels*. 1946. McGraw Hill. 1st/3rd. 496p. VG. H1. $20.00.

GRISWOLD, John. *Fuels, Combustion & Furnaces*. 1946. McGraw-Hill. 3rd. sm4to Some marks on ffep. 496p. VG. H1. $20.00.

GRIVAS, Theodore. *Military Governments In California, 1846 – 1850*. 1963. Clark. 1st. 247p. VG. J2. $165.00.

GRIZZARD & SMITH. *Glory, Glory*. 1981. Atlanta. 1st. VG/VG. B5. $35.00.

GROAT, Dick. *World Champion Pittsburgh Pirates*. 1961. NY. 1st. sgn. VG/dj. B5. $40.00.

GROBANI, Anton. *Guide to Football Literature*. 1975. Gale. 1st. VG+. P8. $65.00.

GROGNARD, C. *Tattoo: Graffiti for the Soul*. 1994. Sanford. ils/photos. 132p. F/dj. M4. $30.00.

GROMME, Owen J. *Birds of Wisconsin*. 1963. Madison. sgn. 220p. gr cloth. B11. $75.00.

GRONDAL, Florence Armstron G. *Romance of Astronomy*. 1942 (1926). Macmillan. 24 pl. 334p. K5. $18.00.

GRONOWICZ, A. *Orange Full of Dreams*. 1971. Dodd Mead. 1st. F/dj. B4. $200.00.

GROOM, Bob. *The Blues Revival*. 1971. London. Studio Vista. 1st. wrps. F. clear plastic reinforcement at spine. B2. $40.00.

GROOM, Bob. *The Blues Revival*. 1971. London. Studio Vista. 1st. F/wrp. B2. $40.00.

GROOM, Winston. *Better Times Than These*. 1978. NY. Summit. 1st. author's 1st book. NF in dj. B2. $50.00.

GROOM, Winston. *Forrest Gump*. 1986. NY. Doubleday. 1st. F/F. D10. $250.00.

GROOM, Winston. *Gone the Sun*. 1988. NY. Doubleday. 1st. F/F. N11. $30.00.

GROOMS, Red. *Ruckus Rodeo*. 1988. Abrams. 6 popups. 4to. P2. $40.00.

GROSE, Francis. *Olio: Being a Collection of Essays, Dialogues, Letters*. 1793. London. Hooper. 1st. 8vo. 321p. $13.00.

GROSE, Francis. *Provincial Glossary, with a Collection of Local Proverbs.* 1811. London. Edward Jeffrey. tall 12mo. H13. $245.00.

GROSS, Joel. *Sarah.* 1987. Morrow. 1st. F/F. H11. $25.00.

GROSS, Kenneth. *Talk Show Defense.* 1997. Forge. 1st. F/F. G8. $10.00.

GROSS, Leonard. *Last Jews in Berlin.* 1982. S&S. 1st. F/VG+. S3. $22.00.

GROSS, Leslie. *Housewives' Guide to Antiques.* 1959. Exposition. 1st. ils. 180p. VG/G. S14. $10.00.

GROSS, Louis S. *Redefining the American Gothic.* 1989. Umi Research. 1st. F/dj. P3. $35.00.

GROSS, Milt. *Dear Dollink.* 1945. NY. 1st. w/orig ink drawing. VG/VG. A11. $135.00.

GROSS, Milton. *Yankee Doodles.* 1948. House of Kent. 1st. photos. VG/G. P8. $15.00.

GROSS, Robert. *Elements of Pathological Anatomy.* 1845. Phil. 2nd. ils. 822p. full leather. A13. $400.00.

GROSS, Robert. *Surgery of Infancy & Childhood.* 1953. Phil. 1st/2nd prt. 1000p. A13. $125.00.

GROSS, S. *I am Blind & My Dog Is Dead.* 1977. Dodd Mead. 1st. VG/VG. P3. $18.00.

GROSS, Samuel W. *Practical Treatise on Tumors of the Mammary Gland.* 1880. NY. 246p. gr cloth. B14. $350.00.

GROSSBACK, Robert. *Never Say Die.* 1979. Harper. 1st. F/dj. M2. $12.00.

GROSSHOLTZ, Jean. *Politics in the Philippines.* 1964. Boston. Little, Brn. 1st prt. 293p. G. P1. $2.00.

GROSSMAN, Harold J. *Grossman's Guide to Wines, Spirits, and Beers.* 1964. NY. Scribner's. 4th. VG/G. A28. $12.95.

GROSVENOR, Graeme. *Growing Irisis.* 1984. Kenthurst. Australia. sc. 192 color photos+b&w ils. New. B26. $12.95.

GROTE, L. R. *Medizin In Der Gegenwart In Selbstdarstellungen.* 1927. Leipzig. Felix Meiner. photos. 251p. gray linen. G1. $175.00.

GROTIUS, Hugo. *Freedom of the Seas; or, Right which Belongs to Dutch.* 1916. NY. OUP. 1st Eng trans. modern sheep. M11. $150.00.

GROTZ, George. *The Antique Restorer's Handbook.* 1976. NY. Doubleday. 8vo faded spine. 206p. AN/VG. H1. $12.00.

GROUNDS, Roger. *Ornamental Grasses.* 1989. London. 232p. New in dj. B26. $39.00.

GROUNDS, Vernon. *Radical Commitment: Getting Serious About Christian Growth.* 1984. Multnomah. 124p. VG/VG. B29. $7.00.

GROUP, Larry. *Treat American Deer Hunt.* 1992. Boulder. 1st. 226p. M/dj. A17. $27.50.

GROUSSET, R. *Empire of the Steppes: History of Central Asia.* 1970. Rutgers. 687p. NF. M4. $25.00.

GROUT, Donald Jay. *History of Western Music.* 1980. Norton. 3rd. ils. 849p. VG/dj. S14. $15.00.

GROVE, Fred. *Running Horses.* 1980. Doubleday. 1st. VG/G. O3. $25.00.

GROVE, Harriet Pyne. *Betty Lee, Freshman.* 1931. Cleveland. World. 1st. 254p. VG/dj. A25. $20.00.

GROVE, Lee Edmonds. *Of Brooks & Books.* 1945. 1/1500. VG/dj. K3. $20.00.

GROVER, Eulalie Osgood. *Mother Goose.* 1915. Volland. 1st. ils Frederick Richardson. lg 4to. bl cloth. M5. $250.00.

GROVER, Eulalie Osgood. *Overall Boys.* (1905). Chicago. ils Bertha Corbett. 123p. VG. B18. $37.50.

GROVER, Eulalie Osgood. *Sunbonnet Babies in Holland.* 1929. 1st thus. ils Melcher. VG+. S13. $55.00.

GROVES, J. Walton. *Edible & Poisonous Mushrooms of Canada.* 1962. Ottawa. Canada Dept Agric. 298p. VG/dj. A10. $28.00.

GROVES, William Henry. *Rational Memory.* 1912. NY. Cosmopolitan. 2nd. 12mo. 172p. prt panelled gr cloth. VG. G1. $37.50.

GROW, Lawrence. *The Warner Collector's Guide to Pressed Glass.* 1982. Warner Books. 1st. 8vo wraps. upper right corner of covers & pages bent. 256p. VG/VG. H1. $27.50.

GRUBB, Davis. *Golden Sickle.* 1968. World. 1st. ils Vosburgh. F/dj. Q1. $75.00.

GRUBB, Davis. *Night of the Hunter.* 1953. Harper. Advance pres. sgn. VG/sans. B30. $200.00.

GRUBB, Davis. *Shadow of My Brother.* 1966. Hutchinson. 1st. NF/dj. P3. $25.00.

GRUBB, Davis. *The Voices of Glory.* 196? NY. Scribner's. 1st. F/lightly used d owner's stp. B2. $35.00.

GRUBB, Davis. *Voices of Glory.* 196? Scribner. 1st. F/NF. B2. $35.00.

GRUBB, Davis. *Voices of Glory.* 1962 Scribner. 1st. F/NF. Q1. $60.00.

GRUBB, Edward. *Christ in Christia Thought.* James Clarke. revision of 1912 ec 161p. G. ex lib. B29. $4.50.

GRUBB, Edward. *What Is Quakerism? c* 1917. London. Headley Bros. 244p. worr V3. $10.00.

GRUBB, Kenneth. *World Christia Handbook.* 1949. World Dominion. 495p. VC B29. $10.00.

GRUBER, Frank. *Brass Knuckles.* 1977 Sherbourne. 1st. VG/dj. P3. $45.00.

GRUBER, Frank. *Buffalo Grass.* 1956. NY Rhinehart. 1st. F/rpr. M15. $45.00.

GRUBER, Frank. *Pulp Jungle.* 1967 Sherbourne. 1st. F/dj. M2. $50.00.

GRUBER, Frank. *Simon Lash.* 1944. NY Avon. pb edition No. 23. In wrp. VG. M15 $45.00.

GRUDIN, Robert. *Time & Art of Living* 1982. SF. VG/dj. M17. $17.50.

GRUELLE, Johnny. *Adventures of Raggedy Ann.* nd. NY. Avenel Books. F/F. A16 $12.00.

GRUELLE, Johnny. *Friendly Fairies.* 1919 Volland. 27th. 8vo. mc pict brd. R5. $125.00.

GRUELLE, Johnny. *Funny Little Book.* 1917 Volland. Sunny Book. 8vo. VG+. M5. $75.00

GRUELLE, Johnny. *Little Sonny Stories.* 1919. Volland. 30th. pict brd. R5. $125.00.

GRUELLE, Johnny. *Orphant Annie Story Book.* (1921). Bobbs Merrill. ils. VG. B15. $175.00.

GRUELLE, Johnny. *Paper Dragon.* (1926). Volland. 3rd. unp. pict brd. M20. $16.00.

GRUELLE, Johnny. *Raggedy Ann & Andy & the Nice Fat Policeman.* 1942. Johnny Gruelle. 8vo. 95p. VG/torn. D1. $100.00.

GRUELLE, Johnny. *Raggedy Ann & Betsy Bonnet String.* 1943. NY. Gruelle. 1st. 8vo. 95p. VG. T10. $50.00.

RUELLE, Johnny. *Raggedy Ann in the Deep Woods*. 1930. Donohue. 8vo. unp. VG/G. D1. \00.00.

RUELLE, Johnny. *Raggedy Ann's Wishing ~bble*. 1925. Volland. later prt. 8vo. VG+. 5. $55.00.

RUEN, John. *Erik Bruhn Danseur Noble.* ~79. Viking. 1st. sgn Erik Bruhn. VG/VG. 23. $30.00.

RUENBERG, Sidonie Mastner. *Let's Hear Story.* (1961). Doubleday. ils Dagmar ilson. 160p. beige cloth. VG. T5. $24.00.

RUENFELD, Lee. *Irreparable Harm.* 1993. Y. Warner. 1st. author's 1st book. F/F. 11. $25.00.

RUENING, Ernest. *Battle for Alaska atehood.* 1967. U AK. inscr. 8vo. blk cloth. F/VG. P4. $30.00.

RUMMOND, J. L. *Baratarians & the Battle New Orleans.* 1961. LA U. 1st. 180p. F/dj. 14. $35.00.

RUNDY, Isabel. *Samuel Johnson & the cale of Greatness.* 1986. Leicester. 1st. F/dj. 13. $65.00.

RUNES, Barbara. *Lunch & Brunch ookbook.* 1985. Ideal. G/dj. A16. $8.00.

RUNFELD, Frederic V. *Vienna.* 1981. NY. ewsweek. dj. A19. $20.00.

RUNSKY, Carl Ewald. *Stockton Boyhood: eing Reminiscences Of...From 1855 – 1877.* ~959. Friends Bancroft Lib. 1/800. 154p. gr oth. F. P4. $65.00.

RUNWALD, Henry Anatole. *Salinger: A ritical & Personal Portrait.* 1962. Harper. 1st. /clip. Q1. $100.00.

RUTER, Margaret. *Law & the Mind, iological Origins of Human Behavior.* 1991. age Pub. 157p. prt wrp. M11. $25.00.

RUZINSKI, Serge. *Painting the Conquest.* ~992. France. Flammerion. 1st. 239p. dj. F3. 65.00.

RZIMEK, H. C. B. *Grzimek's Animal Life ncyclopedia. Vol 3.* 1972. Van Nostrand. 41p. F/dj. B1. $60.00.

RZIMEK & GRZIMEK. *Serengeti Shall Not Die.* 1961. NY. 1st Am. 344p. F. S15. 13.50.

RZYBOWSKI, Kazimierz. *Soviet Legal nstitutions, Doctrines & Social Functions.* ~962. Ann Arbor. M11. $35.00.

GUALINO, Lorenzo. *Storia Medica Dei Romani Pontefici.* 1934. Torino. 1st. 589p. quarter leather. A13. $100.00.

GUDDE, Erwin G. *California Place Names.* 1962. Berkeley. 2nd. NF/VG. O4. $25.00.

GUEDEL, Arthur. *Inhalation Anesthesia.* 1947. NY. 1st. 172p. A13. $30.00.

GUENON, F. *Treatise on Milch Cows.* 1856. 63rd thousand. 88p. VG. E6. $60.00.

GUENTHER, Leonhard. *A German Ace Tells Why. From Kaiserdom to Hitlerism.* 1942. Cambridge. Sci-Art. 2nd. sgn. VG. B2. $25.00.

GUERARD, Michael. *Cruisine Minceur.* 1976. Morrow. 1st. VG/dj. A16. $10.00.

GUERBER, H. A. *Yourself and Your House Wonderful.* 1913. Philadelphia. Uplift Publishing Co. ils by Eugenie Wireman. sm 4to. green cloth numerous ils. 301p. VG. D6. $30.00.

GUERNSEY, Paul. *Unhallowed Ground.* 1986. NY. Morrow. 1st. author's 1st book. F/F. H11. $20.00.

GUERRA, Tonino. *Equilibrium.* 1970. NY. Walker. 1st Am. F/NF. B4. $100.00.

GUEST, Barbara. *Moscow Mansions.* 1973. NY. Viking Press. 1st. review copy w/slip and publicity sheet. F/NF. V1. $30.00.

GUEST, C. Z. *First Garden.* nd. ils/sgn Cecil Beaton. intro Truman Capote. VG/VG. M17. $35.00.

GUEST, Judith. *Killing Time in St. Cloud.* 1988. Delacorte. 1st. F/NF. T11. $10.00.

GUEST, Judith. *Ordinary People.* 1976. NY. Viking. 2nd prt before pub. 263p. F/faded dj. D4. $20.00.

GUIDONI, Enrico & Robert Magni. *Monuments of Civilization: The Andes.* 1977. NY. Grosset & Dunlap. 1st. ex lib. sm folio. color photo ils. glossary. map. 189p. G. F3. $15.00.

GUIDROZ, Myriam. *Adventures in French Cooking.* 1970. London. Macmillan. G/dj. A16. $7.50.

GUILD, Curtis. *Abroad Again; or, Fresh Foray in Foreign Lands.* 1879. Boston/NY. Lee Shepard/Dillingham. sm 8vo. 474p. VG. W1. $18.00.

GUILD, Curtis. *Over the Ocean.* 1884. Lee Shepard. 558p. VG. S17. $7.50.

GUILD, Marion Pelton. *Selected Poems of Katharine Lee Bates.* 1930. Houghton Mifflin. 1st. 230p. VG+. A25. $22.00.

GUILD, Nicholas. *Chain Reaction.* 1983. St Martin. 1st. VG/dj. P3. $15.00.

GUILD, Nicholas. *Favor.* 1981. St. Martin. 1st. VG+/VG+. G8. $10.00.

GUILLAIN, Georges. *J – M Charcot 1825 – 1893: His Life — His Work.* 1959. NY. Hoeber. 1st Eng-language. 202p. tan naugahide. G1. $65.00.

GUILLAUME, Paul. *La Psychologie Des Singes.* 1941. Paris. 1st separate. ils. 335p. prt gr wrp. G1. $28.50.

GUILLEMIN, Amedee. *Heavens: An Ils Yearbook of Popular Astronomy.* 1868. London. Richard Bentley. 3rd. rebacked. K5. $100.00.

GUILLEMIN, Amedee. *Le Ciel: Notions D'Astronomie A L'Usage Des Gens Du Monde...* 1866 (1864). Paris. Hatchette. 3rd. 4to. ils/pl. 632p. half leather. K5. $250.00.

GUILLEMIN, Amedee. *Sun.* 1870. Scribner. Ils Lib of Wonder series. 8vo. gilt cloth. K5. $70.00.

GUILLEN, Michael. *Five Equations that Changed the World.* 1995. NY. Hyperion. 8vo. 277p. VG/dj. P4. $15.00.

GUINEY, Corinne. *Beauty & the Beast. Classic Fairytale Retold...* 1982. Berkeley. Wild Hare. mini. 1/100. 30p. marbled brd. B24. $125.00.

GUINN, J. M. *A History of California and an Extended History of Los Angeles and Environs....* 1915. Los Angeles. Historic Record Co. 3 vols. 4to. orig brown morocco over burgundy silk. 466; 480; (481)-936p. extremities lightly rubbed. minor chip top of spine. K1. $150.00.

GUINNESS, Alex. *Blessings in Disguise.* 1986. London. Hamish Hamilton. 1st/7th imp. 242p. F/clip. M7. $32.50.

GUINNESS, Benjamin. *Guinness Book of World Records.* 1988. Sterling. special ed. 447p. F. W2. $45.00.

GUINNESS & SEEL. *No God But God: Breaking with Idols of Our Age.* 1992. Moody. 223p. F/wrp. B29. $8.00.

GUION, Lady. *Exemplary Life of Pious Lady Guion...* 1804. Phil. Crukshank. 503p. leather. V3. $60.00.

GUITERMAN, Arthur. *Ballads of Old New York.* 1920. Harper. sgn. 12mo. G. B11. $18.00.

GULLION, Gordon. *Grouse of the North Shore.* 1984. Oshkosh. Willowcreek. 144p. F. A17. $40.00.

GULLIVER, P. H. *Social Control in an African Society.* 1963. Boston. 1st. 8vo. VG/dj. W1. $18.00.

GULSTON, Charles. *Jerusalem: The Tragedy and the Triumph.* 1978. Zondervan. 298p. VG/VG. B29. $10.50.

GULVIN, Harold E. *Farm Engines & Tractors.* 1953. McGraw Hill. later prt. 397p. gilt cloth. VG. H1. $20.00.

GULVIN, Jeff. *Close Quarters.* 1997. London. Headline. 1st. VF/VF. T2. $25.00.

GUMMERE, Amelia Mott. *Friends in Burlington.* 1884. Phil. Collins. 100p. VG. V3. $25.00.

GUMMERMAN, Jay. *We Find Ourselves in Moontown.* 1989. Knopf. 1st. author's 1st book. F/dj. R14. $35.00.

GUMMERMAN, Jay. *We Find Ourselves in Moontown.* 1989. Knopf. 1st. sgn. F/dj. B4. $85.00.

GUNDRY, Robert. *A Survey of the New Testament.* 1970. Academie. 379p. VG/torn dj. B29. $11.00.

GUNN, Elizabeth. *Par Four.* 1999. NY. Walker. 1st. sgn. VF/VF. T2. $25.00.

GUNN, James. *Alternate Worlds.* 1975. Prentice Hall. VG/dj. P3. $35.00.

GUNN, James. *Breaking Point.* 1972. Walker. 1st. F/dj. M2. $25.00.

GUNN, James. *Dreamers.* 1980. S&S. 1st. VG/dj. N4. $17.50.

GUNN, James. *The Listeners.* 1972. NY. Scribners. 1st. F/F. T2. $25.00.

GUNN, T. *Moly.* 1971. London. Faber. 1st. sgn. F/NF. R14. $100.00.

GUNN, T. *Poem After Chaucer.* 1971. Albondocani. 1/300. sgn/dtd April 1997. F/wrp. R14. $75.00.

GUNNARSSON, Gunnar. *The Good Shepherd.* 1940. Bobbs Merrill. 84p. VG. B29. $6.50.

GUNSTON, Bill. *Illustrated Guide to Modern Airborne Missiles.* nd. NY. Arco. 8vo. 159p. VG. K5. $15.00.

GUNTHART, Lotte. *Linger Golden Light.* 1984. Pittsburgh. Hunt Botanical Inst. 250p. A10. $25.00.

GUNTHER, John. *Eden for One.* 1927. Harper. 1st. VG. M2. $27.00.

GUNTHER, Max. *Doom Wind.* 1986. Contemporary. 1st. VG/dj. P3. $18.00.

GUPPY, Estella L. *Cypress of Monterey: Historical Sketch.* 1922. np. 1st. ils M DeNeale Morgan. F/stiff tan wrp. B26. $35.00.

GUR, Batya. *Murder Diet: A Musical Case.* 1999. NY. Harper Collins. 1st. sgn. VF/VF. T2. $26.00.

GUR, Batya. *Murder on a Kibbutz.* 1994. Harper & Row. 1st. F/F. G8. $20.00.

GURALNICK, Peter. *Searching for Robert Johnson.* 1989. Dutton. 1st. F/dj. B2. $75.00.

GURDJIEFF, G. I. *Meetings with Remarkable Men.* 1963. Dutton. 1st. F/NF. B2. $50.00.

GURDON, J. E. *Secret of the South.* 1950. London. 1st. NF/dj. M2. $25.00.

GURGANUS, Allan. *Oldest Living Confederate Widow Tells All.* 1989. Knopf. 1st. author's 1st book. F/dj. Q1. $35.00.

GURGANUS, Allan. *White People.* 1991. Knopf. 1st. F/F. A20. $20.00.

GURGANUS, Allan. *White People.* 1991. Knopf. AP. sgn. F/prt wrp. R13. $35.00.

GURION, Itzhak. *Triumph on the Gallows.* Sept 1950. Brooklyn. ils Arthur Szyk. 200p. bl cloth. VG. B14. $45.00.

GURLEY, Ralph Randolph. *Life of Jehudi Ashun.* 1969 (1835). Negro U. rpt. 2 parts in 1. 8vo. cloth. VG. W1. $25.00.

GURNEY, C. S. *Portsmouth: Historic & Picturesque.* 1902. ils. VG. M17. $75.00.

GURNEY, David. *F Certificate.* 1968. Bernard Geis. 1st. F. P3. $10.00.

GURNEY, E. R. *Messages to Boys.* 1929. Yankton, SD. private prt. A19. $30.00.

GURNEY, Gene. *Rocket & Missile Technology.* 1964. Franklin Watts. 1st. 394p. VG/dj. K5. $50.00.

GURNEY, Gene. *Space Technology Spinoffs.* 1979. Franklin Watts. 1st. 8vo. 88p. VG. K5. $12.00.

GURNEY, Gene & Clare. *Cosmonauts [in] Orbit: The Story of the Soviet Manned Spa[ce] Program.* 1972. NY. Franklin Watts. ex lib [w] dj. lt foxing. G. K5. $30.00.

GURNEY, John. *Margaret Tarrant and H[er] Pictures.* 1982. London. The Medici Socie[ty] Ltd. 1997 ed. ils by Tarrant. oblong 12m[o]. color ils pict wrp. 24p. AN. D6. $6.00.

GURNEY, Joseph John. *Baptism & Suppe[r] Disuse of Typical Rites of Worship of God.* 187[ ] Phil. Lewis. 12mo. 96p. V3. $35.00.

GURNEY, Joseph John. *Four Lectures [on] Evidences of Christianity.* 1859. Longstret[h] 2nd. 12mo. 176p. G. V3. $22.00.

GURNEY, Joseph John. *Observations [on] Religious Pecularities of Society Friends.* 183[ ] Phil. Nathan Kite. 2nd Am. 331p. G. V[3] $50.00.

GURR, David. *Troika.* 1979. NY. Methue[n] 1st. author's 1st book. F/NF wht dj. H1[ ] $25.00.

GUSSOW, H. T. & W. S. Odell. *Mushroo[ms] and Toadstools. An Account of the Mo[st] Common Edible and Poisonous Fungi [of] Canada.* 1927. Ottawa. sm 4to. 274p. 2 col[or] & 126 b&w plates. corner bumped. els[ ] VG+. B26. $27.50.

GUSSOW, Mel. *Don't Say Yes Until I Finis[h] Talking.* 1971. Doubleday. 318p. VG/dj. C[ ] $12.50.

GUSTAFSON, A. F. *Conservation of the So[il]* 1937. McGraw Hill. ils/index. 312p. xl. V[G] H10. $15.00.

GUSTAV VON BERG, Baron. *Fro[m] Kapuvar to California.* 1893. 1979. SF. BC [of] CA. 1/500. 73p. P4. $75.00.

GUTERSON, David. *East of the Mountain[s]* 1999. NY. Harcourt Brace. 1st. sgn. F/[ ] D10. $40.00.

GUTERSON, David. *Family Matters: Wh[y] Home Schooling Makes Sense.* 1992. HBJ. 1s[t] author's 2nd book. F/NF. R13. $25.00.

GUTERSON, David. *Snow Falling o[n] Cedars.* 1994. Harcourt Brace. 1st. F/F. M2[ ] $150.00.

GUTERSON, David. *The Country Ahead [of] Us, the Country Behind.* 1989. NY. Harper [&] Row. 1st. author's 1st book. F/F. H1[ ] $240.00.

GUTERSON, David. *The Drowned So[n]* (1996). London. Bloomsbury. 1st British ed[ ] pb orig. pict wrp. 50p. F. B3. $15.00.

GUTHELIM, F. *Illustrated Rivers of America: the Potomac.* 1968. Grosset Dunlap. revised. ls/maps. pict brd. NF/VG+. M12. $25.00.

GUTHELIM, Frederick. *In the Cause of Architecture.* 1975. 1st/2nd prt. 246p. VG/VG. A8. $35.00.

GUTHORN, Peter J. *Sea Bright Skiff & Other New Jersey Shore Boats.* 1971. Rutgers. VG/G. R8. $35.00.

GUTHRIE, A. B. *Big Sky.* 1947. NY. Sloane. 1st. NF/VG clip. H11. $80.00.

GUTHRIE, A. B. *Last Valley.* 1975. Houghton Mifflin. 1st. F/NF. T11. $40.00.

GUTHRIE, A. B. *Murder in the Cotswolds.* 1989. Houghton Mifflin. 1st. F/F. D10. $30.00.

GUTHRIE, A. B. *The Genuine Article.* 1977. Boston. Houghton Mifflin. 1st. F/F. D10. $55.00.

GUTHRIE, A. B. *The Way West.* 1949. NY. Sloane. author's 2nd book. G/G-. R16. $40.00.

GUTHRIE, A. B. *These Thousand Hills.* 1956. Boston. Houghton Mifflin. 1st. NF/VG. D10. $45.00.

GUTHRIE, Donald. *New Testament Introduction.* 1970. IVP. 1054p. VG. B29. $15.00.

GUTHRIE, Donald. *New Testament Theology.* 1981. IVP. 1064p. VG/dj. B29. $18.00.

GUTHRIE, Douglas. *Lord Lister, His Life & Doctrine.* 1949. Edinburgh. 1st. 128p. A13. $60.00.

GUTHRIE, George. *On Diseases & Injuries of Arteries.* 1830. London. 1st. 416p. half leather. xl. A13. $1.000.00.

GUTHRIE, George. *On Wounds & Injuries of the Abdomen & Pelvis.* 1847. London. 1st. 73p. xl. A13. $200.00.

GUTHRIE, Jill, editor. *The Olmec World: Ritual & Rulership.* 1995. NJ. Art Museum. Princeton Univ. 1st. 4to. photo ils. maps. drawings. 344p. G/G. F3. $75.00.

GUTHRIE, Lord. *Robert Louis Stevenson. Some Personal Reflections.* 1920. Edinburgh. W. Green. 1/500 ltd. ils. F/F. R3. $60.00.

GUTHRIE, MOTYER & STIBBS. *New Bible Commentary Revised.* 1976. IVP. 1310p. VG/dj. B29. $12.50.

GUTHRIE, Tyrone. *In Various Directions.* 1963. NY. Macmillan. 1st. sgn. F/F. D10. $50.00.

GUTKIND, Lee. *Best Seat in Baseball, But You Have to Stand.* 1975. NY. Dial. 1st. VG/VG+ clip. R16. $35.00.

GUTMAN, Bill. *Pistol Pete Maravich.* 1972. Grosset Dunlap. 1st. photos. VG/G. P8. $22.50.

GUTTERIDGE, Lindsay. *Killer Pine.* 1973. Putnam. 1st. VG/dj. P3. $18.00.

GUTZKE, Manford George. *Plain Talk About Christian Words.* 1965. Zondervan. 234p. VG/VG. B29. $7.00.

GUY, Joseph & Thomas Keith. *Guy's Elements of Astronomy, and an Abridgement of Keith's New Treatise on the Use of Globes.* 1835. Philadelphia. Key & Biddle. 13th ed. 173p. worn & scuffed cloth. lt foxing. hinges rpr. K5. $65.00.

GUY, Rosa. *The Sun, the Sea, a Touch of the Wind.* 1995. NY. Dutton. AP. wrps. F. B2. $25.00.

GUZINA, Vijislav. *Genetics of European Aspen.* 1981. Aagreb. map. 38p. wrp. B26. $15.00.

GWALTNEY, John Langston. *Drylongso: A Self-Portrait of Black America.* 1980. NY. Random. 1st. F/F. B2. $35.00.

GWYNNE, Fred. *Chocolate Moose for Dinner.* 1976. Prentice Hall. 1st. 4to. NF/NF. C8. $50.00.

— H —

HABEK, James R. *The Vegetation of Northwestern Montana. A Preliminary Report.* 1967. Missoula. 57p + 6p of maps & 19 tables. VG. B26. $15.00.

HABERLY, Loyd. *Pursuit of the Horizon. A Life of George Catlin Painter & Recorder of the American Indian.* 1948. NY. Macmillan. 1st printing. F/F. R3. $22.50.

HADDAD, C. A. *Caught in the Shadows.* 1992. St. Martin. 1st. NF/NF. G8. $12.50.

HADINGHAM, Evan. *Early Man and the Cosmos.* 1984. NY. Walker. 1st printing. b/w photos. diagrams. foxing to fore edge. inscr on ffep. 271p. VG/VG. K5. $30.00.

HADINGHAM, Evan. *Lines to the Mountain Gods.* 1988. Norman. Univ of Oklahoma Press. 1st. 307p. G/chipped dj. F3. $20.00.

HADLEY, Joan Hess. *Deadly Ackee.* 1988. St. Martin. 1st. sgn. NF/VG+. G8. $30.00.

HAGER, Jean. *Fire Carrier.* 1st. NY. Mysterious Press. 1st. sgn. VF/VF. T2. $25.00.

HAGER, Jean. *Ghostland.* 1992. NY. St. Martin. 1st sgn & dated. F/NF. A24. $40.00.

HAGER, Jean. *Night Walker.* 1990. NY. St. Martin. 1st. sgn. VF/VF. T2. $50.00.

HAGER, Jean. *Seven Black Stones.* 1995. NY. Mysterious Press. 1st. sgn. VF/VF. T2. $25.00.

HAGER, Jean. *The Fire Carrier.* 1996. NY. Mysterious. 1st. VF/VF. H11. $15.00.

HAGUE, William E. *Complete Basic Book of Home Decorating.* 1976. NY. Doubleday. G. A28. $6.50.

HAHN, Emily. *The Islands: America's Imperial Adventure in the Philippines.* 1981. NY. C M G. 285p. F/VG. P1. $15.00.

HAHN, Robert. *All Clear.* 1996. Columbia. Univ of SC. 1st. inscr. F/F. B2. $30.00.

HAILEY, Arthur. *Detective.* 1997. NY. Crown. 1st. book has one lightly bumped corner. F/F. H11. $15.00.

HAILEY, Arthur. *The Evening News.* 1990. NY. Doubleday. 1st. 564p. F/F. D4. $20.00.

HAILEY, J. P. *The Underground Man.* 1990. NY. Fine. 1st. Inscribed on half-title page. F/F. H11. $40.00.

HAINES, John. *New Poems 1980 – 1988.* 1990. Brownsville, OR. Story Line Press. 1st. F/F. O11. $40.00.

HAINES, John. *The Owl in the Mask of the Dreamer: Collected Poems.* 1993. St. Paul. Graywolf Press. 1st. sgn. F/F. O11. $40.00.

HAINES, Pamela. *The Kissing Gate.* 1981. Doubleday & Co. 1st. F/chip dj. S19. $30.00.

HAINING, Peter. *The Dream Machines.* 1973. np. World Pub. 1st Am. gilt decor brds. 180p. F/chip dj. B18. $47.50.

HALBERSTAM, David. *Summer of '49.* 1989. NY. Morrow. 1st. NF/NF. R16. $25.00.

HALDEMAN, Joe. *Worlds Apart.* 1983. NY. Viking. 1st. F/F. M23. $40.00.

HALE, John P. *Trans Allegheny Pioneers. Historical Sketches of the First White Settlements West of the Alleghenies 1748 and After.* 1931. Charleston. WV. 2nd ed. ils. 340p. F. B18. $125.00.

HALE, T. J., ed. *Great French Detective Stories*. 1984. Vanguard. 1st Am ed. VG+/VG+. G8. $15.00.

HALEY, Alex. *A Different Kind of Christmas*. 1988. Doubleday. 1st. NF/clip dj. M25. $35.00.

HALEY, Alex. *Roots*. 1976. Doubleday. 1st. warmly inscribed. F/F. M25. $200.00.

HALEY, Alex. *Roots*. 1976. Doubleday. later ed. sgn & inscr. author bio from publisher laid in. NF/lightly browned dj. M25. $60.00.

HALEY, Richard. *When Beggars Die*. 1996. London. Headline. 1st. VF/VF. T2. $25.00.

HALL, David C. *Return Trip Ticket*. 1992. NY. St. Martin. 1st. F/F. G8. $15.00.

HALL, Frederick. *Bible Quizzes for Everybody*. 1941. Wilde. 148p. VG. B29. $5.50.

HALL, Gregory. *Dark Backwards*. 1995. Viking. 1st Am ed. F/F. G8. $25.00.

HALL, James W. *Bones of Coral*. (1991). NY. Knopf. 1st. author's 4th book. F/F. B3. $30.00.

HALL, James W. *Buzz Cut*. 1995. Delacorte. ARC. NF. decor wrp. short crease on front cover. M25. $35.00.

HALL, James W. *Gone Wild*. 1995. Delacorte. ARC. F. decor wrp. M25. $25.00.

HALL, James W. *Mean High Tide*. 1994. NY. Delacorte. 1st. VF/VF. T2. $25.00.

HALL, James W. *Red Sky at Night*. 1997. NY. Delacorte. 1st. VF/VF. T2. $25.00.

HALL, James W. *Tropical Freeze*. 1989. np. Norton. 1st. F/F dj. M19. $17.50.

HALL, James W. *Under Cover of Daylight*. 1987. NY. Norton. 1st. author's 1st novel. sgn. VF/VF. T2. $100.00.

HALL, John. *Sidelights on Holmes*. 1998. Ashcroft. Calabash Press. 1st trade pb orig. VF/pict wrp. T2. $22.00.

HALL, John. *To Mexico with Love. San Miguel With Side Dishes*. 1966. NY. Exposition. 1st. 219p. G/chipped dj. F3. $20.00.

HALL, Karen. *Dark Debts*. 1996. NY. Random House. 1st. author's 1st novel. VF/VF. T2. $24.00.

HALL, Mary Bowen. *Emma Chizzit and the Mother Lode Marauder*. 1993. Walker. 1st. F/VG+. G8. $12.50.

HALL, Mary Bowen. *Emma Chizzit and the Napa Nemesis*. 1992. Walker. 1st. F/F. G8. $15.00.

HALL, Matthew. *The Art of Breaking Glass*. 1997. Boston. Little, Brn. 1st. F/VF. H11. $20.00.

HALL, Oakley. *Ambrose Bierce and the Queen of Spades*. 1998. Univ of California. 1st. F/F. G8. $25.00.

HALL, Parnell. *Blackmail*. 1994. NY. Mysterious. 1st. VF/VF. H11. $25.00.

HALL, Parnell. *Juror*. 1990. NY. Fine. 1st. F/F. H11. $20.00.

HALL, Parnell. *Scam*. 1997. NY. Mysterious. 1st. VF/F. H11. $20.00.

HALL, Patricia. *Death by Election*. 1994. St. Martin. 1st Am ed. NF/VG. G8. $15.00.

HALL, Patricia. *Poison Pool*. 1993. St. Martin. 1st Am ed. NF/NF. G8. $20.00.

HALL, Trevor H. *The Later Mr. Sherlock Holmes and Other Literary Studies*. 1971. NY. St. Martin. 1st. F/dj. M15. $45.00.

HALLBERG, William. *The Rub of the Green*. 1988. NY. Doubleday. 1st. NF/F. H11. $25.00.

HALLESBY, O. *Religious or Christian*. 1947. Augsburg. 198p. VG. ex lib. B29. $5.00.

HALLINANA, Timothy. *Incinerator*. 1992. NY. Morrow. 1st. VF/VF. H11. $30.00.

HALLINANA, Timothy. *The Man with No Time*. 1993. NY. Morrow. 1st. inscr. Also has a signed letter laid in. F/F. H11. $40.00.

HALLION, Richard P. *Test Pilots; The Frontiersmen of Flight. An Illustrated History*. 1981. NY. Doubleday. b/w photos. 8vo. 347p. VG/chipped. worn dj. K5. $25.00.

HALPER, John. *Gary Snyder: Dimensions of a Life*. 1991. San Francisco. Sierra Club Books. 1st. F/F. O11. $30.00.

HAMILL, Pete. *A Drinking Life*. 1994. Boston. Little, Brn. 1st. sgn. F/F. D10. $40.00.

HAMILL, Peter. *Flesh and Blood*. 1977. NY. Random. 1st. VF/VF. H11. $30.00.

HAMILTON, Charles. *Early Day Oil Tales o Mexico*. 1966. Houston. gulf pub co. 1st 246p. G/chipped dj. F3. $20.00.

HAMILTON, Floyd. *The Basis of Christia Faith*. 1946. Harper. 354p. VG. B29. $8.00.

HAMILTON, J. Wallace. *Ride the Wil Horses*. 1952. Revell. sgn. 160p. G/worn dj B29. $4.50.

HAMILTON, James. *Observations on the Utility and Administration of Purgative Medicines*. 1809. Philadelphia. for Benjamir Johnson. 1st Am from 2nd Edinburgh ed contemp. sheepskin. binding rubbed cracked at front spine. 272p. B14. $125.00.

HAMILTON, Jane. *A Map of the World* 1994. NY. Doubleday. 1st. VF/VF. H11 $50.00.

HAMILTON, Jane. *The Book of Ruth*. (1988) NY. Ticknor & Fields. 1st. author's 1st book F/F. B3. $400.00.

HAMILTON, Morse. *Effie's House*. 1990 NY. Greenwillow Books. 1st. NF/NF. A28 $7.95.

HAMILTON, Peter F. *A Second Chance a Eden*. 1998. London. Macmillan. 1st. VF/VF T2. $38.00.

HAMILTON, Virginia. *Cousins*. (1991) London. Gollancz. 1st British ed. sgn by author. F/F. B3. $30.00.

HAMILTON, Virginia. *The Dark Way, Stories from the Spirit World*. (1990). San Diego. HBJ. 1st. ils Lambert Davis. children's ils. NF. lt shelfwear/NF. sm crease to top of spine. B3. $25.00.

HAMILTON-PATERSON, James. *Ghosts of Manila*. (1994). London. Jonathan-Cape. 1st. F/F. B3. $20.00.

HAMMETT, Dashiell. *The Continental Op*. 1974. NY. Random House. 1st. F/dj. M15. $80.00.

HAMMOND, Diana. *The Impersonator*. 1992. NY. Doubleday. 1st. VF/VF. H11. $25.00.

HAMMOND, Gerald. *Carriage of Justice*. 1996. St. Martin. 1st Am ed. NF/NF. G8. $15.00.

HAMMOND, Gerald. *Hook or Crook*. 1994. London. Macmillan. 1st. VF/VF. T2. $30.00.

HAMMOND, Gerald. *Thin Air*. 1994. St Martins. 1st Am ed. NF/VG+. G8. $12.50.

HAMPTON, Taylor. *The Nickel Plate Road, The History of a Great Railroad.* 1949. Cleveland. 2nd printing. buckram. map ep. ls. 366p. F in taped dj. B18. $22.50.

HANAFORD, Jeremiah Lyford. *History of Princeton, Worcester County, Massachusetts, Civil and Ecclesiastical; From Its 1st Settlement n 1739, to April 1852.* Worcester. C. Buckingham Webb. 1852. 12mo. 204p. red cloth. 1st ed. minor wear. occasional minor stain & foxing. VG. L5. $60.00.

HANBURY-TENISON, Robin. *Worlds Apart. An Explorer's Life.* 1984. Boston. Little, Brn. 1st Am ed. sm 4to. G/G. F3. $20.00.

HANCOCK, H. Irving. *The Motor-Boat Club in Florida.* 1909. PA. Henry Altemus. G. A16. $12.00.

HANDLER, David. *Man Who Loved Women to Death.* 1997. Doubleday. 1st Am ed. NF/NF. G8. $20.00.

HANNAH, Barry. *Bats Out of Hell.* 1993. Boston. Houghton Mifflin. 1st. sgn. F/F. D10. $35.00.

HANNAH, Barry. *Captain Maximus.* 1985. NY. Knopf. 1st. F/F. H11. $30.00.

HANNAH, Barry. *High Lonesome.* 1996. NY. Atlantic Monthly. 1st. sgn. F/F. D10. $35.00.

HANNAH, Barry. *Ray.* 1980. NY. Knopf. 1st. sgn. F/F. clip. O11. $60.00.

HANSEN, Brooks. *Perlman's Ordeal.* 1999. NY. Farrar. ARC. wrp. F. B2. $25.00.

HANSEN, Joseph. *Backtrack.* 1982. Woodstock. Countryman Press. 1st. VF/VF. T2. $25.00.

HANSEN, Joseph. *Boy Who was Buried this Morning.* 1990. NY. Viking. 1st. VG/VG. G8. $10.00.

HANSEN, Joseph. *Nightwork.* 1984. Holt. 1st. F/dj. M25. $25.00.

HANSEN, Ron. *Atticus.* 1996. NY. Harper Collins. 1st. sgn. F/F. O11. $35.00.

HANSEN, Ron. *Nebraska.* 1989. NY. Atlantic Monthly. 1st. F in F dj. D10. $50.00.

HARAN, Menahem. *Temples and Temple Service in Ancient Israel.* 1985. Eisenbrauns. 394p. VG. B29. $21.00.

HARDING, Paul. *Red Slayer.* 1993. NY. Morrow. 1st Am ed. VF/VF. T2. $15.00.

HARDING, Paul. *The Nightingale Gallery.* 1991. NY. Morrow. 1st Am ed. VF/VF. T2. $20.00.

HARDWICK, Michael. *Prisoner of the Devil.* 1979. London. Proteus. 1st. F/dj. M15. $45.00.

HARDWICK, Michael. *Sherlock Holmes My Life and Crimes.* 1984. London. Harvill. 1st. F/dj. M15. $45.00.

HARDWICK, Michael. *The Private Life of Dr. Watson.* 1983. NY. Dutton. 1st. VF/VF. T2. $25.00.

HARDWICK, Mollie. *Perish in July.* 1989. St. Martin. 1st Am ed. NF/NF. G8. $15.00.

HARDY, Lindsay. *Requiem for a Redhead.* 1953. NY. Appleton-Century-Crofts. 1st. VG dj. M15. $45.00.

HARE, Cyril. *An English Murder.* 1951. Boston. Little, Brn. 1st Am ed. F dj. M15. $70.00.

HARE, Cyril. *Suicide Excepted.* 1954. NY. Macmillan. 1st Am ed. F w/dj some wear. M15. $45.00.

HARINGTON, Donald. *When Angels Rest.* 1998. Washington. counterpoint. 1st. sgn. VF/VF. T2. $25.00.

HARMETZ, Aljean. *Off the Face of the Earth.* 1997. NY. Scribner. 1st. author's 1st novel. sgn. VF/VF. T2. $25.00.

HARO, Robert. *Latin Americana Research in the United States and Canada; A Guide and Directory.* 1971. ALA. Chicago. 1st. 111p. G. F3. $25.00.

HARPER, Karen. *The Poyson Garden: An Elizabethan Mystery.* 1999. NY. Delacorte. 1st. author's signature laid in. VF/VF. T2. $25.00.

HARRAL, Stewart. *Handbook of Effective Church Letters.* 1965. Abingdon. 208p. VG. B29. $3.00.

HARRINGTON, Kent. *Dark Side.* 1996. NY. St. Martin. 1st. sgn. author's 1st novel. VF/VF. T2. $35.00.

HARRINGTON, Kent. *Dia De Los Muertos.* 1997. Tucson. Dennis McMillan. 1st. sgn. VF/VF. T2. $30.00.

HARRINGTON, William. *Which the Justice Which the Thief.* 1963. Bobbs Merrill. 1st. VG/VG. G8. $10.00.

HARRIS, Charlaine. *Dead Over Heels.* 1996. Scribners. 1st. sgn. F/F. G8. $20.00.

HARRIS, Charlaine. *Julius House.* 1995. Scribners. 1st. sgn. NF/NF. G8. $15.00.

HARRIS, Fred. *Coyote Revenge.* 1999. NY. Harper Collins. 1st. author's 1st novel. sgn. VF/VF. T2. $26.00.

HARRIS, Jana. *The Pearl of Ruby City.* 1998. NY. St. Martin. 1st. sgn. VF/VF. T2. $25.00.

HARRIS, John. *Dragonfly.* (1995). NY. Forge. 1st. F/F. B3. $15.00.

HARRIS, Mark. *A Ticket For A Seamstitch.* 1957. Knopf. 1st. VG/worn dj. M25. $60.00.

HARRIS, Robert. *Archangel.* 1998. London. Hutchinson. 1st. VF/dj. M15. $55.00.

HARRIS, Robert. *Enigma.* 1995. London. Hutchinson. 1st. VF/dj. M15. $100.00.

HARRIS, Robert. *Fatherland.* 1992. NY. Random House. 1st Am ed. VF/VF. T2. $15.00.

HARRIS, Thomas. *Red Dragon.* 1981. NY. Putnam. 1st. VF/F+. H11. $85.00.

HARRIS, Thomas. *The Silence of the Lambs.* 1988. NY. St. Martin. 1st. VF/dj. M15. $85.00.

HARRISON, Colin. *Bodies Electric.* 1993. NY. Crown. 1st. VF/VF. T2. $15.00.

HARRISON, Colin. *Break and Enter.* 1990. NY. Crown. 1st. author's 1st novel. VF/VF. T2. $20.00.

HARRISON, Everett F. *Introduction to the New Testament.* 1977. Eerdmans. 508p. VG/VG. B29. $11.50.

HARRISON, Harry. *Tunnel Through the Deeps.* 1972. NY. Putnam. 1st. F. spot on text block/F. T2. $15.00.

HARRISON, Jamie. *The Edge of the Crazies.* 1995. NY. Hyperion. 1st. author's 1st novel. F/F. D10. $35.00.

HARRISON, Janie. *Roots of Murder: A Gardening Mystery.* 1999. NY. St. Martin. 1st. author's 1st novel. sgn. VF/VF. T2. $25.00.

HARRISON, Jim. *Julip.* (1994). Boston. Houghton Mifflin. 1st. sgn by author. NF/NF slight creasing. B3. $45.00.

HARRISON, Jim. *Just Before Dark.* 1991. Livingston. Clark City Press. 1st trade ed. F/F. O11. $35.00.

HARRISON, Jim. *Legends of the Fall.* (1980). London. Collins. 1st British ed. F/NF lt edgewear. B3. $100.00.

HARRISON, Jim. *Sundog*. 1984. NY. Dutton. 1st. F/F. H11. $55.00.

HARRISON, Jim. *Warlock*. 1981. NY. Delacorte. 1st. F/F. H11. $70.00.

HARRISON, Kathryn. *The Kiss*. 1997. Random House. 1st. F/G. S19. $35.00.

HARRISON, Kathryn. *Thicker than Water*. 1991. NY. Random. 1st. VF/VF. H11. $50.00.

HARRISON, M. John. *Viriconium Nights*. 1985. London. Gollancz. 1st hd ed. VF/VF. T2. $25.00.

HARRISON, Michael. *A Study in Surmise: The Making of Sherlock Holmes*. 1984. Bloomington. Gaslight Publications. 1st. VF/VF. T2. $25.00.

HARRISON, Payne. *Thunder of Erebus*. 1991. NY. Crown. 1st. F/F. H11. $25.00.

HARRISON, Ray. *Deathwatch*. 1985. Scribners. 1st Am ed. NF/NF. G8. $10.00.

HARRISON, Richard E. *Know Your Lilies*. 1970. Cape Town. sm4to. F in dj. B26. $27.50.

HARRISON, Roland KI. *Introduction to the Old Testament*. 1977. Eerdmans. 1325p. VG/torn dj. B29. $17.50.

HARRISON, Sue. *Mother Earth, Father Sky*. (1990). NY. Doubleday. 1st. F/F. B3. $30.00.

HARRISS, Will. *Noble Rot*. 1993. NY. St. Martin. 1st. F/F. A24. $15.00.

HARROD-EAGLES, Cynthia. *Death to Go*. 1994. Scribners. 1st Am ed. sgn. VG/VG. G8. $25.00.

HARROD-EAGLES, Cynthia. *Killing Time*. 1998. Scribners. 1st Am ed. sgn. VG/VG. G8. $25.00.

HART, Carolyn G. *Scandal in Fair Haven*. 1994. NY. Bantam. 1st. inscr by author. NF in F dj. B2. $35.00.

HART, Frances Noyes. *Crooked Lane*. 1934. Doubleday. 1st. VG. G8. $30.00.

HART, Gary. *The Good Fight*. (1993). NY. Random House. 1st. sgn by author. F/F. B3. $40.00.

HART, Roy. *Final Appointment*. 1993. NY. St. Martin. 1st Am ed. F/NF. G8. $15.00.

HARTE, Bret. *Dickens in Camp*. 1923. San Francisco. brds. decor paper. lt soil to cover. wear. VG. B18. $150.00.

HARTLAND, Michael. *Down Among the Dead Men*. 1983. London. Hodder & Stoughton. 1st. sgn. VF in dj. M15. $75.00.

HARTLAND, Michael. *The Third Betrayal*. 1986. London. Hodder & Stoughton. 1st. F in dj w/crease on spine. M15. $65.00.

HARTZMARK, Gini. *Bitter Business*. 1995. Fawcett. 1st. inscr. NF/NF. G8. $20.00.

HARUF, Kent. *Plainsong*. 1999. NY. Knopf. 1st. ARC. VF/pict wrp. T2. $20.00.

HARVEY, Clay. *A Whisper of Death*. 1997. NY. Putnam's. 1st. F in dj. M15. $35.00.

HARVEY, John. *Cutting Edge*. 1991. Holt. 1st Am ed. NF/NF. G8. $20.00.

HARVEY, John. *Easy Meat*. 1996. NY. Henry Holt. 1st Am ed. sgn. VF/VF. T2. $25.00.

HARVEY, John. *Off Minor*. 1992. NY. Henry Holt. 1st Am ed. sgn. VF/VF. T2. $25.00.

HARVEY, John. *Still Waters*. 1997. Holt. 1st Am ed. sgn. F/F. G8. $25.00.

HASKINS, James. *Mabel Mercer: A Life*. 1987. NY. Atheneum. 1st. F/F. M25. $25.00.

HASKINS, Jim. *The Cotton Club*. 1977. NY. Random House. 1st. F/F. B2. $35.00.

HASSAUAREK, F. *Four Years Among Spanish Americans*. 1868 (1867). NY. Hurd & Houghton. 401p. G/gilt on spine. shelf wear on corners. F3. $65.00.

HASSRICK, Royal B. *Cowboys: The Real Story of Cowboys and Cattlemen*. 1974. London. Octopus. 1st ed. 4to. color ils. F/F. O3. $25.00.

HASTE, Steve. *Criminal Sentences: True Crime in Fiction and Drama*. 1997. London. Cygnus Arts. 1st. VF/VF. T2. $30.00.

HATCH, Eric. *The Hatch Way — A Rapid Transit Omnibus*. 1936. np. Little, Brn. 1st. VG/VG. M19. $35.00.

HAUERWAS, Stanley. *Dispatches from the Front; Theological Engagements with the Secular*. 1994. Duke Univ. 235p. VG/VG. B29. $12.50.

HAUGHTON, Rosemary. *Paul and the World's Most Famous Letters*. 1970. Abingdon. 110p. VG/VG. B29. $10.00.

HAUPTMAN, William. *The Storm Season*. 1992. NY. Bantam. 1st. F/F. H11. $20.00.

HAUPTMANN, Tatjana. *Adelima Schlim*. 1981. London. Ernest Benn. 1st English ed. 4to. color pict bds. ils by author throughou. 32p. NF. D6. $35.00.

HAUTMAN, Pete. *Drawing Dead*. (1993. NY. S&S. 1st. author's 1st novel. sgn. F/I. B3. $75.00.

HAUTMAN, Pete. *Ring Game*. (1997). NY. S&S. 1st. sgn & dated by author. F/F. B3. $35.00.

HAUTMAN, Pete. *The Mortal Nuts*. 1996. NY. S&S. 1st. sgn. VF/VF. T2. $30.00.

HAVIGHURST, Walter. *Land of Promise. The Story of the Northwest Territory*. 1946. NY. 1st. inscr. map ep. VG in dj. slight wear. B18. $17.50.

HAVILL, Steven F. *Out of Season*. 1999. NY. St. Martin. 1st. sgn. VF/VF. T2. $25.00.

HAVILL, Steven F. *Privileged to Kill*. 1997. NY. St. Martin. 1st. sgn. VF/VF. T2. $25.00.

HAWKES, John. *Death, Sleep & the Traveler*. 1974. NY. New Directions. 1st. F in F dj. D10. $50.00.

HAWKES, John. *Virginie. Her Two Lives*. 1982. NY. Harper & Row. 1st. F in F dj. D10. $40.00.

HAWKINS, Dean. *Walls of Silence*. 1943. Crime Club. 1st. G. G8. $17.50.

HAWLEY, R. C. & P. W. Stickel. *Forest Protection*. 1956. NY. 2nd ed. 4th prt. B26. $19.00.

HAWORTH-BOOTH, Michael. *The Moutan or Tree Peony*. 1963. NY/London. VG in dj. B26. $29.00.

HAWTHORNE, Nathaniel. *Wonder Book*. (1922). Doubleday Doran. 8vo. 206p. maroon cloth. T5. $70.00.

HAY, Roy & Patrick M. Synge. *The Dictionary of Garden Plants in Colour with House and Greenhouse Plants*. 1971 (1969). 2048 color photos. 4to. 373p. VG in dj. B26. $25.00.

HAYDEN, Robert (ed). *Kaleidoscope — Poems by American Negro Poets*. 1967. np. HBW. 1st. F/VG dj. M19. $35.00.

HAYDEN, Tom. *Love of Possession Is a Disease with Them*. 1972. HRW. 1st. 134p. VG/clip. R11. $15.00.

HAYE, M. Horace. *Veterinary Notes for Horse Owners...* 1987. S&S. 17th/revised. ils/index. 740p. F/dj. H10. $27.50.

HAYES, Billy. *Midnight Express.* 1977. Dutton. 1st. F/NF. M23. $20.00.

HAYES, Captain M. Horace. *Stable Management & Exercise.* 1974. NY. Arco reprint. VG/VG. O3. $18.00.

HAYES, Colonel Thomas J. *Elements of Ordnance....* (1938). NY. Wiley & Sons. 1st. gilt on gray cloth. 377 ils. 715p. NF. B14. $150.00.

HAYES, Florence. *Arctic Gateway.* 1940. NY. Friendship. dbl-p map/phtos. P4. $20.00.

HAYGOOD, T. M. *Henry William Ravenel 1814 – 1887.* 1987. AL U. 204p. F/dj. M4. $25.00.

HAYMAN, Ronald. *Proust: A Biography.* 1990. NY. 1st. dj. T9. $25.00.

HAYNES, David. *Live at Five.* 1996. Minneapolis. Milkweed. 1st. F/dj. O11. $30.00.

HAYNES, David. *Right by My Side.* 1993. Minneapolis. New Rivers Press. pb original. 1/2500. NF in wrp. M23. $65.00.

HAYNES, Roy. *Hungarian Game.* 1973. S&S. 1st. author's 1st book. H11. $20.00.

HAYS, Denys. *Age of the Renaissance.* 1968. McGraw Hill. VG/dj. M20. $45.00.

HAYS, Helen Ashe. *Little Maryland Garden.* 1909. NY. ils. 201p. NF. B26. $37.50.

HAYS, P. *Electricity & Methods of Employment in Removing...* 1889. 1st. ils. xl. VG. E6. $85.00.

HAYTER, Sparkle. *Nice Girls Finish Last.* 1996. NY. Viking. 1st. VF/VF. T2. $20.00.

HAYTER, Sparkle. *What's a Girl Gotta Do?* 1994. NY. Soho. 1st. VF/F. H11. $65.00.

HAYTHORNTHWAITE, Philip. *Uniforms of the Civil War.* 1990. Sterling Pub. 1st Am. F/wrp. A14. $14.00.

HAYWARD, A. *Vital Magnetic Cure & Exposition of Vital Magnetism...* 1873 (1871). VG. E6. $65.00.

HAYWARD, Charles B. *Building and Flying an Aeroplane.* 1918. Chicago. photos. ils. 142p. G+. some wear. B18. $95.00.

HAYWOOD, A. *Autobiography.* Letters & Literary Remains. 1861. London. Longman. 2 vol. 1st/revised. 8vo. VG. H13. $295.00.

HAYWOOD, Carolyn. *Halloween Treats.* 1981. Morrow. 1st. 8vo. 175p. orange brd. NF/VG. T5. $25.00.

HAYWOOD, Gar Anthony. *Bad News Travels Fast.* (1995). NY. Putnam. 1st. F/F. B3. $20.00.

HAYWOOD, Gar Anthony. *Going Nowhere Fast.* 1994. NY. Putnam. 1st. sgn. VF/VF. T2. $25.00.

HAYWOOD, Gar Anthony. *Not Long for This World.* 1990. St. Martin. 1st. F/NF. M23. $40.00.

HAZELTON, Roger. *A Theological Approach to Art.* 1967. Abingdon. 158p. VG/VG. B29. $6.50.

HEAD, Michael G. *Foot Regiments of the Imperial Guard.* 1973. Almark. 1st. 124p. VG/stiff wrp. S16. $35.00.

HEAD, Michael G. *French Napoleonic Lancer Regiments.* 1971. Almark. 1st. 72p. VG/stiff wrp. S16. $35.00.

HEADLAND, Helen. *Swedish Nightingale: Biography of Jenny Lind.* 1940. Rock Island, IL. ils. VG. w/sgn note. M17. $20.00.

HEALD, Tim. *Business Unusual.* 1989. Crime Club. 1st Am ed. NF/VG+. G8. $15.00.

HEALD, Tim. *Deadline.* 1975. Stein & Day. 1st Am ed. VG/VG. G8. $15.00.

HEALEY, Ben. *Midnight Ferry to Venice.* 1981. Walker. 1st Am ed. NF/NF. G8. $15.00.

HEALY, Jeremiah. *Act of God.* 1994. Pocket. 1st. sgn. NF/NF. G8. $20.00.

HEALY, Jeremiah. *Invasion of Privacy.* 1996. Pocket. 1st. sgn. F/F. G8. $20.00.

HEALY, Jeremiah. *Only Good Lawyer.* 1998. Pocket. 1st. sgn. F/F. G8. $25.00.

HEALY, Jeremiah. *So Like Sleep.* 1987. NY. Harper & Row. 1st. sgn. F/F. A24. $40.00.

HEANEY, Seamus. *Door into Dark.* 1969. Oxford. 1st. F/F. B2. $200.00.

HEANEY, Seamus. *Field Work.* 1979. NY. FSG. 1st Am ed. sgn. F/NF. O11. $125.00.

HEANEY, Seamus. *The Redress of Poetry.* 1995. NY. FSG. 1st Am ed. sgn. F/F. O11. $60.00.

HEARD, H. F. *Taste of Honey.* 1941. NY. Vanguard. 1st. F/VG. M15. $150.00.

HEATH, Eric & R. J. Chinnock. *Ferns and Fern Allies of New Zealand.* 1974. Wellington. VG in dj. B26. $17.50.

HEBDEN, Mark. *Pel and the Bombers.* 1982. Walker. 1st Am ed. NF/F. G8. $10.00.

HEBERT, A. G. *The Bible from Within.* 1950. Oxford. 192p. G. ex lib. B29. $6.00.

HEBERT, Anne. *Silent Rooms.* 1974. Toronto. Musson. 1st. F/NF dj. A26. $20.00.

HECHT, Daniel. *Skull Session.* 1998. NY. Viking. 1st. author's 1st novel. sgn. VF/VF. T2. $25.00.

HEDGES, Peter. *What's Eating Gilbert Grape.* 1991. NY. Poseidon. 1st. F/F. M23. $40.00.

HEDRICK, U. P. *A History of Horticulture in America to 1860.* 1950. NY. 1st. 551p. VG. B26. $75.00.

HEGARTY, Frances. *Playroom.* 1991. Pocket. 1st Am ed. NF/F. G8. $15.00.

HEGI, Gustav. *Alpenflora. Die Verbreitetsten Alpenfanzen Von Bayern, Osterreich Und Der Schweiz.* 1952. Munchen. 11th ed. dj. B26. $32.50.

HEIDEN, Konrad. *Der Fuehrer.* 1944. Houghton Mifflin Co. 1st. trans by Ralph Manheim. G+/chip. S19. $40.00.

HEINEMANN, Larry. *Cooler by the Lake.* 1992. NY. FSG. 1st. VF/VF. H11. $30.00.

HEINL, Lt. Col. Robert D & Lt. Col. John A. Crown. *The Marshalls: Increasing the Tempo.* 1954. pict brds. many ils. 11 foldout maps. 188p. G+. B18. $95.00.

HEINLEIN, Robert A. *Heretics of Dune.* 1984. NY. Putnam. 1st Am ed. VF/VF. T2. $10.00.

HEINLEIN, Robert A. *Job: A Comedy of Justice.* 1984. Ballantine. 1st. 376p. F/dj. M21. $25.00.

HEINLEIN, Robert A. *Revolt in 2100.* 1953. Shasta. 1st. F/NF. P3. $500.00.

HEINLEIN, Robert A. *Stranger in a Strange Land.* 1991. Ace Putnam. 1st. F/dj. P3. $30.00.

HEISENFELT, Kathryn. *Ann Sheridan and the Sign of the Sphinx.* 1943. WI. Whitman Pub. paper yellowing. G in chip dj. A16. $6.00.

HELD, Peter; see Vance, Jack.

HELLE, Andre. *French Toys.* 1915. Paris. L'Avenir Feminin. 8vo. stiff paper wrp/pict dj. R5. $200.00.

HELLENGA, Robert R. *The Sixteen Pleasures.* 1994. NY. Soho. 1st. 8vo. 327p. AN/dj. P4. $25.00.

HELLENGA, Robert R. *The Sixteen Pleasures.* 1994. Soho. 1st. F/F. M25. $35.00.

HELLENTHAL, J. A. *Alaskan Melodrama.* 1936. Liveright. 1st. photos/maps. 312p. G. S14. $20.00.

HELLER, Joseph. *Catch-22.* 1961. NY. S&S. ARC in wht pict wrp printed in bl. spine curled & creased. G/VG. A24. $500.00.

HELLER, Joseph. *Catch-22.* 1989. NY. S&S. sgn ltd ed #61/750. bl cloth w/gilt lettering on spine. red slipcase w/gilt. F in slipcase. A24. $125.00.

HELLER, Joseph. *Closing Time.* 1994. S&S. 1st. sgn. F/dj. R14. $40.00.

HELLER, Joseph. *God Knows.* 1984. NY. Knopf. 1st. F/F. A24. $20.00.

HELLER, Joseph. *Good as Gold.* 1979. NY. S&S. 1st. F/F. A24. $20.00.

HELLER, Joseph. *Picture This.* 1988. Putnam. 1st. F/dj. T12. $25.00.

HELLER, Keith. *Man's Illegal Life.* 1984. Scribners. 1st. NF/NF. G8. $15.00.

HELLMAN, Hal. *Light and Electricity in the Atmosphere.* 1968. NY. Holiday House. b/w drawings & photos. 8vo. 223p. G/chipped dj. K5. $20.00.

HELLMAN, Lillian. *Maybe.* 1980. Boston. Little, Brn. F/F. A24. $20.00.

HELPRIN, Mark. *Refiner's Fire.* 1977. NY. Knopf. 1st. NF in dj. D10. $50.00.

HELPRIN, Mark. *Winter's Tale.* 1983. HBJ. 1st. F/dj. M23. $50.00.

HEMINGWAY, Ernest. *A Moveable Feast.* 1964. NY. Scribner. 1st. VNF/NF. D10. $85.00.

HEMINGWAY, Ernest. *Islands in the Stream.* 1970. NY. Scribner's. 1st. F in NF dj. D10. $65.00.

HEMINGWAY, Ernest. *Men Without Women.* 1955. London. VG/G. M17. $25.00.

HEMINGWAY, Ernest. *Old Man & The Sea.* 1954 (1952). NY. Scribner. VG/F. T12. $40.00.

HEMINGWAY, Ernest. *Torrents of Spring.* 1926. Scribner. 1st. F/dj. B24. $4. 500.00.

HEMMINGER, Jane M. *Recipes of Madison County.* 1995. Oxmoor. 1st. F/dj. W2. $35.00.

HEMPHILL, Paul. *Long Gone.* 1979. Viking. 1st. inscr. VG/dj. P8. $50.00.

HENDERSON, Andrew. *Field Guide to the Palms of the Americas.* 1995. Princeton. ils/maps. 376p. sc. AN. B26. $30.00.

HENDERSON, Beverly Manist. *History of Osnaburg Township 1804 – 1976.* 1976. Ohio. pict wrp. ils photos. 118p. VG. B18. $25.00.

HENDERSON, G. F. R. *Civil War: A Soldier's View.* 1958. U Chicago. VG. M17. $17.50.

HENDERSON, William Cranor. *I Killed Hemingway.* 1993. NY. St. Martin. ARC. F in wrp. B2. $35.00.

HENDERSON, William McCranor. *Stark Raving Elvis.* 1984. NY. Dutton. 1st. VF/F. H11. $25.00.

HENDRICK, Basil. *North Mexican Frontier.* 1971. Carbondale. 1st. 255p. dj. F3. $20.00.

HENDRICKS, George D. *Bad Man of the West.* 1970. San Antonio, TX. Naylor. F/dj. A19. $35.00.

HENDRICKS, Vicki. *Miami Purity.* 1995. Pantheon. 1st. sgn. VG/dj. B30. $22.50.

HENDRIE, Laura. *Stygo.* 1994. Aspen. MacMurray Beck. 1st. F/dj. M23. $25.00.

HENDRY, George. *The Holy Spirit in Christian Theology.* 1956. Westminster. 128p. VG/worn dj. B29. $6.50.

HENFREY, Colin. *Through Indian Eyes.* 1965. Holt. 1st Am. 286p. F3. $20.00.

HENIE, Sonja. *Wings on My Feet.* 1940. NY. 1st. sgn. G/dj. B5. $45.00.

HENLEY, Patricia. *Hummingbird House.* 1999. Denver. MacMurray & Beck. 1st. author's 1st novel. VF/VF. T2. $22.00.

HENNIPMAN, E. & M. C. Roos. *A Monograph of the Fern Genus Playtcerium.* 1982. Amsterdam, SC. glossy photo cover. 126p. VG. B26. $34.00.

HENRY, April. *Circles of Confusion.* 1999. NY. Harper Collins. 1st. author's 1st novel. VF/VF. T2. $10.00.

HENRY, Marguerite. *Born to Trot.* 1950. NY. Rand McNally. 1st. decor cloth. 221p. spine faded. sm tears to dj. VG. B18. $25.00.

HENRY, Marguerite. *San Domingo.* 1972. Rand McNally. 1st. ils Robert Lougheed. VG/dj. A21. $45.00.

HENRY, O. *Cabbages & Kings.* 1904. NY. McClure Phillis. 1st. prt cloth. VG. H4. $150.00.

HENRY, O. *Postscripts.* 1923. Harper. 1st. VG/clip. B4. $400.00.

HENRY, Sue. *Murder on the Iditarod Trail.* 1991. Atalantic Monthly. 1st. F/dj. M15. $250.00.

HENRY, Thomas R. *Strangest Things in the World...* 1958. WA. 200p. dj. A17. $10.00.

HENRY, Will. *Maheo's Children.* 1968. Phil. Chilton. 1st. gray cloth. F/clip. T11. $80.00.

HENRY, Will. *To Follow a Flag.* 1953. Random. 1st. NF/VG. T11. $65.00.

HENTOFF, Nat, and Albert McCarthy, eds. *Jazz.* 1959. NY. Rinehart. 1st. F. owner's label/lightly chip dj. B2. $30.00.

HEPBURN, Katherine. *Me. Stories of My Life.* 1991. Knopf. 1st. F/dj. T11/W2. $35.00.

HEPPENHEIMER, T. A. *Toward Distant Suns.* 1979. Stackpole. ils/diagrams. 256p. VG/dj. K5. $16.00.

HEPPER, F. N. *Wild African Herbaria of Isert & Thonning.* 1976. Kew. ils/maps. 227p. VG/dj. B26. $30.00.

HERBERT, Frank. *Chapterhouse: Dune.* 1985. Putnam. 1st. 464p. F/NF. M21. $15.00.

HERBERT, Frank. *Eye.* 1985. Masterworks. ils Jim Burns. 328p. F. W2. $15.00.

HERBERT, James. *Moon.* 1985. Crown. 1st Am. F/dj. S18. $40.00.

HERBERT, James. *Sepulchre.* 1987. London. Hodder Stoughton. 1st. F/dj. M21. $30.00.

HERBST, Josephine. *New Green World.* 1954. Hastings. 272p. cloth. VG. A10. $38.00.

HERGESHEIMER, Joseph. *Sheridan. A Military Narrative.* 1931. Boston. Houghton Mifflin. 1st. orig cloth. plates. maps. 382p. VG. M8. $45.00.

HERIHY, James Leo. *Midnight Cowboy.* 1965. S&S. 1st. VG/VG clip. R14. $50.00.

HERLEY, Richard. *The Penal Colony.* 1988. NY. Morrow. 1st. F/F. H11. $50.00.

HERMAN, Pauline W. *The Family Horse.* 1959. Princeton. Van Norstrand. VG/VG. D3. $20.00.

HERMAN, Zvi. *Peoples, Seas & Ships.* 1967. np. Putnam. 1st. w/foldout ils plates. F/NF dj. M19. $25.00.

HERNANDEZ, Xavier. *San Rafael. A Central American City Through the Ages.* 1992. Boston. Houghton Mifflin. 1st Am ed. 4to. drawings. G/G. F3. $10.00.

HERNDON, James. *Sorrowless Times. A Narrative.* 1981. NY. S&S. AP. wrps. F. lt soiling. B2. $35.00.

HERR, Michael. *Dispatches.* 1977. NY. Knopf. 1st. F in F dj w/darkened spine. B2. $125.00.

HERRICK, Christine. *Chafing Dish Supper.* 1906 (1894). E6. $45.00.

HERRICK, James. *Short History of Cardiology.* 1942. Springfield. 1st. sgn. 258p. cl. A13. $150.00.

HERRIGEL, Eugene. *Zen & the Art of Archery.* 1953. Pantheon. 1st. NF/dj. B2. $40.00.

HERRIN, Lamar. *Rio Loja Ringmaster.* 1977. Viking. 1st. VG/dj. P8. $50.00.

HERRON, Don. *Dark Barbarian: Writings of Robert E Howard.* 1984. Greenwood. ils. 261p. F. A4. $45.00.

HERRON, Francis. *Letters from the Argentine.* 1943. NY. Putnam. 1st. 307p. G/chipped. F3. $20.00.

HERRON, Shaun. *Bird in Last Year's Nest.* 1974. ARC. F/NF. M19. $25.00.

HERSCHEL, William. *Scientific Papers of Sir William Herschel...* 1912. London. Royal Soc/ Royal Astronomical Soc. 2 vol. K5. $1,200.00.

HERSEY, Jean. *A Widow's Pilgrimage.* 1980. Continuum. 114p. VG/VG. B29. $4.50.

HERSEY, John. *The Wall.* 1950. np. Knopf. 1st. F/NF dj. M19. $25.00.

HERSEY, John. *Walnut Door.* 1977. Knopf. 1st. F/NF. A24. $25.00.

HERZOG, Arthur. *Earthsound.* 1975. NY. S&S. 1st. VF/F. H11. $20.00.

HESS, Joan. *Closely Akin to Murder.* 1996. Dutton. 1st. sgn. F/F. G8. $22.50.

HESS, Joan. *Death by the Light of the Moon.* 1992. St. Martin. 1st. sgn. NF/NF. G8. $22.50.

HESS, Joan. *Martians in Maggody.* 1994. Dutton. 1st. sgn. F/F. G8. $20.00.

HESS, Joan. *Mischief in Maggody.* 1988. St. Martin. 1st. VG/VG. G8. $20.00.

HESS, Joan. *Roll Over and Play Dead.* 1991. St. Martin. 1st. VG+/VG. G8. $15.00.

HEUER, Kenneth. *Men of Other Planets.* 1951. NY. Pellegrini Cudahy. ils. 160p. K5. $20.00.

HEUMAN, William. *Little League Champs.* 1953. Lippincott. 1st. VG. P8. $17.50.

HEUVELMANS, Bernard. *In the Wake of the Sea-Serpents.* 1968. NY. Zoological UFOs. ils. 645p. VG. S15. $18.00.

HEWITT, E. J. *Sand & Water Culture Methods Used Study of Plant Nutrition.* 1952. E Malling. Kent. 241p. dj. A10. $20.00.

HEWITT, Lawrence Lee. *Port Hudson: Confederate Bastion on the Mississippi.* 1987. LSU. 1st. NF/dj. A14. $21.00.

HEWITT, R. *Bird Malaria.* 1940. John Hopkins. 1st. 8vo. gilt cloth. F. C12. $45.00.

HEYDEN, Doris & Paul Gendrop. *Pre-Columbian Architecture of Mesoamerica.* 1988. NY. Rizzoli. 1st pb ed. 235p. G. F3. $35.00.

HEYER, Carol. *Beauty & the Beast.* 1989. Ideals. 1st. sgn. 32p. F/dj. D4. $30.00.

HEYER, Georgette. *Civil Contract.* 1961. NY. 1st Am. VG. M17. $15.00.

HEYER, Georgette. *Death in the Stocks.* 1970. Dutton. 1st Am. VG/clip. S13. $14.00.

HEYERDAHL, Thor. *Tigris Expedition: In Search of Our Beginnings.* 1981. Doubleday. 1st. 8vo. ils/map ep. 349p. NF/dj. W1. $22.00.

HEYLINGER, William. *Bean-Ball Bill & Other Stories.* 1930. Grosset Dunlap. 1st. VG. P8. $40.00.

HEYWOOD, Eddie. *Modern Piano Transcriptions.* 1946. NY. Robbins. 1st. wrp. 32p. VG w/creases. B2. $35.00.

HIAASEN, Carl. *Double Whammy.* 1987. NY. Putnam. 1st. VF/dj. M15. $165.00.

HIAASEN, Carl. *Lucky You.* 1997. NY. Knopf. 1st. VF/VF. H11. $25.00.

HIAASEN, Carl. *Naked Came the Manatee.* 1996. NY. Putnam. 1st. VF/VF. H11. $25.00.

HIAASEN, Carl. *Skin Tight.* 1989. NY. Putnam. 1st. F/VF. H11. $80.00.

HIAASEN, Carl. *Stormy Weather.* 1995. NY. Knopf. 1st. VF/VF. T2. $20.00.

HIAASEN, Carl. *Strip Tease.* (1993). NY. Knopf. 1st. F/NF. scratches on rear panel. B3. $20.00.

HIASSEN, Carl. *Stormy Weather.* 1995. NY. Knopf. 1st. NF/NF. R16. $25.00.

HIBBERT, Christopher. *Personal History of Samuel Johnson.* 1971. London. Longman. H13. $45.00.

HIBBERT, Christopher. *Popes.* 1982. Stonehenge. 1st. Treasures of World series. 176p. NF. S14. $19.00.

HIBBERT, Eleanor Alice. *Captive.* 1989. Doubleday. 1st. F/dj. T12. $20.00.

HIBBERT, Eleanor Alice. *Lion Triumphant.* 1974. Putnam. 1st. NF/VG. M19. $17.50.

HIBBERT, Eleanor Alice. *Sun in Splendor.* 1983. Putnam. 1st. F/NF. M19. $17.50.

HICKEY, D. R. *War of 1812: Forgotten Conflict.* 1989. IL U. ils/maps. 457p. NF/dj. M4. $27.00.

HICKS, Edward. *Memoirs of Life & Religious Labors of Edward Hicks...* 1851. Phil. Merrihew Thompson. 12mo. 365p. V3. $125.00.

HIGGINBOTHAM, Don. *Atlas of the American Revolution.* 1974. Rand McNally. 50 period maps. 217p. F/clip. T11. $125.00.

HIGGINS, George V. *A Year Or So with Edgar.* 1979. NY. Harper & Row. 1st. F/F. H11. $35.00.

HIGGINS, George V. *Cogan's Trade.* 1974. NY. Knopf. 1st. F/F. H11. $30.00.

HIGGINS, George V. *Friends of Eddie Coyle.* 1972. NY. Knopf. 1st. VG+/VG+. G8. $10.00.

HIGGINS, George V. *Rat of Fire.* 1981. Knopf. 1st. sgn. NF/VG. R14. $40.00.

HIGGINS, George V. *Victories.* 1991. Andre Deutsch. 1st. F/dj. P8. $25.00.

HIGGINS, Jack. *A Season in Hell.* 1989. NY. S&S. 1st. F/F. H11. $25.00.

HIGGINS, Jack. *Angel of Death.* 1995. NY. Putnam. 1st. VG/VG+. R16. $20.00.

HIGGINS, Jack. *Confessional.* 1985. NY. Stein. 1st. F/F. H11. $30.00.

HIGGINS, Jack. *Eye of the Storm.* 1992. London. Chapmans. 1st. F/dj. M15. $45.00.

HIGGINS, Jack. *Luciano's Luck.* 1981. NY. Stein & Day. 1st. VF/VF. T2. $9.00.

HIGGINS, Jack. *Night of the Fox.* 1986. S&S. F/VG. L4. $15.00.

HIGGINS, Jack. *Sheba.* 1994. London. Michael Joseph. 1st. VF/dj. M15. $75.00.

HIGGINS, Jack. *Solo.* 1980. NY. Stein & Day. 1st. VF/VF. T2. $9.00.

HIGGINS, Jack. *The Last Place God Made.* 1971. London. Collins. 1st. F/dj. M15. $250.00.

HIGGINSON, A. Henry. *British & American Sporting Authors.* 1951. Hutchinson. ils. VG/dj. A21. $225.00.

HIGHSMITH, Patricia. *A Dog's Ransom.* 1972. London. Heinemann. 1st. NF/NF. A24. $25.00.

HIGHSMITH, Patricia. *Mermaids on the Golf Course.* 1988. Penzler. 1st. F/dj. R8. $9.00.

HIGHSMITH, Patricia. *Ripley Under Water.* 1992. NY. 1st. VG/dj. M17. $15.00.

HIGHSMITH, Patricia. *The Boy Who Followed Ripley.* 1980. London. Heinemann. 1st. F/dj. M25. $60.00.

HIGHSMITH, Patricia. *This Sweet Sickness.* 1961. London. Heinemann. 1st Eng. VG/clip. M15. $65.00.

HIGHWATER, Jamake. *Kill Hole.* 1992. NY. Grove. ARC. F/wrp. B2. $25.00.

HIGHWATER, Jamake. *Legend Days.* 1984. Harper Row. 1st. F/NF. D10. $40.00.

HIJUELOS, Oscar. *Empress of the Splendid Season.* (1999). NY. Harper Collins. 1st. sgn by the author. F/F. B3. $35.00.

HIJUELOS, Oscar. *Fourteen Sisters of Emilio Montez O'Brien.* 1993. FSG. 1st. sgn. F/dj. D10. $40.00.

HIJUELOS, Oscar. *Mambo King Plays Songs of Love.* 1989. FSG. 1st. F/F. H11. $45.00.

HILDEBRANDT, Greg. *Dragons.* 1994. Little, Brn. 1st. folio. popups/engineer Keith Moseley. F. B17. $15.00.

HILL, Benjamin L. *Lectures on American Eclectic System of Surgery.* 1850. Cincinnati. Phillips. 100 ils. 671p. sheep. G7. $175.00.

HILL, Clara c. *Spring Flowers of the Lower Columbia Valley.* 1958. Seattle. VG in dj. B26. $15.00.

HILL, David. *Sacred Dust.* 1996. NY. Delacorte. 1st. author's 1st novel. VF/VF. T2. $23.00.

HILL, Eileen. *Candle Shop Mystery.* 1967. Whitman. ils. 192p. VG/dj. B36. $7.50.

HILL, Porter. *War Chest.* 1988. NY. Walker. 1st Am. rem mk. NF/dj. T11. $20.00.

HILL, R. B. *Hanta Yo.* 1979. Garden City. 834p. NF/dj. M4. $18.00.

HILL, Reginald. *A Pinch of Snuff.* 1978. Harper & Row. 1st Am. F/dj. M25. $50.00.

HILL, Reginald. *Blood Sympathy.* 1994. St. Martin. 1st Am ed. NF/NF. G8. $20.00.

HILL, Reginald. *Born Guilty.* 1995. London. Harper Collins. 1st. sgn. VF/VF. T2. $35.00.

HILL, Reginald. *Fairly Dangerous Thing.* 1972. Foul Play. 1st Am ed. F/F. G8. $35.00.

HILL, Reginald. *Pascoe's Ghost.* 1979. London. Collins Crime Club. 1st. F in dj. M15. $250.00.

HILL, Reginald. *Recalled to Life.* 1992. Delacorte. 1st. F/F. G8. $10.00.

HILL, Reginald. *Very Good Hater.* 1974. Foul Play. 1st Am ed. NF/VG. G8. $22.50.

HILLERMAN, Tony. *A Thief of Time.* 1988. NY. Harper & Row. 1st. sgn. VF/VF. T2. $65.00.

HILLERMAN, Tony. *Coyote Waits.* 1990. NY. Harper & Row. 1st. sgn. VF/VF. T2. $45.00.

HILLERMAN, Tony. *Dark Wind.* 1982. Harper Row. 1st. VG+/dj. A14. $140.00.

HILLERMAN, Tony. *People of Darkness.* 1980. NY. Harper & Row. 1st. sgn. NF/NF. A24. $300.00.

HILLERMAN, Tony. *Rio Grande.* 1975. Portland. Charles H. Beeding. 1st. F/dj. M15. $250.00.

HILLERMAN, Tony. *Sacred Clowns.* 1993. NY. Harper Collins. 1st. VG+/NF. R16. $30.00.

HILLERMAN, Tony. *Skinwalkers.* 1988. London. Michael Joseph. 1st. F/clip. A24. $50.00.

HILLERMAN, Tony. *Talking God.* 1989. NY. Harper & Row. 1st. sgn. VF/VF. T2. $50.00.

HILLERMAN, Tony. *The First Eagle.* 1998. NY. Harper Collins. 1st. sgn. VF in dj. M15. $55.00.

HILLERMAN, Tony. *The Spell of New Mexico.* 1976. Albuquerque. U of NM. 1st. F in dj clip. M15. $150.00.

HILLES, Frederick W. *New Light on Dr. Johnson: Essays...* 1959. Yale. 1st. inscr. H13. $125.00.

HILLIER, Bevis. *Cartoons & Caricatures.* 1976. NY/London. Studio Vista/Dutton. 1st. VG/wrp. C9. $48.00.

HILLMAN, William S. *The Physiology of Flowering.* 1963 (1962). NY. VG. B26. $9.00.

HILTON, James. *Goodbye, Mr. Chips.* 1935. Little, Brn. 1st. inscr. ils. gr cloth. VG/dj. J3. $100.00.

HILTON, James. *Time and Time Again.* 1953. Boston. Little, Brn. 1st. F/VG. A24. $25.00.

HILTON, John. *Senora Sketch Book.* 1947. NY. Macmillan. 1st. ils. 333p. G/chipped. tattered dj. F3. $20.00.

HILTON, John Buxton. *Asking Price.* 1983. London. Collins Crime Club. 1st. F/NF. M15. $40.00.

HILTON, John Buxton. *Death in Midwinter.* 1969. London. Cassell. 1st. inscr. author's 2nd mystery. F/dj. M15. $75.00.

HIMES, Chester. *A Case of Rape.* 1984. Washington, DC. Howard U. 1st. ps by Calvin Hernton. F in dj. M15. $45.00.

HIMES, Chester. *If He Hollers Let Him Go.* 1947. London. Falcon. 1st Eng. author's 1st novel. F/NF. M15. $300.00.

HIND, Arthur. *Catalogue of Rembrandt's Etchings...* 1923. London. Vol 1 (of 2) only. ils. VG. A4. $175.00.

HINDE, Thomas. *Games of Chance.* 1965. Vanguard. 1st. F/G. T12. $30.00.

HINDMARSH, W. A. *Magnetism & the Cosmos.* 1967. NY. Am Elsevier. 1st. ils. 8vo. VG/dj. A2. $15.00.

NDS, Harold R. *Wildflowers of Cape Cod.* 48. Chatham, MA. sc. B26. $16.00.

NES, Earl. *Ivory Icing.* 1944. NY. Harms. t. wrps. VG+. $40.00.

NN, Benny. *Good Morning, Holy Spirit.* 90. Nelson. 177p. F/F. B29. $7.00.

RSHSON, Stanley P. *Lion of the Lord: ography of Brigham Young.* 1969. Knopf. /notes/biblio. 391p. G. H10. $25.00.

RST-FISCHE, Robin. *Intermediate Riding ills.* 1990. NY. Howell. 1st. VG/VG. O3. 0.00.

ITCHCOCK, Alfred. *Daring Detectives.* 69. Random. VG/dj. P3. $20.00.

ITCHCOCK, Roswell D. *Baker's Topical le.* 1977. Baker. 685p. VG. B29. $13.00.

ITCHMAN, Janet. *Such a Strange Lady.* 75. NEL. 1st Eng. VG/dj. G8. $30.00.

ITTI, Philip K. *Arabs: Short History.* 1943. inceton. 224p. cloth. VG. Q2. $24.00.

ITTI, Philip K. *Near East in History: 5000-ar Story.* 1961. Van Nostrand. 1st. ils. 574p. G/torn. W1. $30.00.

JORTBERG, William. *Nevermore.* 1994. Y. Atlantic Monthly. 1st. F/F. B2. $25.00.

JORTSBERG, William. *Falling Angel.* 78. HBJ. 1st. F/dj. M21. $75.00.

JORTSBERG, William. *Nevermore.* (1994). Y. Atlantic Monthly Press. 1st. F/F. B3. 0.00.

OAG, Tami. *A Thin Dark Line.* 1997. NY. ntam. 1st. VF/F. H11. $15.00.

OBAN, Russell. *Kleinzeit.* 1974. NY. iking. 1st Am. NF/dj. A14. $25.00.

OBAN, Russell. *Lion of Boaz-Jachin & chin-Boaz.* 1973. Stein Day. 1st. F/F. D10. 0.00.

OBSON, Linda Whitney. *Walker Percy. A mprehensive Descriptive Bibliography.* 1988. ton Rouge. LSU Press. 1st. 2 p intro by rcy. F. B2. $25.00.

OCKING, William Ernest. *Science and the ea of God.* 1944. Chapel Hill. 124p. G. B29. .00.

OCKNEY, David. *Cameraworks.* 1984. nopf. 1st. ils. NF. S14. $75.00.

HODES, Art, and Chadwick Hansen. *Hot Man. The Life of Art Hodes.* 1992. Urbana. Univ of Illinois Press. 1st. F/F. B2. $25.00.

HODGE, Charles. *Commentary on Ephesians.* 1856. Hodder & Stoughton. 398p. G. B29. $9.50.

HODGE, Charles. *Commentary on Romans.* 1964. Eerdmans. 457p. G. B29. $12.00.

HODGSON, Sheila. *The Fellow Travellers and Other Ghost Stories.* 1998. Ashcraft, BC. Ash Tree Press. 1st. VF/VF. T2. $40.00.

HODIER, Andre. *Toward Jazz.* 1962. NY. Grove. 1st Am ed. F/F. B2. $35.00.

HOEG, Peter. *Border Liners.* 1994. NY. FSG. F/F. A24. $20.00.

HOEG, Peter. *Smilla's Sense of Snow.* 1993. FSG. 1st Am. F/dj. M15. $50.00.

HOEG, Peter. *Tales of the Night.* 1998. FSG. UP. NF/purple wrps. one corner wrinkled. M25. $25.00.

HOEHLING, A. A. *Great War at Sea: History of Naval Action 1914 – 1918.* 1965. NY. 1st. ils/maps. VG/dj. E1. $35.00.

HOFFECKER, Carol E. *Delaware: A Bicentennial History.* 1977. NY. Norton. 1st. 8vo. cloth. F/dj. O10. $25.00.

HOFFMAN, Alice. *Fortune's Daughter.* 1985. NY. Putnam. 1st. sgn. F/F. D10. $50.00.

HOFFMAN, Alice. *Practical Magic.* 1995. Putnam. ARC. F/wrp. M25. $45.00.

HOFFMAN, Alice. *Property Of....* 1977. NY. FSG. 1st. author's 1st book. sgn. NF/NF. lt fading. D10. $110.00.

HOFFMAN, Alice. *The Drowning Season.* 1979. NY. Dutton. 1st. sgn. F/F. D10. $95.00.

HOFFMAN, Alice. *Turtle Moon.* 1992. Putnam. 1st. F/dj. B4. $45.00.

HOFFMAN, Alice. *White Horses.* 1982. NY. Putnam. 1st. F/F. D10. $65.00.

HOFFMAN, Charles Fenno. *Winter in the West.* 1966. np. 2 vol. rpt (1835). VG. B18. $19.50.

HOFFMAN, Daniel. *City of Satisfactions.* 1963. Oxford. 1st. F/NF clip. R14. $30.00.

HOFFMAN, Hans. *Theology of Reinhold Neibuhr.* 1956. NY. 1st. VG/G. B5. $20.00.

HOFFMAN, John. *Hank Sauer.* 1953. Barnes. 1st. VG/dj. P8. $75.00.

HOFFMAN, Malvina. *Sculpture Inside & Out.* 1939. NY. Norton. 1st. photos. 300p. VG+/VG. A25. $30.00.

HOFFMAN, Paul. *The Man Who Loved Only Numbers.* 1998. NY. Hyperion. 1st. F/F. M23. $35.00.

HOFFMAN, William. *Tidewater Blood.* 1998. Chapel Hill. Algonquin. 1st. VF/VF. T2. $20.00.

HOGAN, Linda. *Dwellings.* 1995. NY. Norton. 1st. author's 1st novel. 159p. F/F. O11. $25.00.

HOGAN, Linda. *Mean Spirit.* 1990. NY. Atheneum. 1st. author's 1st novel. sgn. F/F. O11. $40.00.

HOGG, Ian V. *Complete Illustrated Encyclopedia of World's Firearms.* 1978. NY. ils. 320p. F/dj. A17. $30.00.

HOGG, Ian V. *History of Fortification.* 1981. NY. ils. F/dj. M4. $45.00.

HOKE, Helen. *Major & the Kitten.* 1941. Franklin Watts. ils Diana Thorne. G. A21. $35.00.

HOKE, Helen. *Mr. Sweeney.* 1940. Henry Holt. 1st. VG/G. P2. $15.00.

HOLBROOK, Richard. *Handbook of Co K 7th Regiment 107 Infantry NYNG.* 1940. 1st. lg 8vo. VG. E6. $40.00.

HOLDEN. *The River Sorrow.* 1994. NY. Delacorte. 1st. F/F. H11. $30.00.

HOLDSTOCK, Robert. *Earthwind.* 1977. London. Faber & Faber. 1st. VF/VF. T2. $25.00.

HOLDSTOCK, Robert. *Lavondyss.* 1988. NY. Morrow. 1st. F/F dj. M19. $25.00.

HOLLAND, Cecelia. *Two Ravens.* 1977. np. Knopf. 1st. rem mk. F/F dj. M19. $25.00.

HOLLAND, Isabelle. *Marchington Inheritance.* 1979. Rawson Wade. 1st. VG/VG. G8. $10.00.

HOLLAND, Rupert Sargent. *Drake's Lad.* 1929. np. Century. 1st. bookplate. VG. M19. $25.00.

HOLLAND, Rupert Sargent. *Historic Railroads.* 1927. Phil. ils. 343p. G. B18. $22.50.

HOLLAND, Rupert Sargent. *Historic Ships.* 1926. Phil. MaCrae Smith. 1st. 8vo. 390p. F/fair box. B11. $50.00.

HOLLAND, Tom. *Lord of the Dead.* 1995. Pocket. 1st. VG/dj. L1. $35.00.

HOLLANDER, Bernard. *Mental Functions of the Brain: An Investigation...* 1901. Putnam. Pres. 38 pl. 512p. panelled gr cloth. G. G1. $100.00.

HOLLANDER, E. *Plastic Und Medizin.* 1912. Enke. 576p. new cloth. G7. $125.00.

HOLLANDER, John. *Head of the Bed.* 1974. Boston. Godine. 1st. sgn. VG/sans. R14. $35.00.

HOLLENSTEINER, Mary. *The Dynamics of Power in a Philippine Municipality.* 1963. Quezon City. Univ of the Philippines. 2nd prt. stiff wrp. 227p. F. P1. $25.00.

HOLLING, Clancy. *Claws of the Thunderbird: A Tale of Three Lost Indians.* 1928. Joliet, IL. P. F. Volland & Co. 1st. ils by author. 8vo. dk bl cloth. 128p. G. D6. $25.00.

HOLLINGSHEAD, Greg. *The Roaring Girl.* 1995. NY. Putnam. ARC. F/wrp. B2. $25.00.

HOLM, Bill. *Northwest Coast Indian Art: Analysis of Form.* 1978. Vancouver. Douglas McIntyre. later prt. 115p. VG/dj. P4. $35.00.

HOLMAN, Sheri. *Stolen Tongue.* 1997. Atlantic. 1st. NF/NF. G8. $20.00.

HOLMAN, Sheri. *The Dress Lodger.* 1999. London. Hodder & Stoughton. 1st. trade pb orig. VF/pict wrp. T2. $20.00.

HOLMBERG, Rita. *Farm Journal's Greatest Dishes from the Oven.* 1977. S&S. G/dj. A16. $7.00.

HOLME, Bryan. *The Enchanted Garden: Images of Delight.* 1982. NY. Oxford Univ Press. F in dj. B26. $12.50.

HOLMES, Oliver Wendell. *Dissertation of Acute Pericarditis.* 1937. Boston. 1st. 12mo. 39p. full vellum. A13. $75.00.

HOLMES, Oliver Wendell. *Professor at the Breakfast Table.* 1860. Ticknor Fields. 1st/1st issue. 410p. brn pebbled cloth. VG. G7. $125.00.

HOLMES, Oliver Wendell. *Urania: A Rhymed Lesson.* 1846. Boston. William D. Ticknor. 1st. thin octavo. orig bl cloth. NF. R3. $50.00.

HOLSTROM, J. E. *Modern Blacksmithing and Horseshoeing.* 1938. Chicago. Frederick J. Drake & Co. 1st. VG. O3. $25.00.

HOLT, Hazel. *Mrs. Mallory Wonders Why.* 1995. Dutton. 1st Am ed. NF/NF. G8. $15.00.

HOLT, Hazel. *Mrs. Mallory's Shortest Journey.* 1994. St. Martin. 1st Am ed. NF/NF. G8. $15.00.

HOLT, Samuel; see Westlake, Donald E.

HOLT, Stephen. *Whistling Stallion.* nd. Grosset Dunlap. Famous Horse Stories series. VG. O3. $15.00.

HOLT, Victoria; See Hibbert, Eleanor Alice.

HOLTON, Hugh. *Chicago Blues.* 1996. Forge. 1st. sgn. F/F. G8. $20.00.

HOLTON, Hugh. *Left Hand of God.* 1999. Forge. 1st. sgn. F/F. G8. $25.00.

HOLTON, Hugh. *Red Lightning.* 1998. Forge. 1st. sgn. F/F. G8. $25.00.

HOLTZER, Susan. *Bleeding Maize and Blue.* 1996. NY. St. Martin. 1st. sgn. VF/VF. T2. $25.00.

HOLWAY, John. *Voices from the Great Black Baseball Leagues.* 1975. Dodd Mead. 1st. photos/stats. F/VG. P8. $125.00.

HOLZER, Erika. *Eye for an Eye.* 1993. NY. Tor. 1st. F/F. H11. $30.00.

HOLZER, Hans. *The New Pagans.* 1972. Doubleday. 203p. VG. B29. $8.00.

HOM, Ken. *Quick and Easy Cooking.* 1990. San Francisco. Chronicle Books. 1st. 8vo. VG/VG. A28. $15.95.

HOME, Jessie. *Happiest Christmas.* 1955. Racine, WI. Whitman. ils Irma Wilde. VG+. B36. $7.00.

HOMES, A. M. *The Safety of Objects.* 1990. NY. Norton. 1st. F/F. H11. $25.00.

HOMEWOOD, Harry. *O God of Battles.* 1983. NY. Morrow. 1st. F/F. H11. $25.00.

HONG, Lily and Mary. *Microwave to the Orient.* 1976. CA. Self published. 1st. 24mo. spiral. sgn by authors. VG. A28. $9.95.

HONGXUN, Yang. *Classical Gardens of China.* 1982. Van Nostrand Reinhold. 1st. ils/index. 128p. VG/dj. H10. $27.50.

HONIG, Donald. *Baseball When the Grass Was Real.* 1975. Coward McCann. 1st. photos. VG/G. P8. $30.00.

HONIG, Donald. *Illusions.* 1974. Doubleday & Co. 1st. G+/chip. S19. $30.00.

HONIG, Donald. *Sword of General Englund.* 1996. Scribner. 1st. NF/NF. G8. $17.50.

HOOD, Margaret Page. *Scarlet Thread.* 1956. Coward. 1st. VG/VG. G8. $25.00.

HOOD, William. *Spy Wednesday.* 1986. NY. WW Norton. 1st. VF in dj. M15. $50.00.

HOOKER, Worthington. *Natural History for the Use of Schools & Families.* 1864. NY. 382p. G. A17. $15.00.

HOOPES, Donelson F. *American Watercolor Painting.* 1977. Watson Guptill. 1st. ils/biographies. 208p. F/dj. D2. $70.00.

HOORMAN, Ferdinand. *Rivals on the Ridge.* 1930. NY. Frederick Pustet. 1st. NF/dj. M15. $65.00.

HOOTON, Earnest Albert. *Up from the Ape.* 1946. Macmillan. revised. 788p. xl. G. S5. $15.00.

HOPE, Bob. *Five Women I Love.* 1966. Doubleday. 1st. 255p. F. W2. $15.00.

HOPE, Laura Lee. *The Bobbsey Twins in the Country.* 1950. NY. Grosset & Dunlap. G in torn dj. A16. $7.00.

HOPE, Laura Lee. *The Bobbsey Twins in Tulip Land.* 1949. NY. Grosset & Dunlap. G in chip dj. A16. $8.00.

HOPE, Laura Lee. *The Bobbsey Twins on an Airplane Trip.* 1933. NY. Grosset & Dunlap. G in chip dj. A16. $8.00.

HOPE, Laura Lee. *The Bobbsey Twins Solve a Mystery.* 1934. NY. Grosset & Dunlap. G in chip dj. A16. $8.00.

HOPKINS, J. Castell. *Canadian Annual Review of Public Affairs: 1916.* (1917). Toronto. Annual Review Pub. 929p. half morocco/marbled brd. A26. $65.00.

HOPKINS, Lee Bennett. *To Look at Any Thing.* 1978. HBJ. 1st. VG/dj. S5. $8.00.

HOPKINS, Mary Alden. *Dr. Johnson's Lichfield.* 1952. Hastings. 1st. inscr. dj. H13. $45.00.

HOPKINS, Robert. *Darwin's South America.* 1969. John Day. 1st. 224p. dj. F3. $20.00.

HORGAN, Paul. *Great River: Rio Grande in North American History.* 1954. Rinehart. 1st. ils/maps. NF/NF case. B19. $65.00.

HORGAN, Paul. *Of America East & West: Selections from Writings Of...* 1982. FSG. 1st. 393p. F/F. B19. $25.00.

HORLER, Sydney. *Curse of Doone.* 1930. Mystery League. 1st Am. VG. G8. $10.00.

HORN, Barbar Lee. *Joseph Papp: A Bio-Biography.* 1992. NY. Greenwood. 409p. VG. C5. $20.00.

HORN, Maurice. *Comics of the American West.* 1977. Winchester. G/dj. A19. $25.00.

HORNBY, Nick. *About a Boy.* (1998). NY. Riverhead. 1st Am ed. F/F. B3. $15.00.

HORNBY, Nick. *High Fidelity.* 1995. NY. Riverhead. 1st. Author's first novel. F/F. H11. $20.00.

HORNIG, Doug. *Dark Side.* 1986. Mysterious. 1st. inscr. NF/NF. G8. $12.50.

HORNIG, Doug. *Deep Dive.* 1988. Mysterious. 1st. F/NF. G8. $10.00.

HORNSBY, Wendy. *Midnight Baby.* 1993. NY. Dutton. 1st. VF/VF. T2. $20.00.

HORNSBY, Wendy. *Telling Lies.* 1992. NY. Dutton. AP. F in wrp. B2. $20.00.

HORNUNG, E. W. *Camera Fiend.* 1911. Scribner. 1st Am ed. G-VG. G8. $35.00.

HORRICKS, Raymond. *Dizzy Gillespie & The Be-Bop Revolution.* 1984. Spellmount/Hippocrene. 1st. ils brd. NF/sans. A14. $10.50.

HORSMAN, R. *War of 1812.* 1969. NY. 1st. 286p. NF/dj. M4. $28.00.

HORSTING, Jessica. *Midnight Graffiti.* 1992. Warner. 1st. F/VG. S18. $15.00.

HORTON, Andrew. *The Films of George Roy Hill.* 1984. NY. Columbia Univ Press. 1st. F/NF. O11. $25.00.

HOSKYNS, Tam. *The Talking Cure.* 1997. London. Hamish Hamilton. 1st. author's 1st novel. sgn. VF/VF. T2. $30.00.

HOSMER, James K. *Color Guard: Being a Corporal's Notes...* 1864. Boston. Walker Wise. 1st. 244p. G. M10. $32.50.

HOSPITAL, Janette Turner. *Charades.* 1989. Toronto. McClelland & Stewart. 1st. F/VG dj. A26. $20.00.

HOUGH, Emerson. *Purchase Price.* 1919. Bobbs Merrill. 415p. G. G11. $18.00.

HOUGH, Emerson. *Story of the Cowboy.* 1897. NY. Appleton. 1st. ils. 349p. cloth. D11. $50.00.

HOUGH, Lt. Col. Frank O. & Major John A. Crown. *The Campaign on New Britain.* 1952. Washington. pict brds. photos. maps. 220p. G+. B18. $95.00.

HOUGH, S. B. *Bronze Perseus.* 1959. Walker. 1st Am ed. VG/VG. G8. $10.00.

HOUGH, S. B. *Dear Daughter Dead.* 1965. Gollancz. 1st British ed. VG/VG. G8. $20.00.

HOUGHTON, Claude. *This Was Ivor Trent.* 1935. London. Heinemann. 1st. F in dj w/chip at spine. M15. $150.00.

HOURANI, Albert. *History of the Arab People.* 1991. Cambridge. 1st. 8vo. ils/maps. NF/dj. Q2/W1. $30.00.

HOURANI, George Faldo. *Arab Seafaring in the India Ocean in Ancient & Medieval...* 1951. Princeton. 1st. ils/maps. 131p. cloth. VG/dj. Q2. $33.00.

HOUSE, Home D. *Wildflowers...* 1935. Macmillan. 4to. 362p. VG. H10. $65.00.

HOUSE, Julius T. *John G. Neihardt: Man & Poet.* 1920. Wayne. NE. FH Jones. 1st. ftspc. F. A18. $25.00.

HOUSEHOLD, Geoffrey. *Courtesy of Death.* nd. Atl. Little, Brn. 1st Am ed. VG+/VG. G8. $10.00.

HOUSEHOLD, Geoffrey. *The Days of Your Fathers.* 1987. London. Michael Joseph. 1st. F/dj. M15. $45.00.

HOUSEHOLD, Geoffrey. *The Last Two Weeks of Georges Rivac.* 1978. London. Michael Joseph. 1st. F/dj. M15. $45.00.

HOUSEHOLD, Geoffrey. *The Third Hour.* 1938. Boston. Little, Brn. 1st Am ed. F in dj. M15. $150.00.

HOUSEWRIGHT, David. *Penance.* 1995. Woodstock. Countryman. 1st. sgn. VF in dj. M15. $80.00.

HOUSEWRIGHT, David. *Penance.* 1995. Coup. 1st. sgn. F/F. G8. $70.00.

HOUSTON, James. *Running West.* 1989. NY. Crown. 1st. NF/clip. T11. $25.00.

HOUSTON, Pam. *Cowboys Are My Weakness.* 1992. Norton. 1st. F/dj. M25. $150.00.

HOUSTON, S. D. *Maya Glyphs.* 1990. Berkley. 2nd. 4to. wrp. F3. $15.00.

HOUZE, Robert A., Jr. *Cloud Dynamics.* 1993. San Diego. Academic Press. 2nd printing. b/w photos & figures. 8vo. 573p. VG/gilt ils cloth. K5. $75.00.

HOWARD, Cecil. *Pizarro & The Conquest of Peru.* 1968. Harper. Am Heritage Pub. 2nd. 153p. F3. $15.00.

HOWARD, Clark. *Arm.* 1967. LA. Sherbourne. 1st. F/F. H11. $40.00.

HOWARD, Denis. *New South Wales System.* 1970. VG/wrp. S1. $10.00.

HOWARD, James L. *Seth Harding, Mariner: Naval Picture of the Revolution.* 1930. New Haven. 8vo. 301p. bl cloth. VG. S17. $15.00.

HOWARD, Maureen. *Facts of Life.* 1978. Little, Brn. 1st. NF/dj. S13. $12.00.

HOWARD, Maureen. *Natural History.* 1992. Norton. 1st. 393p. F/NF. S15. $10.00.

HOWARD, Robert E. *Black Vulmea's Vengeance.* 1976. West Kingston. Donald m. grant. 1st hc ed. VF/VF. T2. $25.00.

HOWARD, Robert E. *Robert E. Howard: Selected Letters 1923 – 1930.* 1989. West Warwick. Necronomicon Press. 1st. Glenn Lord. editor. VF/pict wrp. T2. $12.00.

HOWARD, Robert E. *The Tower of the Elephant.* 1975. West Kingston. Donald M. Grant. 1st hc ed. VF/VF. T2. $45.00.

HOWARD, Robert West. *Great Iron Trail: Story of 1st Transcontinental Railroad.* 1962. Putnam. 376p. VG/dj. J2. $45.00.

HOWARD, Sanford. *Seventh Annual Report State Board Agriculture of Michigan.* 1868. Lansing. Kerr. 490p. cloth. VG. A10. $30.00.

HOWE, Julia Ward. *Reminiscences 1819 – 1899...* 1900. Boston. Houghton Mifflin. 8vo. 465p. tan cloth. F. B14. $55.00.

HOWE, Lucien. *Bibliography of Hereditary Eye Defects.* 1928. Cambridge. 58p. wrp. A13. $40.00.

HOWE, Mark DeWolfe. *Harvard Volunteers in Europe: Personal Records...* 1916. Cambridge. Harvard. 1st. 12mo. 263p. gilt cloth. VG. C14. $22.00.

HOWELLS, William Dean. *The Leatherwood God.* 1916. NY. Century. 1st. octavo. orig brick red cloth. ils Henry Raleigh. F. spine browned. R3. $30.00.

HOWES, Barbara. *From the Green Antilles. Writings of the Caribbean.* nd. NY. Macmillan. 1st. ep maps. 368p. G. F3. $10.00.

HOWLETT-WEST, Stephanie. *The Inter Galactic Price Guide to Science Fiction, Fantasy and Horror 1997.* 1997. Modesto. T2. $38.00.

HOWSDEN, Gordon. *Collecting Cigarette & Trade Cards.* 1995. London. New Cavendish books. 1st. 4to. 152p. AN. H1. $25.00.

HOYLE, Fred. *On Stonehenge.* 1977. San Francisco. W. H. Freeman. 1st. b/w photos. text figures. folding map. 8vo. 157p. VG in pict cloth. K5. $15.00.

HOYT, Edwin P. *The Battle for Leyte Gulf. The Death Knell of the Japanese Fleet.* 1972. NY. Weybright and Talley. cloth. 375p. VG. P1. $10.00.

HOYT, Richard. *Bigfoot.* 1993. NY. Tor. 1st. NF/VG+. G8. $10.00.

HOYT, Richard. *Marimba.* 1962. NY. Tor. 1st. NF/NF. G8. $12.50.

HUBIN, Allen J., editor. *Best Detective Stories of the Year 1973.* 1973. Dutton. 1st. VG+/VG+. G8. $15.00.

HUDDLE, David. *The High Spirits.* (1989). Boston. Godine. 1st. F/F. B3. $40.00.

HUDDLE, David. *The Tenorman.* (1995). San Francisco. Chronicle. 1st. F/F. B3. $25.00.

HUDSON, Arthur Palmer. *Folksongs of Mississippi.* 1936. Chapel Hill. U of NC Press. 1st. uncommon wk. especially in dj. NF in chip dj. B2. $175.00.

HUDSON, W. H. *Birds in Town and Village.* 1920. NY. Dutton. 1st Am ed. ils by E.J. Detmold. 323p. G+. D6. $65.00.

HUEBNER, Fredrick D. *Methods of Execution.* 1994. S&S. 1st. NF/NF. G8. $12.50.

HUGHART, Barry. *Bridge of Birds: A Novel of an Ancient China that Never Was.* 1984. NY. St. Martin. 1st. VF/VF. T2. $35.00.

HUGHES, Langston. *Not Without Laughter.* 1930. Knopf. 1960s reprint of early Hughes title. NF/clip dj. M25. $35.00.

HUGHES, Langston. *The Best of Simple.* 1961. Hill and Wang. simultaneous pb issue. VG/lightly soiled wrps. M25. $25.00.

HUGHES, Langston. *The Langston Hughes Reader.* 1958. NY. Braziller. 1st. VF in VG dj. D10. $40.00.

HUGHES, Ted. *Birthday Letters.* 1998. NY. FSG. 1st. F/F. M23. $35.00.

HUGO, Richard. *The Real West Marginal Way.* 1986. NY. Norton. 1st. sgn. F/F. O11. $75.00.

HUME, H. Harold. *Azaleas and Camellias.* 1954 (1953). NY. rev ed. VG in chip dj. B26. $12.50.

HUMMEL, Roy O. Jr. *More Virginia Broadsides Before 1877.* 1975. Richmond. Virginia State Library. 1st. orig printed wrp. 106p. VG. M8. $37.50.

HUMPHREY, Derek. *Dying with Dignity: Understanding Euthanasia.* 1992. NY. Carol Publishing. 1st. NF/NF. A28. $8.95.

HUMPHREY, William. *Farther Off from Heaven.* 1977. NY. Knopf. 1st. F/F. D10. $45.00.

HUMPHREY, William. *My Moby Dick.* 1978. NY. Doubleday. 1st. F/F. D10. $45.00.

HUMPHREYS, Josephine. *Dreams of Sleep.* 1984. NY. Viking. 1st. author's 1st novel. NF/VG+ some wear. M23. $25.00.

HUMPHREYS, Martha. *Until Whatever.* 1991. NY. Clarion Books. VG/VG. A28. $7.95.

HUNGERFORD, Edward. *Wells Fargo. Advancing the American Frontier.* 1949. NY. Random House. 1st prt. G/G. O3. $45.00.

HUNSAKER, Phillip. *Art of Managing People.* 1980. NY. Prentice Hall. sc. G+. A28. $5.95.

HUNT, E. Howard. *Ixtapa.* 1994. Fine. 1st. review. photo. NF/NF. G8. $12.50.

HUNT, Rachel McMaster Miller. *William Penn. Horticulturist.* 1953. Pittsburgh. Univ of Pittsburgh Press. ltd ed of 999 copies. ils. VG. B26. $16.00.

HUNT, Violet. *The Wife of Rossetti: Her Life and Death.* (1932). London. The Bodley Head Ltd. rubs on top of spine. G. B15. $90.00.

HUNTER, David. *The Dancing Savior.* 1999. Nashville. Cumberland House. 1st. sgn. VF/VF. T2. $25.00.

HUNTER, Evan. *Find the Feathered Serpent.* 1979. Boston. Gregg Press. reissue. 1st thus. author's 1st novel. sgn. VF/VF. T2. $35.00.

HUNTER, Evan. *Privileged Conversation.* 1996. NY. Warner Books. 1st. ARC. sgn. VF/VF. T2. $20.00.

HUNTER, Fred. *Presence of Mind.* 1994. NY. Walker. 1st. author's 1st novel. sgn. VF/VF. T2. $35.00.

HUNTER, Fred. *Ransom for an Angel.* 1995. NY. Walker. 1st. VF/VF. T2. $25.00.

HUNTER, Stephen. *Black Light.* 1996. Doubleday. 1st. NF/NF. G8. $15.00.

HUNTER, Stephen. *Dirty White Boys.* 1994. Harper & Row. 1st. F/F. G8. $17.50.

HUNTER, Stephen. *The Day Before Midnight.* 1989. NY. Bantam. 1st. VF/dj. M15. $100.00.

HUNTER, Stephen. *The Second Saladin.* 1982. NY. Morrow. 1st. NF/NF dj. M19. $25.00.

HUNTER, Stephen. *Time to Hunt.* 1998. NY. Doubleday. 1st. sgn. VF/VF. T2. $25.00.

HURSTON, Zora Neale. *Seraph on the Suwanee.* 1948. Scribners. ARC. VF in worn wrps. M25. $400.00.

HURT, Wesley. *The Interrelationships Between the Natural Environment & Four Sambaquies, Coast of Santa Catarina, Brazil.* 1974. Bloomington, IN. Indiana Univ Museum. 1st. 4to. 42p. G/wrp. F3. $10.00.

HURWITZ, Greg Andrew. *The Tower.* 1999. NY. S&S. ARC. F in wrp. B2. $25.00.

HUTCHCRAFT, Ronald. *Peaceful Living in a Stressful World.* 1985. Guideposts. 209p. VG/VG. B29. $7.50.

HUXLEY, Aldous. *Heaven and Hell.* 1956. London. Chatto & Windus. 1st English ed. NF/NF. M25. $75.00.

HUXLEY, Aldous. *Music at Night & Other Essays.* 1931. np. Chatto & Windus. 1st English ed. NF/NF dj. M19. $85.00.

HUXLEY, Aldous. *The Devils of Loudun.* 1952. Harper & Bros. 1st Am ed. sgn on ffep. NF/chipped dj. M25. $45.00.

HUXLEY, Aldous. *The Genius and the Goddess.* 1955. London. Chatto & Windus. 1st. NF/lightly worn dj. M25. $75.00.

HUXLEY, Aldous. *The Perennial Philosophy.* 1945. Harper. 1st Am ed. NF/rubbed. sunned dj. M25. $45.00.

HUXLEY, Julian. *The Living Thoughts of Darwin.* 1939. Philadelphia. red cloth. VG. B26. $17.50.

HUXLEY, Laura Archera. *Between Heaven and Earth: Recipes for Living and Loving.* 1975. FSG. 1st. NF/clip dj. M25. $25.00.

HUYGEN, Wil. *Gnomes.* 1976. NY. Harry Abrams. folio. VG/VG. A28. $37.95.

YAMS, E. *Great Botanical Gardens of the World.* 1969. 1st Am ed. decor cloth. folio. G. B26. $37.50.

YATT, J. Philip. *The Heritage of Biblical ith.* 1965. Bethany. 361p. VG/VG. B29. .50.

YDER, William. *From Baltimore to Baker reet: Thirteen Sherlockian Studies.* 1996. oronto. Metropolitan Toronto Reference brary. 2nd printing. VF/VF. T2. $24.00.

YER, Richard. *Riceburner.* 1986. NY. ribners. 1st. F/F. T2. $8.00.

YMAN, Laurence J, Publisher. *Atlanta 996 Official Commemorative Book of the entennial Olympic Games.* 1996. San rancisco. Woodford Pub. 1st. sc. AN. A28. 2.95.

YNE, Cutcliffe. *The Lost Continent.* 1974. hiladelphia. Oswald Train. reissue. 1st us. VF/VF. T2. $20.00.

— I —

ACOCCA & NOVAK, Iacocca. *1984.* antam. 1st Canadian/14th prt. F/NF. T12. 5.00.

ACOPI, Robert. *Earthquake Country.* 1973. ane Books. A19. $20.00.

BANEZ, V. *Blasco. Sonnica.* 1918. Duffield. F. M2. $10.00.

BERLIN, Dollie. *Basque Web.* 1982. Buffalo. NY. sgn. photos. A19. $35.00.

BUSE, Masuji. *Black Rain.* 1987. Tokyo. pb. 00p. K3. $20.00.

DONE, Christopher. *Glorious American ood.* 1985. NY. Random. 1st. VG/dj. A16. 37.50.

GLEHART, Charles W. *A Century of rotestant Christianity in Japan.* 1959. Charles . Tuttle. 1st. 384p. VG/worn dj. B29. $29.00.

LES, Greg. *The Quiet Game.* 1999. NY. utton. 1st. sgn. VF/VF. T2. $26.00.

LLER, Lawrence R. *Shots at Whitetails.* 1970. nopf. dj. A19. $20.00.

LLMAN, Harry R. *Unholy Toledo.* 1985. olemic. 361p. cloth. VG+/dj. M20. $45.00.

LOWITE, Sheldon. *Centerman from Quebec.* 974. Hastings. 1st. ils. F/F. P8. $25.00.

MPEY, Oliver. *Chinoiserie: Impact of Oriental Styles on Western Art.* 1977. Scribner. ls. 208p. F. W3. $52.00.

ING, Dean. *Ransom of Black Stealth One.* 1989. St Martin. 1st. F/dj. M2. $22.00.

INGALLS, Eleazar Stillman. *Journal of a Trip to California by Overland Route.* 1979. Ye Galleon. 1st thus. F/sans. A18. $17.50.

INGE, William. *Faith & Its Psychology.* 1910. Scribner. 248p. VG. B29. $6.50.

INGE, William. *Four Plays.* 1958. Random. 1st. F/VG. M19. $35.00.

INGE, William. *Summer Brave: and Eleven Short Plays.* 1962. Random. 1st. F/dj. Q1. $60.00.

INGERSOL, R. *Battle Is the Pay Off.* 1943. TN. 1st. 217p. VG/G. S16. $18.50.

INGERSOLL, Ernest. *Crest of the Continent.* 1885. Chicago. ils. 344p. O8. $18.50.

INGHAM, Vicki. *Christmas with Southern Living.* 1991. Oxmoor. VG. A16. $15.00.

INGHAM, Vicki (ed). *Christmas with Southern Living 1991.* 1991. AL. Oxmoor House. VG. A28. $10.95.

INGLIS, William. *George F. Johnson & His Industrial Democracy.* 1935. Huntington. 1st. 306p. gr cloth. F/dj. B22. $6.50.

INGOLD, C.T. *Spore Discharge in Land Plants.* 1939. London. Oxford. 1st. 12mo. ils. NF. A22. $15.00.

INGRAM, Rex. *Mars in the House of Death.* 1939. Knopf. 1st. ils Carlos Ruano Llopis. VG. P8. $25.00.

INGWERSEN, Will. *Classic Garden Plants.* 1975. London. Hamlyn. 192p. dj. A10. $35.00.

INNES, Clive. *Cacti & Succulents.* 1990. NY. ils/28 photos. M. B26. $20.00.

INNES, Hammond. *North Star.* 1974. London. Collins. 1st. VG/VG. P3. $22.00.

INNES, Hammond. *Sea & Island.* 1967. Knopf. 1st. 288p. cloth. VG+/dj. M20. $15.00.

INNES, Hammond. *Strange Land.* 1954. London. 1st. VG/dj. T9. $25.00.

INNES, Michael. *Appleby & Honeybath.* 1983. NY. Dodd. 1st. F/F. H11. $30.00.

INNES, Michael. *Appleby Intervenes.* 1965. Dodd Mead. Omnibus ed. F/dj. M15. $35.00.

INNES, Michael. *The Ampersand Papers.* 1978. NY. Dodd. Mead. 1st Am ed. F/F. T2. $8.00.

INNES, Michael. *Weight of the Evidence.* 1943. Dodd Mead. 1st (precedes Eng). F/NF. M15. $85.00.

IONIDES, C. J. P. *Mambas & Man Eaters.* 1965. NY. 1st. VG/dj. B5. $35.00.

IRELAND, Orlin L. *Plants of the Three Sisters Region.* Oregon Cascade Range. 1968. Eugene. photos/drawings. 130p. sc. F. B26. $15.00.

IRELAND, Tom. *Great Lakes — St. Lawrence: Deep Waterway to the Sea.* 1934. Putnam. 1st. 223p. cloth. NF/dj. M20. $40.00.

IRONSIDE, H. A. *Epistles to the Galatians.* 1950. Loizeaux. 235p. VG. B29. $9.00.

IRONSIDE, H. A. *Notes on the Minor Prophets.* 1950. Loizeaux. 464p. G. B29. $9.00.

IRONSIDE, H. A. *The Mission of the Holy Spirit and Praying in the Holy Spirit.* 1950. Loizeaux. 64p. VG. B29. $9.00.

IRVINE, Joan. *How to Make Pop-Ups.* 1987. 4to. ils. F/F. A4. $65.00.

IRVINE, Van. *Anybody Can be Slow.* 1989. NY. Irvine Pub. dj. A19. $35.00.

IRVING, David. *Trail of the Fox: Search for True Field Marshal Rommel.* 1977. NY. 1st. photos/biblio/index. 496p. xl. dj. S16. $20.00.

IRVING, John. *A Prayer for Owen Meany.* 1989. Morrow. 1st. F/F. T11. $35.00.

IRVING, John. *A Prayer for Owen Meany.* 1989. NY. Morrow. 1st. F/F. H11. $80.00.

IRVING, John. *A Son of the Circus.* 1994. NY. Random. 1st. F/F. H11. $35.00.

IRVING, John. *Cider House Rules.* (1985). NY. Morrow. F/F. B3. $50.00.

IRVING, John. *Hotel New Hampshire.* 1981. NY. Dutton. 1st. sgn. F/F. T11. $65.00.

IRVING, John. *Trying to Save Piggy Sneed.* 1993. Toronto. Knopf. 1st. F/F. D10. $110.00.

IRVING, Washington. *Crayon Miscellany.* 1895. Putnam. Holly Ed. 2 vol. ils. teg. maroon cloth. NF. $10.00.

IRVING, Washington. *Legend of Sleepy Hollow.* 1906. Indianapolis. 1st. ils Arthur Keller. VG/dj/worn mc box. B5. $45.00.

IRVING, Washington. *Tales from Washington Irving's Traveller.* 1913. Lippincott. 1st. ils George Hood. 235p. G+. P2. $65.00.

IRVING, Washington. *Washington Irving's Tales of the Supernatural.* 1982. Stemmer. 1st. F/dj. M2. $18.00.

IRVWIN, Wallace. *North Shore.* 1932. Houghton Mifflin. 1st. inscr. bl cloth. NF/VG. B4. $150.00.

IRWIN, Constance. *Fair Gods & Stone Faces.* 1963. St Martin. 1st. 346p. dj. F3. $25.00.

IRWIN, Hale. *Play Better Golf than Hale Irwin.* 1980. London. Octopus. 1st. inscr. VG. A23. $45.00.

IRWIN, R. *British Bird Books: An Index to British Ornithology AD 1481.* 1951. London. Grafton. 8vo. 398p. cloth spine. VG+. M12. $60.00.

IRWIN, Robert. *The Arabian Nightmare.* 1987. London. Viking. 1st hc ed. VF/VF. T2. $35.00.

ISAACS, A.C. *Ascent of Mount Shasta: 1856.* 1952. LA. Glen Dawson. 1/250. decor brd/cloth spine. D11. $125.00.

ISAACS, Edith J.R. *Negro in the American Theatre.* 1947. Theatre Arts. 1st. VG/dj. M25. $125.00.

ISADORA, Rachel. *Lili on Stage.* 1995. NY. Putnam. 1st. sm 4to. F/F. C8. $25.00.

ISH-KISHOR, Shulamith. *Boy of Old Prague.* 1963. Pantheon. 1st. 8vo. F/NF. C8. $75.00.

ISHAM, Fredric A. *Social Buccaneer.* 1910. Grosset Dunlap. VG. M2. $12.00.

ISHERWOOD, Christopher. *Christopher and His Kind 1929 – 1939.* 1976. FSG. 1st. sgn. VF/VF. M25. $75.00.

ISHERWOOD, Christopher. *Condor & the Cows.* 1949. Random. 1st. xl. F/NF. B2. $35.00.

ISHERWOOD, Christopher. *Memorial.* 1946. New Directions. 1st. F/VG. M19/T9. $65.00.

ISHIGURO, Kazuo. *Pale View of the Hills.* 1982. Putnam. 1st Am. author's 1st book. F/F. B3. $225.00.

ISHIGURO, Kazuo. *The Remains of the Day.* 1989. NY. Knopf. 1st Am ed. F/F. B2. $85.00.

ISHIGURO, Kazuo. *The Unconsoled.* 1995. London. Faber & Faber. 1st. sgn. VF/VF. T2. $65.00.

ISLER, Alan. *The Bacon Fancier.* 1997. NY. Viking. 1st. UP. F. D10. $10.00.

ISSAWI, Charles. *Egypt: An Economic & Social Analysis.* 1947. London/NY/Toronto. Oxford. 1st. 219p. G. W1. $25.00.

ITTEN, Hans. *Alpine Garden of Schynige Platte.* 1955. Berne. photos. 48p. sc. dj. B26. $15.00.

IVES, Morgan; See Bradley, Marion Zimmer.

IVES, Paul. *Domestic Geese & Ducks.* 1947. Orange Judd. 372p. cloth. VG. A10/M12. $25.00.

IZENBERG, Jerry. *Great Latin Sports Figures.* 1976. Doubleday. 1st. F/VG. P8. $20.00.

IZZI, Eugene. *Bad Guys.* 1988. NY. St. Martin. 1st. sgn & inscr. F/F. A24. $80.00.

IZZI, Eugene. *Invasions.* 1990. Bantam. 1st. NF/NF. G8. $17.50.

IZZI, Eugene. *Matter of Honor.* 1997. Avon. 1st. F/F. G8. $20.00.

IZZI, Eugene. *The Take.* 1987. NY. St. Martin. 1st. author's 1st novel. sgn. F/VG+. A24. $60.00.

— J —

JACKSON, Everett. *Burros & Paintbrushes; a Mexican Adventure.* 1985. College Station. Texas A & M Univ Press. 1st. 151p. G/G. F3. $15.00.

JACKSON, Giles. *Witch's Moon.* 1941. NY. Dial. 1st. F in VG dj. M15. $45.00.

JACKSON, Jon A. *Dead Folks.* 1996. NY. Atlantic Monthly Press. 1st. sgn. VF/VF. T2. $25.00.

JACKSON, Jon A. *Deadman.* 1994. NY. Atlantic Monthly Press. 1st. sgn. VF/VF. T2. $30.00.

JACKSON, Jon A. *Go by Go.* 1998. Tucson. Dennis McMillan. 1st. sgn. VF in dj. M15. $35.00.

JACKSON, Jon A. *The Blind Pig.* 1978. NY. Random House. 1st. VF/dj. M15. $250.00.

JACKSON, Richard. *Black Literature & Humanism in Latin America.* 1988. Athens. Univ of Ga Press. 1st. 166p. G/G. F3. $15.00.

JACOB, Dorothy. *Flowers in the Garden. Personal Reminiscence of 70 Years Gardening.* 1969. NY. VG in dj. B16. $9.00.

JACOB, Helen Pierce. *The Secret of th Strawbridge Place.* 1976. NY. Atheneum. VG in dj. A16. $5.00.

JACOBS, Jonnie. *Evidence of Guilt.* 1997 Kensington. 1st. sgn. F/F. G8. $17.50.

JACOBS, Jonnie. *Murder Among Neighbors* 1994. Kensington. 1st. sgn. F/F. G8. $25.00.

JACOBS, Jonnie. *Murder Among Neighbors* 1994. Kensington. 1st. sgn. F/F. G8. $25.00.

JACOBS, Jonnie. *Shadow of a Doubt.* 1996 Kensington. 1st. sgn. F/F. G8. $20.00.

JACOBS, Nancy Baker. *The Silver Scalpe* 1993. NY. Putnam. 1st. VF/VF. T2. $7.00.

JAFFE, Rona. *An American Love Story.* 1990 Delacorte Press. 1st. sgn. F/F. S19. $35.00.

JAHN, Janheinz. *Neo African Literature. History of Black Writing.* 1969. NY. Grove 1st. F/F. B2. $25.00.

JAKEMAN, Jane. *Let There be Blood.* 1997 London. Headline. 1st. author's 1st novel VF/VF. T2. $25.00.

JAMES, Hartwell. *The Man Elephant, A Book of African Fairy Tales.* 1906. Philadelphia Henry Altemus co. ils by John R. Neill 12mo. gray cloth w/pict designs. 103p. NF D6. $65.00.

JAMES, J. Robert. *Sandman.* 1997. Soho. 1st Am ed. sgn. F/F. G8. $25.00.

JAMES, Neill. *Dust on My Heart. Petticoa Vagabond in Mexico.* 1951. NY. Scribner. sgn 310p. G/G. F3. $20.00.

JAMES, P. D. *Certain Justice.* 1997. Knopf 1st Am ed. VG+/NF. G8. $15.00.

JAMES, P. D. *Children of Men.* nd. Knopf 1st Am ed. VG+/VG+. G8. $15.00.

JAMES, P. D. *Death of an Expert Witness.* 1977. NY. Scribners. 1st. F/F. H11. $70.00.

JAMES, P. D. *Devices & Desires.* 1990. NY Knopf. 1st. F/F. H11. $20.00.

JAMES, P. D. *Original Sin.* 1995. NY. Knopf. 1st Am ed. NF/NF. G8. $10.00.

JAMES, P. D. *Unnatural Causes.* 1967. NY Scribners. 1st. NF/NF. H11. $125.00.

JAMES, Robert. *Board Stiff.* 1951. Crime Club. 1st. VG/G. G8. $20.00.

MES, Russell. *Count Me Out.* 1997. NY. ul Play. 1st. F/F. H11. $20.00.

MES, William. *The Varieties of Religious xperience.* 1929. Modern Library. 526p. G/torn dj. B29. $5.00.

NCE, J. A. *Failure to Appear.* 1993. NY. orrow. 1st. sgn. VF/VF. T2. $30.00.

NCE, J. A. *Name Withheld.* 1996. NY. orrow. 1st. sgn. VF/VF. T2. $25.00.

NCE, J. A. *Tombstone Courage.* 1994. NY. orrow. 1st. sgn. F/NF. A24. $30.00.

NOWITZ, Tama. *American Dad.* 1981. Y. Putnam. 1st. F/F. H11. $65.00.

RDINE, Quintin. *Skinner's Festival.* 1995. Martin. 1st Am ed. NF/NF. G8. $15.00.

Y, Dave. *The Irving Berlin Songography, 07 – 1966.* 1969. New Rochelle. Arlington ouse. 1st. NF/wrps. B2. $50.00.

AN, Marcel, Ed. *The Autobiography of rrealism.* 1980. NY. Viking. 450p. F/F. B2. 0.00.

CKS, Michael. *Belladonna at Belstone.* 99. London. Headline. 1st. sgn. VF/VF. 2. $38.00.

CKS, Michael. *Squire Throwleigh's Heir.* 99. London. Headline. 1st. sgn. VF/VF. 2. $38.00.

FFERS, H. Paul. *The Adventure of the alward Companions.* 1978. NY. Harper & ow. 1st. F/VF. T2. $25.00.

FFREYS, J. G. *Thistlewood Plot.* 1987. alker. 1st Am ed. F/NF. G8. $10.00.

FFRIES, Roderic. *Benefits of Death.* 1964. odd. Mead. 1st Am ed. G/G. G8. $17.50.

NKINS, J. Geraint. *The English Farm agon, Origins and Structure.* 1981. Newton bbott. David & Charles. F in dj. O3. $45.00.

NKINS, Peter. *A Walk Across America.* 79. NY. Morrow. 1st. F/NF. M23. $25.00.

NKINSON, Michael. *Beasts Beyond the re.* 1980. NY. Dutton. 1st. F/F. H11. $30.00.

NNINGS, Jessie & Edward Norbeck, ditors. *Prehistoric Man in the New World.* 64. IL. Univ of Chicago Press. 1st. 633p. /chipped dj. F3. $30.00.

NNINGS, Maureen. *Except the Dying.* 97. NY. St. Martin. 1st. VF in dj. M15. 5.00.

JENSEN, Jens. *Siftings.* 1939. Chicago. Ralph Fletcher Seymour. 1st. issued in plain tissue dj (lacking here). folding maps. NF. B2. $50.00.

JEPSEN, Glenn L. *Genetics, Paleontology, and Evolution.* 1949. Princeton. ils. 474p. VG in spine faded dj. B26. $27.50.

JEPSON, Willis Linn. *A Flora of Western Middle California.* 1901. Berkeley. 1st. several tears. else VG. B26. $49.00.

JETER, K. W. *Death Arms.* 1987. Bath. Avon. Morrigan Publications. 1st. VF/VF. T2. $30.00.

JETER, K. W. *In the Land of the Dead.* 1989. Bath. Avon. Morrigan Publications. 1st. VF/VF. T2. $30.00.

JHABVALA, Ruth Prawer. *Heat & Dust.* 1976. NY. Harper & Row. 1st. F/dj. D10. $55.00.

JICKLING, David & Elaine Elliott. *Facades & Festivals of Antigua: A Guide to Church Fronts & Celebrations.* 1989. Antigua. Casa Del Sol. 1st. b/w photos ils. biblio. drawings. 75p. G/wrp. F3. $10.00.

JOBSON, Hamilton. *Evidence You Will Hear.* 1975. Scribners. 1st Am ed. VG+/VG+. G8. $15.00.

JOHNSON, Brian. *With Mallets Aforethought.* 1994. Otto Penzler. 1st. review copy. F/F. G8. $20.00.

JOHNSON, Charles and Patricia Smith. *Africans in America: America's Journey Through Slavery.* 1998. Harcourt Brace. UP. F/wrp. M25. $45.00.

JOHNSON, Denis. *Fiskadoro.* 1985. NY. Knopf. 1st. VF/F. H11. $40.00.

JOHNSON, Denis. *Resuscitation of a Hanged Man.* (1990). NY. FSG. 1st. F/F. B3. $40.00.

JOHNSON, George Clayton. *Twilight Zone: Scripts & Stories.* 1996. Santa Monica. Streamline pictures. 1st trade ed. sgn. VF/pict wrp. T2. $20.00.

JOHNSON, H. U. *Western Reserve Centennial Souvenir.* 1896. Cleveland. 1st. 100p. VG. B18. $37.50.

JOHNSON, Harold and Grace. *Broken Rosary.* 1959. Bruce. 1st. VG/VG+. G8. $10.00.

JOHNSON, Joyce. *In the Night Cafe.* 1989. Dutton. ARC. NF/decor wrps. M25. $25.00.

JOHNSON, Paul E. *Personality and Religion.* 1957. Abingdon. 297p. VG/ ex lib. B29. $8.50.

JOHNSTON, Annie Fellows. *Little Colonel Stories: Second Series.* 1933. Boston. L. C. Page. VG in poor dj. A16. $12.00.

JOHNSTON, Isabel. *The Jeweled Toad.* (1907). Bobbs-Merrill. spine wear. slight soil; ils W.W. Denslow. G+. B15. $250.00.

JOHNSTON, Paul. *The Bone Yard.* 1998. London. Hodder & Stoughton. 1st. VF/VF. T2. $45.00.

JONES, Bradshaw. *Death Deals in Diamonds.* 1965. Walker. 1st Am ed. VG/VG. G8. $10.00.

JONES, Chester. *Costa Rica & Civilization in the Caribbean.* 1935. Madison. Univ of Wisconsin. 172p. G/wrp. F3. $30.00.

JONES, David. *In Parenthesis.* 1961. NY. Chilmark Press. 1st Am ed. intro by T.S. Elliot. F in NF dj. B2. $50.00.

JONES, Diana Wynne. *Deep Secret.* 1997. London. Gollancz. 1st. VF/VF. T2. $35.00.

JONES, Diana Wynne. *Minor Arcana.* 1996. London. Gollancz. 1st. VF/VF. T2. $35.00.

JONES, Gayl. *The Healing.* 1998. Boston. Beacon Press. 1st. Natl Book Award finalist. F/F. M23. $40.00.

JONES, Hettie. *How I Became Hettie Jones.* 1990. Dutton. 1st. F/dj. M25. $25.00.

JONES, James. *Go to the Widowmaker.* 1967. NY. Delacorte. 1st. F/NF. H11. $35.00.

JONES, James. *The Merry Month of May.* 1970. NY. Delacorte. octavo. blk cloth. ines in green. top edge stained yellow. gr ep. pict dj. F/F. R3. $40.00.

JONES, John Beauchamp. *Rebel War Clerk's Diary at Confederate States Capital.* 1866. Lippincott. 2 vol in 1. 1st. cloth. M8. $450.00.

JONES, Johnny. *Now Let Me Tell You....* 1950. Columbus, OH. Dispatch Printing. sgn by author. 212p. VG in soiled dj. B18. $12.50.

JONES, Le Roi. *Home: Social Essays.* 1966. Morrow. ARC. w/review slip. NF/torn dj. M25. $100.00.

JONES, Matthew. *Blind Pursuit.* 1997. FSG. UP. F/decor wrp. M25. $25.00.

JONES, Matthew. *The Cooter Farm.* 1992. NY. Hyperion. 1st. author's 1st book. UP. F. F10. $10.00.

JONES, Stephen, editor. *Shadows Over Innsmouth*. 1994. Minneapolis. Fedogan & Bremer. 1st. collection of 17 stories. VF/VF. T2. $35.00.

JONES, Thom. *Cold Snap*. (1995). Boston. Little, Brn. 1st. author's second book. F/F. B3. $15.00.

JONES, Thom. *Cold Snap*. 1995. Boston. Little, Brn. 1st. F/F. B2. $30.00.

JONES, Thom. *The Pugilist at Rest*. (1993). Boston. Little, Brn. 1st. author's 1st book. F/F. B3. $40.00.

JONES, Walter. *Sandbar*. 1982. Casper, WY. Basco Inc. AN. A19. $30.00.

JONG, Erica. *How to Save Your Own Life*. 1977. HRW. 1st. F/dj. B4. $65.00.

JONG, Erica. *Loveroot*. 1975. HRW. 1st. F/dj. R14. $35.00.

JONSSON, Reidar. *My Life as a Dog*. 1990. FSG. 1st Am. F/dj. C9. $30.00.

JORDAN, Lee. *Chain Reaction*. 1993. Walker. 1st Am ed. F/F. G8. $15.00.

JORDAN, Lee. *Deadly Side of the Square*. 1988. Walker. 1st Am ed. F/F. G8. $15.00.

JORDAN, Neil. *Night in Tunesia*. 1980. NY. George Braziller. 1st Am ed. F/NF. O11. $45.00.

JORDAN, Neil. *The Past*. 1992. NY. Knopf. 1st Am ed. F in F dj. D10. $50.00.

JORDAN, Pat. *A False Spring*. 1975. NY. Dodd Mead. VG+/VG clip. R16. $45.00.

JORDAN, Steve; Tom Scanlan. *Rhythm Man. Fifty Years in Jazz*. 1991. Ann Arbor. Univ of Michigan Press. ARC w/slip. F/F. B2. $35.00.

JORGGENSEN, Christine. *Curl Up and Die*. 1996. Walker. 1st. sgn. F/F. G8. $20.00.

JOSCELYN, Archie. *The Golden Bowl*. 1931. Internat Fiction Lib. VG/fair. P3. $25.00.

JOSCELYN, Archie. *The Golden Bowl*. 1931. Cleveland. Int Fiction Library. 1st. VG w/chip. M15. $35.00.

JOSEPH, Alison. *The Hour of Our Death*. 1995. London. Headline. 1st. VF/VF. T2. $25.00.

JOSEPH, Mark. *Typhoon*. 1991. S&S. 1st. sm 4to. 300p. F/dj. W2. $30.00.

JOSEPH, Michael. *Charles, The Story of a Friendship*. 1952. NY. Prentice Hall. 1st Am. 110p. NF/dj. D4. $35.00.

JOSEPHY, Alvin M., Jr. *Red Power. The American Indians' Fight for Freedom*. 1971. NY. American Heritage Press. 1st. F in NF dj. B2. $25.00.

JOSLIN, E. P. *The Treatment of Diabetes Mellitus with Observations on the Disease Based Upon Thirteen Hundred Cases*. 1917. Philadelphia. np. 2nd. ils in color and b&w. 559p. VG. B14. $75.00.

JOSS, Morag. *Fearful Symmetry*. 1999. London. Hodder & Stoughton. 1st. VF/VF. T2. $38.00.

JUDD, Bob. *Indy*. 1990. London. Pan books. 1st. sgn. VF/VF. T2. $25.00.

JUDD, Bob. *Monza*. 1992. NY. Morrow. 1st. F/F. H11. $25.00.

JUDD, Bob. *Silverstone*. 1993. NY. Morrow. 1st Am ed. sgn inscr by Judd. VF/VF. T2. $20.00.

JUNG, C. G. *Psychology & Alchemy*. 1953. NY. 1st Eng trans. 563p. A13. $100.00.

JUNGER, Ernst. *Details of Time*. 1995. NY. 1st. trans Neugroschel. edit Hervier. dj. T9. $10.00.

JUST, Ward. *The Congressman Who Loved Flaubert*. 1973. Atlantic. Little, Brn. 1st. Jacket lightly worn. F/dj. M25. $45.00.

JUST, Ward. *To What End: Report from Vietnam*. 1968. Houghton Mifflin. 3rd. 209p. NF/dj. R11. $20.00.

JUSTICE, Donald. *Donald Justice Reader*. 1991. Middlebury College. 1st. VG/dj. M17. $15.00.

JUSTIS, May. *Big Log Mountain*. 1958. Henry Holt. stated 1st. 184p. xl. VG. B36. $16.00.

— K —

KABERRY, Charles. *Our Little Neighbors*. 1921. London. Milford/Oxford. 1st. ils Detmold. 4to. blk lettered rose cloth. R5. $375.00.

KAEWERT, Julie Wallin. *Unsolicited*. 1994. St Martin. 1st. sgn. author's 1st book. F/F. B3. $35.00.

KAFAROFF, Bruce. *Deadwood Gulch*. 1941. Knopf. dj. A19. $35.00.

KAGAWA, Toyohiko. *Before the Daw* 1924. Doran. 1st Am. F/VG+. B4. $175.00.

KAGAWA, Toyohiko. *Grain of Wheat*. 191 Harper. 150p. VG/dj. W3. $38.00.

KAHANE, Meir. *They Must Go*. 198 Grosset Dunlap. 1st. 282p. VG/G+. S $25.00.

KAHL, Virginia. *Gunhilde's Christmas Boc* 1972. NY. Scribners. 1st ed. sm 4to. gree cloth w/color ils same dj. ils by Kahl. 32 NF/NF. D6. $60.00.

KAHL, Virginia. *How Many Dragons a Behind the Door*. 1977. NY. Scribners. Week Reader book club ed. sm 4to. green clo w/color ils. 32p. NF/VG. D6. $65.00.

KAHL, Virginia. *Maxie*. 1956. Scribner. 1s VG/dj. M5. $30.00.

KAHLER, Heinz. *The Art of Rome and H Empire*. 1964. Greystone. 256p. VG/VG. B2 $16.00.

KAHN, Arthur. *Brownstone. A Novel of Ne York*. 1953. NY. Independence Pub. 1st. wr 370p. lightly worn. B2. $30.00.

KAHN, David. *Codebreakers*. 1967. NY. 1s VG/VG. B5. $40.00.

KAHN, E. J. Jr. *Fighting Divisions: Histori of Each US Army Combat....* 1980. W maps/order of battle. 218p. VG. S16. $30.0

KAHN, Edgar M. *Cable Car Days in Sa Francisco*. 1940. Stanford. 8vo. 124p. AN/d K7. $35.00.

KAHN, James. *Timefall*. 1987. St Martin. 1s F/dj. M2. $15.00.

KAHN, Michael. *Due Diligence*. (1995). N Dutton. 1st. F/F. B3. $10.00.

KAHN, Roger. *Boys of Summer*. 1972. N Harper & Row. 1st. VG/VG. R16. $50.00.

KAI-SHEK, Chaing. *Soviet Russia in Chin* 1957. FSC. 1st. NF/dj. B35. $22.00.

KAINS, Josephine; See Goulart, Ron.

KAINS, M. G. *Plant Propagation*. 192 Orange Judd. 322p. VG. A10. $24.00.

KAKONIS, Tom. *Criss Cross*. 1990. NY. S Martin. 1st. VF/VF. T2. $15.00.

KAKONIS, Tom. *Double Down*. 1991. N Dutton. 1st. F/F. D10. $35.00.

KAKONIS, Tom. *Shadow Counter*. 1993 NY. Dutton. 1st. F/F. H11. $25.00.

KALER, Anne K. *Cordially Yours, Brother Cadfael.* 1998. Bowling Green. Bowling Green State Univ Popular Press. 1st. VF/VF. T2. $36.00.

KALPAKIAN, Laura. *Beggars & Choosers.* 1978. Little, Brn. 1st. F/F. H11. $15.00.

KALTON, M. *To Become a Sage: 10 Diagrams on Sage Learning by Yi Yoegye.* 1988. Columbia. 1st. annotated trans. 278p. F/dj. W3. $52.00.

KAMAU, Agymah. *Pictures of a Dying Man.* 1999. Minneapolis. Coffee House. ARC. wrp. F. B2. $25.00.

KAMINSKY, Stuart M. *A Fine Red Rain.* 1987. NY. Scribners. 1st. VF/dj. M15. $45.00.

KAMINSKY, Stuart M. *Buried Caesars.* 1989. NY. Mysterious Press. 1st. VF/VF. T2. $15.00.

KAMINSKY, Stuart M. *Exercise in Terror.* 1985. St Martin. 1st. F/dj. M15. $45.00.

KAMINSKY, Stuart M. *Lieberman's Folly.* 1991. NY. St. Martin. 1st. F/F. A24. $15.00.

KAMINSKY, Stuart M. *Poor Butterfly.* 1990. NY. Mysterious Press. 1st. inscr. VF in dj. M15. $45.00.

KAMINSKY, Stuart M. *Rostnikov's Vacation.* 1991. NY. Scribners. 1st. VF/VF. T2. $15.00.

KAMINSKY, Stuart M. *The Man Who Walked Like a Bear.* 1990. NY. Scribners. 1st. VF/VF. T2. $15.00.

KAMINSKY, Stuart M. *Tomorrow Is Another Day.* 1995. NY. Mysterious Press. 1st. VF/VF. T2. $15.00.

KAMINSKY, Stuart M. *You Bet Your Life.* 1978. St Martin. 1st. F/VG. M19. $25.00.

KAMM, Minnie Watson. *Fifth Pitcher Book.* 1956. Century. 2nd/2nd prt. 209p. VG. H1. $32.50.

KANAMATSU, Kenryo. *Amitabha: Life of Naturalness.* 1949. Kyoto. Otani. sgn. 75p. navy brd. VG. B11. $35.00.

KANE, Elisha Kent. *Adrift in the Arctic Ice Pack.* 1916. Outing. 420p. F. A17. $20.00.

KANE, Frank. *Bullet Proof.* 1951. Washburn. 1st. VG/VG. M22. $55.00.

KANE, Harnet T. *New Orlean's Woman.* 1946. Doubleday. sgn. VG/VG. B11. $20.00.

KANE, Henry. *Report for a Corpse.* 1948. S&S. 1st. 245p. VG/dj. M20. $15.00.

KANE, Ruth. *Wheat, Glass, Stone and Steel. The Story of Massillon.* 1976. np. 1st. ils. sm dent to cover edge. 194p and 13p appendix. VG+. dj rubbed. B18. $35.00.

KANE, Stephanie. *The Phantom Gringo Boat.* 1994. DC. Smithsonian Institution Press. 1st. b/w photo ils. 241p. G/G. F3. $30.00.

KANIEL, Michael. *Judaism.* 1979. Blandford. 160p. VG/dj. S3. $23.00.

KANON, Joseph. *Los Alamos.* 1997. NY. Broadway. 1st. VF/VF. H11. $45.00.

KANON, Joseph. *The Prodigal Spy.* 1998. NY. Broadway. 1st. sgn. VF/VF. T2. $26.00.

KANTOR, Alfred J. *Book of Alfred J. Kantor.* 1971. McGraw Hill. 1st. F/F. B35. $15.00.

KANTOR, MacKinlay. *Andersonville.* 1955. 1st. full-p map. 279p. O8. $12.50.

KANTOR, MacKinlay. *Lobo.* 1957. NF/NF. A4. $20.00.

KANTOR, MacKinlay. *Signal 32.* 1950. Random. 1st. NF/VG. M22. $20.00.

KAO, George. *Chinese Wit & Humor.* 1974. NY. intro Lin Yutang. 347p. F. W3. $45.00.

KAPLAN, Howard. *Chopin Express.* 1978. Dutton. 1st. author's 2nd book. F/F. H11. $25.00.

KAPUSCINSKI, Ryszard. *Shah of Shahs.* 1985. HBJ. 1st Am. 8vo. 152p. VG/dj. W1. $18.00.

KARDINER, Abram. *Bio-Analysis of the Epileptic Reaction.* 1932. NY. Psychoanalytic Quarterly. 1st separate. inscr. VG. G1. $75.00.

KAREN, Ruth. *Questionable Practices.* 1980. NY. Harper & Row. 1st. F/F. H11. $20.00.

KARIG, Walter. *War in the Atomic Age.* 1946. Wm Wise. 63p+ads. VG/wrp. K3. $10.00.

KARLIN, Wayne. *Us.* 1993. NY. Holt. 1st. F/F. H11. $25.00.

KAROLEVITZ, Robert F. *Yankton: A Pioneer Past.* 1972. Aberdeen, SD. North Plains. dj. A19. $65.00.

KARP, Larry. *Music Box Murders.* 1999. write way. 1st. sgn. F/F. G8. $25.00.

KARPINSKI, Louis Charles. *History of Arithmetic.* 1925. Rand McNally. 1st. 8vo. 200p. VG/dj. K3. $50.00.

KARR, Mary. *Liar's Club.* 1995. Viking. 1st. sgn. F/F. A23. $50.00.

KARR, Mary. *The Liars' Club.* 1995. Viking. 1st. NF/NF. M25. $60.00.

KARSH, Yousuf. *Faces of Our Time.* 1971. Toronto. 1st. 48 portraits. 203p. G/G. A8. $50.00.

KARSH, Yousuf. *Karsh: Fifty Year Perspective.* 1983. Boston. 1st. sgn. VG/VG. B5. $75.00.

KARSNER, David. *Debs: His Authorized Life & Letters from Woodstock Prison...* 1919. Boni Liveright. 1st. VG. V4. $50.00.

KARTUN, Derek. *Tito's Plot Against Europe.* 1950. NY. International. 1st. VG in wrp. B2. $30.00.

KASDAN, Sara. *Mazel Tov Y'All.* 1968. Vanguard. G/dj. A16. $15.00.

KASHNER, Rita. *Bed Rest.* 1981. Macmillan. 1st. author's 1st novel. F/F. R13. $25.00.

KASMINOFF, Ross. *The Sentry.* 1995. NY. Crown. 1st. VF/VF. H11. $35.00.

KASTNER, Erich. *Puss in Boots.* 1957. Messner. 1st Am. ils Walter Trier. 66p. VG+/VG-. P2. $55.00.

KATES, George. *Chinese Household Furniture.* 1948. Harper. 1st. 125p. VG. W3. $86.00.

KATO, Ken. *Yamata: A Rage in Heaven.* 1990. NY. Warner. 1st. F/F. T12. $15.00.

KATZ, D. Mark. *Custer in Photographs.* 1990. NY. Bonanza. 2nd. ils. 141p. brd. dj. D11. $60.00.

KATZ, Friedrich. *Ancient American Civilizations.* 1972. NY. Praeger. 1st Eng. 386p. dj. F3. $30.00.

KATZ, John. *Death by Station Wagon.* 1993. Doubleday. 1st. F/dj. M15. $45.00.

KATZ, Michael J. *Last Dance in Redondo Beach.* 1989. NY. Putnam. 1st. inscr. VG/VG. G8. $10.00.

KATZENBACH, John. *Day of Reckoning.* 1989. Putnam. 1st. NF/F. T12. $15.00.

KAUFFMAN, Erle. *Trees of Washington. The Man — The City.* 1932. Washington, DC. sgn. spine. edges faded. else VG. B26. $21.00.

KAUFFMAN, Henry J. *American Pewterer.* 1970. NY. Nelson. 1st. sgn. F/F. B11. $35.00.

KAUFFMAN, Janet. *Body in Four Parts.* 1993. Graywolf. 1st. F/F. R13. $20.00.

KAUFFMAN, Janet. *Collaborators.* 1986. Knopf. 1st. F/F. R13. $20.00.

KAUFFMAN, Reginald Wright. *Share & Share Alike.* 1925. Chelsea. 1st. VG/dj. M2. $25.00.

KAUFFMAN, Russell. *Chihuahua.* 1952. Judy. 1st. 158p. dj. A17. $15.00.

KAUFMANN, Yehezkel. *The Religion of Israel.* 1960. Univ of Chicago. 486p. VG/torn dj. B29. $10.00.

KAVANAGH, Dan; See Barnes, Julian.

KAVANAUGH, James. *Crooked Angel.* 1970. LA. Nash. 1st. ils Elaine Havelock. 48p. F/F. D4. $30.00.

KAWABATA, Yasunari. *Snow Country & Thousand Cranes.* 1969. Knopf. Novel Prize ed. 147p. VG/dj. W3. $52.00.

KAY, Gertrude Alice. *Helping the Weatherman.* 1920. Volland. 1st. 8vo. ils brd/matching pub box. R5. $200.00.

KAY, Terry. *After Eli.* 1981. Houghton Mifflin. 1st. inscr. F/F. B4. $100.00.

KAY, Terry. *To Dance with the White Dog.* 1990. Peachtree. 1st. F/F. B4. $65.00.

KAY, William J. *Complete Book of Dog Health.* 1985. Macmillan. 1st. F/F. W2. $30.00.

KAYE, M. M. *Golden Afternoon.* 1998. NY. St. Martin. ARC. F. B2. $30.00.

KAYS, D. J. *The Horse.* 1953. NY. Barnes. VG. O3. $15.00.

KAYSER, Jacques. *Dreyfus Affair.* 1931. Covici Friede. 1st. 432p. G. B14. $45.00.

KAZAN, Elia. *Acts of Love.* 1978. Knopf. sgn. NF/dj. C9. $75.00.

KAZANTZAKIS, Nikos. *Symposium.* 1974. Crowell. 1st. F/F. B35. $18.00.

KEARNEY, Julian; See Goulart, Ron.

KEATING, Bern. *Invaders of Rome.* 1966. Putnam. dj. A19. $15.00.

KEATING, H. R. F. *Cheating Death.* 1994. NY. Mysterious Press. 1st Am ed. sgn. VF/VF. T2. $20.00.

KEATING, H. R. F. *Sherlock Holmes: The Man and His World.* 1979. London. Thames & Hudson. 1st. F/dj. M15. $45.00.

KEATING, H. R. F. *The Good Detective.* 1995. NY. Scribner. 1st Am ed. sgn. VF/VF. T2. $20.00.

KEATING, H. R. F. *Underside.* 1974. London. Macmillan. 1st. F/F. T12. $20.00.

KEATINGE, Maurice. *True History of Conquest of Mexico.* 1927. rpt 1800 London 1st. ils. 562p. cloth. F3. $25.00.

KEATS, Ezra Jack. *Snowy Day.* 1962. Viking. 1st/12th prt. obl 4to. VG. T5. $17.00.

KECK, L. Robert. *The Spirit of Synergy: God's Power and You.* 1978. Abingdon. 159p. VG/VG. B29. $5.50.

KEEL, B. C. *Cherokee Archaeology: Study of Appalachian Summit.* 1987. TN U. ils/maps. 312p. F. M4. $25.00.

KEELING, J. *Ask of the Beasts.* 1960. London. Blond. ils/photos. 203p. NF/VG. M12. $15.00.

KEEN, Mary. *Glory of the English Garden.* 1989. 1st Am. photos. VG/VG. M17. $30.00.

KEEN, Sam. *Faces of the Enemy: Reflections of the Hostile Imagination.* 1986. Harper Row. 1st. VG/VG. V4. $17.50.

KEENAN, Brian. *Evil Cradling: Five-Year Ordeal of a Hostage.* 1992. Viking. 1st Am. 297p. VG/dj. W1. $18.00.

KEENE, Carolyn. *Dana Girls: In the Shadow of the Tower (#3).* 1934. Grosset Dunlap. 1st. purple cloth. VG/ragged. M20. $95.00.

KEENE, Carolyn. *Nancy Drew Cookbook.* 1973. Grosset Dunlap. 1st. F. A16/T12. $20.00.

KEENE, Carolyn. *Nancy Drew: Mystery at the Ski Jump (#29).* 1952. Grosset Dunlap. 1st. 212p. VG/dj. M20. $60.00.

KEENE, Carolyn. *Nancy Drew: Secret of the Old Clock (#1).* 1930. Grosset Dunlap. 4th (1930D)/blank ep format. VG/tattered. M20. $350.00.

KEENE, John. *Pettibone's Law.* 1991. NY. Linden. 1st. F/F. H11. $30.00.

KEEP, Rosalind A. *Fourscore Years: History of Mills College.* 1932. Mills College. 1st. 1/990. inscr. F. O4. $30.00.

KEEPING, Charles. *Joseph's Yard.* 1969 Franklin Watts. 1st Am. ils. 4to. VG+/VG P2. $35.00.

KEHRER, Daniel M. *Profits in Precious Metals.* 1985. Times. 1st. 302p. NF/NF. W2 $30.00.

KEIFFER, Elisabeth. *Year in the Sun.* 1956 Indianapolis. Bobbs Merrill. 1st. 275p. G. F3 $15.00.

KEILLOR, Garrison. *Book of Guys.* 1993. Viking. 1st. sgn. F/F. R13. $35.00.

KEILLOR, Garrison. *Lake Wobegon Days* 1985. Viking. 1st. F/dj. N4/R14. $40.00.

KEITH, Agnes. *Bare Feet in the Palace.* 1955 Little, Brn. 370p. NF/VG. W3. $38.00.

KEITHLEY, George. *Donnor Party.* 1972 Braziller. 1st. VG/G+. O4. $15.00.

KELEMEN, P. *Art of the Americas.* 1969. NY. Crowell. G. A19. $15.00.

KELLAND, Clarence B. *Thirty Pieces of Silver.* 1913. Harper. 32p. VG. B29. $8.50.

KELLER, A. G. *Theatre of Machine.* 1965. Macmillan. 1st thus. 52 woodcuts. xl. K3. $30.00.

KELLER, David H. *Death & the Doctor.* 1940. S&S. 1st. VG. M2. $45.00.

KELLER, Nora Okja. *Comfort Woman.* (1997). NY. Viking. 1st. author's 1st book. F/F. B3. $15.00.

KELLER, W. Phillip. *Salt for Society.* 1981. Word. 151p. VG/VG. B29. $7.00.

KELLERMAN, Faye. *Day of Atonement.* 1991. NY. Morrow. 1st. VF/VF. T2. $20.00.

KELLERMAN, Faye. *Ritual Bath.* 1986. Arbor. 1st. author's 1st book. F/F. N4. $125.00.

KELLERMAN, John. *Billy Straight.* 1999. Random House. 1st. F/F. G8. $15.00.

KELLERMAN, Jonathan. *Bad Love.* 1994. NY. Bantam. 1st. VF/F. H11. $25.00.

KELLERMAN, Jonathan. *Blood Test.* 1986. NY. Atheneum. 1st. VF/VF. T2. $45.00.

KELLERMAN, Jonathan. *Over the Edge.* 1987. NY. Atheneum. 1st. F/VF. T2. $35.00.

KELLERMAN, Jonathan. *The Clinic.* 1997. NY. Bantam. 1st. F/VF. H11. $15.00.

ELLERMAN, Jonathan. *The Web.* 1996. Y. Bantam. 1st. VF/VF. T2. $9.00.

ELLERMAN, Jonathan. *Time Bomb.* 1990. Y. Bantam. 1st. F/F. T2. $7.00.

ELLERMAN, Jonathan. *When the Bough Breaks.* 1985. NY. Atheneum. 1st. author's 1st novel. F/VF. T2. $125.00.

ELLEY, Kitty. *Nancy Reagan.* 1991. S&S. 1st. NF/NF. W2. $35.00.

ELLEY, William Melvin. *Different Drummer.* 1962. Garden City. 1st. F/NF. L11. $125.00.

KELLOGG, Charles. *Driving the Horse in Harness.* 1980. Brattleboro. Stephen Greene. VG/VG. O3. $18.00.

KELLOGG, Mame Davis. *Tramp.* 1997. NY. Doubleday. 1st. sgn. VG/NF. G8. $12.50.

KELLOGG, Steven. *Liverwurst Is Missing.* 1981. Four Winds. 1st. VG+/VG. P2. $30.00.

KELLOGG, Vernon. *Muova the Bee.* 1920. Houghton Mifflin. ils Milo Winter/14 b&w pl. VG-. P2. $40.00.

KELLY, Celsus, ed. *La Australia Del Espiritu Santo. Two Volumes.* 1966. Cambridge. Hakluyt Society. 2nd series. No. 126 &127. plates. sketches. maps. pp272-446. VG. P4. $75.00.

KELLY, Dr. Fred. *America's Astronauts and Their Indestructible Spirit.* 1986. Blue Ridge Summit, PA. Aero. 1st ed. b/w photos. sm 4to. 179p. VG/chipped. torn dj. K5. $25.00.

KELLY, Edmond. *The Elimination of the Tramp.* 1908. NY. Putnam. 1st. NF. ex lib labels on ep. B2. $40.00.

KELLY, Eric. *Treasure Mountain.* 1937. Macmillan. 1st. 211p. VG/G. P2. $20.00.

KELLY, J. Reaney. *Quakers in the Founding of Anne Arundel County.* MD. 1963. Baltimore. MD Hist Soc. 1st. 146p. VG/dj. V3. $40.00.

KELLY, Nora. *Bad Chemistry.* 1994. St. Martin. 1st. NF/VG. G8. $15.00.

KELLY, Susan. *The Summertime Soldiers.* 1988. NY. Walker. 1st. F/F. T2. $20.00.

KELLY, Susan. *Trail of the Dragon.* 1988. NY. Walker. 1st. F/F. T2. $20.00.

KELLY, Susan B. *Kid's Stuff.* 1994. Scribners. 1st Am ed. NF/NF. G8. $17.50.

KELLY, Walt. *Deck Us All with Boston Charlie.* 1962. NY. 1st. NF/wrp. A11. $50.00.

KELLY, Walt. *Pogo Primer for Parents.* 1961. WA. 1st. 24p. VG+/wrp. A11. $60.00.

KELMAN, James. *Chancer.* 1985. Polygon. 1st. sgn. F/F. A24. $85.00.

KELNER, Toni L. P. *Tight as a Tick.* 1998. Kensington. 1st. sgn. F/F. G8. $22.50.

KELWAY, Christine. *Gardening on the Coast.* 1970. Abbot. England. VG in dj. B26. $15.00.

KEMAL, Yashar. *Seagull.* 1981. NY. 250p. F/dj. W3. $30.00.

KEMBLE, Edward W. *Blackberries & Their Adventures.* 1897. NY. Russell. 1st. obl 4to. pict brd. R5. $975.00.

KEMELMAN, Harry. *Nine Mile Walk.* 1967. Putnam. 1st. F/dj. M15. $60.00.

KEMELMAN, Harry. *Saturday the Rabbi Went Hungry.* 1966. Crown. 1st. sgn. VG/VG. G8. $12.50.

KEMELMAN, Harry. *Sunday the Rabbi Stayed Home.* 1969. Putnam. 1st. VG/VG-. G8. $12.50.

KEMELMAN, Harry. *Wednesday the Rabbi Got Wet.* 1976. Morrow. 1st. VG/VG. G8. $15.00.

KEMP, J. F. *Handbook of Rocks for Use without the Microscope...* 1911. Van Nostrand. 272p. G. D8. $22.00.

KEMPERMANN, Steve. *Lord of the Second Advent: A Rare Look Inside the Terrifying World of the Moonies.* 1981. regal. 175p. VG/VG. B29. $7.00.

KENAN, Randall. *Visitation of Spirits.* 1989. Grove. 1st. author's 1st book. dj. A24/L1. $35.00.

KENDALL, Charles Wye. *Private Men of War.* 1932. NY. McBride. 1st. ils. 308p. VG. B18. $35.00.

KENDRAKE, Carleton; See Gardner, Erle Stanley.

KENEALLY, Thomas. *A River Town.* (1995). NY. Talese. 1st Am ed. sgn by author. F/F. B3. $30.00.

KENEALLY, Thomas. *Gossip from the Forest.* 1976. NY. HBJ. 1st Am. NF/NF. D10. $60.00.

KENEALLY, Thomas. *Schindler's List.* 1982. S&S. 1st Am. F/clip. D10. $125.00.

KENEALLY, Thomas. *Victim of the Aurora.* 1978. NY. HBJ. 1st Am. NF/NF. D10. $45.00.

KENG, Hsuan. *Orders & Families of Malayan Seed Plants.* 1978. Singapore. revised. 8vo. 437p. A22. $35.00.

KENNEDY, Adam. *Debt of Honor.* 1981. NY. Delacorte. 1st. F/F. H11. $30.00.

KENNEDY, Hugh. *Everything Looks Impressive.* 1993. NY. Doubleday. 1st. F/F. H11. $30.00.

KENNEDY, John F. *Burden & The Glory.* 1964. Harper. 1st. VG+/dj. A20. $25.00.

KENNEDY, R. Emmet. *Black Cameos.* 1924. NY. Albert and Charles Boni. 1st. NF. slight spine wear. B2. $40.00.

KENNEDY, William. *Ink Truck.* 1984. Viking. 1st thus. sgn. F/F. B3. $40.00.

KENNEDY, William. *Legs.* 1975. CMG. 1st. author's 2nd novel. VG/G. M22. $50.00.

KENNEDY, William. *Riding the Yellow Trolley Car.* 1993. NY. Viking. 1st. sgn. F/F. D10. $40.00.

KENNEDY, William. *Very Old Bones.* 1992. Viking. 1st. sgn. F/F. R13. $45.00.

KENNEDY, X. J. *Forgetful Wishing Well.* 1985. Atheneum. 1st. ils Monica Incisa. NF/dj. D4. $35.00.

KENNEY, Susan. *In Another Country.* 1984. Viking. 1st. VG. T12. $15.00.

KENNEY, Susan. *One Fell Sloop.* 1990. NY. Viking. 1st. VF/F. H11. $20.00.

KENNINGTON, Donald, and Danny L. Read. *The Literature of Jazz. A Critical Guide.* 1980. Chicago. Am Lib Assoc. 2nd ed. wrps. F. clear plastic strip on spine. B2. $30.00.

KENRICK, Tony. *Faraday's Flowers.* 1985. Garden City. Doubleday. 1st. VF/dj. M15. $45.00.

KENT, Alexander. *A Tradition of Victory.* 1981. London. Hutchinson. 1st. F/dj. M15. $50.00.

KENT, Alexander. *Stand Into Danger.* 1980. London. Hutchinson. 1st. F/dj. M15. $50.00.

KENT, Bill. *Under the Boardwalk.* 1988. NY. Arbor. 1st. F/F. H11. $30.00.

KENT, Patricia. *American Woman & Alcohol.* 1967. HRW. 1st. 184p. VG/dj. A25. $18.00.

KENYON, Jane. *A Hundred White Daffodils.* 1999. St. Paul. Graywolf. ARC. wrp. F. B2. $25.00.

KEPHART, Horace. *Camp Cookery.* 1910. Outing. 1st. 154p. VG. E6. $25.00.

KERASOTE, Ted. *Bloodties.* (1993). NY. Random House. 1st. F/F. B3. $30.00.

KERFOOT, J. B. *American Pewter.* 1924. Houghton Mifflin. 1st. 4to. 239p. VG. T10. $125.00.

KERNODLE, George. *From Art to Theatre: Form & Convention in the Renaissance.* 1947. Chicago. 3rd. 255p. A17. $20.00.

KEROUAC, Jack. *Book of Dreams.* 1961. San Francisco. 1st. 1/5000. VG+. A11. $115.00.

KEROUAC, Jack. *On the Road.* 1957. Viking. 2nd. sgn. silvered blk cloth. G. B11. $150.00.

KERR, Baine. *Harmful Intent.* 1999. NY. Scribner. 1st. author's 1st novel. sgn. VF/VF. T2. $26.00.

KERR, Graham. *Galloping Gourmet.* 1970. Fremantle Internat. G. A16. $7.00.

KERR, Jessica. *Shakespeare's Flowers.* 1969. ils AO Dowden. ils. VG/VG. M17. $20.00.

KERR, Philip. *A Five Year Plan.* 1997. London. Hutchinson. 1st. sgn. VF in dj. M15. $85.00.

KERR, Philip. *Dead Meat.* 1993. London. Chatto & Windus. 1st. VF in dj. M15. $75.00.

KERR, Philip. *Gridiron.* 1995. London. Chatto & Windus. 1st. VF in dj. M15. $65.00.

KERR, Philip. *March Violets.* 1989. London. Viking. 1st. F in dj. M15. $200.00.

KERR, Philip. *Philosophical Investigation.* 1992. FSG. 1st Am. F/F. M25. $25.00.

KESEY, Ken. *Demon.* 1986. NY. Viking. 1st. VF/F. H11. $35.00.

KESEY, Ken. *Further Inquiry.* 1990. Viking. 1st. F/F. B35. $25.00.

KESEY, Ken. *Sailor Song.* 1992. np. Viking. 1st. inscr. F/F dj. M19. $35.00.

KESEY, Ken. *Sailor Song.* 1992. NY. Viking. 1st. sgn. F/F. O11. $50.00.

KESHISHIAN, Mark. *Guide to Oriental Rugs.* 1970. self pub. 1st. sgn pres. ils/maps. 134p. VG/dj. W1. $65.00.

KESSELL, John L. *Good News from Outer Space.* 1989. Tor. 1st. F/dj. M2. $27.00.

KESSLER, Edward. *Flannery O'Connor and the Language of the Apocalypse.* 1986. Princeton. 163p. VG. B29. $13.50.

KETCHUM, Richard. *Will Rogers: The Man & His Times.* 1973. Am Heritage. 415p. paisley bdg. AN/dj. H1. $20.00.

KETTER, David. *Imprisoned in a Tesseract: Life & Works of James Blish.* 1987. Kent State. 1st. F/dj. M2. $35.00.

KEUTNER, Herbert. *Sculpture: Renaissance to Rococo.* 1969. ils. VG/VG. M17. $25.00.

KEY, Alexander. *The Red Eagle.* 1930. NY. Wise Parslow. color ils by author. pict cloth. some edgewear. 120p. VG. B18. $25.00.

KEY, Alexander. *Wrath & the Wind.* 1949. Bobbs Merrill. 1st. F/VG+. B4. $75.00.

KEYES, Frances Parkinson. *Joy Street.* 1950. Messner. 1st. 490p. cloth. VG/dj. M20. $25.00.

KEYES, Frances Parkinson. *The Royal Box.* 1954. NY. Messner. 1st. F/F. H11. $45.00.

KEYES, Thomas E. *History of Surgical Anesthesia.* 1945. ils. VG. M17. $25.00.

KEYNES, Geoffrey. *Apologie & Treatise of Ambroise Pare.* 1952. Chicago. 1st. 8vo. 227p. VG/dj. K3. $45.00.

KEYNES, Geoffrey. *Blood Transfusion.* 1949. Baltimore. 1st Am. 574p. A13. $75.00.

KGOSITILE, Keorapetse. *My Name Is Afrika.* 1971. Doubleday. 1st. F/NF. B4. $125.00.

KHOSLA, G. *Himalayan Circuit.* 1956. London. ils/fld map. 233p. VG/dj. W3. $48.00.

KICH, C. J. *Year of Living Dangerously.* 1978. St. Martin. 1st Am. F/NF. B4. $125.00.

KIDDER, Tracy. *House.* 1984. Boston. Houghton Mifflin. 1st. 341p. F/F. D4. $25.00.

KIDDER, Tracy. *Old Friends.* 1993. Boston. Houghton Mifflin. 1st. F/F. A24. $20.00.

KIERAN, John. *American Sporting Scene.* 1941. NY. 1st. 212p. F/G. A17. $15.00.

KIGER, Robert. *Kate Greenaway: Catalogue of Exhibition...* 1980. Pittsburgh. Hunt. 106p. VG. A10. $35.00.

KIJEWSKI, Karen. *Copy Kat.* 1992. NY. Doubleday. 1st. F/F. D10. $50.00.

KIJEWSKI, Karen. *Honky Tonk Kat.* 1996. NY. Putnam. 1st. sgn. VF/VF. T2. $25.00.

KIJEWSKI, Karen. *Wild Kat.* 1994. Doubleday. 1st. sgn. VG/VG. A23. $40.00.

KIJIMA, Takashi. *Orchids.* 1989. NY. 203 pl. F/dj. S15. $12.00.

KIKUCHI, Sadao. *Treasury of Japanese Wood Block Prints: Ukiyo-E.* 1969. NY. Crown. ils. 423p. F/VG. W3. $165.00.

KILBOURN, Timothy. *The Triumphant Ministry.* 1914. Westminster. 107p. G. B29. $3.00.

KILDUFF, Peter. *That's My Bloody Plane.* 1975. Chester. Pequot. 1st. NF/VG+. T11. $40.00.

KILGO, James. *Inheritance of Horses.* 1994. Athens, GA. Univ of GA Press. sgn 1st ed. F/F. M23. $45.00.

KILLENS, John O. *Youngblood.* 1954. Dial. 1st. inscr/dtd 1955. VG/VG. B4. $225.00.

KILMER, Joyce. *Trees.* 1925. Doran. 1st thus. ils Elizabeth MacKinstry. F/VG. M5. $85.00.

KILMER, Nicholas. *A Place in Normandy.* 1997. NY. Henry Holt. 1st. sgn. VF/VF. T2. $25.00.

KILMER, Nicholas. *Dirty Linen.* 1999. NY. Henry Holt. 1st. sgn. F/F. T2. $25.00.

KILMER, Nicholas. *Man with a Squirrel.* 1996. NY. Henry Holt. 1st. sgn. VF/VF. T2. $20.00.

KILWORTH, Garry. *In Solitary.* 1977. London. Faber & Faber. 1st. author's 1st book. VF/VF. T2. $25.00.

KIMBER, Clarissa. *Martinique Revisited.* 1988. TX A&M. 458p. F. S15. $15.00.

KIMBROUGH, Emily. *Floating Island.* 1968. Harper. 1st. sgn. ils Vasiliu. 243p. VG/dj. A25. $20.00.

KIMBROUGH, Emily. *Now & Then.* 1972. Harper Row. 1st. sgn. ils Vasiliu. 176p. VG/dj. A25. $22.00.

KIMMEL, Eric A. *Boots and His Brothers.* 1992. NY. Holiday House. ils Kimberly Bulcken Root. AN. A28. $7.95.

KIMMEL, Stanley. *Kingdom of Smoke.* 1932. NY. Nicholas Brn. 1st. sgn. VG/VG. B2. $60.00.

KINCAID, Jamaica. *A Small Place.* (1988). NY. FSG. 1st. F/NF. lt edgewear. B3. $50.00.

KINCAID, Jamaica. *Annie John.* 1985. FSG. 1st. author's 2nd book. F/NF. B3. $100.00.

KINCAID, Jamaica. *At the Bottom of the River.* 1983. FSG. 1st. author's 1st book. F/F. L3. $75.00.

KINCAID, Paul. *Camellia Treasury.* 1964. NY. Hearthside. 8vo. 224p. A22. $25.00.

KINCK, Richard E. *Land of Room Enough & Time Enough.* 1953. Albuquerque. 1st. 135p. map ep. pict brd. VG+. F7. $35.00.

KINDER, Gary. *Ship of Gold in the Deep Blue Sea.* 1998. NY. Atlantic Monthly Press. 1st. VF/VF. T2. $27.50.

KING, Alexander. *Peter Altenberg's Evoctation of Love.* 1960. S&S. 1st. 175p. F/F. H1. $22.50.

KING, Bernard. *Strakadder.* 1985. London. 1st. F/dj. M2. $17.00.

KING, Billie Jean. *Billie Jean.* 1974. Harper Row. 1st. photos. VG/VG. P8. $20.00.

KING, Blanche Busey. *Under Your Feet: Story of American Mound Builders.* 1948. Dodd Mead. rpt. sgn. VG. B11. $30.00.

KING, Captain Charles. *Campaigning with Crook and Stories of Army Life.* 1890. NY. Harper & Bros. later printing. ils. lt soiling. edgewear. 295p. G. B18. $25.00.

KING, Charles. *Initial Experience.* 1909. Phil. Lippincott. A19. $35.00.

KING, Charles. *War Time Wooing.* 1888. NY. Harper & Bros. 1st. orig cloth. plates. historical novel. 195p. VG. M8. $25.00.

KING, Constance Eileen. *Encyclopedia of Toys.* 1978. Crown. 1st. 272p. NF/clip. C14. $25.00.

KING, Coretta Scott. *My Life with Martin Luther King.* Jr. 1969. HRW. 1st. NF/dj. M25. $25.00.

KING, Dick. *Ghost Towns of Texas.* 1953. Naylor. 1st. cloth. VG/dj. M20. $25.00.

KING, Elizabeth T. *Memoir with Extracts from Her Letters & Journal.* 1859. Baltimore. 1st. 128p. G. V3. $18.50.

KING, Laurie R. *A Darker Place.* (1999). NY. Bantam. 1st. sgn by author. F/F. B3. $40.00.

KING, Laurie R. *A Grave Talent.* 1995. London. Collins. 1st. VF/VF. H11. $100.00.

KING, Laurie R. *Letter of Mary.* 1996. St. Martin. 1st. NF/NF. G8. $30.00.

KING, Laurie R. *O Jerusalem.* 1999. NY. Bantam. 1st. sgn. VF/VF. T2. $28.00.

KING, M. J. *William Orlando Darby.* 1981. CT. 1st. ils. 219p. VG/VG. S16. $17.50.

KING, Martin Luther, Jr. *Why We Can't Wait.* 194. NY. Harper. 1st. F/F. B2. $40.00.

KING, Mrs. Francis. *Flower Garden Day by Day.* 1927. NY. Stokes. 1st. 209p. VG+/remnant. A25. $10.00.

KING, P. B. *Evolution of North America.* 1977. Princeton. fld map. 197p. NF/dj. D8. $30.00.

KING, Ross. *Domino.* 1995. London. Sinclair-Stevenson. 1st. VF in dj. M15. $100.00.

KING, Rufus. *Deadly Dove.* 1945. Crime Club. 1st. VG. G8. $12.50.

KING, Rufus. *Murder by Latitude.* 1930. Garden City. Doubleday. 1st. NF in dj. M15. $35.00.

KING, Stephen. *Carrie.* 1974. Doubleday. 1st. F/NF. B4. $750.00.

KING, Stephen. *Christine.* 1983. NY. Viking. 1st. F/F. H11. $55.00.

KING, Stephen. *Cujo.* 1981. NY. Viking. 1st. VF/VF. H11. $70.00.

KING, Stephen. *Dark Half.* 1989. Viking. 1st. F/F. M22. $30.00.

KING, Stephen. *Different Seasons.* 1982. Viking. 1st. F/dj. M2. $75.00.

KING, Stephen. *Dolores Claiborne.* 1993. NY. Viking. 1st. VF/VF. T2. $11.00.

KING, Stephen. *Firestarter.* 1980. NY. Viking. 1st. F/F. H11. $70.00.

KING, Stephen. *Four Past Midnight.* 1990. Viking. 1st. F/F. P3. $25.00.

KING, Stephen. *It.* 1986. NY. Viking. 1st. F/F. H11. $50.00.

KING, Stephen. *Misery.* 1987. NY. Viking. 1st. F/F. A24. $25.00.

KING, Stephen. *Needful Things.* 1991. NY. Viking. 1st. VF/VF. T2. $12.00.

KING, Stephen. *Night Shift.* 1978. Doubleday. 1st. F/F. M2. $675.00.

KING, Stephen. *Pet Cemetery.* (1983). Garden City. Doubleday. 1st. F/NF. lt rubbing. wear to corners. B3. $45.00.

KING, Stephen. *Pet Cemetery.* 1983. Doubleday. 1st. NF/dj. M21/R14. $30.00.

KING, Stephen. *Skeleton Crew.* 1985. NY. Putnam. 1st. VF/VF. H11. $60.00.

KING, Stephen. *The Eyes of the Dragon.* 1987. NY. Viking. 1st. F/F. D10. $45.00.

KING, Stephen. *The Eyes of the Dragon.* 1987. Viking. 1st. F/NF. Q1. $35.00.

KING, Stephen. *The Girl Who Loved Tom Gordon.* 1999. Scribner. 1st. F/F. S19. $40.00.

KING, Stephen. *The Green Mile, Parts 1 – 6.* 1996. NY. signet. 1st eds. pb orig. six volumes. VF/pict wrp. T2. $25.00.

KING, Stephen. *The Stand.* 1978. NY. Doubleday. 1st. NF/VG+. D10. $135.00.

KING, Stephen. *Thinner.* 1984. NAL. 1st. VG/VG. M22. $35.00.

KING, Stephen. *Tommyknockers.* 1987. NY. Putnam. 1st. F/F. H11. $40.00.

KING, Tabitha. *Small World.* 1981. NY. Macmillan. 1st. F/NF. T12. $40.00.

KING, W. C. *Campfire Sketches & Battlefield Echoes of '61 – 65.* 1889. 624p. ils red bdg. O8. $42.50.

KINGMAN, Lee. *Ilenka.* 1945. Boston. Houghton Mifflin. 1st. ils by Arnold Edwin Bare. sm 4to. red cloth w/blk map. 46p. VG/Fair dj. D6. $75.00.

KINGSBURN, Emart. *Gems of Promise.* 1924. Chelsea. 1st. F/dj. M2. $27.00.

KINGSLEY, Charles. *Hypatia.* 1897. Crowell. ils EH Garrett. 477p. VG+. M20. $35.00.

KINGSLEY, Charles. *Two Years Ago.* 1887. Macmillan. 1st. VG. M19. $45.00.

KINGSLEY, Charles. *Water Babies.* 1961. Gollancz. 1st thus. 222p. gr brd. VG. T5. $35.00.

KINGSMILL, Hugh. *Return of William Shakespeare.* 1929. Bobbs Merrill. 1st. VG/dj. M2. $40.00.

KINGSOLVER, Barbara. *Animal Dreams.* 1990. NY. Harper Collins. 1st. sgn. VF/VF. T2. $65.00.

KINGSOLVER, Barbara. *Homeland.* (1993). NY. Harper & Row. 1st. sgn by author. NF/F. B3. $150.00.

KINGSOLVER, Barbara. *Pigs in Heaven.* 1993. NY. Harper Collins. 1st. sgn. VF/VF. T2. $35.00.

KINGSOLVER, Barbara. *The Bean Trees.* 1989. London. Virago. 1st British ed. sgn. author's 1st book. F/F. O11. $125.00.

KINGSOLVER, Barbara. *The Poisonwood Bible.* 1998. NY. Harper Flamingo. ARC. wrp. F. B2. $30.00.

KINNELL, Galway. *Black Light.* 1966. Houghton Mifflin. 1st. sgn. VG/VG. R14. $60.00.

KINNELL, Galway. *Cemetary Angels.* 1980. Graywolf Broadside. author sgn. NF. V1. $65.00.

KINNEY, Charles; See Gardner, Erle Stanley.

KINO, Father. *Kino & the Cartography of Northwestern New Spain.* 1965. AZ Pioneers Hist Soc. 1/750. sm folio. ils. gilt red cloth. AN. R3. $385.00.

KINSELLA, W. P. *Dance Me Outside.* (1977). Boston. Godine. 1st. F/F. B3. $60.00.

KINSELLA, W. P. *Dixon Cornbelt League.* 1993. Harper Collins. 1st. sgn. F/F. A23. $40.00.

KINSELLA, W. P. *Iowa Baseball Confederacy.* 1986. Houghton Mifflin. 1st. F/F. T11. $30.00.

KINSELLA, W. P. *Shoeless Joe.* 1982. Boston. Houghton Mifflin. 1st ed. sgn & inscr. F/F. M25. $250.00.

KINSEY, Alfred C. *Sexual Behavior in the Human Female.* 1953. Phil. WB Saunders. 1st. F/dj. Q1. $125.00.

KINSOLVING, William. *Born with the Century.* 1979. NY. Putnam. 1st. F/F. H11. $25.00.

KINYON, Jeannette K. *Incredible Gladys Pyle.* 1985. Vermillion, SD. SD U. A19. $15.00.

KINZIE, Mary. *Autumn Eros & Other Poems.* 1991. Knopf. 1st. F/NF. R13. $15.00.

KIPLING, Rudyard. *Captains Courageous.* 1897. London. 1st. VG. T9. $100.00.

KIPLING, Rudyard. *Diversity of Creatures.* 1917. Macmillan. 1st. NF. Q1. $75.00.

KIPLING, Rudyard. *Jungle Book.* 1894. Century. 1st Am. 303p. VG+. P2. $100.00.

KIPLING, Rudyard. *Just-So Stories.* 1929. Doubleday Doran. mc pl. NF. M19. $35.00.

KIPLING, Rudyard. *Soldier Tales.* 1896. London. Macmillan. 1st. NF. Q1. $250.00.

KIRBY, Michael. *Happenings.* 1965. Dutton. 1st. F/NF. B2. $35.00.

KIRBY-PARRISH, L. *Greta & Peter in the Tea Cup.* 1915. Volland. ils. VG. M5. $38.00.

KIRK, Russell. *A Creature of the Twilight: His Memorials.* 1966. NY. Fleet Publishing. 1st. VG/VG. T2. $5.00.

KIRK, Russell. *Watchers at the Strait Gate.* 1984. Arkham. 1st. F/F. R10. $15.00.

KIRKEBY, Ed. *Ain't Misbehavin'. The Story of Fats Waller.* 1966. NY. Dodd. 1st. F/lightly used. clip dj. B2. $40.00.

KIRKWOOD, Edith Brown. *Animal Children.* 1913. Volland. 10th. ils MT Ross. 8vo. mc pict brd. pub box. R5. $250.00.

KIRKWOOD, J. E. *Northern Rocky Mountain Trees and Shrubs.* 1930. Stanford. 340p. 35 full pg photo plates. 87 other ils. remains of bookplate. else VG. B26. $37.50.

KIRKWOOD, James. *PS Your Cat Is Dead.* 1972. Stein Day. 1st. VG/dj. M25. $25.00.

KIRN, Walter. *My Hard Bargain.* 1990. Knopf. 1st. F/F. B35. $30.00.

KIRSHENBAUM, Binnie. *A Disturbance in One Place.* 1994. NY. Fromm. 1st. F/F w/pub postcard. A24. $25.00.

KIRSHENBAUM, David. *Mixed Marriage & the Jewish Future.* 1958. Bloch. 2nd. 144p. VG/VG. S3. $25.00.

KIRST, Hans Hellmut. *A Time for Truth.* 1974. NY. Coward. 1st. F/NF. H11. $25.00.

KIRST, Hans Hellmut. *Nights of the Long Knives.* 1976. London. 1st. dj. T9. $18.00.

KIRST, Hans Hellmut. *The 20th of July.* 1966. London. Collins. 1st. VF/dj. M15. $65.00.

KISSELL, M. L. *Basketry of the Papago & Pima Indians.* 1972. Rio Grande Classic. ils/photos. 264p. F. M4. $25.00.

KISSINGER, Henry. *Years of Upheaval.* 1982. Little, Brn. 1st. NF/NF. W2. $45.00.

KITELEY, Brian. *Still Life with Insects.* 1990. London. Bodley Head. 1st British ed. F/F. A24. $40.00.

KITTREDGE, Mary. *Dead and Gone.* 1989. Walker. 1st. F/NF. G8. $25.00.

KITTREDGE, Mary. *Rigor Mortis.* 1991. NY. St. Martin. 1st. NF/VG. G8. $10.00.

KITTREDGE, William. *Hole in the Sky.* 1992. NY. Knopf. 1st. sgn. F/F. O11. $50.00.

KITZINGER, Shelia. *Experience of Childbirth.* 1962. London. Gollancz. 1st. ils. VG/G. A25. $12.00.

KIZER, Carol. *The Ungrateful Children.* 1961. Bloomington. Indiana Univ Press. 1st. author's 1st book. inscr by author. NF/VG. O11. $35.00.

KJELGAARD, Jim. *Explorations of Pere Marquette.* (1951). Random/Landmark. 6th. 8vo. 179p. rebound. xl. G+. T5. $12.00.

KLAR, M. *Technology of Wood Distillation.* 1925. Van Notrand. 496p. VG. H1. $25.00.

KLARMANN, Andrew. *Fool of God.* 1912. Pustet. 1st. VG. M2. $10.00.

KLAUBER, L. M. *Rattlesnakes: Their Habits. Life Histories. Etc.* 1956. Berkeley. ils/figures/tables. 476p. cloth. VG+/G+. M12. $375.00.

KLAUSNER, Betty. *Focus Santa Barbara.* 1985. Santa Barbara. Santa Barbara Contemporary Arts Forum. 58p. wrp. D11. $25.00.

KLAVAN, Andrew. *Darling Clementine.* 1988. Sag Harbor. Permanent Press. 1st. sgn. VF/VF. T2. $30.00.

KLAVAN, Andrew. *Face of the Earth.* 1980. Viking. 1st. F/F. H11. $35.00.

KLAVAN, Andrew. *Son of Man.* 1988. Sag Harbor. Permanent Press. 1st. sgn. VF/VF. T2. $30.00.

KLAVAN, Andrew. *The Animal Hour.* 1993. NY. Pocket Books. 1st. sgn. VF/VF. T2. $25.00.

KLEES, F. *Pennsylvania Dutch.* 1950. NY. 1st. VG/VG. B5. $32.50.

KLEHR, Harvey. *Secret World of American Communism.* 1995. Yale. 1st. F/F. V4. $15.00.

KLEIN, Herman. *Herman Klein & the Gramophone.* 1990. Portland. Amadeus. 618p. F/dj. A17. $25.00.

KLEIN, Herman. *Star Altas.* 1893. London. 2nd. trans Edmund McClure. 72p. disbound. K5. $20.00.

KLEIN, T. E. D. *Dark Gods.* 1985. NY. Viking. 1st. F/F. H11. $25.00.

KLIMA, Ivan. *Love & Garbage.* 1991. Knopf. 1st. F/F. A20. $15.00.

KLIMA, Ivan. *My Merry Mornings.* 1985. London. Readers International. 1st. sgn. NF/NF. O11. $45.00.

KLIMA, Ivan. *Waiting for the Dark, Waiting For The Light.* 1995. NY. Grove. 1st Am ed. sgn. F/F. O11. $40.00.

KLIMKE, Reiner. *Basic Training of the Young Horse.* 1993. London. Allen. brd. VG. O3. $30.00.

KLINEFELTER, Lee M. *Bookbinding Made Easy.* 1952. Milwaukee. WI. dj. A19. $20.00.

KLINGER, Leslie S. *The Adventures of Sherlock Holmes.* 1998. Indianapolis. Gasogene Books. 1st. trade pb. VF/pict wrp. T2. $27.00.

KLIPPART, John. *Wheat Plant.* 1860. Cincinnati. Moore. 706p. G+. A10. $50.00.

KLOPPENBURG, Jack R. *Seeds & Sovereignty.* 1988. Durham. 368p. F/dj. B26. $40.00.

KLOTZ, John W. *Genes, Genesis, and Evolution.* 1955. Concordia. 575p. VG. B29. $11.00.

KNAPP, Arthur Jr. *Race Your Boat Right.* 1952. Van Nostrand. 1st. sgn. 296p. VG. B11. $35.00.

KNAPP, H. S. *History of the Maumee Valley.* 1872. Toledo. ils. 667p. rebound. B18. $95.00.

KNEBEL, Fletcher. *Bottom Line.* 1974. Doubleday. 1st. G+/dj. N4. $17.50.

KNEBEL, Fletcher. *Night of Camp David.* 1965. Harper & Row. 1st. G+. S19. $30.00.

KNIGHT, Charles. *Half Hours with the Best Authors.* (1859). London. 4 vol. 12mo. woodcuts. 3-quarter leather. VG. H3. $125.00.

KNIGHT, Damon. *In Deep.* 1964. London. Gollancz. 1st hc. sgn. F/NF. T2. $45.00.

KNIGHT, Damon. *Off Centre.* 1969. London. Victor Gollancz. 1st hc ed. F. lt foxing/VG. T2. $35.00.

KNIGHT, Damon. *Orbit 20.* 1978. Harper. 1st. F/dj. M2. $20.00.

KNIGHT, Damon. *Other Foot.* 1966. London. Whiting Wheaton. 1st hc. F/clip. T2. $50.00.

KNIGHT, Damon. *The Man in the Tree.* 1985. London. Victor Gollancz. 1st hc ed. VF/VF. T2. $20.00.

KNIGHT, Damon. *Turning On.* 1967. London. Victor Gollancz. 1st British ed. F/F. T2. $25.00.

KNIGHT, Edward H. *Knight's American Mechanical Dictionary....* 1884. Boston. Houghton Mifflin/Hurd & Houghton. 4 vols. rebound in buckram. ils. some foldout. G. B18. $250.00.

KNIGHT, Etheridge. *Poems from Prison.* 1968. Detroit. Broadside Press. wrps. owner's name. minor pencilings. VG. B2. $30.00.

KNIGHT, Frank. *Clipper Ship.* 1973. London. Collins. photos/maps. 95p. dj. T7. $35.00.

KNIGHT, Kathleen Moore. *Death Goes to a Reunion.* 1952. Crime Club. 1st. VG/VG-. G8. $25.00.

KNIGHT, Marjorie. *Land of Lost Hankerchiefs.* 1954. Dutton. stated 1st. ils Rosalie K Fry. VG/dj. M5. $45.00.

KNIGHT, Oliver. *Frontier Army.* 1978. Norman, OK. dj. A19. $25.00.

KNIGHT, R. Baker. *Chronicle of Kings of England.* 1660. London. 3rd. 500p+catalog of nobility/index. A15. $50.00.

KNIGHT, Steven. *Out of the Blue.* 1996. London. Viking. 1st ed. trade pb orig. VF/VF. T2. $10.00.

KNOPF, Mildred O. *Around the World Cookbook for Young People.* 1966. Knopf. G/dj. A16. $10.00.

KNOPF, Olga. *Successful Aging: Facts & Fallacies of Growing Old.* 1975. Viking. 1st. 229p. VG/dj. A25. $18.00.

KNOWLES, John. *Separate Peace.* 1960. Macmillan. 1st Am. NF/2nd state. T11. $150.00.

KNOWLES, Robert E. *The Dawn at Shanty Bay.* 1907. np. Fleming Revell. 1st. ils by Griselda McClure; bookplate. NF. M19. $25.00.

KNOX, Calvin; see Silverberg, Robert.

KNOX, Dudley W. *Naval Sketches of the War in California.* 1939. Random. sm folio. ils. marbled brd/vellum spine. F. R3. $300.00.

KNOX, Rawle. *Work of EH Shepard.* (1980). NY. Schocken. 1st. ils Shepard. 256p. VG/VG. D1. $65.00.

KNOX, Ronald. *Memories of the Future.* 1923. London. 1st. F/dj. M2. $50.00.

KNOX, Thomas. *Overland Through Asia...Siberian, Tartar & Chinese Life.* 1870. Hartford. 1st. 200 engravings/map. 608p. VG. W3. $275.00.

KNYSTAUTAS, A. *Natural History of the USSR.* 1987. McGraw Hill. 275 mc photos. cloth. F/F. B1. $38.50.

KOCH, Dorothy. *I Play at the Beach.* 1955. Holiday House. 1st. ils Rojankovsky. 8vo. VG/dj. P2. $110.00.

KOCH, Robert. Louis. *Tiffany: Rebel in Glass.* 1964. Crown. 1st/1st prt. sgn. 4to. 246p. AN/F. H1. $65.00.

KOCHER, Theodor. *Text-Book of Operative Surgery.* 1895. London. 1st Eng trans. 303p. A13. $350.00.

KOEBEL, W. H. *Argentina, Past & Present.* 1914. London. A & C Black. 2nd ed. 465p. G/pict cloth. chipped & torn. F3. $20.00.

KOEBEL, W. H. *Central America.* 1925. London. Fisher Unwin. 3rd. 382p. F3. $20.00.

KOESTLER, Arthur. *Act of Creation.* 1964. Macmillan. 1st Am. NF/clip. Q1. $60.00.

KOFSKY, Frank. *Black Nationalism and the Revolution in Music.* 1970. NY. Pathfinder Press. 1st. wrp. F. B2. $40.00.

KOHN, Harold. *A Touch of Greatness.* 1965. Eerdmans. 205p. VG. B29. $5.00.

KOHN, Marek. *Narcomania. On Heroin.* 1987. London. Faber. 1st. VG+/wrp. B2. $25.00.

KOHN, Susan E. *Conduction Aphasia.* 1992. Hillsdale, NJ. Lawrence Erlbaum Assoc. bl cloth. G1. $38.00.

KOHOUT, Pavel. *The Widow Killer.* 1998. NY. St. Martin. ARC. F/wrp. B2. $25.00.

KOLB, E. L. *Through the Grand Canyon from Wyoming to Mexico.* 1946. NY. Macmillan. inscr/dtd 1947. 76 pl. F. B14. $55.00.

KOMAN, Victor. *Solomon's Knife.* (1989). NY. Franklin Watts. 1st. F/F. B3. $15.00.

KONCZEWSKA, Florence L. *Argentine Flowers.* 1976. Buenos Aires. sc. OP. F. B26. $19.00.

KONDO, Yumiko. *Moontoo the Cat.* 1978. Barron's. 1st Am. ils. F/F. P2. $25.00.

KONVITZ, Jeffrey. *Sentinel.* 1974. S&S. 1st. sgn. F/F. M21. $55.00.

KOONTZ, Dean. *Cold Fire.* 1991. NY. Putnam. 1st trade ed. VF/VF. T2. $25.00.

KOONTZ, Dean. *Cold Fire.* 1991. London. Headline. 1st British ed. VF/VF. T2. $75.00.

KOONTZ, Dean. *Dark Rivers of the Heart.* 1994. NY. Knopf. 1st. sgn. VF/VF. T2. $45.00.

KOONTZ, Dean. *Demon Seed.* 1997. London. Headline. 1st hc ed. VF/VF. T2. $38.00.

KOONTZ, Dean. *Dragon Tears.* 1993. NY. Putnam. 1st. 1/750 # copies. sgn. VF/VF in dj & matching pict slipcase. T2. $175.00.

KOONTZ, Dean. *Dragon Tears.* 1993. NY. Putnam. 1st trade ed. VF/VF. T2. $25.00.

KOONTZ, Dean. *False Memory.* 1999. London. Headline. 1st. VF/VF. T2. $36.00.

KOONTZ, Dean. *Hideaway.* 1991. NY. Putnam. 1st. VF/VF. T2. $25.00.

KOONTZ, Dean. *Hideaway.* 1991. NY. Putnam. 1st. UP. sgn. VF/printed wrp. T2. $200.00.

KOONTZ, Dean. *How to Write Best Selling Fiction.* 1981. Cincinnati. Writers Digest Books. 1st. VF/VF. T2. $150.00.

KOONTZ, Dean. *Intensity.* 1995. London. Headline. 1st British ed. VF/VF. T2. $45.00.

KOONTZ, Dean. *Lightning.* 1988. NY. Putnam. 1st. F/F. T2. $35.00.

KOONTZ, Dean. *Lightning.* 1988. NY. Putnam. 1st. UP. sgn. VF/printed wrp. T2. $250.00.

KOONTZ, Dean. *Lightning.* 1988. London. Headline. 1st British ed. VF/VF. T2. $60.00.

KOONTZ, Dean. *Midnight.* 1989. London. Headline. 1st British ed. VF/VF. T2. $45.00.

KOONTZ, Dean. *Midnight.* 1989. NY. Putnam. 1st. VF/VF. T2. $45.00.

KOONTZ, Dean. *Oddkins: A Fable for All Ages.* 1988. NY. Warner. 1st. VF/VF. T2. $75.00.

KOONTZ, Dean. *Santa's Twin.* 1996. NY. Harper Prism. 1st. VF/VF. T2. $25.00.

KOONTZ, Dean. *Seize the Night.* 1999. NY. Bantam. 1st Am ed. sgn. VF/VF. T2. $35.00.

KOONTZ, Dean. *Sole Survivor.* 1997. London. Headline. 1st. VF/VF. T2. $38.00.

KOONTZ, Dean. *Strangers.* 1986. NY. Putnam. 1st. VF/VF. T2. $50.00.

KOONTZ, Dean. *The Bad Place.* 1990. London. Headline. 1st British ed. VF/VF. T2. $50.00.

KOONTZ, Dean. *The Bad Place.* 1990. NY. Putnam. 1st. F/F. H11. $20.00.

KOONTZ, Dean. *The Eyes of Darkness.* 1989. Arlington Heights. Dark Harvest. 1st hc ed. VF/VF. T2. $45.00.

KOONTZ, Dean. *The Face of Fear.* 1989. London. Headline. reissue. 1st thus. VF/VF. T2. $45.00.

KOONTZ, Dean. *The Mask.* 1989. London. Headline. 1st British ed. VF/VF. T2. $65.00.

KOONTZ, Dean. *The Servants of Twilight.* 1991. London. Headline. 1st British hc ed. VF/VF. T2. $65.00.

KOONTZ, Dean. *The Vision.* 1997. NY. Putnam. 1st. sgn. VF/VF. T2. $250.00.

KOONTZ, Dean. *Ticktock.* 1996. London. Headline. 1st. VF/VF. T2. $65.00.

KOONTZ, Dean. *Watchers.* 1987. NY. Putnam. 1st. VF/VF. T2. $65.00.

KOOP, C. Edward. *Memoirs of America's Family Doctor.* 1991. Random. 1st. sgn. F/F. A23. $40.00.

KORCZAK, Janusz. *Ghetto Diary.* 1978. Holocaust Lib. ils. 181p. VG/G+. S3. $26.00.

KOREIN, Julius. *Brain Death: Interrelated Mecial & Social Issues.* 1978. NY. Academy of Sciences. 454p. prt bl wrp. G1. $42.00.

KORNBLATT, Joyce Reiser. *White Water.* 1985. Dutton. 1st. author's 2nd book. F/NF. R13. $20.00.

KORTH, William W. *Tertiary Record of Rodents in North America.* 1994. Plenum. 319p. F. S15. $35.00.

KOSINSKI, Jerzy. *Being There.* 1970. Harcourt Brace. 1st. F/NF. B4. $85.00.

KOSINSKI, Jerzy. *Cockpit.* 1975. Boston. Houghton. 1st. F/NF. H11. $35.00.

KOSINSKI, Jerzy. *Steps.* 1968. Random. 1st. F/NF. M19. $35.00.

KOSINSKI, Jerzy. *The Hermit of 69th Street.* (1988). NY. Seaver Books. 1st. F/F. B3. $10.00.

KOSTER, R. M. *Carmichael's Dog.* 1992. NY. Norton. 1st. VF/F. H11. $30.00.

KOTSUJI, Abram. *Origin & Evolution of Semitic Alphabets.* 1937. Tokyo. sgn pres. ils/bibliography/index. 229p. VG/dj. W3. $125.00.

KOTZWINKLE, William. *E T the Extra-Terrestrial.* 1982. Putnam & Sons. 4th imp. F/chip dj. S19. $35.00.

KOTZWINKLE, William. *Great World Circus.* 1983. np. Putnam. 1st. F/F dj. M19. $17.50.

KOTZWINKLE, William. *Great World Circus.* 1983. Putnam. 1st. ils Joe Sefello. F/F. R14. $30.00.

KOTZWINKLE, William. *Queen of Swords.* 1983. Putnam. 1st. F/F. R14. $30.00.

KOTZWINKLE, William. *Swimmer in the Secret Sea.* (1994). np. Chronicle. 1st. F/F. B3. $20.00.

KOTZWINKLE, William. *The Exile.* (1987). NY. Dutton. 1st. sgn by author. F/F. B3. $55.00.

KOVACS, Ernie. *Zoomar.* 1957. Doubleday. 1st. NF/dj. M25. $60.00.

KOVEL, Joel. *Against the State of Nuclear Terror.* 1984. Boston. South End Pr. 1st Am. VG/wrp. K3. $5.00.

KOVIC, Ron. *Around the World in Eight Days.* 1984. San Francisco. City Lights. 1st. VF/VF. H11. $175.00.

KOVIC, Ron. *Born on the Fourth of July.* 1976. McGraw Hill. 1st. F/F. H11. $80.00.

KOWAGA, Joy. *Obasan.* 1981. Toronto. Lester & Orpen Dennys. 1st. sgn. author's 1st novel. F/VG dj. A26. $45.00.

KOWALKSI, Robert. *8 Week Cholesterol Cure, The.* nd. NY. Harper & Row. VG/VG. A28. $4.95.

KRAEMER, Henry. *A Course in Botany and Pharmacognosy.* 1902. Philadelphia. 1st. scarce. cloth rubbed. corners worn. B26. $32.50.

KRAEPELIN, Emil. *General Paresis: Nervous & Mental Disease...* 1913. NY. Monograph 14/Journal Nervous Mental Disease Pub. G1. $150.00.

RAHN, Fernanco. *Mr. Top.* 1983. NY. Morrow. VG/VG. A28. $10.95.

RAMER, Dale. *Ross & the New Yorker.* 1951. Doubleday. 1st. F/VG+ clip. B4. $35.00.

RAMER, Jack. *Philodendrons.* 1974. NY. ils. 7p. VG/dj. B26. $14.00.

RAMER, Jerry. *Distant Replay.* 1985. Putnam. 1st. 236p. F/NF. W2. $25.00.

RAMER, Kathryn. *Rattlesnake Farming.* 1992. Knopf. 1st. author's 2nd novel. F/dj. 24. $20.00.

RAMISH, Arnold. *Atomic Energy in the Soviet Union.* 1959. Stanford. 1st. xl. VG/dj. 3. $50.00.

RANTZ, Judith. *Dazzle.* 1990. Crown. 1st. F/F. W2. $30.00.

RASNEY, Samuel A. *Homicide Call.* 1962. NY. William Morrow. 1st. F in dj. M15. $45.00.

RASNEY, Samuel A. *Homicide West.* 1961. NY. Morrow. 1st. VG/VG. G8. $10.00.

RAUS, George. *High Road to Promontory, Building the Central Pacific Across the High Sierra.* 1969. Palo Alto, CA. 1st. ils. 317p. F/VG. B18. $25.00.

RAUS, H. *Work Relief in Germany.* 1934. NY. Russell Sage Found. 1st. photos. VG. 25. $18.00.

RAUSE, Lawrence A. *Money Go Round.* 1985. S&S. 1st. 202p. F/F. W2. $30.00.

RAUSS, Ruth. *Big World & the Little House.* 1949. Henry Schuman. 1st. ils Marc Simont. G+/VG. P2. $50.00.

RAUSS, Ruth. *Cantilever Rainbow.* 1965. Pantheon. probable 1st. VG+/VG. P2. $35.00.

RAUSS, Ruth. *Open House for Butterflies.* 1960. Harper. 1st. VG+/VG. B3. $75.00.

RAVITZ, Nathaniel L. *3000 Years of Hebrew Literature from Earliest Time...* 1972. Swallow. biblio/index. 586p. VG/G+. S3. 28.00.

REDENSER, Gail. *ABC of Bumptious Beasts.* 1966. Harlin Quest. 1st. sgn. ils/sgn Stanley Mack. VG+/VG. P2. $30.00.

REIG, Margaret B. *Green Medicine. Search for Plants that Heal.* 1964. Chicago. Rand McNally. 1st. 8vo. cloth. F/VG. A22. $30.00.

KREISLER, Fritz. *Four Weeks in the Trenches.* 1915. Houghton Mifflin. 1st. inscr. gr cloth. F. B14. $200.00.

KREMENTZ, Jill. *How it Feels When a Parent Dies.* 1981. Knopf. 1st. sm 8vo. F/F. C8. $30.00.

KRENTZ, Jayne Ann. *Sharp Edges.* 1998. Pocket. 1st. F/F. G8. $12.50.

KRESS, Nancy. *Dancing on Air.* 1997. San Francisco. Tachyon Publications. 1st. 1/26 lettered copies. sgn. VF/VF dj & slipcase. T2. $60.00.

KRESS, Nancy. *Maximum Light.* 1998. NY. Tor. sgn 1st ed. F/F. M23. $30.00.

KRICH, Rochelle Majer. *Fair Game.* 1993. NY. Mysterious Press. 1st. sgn. F. stains/VF. T2. $20.00.

KRICH, Rochelle Majer. *Fertile Ground.* 1998. Avon. 1st. sgn. F/F. G8. $25.00.

KROLL, Harry Harrison. *Their Ancient Grudge.* 1946. Bobbs Merrill. 1st. 8vo. bl cloth. VG/dj. T10. $25.00.

KROLL, Steven. *Hand-Me-Down Doll.* 1983. Holiday. 1st. sq 8vo. unp. lilac brd/bl spine. F/NF. T5. $30.00.

KRUGER, Paul. *Finish Line.* 1968. NY. S&S. 1st. VG/VG. G8. $10.00.

KRUGER, Paul. *Weep for the Willow Green.* 1966. NY. S&S. 1st. VG/VG. G8. $10.00.

KRUGER, Rayne. *Goodbye Dolly Gray.* 1960. Phil. VG/VG. B5. $30.00.

KUBASTA, V. *Jolly Jim.* 1969. Frick. 1st Am. popup. obl 4to. VG. P2. $125.00.

KUBE-MCDOWELL, Michael. *Quiet Pools.* 1990. Ace. 1st. F/dj. M2. $25.00.

KUHLKEN, Ken. *The Angel Gang.* 1994. NY. St. Martin. 1st. sgn. F/F. T2. $20.00.

KUHLKEN, Ken. *The Venus Deal.* 1993. NY. St. Martin. 1st. sgn. dj sgn by artist John Dawson. VF/VF. T2. $30.00.

KUKLA, Barbara J. *Swing City. Newark Nightlife, 1925 – 1950.* 1991. Philadelphia. Temple Univ Press. 1st. sm 4to. F/F. B2. $25.00.

KUMIN, Maxine. *Connecting the Dots.* 1996. NY. Norton. 1st. sgn. F/F. V1. $30.00.

KUMIN, Maxine. *Our Ground Time Here Will be Brief.* 1983. Viking. AP. F/wrp. R14. $35.00.

KUMIN, Maxine. *Why Can't We Live Together Like Civilized Human Beings.* 1982. Viking. 1st. inscr. NF/VG. B3. $45.00.

KUMMER, Frederic Arnold. *Gentlemen in Hades.* 1930. Sears. 1st. VG. M2. $22.00.

KUNDEERA, Milan. *Life Is Elsewhere.* 1974. Knopf. 1st Eng trans. author's 3rd book. F/F. D10. $85.00.

KUNDERA, Milan. *Art of the Novel.* 1988. NY. Grove. 1st Eng language. F/F. R14. $35.00.

KUNDERA, Milan. *Life Is Elsewhere.* 1974. NY. Knopf. 1st Eng trans. F in F dj. D10. $85.00.

KUNDERA, Milan. *The Joke.* 1969. NY. Coward. 1st Am ed. F in NF clip dj. B2. $85.00.

KUNDERA, Milan. *The Unbearable Lightness of Being.* 1984. NY. Harper & Row. 1st Am & 1st Eng trans. F in F dj. D10. $60.00.

KUNG, Hans. *Signposts for the Future: Contemporary Issues Facing the Church.* 1978. Doubleday. 204p. VG/VG. B29. $6.00.

KUNHARDT, C. P. *Steam Yachts & Launches: Their Machinery & Management.* 1887. Forest Stream. 1st. 239p+ads. G. A17. $45.00.

KUNHARDT, Dorothy. *Brave Mr Buckingham.* 1935. Harcourt Brace. 1st. 8vo. unp. VG. D1. $95.00.

KUNTZLEMAN, Charles T. *Well Family Book.* 1985. Here's Life. 266p. F/dj. B29. $7.50.

KUNZ, George Frederick. *Rings for the Finger.* 1917. Lippincott. 1st. ils. 381p. F. B14. $275.00.

KUNZ, Jeffrey R. M. *AMA Family Medical Guide.* 1982. Random. ne. 832p. F. W2. $75.00.

KUPFERBERG, Tuli. *1001 Ways to Live without Working.* 1961. NY. Birth Press. 1st. tall bl wrp. F. B2. $35.00.

KUPFERBERG, Tuli. *Newspoems.* 1971. NY. Birth Press. 1st. wrp. F. B2. $35.00.

KUREISHI, Hanif. *Black Album.* 1995. London. Faber. 1st. F/F. A24. $35.00.

KURGER, Mary. *Death on the Cliff Walk.* 1994. NY. Kensington. 1st. author's 1st book. VF/VF. H11. $25.00.

KURLAND, Michael. *Too Soon Dead.* 1997. St. Martin. 1st. F/F. G8. $17.50.

KUROSAWA, Akira. *Something Like an Autobiography.* 1982. Knopf. ils. 205p. F/F. W3. $38.00.

KURZ, Ron. *Lethal Gas.* 1974. np. Evans. 1st. author's 1st book. F/F dj. M19. $25.00.

KURZWELL, Allen. *A Case of Curiosities.* 1992. NY. HBJ. 1st. F/F. H11. $35.00.

KUSHNER, Ellen. *Thomas the Rhymer.* 1990. Morrow. 1st. F/F. M21. $40.00.

KUSKIN, Karla. *Near the Window Tree.* 1975. Harper Row. 1st. 63p. F/VG. D4. $30.00.

KUSKIN, Karla. *Roar & More.* 1956. Harper. early ed. inscr. 48p. pict brd. D4. $75.00.

KUTTNER, Henry. *Man Drowning.* 1952. Harper. 1st. F/dj. M2. $50.00.

KWANT, Remy C. *Philosophy of Labor.* 1960. Philadelphia. Duquesne. 1st. F/issued w/o dj?. B2. $45.00.

— L —

L'AMOUR, Louis. *The Lonesome Gods.* 1983. NY. Bantam Books. 1st. inscr on ffep. F/NF. D10. $50.00.

L'AMOUR, Louis. *The Sackett Companion.* 1988. NY. Bantam. 1st. Book has bumped top corners. F-/F. H11. $25.00.

L'ENGLE, Madeleine. *A Wrinkle in Time.* 1962. NY. Farrar. 1st. VG. spine wear. bookplate on ffep/G. B2. $200.00.

LA FOUNTAINE, George. *Falshpoint.* 1976. NY. Coward. 1st. F/NF. H11. $20.00.

LABIN, Suzanne. *Hippies, Drugs and Promiscuity.* 1972. New Rochelle. Arlington House. 1st. NF/chip dj. B2. $25.00.

LAETSCH, Theo. *The Minor Prophets.* 1956. Concordia. 566p. G. B29. $17.50.

LAFFERTY, R. A. *East of Laughter.* 1988. Bath. Avon. Morrigan Publications. 1st. VF/VF. T2. $58.00.

LAFFERTY, R. A. *Serpent's Egg.* 1987. Bath. Avon. Morrigan Publications. 1st. VF/VF. T2. $30.00.

LAKE, Deryn. *Death in the Peerless Pool.* 1999. London. Hodder & Stoughton. 1st. sgn. VF/VF. T2. $38.00.

LAMANTIA, Philip. *Touch of the Marvelous.* 1966. Berkeley. Oyez. 1st. NF/wrp. B2. $25.00.

LAMB, Wally. *She's Come Undone.* 1992. NY. Pocket Books. 1st. author's 1st book; sgn. F in dj. D10. $65.00.

LAMBERT, Derek. *Angels in the Snow.* 1969. London. Joseph. 1st. Author's first novel. F/F. H11. $40.00.

LAMBERT, Gavin. *The Dangerous Edge.* 1975. London. Barrie & Jenkins. 1st. F/dj. M15. $65.00.

LAMBERT, Mercedes. *Soultown.* 1996. NY. Viking. 1st. VF/VF. H11. $15.00.

LAMBERT, Mercedes. *Soultown.* 1996. NY. Viking. 1st. VG/VG. G8. $10.00.

LAMONT, Hammond. *Burke's Speech on Conciliation with America.* 1897. Ginn. 152p. VG. B29. $7.00.

LAMOTT, Anne. *Operating Instructions.* 1993. Pantheon Nonfiction Reader. 12 pg excerpt. F/decor wrp. M25. $10.00.

LAMOTT, Anne. *Traveling Mercies.* 1999. NY. Pantheon. 1st. F/F. M23. $40.00.

LANDON, Herman. *Three Brass Elephants.* 1930. Liveright. 1st. VG. G8. $30.00.

LANDORF, Joyce. *His Stubborn Love.* 1972. Zondervan. 144p. VG/VG. B29. $3.50.

LANDRETH, Marsha. *Vial Murders.* 1994. NY. Walker. 1st. VF/VF. T2. $15.00.

LANG, Andrew. *The True Story Book.* 1893. London. Longmans, Green & Co. 1st ed. 2nd issue. ils by H. J. Ford. 8vo. 337p. VG. D6. $50.00.

LANG, Maria. *Wreath for the Bride.* 1966. H&S. 1st British ed. VG/VG-. G8. $15.00.

LANGFORD, R. H. *Thoughts in Prose and Rhyme.* 1904. East St. Louis, IL. ils. 310p. VG. B18. $22.50.

LANGTON, Jane. *Murder at the Gardner.* 1988. St. Martin. 1st. VG/VG+. G8. $35.00.

LANIER, Virginia. *The House on Bloodhound Lane.* (1996). NY. Harper Collins. 1st. F/F. B3. $40.00.

LANKES, J. J. *Brief History of Aeronautics.* 1946. Langley Field. Langley Memorial Aeronautic Library. ils. inscr by author. 14p. VG. B18. $47.50.

LANSDALE, Joe R. *Act of Love.* 1992 Baltimore. C D Publications. 1st. 1/750 # copies. sgn by author & artist Mark Nelson VF/VF dj & slipcase. T2. $50.00.

LANSDALE, Joe R. *Act of Love.* 1992 London. Kinnell. 1st hc ed. sgn. author's 1s novel. F/F. T2. $35.00.

LANSDALE, Joe R. *Bad Chili.* 1997. NY Mysterious Press. 1st. sgn. VF/VF. T2 $25.00.

LANSDALE, Joe R. *Cold in July and Savage Season.* 1990. Shingletown. Mark V. Ziesing 1st hc ed. sgn by Lansdale & artist Terry Lee. VF/VF. T2. $25.00.

LANSDALE, Joe R. *Dead in the West.* 1990 London. Kinnell. 1st hc ed. sgn. VF/VF. T2 $35.00.

LANSDALE, Joe R. *Freezer Burn.* 1999 Holyoke. Crossroads Press. 1st. 1/400 # copies. sgn. VF/VF. T2. $60.00.

LANSDALE, Joe R. *Freezer Burn.* 1999. NY Mysterious Press. 1st trade ed. sgn. VF/VF T2. $25.00.

LANSDALE, Joe R. *Mucho Mojo.* 1995 London. Gollancz. 1st British ed. sgn VF/VF. T2. $25.00.

LANSDALE, Joe R. *Rumble Tumble.* 1998 Mysterious. 1st. NF/F. G8. $15.00.

LANSDALE, Joe R. *Something Lumber thi Way Comes.* 1999. Burton. Subterranean Press. 1st. 1/500 # copies. sgn. VF/VF. T2 $35.00.

LANSDALE, Joe R. *The Boar.* 1998. Burton Subterranean Press. 1st. 1/750 # copies. sgn VF/VF. T2. $50.00.

LANSDALE, Joe R. *Two Bear Mambo.* 1995 Mysterious. 1st. F/F. G8. $12.50.

LANTIGUA, John. *Heat Lightning.* 1987 NY. Putnam. 1st. author's 1st book. F. wear/NF. T2. $20.00.

LAPIERRE, Janet. *Children's Games.* 1989 NY. Scribner's. 1st. NF/NF. G8. $17.50.

LAPIERRE, Janet. *Grandmother's House* 1991. NY. Scribners. 1st. F/F. T2. $15.00.

LARKIN, Philip. *All What Jazz.* 1985. NY Farrar. 1st Am ed of revised ed. F/F. B2 $35.00.

LARSON, Edward J. *Summer for the Gods* 1997. NY. Basic Books. 1st. winner o Pulitzer Prize. F/F. M23. $50.00.

LARSON, Edward J. *Trial and Error.* 1985. Oxford. 222p. VG. ex lib. B29. $8.00.

LASSERRE, Jean. *War and the Gospel.* 1962. Herald. 243p. VG/VG. B29. $6.00.

LATHEN, Emma. *A Stitch in Time.* 1968. NY. Macmillan. 1st. F in dj. M15. $75.00.

LATIMER, Jonathan. *Black Is the Fashion for Dying.* 1959. NY. Random House. 1st. VG in soiled dj. M15. $40.00.

LATREILLE, Stan. *Perjury.* 1998. NY. Crown. 1st. author's 1st novel. sgn. VF/VF. T2. $25.00.

LATTING, J. (ed). *Plant Communities of Southern California.* 1976. Berkeley. CNPS. 4to. sc. VG. B26. $15.00.

LAUBENSTEIN, William. J. *The Emerald Whaler.* Indianapolis. Bobbs Merrill Company. (1980). 8vo. 239p. ils. gr cloth spine & gr brd. dj. 1st ed. VG/VG. few nicks. L5. $25.00.

LAURENCE, Janet. *Canaletto and the Case of Westminster Bridge.* 1997. London. Macmillan. 1st. sgn. VF/VF. T2. $40.00.

LAURENCE, Margaret. *The Diviners.* 1974. Toronto. McClelland & Stewart. 1st. F/NJ dj. A26. $30.00.

LAW, Deborah. *Growing Fuchsias.* 1988. Kenthurst. Australia. 2nd ed. sc. New. B26. $12.00.

LAWRENCE, Ann T. & Joan M. Schattinger. *Cleveland's Flats: The Incredible City Under the Hill.* 1979. Cleveland. Historical Society. 1/100 copies. pict wrps. photos. sgn by both authors. 140p. VG. B18. $25.00.

LAWRENCE, Josephine. *The Berry Patch.* 1925. NY. Cupples & Leon. G. A16. $7.50.

LAWS, Stephen. *The Frighteners.* 1990. London. Souvenir Press. 1st. sgn. VF/VF. T2. $35.00.

LAWSON, Philip. *Would It Kill You to Smile?* 1998. Atlanta. Longstreet Press. 1st. review copy w/promo materials. author's 1st novel. VF/VF. T2. $20.00.

LAWSON, Steven J. *Men Who Win: Pursuing the Ultimate Prize.* 1992. Navpress. 223p. VG/VG. B29. $6.50.

LAWTON, John. *A Little White Death.* 1998. London. Weidenfeld & Nicolson. 1st. VF/dj. M15. $65.00.

LAWTON, John. *Black Out.* 1995. NY. Viking. 1st. F/VF. H11. $25.00.

LAWTON, John. *Old Flames.* 1996. London. Weidenfeld & Nicolson. 1st. VF/dj. M15. $100.00.

LAYMON, Richard. *After Midnight.* 1997. London. Headline. 1st. VF/VF. T2. $35.00.

LAYMON, Richard. *Alarms.* 1992. Shingletown. Mark V. Ziesing. 1st. VF/VF. T2. $25.00.

LAYMON, Richard. *Come Out Tonight.* 1999. London. Headline. 1st. VF/VF. T2. $35.00.

LAYMON, Richard. *Come Out Tonight.* 1999. Baltimore. Cemetery Dance Publications. 1st Am ed. sgn. VF/VF. T2. $40.00.

LAYMON, Richard. *Cuts.* 1999. Baltimore. Cemetery Dance Publications. 1st. sgn. VF/VF. T2. $40.00.

LAYMON, Richard. *Flesh.* 1987. London. W. H. Allen. 1st. sgn. F/F. T2. $100.00.

LAYMON, Richard. *Savage.* 1994. NY. St. Martin. 1st Am ed. sgn. F/VF. T2. $35.00.

LAYMON, Richard. *The Midnight Tour.* 1998. London. Headline. 1st. VF/VF. T2. $35.00.

LAYNG, Charles. *The Game Is Afoot!* 1995. Toronto. Metropolitan Toronto Reference Library. 1st. VF/VF. T2. $24.00.

LE CARRE, John. *A Perfect Spy.* 1986. NY. Knopf. 1st. F/F. H11. $25.00.

LE CARRE, John. *Our Game.* 1995. London. Hodder & Stoughton. 1st Eng. F/dj. M15. $300.00.

LE CARRE, John. *Smiley's People.* 1980. NY. Knopf. 1st Am ed. VF/VF. T2. $15.00.

LE CARRE, John. *The Honourable Schoolboy.* 1977. Knopf. 1st. F/dj. M25. $35.00.

LE CARRE, John. *The Little Drummer Girl.* 1983. NY. Knopf. 1st. F/F. H11. $45.00.

LE CARRE, John. *The Looking Glass War.* 1965. Coward - McCann. 1st. G. S19. $70.00.

LE CARRE, John. *The Night Manager.* 1993. NY. Knopf. 1st Am ed. VF/VF. T2. $15.00.

LE CARRE, John. *The Russia House.* 1989. NY. Knopf. 1st Am ed. VF/VF. T2. $15.00.

LE GUIN, Ursula K. *Fish Soup.* (1992). NY. Atheneum. 1st. ils Patrick Wynne. F/F. B3. $25.00.

LE GUIN, Ursula K. *The Wind's Twelve Quarters.* 1975. np. 1st. F/VG. M19. $35.00.

LEA, Tom. *The Wonderful Country.* 1952. Boston. Little, Brn. 1st. VG+/NF. some soiling. fading. price clip. A24. $40.00.

LEAR, Edward. *How Pleasant to Know Mr. Lear.* 1994. MD. Stemmer House Publishers. 1st. New. A28. $9.50.

LEARY, Paris and Robert Kelly, eds. *A Controversy of Poets.* 1965. Garden City. Anchor. PBO. anthology. NF/wrp. B2. $25.00.

LEARY, Timothy. *Flashbacks.* 1983. Tarcher. 1st. sgn & inscr. F/F. M25. $75.00.

LEATHER, Edwin. *Mozart Score.* nd. Macmillan. 1st British ed. VG/VG. G8. $30.00.

LEE, Chang Rae. *A Gesture Life.* 1999. NY. Riverhead Books. 1st. sgn. VF/VF. T2. $26.00.

LEE, Chang-Rae. *Native Speaker.* 1995. NY. Riverhead Books. 1st. F/F. D10. $45.00.

LEE, Douglas H. K. *Climate and Economic Development in the Tropics.* 1957. NY. Harper. Council on Foreign Relations. 8vo. 182p. VG/chipped dj. K5. $20.00.

LEE, Gus. *China Boy.* 1991. NY. Dutton. 1st. remainder mark. F/F. H11. $20.00.

LEE, Li Young. *The City in Which I Love You.* 1990. Boa Editions. F/F. V1. $25.00.

LEE, Sally. *Predicting Violent Storms.* 1989. NY. Franklin Watts. 1st. b/w photos & diagrams. 8vo. 128p. VG/VG. K5. $20.00.

LEE, Tanith. *Louisa the Poisoner.* 1995. Berkeley Heights. Wildside Press. 1st. 1/300 # copies. sgn. VF/VF. T2. $35.00.

LEHANE, Dennis. *A Drink Before the War.* 1994. NY. Harcourt. 1st. Signed on title page. F/VF. H11. $100.00.

LEHANE, Dennis. *A Drink Before the War.* (1994). NY. HBJ. 1st. sgn by author. F/F. B3. $75.00.

LEHANE, Dennis. *Darkness, Take My Hand.* 1996. NY. Morrow. 1st. F/F. H11. $35.00.

LEHANE, Dennis. *Sacred.* (1997). NY. Morrow. 1st. sgn by author. F/F. B3. $40.00.

LEIB, Franklin A. *Fire Arrow.* 1988. np. Presidio. 1st. author's 1st novel. VG/VG+. R16. $30.00.

LEIBER, Fritz. *Heroes and Horrors.* 1978. Chapel Hill. Whispers Press. 1st. sgn. VF/VF. T2. $35.00.

LEIBER, Fritz. *The Dealings of Daniel Kesserich.* 1997. NY. Tor. 1st. VF/VF. T2. $19.00.

LEIBER, Fritz. *The Knight and Knave of Swords.* 1988. NY. Morrow. 1st. VF/VF. T2. $25.00.

LEIBOLD, Jay. *Secret of the Ninja.* 1987. NY. Bantam. Choose Your Own Adventure #66. sc. G. A28. $1.75.

LEIGH, Norman. *Thirteen Against the Bank.* 1976. NY. Morrow. 1st. F/VF. H11. $25.00.

LEIGHTON, Marie & Robert. *Convict 99.* 1989. London. Grant Richards. 1st. pict. cloth brd. VG. M15. $175.00.

LELY, H. V. *The Useful Trees of Northern Nigeria.* 1925. London. gr leather bdg w/raised bands. marbled brds. some tanning. B26. $89.00.

LEMARCHAND, Elizabeth. *Death of an Old Girl.* 1967. Walker. 1st Am ed. NF/NF. G8. $12.50.

LEMARCHAND, Elizabeth. *Light Through Glass.* 1984. Walker. 1st Am ed. NF/VG-. G8. $15.00.

LEMLEY, John. *Autobiography and Personal Recollections of John Lemley....* 1875. Rockford, IL. later ed. some wear to cover. hinge damage. 400p. G. B18. $35.00.

LEMMON, Kenneth. *The Golden Age of Plant Hunters.* 1969. London/So. Brunswick. VG in dj. B26. $41.00.

LENARD, Alexander. *The Valley of the Latin Bear.* 1965. NY. Dutton. 1st. 219p. G/chipped dj. F3. $15.00.

LENNON, John and Yoko Ono. *The Playboy Interviews with John Lennon and Yoko Ono.* 1981. NY. Playboy Press. 1st. F in F dj. B2. $25.00.

LENZ, Lee. *An Annotated Catalog of Plants of the Cape Region, Baha California Sur, Mexico.* 1992. Claremont, CA. sc. 7 x 10". New. B26. $17.50.

LEON-PORTILLO, Miguel. *Native Mesoamerican Spirituality.* 1980. NY. Paulist Press. 1st. 300p. G. pict cloth. F3. $30.00.

LEONARD, Elmore. *Bandits.* 1987. NY. Arbor House. 1st. sgn. F/F. T2. $30.00.

LEONARD, Elmore. *Bandits.* 1987. NY. Arbor House. 1st. VF in dj. M15. $45.00.

LEONARD, Elmore. *Be Cool.* 1999. NY. Delacorte Press. 1st. sgn. F/F. O11. $35.00.

LEONARD, Elmore. *City Primeval.* 1980. NY. Arbor House. 1st. F/NF. B2. $25.00.

LEONARD, Elmore. *Freaky Deaky.* 1988. NY. Arbor. 1st. VG/VG. R16. $30.00.

LEONARD, Elmore. *Get Shorty.* 1990. NY. Delacorte Press. 1st. sgn. F/F. O11. $45.00.

LEONARD, Elmore. *Gunsights.* 1979. NY. Bantam. 1st. pb orig. VF in wrp. M15. $85.00.

LEONARD, Elmore. *Killshot.* 1989. NY. Arbor House. 1st. sgn. F/F. O11. $35.00.

LEONARD, Elmore. *Maximum Bob.* 1991. NY. Delacorte Press. 1st. sgn. F/F. O11. $35.00.

LEONARD, Elmore. *Mr. Majestyk.* 1974. NY. Dell. 1st. pb orig. F in wrp. M15. $65.00.

LEONARD, Elmore. *Out of Sight.* 1996. Delacorte. UP. F/WRP. M25. $75.00.

LEONARD, Elmore. *Pronto.* 1993. NY. Delacorte Press. 1st. sgn. F/F. O11. $35.00.

LEONARD, Elmore. *Rum Punch.* 1992. NY. Delacorte. 1st. VF/dj. M15. $45.00.

LEONARD, Elmore. *The Big Bounce.* 1989. NY. Armchair Detective. 1st Am. F/dj. M15. $45.00.

LEONARD, Elmore. *The Switch.* 1979. London. Secker and Warburg. 1st hc ed. VF in dj. M15. $300.00.

LEONARD, Elmore. *Touch.* 1987. NY. Arbor House. 1st. sgn. F. corners bumped/F. T2. $20.00.

LEONARD, Elmore. *Valdez Is Coming.* 1970. NY. Fawcett. 1st. PBO. Gold Medal Book #R1228. VNF. O11. $55.00.

LEPPECK, Christopher. *The Surrogate Assasin.* 1998. Aurora. Write Way Publishing. 1st. sgn. VF/VF. T2. $25.00.

LESCROART, John T. *Son of Holmes.* 1986. NY. Fine. 1st. F/F. H11. $30.00.

LESLEY, Craig. *River Song.* (1989). Boston. Houghton Mifflin. 1st. author's 1st book. NF. prev owner's emb stp on ffep/F. B3. $100.00.

LESLIE, Peter. *Gay Deceiver.* 1967. Stein & Day. 1st Am ed. VG/VG. G8. $12.50.

LESSING, Doris. *The Good Terrorist.* 1985. NY. Knopf. 1st Am ed. F/F. A24. $20.00.

LESTER, Mary. *Hand Me that Corkscrew, Bacchus.* 1973. CA. Piper Company. sgn. VG/G. A28. $17.95.

LETHEM, Jonathan. *Amnesia Moon.* 1995. NY. Harcourt. 1st. VF/VF. H11. $30.00.

LETHEM, Jonathan. *The Wall of the Sky, the Wall of the Eye.* 1996. NY. Harcourt Brace. 1st. sgn. VF/VF. T2. $25.00.

LETTS, Billie. *Where the Heart Is.* 1995. NY. Warner. sgn 1st ed. author's 1st novel. F/F. M23. $40.00.

LEVI, Peter. *Knit One, Drop One.* 1986. Walker. 1st Am ed. NF/NF. G8. $10.00.

LEVIN, Ira. *The Boys from Brazil.* 1976. NY. Random. 1st. Front corners lightly bumped. F/F. H11. $45.00.

LEVIN, Ira. *The Stepford Wives.* 1972. NY. Random House. 1st. F/F. D10. $75.00.

LEVIN, Lee. *King Tut's Private Eye.* 1996. THDU. 1st. F/F. G8. $25.00.

LEVINE, Paul. *False Down.* 1993. Bantam. 1st. NF/NF. G8. $12.50.

LEVINE, Robert. *Historical Dictionary of Brazil.* 1979. NJ. Scarecrow Press. 1st. extensive biblio. 297p. G. F3. $35.00.

LEVIS, Larry. *The Afterlife.* 1977. Iowa City. Univ. of Iowa Press. 1st. F/NF. V1. $45.00.

LEVITSKY, Ronald. *Innocence that Kills.* 1994. Scribner. 1st. NF/NF. G8. $12.50.

LEVITSKY, Ronald. *Stone Boy.* 1993. Scribner. 1st. NF/NF. G8. $15.00.

LEVITSKY, Ronald. *The Innocence that Kills.* 1994. NY. Scribners. 1st. sgn. VF/VF. T2. $20.00.

LEVY, David H. *The Man Who Sold the Milky Way; A Biography of Bart Bok.* 1993. Tucson. Univ. of Arizona Press. sgn by author. b/w photo ils. 8vo. 246p. VG in pb. K5. $12.00.

LEVY, Harry. *Chain of Custody.* 1998. Random House. 1st. NF/NF. G8. $15.00.

LEWIN, Michael Z. *And Baby will Fall.* 1988. Morrow. 1st. sgn. VG+/VG+. G8. $20.00.

LEWIN, Michael Z. *Hard Line.* 1982. Morrow. 1st. sgn. NF/NF. G8. $25.00.

LEWIN, Michael Z. *Silent Salesman*. 1978. Knopf. 1st. sgn. VG+/VG+. G8. $22.50.

LEWIN, Michael Z. *Underdog*. 1993. NY. Mysterious Press. 1st. VF/VF. T2. $8.00.

LEWIS, David Levering. *When Harlem Was in Vogue*. 1981. Knopf. 1st. NF/NF. M25. $45.00.

LEWIS, Flannery. *Suns Go Down*. 1937. np. Macmillan. 1st. sgn. ES. scarce because book was censored. NF/NF dj. M19. $65.00.

LEWIS, Gregg. *The Power of a Promise Kept*. 1995. Focus on the Family. 186p. VG. B29. $8.00.

LEWIS, Margaret. *Ngaio Marsh: A Life*. 1998. Scottsdale. Poisoned Pen Press. 1st. sgn. VF/VF. T2. $28.00.

LEWIS, Richard S. *A Continent for Science; The Antarctic Adventure*. 1965. NY. Viking. 4to. b/w photos. 300p. VG/chipped dj. K5. $20.00.

LEWIS, Roy. *Suddenly as a Shadow*. 1997. London. Harper Collins. 1st. VF/VF. T2. $25.00.

LEWIS, Sinclair. *Ann Vickers*. 1932. 1933. np. Collier & Son. ne. emb. G. S19. $30.00.

LEWIS, Terry. *Conflict of Interest*. 1997. Sarasota. Florida. Pineapple Press. 1st. sgn. author's 1st novel. VF/VF. T2. $25.00.

LICHFIELD, Patrick. *The Most Beautiful Women*. 1983. NY. Crescent Books. 4to. 159p. NM/F. H1. $18.00.

LIEBERG, Carolyn. *Calling Midwest Home*. 1996. CA. Wildcat Canyon Press. 1st trade pb. F. F6. $4.00.

LIENHARD, Marc. *Luther: Witness to Jesus Christ*. 1982. Augsburg. 412p. VG/VG. B29. $11.50.

LIGHTMAN, Alan. *Einstein's Dreams*. 1993. NY. Pantheon. 1st. book store stamp on bottom edges. F/F. H11. $30.00.

LIGNELL, Lois. *Three Japanese Mice and Their Whiskers*. 1934. NY. Farrar & Rinehart. G in torn dj. A16. $40.00.

LIGOTTI, Thomas. *Grimscribe: His Lives and Works*. 1991. NY. Carroll & Graf. 1st. F/F. H11. $30.00.

LIMON, Martin. *Slicky Boys*. 1997. NY. Bantam. 1st. sgn. VF/VF. T2. $25.00.

LINCOLN, C. Eric. *The Avenue, Clayton City*. 1988. Morrow. UP. NF/gray wrps. M25. $25.00.

LINDBERG, Carter. *The Third Reformation: Charismatic Movements and the Lutheran Tradition*. 1983. Mercer Univ. 345p. VG/VG. B29. $10.00.

LINDSAY, Howard. *The Great Sebastians*. 1956. NY. Random House. 1st. co-written by Russel Crouse. NF/VG+. lt wear. A24. $30.00.

LINDSAY, Paul. *Code Name: Gentkill*. 1995. NY. Villard. 1st. VF/VF. T2. $25.00.

LINDSAY, Paul. *Freedom to Kill*. 1997. NY. Villard. 1st. ARC. VF/pict wrp. T2. $10.00.

LINDSEY, David. *Body of Truth*. 1992. NY. Doubleday. 1st. VF/VF. T2. $20.00.

LINDSEY, David. *Heat from Another Sun*. 1984. NY. Harper & Row. 1st. F/F. A24. $28.00.

LINDSEY, David. *Ibody of Truth*. 1992. NY. Doubleday. 1st. F/F. H11. $20.00.

LINDSEY, Hal. *The 1980s: Countdown to Armageddon*. 1980. Westgate. 195p. VG. B29. $4.00.

LINDSEY, Hal. *The Final Battle*. 1995. Western Front. 286p. VG. B29. $4.00.

LINGARD, Joan. *Tug of War*. 1990. NY. Lodestar Books. VG/NF. A28. $7.95.

LIPINSKI, Thomas. *Picture of Her Tombstone*. 1996. THDU. 1st. sgn. F/F. G8. $20.00.

LIPSCOMBE VINCETT, Betty A. *Wild Flowers of Central Saudi Arabia*. 1977. Milan. 4to. ep maps. owner's stp. dj. B26. $31.00.

LISTER, Michael. *Power in the Blood*. 1997. Sarasota, Florida. Pineapple Press. 1st. sgn. author's 1st novel. VF/VF. T2. $25.00.

LITTAUER, Vladimir S. *Be a Better Horseman*. 1941. NY. Duell Sloan & Pearce. G. O3. $35.00.

LITTELL, Robert. *The Debriefing*. 1979. NY. Harper & Row. 1st. F/F. H11. $30.00.

LITTLE, Constance & Gwenyth. *Black Shrouds*. nd. Triangle. reprint. VG/G. G8. $35.00.

LITTLE, Eddie. *Another Day in Paradise*. 1997. NY. Viking. 1st. author's 1st novel. sgn. VF/VF. T2. $25.00.

LIVELY, Penelope. *City of the Mind*. 1991. NY. Harper Collins. 1st Am ed. sgn. F/F. O11. $30.00.

LIVELY, Penelope. *Heat Wave*. 1996. NY. Harper Collins. 1st Am ed. sgn. F/F. O11. $30.00.

LIVELY, Penelope. *Oleander, Jacaranda: A Childhood Perceived*. 1994. NY. Harper Collins. 1st Am ed. sgn. memoir. F/F. O11. $30.00.

LIVELY, Penelope. *Passing On*. 1989. NY. Grove Weidenfeld. 1st Am ed. sgn. F/F. O11. $35.00.

LLEWELLYN, Sam. *Clawhammer*. 1993. London. Michael Joseph. 1st. VF/VF. T2. $25.00.

LLOSA, Mario Vargas. *Aunt Julia & the Scriptwriter*. 1982. np. FSG. 1st. F/F dj. M19. $25.00.

LOBO, Jeronimo. *The Itinerario of Jeronimo Lobo*. 1984. London. Hakluyt Society. 2nd series. vol. 12. bl cloth 8vo. 4 maps. 9 ils. 417p. NF in lightly worn dj. P4. $55.00.

LOCHTE, Dick. *Blue Bayou*. 1992. S&S. 1st. sgn. NF/NF. G8. $25.00.

LOCHTE, Dick. *Sleeping Dog*. 1985. NY. Arbor House. 1st. sgn. author's 1st novel. F/F. T2. $35.00.

LOCKE, Alain & Montgomery Gregory. *Plays of Negro Life*. 1927. Harper & Bros. 1st. VG/chipped dj. M25. $350.00.

LOCKRIDGE, Richard. *Death on the Hour*. 1974. NY. Lippincott. 1st. VF/VF. T2. $5.00.

LOCKRIDGE, Richard. *The Empty Day*. 1964. NY. Lippincott. 1st. F/F. T2. $10.00.

LOCKYER, Herbert. *All the Promises of the Bible*. 1964. Zondervan. 351p. VG/torn dj. B29. $11.50.

LOCKYER, Herbert. *Death and the Life Hereafter*. 1977. Baker. 110p. G. B29. $4.00.

LOCKYER, Herbert. *The Holy Spirit of God*. 1981. Nelson. 246p. VG/VG. B29. $11.00.

LOEFFLER, Jack. *Headed Upstream: Interviews with Iconoclasts*. (1989). Tucson. Harbinger House. 1st pb orig. pict wrp sgn by Loeffler. F. B3. $35.00.

LOEWENICH, Walther. *Luther's Theologies of the Cross*. 1976. Augsburg. 223p. VG/VG. B29. $10.00.

LOFTING, Hugh. *Doctor Doolittle in the Moon.* 1938 print (1928). Frederick A. Stokes. ils by author. VG. B15. $75.00.

LOFTING, Hugh. *The Story of Doctor Doolittle.* 1923 14th print (1920). Frederick A. Stokes. intro to 10th prt by Hugh Walpole; ils by author. VG. spine poor rpr & top fray. B15. $100.00.

LOFTING, Hugh. *The Story of Mrs. Tubbs.* 1931. NY. Frederick A. Stokes. G. A16. $40.00.

LOGAN, Chuck. *The Big Law.* 1998. NY. Harper Collins. 1st. sgn on tipped in bkplt. VF/VF. T2. $20.00.

LOGUE, Mary. *Blood Country.* 1999. NY. Walker. 1st. sgn. VF/VF. T2. $25.00.

LOMAX, John A. *Adventures of a Ballad Hunter.* 1947. NY. Macmillan. 1st. owner's inscr. F in VG clip dj. B2. $40.00.

LOMBREGLIA, Ralph. *Men Under Water.* 1990. NY. Doubleday. 1st. NF. mild foxing/NF. sm tear. M23. $25.00.

LONDON, David. *Sun Dancer.* 1996. NY. S&S. 1st. author's 1st book. F. B3. $15.00.

LONG, David. *Blue Spruce.* 1994. NY. Scribner's. 1st. author's 1st book. F/F. B3. $25.00.

LONG, Frank Belknap. *The Darkling Tide: Previously Uncollected Poetry.* 1995. West Hills. Tsathoggua Press. 1st. Perry M. Grayson. editor. VF/pict wrp. T2. $7.00.

LONG, Frank Belknap. *The First World Fantasy Convention: The Interviews.* 1995. West Hills. Tsathoggua Press. 1st. VF/pict wrp. T2. $7.00.

LONG, Trevor & Elizabeth Bell. *Antigua, Guatemala, An Illustrated History of the City and its Monuments.* 1989. np. Guatemala. biblio. maps. 12mo. b/w photos. 101p. G/wrp. F3. $10.00.

LONGYEAR, Barry B. *The Homecoming.* 1989. NY. Walker. 1st. VF/VF. T2. $8.00.

LOOS, Anita. *Kiss Hollywood Good-By.* 1974. Viking. 1st. picts. clip. F/chip dj. S19. $40.00.

LOPEZ, Barry. *Crossing Open Ground.* 1988. London. Macmillan. 1st British ed. sgn by author. F/F. B3. $35.00.

LOPEZ, Barry Holstun. *About this Life: Journeys on the Threshold of Memory.* 1998. NY. Knopf. 1st. sgn. F/F. O11. $30.00.

LOPEZ, Barry Holstun. *Of Wolves and Men.* 1978. NY. Scribner. 1st. sgn. F/F. price clip. O11. $200.00.

LOPEZ, Barry Holstun. *Winter Count.* 1981. NY. Scribner. 1st. sgn. F/NF. O11. $85.00.

LOPEZ, Steve. *The Sunday Macaroni Club.* 1997. NY. Harcourt Brace. 1st. F/F. B3. $15.00.

LOPEZ, Steve. *Third and Indiana.* 1994. NY. Viking. 1st. UP. F. D10. $10.00.

LORAINE, Philip. *A Mafia Kiss.* 1969. NY. Random. 1st. F/F. H11. $15.00.

LORD, Graham. *Dick Francis: A Racing Life.* 1999. London. Little, Brn. 1st. VF/VF. T2. $38.00.

LORENZ, Lee. *A Weekend in the City.* 1991. NY. Pippin Press. 1st. New. A28. $8.50.

LORING, Laurie. *Cassy.* 1875. Boston. D. Lothrop. F. A16. $5.00.

LOTT, Bret. *Jewel.* 1991. NY. Pocket Books. 1st. F/NF. M23. $20.00.

LOUGANIS, Greg. *Breaking the Surface.* 1994. NY. Random House. 1st. F/F. crease. M23. $35.00.

LOUGHERY, John. *Alias S. S. Van Dine.* 1992. NY. Scribner. 1st. VF/dj. M15. $45.00.

LOUGHERY, John. *Alias S. S. Van Dine: The Man Who Created Philo Vance.* 1992. NY. Scribners. 1st. VF/VF. T2. $15.00.

LOVE, William F. *Bloody Ten.* 1992. Fine. 1st. NF/NF. G8. $10.00.

LOVELESS, Dashiell. *By the Balls.* 1998. Los Angeles. Uglytown Productions. 1st. pb orig. VF/pict wrp. T2. $6.00.

LOVELL, Jim & Jeffrey Kluger. *Lost Moon: The Perilous Voyage of Apollo 13.* 1994. Boston. Houghton Mifflin. 1st. inscr by Lovell. F/F. O11. $60.00.

LOVESEY, Peter. *Bertie and the Seven Bodies.* 1990. Mysterious. 1st Am ed. VG/VG. G8. $12.50.

LOVESEY, Peter. *Do Not Exceed the Stated Dose.* 1998. Norfolk. Crippen & Landru. 1st. 1/250# copies. sgn. VF/VF. T2. $50.00.

LOVESEY, Peter. *On the Edge.* 1989. NY. Mysterious Press. 1st Am ed. VF/VF. T2. $12.00.

LOVESEY, Peter. *Rough Cider.* 1987. NY. Mysterious Press. 1st Am ed. VF/VF. T2. $14.00.

LOVESEY, Peter. *The Last Detective.* 1991. NY. Doubleday. 1st. VF/VF. T2. $15.00.

LOVESEY, Peter. *The Vault.* 1999. London. Little, Brn. 1st. sgn. VF/VF. T2. $38.00.

LOWELL, Amy. *John Keats.* 1925. Boston. Houghton Mifflin. 1st. 2 vol set. NF. D10. $98.00.

LOWRY, Lois. *The Giver.* 1993. Boston. Houghton Mifflin. 1st. winner of Newbery Medal. F/F. M23. $75.00.

LOWRY, Malcolm. *Dark as the Grave Wherein My Friend Is Laid.* 1968. np. General Publishing. 1st. NF/G dj. M19. $25.00.

LUCAS, Robert Irwin. *Tarentum Pattern Glass.* 1981. self-published. 1st. sm4to. 422p. AN/AN. H1. $48.00.

LUCCOCK, Halford. *Marching Off the Map and Other Sermons.* 1952. Harper. 192p. G. B29. $4.50.

LUCKERT, Karl. *Olmec Religion. A Key to Middle America & Beyond.* 1976. Norman. Univ. of Oklahoma Press. 1st. b/w photo ils. drawings. 185p. G/G. F3. $35.00.

LUDLUM, Robert. *Road to Omaha.* 1992. NY. Random House. 1st. VG+/VG. R16. $25.00.

LUDLUM, Robert. *The Aquitaine Progression.* 1984. NY. Random. 1st. F/F. H11. $35.00.

LUDLUM, Robert. *The Bourne Supremacy.* 1986. Random House. 1st trade ed. F/chip dj. S19. $35.00.

LUDLUM, Robert. *The Chancellor Manuscript.* 1977. NY. Dial Press. 1st. F/VG. T2. $15.00.

LUDLUM, Robert. *The Holcroft Covenant.* 1978. NY. Marek. 1st. light edge wear. F/F. H11. $55.00.

LUDLUM, Robert. *The Icarus Agenda.* 1988. Random House. 1st. F/F. S19. $35.00.

LUDLUM, Robert. *The Matarese Circle.* 1979. NY. Marek. 1st. F/F. H11. $35.00.

LUDLUM, Robert. *The Parsifal Mosaic.* 1982. NY. Random. 1st. F/F. H11. $35.00.

LUDLUM, Robert. *The Rhinemann Exchange.* 1974. NY. Dial. 1st. F/F. H11. $45.00.

LUDWIGSON, R. *Bible Prophecy Notes.* 1961. Zondervan. 172p. G. ex lib. B29. $5.00.

LUMLEY, Brian. *Necroscope: The Lost Years Volume 1.* 1995. London. Hodder & Stoughton. 2nd printing. VF/VF. T2. $15.00.

LUPICA, Mike. *Dead Air.* 1986. Villard. 1st. VF/NF. G8. $15.00.

LUPOFF, Richard. *The Forever City.* 1987. NY. Walker. 1st. sgn. VF/VF. T2. $25.00.

LUPOFF, Richard A. *The Bessie Blue Killer.* 1994. NY. St. Martin. 1st. VF/VF. T2. $15.00.

LUPOFF, Richard A. *The Sepia Siren.* 1994. NY. St. Martin. 1st. VF/VF. T2. $15.00.

LUSTBADER, Eric V. *Angel Eyes.* 1991. NY. Fawcett Columbine. 1st. VF/VF. T2. $9.00.

LUSTBADER, Eric V. *Black Blade.* 1993. NY. Fawcett Columbine. 1st. VF/VF. T2. $10.00.

LUTHER, Martin. *Commentary on the Epistle to the Galatians.* nd. Revell. 567p. VG. B29. $14.00.

LUTHER, T. N. *Collecting Taos Authors.* 1993. Taos, NM. New Mexico Book League. 1st. 1/400 copies in paper. sgn. 90p. F. B19. $15.00.

LUTZ, John. *Death by Jury.* 1995. NY. S M P. 1st. F/F. H11. $20.00.

LYLE, Sparky and Peter Golenbock. *The Bronx Zoo.* 1979. NY. Crown. VG+/VG. R16. $30.00.

LYMAN, Chester S. *Around the Horn to the Sandwich Islands and California. 1845 – 1850.* 1924. New Haven. Yale U Press. blk cloth. gilt spine titles. map ep. 16 plates. VG. minor shelfwear. P4. $125.00.

LYNDS, Gayle. *Masquerade.* 1996. NY. Doubleday. 1st. author's 1st book under her own name. sgn & dated. F/F. B3. $35.00.

LYONS, C. P. *Trees, Shrubs, and Flowers to Know in British Columbia.* 1959 (1952). 2nd. 194p. VG. B26. $12.50.

LYONS, Nan & Ivan. *Someone Is Killing the Great Chefs of America.* (1993). Boston. Little, Brn. 1st. F/F. B3. $25.00.

LYSAGHT, A. M. *Joseph Banks in Newfoundland and Labrador, 1766, His Diary, Manuscripts and Collections.* 1971. Berkeley. U of California Press. 1st Am ed. rem mk on heel. bookplates on front pastedown. thick 4to. rust cloth. 512p. VG w/ minor wear in worn dj. P4. $145.00.

LYTTELTON, Humphrey. *The Best of Jazz 2. Enter the Giants 1931 – 1944.* 1983. NY. Taplinger. ARC w/ slip. 1st paper ed. F. B2. $25.00.

— M —

MAAS, Peter. *Father and Son.* 1989. NY. S&S. 1st. rem. F/VF. H11. $20.00.

MAAS, Peter. *King of the Gypsies.* 1975. NY. Viking. 1st. top of jacket spine a bit frayed. F/NF+. H11. $40.00.

MACARTNEY, Clarence E. *Not Far from Pittsburgh.* 1936. Pittsburgh. Gibson Press. 2nd. 12mo Bookseller's label on endpaper. Minor edge chips. 138p. F/F. H1. $22.50.

MACBRIDE, J. Francis. *Flora of Peru, Part 3, No. 1 Leguminosae.* 1943. Chicago. Field Museum of History. Botany Series. Vol XIII. OP. wrp tanned. B26. $75.00.

MACCAULEY, Clay. *Memories and Memorials; Gatherings from an Eventful Life.* 1914. Tokyo, Japan. Fukuin Printing Co. 1st. orig cloth. spine sunned. inner hinges starting. scarce. 781p. VG. M8. $125.00.

MACDONAGH, Donagh. *A Warning to Conquerors.* 1968. Dolmen Press. 1st. F/NF. V1. $25.00.

MACDONALD, Betty. *Mrs. Piggle Wiggle.* 1947. Philadelphia. J. B. Lippincott. 1st. ils by Richard Bennett. 8vo. teal bl cloth. 119p. VG/G+. D6. $125.00.

MACDONALD, Betty. *Mrs. Piggle Wiggle's Magic.* 1949. Philadelphia. J. B. Lippincott. 4th ed. ils by Kurt Wiese. 8vo. maroon cloth w/blk design & lettering. 119p. NF/VG few chips at corners. D6. $35.00.

MACDONALD, Betty. *Mrs. Piggle Wiggle's Magic.* 1957. Philadelphia. J. B. Lippincott. 10th ed w/these ils. ils by Hilary Knight. 8vo. gr cloth w/blk design & lettering. lavender & navy dj w/different ils. 126p. NF/NF. D6. $25.00.

MACDONALD, Gordon. *Restoring Your Spiritual Passion.* 1986. Oliver. 223p. VG/VG. B29. $5.50.

MACDONALD, Gordon. *There's No Place Like Home: Faith and Inspiration for the Tough and Tender Moments of Life.* 1990. Tyndale. 305p. F/F. B29. $5.50.

MACDONALD, John D. *A Purple Place for Dying.* 1976. Philadelphia. Lippincott. 1st Am. jacket has short closed tear. F/dj. M15. $200.00.

MACDONALD, John D. *Barrier Island.* 1986. NY. Knopf. 1st. F/NF. T2. $7.00.

MACDONALD, John D. *Cinnamon Skin.* 1982. NY. Harper & Row. 1st. F/NF. T2. $20.00.

MACDONALD, John D. *Free Fall in Crimson.* 1981. NY. Harper & Row. 1st. F/F. T2. $25.00.

MACDONALD, John D. *Good Old Stuff.* 1982. NY. Harper & Row. 1st. VG/VG. G8. $20.00.

MACDONALD, John D. *One More Sunday.* 1984. NY. Knopf. 1st. VG/VG. G8. $10.00.

MACDONALD, John D. *The Empty Copper Sea.* 1978. Philadelphia. Lippincott. 1st. F/F. H11. $55.00.

MACDONALD, John D. *The Green Ripper.* 1979. NY. Lippincott. 1st. F/F. T2. $25.00.

MACDONALD, John D. *The Lonely Silver Rain.* 1985. NY. Knopf. 1st. F/F. H11. $30.00.

MACDONALD, John Ross. *Find a Victim.* 1954. Knopf. 1st. NF. burgundy paper bds. lt wear at spine ends. missing dj. stp on ffep. M25. $75.00.

MACDONALD, John Ross. *The Name Is Archer.* 1955. Bantam. 1st. VG to NF in pb. upper corner of corner creased. M25. $60.00.

MACDONALD, Marianne. *Death's Autograph.* 1997. NY. St. Martin. 1st. F/F. M23. $60.00.

MACDONALD, Marianne. *Ghost Walk.* 1997. London. Hodder & Stoughton. 1st. VF in dj. M15. $60.00.

MACDONALD, Patricia J. *Mother's Day.* 1994. NY. Warner. 1st. NF/NF. G8. $12.50.

MACDONALD, Patricia J. *No Way Home.* nd. NY. Delacorte. 1st. sgn. NF/VG. G8. $12.50.

MACDONALD, Philip. *Death and Chicanery.* 1962. Garden City. Doubleday. 1st. inscribed. agent's label on front endpaper. F/dj. M15. $100.00.

MACDONALD, Ross. *Archer at Large.* 1970. Knopf. 1st. F/dj. yellow stain on top of book block. M25. $50.00.

MACDONALD, Ross. *Archer in Jeopardy.* 1979. Knopf. 1st. F/clip dj. spine very lightly sunned. M25. $25.00.

MACDONALD, Ross. *Black Money.* 1966. NY. Knopf. 1st. stain on top of colored page edges. jacket has a short closed tear. F/dj. M15. $250.00.

MACDONALD, Ross. *Self Portrait.* 1981. Capra. 1st. foreword by Eudora Welty. essays. F/dj. M25. $25.00.

MACDONALD, Ross. *The Blue Hammer.* 1976. Knopf. 1st. NF/F. top of bds faded. wrinkle at head of spine.dj. M25. $25.00.

MACDONALD, Ross. *The Far Side of the Dollar.* 1965. Knopf. 1st. VG+/stained dj. M25. $90.00.

MACDONALD, Ross. *The Goodbye Look.* 1969. Knopf. 1st. F/clip dj. lt sunned on spine. M25. $50.00.

MACDONALD, Ross. *The Instant Enemy.* 1968. Knopf. 1st. NF/stained dj. M25. $75.00.

MACDOUGAL, Bonnie. *Breach of Trust.* 1996. np. Pocket. 1st. author's 1st novel. NF/NF. R16. $35.00.

MACE, Elizabeth. *Under Siege.* 1990. NY. Orchard Books. 1st Am ed. NF/VG. A28. $7.50.

MACFALL, Haldane. *The French Pastellists of the 18th Century: Their Lives, Their Times, Their Art and Their Significance.* 1909. London. Macmillan. lg 4to. xvi. 52 ils. mtd color plates. 212p. orig aqua cloth. gilt. K1. $100.00.

MACINNES, Colin. *City of Spades.* 1958. Macmillan. 1st. NF/blk bds. missing dj. M25. $40.00.

MACINNES, Helen. *Ride a Pale Horse.* 1984. NY. HBJ. 1st. F/F. H11. $20.00.

MACK, Robert Ellice. *All Things Bright and Beautiful.* c.1890. np. Ernest Nister. 1st. beautiful plates. folio. VG. M19. $85.00.

MACKAY, Charles. *Extraordinary Popular Delusions and the Madness of Crowds.* 1954. L. c. page. 724p. G/broken hinge. B29. $19.50.

MACKINNON, Col. *Origin and Sevices of the Cold Stream Guards.* 1833. London. 2 vols. ils. full leather. aeg. edgewear. some browning. 488/522p. VG. B18. $95.00.

MACKINTOSH, H. R. *The Doctrine of the Person Jesus Christ.* 1912. T&T Clark. 540p. Fair/ broken back. ex lib. B29. $9.50.

MACKINTOSH, Hugh Ross. *Types of Modern Theology: Schleiermacher to Barth.* nd. Scribner's. 333p. VG/VG. B29. $9.00.

MACKLER, Tasha. *Murder by Category: A Subject Guide to Mystery Fiction.* 1991. Metuchen. Scarecrow. 1st. Inscribed. VF/. M15. $50.00.

MACLAY, John. *Mindwarps.* 1991. Baltimore. Maclay. 1st. sgn. 500 copies printed. VF/no dj as issued. T2. $12.00.

MACLAY, John. *Other Engagements.* 1987. Madison. Dream House. 1st. sgn. 1000 copies printed. VF/no dj as issued. T2. $12.00.

MACLAY, John. *Tom Rudolph PI.* 1991. Baltimore. Maclay. 1st. sgn. VF/pict wrp. T2. $5.00.

MACLEAN, Alistair. *Athabasca.* 1980. London. Collins. 1st. F/dj. M15. $45.00.

MACLEAN, Alistair. *Bear Island.* 1971. London. Collins. 1st. F/dj. M15. $45.00.

MACLEAN, Alistair. *Flood Gate.* 1984. NY. Doubleday. 1st. VG+/dj clip. R16. $30.00.

MACLEAN, Alistair. *Goodbye California.* 1978. Garden City. Doubleday. 1st. VF/F. H11. $30.00.

MACLEAN, Alistair. *San Andreas.* 1985. NY. Doubleday. 1st. NF/VG. R16. $35.00.

MACLEAN, Charles. *The Watcher.* 1982. NY. S&S. 1st. F/F. B3. $30.00.

MACLEAN, Norman. *A River Runs Through It.* 1983. Chicago. U of Chicago. F in NF dj. D10. $55.00.

MACLEAN, Norman. *Young Men and Fire.* (1992). Chicago. U of Chicago. 1st. F/F. B3. $60.00.

MACLEISH, Archibald. *J. B.* 1957. Houghton Mifflin. 153p. G/G. B29. $4.50.

MACLEOD, Charlotte. *Had She But Known: A Biography of Mary Roberts Rinehart.* 1994. NY. Mysterious Press. 1st. VF/VF. T2. $15.00.

MACLEOD, Charlotte. *Rest You Merry.* 1978. Garden City. Doubleday. 1st. some spotting on page edges. F/dj. M15. $100.00.

MACLEOD, Charlotte. *The Corpse in Oozak's Pond.* 1987. NY. Mysterious Press. 1st. F/F. T2. $14.00.

MACLEOD, Charlotte. *The Resurrection Man.* 1992. NY. Mysterious Press. 1st. VF/VF. T2. $14.00.

MACLEOD, Charlotte. *The Silver Ghost.* 1988. NY. Mysterious Press. 1st. VF/VF. T2. $14.00.

MACLEOD, Charlotte. *Vane Pursuit.* 1989. Mysterious. 1st. NF/NF. G8. $10.00.

MACMILLAN, H. F. *Tropical Planting and Gardening with Special Reference to Ceylon.* 1962 (1949). London. 5th (& last) ed. upper corners bumped. B26. $49.00.

MACNEIL, Alan & Esther. *Garden Lilies.* 1946. NY. 226p w/34 plates & ep charts. ep tanned. B26. $17.50.

MACOBOY, Sterling. *What Shrub Is That?* 1990. NY. 4to. 268p. ils color photos. AN in dj. B26. $39.00.

MACPHERSON, Rett. *Family Skeletons.* 1997. NY. St. Martin. 1st. author's 1st novel. VF/VF. T2. $35.00.

MACSELF, A. J. *French Intensive Gardening.* nd. London. 128p. 25 text ils. 15 b&w photos. faded orange cloth. B26. $29.00.

MACSHANE, Frank. *The Life of Raymond Chandler.* 1976. Dutton. 1st. F in dj. M25. $45.00.

MACVICAR, Angus. *The Dancing Horse.* 1961. London. John Long. 1st. jacket has tiny wear at spine ends and a couple of tiny tears. F/dj. M15. $60.00.

MADDEN, E. S. *Craig's Spur.* 1961. NY. Vanguard. 1st Am. F/dj. M15. $50.00.

MADISON, Michael. *A Revision of Monstera.* 1977. Gray Herbarium of Harvard Univ. No. 207. lt gr cloth. inscr by author to Paul Hutchinson. F. B26. $39.00.

MAETERLINCK, Maurice. *The Swarm, from the Life of the Bee.* 1906. np. Dodd Mead. 1st. ils by Anthony Euwer. VG. M19. $25.00.

MAFFITT, John Newland. *Nautilus Or Cruising Under Canvas.* 1872. NY. United States Publishing Co. 1st. orig cloth. bi rubbed with weat to extremities. scarce historical novel. 352p. VG. M8. $450.00.

MAGNER, D. *Magner's A B C Guide to Sensible Horse-Shoeing.* 1899. Akron. Warner. 1st. sm 4to. G. O3. $95.00.

MAGUIDOVICH, I. P. *Historia De Descubrimiento Y Exploracion De Latinoamerica.* 1979. Cuba. Casa de las Americas. 285p. VG/bds worn. dj chipped. F3. $35.00.

MAGUIRE, Gregory. *Wicked, the Life and Times of the Wicked Witch of the West.* 1995. NY. Regan Books. 1st. ils by Douglas Smith. F/F. B3. $40.00.

MAGUIRE, Rochfort. *The Journal of Rochfort Maguire 1852 – 1854.* 1988. London. Hakluyt Society. 1st. 2 vol set. second series vols 169. 170. ed by John Bockstoce w/extensive intro. 318. 584p. NF in rubbed dj. P4. $75.00.

MAHFOUZ, Naguib. *The Journey of Ibn Fattouma.* 1992. NY. Doubleday. 1st. trans by Denys Johnson-Davies. author Is a Nobel prize winner. F/F. B3. $20.00.

MAHONEY, Dan. *Detective First Grade.* 1993. NY. St. Martin. 1st. author's 1st novel. VF/VF. T2. $35.00.

MAIKEN, Peter T. *Night Trains, the Pullman System in the Golden Years of American Rail Travel.* 1989. Chicago. 1st. ils ep. ils and maps. 415p. VG in dj. B18. $35.00.

MAILER, Norman. *An American Dream.* 1965. London. Deutsch. 1st. jacket has minor chipping at top of spine and rubbing at top of rear flap fold. F/NF. H11. $45.00.

MAILER, Norman. *Harlot's Ghost.* 1991. NY. Random. 1st. jacket has Canadian price sticker on front flap. F/F. H11. $30.00.

MAILER, Norman. *The Executioner's Song.* 1979. Boston. Little, Brn. 1st. F/F. H11. $60.00.

MAILER, Norman. *The Gospel According to the Son.* 1997. NY. Random House. 1st. F/F. B3. $15.00.

MAILER, Norman. *Tough Guys Don't Dance.* 1984. NY. Random House. 1st trade ed. F/VF. T2. $8.00.

MAILING, Arthur. *Decoy.* 1969. Harper & Row. 1st. yellowing. G-. S19. $18.00.

MAINS, Karen. *Open Heart Open Home.* 1977. Cook. 199p. G/G. ex lib. B29. $7.00.

MAITLAND, Barry. *The Chalon Heads.* 1999. London. Orion. 1st. VF/VF. T2. $38.00.

MAJOR, Clarence, Ed. *The New Black Poetry.* 1969. NY. International. 1st. F/lightly used dj. B2. $50.00.

MAJOR, Reginald. *Justice in the Round, The Trial of Angela Davis.* 1973. NY. Third Press. 1st. NF/used dj. B2. $30.00.

MALAMUD, Bernard. *Dubin's Lives.* 1979. NY. Farrar. 1st. F/F. H11. $30.00.

MALAMUD, Bernard. *Dubin's Lives.* 1979. NY. FSG. 2nd issue w/pg 231 tipped in. VG+/NF. A24. $25.00.

MALAMUD, Bernard. *God's Grace.* 1982. NY. FSG. 1st. F/F. lt wear to corners. A24. $25.00.

MALAMUD, Bernard. *The Assistant.* 1957. NY. Farrar. 1st. book has a very slight slant. name and date on front fep. jacket spine Is faded. NF/NF. H11. $230.00.

MALAMUD, Bernard. *The Fixer.* 1966. NY. F S G. 1st. White jacket Is slightly soiled and price clipped. F/F. H11. $35.00.

MALCOLM, John. *Godwin Sideboard.* 1984. NY. Scribner's. 1st Am ed. NF/NF. G8. $12.50.

MALCOLM, John. *Hungover.* 1995. NY. St. Martin. 1st Am ed. sgn. VF/VF. T2. $20.00.

MALCOLM, John. *Hungover.* 1994. London. Harper Collins. 1st. sgn. VF/VF. T2. $35.00.

MALCOLM, John. *Mortal Ruin.* 1988. NY. Scribners. 1st Am ed. sgn. VF/VF. T2. $25.00.

MALCOLM, John. *Sheep, Goats and Soap.* 1991. NY. Scribners. 1st Am ed. sgn. VF/VF. T2. $20.00.

MALCOLM, John. *The Godwin Sideboard.* 1985. NY. Scribners. 1st Am ed. VF/VF. T2. $15.00.

MALING, Arthur. *A Taste of Treason.* 1983. NY. Harper & Row. 1st. F/F. H11. $20.00.

MALLALIEU, J. P. W. *Extraordinary Seaman.* 1957. np. np. 1st. NF/G dj. M19. $25.00.

MALLIOL, William. *Slave.* 1986. NY. Norton. 1st. VF/VF. H11. $25.00.

MALMONT, Valerie S. *Death, Lies, and Apple Pies.* 1997. NY. S&S. 1st. sgn. F/F. G8. $25.00.

MALMONT, Valerie S. *Death Pays the Rose Rent.* 1994. NY. S&S. 1st. sgn. NF/NF. G8. $25.00.

MALONE, Michael. *Foolscap.* 1991. Boston. Little, Brn. 1st. F/VF. H11. $35.00.

MALONE, Michael. *Handling Sin.* 1986. Boston. Little, Brn. 1st. Top corners are bumped. Jacket has several short edge tears. F-/NF. H11. $25.00.

MALONE, Michael. *Time's Witness.* 1989. Boston. Little, Brn. 1st. VF/dj. M15. $75.00.

MALONEY, Shane. *The Brush-Off.* 1998. NY. Arcade. 1st author's 1st book. VF/VF. H11. $30.00.

MALOUF, David. *Remembering Babylon.* 1993. London. Chatto & Windus. 1st British ed. F/F. B3. $30.00.

MALRAUX, Andre. *Anti-Memoirs.* 1968. NY. HRW. 1st. F/F. B3. $10.00.

MALZBERG, Barry N. *The Passage of the Light: The Recursive Science Fiction of Barry N. Malzberg.* 1994. Framingham. Nesfa Press. 1st. Mike Resnick. Anthony R. Lewis. editors. VF/pict wrp. T2. $15.00.

MAMET, David. *Make Believe Town.* 1996. Boston. Little, Brn. 1st. sgn. F/F. D10. $35.00.

MAMET, David. *Some Freaks.* 1989. NY. Viking. 1st. sgn. F/F. D10. $45.00.

MAMET, David. *The Cabin, Reminiscence and Diversions.* 1992. NY. Turtle Bay Books. 1st. sgn. F/F. D10. $45.00.

MAMET, David. *The Village.* 1994. Boston. Little, Brn. 1st. F/F. B3. $30.00.

MAMET, David. *Warm and Cold.* 1988. NY. Grove Press. 1st. author's 2nd children's book. ils Donald Sultan. F/F. D10. $45.00.

MAMET, David. *We're No Angels, A Screenplay.* 1990. NY. Grove Weidenfeld. PBO. sgn. NF in pict wrp. D10. $35.00.

MAMET, David. *Writing in Restaurants.* 1986. NY. Viking. 1st. sgn. F/F. D10. $50.00.

MANALANG, Priscilla S. *A Philippine Rural School; Its Cultural Dimension.* 1977. Quezon City. Univ. of the Philippines Press. cloth. 255p. F/F. P1. $20.00.

MANCHESTER, William. *Portrait of a President.* 1962. Little, Brn. 1st. 8vo. 238p. AN/F-. H1. $18.00.

MANCHESTER, William. *The Death of a President.* 1967. Harper & Row. 1st. NF/worn dj. M25. $50.00.

MANDERINO, John. *Sam and His Brother Len.* 1994. Chicago. Academy. 1st. author's 1st book. VF/VF. H11. $40.00.

MANES, Stephen. *Comedy High.* 1992. NY. Scholastic Hardcover. F/VG. A28. $6.95.

MANFRED, Frederick. *Lord Grizzly.* 1954. McGraw Hill. 1st. VG/chipped dj. M25. $45.00.

MANIER, Edward. *The Young Darwin and His Cultural Circle.* 1978. Dordrecht. Holland. sc. F. B26. $21.00.

MANLEY, Frank. *The Cockfighter.* 1998. Minneapolis. Coffee House Press. 1st. VF/VF. T2. $20.00.

MANN, Graciela. *The 12 Prophets of Aleijahinho.* 1967. Austin. Univ. of Texas Press. 1st. 4to. 131p. G/chipped dj. F3. $25.00.

MANN, Jessica. *Faith, Hope and Homicide.* 1991. NY. St. Martin. 1st Am ed. F/NF. G8. $10.00.

MANN, Jessica. *Grave Goods.* 1985. Crime Club. 1st Am ed. NF/NF. G8. $10.00.

MANN, Jessica. *The Survivor's Revenge.* 1998. London. Constable. 1st. sgn. VF/VF. T2. $35.00.

MANN, Patrick. *Dog Day Afternoon.* 1974. NY. Delacorte. 1st. Book has lightly bumped corners. White jacket Is lightly soiled and has light chippings at extremities. NF/VG+. H11. $80.00.

MANN, Paul. *Season of the Monsoon.* 1993. NY. Fawcett. 1st. F/F. H11. $25.00.

MANN, Phillip. *The Eye of the Queen.* 1983. NY. Arbor. 1st. VF/F. H11. $40.00.

MANNING, Thomas G. *U S Coast Survey vs Naval Hydrographic Office; A 19th Century Rivalry in Science and Politics.* 1988. Tuscaloosa. Univ. of Alabama Press. 8vo. 202p. F/F. K5. $30.00.

MANNIX, Daniel P. *Black Cargoes: A History of the Atlantic Slave Trade.* 1962. Viking. later printing. in collaboration with Malcolm Cowley. NF/sunned dj. M25. $15.00.

MANRIQUE, Manuel. *Island in Harlem.* 1966. NY. day. 1st. F/F. H11. $50.00.

MANTLE, Mickey. *All My Octobers.* 1994. NY. Harper Collins. 1st. NF/VG. R16. $30.00.

MANTLE, Mickey. *The Mick.* 1985. NY. Doubleday. VG/VG. R16. $25.00.

MANUEL, David. *A Matter of Roses.* 1999. Brewster. Paraclete Press. 1st. author's 1st novel. sgn. VF/VF. T2. $25.00.

MAPSON, Jo-Ann. *Shadow Ranch.* 1996. NY. Harper Collins. 1st. F/F. B3. $25.00.

MARCUS, Alan. *Of Streets and Stars.* 1960. Manzanita Press. 1st. Jacket Is browned on the rear panel and sunned at the spine; sgn; inscr. F/dj. M25. $100.00.

MARCUS, J. S. *The Art of Cartography.* 1991. NY. Knopf. 1st. author's 1st book. F/F. A24. $35.00.

MARCUS, J. S. *The Captain's Fire.* 1996. NY. Knopf. 1st. author's 1st novel. F/F. B3. $25.00.

MARCUS, Joyce & Kent Flannery. *Zapotec Civilization. How Urban Society Evolved In Mexico's Oaxacan Valley.* 1996. NY. Thames & Hudson. 1st. 4to. 255p. G/G. F3. $60.00.

MARDEN, Orison Swett. *Prosperity: How to Attract It.* 1924. NY. Success Magazine corp. 3rd. 12mo. 325p. VG. H1. $15.00.

MARDER, Norma. *An Eye for Dark Places.* 1993. Boston. Little, Brn. 1st. author's 1st book. F/F. H11. $25.00.

MARGOLIN, Phillip. *After Dark.* 1995. NY. Doubleday. UP. F in pict wrp w/pub letter. A24. $15.00.

MARGOLIN, Phillip. *Gone, but Not Forgotten.* 1993. NY. Doubleday. 1st. sgn. F/F. A24. $35.00.

MARGOLIN, Phillip. *The Burning Man.* 1996. NY. Doubleday. 1st. sgn by author. F/F. B3. $35.00.

MARIUS, Richard. *Bound for the Promised Land.* 1976. NY. Knopf. 1st. inscribed on the front fep. Book has a slight slant and a rubbed spine. NF/F. H11. $40.00.

MARK, Harry. *Patterns for Preaching.* 1959. Zondervan. 183p. VG. B29. $7.00.

MARKHAM, Sir Clements R. *The Lands of Silence, A History of Arctic and Antarctic Exploration.* 1998. Mansfield Centre. Martino Fine Books. 1 of 150 copies. issued w/o dj. rpt of 1921 Cambridge Univ. Press. 8vo. 539p. New. P4. $75.00.

MARKMAN, Sidney. *Arquitectura Y Urbanizacion En El Chiapas Colonial.* 1993. Mexico. np. 1st ed Spanish. inscr. wrp. 604p. VG. corners bent. F3. $50.00.

MARKMAN, Sidney. *Colonial Architecture of Antigua, Guatemala.* 1966. Philadelphia. Am Philosophical Society. 1st. lg 4to. index. biblio. b/w photo ils. maps. 335p. G/G. F3. $75.00.

MARKSON, David. *Springer's Progress.* 1977. NY. HRW. 1st. Full page inscription. lightly sunned. F/F. D10. $65.00.

MARLETT, Melba. *Escape While I Can.* 1944. Crime Club. 1st. VG/VG. G8. $10.00.

MARLOWE, Derek. *A Dandy in Aspic.* 1966. London. Victor Gollancz. 1st. author's 1st novel. F in dj. M15. $90.00.

MARLOWE, Derek. *A Dandy in Aspic.* 1966. NY. Putnam. 1st Am ed. author's 1st book. NF/NF. D10. $45.00.

MARLOWE, George Francis. *Coaching Roads of Old New England.* 1945. NY. Macmillan. VG. O3. $30.00.

MARON, Margaret. *Bootlegger's Daughter.* 1992. NY. Mysterious Press. 1st. Edgar Award for best novel. VF/VF. T2. $85.00.

MARON, Margaret. *Corpus Christmas.* 1989. NY. Doubleday. 1st. F/dj. M15. $65.00.

MARON, Margaret. *Home Fires.* 1998. Warner. 1st. sgn. F/F. G8. $22.50.

MARON, Margaret. *Killer Market.* 1997. Mysterious. 1st. sgn. NF/NF. G8. $22.50.

MARON, Margaret. *Shooting at Loons.* 1994. NY. Mysterious Press. 1st. VF/VF. T2. $25.00.

MAROT, Helen. *American Labor Unions.* 1914. NY. Macmillan. ex lib. G/VG. B2. $25.00.

MARQUAND, John P. *Sincerely, Willis Wayde.* 1955. Little, Brn. G. S19. $20.00.

MARQUETTE, Arthur F. *Brands, Trademarks and Good Will, the Story of the Quaker Oats Company.* 1967. NY. 1st. ils. 274p. VG in dj. B18. $15.00.

MARSH, F. E. *Fully Furnished: The Christian Worker's Equipment.* 1973. Kregel. 390p VG/VG. B29. $9.00.

MARSH, Ngaio. *Hand in Glove.* 1962. London. Collins Crime Club. 1st. VF in dj M15. $95.00.

MARSH, Ngaio. *Swing Brother Swing.* 1949 London. Collins Crime Club. 1st. page edges spotted. Jacket has long closed crease tear on front panel. a couple of short closed tears and wear at spine ends. VG/dj. M15 $75.00.

MARSH, Richard. *The Haunted Chair and Other Stories.* 1997. Ashcroft, BC. Ash Tree Press. 1st. Richard Dalby, editor. VF/VF T2. $50.00.

MARSHALL, L. H. *The Challenge of New Testament Ethics.* 1956. Macmillan. 363p VG/torn dj. B29. $7.50.

MARSHALL, Logan. *The Story of the Panama Canal.* 1913. np. color frontis. b/w photo ils. 86p. G/lt shelf wear. F3. $20.00.

MARSHALL, Paule. *Soul Clap Hands and Sing.* 1961. NY. Atheneum. 1st. NF/lightly soiled dj. chips. M25. $125.00.

MARSHALL, Paule. *The Chosen Place, The Timeless People.* 1969. HBW. 1st. NF/chipped dj. M25. $200.00.

MARSHALL, Sidney. *Some Like it Hot.* 1941. NY. William Morrow. 1st. sgn. F in dj. M15. $50.00.

MARSTON, A. E. *The Dragons of Archenfield.* 1995. London. Headline. 1st. sgn. VF/dj. M15. $55.00.

MARSTON, Edward (Keith Miles). *The King's Evil.* 1999. London. Headline. 1st. sgn. VF/VF. T2. $40.00.

MARSTON, Edward (Keith Miles). *The Nine Giants.* 1991. London. Bantam Press. 1st. sgn. VF/VF. T2. $30.00.

MARTI, Samuel. *Music Before Columbus.* 1978. np. Mexico. 2nd ed. bibio. b/w photo ils. English/ Spanish. 95p. G/ wrp. F3. $20.00.

MARTIN, Ann M. *Babysitter's Club, The Portrait Collection, Claudia's Book.* 1995. Apple Paperbacks. Scholastic Edition. G. A28. $2.95.

MARTIN, Dannie. *In the Hat.* 1997. NY. S&S. 1st. sgn by Martin aka Red Hog. VF/VF. T2. $25.00.

MARTIN, David. *Bring Me Children.* 1992. NY. Random House. 1st. VF/VF. T2. $8.00.

MARTIN, David. *Lie to Me.* 1990. NY. Random House. 1st. VF/VF. T2. $9.00.

MARTIN, George R. R. *Portraits of His Children.* 1987. Arlington Heights. Dark Harvest. 1st. sgn. VF/VF. T2. $35.00.

MARTIN, George R. R. *The Armageddon Rag.* 1983. NY. Poseidon Press. 1st. sgn. VF/VF. T2. $30.00.

MARTIN, Percy F. *Mexico's Treasure House (Guanajuato). An Ils and Descriptive Account of the Mines and their Operations in 1906.* NY. The Cheltenham Press. 1906. 8vo. 259p. ils including folding plates. red cloth. 1st ed. ex lib with library markings (discard stamp). cloth soiled. G. L5. $30.00.

MARTIN, Valerie. *Italian Fever.* 1999. NY. Knopf. 1st. sgn. VF/VF. T2. $25.00.

MARTIN, Walter R. *The Kingdom of the Cults.* 1977. Bethany. 443p. VG/VG. B29. $5.50.

MARTIN, William. *Back Bay.* 1979. NY. Crown. 1st. author's 1st book. F/F. H11. $35.00.

MARTIN, William. *Nerve Endings.* 1984. NY. Crown. 1st. F/F. H11. $20.00.

MARTIN, William. *The Rising of the Moon.* 1987. NY. Crown. 1st. F/VF. H11. $30.00.

MARTINEAU, Mrs. Philip. *Gardening in Sunny Lands. The Riviera, California, Australia.* 1924. London. lt foxing throughout. B26. $39.00.

MARTINEAU, Robert A. S. *Rhodesian Wild Flowers.* 1953. London. orig blk cloth. paintings by Margaret H. Phear. ep tanned. B26. $56.00.

MARTINEZ, Demetria. *Mother Tongue.* (1993). Tempe. Bilingual Press. 1st. F/F. B3. $30.00.

MARTINI, Steve. *Compelling Evidence.* 1992. NY. Putnam. 1st. F/F. H11. $25.00.

MARTINI, Steve. *Prime Witness.* 1993. NY. Putnam. 1st. sgn. VF/VF. T2. $30.00.

MARTINI, Steve. *The Judge.* (1996). NY. Putnam. 1st. sgn by author. F/F. B3. $40.00.

MARTINI, Steve. *The List.* 1997. NY. Putnam. 1st. F/F. H11. $15.00.

MARTONE, Michael. *Alive and Dead in Indiana.* 1984. NY. Knopf. 1st. author's 1st book. VF/F. H11. $35.00.

MARTYN, Wyndham. *Secret of the Silver Car.* 1922. Herbert Jenkins. 1st British ed. VG. G8. $12.50.

MARX, Robert. *In Quest of the Great White Gods.* 1992. NY. Crown. 1st. 343p. G/G. F3. $25.00.

MARZANI, Carl. *The Survivor.* 1958. NY. Marzani & Munsell. 1st. VG/orig wrp. B2. $30.00.

MASCALL, E. L. *Christ, The Christian and the Church, A Study of the Incarnation and its Consequences.* 1946. Longmans. Green and Co. 257p. VG. ex lib. B29. $9.50.

MASO, Carole. *Ghost Dance.* (1986). San Francisco. North Point Press. 1st. author's first novel. VF/F. B3. $35.00.

MASON, A. E. W. *Fire Over England.* 1936. London. Hodder & Stoughton. 1st. VG in dj. M15. $75.00.

MASON, A. E. W. *The House in Lordship Lane.* 1946. London. Hodder & Stoughton. 1st. some slight spotting. F in soiled dj. M15. $85.00.

MASON, A. E. W. *The Prisoner in the Opal.* 1928. Garden City. Doubleday Crime Club. 1st Am ed. F in dj. M15. $35.00.

MASON, Bobbie Ann. *Feather Crowns.* 1993. NY. Harper Collins. 1st. sgn. F/F. O11. $30.00.

MASON, Bobbie Ann. *In Country.* 1985. NY. Harper & Row. 1st. VF/F. H11. $40.00.

MASON, Bobbie Ann. *Love Life.* (1989). NY. Harper & Row. 1st. sgn. F/F. O11. $30.00.

MASON, Clifford. *Jamaica Run.* 1987. NY. St. Martin. 1st. VF in dj. M15. $65.00.

MASON, Clifford. *The Case of the Ashanti Gold.* 1985. NY. St. Martin. 1st. Author's first novel. F/dj. M15. $45.00.

MASON, F. Van Wyck. *Brimstone Club.* 1971. Boston. Little, Brn. 1st. F/F. H11. $35.00.

MASON, Francis Van Wyck. *Hang My Wreath. By Ward Weaver (pseud).* 1941. NY. Wilfred Funk. Inc. 1st. orig cloth. author's 1st book. historical novel. 358p. VG. chipped slightly dj. M8. $25.00.

MASON, Francis Van Wyck. *Proud New Flags.* 1951. Philadelphia. Lippincott. BCE. orig cloth. 492p. VG/VG. M8. $151.00.

MASON, Hamilton. *Your Garden in the South.* 1961. Princeton. turquoise cloth & wht brds. VG. B26. $27.50.

MASON, John. *Papermaking as an Artistic Craft, with a Foreword by Dr. Dard Hunter, Illustrated by Rigby Graham.* (1963). Leicester. twelve by eight. sm 8vo. 86 line-block drawings. 8 samples of handmade paper tipped in. insert sgn by Mason. 96p. wht limp Linson cloth. gilt. K1. $150.00.

MASON, Miriam E. *Caroline and Her Kettle Named Maud.* 1951. NY. Macmillan. G. child's writings on ep. A16. $5.00.

MASON, Otis Tufton. *Aboriginal American Harpoons: A Study in Ethnic Distribution and Invention.* 1902. Washington. US Natl. Museum. removed from the Annual Rpt of the Smithsonian for 1900. 92 ils. 19 plates. pp189-304. VG. marginal holes from orig stitching. P4. $60.00.

MASON, Redfern. *The Song Lore of Ireland. Erin's Story in Music and Verse.* NY. Wessel & Russell. 1910. 8vo. 329p. ils with music. gr cloth. 1st Am ed. Endpapers foxed. minor wear. G to VG. L5. $35.00.

MASON, Richard. *The Fever Tree.* 1962. Cleveland. World. 1st. F in NF dj. B2. $25.00.

MASON, Sara Elizabeth. *Crimson Feather.* 1945. Crime Club. 1st. VG. G8. $15.00.

MASON, Van Wyck. *Maracaibo Mission.* 1965. Garden City. Doubleday. 1st. F in dj. M15. $45.00.

MASON, Van Wyck. *The Rio Casino Intrigur.* 1941. NY. Reynal & Hitchcock. 1st. wear along cover edges and light spotting on page edges. Jacket has lightly soiled spine. VG/dj. M15. $100.00.

MASON, Van Wyck. *Trouble in Burma.* 1962. Garden City. Doubleday. 1st. F in dj. M15. $45.00.

MASSEE, William W. *Just Tell Me What I Want to Know About Wine.* 1981. NY. Grosset & Dunlap. trade pb. VG. A28. $6.50.

MASSEY, A. B. *The Ferns and Fern Allies of Virginia.* 1958. staplebound pamphlet. Ira L. Wiggins stp on front. B26. $11.00.

MASSIE, Chris. *The Green Circle.* 1943. NY. Random House. 1st Am ed. F in worn dj. M15. $65.00.

MASTERS, John. *Bhowani Junction.* 1954. Michael Joseph. 1st. Rubbed jacket. VG/dj. M25. $50.00.

MASTERS, John. *Heart of War.* 1980. McGraw-Hill. 1st. tall 8vo. 617p. G+/G. H1. $20.00.

MASTERS, Priscilla. *And None Shall Sleep.* 1997. London. Macmillan. 1st. sgn. VF/VF. T2. $30.00.

MATEER, Florence. *Just Normal Children.* 1929. NY. Appleton. 1st. paper browning. 294p. VG. B18. $12.50.

MATERA, Lia. *A Hard Bargain.* 1992. NY. S&S. 1st. VF/VF. T2. $15.00.

MATERA, Lia. *Prior Convictions.* 1991. NY. S&S. 1st. VF/VF. H11. $25.00.

MATHER, Berkely. *A Spy for a Spy.* 1968. NY. Scribners. 1st. Jacket has 1" closed tear at top of rear panel. VF/F. H11. $35.00.

MATHESON, Richard. *7 Steps to Midnight.* 1993. NY. Forge. 1st. VF/VF. T2. $11.00.

MATHESON, Richard. *Earthbound.* 1989. London. Robinson Publishing. 1st hc ed. restores author's preferred text cut from the orig pb ed written as by Logan Swanson. VF/VF. T2. $40.00.

MATHESON, Richard. *Hell House.* 1971. NY. Viking. 1st. NF/NF. fading. mild soiling. A24. $200.00.

MATHESON, Richard. *I Am Legend: The 40th Anniversary Edition.* 1995. Springfield. Gauntlet Press. ltd ed. 1/500 # copies. sgn by author. George Clayton Johnson. Dan Simmons. & Dennis Etchison. VF/no dj in slipcase as issued. T2. $75.00.

MATHESON, Richard. *What Dreams May Come: 20th Anniversary Edition.* 1998. Springfield. Gauntlet Press. ltd ed. 1/500 # copies. sgn. VF/VF dj in slipcase. T2. $60.00.

MATHESON, Richard Christian. *Created By.* 1993. NY. Bantam. 1st. VF/VF. T2. $10.00.

MATHEWS, Harry. *Cigarettes.* 1987. NY. Weidenfeld. 1st. F/F. H11. $30.00.

MATHEWSON, R. Duncan. *Treasure of the Atocha.* 1986. NY. Dutton. 1st. 190p. G/chipped dj. F3. $25.00.

MATOS MOCTEZUMA, Eduardo. *The Aztecs.* 1989. NY. Rizzoli. 1st. folio. color & b/w photo ils. 239p. G/G. F3. $85.00.

MATTESON, Stefanie. *Murder Among the Angels.* 1996. Berkeley. 1st. sgn. F/F. G8. $15.00.

MATTHEWS, Alex. *Satan's Silence.* 1997. Intrigue. 1st. sgn. NF/NF. G8. $15.00.

MATTHEWS, Brander. *Tales of Fantasy and Fact.* 1896. NY. Harper & Brothers. 1st. rust cloth-covered boards with gold-stamped titles and figures. F/. M15. $100.00.

MATTHEWS, I. G. *The Religious Pilgrimage.* 1947. Harper. 304p. G/torn dj. B29. $13.00.

MATTHIESSEN, Peter. *African Silences.* 1991. NY. Random House. 1st. sgn. F in F dj. D10. $50.00.

MATTHIESSEN, Peter. *At Play in the Fields of the Lord.* 1965. NY. Random House. 1st. sgn. F/NF. slight darkening on spine. shallow chip. O11. $300.00.

MATTHIESSEN, Peter. *Bone by Bone.* 1999. NY. Random House. 1st. sgn. F/F. O11. $40.00.

MATTHIESSEN, Peter. *Far Tortuga.* (1975). NY. Random House. 1st. VG. sunning to edges/VG. price clip. stain. creasing to front flap. B3. $30.00.

MATTHIESSEN, Peter. *In the Spirit of Crazy Horse.* 1983. Viking. 1st. this book was withdrawn from sale due to libel suits. F/F. M25. $150.00.

MATTHIESSEN, Peter. *Indian Country.* 1986. NY. Viking. 1st. NF. lt sunning to edges/NF. closed tear at bottom of spine. B3. $85.00.

MATTHIESSEN, Peter. *Killing Mr. Watson.* 1990. NY. Random House. 1st. sgn. F in F dj. D10. $50.00.

MATTHIESSEN, Peter. *Lost Man's River.* 1997. NY. Random House. 1st. sgn on tip in p. F in F dj. D10. $50.00.

MATTHIESSEN, Peter. *On the River Styx and Other Stories.* 1986. NY. Random House. 1st. sgn. F/F. clip. O11. $35.00.

MATTHIESSEN, Peter. *Sand Rivers.* 1981. NY. Viking. 1st. color photos by Hugo Van Lawick. F/NF. minor wear & soiling. A24. $32.00.

MATTHIESSEN, Peter. *The Snow Leopard.* 1978. Viking. 1st. F/torn dj. M25. $30.00.

MAUDSLEY, Athol. *Highways and Horses.* 1888. London. Chapman & Hall. 1st ed. spine faded. ftspc detached but present. O3. $165.00.

MAUGHAM, Robin. *The Link: A Victorian Mystery.* 1969. NY. McGraw Hill. 1st. VF/VF. T2. $15.00.

MAUPIN, Armistead. *Sure of You.* (1989). NY. Harper. 1st. sgn by author. F/F. B3. $35.00.

MAURICE, Rene L & Ken Follett. *Gentlemen of 16 July.* 1978. Arbor. 1st Am ed. VG+/VG. G8. $20.00.

MAUROIS, Andre. *September Roses.* 1958. London. Bodley Head. 1st English. F/F dj. M19. $25.00.

MAUS, Cynthia P. *Christ and the Fine Arts.* 1938. Harper. 764p. G/torn dj. B29. $7.50.

MAXWELL, A. E. *Just Enough Light to Kill.* 1988. NY. Doubleday. 1st. F/VF. T2. $15.00.

MAXWELL, A. E. *Money Burns.* 1991. NY. Villard. 1st. VF/VF. T2. $15.00.

MAXWELL, Evan. *Season of the Swan.* 1997. NY. Harper Collins. 1st. sgn. VF/VF. T2. $25.00.

MAXWELL, Thomas. *The Suspense Is Killing Me.* 1990. NY. Mysterious. 1st. F/F. H11. $15.00.

MAY, Robin. *Gold Rushes: From California to the Klondike.* 1977. London. Wm Luscombe. 1st. sm 4to. ils. F/dj. O4. $20.00.

MAYBURY-LEWIS, David. *The Savage and the Innocent.* 1965. Cleveland. World Pub Co. 1st. 270p. G/chipped dj. F3. $20.00.

MAYERS, Edward. *Lucius Q. C. Lamar; His Life, Times and Speeches, 1825 – 1893.* 1896. Nashville. Methodist Episcopal Church. 2nd ed. photos. lt wear to cover. rebound. 820p. VG. B18. $37.50.

MAYERSON, Evelyn Wilde. *Sanjo.* 1979. Lippincott. 1st. 8vo. 274p. NF/dj. W2. $20.00.

MAYES, Vernon O. *Nanise: A Navajo Herbal.* 1989. Tsaile, AZ. Navajo Comm. College. sc. F. A19. $25.00.

MAYES, Willie. *Danger in Centerfield.* 1963. Argonaut. 1st. VG/dj. P8. $75.00.

MAYNARD, Joyce. *At Home in the World, A Memoir.* 1998. NY. Picador USA. ARC in trade dj. wrp. F in F dj. B2. $45.00.

MAYNARD, Joyce. *Baby Love.* 1981. NY. Knopf. 1st. F/F. H11. $40.00.

MAYNARD, Joyce. *Where Love Goes.* 1995. Crown. UP. F/WRP. M25. $45.00.

MAYO, C. M. *Sky Over El Nido.* 1995. Athens. U GA. 1st. F/dj. M23. $35.00.

MAYO, Jim; see L'Amour, Louis.

MAYONE DIAS, Eduardo. *Cantares De Alem-Mar.* 1982. Coimbre. Ordem. 1/1000. 4to. 223p. wrp. F3. $10.00.

MAYOR, Archer. *Occam's Razor.* 1999. NY. Mysterious Press. 1st. sgn. VF/VF. T2. $25.00.

MAYOR, Archer. *The Disposable Man.* 1998. NY. Mysterious Press. 1st. sgn. VF/VF. T2. $25.00.

MAYOR, Susan. *Collecting Fans.* 1980. Christies Internat Collectors. photos. VG/dj. M17. $22.50.

MAYS, James L. *Hosea.* 1969. SCM. 190p. VG/VG. B29. $17.50.

MAZEL, Henry F. *Murderously Incorrect.* 1999. NY. Crime and Again Press. 1st. trade pb orig. author's 1st novel. VF/pict wrp. T2. $12.00.

MAZEL, Henry F. *Murderously Incorrect.* 1999. NY. Crime and Again Press. 1st. trade pb orig. author's 1st novel. VF/pict wrp. T2. $12.00.

MAZUR, Gail. *Nightfire.* 1978. Boston. Godine. 1st. inscr. G/sans. L3. $25.00.

MAZZANOVICH, Anton. *Trailing Geronimo.* 1931. NY. 3rd. ils. 322p. VG/dj. B18. $50.00.

MCADAM, E. L. *Dr. Johnson & the English Law.* 1951. Syracuse. 1st. VG. H13. $65.00.

MCADIE, Alexander G. *Climatology of California.* 1903. Washington, DC. GPO. ils/pl. cloth. G. K5. $45.00.

MCAFEE, John P. *Slow Walk in a Sad Rain.* 1993. NY. Warner. 1st. F/F. H11. $30.00.

MCANDREWS, Anita. *Conquistador's Lady.* 1990. Santa Barbara. Fithian Press. 1st. 226p. G/wrp. F3. $10.00.

MCAULEY, Paul J. *Pasquale's Angel.* 1994. London. 1st. dj. T9. $10.00.

MCBAIN, Ed. *Another Part of the City.* (1986). NY. Mysterious Press. 1st. F/F. B3. $25.00.

MCBAIN, Ed. *Cinderella.* 1986. NY. Holt. 1st. F/F. H11. $35.00.

MCBAIN, Ed. *Guns.* 1976. NY. Random House. 1st. VG in dj. M15. $45.00.

MCBAIN, Ed. *Ice.* 1983. NY. Arbor. 1st. F/F. H11. $40.00.

MCBAIN, Ed. *Kiss.* (1992). NY. William Morrow. 1st. sgn by author. F/F. B3. $35.00.

MCBAIN, Ed. *The Big Bad City.* 1999. NY. S&S. 1st. sgn. VF in dj. M15. $40.00.

MCBAIN, Ed. *There Was a Little Girl.* (1994). NY. Warner. 1st. sgn by author. F/F. B3. $30.00.

MCBAIN, Ed. *Widows.* 1991. NY. Morrow. 1st. F/F. H11. $25.00.

MCBRIDE, Bill. *A Pocket Guide to the Identification of First Editions.* nd. West Hartford, McBride, publisher. T2. $10.00.

MCBRIDE, Bill. *Points of Issue.* nd. West Hartford, McBride, publisher. 3rd ed. book collecting. T2. $13.00.

MCBRIDE, Bill. *Points of Issue.* nd. West Hartford, McBride, publisher. 3rd ed. book collecting. T2. $13.00.

MCBRIDE, H. W. *Rifleman Went to War.* 1987. Mt. Ida. 398p. F/G. M4. $25.00.

MCCABE, James D. *Our Young Folks Abroad, Adventures of Four American Boys.* 1886 (1881). Lippincott. 312p. rust-red cloth. NF. B20. $50.00.

MCCABE, John. *Cagney: A Biography.* 1997. Knopf. ARC/1st. 8vo. F/dj. w/pub slip & fld poster. S9. $35.00.

MCCABE, Peter. *City of Lies.* 1993. NY. Morrow. 1st. F/F. H11. $25.00.

MCCALL, Wendell (Ridley Pearson). *Concerto in Dead Flat: A Chris Klick Mystery.* 1999. Scottsdale. Poisoned Pen Press. 1st. sgn. VF/VF. T2. $25.00.

MCCALL's, Elaine Prescott Wonsavage, editor. *No Time to Cook: Meals in Minutes.* nd. Ohio. Field Publications. VG/VG. A28. $10.95.

MCCAMMON, Robert R. *Bethany's Sin.* 1989. London. Kinnell. 1st hc ed. VF/VF. T2. $40.00.

MCCAMMON, Robert R. *Boy's Life.* 1991. Pocket. 1st. F/dj. N4. $35.00.

MCCAMMON, Robert R. *Gone South.* 1992. Pocket. 1st. AN/dj. S18. $25.00.

MCCAMMON, Robert R. *Mine.* 1990. NY. Pocket. 1st. F/F. H11. $30.00.

MCCAMMON, Robert R. *Night Boat.* 1990. London. Kinnell. 1st hc. NF/dj. A14. $35.00.

MCCAMMON, Robert R. *Swan Song.* 1989. Arlington Heights. Dark Harvest. 1st hc ed. VF/VF. T2. $55.00.

MCCAMMON, Robert R. *The Night Boat.* 1990. London. Kinnell. 1st. VF/VF. H11. $50.00.

MCCAMMON, Robert R. *They Thirst.* 1991. Dark Harvest. 1st. VG/dj. L1. $50.00.

MCCANN, Colum. *Songdogs.* 1995. NY. Metropolitan Books. 1st Am ed. author's 1st novel. sgn. F/F. D10. $40.00.

MCCANN, Colum. *This Side of Brightness.* 1998. NY. Metropolitan Books. 1st Am ed. author's 2nd novel. sgn. F/F. D10. $35.00.

MCCANN, Rebecca. *About Annabel: Her Strange & Wonderful Adventures Plus Annabel & Davy Jones.* (1922). John Martin's Book House. ils by author. VG. B15. $150.00.

MCCARRY, Charles. *Shelley's Heart.* 1995. NY. Random. 1st. F/F. H11. $25.00.

MCCARTHY, Albert. *Big Band Jazz.* 1974. NY. Putnam. 1st Am ed. 4to. lightly soiled/used dj. B2. $65.00.

MCCARTHY, Albert. *The Dance Band Era.* 1971. Philadelphia. Chilton. 1st. 4to. F/F. B2. $65.00.

MCCARTHY, Cormac. *All the Pretty Horses.* 1992. NY. Knopf. 1st. F/F. D10. $250.00.

MCCARTHY, Cormac. *Cities of the Plains.* (1998). NY. Knopf. 1st. F/F. B3. $15.00.

MCCARTHY, Cormac. *Crossing.* 1994. London. Picador. 1st. F/dj. O11. $30.00.

MCCARTHY, Cormac. *The Stonemason.* (1994). NY. Ecco. 1st. play. F/F. B3. $40.00.

MCCARTHY, Elaine Clark. *The Falconer.* (1996). NY. Random House. 1st. F/F. B3. $15.00.

MCCARTHY, Joe. *McCarthyism: Fight for America.* 1952. NY. Devin Adair. 1st. 4to. photos. 104p. VG. B14. $40.00.

MCCARTHY, Justin. *Muslims & Minorities: Population of Ottoman Anatolia...* 1983. NY U. 248p. cloth. VG. Q2. $47.00.

MCCARTHY, Mary. *Oasis.* 1949. NY. Random. 1st. 181p. NF/dj. B20. $165.00.

MCCARTNEY, Clarence Edward Noble. *Grant and His Generals.* 1953. NY. The McBride Co. 2nd printing. orig cloth. 352p. VG/VG. M8. $25.00.

MCCARTNEY, John. *Story of a Great Horse.* 1902. Indianapolis. 1st. sgn pres. B5. $45.00.

MCCARTY, John L. *Maverick Town: Story of Old Tascosa.* 1946. Norman. OK U. 2nd. 8vo. 277p. VG/dj. P4. $40.00.

MCCARTY, Tom. *Tom McCarthy's Own Story.* 1986. Hamilton, MT. Rocky Mtn. House. sgn. sc. F. w/ephemera. A19. $75.00.

MCCHRISTIAN, Douglas C. *US Army in the West 1870 – 1880.* 1995. U. OK. 1st. photos. 315p. J2. $85.00.

MCCLANE, A. J. *American Angler.* 1954. Holt. 1st. F/VG clip. T11. $25.00.

MCCLANE, A. J. *McClane's New Standard Fishing Encyclopedia.* 1974. HRW. 1st. 4to. 1156p. F/NF clip. T11. $55.00.

MCCLELLAN, Henry Brainerd. *Life & Campaigns of Major-Genral JEB Stuart.* 1885. Houghton Mifflin. 1st. 7 fld maps. 468p. half leather. M8. $1. 250.00.

MCCLELLAN, J. *Regional Anatomy in its Relation to Medicine & Surgery.* 1891. 2 vol. 4to. 97 mc pl. VG. E6. $250.00.

MCCLELLAN, John L. *Crime Without Punishment.* 1962. DSP. 1st. VG/dj. N2. $10.00.

MCCLELLAND, Doug. *Golden Age of B Movies.* 1978. NY. Bonanza. 216p. VG. C5. $12.50.

MCCLENDON, Lise. *Painted Truth.* 1995. Walker. 1st. sgn. F/F. G8. $20.00.

MCCLINTOCK, E. & V. Moore. *Trees of the Panhandle. Golden Gate Park, San Francisco.* 1973 (1965). San Fran. California Academy of Sciences. 4th ed. Misc. Paper No. 1. sc. B26. $14.00.

MCCLINTON, Katherine Morrison. *Lalique for Collectors.* 1975. NY. Scribner. 1st. sm4to. 152p. AN/F. H1. $37.50.

MCCLOSKEY, Robert. *Lentil.* 1940. Viking. 1st. author's 1st book. red-lettered gray cloth. dj. R5. $475.00.

MCCLUNG, Nellie. *Leaves from Lantern Lane.* 1936. Toronto. Thomas Allen. 1st. sgn & inscr. scarce dj. VG/VG dj. A26. $75.00.

MCCLURE, James. *Four and Twenty Virgins.* 1973. London. Victor Gollancz. 1st. F/dj. M15. $150.00.

MCCLURE, James. *Snake.* 1975. London. Victor Gollancz. 1st. F/dj. M15. $65.00.

MCCLURE, James. *The Artful Egg.* 1984. NY. Pantheon. 1st. F/F. H11. $25.00.

MCCLURE, Michael. *Gargoyle Cartoons.* 1971. NY. Delacorte Press/Seymour Lawrence. 1st. sgn. F/F. lt edgewear. O11. $45.00.

MCCLURE, Michael. *Gorf.* 1976. NY. New Directions. 1st. sgn. F/F. O11. $30.00.

MCCLURE, Michael. *Scratching the Beat Surface.* 1982. San Francisco. North Point Press. 1st. sgn. F/F. O11. $40.00.

MCCLURE, Michael. *Selected Poems.* 1986. NY. New Directions. 1st. sgn. F/F. price clip. O11. $35.00.

MCCLURE, Michael. *Star.* 1970. NY. Grove. 1st. F/F. B2. $25.00.

MCCLUSKEY, John. *Look What They Done to My Song.* 1974. NY. Random House. 1st. F/F. B2. $35.00.

MCCOLLEY, Kevin. *Praying to a Laughing God.* 1998. NY. S&S. 1st. sgn. VF/VF. T2. $25.00.

MCCONNELL, Frank. *Blood Lake.* 1987. NY. Walker. 1st. VF/F. H11. $25.00.

MCCONNELL, Frank. *Liar's Poker.* 1993. NY. Walker. 1st. F/F. H11. $20.00.

MCCONNELL, Frank. *The Frog King.* 1990. NY. Walker. 1st. VF/VF. H11. $30.00.

MCCONNELL, Malcolm. *Into the Mouth of the Cat: Story of Lance Sijan.* 1985. NY. Norton. 1st. 253p. F/NF. R11. $25.00.

MCCOOL, J. M. *Cooling Off.* 1984. Boston. Little, Brn. 1st. author's 1st book. F/F. H11. $20.00.

MCCORD, David. *Notes from Four Cities.* 1969. Worcester. St. Onge. mini. 1/1500. aeg. gilt stp brn leather. B24. $35.00.

MCCORD, Eugene (ed). *The History of the 125th Evacuation Hospital, from Activation to Occupation.* 1945. Germany. Ablassmayer and Penninger. 1st. ils. slightly musty. 56p. VG. B18. $75.00.

MCCORKLE, Jill. *Carolina Moon.* 1996. Chapel Hill. 1st. 8vo. 260p. NF/dj. P4. $25.00.

MCCORKLE, Jill. *Crash Diet.* (1992). Chapel Hill. Algonquin. 1st. F/F. B3. $30.00.

MCCORKLE, Jill. *Ferris Beach.* 1990. Algonquin. 1st. sgn. F/dj. A24. $47.50.

MCCORKLE, Jill. *Tending to Virginia.* 1987. Algonquin. 1st. rem mk. NF/NF. B3. $20.00.

MCCORMAC, Billy M. *Aurora & Airglow.* 1967. NY. Reinhold. 8vo. 689p. xl. K5. $50.00.

MCCORMAC, Billy M. *Radiating Atmosphere.* 1971. NY. Springer. sm 4to. 455p. xl. K5. $30.00.

MCCORMACK, Eric. *Paradise Motel.* 1989. Markham. Viking. 1st. F/F. H11. $15.00.

MCCORMICK, Claire. *Club Paradis Murders.* 1983. Walker. 1st. NF/VG. G8. $10.00.

MCCORMICK, Patricia. *Lady Bullfighter.* (1954). Holt. 1st. photos/ils. 209p. dj. F3. $12.50.

MCCORMICK, Robert R. *War Without Grant.* 1950. NY. Bond Wheelwright. 1st. VG/G. A14. $14.00.

MCCORQUODALE, Robin. *Dansville.* 1986. NY. Harper & Row. 1st. F/F. H11. $30.00.

MCCOURT, Frank. *Angela's Ashes.* 1996. Scribner. sgn. F/dj. M25. $35.00.

MCCOURT, Malachy. *A Monk Swimming.* 1998. NY. Hyperion. 1st. ARC. F. D10. $10.00.

MCCOY, Horace. *Black Box Thrillers: 4 Novels by Horace McCoy.* 1983. London. Zomba Books. 1st hc ed. VF/VF. T2. $35.00.

MCCOY, Horace. *No Pockets in a Shroud.* 1948. NY. Signet. 1st Am ed. revised from 1937 UK ed. VG/wrps. B2. $35.00.

MCCOY, Maureen. *Divining Blood.* 1992. Poseiden. 1st. F/F. H11. $20.00.

MCCRACKEN, Elizabeth. *Here's Your Hat What's Your Hurry.* (1993). NY. Turtle Bay Books. 1st. author's 1st book. F/F. B3. $125.00.

MCCRACKEN, Elizabeth. *The Giant's House.* 1996. NY. Dial. 1st. sgn. F/F. D10. $60.00.

MCCRACKEN, Harold. *Charles M. Russell Book.* 1957. Doubleday. rpt. ils. 236p. NF/poor. T11. $40.00.

MCCRACKEN, Harold. *George Catlin & the Old Frontier.* 1959. NY. Dial. 1st trade. 216p. VG/dj. P4. $75.00.

MCCRACKEN, Harold. *Sentinal of the Snow Peaks: Story of the Alaskan Wild.* (1945). Phil. Lippincott. 1st. 151p. bl cloth. P4. $18.00.

MCCRUMB, Sharyn. *If I'd Killed Him When I Met Him.* (1995). NY. Ballantine. 1st. sgn by author. F/F. B3. $50.00.

MCCRUMB, Sharyn. *Missing Susan.* 1991. NY. Ballantine. 1st. sgn. VF/VF. T2. $35.00.

MCCRUMB, Sharyn. *She Walks Through These Hills.* 1994. NY. Scribner's. sgn 1st ed. F/F. M23. $50.00.

MCCRUMB, Sharyn. *The Ballad of Frankie Silver.* 1998. NY. Dutton. sgn 1st ed. F/F. M23. $20.00.

MCCRUMB, Sharyn. *The Hangman's Beautiful Daughter.* 1992. NY. Scribner. 1st. F/F. D10. $45.00.

MCCRUMB, Sharyn. *The Rosewood Casket.* (1996). NY. Ballantine. 1st. sgn & dated by author. F/F. B3. $35.00.

MCCRUMB, Sharyn. *The Windsor Knot.* (1990). NY. Ballantine. 1st. sgn by author. F/F. B3. $65.00.

MCCRUMB, Sharyn. *Zombies of the Gene Pool.* 1992. S&S. 1st. F/dj. D10. $45.00.

MCCUE, Andy. *Baseball by the Book.* 1991. Wm Brn. 1st. AN/sans. P8. $25.00.

MCCUEN, Gary E. *Religion and Politics: Issues in Religious Liberty.* 1989. Gem. 172p. VG. B29. $5.50.

MCCULLERS, Carson. *Member of the Wedding.* 1946. New Directions. 118p. VG. C5. $12.50.

MCCULLOUGH, Colleen. *Caesar's Women.* 1996. Morrow. ne. ils. inscr. F/F. S19. $25.00.

MCCULLOUGH, David. *The Path Between the Seas. The Creation of the Panama Canal, 1870 – 1914.* 1977. NY. S&S. BCE. index. biblio. b/w photos. 698p. G/G. F3. $15.00.

MCCULLOUGH, David Willis. *Think on Death.* 1991. NY. Viking. 1st. F/F. G8. $10.00.

MCCULLOUGH, John G. *Dark Is Dark.* 1947. NY. William R. Scott. 1st. ils by Charles G. Shaw. sm 4to. gray faux cloth w/bl lettering. gray/bl/yellow dj. 34p. VG/G. D6. $65.00.

MCCULLOUGH, Robert & Walter Leuba. *The Pensylvania Main Line Canal.* 1973. York. PA. The American Canal & Transportation Center. 1st. 8vo. 184p. VG. H1. $22.50.

MCCULLY, Waldridge. *Death Rides Tandem.* 1942. NY. Doubleday. 1st. Some darkening on endpapers. Jacket has tiny wear at spine ends. at corners and along edges. F/dj. M15. $65.00.

MCCURDY, F. Earl & Jane A. *A Collector's Guide & History of Uhl Pottery.* 1988. Evansville, IN. Ohio Valley Books. 1st. 4to Separate 1988 price guide. 84p. F. H1. $45.00.

MCCUTCHAN, Philip. *Cameron in Command.* 1983. London. Barker. 1st. NF/dj. A14. $28.00.

MCCUTCHAN, Philip. *Cameron's Crossing.* 1993. St. Martin. 1st Am. Cameron #12. F/NF. T11. $35.00.

MCCUTCHAN, Philip. *Convoy of Fear.* 1990. St. Martin. 1st Am. F/dj. T11. $25.00.

MCCUTCHEON, George Barr. *Cowardice Court.* 1907. Dodd Mead. ils Harrison Fisher. 140p. G. G11. $12.00.

MCCUTCHEON, George Barr. *Graustark: Story of a Love Behind a Throne.* 1901. Chicago. Herbert Stone. 1st. VG. N2. $65.00.

MCDANIEL, William H. *The History of Beech.* 1971. Wichita. 1st. ils by photos. some in color. presentation slip. 336p. VG. B18. $65.00.

MCDERMID, Val. *Kickback.* 1993. NY. St. Martin. 1st Am ed. F/NF. T2. $10.00.

MCDERMID, Val. *The Wire in the Blood.* 1998. Scottsdale. Poisoned Pen Press. 1st Am ed. 1/300 # copies. sgn. VF/VF acetate dj. T2. $50.00.

MCDERMOTT, Alice. *At Weddings and Wakes.* (1992). NY. FSG. 1st. F/F. B3. $50.00.

MCDERMOTT, Alice. *Charming Billy.* 1998. NY. FSG. 1st. sgn. F in dj. D10. $55.00.

MCDERMOTT, Alice. *That Night.* 1987. NY. FSG. 1st. NF/NF. M23. $20.00.

MCDERMOTT, John Francis, editor. *Western Journals of Dr. George Hunter. 1796-1805.* 1963. am phil society. ils. notes. bib. index. 133p. VG+. B19. $20.00.

MCDEVITT, Jack. *A Talent for War.* 1989. London. Kinnell. 1st British hc ed. author's 2nd book. VF/VF. T2. $35.00.

MCDEVITT, Jack. *Standard Candles.* 1996. San Francisco. Tachyon publications. 1st. VF/VF. T2. $25.00.

MCDONALD, Frank. *Provenance.* 1979. np. Atlantic-Little, Brn. 1st. author's 1st novel. NF/NF-. R16. $95.00.

MCDONALD, Gregory. *Fletch, Too.* 1986. Warner. 1st. F/dj. N4. $25.00.

MCDONALD, Gregory. *Flynn's In.* 1985. 1st Eng. F/NF. M19. $17.50.

MCDONALD, H. D. *Theories of Revelation: An Historical Study 1700 – 1960.* 1979. Baker. VG/wrp. B29. $13.00.

MCDONALD, Scott. *Complete Jobfinder's Guide for the 90s. Marketing Yourself in the New Job Market.* 1993. VA. Impact Publications. trade sc. VG. A28. $7.50.

MCDONALD, T. H. *Exploring the Northwest Territory: Sir Alexander Mackenzie.* 1966. Norman, OK. 1st. 133p. F/torn. B20. $45.00.

MCDONALD, Walter. *Caliban in Blue & Other Poems.* 1976. Texas Tech. 1st. NF. R11. $20.00.

MCDONOUGH, Nancy. *Garden Sass: Catalog of Arkansas Folkways.* 1975. NY. photos. 319p. F/dj. M4. $18.00.

MCDOUGAL, A. *Secret of Sucessful Restaurants.* 1929. 1st. VG. E6. $25.00.

MCDOUGALL, John A. *McDougall Program for Maximum Weight Loss, The.* 1994. NY. Dutton. 1st. NF/NF. A28. $12.50.

MCDOWELL, Jack, editor. *Mexico.* 1973. California. lane. 1st. 256p. G/chipped dj. F3. $20.00.

MCDOWELL, Michael. *Toplin.* 1987. Scream. 1/250. sgn. ils/sgn Harry O Morris. AN/box. T12. $125.00.

MCELFRESH, Adeline. *Murder with Roses.* 1950. Phoenix. 1st. VG. G8. $15.00.

MCELROY, Joseph C., compiler. *Chickamauga Record of the Ohio Chickamauga and Chattanooga National Park Commission.* 1896. Cincinnati. Earhart & Richardson. 1st. orig cloth. Pocket map lacking. 55 plates. 199p. NF. M8. $150.00.

MCELROY, Susan Chernak. *Animals as Teachers & Healers.* 1997. Ballantine. 1st. 8vo. 253p. F/dj. S14. $10.00.

MCEWAN, Ian. *Black Dogs.* 1992. London. Cape. 1st. sgn. F/dj. O11. $35.00.

MCEWAN, Ian. *Black Dogs.* 1992. NY. Doubleday. 1st. VF/VF. H11. $25.00.

MCEWAN, Ian. *Enduring Love.* 1998. NY. Doubleday. 1st. sgn. F in F dj. D10. $40.00.

MCEWAN, Ian. *First Love, Last Rites.* 1975. NY. Random House. 1st. F in dj. D10. $125.00.

MCEWAN, Ian. *Innocent.* 1990. Lester. 1st Canadian. AN/dj. S18. $25.00.

MCEWEN, Inez Puckett. *So This Is Ranching.* 1948. Caxton. 1/1000. sgn. 270p. red cloth. VG+. B20. $50.00.

MCFALL, Patricia. *Night Butterfly.* 1992. NY. SMP. 1st. author's 1st book. sgn. F/F. H11. $40.00.

MCFARLAND, Dennis. *School for the Blind.* 1994. Boston. Houghton Mifflin. 1st. sgn. F/dj. D10. $45.00.

MCFARLAND, Dennis. *The Music Room.* (1990). NY. Houghton Mifflin. 1st. author's 1st book. F/F. B3. $60.00.

MCGARRITY, Michael. *Serpent Gate.* 1998. Scribners. 1st. sgn. F in dj. M25. $45.00.

MCGAUGHEY, Neil. *And Then There Were Ten.* 1995. NY. Scribners. 1st. UP. VF/pict wrp. T2. $5.00.

MCGAUGHEY, Neil. *Otherwise Known as Murder.* 1994. NY. Scribner. 1st. F/dj. M23. $35.00.

MCGAVRAN, S. B. *A Brief History of Harrison County, Ohio.* 1894. Cadiz, OH. ils. wrps. browning. fading. 55p. G. B18. $45.00.

MCGEE, D. H. *Famous Signers of the Declaration.* 1955. NY. inscr/sgn. 307p. F/dj. M4. $20.00.

MCGEE, J. Vernon. *Through the Bible with J. Vernon McGee.* 1981. Thos Nelson. 5 vol. hc. VG. B29. $70.00.

MCGINLEY, Patrick. *Bogmail.* 1981. NY. Ticknor. 1st. F/F. H11. $30.00.

MCGINLEY, Patrick. *Goosefoot.* 1982. NY. Dutton. 1st Am. F/dj. Q1. $35.00.

MCGINNIS, Joe. *Cruel Doubt.* 1991. S&S. 1st. G+. S19. $20.00.

MCGOVERN, James. *Crossbow and Overcast.* 1965. Chicago. combined registry company. 2nd printing. b/w photo ils. 8vo. 279p. VG/rubbed. chipped dj. clip. bkplt on ffep. K5. $30.00.

MCGOWAN, Harold. *Another World for Christmas.* 1984. Central Islip. NY. Metaprobe Inst. 1st. VG/dj. M21. $15.00.

MCGRADY, Mike. *Dove in Vietnam.* 1968. Funk Wagnall. 245p. NF/dj. R11. $25.00.

MCGRATH, Harold. *The Lure of the Mask.* 1908. Indianapolis. Bobbs-Merrill. 1st. ils by Harrison Fisher/Karl Ander. F in dj. M15. $150.00.

MCGRATH, Patrick. *Grotesque.* 1989. Poseidon. 1st. F/dj. M23. $20.00.

MCGRATH, Patrick. *Spider.* 1990. Poseidon. 1st. F/dj. M23. $10.00.

MCGREGOR, Miriam. *Weeds in My Garden.* (1986). Lorson's Books & Prts. mini. 1/50 (175 total). sgn. w/extra proof set. B24. $275.00.

MCGRILLIS, John O. C. *Printer's Abecedarium.* 1974. Boston. Godine. 1st. 8vo. unp. F/dj. O10. $25.00.

MCGUANE, Thomas. *Keep the Change.* 1989. Houghton Mifflin. 1st. sgn & dated. F/F. M25. $60.00.

MCGUANE, Thomas. *Ninety-Two in the Shade.* 1973. NY. FSG. 1st. NF/NF. D10. $75.00.

MCGUANE, Thomas. *Nobody's Angel.* 1981. NY. Random House. 1st. F/F. D10. $60.00.

MCGUANE, Thomas. *Panama.* 1978. NY. FSG. 1st. F/F. D10. $65.00.

MCGUIRE, Christine. *Until Proven Guilty.* 1993. Pocket. 1st. VG/VG. G8. $10.00.

MCGUIRE, Paul. *Murder at High Noon.* 1935. Garden City. Doubleday Crime Club. 1st Am ed. VG. M15. $35.00.

MCHALE, Tom. *Farragan's Retreat.* 1971. NY. Viking. 1st. F/NF. H11. $50.00.

MCHATTON, Thomas H. *Armchair Gardening. Some of the Spirit, Philosophy, & Psychology of the Art of Gardening.* 1947. Athens. Univ. of Georgia. F in chip dj. B26. $19.00.

MCHUGH, Maureen F. *Half the Day Is Night.* 1994. NY. Tor. 1st. F/F. M23. $20.00.

MCINERNEY, Jay. *Bright Lights, Big City.* 1984. NY. Vintage Contemporaries. 1st. wrp. pb orig. F. B2. $40.00.

MCINERNEY, Jay. *Ransom.* 1985. NY. Vintage. 1st. F/F. H11. $50.00.

MCINERNY, Ralph. *Bishop as Pawn.* 1978. NY. Vanguard Press. 1st. F/F. T2. $25.00.

MCINERNY, Ralph. *Body and Soil.* 1989. NY. Atheneum. 1st. VF/VF. T2. $6.00.

MCINERNY, Ralph. *Easeful Death.* 1991. NY. Atheneum. 1st. VF/VF. T2. $6.00.

MCINERNY, Ralph. *Her Death of Cold.* 1977. NY. Vanguard Press. 1st. F/VG. T2. $25.00.

MCINERNY, Ralph. *Second Vespers.* 1980. NY. Vanguard Press. 1st. F/F. T2. $20.00.

MCINERNY, Ralph. *The Search Committee.* 1991. NY. Atheneum. 1st. VF/VF. T2. $6.00.

MCINTYRE, Ruth A. *Debts Hopeful & Desperate: Financing Plymouth Colony.* 1963. Plymouth Plantation. 1st? sgn. 8vo. w/inscr postcard. F/dj. A2. $17.50.

MCINTYRE, Vonda N. *The Moon and the Sun.* 1997. NY. Pocket Books. 1st. VF/VF. T2. $25.00.

MCKAY, Claude. *Selected Poems of Claude McKay.* 1953. NY. Bookman Association. 1st. NF/torn dj. M25. $100.00.

MCKEAN, Hugh F. *Lost Treasures of Louis Comfort Tiffany.* 1980. Doubleday. 1st. 4to. 304p. NF/plastic. H1. $90.00.

MCKEARIN, Helen & Kenneth M. Wilson. *American Bottles & Flasks & Their Ancestry.* 1978. NY. Crown. 1st. 4to A few minor edge tears. 779p. F/VG. H1. $150.00.

MCKEE, Edwin D. *Ancient Landscapes of the Grand Canyon Region.* 1931. Lockwood-Hazel. 1st. ils Russell Hastings. VG/dj. F7. $55.00.

MCKEE, Russell. *Last West: History of the Great Plains of North America.* 1974. Crowell. ils/maps/photos. VG/dj. J2. $40.00.

MCKEEVER, William. *Farm Boys & Girls.* 1913. Macmillan. 326p. cloth. A10. $15.00.

MCKELVEY, Jean T. *Changing Law of Fair Representation.* 1985. Ithaca. ILR Pr. M11. $35.00.

MCKENDRY, Maxime. *Seven Centuries Cookbook.* 1973. McGraw Hill. G/dj. A16. $25.00.

MCKENNEY, Ruth. *Industrial Valley.* 1939. NY. Harcourt. 1st. NF. owner's name/VG. B2. $35.00.

MCKENZIE, John L. *The Two Edged Sword.* 1956. Bruce. 317p. VG/VG. B29. $9.50.

MCKINLEY, Carolyn. *Goofus Glass.* 1984. Paducah. Collector Books. 8vo. 128p. F. H1. $48.00.

MCKINLEY, Robin. *Deerskin.* 1993. NY. Ace Books. BCE. VG/VG. A28. $6.50.

MCKINLEY, Robin. *Hero & the Crown.* 1985. Greenwillow. 1st. F/dj. M25. $45.00.

MCKINLEY, Robin. *Outlaws of Sherwood.* 1988. Greenwillow. 1st. F/dj. M25. $25.00.

MCKINLEY, William. *Speeches & Addresses Of...* 1894. NY. Appleton. ils. 664p. B18. $27.50.

MCKINNEY, E. L. *King of Indoor Sports.* 1963. Chicago. Petit Oiseau. mini. 1/50. 21p. bl brd. B24. $175.00.

MCKINNEY, Sam. *Bligh, A True Account of Mutiny Aboard His Majesty's Ship Bounty.* 1989. Camden. International Marine Publishing. 1st. bl cloth. gilt titles. map ep. 210p. NF in price clipped dj. P4. $90.00.

MCKINNEY, William M. *Treatise on the Law of Fellow-Servants.* 1890. Northport. Edward Thompson. sheep. M11. $75.00.

MCKINNEY-WHETSTONE, Diane. *Tumbling.* 1996. NY. Morrow. 1st. author's 1st book. F/F. H11. $20.00.

MCKREADY, Kelvin. *A Beginner's Star Book.* 1929. NY. Putnam. 3rd ed. revised by Maud King Murphy. 4to. photos & charts. some wear. 154p. ex lib in worn & scuffed cloth. K5. $20.00.

MCLEAN, Duncan. *Bucket of Tongues.* 1999. NY. Norton. 1st Am ed. F in pict wrp. D10. $35.00.

MCLEAN, Ruari. *Typographers on Type: Illustrated Anthology.* 1995. NY. Norton. 1st. tall 8vo. F/dj. O10. $27.00.

MCLENDON, James. *Eddie Macon's Run.* 1980. NY. Viking. 1st. F/F. H11. $35.00.

MCLENNAN, Rob. *Growing Proteas.* 1993. Kenhurst. Australia. photos. sc. AN. B26. $14.00.

MCLEOD, Alexander. *Pigtails & Gold Dust.* 1947. Caxton. 1st. VG/sans. O4. $35.00.

MCLEOD, James Richard. *Theodore Roethke: A Manuscript Checklist.* (1971). Kent State. 1st. index. F/sans. A18. $25.00.

MCLINTIC, Guthrie. *Me & Kit.* 1955. Little, Brn. 1st. 341p. F/NF. B20. $90.00.

MCLINTOCK, F. L. *Narrative of Discovery of Fate of Sir John Franklin.* 1859. London. Murray. 3 fld maps/2 pocket maps. 403p. rb. NF. M4. $400.00.

MCLINTON, Katherine Morrison. *Collecting American Glass.* (1950). Granmercy. 2nd. sm 8vo. 64p. F/VG plastic. H1. $22.50.

MCLOUGHLIN, Denis. *Wild & Woolly: An Encyclopedia of the Old West.* 1975. Barnes Noble. 2500 entries. VG/dj. A4. $65.00.

MCLUHAN, Marshall. *Culture Is Our Business.* (1970). McGraw Hill. 3rd. ils. F/dj. A26. $35.00.

MCMAHON, Jo. *Deenie Folks & Friends of Theirs.* (1925). Volland. 1st (so stated). ils John Gee. 8vo. ils brd/pub box. R5. $200.00.

MCMEEKIN, Clark. *Old Kentucky Country.* 1957. DSP. 1st. 214p. VG/fair. B10. $45.00.

MCMEEKIN, Isabel McLennan. *Kentucky Derby Winner.* 1949. Grosset Dunlap. later prt. bl tweed brd. G+. B36. $9.00.

MCMICHAEL, Robert. *One Man's Obsession.* 1986. Prentice Hall. 1st. rem mk. VG/dj. N2. $12.50.

MCMILLAN, Ann. *Angel Trumpet: A Civil War Mystery.* 1999. NY. Viking. 1st. sgn. VF/VF. T2. $25.00.

MCMILLAN, Ann. *Angel Trumpet: A Civil War Mystery.* 1999. NY. Viking. 1st. sgn. VF/VF. T2. $25.00.

MCMILLAN, Terry. *Disappearing Acts.* 1989. NY. Viking. 1st. F/F. D10. $85.00.

MCMILLAN, Terry. *How Stella Got Her Groove Back.* 1996. NY. Viking. 1st. NF/NF. R16. $35.00.

MCMILLAN, Terry. *Waiting to Exhale.* 1992. NY. Viking. 1st. F/F. H11. $65.00.

MCMINN, Howard E. *An Illustrated Manual of California Shrubs.* 1939. San Francisco. 1st. B26. $42.50.

MCMURTRIE, Douglas C. *Pioneer Printing in North Carolina.* 1932. Springfield, IL. 1st. 1/200. 4p. VG/wrp. M8. $75.00.

MCMURTRIE, Douglas C. *Preliminary Short-Title Check List of Books, 1784 – 1860.* 1937. Jacksonville. 1st. 15p. VG/wrp. M8. $75.00.

MCMURTRY, Larry. *Anything for Billy.* (1988). NY. S&S. 1st. sgn by the author. F/F. B3. $60.00.

MCMURTRY, Larry. *Buffalo Girls.* 1990. NY. S&S. 1st. VG+/VG. R16. $45.00.

MCMURTRY, Larry. *Cadillac Jack.* 1982. NY. S&S. 1st. F/NF. B2. $40.00.

MCMURTRY, Larry. *Dead Man's Walk.* 1995. NY. S&S. 1st. VG+/VG+. R16. $30.00.

MCMURTRY, Larry. *Lonesome Dove.* 1985. NY. S&S. 1st. F/F. soiling to pg ends. minor creases. A24. $225.00.

MCMURTRY, Larry. *Some Can Whistle.* 1989. NY. S&S. 1st. F/F. H11. $30.00.

MCMURTRY, Larry. *Streets of Laredo.* 19903. NY. S&S. 1st. VG+/NF. R16. $30.00.

MCMURTRY, Larry. *Terms of Endearment.* 1975. NY. S&S. 1st. sgn. F/F. darkening to top edge. O11. $175.00.

MCMURTRY, Larry. *Texasville.* 1987. S&S. 1st. rem mk. F/NF. H11. $15.00.

MCMURTRY, Larry. *The Desert Rose.* 1983. NY. S&S. 1st. F/VF. H11. $75.00.

MCMURTRY, Larry & Diana Ossana. *Pretty Boy Floyd.* 1994. NY. S&S. 1st. F/F. G8. $15.00.

MCNABB, R. L. *The Women of the Middle Kingdom.* (1903). Cincinnati. Jennings and Fye. 12mo. 160p. ils. gr cloth. 1sted. Minor wear. VG. L5. $25.00.

MCNAGNY, Bob. *Noah's Nightmare with Illustrations and Other Nonsense by the Author.* 1926. Indianapolis. Bobbs Merrill. 1st. sm 4to. red cloth w/bl rules & lettering. dj diff in bl and gold. 128p. VG/G+. D6. $95.00.

MCNALLY, Tom. *Fisherman's Bible.* 1976. Chicago. 1st. photos/ils. 444p. F/dj. A17. $20.00.

MCNAMARA, Eugene. *Interior Landscape: Literary Criticism of Marshall McLuhan.* 1969. McGraw Hill. stated 1st. VG/dj. N2. $10.00.

MCNAMARA, Joseph D. *Fatal Command.* 1987. NY. Arbor. 1st. F/F. H11. $25.00.

MCNAMEE, Eoin. *Resurrection Man.* 1994. London. Picador. 1st. author's 1st novel. VF/VF. T2. $65.00.

MCNAUGHTON, Brian. *The Throne of Bones.* 1997. Black River. Terminal Flight. 1st. VF/VF. T2. $35.00.

MCNEAL, Tom. *Goodnight, Nebraska.* 1998. NY. Random House. 1st. F/F. M23. $30.00.

MCNEIL, John. *Spy Game.* 1980. NY. Coward McCann. 1st. author's 2nd book. F/F. H11. $25.00.

MCNEIL, John. *Spy Game.* 1980. NY. Coward. 1st. F/F. H11. $25.00.

MCNEILL, Elizabeth. *Nine and a Half Weeks.* 1978. Dutton. 1st. F/F. M25. $50.00.

MCNEILL, William. *Plagues & Peoples.* 1976. Garden City. NY. 1st. 369p. A13. $30.00.

MCNICHOLS, Charles. *Crazy Weather.* 1944. Macmillan. 1st. 195p. F/NF. D4. $30.00.

MCNITT, Frank. *Indian Traders.* 1962. Norman, OK. 1st. 8vo. red cloth. dj. F7. $75.00.

MCPHEE, John. *In Suspect Terrain.* 1983. FSG. 1st. F/NF clip. H11. $35.00.

MCPHEE, John. *Levels of the Game.* 1969. FSG. 1st. F/NF. B3. $85.00.

MCPHEE, John. *Looking for a Ship.* 1990. FSG. 1st. F/dj. R14. $25.00.

MCPHEE, John. *Outcroppings.* 1988. Gibbs Smith. 1st. photos Tom Till. 130p. F/F. B19. $35.00.

MCPHEE, John. *Sense of Where You Are.* 1965. FSG. 1st. author's 1st book. F/G+. B4. $250.00.

MCPHEE, John. *The Headmaster.* (1966). NY. FSG. 1st. author's 2nd book. NF+. very slight shelfwear/VF. B3. $300.00.

MCPHEE, John. *Wimbledon, A Celebration.* (1972). NY. Viking. 1st. photography by Alfred Eisenstaedt. F/VG. closed tear at top front gutter. rubbing to top corners. B3. $85.00.

MCPHERSON, Flora. *Watchman Against the World: Story of Norman McLeod.* 1962. London. Robert Hale. 1st. VG/clip. N2. $12.50.

MCPHERSON, William. *To the Sargasso Sea.* 1978. S&S. 1st. F/F. H11. $20.00.

MCQUEEN, Cyrus B. *Field Guide to Peat Mosses of Boreal North America.* 1990. U New Eng. 138p. F. S15. $7.00.

MCQUILLAN, Karin. *The Cheetah Chase.* 1994. NY. Ballentine. 1st. F/F+. H11. $20.00.

MCQUINN, Donald E. *Targets.* 1980. Macmillan. 1st. sgn. F/NF. R11. $45.00.

MCQUOWN, F. R. *Carnations and Pinks.* 1965. London. VG in dj. B26. $14.00.

MCQUOWN, F. R. *Pinks, Selection and Cultivation.* 1955. London. GBC. VG. B26. $12.50.

MCREA, Ruth. *ABC of Gourmet Cookery.* 1956. Mount Vernon. NY. Peter Pauper Press. reprint ed. 12mo. 61p. G+/G. clip. edgewear. S14. $5.00.

MCREA EATON, Flora. *Memory's Wall.* 1956. Toronto. Clarke Irwin. 1st. ils. 214p. F/VG dj. A26. $35.00.

MCREYNOLDS, Robert. *Thirty Years on the Frontier.* 1906. Colorado Springs, CO. E Paso Pub. G. A19. $95.00.

MCSHANN, Jay. *5 Boogie Woogie and Blues Piano Solos.* 1942. NY. Leeds. 1st. wrp. 24p. VG w/reattached wrp. B2. $25.00.

MCSHERRY, Frank Jr. *Nightmares in Dixie.* 1987. Little Rock, AR. August House. 1st. VG/dj. L1. $35.00.

MCSPADDEN, J. Walker. *Animals of the World.* 1947. Garden City. G. A19. $30.00.

MEACHAM, Ellis K. *East Indianman.* 1976. Boston. Little, Brn. 1st. gilt bl cloth. F/VG. T11. $85.00.

MEAD, Frank. *The Encyclopedia of Religious Quotations.* 1965. Revell. 534p. VG/VG. B29. $9.50.

MEAD, Margaret. *Culture & Commitment: A Study of the Generation Gap.* 1970. NY Nat Hist/Doubleday. sm 8vo. 91p. F/dj. H4. $12.50.

MEAD, Shepherd. *The Admen.* 1958. NY. S&S. 1st. F-/F-. H11. $45.00.

MEADE, L. T. & Robert Eustace. *The Detections of Miss Cusack.* 1998. Shelburne. Ontario. Battered Silicon Dispatch Box. 1st. VF/VF. T2. $22.00.

MEADE, Martha L. *Recipes from the Old South.* 1961. Bramhall. G/dj. A16. $12.00.

MEAGHER, John R. *RCA Television Pict-O-Guide.* 1949. Harrison, NJ. RCA Television. 3 vol. 1st. obl 12mo. sbdg. F. B20. $50.00.

MEAKIN, Budgett. *Moors: A Comprehensive Description.* 1902. London. Sonnenschein. 8vo. 503p. gilt gr cloth. NF. H4. $100.00.

MEANS, James. *Aeronautical Annual 1895.* 1895 (1894). Boston. 172p. wrp. B18. $195.00.

MEANS, Philip Ainsworth. *Ancient Civilizations of the Andes.* 1931. Scribner. 1st. 586p. F3. $45.00.

MEANS, Russell. *Where White Men Fear to Tread.* 1995. St. Martin. 1st. sgn. F/dj. O11. $50.00.

MEANY, Edmond S. *Mt. Rainier: A Record of Exploration.* 1957. Binfords & Mort. rpt. 8vo. 325p. F/VG+. B20. $40.00.

MEDVED, Michael. *Hollywood Vs. America.* 1992. Zondervan. 1st. 386p. VG/VG. B29. $10.00.

MEEK, M. R. D. *This Blessed Plot.* 1990. NY. Scribner's. 1st Am ed. VG/NF. G8. $10.00.

MEEK, M. R. D. *Touch and Go.* 1993. NY. Scribner's. 1st Am ed. F/F. G8. $10.00.

MEEK, S. P. *Jerry: The Adventures of An Army Dog.* 1942. NY. Appleton Century. ils Clinton Balmer. VG/dj. A21. $40.00.

MEEK, S. P. *Omar: A State Police Dog.* 1953. Knopf. 1st. rb. VG. P12. $15.00.

MEEKER, Arthur. *Prairie Avenue.* 1949. Knopf. BC. NF/VG. H4. $10.00.

MEEKER, Ezra. *Pioneer Reminiscenes of Puget Sound: A Tragedy of Leshi.* 1905. Lowman Hanford. 1st. 8vo. 555p. bl cloth. VG+. B20. $135.00.

MEEN & TUSHINGHAM. *Crown Jewels of Iran.* 1974. Toronto/Buffalo. U Toronto. 2nd. folio. ils 159p. VG. W1. $65.00.

MEESE, Edwin III. *With Reagan.* 1992. Regnery Gateway. 1st. sgn. F/F. W2. $35.00.

MEGARGEE, Edwin. *Horses.* 1946. Messner. 1st. obl 4to. ils. VG. H4. $20.00.

MEGGENDORFER, Lothar. *International Circus.* 1979. Penguin Books. repro of 1887 ed. VG. A16. $25.00.

MEGGERS, Betty. *Ecuador.* 1966. NY. Praeger. 1st. 220p. G/chipped dj. F3. $25.00.

MEIER, Leslie. *Mail-Order Murder.* 1991. NY. Viking. 1st. VF/dj. M15. $45.00.

MEIGS, Cornelia. *Wind in the Chimney.* 1934. NY. Macmillan. 1st. 144p. VG. D4. $35.00.

MEIGS, John. *Cowboy in American Prints.* 1972. Sage. xl. VG/dj. A21. $45.00.

MEIGS, Peveril. *Dominican Mission Frontier of Lower California.* 1935. U. CA. 1st. photos/maps. VG. S14. $75.00.

MEIJERING, Piet. *Signed with their Honor: Air Chivalry During Two World Wars.* 1988. NY. 1st. photos/biblio/index. VG/dj. S16. $25.00.

MEILACH, D. Z. *Creating Art from Anything.* 1968. Reilly Lee. ils/pl. 119p. cloth. dj. D2. $25.00.

MEIR, Golda. *My Life.* 1975. NY. Putnam. 1st Am. tall 8vo. bookplate. 480p. NM/F. H1. $18.00.

MEISSNER, Bill. *Hitting into the Wind.* 1994. Random. 1st. F/dj. P8. $15.00.

MELANSON, Philip H. *Spy Saga: Lee Harvey Oswald & US Intelligence.* 1990. Praeger. 1st. VG/dj. N2. $12.50.

MELBER, Jehuda Hermann. *Cohen's Philosophy of Judaism.* (1968). NY. Jonathan. 8vo. 593p. NF/VG. H4. $18.50.

MELENDY, Mary Ries Dr. *The Science of Eugenics & Sex Life.* 1917. W. R. Vansant. sm4to. 596p. F. H1. $20.00.

MELLEN, Joan. *Privilege: Enigma of Sasha Bruce.* (1982). Dial. BC. photos. 306p. VG/dj. B10. $10.00.

MELLERSH, H. E. L. *Destruction of Knossos: Rise & Fall of Minoan Crete.* 1993. VG/dj. M17. $15.00.

MELLIN, Jeanne. *The Morgan Horse Handbook.* 1976. Brattleboro. Stephen Greene. VG/VG. O3. $40.00.

MELLY, George. *Don't Tell Sybil: Intimate Memoir of E.L.T. Mesens.* 1997. Heinemann. 1st. F/dj. P3. $35.00.

MELNYK, Eugenie. *My Darling Elia.* 1999. NY. St. Martin. ARC. F/wrp. B2. $25.00.

MELODY, Michael E. *Apaches: Critical Bibliography.* 1977. IN U. 1st. 86p. VG+. B19. $10.00.

MELONEY, William Brown. *Rush to the Sun.* 1937. Farrar. 1st. sgn. VG/dj. S13. $20.00.

MELTZER, Brad. *The Tenth Justice.* 1997. London. Hodder & Stoughton. 1st. author's 1st novel. VF/VF. T2. $35.00.

MELTZER, David. *Tens, Selected Poems 1961 – 1971.* 1973. NY. McGraw Hill. 1st. review copy. intro by Kenneth Rexroth. F/NF. V1. $30.00.

MELVILLE, Herman. *Moby Dick.* 1930. NY. Random. 1st trade. ils Rockwell Kent. H4. $30.00.

MELVILLE, Herman. *Omoo: Narrative of Adventures in South Seas.* 1847. London. 1st (precedes Am). map. brn leather. M17. $600.00.

MELVILLE, Jennie. *Death in the Family.* 1995. NY. St. Martin. 1st Am ed. VG/VG. G8. $12.50.

MELVILLE, Jennie. *Morbid Kitchen.* 1996. NY. St. Martin. 1st Am ed. NF/NF. G8. $15.00.

MELVILLE, Jennie. *Witching Murder.* 1994. NY. St. Martin. 1st Am ed. NF/NF. G8. $15.00.

MELVILLE, John. *Guide to California Wines: A Practical Reference Book for Wine Lovers.* 1960. CA. Nourse Publishing. sc. G. A28. $6.50.

MELVILLE, Lewis. *Life & Letters of Tobias Smollett.* 1927. Houghton Mifflin. VG. H4. $15.00.

MELVIN, A. Gordon. *Seashell Parade: Fascinating Facts, Pictures & Stories.* 1973. Tuttle. 1st. ils. F/dj. A2. $22.50.

MELVIN, Floyd F. *Socialism as the Sociological Ideal. A Broader Basis for Socialism.* 1915. NY. Sturgis & Walton. 1st. VG+. owner's name. B2. $30.00.

MENCKEN, H. L. *Days of HL Mencken: Three Volumes in One.* (1947). Dorset. 8vo. F/dj. H4. $25.00.

MENCKEN, H. L. *In Defence of Women.* 1927. NY. 10th. VG. M17. $20.00.

MENDELSOHN, Felix. *Superbaby.* 1969. Nash. 1st. F/VG. P8. $85.00.

MENDELSOHN, Jane. *I Was Amelia Earhart.* 1996. NY. Knopf. 1st. F/F. D10. $55.00.

MENHENNET, Alan. *Order & Freedom: German Literature & Society 1720 – 1805.* 1973. NY. 1st. VG/dj. M17. $17.50.

MENNINGER, Edwin A. *Flowering Trees of the World.* 1962. NY. ils/photos. 336p. dj. B26. $90.00.

MENOTTI, G. C. *Last Savage.* 1964. NYGS. 1st. 48p. NF/VG. D4. $35.00.

MENPES, Mortimer. *Whistler as I Knew Him.* 1904. London. Blk. ils. 153p. 3-quarter bl calf/cloth. VG+. B20. $175.00.

MERCEIN, Eleanor. *The Booke of Bette.* 1929. NY. Grosset & Dunlap. G in chip dj. A16. $5.00.

MERCER, Judy. *Fast Forward.* 1995. NY. Pocket. 1st. author's 1st book. VF/VF. H11. $25.00.

MERCHANT, Paul; see Ellison, Harlan.

MERCHANT, R. A. *Man & Beast.* 1968. Macmillan. 1st. ils. VG/dj. A2. $12.00.

MERCIA, Leonard S. *Raising Poultry the Modern Way.* 1980. VT. Garden Way. 220p. VG. A10. $6.00.

MEREDITH, Robert. *Around the World on Sixty Dollars.* 1895. Chicago. Laird Lee. 1st. dk olive cloth. G+. M21. $20.00.

MEREDITH, William. *The Wreck of the Thresher.* 1964. NY. Knopf. 1st. F/NF. wear at top edge. B2. $25.00.

MERRIAM, Alan P. and Robert J. Benford. *A Bibliography of Jazz.* 1954. NY. Philadelphia. American Folklore Society. over 3300 entries. NF w/sunned spine (issued w/o dj). B2. $75.00.

MERRILL, William. *Raramuri Soulds.* 1988. DC. Smithsonian Institution Press. 1st. 237p. G/G. F3. $20.00.

MERRIMAN, Roger Bigelow. *Suleiman the Magnificent, 1520 – 1566.* 1966. NY. Cooper Sq. ils. 325p. cloth. VG. Q2. $40.00.

MERRINGTON, M. *Custer Story.* 1950. NY. NY. Devin Adair. F. A19. $45.00.

MERRITT, A. *The Ship of Ishtar.* 1973. London. Tom Stacey. reprint. 1st thus. F/F. clip. T2. $25.00.

MERTON, Thomas. *The Silent Life.* (1957). NY. FSC. 1st. F/NF. lt wear to extremities. B3. $60.00.

MERTZ, Barbara Gross. *Hippopotamus Pool.* 1996. Warner. 1st. sgn. NF/dj. G8. $25.00.

MERTZ, Barbara Gross. *Naked Once More.* 1989. NY. Warner. 1st. F/F. H11. $25.00.

MERTZ, Barbara Gross. *Vanish with the Rose.* 1992. S&S. 1st. sgn. NF/dj. G8. $22.50.

MERWIN, W. S. *The Vixen.* 1996. NY. Knopf. 1st. sgn on ffep. F/F. V1. $45.00.

MESSICK, H. *King's Mountain: Epic of Blue Ridge Mountain Men.* 1976. Boston. 1st. inscr. F/dj. M4. $25.00.

METCALF, C. L. *Destructive & Useful Insects: Their Habits & Control.* 1939 (1928). NY. 2nd. 981p. B26. $20.00.

METCALF, L. J. *The Cultivation of New Zealand Trees & Shrubs.* 1972. Wellington. 1st. F in dj. B26. $24.00.

METCALF, Z. P. *General Catalog of Homoptera, Fascicili VI Cicadelloidea.* 1964. USDA. 348p. xl. VG. S5. $15.00.

METCALFE, John. *Nightmare Jack and Other Tales: The Best Macabre Short Stories of Jack Metcalfe.* 1998. Ashcroft. BC. Ash Tree Press. 1st. VF/VF. T2. $45.00.

METHUEN, Eyre. *The Brand New Monty Python Book.* nd. Python. assumed 1st ed. no copyright pg. F/lightly browned dj. M25. $45.00.

METTHIESSEN, Peter. *Race Rock.* 1954. Harper. 1st. author's 1st book. VG+/chipped dj. M25. $100.00.

MEYER, B. S. *Plant Physiology.* 1952 (1939). NY. 2nd ed. occasional underlining in text. B26. $12.50.

MEYER, Charles A. *Whaling and the Art of Scrimshaw.* 1976. NY. David McKay Co. Inc. photo ils. glossary and index. 271p. VG in lightly worn. clipped dj. P4. $75.00.

MEYER, Charles R. *How to Be an Acrobat: A Ringling Bros. and Barnum & Bailey Book.* 1978. NY. David McKay Company Inc. 1st. VG-/no dj. A28. $8.95.

MEYER, Lorenzo. *Mexico & the United States in the Oil Controversy 1917 – 1942.* 1977. Austin. Univ. of Texas. 1st. 367p. G/G. F3. $20.00.

MEYER, Nicholas. *West End Horror.* 1976. Dutton. 1st. F/F. H11. $20.00.

MEYER, William R. *Film Buff's Catalog.* 1978. Arlington House. 432p. VG. C5. $12.50.

MEYERS, Annette. *Blood on the Street.* 1992. NY. Doubleday. 1st. VF/VF. H11. $25.00.

MEYERS, Annette. *Tender Death.* 1990. NY. Bantam. 1st. Jacket has small scrape on the front panel. wear at spine ends. VF/NF. H11. $20.00.

MEYERS, Annette. *The Big Killing.* 1989. NY. Bantam. 1st. author's 1st book. VF/F. H11. $35.00.

MEYNELL, Alice. *Wares of Autolycus: Selected Literary Essays Of.* 1965. London. OUP. 1st. F/VG. O4. $15.00.

MEYNELL, Laurence. *Fatal Flaw.* 1973. Macmillan. 1st Eng. VG/dj. G8. $12.50.

MEYNELL, Laurence. *Hooky & the Prancing Horse.* 1980. Macmillan. 1st British ed. VG+/VG+. G8. $12.50.

MEYNELL, Viola. *Letters of J. M. Barrie.* 1947. Scribner. 1st. 311p. cloth. F/dj. O10. $20.00.

MEZEY, Robert. *The Lovemaker.* 1961 Cummington Press. 1st. F/F. V1. $35.00.

MIANO, Mark. *Flesh and Stone.* 1997. NY Kensington. 1st author's 1st novel. VF/VF T2. $20.00.

MICHAEL, Bryan; see Moore, Brian.

MICHAEL, Judith. *Tangled Web.* 1994. S&S 1st. F/dj. W2. $25.00.

MICHAEL, M. A. *Traveller's Quest: Origina Contributions.* 1950. London. Wm Hodge 1st. 8vo. F/VG. A2. $30.00.

MICHAELS, Anne. *Fugitive Pieces.* 1997 NY. Knopf. 1st. F/F. M23. $40.00.

MICHAELS, Barbara. *Into the Darkness* 1990. NY. S&S. 1st. NF/NF. G8. $20.00.

MICHAELS, Barbara. *Other Worlds.* 1999 NY. Harper Collins. 1st. sgn by Michaels VF/VF. T2. $25.00.

MICHAELS, Barbara. *Stitches in Time.* 1995 NY. Harper & Row. 1st. sgn. NF/NF. G8 $20.00.

MICHAELS, Barbara. *Vanish with the Rose* 1992. NY. S&S. 1st. sgn. NF/NF. G8. $20.00

MICHENER, James. *A Century of Sonnets* (1997). Austin. State House Press. ltd to 250 copies. in celebration of author's 90th birth day. sgn by author. spine Is in leather w/ brd in pict cloth designed by David Timmons. F/in pict slipcase. B3. $250.00.

MICHENER, James A. *Centennial.* 1974 Random. 1st. 1/500. #d/sgn. 909p. dk b cloth. F/case. H5. $300.00.

MICHENER, James A. *Drifters.* 1971 Random. 1st. NF/dj. A24. $60.00.

MICHENER, James A. *Floating World.* 1954 NY. 1st. VG/dj. B5. $105.00.

MICHENER, James A. *Hawaii.* 1959 Random. 1st. VG/G. B5. $50.00.

MICHENER, James A. *Hawaii.* 1959. Random. 1st. 8vo. NF/dj. S9. $150.00.

MICHENER, James A. *Kent State: What Happened & Why.* 1971. NY. Random. 1st. VG+/dj. A14. $52.50.

MICHENER, James A. *Legacy.* 1987. NY. Random. 1st. F/F. H11. $20.00.

MICHENER, James A. *Mexico.* 1992. NY. Random. 1st. F/F. H11. $25.00.

ICHENER, James A. *Poland*. 1983. ndom House. 1st. F/chip dj. S19. $35.00.

ICHENER, James A. *Return to Paradise*. 51. np. Random House. 1st. F/G dj. M19. 00.00.

ICHENER, James A. *Six Days in Havana*. '89. Austin, TX. 1st. F/F. B3. $40.00.

ICHENER, James A. *Source*. 1965. ndom. 1st. VG. S13. $15.00.

ICHENER, James A. *Tales of the South acific*. 1947. NY. 1st. VG. A14. $140.00.

ICHENER, James A. *The Covenant*. 1982. wcett Crest. pb. G. F6. $1.25.

ICHENER, James A. *The Fires of Spring*. '49. Fawcett Crest. pb. G. F6. $1.35.

IDDLECOFF, Cary. *Golf Doctor*. 1950. NY. t. inscr. VG. B30. $15.00.

IDDLEKAUFF, R. *Glorious Cause: merican Revolution 1763 – 1789*. 1982. xford. 1st. ils/maps. F/dj. M4. $25.00.

IDDLETON, Faith. *Goodness of Ordinary ople*. 1996. Crown. 1st. F/dj. T11. $25.00.

IDDLETON, W. E. Knowles. *Invention of e Meteorological Instruments*. 1969. altimore. 1st. 362p. A13. $45.00.

IDDLETON, William D. *Interurban Era*. '78. Milwaukee. ils. 432p. F/VG+. B18. 55.00.

IELCHE, Hakon. *Lands of Aladdin*. 1955. ondon. Hodge. ils/pl. cloth. VG+/dj. Q2. 30.00.

IKEL, John T. *A Monographic Study of the ern Genus Anemia, Subgenus Coptophyllum*. '62. Amsterdam. wrp. B26. $22.50.

IIKES, George. *The Spy Who Died of oredom*. 1973. NY. Harper & Row. 1st. F/F. 11. $25.00.

MIKESH, Robert C. *Japan's World War II alloon Attacks on North America*. 1978. mithsonian. 3rd. photos. VG/wrp. M17. 20.00.

IILAN, Victor. *Cybernetic Shogun*. 1990. orrow. 1st. F/dj. M25. $15.00.

IILBURN, Frank. *Polo: Emperor of Games*. '94. NY. Knopf. 1st. F/dj. O3. $25.00.

IILBURN, Frank. *Sheltered Lives*. 1986. oubleday. 1st. rem mk. NF/dj. R11. $15.00.

MILCH, Henry & R. A. Milch. *Fracture Surgery a Textbook of Common Fractures*. (1959). NY. Hoeber. 1st. 671 ils. 470p. F. B14. $55.00.

MILES, Keith. *Bullet Hole*. 1986. London. Andre Deutsch. 1st. sgn. VF/VF. T2. $35.00.

MILES, Keith. *Double Eagle*. 1987. London. Andre Deutsch. 1st. sgn. VF/VF. T2. $35.00.

MILES, Keith; see Tralins, Bob.

MILES, Manly. *Stock-Breeding: Practical Treatise*. 1879. NY. Appleton. 1st. G. O3. $20.00.

MILL, John Stuart. *Autobiography*. 1873. London. Longman Gr. sm 4to. list of author's works at end. cloth. R12. $375.00.

MILL, John Stuart. *Principls of Political Economy with Some of Their Applications to Social Philosophy*. 1895. London. Routledge. ne. gilt decor spine in blue cloth. 640p. VG. B14. $55.00.

MILLAIS, J. G. *Newfoundland & Its Untrodden Ways*. 1967. Abercrombie Fitch. rpt. 340p. F/torn. M4. $30.00.

MILLAN, Verna. *Mexico Reborn*. 1939. Boston. Houghton Mifflin. 1st. 312p. G/chipped dj. F3. $20.00.

MILLAR, Andree. *Orchids of Papua New Guinea. An Introduction*. 1978. Canberra. over 200 color photos. ep maps. VG in dj. B26. $34.00.

MILLAR, John F. *American Ships of the Colonial & Revolutionary Periods*. 1978. NY. Norton. 1st. ils. 356p. VG/dj. M10. $45.00.

MILLAR, Kenneth. *Black Money*. 1966. NY. Knopf. 1st. NF/dj. M15. $250.00.

MILLAR, Margaret. *An Air that Kills*. 1957. NY. Random House. 1st. F in clip dj. M15. $45.00.

MILLAR, Margaret. *The Fiend*. 1964. NY. Random House. 1st. F in dj. M15. $40.00.

MILLAR, Margaret. *The Iron Gates*. 1945. NY. Random House. 1st. VG in dj. M15. $45.00.

MILLARD, Alan. *Treasures from Bible Times*. 1985. Lion. 189p. VG. B29. $8.50.

MILLARES CARLO, Agustin. *Introduccion A La Historia Del Libro Y De Las Bibliotecas*. 1988. FCE. Mexico. 4th printing. b/w photo ils. 399p. F/wrp. F3. $30.00.

MILLAY, Edna St. Vincent. *Mine the Harvest*. 1954. Harper. 1st. 8vo. 140p. VG/dj. H1. $30.00.

MILLAY, Edna St Vincent. *Princess Marries the Page*. 1932. Harper. 1st. ils. cloth/brd. G. B27. $25.00.

MILLEN, Gilmore. *Sweet Man*. 1930. Viking. later printing. VG in faded blk cloth. missing dj. M25. $15.00.

MILLER, Arthur. *Creation of the World & Other Business*. 1973. NY. Viking. 1st. NF/clip. A24. $30.00.

MILLER, Arthur. *Death of a Salesman*. 1949. Viking. 139p. VG. C5. $12.50.

MILLER, Arthur. *Death of a Salesman*. 1981. Viking. special ils ed. sgn. NF/dj. R14. $60.00.

MILLER, Arthur. *Focus*. 1945. Reynal Hitchcock. 1st. 8vo. F/NF. S9. $375.00.

MILLER, Charles. *Raggedy Ann's Joyful Songs*. 1937. NY. Miller Music Inc. 1st. oblong 8vo. ils by Johnny Gruelle. full color pict wrps. 14 b/w ils. 48p. NF. D6. $75.00.

MILLER, Denning. *Wind, Storm and Rain; The Story of Weather*. 1952. NY. Coward McCann. 2nd printing. b/w photos. 8vo. 177p. G/chipped dj. K5. $15.00.

MILLER, Dorothy Ruth. *A Handbook of Ancient History in Bible Light*. 1922. Revell. 286p. VG. B29. $4.50.

MILLER, Dr. Richard Gordon. *A History and Atlas of the Fishes of the Antarctic Ocean*. 1993. Carson City. Foresta Institute for Ocean and Mountain Studies. 1st. dk bl cloth w/ wht spine and cover titles. decor ep. 792p+21. New in dj. P4. $125.00.

MILLER, Everett R. & Addie R. *The New Martinsville Glass Story*. 1972. Marietta, OH. Richardson Publishing. 1st. 4to sgn. 62p. VG. H1. $45.00.

MILLER, Francis Trevelyan. *Photographic History of the Civil War*. 1911. 10 vol. bl cloth. VG. E6. $225.00.

MILLER, Harry. *Gallery of American Dogs*. 1950. NY. McGraw Hill. ils w/photos and w/drawings by Paul Brown. VG/F. O3. $25.00.

MILLER, Helen Hill. *Case for Liberty*. 1965. Chapel Hill. VG/dj. M11. $65.00.

MILLER, Henry. *A Devil in Paradise*. 1956. NY. Signet. 1st. wrp. pb orig. F. B2. $30.00.

MILLER, Henry. *Letters of Henry Miller & Wallace Fowlie*. 1975. Grove. 1st. F/dj. M19. $17.50.

MILLER, Henry. *Nexus*. 1965. NY. Grove. 1st Am ed. Book 3 of the Rosy Crucifixion. F/F. B2. $40.00.

MILLER, Henry. *The Colossus of Maroussi*. 1941. np. Colt Press. 1st. F/G dj. M19. $250.00.

MILLER, J. Hillis. *Illustration*. 1992. Harvard. ils. VG/dj. M17. $20.00.

MILLER, James. *Passion of Michel Foucault*. 1993. NY. 1st. dj. T9. $18.00.

MILLER, Jimmy. *The Big Win*. 1969. NY. Knopf. 1st. F/F. H11. $25.00.

MILLER, Joaquin. *Building of the City Beautiful*. 1905. Albert Brandt. 1st complete. NF. M19. $45.00.

MILLER, John A. *Causes of Action*. 1999. NY. Pocket Books. 1st. sgn. VF/VF. T2. $25.00.

MILLER, John A. *Cutdown*. 1997. NY. Pocket Books. 1st. sgn. author's 1st novel. VF/VF. T2. $30.00.

MILLER, Laurence. *Jesus Christ Is Alive*. 1949. Wilde. 89p. VG. B29. $3.00.

MILLER, Marc. *Widow, Weep for Me*. 1960. Arcadia. 1st. VG/VG. G8. $12.50.

MILLER, Mark. *Wine: A Gentleman's Game*. 1984. Harper Row. 1st. ils. VG/dj. M17. $20.00.

MILLER, Mary Britton. *Menagerie*. 1928. NY. Macmillan. 1st. ils by Helen Sewell. sm 8vo. brick cloth w/gr & blk title. designs. ils throughout. 124p. VG. D6. $78.00.

MILLER, Max. *Mexico Around Me*. 1937. NY. Reynal & Hitchcock. 1st. ils by Everett Jackson. ep maps. 305p. G/chipped dj. F3. $20.00.

MILLER, Merle. *What Happened*. 1972. Harper Row. 1st. NF/NF. H11. $15.00.

MILLER, Olive Beaupre. *The Latch Key of Bookhouse*. (1921). The Bookhouse for Children. blk binding; ils Donn P. Crane & others. VG. B15. $55.00.

MILLER, Rabbi David. *The Secret of the Jew; His Life, His Family*. 1938. Miller. 253p. VG. B29. $6.00.

MILLER, Rex. *St. Louis Blues*. 1995. Baltimore. Maclay & Associates. 1st. 1/500 # copies. sgn. VF/no dj in slipcase as issued. T2. $40.00.

MILLER, Robert M. *Ranchin', Ropin', an' Doctorin': A Book of Cowboy and Veterinary Cartoons*. 1993. Vet Data. 1st. ils. 123p. F. B19. $10.00.

MILLER, Samuel. *The Dilemma of Modern Belief*. 1963. Harper. 113p. G. B29. $6.50.

MILLER, Stephen. *The Woman in the Yard*. 1999. NY. Picador/USA. ARC. F in wrp. B2. $25.00.

MILLER, Stephen E. *The Woman in the Yard*. 1999. NY. Picador. 1st. author's 1st novel. sgn. VF/VF. T2. $25.00.

MILLER, Sue. *Family Pictures*. (1990). NY. Harper & Row. 1st. sgn by author. F/NF. lt wear. B3. $35.00.

MILLER, Sue. *For Love*. (1993). NY. Harper Collins. 1st. sgn by author. F/F. B3. $30.00.

MILLER, Sue. *Inventing the Abbotts*. (1987). London. Gollancz. 1st British ed. author's 2nd book. F/NF. very lt wear. B3. $20.00.

MILLER, Sue. *The Distinguished Guest*. (1995). NY. Harper Collins. 1st. sgn by author. F/F. B3. $35.00.

MILLER, Wade. *Dead Fall*. 1954. NY. Mystery House. 1st. Price clipped jacket. F/dj. M15. $125.00.

MILLER, Walter M. Jr. *Saint Leibowitz and the Wild Horse Woman*. 1997. London. Orbit. 1st. VF/VF. T2. $35.00.

MILLER, William. *Ottoman Empire & Its Successors 1801 – 1927*. 1936. Cambridge. 8vo. ils/5 maps. 644p. cloth. VG. Q2. $40.00.

MILLER, William J. *Training of an Army: Camp Curtin & North's Civil War*. 1990. Wht. Mane Pub. 1st. F/dj. A14. $21.00.

MILLER & MORATH. *Chinese Encounter*. 1979. FSG. 1st. 8vo. 255p. VG/dj. B11. $15.00.

MILLETT, Larry. *Sherlock Holmes and the Ice Palace Murders*. 1998. NY. Viking. 1st. VF/VF. T2. $24.00.

MILLETT, Larry. *Sherlock Holmes and the Rune Stone Mystery*. 1999. NY. Viking. 1st. sgn. VF/VF. T2. $25.00.

MILLHAUSER, Steven. *Little Kingdoms*. 1993. NY. Poseidon. 1st. rem mk. NF/dj. R14. $30.00.

MILLHAUSER, Steven. *Martin Dressle The Tale of an American Dreamer*. 1996. N Crown. 1st. F in F dj. D10. $85.00.

MILLHAUSER, Steven. *Portrait of Romantic*. 1977. Knopf. 1st. sgn. rem m VG+/dj. B30. $75.00.

MILLHAUSER, Steven. *The Barnu Museum*. 1990. NY. Poseidon. 1st. F/F. D1 $50.00.

MILLHISER, Marlys. *Death of the Offic Witch*. (1993). NY. Otto Penzler. 1st. sgn b author. F/F. B3. $40.00.

MILLIGAN, David. *All Color Book of Win 1974. NY. Octopus Books. hc. VG/G+. A2 $16.00.

MILLIKAN, Robert A. *Science & the Ne Civilization*. 1930. Scribner. 1st. 194p. VG+ A25. $20.00.

MILLIKIN, Stephen F. *Chester Himes: / Critical Appraisal*. 1976. Columbia University of Missouri. 1st. price clippe jacket. F/dj. M15. $75.00.

MILLON, Theodore. *Handbook of Clinica Health Psychology*. 1982. NY. Plenum. heav 8vo. 608p. prt gr cloth. VG. G1. $65.00.

MILLS, C. Wright. *The Sociologica Imagination*. 1959. NY. Oxford U. Press. 1st 8vo. 234p. F/VG. H1. $22.50.

MILLS, Charles. *Choice*. 1943. Macmillan 1st. inscr. VG/dj. S13. $35.00.

MILLS, Charles. *Harvest of Barren Regret Army Career, FW Benteen*. 1985. Clark. ils VG. J2. $295.00.

MILLS, Charles A. *The Sherlock Holmes Boo of Wines and Spirits*. 1998. Alexandria. Appl Cheeks Press. 1st. VF/pict wrp. T2. $8.00.

MILLS, James. *Underground Empire*. 1986 Doubleday. 1st. sgn. 1165p. NF/dj. W2 $40.00.

MILLS, Kyle. *Riding Phoenix*. 1997. NY Harper Collins. ARC. wrp. NF. B2. $25.00.

MILLS, Kyle. *Rising Phoenix*. 1997. np Harper Collins. 1st. author's 1st novel NF/NF rem mk. R16. $30.00.

MILLS, Lennox A. *Southeast Asia: Illusio and Reality in Politics and Economics*. 1964 Minneapolis. Univ. of Minnesota Press sm4to. cloth. 365p. F. P1. $20.00.

MILLSON, Larry. *Ballpark Figures*. 1987 Toronto. McClelland Stewart. 1st. F/VG+ P8. $45.00.

ILNE, A. A. *Chloe Marr.* 1946. Dutton. 1st m. 8vo. VG/G. A2. $12.00.

ILNE, A. A. *Christopher Robin Birthday ook.* 1930. London. Methuen. 1st. ils epherd. VG. B14. $300.00.

ILNE, A. A. *Four Days Wonder.* 1933. ndon. Metheun. 1st. F in dj. M15. $75.00.

ILNE, A. A. *House at Pooh Corner.* (1928). ondon. Methuen. 1st. 12mo. ils EH epherd. teg. gilt salmon cloth. dj. R5. 50.00.

ILNE, A. A. *Now We Are Six.* 1927. ondon. Methuen. 1st. aeg. bl leather. box. B4. $1. 500.00.

ILNE, A. A. *When We Were Very Young.* 50. Dutton. 8vo. VG/dj. B17. $25.00.

ILNE, A. A. *Winnie the Pooh.* (1926). ndon. Meuthuen. 1st. 12mo. teg. gilt gr oth. R5. $600.00.

ILNE, A. A. *Winnie the Pooh.* 1955 (1926). utton. 1st. ils Ernest Shepherd. G. M5. 0.00.

ILOSZ, Czeslaw. *The Land of Ulro.* (1984). Y. FSG. 1st. trans by Louis Iribarne. author a Nobel Prize winner. F/F. B3. $45.00.

ILTON, John R., ed. *The American Indian* peaks. 1969. Vermillion. U of South Dakota. t. wrp. 194p. NF. B2. $40.00.

IN, Anchee. *Katherine.* (1995). NY. iverhead. 1st. author's 2nd book. F/F. B3. 20.00.

INARIK, Else Holmelund. *Little Bear.* 57. NY. Harper & Bros. G. A16. $15.00.

INCHIN, C. O. *Sea Fishing.* 1911. London. k. 1st. F. B9. $85.00.

INGUS, Charles. *Beneath the Underdog.* 971. NY. Knopf. 1st. F/lightly chip dj. B2. 30.00.

INOR, Robert. *Lynching and Frame Up in* ennessee. 1946. NY. New Century. 1st. 96p. G+wrp. B2. $25.00.

INOR, Robert. *One War to Defeat Hitler.* 941. NY. Workers Library. 1st. F. wrp. stp n front. B2. $25.00.

INOT, Stephen. *Chill of Dusk.* 1964. arden City. Doubleday. 1st. Jacket has ght wear at extremities. F/NF. H11. $35.00.

INOT, Susan. *Evening.* 1998. Knopf. ARC. F/decor wrp. M25. $45.00.

MINOT, Susan. *Lust & Other Stories.* 1989. Boston. Houghton. 1st. F/VF. H11. $30.00.

MINOT, Susan. *Monkeys.* 1986. NY. Dutton. 1st. author's 1st book. F/F. H11. $70.00.

MISHIMA, Yukio. *Decay of the Angel.* 1974. Knopf. 1st Am. NF/dj. M25. $25.00.

MISHIMA, Yukio. *Spring Snow.* 1972. Knopf. 1st Am. NF/clip. M25. $25.00.

MISTRY, Rohinton. *Swimming Lessons and Other Stories.* 1989. Boston. Houghton Mifflin. 1st. F/dj. D10. $50.00.

MITCHARD, Jacquelyn. *The Deep End of the Ocean.* 1996. NY. Viking. 1st. author's 1st novel. F/VF. H11. $65.00.

MITCHELL, Don. *Thumb Tripping.* 1970. np. Little, Brn. 1st. a hippie classic. F/VG dj. M19. $25.00.

MITCHELL, Donald. *Wet Days at Edgewood.* 1865. Scribner. 324p. A10. $45.00.

MITCHELL, Edwin Valentine. *Morocco Bound: Adrift Among Books.* 1929. Farrar Rinehart. 1st/2nd prt. 232p. cloth. F/dj. O10. $25.00.

MITCHELL, Ehrman B. *MFH: Ponies for Young People.* 1960. Van Nostrand. VG/fair. O3. $12.00.

MITCHELL, George. *I'm Somebody Important, Young Black Voices from Rural Georgia.* 1973. Urbana. Univ. of Illinois Press. 1st. sm 4to. F/F. B2. $45.00.

MITCHELL, Gladys. *Here Lies Gloria Mundy.* 1982. London. Michael Joseph. 1st. F/dj. M15. $50.00.

MITCHELL, Gladys. *Nest of Vipers.* 1979. London. Michael Joseph. 1st. F/dj. M15. $65.00.

MITCHELL, Gladys. *Noonday and Night.* 1977. London. Michael Joseph. 1st. F in dj. M15. $75.00.

MITCHELL, Gladys. *Winking at the Brim.* 1974. McKay Washburn. 1st Am ed. NF/NF. G8. $10.00.

MITCHELL, Joni. *Complete Poems & Lyrics.* 1997. NY. Crown. 1st. F/dj. R14. $35.00.

MITCHELL, Julian. *Undiscovered Country.* 1969. Grove. 1st. VG/dj. B30. $20.00.

MITCHELL, Juliet. *Woman's Estate.* 1971. NY. Pantheon. 1st. jacket rubbed spots on front panel and minor wear at spine ends. F/F. H11. $35.00.

MITCHELL, M. H. *Passenger Pigeon in Ontario.* 1935. Toronto. lg 8vo. ils/maps. 181p. NF. C12. $160.00.

MITCHELL, Margaret. *Gone with the Wind.* 1936. Macmillan. 2nd issue (June 1936). gray cloth. VG. B20. $85.00.

MITCHELL, Peter. *Great Flower Painters: Four Centuries of Floral Art.* 1973. Woodstock. NY. 4to. VG in dj. B26. $40.00.

MITCHELL, Sidney Alexander. *S.Z. Mitchell & the Electrical Industry.* 1960. FSC. 1st. VG. N2. $10.00.

MITCHELL, Stephen. *The Gospel According to Jesus.* 1990. Harper. 310p. F/F. B29. $6.50.

MITCHELL, Sydney B. *Iris for Every Garden.* 1960 (1949). NY. BC. rev ed. VG in dj. B26. $10.00.

MITCHELL-HEDGES, F. A. *Danger My Ally.* 1954. London. Elek Books. 1st. 255p. F/dj. F3. $35.00.

MITCHELTREE, Tom. *Katie's Will.* 1997. Aurora. Write Way Publishing. 1st. sgn. VF/VF. T2. $25.00.

MITCHISON, Naomi. *Blood of the Martyrs.* 1948. McGraw Hill. 375p. G. W2. $30.00.

MITFORD, Jessica. *Faces of Philip.* 1984. NY. 1st. dj. T9. $12.00.

MITFORD, Nancy. *Blessing.* 1951. London. 1st. dj. T9. $35.00.

MOATS, Alice. *Thunder in their Veins.* 1932. NY. Century Co. 1st. 279p. G/chipped dj. F3. $25.00.

MOATS, Leone & Alice. *Off to Mexico.* 1940. NY. Scribners. 2nd printing. 172p. G/lt shelf wear. front hinge cracked. F3. $10.00.

MOFFAT, Gwen. *Cue the Battered Wife.* 1994. London. Macmillan. 1st. VF/VF. T2. $20.00.

MOFFAT, Gwen. *The Outside Edge.* 1993. London. Macmillan. 1st. VF/VF. T2. $20.00.

MOFFAT, Gwen. *Veronica's Sisters.* 1992. London. Macmillan. 1st. VF/VF. T2. $20.00.

MOHLENBROCK, Robert H. *The Illustrated Flora of Illinois: Ferns.* 1967. Carbondale. SIU Press. OP. VG in faded dj. B26. $37.50.

MOHR, Nancy L. *Lady Blows a Horn*. 1995. Unionville, PA. Sevynmore. 1st. sgn. VG/dj. O3. $25.00.

MOHR, Nicolas. *Excursion Through America*. 1973. Lakeside Classic. 1st thus. 2 fld maps. teg. NF. T11. $40.00.

MOLDENKE, Harold N. *American Wild Flowers*. 1949. NY. photos. 453p. F. B26. $17.50.

MOLE, William. *Skin Trap*. 1957. London. Eyre & Spottiswoode. 1st. F/dj. M15. $75.00.

MOLES, Robert N. *Definition & Rule in Legal Theory*. 1987. Oxford. VG/dj. M11. $45.00.

MOLEY, Raymond. *Our Criminal Courts*. 1930. Minton Balch. M11. $75.00.

MOLLOY, Paul. *Pennant for the Kremlin*. 1964. Doubleday. 1st. inscr. VG/dj. P8. $35.00.

MOLSEED, Elwood. *Genus Trigidia (Iridaceae) of Mexico & Central America*. 1970. Berkeley. ils. 127p. wrp. B26. $15.00.

MOMADAY, N. Scott. *House Made of Dawn*. 1968. NY. Harper. 1st. F/dj. B4. $450.00.

MOMADAY, N. Scott. *The Ancient Child*. 1989. NY. Doubleday. ARC. sgn. F in F dj. D10. $50.00.

MOMADAY, N. Scott. *The Gourd Dancer*. 1976. NY. Harper & Row. 1st pb ed. sgn. F. V1. $75.00.

MOMADAY, N. Scott. *The Man Made of Words*. 1997. NY. St. Martin. 1st. sgn. F in F dj. D10. $40.00.

MOMADAY, N. Scott. *Way to Rainy Mountain*. 1969. NM U. ils Al Momaday. 88p. NF/rpr. M4. $20.00.

MONACHAN, John; see Burnett, W. R.

MONAGHAN, James Jay. *Civil War on the Western Border 1854 – 1865*. 1955. Boston. Little, Brn. 3rd printing. orig cloth. 454p. NF/VG. M8. $35.00.

MONAGHAN, Jay. *Book of the American West*. 1963. NY. Messner. 1st. 4to. 607p. VG. O3. $35.00.

MONAGHAN, Jay. *Civil War on the Western Border*. 1955. Bonanza. 454p. NF/dj. E1. $35.00.

MONAGHAN, Tom. *Pizza Tiger*. 1986. Random. ils. 346p. dj. H6. $24.00.

MONDEY, David. *Rockets and Missiles*. 1971. NY. Grosset & Dunlap. ils by Gordon Davies. 75p. G in pict cloth. wear. some foxing. K5. $9.00.

MONES, Nicole. *Lost in Translation*. 1998. NY. Delacorte. 1st. author's 1st novel. sgn. VF/VF. T2. $25.00.

MONETTE, Paul. *Last Watch of the Night*. (1993). NY. Harcourt Brace. 1st. F/F. B3. $25.00.

MONFREDO, Miriam Grace. *Blackwater Spirits*. 1995. NY. St. Martin. 1st. sgn. VF/VF. T2. $30.00.

MONFREDO, Miriam Grace. *North Star Conspiracy*. 1993. NY. St. Martin. 1st. sgn. VF/VF. T2. $35.00.

MONIG, Christopher. *Abra-Cadaver*. 1958. Dutton. 1st. VG/dj. M19. $17.50.

MONK, Samuel H. *Sublime: Study of Critical Theories in XVII Century England*. 1935. NY. Mod Lang Assn. inscr. VG. H13. $95.00.

MONK, Thelonious. *Thelonious Monk's Piano Originals Revealing Instincts of the Genius on Jazz*. 1958? NY. Charles Colin. 1st. 24p. VG/wrps. B2. $65.00.

MONKMAN, Noel. *From Queensland to the Great Barrier Reef*. 1958. NY. 1st. 182p. F/VG clip. H3. $30.00.

MONRO, Thomas. *Physician as Man of Letters*. Science & Action. 1933. Glasgow. 1st. 212p. A13. $90.00.

MONROE, Harriet. *Valeria and Other Poems*. 1892. Chicago. McClurg. trade ed. author's 1st book. VG+ w/date and owner's name. B2. $60.00.

MONROE, Marilyn. *My Story*. 1974. Stein Day. 1st. NF/VG. M19. $17.50.

MONSARRAT, Nicholas. *Fair Day's Work*. 1964. London. Cassell. 1st. bl cloth. NF/VG. T11. $20.00.

MONSARRAT, Nicholas. *Ship that Died of Shame & Other Stories*. 1974. NY. Wm Sloane. 1st. VG/dj. T11. $10.00.

MONSER, Harold E. *Monser's Topical Index and Digest of the Bible*. 1960. Baker. 681p. VG/torn dj. B29. $12.50.

MONSMAN, G. *Olive Schreiner's Fiction: Landscape & Power*. 1991. rpt. ils. F/dj. M4. $15.00.

MONTAGUE, John. *Bitter Harvest: A Anthology*. 1989. NY. 1st. VG/dj. M1? $25.00.

MONTECINO, Marcel. *Big Time*. 1990. NY Morrow. 1st. VF/VF. H11. $35.00.

MONTECINO, Marcel. *The Crosskiller* 1988. NY. Arbor House. 1st. VNF/dj. D1? $65.00.

MONTGOMERY, Ione. *The Golden Dress* 1940. NY. Doubleday Crime Club. 1st. F in dj/worn. bookplate. M15. $50.00.

MONTGOMERY, John Warwick *Principalities and Powers: The World of th Occult*. 1973. Bethany. 224p. VG. B29. $6.00

MONTGOMERY, L. M. *Anne of Green Gables*. 1960. Toronto. Ryerson. Canadian ed. G in F dj. A16. $20.00.

MONTGOMERY, L. M. *Rilla of Ingleside* 1947. Toronto. Ryerson. Canadian ed. VG in chip dj. A16. $20.00.

MONTGOMERY, L. M. *The Golden Road* 1913. NY. Grosset & Dunlap. G in chip dj A16. $25.00.

MONTGOMERY, Richard G. *Pechuck Lorne Knight's Adventure in the Arctic*. 1932 Dodd Mead. inscr. 8vo. 219p. VG/dj. P4 $65.00.

MONTGOMERY, Rutherford. *Golden Stallion to the Rescue*. 1954. Little, Brn. 1st VG. O3. $35.00.

MONTGOMERY, Rutherford. *Snowman* 1964. NY. Duell. Sloan & Pearce. 1st ed VG/VG. O3. $45.00.

MONTUNO MORENTE, Vicente. *Nuestra Senora De La Capilla*. 1950. Madrid. Ensayo Historico. 1st. sgn Charles Gibson. 424p G/wrp. foxing. F3. $20.00.

MOODY, Bill. *Bird Lives!* 1999. NY. Walker. 1st. sgn. VF/VF. T2. $25.00.

MOODY, Bill. *Death of a Tenor Man*. 1995 NY. Walker. 1st. F/dj. M23. $40.00.

MOODY, Ralph. *Horse of a Different Color*. 1968. NY. Norton. 1st prt. VG/VG. O3. $25.00.

MOODY, Richard. *Kit Carson & the Wild Frontier*. 1955. Random. 5th. Landmark #53. ils Galli. 184p. VG. B36. $9.00.

MOODY, Rick. *Ice Storm*. 1994. Little, Brn. 1st. F/dj. B30. $25.00.

MOODY, Rick. *Purple America.* 1997. Boston. Little, Brn. 1st. sgn. F/F. D10. $35.00.

MOODY, Rick. *The Ice Storm.* 1994. Boston. Little, Brn. 1st. sgn. F/F. D10. $55.00.

MOODY, Rick. *The Ring of Brightest Angels Around Heaven.* 1995. Boston. Little, Brn. 1st. sgn. F/F. D10. $45.00.

MOODY, Susan. *Falling Angel.* 1998. London. Hodder & Stoughton. 1st. VF/VF. T2. $30.00.

MOODY, Susan. *Mosaic.* (1991). NY. Delacorte. 1st. sgn by author. F/F. B3. $35.00.

MOODY, Susan. *Playing with Fire.* (1990). London. MacDonald. 1st British ed. the true first. F/F. B3. $30.00.

MOORCOCK, Michael. *The Fortress of the Pearl.* 1989. NY. Ace Books. 1st Am ed. F/F. T2. $8.00.

MOORE, Alexander. *Life Cycles in Atchalan.* 1973. NY. Teachers College Press. 1st. 220p. G/chipped dj. F3. $15.00.

MOORE, Anne Carroll. *Nicholas, a Manhattan Christmas Story.* 1924. NY. Putnam. 2nd printing. ils by Jay Van Everen. red cloth w/gilt. map ep. 332p. G+. D6. $20.00.

MOORE, Brian. *An Answer from Limbo.* 1962. Boston. Atlantic-Little, Brn. 1st. sgn. F/NF. price clip by pub. D10. $90.00.

MOORE, Brian. *Black Robe.* 1985. NY. Dutton. 1st. VF/VF. H11. $45.00.

MOORE, Brian. *Fergus.* 1970. NY. Holt. 1st. VF/F. H11. $40.00.

MOORE, Brian. *Lies of Silence.* 1990. London. 1st. sgn. F/dj. T9. $45.00.

MOORE, Brian. *The Color of Blood.* 1987. NY. Dutton. 1st. sgn. F/F. D10. $50.00.

MOORE, C. L. *Black God's Shadow.* 1977. Donald Grant. 1st. VG/dj. L1. $40.00.

MOORE, Carman. *Somebody's Angel Child: Story of Bessie Smith.* 1969. Crowell. 1st. F/NF. B2. $45.00.

MOORE, Charles. *Northwest Under Three Flags, 1635–1796.* 1900. NY. Harper. 1st. pict cloth. many b&w ils & maps. paper slightly browning. soiled. 402p. VG. B18. $35.00.

MOORE, Christopher. *Coyote Blue.* 1994. NY. S&S. 1st. F/F. H11. $30.00.

MOORE, Christopher. *Island of the Sequined Love Nun.* 1997. NY. Avon. 1st. F/VF. H11. $25.00.

MOORE, Christopher. *Practical Demonkeeping: A Comedy of Horrors.* 1991. NY. St. Martin. 1st. sgn. author's 1st novel. VF/VF. T2. $45.00.

MOORE, Christopher. *The Big Weird.* 1996. Bangkok. Book Siam. 1st. trade pb orig. VF/pict wrp. T2. $15.00.

MOORE, Clement C. *Night Before Christmas.* (1931). Phil. Lippincott. 1st Am. ils Rackham. gr cloth/pict label. R5. $150.00.

MOORE, Clement C. *Twas the Night Before Christmas.* 1937. Chicago. Merrill. lg 4to. mc pict wrp. R5. $85.00.

MOORE, E. W. *Natchez Under-the-Hill.* 1958. Natchez. 1st. inscr. ils. 131p. F/dj. M4. $23.00.

MOORE, Elaine T. *Winning Your Spurs.* 1954. Boston. Little, Brn. 1st. 4to. ils by Paul Brown. VG/F. O3. $25.00.

MOORE, Gilbert. *A Special Rage.* 1971. Harper & Row. 1st. F/F. M25. $35.00.

MOORE, Joan Andre. *Astronomy in the Bible.* 1981. Nashville. Abingdon. 8vo. b/w photos. drawings. diagrams. 160p. VG/chipped dj. K5. $27.00.

MOORE, Julia. *Sweet Singer of Michigan.* 1928. Chicago. Pascal Covici. 158p. decor brd. VG/dj. B18. $37.50.

MOORE, Laurie. *The Birds of America.* 1998. NY. Knopf. 1st. sgn. F/F. O11. $45.00.

MOORE, Laurie. *Who Will Run the Frog Hospital?* 1994. NY. Knopf. 1st. sgn. F/F. O11. $55.00.

MOORE, Lorrie. *Self-Help.* 1985. Knopf. 1st. author's 1st book. F/dj. D10. $160.00.

MOORE, Norman. *History of Study of Medicine in British Isles.* 1908. Oxford. 1st. 202p. A13. $100.00.

MOORE, Patrick. *Guide to the Planets.* 1954. Norton. 1st Am. ils/pl. 254p. VG/dj. K5. $25.00.

MOORE, Patrick. *Watchers of the Stars.* 1973. Putnam. 1st. NF/dj. O4. $20.00.

MOORE, Susanna. *In the Cut.* 1995. NY. Knopf. 1st. F/F. H11. $25.00.

MOORE, Susanna. *Sleeping Beauties.* (1993). NY. Knopf. 1st. sgn by the author. F/NF. slight creasing on top spine. B3. $40.00.

MOORE, Susanna. *The Whiteness of Bones.* 1989. NY. Doubleday. 1st. F/F. H11. $30.00.

MOORE, Ward. *Lot & Lot's Daughter.* 1996. San Francisco. Tachyon Publications. 1st. 1/100 # copies. sgn by introducer Michael Swanwick. VF/VF. T2. $25.00.

MOOREHEAD, Alan. *Darwin and the Beagle.* 1970 (1969). NY. 7th prt. sm4to. F in dj. B26. $26.00.

MOOREHOUSE, Alfred C. *Triumph of the Alphabet. A History of Writing.* 1953. NY. Henry Schuman. 1st. 8vo. 223p. cloth. F/dj. O10. $45.00.

MOORHEAD, Alan. *March to Tunis.* 1967. Harper. 1st. 592p. VG/dj. M7. $25.00.

MOORHOUSE, G. *India Britannica.* 1983. NY. 1st Am. 288p. F/dj. M4. $20.00.

MOORMAN, Fay. *My Heart Turns Back: Childhood Memories of Rural Virginia.* (1964). Exposition. 1st. 124p. VG/G. B10. $18.00.

MOORMAN, L. J. *Pioneer Doctor.* 1951. OK U. photos. 252p. F/dj. M4. $15.00.

MOORMAN, Lewis. *Tuberculosis & Genius.* 1940. Chicago. 1st. 272p. A13. $60.00.

MOOTO, Shani. *Cereus Blooms at Night.* 1996. NY. Grove. ARC. wrps. F. B2. $25.00.

MORALES, Dr. Eusebio. *Ensayos, Documentos Y Discuros.* circa 1928. Tomo I. Panama. wrp rebound in Library of Congress bdg. 236p. G. F3. $15.00.

MORAN, Bob. *A Closer Look at Catholicism.* 1986. Word. 259p. VG/VG. B29. $8.50.

MORGAN, Alfred Powell. *How to Build a 20 Foot Bi-Plane Glider.* 1912. NY. Spon & Chamberlain. ils. 59p. edgewear. damp stain/G. B18. $37.50.

MORGAN, Alun, and Raymond Horricks. *Modern Jazz. A Survey of Developments Since 1939.* 1956. London. Gollancz. 1st. F/VG. sm chip on rear panel. B2. $50.00.

MORGAN, Conway Lloyd. *Animal Behaviour.* 1900. London. Longman Gr. sm 8vo. 334p+32p ads. panelled bl buckram. G1. $85.00.

MORGAN, Conway Lloyd. *Introduction to Comparative Psychology.* 1894. London. Walter Scott Ltd. 12mo. 382p+18p ads. emb crimson cloth. G1. $250.00.

MORGAN, Dale L. *West of William H. Ashley.* 1964. Rosenstock. ltd ed. VG. J2. $850.00.

MORGAN, Dan. *Complete Baseball Joke Book.* 1953. Stravon. 1st. VG/dj. P8. $50.00.

MORGAN, Dan. *Rising in the West: True Story of an Oakie Family...* 1992. Knopf. stated 1st. photos. NF/dj. P12. $15.00.

MORGAN, DeWolfe. *Before Homer: Boy's Story of the Earliest Greeks.* 1938. Longman Gr. 1st. 261p. VG. C14. $10.00.

MORGAN, Marlo. *Mutant Message Down Under.* 1994. NY. Harper Collins. 1st. author's 1st novel. VG/VG. R16. $35.00.

MORGAN, Mary. *The House at the Edge of the Jungle.* 1999. NY. St. Martin. 1st. sgn. VF/VF. T2. $25.00.

MORGAN, Mary. *Willful Neglect.* 1997. NY. St. Martin. 1st. sgn. author's 1st novel. VF/VF. T2. $30.00.

MORGAN, Michael. *Nine More Lives.* 1947. NY. Random House. 1st. F/NF. T2. $15.00.

MORGAN, Robin. *Monster.* 1972. Random. 1st. inscr/dtd 1972. F/NF. L3. $45.00.

MORGAN, Seth. *Homeboy.* 1990. NY. Random House. 1st. author's 1st book. F/F. D10. $40.00.

MORGAN, Ted. *Maugham: A Biography.* 1980. S&S. 1st. F/NF clip. P3. $25.00.

MORGANSTEIN, Gary. *Take Me Out to the Ballgame.* 1980. St. Martin. 1st. F/dj. P8. $35.00.

MORISON, B. J. *Voyage of the Chianti.* 1987. North County. 1st. NF/NF. G8. $20.00.

MORLEY, Christopher. *The Haunted Bookshop.* 1918. Grosset & Dunlap. ne. inscr. G/chip. S19. $25.00.

MORLEY, John David. *The Case of Thomas N.* 1987. NY. Atlantic Monthly Press. 1st. VF/VF. T2. $7.00.

MOROSO, John A. *The Listening Man.* 1924. NY. D. Appleton. 1st. VG w/o dj. M15. $40.00.

MORREL, M. M. *Young Hickory: Life of President James K. Polk.* 1949. NY. 1st. inscr. 381p. NF/dj. M4. $30.00.

MORRELL, David. *Blood Oath.* 1982. NY. St. Martin. ARC/1st. RS. F/dj. M15. $90.00.

MORRELL, David. *Desperate Measures.* 1994. NY. Warner. 1st. F/F. H11. $20.00.

MORRELL, David. *Double Image.* 1998. NY. Warner Books. 1st. ARC. VF/pict wrp. T2. $15.00.

MORRELL, David. *First Blood.* 1990. Armchair Detective. rpt. AN/dj. S18. $10.00.

MORRELL, David. *Last Reveille.* 1977. M. Evans & Co. 1st. F/G. S19. $30.00.

MORRELL, David. *Testament.* 1975. NY. Evans. 1st. F+/F. H11. $70.00.

MORRELL, David. *The Covenant of the Flame.* 1991. NY. Warner. 1st. F/F. H11. $25.00.

MORRELL, David. *The Fifth Profession.* 1990. NY. Warner. 1st. F/F-. H11. $15.00.

MORRELL, David. *The League of Night and Fog.* (1987). NY. Dutton. 1st. F/F. B3. $20.00.

MORRIS, Donald R. *Warm Bodies.* 1957. NY. S&S. 1st. F/NF. H11. $50.00.

MORRIS, Earl. *The Temple of the Warriors.* 1931. NY. Scribners. 1st. 251p. VG/spine faded. F3. $50.00.

MORRIS, George. *The Trotskyite 5th Column.* 1945. NY. New Century. 1st. 32p. F/wrp. B2. $25.00.

MORRIS, Henry m. *The Bible and Modern Science.* 1951. Moody. 191p. VG. B29. $5.00.

MORRIS, Jan. *Manhattan '45.* 1987. NY. Oxford. 1st. F/F. H11. $30.00.

MORRIS, Jan. *Pleasures of a Tangled Life.* 1989. London. 1st. dj. T9. $15.00.

MORRIS, Joseph. *Reminiscences of Joseph Morris.* 1899. Mt. Gilead, OH. Sentinel Prt House. 2nd. 12mo. 212p. VG. V3. $30.00.

MORRIS, M. E. *The Icemen.* 1988. NY. Presidio. 1st. 330p. NF/dj. R16. $20.00.

MORRIS, Mark. *Mark Morris.* 1993. FSG. 1st. sgn. F/dj. O11. $75.00.

MORRIS, Terry. *Doctor America: The Story of Tom Dooley.* 1963. NY. Hawthorne Books. 1st printing. Credo Book. ils Richard Lewis. G+/G. A28. $9.95.

MORRIS, Walter. *A Millennium of Weaving in Chiapas.* 1984. Mexico. Chiapas. 1st. ltd to 1800. wrp. 56p. G. F3. $25.00.

MORRIS, Walter. *Living Maya.* 1988. NY. Abrams. 2nd printing. 4to. 224p. G/G. F3. $45.00.

ORRIS, Walter. *Luchetik, The Woven Word from Highland Chiapas.* nd. Mexico. wrp. drawings. map. 38p. G. F3. $20.00.

MORRIS, William. *Glass: Artifact and Art.* 1989. Seattle & London. Univ. of Washington Press. 1st. intro Henry Geldzahler. essay Patterson Sims. sgn by artist. F/F. O11. $125.00.

MORRIS, Willie. *After All, It's Only a Game.* (1992). Jackson. U. of Mississippi. 1st. ils Lynn Green Root. F/F. B3. $30.00.

MORRIS, Willie. *My Dog Skip.* 1995. Random. 1st. F/dj. M23. $15.00.

MORRIS, Willie. *North Toward Home.* 1967. Houghton Mifflin. 1st. F/NF. B4. $150.00.

MORRIS, Willie. *Plains Song.* 1980. NY. Harper & Row. 1st. F/F. D10. $40.00.

MORRIS, Willie. *Prayer for the Opening of the Little League Season.* 1993. Northtowne Prts. F. P8. $150.00.

MORRIS, Wright. *Cause of Wonder.* 1963. Atheneum. 1st. VG/dj. B30. $35.00.

MORRIS, Wright. *Home Place.* 1948. Scribner. 1st. author's 1st book to feature photos. F/dj. B4. $300.00.

MORRIS, Wright. *Inhabitants.* 1946. Scribner. 1st. 4to. 112p. olive cloth. dj. K1. $150.00.

MORRIS, Wright. *Life.* 1973. Harper. 1st. inscr. F/NF. B4. $150.00.

MORRIS, Wright. *Love Among the Cannibals.* 1957. NY. Harcourt Brace. 1st. NF/VG+. minor wear. A24. $40.00.

MORRIS, Wright. *Man & Boy.* 1951. Knopf. 1st/2nd prt. 212p. VG. S14. $25.00.

MORRIS, Wright. *Solo.* 1983. NY. Harper & Row. 1st. F/NF. A24. $15.00.

MORRIS, Wright. *The Fork River Space Project.* (1977). NY. Harper & Row. 1st. F/F. B3. $25.00.

MORRISON, A. J. *Travels in Virginia in Revolutionary Times.* (1922). Bell. 138p. VG/dj. B10. $65.00.

MORRISON, Anne Hendry. *Women & Their Careers: A Study of 306 Women in Business.* 1934. NY. Nat. Federation of Business & Professional Women. VG. A25. $20.00.

MORRISON, Dorothy Nafus. *Whisper Again.* 1987. NY. Atheneum. 1st. F/VF. H11. $45.00.

MORRISON, Philip & Phylis and the Office of Charles and Ray Eames. *Powers of Ten; A Book About the Relative Size of Things in the Universe and the Effect of Adding Another Zero.* 1982. NY. Scientific American Library. 4th printing. ils w/ photos. many in color. sm 4to. 150p. VG/chipped dj. K5. $35.00.

MORRISON, Shelly & Richard. *Nineteenth Century Texana: A Priced Checklist — Books & Pamphlets Relating to Texas Published Before 1900.* 1991. W. M. Morrison Books. 1st. sources. index. 136p. NF. B19. $35.00.

MORRISON, Toni. *Beloved.* 1987. NY. Knopf. 1st. VNF/F. D10. $55.00.

MORRISON, Toni. *Jazz.* 1992. NY. Knopf. 1st. F/F. D10. $40.00.

MORRISON, Toni. *Paradise.* 1998. Knopf. UP. F/WRP. M25. $100.00.

MORRISON, Toni. *Song of Solomon.* 1977. Knopf. 1st. sgn. F/F. D10. $300.00.

MORRISON, Toni. *Tar Baby.* 1981. Knopf. 1st trade ed. F/F. M25. $75.00.

MORRISON, Toni. *The Dancing Mind.* 1996. NY. Knopf. 1st. F/F. D10. $30.00.

MORRISON & OWEN. *Planetary System.* 1996 (1988). Reading. MA. Addison-Wesley. 2nd. ils 570p. F. K5. $30.00.

MORROW, Brad. *Trinity Fields.* (1995). NY. Viking. 1st. sgn by author. F/F. B3. $35.00.

MORROW, Bradford. *Giovanni's Gift.* (1997). NY. Viking. 1st. sgn by author. F/F. B3. $35.00.

MORROW, Bradford. *The Almanac Branch.* 1991. NY. Linden. 1st. sgn. F/F. D10. $50.00.

MORROW, Elizabeth. *Shannon.* 1941. Macmillan. 1st. 12mo. ils Helen Torrey. VG+/G. M5. $20.00.

MORROW, James. *Blameless in Abaddon.* (1996). NY. Harcourt Brace. 1st. NF. lt shelfwear/F. B3. $15.00.

MORROW, James. *City of Truth.* 1990. London. Century/Legend. 1st. VF/VF. T2. $25.00.

MORSON, Ian. *Falconer's Crusade.* 1994. London. Gollancz. 1st. author's 1st novel. VF/VF. T2. $30.00.

MORSON, Ian. *Psalm for Falconer.* 1997. NY. St. Martin. 1st Am ed. F/F. G8. $15.00.

MORTIMER, John. *Rumpole on Trial.* 1992. NY. Viking. 1st Am ed. VF/VF. T2. $15.00.

MORTIMER, John. *The Narrowing Stream.* 1989. NY. Viking. 1st Am ed. VF/VF. T2. $12.00.

MORTON, Rosalie Slaughter. *Doctor's Holiday in Iran.* 1940. Funk Wagnall. 1st. 8vo. 15 pl. xl. VG. W1. $18.00.

MORWOOD, William. *Traveler in a Vanished Landscape: The Life and Times of David Douglas.* 1973. NY/London. 1st. 244p w/ maps & ils. F in dj. B26. $19.00.

MOSBY, Henry S. *Wildlife Investigational Techniques.* 1965. Ann Arbor. Wildlife Soc. 2nd. 419p. cloth. A17. $20.00.

MOSELEY, Margaret. *Bonita Faye.* 1996. Dallas. Three Forks Press. 1st. author's 1st novel. VF/VF. T2. $150.00.

MOSER, Barry. *Fly! A Brief History of Flight.* (1993). NY. Willa Perlman. 1st. ils by author. F/F. B3. $30.00.

MOSER, Barry. *Polly Vaughn.* (1992). Boston. Little, Brn. 1st. ils & sgn by author. F/F. B3. $30.00.

MOSLEY, Leonard. *Gideon Goes to War: Story of Wingate.* 1955. London. Barker. 1st. 256p. gilt. red buckram. F/VG. M7. $42.50.

MOSLEY, Walter. *A Little Yellow Dog.* 1996. NY. Norton. 1st. sgn. VF/VF. T2. $30.00.

MOSLEY, Walter. *A Red Death.* 1991. NY. Norton. 1st. VF/F+. H11. $55.00.

MOSLEY, Walter. *Black Betty.* 1994. NY. Norton. 1st. F/F. H11. $20.00.

MOSLEY, Walter. *Blue Light.* 1998. Boston. Little, Brn. 1st. sgn. VF/VF. T2. $30.00.

MOSLEY, Walter. *Gone Fishin'.* 1997. Baltimore. Blk. Classic. 1st. F/dj. B9. $15.00.

MOSLEY, Walter. *R. L.'s Dream.* 1995. NY. Norton. 1st. F/F. A24. $30.00.

MOSLEY, Walter. *Walkin' the Dog.* 1999. Boston. Little, Brn. 1st. sgn. VF/VF. T2. $26.00.

MOSLEY, Walter. *White Butterfly.* 1992. NY. W.W. Norton. 1st. VF in dj. M15. $95.00.

MOSTEL, Zero. *Zero Mostel's Book of Villains.* 1976. Doubleday. 1st. VG/wrp. C9. $48.00.

MOTHER TERESA of Calcutta. *The Love of Christ; Spiritual Counsels.* 1981. Harper. 1st. 115p. VG/VG. B29. $4.00.

MOTLEY, Willard. *Knock on Any Door.* 1947. Appleton Century Crofts. 1st. 504p. VG/dj. R11. $20.00.

MOURELLE, Don Francisco A. *Journal of Voyage of the Sonora: From 1775.* 1987. Ye Galleon. ltd reissue. 1/301. F/sans. B19. $20.00.

MOWAT, Farley. *A Whale for the Killing.* (1972). Toronto. McClelland & Stewart. 1st Canadian ed. F/VG. price clip. moderate creasing. B3. $40.00.

MOWAT, Farley. *Aftermath, Travels in a Post-War World.* (1995). Toronto. Key Porter. 1st Canadian ed. VF/VF. B3. $35.00.

MOWAT, Farley. *And No Birds Sang.* (1979). Toronto. McClelland & Stewart. 1st Canadian ed. NF. very minor bumping to one corner/F. B3. $35.00.

MOWAT, Farley. *Black Joke.* 1963. Little, Brn. 1st Am. VG/dj. T11. $50.00.

MOWAT, Farley. *Born Naked.* 1994. Houghton Mifflin. 1st. F/dj. T11. $25.00.

MOWAT, Farley. *Curse of the Viking Grave.* 1966. Little, Brn. 1st. F/clip. T11. $45.00.

MOWAT, Farley. *My Discovery of America.* 1985. Toronto. McClelland Stewart. 1st Canadian. F/clip. B3. $75.00.

MOWAT, Farley. *Never Cry Wolf.* 1963. Boston. Little, Brn. 1st. NF/VG+. M23. $20.00.

MOWAT, Farley. *Tundra.* 1973. Toronto. McClelland Stewart. 1st. F/dj. A26. $35.00.

MOYE, Catherine. *Asleep at the Wheel.* 1989. London. Bodley. 1st. author's 1st book. F/VF. H11. $35.00.

MOYES, Patricia. *Angel Death.* 1981. HRW. 1st Am. F/dj. N4. $30.00.

MOYES, Patricia. *Death and the Dutch Uncle.* 1968. London. Collins Crime Club. 1st. F in dj. M15. $50.00.

MOYES, Patricia. *Night Ferry to Death.* 1985. London. Collins Crime Club. 1st. F/dj. M15. $45.00.

MUELLER, F. J. H. (trans). *Select Plants Readily Eligible for Industrial Culture or Naturalisation in Victoria.* 1876. Melbourne. 1st. marbled paper over brds. cloth spine w/gold emb leather label. corners. lower edges worn. else VG. B26. $65.00.

MUELLER, Lisel. *The Private Life.* 1976. Baton Rouge. LSU Press. 1st. F in F dj. B2. $30.00.

MUHLBACH, Louise. *Marie Antoinette & Her Son.* 1867. PF Collier. 1st. 8vo. 566p. NF. W2. $195.00.

MUHLBACH, Louise. *Napoleon & Blucher. Vol 9.* 1893. PF Collier. 8vo. 607p. VG. W2. $225.00.

MUIR, Augustus. *Shadow on the Left.* 1928. Bobbs Merrill. 1st Am. VG/dj. M15. $50.00.

MUIR, Augustus. *The Silent Partner.* 1930. Indianapolis. Bobbs-Merrill. 1st Am ed. VG w/o dj. M15. $35.00.

MUIR, John. *Gentle Wilderness: Sierra. Nevada.* 1968 (1967). Sierra Club/Ballantine. 3rd. photos Richard Kauffman. VG/dj. S5. $15.00.

MUIR, John. *Notes on My Journeying in California's Northern Mountains.* 1975. Ashland. OR. 72p. wrp. A17. $15.00.

MUIR, John. *Stickeen.* 1909. Houghton Mifflin. tan cloth. P4. $195.00.

MUJIA, Ricardo. *El Chaco.* 1933. Bolivia. Sucre. Publicacion Oficial. 4to. 172p. G/cover & spine chipped. F3. $45.00.

MUKHERJEE, Bharati. *The Middleman and Other Stories.* 1988. NY. Grove. 1st. F/F. H11. $35.00.

MULFORD, Clarence E. *Bar-20 Days.* 1911. AC McClurg. 1st. ils Maynard Dixon. 412p. decor brn cloth. G+. B20. $35.00.

MULKEEN, Thomas. *My Killer Doesn't Understand Me.* 1973. Stein & Day. 1st. VG+/VG. G8. $10.00.

MULLER, Gilbert. *Chester Himes.* 1989. Boston. Twayne. 1st. VF/dj. M15. $50.00.

MULLER, Marcia. *A Wild and Lonely Place.* 1995. NY. Mysterious Press. 1st. sgn. VF/VF. T2. $25.00.

MULLER, Marcia. *Broken Promise Land.* 1996. Mysterious. 1st. NF/NF. G8. $15.00.

MULLER, Marcia. *Eye of the Storm.* 1988. np. Mysterious Press. UP. F. M19. $25.00.

MULLER, Marcia. *The Cavalier in White.* 1986. NY. St. Martin. 1st. VG/VG+ lt wear. A24. $30.00.

MULLER, Marcia. *Till the Butchers Cut Him Down.* 1994. Mysterious. 1st. VG+/VG+. G8. $15.00.

MULLER, Marcia. *Wolf in the Shadows.* 1993. NY. Mysterious. 1st. Inscribed. F/F. H11. $30.00.

MULLER, Paul. *Slay Time.* 1968. Roy. 1st Am ed. VG/VG. G8. $10.00.

MUMEY, Nolie. *James Pierson Beckwourth 1856 – 1866.* 1957. Denver, CO. Old West Pub. inscr. F. A19. $200.00.

MUMFORD, F. B. *Breeding of Animals.* 1922. Macmillan. 310p. cloth. A10. $12.00.

MUMFORD, James. *Narrative of Surgery: A Historical Sketch.* 1906. Phil. 1st. 983p. A13. $50.00.

MUNRO, Alice. *Moon of Jupiter.* 1983. Knopf. 1st Am. F/NF. M25. $25.00.

MUNRO, Alice. *Progress of Love.* 1986. Knopf. 1st Am. F/dj. O11. $30.00.

MUNRO, Alice. *The Love of a Good Woman.* 1998. NY. Knopf. 1st. F/F. M23. $45.00.

MUNRO, Dana. *A Student in Central America 1914 – 1916.* 1983. New Orleans. Mari. 4to. 75p. G. wrp. F3. $15.00.

MUNROE, Enid. *Artist in the Garden: Guide to Creative & Natural Planting.* 1994. NY. Holt. 262p. F/dj. H10. $25.00.

MUNSON, Douglas Anne. *El Nino.* 1990. Viking. UP. F. tan wrp. M25. $50.00.

MUNSON, Edward L. *Theory & Practice of Military Hygiene.* 1901. NY. Wm Wood. 1st. ils. 971p. NF. E6. $65.00.

MUNSON, Linda Chandler. *Heat Storm.* 1991. Atlanta. Longstreet. 1st. VF/F. H11. $25.00.

MUNSON, Ronald. *Nothing Human.* 1991. NY. Pocket. 1st. VF/F. H11. $25.00.

MUNZ, Philip A. & David D. Keck. *A California Flora and Supplement.* 1973. Berkeley. F in dj. B26. $39.00.

MURAKAMI, Hanuki. *Hard Boiled Wonderland & the End of the World.* 1991. NY. Kodansha. 1st. F/F. M23. $25.00.

MURDOCH, Iris. *The Green Knight.* 1994. NY. Viking. AP. 1st Am ed. wrps. F. B2. $30.00.

MURDOCH, Iris. *Unicorn.* 1963. London Chatto Windus. 1st. VG+/dj. A14. $52.50.

MURDOCK, Eugene C. *Mighty Casey All-American.* 1984. Greenwood. 1st. F. P8. $25.00.

MURDOCK, Harold. *Earl Percy Dines Abroad.* 1924. Houghton Mifflin. 1st. tall 4to. 46p. VG. H13. $95.00.

MURIE, A. *Naturalist in Alaska.* 1961. NY. photos/drawings. F/dj. M4. $18.00.

MURLE, Adolph. *Wolves of Mt. McKinley.* 1971 (1944). Wash. 1st. 238p. VG. S15. $9.00.

MURLOCK, Miss; see Murlock, Dinah.

MURPHY, Dallas. *Apparent Wind.* 1991. NY. Pocket. 1st. F/F. H11. $20.00.

MURPHY, Dallas. *Lush Life.* 1992. NY. Pocket Books. 1st. VF/VF. T2. $8.00.

MURPHY, Earl. *Water Purity: Study of Legal Control of Natural Resources.* 1961. Madison. 1st. 212p. dj. A13. $25.00.

MURPHY, Haughton. *Murders & Acquisitions.* (1988). NY. S&S. 1st. NF. shows lt use/F. B3. $15.00.

MURPHY, Jim. *Boys' War: Confederate & Union Soldiers Talk.* 1990. Clarion. 1st. photos. 110p. NF. P12. $20.00.

MURPHY, Marguerite. *Borrowed Alibi.* 1961. Avalon. 1st. ex lib. VG/G+. G8. $10.00.

MURPHY, Pat. *The Falling Woman.* 1986. NY. Tor. 1st. sgn. 1987 Nebula Award for best novel. F/F. T2. $100.00.

MURPHY, Shirley Rousseau. *Cat in the Dark.* 1999. NY. Harper Collins. 1st. VF/VF. T2. $10.00.

MURPHY, Thos. D. On *Sunset Highways. A Book of Motor Rambles in California.* Boston. The Page Company. 1915. 8vo. 376p & (4)p publisher advertisement. teg. pict tan cloth. 1sted. well ils with both color plates and sepia plates. VG. L5. $45.00.

MURPHY, Virginia Reed. *Across the Plains in the Donner Party.* nd. np. Lewis Osborne. 1st. ltd to 1400 copies; fwd by George R. Stewart. 56p. VG. M19. $35.00.

MURRAY, A. Victor. *Education Into Religion.* 1953. Harper. foreword by Elton Trueblood. 230p. VG/VG. B29. $4.50.

MURRAY, Albert. *Good Morning Blues, The Autobiography of Count Basie.* 1985. NY. Random House. 1st. F/F. B2. $30.00.

MURRAY, Albert. *South to a Very Old Place.* 1971. McGraw Hill. 1st. F/lightly soiled dj. M25. $60.00.

MURRAY, Albert. *Stomping the Blues.* 1976. NY. McGraw. 1st. 4to. F in VG dj w/ tears. B2. $75.00.

MURRAY, Albert. *The Hero and the Blues.* 1973. np. Univ. of Missouri Press. 1st. F/F. B2. $150.00.

MURRAY, Alexander Hunter. *Journal Du Yukon. 1847 – 48.* 1910. Ottawa. Government Printing Bureau. gray/bl wrp. blk cover titles & seal. folding map. 15 plates. 138p. NF. lt shelfwear. P4. $75.00.

MURRAY, Andrew. *The Holiest of All.* 1924. Revell. 552p. G. B29. $9.50.

MURRAY, Beatrice; see Posner, Richard.

MURRAY, George. *The Antarctic Manual for the Use of the Expedition of 1901.* 1994. Plaistow. Explorer Books. facs ed. ltd to 500 copies. bl cloth 8vo. gilt spine titles. 3 folding maps. 586p. new. issued w/o dj. P4. $75.00.

MURRAY, John Fisher. *Picturesque Tour of the River Thames in its Western Course.* 1845. London. Henry G. Bohn. 1st. 8vo. 356p. gr cloth. F. H5. $450.00.

MURRAY, Kenneth. *Down to Earth: People of Appalachia.* (1974). Appalachia Consortium Pr. photos. 128p. VG. B10. $15.00.

MURRAY, Pauli. *Proud Shoes: The Story of an American Family.* 1978. Harper & Row. 1st. F/sunned dj. M25. $150.00.

MURRAY, Sean. *Ireland's Fight for Freedom & the Irish in the USA.* 1934. NY. Irish Workers Club/Workers Lib. NF/wrp. B2. $50.00.

MURRAY, Will. *The First World Fantasy Convention: The Interviews.* 1995. West Hills. Tsathoggua Press. 1st. VF/pict wrp. T2. $7.00.

MURRAY, William. *Tip on a Dead Crab.* 1984. Viking. 1st. inscr/sgn twice. F/dj. D10. $75.00.

MURRAY, William. *When the Fat Man Sings.* 1987. NY. Bantam. 1st. F/F. H11. $25.00.

MURTZ, Harold A. *Gun Digest Book of Exploded Firearms Drawings.* 1974. Northfield, IL. Digest Books. 1st. ils. F. A2. $20.00.

MUSCATINE, Doris. *Book of California Wine.* 1984. U. CA/Sotheby's. 1st. ils. 616p. VG/dj. S14. $30.00.

MUSELER, Wilhelm. *Riding Logic.* 1877. London. Methuen. translated by F.W. Schiller. VG. O3. $22.00.

MUSER, Curt. *Facts & Artifacts of Ancient Middle America.* 1978. NY. Dutton. 1st. 212p. G/wrp. F3. $20.00.

MUTZA, Wayne. *UH1 Huey in Action.* 1986. Carrollton. TX. Squadron/Signal Pub. ils. 49p. VG in torn dj. B18. $35.00.

MUZZEY, David Saville. *Thomas Jefferson.* 1918. Scribner. 1st. 319p. VG. B10. $25.00.

MYERS, Elizabeth P. *Langston Hughes: Poet of His People.* 1970. Champaign, IL. Garrard. 1st. NF/NF. M25. $45.00.

MYERS, Frederick William H. *Human Personality & Its Survival of Bodily Death.* 1920 (1903). Longman Gr. 2 vol. 1st Am/6th prt. panelled navy cloth. G1. $100.00.

MYERS, Jeffrey. *T. E. Lawrence: A Bibliography.* 1974. NY/London. Garland. 48p. cloth. VG. Q2. $27.00.

MYERS, Robert J. *Cross of Frankenstein.* 1975. Lippincott. 1st. rem mk. VG/G. L1. $75.00.

MYERS, Robin & Michael Harris. *Fakes & Frauds: Varieties of Deception in Print and Manuscript.* 1989. Winchester. Hampshire. St. Paul's bibliographies. 1st. VF/pict brds. T2. $35.00.

MYERS, Tamar. *Parsley, Sage, Rosemary, and Crime.* 1995. NY. Doubleday. 1st. F/VF. H11. $25.00.

MYERS, Tamar. *Too Many Crooks Spoil the Broth.* 1994. NY. Doubleday. 1st. VF/VF. H11. $50.00.

MYKEL, A. W. *Windchime Legacy.* 1980. St. Martin. 1st. author's 1st book. NF/dj. A14. $42.00.

MYRER, Anton. *Last Convertible.* 1978. Putnam. 1st. NF/clip. A14. $17.50.

MYRER, Anton. *Violent Shore.* 1962. Little, Brn. 1st. 503p. AN/VG. H1. $15.00.

MYRES, J. Arthur. *Masters of Medicine: Historical Sketch of College.* 1968. St. Louis. 1st. 921p. A13. $45.00.

MYRES, Sandra L. *Westering Women & the Frontier Experience 1800 – 1915.* 1982. U. NM. 1st. VG/dj. R8. $16.00.

MYRICK, Herbert. *Turkeys & How to Grow Them: A Treatise.* (1918). NY. Judd. 12mo. ils. 159p+ads. VG+. M12. $50.00.

— N —

NABAKOV, Vladimir. *Details of a Sunset.* 1976. NY. McGraw-Hill. 1st trans from Russian w/ Dimitri Nabakov. F in F dj. D10. $45.00.

NABB, Magdalen. *Marshal at Villa Torrini.* 1994. NY. Harper. 1st Am ed. NF/NF. G8. $10.00.

NABB, Magdalen. *The Marshall at the Villa Torrini.* 1994. NY. Harper Collins. 1st Am ed. VF/VF. T2. $15.00.

NABOKOV, Vladimir. *Glory.* 1971. NY. McGraw-Hill. 1st English language trans. trans by Dmitri Nabokov. F/F. A24. $50.00.

NABOKOV, Vladimir. *Invitation to a Beheading.* 1960. London. Weidenfeld & Nicolson. 1st British ed. NF/VG+. lt wear. A24. $85.00.

NABOKOV, Vladimir. *Pale Fire.* 1962. NY. Putnam. 1st imp w/ red ep. VG+/VG. minor wear. A24. $185.00.

NADER, Laura. *Harmony Ideology.* 1990. Ca. Stanford Univ. Press. 1st. 343p. G/G. F3. $20.00.

NAGUS, Sylvia. *Dead to Rites.* 1978. NY. Crown. 1st. F/F. H11. $35.00.

NANRY, Charles. *The Jazz Text.* 1979. NY. Van Nostrand. 1st. F/F. B2. $35.00.

NARANJO, Claudio & Robert E. Ornstein. On *The Psychology of Meditation.* 1971. Viking. 1st. NF/dj. M25. $25.00.

NASBY, Gordon. *Treasury of the Christian World.* 1953. Harper. 397p. VG. B29. $4.50.

NASLUND, Sena Jeter. *Ahab's Wife, or The Star Gazer.* 1999. NY. Morrow. 1st. sgn. VF/VF. T2. $45.00.

NATHAN, Robert. *Road of Ages.* 1935. np. Knopf. 1st. F/NF dj. M19. $25.00.

NATIONAL GEOGRAPHIC SOCIETY, editors. *Lost Empire, Living Tribes.* 1982. DC. NGS. 1st. 402p. G/chipped dj. F3. $30.00.

NAVA, Michael. *Hjow Town.* 1990. NY. Harper & Row. 1st. NF/NF. G8. $10.00.

NAVA, Michael. *The Burning Plain.* 1997. NY. Putnam. 1st. sgn. VF/VF. T2. $25.00.

NAYLOR, Gloria. *Linden Hills.* 1985. NY. Ticknor. 1st. F/F. H11. $50.00.

NAYLOR, Gloria. *Mama Day.* 1988. NY. Ticknor & Fields. 1st. sgn. F/F. D10. $50.00.

NEARING, Scott. *The Conscience of a Radical.* 1965. Harborside. Social Science Institute. 1st. NF. wrp. B2. $35.00.

NEARING, Scott. *The Soviet Union as a World Power.* 1945. NY. Social Science Publishers. 1st. wrp. 32p. F. B2. $30.00.

NEARING, Scott. *War.* 1931. NY. Vanguard. 1st. 310p. VG w/darkening on spine. B2. $35.00.

NEARING, Scott. *War on Peace?* 1946. NY. Island Press. 1st. G-VG. wrp. B2. $25.00.

NEELY, Barbara. *Blanche Among the Talented Tenth.* (1994). NY. St. Martin. 1st. author's second book. sgn by author. VF/VF. B3. $40.00.

NEELY, Richard. *The Ridgway Women.* 1975. NY. Crowell. 1st. F/F. H11. $40.00.

NEHRBASS, Arthur F. *Dead Easy.* nd. Dutton. 1st. F/F. G8. $10.00.

NEHRBASS, Richard. *Perfect Death for Hollywood.* 1991. NY. Harper. 1st. F/F. G8. $10.00.

NEIFERT, Marianne. *Dr. Mom's Parenting Guide: Commonsense Guidance for the Life of Your Child.* 1991. NY. Dutton. 1st. VG/VG. A28. $10.50.

NELSON, Antonya. *The Expendables.* 1990. Athens. Univ. of GA Press. 1st. author's 1st book. F/F. A24. $40.00.

NELSON, Arty. *Technicolor Pulp.* 1995. NY. Warner. 1st. author's 1st book. F/NF. R16. $40.00.

NELSON, James. *Great Cheap Wines: A Poorperson's Guide.* 1977. NY. McGraw Hill. VG. A28. $6.50.

NEMEROV, Howard. *The Western Approaches, Poems 1973 – 1975.* 1975. Chicago. U. of Chicago Press. 1st. F/VG dj. M19. $17.50.

NEMESIO, Vitorino. *Campo De Sao Paulo.* 1971. Lisboa. 3rd ed. 417p. G/wrp. F3. $30.00.

NEWELL, Gordon (editor). *The H. W. Mc Curdy Marine History of the Pacific Northwest 1966 – 1976.* 1977. Seattle. The Superior Publishing Company. sgn by editor. b&w ils. 255p. F in slipcase. P4. $95.00.

NEWELL, William. *Hebrews Verse by Verse.* 1947. Moody. 494p. VG. B29. $11.00.

NEWMAN, Kim. *Bad Dreams.* 1991. NY. Carroll & Graf. 1st. F/F. H11. $20.00.

NEWMAN, Kim. *The Quorum.* 1994. NY. Carroll & Graf. 1st Am ed. VF/VF. T2. $10.00.

NEWMAN, Sharan. *Difficult Saint.* 1999. Forge. 1st. sgn. F/F. G8. $25.00.

NEWMAN, Sharan. *The Devil's Door.* 1994. NY. Forge. 1st. sgn. VF/VF. T2. $30.00.

NEWPORT, John P. *Demons, Demons, Demons.* 1972. Broadman. 159p. VG/VG. B29. $4.50.

NEWTH, A. H. And F. W. Owen. *Post-Mortems; What to Look for and How to Make Them with Sections on Infanticide, Poisons, Malformations, Etc.* (1885). Detroit. The Ils Medical Journal Company. 16mo. 136p. brn cloth. revised ed. Cloth worn. G to VG. L5. $90.00.

NEYMAN, Jerzy, editor. *The Heritage of Copernicus; Theories More Pleasing to the Mind.* 1974. MIT Press. Cambridge. photo ils. 542p. VG/chipped dj. K5. $35.00.

NICHOLS, John. *A Ghost in the Music.* 1979. NY. Holt. 1st. F/F. H11. $35.00.

NICHOLS, John. *American Blood.* 1987. NY. Holt. 1st. F/VF. H11. $20.00.

NICHOLSON, Meredith. *The Siege of the Seven Suitors.* 1910. Boston. Houghton Mifflin. 1st. VG in pict cloth brd w/o dj. M15. $40.00.

NICKOLAE, Barbara. *Finders Keepers.* 1989. NY. McGraw Hill. 1st. NF/NF. G8. $10.00.

NICOLA, Toufick. *Atlas of Surgical Approaches to Bones and Joints.* 1945. NY. np. 1st. viii. sm 4to. blue cloth. 218p. VG. B14. $75.00.

NIGGLI, Josephina. *Mexican Village.* 1945. Chapel Hill. Univ. of North Carolina Press. 4th printing. drawings. 491p. G/chipped dj. F3. $15.00.

NILES, D. T. *As Seeing the Invisible: A Study of the Book of Revelation.* 1961. NY. Harper. 1st. 192p. VG/VG. B29. $10.50.

NIN, Anais. *Children of the Albatross.* 1947. NY. Dutton. 1st. G/G. staining to brds & dj. A24. $25.00.

NIN, Anais. *Little Birds.* 1979. np. HBJ. 1st. F/F dj. M19. $25.00.

NIN, Anais. *Naked Under the Mask by Elisabeth Barille.* (1992). London. Lime Tree. 1st British ed. trans by Elfreda Powell. F/F. B3. $25.00.

NISWANDER, Adam. *The Charm.* 1993. Phoenix. Integra Press. 1st. author's 1st novel. VF/VF. T2. $25.00.

NISWANDER, Adam. *The Sand Dwellers.* 1998. Minneapolis. Fedogan & Bremer. 1st. VF/VF. T2. $27.00.

NIVEN, Larry. *The Integral Trees.* 1984. NY. Ballantine. 1st. sgn. F/VF. T2. $35.00.

NIVEN, Larry. *The Smoke Ring.* 1987. NY. Ballantine. 1st. sgn by Niven & artist Michael Whelan. F/VF. T2. $30.00.

NOAKES, Aubrey. *The World of Henry Alken.* 1952. London. Witherby. 1st. VG/F. O3. $45.00.

NOBLE, Hollister. *Woman with a Sword, The Biographical Novel of Anna Ella Carroll of Maryland.* 1948. NY. Doubleday. 1st. orig cloth. fictional bio of woman who advised Lincoln on military strategy. 395p. VG/worn dj. M8. $25.00.

NOLAN, William F. *Look Out for Space.* 1985. NY. International Polygonics. 1st. pb orig. sgn. VF/pict wrp. T2. $10.00.

NOLAN, William F. *Sharks Never Sleep.* 1998. NY. St. Martin. 1st. sgn. VF/printed wrp. T2. $20.00.

NOLAN, William F. *The Black Mask Murders.* 1994. NY. St. Martin. 1st. VF in dj. M15. $35.00.

NOLAN, William F. *The White Cad Cross-Up.* 1969. Los Angeles. Sherbourne Press. 1st. sgn by Nolan w/orig drawing on recto of ffep. F/F. T2. $50.00.

NOON, Jeff. *Pollen.* 1996. NY. Crown. 1st. VF/VF. H11. $40.00.

NOONAN, Michael. *McKenzie's Boots.* 1988. NY. Orchard Books. 1st Am ed. NF/NF. A28. $7.95.

NOOTEBOOM, Cees. *A Song of Truth and Semblance.* 1984. Baton Rouge. LSU Press. 1st Am ed. sgn. F/F. O11. $50.00.

NOOTEBOOM, Cees. *In the Dutch Mountains.* 1987. Baton Rouge. LSU Press. 1st Am ed. sgn. F/F. O11. $50.00.

NOOTEBOOM, Cees. *The Knight Has Died.* 1990. Baton Rouge. LSU Press. 1st Am ed. sgn. F/F. O11. $35.00.

NORDAN, Lewis. *Lightning Song.* (1997). Chapel Hill. Algonquin. 1st. sgn & dated by author. F/F. B3. $35.00.

NORDAN, Lewis. *The Sharp Shooter Blues.* (1995). Chapel Hill. Algonquin. 1st. sgn by author. F/NF. lt creasing to top edge. B3. $35.00.

NORMAN, Howard. *Kiss in the Hotel Joseph Conrad and Other Stories.* 1989. NY. Summit. 1st. F/F. H11. $70.00.

NORMAN, Howard. *The Bird Artist.* 1994. NY. FSG. 1st. F/F. M23. $40.00.

NORRIS, Karen. *The Cloister Walk.* (1996). NY. Riverhead Books. 1st. author's 2nd book. sgn by author. F/F. B3. $40.00.

NORRIS, Kathleen. *Burned Fingers.* 1946. Sun Dial Press. sm8vo. 273p. F/F. H1. $8.00.

NORTH, Darian. *Criminal Seduction.* 1993. NY. Dutton. 1st. author's 1st book. Book has a bumped corner. NF/F. H11. $25.00.

NORTH, Gary. *Unholy Spirits: Occultism and New Age Humanism.* 1986. Dominion. 426p. VG. B29. $11.50.

NORTH, John. *Sherlock Holmes and the German Nanny.* 1990. Romford. Essex. Ian Henry Publications. 1st. VF/VF. T2. $30.00.

NORTHCOTE, Amyas. *In Ghostly Company.* 1997. Ashcroft, BC. Ash Tree Press. reissue. 1st thus. VF/VF. T2. $40.00.

NORTHEN, Rebecca T. *Home Orchid Growing.* 1970 (1950). NY. 3rd ed. 4to. VG in dj. B26. $25.00.

NORTHEND, Mary J. *Remodeled Farmhouses.* 1915. Boston. 1st. pict cloth. ils. spine darkened. mark on spine. 264p. VG. B18. $25.00.

NORTON, Andre. *The Gate of the Cat.* 1987. NY. Ace Books. 1st. F/F. T2. $7.00.

NORTON, Andre. *Ware Hawk.* 1983. np. Atheneum. 1st. F/F dj. M19. $25.00.

NORTON, Doreen M. *The Palomino Horse.* 1949. Los Angeles. Borden. 1st ed. 4to. VG/F. O3. $125.00.

NOSS, John B. *Man's Religions.* 1980. Macmillan. 6th ed. 580p. VG. B29. $13.50.

NOTESTEIN, Lucy Lilian. *Wooster of the Middle West.* 1937. CT. Yale Univ. Press. 1st. photo ils. bdg slightly cocked. VG in dj w/ sm edge tears. B18. $22.50.

NOTH, Martin. *The History of Israel.* 1960. Harper. 486p. VG/VG. B29. $15.00.

NOVO, Salvador. *New Mexican Grandeur.* 1967. np. Mexico. 1st English ed. 4to. 140p text + b/w photo ils. ep map. G/G. F3. $15.00.

NUNEZ, Sigrid. *A Feather on the Breath of God.* (1995). NY. Harper Collins. 1st. author's 1st book. F/F. B3. $30.00.

NUNEZ, Sigrid. *Naked Sleeper.* (1996). NY. Harper Collins. 1st. author's 2nd book. F/F. B3. $20.00.

NUNEZ CHINCHILLA, Jesus. *Copan Ruins, Complete Guide to Tegucigalpa.* 1975. np. 4th ed. b/w photo ils. foldout map. 111p. G. F3. $15.00.

NUNN, Kem. *Dogs of Winter.* 1997. NY. Scribner's. 1st. F/F. G8. $12.50.

NUNN, Kem. *Unassigned Territory.* 1987. NY. Delacorte. 1st. F/NF. H11. $35.00.

NURGE, Ethel. *Life in a Leyte Village.* 1965. Seattle. Univ. of Washington. sm4to. cloth. 157p. VG/VG. P1. $18.00.

NUTTALL, R. Preston. *Warriors of the Triple Chevron, A Story of the American Civil War.* 1999. Richmond, VA. Dietz Press. 1st. privately pub. ltd to 1000 numbered copies. orig cloth. 454p. NF/NF. M8. $30.00.

NUTTALL, Zelia. *The Codex Nuttall.* 1975. NY. Dover. oblong 4to. VG/cover faded. lt corner wear. F3. $15.00.

NYE, Nelson C. *Your Western Horse.* 1968. NY. Barnes. VG/VG. O3. $18.00.

— O —

O'BRIAN, Patrick. *Clarissa Oakes.* (1992). London. Harper Collins. 1st British ed. true first. F/F. B3. $75.00.

O'BRIAN, Patrick. *Men-Of-War.* 1974. London. Collins. 1st. F/F clip. w/pub price label present. B4. $375.00.

O'BRIAN, Patrick. *The Commodore.* (1994). London. Harper Collins. 1st British ed. true first. NF. sm rem dot at base of spine/F. B3. $35.00.

O'BRIAN, Patrick. *The Far Side of the World.* 1984. London. Collins. 1st. F/F. clip. B2. $500.00.

O'BRIAN, Patrick. *Treason's Harbour.* 1983. London. Collins. 1st. F/F. B2. $600.00.

O'BRIEN, Andy. *Fire-Wagon Hockey.* 1967. Ryerson. 1st. photos. VG+/VG+. P8. $35.00.

O'BRIEN, Dan. *Eminent Domain.* 1987. Iowa City. U of Iowa Press. author's 1st book. NF in F dj. D10. $60.00.

O'BRIEN, Edna. *August Is a Wicked Month.* 1965. S&S. 1st Am. author's 3rd novel. F/NF. D10. $60.00.

O'BRIEN, Edna. *Girls in their Married Bliss.* 1965. S&S. 1st Am. F/F. D10. $50.00.

O'BRIEN, Edna. *High Road.* 1988. FSG. 1st. F/F. R14. $30.00.

O'BRIEN, Flann. *Poor Mouth.* 1974. Viking. 1st. trans PC Power. Ils Ralph Steadman. F/dj. Q1. $75.00.

O'BRIEN, Frederick. *Atolls of the Sun.* 1922. NY. Century. 60 photos/map. 508p. T7. $25.00.

O'BRIEN, Jack. *Valiant, Dog of the Timberline.* (1935). Grosset Dunlap. pre-1963 prt. ils Kurt Wiese. VG+/dj. C8. $22.50.

O'BRIEN, John. *Leaving Las Vegas.* 1990. Wichita. Watermark. 1st. sgn. author's 1st novel. F/dj. B3/L3. $500.00.

O'BRIEN, John. *Twelve Days of Christmas.* 1991. Honesdale. Boyds Mill. 4th. sgn. F/F. A23. $32.00.

O'BRIEN, Meg. *Thin Ice.* 1993. NY. Doubleday. 1st. review copy. F/F. G8. $10.00.

O'BRIEN, Robert. *This Is San Francisco.* 1948. McGraw Hill. ils Antonio Sotomayor. blk cloth. NF/dj. K7. $15.00.

O'BRIEN, Tim. *Going After Cacciato.* 1978. London. Cape. 1st. F/NF clip. B3. $125.00.

O'BRIEN, Tim. *In the Lake of the Woods.* (1994). Boston. Houghton Mifflin. 1st. sgn by author. F/F. B3. $75.00.

O'BRIEN, Tim. *Speaking of Courage.* 1980. Santa Barbara. Neville. ltd ed. 1/326. sgn. F/sans. R14. $225.00.

O'BRIEN, Tim. *The Nuclear Age.* 1985. NY. Knopf. 1st. F/F. H11. $40.00.

O'BRIEN, Tim. *The Things They Carried.* (1990). Boston. Houghton Mifflin. 1st. sgn by author. F/F. B3. $125.00.

O'BRIEN, Tim. *Tomcat in Love.* 1998. NY. Broadway Books. 1st. sgn. F in F dj. D10. $45.00.

O'CASEY, Sean. *Silver Tassie: A Tragi-Comedy in Four Acts.* 1928. Macmillan. 1st. 140p. gr cloth. VG+/F. B22. $10.00.

O'CONNELL, Carol. *Killing Critics.* 1996. NY. Putnam. 1st. F/F. H11. $20.00.

O'CONNELL, Carol. *Mallory's Oracle.* 1994. London. Hutchinson. 1st. author's 1st novel. VF/VF. T2. $75.00.

O'CONNELL, Carol. *Mallory's Oracle.* 1994. NY. Putnam. 1st Am ed. author's 1st novel. sgn. VF/VF. T2. $35.00.

O'CONNELL, Carol. *Shell Game.* 1999. NY. Putnam. 1st. sgn. VF/VF. T2. $26.00.

O'CONNELL, Carol. *Stone Angel.* 1997. NY. Putnam. 1st. sgn. VF/VF. T2. $30.00.

O'CONNELL, Carol. *The Man Who Lied to Women.* (1995). London. Hutchinson. 1st British ed. F/F. B3. $75.00.

O'CONNELL, Jack. *Box Nine.* 1992. Mysterious. 1st. author's 1st novel. F/F. P3. $40.00.

O'CONNOR, Elizabeth. *Call to Commitment.* 1963. Harper. 205p. G. B29. $4.50.

O'CONNOR, Flannery. *Everything that Rises Must Converge.* 1965. NY. Farrar. 1st. F/F. B2. $175.00.

O'CONNOR, Flannery. *Memoir of Mary Ann.* 1961. FSG. 1st. VG/VG. S13. $85.00.

O'CONNOR, Flannery. *Running in the Family.* 1982. FSG. 1st. NF/VG+. S13. $30.00.

O'CONNOR, J. Regis. *The Sacred Seal.* 1998. Shelburne. Ontario. battered silicon dispatch box. 1st. VF/VF. T2. $24.00.

O'CONNOR, Jack. *Hunting Rifle.* 1970. Winchester. 1st. 314p. cloth. VG+/worn. M20. $25.00.

O'CONNOR, John. *Adobe Book.* 1973. Santa Fe. 1st. 130p. VG/dj. B5. $45.00.

O'CONNOR, Richard. *Sheridan the Inevitable.* 1953. Bobbs Merrill. 1st. 24 pl/7 maps. 400p. F/VG. H1. $60.00.

O'DAY, Anita. *High Times, Hard Times.* 1981. NY. Putnam. 1st. F/lightly worn dj. B2. $40.00.

O'DONNELL, Barrett; see Malzberg, Barry.

O'DONNELL, E.P. *Great Big Doorstep.* 1941. Boston. Houghton Mifflin. 1st. F/NF. B4. $250.00.

O'DONNELL, K.M.; see Malzberg, Barry.

O'DONNELL, Lillian. *Falling Star.* 1979. Putnam. 1st. F/dj. P3. $20.00.

O'DONNELL, Lillian. *Ladykiller.* 1984. Putnam. 1st. VG/dj. P3. $18.00.

O'DONNELL, Lillian. *The Phone Calls.* 1972. NY. Putnam. 1st. F/F. H11. $60.00.

O'DONNELL, Peter. *Modesty Blaise.* 1965. Souvenir. 1st. NF/dj. P3. $30.00.

O'DONNELL, Peter. *Silver Mistress.* 1973. Archival. 1st Am ed. ils. NF/NF. G8. $50.00.

O'FAOLAIN, Nuala. *Are You Somebody.* 1998. NY. Henry Holt. 1st. dj has a closed tear to head of spine. F/F. M23. $35.00.

O'FAOLAIN, Sean. *Talking Trees & Other Stories.* 1970. Boston. 1st. F/F. A17. $20.00.

O'FARRELL, William. *Grow Young and Die.* 1952. Crime Club. 1st. VG/VG+. G8. $10.00.

O'FLAHERTY, Joseph S. *Those Powerful Years: South Coast & Los Angeles 1887 – 1917.* 1978. Hicksville, NY. 1st. F/F. O4. $15.00.

O'FLAHERTY, Liam. *Insurrection.* 1950. London. 1st. VG/VG. T9. $45.00.

O'FLAHERTY, Liam. *Land.* 1946. NY. Random House. 1st. F in NF dj. D10. $45.00.

O'GRADY, Timothy. *Motherland.* 1989. Holt. 1st. F/F. A20/W2. $25.00.

O'HAGAN, Andrew. *Our Fathers.* 1999. Harcourt Brace. ARC. F/WRP. M25. $35.00.

O'HANLON, Redmond. *Joseph Conrad & Charles Darwin.* 1984. Atlantic Highlands. 1st Am. author's 1st book. NF/VG. L3. $200.00.

O'HARA, Frank. *Homage to Frank O'Hara.* 1980. Creative Age. revised. photos. V1. $15.00.

O'HARA, John. *Farmer's Hotel.* 1951. Random. 1st. VG/VG. P3. $60.00.

O'HARA, John. *From the Terrace.* 1958. Random. 1st. F/NF. D10. $50.00.

O'HARA, John. *Lockwood Concern.* 1965. NY. 1st. 1/300. sgn. F/case. C2. $150.00.

O'HARA, John. *Ourselves to Know.* 1963. Random. 1st. NF/VG. R14. $35.00.

O'HARA, John. *Pipe Night.* 1946. Faber. 1st. F/F. M19. $85.00.

O'HARA, Kenneth. *Bird Cage.* 1968. Random. 1st. 184p. VG/dj. M20. $15.00.

O'HARA, Mary. *My Friend Flicka.* 1969. Philadelphia. Lippincott. 44th prt. VG/VG. O3. $15.00.

O'HARE, Kate Richards. *In Prison.* 1920. St. Louis. Frank P. O'Hare. 1st. 64p. soiled. bit worn. B2. $75.00.

O'HARRA, Cleophas. *White River Badlands.* 1920. Rapid City, SD. scarce. A19. $40.00.

O'LEARY, Brian. *Mars 1999.* 1987. Stackpole. 1st. 8vo. 160p. VG/VG. K5. $30.00.

O'LEARY, Patrick. *Door Number Three.* 1995. NY. Tor. sgn 1st. author's 1st book. F/NF. M23. $60.00.

O'MALLEY, C.D. *Andreas Vesalius of Brussels.* 1964. Berkeley. 1st. 480p. A13. $100.00.

O'MALLEY, M. *Gone Away With O'Malley.* 1944. Garden City. 1st. ils Paul Brn. VG/VG. B5. $20.00.

O'MARIE, Sister Carol Anne. *Advent of Dying.* 1986. np. Delacorte. 1st. inscr. F/VG dj. M19. $25.00.

O'MARIE, Sister Carol Anne. *Murder Makes a Pilgrimage.* 1993. NY. Delacorte. 1st. VF/VF. T2. $7.00.

O'MEARA, W. *Guns at the Forks.* 1965. Englewood Cliffs. American Fort series. 273p. F/dj. M4. $25.00.

O'NAN, Stewart. *A Prayer for the Dying.* (1999). NY. np. 1st sgn by author. F/F. B3. $40.00.

O'NAN, Stewart. *The Names of the Dead.* (1996). NY. Doubleday. 1st. F/F. B3. $30.00.

O'NEAL, Bill. *Encyclopedia of Western Gun-Fighters.* 1983. Norman, OK. dj. A19. $20.00.

O'NEIL, Dennis. *Secret Origins of the Super DC Heroes.* 1976. Harmony. 1st. F/dj. M2. $25.00.

O'NEIL, George. *American Dream.* 1933. NY. Samuel French. 1st. F/VG. B4. $125.00.

O'NEILL, Eugene. *All God's Chillun Got Wings & Welded.* 1924. NY. 1st. NF. B4. $75.00.

O'NEILL, Eugene. *Dynamo.* 1929. Horace Liveright. 1st. NF/VG. M23. $25.00.

O'NEILL, Eugene. *Hughie.* 1959. New Haven. Yale. 1st. F/F. B4. $200.00.

O'NEILL, Eugene. *Marco Millions.* 1927. Boni Liveright. 1st. F/F. B4. $275.00.

O'NEILL, Eugene. *Mourning Becomes Electra: A Trilogy.* 1931. Horace Liveright. 1st. glazed teal cloth. F/dj. B24. $100.00.

O'NEILL, Eugene. *Strange Interlude.* 1928. Boni Liveright. 1st. F/NF. D10. $225.00.

O'NEILL, Eugene. *The Iceman Cometh.* 1946. NY. Random House. 1st. VG in dj. D10. $55.00.

O'NEILL, Moira. *Songs of the Glens of Antrim.* 1911. Portland, ME. Thomas B. Mosher. 1st. 1/950. 16mo. VG. $1.00.

O'NEILL, Tip. *Man of the House.* 1987. Random. 1st. VG. W2. $20.00.

O'NEILL, William L. *Everyone was Brave: Rise & Fall of Feminism in America.* 1969. Quadrangle. 1st. F/F. B35. $35.00.

O'REILLY, Tim. *Frank Herbert: Maker of Dune.* 1987. Berkley. 1st. F. M2. $15.00.

O'REILLY, Victor. *Games of the Hangman.* 1991. Grove Weidenfeld. 1st. NF/dj. P3. $20.00.

O'SHAUGHNESSY, Michael. *Monster Book of Monsters.* 1988. Bonanza. 1st. F/F. P3. $15.00.

O'SHAUGHNESSY, Perri. *Motion to Suppress.* 1995. np. Delacorte. 1st. author's 1st novel. F/NF. R16. $35.00.

O'SHEA, Sean; see Tralins, Bob.

O'SHELL, Patrick. *Semper Fidelis: US Marines in the Pacific 1942 – 1945.* 1947. NY. 1st. maps/photos. 360p. VG. S16. $45.00.

O'SULLIVAN, Bill. *Precious Blood.* 1992. NY. Soho. 1st. author's 1st book. VF/VF. H11. $25.00.

O'SULLIVAN, J.B. *Don't Hang Me too High.* 1954. Mill Morrow. 1st. 222p. VG/dj. M20. $12.00.

O'SULLIVAN, Maurice. *Twenty Years A-Growing.* 1933. 1st. VG/VG. M17. $20.00.

OAKENFULL, J. C. *Brazil.* 1913. Frome. England. 604p. G. F3. $30.00.

OAKESHOTT, E. *Dark Age Warrior.* 1974. Lutterworth. ils/map ep. 135p. brd. F/F. M12. $27.50.

OAKLEY, Giles. *The Devil's Music, A History of the Blues.* 1976. NY. Taplinger. 1st Am ed. sm 4to. F/F. B2. $75.00.

OATES, Joyce Carol. *American Appetites.* 1989. Dutton. 1st. F/dj. Q1. $30.00.

OATES, Joyce Carol. *Angel of Light.* 1981. NY. Dutton. 1st. F/F. H11. $30.00.

OATES, Joyce Carol. *Assassins.* 1975. Vanguard. 1st. F/F. H11. $35.00.

OATES, Joyce Carol. *Black Water.* (1992). NY. Dutton. 1st. F/F. B3. $15.00.

OATES, Joyce Carol. *Fabulous Beasts.* 1975. LSU. 1st. ils AG Smith. F/F. B4. $125.00.

OATES, Joyce Carol. *Hungry Ghosts.* 1974. Blk Sparrow. 1st issue in wrp. F. Q1. $35.00.

OATES, Joyce Carol. *I Lock My Door Upon Myself.* 1990. Ecco. 1st. sgn. F/F. B4. $85.00.

OATES, Joyce Carol. *Mysteries of Winterhurn.* 1984. Dutton. 1st. NF/NF. A20. $25.00.

OATES, Joyce Carol. *Poisoned Kiss & Other Stories.* 1976. Gollancz. 1st. F/F. P3. $20.00.

OATES, Joyce Carol. *Snake Eyes.* 1992. NY. Dutton. 1st. F/F. B4. $45.00.

OATES, Joyce Carol. *Son of the Morning.* 1978. Vanguard. 1st. VG/dj. P3. $30.00.

OATES, Joyce Carol. *Soul/Mate.* 1989. Dutton. 1st. VG/dj. P3. $20.00.

OATES, Joyce Carol. *The Assignation.* (1988). NY. Ecco Press. 1st. F/F. B3. $20.00.

OATES, Joyce Carol. *Wonderland.* 1971. Vanguard. 1st. F/F. H11. $45.00.

OATES, Wayne. *The Revelation of God in Human Suffering.* 1959. Westminster. 143p. VG/VG. B29. $7.50.

OBER, Frederick. *Travels in Mexico & Life Among the Mexicans.* (1887). Boston. Estes Lauriat. revised. ils/lacks fld map. 732p. F3. $65.00.

OBERG, James E. *Red Star in Orbit.* 1981. NY. Random House. 2nd printing. b/w photo ils. 8vo. inscr/sgn on ffep. 272p. VG/VG. K5. $50.00.

OBERHOSLER, Harry C. *Birds of the Natuna Islands.* 1932. Smithsonian. Bulletin 159. 137p. VG. S15. $15.00.

OBLIGADO, George. *Gaucho Boy.* 1961. Viking. 1st. ils Lilian Obligado. 63p. VG/G+. P2. $20.00.

OBREGON, Mauricio. *Argonauts to Astronauts.* 1980. Harper. 1st. 205p. dj. F3. $15.00.

OCHROCH, Ruth. *Diagnosis & Treatment of Minimal Brain Dysfunction.* 1981. NY. Human Sciences. 304p. gray cloth. VG/dj. G1. $25.00.

OCHSNER, Albert. *Clinical Surgery.* 1904. Chicago. 2nd. 757p. A13. $75.00.

ODDO, Sandra. *Home Made.* 1972. Atheneum. VG/dj. A16. $12.00.

ODENS, Peter. *Outlaws, Heroes, and Jokers of the Old Southwest.* 1984. Cambray Enterprises. 3rd printing. ils. 76p. NF. B19. $4.50.

ODETS, Clifford. *North Star.* 1963. Culver City. Classic Films. 1st revised screenplay. F/wrp. B2. $150.00.

ODETS, Clifford. *Paradise Lost.* 1936. NY. Random House. 1st. 204p. lt spots. VG/dj chipped spine. B18. $35.00.

ODLUM, Jerome. *Morabilis Diamond.* 1945. Scribner. 1st. NF/dj. M25. $60.00.

OEHLER, C.M. *Great Sioux Uprising.* 1959. Oxford. 1st. sgn pres. ils/map/drawings. 272p. VG/VG. J2. $110.00.

OELLRICHS, Inez. *Murder Comes at Night.* 1940. Doubleday Crime Club. 1st. F/VG. M15. $40.00.

OERTEL, Horst. *Special Pathological Anatomy & Pathogenesis of Circulatory.* 1838. Montreal. 1st. 640p. Buckram. A13. $40.00.

OFFENBERG, Bernice Weitzel. *Over the Years in Olmstead.* 1964. np. ils. wrp. 153p. VG. B18. $35.00.

OFFUTT, Chris. *Out of the Woods.* (1999). NY. S&S. 1st. sgn by author. F/F. B3. $75.00.

OFFUTT, Chris. *Same River Twice.* 1993. S&S. 1st. author's 2nd book. F/dj. A24. $65.00.

OFFUTT, Chris. *The Good Brother.* 1997. NY. S&S. sgn 1st ed. F/F. M23. $25.00.

OGBURN, C. *Marauders.* 1959. NY. ils/maps. 307p. VG/VG. S16. $23.50.

OGDEN, A. *California Sea Otter Trade 1784 – 1848.* (1975). Berkeley. 251p. cloth. VG+. M12. $30.00.

OGDEN, Peter Skeene. *Portraits of American Indian Life & Character.* 1933. Grabhorn. 1st ltd. 1/500. 6 pl. 107p. VG. J2. $175.00.

OGDEN, Robert Morris. *Hearing: Illustrated With Diagrams.* 1924. London. Cape. 1st. buckram. G1. $35.00.

OGILVIE, Lloyd J. *Falling into Greatness.* 1984. Guideposts. 220p. VG/worn dj. B29. $8.00.

OGILVIE, Lloyd J. *Life as it Was Meant to Be.* 1980. Regal. 157p. VG/VG. B29. $5.50.

OGRIZEK, Dore. *United States.* 1950. NY. 418p. The World in Color series. G. A17. $10.00.

OHIE, Howard Pitcher. *Old Silver & Old Sheffield Plate.* 1928. Doubleday Doran. 1st. 12 full-p ils. 420p. teg. blk buckram. T10. $125.00.

OKRI, Ben. *Dangerous Love.* (1996). London. Phoenix House. 1st British ed. F/F. B3. $35.00.

OKRI, Ben. *Incidents at the Shrine.* 1986. Heinemann. 1st. author's 3rd book. F/dj. A24. $45.00.

OKRI, Ben. *Songs of Enchantment.* (1993). NY. Doubleday. 1st. F/F. B3. $25.00.

OKRI, Ben. *Stars of the Curfew.* (1988). NY. Viking. 1st Am ed. F/F. B3. $35.00.

OKUDAIRA, Hideo. *Emaki: Japanese Picture Scrolls.* 1962. Tuttle. 1st. 241p. F/NF. W3. $150.00.

OLAJUWON, Hakeem. *Living the Dream.* 1996. Little, Brn. 1st. sgn. F/F. A23. $75.00.

OLCOTT, William T. *Field Book of the Stars.* nd (1907). Putnam. 8vo. VG/dj. K5. $20.00.

OLDEROGGE, D. A. *Kamus Na Hausa Rashaci (Hausa-Russian Dictionary).* 1963. Moscow. Foreign & Internat Dictionaries. 12mo. 459p. VG. W1. $20.00.

OLDFELD, Peter. *Alchemy Murder.* 1929. Washburn. 1st. VG. N4. $22.50.

OLDRIN, John. *Chipmunk Terrace.* 1958. Viking. sgn. ils Kurt Wiese. 79p. cloth. VG/dj. M20. $20.00.

OLDROYD, Ida Shepherd. *Marine Shells of the West Coast of North America.* 1924 & 1927. Stanford. 4 vol. ils. cloth. D11. $125.00.

OLDROYD, Osborn. *Assassination of Abraham Lincoln.* 1901. 1st. O8. $47.50.

OLDS, Bruce. *Raising Holy Hell.* (1995). NY. Henry Holt. ARC. author's 1st novel. pict wrp. sgn by author. NF. lt edgewear. B3. $40.00.

OLDS, Helen Diehl. *Joan of the Journal.* 1930. NY. 1st. ils Robb Beebe. VG/dj. A25. $15.00.

OLIVER, Chad. *Another Kind.* 1955. Ballantine. 1st. F/rpr. M2. $150.00.

OLIVER, Chad. *Shadows in the Sun.* 1985. Crown. 1st. F/dj. P3. $14.00.

OLIVER, Douglas. *Return to Tahiti: Bligh's Second Breadfruit Voyage.* 1988. Honolulu. 281p. M/dj. P4. $40.00.

OLIVER, James. *Abdominal Tumours & Abdominal Dropsy in Women.* 1895. London. 1st. 289p. A13. $100.00.

OLIVER, Katherine Elspeth. *Claw.* 1914. Los Angeles. Out West Magazine. 1st. 384p. gilt red cloth. VG. T10. $45.00.

OLIVER, Martha Capps. *A Year of Sacred Song.* 1895. NY. Raphael Tuck & Sons. spotted & stained pict gilt cover. browning. 366p. G. B18. $37.50.

OLIVER, Paul. *Aspects of the Blues Tradition.* 1968. NY. Oak. 1st Am ed of Screening the Blues. F/VG. torn. B2. $50.00.

OLIVER, Paul. *Blues Off the Record.* 1984. NY. Hippocrene. 1st. sm 4to. F/F. B2. $50.00.

OLIVER, Paul. *Screening the Blues.* 1968. London. Cassell. correct 1st ed. F/F. B2. $100.00.

OLIVER, Raymond. *La Cuisine: Secrets of Modern French Cooking.* 1969. Tudor. 1st Am. 896p. bl cloth. F/dj. H1. $32.00.

OLIVER, Steve. *Moody Gets the Blues.* 1996. Seattle. off by one Press. 1st. sgn. author's 1st book. VF/VF. T2. $30.00.

OLIVIER, Charles P. *Meteors.* 1925. Baltimore. Williams Wilkins. assn copy. 276p. VG. K5. $150.00.

OLLARD, Richard. *Escape of Charles II After Battle of Worcester.* 1966. ils. VG/VG. M17. $15.00.

OLMSTEAD, Denison. *Letters on Astronomy.* 1841 (1841). Boston. Marsh Capen Lyon Webb. 419p. G. K5. $90.00.

OLMSTEAD, Robert. *America by Land.* 1993. Random. 1st. F/F. R14. $30.00.

OLMSTEAD, Robert. *Trail of Heart's Blood Wherever We Go.* 1990. London. Secker Warburg. 1st Eng. F/F. R14. $35.00.

OLNEY, Andy. *Rocket Richard.* 1961. Ryerson. later prt. photos. VG. P8. $20.00.

OLNEY, Ross. *Out to Launch.* 1979. Lee Shepherd. 8vo. 125p. xl. K5. $15.00.

OLNEY, Ross. *Winners! Super Champions of Ice Hockey.* 1982. Clarion. 1st. photos. F/VG+. P8. $20.00.

OLSEN, D.B. *Bring the Bride a Shroud.* 1945. Doubleday Crime Club. 1st. F/NF. M15. $40.00.

OLSEN, D.B. *Death Walks on Cat Feet.* 1956. Doubleday Crime Club. 1st. NF/dj. M15. $45.00.

OLSEN, Jack. *Silence on Monte Sole: Italy's Mountain of the Sun.* 1968. NY. 374p. VG/G. S16. $28.50.

OLSHAUSEN, George. *American Slavery & After.* 1983. Olema. 1st. VG. V4. $20.00.

OLSON, Albert. *Picture Painting for Young Artists.* 1906. Chicago. Thompson Thomas. 1st. 8vo. ils. D1. $65.00.

OLSON, Charles. *Charles Olson & Ezra Pound.* 1975. Grossman. 1st. F/dj. V1. $30.00.

OLSON, Charles. *Mayan Letters.* 1953. np. Divers Press. 1st. F/wrp. lt staining to upper corner. B2. $200.00.

OLSON, Charles. *Reading at Berkeley.* 1966. San Francisco. Coyote. 1st. wrp. F. B2. $30.00.

OLSON, Reuel Leslie. *Colorado River Compact.* 1926. Los Angeles. Neuner Corp. 2nd. 8vo. bl cloth. VG+. F7. $55.00.

OLSON, Ted. *Ranch on the Laramie.* 1973. Boston/Toronto. Little, Brn. dj. A19. $25.00.

OLSON, Toby. *Changing Appearance: Poems 1965 – 1970.* 1975. Membrane. NF/wrp. V1. $20.00.

OLSON, Toby. *Seaview*. 1982. New Directions. 1st. F/dj. A24. $40.00.

OLSON, Toby. *Utah*. 1987. Linden/S&S. 1st. F/NF. A24. $85.00.

OLSVANGER, Immanuel. *L'Chayim — Jewish Wit & Humor*. 1949. Schocken. index. 192p. VG/G+. S3. $21.00.

OMMANNEY, F.D. *Shoals of Capricorn*. 1952. NY. Harcourt Brace. 1st Am. 8vo. 322p. map ep. gray cloth. $4.00.

OMORI, Annie Shepley. *Diaries of Court Ladies of Old Japan*. 1920. Houghton Mifflin. 1st. ils. 199p. VG+. A25. $45.00.

OMWAKE, John. *Conestoga Six-Horse Bell Teams of Eastern Pennsylvania*. 1930. Cincinnati. sm 4to. G. O3. $145.00.

ONASSIS, Jacqueline. *Firebird & Other Russian Fairy Tales*. 1978. Viking. 1st Am. ils Boris Zvorykin. 112p. F/dj. T10. $50.00.

ONDAATJE, Michael. *Coming Through Slaughter*. 1976. Norton. 1st. sgn. author's 1st novel. F/NF. D10. $125.00.

ONDAATJE, Michael. *Coming Through Slaughter*. 1979. London. Marion Boyars. 1st Eng. F/F. B2. $85.00.

ONDAATJE, Michael. *In the Skin of a Lion*. 1987. Toronto. McClelland & Stewart. 1st. F/F. B2. $75.00.

ONDAATJE, Michael. *Running in the Family*. 1982. Norton. 1st. F/F. D10. $75.00.

ONDAATJE, Michael. *The English Patient*. 1992. NY. Knopf. 1st Am ed. sgn. F in F dj. D10. $110.00.

ONDER, Eleanor Fox. *Plantation Shadows*. 1949. Pelican. 1st. inscr assn copy. G. B11. $65.00.

ONEAL, Cora M. *Gardens and Homes of Mexico*. 1947 (1945). Dallas. rev 2nd prt. scarce dj. dj chipped & torn. B26. $47.50.

ONIONS, Oliver. *Whom God Hath Sundered*. 1947. London. VG/dj. M2. $25.00.

ONIS, Harriet De. *The Golden Land, An Anthology of Latin American Folklore in Literature*. 1948. NY. Knopf. 1st. 395p. G/chipped dj. F3. $15.00.

OPEKE, Lawrence K. *Tropical Tree Crops*. 1982. Chichester. ils. 312p. VG/dj. B26. $49.00.

OPERATION CROSSROADS. *The Official Record*. 1946. NY. pict imitation leather. many ils. color ftspc. brds warped. VG. B18. $22.50.

OPIE, Iona and Tatem, Moira (eds). *A Dictionary of Superstitions*. 1990. NY. Oxford. trade sc. VG+. A28. $7.95.

OPIE, John Newton. *Rebel Cavalryman with Lee*. Stuart & Jackson. 1899. Chicago. WB Conkey. 1st. 336p. cloth. VG. $8.00.

OPLER, Morris E. *Grenville Goodwin Among the Western Apaches*. 1973. AZ U. ils. 103p. F/F. B19. $25.00.

OPPENHEIM, E. *Phillips, Lost Leader*. 1907. Little, Brn. 1st. VG. M2. $25.00.

OPPENHEIM, E. *Phillips, Secret Service Omnibus*. 1941. Blue Ribbon. 1st. F/dj. M2. $12.00.

OPPENHEIM, E. *Phillips, Shy Plutocrat*. 1941. Little, Brn. 1st. VG. P3. $25.00.

OPPENHEIM, E. *Phillips, Tempting of Tavernake*. 1912. Little, Brn. 1st. VG. P3. $20.00.

OPPENHEIM, Hermann. *Diseases of the Nervous System: Text-Book for Students*. 1900. Lippincott. 1st Eng-language. ils. 899p. panelled bl buckram. G1. $250.00.

OPPENHEIMER, Jane. *New Aspects of John & William Hunter*. 1946. NY. 1st. 188p. A13. $50.00.

OPPENHEIMER, Joel. *Pan's Eyes*. 1974. Amherst. Mulch Press. 1st. wrp. F. B2. $25.00.

OPTIC, Oliver. *Blue & the Gray: On the Blockade*. 1891 (1890). Lee Shepherd. 355p. VG. M20. $30.00.

ORCUTT, William. *The Princess Kalister and Tales of the Fairies*. 1902. Little, Brn. 1st. chip near spine. ils Harriette Amsden. VG. B15. $145.00.

ORCUTT, William Dana. *Kingdom of Books*. 1927. Little, Brn. 1st trade. 8vo. brn cloth. F. T10. $45.00.

ORCZY, Baroness. *Bronze Eagle*. 1915. Doran. 1st. NF. P3. $30.00.

ORD, Angustias De La Guerra. *Occurences in Hispanic California*. 1956. Washington, DC. Academy Am. Franciscan Hist. 98p. navy cloth. F. K7. $50.00.

ORDE, A. J. *Little Neighborhood Murder*. 1989. Doubleday. 1st. author's 1st book. F/F. H11/T2. $25.00.

ORDWAY, Frederick I. *Advances in Space Science & Technology*. 1962. Academic. 8vo. 431p. xl. K5. $35.00.

ORE, Rebecca. *Alien Bootlegger & Other Stories*. 1993. NY. Tor. 1st. F/NF. G10. $15.00.

OREN, Dan A. *Joining the Club: History of Jews & Yale*. 1985. New Haven. Yale. 1st. 8vo. VG/dj. A2. $20.00.

ORFIELD, Didrick. *Uncle Didrick's Stories*. 1954. MN Pub Co. revised. sgn. 96p. VG/worn. D4. $30.00.

ORGAIN, Kate Alma. *Southern Authors in Poetry & Prose*. 1908. Neale Pub. 1st. 233p. cloth. VG. M8. $85.00.

ORGILL, D. *Gothic Line: Autumn Campaign in Italy 1944*. 1967. London. 1st. ils/maps. 257p. VG/VG. S16. $21.50.

ORIARD, Michael. *End of Autumn*. 1982. Doubleday. 1st. VG/G+. P8. $15.00.

ORITA, Zenji. *I-Boat Captain*. 1976. Canoga Park, CA. Major Books. 8vo. 317p. VG/dj. B11. $35.00.

ORLANDO, Guido. *Confessions of a Scoundrel*. 1954. Winston. 1st. VG/dj. N2. $10.00.

ORLINSKY, Harry M. *Notes on the New Translation of the Torah*. 1969. JPS. biblio/indexes. 288p. VG/G+. S3. $22.00.

ORME, B. *Anthropology for Archaeologists: An Introduction*. nd. Ithaca. Cornell. ils. 300p. cloth. VG+/VG. M12. $22.50.

ORNDUFF, Robert. *Papers on Plant Systematics*. 1967. Boston. sc. ils. B26. $17.50.

ORNISH, Dean. *Eat More, Weigh Less*. 1993. NY. Harper Collins. rem mk. VG/VG. A28. $12.50.

ORR, A. *In the King's Palace*. 1986. Tor. 1st. F/F. P3. $16.00.

ORR, A. *World in Amber*. 1985. Bluejay. 1st. VG/dj. P3. $20.00.

ORR, Bobby. *Bobby Orr: My Game*. 1974. Little, Brn. 1st. F/VG. P8. $30.00.

ORR, Frank. *Puck Is a Four Letter Word*. 1983. Morrow. 1st. F/VG. P8. $25.00.

ORR, James. *International Standard Bible Encyclopedia*. 1937. Howard Severance. 5 vol. VG. B29. $50.00.

ORR, James. *Resurrection of Jesus.* nd. Hodder Stoughton. 292p. G. B29. $9.50.

ORSTEIN, Robert Evan. *New World New Mind.* 1989. Doubleday. 1st. 302p. F/F. W2. $30.00.

ORTIZ, Elisabeth Lambert. *Complete Book of Caribbean Cooking.* 1973. Evans. G+/dj. A16. $10.00.

ORTIZ, Fernando. *Cuban Counterpoint; Tobacco & Sugar.* 1947. NY. Knopf. 1st. 312p. G/G. chipped. F3. $30.00.

ORTIZ, Simon J. *Going for the Rain.* 1976. Harper Row. 1st. author's 1st book. NF/NF. L3. $175.00.

ORTLOFF, Henry Stuart. *Garden Bluebook of Annuals & Biennials.* 1931. Doubleday. VG. P3. $8.00.

ORTON, Helen Fuller. *Mystery Over the Brick Wall.* 1951. Lippincott. 1st. ils Robert Doremus. 114p. G+/dj. P2. $15.00.

ORTON, Joe. *Head to Toe.* 1971. St. Martin. 1st. 186p. VG/dj. M20. $25.00.

ORTZEN, Len. *Guns at Sea.* 1976. NY. Galahad. 160p. dj. T7. $35.00.

ORWELL, George. *Animal Farm.* 1946. Harcourt Brace. 1st Am. VG/dj. M25. $75.00.

ORWELL, George. *Coming Up for Air.* 1950. Harcourt Brace. 1st Am. F/NF. A24. $70.00.

ORWELL, George. *Lost Writings.* 1985. Arbor. 1st Am. F/F. B4. $45.00.

ORWELL, George. *Nineteen Eighty-Four.* 1949. Harcourt Brace. 1st Am. F/dj. Q1. $125.00.

OSBORN, Albert S. *Mind of the Juror as Judge of the Facts.* 1938. Albany. Boyd Prt. dk maroon cloth. M11. $150.00.

OSBORN, David. *Love & Treasure.* 1982. NAL. 1st. VG/dj. P3. $15.00.

OSBORN, John Jay. *Paper Chase.* 1971. Houghton Mifflin. 1st. F/clip. B4. $300.00.

OSBORN, Paul. *Point of No Return.* 1952. Random. 1st. F/VG. A24. $35.00.

OSBORN, Ronald E. *The Spirit of American Christianity.* 1958. Harper. 241p. G/G. B29. $6.50.

OSBORNE, Charles. *Life & Crimes of Agatha Christie.* 1984. Agatha Christie Mystery Collection. VG/dj. P3. $20.00.

OSBORNE, H. *Oxford Companion of Art.* 1970. NY. 1st. dj. T9. $22.00.

OSBORNE, J. *Cardinal.* 1992. Austin, TX. ils/photos G Barland. 108p. cloth. F/F. M12. $17.50.

OSBORNE, John. *Better Class of Person.* 1981. Dutton. 1st Am. NF/NF. R14. $25.00.

OSBORNE, John. *Look Back in Anger.* 1957. London. Faber. 1st Eng. NF/dj. Q1. $100.00.

OSBORNE, John. *Patriot for Me.* 1966. London. Faber. 1st. F/dj. B4. $125.00.

OSBORNE, Walter. *Thoroughbred World.* nd. np. Amiel. 4to. VG/fair. O3. $20.00.

OSGOOD, Henry O. *So This Is Jazz.* 1926. Boston. Little, Brn. 1st. one of the earliest books on jazz. VG+/NF. B2. $50.00.

OSGOOD, Kate Putnam. *Driving the Cows Home.* nd. Boston. D. Lothrop & Co. G. A16. $5.00.

OSHIKAWA, Josui. *Manual of Japanese Flower Arrangement.* 1936. Tokyo. 1st. ils. 322p. VG/VG. B5. $45.00.

OSIER & WOZNIAK. *Century of Serial Publications in Psychology 1850 – 1950.* 1984. NY. Kraus. 806p. gray buckram. G1. $75.00.

OSLER, Jerry. *Saint Mike.* 1987. Harper Row. 1st. F/F. A20. $20.00.

OSLER, W. *An Alabama Student & Other Biographical Addresses.* 1909. London. 1st/2nd prt. 334p. A13. $100.00.

OSLER, W. *Way of Life.* nd. Baltimore. Remington Putnam. ils. 47p. NF/dj. K3. $20.00.

OSLER, William. *Concise History of Medicine.* 1919. Baltimore. 1st. 66p. xl. A13. $100.00.

OSLEY, A. S. *Scribes & Sources.* 1980. Boston. Godine. 1st. ils. VG/dj. K3. $15.00.

OSOFSKY, Gilbert. *Puttin' on Ole Massa.* 1969. Harper Row. 1st. 8vo. 409p. F/dj. H1. $35.00.

OSSOLI, Margaret Fuller. *Woman in the Nineteenth Century, and Kindred Papers Relating to the Sphere, Condition, and Duties of Woman.* Boston. Roberts Brothers. 1875. 12mo. 420p. gr cloth. 1st ed. 8th prt. Minor wear & rubbing. G to VG. L5. $80.00.

OSTER, Harry. *Living Country Blues.* 1969. Detroit. Folklore Associates. 1st. F/slight slant/NF. clip. B2. $85.00.

OSTER, Jerry. *Club Dead.* 1988. NY. Harper & Row. 1st. VF/VF. T2. $12.00.

OSTER, Jerry. *Nowhere Man.* 1987. NY. Harper & Row. 1st. VF/VF. T2. $12.00.

OSTERGAARD, Vilhelm. *Tycho Brahe.* 1907 (1895). Copenhagen. Glydendalske Boghandel Nordisk Forlag. 273p. VG. K5. $40.00.

OSTERWEIS, Rollin G. *Rebecca Gratz: Study in Charm.* 1935. Putnam. ils/biblio/index. 244p. VG. S3. $27.00.

OSTRANDER, Isabel. *Crimson Blotter.* 1921. White House. G+. M2. $12.00.

OSTRANDER, Isabel. *Twenty-Six Clues.* 1919. WJ Watt. 277p. VG/VG. M20. $45.00.

OSTRANSKY, Leroy. *The Anatomy of Jazz.* 1960. Seattle. Univ. of Washington Press. 1st. f/chip. B2. $35.00.

OSTROGORSKY, George. *History of the Byzantine State.* 1957. Rutgers. 1st Am. maps. 548p. AN/dj. H1. $48.00.

OSTROW, Joanna. *In the Highlands Since Time Immemorial.* 1970. Knopf. 1st. author's 1st book. F/NF. H11. $30.00.

OSWALD, F.L. *Zoological Sketches: A Contribution to Outdoor Study.* 1883. Phil. Lippincott. pres. ils H Faber. 266p. pict cloth. G+. $12.00.

OSWALD, John Clyde. *Printing in the Americas.* 1937. London. Gregg. 1st. VG/dj. K3. $85.00.

OSWALT, Wendell H. *Mission of Change in Alaska: Eskimos & Moravians...* 1963. San Marino. Huntington Lib. 8vo. 170p. gr cloth. NF/dj. P4. $40.00.

OTTEN, George. *Tuberous-Rooted Begonias.* 1949 (1935). NY. VG/dj minor wear. B26. $16.00.

OTTLEY, Roi. *No Green Pastures.* 1951. Scribner. 1st. 234p. VG/VG. B4. $85.00.

OTTLEY, Roi. *White Marble Lady.* 1965. FSG. 1st. F/NF. M25. $60.00.

OTTMAN, Jim. *Hunting on Horseback.* 1987. Paladin. F/F. O3. $15.00.

OTTO, Margaret. *Great Aunt Victoria's House.* 1957. Holt. 1st. 122p. VG/G+. P2. $25.00.

OTTO, Whitney. *How to Make an American Quilt.* 1991. NY. Villard. 1st. sgn. author's 1st novel. F/F. L3. $85.00.

OURSLER, Will. *Folio on Florence White.* 1942. NY. S&S. 1st. F in dj. M15. $75.00.

OUSPENSKY, P.D. *Strange Life of Ivan Osokin.* 1955 (1966). Hermitage. rpt. VG/clip. M25. $35.00.

OUSTALET, M. E. *Revision De Queloques Especes D'Oiseaux De La Chine.* 1901. Paris. sm folio. ils. 27p. new cloth. C12. $95.00.

OUTLAND, Charles. *Stagecoaching on El Camino Real.* Los Angeles. 1973. Clark. 1st. ils/maps. 339p. VG/VG. J2. $195.00.

OUTLAND, Charles F. *Mines, Murders & Grizzlies: Tales of California.* 1986. Ventura Hist. Soc. revised. ils/notes/index. 151p. NF/NF. B19. $25.00.

OVERMIER & SENIOR. *Books & Manuscripts of the Bakken.* 1992. ils. 5000+entries. 525p. F. A4. $85.00.

OVERTON, Grant. *American Nights Entertainment.* 1923. Scribner. 1st. 12mo. 386p. gr cloth/gold labels. NF/dj. J3. $50.00.

OVINGTON, Ray. *Tactics on Trout.* 1969. Knopf. 1st. ils/index. 327p. F/dj. A17. $15.00.

OWEN, Catherine. *Catherine Owen's New Cookbook.* Part 1 & Part 2. 1883. revised. pict bdg. G+. E6. $60.00.

OWEN, Catherine. *Choice Cookery: Not for Those Seeking Economy.* 1889. 1st. VG. E6. $85.00.

OWEN, David. *Fantastic Planets.* 1979. Addison. 1st. VG/dj. M2. $12.00.

OWEN, Howard. *Littlejohn.* 1993. NY. Villard. 1st thus. F/dj. M23. $40.00.

OWEN, Iris M. *Conjuring Up Philip.* 1976. Harper Row. 1st. VG. P3. $15.00.

OWEN, Joseph R. *Colder than Hell, a Marine Rifle Company at Chosen Reservoir.* 1996. Annapolis. Naval Institute Press. 1st. 237p. F/F. B18. $15.00.

OWEN, Maggie. *Book of Maggie Owen.* 1944. NY. VG/VG. M17. $15.00.

OWEN, Richard. *On The Nature of Limbs.* 1849. London. 1st. fld pl. 119p. A13. $300.00.

OWEN, Richard. *The Eye of the Gods.* 1978. NY. Dutton. 1st. F/F. H11. $55.00.

OWEN-SMITH, R.N. *Megaherbivores.* 1992. Cambridge. 369p. F. S15. $18.50.

OWENS, Bill. *Our Kind of People: American Groups & Rituals.* 1975. SF. Straight Arrow. sgn/dtd. photos. wrp. D11. $75.00.

OWENS, George. *The Judas Pool.* 1994. NY. Putnam. 1st. VF/VF. H11. $30.00.

OWENS, J. Garfield. *All God's Chillun. Meditations on Negro Spirituals.* 1971. Nashville. Abingdon. 1st. blk cloth w/ ribbon marker. F in F dj. B2. $25.00.

OWENS, Janis. *My Brother Michael.* 1997. Sarasota. Pineapple Press. 1st. sgn. author's 1st novel. VF/VF. T2. $30.00.

OWENS, Janis. *Myra Sims.* 1999. Sarasota. Pineapple Press. 1st. sgn. VF/VF. T2. $25.00.

OWENS, Louis. *Nightland.* 1996. NY. Dutton. 1st. sgn. VF/VF. T2. $25.00.

OWENS, Robert Dale. *Wrong of Slavery. Right of Emancipation.* 1864. Lippincott. VG+. B2. $100.00.

OXBERRY, William. *Actor's Budget of Wit & Merriment.* nd (1820). London. Simpkin Marshall. 1st thus. Morrell bdg. H13. $195.00.

OXENHORN, Harvey. *Tuning the Rig: A Journey to the Arctic.* 1990. Harper. 281p+2p ship drawings. M/wrp. A17. $10.00.

OZ, Amos. *Hill of Evil Council.* 1978. HBJ. 1st Am. sgn. author's 5th book. F/clip. D10. $60.00.

OZ, Amos. *In the Land of Israel.* 1983. HBJ. 1st. F/F. B35. $20.00.

OZAKI, Yukio. *Romances of Old Japan.* 1920. NY. Brentano. 32 full-p ils. 278p. pict cloth. W3. $48.00.

OZICK, Cynthia. *Bloodshed.* 1976. Knopf. 1st. sgn. F/clip. D10. $50.00.

OZICK, Cynthia. *Messiah of Stockholm.* 1987. Knopf. 1st. F/dj. A24. $25.00.

OZICK, Cynthia. *Pagan Rabbi & Other Stories.* 1971. Knopf. 1st. author's 1st book. F/dj. B4. $85.00.

OZICK, Cynthia. *Shawl.* 1989. Knopf. 1st. F/NF. B4. $35.00.

— P —

PACK, Charles Lathrop. *The War Garden Victorious.* 1919. Phila. teg. ils. 179p. VG. B18. $25.00.

PACKER & HOWARD. *Christianity; The True Humanism.* 1985. Word. 242p. VG/VG. B29. $9.00.

PADEV, Michael. *Escape from the Balkans.* 1943. NY. Bobbs & Merrill. 1st. G+/G. R16. $30.00.

PADGETT, Abigail. *Child of Silence.* 1993. NY. Mysterious Press. 1st. sgn. author's 1st novel. VF/VF. T2. $85.00.

PADGETT, Abigail. *Strawgirl.* 1994. NY. Mysterious. 1st. VF/VF. H11. $50.00.

PADILLA, Heberto. *Heroes are Grazing in My Garden.* 1984. NY. F S G. 1st. VF/F. H11. $20.00.

PADILLA, Victoria. *Southern California Gardens. An Illustrated History.* 1961. Berkeley. 1st. sm4to. B26. $55.00.

PAGE, Jake. *The Deadly Canyon.* 1994. NY. Ballantine Books. 1st. VF/VF. T2. $20.00.

PAGE, Katherine Hall. *The Body in the Vestibule.* 1992. NY. St. Martin. 1st. VF/VF. T2. $25.00.

PAGE, Martin. *Man Who Stole the Mona Lisa.* 1984. Pantheon. 1st Am ed. NF/NF. G8. $10.00.

PAGE, Thomas Nelson. *Meh Lady. A Story of the War.* 1909. NY. Scribners. early printing. orig cloth. bit rubbed. written in Black dialect. 70p. VG. M8. $22.50.

PAGET, Guy. *Sporting Pictures of England.* 1987. London. Bracken Books. Sporting Pictures of England series. brd. F. O3. $15.00.

PAIGE, Satchel. *Maybe I'll Pitch Forever.* 1962. NY. Doubleday. NF/VG+. R16. $40.00.

PALEY, Grace. *Just as I Thought.* 1997. FSG. UP. F in lt yellow wrp. M25. $60.00.

PALEY, Grace. *Later the Same Day.* 1985. NY. FSG. 1st. sgn. F in F dj. D10. $50.00.

PALMER, Michael. *Silent Treatment.* 1995. NY. Bantam. 1st. VF/VF. T2. $9.00.

PALMER, Robert. *Deep Blues.* 1981. NY. Viking. 1st. F/F. B2. $35.00.

PALMER, Thomas. *Dream Science.* 1990. NY. ticknor. 1st. VF/F. H11. $25.00.

PALMER, William J. *The Highwayman and Mr. Dickens.* 1992. NY. St. Martin. 1st. VF/VF. T2. $15.00.

PALOU, Fray Francisco. *La Vida De Fray Junipero Serra.* 1972. Mexico. drawings. 300p. G/wrp. F3. $20.00.

PAMUK, Orhan. *The New Life.* 1997. NY. FSG. 1st Am ed. trans Guneli Gun. sgn by author. F/F. O11. $45.00.

PANASSIE, Hugues. *The Real Jazz.* 1942. NY. Smith and Durrell. 1st. NF/VG. B2. $50.00.

PANEK, Richard. *Seeing and Believing.* 1998. NY. Viking. 1st. F/F. M23. $45.00.

PANG, Eul Soo. *In Pursuit of Honor and Power.* 1988. Tuscaloosa. Univ. of Alabama Press. 1st. 341p. G/G. F3. $20.00.

PANGBORN, Georgia Wood. *The Wind at Midnight.* 1999. Ashcroft, BC. Ash Tree Press. 1st. VF/VF. T2. $40.00.

PANSHIN, Alexei. *Farewell to Yesterday's Tomorrow.* 1975. NY. Berkley/Putnam. 1st. F/F. T2. $25.00.

PAPPAS, Nick. *The Bloody Dagger Price Guide to Science Fiction, Fantasy & Horror: 1998 Edition.* 1998. San Diego. Bloody Dagger Books. T2. $45.00.

PARETSKY, Sara. *Bitter Medicine.* 1987. NY. Morrow. 1st. sgn. F/F. D10. $90.00.

PARETSKY, Sara. *Blood Shot.* 1988. NY. Delacorte. 1st. sgn. VF/VF. T2. $35.00.

PARETSKY, Sara. *Burn Marks.* 1990. NY. Delacorte. 1st. F/F. H11. $35.00.

PARETSKY, Sara. *Guardian Angel.* 1992. NY. Delacorte. 1st. sgn. F/F. O11. $35.00.

PARETSKY, Sara. *Killing Orders.* 1985. NY. Morrow. 1st. F/F. D10. $125.00.

PARETSKY, Sara. *Windy City Blues.* 1995. NY. Delacorte. 1st. sgn. VF/VF. T2. $25.00.

PARKER, Barbara. *Suspicion of Innocence.* 1994. NY. Dutton. 1st. author's 1st novel. sgn. T2. $35.00.

PARKER, Gwendolyn. *These Same Long Bones.* 1994. Boston. Houghton. 1st. F/F. H11. $35.00.

PARKER, Phyllis. *Brazil & the Quiet Intervention.* 1979. Austin. Univ. of Texas Press. 1st. 147p. G/G. F3. $20.00.

PARKER, Richard. *Kind of Misfortune.* 1955. NY. Scribner. 1st. VG/VG. G8. $10.00.

PARKER, Robert B. *A Catskill Eagle.* 1985. NY. Delacorte/Seymour Lawrence. 1st. VF in dj. M15. $45.00.

PARKER, Robert B. *All Our Yesterdays.* 1994. NY. Delacorte. 1st. NF/NF. G8. $15.00.

PARKER, Robert B. *Ceremony.* 1982. NY. Delacorte/Seymour Lawrence. 1st. VF in dj. M15. $65.00.

PARKER, Robert B. *Crimson Joy.* 1998. NY. Delacorte. 1st. VG/VG. G8. $12.50.

PARKER, Robert B. *Double Deuce.* 1992. NY. Putnam. 1st. sgn. VF/VF. T2. $25.00.

PARKER, Robert B. *Double Deuce.* 1992. NY. Putnam. 1st. F/F. G8. $15.00.

PARKER, Robert B. *Night Passage.* 1997. NY. Putnam. 1st. sgn. VF/VF. T2. $25.00.

PARKER, Robert B. *Paper Doll.* 1993. NY. Putnam. 1st. sgn. VF/VF. T2. $25.00.

PARKER, Robert B. *Pastime.* 1991. NY. Putnam. 1st. sgn. VF/VF. T2. $25.00.

PARKER, Robert B. *Playmates.* 1989. NY. Putnam. 1st. sgn. VF/VF. T2. $25.00.

PARKER, Robert B. *Stardust.* 1990. NY. Putnam. 1st. NF/NF. G8. $15.00.

PARKER, Robert B. *Sudden Mischief.* 1998. NY. Putnam. 1st. NF/NF. G8. $15.00.

PARKER, Robert B. *Taming a Sea Horse.* 1986. NY. Delacorte/Lawrence. 1st. sgn. VF/VF. T2. $30.00.

PARKER, Robert B. *The Judas Goat.* 1978. Boston. Houghton Mifflin. 1st. VF/dj. M15. $125.00.

PARKER, Robert B. *Trouble in Paradise.* 1998. NY. Putnam. 1st. sgn. VF/VF. T2. $25.00.

PARKER, Robert B. *Wilderness.* 1979. NY. Delacorte/Seymour Lawrence. 1st. VF in dj. M15. $85.00.

PARKER, Robert B. & Raymond Chandler. *Poodle Springs.* 1989. NY. Putnam. 1st. sgn by Parker. VF/VF. T2. $25.00.

PARKER, Robert M. Jr. *Bordeaux: The Definitive Guide for the Wines Produced Since 1961.* 1985. NY. S&S. VG/VG. A28. $14.95.

PARKER, T. Jefferson. *Little Saigon.* 1988. NY. St. Martin. 1st. sgn. VF/VF. T2. $35.00.

PARKER, T. Jefferson. *Pacific Beat.* 1991. NY. St. Martin. 1st. sgn. VF/VF. T2. $25.00.

PARKER, T. Jefferson. *Summer of Fear.* 1993. NY. St. Martin. 1st. sgn. VF/VF. T2. $25.00.

PARKS, Gordon. *The Learning Tree.* 1963. NY. Harper & Row. 1st. VG w/dj. D10. $90.00.

PARRISH, Frank. *Bait on the Hook.* 1983. Dodd, Mead. 1st Am ed. NF/VG+. G8. $10.00.

PARRISH, Randall. *The Red Mist, A Tale of Civil Strife.* 1914. NY. A. L. Burt Co. 1st. orig. cloth. one plate lacking. plates. 401p. VG. M8. $12.50.

PARROTT, Bob W. *Earth, Moon and Beyond.* 1969. Waco, TX. Word Books. 8vo. color photo ils. 176p. G/chipped dj. clip. K5. $9.00.

PARRY, Owen. *Faded Coat of Blue.* 1999. NY. Avon Books. 1st. author's 1st novel. sgn. VF/VF. T2. $25.00.

PARSONS, Julie. *Mary, Mary.* 1998. London. Macmillan. 1st. author's 1st novel. VF/VF. T2. $35.00.

PARTRIDGE, Norman. *Red Right Hand.* 1998. Burton. Subterranean Press. 1st. 1/26 lettered copies. sgn. VF no dj as issued. T2. $50.00.

PARTRIDGE, Norman. *Wildest Dreams.* 1998. Burton. Subterranean Press. 1st. 1/500 # copies. sgn. VF/VF. T2. $50.00.

PASACHOFF, Jay M. *Astronomy; from the Earth to the Universe.* 1979. Philadelphia. W. B. Saunders. 1st. photos ils. some color. & diagrams. 476p. G in glossy wrp. K5. $6.00.

PASCOE, David. *Fox on the Run.* 1999. London. Orion. 1st. author's 1st novel. VF/VF. T2. $35.00.

PASTERNAK, Boris. *Doctor Zhivago.* 1958. NY. Signet. 21st prt pb. VG. F6. $1.50.

PASZTORY, Esther. *Aztec Stone Sculpture.* 1977. NY. np. 1st. wrp. 46p. F. F3. $10.00.

PATCHETT, Ann. *Taft.* (1994). NY. Houghton Mifflin. 1st. F/F. B3. $25.00.

PATCHETT, Ann. *The Patron Saint of Liars.* (1992). Boston. Houghton Mifflin. 1st. sgn by author. F/F. B3. $75.00.

PATRICK, Millar. *Four Centuries of Scottish Psalmody.* 1950. Oxford. 234p. VG. B29. $36.00.

PATTERSON, Harry. *Dillinger.* 1983. NY. Stein & Day. 1st. VF/VF. T2. $15.00.

PATTERSON, Harry. *To Catch a King.* 1979. NY. Stein & Day. 1st. F/F. T2. $15.00.

PATTERSON, James. *Cat & Mouse.* 1997. Boston. Little, Brn. 1st. sgn. VF in dj. M15. $40.00.

PATTERSON, James. *Jack and Jill.* (1996). Boston. Little, Brn. 1st. F/F. B3. $25.00.

PATTERSON, James. *Kiss the Girls.* 1995. Boston. Little, Brn. 1st. sgn. VF/VF. T2. $25.00.

PATTERSON, James. *Pop Goes the Weasel.* 1999. Boston. Little, Brn. 1st. sgn. VF/VF. T2. $27.00.

PATTERSON, James. *See How They Run.* (1997). 1979. Warner Books. ne. originally pub as The Jericho Commandment. F/chip dj. S19. $25.00.

PATTERSON, James. *Virgin.* 1980. NY. McGraw-Hill. 1st. F in dj. M15. $150.00.

PATTERSON, Richard North. *Degree of Guilt.* 1993. NY. Knopf. 1st. F/F. H11. $30.00.

PATTERSON, Richard North. *Eyes of a Child.* 1995. NY. Knopf. 1st. F/F. H11. $20.00.

PATTERSON, Richard North. *Silent Witness.* 1997. NY. Knopf. 1st. sgn. VF/VF. T2. $25.00.

PATTERSON, Richard North. *The Final Judgment.* 1995. NY. Knopf. 1st. sgn. VF/VF. T2. $30.00.

PAUCH, Wilhelm. *The Heritage of the Reformation.* 1950. Beacon. sgn by author. 312p. VG/VG. B29. $12.00.

PAUL, Barbara. *Cadenza for Caruso.* 1984. NY. St. Martin. 1st. VG+/VG+. G8. $15.00.

PAUL, Barbara. *In Laws and Outlaws.* 1990. NY. Scribners. 1st. VF/VF. T2. $14.00.

PAULOS, John Allen. *Beyond Numeracy.* (1991). NY. Knopf. 1st. F/F. B3. $5.00.

PAULSEN, Gary. *Night Rituals.* 1989. NY. Donald I. Fine. 1st. VF/VF. T2. $6.00.

PAULSEN, Gary. *The Rifle.* (1995). San Diego. HBJ. 1st. F/F. B3. $25.00.

PAYNE, David. *Confessions of a Taoist on Wall Street.* 1984. np. 1st. F/VG dj. M19. $17.50.

PAYNE, David. *Ruin Creek.* 1993. NY. Doubleday. 1st. F/VF. H11. $25.00.

PAYNE-GAPOSCHKIN, Cecilia. *Introduction to Astronomy.* 1954. NY. Prentice Hall. b/w photos & figures. 8vo. 508p. VG/chipped & torn dj. K5. $20.00.

PAZ, Octavio. *Convergences: Essays on Art and Literature.* 1987. NY. HBJ. 1st Am ed. F/F. O11. $50.00.

PAZ, Octavio. *The Double Flame: Essays on Love and Eroticism.* 1995. Harcourt Brace. UP of Am ed. F in wrp. M25. $35.00.

PEARCE, Michael. *Mamur Zapt and the Girl in the Nile.* 1994. Warner/ Mysterious. 1st Am ed. NF/NF. G8. $12.50.

PEARCE, Michael. *The Mamur Zapt and the Donkey-Vous.* (1992). NY. Mysterious Press. 1st. F/F. B3. $15.00.

PEARS, Iain. *Death and Restoration.* 1996. London. Harper Collins. 1st. VF/dj. M15. $50.00.

PEARS, Iain. *Giotto's Hand.* (1994). NY. Scribner's. 1st Am ed. F/F. B3. $15.00.

PEARS, Iain. *The Titian Committee.* 1991. London. Victor Gollancz. 1st. VF/dj. M15. $65.00.

PEARS, Tim. *In the Place of Fallen Leaves.* (1995). NY. Donald I. Fine. 1st Am ed. author's 1st novel. F/F. B3. $35.00.

PEARSON, Nathan W. *Goin' to Kansas City.* 1988. Ann Arbor. Univ. of Michigan Press. ARC w/slip. F. soiled/F. B2. $30.00.

PEARSON, Ridley. *Beyond Recognition.* 1997. NY. Hyperion. 1st. sgn. VF/VF. T2. $25.00.

PEARSON, Ridley. *Chain of Evidence.* 1995. NY. Hyperion. 1st. F/F. H11. $20.00.

PEARSON, Ridley. *No Witnesses.* 1994. NY. Hyperion. 1st. sgn. VF/VF. T2. $25.00.

PEARSON, Ridley. *The Angel Maker.* 1993. NY. Delacorte Press. 1st. sgn. VF/VF. T2. $25.00.

PEARSON, Ridley. *The Seizing of Yankee Green Mall.* 1987. NY. St. Martin. 1st. sgn. VF/VF. price clip. T2. $45.00.

PEARSON, T. R. *A Short History of a Small Place.* 1985. NY. Linden. 1st. author's 1st book. F/F. D10. $60.00.

PEARSON, William. *Chessplayer.* 1984. NY. Viking. 1st. VF/VF. H11. $40.00.

PEATTIE, Donald C. *A Natural History of Trees of Eastern and Central North America.* 1950. Boston. 1st. 606p w/numerous woodcuts by Paul Landacre. VG+/sm chip in dj. B26. $32.50.

PEATTIE, Roderick (ed). *The Pacific Coast Ranges.* 1946. NY. 408p w/18 b&w plates & 4 maps. dj. B26. $19.00.

PECK, Anne. *Young Mexico.* 1934. NY. McBride Co. 1st. b/w photo ils. map. drawings. 270p. G. F3. $15.00.

PECK, Dale. *Now it's Time to Say Goodbye.* 1998. FSG. ARC. F in decor wrp. M25. $45.00.

PECKER, Jean Claude. *The Orion Book of the Sky.* 1960. NY. Orion. translated by William D. O'Gorman. Jr. 50 ils. 12 in color. 112p. VG/chipped. clipped dj. K5. $13.00.

PEERY, Janet. *The Alligator's Dance.* (1993). Dallas. Southern Methodist U. 1st. author's 1st book. sgn by author. F/F. B3. $50.00.

PEERY, Janet. *The River Beyond the World.* 1996. NY. Picador USA. ARC. F/wrp. B2. $35.00.

PEISSEL, Michel. *The Lost World of Quintana Roo.* 1963. NY. Dutton. 1st. chipped dj (2nd pr). 306p. G. F3. $20.00.

PELECANOS, George P. *Shame the Devil.* 1999. Tucson. Dennis McMillan. 1st ed. 1/400 # copies. sgn. VF/VF dj & slipcase. T2. $125.00.

PELECANOS, George P. *Shame the Devil.* 1999. Boston. Little, Brn. 1st trade ed. sgn. VF/VF. T2. $26.00.

PELECANOS, George P. *Shoedog.* 1994. NY. St. Martin. 1st. VF in dj. M15. $90.00.

PELECANOS, George P. *The Big Blowdown.* 1996. NY. St. Martin. 1st. sgn. VF/VF. T2. $35.00.

PELECANOS, George P. *The Sweet Forever.* 1998. Boston. Little, Brn. 1st trade ed. sgn. VF/VF. T2. $25.00.

PEMBERTON, Ralph & Robt. B. Osgood. *The Medical & Orthopaedic Management of Chronic Arthritis.* 1934. Macmillan Co. 1st. 8vo. 403p. VG. H1. $15.00.

PENMAN, Sharon Kay. *Cruel as the Grave.* 1998. Holt. 1st. sgn. F/F. G8. $25.00.

PENMAN, Sharon Kay. *The Queen's Man: A Medieval Mystery.* 1996. NY. Holt. 1st. F/F. H11. $20.00.

PENNYBACKER, Morton. *The Two Spies, Nathan Hale and Robert Townsend.* 1930. Boston. Houghton Mifflin. 1st. 1/780. b&w ils. 115p. G. soiling. wear. B18. $25.00.

PENTECOST, Hugh. *Death by Fire.* 1986. NY. Dodd. 1st. F/F. H11. $20.00.

PENZLER, Otto. *Earl Derr Biggers' Charlie Chan: A Descriptive Bibliography and Price Guide.* 1999. NY. Mysterious Bookshop. 1st. 1/250. chapbook. VF/printed wrp. T2. $10.00.

PENZLER, Otto. *Mickey Spillane: A Descriptive Bibliography and Price Guide.* 1999. NY. Mysterious Bookshop. 1st. 1/250. chapbook. VF/printed wrp. T2. $13.00.

PEPENOE, Paul B. *Date Growing in the Old and New Worlds.* 1913. Altadena, CA. pict cloth cover. index. 316p+40 full pg b&w photos. VG-. B26. $65.00.

PEPPER, Art and Laurie. *Straight Life, The Story of Art Pepper.* 1979. NY. Schirmer. 1st. F/lightly used dj. B2. $50.00.

PERCY, Walker. *Love in the Ruins.* 1971. NY. FSG. 1st. F/F. O11. $50.00.

PERDUE, Virginia. *Alarum and Excursion.* 1944. Garden City. Doubleday. 1st. F/NF. T2. $25.00.

PERELMAN, S. J. *The Swiss Family Perelman.* 1950. NY. S&S. 1st. drawings by Hirschfeld. F in used dj. B2. $60.00.

PERES DE COSTA, Suneeta. *Homework.* 1999. NY. Bloomsbury USA. ARC. F/wrp. B2. $25.00.

PEREZ-REVERTE, Arturo. *The Fencing Master.* 1998. NY. Harcourt. ARC. F/wrps. B2. $35.00.

PEREZ-REVERTE, Arturo. *The Flanders Panel.* 1990. NY. Harcourt. 1st. F/F. H11. $45.00.

PEREZ-REVERTE, Arturo. *The Seville Communion.* 1998. London. Harvill. 1st Eng. VF/dj. M15. $75.00.

PERKINS, Frances. *People at Work.* 1834. NY. John Day. 1st. by 1st woman cabinet member & Sec. of Labor. F/VG. slight chips. B2. $35.00.

PERLIN, Doris. *Eight Bright Candles. Courageous Women of Mexico.* 1995. Plano. Texas. Republic of Tx Press. 1st. 162p. G. F3. $15.00.

PERRET, Patti. *The Faces of Fantasy.* 1996. NY. Tor. 1st. sgn by contributor Barbara Hambly. VF/VF. T2. $35.00.

PERRY, Anne. *Bedford Square.* 1999. Ballantine. 1st. sgn. F/F. G8. $32.50.

PERRY, Anne. *Pentecost Alley.* 1996. NY. Fawcett Columbine. 1st. sgn. VF/VF. T2. $35.00.

PERRY, Anne. *Traitors Gate.* 1995. NY. Fawcett Columbine. 1st. sgn. VF/VF. T2. $35.00.

PERRY, Anne. *Twisted Root.* 1999. Ballantine. 1st. sgn. F/F. G8. $32.50.

PERRY, Charles. *The Haight Asbury, A History.* 1984. NY. Random House. 1st. ils w/ photos. F/F. B2. $35.00.

PERRY, Thomas. *Big Fish.* 1985. NY. Scribners. 1st. F/F. H11. $50.00.

PERRY, Thomas. *Dance for the Dead.* 1996. NY. Random. 1st. F/F. H11. $25.00.

PERRY, Thomas. *Island.* (1987). NY. Putnam. 1st. F/F. B3. $20.00.

PERRY, Thomas. *Sleeping Dogs.* 1992. NY. Random House. 1st. sgn. VF/VF. T2. $35.00.

PETERS, Daniel. *Rising from the Ruins.* 1995. NY. Random House. 1st ed. maps. 316p. G/G. F3. $20.00.

PETERS, Daniel. *The Luck of Huemac.* 1981. NY. Random House. 1st ed. glossary. map. 659p. G/G. F3. $20.00.

PETERS, Elizabeth. *The Deeds of the Disturber.* 1988. NY. Atheneum. UP. NF. B2. $35.00.

PETERS, Ellis. *An Excellent Mystery.* 1985. London. Macmillan. 1st. VF/dj. M15. $150.00.

PETERS, Ellis. *City of Gold and Shadows.* 1973. London. Macmillan. 1st. F/dj. M15. $250.00.

PETERS, Ellis. *Mourning Raga.* 1967. London. Macmillan. 1st. F/dj. M15. $200.00.

PETERS, Ellis. *The Pilgrim of Hate.* 1984. London. Macmillan. 1st. VF/dj. M15. $150.00.

PETERS, Ellis. *The Raven in the Foregate.* 1986. London. Macmillan. 1st. F/dj. M15. $85.00.

PETERSEN, William. *Those Curious New Cults.* 1973. Keats. 214p. VG/VG. B29. $7.50.

PETERSON, Frederick. *Ancient Mexico, An Introduction to the Pre-Hispanic Cultures.* 1961. NY. Putnam. 2nd pr. b/w photo ils. drawings. map. 313p. G/chipped dj. F3. $20.00.

PETIEVICH, Gerald. *Money Men and One Shot Deal.* 1981. HBJ. 1st. star stamp. NF. dj. M25. $75.00.

PETIEVICH, Gerald. *The Quality of the Informant.* 1985. NY. Arbor House. 1st. VF. dj. M25. $25.00.

PETIEVICH, Gerald. *To Die in Beverly Hills.* 1983. NY. Arbor House. 1st. sgn. F/F. T2. $30.00.

PETIT, Chris. *The Psalm Killer.* 1997. NY. Knopf. 1st. VF/F. H11. $20.00.

PETRAKIS, Harry Mark. *The Waves of Night & Other Stories.* 1969. np. David McKay. 1st. sgn. pc. F/VG dj. M19. $25.00.

PETRY, Ann. *Tituba of Salem Village.* 1964. NY. Crowell. 1st. F/VG+. clip w/lt edgewear. O11. $35.00.

PFEIFFER, Lee & Dave Worral. *The Essential Bond: The Authorized Guide to the World of 007.* 1998. London. Boxtree. 1st. VF/VF. T2. $35.00.

PHILBRICK, R. N. (ed). *Proceedings of the Symposium on the Biology of the California Islands.* 1967. Santa Barbara. 363p w/numerous photos & text figures. New. B26. $15.00.

PHILBRICK, W. R. *Walk on the Water.* 1991. NY. St. Martin. 1st. NF/NF. G8. $12.50.

PHILBY, Kim. *My Silent War.* 1968. NY. Grove. 1st. VF/F. H11. $50.00.

PHILLIPS, Gary. *Violent Spring.* 1994. Portland. West Coast Crime. 1st. trade pb orig. sgn. author's 1st novel. VF/pict wrp. T2. $15.00.

PHILLIPS, Jayne Anne. *Fast Lanes.* 1987. NY. Dutton. 1st. F/F. H11. $30.00.

PHILLIPS, Jayne Anne. *Machine Dreams.* (1948). NY. Dutton. 1st. F. very lt use/F. B3. $30.00.

PHILLIPS, Julia. *You'll Never Eat Lunch in this Town Again.* 1991. Random House. 1st. F/chip dj. S19. $35.00.

PHILLIPS, W. Glasgow. *Tuscaloosa.* 1994 np. Morrow. 1st. F/F dj. M19. $17.50.

PICANO, Felice. *The Book of Lies.* 1998. Los Angeles. Alyson Books. ARC. wrp. F. B2. $25.00.

PICKARD, Nancy. *Bum Steer.* 1990. NY. Pocket Books. 1st. sgn. VF/VF. T2. $25.00.

PICKARD, Nancy. *Confession.* 1994. NY. Pocket Books. 1st. sgn. VF/VF. T2. $25.00.

PICKARD, Nancy. *Generous Death.* 1992. Arlington Heights. Dark Harvest. 1st hc ed. sgn. VF/VF. T2. $25.00.

PIERCE, Julian R. *Speak Rwanda.* 1999. NY. Picador. ARC. F in wrps. B2. $25.00.

PIERCY, Marge. *Summer People.* 1989. NY. Summit. 1st. F/F. H11. $30.00.

PIERSON, Robert L. *Riots Chicago Style.* 1984. Great Neck. Todd & Honeywell. 1st. sgn by author. F/F. B2. $35.00.

PIKE, Christopher. *Road to Nowhere.* 1993. Archway Paperback. G. A28. $1.95.

PILCHER, Rosamunde. *The Shell Seekers.* (1988). NY. St. Martin. 1st. NF. slight bumps/F. B3. $20.00.

PILKINGTON, James. *The Artist's Guide and Mechanic's Own Book...A Variety of Useful Receipts, Extending to Every Profession and Occupation of Life.* NY. Alexander V. Blake. 1843. 12mo. 492. (36)p. illus. full calf. later printing (copyright 1841). calf very worn & rubbed. leather at top of spine torn. relatively minor damp stain. soiling. fair to G. L5. $30.00.

PINA CHAN, Roman. *The Olmec, Mother Culture of Mesoamerica.* 1989. NY. Rizzoli. 1st. sm folio. color & b/w photos. maps. 240p. G/G. F3. $85.00.

PINEDA, Ceceil. *The Love Queen of the Amazon.* 1992. Boston. Little, Brn. 1st. UP. F. D10. $10.00.

PINTER, Harold. *Mountain Language.* 1989. NY. Grove Press. true 1st ed. F/F. D10. $35.00.

PINTER, Harold. *The French Lieutenant's Woman.* 1981. Boston. Little, Brn. 1st. top edges lightly foxed. F/VF. H11. $35.00.

PINTER, Harold. *The Hothouse.* 1980. NY. Grove Press. 1st Am ed. F/F. D10. $45.00.

PIOUS, Richard M. *Richard Nixon: A Political Life.* 1991. NJ. Julian Messner. 1st. VG. no dj as issued. A28. $9.95.

PIPER, H. Beam. *Murder in the Gunroom.* 1953. NY. Knopf. 1st. F in VG dj. B2. $150.00.

PIVER, Steven M. with Gene Wilder. *Gilda's Disease, Sharing Personal Experiences and a Medical Perspective on Ovarian Cancer.* 1996. NY. Prometheus Books. VG/VG. A28. $9.95.

PLATH, Sylvia. *The Bell Jar.* nd. np. Harper & Row. 1st. prev inscr. VG/NF dj. M19. $75.00.

PLATH, Sylvia. *Winter Trees.* 1971. Faber. 1st. VG+/F. edges of book rubbed. M25. $75.00.

PLENN, Abel. *The Southern Americas, A New Chronicle.* 1948. NY. Creative Age Press. 1st. 455p. G/chipped dj. F3. $15.00.

PLIMPTON, George. *The Curious Case of Sidd Finch.* 1987. NY. Macmillan. 1st. jacket Is price clipped. VF/VF. H11. $25.00.

PODRUG, Junius. *Frost of Heaven.* 1992. Arlington Heights. Dark Harvest. 1st. sgn. author's 1st novel. VF/VF. T2. $25.00.

POHL, Frederick. *Midas World.* 1983. NY. St. Martin. 1st. sgn. F/F. closed tears. T2. $25.00.

POLLACK, Rachel. *Temporary Agency.* 1994. NY. St. Martin. sgn 1st ed. Nebula Award finalist. F/F. M23. $40.00.

POLLAK, J. C. *Crossfire.* 1985. NY. Crown. 1st. VF/F. H11. $20.00.

POLLARD, Edward Alfred. *Southern History of the War, Two Volumes in One.* 1866. NY. Charles R. Richardson. 1st. thus. orig cloth. minor wear to extremities. 20 plates of Confederate generals. 1258p. VG. M8. $150.00.

POND, Jonathan D. *1001 Ways to Cut Your Expenses.* 1992. NY. Dell. hb. NF/NF. A28. $6.95.

PONS, Maurice. *The Seasons of the Ram.* 1977. St. Martin. ne. trans by Frances Frenaye. F/G. S19. $25.00.

PONSOT, Georges. *The Romance of the River.* 1924. NY. Dodd, Mead. 8vo. ils by E. J. Detmold. gr cloth w/gilt. 290p. VG. D6. $20.00.

POOLE, Ernest. *Great Winds.* 1933. np. Macmillan. 1st. NF/VG dj. M19. $25.00.

POOLE, Ernest. *The Hunter's Moon.* 1925. np. Macmillan. 1st. NF/G dj. M19. $35.00.

POPE, Dudley. *Buccaneer.* 1981. London. Secker & Warburg. 1st. F/dj. M15. $45.00.

POPE, Dudley. *Corsair.* 1987. London. Secker & Warburg. 1st. F/dj. M15. $45.00.

POPKIN, Michael, editor. *Modern Black Writers.* 1978. Ungar. later printing. NF/torn dj. M25. $35.00.

PORT, Weimar. *Chicago the Pagan.* 1953. Chicago. Judy Publishing Co. 1st. orange cloth. VG. B2. $45.00.

PORTER, Connie. *All Bright Court.* 1991. Boston. Houghton Mifflin. 1st. author's 1st novel. F/F. A24. $35.00.

PORTER, Eliot. *Nature's Chaos.* (1990). NY. Viking. 1st. text by James Gleick. photography. F/F. B3. $30.00.

PORTER, Elizabeth & Ellen Auerbach. *Mexican Celebrations.* 1990. Albuquerque. Univ. of New Mexico Press. 1st. sq 4to. 115p w/90 color plates. F3. $40.00.

PORTER, Joyce. *Dover Three.* 1966. NY. Scribner's. 1st Am ed. F/F. B2. $25.00.

PORTER, Katherine Anne. *The Never-Ending Wrong.* 1977. Boston. Atlantic/Little, Brn. 1st. F/F. minor edgewear. A24. $28.00.

PORTER, Lewis. *Lester Young.* 1985. NY. Twayne. 1st. inscr by author. F in lightly chip dj. B2. $65.00.

POST, Charles. *The Cuyahoga, The Crooked River that Made a City Great.* 1941. np. privately printed. photos and maps. wrps. 44p. VG. B18. $22.50.

POST, Melville Davisson. *The Methods of Uncle Abner.* 1974. Boulder. Aspen. 1st. VF in dj. M15. $45.00.

POSTGATE, Raymond. *The Ledger Is Kept.* 1953. London. Michael Joseph. 1st. F/dj. M15. $65.00.

POSTMA, C. *Plant Marvels in Miniature. A Photographic Study.* 1961. NY. Folio. VG in dj. B26. $17.50.

POTOK, Chaim. *The Book of Lights.* 1982. Fawcett Crest. pb. VG. F6. $1.15.

POTT, William H. *Stories from Dream Land.* 1900. NY. James Pott & Co. 1st. sm 8vo. ils by George W. Bardwell. 206. NF. D6. $20.00.

POTTER, Beatrix. *The Tale of Benjamin Bunny.* nd. NY. Avenel Books. F in F dj. A16. $12.00.

POTTER, Beatrix. *The Tale of Mrs. Tiggy Winkle.* 1992. NY. Derrydale Books. VG in dj. A16. $10.00.

POTTER, Beatrix. *The Tale of Squirrel Nutkin.* nd. NY. Avenel Books. F in F dj. A16. $12.00.

POTTINGER, Stanley. *The Fourth Procedure.* 1995. np. Ballantine. 1st. author's 1st novel. NF/NF-. R16. $40.00.

POTTLE, Frederick A. *Pride & Negligence: History of the Boswell Papers.* 1982. McGraw Hill. 1st. 8vo. 290p. linen spine/gray brd. F/dj. H13. $85.00.

POTTLE & WIMSATT. *Boswell for the Defense, 1769 – 1744.* 1959. McGraw Hill. 1st. fld map/ils. NF. H13. $85.00.

POURADE, Richard. *Silver Dons, Volume Three, History of San Diego.* 1963. San Diego. Union-Tribune. special ed. sgn. case. w/ephemera. P4. $60.00.

POVERMAN, C. E. *On the Edge.* 1997. Princeton. Ontario Review Press. 1st. sgn. VF/VF. T2. $25.00.

POVERMAN, C. E. *Skin.* 1992. Princeton. Ontario Review Press. 1st. sgn. VF/VF. T2. $25.00.

POWELL, Anthony. *Soldier's Art.* 1966. Little, Brn. 1st Am. F/dj. Q1. $40.00.

POWELL, Edward Alexander. *By Camel & Car to the Peacock Throne.* 1923. NY. Century. 1st. sm 8vo. 392p. VG+. M7. $35.00.

POWELL, El Sea. *Sea as Seen by El Sea Powell.* 1962. Malibu. Dawson/Cheney. mini. 1/200. sgn. 8p. Bela Blau bdg. F/dj. B24. $85.00.

POWELL, Hickman. *Lucky Luciano.* 1975. Secaucus. Citadel. 1st. VG/dj. B5. $15.00.

POWELL, Ivor. *This I Believe: The Essential Truths in Christianity.* 1961. Zondervan. 222p. VG/VG. B29. $7.50.

POWELL, J. W. *Report on Lands of the Arid Region of the US: Lands of UT.* 1879. GPO. 2nd. 4to. 3 maps. rb orig brd/spine. new ep. VG. F7. $225.00.

POWELL, Richard. *Tickets to the Devil.* 1968. NY. Scribner's. 1st. G/VG. G8. $10.00.

POWER, Susan. *The Grass Dancer.* 1994. NY. Putnam. 1st. author's 1st book. F/F. D10. $40.00.

POWERS, Edwin. *Crime & Punishment in Early Massachusetts 1620 – 1692.* 1966. Boston. VG/dj. M17. $30.00.

POWERS, R. *Far From Home: Life & Loss in Two American Towns.* 1991. NY. 1st. F/dj. M4. $15.00.

POWERS, Richard. *Prisoner's Dilemma.* 1988. Morrow. 1st. author's 2nd book. F/VG. B3. $75.00.

POWERS, Richard. *The Gold Bug Variations.* 1991. NY. Morrow. 1st. F/F. O11. $100.00.

POWERS, Ron. *Toot Toot Tootsie Goodbye.* 1981. Delacorte. 1st. F/dj. P8. $15.00.

POWERS, Susan. *Grass Dancer.* 1994. Putnam. 1st. sgn. author's 1st book. F/dj. A24. $35.00.

POWERS, Tim. *Last Call.* 1992. NY. Morrow. 1st. sgn. VF/VF. T2. $65.00.

POWTER, Susan. *Stop the Insanity!* nd. NY. S&S. VG/VG. A28. $9.95.

POWYS, John Cowper. *Three Fantasies.* 1985. Manchester. Carcanet Press. 1st. VF/VF. T2. $20.00.

PRADO, Benjamin. *Never Shake Hands with a Left-Handed Gunman.* 1999. NY. St. Martin. ARC. F/wrps. B2. $25.00.

PRANTERA, Amanda. *The Cabalist.* 1986. NY. Atheneum. 1st. F/F. M23. $20.00.

PRATCHETT, Terry. *A Tourist Guide to Lancre: A Discworld Mapp.* 1998. London. Corgi Books. 1st printing. VF book & map in pict wrp. T2. $15.00.

PRATCHETT, Terry. *Carpe Jugulum.* 1998. London. Doubleday. 1st. VF/VF. T2. $38.00.

PRATCHETT, Terry. *Jingo.* 1997. London. Gollancz. 1st. VF/VF. T2. $38.00.

PRATSON, F. *Land of the Four Directions.* 1970. Old Greenwich. Chatham Press. 1st. oblong 8vo. F. owner's name/VG. B2. $30.00.

PRATT, Fletcher. *Stanton Lincoln's Secretary of War.* 1953. NY. Norton. 1st. orig cloth. 520p. VG/VG. M8. $35.00.

PRATT, Kristin Joy. *Walk in the Rain Forest.* 1992. CA. Dawn Pub. 1st. 30p. NF/dj. T5. $30.00.

PRATT, Mayans, Miguel & Carlos Pusineri Scala. *Paraguay Paper Money.* 1990. Paraguay. Catalogo. 1st. Eng/Spanish. 162p. G. wrp. F3. $10.00.

PRAWER, J. *World of the Crusaders.* 1972. Weidenfeld Nicolson. ils/3 maps. gilt cloth. VG. Q2. $18.00.

PREJEAN, Helen. *Dead Man Walking: An Eyewitness Account.* 1993. Random. 1st. rem mk. F/dj. B4. $85.00.

PRELUTSKY, Jack. *Beneath a Blue Umbrella.* 1990. NY. Greenwillow. 1st. ils. F/dj. D4. $30.00.

PRENTICE, Helaine K. *The Gardens of Southern California.* 1990. San Francisco. over 200 color photos by Melba Levick. AN. B26. $29.00.

PRESCOTT, H. F. M. *Lost Fight.* 1956. NY. VG/dj. M17. $15.00.

PRESCOTT, Samuel. *When MIT Was Boston Tech 1861 – 1916.* 1954. Cambridge. 1st. 350p. VG/G. B5. $25.00.

PRESCOTT, William H. *Conquest of Mexico.* 1981. McKay. 3 vol. rpt. 12mo. gr cloth. G. S17. $7.50.

PRESS, Margaret. *Elegy for a Thief.* 1993. NY. Carroll & Graf. 1st. F/F. H11. $20.00.

PRESS, Margaret. *Requiem for a Postman.* 1992. NY. Carroll & Graf. 1st. VF/F. H11. $30.00.

PRESTON, Douglas. *Riptide.* 1998. NY. Warner. 1st. F-/VF. H11. $15.00.

PRESTON, J. H. *Gentleman Rebel: Mad Anthony Wayne.* 1930. Garden City. ils. 370p. G. M4. $20.00.

PRESTON, Jennifer. *Queen Bess: Unauthorized Biography of Bess Myerson.* 1990. Contemporary Books. 1st. F/dj. W2. $30.00.

PRESTON, Richard J. *Rocky Mountain Trees.* 1947 (1940). Ames. 2nd. ils/maps. 285p. VG. B26. $17.50.

PRICE, Alfred. *Battle of Britain.* 1980. Scribner. BC. 12mo. photos. 246p. VG/dj. M7. $15.00.

PRICE, Anthony. *Memory Trap.* 1989. London. Gollancz. 1st. F/dj. M15. $45.00.

PRICE, Byron. *Cowboys of the American West.* 1996. Thunder Bay. 205p. VG. J2. $65.00.

PRICE, D. J. *Equatorie of the Planetis.* 1955. Cambridge. 4to. pl. 214p. dj. K5. $65.00.

PRICE, Eugenia. *Beauty from the Ashes.* 1995. Doubleday. 1st. F/dj. B30. $24.00.

PRICE, Eugenia. *New Moon Rising.* 1969. Lippincott. 1st. 281p. VG/worn dj. B29. $12.00.

PRICE, George F. *Across the Continent with the Fifth Cavalry.* 1959. Antiquarian. 1/750. 706p. NF. B19. $35.00.

PRICE, Margaret Evans. *Hansel and Gretel.* 1916. NY. Stecher Lithographic Co. wrp. VG. A16. $120.00.

PRICE, Nancy. *Sleeping with the Enemy.* 1987. NY. S&S. 1st. F/F. H11. $40.00.

PRICE, Reynolds. *Clear Pictures.* (1989). NY. Atheneum. 1st. sgn by author. F/F. B3. $60.00.

PRICE, Reynolds. *Good Hearts.* (1988). NY. Atheneum. 1st. F/F. B3. $25.00.

PRICE, Reynolds. *The Promise of Rest.* 1995. NY. Scribner's. sgn 1st ed. F/F. M23. $50.00.

PRICE, Richard. *Clockers.* 1992. Boston. Houghton. 1st. F/F. H11. $40.00.

PRICE, Richard. *Freedomland.* 1998. NY. Broadway. 1st. VF/VF. H11. $20.00.

PRICE, Sammy. *What Do They Want? A Jazz Autobiography.* 1990. Urbana. Univ. of Illinois Press. 1st. OP. F/F. B2. $25.00.

PRIEST, Christopher. *An Infinite Summer.* 1979. NY. Scribners. 1st. Book has shelf wear and bumped spine ends. Jacket has crease on front flap. NF/F. H11. $15.00.

PRIEST, John Michael. *Captain James Wren's Diary: From New Bern to Fredricksburg.* 1990. Wht. Mane Pub. 1st. F/dj. A14. $25.00.

PRIESTLEY, J. B. *Three Men in New Suits.* 1945. London. Heinemann. 1st. NF/dj. A24. $30.00.

PRIHARA, Maria. *Cossack Holota: Stories Based on Ancient Ukrainian Ballads.* 1985. Biev. ils Heorhiy Yakutovich. trans Mary Skrypnyk. VG. M17. $20.00.

PRINCE, Leslie B. *The Farrier and His Craft; The History of the Worshipful Company of Farriers.* 1980. London. Allen. 1st prt. VG. O3. $35.00.

PRINCE, Morton. *Dissociation of a Personality: Biographical Study.* 1992. NY. Classics of Psychiatry & Behavioral Sciences Lib. F. G1. $75.00.

PRINGLE, David. *Ultimate Guide to Science Fiction.* 1990. NY. Pharos. 1st thus. F/wrp. G10. $15.00.

PRINGLE, Terry. *The Preacher's Boy.* 1988. Chapel Hill. Algonquin. 1st. author's 1st novel. F/F. D10. $40.00.

PRINGLE, Terry. *Tycoon.* 1990. Chapel Hill. Algonquin. F/F. H11. $25.00.

PRITCHARD, Alan. *Alchemy: Bibliography of English-Language Writings.* 1980. London. 1st. 439p. dj. A13. $150.00.

PRITCHARD, James. *Archaeology & the Old Testament.* 1958. Princeton. 263p. VG/dj. B29. $17.00.

PROCTOR, Mary. *Romance of the Planets.* 1929. NY. Harper. 8vo. 272p. VG/dj. K5. $30.00.

PROCTOR, Richard A. *Half Hours with the Telescope.* 1889 (1868). London. WH Allen. 10th. ils. 109p. gilt cloth. K5. $70.00.

PROCTOR, Richard A. *Spectroscope & Its Work.* 1877. London. 128p. cloth. VG. K5. $45.00.

PROKOSCH, Frederic. *Death at Sea.* 1940. np. Harper. 1st. F/VG dj. M19. $35.00.

PROKSCH, J. K. *Geschichte Der Geschlechtskrankheiten.* 1910. Vienna. 1st. 140p. A13. $50.00.

PRONZINI, Bill. *Breakdown.* 1991. NY. Delacorte. 1st. VF/F. T2. $14.00.

PRONZINI, Bill. *Epitaphs.* (1992). NY. Delacorte. 1st. sgn by the author. F/F. B3. $40.00.

PRONZINI, Bill. *Invitation to Murder.* 1991. Arlington Heights. Dark Harvest. 1st. VF in dj. M15. $45.00.

PRONZINI, Bill. *Jackpot.* (1990). NY. Delacorte. 1st. F/F. B3. $25.00.

PRONZINI, Bill. *Masques.* 1981. NY. Arbor House. 1st. F/F. T2. $15.00.

PRONZINI, Bill. *Nightshades.* 1984. NY. St. Martin. 1st. F/F. T2. $15.00.

PRONZINI, Bill. *Quarry.* (1992). NY. Delacorte. 1st. F/F. B3. $30.00.

PRONZINI, Bill. *Starvation Camp.* 1984. Doubleday. 1st. F/dj. M15. $75.00.

PROSKE, Beatrice G. *Brookgreen Gardens: Sculpture.* 1943. Brookgreen, SC. VG. B26. $17.50.

PROSKOURIAKOFF, Tatiana. *An Album of Maya Architecture.* 1983. Norman. Univ. of Oklahoma Press. 1st. wrp. 142p. G. F3. $20.00.

PROULX, E. Annie. *Accordion Crimes.* 1982. NY. Scribner's. 1st. sgn. F/F. O11. $55.00.

PROULX, E. Annie. *Heart Songs.* (1995). NY. Scribner's. 1st Am ed. sgn by the author. unread copy. outstanding. VF/VF. B3. $600.00.

PROUST, Marcel. *Letters of Marcel Proust.* 1949. NY. Random House. 1st. trans/ed Mina Curtiss. F/VG. B2. $35.00.

PROUST, Marcel. *Selected Letters, Vol. 2 1904 – 09.* 1989. NY. 1st. trans T Kilmartin. edit P Kolb. dj. T9. $15.00.

PROUTY, Amy. *Mexico and I.* 1951. Philadelphia. Dorrance. 1st. 258p. G. F3. $15.00.

PROVENSEN, Alice & Martin. *An Owl and Three Pussycats.* 1981. NY. Atheneum. 1st Am ed. ils by authors. 4to. bl cloth w/bl lettering. color ils dj different. 32p. NF/NF. D6. $40.00.

PROWELL, Sandra West. *By Evil Means.* 1993. NY. Walker. 1st. author's 1st book. F/F. O11. $125.00.

PROWELL, Sandra West. *The Killing of Monday Brown.* 1994. NY. Walker. 1st. sgn. VF/VF. T2. $30.00.

PROWELL, Sandra West. *When Wallflowers Die.* 1996. NY. Walker. 1st. sgn. VF/VF. T2. $25.00.

PRUDHOMME, Paul. *Chef Paul Prudhomme's Louisiana Kitchen.* 1984. photos. F/F. E6. $12.00.

PRYOR, Larry. *The Viper.* 1978. NY. Harper & Row. 1st. author's 1st book. F/F. H11. $30.00.

PUGMIRE, W. H. *Tales of Sesqua Valley.* 1997. Westborough. Necropolitan Press. 1st. VF/pict wrp. T2. $5.00.

PUHARICH, Andrija. *Sacred Mushroom: Key to the Door of Eternity.* 1959. Garden City. 1st. 262p. A13. $20.00.

PUHARICH, Andrija. *Uri: A Journal of the Mystery of Uri Geller.* 1974. NY. Anchor. 1st. NF/dj. H11. $20.00.

PUIG, Manuel. *Eternal Curse on the Reader of These Pages.* 1992. Random. 1st. VG/dj. B30. $22.50.

PUIG, Manuel. *Heartbreak Tango.* 1973. NY. Dutton. 1st. F in F dj. B2. $25.00.

PUJOL, Valero. *Compendio De La Historia Universal.* 1879. Guatemala. Tercera Parte. Edad Moderna. 560p. G/wrp. F3. $65.00.

PULLEN, H. F. *Atlantic Schooners.* 1967. Brunswick. 1st Canadian. F/sans. T12. $15.00.

PULSFORD, Petronella. *Lee's Ghost.* 1990. London. Constable. 1st. F/dj. G10. $22.00.

PUNSHON, E. R. *Conqueror Inn.* nd. Gollancz. 5th British. VG. G8. $15.00.

PUNSHON, E. R. *So Many Doors.* 1949. Macmillan. 1st Am ed. VG. G8. $15.00.

PURDY, James. *Color of Darkness.* 1957. New Directions. 1st. sgn. VG/dj. R14. $50.00.

PURDY, James. *Day After the Fair.* 1977. NY. Note of Hand. 1st. sgn. F/NF. R14. $40.00.

PURDY, James. *Dream Palaces.* 1980. NY. Viking. 1st. Jacket has creases on front flap. F/F. H11. $30.00.

PURDY, John C. *Parables at Work.* 1985. Westminster. 132p. VG/VG. B29. $5.00.

PURI, A. N. *Soils: Their Physics & Chemistry.* 1949. Reinhold. 550p. xl. G. S5. $12.00.

PUSATERI, Samuel J. *Flora of Our Sierran National Parks — Yosemite, Sequoia and Kings Canyon (Including Many Valley and Foothill Plants).* 1963. Three Rivers. VG in chip dj. B26. $34.00.

PUTNAM, James Jackson. *A Memoir of Dr. James Jackson with Sketches of His Father Hon. Jonathan Jackson, and His Brothers Robert, Henry, Charles, and Patrick Tracy Jackson; and Some Account of their Ancestry.* Boston and NY. Houghton, Mifflin and Company. 1905. 8vo. 456p. ils. gr cloth. 1st ed. Very minor wear. VG. L5. $50.00.

PUZO, Mario. *Fools Die.* 1978. NY. Putnam. 1st. F/F. H11. $40.00.

PUZO, Mario. *The Dark Arena.* 1955. NY. Random. 1st. author's 1st book. Jacket spine Is slightly faded. F/F. H11. $130.00.

PUZO, Mario. *The Fourth K.* 1990. NY. Random. 1st. F/F. H11. $25.00.

PUZO, Mario. *The Last Don.* 1996. NY. Random House. 1st. NF/VG+. R16. $40.00.

PYLE, A. M. *Murder Moves in.* 1986. Walker. 1st. NF/NF. G8. $15.00.

PYLE, A. M. *Trouble Making Toys.* 1985. Walker. 1st. F/F. G8. $15.00.

PYLE, Howard. *Howard Pyle's Book of Pirates.* 1921. NY. Harper. later issue. folio. 36 pl. 246p. teg. F. H5. $500.00.

PYLE, Howard. *Otto of the Silver Hand.* 1888. Scribner. 1st. lg 8vo. new leather spine. VG. M5. $245.00.

PYLE, Robert Michael. *Audubon Society Handbook for Butterfly Watchers.* 1984. NY. 1st. ils. VG/dj. M17. $15.00.

PYLE, Robert Michael. *Thunder Tree: Lessons from an Urban Wildland.* 1993. Houghton Mifflin. 1st. 220p. S15. $9.00.

PYNCHON, Thomas. *Mason and Dixon.* 1997. Henry Holt. ARC. F/WRP. M25. $200.00.

PYNCHON, Thomas. *The Crying of Lot 49.* 1966. Philadelphia. Lippincott. 1st. VG+ lt soiling. no dj. D10. $125.00.

PYNCHON, Thomas. *Vineland.* 1990. Boston. Little, Brn. 1st. VF/VF. H11. $40.00.

PYRNELLE, Louise Clarde. *Miss Lil Tweety.* 1918. NY. Harper. 1st. ils by Wm Mead Prince. 255p. VG. minor rubbing. D6. $45.00.

— Q —

QUACKENBOS, John D. *Geological Ancestors of the Brook Trout.* 1916. NY Anglers Club. 1st. inscr. 10 pl. 50 p.

QUAIFE, Milo. *Absolom Grimes: Confederate Mail Runner.* 1926. Yale. 1st. xl. VG. E6. $30.00.

QUAIFE, Milo. *Chicago's Highways Old & New.* 1923. Chicago. DF Keller. 1st. ils/fld map. 278p. G. B18. $25.00.

QUAIFE, Milo. *Pictures of Gold Rush California.* 1949. Lakeside Classic. 1st thus. teg. dk red cloth. VG/sans. T11. $35.00.

QUAMMEN, David. *Natural Acts.* 1985. NY. Lyons. 1st. F/NF. B3. $50.00.

QUAMMEN, David. *Song of the Dodo: Island Biogeography in Age Extinctions.* 1996. Scribner. 702p. xl. VG. S5. $20.00.

QUAMMEN, David. *Soul of Victor Tronko.* 1987. NY. Doubleday. 1st. sgn. F/NF. B3. $40.00.

QUAMMEN, David. *To Walk the Line.* 1970. NY. Knopf. 1st. 1/225. sgn. author's 1st book. F/F. $3.00.

QUANTIC, Diane Dufva. *Nature of the Place: A Study of Great Plains Fiction.* 1995. NE U. 1st. M/dj. A18. $25.00.

QUARLES, Benjamin. *Frederick Douglass.* 1948. Washington, DC. Assoc Pub. 1st. F/NF clip. B4. $185.00.

QUARLES, E. A. *American Pheasant Breeding & Shooting.* 1916. Wilmington, DE. Hercules Powder. 1st. ils. 132+8P.

QUARLES, Garland R. *Some Worthy Lives: Mini-Biographies.* 1988. Winchester-Frederick Co Hist. Soc. 280p. AN. B10. $25.00.

QUARRINGTON, Paul. *Home Game.* 1983. Canada. Doubleday. 1st. VG/dj. P8. $30.00.

QUARRY, Nick; see Albert, Marvin H.

QUASHA, George. *Somapoetics.* 1973. Fremont. Sumac. 1st. 1/1000. inscr. NF. L3. $35.00.

QUAYLE, Eric. *Magic Ointment & Other Cornish Legends.* 1986. London. Andersen. 1st. 108p. F/sans. D4. $30.00.

QUAYLE, Eric. *Shining Princess.* 1989. Arcade. 1st. 8vo. ils Michael Forman. VG/dj. B17. $15.00.

QUAYLE, Eric. *The Collector's Book of Books.* 1971. NY. Clarkson N. Potter Inc. 4to. navy cloth w/gilt lettering. 144p. VG/NF. D6. $45.00.

QUEEN, Ellery. *Ellery Queen's Aces of Mystery.* 1975. NY. Dial. 1st. 8vo. cloth. F/dj. O10. $17.00.

QUEEN, Ellery. *Ellery Queen's Bureau of Investigation.* 1954. Little, Brn. 1st. F/clip. M15. $45.00.

QUEEN, Ellery. *Ellery Queen's Champions of Mystery.* 1977. Dial. 1st. F/F. N4. $25.00.

QUEEN, Ellery. *Ellery Queen's Circumstantial Evidence.* 1980. Dial. 1st. VG/dj. P3. $16.00.

QUEEN, Ellery. *Ellery Queen's Doors to Mystery.* 1981. Dial. 1st. VG/dj. P3. $15.00.

QUEEN, Ellery. *Literature of Crime.* 1950. Little, Brn. 1st. F/G. M19. $25.00.

QUEEN, Ellery. *The King Is Dead.* 1952. Little, Brn. 1st. G+. S19. $40.00.

QUEEN, Ellery. *To the Queen's Taste.* 1946. Little, Brn. 1st. VG. P3. $30.00.

QUEKETT, John. *Lectures on Histology.* 1852. London. 1st. 215p. A13. $75.00.

QUENNELL, Peter. *Mayhew's Characters.* nd. London. Spring Books. 360p. cloth. VG/dj. M20. $15.00.

QUENNELL, Peter. *Prodical Rake: Memoirs of William Hickey.* 1962. Dutton. 1st/3rd prt. 8vo. 452p. VG. W2. $12.00.

QUENNELL, Peter. *Shakespeare.* 1963. World. 1st. 8vo. 352p. rust cloth. F/VG. H1. $12.00.

QUENTIN , Patrick. *Puzzle for Fiends.* 1946. NY. S&S. 1st. F/NF. M15. $45.00.

QUENZEL, Carrol H. *Belmont.* 1960. Mary WA College. VG. B10. $5.00.

QUERRY, Ron. *Bad Medicine.* 1998. NY. Bantam. 1st. sgn. VF/VF. T2. $25.00.

QUERRY, Ron. *The Death of Bernadette Lefthand.* 1993. Santa Fe. Red Crane Books. 1st. sgn. author's 1st novel. VF/VF. T2. $90.00.

QUERRY, Ronald B. *Growing Old at Willie Nelson's Picnic.* 1983. TX A&M. 1st. sgn. F/F. B3. $75.00.

QUICK, Armand. *Physiology & Pathology of Hemostasis.* 1951. Phil. 1st. 188p. A13. $75.00.

QUICK, Arthur C. *Wild Flowers of the Northern States and Canada.* 1939. Chicago. foreword by L. H. Bailey. ep tanned. else VG. B26. $24.00.

QUICK, Herbert. *Brown Mouse.* 1915. Bobbs Merrill. 1st. ils JA Coughlin. 310p. G. G11. $12.00.

QUICK, Herbert. *Invisible Woman.* 1924. Bobbs Merrill. 1st. F/VG. A18. $30.00.

QUICK, Jim. *Fishing the Nymph.* 1960. Ronald. G. A19. $25.00.

QUIGLEY, Martin. *Original Colored House of David.* 1981. Houghton Mifflin. 1st. F/VG. P8. $30.00.

QUIGLEY, Martin. *Today's Game.* 1965. Viking. 1st. 176p. VG+/dj. B18. $22.50.

QUILL, Monica. *The Veil of Ignorance.* 1988. NY. St. Martin. 1st. VF/dj. M15. $35.00.

QUILLER-COUCH, Arthur. *New Oxford Book of English Verse.* 1961. OUP. new ed. sm 8vo. 1166p. F/VG. W2. $360.00.

QUIN, Bernetta. *Introduction to the Poetry of Ezra Pound.* 1972. Columbia. 1st. F/VG+. V1. $15.00.

QUINCY, Josiah. *Essays on the Soiling of Cattle.* 1866. Boston. Williams. 121p. cloth. A10. $35.00.

QUINCY, Josiah. *Memoir of the Life of John Quincy Adams.* 1858. Boston. Philips Sampson. 429p. VG. B14. $99.00.

QUINCY, William S. *Three-Masted Schooner James Miller.* 1986. Mystic Seaport Mus. ils/3 fld plans. 48p. wrp. T7. $17.00.

QUINDLEN, Anna. *Black and Blue.* (1998). NY. Random. 1st. inscr by author. F/F. B3. $60.00.

QUINDLEN, Anna. *Object Lessons.* (1991). NY. Random House. 1st. author's 1st novel. F/F. B3. $50.00.

QUINN, Dan; see Lewis, Alfred Henry.

QUINN, David. *North America from Earliest Discovery to First Settlements.* 1977. Harper Row. New Am Nation series. 1st. 81 ils/maps. F/dj. O7. $45.00.

QUINN, David. *Roanoke Voyages 1584 – 1590.* 1955. London. Hakluyt Soc. 1st. 2 vol. 8vo. gilt bl cloth. NF. P4. $165.00.

QUINN, P. T. *Pear Culture For Profit.* 1869. NY. Tribune. 136p. A10. $38.00.

QUINN, Seabury. *Phantom-Fighter.* 1966. Arkham. 1st. VG/dj. P3. $60.00.

QUINN, Vernon. *Leaves: Their Place in Life & Legend.* 1937. NY. Stokes. 211p. VG. A10. $32.00.

QUINTANILLA, Luis. *Franco's Black Spain.* 1946. Reynal Hitchcock. 1st. 4to. VG/VG. B2. $85.00.

QUIRK, Joe. *The Ultimate Rush.* 1998. NY. Rob Weisbach Books/ Morrow. 1st. author's 1st novel. sgn. VF/VF. T2. $25.00.

QUIRK, John. *Hard Winners.* 1965. Random. 1st. VG/VG. P3. $22.00.

QUISUMBING, E. A. *Complete Writings Of… On Philippine Orchids.* 1981. Manila. 2 vol. ils/pl. edit HI Valmayor. AN. B26. $45.00.

QUOGAN, Anthony. *Fine Art of Murder.* 1988. St. Martin. 1st. VG/VG. P3. $16.00.

— R —

RABAN, Jonathan. *Coasting.* 1986. London. Collins Harvill. 1st. NF/dj. A14. $28.00.

RABASA, George. *Floating Kingdom.* (1997). Minneapolis. Coffee House Press. 1st. author's first novel. sgn by author. F/ F. B3. $35.00.

RABB, Kate Milner. *Tour Through Indiana in 1840: Diary of John Parsons.* 1920. NY. McBride. 1st. 391p. VG. $7.00.

RABBITT, Mary C. *Colorado River Region & John Wesley Powell.* 1969. GPO. 1st. ils. NF. B19. $50.00.

RABI, S. S. *Boatbuilding in Your Own Backyard.* 1958. Cambridge, MA. Cornell Maritime. 2nd. 223p. T7. $30.00.

RABINOWICZ, Oskar K. *Winston Churchill on Jewish Problems.* 1960. Yoseloff. 231p. VG+/G. S3. $26.00.

RABKIN, Eric S. *Fantastic Worlds.* 1979. Oxford. 1st. VG/dj. P3. $20.00.

RACINA, Thom. *Hidden Agenda.* 1999. NY. Dutton. 1st. VG+/VG+. G8. $10.00.

RACKHAM, Arthur. *Peter Pan Portfolio.* 1912. London. Hodder Stoughton. 1/500. sgns. 12 mtd pl. half vellum/gr cloth. F. $24.00.

RACKHAM, Arthur. *Some British Ballads.* 1919. London. Constable. 1st. 1/575. sgn. 170p. teg. gilt bdg. case. B24. $1.800.00.

RACKHAM, Arthur. *Vicar of Wakefield.* 1929. London. Harrap. 1st. 12 mc pl. VG/dj. B5. $150.00.

RACKHAM, Bernard. *Guide to Collections of Stained Glass.* Victoria/Albert Mus. 1936. London. 62 pl. bl cloth. VG. $14.00.

RACKHAM, John. *Time to Live.* 1969. Lodnon. 1st. NF/dj. M2. $20.00.

RADER, Dotson. *Tennessee: Cry of the Heart.* 1985. Doubleday. 1st. VG/dj. M20. $15.00.

RADIGUET, Raymond. *Devil in the Flesh.* 1948. Blk Sun. 1st thus. trans Kay Boyle. VG/VG. M22. $35.00.

RADIN, Max. *Day of Reckoning.* 1943. Knopf. VG/dj. M11. $75.00.

RADIN, Paul. *Story of the American Indian.* 1937. Garden City. 383p. F3. $15.00.

RADL, Emanuel. *History of Biological Theories.* 1930. Oxford. 408p. xl. VG. S5. $45.00.

RADLEY, Sheila. *Cross My Heart & Hope to Die.* 1992. NY. Scribners. 1st. F/F. H11. $15.00.

RADOFF, Morris L. *Buildings of the State of Maryland at Annapolis.* 1954. Hall of Records Comm. ils/plans. 173p. VG. B10. $45.00.

RAE, Hugh C. *Harkfast: Making of a King.* 1976. St. Martin. 1st. NF/dj. M21. $35.00.

RAEDER, Erich. *My Life.* 1960. Annapolis. 1st. VG/VG. B5. $50.00.

RAEPER, William. *George MacDonald.* (1987). Lion. 1st Eng. photos/notes. AN/dj. A27. $27.00.

RAFFELOCK, David. *Echo Anthology of Verse.* (1927). Denver. Echo. 1st. 1/350. fancy brd. VG. A18. $20.00.

RAFIZADEH, Mansur. *Witness: From the Shah to the Secret Arms Deal.* 1987. Morrow. 1st. 8vo. ils. 396p. VG/dj. W1. $18.00.

RAGEN, Naomi. *Jephte's Daughter.* 1989. NY. Warner. 1st. author's 1st novel. F/F. M23. $25.00.

RAGLAND, J. Farley. *Little Slice of Living.* 1953. Richmond. Quality Pr. 1st. inscr. F/prt wrp. B4. $175.00.

RAIDL, R. R. & D. R. Leslie. *Nazi Daggers and Dress Bayonets.* 1959. Cleveland, OH. R & L Enterprises. wrp. ils. 60p. VG. B18. $22.50.

RAIGERSFELD, Jeffrey. *Life of a Sea Officer.* 1929. London. Cassell. 8 pl. 210p. T7. $60.00.

RAIM, Ethel. *Freedom Is a Constant Struggle: Songs of Freedom Movement.* 1968. Oak Pub. 2nd. VG/VG. V4. $20.00.

RAINE, James. *Wills & Inventories Illustrative of History, Manners.* 1835. London. 1/400. gilt olive cloth. M11. $150.00.

RAINE, William McLeod. *Justice Comes to Tomahawk.* 1952. Houghton Mifflin. 1st. F/VG. B4. $200.00.

RAINGER, Ronald. *Agenda for Antiquity.* 1991. AL U. 360p. F/F. S15. $13.50.

RAINS, Mane. *Lazy Liza Lizard.* 1938. Winston. 1st. sgn. ils V Neville. 184p. VG. P2. $75.00.

RAINSFORD, Marcus. *Our Lord Prays for His Own.* 1950. Moody. 476p. G. B29. $8.50.

RAINSFORD, W. S. *Story of a Varied Life.* 1922. Doubleday Page. 481p. NF/dj. H7. $25.00.

RAISIN, Jacob S. *Haskalah Movement in Russia.* 1913. JPS. ils. 355p. G+. S3. $24.00.

RAISOR, Gary. *Obsessions.* 1991. Dark Harvest. 1st. F/dj. S18. $35.00.

RAKOSI, Carl. *Collected Prose of Carl Rakosi.* 1983. Orono. Nat Poetry Found. 1st. inscr. F/wrp. L3. $75.00.

RAKOVAC, Milan. *Croatia.* 1987. photos. VG/dj. M17. $20.00.

RALEIGH, Walter. *Johnson on Shakespeare: Essays & Notes.* 1908. OUP. sm 8vo. gilt blk cloth. H13. $25.00.

RALLI, Paul. *Nevada Lawyer: Story of Life & Love in Las Vegas.* 1949. Murry Gee. 2nd. inscr. 320p. VG/G. B19. $35.00.

RAMANUJAN, A. K. *The Striders.* 1966. London. Oxford Univ. Press. 1st. poet's first book. F/VG+. V1. $85.00.

RAMIREZ, Anthony Jr. *Romualdo Pacheco: Governor of California.* 1974. SF Pr. 1st. inscr. ils Victor R. Anderson. NF. O4. $15.00.

RAMIREZ, Jose F. *Statement of the Right & Just Reasons on Part of Government.* 1852. Mexico. Sullivan Nolan. 40p. 2 Lib Congress stps. wrp. F3. $125.00.

RAMM, Bernard. *Varieties of Christian Apologetics.* 1965. Baker. 199p. G. ex lib. B29. $8.00.

RAMOS, Manuel. *Blues for the Buffalo.* (1997). NY. St. Martin. 1st. sgn by the author. F/F. B3. $40.00.

RAMOS, Manuel. *The Ballad of Gato Guerrero.* 1994. NY. St. Martin. 1st. sgn. VF/VF. T2. $30.00.

RAMPERSAD, Arnold. *The Life of Langston Hughes: Volume 2: 1941 – 1967.* 1988. Oxford. 1st. F/F. M25. $35.00.

RAMPLING, Anne; see Rice, Anne.

RAMSAY, Jay; see Campbell, Ramsey.

RAMSAY, Robert. *Rough & Tumble on Old Clipper Ships.* 1930. NY. Appleton. 1st. NF/G. T11. $65.00.

RAMSDEN, Charles. *French Bookbinders 1789 – 1848.* 1989. London. B. T. Batsford Ltd. rpt. 228p. new in dj. P4. $85.00.

RAMSEY, Frederic. *Where the Music Started.* 1970. New Brunswick. Rutgers Inst Jazz Studies. F/wrp. B2. $45.00.

RAMSEY, Frederic Jr. *Been Here & Gone.* 1960. Rutgers. 1st. F/NF. M25. $60.00.

RAMSEY, Fredric & Charles Edward Smith. *Jazzmen.* 1939. NY. Harcourt. 1st. VG. B2. $35.00.

RAMSEY, Paul. *Basic Christian Ethics.* 1950. Scribner's. 404p. VG/worn dj. B29. $8.50.

RAMSLAND, Katherine. *Prism of the Night.* 1991. Dutton. 1st. F/dj. P3. $23.00.

RAMUS, David. *The Gravity of Shadows.* 1998. NY. Harper Collins. 1st. sgn on tipped in bkplt. VF/VF. T2. $20.00.

RAND, Ayn. *Anthem.* 1953. Caxton. 1st hc. F/VG. M19. $250.00.

RAND, Ayn. *Atlas Shrugged.* 1957. Random House. 1st. NF/gr cloth bds. lacking dj. M25. $150.00.

RAND, Ayn. *Capitalism: The Unknown Ideal.* 1966. NY. NAL. 1st. F in NF dj. B2. $85.00.

RAND, Clayton. *Sons of the South.* 1961. HRW. 1st. inscr. 212p. NF. T10. $35.00.

RAND, Paul. *Paul Rand: A Designer's Art.* 1985. Yale. 1st. ils. F/NF. C9. $150.00.

RANDALL, Bob. *Calling.* 1981. S&S. 1st. VG/dj. S18. $5.00.

RANDALL, Charles A. *Extra-Terrestrial Matter.* 1969. DeKalb. IL. N IL U. 331p. VG. K5. $40.00.

RANDALL, E. O. *Serpent Mound & Adams County Ohio Mystery.* 1907. Columbus. 2nd. ils. 125p. VG. B5. $50.00.

RANDALL, J. G. *Mid-Stream: Lincoln the President.* 1952. Dodd Mead. 1st. 467p. bl cloth. F/dj. H1. $25.00.

RANDALL, Marta. *Sword of Winter.* 1983. Timescape. 1st. F/dj. M2. $20.00.

RANDALL, Ruth Painter. *Lincoln's Sons.* 1956. Boston. 2nd. ils. VG/dj. M17. $20.00.

RANDALL, W. S. *Benedict Arnold: Patriot & Traitor.* 1990. NY. 1st. ils. 667p. F/dj. M4. $25.00.

RANDIER, Jean. *Men and Ships Around Cape Horn. 1616 – 1939.* 1969. NY. David McKay Company. Inc. 1st Am ed. bl cloth 4to. decor ep. ils. trans from French by MWB Sanderson. 360p. VG in worn dj. P4. $65.00.

RANDIER, Jean. *Nautical Antiques for the Collector.* 1977. photos. VG/VG. M17. $25.00.

RANDISI, Robert J. *Eyes Still Have It.* 1995. Dutton. 1st. NF/dj. G8. $20.00.

RANDISI, Robert J. *Full Contact.* 1984. St. Martin. 1st. sgn. F/NF. A24. $30.00.

RANDISI, Robert J. *No Exit from Brooklyn.* 1987. NY. St. Martin. 1st. sgn. F/F. T2. $35.00.

RANDISI, Robert J. *The Dead of Brooklyn.* 1991. NY. St. Martin. 1st. sgn. VF/VF. T2. $30.00.

RANDOLPH, Clare. *Nautical Ned.* 1948. Chicago. Hollow-Tree House. 1st probable. NF/VG+. C8. $20.00.

RANDOLPH, Cornelia. *Parlor Gardener: Treatise on House Culture.* 1861. Boston. Tilton. 158p. VG. A10. $55.00.

RANDOLPH, E. *Hell Among the Yearlings.* 1978. Lakeside Classic. photos. F. M4. $15.00.

RANDOLPH, Helen. *Mystery of Carlitos (#1).* 1936. AL Burt. lists 3 titles. VG/dj. M20. $40.00.

RANDOLPH, Vance. *Ozark Folksongs.* 1946. Columbia. MO. 4 vol. 1st. ils Benton. VG. B5. $145.00.

RANKIN, Ian. *Dead Souls.* 1999. NY. St. Martin. 1st Am ed. sgn. VF/VF. T2. $25.00.

RANKIN, Ian. *Dead Souls.* 1999. Orion. 1st British. sgn. F/F. G8. $35.00.

RANKIN, Ian. *Death Is Not the End.* 1998. London. Orion. 1st. sgn. VF in dj. M15. $55.00.

RANKIN, Ian. *The Hanging Garden.* 1998. London. Orion. 1st. sgn. VF/VF. T2. $60.00.

RANKIN, Ian. *Wolfman.* 1992. London. Century. 1st. F/dj. M15. $85.00.

RANKIN, James. *Sixteen Years' Experience in Artificial Poultry Raising.* 1889. Springfield. MA. Homestead. 65p. wrp. A10. $25.00.

RANKIN, John. *Letters on American Slavery.* 1833. Boston. Garrison Knapp. 1st. 12mo. 118p.

RANSOM, J. E. *Fossils in America.* 1964. Harper Row. 1st. 402p. F/dj. D8. $18.00.

RANSOM, J. H. *History of American Saddle Horses.* 1952. Lexington. Ransom. 1st. VG. O3. $195.00.

RANSOM, John Crowe. *Chills & Fever: Poems.* 1924. Knopf. 1st. G/dj. Q1. $200.00.

RANSOM, Will. *Private Presses & Their Books.* 1929. NY. RR Bowker. 1st. 1/1200. 193p. F/NF. O10. $225.00.

RANSOME, Arthur. *Bohemia in London.* 1907. London. Chapman Hall. 1st. ils Fred Taylor. VG. Q1. $150.00.

RAPAPORT, David. *Organization & Pathology of Thought.* 1951. Columbia. thick 8vo. 786p. bl cloth. VG/dj. G1. $65.00.

RAPHAEL, Arthur Michael. *Great Jug.* 1936. Reilly Lee. ils Clifford Benton. VG/ragged edged dj. M20. $27.00.

RAPHAEL, Frederic. *Latin Lover & Other Stories.* 1994. London. Orion. 1st. NF/dj. A14. $21.00.

RAPHAEL, Ray. *Edges: Human Ecology of the Backcountry.* 1986. U NE. 233p. F/wrp. S15. $4.50.

RAPPLEYE, Willard. *Graduate Medical Education.* 1940. Chicago. 1st. 304p. A13. $40.00.

RASA, A. *Mongoose Watch.* 1985. London. John Murray. 298p. NF/F. B1. $25.00.

RASCHOVICH, Mark. *Bedford Incident.* 1963. Atheneum. 1st. F/dj. T12. $50.00.

RASHKE, Richard. *Escape from Sobibor: Heroic Escape of Jews.* 1982. Boston. ils. VG/dj. M17. $15.00.

RASKIN, Ellen. *Westing Game.* (1978). Dutton. 2nd. sgn. 185p. VG/G. T5. $45.00.

RASWAN, Car;. *Drinkers of the Wind.* 1942. NY. Creative Age. VG/G. O3. $35.00.

RASWAN, Carl R. *Black Tents of Arabia.* nd. London. Hurst Blackett. 8vo. ils/pl/tables. 256p. cloth. VG. $2.00.

RATHBONE, Basil. *In & Out of Character.* 1962. Doubleday. ils. 278p. VG/dj. B5. $60.00.

RATHBONE, Hannah Mary. *Letters of Richard Reynolds with a Memoir.* 1855. Phil. Longstreth. 12mo. 285p. G. $3.00.

RATTIGAN, Terence. *French without Tears: A Play in Three Acts.* nd. London. 1st. VG/wrp. M17. $20.00.

RATTRAY, R. F. *Bernard Shaw: A Chronicle.* 1950. Leagrave. 1st. VG/dj. V4. $20.00.

RAU, M. A. *High Altitude Flowering Plants of West Himalaya.* 1975. Howrah. VG. B26. $44.00.

RAUCAZ, L. M. *In the Savage Solomons: Story of a Mission.* 1928. Lyon. 1st. ils. 270p. simulated leather. B14. $45.00.

RAUCHER, Herman. *Summer of '42.* 1971. Putnam. 1st. F/F. B4. $150.00.

RAUH, Werner. *Die Grossartige Welt Der Sukkulenten.* 1967. Hamburg. sgn. ils/96 pl. F/dj. B26. $50.00.

RAUH, Werner. *Schone Kakteen Und Sukkulenten.* 1967. Heidelberg. ils/photos/pl. 221p. F/dj. B26. $22.00.

RAVEN, Charles E. *Teilhard De Chardin: Scientist & Seer.* 1962. NY. Harper Row. 1st. VG/dj. M20. $15.00.

RAVEN, Charles P. *Oogenesis: Storage of Developmental Information.* 1961. Pergamon. 274p. xl. VG. S5. $12.00.

RAVEN, Neil. *Evidence.* 1987. NY. Scribners. 1st. VF/F. H11. $35.00.

RAVEN, Simon. *English Gentleman: Essay in Attitudes.* 1961. London. 1st. dj. T9. $30.00.

RAWLINGS, Marjorie Kinnan. *Cross Creek.* 1942. Scribner. 1st. 8vo. VG/dj. B17. $35.00.

RAWLINGS, Marjorie Kinnan. *Cross Creek Cookery.* 1942. NY. 1st. VG/VG. P3. $50.00.

RAWLINGS, Marjorie Kinnan. *Cross Creek Cookery.* 1960. Hammond. 1st Eng. 12mo. F/NF clip. T10. $100.00.

RAWLINGS, Marjorie Kinnan. *Secret River.* 1955. Scribner. 1st. ils Leonard Weisgard. VG+/dj. P2. $125.00.

RAWLINGS, Marjorie Kinnan. *Sojourner.* 1953. Scribner. 1st. NF/VG+. A24. $75.00.

RAWLINGS, Marjorie Kinnan. *Yearling.* 1939. Scribner. Pulitzer Prize ed. ils NC Wyeth. oatmeal buckram. dj. R5. $200.00.

RAWLINSON, Peter. *The Caverel Claim.* 1998. London. Constable. 1st. VF/VF. T2. $35.00.

RAY, Cyril. *Lancashire Fusiliers: 20th Regiment of Foot.* 1971. Leo Cooper. 1st. photos/chronology. 135p. VG/dj. $16.00.

RAY, Isaac. *Contribution to Mental Pathology.* 1873. Boston. 558p. gr cloth. VG. B14. $275.00.

RAY, Man. *Man Ray: Self Portrait.* 1963. Boston. 1st. 398p. dj. A17. $65.00.

RAY, Michelle. *Two Shores of Hell: A French Journalist's Life.* 1968. McKay. trans Elizabeth Abbott. VG/G+. R11. $24.00.

RAY, R. & M. MacCaskey. *Roses: How to Select, Grow & Enjoy.* 1981. Tucson. 4to. sc. F. B26. $17.50.

RAY, Robert. *Cage of Mirrors.* 1980. Lippincott/Crowell. 1st. VG/VG. A20. $20.00.

RAYMO, Chet. *Honey from a Stone: A Naturalist's Search for God.* 1987. NY. 1st. ils Bob O'Cathail. VG/dj. M17. $15.00.

RAYMOND, Alex. *Flash Gordon in the Planet Mongo.* 1974. Nostalgia. 1st. F/dj. M2. $50.00.

RAYMOND, Derek. *I Was Dora Suarez.* 1990. London. Scribner. 1st. F/dj. M15. $45.00.

RAYMOND, Ernest. *Late in the Day.* 1964. London. 1st. VG/VG. T9. $8.00.

RAYMOND, Linda. *Rocking the Babies.* (1994). NY. Viking. 1st. author's 1st book. F/F. B3. $20.00.

RAYMOND, Louise. *Child's Book of Prayers.* (1941). Random. ils Masha. unp. pict brd/gray cloth spine. G. T5. $20.00.

RAYNAL, Maurice. *Picasso: Biographical & Critical Studies.* 1959. Lausanne. Skira. ils/bibliography/index. 136p. cloth. dj. D2. $30.00.

RAYNER, John. *Wood Engravings by Thomas Beswick.* 1947. London/NY. King Penguin. VG. M20. $20.00.

RAYZER, G. *Flowering Cacti: A Color Guide.* 1984. NY. 181p. photo brd. F. B26. $9.00.

REA, John. *Layman's Commentary on the Holy Spirit.* 1974. Logos. 281p. VG. B29. $8.00.

READ, Daisy I. *New London: Today & Yesterday.* 1950. JP Bell. 1st. photos. 129p. G/G. B10. $45.00.

READ, George H. *Last Cruise of the Saginaw.* 1912. Houghton Mifflin. 1/150. 127p. P4. $70.00.

READ, Opie. *Harkriders.* 1903. Laird Lee. 1st. ils. VG. M19. $45.00.

READ, Piers Paul. *On the Third Day.* 1990. Random. 1st. F/F. B35. $16.00.

READ, Piers Paul. *Season in the West.* 1988. NY. 1st. dj. T9. $15.00.

READ, Robert W. *Genus Thrinax.* 1975. Washington, DC. photos. 98p. VG. B26. $20.00.

READE, Aleyn Lyell. *Johnsonian Gleanings.* 1968. NY. Octagon. 11 vol in 10. lg 8vo. red cloth. F. H13. $395.00.

READER'S DIGEST. *Family Encyclopedia of American History.* 1975. Pleasantville, NY. RD. sm4to. 1370p. VG. S14. $9.00.

READER'S DIGEST. *Family Guide to the Bible.* 1984. Pleasantville, NY. RD. 832p. VG+/G. S14. $15.00.

READER'S DIGEST. *Great Recipes for Good Health.* 1990 (1988). Pleasantville, NY. RD. 4th printing. sm4to. 304p. VG+. S14. $11.00.

READING, Joseph H. *Ogowe Band: Narrative of African Travel.* 1890. Phil. Reading. 1st. ils/map. 278p. G. H7. $30.00.

READING, Joseph H. *Voyage Along the Western Coast of Newest Africa.* 1901. Phil. Reading. 1st. photos. 211+2p. $0.00.

REAGAN, Michael. *On the Outside Looking In.* 1988. Zebra. 1st. sm 4to. 286p. F/dj. W2. $25.00.

REAGAN, Nancy. *My Turn.* 1989. Random. 1st. sm 4to. 384p. F/dj. W2. $75.00.

REAGAN, Nancy. *My Turn.* 1989. Random. 1st. inscr. F/F. A23. $75.00.

REAGAN, Ronald W. *American Life.* 1990. S&S. 1st. inscr/sgn. 748p. F/dj. W2. $150.00.

REAGE, Pauline. *Story of O.* 1965. Grove. 1st Am. F/NF. R14. $75.00.

REAMY, Tom. *Blind Voices.* 1978. Berkley. 1st. F/dj. M2. $25.00.

REARDON, Lisa. *Billy Dead.* 1998. NY. Viking. 1st. author's 1st novel. VF/VF. T2. $23.00.

REAVES, Michael. *Street Magic.* 1991. NY. Tor. 1st. F/NF. G10. $15.00.

REAVES, Sam. *Fear Will Do It.* 1992. NY. Putnam's. 1st. ARC. F in dj. M15. $35.00.

RECHY, John. *City of Night.* 1963. Grove. 1st. F/NF. B2. $40.00.

RECORD, Paul. *Tropical Frontier.* 1969. Knopf. 1st. 325p. dj. F3. $15.00.

RECORD, S. J. *Economic Woods of the United States.* 1912. John Wiley. 117p. cloth. B1. $25.00.

RECTOR, Carolyn K. *How to Grow African Violets.* 1951. SF. ils. 94p. sc. B26. $15.00.

REDDING, David. *Miracles of Christ.* 1964. Revell. 186p. VG/dj. B29. $10. 50.

REDDING, David. *The Parables He Told.* 1962. Revell. 177p. G/worn dj. B29. $6.00.

REDFIELD, James. *The Celestine Prophecy.* 1994. NY. Warner. 1st. F/F. H11. $50.00.

REDFIELD, Robert. *Folk Culture of Yucatan.* 1959. Chicago. 7th. 416p. F3. $20.00.

REDMAN, L. A. *Einstein Delusion & Other Essays.* 1926. SF. Robertson. 1st. 217p. VG. K3. $20.00.

REDMOND, Christopher. *Canadian Holmes: The First 25 Years.* 1997. Ashcroft. Calabash Press. 1st. VF/VF. T2. $40.00.

REDMOND, Juanita. *I Served on Bataan.* 1943. Lippincott. 10th imp. 12mo. 167p. VG/G clip. M7. $20.00.

REDMOND, Patrick. *The Wishing Game.* 1999. London. Hodder & Stoughton. 1st. VF/dj. M15. $85.00.

REDOUTE, P. J. *Redoute's Roses.* 1990. London. Wellfleet. 342p. dj. A10. $50.00.

REDPATH, James. *Echoes of Harper's Ferry.* 1860. Boston. Thayer Eldridge. 1st. gilt brn cloth. M24. $225.00.

REECE, N. C. *Cultured Pearl: Jewel of Japan.* 1958. Rutland. Tuttle. ils/photos/maps. 107p. F/VG. M12. $25.00.

REED, Alma. *The Ancient Past of Mexico.* 1966. NY. Crown. 1st. 388p. G/chipped dj. F3. $25.00.

REED, Frank A. *Lumberjack Sky Pilot.* 1965. Old Forge, NY. N. Country Books. 2nd. sgn. VG/dj. A2. $12.00.

REED, Ishmael. *Airing Dirty Laundry.* 1993. MA. Addison Wesley. 1st. F/F. mild rubbed corners. A24. $20.00.

REED, Ishmael. *Conjure.* 1972. Amherst. 1st. F/clip. V1. $20.00.

REED, Ishmael. *Japanese by Spring.* 1993. Atheneum. 1st. sgn. F/dj. D10. $45.00.

REED, Ishmael. *Last Days of Louisiana Red.* 1974. Random. 1st. F/dj. D10. $50.00.

REED, Marjorie. *Butterfield Overland Stage Across Arizona.* 1981. Old Adobe Gallery. 4th. ils. F/sans. B19. $20.00.

REED, Myrtle. *Book of Clever Beasts.* 1904. Putnam. 1st. ils Peter Newell. VG. B5. $35.00.

REED, Myrtle. *Weaver of Dreams.* 1911. Putnam. 1st. 8vo. 374p. decor lavender cloth. NF/dj. J3. $95.00.

REED, Philip. *Bird Dog.* 1997. London. Hodder & Stoughton. 1st. author's 1st book. VF/dj. M15. $65.00.

REED, Robert. *Black Milk.* 1989. NY. Donald I. Fine. 1st. VF/VF. T2. $9.00.

REED, Ronald. *Nature & Making of Parchment.* 1975. Leeds. Elmete. 1st. 1/450. reg. gilt quarter vellum/label. F. $24.00.

REED, Walt. *Harold Von Schmidt Draws the Old West.* 1972. AZ. 1st. 230p. F/dj. E1. $75.00.

REED, Walt. *Illustrator in America 1900 – 1960s.* 1966. NY. 1st. VG/G. B5. $35.00.

REEDER, Red. *Sheridan: General Who Wasn't Afraid to Take a Chance.* 1962. DSP. 1st. 238p. VG/fair. S17. $6.00.

REEDSTROM, Ernest L. *Scrapbook of the American West.* 1991. Caxton. ils/index. 259p. NF/wrp. B19. $10.00.

REEDY, William. *Impact: Photography for Advertising.* 1973. 1st/1st prt. inscr. ils. 323p. F/VG. A8. $45.00.

REEMAN, Douglas. *Badge of Glory.* 1984. NY. Morrow. 1st Am. NF/VG clip. T11. $30.00.

REEMAN, Douglas. *HMS Saracen.* 1965. London. Jarrolds. 1st Eng. F/F. T11. $145.00.

REEMAN, Douglas. *Rendezvous: South Atlantic.* 1972. London. Hutchinson. 1st. sgn. VG/dj. A14. $63.00.

REEMAN, Douglas. *Surface with Daring.* 1976. London. Hutchinson. 1st Eng. inscr. NF/NF. T11. $85.00.

REES, Arthur. *Threshold of Fear.* 1926. Dodd Mead. VG. M2. $20.00.

REES, Ronald. *New and Naked Land: Making the Prairies Home.* 1988. Saskatoon, Canada. Western Producer Prairie Books. 1st. F. A26. $20.00.

REESE, A. M. *Alligator & its Allies.* 1915. Putnam. ils/figures/pl. 358p. cloth. G. M12. $75.00.

REESE, H. H. *Horses of Today.* 1960. Pomona. Reese. 2nd. VG/fair. O3. $30.00.

REESE, John. *Big Hitch.* 1972. Garden City. Doubleday. 1st. F/dj. M15. $35.00.

REESE, John. *Maximum Range.* 1981. Garden City. Doubleday. 1st. F/dj. M15. $35.00.

REEVE, Arthur B. *Clutching Hand.* 1934. Reilly Lee. 1st. VG. M2. $25.00.

REEVES, James. *Blackbird in the Lilac.* 1959. EP Dutton. 1st Am. 8vo. blk-lettered lilac cloth. R5. $100.00.

REEVES, Robert. *Doubting Thomas.* 1985. NY. Arbor. 1st. author's 1st novel. F/NF. H11. $25.00.

REEVES-STEVENS, Garfield. *Dark Matter.* 1990. Doubleday. 1st. F/F. M21. $25.00.

REGAN, Michael. *Mansions of Los Angeles.* 1965. Regan Pub. photos. 80p. gilt fabricoid. D11. $75.00.

REGAN, Robert. *Poe: Collection of Critical Essays.* 1967. Prentice Hall. 1st. NF/wrp. M2. $10.00.

REGIS, Ed. *Who Got Einstein's Office.* 1987. Reading, MA. Addison-Wesley. 8vo. 316p. F/dj. K5. $20.00.

REGLI, Adolph. *Mayos: Pioneers In Medicine.* 1942. NY. 248p. A13. $35.00.

REGNERY, Dorothy F. *Enduring Heritage.* 1976. Stanford. 124p. xl. F/dj. K7. $35.00.

REICH, Christopher. *Numbered Account.* 1998. NY. Delacorte. 1st. author's 1st book. VF/VF. H11. $25.00.

REICH, Warren. *Encyclopedia of Bioethics.* 1978. NY. 1st. A13. $250.00.

REICH, Wilhelm. *Character Analysis.* 1949. Orgone Institute Press. 3rd. F. M25. $50.00.

REICHLER, Joseph. *30 Years of Baseball's Great Moments.* 1974. Crown. 1st. photos. F/VG. P8. $15.00.

REICHS, Kathy. *Deja Dead.* 1997. NY. Scribners. 1st. author's 1st novel. VF/VF. T2. $24.00.

REID, Alastair. *Supposing.* 1960. Little, Brn. 1st. 8vo. 48p. VG+/G+. C14. $9.00.

REID, Alastair. *To Be Alive.* 1966. Macmillan. 1st. VG/dj. C9. $60.00.

REID, Ed. *Mafia.* 1957. NY. Random. 1st. VG/dj. B5. $15.00.

REID, Robin Anne. *Arthur C. Clarke: A Critical Companion.* 1997. Greenwood. decor brd. F. P3. $30.00.

REIGER, Barbara. *Zane Grey Cookbook.* 1976. Prentice Hall. xl. G/dj. A16. $15.00.

REILLY, Helen. *The Day She Died.* 1962. NY. Random House. 1st. F in dj. M15. $45.00.

REILLY, John M. Ed. *Twentieth Century Crime and Mystery Writers.* 1985. NY. St. Martin. 2nd ed. VG/used dj. B2. $65.00.

REINHARDT, Hans. *Holbien.* 1938. French/European Pub. ils/pl. VG. M17. $25.00.

REISER, Stanley. *Medicine & the Region of Technology.* 1978. Cambridge. 1st. 317p. A13. $50.00.

REIT, Sy. *Canvas Confidential.* 1963. Dial. 1st. ils Kelly Freas. G+. P3. $30.00.

RELLING, William Jr. *Deadly Vintage.* 1995. NY. Walker. 1st. sgn. VF/VF. T2. $30.00.

RELLING, William Jr. *Sweet Poison.* 1998. NY. Walker. 1st. sgn. VF/VF. T2. $25.00.

REMARQUE, Erich Maria. *All Quiet on the Western Front.* 1929. Little, Brn. VG+. S13. $15.00.

REMARQUE, Erich Maria. *All Quiet on the Western Front.* 1929. London. Putnam. 1st Eng. NF/NF. M23. $200.00.

REMINGTON, Frederic. *Cuba in War Time.* 1897. NY. Russell. 1st. 23 pl/ftspc. tan brd. NF/dj. J3. $1.00.

REMINGTON, Frederic. *Frederic Remington Memorial Collection.* 1954. Knoedler Gallery. 1st. ils. F/sans. T11. $60.00.

REMINGTON, Frederic. *Frederic Remington's Own West.* 1960. NY. ils. F/NF. E1. $50.00.

RENAULT, Mary. *Fire from Heaven.* 1969. Pantheon. 1st. F/VG. M19. $17.50.

RENAULT, Mary. *Praise Singer.* 1978. Pantheon. 1st. F/dj. Q1. $35.00.

RENDELL, Ruth. *A Sight for Sore Eyes.* 1998. London. Hutchinson. 1st. VF/dj. M15. $50.00.

RENDELL, Ruth. *An Unkindness of Ravens.* 1985. NY. Pantheon. 1st Am ed. VF/F. T2. $14.00.

RENDELL, Ruth. *Best Man to Die.* 1970. Doubleday. 1st. NF/NF. H11. $60.00.

RENDELL, Ruth. *Bridesmaid.* 1989. London. Hutchinson. 1st. sgn. F/NF. B3. $70.00.

RENDELL, Ruth. *Crocodile Bird.* 1993. Crown. 1st Am. sgn. F/NF. N4. $40.00.

RENDELL, Ruth. *Fever Tree*. 1983. Pantheon. 1st Am. F/NF. N4. $40.00.

RENDELL, Ruth. *Guilty Thing Surprised*. 1970. Hutchinson. 1st. VG/VG+ clip. A24. $250.00.

RENDELL, Ruth. *Harm Done*. 1999. London. Hutchinson. 1st. VF/dj. M15. $50.00.

RENDELL, Ruth. *Killing Doll*. 1984. London. Hutchinson. 1st. F/dj. A24. $40.00.

RENDELL, Ruth. *Killing Doll*. 1984. Pantheon. 1st Am. F/F. W2. $40.00.

RENDELL, Ruth. *Lake of Darkness*. 1980. Doubleday. 1st Am. NF/VG+. A24. $25.00.

RENDELL, Ruth. *Live Flesh*. 1986. London. Hutchinson. 1st. sgn. F/dj. A24. $50.00.

RENDELL, Ruth. *Make Death Love Me*. 1979. NY. Doubleday. 1st. F/F. D10. $55.00.

RENDELL, Ruth. *Speaker of Mandarin*. 1983. Pantheon. 1st Am. sgn. F/F. B3. $50.00.

RENDELL, Ruth. *The Chimney Sweeper's Boy*. 1998. London. Viking. 1st. VF/dj. M15. $50.00.

RENDELL, Ruth. *The Lake of Darkness*. 1980. NY. Doubleday. 1st Am ed. NF/VG+. minor wear. A24. $25.00.

RENDELL, Ruth. *The New Girlfriend*. (1986). NY. Pantheon. 1st. sgn by author. F/F. B3. $35.00.

RENDELL, Ruth. *The Veiled One*. 1988. London. Hutchinson. 1st. F/F. some wear. A24. $30.00.

RENDELL, Ruth. *Tree of Hands*. 1985. Pantheon. 1st Am. F/dj. A24. $15.00.

RENEHAN, E. J. *John Burroughs: An American Naturalist*. 1992. Post Mills. Chelsea Gr. 1st. 356p. F/F. B1. $35.00.

RENICK, Marion. *Dooley's Play Ball*. 1949. Scribner. 1st. G. P8. $10.00.

RENNER, Clayton L. *Ragersville Centennial History*. 1930. 32p. G/wrp. B18. $25.00.

RENNER, G. K. *Joplin from Mining Town to Urban Center: Ils History*. 1985. Joplin Hist. Soc. 1st. ils. 128p. F/dj. M4. $25.00.

RENZI, Thomas C. *H. G. Wells: Six Scientific Romances Adapted for Film*. 1992. Metuchen. Scarecrow. 238p. VG. C5. $15.00.

REPS, Paul. *Letters to a Friend: Writings & Drawings 1939 – 1980*. 1981. Stillgate. 1st. ils/2 fld ils. VG/dj. M17. $60.00.

REPTON, Humphrey. *Art of Landscape Gardening*. 1907. Boston. 22 pl. 253p. brd. B26. $76.00.

RESSMEYER, Roger. *Space Places*. 1990. SF. Collins. 1st. VG/VG. K5. $45.00.

RESTON, James. *Collision at Home Plate*. 1991. Burlingame. 1st. VG/dj. P8. $25.00.

RETELI, Ernest. *Captain Knickerbocker*. 1938. London. Edward Arnold. 1st. 4to. pict brd. dj. R5. $250.00.

REUBEN, Shelly. *Julian Solo*. 1988. NY. Dodd Mead. 1st. sgn. F in clip dj. M15. $45.00.

REUBEN, Shelly. *Origin & Cause*. 1994. Scribner. 1st. F/NF. A23. $30.00.

REUTTER, Winifred. *Early Dakota Days*. 1962. Stickney. SD. Argus. A19. $40.00.

REVESZ, Geza. *Die Menschliche Hand: Eine Psychologische*. 1944. Basel. Von S Karger. ils. 122p. prt gray cloth. G1. $25.00.

REVESZ, Geza. *Psychology of a Musical Prodigy*. 1925. London. Kegan Paul. 1st/Am issue. 180p. gr cloth. VG. G1. $50.00.

REVI, Albert Christian. *American Art Nouveau*. 1981. Schiffer. 5th. 476p. F/dj. H1. $85.00.

REVI, Albert Christian. *American Art Nouveau*. 1968. Thomas Nelson. 1st. 4to. 476p. NF/G. H1. $95.00.

REXROTH, Kenneth. *American Poetry in the Twentieth Century*. (1971). NY. Herder. 1st. F/clip. A18. $30.00.

REXROTH, Kenneth. *Autobiographical Novel*. 1966. Doubleday. 1st. F/dj. L3. $35.00.

REXROTH, Kenneth. *Morning Star*. (1979). New Directions. 1st. F/dj. A18. $30.00.

REXROTH, Kenneth. *Phoenix & the Tortoise*. 1944. New Directions. 1st. VG. M19. $45.00.

REY, H. A. *Where's My Baby*. (1943). Houghton Mifflin. 1st. G+/pict wrp. D1. $50.00.

REY, Margaret. *Pretzel*. 1944. Harper. 1st. ils HA Rey. 4to. VG+/G. P2. $125.00.

REYNOLDS, Alfred. *Kiteman of Karanga*. 1985. Knopf. 1st. F/dj. M2. $10.00.

REYNOLDS, Barbara Leonard. *Hamlet & Brownswiggle*. 1954. Scribner. ils. tan cloth. VG. B36. $20.00.

REYNOLDS, Chang. *Pioneer Circuses of the West*. 1966. LA. Westernlore. ils. 212p. cloth. dj. D11. $40.00.

REYNOLDS, James. *Ghosts in American Houses*. 1955. NY. FSC. 1st. VG/dj. M20. $30.00.

REYNOLDS, Mack. *Compounded Interests*. 1983. Cambridge. NEFSA. 1st. RS. F/dj. G10. $24.00.

REYNOLDS, Michael. *Young Hemingway*. 1986. Basil Blackwell. photos. VG/dj. M17. $25.00.

REYNOLDS, Quentin. *Fiction Factory: From Pulp Row to Quality Street*. 1955. Random. 1st. VG/dj. P3. $100.00.

REYNOLDS, Quentin. *Officially Dead*. 1945. NY. 244p. VG. S16. $16.50.

REYNOLDS, Quentin. *They Fought for the Sky*. 1957. NY. 1st. VG/VG. B5. $20.00.

REYNOLDS, V. *Apes*. 1967. Dutton. 1st. 296p. VG/VG. B1. $30.00.

REYNOLDS, W. F. R. *Fly & Minnow: Common Problems of Trout & Salmon Fishing*. (1930). Country Life. 1st. sm 4to. 156p. VG. H7. $25.00.

REYNOLDS, William. *Theory of the Law of Evidence*. 1883. Chicago. Callaghan. cloth. M11. $125.00.

REYNOLDS, William J. *Things Invisible*. 1989. Putnam. 1st. sgn. F/F. B2. $40.00.

RHEINHARDT, E. A. *Josephine: Wife of Napoleon*. 1934. Knopf. 3rd. 8vo. VG/G. A2. $16.00.

RHINE, J. B. *New Frontiers of the Mind*. 1937. Farrar. 1st. VG/dj. M2. $20.00.

RHINE, Joseph Banks. *Extra-Sensory Perception*. 1935. Soc. Psychical Research. 1st/1st issue. inscr. 169p. panelled red cloth. G1. $85.00.

RHINE, Joseph Banks. *New Frontiers of the Mind: Story of Duke Experiments*. 1937. Farrar Rinehart. inscr/dtd 1948. photos. 275p. VG/dj. G1. $65.00.

RHINEHART, Mary Roberts. *Dangerous Days*. 1919. NY. Doran. 1st. 400p. G. G11. $10.00.

RHODE, John. *Telephone Call.* 1948. London. Bles. 1st. VG/clip. M15. $45.00.

RHODE, John. *Three Cousins Die.* 1960. Dodd Mead. 1st. F/NF. N4. $35.00.

RHODES, Arnold. *Psalms.* 1966. John Knox. 92p. VG/torn dj. B29. $3.50.

RHODES, Dennis. *Bookbindings & Other Bibliography.* 1994. Verona. Valdonega. 1st. decor cloth. F. w/pub flyer. M24. $125.00.

RHODES, Eugene Manlove. *Desire of the Moth.* 1916. Henry Hold. 1st. 155p. VG. J2. $225.00.

RHODES, Jewel Parker. *Voodoo Dreams.* 1993. St. Martin. 1st. author's 1st book. VG/dj. L1. $55.00.

RHODES, Richard. *Making of the Atomic Bomb.* 1986. ils. NF/wrp. K3. $20.00.

RIALA, John L. *Flowering Crabapples: Genus Malus.* 1995. Portland. photos. 272p. AN/dj. B26. $50.00.

RIBOT, Theodule Armand. *Diseases of Memory.* 1882. Appleton. 1st Am. 12mo. 209p. decor red cloth. VG. G1. $75.00.

RICARD, Robert. *La Conquete Spirituelle Du Mexique.* 1933. Paris Inst d'Ethnologie. 1st in French. 404p. F3. $65.00.

RICCIOTTI, Giuseppe. *Life of Christ.* 1951. Milwaukee, WI. Bruce. 5th. 8vo. ils. cloth. VG. W1. $10.00.

RICCIUTI, E. R. *American Alligator: Its Life in the Wild.* 1972. Harper Row. ils/photos. 71p. cloth. NF/VG. M12. $15.00.

RICCIUTI, E. R. *Devil's Garden.* 1978. NY. ils. 172p. VG+/dj. B26. $27.50.

RICCIUTI, Edward R. *Wildlife of the Mountains.* 1979. Abrams. 232p. VG/box. A17. $17.50.

RICE, Alice Hegan. *Lovey Mary.* 1903. NY. Century Co. 1st ed. VG. A16. $40.00.

RICE, Anne. *Cry to Heaven.* 1982. Knopf. 1st. F/NF. B2. $85.00.

RICE, Anne. *Exit to Eden.* 1985. Arbor. 1st. sgn. F/F. A23. $150.00.

RICE, Anne. *Feast of all Saints.* 1979. S&S. 1st. NF/NF. M19. $85.00.

RICE, Anne. *Feast of all Saints.* 1979. S&S. 1st. VG/VG. B5. $50.00.

RICE, Anne. *Interview with the Vampire.* 1976. Knopf. 1st. author's 1st book. VG+/VG+. A14. $525.00.

RICE, Anne. *Lasher.* (1993). NY. Knopf. 1st. sgn by author. F/F. B3. $65.00.

RICE, Anne. *Memnoch the Devil.* 1995. Knopf. 1/425. sgn. BE Trice bdg. F/cloth case. B3. $150.00.

RICE, Anne. *Memnoch the Devil.* 1995. Knopf. 1st. sgn. F/F. A23. $45.00.

RICE, Anne. *Queen of the Damned.* 1988. Knopf. 1st. NF/NF. H11. $35.00.

RICE, Anne. *Queen of the Damned.* 1988. Knopf. 1st. VG/dj. P3. $25.00.

RICE, Anne. *Servant of the Bones.* 1996. Knopf. 1st. sgn. VG/dj. L1. $65.00.

RICE, Anne. *Servant of the Bones.* 1996. Toronto. Knopf. 1st Canadian. F/NF. T12. $40.00.

RICE, Anne. *Taltos.* 1994. Knopf. 1st. F/dj. M21. $20.00.

RICE, Anne. *Taltos.* 1994. Knopf. 1st. sgn. VG/VG. A23. $60.00.

RICE, Anne. *The Feast of all Saints.* 1979. NY. S&S. 1st. author's 2nd book. sgn twice by author. on ffep and on title pg. F/F. D10. $175.00.

RICE, Anne. *The Tale of the Body Thief.* 1992. NY. Knopf. 1st. VF/VF. T2. $12.00.

RICE, Anne. *Vampire Chronicles.* 1990. Knopf. 3 vol. special reissue. sgn. blk cloth. NF/box. A14. $210.00.

RICE, Anne. *Vampire Lestat.* 1985. Knopf. 1st. VG/VG. M19. $75.00.

RICE, Anne. *Violin.* 1997. Knopf. 1st Am. sgn Mayfair House bookplate. F/dj. R14. $35.00.

RICE, Anne. *Violin.* 1997. Knopf. ARC. F/decor wrp. M25. $45.00.

RICE, Anne. *Witching Hour.* 1990. Knopf. 1st. sgn. VG/dj. L1. $125.00.

RICE, Anne. *Witching Hour.* 1990. Knopf. 1st. 965p. F/F. W2. $65.00.

RICE, Anne (as Anne Rampling). *Belinda.* 1986. NY. Arbor House. 1st. sgn as Rice. F/F. D10. $75.00.

RICE, Craig. *Fourth Postman.* 1948. S&S. 1st. F/NF. M15. $85.00.

RICE, Damon. *Seasons Past.* 1976. Praeger. 1st. F/VG. P8. $30.00.

RICE, Elmer. *Two on an Island.* 1940. Coward McCann. 1st. F/NF. B2. $45.00.

RICE, Helen Steiner. *Heart Gifts.* 1968. Revell. 96p. VG. B29. $2.00.

RICE, Josiah M. *Cannoneer in Navajo Country.* 1970. Denver. Old West Pub. ils. F/dj. A19. $35.00.

RICE, Lawrence D. *Negro in Texas, 1874 – 1900.* 1971. LSU. 1st. rem mk. F/NF. B2. $25.00.

RICE, Luanne. *Stone Heart.* 1991. London. Michael Joseph. 1st. F/F. B3. $15.00.

RICH, Adrienne. *A Wild Patience has Taken Me this Far: Poems 1978 – 1981.* 1981. NY. Norton. 1st. F/F. O11. $35.00.

RICH, Adrienne. *Midnight Salvage: Poems 1995 – 1998.* 1999. NY. Norton. 1st. review copy w/pub info. sgn. F/F. O11. $40.00.

RICH, Adrienne. *Necessities of Life.* 1966. NY. Norton. 1st. sgn & inscr to fellow poet. F/VG. V1. $140.00.

RICH, Adrienne. *Wild Patience has Taken Me this Far.* 1981. Norton. 1st. assn copy. F/dj. V1. $45.00.

RICH, Daniel Catton. *Seurat: Paintings & Drawings.* 1958. Chicago Art Inst. ils. 192p. VG. M10. $4.50.

RICH, Doris. *Amelia Earhart: A Biography.* 1990. London/WA. Smithsonian. ils/notes. 321p. AN/dj. P4. $22. $50.00.

RICH, Louise Dickinson. *We Took to the Woods.* 1942. Lippincott. 1st. photos. 322p. VG+. A25. $8.00.

RICH, Virginia. *The Cooking School Murders.* 1982. NY. Delacorte. 1st. VF/dj. M15. $55.00.

RICHARD, Adrienne. *Accomplice.* 1973. Little, Brn. 1st. 174p. F/VG. C14. $14.00.

RICHARD, Lionel. *Concise Encyclopedia of Expressionism.* 1978. Chartwell. ils. VG/dj. M17. $17.50.

RICHARD, Mark. *Ice at the Bottom of the World.* 1989. Knopf. 1st. author's 1st book. F/dj. A24. $35.00.

RICHARDS, A. *Ennal's Point.* 1977. London. Michael Joseph. 1st Eng. F/F. T11. $45.00.

RICHARDS, Alan. *Birds of Prey: Hunters of the Sky.* 1992. Phil. photos. 144p. F/F. S15. $15.00.

RICHARDS, Edward A. *Shadows: Selected Poems.* 1933. St Thomas, Virgin Islands. 1st. sm 8vo. 20p. cloth. NF. B4. $275.00.

RICHARDS, Eugene. *Knife & Gun Club: Scenes from an Emergency Room.* 1989. Altantic Monthly. 1st. VG/dj. S5. $30.00.

RICHARDS, G. M. *Pied Piper of Hamelin.* 1934 (1927). Macmillan. 12mo. VG. P2. $40.00.

RICHARDS, Kel. *Sherlock Holmes' Tales of Terror: The Curse of the Pharaohs.* 1997. NSW. Australia. BEacon Communications. 1st. VF/pict wrp. T2. $8.00.

RICHARDS, Kel. *Sherlock Holmes' Tales of Terror: The Vampire Serpent.* 1997. NSW. Australia. Beacon Communications. 1st. VF/pict wrp. T2. $8.00.

RICHARDS, Larry. *Dictionary of Basic Bible Truths.* 1987. Lamplighter. 384p. AN. B29. $7.50.

RICHARDS, Laura E. *Captain January.* Dana Estes. 3rd. 78p. VG. B36. $10.00.

RICHARDS, Lawrence O. *Practical Theology of Spirituality.* 1987. Zondervan. 253p. VG/dj. B29. $9. 50.

RICHARDSON, A. E. *Old Inns of England, 1035.* London. 2nd/revised. G. O3. $40.00.

RICHARDSON, Alan. *Bible in the Age of Science.* 1961. Westminster. 192p. VG/dj. B29. $8. 50.

RICHARDSON, Alan. *Science, History, and Faith.* 1956. Oxford. 210p. VG. B29. $4.50.

RICHARDSON, Bobby. *Bobby Richardson Story.* 1965. Revell. 1st. sgn. photos. VG/G. P8. $50.00.

RICHARDSON, C. *Practical Farriery: A Guide for Apprentices.* 1950. London. Pitman. 1st. VG/VG. O3. $25.00.

RICHARDSON, Charles. *Chancellorsville Campaign.* 1907. Neale Pub. 124p. NF. A4. $200.00.

RICHARDSON, Edward. *Standards & Colors of the American Revolution.* 1982. U. PA. 1st. 341p. VG/dj. S16. $40.00.

RICHARDSON, R. S. *Fascinating World of Astronomy.* 1960. McGraw Hill. 1st. 274p. F/dj. D8. $10.00.

RICHARDSON, Robert. *Book of the Dead.* 1989. London. Vollancz. 1st. sgn. F/dj. M15. $75.00.

RICHARDSON, Robert. *Murder in Waiting.* 1991. St. Martin. 1st Am ed. NF/NF. G8. $10.00.

RICHARDSON, Robert. *Sleeping in the Blood.* 1991. Bristol. Scorpion. 1st. 1/75. sgn. F/dj. T2. $125.00.

RICHARDSON, Rupert Norval. *Frontier of Northwest Texas.* 1963. Arthur H. Clark. 332p. cloth. D11. $100.00.

RICHARDSON, S. C. *In Desert Arizona.* 1938. Zion Prt/Pub. inscr. ils. 186p. NF. B19. $75.00.

RICHARDSON, Samuel. *History of Sir Charles Grandison. 1762.* London. Rivington. 7 vol. 4th. 12mo. contemporary bdg. H13. $395.00.

RICHLER, Mordecai. *Incomparable Atuk.* 1963. Toronto. McClelland Stewart. 1st. NF/dj. M25. $45.00.

RICHLER, Mordecai. *Joshua Then & Now.* 1980. Knopf. 1st. VG/dj. C9. $25.00.

RICHTER, Conrad. *Aristocrat.* 1968. Knopf. 1st. F/clip. A24. $18.00.

RICHTER, Conrad. *Tacey Cromwell.* 1942. Knopf. 1st. 208p. VG/G. B19. $20.00.

RICHTER, N. B. *Nature of Comets.* 1963. London. Methuen. revised/trans. 8vo. 221p. G/dj. K5. $45.00.

RICKARD, T. A. *Mines: A History of American Mining.* 1932. 1st. ils. 419p. O8. $21.50.

RICKETT, Harold W. *Wildflowers of the US: The Northeastern States.* 1966. McGraw Hill. 1st ed. 2 vol. folio. A10. $200.00.

RICKETTS, Charles. *Defence of the Revival of Printing.* 1899. London. Vale. 1st. 1/250. lt bl brd/label/rb. M24. $200.00.

RICKETTS, Charles. *Letters to Michael Field.* 1981. Edinburgh. Tragara. 1st. 1/145. VG/VG. T9. $65.00.

RICKETTS, R. L. *First Class Polo.* 1928. Aldershot. Gale Polden. 1st. VG. O3. $125.00.

RICKMAN, Phil. *Curfew.* 1993. NY. Putnam. 1st. F/F. H11. $20.00.

RIDDELL, James. *In the Forests of the Night.* 1946. NY. 1st. 228p. VG. A17. $15.00.

RIDDELL, John. *John Riddell Murder Case: Philo Vance Parody.* 1930. Scribner. 1st. VG/dj. M15. $75.00.

RIDEAL, Samuel. *Disinfection & Disinfectants.* 1895. London. ils/lg fld plan. red cloth. VG. B14. $125.00.

RIDEOUT, Henry Milner. *Dulcarnon.* 1925. Duffield. 1st. VG. M2. $12.00.

RIDER, J. W. *Hot Tickets.* 1987. NY. Arbor. 1st. author's 2nd book. F/F. H11. $25.00.

RIDER, J. W. *Jersey Tomatoes.* 1986. NY. Arbor. 1st. author's 1st book. F/F. H11. $50.00.

RIDGWAY, Matthew. *Soldier: Memoirs of Matthew B. Ridgway.* 1956. Harper. 1st. inscr. 371p. G+. B11. $100.00.

RIDLEY, John. *Stray Dogs.* 1997. NY. Ballantine. 1st. author's 1st book. F/NF. R16. $45.00.

RIDLON, Marci. *That was Summer.* 1969. Chicago. Follett. 1st. 80p. cloth. F/dj. D4. $25.00.

RIDOLFI, Roberto. *Life of Francesco Guicciardini.* 1968. Knopf. 1st Am. 336p. VG+/dj. M20. $18.00.

RIDPATH, Ian. *Messages from the Stars.* 1978. Harper Row. 1st. ils. 241p. VG/dj. K5. $15.00.

RIDPATH, Ian. *Stars & Planets.* 1979 (1978). London. Hamlyn. 2nd. 4to. 96p. VG/dj. K5. $12.00.

RIEFE, Barbara. *Women Who Fell from the Sky.* 1992. Forge. 1st. NF/dj. S13. $10.00.

RIESE, Randall. *All About Bette.* 1993. Chicago. Contemporary Books. 504p. VG/dj. C5. $15.00.

RIESEN, Rene. *Jungle Mission.* 1957. NY. 1st. 204p. VG/dj. B5. $30.00.

RIESENBERG, Felix. *Golden Gate: Story of San Francisco Harbor.* 1940. Knopf. 1st. NF/VG. O4. $15.00.

RIGBY, Douglas & Elizabeth. *Lock, Stock and Barrel, The Story of Collecting.* 1944. Lippincott. 1st. 8vo. worn & chipped edges. 570p. F/dj. H1. $12.50.

RIGBY, Ray. *Hill.* 1965. John Day. 1st Am. F/VG+. B4. $75.00.

RIGG, Robert B. *Red China's Fighting Hordes.* 1952. Harrisburg. 1st revised. ils/index. 378p. VG/VG. B5. $35.00.

RIGGS, S. R. *Dakota-English Dictionary.* 1992. NM Hist. Soc. rpt 1890 ed. M/wrp. A17. $25.00.

RIIS, Jacob A. *Old Town.* 1909. Macmillan. 1st. VG. B2. $75.00.

RIKER, Ben. *Pony Wagon Town.* 1948. Indianapolis. 1st. sgn. 312p. G+/dj. B18. $22.50.

RIKHOFF, Jean. *One of the Raymonds.* 1974. Dial Press. 2nd prt. G/G. S19. $20.00.

RILEY, Herbert P. *Families of Flowering Plants of Southern Africa.* 1963. (Lexington). 4to. VG in dj. edge spotted. B26. $59.00.

RILEY, J. H. *Birds from Siam & the Malay Penninsula.* 1938. Smithsonian. ils 579p. VG. S15. $30.00.

RILEY, James A. *Biographical Encyclopedia of the Negro Baseball Leagues.* 1994. Carroll Graf. 1st. ils. F/VG. A2. $25.00.

RILEY, James Whitcomb. *Flying Islands of the Night.* 1913. Bobbs Merrill. 4to. dj. R5. $250.00.

RILEY, James Whitcomb. *Home Folks.* (1900). Bowen Merrill. sm 8vo. ftspc. sgn w/6-line poem/dtd 1905. fld/case. K1. $250.00.

RILEY, James Whitcomb. *Old Sweetheart of Mine.* 1902. Bobbs Merrill. ils H.C. Christy. VG. M17. $25.00.

RILEY, James Whitcomb. *Riley Farm-Rhymes. 1883 – 1901.* Bobbs Merrill. 187p. gilt cloth. VG. M20. $20.00.

RILEY, James Whitcomb. *While the Heart Beats Young.* 1906. Bobbs Merrill. 8vo. 110p. VG. D1. $75.00.

RILEY, Jocelyn. *Crazy Quilt.* 1984. NY. Morrow. 1st. sgn. on title page. Jacket has minor wear at spine and flap fold ends. F/F. H11. $65.00.

RILEY, Morgan T. *Dahlias. What Is Known About Them.* 1948(1947). NY. 213p w/29 b&w ils. spine faded. ep tanned. B26. $14.00.

RILEY, Pat. *Show Time.* 1988. Bantam. 1st. sgn. photos. F/F. P8. $65.00.

RILEY, Ridge. *Road to Number One.* 1977. Doubleday. 1st. VG/G+. P8. $25.00.

RILKE, Rainer Maria. *Letters to Merline 1919 – 1922.* 1951. London. 1st Eng. F/VG. M19. $35.00.

RIMMER, Harry. *The Harmony of Science & Scripture.* 1964. Eerdmans. 283p. VG/VG. B29. $12.00.

RINEHART, Mary Roberts. *Out Trail.* 1932. NY. McBride. 8vo. 246p. red cloth. F7. $25.00.

RING, Douglas; see Prather. Richard.

RING, Ray. *Arizona Kiss.* 1991. Boston. Little, Brn. 1st. VF/VF. T2. $15.00.

RING, Ray. *Telluride Smile.* 1988. Dodd Mead. 1st. author's 1st book. F/NF. H11. $65.00.

RINGER, Robert. *Million Dollar Habits.* 1990. np. Wynwood. NF/NF. A28. $6.95.

RINK, Paul. *To Steer by the Stars: Story of Nathaniel Bowditch.* 1969. NY. Doubleday. 8vo. 189p. VG/dj. K5. $14.00.

RINTOUL, William. *Drilling Ahead: Tapping California's Richest Oil Fields.* 1981. Santa Cruz. Valley Pub. 289p. cloth. dj. D11. $30.00.

RINTOUL, William. *Spudding in: Recollections of Pioneer Days.* 1978. Fresno. Valley Pub. 2nd. 240p. cloth.

RINZLER, Carol Eisen. *Girl Who Got all the Breaks.* 1980. NY. Putnam. ARC/1st. 191p. F/dj. O10. $20.00.

RIOS, Eduardo Enrique. *Life of Fray Antonio Margil.* OFM. 1959. Academy of Am. Franciscan Hist. 1st. 159p. NF/sans. B19. $30.00.

RIPLEY, Alexandra. *Dreamsicle.* 1993. Boston. Little, Brn. 1st. VF/VF. H11. $30.00.

RIPLEY, Alexandra. *Electric Country Roulette.* 1996. NY. Holt. 1st. F/F. H11. $15.00.

RIPLEY, Alexandra. *Scarlett.* 1991. NY. Warner. 1st. F/F. H11. $30.00.

RIPLEY, Dillon. *Paddling of Ducks.* 1957. 1st. ils. VG/G+. M17. $15.00.

RIPPERGER, H. *Coffee Cookery.* 1940. 1st. 94p. VG. E6. $15.00.

RISTER, C. C. *Southern Plainsmen.* 1939. OK U. 1st. photos/map. 289p. NF. M4. $35.00.

RITCHIE, Rita. *Pirates of Samarkand.* 1967. Norton. 1st. sm 8vo. 158p. VG. C14. $13.00.

RITCHIE, Rita. *Year of the Horse.* 1957. Dutton. 1st. ils LF Bjorklund. VG/G. O3. $25.00.

RITTER, Ema I. *Life at the Old Amphibian Airport.* 1970. Santa Ana, CA. 1st. NF/dj. H1. $30.00.

RITTER, Gerhard. *Luther: His Life & Work.* 1963. Harper Row. 256p. VG/dj. H10. $15.00.

RITTER, L. *Glory of their Times.* 1966. Macmillan. 1st sgn Harry Hooper. VG/dj. P8. $150.00.

RITTER, L. *Lost Ballparks.* 1992. NY. Viking/ Studio. 1st. ils/drawings. VG. B27. $45.00.

RITTER, Lawrence. *Glory of their Times.* 1966. NY. Macmillan. 1st. photos. VG/G clip. R16. $35.00.

RITTERHAUSEN, Brian & Wilma. *Popular Orchids.* 1971. South Brunswick. 240p w/color ftspc. & 92 photos & line drawings. F in dj. B26. $12.50.

RITZ, David. *Blue Notes Under a Green Felt Hat.* 1989. NY. DIF. 1st. NF/F. H11. $20.00.

RIVERS, Joan. *Still Talking.* 1991. Turtle Bay. 1st. sgn. F/F. A23. $32.00.

RIVERS, William Halse. *Psychology & Politics & Other Essays.* 1923. Harcourt Brace. 180p. gr cloth. G1. $85.00.

RIZK, Salom. *Syrian Yankee.* 1952. Doubleday. sgn. 317p. cloth. VG/torn. W1. $10.00.

RIZZI, Timothy. *Night Stalker.* 1992. np. Donald Fine. 1st sgn. author's 1st novel. NF/NF-. R16. $55.00.

ROARK, R. J. *Formulas for Stress & Strain.* 1938. McGraw Hill. 1st. 326p. G. D8. $9.00.

ROAT, Ronald Clair. *Close Softly the Doors.* 1991. Story Line. 1st. F/F. G8. $10.00.

ROBACK, Abraham Aaron. *Il Peretz: Psychologist of Literature.* 1935. Cambridge. Sci-Art Pub. pres. 457p. gr cloth. G1. $75.00.

ROBACKER, Earl F. *Touch of the Dutchland.* 1965. London. Yoseloff/Barnes. 1st. 100+ photos. 240p. F/dj. H1. $22.00.

ROBB, Candace. *A Spy for the Redeemer.* 1999. London. William Heinemann. 1st. sgn. VF/VF. T2. $35.00.

ROBB, Candace. *King's Bishop.* 1995. St. Martin. 1st. sgn. F/dj. O11. $20.00.

ROBB, Charles. *Red O'Leary Wins Out.* 1927. NY. 1st. ils. 287p. VG/dj. B5. $25.00.

ROBB, Mary Cooper. *William Faulkner: Estimate of His Contribution to Am. Novel.* (1961). Pittsburgh. 3rd. tall 8vo. VG/wrp. H4. $35.00.

ROBBINS, Clifton. *Mystery of Mr. Cross.* 1933. Appleton. VG. N4. $20.00.

ROBBINS, Jhan. *Bess & Harry.* 1980. NY. Putnam. 1st. F/VG+. M23. $10.00.

ROBBINS, John. *Tooth Fairy Is Broke.* 1988. Darnstown. MD. Clark-Davis. 1st. ils/sgn Rae Owings. lg 8vo. F/F. C8. $45.00.

ROBBINS, Maria P. *Puss in Books: A Collection of Great Cat Quotations.* 1994. ils. 270p. F/F. A4. $25.00.

ROBBINS, Tom. *Another Roadside Attraction.* 1971. Doubleday. 1st. author's 1st book. NF/dj. D10. $450.00.

ROBBINS, Tom. *Jitterbug Perfume.* 1984. Bantam. 1st. F/NF. B3. $50.00.

ROBBINS, Tom. *Skinny Legs and All.* 1990. NY. Bantam. 1st. F/F. D10. $45.00.

ROBBINS, Tom. *Still Life with Woodpecker.* 1980. Bantam. 1st. VG/G. M19. $45.00.

ROBERTS, Barrie. *Sherlock Holmes and the Devil's Grail.* 1995. London. Constable. 1st. VF/dj. M15. $45.00.

ROBERTS, Brian B. *Chronological List of Antarctic Expeditions.* 1958. Cambridge. Scott Polar Research Inst. prt wrp. P4. $75.00.

ROBERTS, Daniel. *Some Account of the Persecutions & Sufferings of People.* 1832. NY. Daniel Cooledge. 24mo. 256p. cloth. $3.00.

ROBERTS, Daniel. *Some Memoirs of the Life of John Roberts.* nd. Phil. Friends Book Store. 16mo. 86p. VG. V3. $15.00.

ROBERTS, David. *Cattle Breeds & Origin.* 1916. Waukesha, WI. self pub. 177p. cloth. VG. A10. $48.00.

ROBERTS, E. & E. Rehmann. *American Plants for American Gardens.* 1929. NY. ex lib. 131p. 11 photos. B26. $15.00.

ROBERTS, Edwards. *Shoshone & Other Western Wonders.* 1888. Harper. A19. $35.00.

ROBERTS, Gilliam. *I'd Rather be in Philadelphia.* 1992. NY. Ballentine. 1st. F/F. H11. $25.00.

ROBERTS, Henry W. *Aviation Radio.* 1945. Morrow. 1st. inscr. ils. VG/dj. K3. $25.00.

ROBERTS, James A. *New York in the Revolution as Colony & State.* 1897. Albany. Weed Parsons. 1st ed. ils/fld map. 261p. VG. B18. $125.00.

ROBERTS, Jim. *Gene Autry & the Prairie Fire.* 1950s. London. Adprint Ltd. pub file copy. AN. R5. $200.00.

ROBERTS, Keith. *Kiteworld.* 1985. London. Gollancz. 1st. sgn. VF/VF. T2. $35.00.

ROBERTS, Keith. *Winterwood and Other Hauntings.* 1989. Scotforth. Lancaster. Morrigan Publications. 1st. VF/VF. T2. $25.00.

ROBERTS, Kenneth. *Boon Island.* 1956. Doubleday. 1st. F/NF. H11. $25.00.

ROBERTS, Kenneth. *Lively Lady.* 1931. Doubleday Doran. 1st. 1/5560. VG. T11. $45.00.

ROBERTS, Kenneth. *Water Unlimited.* 1957. Doubleday. 1st. NF/dj. T11. $70.00.

ROBERTS, Kenneth. *Why Europe Leaves Home.* 1922. Bobbs Merrill. 1st. 1/2011. NF/VG. T11. $700.00.

ROBERTS, L. *MacKenzie.* 1949. NY. Rivers of Am. 1st. ils. F/dj. M4. $25.00.

ROBERTS, Lee; see Martin, Robert.

ROBERTS, Les. *An Infinite Number of Monkeys.* 1987. NY. St. Martin. 1st. author's 1st novel. sgn. VF/VF. T2. $45.00.

ROBERTS, Les. *Not Enough Horses.* 1988. NY. St. Martin. 1st. F/dj. M15. $40.00.

ROBERTS, Les. *Seeing the Elephant.* 1992. NY. St. Martin. 1st. VF/VF. T2. $15.00.

ROBERTS, Les. *The Lemon Chicken Jones.* 1994. NY. St. Martin. 1st. VF/VF. T2. $15.00.

ROBERTS, Monte. *The Man Who Listens to Horses.* 1996. London. Hutchinson. 1st UK ed. sgn presentation copy. F/F. O3. $45.00.

ROBERTS, Ned H. *Muzzle-Loading Cap Lock Rifle.* 1958. Stackpole. 5th. 308p. VG. A17. $32.50.

ROBERTS, Norman C. *Baja California Plant Field Guide.* 1989. La Jolla. ils/map/photos. AN/photo wrp. B26. $23.00.

ROBERTS, S. C. *Holmes and Watson.* 1953. London. Oxford University. 1st. Jacket has chipping along top edge of front panel. F/VG. M15. $45.00.

ROBERTS, Susan. *Magician of the Golden Dawn: Story of Aleister Crowley.* 1978. Contemporary Books. 1st. NF/F. R10. $15.00.

ROBERTS, Thomas. *Birds of Minnesota.* 1932. Minneapolis. 2 vol. 1st. 4to. ils. F. C6. $185.00.

ROBERTS, W. Adolphe. *Haunting Hand.* 1926. Macaulay. 1st. VG/VG. B4. $1,000.00.

ROBERTS, W. Adolphe. *Single Star.* 1949. Bobbs Merrill. 1st. F/VG+. B4. $175.00.

ROBERTSON, Don. *Ideal Genuine Man.* 1987. Bangor, ME. Philtrum. 1st. intro Stephen King. F/NF. G10. $25.00.

ROBERTSON, Frederick. *Sermons on Religion & Life.* 1912. Dent. 332p. VG. B29. $3.00.

ROBERTSON, Gavin. *Thousand.* 1998. London. Headline. 1st. author's 1st novel. VF/VF. T2. $30.00.

ROBERTSON, Heather. *Terrible Beauty: Art of Canada at War.* 1977. Toronto. Lorimer. 1st. F/NF. T12. $40.00.

ROBERTSON, James Alexander. *Louisiana Under the Rule of Spain.* France & United States. 1911. Cleveland. AH Clark. 2 vol. 1st. $8.00.

ROBERTSON, John. *Rusty Staub of the Expos.* 1971. Prentice Hall. 1st. photos. F/VG+. P8. $85.00.

ROBERTSON, Mary Elsie. *Clearing.* 1982. Atheneum. 1st. F/F. B4. $45.00.

ROBERTSON, Mary Elsie. *What I Have to Tell You.* 1989. Doubleday. 1st. 322p. F/F. W2. $25.00.

ROBERTSON, R. B. *Of Whales & Men.* 1954. Knopf. ils. gilt bl cloth. VG. P12. $15.00.

ROBERTSON, Terrence. *Dieppe: Shame & the Glory.* 1962. Little, Brn. 1st. 432p. VG/dj. S16. $22.00.

ROBERTSON, William. *The Life of Miranda.* 1929. Chapel Hill. Univ. of North Carolina Press. 1st. 2 vols. ex lib. b/w photo ils. 372p. 306p. G. F3. $30.00.

ROBESON, Kenneth; see Goulart, Ron.

ROBEV, Melvin J. *African Violets: Queens of the Indoor Gardening Kingdom.* 1980. San Diego. 199p w/8 color plates. 71 photos & drawings. dj. B26. $20.00.

ROBICSEK, Francis. *The Smoking Gods.* 1978. Norman. Univ. of Oklahoma Press. 1st. 4to. photo ils. drawings. maps. 233p. /chipped dj. F3. $135.00.

ROBIN, Jeff. *Adventure Heroes.* 1994. Facts on File. 1st. F/dj. M2. $35.00.

ROBIN, Robert. *Above the Law.* 1992. Pocket. 1st. VG/dj. A28. $8.00.

ROBINSON, Albert G. *Old New England Houses.* 1920. NY. Scribner's. 1st. color pict cloth. water stain on cover. lt foxing. 29p of text. 103 plates. G. B18. $32.50.

ROBINSON, Bill. *Islands.* 1985. NY. photos. VG/dj. M17. $15.00.

ROBINSON, Bruce. *The Peculiar Memories of Thomas Penman.* 1999. NY. Overlook. 1st. F/F. M23. $40.00.

ROBINSON, C. *View from Chapultepec: Mexican Writers on Mexican War.* 1989. U AZ. 1st. 223p. F/dj. M4. $25.00.

ROBINSON, Charles N. *Old Naval Prints: Their Artists & Engravers.* 1924. London. The Studio. 1/1500. 4to. 96 pl. teg. gilt buckram. F. B24. $250.00.

ROBINSON, Conway. *Account of Discoveries in the West.* 1848. Richmond. Shepherd Colin. 491p. T7. $180.00.

ROBINSON, Edwin Arlington. *Sonnets 1889 – 1927.* 1928. Macmillan. 1st collected. paper brd/cloth spine. F/NF. T10. $50.00.

ROBINSON, Frank. *Frank: The First Year.* 1976. Holt Rinehart. 1st. sgn. VG/dj. P8. $150.00.

ROBINSON, George O. *Oak Ridge Story.* 1950. Kingsport. Southern Pub. 1st. VG/dj. K3. $35.00.

ROBINSON, H. N. *A Treatise on Astronomy.* 1850. Albany. NY. Erastus H. Pease. 57 text ils. 8vo. 302p+54p tables. worn & scraped leather. joints cracked. chips. stains & overall wear. K5. $50.00.

ROBINSON, Heath. *Heath Robinson at War.* 1942. London. Methuen. 1st. 48p. prt paper wrp. paper dj. R5. $275.00.

ROBINSON, Heath. *Inventions.* 1973. Duckworth. 1st. ils. 147p. VG/VG. D1. $30.00.

ROBINSON, Jackie. *Breakthrough to the Big League.* 1965. Harper Row. 1st. VG/dj. P8. $45.00.

ROBINSON, James M. *New Quest of the Historical Jesus.* 1966. SCM. 128p. VG/wrp. B29. $11.00.

ROBINSON, Jeffers. *Such Counsels You Gave to Me.* (1937). Random. 1st. NF. A18. $40.00.

ROBINSON, Judith. *Tom Cullen of Baltimore.* 1949. NY. 1st. 453p. A13. $30.00.

ROBINSON, Kim Stanley. *Blue Mars.* 1996. London. Harper Collins. 1st. sgn. F/dj. M23. $100.00.

ROBINSON, Kim Stanley. *Remaking History.* 1991. NY. Tor. 1st. F/NF. G10. $27.00.

ROBINSON, Kim Stanley. *The Gold Coast.* 1988. NY. Tor. 1st. sgn. VF/ VF. T2. $35.00.

ROBINSON, Lynda S. *Eater of Souls.* (1997). NY. Walker. 1st. sgn by author. F/F. B3. $35.00.

ROBINSON, Lynda S. *Murder at the Feast of Rejoicing.* (1996). NY. Walker. 1st. sgn by author. F/F. B3. $35.00.

ROBINSON, Lynda S. *Murder at the God's Gate.* 1995. NY. Walker. 1st. F/F. M23. $40.00.

ROBINSON, Mabel L. *Blue Ribbon Stories: Best Current Stories.* 1932. Macmillan. 1st. ils. cloth. VG. $27.00.

ROBINSON, Peter. *Final Account.* 1994. Toronto. Viking. 1st. sgn. VF/pict wrp. T2. $25.00.

ROBINSON, Peter. *In a Dry Season.* 1999. NY. Avon Books. 1st. sgn. VF/VF. T2. $26.00.

ROBINSON, Peter. *Past Reason Hated.* 1993. NY. Scribners. 1st Am ed. sgn. VF/VF. T2. $25.00.

ROBINSON, Tom. *In & Out.* 1943. Viking. 1st. ils Marguerite deAngeli. 140p. G+. T5. $25.00.

ROBINSON, Victor. *Pathfinders in Medicine.* 1929. NY. 2nd. 810p. A13. $125.00.

ROBINSON, W. W. *Lawyers of Los Angeles.* 1959. Los Angeles. 1st. F/G. O4. $15.00.

ROBISON, Mary. *Amateur's Guide to the Night.* 1983. Knopf. 1st. F/F. R13. $25.00.

ROCHE, Henri-Pierre. *Jules & Jim.* 1963. London. Caldar. 1st Eng. F/NF clip. B4. $150.00.

ROCK, J. F. *Amnye Ma-Chen Range & Adjacent Regions.* 1956. Rome. 1st. 80 photos/5 fld maps. 194p. NF. W3. $485.00.

ROCK, J. F. *Sandalwoods of Hawaii.* 1916. Honolulu. ils. 43p. F/wrp. B26. $26.00.

ROCKEFELLER, John D. Jr. *Last Rivet: Story of Rockefeller Center.* 1940. NY. 1st. ils. suede cloth. F. B5. $40.00.

ROCKFELLOW, John A. *Log of an Arizona Trail Blazer.* 1933. Acme. 1st. ils. 201p. B19. $55.00.

ROCKNE, Dick. *Bow Down to Washington.* 1975. Strode. 1st. VG/VG. P8. $30.00.

ROCKWELL, F. F. *Gardening Under Glass.* 1923. Doubleday. 297p. VG. A10. $25.00.

ROCKWELL, Robert F. *Frederick Carder & His Steuben Glass 1903 – 1933.* 1966. Dexter. sm 4to. 35p. VG. H1. $22.50.

ROCKWOOD, Roy. *Great Marvel Series: Lost on the Moon (#5).* 1911. Cupples Leon. lists 7 titles. 248p. orange cloth. VG/2nd dj art. M20. $125.00.

RODEN, Christopher & Barbara. *The Case Files of Sherlock Holmes: The Blue Carbuncle.* 1999. Ashcroft. Calabash Press. 1st. VF/acetate dj. T2. $32.00.

RODEN, Christopher & Barbara. *The Case Files of Sherlock Holmes: The Dying Detective.* 1998. Ashcroft. Calabash Press. 1st. VF/acetate dj. T2. $30.00.

RODEN, Christopher & Barbara. *The Case Files of Sherlock Holmes: The Musgrave Ritual.* 1996. Ashcroft. Calabash Press. 1st. VF/acetate dj. T2. $40.00.

RODGERS, Alan. *Night.* 1991. Newark. Wildside Press. 1st. 1/250 # copies. sgn. VF/no dj as issued. T2. $35.00.

RODGERS, Andrew D. *Noble Fellow: William Starling Sullivant.* 1940. NY. 1st. 14 pl/3 maps. 361p. VG/dj. B26. $25.00.

RODMAN, Seldan. *The Peru Traveler. A Concise History and Guide.* 1967. NY. Meredith Press. 1st. ep maps. photo il. 189p. G/chipped dj. F3. $15.00.

RODMAN, Seldon. *Caribbean.* 1968. Hawthorne. 1st. 4to. 320p. dj. F3. $15.00.

RODRIQUEZ, Manuel. *Rum & Roosters.* (1957). Crowell. 1st. 256p. dj. F3 $15.00.

ROE, Francis. *Doctors & Doctor's Wives.* 1990. NAL. 1st. author's 1st book. F/F. W2. $75.00.

ROEDER, Ralph. *Juarez and His Mexico.* 1948. NY. Viking. 2nd. 761p. G. F3. $15.00.

ROESLER, Hugo. *Atlas of Cardio-Roentgenology.* 1940. Springfield. 1st. 124p. A13. $100.00.

ROETHKE, Theodore. *Straw for the Fire.* 1972. Doubleday. 1st. NF/NF. R14. $35.00.

ROFES, Eric. *Kids Book of Divorce.* 1981. Lexington, MA. Lewis Pub. 3rd. 8vo. F/F. C8. $15.00.

ROGAN, Barbara. *Suspicion.* 1999. NY. S&S. ARC. F/wrp. B2. $25.00.

ROGAN, Helen. *Mixed Company: Women in the Modern Army.* 1981. NY. Putnam. 1st. 333p. rem mk. VG/dj. A25. $18.00.

ROGER, J. E. *Shell Book.* 1951. Boston. Branford. revised. 503p. cloth. B1. $35.00.

ROGERS, David Banks. *Prehistoric Man of the Santa Barbara Coast.* 1929. Santa Barbara. Mus Nat Hist. ils/fld map. 452p. D11. $175.00.

ROGERS, Ernest E. *Connecticut's Naval Office at New London.* 1933. New London. CT. New London Co Hist. Soc. 1/750. ils. 357p. teg. T7. $55.00.

ROGERS, Francis M. *Europe Informed: An Exhibition of Early Books.* 1966. Harvard/Columbia. ils/index. F/wrp. O7. $45.00.

ROGERS, H. C. B. *Mounted Troops of the British Army 1066–1945.* 1959. London. 1st. ils. 256p. VG/poor. M4. $20.00.

ROGERS, Mary. *Rotten Book.* 1969. Harper Row. 1st. ils Steven Kellogg. F/VG. T5. $30.00.

ROGERS, Samuel. *Pleasures of Memory. In Two Parts.* 1805. Portland, ME. Prt for Daniel Johnson. 12mo. 127p. M1. $175.00.

ROGERS, Stanley. *Ships & Sailors.* 1928. Little, Brn. 1st. 8vo. VG. T10. $45.00.

ROGERS, Will. *Illiterate Digest.* 1924. Boni. 1st author's 2nd book. VG. L3. $85.00.

ROGERS, Will. *Letters of a Self-Made Diplomat to His President.* 1926. NY. Boni. 1st. NF/pict dj. L3. $250.00.

ROGERS, Will. *Wit & Wisdom.* 1936. NY. Stokes. 1st/2nd prt. photos. NF. L3. $45.00.

ROGIN, Gilbert. *Fencing Master & Other Stories.* 1965. Random. 1st. rem mk. NF/F. B4. $50.00.

ROGOW, Roberta. *Futurespeak: A Fan's Guide to the Language of Science Fiction.* 1991. NY. Paragon House. 1st. sgn. VF/VF. T2. $25.00.

ROGOW, Roberta. *The Problem of the Missing Miss.* 1998. NY. St. Martin. 1st. sgn by Rogow. VF/VF. T2. $30.00.

ROHAN, Michael Scott. *Cloud Castles.* 1993. London. Gollancz. 1st. VF/VF. T2. $20.00.

ROHAN, Michael Scott. *The Gates of Noon.* 1992. London. Gollancz. 1st. VF/VF. T2. $25.00.

ROHAN, Michael Scott. *The Lord of Middle Air.* 1994. London. Gollancz. 1st. VF/VF. T2. $20.00.

ROHDER, Regis. *Padre to the Papagos: Father Bonaventure Oblasser.* 1982. OFM Oblasser Library. 1st ed. ils. 72p. F. B19. $10.00.

ROHMER, Sax. *Brood of the Witch Queen.* 1924. Doubleday. 1st. G. P3. $45.00.

ROHMER, Sax. *Dope.* 1925. London. VG. M2. $12.00.

ROHMER, Sax. *Drums of Fu Manchu.* 1939. Doubleday Crime Club. 1st. F/NF. M15. $400.00.

ROHMER, Sax. *Emperor Fu Manchu.* 1959. London. Herbert Jenkins. 1st. F/dj. M15. $250.00.

ROHMER, Sax. *She Who Sleeps.* 1928. Doubleday Doran. 1st. VG. M19. $35.00.

ROJANKOVSKY, Feodor. *Tall Book of Nursery Tales.* 1944. Harper. 1st. 120p. VG/dj. D1. $95.00.

ROLLINI, Arthur. *Thirty Years With the Big Bands.* 1987. Urbana. Univ. of Illinois Press. 1st. F/F. B2. $35.00.

ROLTZ, L. T. C. *Picture History of Motoring.* 1956. Macmillan. 1st. 160p. cloth. VG/dj. M20. $25.00.

ROMAN, Catherine. *Foreplay.* 1989. NY. Random. 1st. F/F. H11. $35.00.

ROMBAUER, Irma S. *Joy of Cooking.* 1972. Bobbs Merrill. G. A16. $20.00.

ROME, Anthony; see Albert, Marvin H.

ROMERO, George A. *Dawn of the Dead.* 1978. St. Martin. 1st. F/dj. M2. $35.00.

ROMILLY, Eric. *Bleeding from the Roman.* 1949. London. 1st. F/dj. M2. $15.00.

ROMOLI, Kathleen. *Colombia: Gateway t South America.* 1941. Doubleday. 1st. 4t 364p. G. M20. $15.00.

ROMULO, Carlos P. *Mother America, Livin Story of Democracy.* 1943. NY. Garden City 1st. cloth. sm4to. 234p. G+. P1. $10.00.

RONAN, Colin. *Edmund Halley: Genius i Eclipse.* 1970. London. MacDonald. 1st Eng ils. 251p. VG/dj. K3. $25.00.

ROONEY, Andy. *Word for Word.* 1986 Putnam. 1st. F/F. B35. $20.00.

ROONEY, Mickey. *Life Is too Short.* 1991 Villard. 1st. sgn. F/F. $50.00.

ROOSEVELT, Nicholas. *A Front Row Sea* 1953. Norman. Univ. of Oklahoma. 1s cloth. ils. 304p. F/G. P1. $5.00.

ROOSEVELT, Robert Barnwell. *Game Bir of the North Carleton.* 1866. NY. A19. $75.00.

ROOSEVELT, Theodore. *African Gam Trails.* 1910. Scribner. 1st. gilt gr bdg. VG+ B5. $95.00.

ROOSEVELT, Theodore. *Ranch Life & th Hunting-Trail.* 1907. Century. sm 4to. il Remington. teg. stp City of Boston. H7 $55.00.

ROOSEVELT, Theodore. *Stories of the Grea West.* 1913. Century. sm 8vo. 254p. G. H1 $20.00.

ROOT, Ralph Rodney. *Camouflage wit Planting.* 1942. Chicago. Seymour. 79p VG/self wrp. A10. $35.00.

ROPER, Robert. *Royo Country.* 1973. Wn Morrow. 1st. F/dj. A23. $32.00.

ROQUELAURE, A.N.; see Rice, Anne.

ROREM, Ned. *Other Entertainment.* 1996 S&S. 1st. F/F. H11. $30.00.

RORER, Sarah Tyson. *My Best 250 Recipes* (1907). Phil. 162p. G. B18. $15.00.

ROSA, Joseph. *West of Wild Bill Hickok* 1982. Norman. OK. 1st. 223p. VG/VG. J2 $195.00.

ROSE, Barbara. *Alexander Liberman.* 1981 NY. Abbeville. rem mk. VG. H4. $75.00.

ROSE, Elizabeth. *Socerer's Apprentice.* 1968 NY. Walker. 1st Am. sm 4to. unp. VG. C14 $12.00.

ROSE, James C. *Creative Gardens.* 1958. NY 1st. folio. VG. B26. $34.00.

ROSE, Jasper. *Lucy Boston.* 1966. NY. Walck. 1st Am. sm 8vo. 71p. VG/dj. T5. $25.00.

ROSE, Lois. *Shattered Ring.* 1970. John Knox. 1st. NF/dj. P3. $30.00.

ROSE, Mark. *Science Fiction.* 1976. Prentice Hall. 1st. NF/dj. M2. $22.00.

ROSE, Pete. *Pete Rose Story.* 1970. World. 1st. VG/dj. P8. $45.00.

ROSE, Robert T. *Advocates & Adversaries.* 1977. Lakeside Classics. 1st thus. teg. dk bl cloth. F. T11. $30.00.

ROSE, William Ganson. *Cleveland, the Making of a City.* 1950. Cleveland. 1272p. VG/dj. B18. $35.00.

ROSEBAUM, Thane. *Second Hand Smoke.* 1999. NY. St. Martin. AP. F/wrp. B2. $25.00.

ROSEMONT, Penelope. *Surrealist Women. An International Anthology.* 1998. Austin. Univ. of Texas Press. 1st. 600p. F in wrps. B2. $25.00.

ROSEN, Edward. *Naming of the Telescope.* 1947. NY. Schuman. 1st. 110p. dj. K5. $45.00.

ROSEN, Richard. *Fadeaway.* 1986. NY. Harper & Row. 1st. F/F. H11. $30.00.

ROSEN, Richard. *Fadeaway.* 1986. Harper & Row. 1st. NF/NF. G8. $10.00.

ROSEN, Richard. *Saturday Night Dead.* 1988. NY. Viking. 1st. VF/VF. T2. $15.00.

ROSENBACH, A. S. W. *Books & Bidders: Adventures of a Bibliophile.* 1927. 77 pl. 402p. VG/dj. A4. $65.00.

ROSENBAUM, David. *Sasha's Trick.* 1995. NY. Mysterious. 1st. F/F. H11. $25.00.

ROSENBAUM, David. *Zaddick.* 1993. NY. Mysterious. 1st. F/F. H11. $30.00.

ROSENBERG, David. *Movie that Changed My Life.* 1991. Viking. 304p. VG/dj. C5. $15.00.

ROSENBERG, Nancy. *Interest of Justice.* 1993. Dutton. 1st. 368p. F/F. W2. $35.00.

ROSENBERG, Nancy Taylor. *Interest of Justice.* 1993. NY. Dutton. 1st. sgn. VF/VF. T2. $22.00.

ROSENBERG, Nancy Taylor. *Mitigating Circumstances.* 1993. Dutton. 1st. rem mk. F/F. H11. $25.00.

ROSENBERG, Philip. *Tygers of Wrath.* 1991. St. Martin. 1st. F/dj. S18. $25.00.

ROSENBERG, Robert. *The Cutting Room.* 1993. NY. S&S. 1st. sgn bkplt laid in. VF/VF. T2. $25.00.

ROSENE, Walter. *Bobwhite Quail: Its Life & Management.* 1969. Rutgers. 418p+65 photos+5 mc pl+2 maps. F/dj. A17. $50.00.

ROSENFELD, Lulla. *Death and the I Ching.* 1981. NY. Potter. 1st. author's 1st mystery. F/F. H11. $20.00.

ROSS, D. A. *Introduction to Oceanography.* 1970. NY. Appleton Century Crofts. 384p. VG. D8. $8.50.

ROSS, David. *Letters from Foxy.* 1966. Pantheon. 1st Am. 103p. cloth. VG/clip. M20. $18.00.

ROSS, Diana. *Secrets of a Sparrow.* 1993. Villard Books. 1st. pics. F/F. S19. $35.00.

ROSS, Edward Alsworth. *Sin & Society: Analysis of Latter-Day Iniquity.* 1907. Houghton Mifflin. 1st. VG. N2. $15.00.

ROSS, James. *They Don't Dance Much.* 1940. Houghton Mifflin. 1st. F/F. B4. $500.00.

ROSS, Kate. *Devil in Music.* 1997. NY. Viking. 1st. sgn. F/dj. T2. $35.00.

ROSS, Kate. *Whom the Gods Love.* 1995. NY. Viking. 1st. VF/VF. H11. $20.00.

ROSS, Lillian. *Portrait of Hemingway.* 1961. S&S. 1st. G/G. B35. $16.00.

ROSS, Norman. *Epic of Man.* 1961. NY. Time. 1st. folio. 307p. dj. F3. $10.00.

ROSS, Patricia. *In Mexico They Say.* 1946. Knopf. 3rd. 211p. dj. F3. $15.00.

ROSS, Paul. *4 Corners on Main Street.* 1990. Toronto. 1st. F/NF. T12. $15.00.

ROSS, Sam. *He Ran all the Way.* 1947. NY. 1st. NF/VG clip. B4. $150.00.

ROSS, W. Gillies. *Arctic Whalers Icy Seas.* 1985. Tor. 1st. 263p. F/dj. A17. $25.00.

ROSSELLINI, Roberto. *War Trilogy.* 1973. Grossman. 1st. 467p. F/dj. A17. $15.00.

ROSSETTI, Christina. *Goblin Market.* nd. Lippincott. ils Rackham/4 mc pl. 42p. cloth. VG+/dj. M20. $200.00.

ROSSI, Agnes. *Quick.* 1992. Norton. 1st. author's 1st book. F/dj. A24. $30.00.

ROSSI, Carlo. *In the Dungeons of Mussolini.* 1936. NY. Italian Patronati. 1st. wrp. 32p. VG. B2. $25.00.

ROSSMAN, Douglas A. *Garter Snakes: Evolution & Ecology.* 1996. U. OK. ils/maps. 332p. AN/dj. S15. $40.00.

ROSSNER, Judith. *August.* 1983. Boston. Houghton. 1st. F/F. H11. $20.00.

ROSSNER, Judith. *Emmeline.* 1980. NY. S&S. 1st. F/F. H11. $25.00.

ROSSNER, Judith. *Looking for Mr. Goodbar.* 1975. S&S. 1st/MTI. F/dj. M25. $35.00.

ROSTAND, Edmund. *Story of Chanticleer.* 1913. Stokes. 1st. ils J. A. Shepherd. VG. M5. $60.00.

ROSTEN, Leo. *Treasury of Jewish Quotations.* 1972. NY. 1st. 716p. VG/dj. B5. $25.00.

ROSTENBERG, Leona. *Minority Press & the English Crown: A Study in Repression.* 1971. Nieuwkoop. De Graaf. 4to. ils. cloth. R12. $75.00.

ROSTENBERG, Leona & Madeleine Stern. *Old Books, Rare Friends: Two Literary Sleuths and Their Shared Passion.* 1997. NY. Doubleday. 1st. VF/VF. T2. $22.00.

ROSTOV, Mara. *A Careless Feast.* 1985. NY. Putnam. 1st. F/F. H11. $30.00.

ROSTRON, Richard. *Sorcerer's Apprentice.* 1941. NY. Morrow. 1st thus. 41p. VG. D4. $25.00.

ROSVALL, Toivo David. *Very Stupid Folk.* 1938. Dutton. 1st. ils Tibor Gergely. VG+/VG. C8. $45.00.

ROTH, Barry. *Annotated Bibliography of Jane Austen Studies.* 1985. VA U. 1st. AN. V4. $25.00.

ROTH, Philip. *American Pastoral.* 1977. Houghton Mifflin. UP. F/buff colored wrp. F/buff colored w. $50.00.

ROTH, Philip. *Anatomy Lesson.* 1983. FSG. 1st. NF/NF. H11. $30.00.

ROTH, Philip. *Great American Novel.* 1973. HRW. 1st. F/VG. P8. $22.50.

ROTH, Philip. *Our Gang.* 1971. Random. 1st. F/F. B35. $35.00.

ROTH, Philip. *Portnoy's Complaint.* 1969. Random. 1st. F/dj. B35. $38.00.

ROTH, Robert. *Sand in the Wind.* 1973. Boston. Little, Brn. 1st. F/NF. B2. $30.00.

ROTH, Susan. *Weekend Garden Guide.* 1991. Emmaus. Rodale. 358p. VG. A10. $18.00.

ROTHENBERG, Jerome. *Shaking the Pumpkin.* 1972. Doubleday. F/dj. A19. $35.00.

ROTHENBERG, Rebecca. *The Dandelion Murders.* 1994. NY. Mysterious. 1st. VF/VF. H11. $35.00.

ROTHERT, Otto A. *Outlaws of Cave-In-Rock.* 1924. Cleveland. AH Clark. 1st. ils. 364p. maroon cloth. B11. $450.00.

ROTHERY, Agnes. *Central American Roundabout.* 1944. Dodd Mead. 1st. 248p. dj. F3. $15.00.

ROTHERY, Agnes. *South America. The West Coast & the East.* 1930. Boston. Houghton Mifflin. 1st. 294p. G/chipped dj. F3. $20.00.

ROTHERY, Agnes. *South America. The West Coast & the East.* 1930. Boston. Houghton Mifflin. 1st. 294p. G/no dj. F3. $15.00.

ROTHSCHILD, Michael. *Wonder Monger.* 1990. NY. Viking. 1st. F/dj. A23. $32.00.

ROTHWELL, H. T. *Duet for Three Spies.* 1967. Roy. 1st. F/F. P3. $10.00.

ROTSLER, William. *Zandra.* 1973. Doubleday. 1st. F/dj. M2. $25.00.

ROTTENSTEINER, Franz. *Science Fiction Book: Illustrated History.* 1975. Seabury. 1st. F/dj. M2. $15.00.

ROUECHE, Berton. *Last Enemy.* nd. Harper & Row. 1st hc ed. VG/VG. G8. $10.00.

ROUNDS, Glen. *Stolen Pony.* 1948. Holiday House. sgn/sketch. VG/VG. O3. $25.00.

ROURKE, Thomas. *Gomez: Tyrant of the Andes.* 1936. Morrow. 1st. 320p. dj. F3. $15.00.

ROUSE, John. *Criollo: Spanish Cattle in the Americas.* 1977. Norman, OK. 303p. AN/dj. A10. $40.00.

ROUSE, Parke Jr. *Great Wagon Road: From Philadelphia to the South.* 1973. McGraw Hill. VG/VG. O3. $65.00.

ROUSSEAU, Victor. *Messiah of the Cylinder.* 1917. McClurg. 1st. ils Joseph Clement Coll. VG. M2. $150.00.

ROVIN, Jeff. *Vespers.* 1998. NY. St. Martin. ARC. F/wrp. B2. $25.00.

ROVINSON, H. Wheeler. *The Religious Ideas of the Old Testament.* 1956. Duckworth. 246p. G. B29. $7.50.

ROWAN, A. N. *Of Mice, Models & Men.* 1984. Albany. 8vo. 323p. VG. B1. $26.50.

ROWE, John. *Introduction to Archaeology of Cuzco.* 1944. Cambridge. ils. VG/wrp. O7. $45.00.

ROWE, John. *Long Live the King.* 1984. Stein Day. VG/VG. P3. $15.00.

ROWE, Richard. *Jack Afloat & Ashore.* 1875. London. Smith Elder. 268p. T7. $45.00.

ROWELL, Galen. *Mountains of the Middle Kingdom: Exploring. China & Tibet.* 1983. Sierra Club. 1st. photos. VG/VG. M17. $30.00.

ROWELL, Raymond J. *Ornamental Flowering Shrubs in Australia.* 1991. Kensington. NSW. 28 mc photos. 334p. AN. B26. $36.00.

ROWLAND, B. *Birds with Human Souls: A Guide to Bird Symbolism.* 1978. Knoxville. ils. 213p. pict cloth. NF/NF. M12. $30.00.

ROWLAND, John. *Rutherford: Atom Pioneer.* 1957. NY. VG/dj. K3. $12.00.

ROWLAND, Peter. *Disappearance of Edwin Drood.* 1992. St. Martin. 1st Am. F/NF. N4. $25.00.

ROWLAND, Phyllis. *Every Day in the Year.* 1959. Little, Brn. 1st. sm 4to. unp. VG. C14. $17.00.

ROWLANDS, John J. *Cache Lake Country.* 1990. Lyons Burford. rpt. 272p. AN/dj. S15. $15.00.

ROWLEY, Gordon D. *Caudiciform & Pachycaul Succulents.* 1987. Mill Valley. ils/photos. 282p. M/dj. B26. $85.00.

ROWLEY, H. H. *The Faith of Israel: Aspects of Old Testament Thought.* 1956. Westminster. 220p. G/torn dj. B29. $9.00.

ROWLING, J. K. *Harry Potter and the Chamber of Secrets.* 1999. NY. Scholastic Press. 1st. F/F. M23. $20.00.

ROWLING, J. K. *Harry Potter and the Sorcerer's Stone.* 1998. NY. Scholastic Press. sgn 1st. scarce. F/F. M23. $1000.00.

ROWNDREE, Lester. *Flowering Shrubs of California & Their Value.* 1948 (1939). Stanford. 2nd. ils. VG+/torn. B26. $45.00.

ROWSE, A. L. *Shakespeare's Southampton.* 1965. Harper Row. 1st Am. 323p. VG/dj. M20. $25.00.

ROWSOME, Frank. *Verse by the Side of the Road.* 1965. Brattleboro. 2nd. lg 12mo. cloth F/F. C8. $20.00.

ROXAS, Manuel. *Problems of Philippine Rehabilitation & Trade Relations.* 1947 Manila. Bureau of Prt. 208p. VG. P1. $10.00.

ROXBOROUGH, Henry. *Stanley Cup Story.* 1966. Follett. revised/1st prt. photos. VG P8. $20.00.

ROXBURGH, Ronald. *Origins of Lincoln's Inn.* 1963. Cambridge. M11. $85.00.

ROY, Arundhali. *God of Small Things.* 1997. Random. 1st Canadian. AN/as issued. T12. $70.00.

ROY, Gabrielle. *Tin Flute.* 1947. Reynal Hitchcock. 1st. VG. P3. $25.00.

ROY, Maurice. *Dynamics of Satellites.* 1963. Academic. 8vo. 335p. xl. K5. $45.00.

ROZAN, S. J. *Mandarin Plaid.* 1996. NY. St. Martin. 1st. sgn. VF in dj. M15. $45.00.

ROZAN, S. J. *No Colder Place.* 1997. NY. St. Martin. 1st. sgn. VF in dj. M15. $35.00.

RUARK, Robert. *Uhuru.* 1962. McGraw Hill. 1st. 555p. NF. W2. $20.00.

RUBER, Peter. *Last Bookman.* 1968. NY. Candlelight. 1st. sgn. VG/dj. K3. $35.00.

RUBIE, Peter. *Werewolf.* 1991. Longmeadow. 1st. F/F. P3. $16.00.

RUBULIS, Aleksis. *Baltic Literature.* 1970. Notre Dame. 1st. F/clip. O4. $15.00.

RUCKA, Greg. *Finder.* 1997. NY. Bantam. 1st. VF/VF. T2. $20.00.

RUCKA, Greg. *Keeper.* 1996. NY. Bantam. 1st. author's 1st novel. VF/VF. T2. $25.00.

RUCKA, Greg. *Shooting at Midnight.* 1999. NY. Bantam. 1st. sgn. VF/VF. T2. $25.00.

RUCKER, Rudy. *Secret of Life.* 1985. Bluejay. 1st. F/dj. M2. $25.00.

RUCKER, Wilbur. *History of the Opthalmoscope.* 1971. Rochester. 1st. sgn. 127p. A13. $125.00.

RUDD, W. H. *Orrocco Poultry Farm.* 1893. Boston. Rudd. 64p. wrp. A10. $35.00.

RUE, Leonard Lee. *World of the White-Tailed Deer.* 1962. Lippincott. ils. 134p. NF/VG. S15. $14.00.

RUFF, Willie. *Call to Assembly: Autobiography of Musical Storyteller.* 1991. Viking. 1st. 432p. F/F. B4. $45.00.

RUFFNER, Budge. *All Hell Needs Is Water.* 1972. Tucson, AZ. 1st. sgn. 96p. NF/VG+. B19. $35.00.

RUGGERO, Ed. *38 North Yankee.* 1990. NY. Pocket. 1st. F/F. H11. $25.00.

RUGGIERI, Guido. *Secrets of the Sky.* 1969 (1967). London. Hamlyn. trans DD Bayliss. 174p. VG/dj. K5. $15.00.

RUGGLES, R. G. *One Rose.* 1964. Oakland. 1st. sgn. VG/dj. B5. $80.00.

RUHL, Arthur. *Central Americans: Adventures & Impressions.* 1928. Scribner. 1st. 284p. F3. $20.00.

RULE, Ann. *Small Sacrifices.* 1987. NAL. 1st. F/wht dj. A24. $15.00.

RUNDELL, Maria Eliza. *New System of Domestic Cookery, Formed Upon Principles.* 1864. 32mo. 348p. VG. E6. $75.00.

RUNTE, Alfred. *Yosemite: Embattled Wilderness.* 1990. U NE. 1st. ils. F/NF. O4. $30.00.

RUNYAN, Damon. *Guys & Dolls.* 1931. Stokes. 1st. blk-lettered red cloth. VG. C15. $100.00.

RUNYAN, Harry. *Faulkner Glossary.* (1954). NY. Citadel. stated 1st. 8vo. 210p. H4. $25.00.

RUNYON, Damon. *Take It Easy.* 1938. Stokes. 1st. VG+/VG+ clip. B4. $350.00.

RUSH, George Herman. *Babe Ruth's Own Book of Baseball.* 1928. Putnam. 1st. photos. G+. P8. $85.00.

RUSH, Hanniford. *Man to the Moon.* 1962. Chicago. Rand McNally. 4to. 96p. VG/wrp. K5. $8.00.

RUSH, Norman. *Whites.* 1986. Knopf. 1st. F/F. B4. $75.00.

RUSHDIE, Salman. *Good Advice Is Rarer Than Rubies.* (1995). NY. Pantheon. adv excerpt from East West. 1/2000 copies. pict wrp. sgn by author. F/in glossy envelope. B3. $40.00.

RUSHDIE, Salman. *Grimus.* 1979. Woodstock. Overlook Press. 1st Am ed. review copy. F/F. D10. $175.00.

RUSHDIE, Salman. *Satanic Verses.* 1988. Viking. 1st. F/dj. S18. $50.00.

RUSHDIE, Salman. *Shame.* 1983. NY. Knopf. 1st Am ed. F/F. O11. $35.00.

RUSHDIE, Salman. *The Ground Beneath Her Feet.* 1999. NY. Henry Holt. 1st. sgn. F in F dj. D10. $55.00.

RUSHDIE, Salman. *The Moor's Last Sigh.* 1995. NY. Pantheon. 1st am ed. sgn. F/F. O11. $65.00.

RUSHER, William A. *Coming Battle for the Media.* 1988. Morrow. 1st. 228p. F/F. W2. $25.00.

RUSHKOFF, Douglas. *Ecstasy Club.* 1997. np. Harper Collins. 1st. author's 1st novel. F/cover art. R16. $35.00.

RUSHO, W. L. *Powell's Canyon Voyage.* 1969. Filter Press. ils. 44p. NF. B19. $3.50.

RUSHTON, Charles. *Furnace for a Foe.* 1957. London. 1st. VG/dj. M2. $20.00.

RUSKIN, John. *Dame Wiggins of Lee & Her Seven Wonderful Cats.* 1980. NY. Crowell. 1t. sm 8vo. 29p. F/dj. W2. $20.00.

RUSS, Joanna. *Two of Them.* 1978. Berkley Putnam. 1st. F/F. P3. $20.00.

RUSSEL, Ross. *Bird Lives! The High Life and Hard Times of Charlie Yardbird Parker.* 1973. NY. Charterhouse. 1st. NF in VG dj w/sunned spine & tears. B2. $85.00.

RUSSELL, Alan. *Shame.* 1998. NY. S&S. 1st. sgn. VF/VF. T2. $25.00.

RUSSELL, Alan. *The Forest Prime Evil.* 1992. NY. Walker. 1st. sgn. VF/VF. T2. $35.00.

RUSSELL, Alan. *The Hotel Detective.* 1994. NY. Mysterious Press. 1st. sgn. VF/VF. T2. $35.00.

RUSSELL, Andy. *Andy Russell's Adventures With Wild Animals.* 1978. NY. Knopf. F/dj. A19. $25.00.

RUSSELL, Austin. *Charles M. Russell, Artist.* 1957. Twayne. 1st. 247p. VG/VG. J2. $145.00.

RUSSELL, Austin. *Mr. Arrow.* 1947. Veechhurst. 1st. VG/dj. M2. $27.00.

RUSSELL, Bertrand. *Authority & the Individual.* 1949. Unwin Bros. 1st. B35. $45.00.

RUSSELL, Bill. *Second Wind.* 1979. Random. 1st. VG+/dj. P8. $15.00.

RUSSELL, Charles Edward. *Outlook for the Philippines.* 1922. NY. Century. 411p. VG+. P1. $10.00.

RUSSELL, Eric Frank. *Men, Martians & Machines: Classics of Modern SF Vol I.* 1984. NY. Crown. 1st thus. F/dj. G10. $14.00.

RUSSELL, Eric Frank. *Sinister Barrier.* 1948. np. Fantasy Press. 1st. VG/VG dj. M19. $75.00.

RUSSELL, Eric Frank. *Sinister Barrier.* 1948. Fantasy. 1st. VG/G. P3. $60.00.

RUSSELL, Franklin. *Secret Islands.* 1966. Hodder Stoughton. 1st. F/VG. A26. $20.00.

RUSSELL, Howard. *Long, Deep Furrow: 3 Centuries of Farming in New England.* 1976. Hanover. 672p. dj. A10. $40.00.

RUSSELL, Howard Lewis. *Iced Tea and Ignorance.* 1989. NY. Fine. 1st. F/VF. H11. $20.00.

RUSSELL, Jacqueline. *If You Like Horses.* 1932. Houghton Mifflin. 1st. 12mo. ils. VG. O3. $25.00.

RUSSELL, Jane. *Jane Russell.* 1985. Franklin Watts. 1st. inscr. F/F. A23. $50.00.

RUSSELL, Martin. *Darker Side of Death.* 1985. Collins Crime Club. 1st. VG/dj. P3. $15.00.

RUSSELL, Paul. *Salt Point.* 1990. Dutton. 1st. author's 1st book. VG/VG. L1. $30.00.

RUSSELL, Randy. *Caught Looking.* 1992. Doubleday. 1st. F/dj. P8. $20.00.

RUSSELL, Ray. *Bishop's Daughter.* 1981. Boston. Houghton Mifflin. 1st. VF/VF. T2. $35.00.

RUSSELL, Ray. *Incubus.* 1976. Morrow. 1st. F/dj. M2. $100.00.

RUST, Brian. *The Dance Bands.* 1974. New Rochelle. Arlington House. 1st Am ed. F/lightly used dj. sm tears at end of spine. B2. $40.00.

RUTHERFORD, Douglas. *Black Leather Murders.* 1966. Walker. 1st. VG/VG. P3. $15.00.

RUTHERFORD, Douglas. *Collision Course.* 1978. Macmillan. 1st. NF/dj. P3. $16.00.

RUTHERFORD, Douglas. *Turbo.* 1980. Macmillan. 1st. NF/NF. P3. $15.00.

RUTHERFORD, Mildred Lewis. *The Assassination of Abraham Lincoln.* 1924. self pub. Athens. GA. 1st. orig printed wrp. VG. M8. $45.00.

RUTHERFURD, Edward. *Russka: Novel of Russia.* 1991. NY. sgn. VG/dj. M17. $20.00.

RUTSALA, Vern. *Window.* 1964. Wesleyan. 1st. poet's 1st book. F/dj. V1. $75.00.

RUTTER, John. *Culture & Diseases of the Peach.* 1880. Harrisburg. 95p. cloth. VG. A10. $50.00.

RYAN, Alan. *Bones Wizard.* 1988. Doubleday. 1st. F/dj. M2. $30.00.

RYAN, Alan. *Night Visions 1: All Original Stories.* 1984. Niles. Dark Harvest. 1st. F/dj. G10. $115.00.

RYAN, Alan. *Penguin Book of Vampire Stories.* 1991. Bloomsbury Books. F/dj. P3. $20.00.

RYAN, Alan. *Reader's Companion to Mexico.* 1995. Harcourt Brace. 1st. 372p. wrp. F3. $15.00.

RYAN, Bob. *Boston Celtics.* 1989. Addison Wesley. 1st. photos. F/F. P8. $27.50.

RYAN, Charles C. *Starry Messenger.* 1979. St. Martin. 1st. F/F. P3. $20.00.

RYAN, Marah Ellis. *Indian Love Letters.* 1911. McClurg. 2nd. 122p. brd. G+. F7. $40.00.

RYAN, Nolan. *Throwing Heat.* 1988. Doubleday. 1st. sgn. F/F. A23. $75.00.

RYAN, Stella. *Death Never Weeps.* 1992. Harper Collins. 1st. VG/dj. P3. $25.00.

RYCROFT, Brian. *Kirstenbosch.* 1980. Cape Town. 4to. F in dj. B26. $29.00.

RYDEN, Hope. *God's Dog.* 1975. NY. photos. 288p. VG/VG. S15. $15.00.

RYDER, Jonathan; see Ludlum, Robert.

RYDER, Tom. *High Stepper.* 1979. London/NY. Allen. VG/G. O3. $25.00.

RYLE, Gilbert. *Concept of Mind.* 1949. London. Hutchinson. 334p. bl cloth. VG/dj. G1. $100.00.

RYMAN, Geoff. *Child Garden.* 1989. London. Unwin Hyman. 1st. sgn. F/dj. M21. $60.00.

— S —

SABERHAGEN, Fred. *A Question of Time.* 1992. NY. Tor. 1st. VF/VF. T2. $8.00.

SABLE, Martin. *Latin American Urbanization; A Guide to the Literature, Organizations, and Personnel.* 1971. NJ. Scarecrow Press. 1st. ex lib. 1077p. F. F3. $20.00.

SABLOFF, Jeremy. *The Cities of Ancient Mexico.* 1989. NY. Thames & Hudson. 1st. b/w photo ils. 224p. G/G. F3. $25.00.

SADOWNICK, Douglas. *Sacred Lips of the Bronx.* 1994. NY. St. Martin. ARC. wrps. F. B2. $25.00.

SAENZ, Benjamin Allire. *Carry Me Like Water.* (1995). NY. Hyperion. 1st. sgn & dated by author. F/F. B3. $30.00.

SAFFRON, Robert. *The Demon Device.* 1979. NY. Putnam. 1st. F+/F. H11. $30.00.

SAGAN, Carl. *Contact.* 1985. NY. S&S. 1st. F/VF. H11. $35.00.

SALK, Jonas. *Man Unfolding.* (1972). NY. Harper & Row. 2nd printing. presentation copy sgn by Salk on ffep. gray cloth. dj. xxii. 118. (4)p. K1. $75.00.

SALLIS, James. *Bluebottle.* 1998. NY. Walker. 1st. sgn. VF/VF. T2. $25.00.

SALLIS, James. *Death Will Have Your Eyes.* 1997. NY. St. Martin. 1st. sgn. VF/VF. T2. $25.00.

SALLIS, James. *Eye of the Cricket.* 1997. NY. Walker. 1st. sgn. VF/VF. T2. $25.00.

SALLIS, James. *Renderings.* 1995. Seattle. Black Heron Press. 1st. sgn. VF/pict wrp. T2. $15.00.

SALLNOW, Michael. *Pilgrims of the Andes.* 1987. DC. Smithsonian. 1st. 351p. G/G. F3. $25.00.

SALMON, George. *Infallibility of the Church.* 1959. Baker. 497p. VG/VG. B29. $14.50.

SALTEN, Felix. *Bambi.* 1931. NY. Grosset & Dunlap. G. A16. $7.00.

SALTER, James. *Light Years.* 1975. NY. Random House. 1st. F. owner's name/NF. B2. $30.00.

SALTER, James. *Solo Faces.* 1979. Boston. Little, Brn. 1st. sgn & dated. F/NF. lt wear. D10. $110.00.

SALZMAN, Mark. *The Soloist.* (1994). NY. Random House. 1st. author's third book. sgn by author. F/F. B3. $45.00.

SANDERS, George. *Memoirs of a Professional Cad.* 1960. np. Putnam. 1st. pc. F/VG dj. M19. $35.00.

SANDERS, John. *The Hat of Authority.* 1965. London. Heinemann. 1st. F/F. H11. $30.00.

SANDERS, Lawrence. *McNally's Gamble.* 1997. NY. Putnam. 1st. F/VF. H11. $15.00.

SANDERS, Lawrence. *The Anderson Tapes.* 1970. NY. Putnam. 1st. F/F. H11. $115.00.

SANDERS, Lawrence. *The Pleasures of Helen.* 1971. NY. Putnam. 1st. author's second novel. F/F. T2. $16.00.

SANDERS, Lawrence. *The Seduction of Peter S.* 1983. NY. Putnam. 1st. F/F. H11. $35.00.

SANDERSON, Ivan. *Book of Great Jungles.* 1965. NY. Messner. 1st. 480p. G/chipped dj. F3. $15.00.

SANDERSON, Jim. *El Camino Del Rio.* 1998. Albuquerque. Univ. of New Mexico Press. 1st. author's 1st novel. sgn. VF/VF. T2. $30.00.

SANDFORD, John. *Eyes of Prey.* 1991. NY. Putnam. 1st. F/F. H11. $35.00.

SANDFORD, John. *Night Crew.* 1997. NY. Putnam. 1st. NF/NF. G8. $10.00.

SANDFORD, John. *Shadow Prey.* 1990. NY. Putnam. 1st. VG/VG. G8. $12.50.

SANDFORD, John. *Silent Prey.* 1992. NY. Putnam. 1st. F/F. H11. $30.00.

SANDFORD, John. *The Empress File.* 1991. NY. Henry Holt. 1st. F in dj. M15. $50.00.

SANDFORD, John. *The Fools Run.* 1989. NY. Henry Holt. 1st. F/dj. M15. $50.00.

SANDFORD, John. *Winter Prey.* 1993. NY. Putnam. 1st. VF/F+. H11. $25.00.

SANDMELL, Samuel. *Judaism and Christian Beginnings.* 1978. Oxford. 510p. VG. B29. $16.50.

SANDOZ, Maurice. *The Pleasures of Mexico.* 1957. NY. Kamin Pub. 1st. 4to. 171p. G/chipped dj. F3. $25.00.

SANDSTROM, Eve K. *Death Down Home.* 1990. NY. Scribners. 1st. author's 1st mystery. sgn. VF/VF. T2. $20.00.

SANFORD, Herb. *Tommy and Jimmy. The Dorsey Years.* 1972. New Rochelle. Arlington House. 1st. F/very lightly used dj. B2. $30.00.

SANGSTER, Jimmy. *Blackball.* 1987. NY. Henry Holt. 1st. VF/VF. T2. $15.00.

SANGSTER, Jimmy. *Snowball.* 1986. NY. Henry Holt. 1st. VF/VF. T2. $16.00.

SANTANGELO, Elena. *By Blood Possessed.* 1999. NY. St. Martin. 1st. sgn. F/F. G8. $25.00.

SARG, Tony. *Tony Sarg's Surprise Book.* 1941. NY. McGraw-Hill. by B. F. Jay. G. A16. $80.00.

SAROYAN, William. *The Adventures of Wesley Jackson.* 1946. NY. Harcourt Brace. 1st. F/NF. D10. $55.00.

SARTON, May. *Anger.* (1982). NY. Norton. 1st. journal. F/F. B3. $40.00.

SARTON, May. *Encore, A Journal of the Eightieth Year.* (1993). NY. Norton. 1st. journal. F/F. B3. $20.00.

SARTON, May. *The Magnificent Spinster.* (1986). London. Women's Press. 1st British ed. F/F. B3. $25.00.

SATTERTHWAIT, Walter. *A Flower in the Desert.* 1992. NY. St. Martin. 1st. VF in dj. M15. $45.00.

SATTERTHWAIT, Walter. *Escapade.* 1995. NY. St. Martin. 1st. sgn. VF in dj. M15. $50.00.

SATTERTHWAIT, Walter. *The Gold of Mayani.* 1995. Gallup. Buffalo Medicine. 1st. VF/dj. M15. $35.00.

SATTERTHWAIT, Walter. *The Hanged Man.* 1993. NY. St. Martin. 1st. VF in dj. M15. $45.00.

SATTERTHWAIT, Walter. *Wilde West.* (1991). NY. St. Martin. 1st. inscr & dated by author. F/F. B3. $50.00.

SAUER, Carl Ortwin. *The Early Spanish Main.* 1966. Berkeley. Univ. of California Press. beige cloth. decor ep. 27 ils. 306p. VG in lightly worn dj. P4. $75.00.

SAUER, Erich. *From Eternity to Eternity.* 1954. Eerdmans. 207p. VG/torn dj. B29. $7.00.

SAUL, John. *Creature.* 1989. NY. Bantam. 1st. VF/VF. T2. $9.00.

SAUL, John. *Darkness.* 1991. NY. Bantam. 1st. VF/VF. T2. $9.00.

SAUL, John. *Guardian.* 1993. NY. Fawcett. 1st. VF/VF. H11. $25.00.

SAUL, John. *Second Child.* 1990. NY. Bantam. 1st. VF/VF. T2. $8.00.

SAUL, John. *The God Project.* 1982. NY. Bantam. 1st. VF/NVF. T2. $12.00.

SAUTER, Eric. *Skeletons.* 1990. NY. Dutton. 1st. F. rem mk/VF. T2. $5.00.

SAVAGE, Marc. *Flamingos.* 1992. NY. Doubleday. 1st. sgn. VF/VF. T2. $25.00.

SAVAGE, Tom. *Precipice.* 1994. Boston. Little, Brn. 1st. author's 1st book. VF/VF. H11. $40.00.

SAWYER, Robert J. *Flashforward.* 1999. NY. Tor. 1st ed. F/F. M23. $24.00.

SAYER, Chloe. *Costumes of Mexico.* 1985. Austin. Univ. of Texas. 1st. wrp. 4to. 240p. F/F. F3. $30.00.

SAYERS, Dorothy. *The Man Born to be King.* 1943. Harper. 339p. G. B29. $8.00.

SAYLOR, Steven. *Catilina's Riddle.* 1993. NY. St. Martin. 1st. sgn. VF/VF. T2. $40.00.

SAYLOR, Steven. *The Venus Throw.* (1995). NY. St. Martin. 1st. F/F. B3. $25.00.

SCARBOROUGH, Dorothy. *Impatient Griselda.* 1927. NY. Harper. 1st. VG/VG. B2. $50.00.

SCHAEFFER, Edith. *A Way of Seeing.* 1977. Revell. 255p. VG/VG. B29. $7.50.

SCHAPIRO, Eleanor Iler (ed). *Wadsworth, Center to City.* 1938. Wadsworth. ils. hc. 203p. VG. B18. $45.00.

SCHIMMEL, Betty. *To See You Again.* 1999. NY. Dutton. 1st. sgn. VF/VF. T2. $25.00.

SCHINE, Cathleen. *The Evolution of Jane.* (1998). Boston. Houghton Mifflin. ARC. pict wrp. F. B3. $20.00.

SCHINE, Cathleen. *The Love Letter.* (1995). Boston. Houghton Mifflin. 1st. F/F. B3. $35.00.

SCHINE, Cathleen. *To the Birdhouse.* (1990). NY. FSG. 1st. author's 2nd book. F/F. B3. $50.00.

SCHLESINGER, Arthur M., Jr. *A Thousand Days: John F. Kennedy in the White House.* 1965. Houghton Mifflin. 1st. NF/lightly chipped & rubbed. clipped dj. M25. $45.00.

SCHNEIDER, Joyce Anne. *Darkness Falls.* 1989. NY. Pocket. 1st. F/NF. H11. $15.00.

SCHOFIELD, Susan Clark. *Telluride.* 1993. Chapel Hill. Algonquin. 1st. F/F. H11. $20.00.

SCHOONMAKER, Frank. *Frank Schoonmaker's Encyclopedia of Wine.* 1965. NY. Hastings House. VG/G. A28. $12.95.

SCHULLER, Gunther. *Early Jazz, Its Roots and Musical Development.* 1968. NY. Oxford. 1st. F/clip. lightly used dj. B2. $45.00.

SCHULMAN, Irving. *Harlow: An Intimate Biography.* 1964. NY. Bernard Geis Associates. 1st. sgn by author. F/NF. O11. $35.00.

SCHULTZ, Samuel J. *The Old Testament Speaks.* 1960. Harper. 436p. VG. B29. $10.00.

SCHUYLER, George. *Black & Conservative — The Autobiography of George S. Schuyler.* 1966. np. Arlington House. 1st. VG/NF dj. M19. $25.00.

SCHWARTZ, John Burnham. *Reservation Road.* (1998). NY. Knopf. 1st. F/F. B3. $40.00.

SCHWARTZ, Randall. *Carnivorous Plants.* 1974. NY. VG in dj. B26. $20.00.

SCHWARTZ, Steven. *Therapy.* (1994). NY. Harcourt Brace. 1st. author's 1st novel. sgn by author. F/F. B3. $45.00.

SCHWEITZER, Albert. *Paul and His Interpreters, A Critical History. Trans by W. Montgomery.* 1912. London. Adam and Charles Black. 1st English ed. xiv. 254p + 2p ads. orig gr cloth. K1. $75.00.

SCHWEITZER, Darrell. *The White Isle.* 1989. Philadelphia. Owlswick Press. 1st. VF/VF. T2. $20.00.

SCHWEIZER, Eduard. *The Good News According to Luke.* 1984. John Knox. 392p. VG. B29. $17.50.

SCHWIEBERT, E. G. *Luther and His Times.* 1950. Concordia. 892p. VG. B29. $19.00.

SCOPPETTONE, Sandra. *Everything You Have Is Mine.* 1991. Boston. Little, Brn. 1st. author's 1st mystery. F/F. A24. $35.00.

SCOPPETTONE, Sandra. *I'll Be Leaving You Always.* 1993. Boston. Little, Brn. 1st. F/F. A24. $20.00.

SCOTT, Hazel. *Boogie Woogie Piano Transcriptions.* 1943. NY. Robbins. 1st. wrp. 28p. VG. B2. $35.00.

SCOTT, Holden. *Skeptic.* 1998. NY. St. Martin. ARC. F/wrp. B2. $25.00.

SEABROOKE, John Paul. *Four Knocks on the Door.* 1925. Chelsea. 1st. VG. G8. $15.00.

SEARLS, Hank. *Blood Song.* 1984. NY. Villard. 1st. F/F. H11. $30.00.

SEE, Lisa. *Flower Net.* 1997. NY. Harper Collins. 1st. sgn. author's 1st novel. VF/VF. T2. $25.00.

SEE, Lisa. *On Gold Mountain: The One Hundred Year Odyssey of a Chinese American Family.* 1995. NY. St. Martin. 1st. author's 1st book. sgn. VF/VF. T2. $30.00.

SEE, Lisa. *The Interior.* 1999. NY. Harper Collins. 1st. UP. sgn. VF/pict wrp. T2. $20.00.

SELF, Will. *Cock & Bull.* 1992. London. Bloomsbury. 1st. sgn. F/F. O11. $65.00.

SELF, Will. *My Idea of Fun.* 1994. NY. Atlantic Monthly Press. 1st. sgn. F/F. O11. $35.00.

SENDAK, Maurice and Lore Segal. *The Juniper Tree and Other Tales from Grimm.* 1973. NY. Farrar. 2 vols. F/F. NF slipcase. B2. $100.00.

SERANELLA, Barbara. *No Human Involved.* 1997. NY. St. Martin. 1st. sgn. VF in dj. M15. $100.00.

SERANELLA, Barbara. *No Offense Intended.* 1999. NY. Harper Collins. 1st. sgn. VF/VF. T2. $25.00.

SETH, Ronald. *In the Name of the Devil.* 1970. NY. Walker. 1st. F/F. H11. $40.00.

SEWART, Alan. *Loop Current.* 1980. Robert Hale. 1st British ed. NF/NF. G8. $10.00.

SEXTON, Anne. *Live or Die.* 1966. Boston. Houghton Mifflin. 1st. wrp. VG+. V1. $12.00.

SEXTON, Anne. *The Complete Poems.* 1981. Boston. Houghton Mifflin. 1st. F/VG+. V1. $35.00.

SEYMOUR, Gerald. *Glory Boys.* 1976. NY. Random House. 1st Am ed. NF/NF. G8. $17.50.

SHACOCHIS, Bob. *Easy in the Islands.* 1985. NY. Crown. 1st. author's 1st book. winner of Natl. Book Award. F/F. A24. $75.00.

SHACOCHIS, Bob. *Swimming in the Volcano.* (1993). NY. Scribner's. 1st. sgn by author. F/F. B3. $60.00.

SHAMES, Laurence. *Scavenger Reef.* 1994. NY. S&S. 1st. VF/VF. H11. $50.00.

SHAMES, Laurence. *Sunburn.* 1995. NY. Hyperion. 1st. F/F. H11. $25.00.

SHAMES, Laurence. *Sunburn.* 1995. NY. Hyperion. 1st. sgn. VF/VF. T2. $30.00.

SHAMES, Laurence. *The Big Time.* 1986. NY. Harper & Row. 1st. author's 1st book. F/VF. H11. $90.00.

SHAMES, Laurence. *Virgin Heat.* 1997. NY. Hyperion. 1st. F/VF. H11. $20.00.

SHANKMAN, Sarah. *She Walks in Beauty.* 1991. NY. Pocket Books. 1st. VF/VF. T2. $15.00.

SHANNON, John. *The Concrete River.* 1996. Salem. John Brown Books. 1st. trade pb orig. sgn. VF/pict wrp. T2. $15.00.

SHANNON, John. *The Taking of the Waters.* 1994. Culver City. John Brown Books. 1st. trade pb. VF/pict wrp. T2. $20.00.

SHAPLEN, Robert. *A Turning Wheel, Thirty Years of the Asian Revolution.* 1979. NY. Random House. 1st. cloth. sm4to. 397p. F/VG. P1. $5.00.

SHARKEY, Jack. *Death for Auld Lang Syne.* 1962. NY. Holt. Rinehart & Winston. 1st. F/dj. M15. $45.00.

SHARP, Paula. *The Woman Who Was Not All There.* 1988. NY. Harper & Row. 1st. author's 1st book. F/F. O11. $25.00.

SHAW, George Bernard. *Quintessence of Bernard Shaw.* 1920. London. Allen Unwin. 1st. VG/dj. A24. $45.00.

SHAW, George Russell. *Pines of Mexico.* 1961 (1909). Jamaica Plain. 22 pl/map. AN/wrp. B26. $45.00.

SHAW, Irwin. *Nightwork.* 1975. NY. Delacorte. 1st. F/NF. H11. $30.00.

SHAW, Irwin. *Top of the Hill.* 1979. Weidenfeld Nicholson. 1st. F/dj. T12. $30.00.

SHAW, Irwin. *Young Lions.* Modern Lib/Random. F/NF. L4. $70.00.

SHECTER, L. *Once Upon the Polo Grounds.* 1970. NY. 1st. VG/dj. B5. $17.50.

SHEDD, Margaret. *Inherit the Earth.* 1944. Harper. 1st. VG/clip. S18. $15.00.

SHEEHAN, William. *The Planet Mars; A History of Observation and Discovery.* 1996. Tucson. Univ. of Arizona. 1st printing. b/w photos ils. 8vo. 270p. F/F. K5. $45.00.

SHELBY, Philip. *Days of Drums.* 1996. NY. S&S. 1st. author's 1st book. F/NF. R16. $35.00.

SHELDON, Gerard P. *Gentle Ways in Japan.* 1989. SF. Saville Photo Arts. photos. VG/dj. S5. $20.00.

SHELDON, Harold P. *Tranquility Revisited.* 1989. Derrydale. 1/2500. 130p. gilt leather. F. A17. $35.00.

SHELDON, Sidney. *Other Side of Midnight.* 1974. Morrow. 1st. F/NF. H11. $35.00.

SHELDON, Sidney. *Stars Shine Down.* 1992. Morrow. 1st. F/F. H11. $20.00.

SHELLEY, Mary. *The Mortal Immortal: The Complete Supernatural Short Fiction.* 1996. San Francisco. Tachyon Publications. 1st. 1/100 # copies. sgn by introducer Michael Bishop. VF/VF. T2. $30.00.

SHELLEY, Percy Bysshe. *Shelley's Complete Poetical Works.* 1901. Boston. teg. half brn leather/marbled brd. F. B30. $40.00.

SHELTON, Connie. *Deadly Game.* 1995. Angel Fire. Intrigue Press. 1st. author's 1st novel. sgn. VF/VF. T2. $22.00.

SHELTON, Louise. *Seasons in a Flower Garden.* 1915. Scribner. 2nd. 117p. VG. A10. $40.00.

SHEPARD, Lucius. *Green Eyes.* 1984. NY. Ace books. 1st. pb orig. author's 1st book. F. lt wear/pict wrp. T2. $15.00.

SHEPARD, Lucius. *Kalimantan.* 1990. London. Century/Legend. 1st. sgn. VF/VF. T2. $35.00.

SHEPARD, Lucius. *Life During Wartime.* 1991. Bantam. 1st. sgn. NF/wrp. R11. $15.00.

SHEPARD, Sam. *Cruising Paradise.* 1996. Knopf. 1st. sgn. F/dj. M25. $50.00.

SHEPERD, John. *History of the Liverpool Medical Institution.* 1979. Liverpool. 1st. 319p. A13. $35.00.

SHEPHERD, Roy E. *History of the Rose.* 1954. NY. 1st prt. biblio lists 75 titles. index. corner bumped. dj. B26. $24.00.

SHERMAN, Harold M. *Hit & Run*. 1929. Grosset Dunlap. 1st. VG/dj. P8. $25.00.

SHERWMAKE, Oscar L. *Honorable George Wythe: Teacher, Lawyer, Jurist, Statesman*. 1954. Wm & Mary. 2nd. 48p. VG. B10. $25.00.

SHERZER, Joel. *Kuna Way of Speaking. An Ethnographic Perspective*. 1983. Austin. Univ. of Texas Press. 1st. color frontis. b/w photo ils. 260p. G/chipped dj. F3. $30.00.

SHIELDS, Carol. *Larry's Party*. 1997. NY. Viking. ARC. sgn. F in F dj. D10. $40.00.

SHIELDS, Carol. *Swann*. 1987. NY. Viking. 1st Am ed. sgn. F in F dj. D10. $75.00.

SHIMWELL, David W. *The Description and Classification of Vegetation*. 1972. Seattle. 1st Am ed. extensive biblio. appendices. indexes. B26. $21.00.

SHIPMAN, David. *Cinema, The First Hundred Years*. 1993. NY. St. Martin. 1st. quarto. blk cloth w/silver spine title. pict ep & dj. F/F. R3. $50.00.

SHIPPEY, Lee. *It's an Old California Custom*. 1948. Vanguard. 1st. Am Customs series. NF/VG. T11. $20.00.

SHIRER, William L. *Collapse of the Third Republic*. 1969. S&S. sm 4to. 1082p. NF/dj. W2. $40.00.

SHIRER, William L. *Rise & Fall of the Third Reich*. 1960. S&S. BC. 1st/13th prt. 584p. F/NF. W2. $35.00.

SHIRLEY, Dame. *California in 1851: Letters of Dame Shirley*. 1933. SF. Grabhorn. 8vo. P4. $120.00.

SHIRLEY, John. *Heatseeker*. 1989. LA. Scream/Press. 1st. sgn inscr by Shirley. VF/VF. T2. $40.00.

SHIRLEY, John. *Silicon Embrace*. 1996. Shingletown. Mark V. Ziesing. 1st. VF/VF. T2. $30.00.

SHIRLEY, John. *Wetbones*. 1991. Shingletown. Mark V. Ziesing. 1st. VF/VF. T2. $25.00.

SHLAIN, Bruce. *Baseball Inside Out*. 1992. Viking. 1st. photos. F/dj. C15. $10.00.

SHOEMAKER, Bill. *Stalking Horse*. 1994. Fawcett. 1st. F/F. H11. $20.00.

SHOEMAKER, Bill and Barney Nagler. *Shoemaker America's Greatest Jockey*. 1988. NY. Doubleday. 1st ed. VG/VG. O3. $25.00.

SHOTWELL, Walter Gaston. *The Civil War in America*. 1923. London. Longmans. Green and Co. 1st. 2 vols. orig cloth. folding map. comprehensive work covering all campaigns. 397p; 379p. NF. M8. $450.00.

SHUMATE, Albert. *The Notorious I. C. Woods of the Adams Express*. 1986. Glendale. Arthur H. Clark. 1st. octavo. red linen cloth. dj. ils. F/F. R3. $25.00.

SHUMWAY, George, Edward Durrel, Howard C. Frey. *Conestoga Wagon 1750 – 1850*. 1964. York, PA. Early Am Industries & George Shumway. 1st. ltd to 1500 copies. VG. O3. $225.00.

SHUMWAY, Larry V. *Frontier Fiddler: Life of N Arizona Pioneer KC Kartchner*. 1990. Tucson, AZ. 1st. ils/music/index. 280p. AN. B19. $10.00.

SHUPTRINE, Hubert. *Jericho, The South Beheld*. 1974. Birmingham. Oxmoor. 1st. VG/dj. B5. $45.00.

SHUTE, Henry A. *Brite & Fair*. 1968. Noone House. rpt. 8vo. ils. VG/G. B17. $45.00.

SHUTE, Nevil. *Old Captivity*. 1940. NY. 1st Am. 333p. VG/dj. B18. $25.00.

SHUTE, Nevil. *On The Beach*. 1957. Heinneman. 1st. VG+/dj. S13. $25.00.

SHUTE, Nevil. *Trustee from the Toolroom*. 1960. NY. Morrow. 1st. VG+/NF. T11. $40.00.

SIAS, Beverlee. *Skier's Cookbook*. 1971. AS Barnes. G/dj. A16. $10.00.

SIBBALD, John. *Career Makers*. 1992. Harper Business. 1st. sm 4to. 408p. F/dj. W2. $30.00.

SIDDONS, Anne Rivers. *King's Oak*. 1990. Harper Collins. 1st Canadian. F/F. T12. $25.00.

SIDDONS, Anne Rivers. *King's Oak*. 1990. Harper Collins. 1st. F/NF. H11. $20.00.

SIDDONS, Dan. *Fires of Eden*. 1994. Putnam. 1st. sgn. AN/dj. S18. $30.00.

SIDDONS, Dan. *Hollow Man*. 1993. Bantam. 1st. sgn. AN/dj. S18. $40.00.

SIDNEY, Margaret. *Five Little Peppers & How They Grew*. 1948. Grosset Dunlap. ils. 275p. VG. B36. $8.50.

SIDRAN, Ben. *Talking Jazz, An Illustrated Oral History*. 1992. Petaluma. Pomegranate. ARC w/slip. 4to. F/F. B2. $45.00.

SIGERIST, Henry. *University at the Crossroads*. 1946. NY. 1st. 162p. A13. $40.00.

SILKO, Leslie Marmon. *Almanac of the Dead*. (1991). NY. np. 1st. sgn by author. F/F. B3. $60.00.

SILKO, Leslie Marmon. *Ceremony*. 1977. NY. Viking. 1st. author's 1st novel. F/NF. writing on ffep. faded dj. A24. $200.00.

SILONE, Ignazio. *Seed Beneath the Snow*. 1965. Atheneum. 1st. VG/dj. B11. $15.00.

SILVA, Daniel. *The Unlikely Spy*. 1997. NY. Villard. 1st Am ed. VF/VF. T2. $20.00.

SILVA, David B. *Best of the Horror Show*. 1987. Chicago. 2am Publications. 1st. trade pb orig. sgn by contrib Joe R. Lansdale. VF/pict wrp. T2. $15.00.

SILVER, George. *Spy in the House of Medicine*. 1976. Germantown, MD. 1st. 308p. A13. $20.00.

SILVER, Jim. *Assumption of Risk*. 1996. NY. S&S. 1st. author's 1st novel. F/F. T2. $22.00.

SILVER, Rollo G. *American Printer 1787 – 1825*. 1967. Charlottesville. 1st. ils. 189p. gilt blk cloth. F. F1. $25.00.

SILVERMAN, Mel. *Good-For-Nothing Burro*. 1958. Cleveland. World. 1st. 8vo. red cloth. G. T5. $10.00.

SILVIS, Randall. *Dead Man Falling*. 1996. NY. Carroll & Graf. 1st. sgn. VF/VF. T2. $30.00.

SILVIS, Randall. *Occasional Hell*. 1993. Sag Harbor. Permanent. 1st. sgn. F/dj. T2. $35.00.

SIMCOX, William Henry. *Language of the New Testament*. 1980. Alpha. reprint. 226p. VG. B29. $8.00.

SIMENON, Georges. *Blue Room & the Accomplices*. 1964. HBW. 1st. NF/NF. H11. $15.00.

SIMENON, Georges. *Danger Ahead*. 1955. London. Hamish Hamilton. 1st Eng. price clipped jacket with nicks at spine ends. a couple of short closed tears and tiny wear along folds. F/dj. M15. $65.00.

SIMENON, Georges. *Girl with a Squint*. 1951. HBJ. 1st Am. NF/dj. G8. $15.00.

SIMENON, Georges. *Maigret and the Spinster*. 1977. London. Hamish Hamilton. 1st Eng. F/dj. M15. $45.00.

SIMENON, Georges. *Maigret in Society.* 1962. London. Hamish Hamilton. 1st. F/clip. M15. $45.00.

SIMENON, Georges. *Rich Man.* 1971. HBJ. 1st AM. F/NF. G8. $25.00.

SIMENON, Georges. *The Man with the Little Dog.* 1965. London. Hamish Hamilton. 1st Eng ed. F in dj. M15. $45.00.

SIMENON, Georges. *The Shadow Falls.* 1945. Harcourt, Brace. 1st Am ed. NF/lightly worn dj. M25. $90.00.

SIMENON, Georges. *The Widower.* 1961. London. Hamish Hamilton. 1st Eng ed. F in dj. M15. $45.00.

SIMENON, Georges. *Tidal Wave.* 1954. Doubleday. 1st Am ed. VG+/reinforced dj. M25. $45.00.

SIMIC, Charles. *Jacstraws.* 1999. Harcourt Brace. UP. F/WRP. M25. $25.00.

SIMIC, Charles. *Return to a Place Lit by a Glass of Milk.* 1974. Braziller. 1st. F/F. B3. $50.00.

SIMMONS, Adelma G. *Herb Gardening in Five Seasons.* 1965. Van Nostrand. BC. 353p. VG/dj. A10. $20.00.

SIMMONS, Dan. *Children of the Night.* 1992. NY. Putnam. 1st. sgn. VF/ VF. T2. $35.00.

SIMMONS, Dan. *Fires of Eden.* 1994. NY. Putnam. 1st. sgn. VF/ VF. T2. $30.00.

SIMMONS, Dan. *Lovedeath.* 1993. NY. Warner Books. 1st. sgn. VF/ VF. T2. $30.00.

SIMMONS, Dan. *Summer of Night.* 1991. NY. Putnam. 1st. F/F. H11. $40.00.

SIMMONS, Dan. *The Hollow Man.* 1992. NY. Bantam. 1st. sgn. VF/ VF. T2. $35.00.

SIMMONS, Richard. *Never Say Diet Book.* 1980. NY. Warner Books. poi on ffep. VG/VG. A28. $7.95.

SIMON, Carly. *The Fisherman's Song.* (1991). NY. Doubleday. 1st. ils Margaret Datz. children's. F/F. B3. $30.00.

SIMON, George T. *Glenn Miller and His Orchestra.* 1974. NY. Crowell. ARC w/slip. inscr by author. F/NF. B2. $50.00.

SIMON, Neil. *Jake's Women.* 1994. Random. 1st. F/dj. A24. $25.00.

SIMON, Neil. *They're Playing Our Songs.* 1980. Random. 1st. VG/dj. C9. $36.00.

SIMON, Roger L. *California Roll.* 1985. NY. Villard. 1st. F/F. H11. $20.00.

SIMON, Roger L. *Wild Turkey.* 1974. np. Straight Arrow Books. 1st. F/NF dj. M19. $17.50.

SIMPSON, Helen. *Four Bare Legs in a Bed.* 1992. NY. Harmony. 1st. author's 1st book. VF/VF. H11. $30.00.

SIMPSON, John E. *Crossed Wires.* 1992. NY. Carroll & Graf. 1st. author's 1st book. F/F. H11. $30.00.

SIMPSON, Louis. *Selected Poems.* 1965. HBW. 1st. sgn. F/dj. L3. $75.00.

SIMPSON, Louis. *Selected Prose.* 1989. NY. VG/dj. M17. $15.00.

SIMPSON, Marc. *Winslow Homer Paintings of the Civil War.* 1988. SF. Fine Arts Mus. ils. VG/dj. M17. $45.00.

SIMPSON, Mona. *Anywhere but Here.* 1987. NY. Knopf. 1st. author's 1st book. F/F. H11. $75.00.

SIMPSON, Mona. *The Lost Father.* 1992. NY. Knopf. 1st. F/F. H11. $25.00.

SIMPSON, Thomas. *Full Moon Over America.* 1994. NY. Warner. 1st. VF/VF. H11. $25.00.

SIMS, George; see Cain, Paul.

SINCLAIR, April. *Ain't Gonna be the Same Fool Twice.* 1996. Hyperion. ARC. F/wrp. R14. $35.00.

SINCLAIR, April. *Coffee Will Make You Black.* (1994). NY. Hyperion. 1st. author's 1st book. sgn by author. F/F. B3. $65.00.

SINCLAIR, Upton. *It Happend to Didymus.* 1958. Sagamore. 1st. NF/NF. H11. $25.00.

SINCLAIR, Upton. *The Jungle.* 1906. NY. Doubleday. Page. 1st. NF w/only lightly faded spine lettering. B2. $125.00.

SINGER, Isaac Bashevis. *Passions.* 1975. FSG. 1st. NF/clip. R14. $35.00.

SINGER, Isaac Bashevis. *Zlateh the Goat.* 1966. Harper Row. 1st. VG/G. P2. $75.00.

SINGER, Kurt. *Laughton Story.* 1954. Winston. 1st. VG/dj. P3. $15.00.

SINGER, Marilyn. *Horsemaster.* 1985. Atheneum. 1st. VG/dj. O3. $25.00.

SINGER, Shelley. *Spit in the Ocean.* 1987. NY. St. Martin. 1st. sgn. NF/VG. G8. $17.50.

SITCHEN, Zecharia. *Lost Realms.* 1990. Santa Fe. Bear & Co. 1st. ils/maps/biblio. 298p. F3. $10.00.

SITWELL, Osbert. *Scarlet Tree.* 1946. Little, Brn. 1st. NF/VG. B9. $50.00.

SITWELL, Sacheverell. *Arabesque & Honeycomb.* 1957. London. Hale. ils/pl. 224p. VG/torn. Q2. $37.00.

SKAL, David J. *Hollywood Gothic.* 1990. Norton. 1st. VG/dj. L1. $85.00.

SKAL, David J. *Monster Show.* 1993. Norton. 1st. VG/dj. L1. $75.00.

SKINNER, H. *American Book of Cookery Containing More Than 500 Receipts.* 1850. Boston. 1st. 110p. G. E6. $65.00.

SKINNER, Henry T. (ed). *Garden Plants in Color, Vol 1: Trees, Shrubs, Vines.* 1958. Portland. 4to. VG. B26. $35.00.

SKINNER, Robert. *Daddy's Gone A-Hunting.* 1999. Scottsdale. Poisoned Pen Press. 1st. sgn. VF/VF. T2. $24.00.

SKINNER, Robert. *Skin Deep, Blood Red.* 1997. NY. Kensington. sgn 1st. F/F. M23. $45.00.

SKLEPOWICH, Edward. *Death in a Serene City.* 1990. NY. Morrow. 1st. VF/VF. H11. $35.00.

SKLEPOWICH, Edward. *Liquid Desires.* 1993. NY. Morrow. 1st. VF/VF. H11. $20.00.

SLADEK, John. *Bugs.* 1989. London. Macmillan. 1st. VF/VF. T2. $20.00.

SLATER, Philip. *How I Saved the World.* 1985. Dutton. 1st. NF/dj. S18. $30.00.

SLATER, Susan. *The Pumpkin Seed Massacre.* 1999. Angel Fire. Intrigue Press. 1st. sgn. VF/VF. T2. $25.00.

SLAUGHTER, Frank G. *Road to Bythinia.* 1951. Peoples. 1st. RS. NF/VG. S18. $17.00.

SLAVITT, David. *Big Nose.* 1983. Baton Rouge. LSU. 1st. sgn. F/dj. R14. $45.00.

SLAVITT, David. *King of Hearts.* 1976. NY. Arbor. 1st. NF/clip. A14. $21.00.

SLOAN, Rick. *Brown Shoe.* 1992. NY. Random House. 1st. author's 1st book. UP. F. D10. $10.00.

SLOANE, Eric. *I Remember America.* 1971. Funk Wagnall. 1st. ils. 184p. VG. B18. $35.00.

SLOANE, Eric. *Museum of Early American Tools*. 1974. NY. ils. 108p. VG/wrp. M4. $10.00.

SLOANE, Eric. *Seasons of America Past*. 1988. NY. 4 mc pl. F/dj. M4. $25.00.

SLOANE, Eric. *Sketches of America's Past*. 1986. NY. ils. 3 books in 1. 336p. F/dj. M4. $35.00.

SLOVO, Gillian. *Death Comes Staccato*. 1987. Crime Club. 1st Am ed. NF/NF. G8. $10.00.

SLUNG, Michelle. *I Shudder at Your Touch*. 1991. NY. NAL/Penguin. 1st. AN/dj. T12. $30.00.

SMALL, David. *Alone*. 1991. NY. Norton. 1st. F/VF. H11. $25.00.

SMELLIE, William. *Philosophy of Natural History*. 1790 & 1799. Edinburgh. Prt for Heirs Chas Elliot. 2 vol. 4to. G1. $750.00.

SMILEY, David. *A Thousand Acres*. 1991. NY. Knopf. 1st. F/F. H11. $90.00.

SMILEY, David. *Moo*. 1995. NY. Knopf. 1st. F/F. H11. $35.00.

SMILEY, Jane. *A Thousand Acres*. 1991. NY. Knopf. 1st. F/F. D10. $85.00.

SMILEY, Jane. *Catskill Crafts*. 1988. Crown. 1st. NF/NF. M25. $35.00.

SMILEY, Jane. *Duplicate Keys*. 1984. Knopf. 1st. VG+/dj. B30. $200.00.

SMILEY, Jane. *Duplicate Keys*. 1984. London. cape. 1st. F/F. H11. $125.00.

SMILEY, Jane. *Ordinary Love & Good Will*. 1989. Knopf. 1st. F/F. B3. $75.00.

SMILEY, Jane. *The All New Travels and Adventures of Lidie Newton*. (1998). NY. Knopf. 1st. F/F. B3. $35.00.

SMILEY, Jane. *The Greenlanders*. 1988. NY. Knopf. 1st. F/VF. H11. $65.00.

SMITH, Alison. *Rising*. 1987. NY. St. Martin. 1st. NF/VG. G8. $10.00.

SMITH, April. *North of Montana*. 1994. NY. Knopf. 1st. VF/VF. H11. $35.00.

SMITH, Audrey. *Current Trends in Cryobiology*. 1970. Plenum. 252p. xl. VG. S5. $10.00.

SMITH, Bernie. *Joy of Trivia, The*. 1976. NY. Bell Publishing co. VG/VG. A28. $9.95.

SMITH, Bradley. *Mexico, A History in Art*. 1967. NY. Gemini Smith. 1st. sm folio. photos ils. 296p. F/F. F3. $35.00.

SMITH, Charlie. *Canaan*. 1984. S&S. 1st. sgn. rem mk. F/dj. D10. $85.00.

SMITH, Charlie. *Cheap Ticket to Heaven*. 1996. NY. Holt. 1st. F/dj. R14. $25.00.

SMITH, Charlie. *Shine Hawk*. 1988. NY. Paris Review. 1st. sgn. F/dj. D10. $75.00.

SMITH, Charlie. *The Lives of the Dead*. 1990. NY. Linden. 1st. F/F. H11. $35.00.

SMITH, Curtis C. *Twentieth Century Science Fiction Writers*. 1981. NY. St. Martin. 1st. NF/VG. B2. $50.00.

SMITH, Daniel. *A Walk in the City*. 1971. NY. World. 1st. F/NF. B2. $25.00.

SMITH, Dave. *Dream Flights*. 1981. Univ. of Illinois Press. 1st. F/VG+. V1. $22.00.

SMITH, Denis O. *The Chronicles of Sherlock Holmes*. 1997. Ashcroft. Calabash Press. 1st. trade pb. VF/pict wrp. T2. $20.00.

SMITH, Ella Williams. *Tears & Laughter in Virginia & Elsewhere*. 1972. McClure. 148p. VG/dj. B10. $15.00.

SMITH, Fay Jackson. *Father Kino in Arizona*. 1966. AZ Hist Found. 1st. maps. 142p. F/sans. B19. $50.00.

SMITH, Florence. *Romancing the Gold*. 1986. Florida. Museum of Archaeology. 1st. wrp. 4to. F. F3. $15.00.

SMITH, Gary. *Happy Hours*. 1987. NY. Harmony. 1st. author's 1st book. F/VF. H11. $40.00.

SMITH, George Gillman. *The Story of Georgia and the Georgia People 1732 – 1860*. 1900. Macon. George G. Smith. marbled page edges. ils. 634p. G. hinge cracks. few pencil marks. B18. $75.00.

SMITH, Grover, editor. *Letter of Aldous Huxley*. 1969. Harper & Row. 1st Am ed. NF/NF. M25. $45.00.

SMITH, Herndon. *Centralia: First Fifty Years 1845 – 1900*. 1942. Centralia. Wash. 1st. VG/dj. N2. $50.00.

SMITH, Jane S. *Elsie DeWolfe: Life in High Style*. 1982. NY. 3rd. photos. VG/dj. M17. $30.00.

SMITH, Jeff. *The Frugal Gourmet*. 1984. NY. Morrow. VG/VG. A28. $8.50.

SMITH, Jeffery A. *Printers & Press Freedom: Ideology of Early Am Journalism*. 1988. OUP. 233p. VG. M10. $15.00.

SMITH, Joan. *A Masculine Ending*. 1988. NY. Scribners. 1st. author's 1st book. F/F. H11. $25.00.

SMITH, Joan. *Why Aren't They Screaming?* 1989. Scribner. 1st Am. VG/dj. R8. $10.00.

SMITH, Joseph. *Book of Mormon*. 1985 (1830). Latter-Day Saints. 12mo. 779p. F. W2. $25.00.

SMITH, Julie. *Huckleberry Fiend*. 1987. Mysterious. 1st. rem mk. F/dj. B2. $30.00.

SMITH, Julie. *Jazz Funeral*. 1993. NY. Fawcett. 1st. F/F. H11. $25.00.

SMITH, Julie. *The Kindness of Strangers*. 1996. NY. Fawcett Columbine. 1st. sgn. VF/VF. T2. $25.00.

SMITH, Ken. *Willie Mays Story*. 1954. Greenberg. 1st. photos. VG+/wrp. P8. $135.00.

SMITH, Lee. *Black Mountain Breakdown*. 1980. Putnam. 1st. author's 4th book. F/F. B3. $125.00.

SMITH, Lee. *Cakewalk*. 1981. Putnam. 1st. sgn. NF/dj. R14. $65.00.

SMITH, Lee. *Fair & Tender Ladies*. 1989. London. Macmillan. 1st. F/F. B3. $35.00.

SMITH, Lee. *Family Linen*. (1985). NY. Putnam. 1st. F/F. B3. $35.00.

SMITH, Lee. *Me and My Baby View the Eclipse*. (1989). NY. Putnam. 1st. F/F. B3. $25.00.

SMITH, Lee. *News of the Spirit*. (1997). NY. Putnam. 1st. sgn by author. F/F. B3. $40.00.

SMITH, Lee. *Saving Grace*. 1995. NY. Putnam. 1st. sgn. F/dj. M23. $40.00.

SMITH, Lee. *Something in the Wind*. 1971. NY. Harper. 1st. F in lightly used dj w/tiny tears. B2. $250.00.

SMITH, Mark. *The Death of the Detective*. 1974. NY. Knopf. 1st. Book has faint smudges on bottom page block. Jacket Is price clipped. F-/F. H11. $40.00.

SMITH, Martin Cruz. *Gorky Park*. 1981. NY. Random. 1st. F/F. H11. $40.00.

SMITH, Martin Cruz. *Gorky Park*. 1990. Ballantine. pb. VG. F6. $1.50.

SMITH, Martin Cruz. *Havana Bay.* 1999. NY. Random House. 1st. sgn. VF/VF. T2. $26.00.

SMITH, Martin Cruz. *Polar Star.* 1989. NY. Random. 1st. F/F. H11. $20.00.

SMITH, Martin Cruz. *Stallion Gate.* 1986. NY. Random House. 1st. sgn. F/F. T2. $30.00.

SMITH, Maurice. *Short History of Dentistry.* 1958. London. 120p. dj. A13. $30.00.

SMITH, Michael. *Stone City.* nd. BC. F/NF. S18. $8.00.

SMITH, Mitchell. *Daydreams.* 1987. McGraw Hill. 1st. F/F. H11. $30.00.

SMITH, Mitchell. *Due North.* 1992. NY. S&S. 1st. VF/VF. H11. $25.00.

SMITH, Nicholas. *Songs from the Hearts of Women.* 1903. Chicago. McClurg. 1st. xl. G. G11. $6.00.

SMITH, Peter J. *Highlights of the Off-Season.* 1986. NY. S&S. 1st. F/F. H11. $40.00.

SMITH, R. Dixon. *Jeremy Brett & David Burke: An Adventure in Canonical Fidelity.* 1998. Cambridge. UK. Rupert Books. reissue. 1st thus. sgn by Smith. VF/pict wrp. T2. $18.00.

SMITH, Richard P. *Deer Hunting.* 1978. Stackpole. 256p. F/dj. A17. $12. 50.

SMITH, Robert. *Babe Ruth's America.* 1974. Crowell. 1st. photos. VG/dj. P8. $40.00.

SMITH, Scott. *A Simple Plan.* 1993. NY. Knopf. 1st. author's 1st novel. VF/VF. T2. $25.00.

SMITH, Wilbur. *Elephant Song.* 1991. NY. Random. 1st. F/F. H11. $25.00.

SMITH, Wilbur. *Gold Mine.* 1970. Doubleday. 1st Am ed. rem spray on bottom edge. NF/worn dj. M25. $25.00.

SMOLLA, Rodney A. *Jerry Falwell vs. Larry Flint.* 1988. St. Martin. 1st. 8vo. F/dj. A2. $12. 50.

SMOLONSKY, Marc. *Dirty Laundry.* 1991. NY. Walker. 1st. F/F. H11. $20.00.

SMULLYAN, Raymond. *The Chess Mysteries of Sherlock Holmes.* 1979. NY. Knopf. 1st. pb orig. VF/pict wrp. T2. $25.00.

SMYTHE, Pat. *Jump for Joy.* 1955. Dutton. 1st. VG/G. O3. $18.00.

SNELL, Roy J. *The Firebug.* 1925. Chicago. Reilly & Lee. G in poor dj. A16. $6.00.

SNOW, William Parker. *Southern Generals: Their Lives & Campaigns.* 1866. Chas Richardson. 500p. cloth. B10. $100.00.

SNYDER, Gary. *Earth House Hold.* 1969. New Directions. 1st. F/dj. O11. $150.00.

SNYDER, Gary. *Mountains and Rivers Without End.* 1996. Washington. DC. Counterpoint Press. 1st. F/F. O11. $25.00.

SNYDER, Gary. *Old Ways.* 1977. City Lights. 1st. sgn. F. O11. $55.00.

SNYDER, Gary. *Regarding Wave.* 1970. New Directions. 1st. F/dj. O11. $140.00.

SNYDER, Gary. *Sours of the Hills.* (1969). np. Samuel Charters. 1/300. sgn. F. O11. $160.00.

SOAMES, Mary. *Clementine Churchill: Biography of a Marriage.* 1979. Houghton Mifflin. 4th. 8vo. 732p. F. W2. $50.00.

SOBEL, Dava. *Longitude.* 1995. NY. Walker. UP. ES. F in pict wrp. M23. $40.00.

SOHMER, Steve. *Favorite Son.* 1987. NY. Bantam. 1st. author's 1st book. VF/VF. H11. $40.00.

SOHMER, Steve. *Patriots.* 1990. NY. Random. 1st. VF/VF. H11. $25.00.

SOLOMITA, Stephen. *Bad to the Bone.* 1991. NY. Putnam. 1st. F/F. H11. $20.00.

SOLZHENITSYN, Alexander. *Noble Lecture.* 1972. Farrar Straus. Bilingual/1st. gr cloth. F. B14. $55.00.

SOLZHENITSYN, Alexander. *One Day in the Life of Ivan Denisovich.* 1963. NY. 1st. F/dj. B2. $65.00.

SOMMER, Joseph. *After the Storm. Landmarks of the Modern Mexican Novel.* 1968. Albuquerque. Univ. of New Mexico Press. 1st. 208p. G/chipped dj. F3. $20.00.

SOMTOW, S. P. *Moon Dance.* 1991. London. Gollancz. 1st. VF/VF. T2. $25.00.

SOMTOW, S. P. *Vanitas: Escape from Vampire Junction.* 1995. London. Gollancz. 1st. VF/VF. T2. $30.00.

SONTAG, Susan. *I, Etcetera.* (1978). NY. FSG. 1st. F/F. B3. $20.00.

SONTAG, Susan. *The Volcano Lover.* 1992. Farrar Straus Giroux. 3rd prt. F/chip dj. S19. $20.00.

SOOS, Troy. *Murder at Ebbets Field.* 1995. NY. Kensington. 1st. F/dj. M15. $50.00.

SOOS, Troy. *The Cincinnati Red Stalkings.* 1998. NY. Kensington. 1st. VF/dj. M15. $45.00.

SOUTHERN, Terry. *Red Dirt Marijuana and Other Tastes.* 1967. NY. NAL. 1st. NF/NF. D10. $75.00.

SOUTHERN, Terry. *Texas Summer.* 1991. NY. Arcade/Little, Brn. 1st. F/F. A24. $20.00.

SOUTHERN LIVING, editors. *1991 Annual Recipes.* 1991. AL. Oxmoor House. hc. NF. A28. $7.95.

SOYINKA, Wole. *Art, Dialogue, and Outrage, Essays on Literature and Culture.* 1993. NY. Pantheon. 1st. sgn. F/F. D10. $50.00.

SOYINKA, Wole. *Isara, A Voyage Around Essay.* 1989. NY. Random House. 1st. sgn. F/F. D10. $55.00.

SOYINKA, Wole. *The Burden of Memory, the Muse of Forgiveness.* 1999. NY. Oxford Univ. Press. 1st. sgn. F/F. D10. $40.00.

SPANGLER, Edward W. *Annals of Families of Casper.* Henry, Baltzer & Spengler. 1896. York. np. 605p. G+. B18. $75.00.

SPANN, J. Richard. *The Christian Faith and Secularism.* 1948. Abingdon. 296p. VG/torn dj. B29. $5.50.

SPARK, Muriel. *Abbess of Crewe.* 1974. London. Macmillan. 1st. NF/dj. A14. $28.00.

SPARK, Muriel. *Driver's Seat.* 1970. London. Macmillan. 1st. NF/VG. A14. $28.00.

SPARK, Muriel. *Far Cry from Kensington.* 1988. Toronto. Viking Penguin. 1st Canadian. NF/dj. A14. $21.00.

SPARK, Muriel. *Not to Disturb.* 1971. London. Macmillan. 1st. NF/VG. A14. $35.00.

SPARK, Muriel. *Public Image.* 1968. Knopf. 1st. 144p. xl. G/dj. S14. $6.00.

SPARKS, Jared. *Writings of George Washington: Being His Correspondence.* (1837). Harper. 12 vol. full leather. G+. B10. $300.00.

SPARKS, Nicholas. *The Notebook.* (1996). NY. Warner. 1st. author's 1st book. F/F. B3. $25.00.

SPARLING, Joyce. *North of Delhi, East of Heaven.* 1988. NY. Walker. 1st. F/F. H11. $20.00.

SPARROW, Walter Shaw. *British Sporting Artists.* 1922. Scribner. 1st. VG. A21. $250.00.

SPAULDING, C. E. *A Veterinary Guide for Animal Owners.* 1976. Emmaus. Rodale. VG/G. O3. $18.00.

SPAULDING, Edward Selden. *Wild Oats and Chaparral.* 1944. np. Quarto. burgundy cloth. pict stp & lettered in blk. ils George Browne & Egmont Rett. NF/NF. R3. $30.00.

SPAYTHE, Jacob A. *History of Hancock County.* Ohio. 1903. Toledo. ils/rosters/biographies. 312p. VG. B18. $70.00.

SPEARMAN, Charles Edward. *Psychology Down the Ages.* 1937. Macmillan. 2 vol. bl cloth. VG. G1. $85.00.

SPEARS, John R. *Story of the New England Whalers.* 1908. NY. 418p. VG. S15. $20.00.

SPECHT, Robert. *Story of a Young Teacher in Alaska Wilderness.* c 1976. NY. St. Martin. 8vo. 358p. VG/dj. P4. $30.00.

SPECTOR, Benjamin. *One Hour of Medical History.* 1931. Boston. 1st. 88p. A13. $20.00.

SPENDER, Stephen. *Poems of Dedication.* 1947. NY. Random House. 1st. F/NF. B2. $35.00.

SPIER, Peter. *Of Dikes and Windmills.* 1969. Garden City. Doubleday. 1st. pict brds. ils by the author. 187p. VG in dj. lt wear. chipping on extremities. B18. $45.00.

SPIKE, Paul. *The Night Letter.* 1979. NY. Signet. 1st pb. NF. F6. $1.50.

SPILLANE, Micky. *The Killing Man.* 1989. NY. Dutton. 1st trade. rem mk. VG+/VG+. R16. $30.00.

SPINAR, Zdenek V. *Life Before Man.* 1981. NY. Crescent. color ils. 4to. NF/VG. R16. $45.00.

SPINRAD, Norman. *The Void Captain's Table.* 1983. NY. Timescape/ S&S. 1st sgn inscr by Spinrad. F/F. short closed tear. T2. $25.00.

SPORES, Ronald. *The Mixtec Kings & Their People.* 1967. Norman. Univ. of Oklahoma Press. 1st. wrp. b/w photos. drawings. 265p. G. F3. $15.00.

SPRING, Michelle. *Every Breath You Take.* 1994. NY. Pocket. 1st. VF/VF. H11. $30.00.

SPYRI, Johanna. *Heidi.* 1923. Philadelphia. David McKay Co. ils Anne Anderson. sm 8vo. dk gr textured cloth. ils by Anne Anderson. 356p. VG. D6. $45.00.

SQUIER, Emma Lindsay. *Gringa, An American Woman in Mexico.* 1934. Boston. Houghton Mifflin. 1st. ep maps. 282p+24b/w plates. G. F3. $20.00.

ST. CLAIR, Robert James. *Neurotics in the Church.* 1963. Revell. 251p. VG/worn dj. B29. $8.50.

STABENOW, Dana. *Blood will Tell.* 1996. NY. Putnam. 1st. sgn. VF/VF. T2. $20.00.

STABENOW, Dana. *Breakup.* (1997). NY. Putnam. 1st. sgn by author. F/F. B3. $25.00.

STABENOW, Dana. *So Sure of Death.* 1999. NY. Dutton. 1st. sgn. VF/VF. T2. $25.00.

STACEY, Susannah. *Knife at the Opera.* 1988. Summit. 1st. F/VG+. N4. $15.00.

STACK, Frederic W. *Wild Flowers Every Child Should Know.* 1909. NY. ils/photo ep. decor cloth. B26. $26.00.

STACKPOLE, Edward J. *Chancellorsville: Lee's Greatest Battle.* 1958. Stackpole. 1st. NF/VG. A14. $25.00.

STACKPOLE, Edward James. *They Met at Gettysburg.* 1956. Harrisburg. Pa. Eagle Books. 3rd printing. orig cloth. 19 maps. 124 ils. 342p. NF/NF. M8. $35.00.

STACTON, David. *Segaki.* 1959. Pantheon. 1st. VG/clip. N2. $10.00.

STADDEN, Charles. *Life Guards: Dress & Appointments 1660 – 1914.* 1971. Almark. 1st. ils/pl. 68p. VG/stiff wrp. S16. $22. $50.00.

STAFFORD, Harry. *Early Inhabitants of the Americas.* 1959. Vantage. VG/dj. A19. $30.00.

STAFFORD, Jean. *Mother in History.* 1966. FSG. 2nd. 121p. VG/G. P12. $15.00.

STAFFORD, William. *Even in Quiet Place.* (1996). Lewiston, ID. Confluence. 1st. AN/dj. A18. $20.00.

STAGNER, Lloyd E. *Rock Island Motive Power, 1933 – 1955.* 1st. pict ep. brds. ils. 206p. F/F. B18. $45.00.

STAHL, Jerry. *Perv, a Love Story.* 1999. NY. Morrow. 1st. author's 1st novel. sgn. VF/VF. T2. $25.00.

STALLMAN, Robert. *The Beast.* 1990. London. Kinnell. 1st hc ed. sgn by jacket artist Don Maitz. VF/VF. T2. $35.00.

STALLMAN, Robert. *The Captive.* 1989. London. Kinnell. 1st hc ed. sgn by jacket artist Don Maitz. VF/VF. T2. $35.00.

STALLWOOD, Veronica. *Death and the Oxford Box.* 1994. NY. Scribners. 1st Am ed. UP. VF/VF. T2. $15.00.

STALLWOOD, Veronica. *Oxford Mourning.* 1996. NY. Scribners. 1st Am ed. UP. VF/pict wrp. T2. $5.00.

STANDIFORD, Les. *Done Deal.* 1993. NY. Harper Collins. 1st. 1st Johnny Deal mystery. sgn. VF/VF. T2. $30.00.

STANDIFORD, Les. *Raw Deal.* 1994. Harper & Row. 1st. NF/NF. G8. $15.00.

STANDIFORD, Les. *Spill.* 1991. Atlantic. 1st. author's 1st book. F/F. H11. $40.00.

STANDING BEAR, Chief. *My People the Sioux.* 1928. Houghton Mifflin. ils/photos. 288p. VG/G. B5. $45.00.

STANDISH, Burt L. *Lefty of Big League: Crossed Signals (#16).* 1928. Barse. 1st. final of series. VG. P8. $200.00.

STANDRING, Lesley. *Doctor Who Illustrated A – Z.* 1985. London. WH Allen. 1st. 121p. NF. M21. $15.00.

STANIER, Sylvia. *Mrs. Houblon's Side-Saddle.* 1986. London. Allen. VG/dj. O3. $25.00.

STANLEY, Charles H. *Confronting Casual Christianity.* 1985. Broadman. 167p. VG/VG. B29. $8.50.

STANLEY, Charles H. *Forgiveness.* 1987. Nelson. 197p. VG. B29. $3.50.

STANSBERRY, Domenic. *Spoiler.* 1987. Atlantic Monthly. 1st. sgn. author's 1st novel. F/dj. T2. $40.00.

STANTON, Carey. *An Island Memoir.* 1984. Los Angeles. The Zamorano Club. 1 of 350 ltd ed. brown cloth 8vo. gilt spine titles & cover decor. ils ep. 38p. F. P4. $50.00.

STANTON, Robert Brewster. *Colorado River Controversies.* 1932. Dodd Mead. 8vo. ils. 232p. red cloth. VG/facs dj. F7. $600.00.

STANTON, Robert Brewster. *Down the Colorado.* 1965. U OK. 1st. intro/edit DL Smith. 237p. VG/dj. F7. $75.00.

STANWOOD, Brooks. *The 7th Child.* 1982. NY. S&S. 1st. VG/VG. R16. $25.00.

STAR, Nancy. *Up Next.* 1998. Pocket. 1st. F/F. G8. $15.00.

STARK, Richard. *The Handle.* 1985. London. Allison & Busby. 1st hc ed. VF in dj. M15. $45.00.

STARK, Richard. *The Mourner.* 1987. London. Allison & Busby. 1st hc ed. F in dj. M15. $45.00.

STARR, Frederick. *Physical Characters of Indians of Southern Mexico.* 1902. Chicago. 1st separate. ils/mc chart. 59p. wrp. F3. $75.00.

STARR, Henry. *Thrilling Events: Life of Henry Starr By Himself.* 1982. Creative. rpt. ils/index. 95p. aeg. leather. F. $1.00.

STARR, Jimmy. *Three Short Biers.* 1946. Hollywood. Murray Gee. 1st. NF/rpr. M15. $125.00.

STARR, Jimmy. *Three Short Biers.* 1945. Murray & Gee. 1st. Lightly chipped jacket. F/dj. M25. $75.00.

STARR, S. Frederick. *Red and Hot, The Fate of Jazz in the Soviet Union 1917 – 1980.* 1983. NY. Oxford. AP. VG+/wrps. B2. $25.00.

STARR, Victor P. *Basic Principles of Weather Forecasting.* 1942. NY. Harper. 1st. 8vo. 125 text ils. 299p. VG/cloth. K5. $17.00.

STARRETT, Vincent. *Bookman's Holiday.* 1943. Random. 1st. inscr. red cloth. VG/dj. J3. $150.00.

STARRETT, Vincent. *Born in a Bookshop.* 1965. Norman. U of OK Press. 1st. F in F dj. B2. $35.00.

STARZL, Thomas E. *Puzzle People: Memoirs of a Transplant Surgeon.* 1992. Pittsburgh. ARC. 8vo. 364p. F/NF. C14. $20.00.

STAUTON, Howard. *Complete Illustrated Shakespeare.* 1989. NY. Gallery. 813p. VG. C5. $25.00.

STAVELEY, Gaylord. *Broken Waters Sing: Rediscovering Two Great Rivers of West.* 1971. Boston. 1st. sgn. ils/index. 283p. gr/wht bdg. VG. $7.00.

STEAD, Robert J. C. *The Copper Disc.* 1930. Garden City. Doubleday Crime Club. 1st. VG w/o dj. M15. $35.00.

STEARNS, Marshall, and Jean Stearns. *Jazz Dance, The Story of American Vernacular Dance.* 1979. NY. Schirmer. reprint. OP in cloth. NF. B2. $25.00.

STEBBINS, R. L & L. Walheim. *Western Fruit Berries & Nuts: How To Select, Grow and Enjoy.* 1981. Tucson. 4to. sc. 192p w/hundreds of color photos. F. B26. $17.50.

STEED, Neville. *Boxed In.* 1991. London. Century. 1st. VF/VF. T2. $25.00.

STEED, Neville. *Clockwork.* 1989. NY. St. Martin. 1st Am ed. F/F. T2. $15.00.

STEED, Neville. *Wind Up.* 1991. NY. St. Martin. 1st Am ed. VF/VF. T2. $15.00.

STEELE, Adison; see Lupoff, Richard.

STEELE, Arthur R. *Flowers for the King, The Expeditions of Ruiz and Pavon and the Flora of Peru.* 1964. Durham. F in dj. B26. $42.50.

STEELE, Danielle. *Message from Nam.* 1990. Delacorte. 1st. F/dj. R11. $25.00.

STEELE, Harold C. *Departmental Laboratory Assistant in Biological Science.* 1966. Dorrance. 213p. xl. G. S5. $12.00.

STEELE, J. Dorman. *Fourteen Weeks in Popular Geology; The Story of the Rocks.* 1877. NY. American Book Company. rev ed. sm 8vo. 121 text figures. 273p. VG/decor cloth. marbled page edges. lt wear. pencil mks on ep. K5. $20.00.

STEENBERG, Elisa. *Swedish Glass.* 1950. NY. Gramercy Pub. Co. 1st. 8vo. 128p. VG/G. H1. $22.50.

STEFFERUD, Alfred. *Crops in Peace & War: Yearbook of Agriculture 1950 – 51.* 1951. GPO. 942p. cloth. A10. $18.00.

STEGNER, Wallace. *A Shooting Star.* 1961. NY. Viking. 1st. F in F pict dj. D10. $125.00.

STEGNER, Wallace. *All the Little Live Things.* 1967. NY. Viking. 1st. NF in dj. D10. $50.00.

STEGNER, Wallace. *Collected Stories of Wallace Stegner.* 1990. Random. 1st. F/dj. R14. $90.00.

STEGNER, Wallace. *Gathering of Zion: Story of the Mormon Trail.* (1964). NY. later prt. ils/maps. F/dj. M4. $25.00.

STEGNER, Wallace. *Mormon Country.* 1942. NY. DSP. 1st. 8vo. 362p. map ep. VG. $7.00.

STEGNER, Wallace. *The Collected Stories of Wallace Stegner.* 1990. NY. Random House. 1st. F in F dj. D10. $60.00.

STEGNER, Wallace. *Where the Bluebird Sings.* 1992. NY. Random House. 1st. F/F. D10. $40.00.

STEIG, William. *Dominic.* (1972). FSG. 8vo. ils. 146p. red cloth. VG. T5. $15.00.

STEIG, William. *Rotten Island.* 1984 (1969). Eng. Viking Kestrel. 1st Eng. 4to. unp. NF. T5. $25.00.

STEIN, Charles Francis. *Origin & History of Howard County.* Maryland. 1972. Baltimore. ils/map ep. 383p. VG/dj. B18. $45.00.

STEIN, Eugene. *Straitjacket & Tie.* 1994. Ticknor. 1st. author's 1st book. F/F. H11. $15.00.

STEIN, Evaleen. *Little Shepherd of Provence.* 1910. LC Page. 1st. 8vo. ils. VG+. M5. $20.00.

STEIN, Gertrude. *Autobiography of Alice B Toklas.* 1933. Harcourt Brace. 1st. NF/VG. B4. $450.00.

STEIN, Gertrude. *Lectures in America.* 1953. Random. 1st/1st state. 8vo. 246p. NF/dj. J3. $225.00.

STEIN, Gertrude. *The World Is Round.* (1988). San Francisco. Northpoint. 1st. F/F. B3. $20.00.

STEIN, Gertrude. *Wars I Have Seen.* 1945. 1st. NF/VG. M19. $45.00.

STEIN, Harry. *Hoopla.* 1983. Knopf. 1st. sgn. F/VG. P8. $85.00.

STEIN, Jean. *Edie: An American Biography.* 1982. Knopf. BC. ils. 455p. VG/G. P12. $8.00.

STEINBECK, John. *East of Eden.* 1952. NY. Viking. 1st. F/F. L3. $750.00.

STEINBECK, John. *Fabulous Redmen.* 1951. Harrisburg. 1st. VG/dj. B5. $35.00.

STEINBECK, John. *Journal of a Novel.* 1969. NY. 1st. F/F. B5. $60.00.

STEINBECK, John. *Red Pony.* 1945. Viking. 1st. ils Wesley Dennis. VG/worn case. S13. $16.00.

STEINBECK, John. *Red Pony.* 1989. Viking. ils Wesley Dennis. NF/dj. A21. $30.00.

STEINBECK, John. *Sweet Thursday.* 1954. Viking. 1st. F/dj. Q1. $175.00.

STEINBECK, John. *The Short Reign of Pippin IV. A Fabrication.* 1957. NY. Viking. 1st. NF in dj. D10. $50.00.

STEINER, Mona Lisa. *Philippine Ornamental Plants and Their Care.* 1952. Manila. 1st. 215p w/color ftspc. many ils. dj. B26. $29.00.

TEINKE, Darcy. *Up Through the Water.* 989. Doubleday. 1st. sgn. F/NF. D10. 5.00.

TEMP, Jane. *Waterbound.* 1996. Dial. 1st m. F/dj. T12. $25.00.

TEN, Maria. *The Mexican Codices & Their xtraordinary History.* 1974. np. Mexico. 1st nglish ed. 142p. G/wrp. F3. $15.00.

TEPANEK, O. *Birds of Heath & Marshland.* 966. London. 4th. 134p. F/dj. A17. $20.00.

TEPANSKY, Paul E. *Memoirs of Margaret Mahler.* 1988. Free Pr. 1st. 8vo. 179p. F/NF. 14. $14.00.

TEPHAN, Leslie. *Reprise.* 1988. St. Martin. st. F/F. H11. $20.00.

TEPHEN, Leslie. *Samuel Johnson.* 1878. Harper. 1st Am. brn cloth. H13. $35.00.

TEPHENS, James. *Crock of Gold.* 1926. Macmillan. 1st. 227p. G. M10. $75.00.

TEPHENS, Robert Neilson. *Captain avenshaw.* 1901. np. L. C. Page Co. 1st. ils y Howard Pyle & others; owner sgn. VG. M19. $25.00.

TEPHENS, Rockwell R. *One Man's Forest.* 974. Brattleboro, VT. ils. VG in torn dj. B26. 12.50.

TEPHENSON, George M. *Puritian Meritage.* 1952. Macmillan. 282p. G/dj. B29. 7.00.

TEPHENSON, Neal. *The Diamond Age.* 1995). NY. Bantam. 1st. F/F. B3. $40.00.

TEPHENSON, Neal. *Zodiac: The Eco Thriller.* 1988. NY. Atlantic Monthly Press. st. PBO. sgn. F. O11. $75.00.

TEPHENSON, Patricia & Alex Jay Kimmelman. *Tom Marshall's Tucson.* 1996. rivately printed. 1st. ils. maps. sgn by uthors. 88p. F. B19. $19.50.

TEPHENSON, Peter H. *The Hutterian People: Ritual and Rebirth in the Evolution of Communal Life.* 1991. University Press. 272p. G. B29. $25.00.

TERLING, Stewart. *Fire on Fear Street.* 958. Lippincott. 1st. VG/VG. G8. $10.00.

TERLING, Stewart. *Nightmare at Noon.* 951. Dutton. 1st. VG/VG. G8. $15.00.

TERLING, Thomas. *Silent Siren.* 1958. &S. 1st. VG/VG. G8. $10.00.

STERN, Louis William. *Psychology of Early Childhood up to Sixth Year of Age.* 1924. London. Allen Unwin. 1st Eng-language. 557p. panelled bl cloth. VG. G1. $65.00.

STERN, Madeleine B. *Behind a Mask: Unknown Thrillers of Louisa May Alcott.* 1995. Morrow. 1st. ils. cloth/brd. dj. R12. $25.00.

STERN, Madeleine B. *Louisa May Alcott.* 1996. Random. 8vo. ils. wrp. R12. $18.00.

STERN, Philip Van Doren. *Robert E Lee: Man & the Soldier.* 1963. McGraw Hill. 1st. 256p. F/dj. H1. $40.00.

STERN, Richard Martin. *Cry Havoc.* 1963. Scribners. 1st. VG/VG. G8. $10.00.

STERN, Richard Martin. *High Hazard.* 1962. Scribners. 1st. VG/G. G8. $10.00.

STERN, Steve. *Lazar Malkin Enters Heaven.* 1986. Viking. 1st. sgn. F/dj. B30. $25.00.

STERNE, Laurence. *A Sentimental Journey Through France & Italy.* 1900. np. Dodd Mead. color ftspc. NF. M19. $45.00.

STETTINIUS, Edw. R., Jr. *Roosevelt & the Russians: The Yalta Conference.* 1949. NY. Doubleday. 1st. 8vo. 367p. F+/G. H1. $9.00.

STEVENS, Brooke. *Circus of the Earth & Air.* 1994. NY. Harcourt. 1st. F/F. H11. $25.00.

STEVENS, P. Gregory. *The Life of Grace.* 1963. Prentice Hall. 118p. VG/VG. B29. $7.50.

STEVENS, Patricia. *God Save Ireland!* 1974. Macmillan. 1st. 200p. F/dj. D4. $30.00.

STEVENS, Shane. *Anvil Chorus.* 1985. Delacorte. 1st. F/dj. M15. $45.00.

STEVENS, Shane. *By Reason of Insanity.* 1979. S&S. 1st. F/NF. M19. $17.50.

STEVENS, Shane. *Dead City.* 1973. HBW. 1st. author's 3rd novel. F/clipped dj. M25. $60.00.

STEVENS, Sheppard. *In the Eagle's Talon.* 1902. Boston. Little, Brn. 1st. 475p. G. G11. $6.00.

STEVENS, William Chase. *Kansas Wild Flowers.* 1948. U KS. 463p. xl. VG. S5. $35.00.

STEVENS-ARROYO, Antonio. *Cave of the Jagua: Mythological World of Tainos.* 1988. U NM. 1st. 282p. F3. $25.00.

STEVENSON, Elizabeth. *Park Maker: Life of Frederick Law Olmsted.* 1977. NY. 484p. VG/dj. B26. $26.00.

STEVENSON, James. *Could be Worse.* nd. NY. Greenwillow Books. VG. no dj as issued. A28. $7.95.

STEVENSON, Richard. *Chain of Fools.* 1996. St. Martin. 1st. NF/NF. G8. $10.00.

STEVENSON, Robert Louis. *A Child's Garden of Verses.* 1930. NY. Saalfield Pub Co. 1st ed thus. ils by Clara M. Burd. 4to. bl cloth spine. color ils & striped paper over bds. 8 color plates. sold together w/picture puzzle box. #575. 38p. VG. edges rubbed. D6. $125.00.

STEVENSON, Robert Louis. *A Child's Garden of Verses.* 1905. NY. Scribners. 1st. ils by Jessie Wilcox Smith. sm 4to. blk cloth w/gilt lettering. color ils ep. color & b/w plates. 125p. G+. spine faded. corners rubbed. D6. $150.00.

STEVENSON, Robert Louis. *Black Arrow.* 1888. Cassell. 1st. red cloth. G. S13. $15.00.

STEVENSON, Robert Louis. *Kidnapped.* 1908. McLoughlin. lg 8vo. ils. 139p. G. M7. $25.00.

STEVENSON, Robert Louis. *Land of Nod.* 1988. Holt. 1st. ils Hague. F. B17. $20.00.

STEVENSON, Robert Louis. *Strange Case of Dr. Jekyll & Mr. Hyde.* 1952. Heritage. lg 8vo. gilt blk cloth. F. M7. $18.00.

STEVENSON, Robert Louis. *Treasure Island.* 1930. Philadelphia. Anderson Books. No. 1. 1st and only book published by Anderson. uncut. beige linen. VG. A16. $50.00.

STEVENSON, Robert Louis. *Treasure Island.* 1947. Grosset & Dunlap. ne. ils. intl. G. s19. $30.00.

STEVENSON, Violet. *Successful Flower Marketing.* 1952. London. Collingridge. 164p. VG/dj. A10. $22.00.

STEWART, Dugald. *Elements of Philosophy of the Human Mind.* 1818. NY. James Eastburn. 420p. G. G1. $75.00.

STEWART, Edgar I. *Penny-An-Acre Empire in the West.* 1968. Norman. OK. 1st. 268p. E1. $35.00.

STEWART, Edward. *Ariana.* 1985. NY. Crown. 1st. F/VF. H11. $15.00.

STEWART, George. *Storm.* 1941. Random House. 1st. bl. cloth. intl. G. s19. $30.00.

STEWART, George. *These Men My Friends.* 1954. np. Caxton. 1st. VG/VG dj. M19. $17.50.

STEWART, James. *The Gates of New Life.* 1964. T & T Clark. 251p. VG. B29. $10.50.

STEWART, Jimmy. *Jimmy Stewart & His Poems.* 1989. np. Crown. sgn 1st ed. photo inlaid. pc. F/F dj. M19. $35.00.

STEWART, John. *Antarctica: An Encyclopedia.* 1990. Jefferson. McFarland & Company. Inc. issued w/o dj. two volumes. 8vo. bl cloth w/ wht spine & cover titles. 1220p. New. P4. $155.00.

STEWART, John Z. *Coasts, Waves and Weather, for Navigators.* 1945. Boston. Ginn. b/w photos & diagrams. 4to. 348p. G/cloth. K5. $15.00.

STEWART, Mary. *Tell Me a True Story.* 1909. NY. Fleming H. Revell Co. Poor. A16. $1.00.

STEWART, Michael. *Far Cry.* 1984. NY. Freundlich. 1st. VF/F. H11. $30.00.

STEWART, Michael. *Monkey Shines.* 1983. Freundlich. 1st. F/F. H11. $30.00.

STEWART, P. *Vintner in the Kitchen: Wine & Cookery in the West.* 1974. ils. easel stand format. VG. E6. $12.00.

STEWART, Robert. *Sam Steele: Lion of the Frontier.* 1979. Toronto. Doubleday. UP. NF/wrp. A26. $50.00.

STEWART, Watt. *Keith & Costa Rica.* 1964. Albuquerque. 1st. 210p. dj. F3. $25.00.

STICKNEY, Brian. *Numismatic History of Republic of Panama.* 1971. Texas. Almanzar's Coins. 1st. 64p. G. wrp. F3. $10.00.

STIERLIN, Henri. *Living Architecture; Ancient Mexican.* 1968. NY. np. 1st. 192p. F/F. F3. $35.00.

STIERLIN, Henri. *Living Architecture; Mayan.* 1976. Mexico. Campania. 1st. 192p. F/F. F3. $35.00.

STILES, Robert. *Four Years Under Marse Robert.* 1903. NY/Washington. Neale Pub Co. 2nd ed. orig cloth. 368p. VG. lightly rubbed & soiled. M8. $150.00.

STILL, Steven M. *Manual of Herbaceous Ornamental Plants.* 1994 (1980). Champaign. 4th expanded. photos. 814p. VG. B26. $35.00.

STILLWELL, Benjamin. *Early Memoirs of the Stillwell Family.* 1878. NY. dk gr half leather/marbled brd. VG. B30. $45.00.

STINE, R. l. *99 Fear Street: The House of Evil, the First Horror.* 1994. NY. Parachute Press. sc. VG. A28. $1.95.

STINE, R. l. *A Shocker on Shock Street.* 1995. NY. Goosebumps. #35 ed sc. G. A28. $2.50.

STINEMAN, Esther Lanigan. *Mary Austin: Song of the Maverick.* 1989. New Haven/London. 1st. 8vo. 269p. AN/dj. P4. $35.00.

STINETORF, L. *La Cina Problana.* 1960. Bobbs Merrill. 1st. 256p. dj. F3. $15.00.

STINETORF, Louisa A. *White Witch Doctor.* 1950. Phil. Westminster. BC. 276p. VG/dj. A25. $15.00.

STINSON, Jim. *TV Safe.* 1991. Scribner. 1st. VG+/VG+. G8. $10.00.

STOCKTON, Frank R. *Pomona's Travels.* 1894. Scribner. 1st. ils AB Frost. F. M19. $45.00.

STODOLA, Jiri. *Encyclopedia of Water Plants.* 1967. Jersey City. 368p w/over 200 color drawings. B26. $29.00.

STOKER, Bram. *Dracula.* nd. Grosset Dunlap. MTI. ils. VG. L1. $40.00.

STOKER, Bram. *Dracula.* 1965. Heritage. 1st thus. VG/dj. L1. $50.00.

STOKES, Terry. *Crimes of Passion.* 1973. Knopf. ARC/1st. inscr. F/dj. L3. $75.00.

STOKES, W. Royal. *The Jazz Scene.* 1991. NY. Oxford. 1st. F/NF. B2. $25.00.

STOKES, W. Royal. *The Jazz Scene.* 1991. NY. Oxford. 1st. F/NF. B2. $25.00.

STOMMELL, Henry. *View of the Sea.* 1987. Princeton. 165p. F/dj. A17. $12. 50.

STONE, Irving. *Adversary in the House.* 1947. np. Doubleday. 1st. pc. NF/G. M19. $25.00.

STONE, Irving. *Greek Treasure.* 1975. Doubleday. 1st. sgn. VG/G. B30. $45.00.

STONE, Joel. *A Town Called Jericho.* 1991. NY. Fine. 1st. author's 1st book. VF/F. H11. $40.00.

STONE, Jonathan. *The Cold Truth.* 1999. NY. St. Martin. ARC. F/wrp. B2. $25.00.

STONE, Josephine Rector. *Praise all the Moons of Morning.* 1979. NY. Atheneum. 1st. VF/VF. T2. $7.00.

STONE, Lee Alexander. *Power of a Symbol.* 1925. Chicago. Pascal Covici. ltd. G. B9. $40.00.

STONE, Martha. *At the Sign of Midnight.* 1975. Tucson. 1st. photos. 262p. F3. $20.00.

STONE, Michael. *A Long Reach.* 1996. NY. Viking. 1st. ARC. sgn. VF/pict wrp. T2. $20.00.

STONE, Michael. *The Low End of Nowhere.* 1996. NY. Viking. 1st. sgn. author's 1st book. VF/VF. T2. $35.00.

STONE, Raymond. *Donald Dare. The Champion Pitcher.* 1914. Graham. 1st. ils. G+. P8. $200.00.

STONE, Raymond. *Tommy Piptop & His Baseball Nine.* 1912. Graham Matlack. 1st. G+. P8. $200.00.

STONE, Robert. *Bear and His Daughter.* 1997. Houghton Mifflin. UP. NF/white wrp. M25. $75.00.

STONE, Robert. *Children of Light.* 1986. NY. Knopf. 1st. F/F. H11. $40.00.

STONE, Robert. *Damascus Gate.* 1998. Boston. Houghton Mifflin. 1st. sgn. F/F. O11. $40.00.

STONE, Robert. *Flag for Sunrise.* 1981. Knopf. 1st. sgn. VG/dj. B30. $45.00.

STONE, Robert. *Outerbridge Reach.* 1992. NY. Ticknor. 1st. F/F. H11. $30.00.

STONE, William L. *Life & Times of Sa-Go-Ye-Wat-Ha or Red Jacket.* 1841. NY. 1/550 ils/5 pl. 484p. gilt cloth. B18. $250.00.

STONE, William L. *Life & Times of Sir William Johnson.* Bart. 1965. Albany. Munsell. 2 vol. 555/544p. B18. $55.00.

STONELY, Jack. *Scruffy.* 1979. Random. 1st (stated). 8vo. 156p. brd/cloth spine. VG/dj. T5. $30.00.

STONG, Phil. *Horses & Americans.* 1946. Garden City. deluxe ed. ils Kurt Wiese. 333p. NF. A17. $22. $50.00.

STONUM, Gary Lee. *The Dickinson Sublime.* (Madison). The Univ of Wisconsin Press. (1990). 8vo. 221p. pink cloth. dj. 1st ed. F/NF. l5. $30.00.

STOOKEY, Lorena Laura. *Robin Cook: A Critical Companion.* 1996. Greenwood. 1st. F. P3. $30.00.

STOREY, Gail Donohue. *God's Country Club*. 1996. NY. Persea. 1st. VF/VF. H11. 25.00.

STORM, Margaret. *Dessert Lover's Cookbook*. 1970. LA. Nash. G/dj. A16. $7.00.

STORM, Robert. *Animal Orientation & Navigation*. 1967. OR State U. 134p. xl. G. S5. $15.00.

STORRING, Gustav. *Mental Pathology in its Relation to Normal Psychology*. 1907. Sonnenschein. 1st Eng-language. 298p. tan cloth. G1. $65.00.

STORY, Alfred T. *Story of Photography*. 1909. NY. McClure. ils. half morocco/cloth. B14. $100.00.

STOTT, John. *Involvement: Being a Responsible Christian in a Non Christian Society*. 1985. Revell. 221p. VG/VG. B29. $9.50.

STOUDT, John Joseph. *Early Pennsylvania Art & Crafts*. (1964). London. Yoseloff/Barnes. 3rd. ils. 364p. F/dj. H1. $30.00.

STOUT, David. *Carolina Skeletons*. 1988. NY. Mysterious Press. 1st. F in F dj. D10. $60.00.

STOUT, Rex. *Alphabet Hicks*. 1941. NY. Farrar & Rinehart. 1st. Jacket has internal tape mends and chips at spine ends. along edges and at corners. VG/dj. M15. $250.00.

STOUT, Rex. *Father Hunt*. 1968. Viking. 1st. rem mk. NF/G. M19. $25.00.

STOUT, Rex. *Final Deduction*. 1961. Viking. 1st. NF. T12. $60.00.

STOUT, Rex. *Mr. Cinderella*. 1938. np. Farrar & Rinehart. 1st in facsimile dj. very scarce title. NF/F. M19. $250.00.

STOUT, Rex. *Please Pass the Guilt*. 1973. NY. Viking. 1st. F/dj. M15. $65.00.

STOUT, Sandra McPhee. *Complete Book of McKee Glass*. 1972. Trojan. 1st. 1/2500. 456p. F/dj. H1. $125.00.

STOWE, Everett. *Communicating Reality Through Symbols*. 1966. Westminster. 158p. VG/VG. B29. $8.00.

STOWELL, Joseph. *The Dawn's Early Light: Daring to Challenge the Deepening Darkness*. 1990. Moody. 178p. VG/VG. B29. $9.00.

STRALEY, John. *The Angels Will Not Care*. (1998). NY. Bantam. 1st. F/F. B3. $15.00.

STRALEY, John. *The Curious Eat Themselves*. 1993. NY. Soho Press. 1st. sgn. VF/VF. T2. $35.00.

STRALEY, John. *The Music of What Happens*. 1996. NY. Bantam. 1st. sgn. VF/VF. T2. $25.00.

STRALEY, John. *The Woman Who Married a Bear*. 1992. NY. Soho. 1st. VF/VF. H11. $60.00.

STRANG, Mrs. Herbert. *The Big Book for Girls*. 1929. London. Oxford U Press. G. A16. $20.00.

STRANGE, John Stephen. *Look Your Last*. 1943. Crime Club. 1st. VG. G8. $15.00.

STRATEMAN, Dr. Klaus. *Negro Bands on Film. Vol. 1: Big Bands 1928 – 1950*. 1981. Lubbecke. Uhle & Kleimann. 1st. wrp. 124p. F. B2. $65.00.

STRATER, Henry. *Henry Strater: American Artist*. 1962. Ogunquit, ME. 1/3000. ils. VG. M17. $30.00.

STRATTON, Charlotte Kimball. *Rug Hooking Made Easy*. 1955. NY. ils. VG/dj. M17. $17. 50.

STRATTON, Clarence. *Swords & Statues*. 1937. Winston. 1st. ils Robert Lawson. VG/G. P2. $25.00.

STRAUB, Peter. *General's Wife*. 1982. Donald Grant. 1st. sgn. VG/sans. L1. $85.00.

STRAUB, Peter. *Houses Without Doors*. 1990. NY. Dutton. 1st Am. rem mk. F/F. G10. $12. $50.00.

STRAUB, Peter. *Koko*. 1988. NY. Dutton. 1st. VF/VF. H11. $40.00.

STRAUB, Peter. *Mystery*. 1990. NY. Dutton. 1st. F/VF. H11. $40.00.

STRAUB, Peter. *Pork Pie Hat*. 1999. London. Orion. 1st. VF/VF. T2. $15.00.

STRAUB, Peter. *The Hellfire Club*. 1996. NY. Random House. 1st. VF/VF. T2. $20.00.

STRAUB, Peter. *The Talisman*. 1984. NY. Viking. 1st. Stephen King, co-writer. sgn Straub. VF/VF. T2. $45.00.

STRAUB, Peter. *The Throat*. 1993. NY. Dutton. 1st. sgn. VF/VF. T2. $45.00.

STREATFEILD, Noel. *Movie Shoes*. 1949. Random House. 1st. ils. F/ chip dj. s19. $25.00.

STREET, David. *Karen Kain: Lady of Dance*. 1978. Toronto. McGraw-Hill Ryerson. 1st. clip. 128p. F/NF dj. A26. $65.00.

STREET, Frederick. *Azaleas*. 1959. London. 1st. 278p. VG. B26. $26.00.

STREET, J. *Goodbye My Lady*. 1954. Phil. Lippincott. 1st. VG/G. B5. $30.00.

STREETER, Brunett Hillman. *Primitive Church Studies with Special Reference*. 1929. NY. Macmillan. 1st. index/map. 323p. VG. H10. $27.00.

STREETER, Thomas W. *Bibliography of Texas 1795 – 1845*. 1996. Stoors-Mansfield. CT. Maurizio Martino. 5 vol. rpt. 1/150. cloth.

STREHL, Dan. *One Hundred Books on California Food & Wine*. 1990. LA. Book Collectors. 1/300. 45p. patterned wrp w/flaps. D11. $40.00.

STRETE, Craig Kee. *Paint Your Face on a Drowning in the River*. 1978. NY. Greenwillow. 1st. F/F. D10. $75.00.

STRIEBER, Whitley. *Billy*. 1990. NY. Putnam. 1st. sgn. VF/VF. T2. $30.00.

STRIEBER, Whitley. *Black Magic*. 1982. NY. Morrow. 1st. sgn. VF/VF. T2. $45.00.

STRIEBER, Whitley. *Majestic*. 1989. NY. Putnam. 1st. sgn. F/VF. T2. $20.00.

STRIEBER, Whitley. *Night Church*. 1983. S&S. 1st. xl. VG/dj. S18. $7.00.

STRIEBER, Whitley. *The Forbidden Zone*. 1993. NY. Dutton. 1st. sgn. VF/VF. T2. $25.00.

STRIEBER, Whitley. *The Wolfen*. 1978. NY. Morrow. 1st. F/dj. M15. $45.00.

STRIEBER, Whitley. *The Wolfen*. (1978). NY. Morrow. 1st. author's 1st novel. sgn by author. F/F. B3. $40.00.

STRIEBER, Whitley. *Transformation*. 1988. Morrow. 1st. F/dj. S18. $25.00.

STRIEBER, Whitley. *Transformation: The Breakthrough*. 1988. NY. Morrow. 1st. sgn. VF/VF. T2. $20.00.

STRIEBER, Whitley. *Unholy Fire*. 1992. NY. Dutton. 1st. sgn. F/dj. T2. $25.00.

STRIEBER, Whitley. *Unholy Fire*. 1992. NY. Dutton. 1st. sgn. VF/VF. T2. $25.00.

STRINGER, Lee. *Grand Central Winter.* 1997. NY. Seven Stories. 1st. sgn & dated. F/F. M23. $50.00.

STRINGFELLOW, William. *An Ethic for Christians & Other Aliens in a Strange Land.* 1973. Word. 156p. VG/VG. B29. $6.00.

STRINGFELLOW, William. *An Ethic for Christians & Other Aliens in a Strange Land.* 1974. Word. 156p. G/G. B29. $4.50.

STROFF, Stephen M. *Discovering Great Jazz. A New Listener's Guide.* 1991. NY. Newmarket Press. ARC w/slip. F/F. B2. $25.00.

STRONG, Augustus H. *Systematic Theology.* 1956. Judson. 3 vols in 1. 1157p. G/broken back hinge. B29. $19.00.

STROUD, Patricia Tyson. *Thomas Say: New World Naturalist.* 1992. U PA. 340p. F/dj. S15. $12. 50.

STROUT, Elizabeth. *Amy and Isabelle.* 1999. NY. Random House. UP. F in pict wrp. M23. $40.00.

STROUT, Elizabeth. *Amy and Isabelle.* 1999. NY. Random House. 1st. F/F. M23. $40.00.

STRUBBERG, Friedreich Armand. *Backwoodsman; or, Life on the Indian Frontier.* ca 1864. London. later prt. 428p. half leather. B18. $125.00.

STRUGATSKY, Arkadi & Boris. *Hard to be a God.* 1973. NY. Seabury Press. 1st English language ed. F/F. T2. $45.00.

STRUGATSKY, Arkadi & Boris. *The Time Wanderers.* 1986. NY. Richardson & Steirman. 1st English language ed. F/F. T2. $20.00.

STRUGHOLD, Hubertus. *Green & Red Planet.* 1954. London. Sidgwick Jackson. ils. 96p. G/dj. $5.00.

STRUIK, Dirk. *Yankee Science in the Making.* 1948. Little, Brn. 430p. VG. A10. $20.00.

STUART, G. A. *Chinese Materia Medica: Vegetable Kingdom, Extensively Revised from Dr. F. Porter Smith's Work.* 1985 (1911). reprint. dj. B26. $45.00.

STUART, Ian. *Satan Bug.* 1962. NY. Scribner. rpt. VG/dj. B11. $25.00.

STUART, Jesse. *Save Every Lamb.* 1964. NY. McGraw. 1st. inscr by author. F/NF. B2. $50.00.

STUART, Jesse. *Thread that Runs So True.* 1950. 293p. NF/VG. A4. $65.00.

STUBER, Stanley. *The Illustrated Bible and Church Handbook.* 1966. Association. 532p. VG/VG. B29. $10.00.

STUCK, G. *Annie McCune: Shreveport Madame.* 1981. Baton Rouge. sgn. photos. 114p. F/dj. M4. $15.00.

STUMP, Al. *Cobb.* 1994. Algonquin. 1st. F/VG+. P8. $25.00.

STURGIS, William Bayard. *Fly-Tying.* 1940. Scribner. ils. G. A19. $30.00.

STUSSMAN, Morton. *Follow Thru 60th Infantry Regiment.* 1945. Stuttgart. Germany. 1st. ils/maps. 127p. VG. S16. $30.00.

STUTZ, Bruce. *Natural Lives, Modern Times.* 1992. Crown. 1st. ils. F/dj. R14. $35.00.

STYRON, William. *A Tidewater Morning.* 1993. NY. Random House. 1st. F/F. D10. $30.00.

STYRON, William. *As He Lay Dead, a Bitter Grief.* 1981. NY. Atheneum. 1st. 1/300. sgn. F/saddle-stiched wrp. B4. $175.00.

STYRON, William. *Darkness Visible.* 1990. Random. UP. sgn. F/wrp. D10. $85.00.

STYRON, William. *Darkness Visible: A Memoir of Madness.* 1990. Random. 1st. F/dj. M23. $30.00.

STYRON, William. *Lie Down in Darkness.* 1951. Bobbs Merrill. 1st. sgn. VG+/dj. D10. $240.00.

STYRON, William. *Set this House on Fire.* 1960. Random. 1st. sgn. F/NF. D10. $110.00.

STYRON, William. *Sophie's Choice.* 1979. Random. 1st trade. thick 8vo. bl cloth. F/wrp. R3. $50.00.

STYRON, William. *The Confessions of Nat Turner.* 1967. NY. Random. 1st. very bright jacket with 1" closed tear at top of rear panel. VF/F. H11. $70.00.

SUAREZ, Virgil. *Havana Thursdays.* (1995). Houston. Arte Publico. 1st. sgn by author. F/F. B3. $25.00.

SUDHALTER, Richard M. and Philip R. Evans. *Bix, Man and Legend.* 1974. New Rochelle. Arlington House. 1st. F/NF. B2. $85.00.

SULLIVAN, J. W. N. *Gallio or the Tyranny of Science.* 1928. Dutton. 57p. G. B29. $10.00.

SULLIVAN, William H. *Mission to Iran: By Last US Ambassador.* 1981. NY. Norton. 1st. 8vo. ils/map. 296p. NF/dj. $1.00.

SULLIVAN, Winona. *Sudden Death at the Norfolk Cafe.* 1993. St. Martin. 1st. AN/dj. N4. $25.00.

SULLY, James. *Human Mind: A Text-Book of Psychology.* 1892. Longman Gr. 2 vol. panelled brn cloth. G1. $150.00.

SULLY, Langdon. *No Tears for the General.* 1974. Palo Alto, CA. 1st. ils/index. 255p. E1. $35.00.

SULMAN, Florence. *A Popular Guide to the Wild Flowers of New South Wales. Vol 1 (of 2).* 1926 (1913). Sydney. ep tanned. B26. $15.00.

SUMMERHAYS, Reginald. *Arabian Horse: Breed in Britain.* 1972. S Brunswick. Barnes. 2nd. VG/dj. O3. $20.00.

SUMMERS, Anthony. *Goddess: Secret Lives of Marilyn Monroe.* 1985. Gollancz. 1st. F/dj. P3. $30.00.

SUMMERS, Anthony. *Goddess: Secret Lives of Marilyn Monroe.* 1985. London. Gollancz. 1st. NF/dj. A14. $25.00.

SUMMERS, Montague. *Vampire: His Kith & Kin.* 1960. U Books. 1st. VG/G. L1. $75.00.

SUMMERS, Richard. *Ball Shy Pitcher.* 1970. Steck Vaughn. 1st. F/dj. P8. $30.00.

SUMNER, Charles. *White Slavery in the Barbary States.* 1853. John P. Jewett & Co. 1st. intl. ils. gilt brown cloth. F. s19. $475.00.

SUMNER, Cid Ricketts. *Traveler in the Wilderness.* 1957. Harper. 8vo. map ep. 248p. VG/dj. F7. $40.00.

SUMPTON, Lois. *Cookies & More Cookies.* 1948. IL. Bennet. G/dj. A16. $10.00.

SWAIN, E. G. *The Stoneground Ghost Tales.* 1996. Penyffordd. Chester. Ash Tree Press. reissue. 1st thus. 400 copies printed. VF/VF. T2. $45.00.

SWAIN, James. *The Man Who Walked Through Walls.* 1989. NY. St. Martin. 1st. VF/VF. T2. $7.00.

SWALLOW, Alan. *The Rinehart Book of Verse.* 1963. NY. HRW. 18th prt. VG+ sc. F6. $7.00.

SWAN, Michael. *The Marches of El Dorado.* 1958. Boston. Beacon Press. 1st. 304p. G. F3. $20.00.

SWAN, Thomas. *The Final Faberge.* 1999. NY. Newmarket Press. 1st. sgn. VF/VF. T2. $26.00.

SWANN, Brian. *The Whale Scars*. 1974. New Rivers Press. 1st pb ed. art by Tom Huffman. VG+. V1. $30.00.

SWANSON, Doug J. *Big Town*. 1994. NY. Harper Collins. 1st. author's 1st book. remainder mark. F/F. H11. $20.00.

SWANSON, Logan; see Matheson, Richard.

SWANSON, Nellie R. *Pioneer Women Teachers of North Dakota*. 1965. Minot, ND. sc. G. A19. $25.00.

SWANTON, John. *Indian Tribes of Mexico, Central America and the West Indies*. 1965. Washington. Shorey Book Store. reprint of 1952 ed. ltd to 100. G/wrp. F3. $15.00.

SWANWICK, Michael. *Gravity's Angels*. 1991. Saulk City. 1st. 13 stories. F/dj. T2. $25.00.

SWANWICK, Michael. *Griffin's Egg*. 1990. London. Century/Legend. 1st. F/dj. T2. $20.00.

SWANWICK, Michael. *Stations of the Tide*. 1991. NY. Morrow. sgn 1st ed. some wear to tail of spine. NF/NF. M23. $100.00.

SWANWICK, Michael. *The Postmodern Archipelago: Two Essays on Science Fiction and Fantasy*. 1997. San Francisco. Tachyon Publications. 1st. VF/pict wrp. T2. $7.50.

SWARTHOUT, Burkes. *The Hills Beyond the Hills: 400 Years in the Ministry*. 1971. North Country Books. 327p. VG/VG. B29. $10.50.

SWARTHOUT, Glendon. *The Homesman*. 1988. NY. Weidenfeld. 1st. F/VF. H11. $25.00.

SWEET, William W. *The Story of Religion in America*. 1950. Harper. 492p. VG/VG. B29. $9.50.

SWEET, William Warren. *Religion in Development of American Culture 1765 – 1840*. 1952. Scribner. 1st. 338p. VG. H10. $25.00.

SWENSON, May. *Nature: Poems Old and New*. (1994). Boston. Houghton Mifflin. 1st. F/F. B3. $20.00.

SWETE, Henry B. *Introduction to the Old Testament in Greek*. 1968. KTAV. 626p. VG. B29. $29.00.

SWETTENHAM, John. *Canada's Atlantic War*. 1979. Canada. Samuel Stevens. 1st. F/dj. T12. $40.00.

SWIFT, Charles F. *Cape Cod: Right Arm of Massachusetts: Historical Narrative*. 1897. Yarmouth. Register Pub. 1st. worn/lacks backstrip. V3. $40.00.

SWIFT, Graham. *Ever After*. 1992. Knopf. 1st Am. sgn. F/dj. M25. $35.00.

SWIFT, Graham. *Ever After*. 1992. London. Picador. 1st. F/dj. M23. $30.00.

SWIFT, Graham. *Learning to Swim*. 1985. London. Picador. 1st hc. F/dj. A24. $40.00.

SWIFT, Graham. *Out of this World*. 1988. Poseidon. 1st Am. rem mk. NF/dj. R14. $25.00.

SWIFT, Graham. *Out of this World*. 1988. NY. Poseidon. 1st Am ed. sgn. F/F. A24. $45.00.

SWIFT, Graham. *Shuttlecock*. 1985. NY. Washington Square Press. 1st. F/. D10. $60.00.

SWIFT, Graham. *The Sweet-Shop Owner*. 1985. NY. Washington Square Press. 1st. author's 1st book. F/. D10. $60.00.

SWIFT, Graham. *Waterland*. 1984. Poseidon. 1st. sgn. rem mk. F/dj. D10. $55.00.

SWIFT, Jonathan. *Gulliver's Travels*. 1945. NY. Doubleday. ils by Jon Corbino. VG in dj. A16. $8.00.

SWIFT, Jonathan. *Gulliver's Travels into Several Remote Regions of World*. nd (1880s). London. ils T Morten. G. M17. $25.00.

SWIGGETT, Howard. *Rebel Raider: Life of John Hunt Morgan*. 1937 (1934). Garden City. map. 341p. fair. B10. $25.00.

SWINBURNE, Algernon Charles. *Midsummer Holiday & Other Poems*. 1884. London. Chatto Windus. 8vo. 189p. gilt brd edges/turn-ins. teg. F. $5.00.

SWINBURNE, Algernon Charles. *The Springtide of Life*. 1918. Philadelphia. Lippincott. 1st Am ed. ils by Arthur Rackham. sm 4to. gr cloth w/gilt. 133p. G+. D6. $95.00.

SWINDLE, Howard. *Jitter Joint*. 1999. NY. St. Martin. ARC. wrp. F. B2. $25.00.

SWINDOLL, Charles R. *Growing Strong in the Seasons of Life*. 1983. Multnomah. 414p. VG/worn dj. B29. $8.50.

SWINDOLL, Charles R. *Improving Your Serve; The Art of Unselfish Living*. 1983. Word. 219p. VG/VG. B29. $7.00.

SWINDOLL, Charles R. *Quest of Character*. 1987. Multnomah. 216p. F/F. B29. $7.50.

SWINGLE, Walter T. *The Botany of Citrus and its Wild Relatives of the Orange Subfamily*. 1943. Berkeley. gilt emb brown cloth. VG. B26. $55.00.

SWITKIN, Abraham. *Hand Lettering Today*. 1976. Harper Row. 1st. 212p. cloth. F/dj. O10. $35.00.

SYKES, Christopher. *High-Minded Murder*. 1944. London. Home & Van Thal. 1st. F in dj. M15. $85.00.

SYKES, Gerald (ed). *Alienation — The Cultural Climate of Our Time*. 1964. np. George Braziller. 1st. 2 vols. includes almost every modern author. F in edgeworn slipcase. M19. $25.00.

SYKES, John. *Mountain Arabs: Window in the Middle East*. 1968. Chicago. 1st. 8vo. 229p. NF/dj. W1. $16.00.

SYLVERSTER, Edward J. *Healing Blade: A Tale of Neurosurgery*. 1993. S&S. 1st. tall 8vo. 240p. F/NF. C14. $20.00.

SYLVESTER, Martin. *Rough Red*. 1989. London. Michael Joseph. 1st. F/dj. M15. $45.00.

SYLVESTER, Martin. *Sour Grapes*. 1992. NY. Villard. 1st. VF/dj. M15. $35.00.

SYLVESTER, Natalie G. *Home-Baking Cookbook*. 1973. Grosset Dunlap. 1st. G/dj. A16. $25.00.

SYMONDS, Craig L. *Joseph E. Johnston: Civil War Biography*. 1992. NY. Norton. 1st. F/dj. A14. $25.00.

SYMONDS, Craig L. *Naval Institute Historical Atlas of US Navy*. 1995. Annapolis. MD. stated 1st. ils. VG/dj. M17. $25.00.

SYMONDS, John. *Hurt Runner*. 1968. London. Baker. 1st. NF/dj. A14. $21.00.

SYMONDS, John. *With a View of the Palace*. 1966. London. 1st. inscr. dj. T9. $28.00.

SYMONDS, John A. *The Autobiography of Benvenuto Cellini*. 1946. Doubleday & Co. ne. ils by Salvador Dali in color & b&w. red cloth. G+. s19. $500.00.

SYMONS, Julian. *A Criminal Comedy*. (1986). NY. Viking. 1st Am prt of the revised ed. F/F. B3. $15.00.

SYMONS, Julian. *Charles Dickens*. 1951. Arthur Baker. 1st. VG/G. P3. $20.00.

SYMONS, Julian. *Detling Secret*. 1992. Viking. 1st Am ed. review copy. NF/NF. G8. $12.50.

SYMONS, Julian. *Horatio Bottomley.* 1955. Cresset. 1st. VG. P3. $15.00.

SYMONS, Julian. *Man Who Killed Himself.* 1967. Harper Row. 1st Am. VG/dj. G8. $15.00.

SYNGE, Patrick M. *Colins Guide to Bulbs.* 1971 (1961). London. 2nd. VG in dj. B26. $29.00.

SZATHMARY, Louis. *Chef's Secret Cook Book.* 1971. Chicago. Quadrangle. VG/dj. A16. $10.00.

— T —

TABER, Gladys. *One Dozen & One.* 1966. Phil. 1st. VG/VG. B5. $30.00.

TABER, Gladys. *Still Cover Journal.* 1981. Harper Row. 1st. 223p. VG/dj. M20. $25.00.

TABER, Mary J. *Just a Few Friends.* 1907. Phil. Winston. 1st. sgn. 166p. V3. $40.00.

TABER, William P. *Eye of Faith: History of Ohio Yearly Meeting.* 1985. Barnesville, OH. VG/dj. V3. $16.00.

TACHOLM, Vivi. *Students' Flora of Egypt.* 1956. Cairo. 1st. 81 pl/map/photos. 649p. VG/dj. B26. $55.00.

TAFT, L. R. *Greenhouse Construction: A Complete Manual.* 1915 (1893). Orange Judd. 210p. cloth. A10. $35.00.

TAFT, Robert. *Artists & Illustrators of the Old West, 1850 – 1900.* nd. Bonanza. rpt 1953 orig. 8vo. brn cloth. dj. F7. $45.00.

TAFT, Robert. *Artists & Illustrators of the Old West, 1850 – 1900.* 1953. NY. 1st. VG/G+. B5. $30.00.

TAGGART, Donald. *History of the 3rd Infantry Division In WWII.* 1947. WA. DC. 1st. photos/maps. 574p. VG. S16. $125.00.

TAIBO, Paco Ingnacio II. *An Easy Thing.* 1990. Viking. 1st Am. F/F. M22. $20.00.

TAINE, John. *Before the Dawn.* 1934. Williams. 1st. VG. M2. $30.00.

TAINE, John. *Cosmic Geoids & One Other.* 1949. Fantasy. 1st. F/VG. M19. $45.00.

TAINE, John. *Gold Tooth.* 1927. Dutton. 1st. VG/fair. P3. $50.00.

TAINE, John. *Seeds of Life.* 1951. Fantasy. ltd. sgn/#d/inscr. F/VG. P3. $100.00.

TAINE, John. *Time Stream.* 1975. Garland. F. M2. $25.00.

TAKAGI, Akimitsu. *Tattoo Murder Case.* 1948. 98. Soho. 1st. F/F. G8. $27.50.

TAKHAJAN, Armen. *Die Evolution Der Angiospermen.* 1959. Jena. sgn. ils. 344p. VG/dj. B26. $45.00.

TALBERT, Bill. *Tennis Observed.* 1967. Barre. 1st. ils. VG/dj. P8. $35.00.

TALBOT, Frederick A. *Lightships & Lighthouses.* 1913. Lippincott. ils. 325p. T7. $50.00.

TALBOT, Godfrey. *Queen Elizabeth: Queen Mother.* 1973. London. Jarrold. F/F. T12. $30.00.

TALBOT, J. S. *Foxes at Home & Reminiscences.* 1906. London. Horace Cox. 1st. VG. O3. $35.00.

TALBOT, Michael. *Bog.* 1986. Morrow. 1st. NF/dj. M2. $15.00.

TALBOT-PONSONBY, J. A. *Art of Show Jumping.* 1955. London. Naldrett. 1st. VG/fair. O3. $15.00.

TALBOYS, W. P. *West India Pickles.* 1876. NY. GW Carlton. 16mo. ils. 209p. new ep. T7. $90.00.

TALESE, Gay. *Kingdom & the Power.* 1969. World. 1st. 555p. AN/dj. H1. $25.00.

TALLANT, Robert. *Mrs. Candy & Saturday.* 1947. Doubleday. 1st. sgn. 269p. VG/clip. M20. $20.00.

TALLENT, Elizabeth. *In Constant Flight.* 1983. Knopf. 1st. author's 1st book. F/F. T11. $30.00.

TALLENT, Elizabeth. *Married Men & Magic Tricks: John Updike's Erotic Heroes.* 1982. Creative Arts. 1st. author's 1st collection of stories. F/NF. L3. $150.00.

TALLIS, David. *Music Boxes.* 1971. 1st. NF/NF. S13. $30.00.

TAMBO, Oliver. *Oliver Tambo Speaks.* 1988. Braziller. 1st. F/F. A20. $30.00.

TAN, Amy. *Chinese Siamese Cat.* 1994. Macmillan. 1st. sgn. ils Gretchen Shields. F/case. B3. $150.00.

TAN, Amy. *The Hundred Secret Senses.* 1995. Putnam. 1st. F/F. s19. $35.00.

TAN, Amy. *The Hundred Secret Senses.* 1995. NY. Putnam. sgn 1st. F/F. M23. $40.00.

TAN, Amy. *The Joy Luck Club.* 1989. NY. Putnam. 1st. F/F. one closed tear. B2. $175.00.

TAN, Amy. *The Kitchen God's Wife.* 1991. NY. Putnam. 1st. F/F. H11. $40.00.

TAN, Amy. *The Kitchen God's Wife.* 1991. NY. Putnam. 1st. NF/NF. R16. $40.00.

TAN, Amy. *The Moon Lady.* (1992). NY. Macmillan. 1st. ils Gretchen Schields. sgn by author and illustrator. children's. F/F. B3. $125.00.

TANCIG, W. J. *Requiem.* 1968. South Brunswick. NJ. Thomas Yoseloff. 1st. orig cloth. ils. 74p. NF/VG. M8. $12.50.

TANENBAUM, Robert K. *No Lesser Plea.* 1987. NY. Watts. 1st. author's 1st book. F/F. H11. $40.00.

TANITCH, Robert. *Peggy Ashcroft.* 1987. Hutchinson. ARC. NF/dj. C9. $45.00.

TANKARD, J. B. & M. R. Van Valkenburgh. *Gertrude Jekyll: A Vision of Garden and Wood.* 1989. NY. foreword by Jane Brown. index. annotated biblio. sq 4to. edges of cloth faded. else. VG in dj. B26. $27.50.

TANNAHILL, Reay. *Flesh & Blood.* 1975. Hamish Hamilton. 1st. VG/dj. P3. $20.00.

TANNENBAUM, Robert K. *Depraved Indifference.* 1989. NAL. 1st. VG/dj. P3. $20.00.

TANNENBAUM, Robert K. *No Lesser Plea.* 1987. NY. Watts. 1st. author's 1st book. F/NF. H11. $30.00.

TANNER, Jake. *Old Black Magic.* 1991. NY. Crown. 1st. VF/VF. T2. $15.00.

TANNER, Jake. *Saint Louie Blues.* 1992. NY. Crown. 1st. VF/VF. T2. $15.00.

TANNER, Ralph E.S. *Transition in African Beliefs.* 1967. Maryknoll. 1st. 8vo. 256p. VG/dj. W1. $18.00.

TANNER, William. *Book of Bond.* 1965. Jonathan Cape. 1st. VG/dj. P3. $35.00.

TAPPAN, Eva. *Robin Hood: His Book.* 1905 (1903). ils Charlotte Harding. VG+. S13. $20.00.

TAPPLY, William G. *Dead Winter.* 1989. NY. Delacorte. 1st. VF/VF. T2. $20.00.

TAPPLY, William G. *Follow the Sharks.* 1985. Scribner. 1st. F/F. P3. $18.00.

TAPPLY, William G. *The Spotted Cats.* 1991. NY. Delacorte. 1st. VF/VF. T2. $15.00.

TARAKANOFF, Vassili P. *Statement of My Captivity Among the Californians.* 1953. LA. Glen Dawson. 1/200. 47p. decor cloth. D11. $75.00.

TARG, William. *Indecent Pleasures: Life & Colorful Times of Wm. Targ.* 1975. Macmillan. 1st. ils. 428p. NF/dj. K3. $25.00.

TARKINGTON, Booth. *Claire Ambler.* 1928. Doubleday. 1st. F/VG. H11. $30.00.

TARKINGTON, Booth. *Penrod and Sam.* 1916. NY. Doubleday Page & Co. 1st. ils by Worth Brehm. VG. M19. $25.00.

TARKINGTON, Booth. *Two Vanrevels.* 1902. McClure Phillips. 1st. VG. A20. $20.00.

TARKOVSKY, Andrey. *Sculpting in Time, Reflections on the Cinema.* 1987. Knopf. ARC/1st am. photos. w/promo material. C9. $50.00.

TARR, Judith. *Dagger & the Cross.* 1991. Doubleday. 1st. F/dj. P3. $22.00.

TARR, Judith. *King and Goddess.* 1996. NY. Forge. 1st. sgn. VF/VF. T2. $25.00.

TARTT, Donna. *Secret History.* 1992. Knopf. 1st. author's 1st book. F/dj. A15. $40.00.

TATE, Carolyn. *Yaxchilan. The Design of a Maya Ceremonial City.* 1993. Austin. Univ of Texas Press. 1st. 306p. G/G. F3. $65.00.

TATE, James. *Riven Doggeries.* 1979. NY. Ecco Press. 1st. sgn. vol 18 in The American Poetry Series. F/F. O11. $55.00.

TATE, James. *Shepherds of the Mist.* 1969. Blk Sparrow. 1/300. sgn/#d. F/sewn wrp. B2. $45.00.

TATE, James & Bill Knott. *Lucky Darryl.* 1977. Brooklyn. Release Press. 1/1000. PBO. sgn. F/F. O11. $60.00.

TATE, Peter. *Faces in the Flames.* 1976. Doubleday. 1st. VG/dj. P3. $13.00.

TATE, Peter. *Greencomber.* 1979. Doubleday. 1st. F/dj. P3. $13.00.

TAUBE, Karl. *Aztec Myths.* 1993. Austin. Univ of Texas Press. 1st. wrp. 4to. 80p. G. F3. $15.00.

TAVES, Isabella. *The Quick Rich Fox.* 1959. Random House. 1st. chipped and rubbed jacket. bookplate on front pastedown. NF/dj. M25. $45.00.

TAWES, Leonard S. *Coasting Captain.* 1967. Newport News. Mariners Mus. ils. 461p. dj. T7. $60.00.

TAX, Meredith. *Rivington Street.* 1982. NY. Morrow. 1st. F/F. H11. $25.00.

TAX, Sol. *Penny Capitalism. A Guatemalan Indian Economy.* 1963 reprint of 1953 ed. Chicago. Univ of Chicago Press. 1st thus. 4to. 230p. VG/cloth cover lightly soiled. shelf wear at edges. F3. $15.00.

TAYLOR, Airutheus Ambush. *Negro in South Carolina During Reconstruction.* 1924. WA. Assn for Study of Negro Hist. xl. VG. B2. $50.00.

TAYLOR, Albert. *Complete Garden.* 1929 (1921). 8vo. 50 pl. VG. E6. $20.00.

TAYLOR, Andrew. *The Judgement of Strangers.* 1998. London. Harper Collins. 1st. review copy w/slip. sgn. Book 2 of Roth trilogy. VF/VF. T2. $40.00.

TAYLOR, Andrew. *The Mortal Sickness.* 1995. Blakeney. Glos. Scorpion Press. 1st. 1/75 # copies. sgn. VF/VF acetate dj. T2. $125.00.

TAYLOR, Bayard. *Journey to Central Africa.* 1859. NY. Putnam. 10th. sm 8vo. 522p. VG. W1. $35.00.

TAYLOR, Baynard. *Story of Kennett.* 1903 (1866). Putnam. 12mo. 469p. gilt bl cloth/photo. G. H1. $20.00.

TAYLOR, Bernard. *Reaping.* 1980. Souvenir. 1st. NF/dj. P3. $20.00.

TAYLOR, Casey. *Game Plan.* 1975. Atheneum. 1st. F/F. P8. $10.00.

TAYLOR, Daniel. *The Myth of Certainty: The Reflective Christian and the Risk of Commitment.* 1986. Jarrell. 154p. VG/VG. B29. $9.00.

TAYLOR, E. G. R. *Tudor Geography 1485 – 1583.* 1968. NY. Octagon. ils. F. O7. $65.00.

TAYLOR, Frank, and Gerald Cook. *A Celebration in Blues.* 1987. NY. McGraw Hill. 1st. F/F. B2. $30.00.

TAYLOR, Geoff. *Court of Honor.* 1966. S&S. 1st. VG/dj. P3. $20.00.

TAYLOR, George. *An Account of the Genus Meconopsis, with Notes on the Cultivation of the Introduced Species By E. H. M. Cox.* 1934. London. 1st. 134p+29 photographic plates & 12 maps. orig cloth. B26. $69.00.

TAYLOR, George F. *Aeronautical Meteorology.* 1938. NY. Pitman. sgn. 429p. gilt bl cloth. VG. B11. $75.00.

TAYLOR, Georgia Elizabeth. *Death of Jason Darby.* 1970. World. 1st. F/dj. M2. $12.00.

TAYLOR, Gordon Rattray. *Natural History of the Mind.* 1979. Dutton. 1st Am. 370p. cloth. VG/dj. G1. $22.50.

TAYLOR, Greyton H. *Treasury of Wine & Wine Cookery.* 1963. Harper. 278p. VG/VG. B10. $25.00.

TAYLOR, Ida Scott. *Little Quaker Meeting.* nd. London. Raphael Tuck. ils Frances Brundage. V3. $75.00.

TAYLOR, James. *Third Reich Almanac.* 1987. NY. photos/maps. 392p. VG/VG. S16. $25.00.

TAYLOR, John Russell. *Hitch.* 1978. Pantheon. 1st. VG/dj. P3. $20.00.

TAYLOR, John W.R. *Combat Aircraft of the World.* 1969. Putnam. VG/dj. P3. $20.00.

TAYLOR, John W.R. *Rockets & Missiles.* 1970. NY. Grosset Dunlap. 8vo. 159p. xl. dj. K5. $8.00.

TAYLOR, Lucy. *Spree.* 1998. Baltimore. Cemetery Dance Publications. 1st. 1/450 # copies. sgn. VF/VF. T2. $35.00.

TAYLOR, Matt & Bonnie. *Black Dutch.* 1991. Walker. 1st. F/F. G8. $10.00.

TAYLOR, Norman. *Vegetation of the Allegheny State Park.* 1928. Albany. 12mo. VG/wrp. A22. $15.00.

TAYLOR, Norman. *Wild Flower Gardening.* 1955. Princeton. 32p mc pl. 128p. VG/dj. B26. $20.00.

TAYLOR, P. Walker. *Murder in the Game Reserve.* 1947. Thornton Butterworth. 1st. VG. P3. $35.00.

TAYLOR, Peter. *Old Forest & Other Stories.* 1985. Dial. 1st. F/clip. D10. $45.00.

TAYLOR, Peter. *Summons to Memphis.* 1986. Knopf. 1st. F/F. D10. $60.00.

TAYLOR, Peter. *The Collected Stories of Peter Taylor.* 1969. NY. FSG. 1st. F in NF dj. D10. $85.00.

TAYLOR, Peter. *The Old Forest and Other Stories.* 1985. NY. Dial Press. 1st. F in F dj. D10. $55.00.

TAYLOR, Phoebe Atwood. *Going, Going, Gone*. 1943. Norton. 1st. VG. P3. $35.00.

TAYLOR, Phoebe Atwood. *Mystery of the Cape Cod Tavern*. nd. Norton. G. P3. $15.00.

TAYLOR, Phoebe Atwood. *Octagon House*. 1937. NY. Norton. ne. F. T12. $60.00.

TAYLOR, Phoebe Atwood. *Spring Harrowing*. 1939. Norton. 1st. F/NF. M15. $200.00.

TAYLOR, R.L. *Vessel of Wrath: Life & Times of Carry Nation*. 1966. NY. 1st. ils. 373p. F/dj. M4. $20.00.

TAYLOR, Raymond Griswold. *Recollection of 60 Years of Medicine in Southern California*. 1953. LA. self pub. typescript. 4 vol in 2. photos. gilt fabricoid. D11. $750.00.

TAYLOR, Richard. *Destruction and Reconstruction: Personal Experiences of the Late War*. 1955. NY. Longmans. Green & Co. 1st thus. orig cloth. 380p. NF/VG. M8. $75.00.

TAYLOR, Richard Cachor. *Trogons of the Arizona Borderlands*. 1994. tr ch pubs. 1st. ils. bib. 101p. NF. B19. $8.50.

TAYLOR, Robert Louis. *Adrift in a Boneyard*. 1947. Doubleday. 1st. NF/dj. M2. $35.00.

TAYLOR, Sam S. *Sleep No More*. 1949. Dutton. 1st. VG/remnant. M25. $50.00.

TAYLOR, Samuel W. *The Grinning Gismo*. 1951. A. A. Wyn. 1st. VG/dj. P3. $35.00.

TAYLOR, Samuel W. *The Grinning Gismo*. 1951. NY. A. A. Wyn. 1st. F in worn dj. M15. $65.00.

TAYLOR, Silas. *History of Gavel-Kind, with Etymology Thereof*. 1663. London. prt John Starkey. modern cloth. M11. $650.00.

TAYLOR, Sydney. *More All-Of-A-Kind Family*. 1957 (1954). Follett. 2nd. sm 4to. 160p. gray brd. VG/G. T5. $20.00.

TAYLOR, T. *Magnificent Mitscher*. 1954. NY. 1st. VG. B5. $35.00.

TAYLOR, T. M. C. *Pea Family (Leguinosae) of British Columbia*. 1974. Victoria. ils/maps. 237p. sc. B26. $12.50.

TAYLOR, Vincent. *Gospel According to Mark*. 1957. Macmillan. 696p. G. B29. $30.00.

TAYLOR, W. Thomas. *Texfake, an Account of Theft & Forgery of Early Texas*. 1991. TX State Hist Assn. 1st. 158p. M. J2. $50.00.

TAYLOR, William. *California Life Illustrated*. 1867. London/NY. Jackson Walford Hodder/Carlton Porter. 1st. 391p. VG. K7. $175.00.

TAYLOR, William. *Our South American Cousins*. 1878. NY. Nelson Phillips. 1st. 12mo. 318p. F3. $30.00.

TAYLOR, William R. *Plants of Bikini and Other Northern Marshall Islands*. 1950. Ann Arbor. VG in dj. B26. $42.50.

TAYLOR & TAYLOR. *Neon Dancers*. 1991. Walker. 1st. F/F. M22. $15.00.

TAYLOR & TILLOTSON. *Grand Canyon Country*. 1929. Stanford. 1st. 8vo. orange cloth. VG+. F7. $35.00.

TAYLOR & VALUM. *Wildflowers 2: Sagebrush Country*. 1974. Beaverton. 189 mc photos. 139p. sc. VG. B26. $15.00.

TAYLOR & WELTY. *Black Bonanza*. 1950. Whittlesey/McGraw Hill. 280p. VG. D8. $35.00.

TAYLOR & WINDLE. *Early Architecture of Madison, IN*. 1986. IN Hist Soc. photos. 230p. F/dj. M4. $35.00.

TAZEWELL, Charles. *The Small One*. 1947. Philadelphia. John C. Winston. ils by Franklin Whitman. VG. A16. $25.00.

TCHITCHINOFF, Zakahar. *Adventures in California of 1818 – 1821*. 1956. LA. Glen Dawson. 1/225. ils. 26p. decor brd/cloth spine. $11.00.

TCHOLAKIAN, Arthur. *Majesty of the Black Woman*. 1971. Van Nostrand Reinhold. 1st. ils. 160p. VG/partial. A25. $45.00.

TEACHOUT, Terry. *City Limits*. 1991. NY. Poseiden. 1st. VF/VF. H11. $30.00.

TEAGLE, Mike. *Murder Over San Silvestro*. 1936. Hillman Curl. 1st. VG. G8. $20.00.

TEAGLE, Mike. *Murders in Silk*. 1938. Hillman Curl. 1st. VG. P3. $25.00.

TEAGUE, Bob. *Flip Side of Soul: Letters to My Son*. 1989. Morrow. 1st. F/F. B4. $45.00.

TEALE, E. W. *Audubon's Wildlife*. 1964. Viking. 1st. F/VG clip. B3. $40.00.

TEALE, E. W. *Autumn Across America*. 1956. NY. photos/map. F/dj. M4. $15.00.

TEALE, E. W. *Dune Boy: Early Years of a Naturalist*. 1957. IU. 275p. F. M4. $22.00.

TEALE, E. W. *Grassroot Jungles*. 1950. photos. VG/VG. M17. $20.00.

TEASDALE-BUCKELL, G. T. *Experts on Guns & Shooting*. 1900. London. Sampson Low. 1st. 4to. ils. 590p. VG. $7.00.

TEATHER, Louise. *Island of Six Names. A History of Belvedere, California 1834 – 1890*. 1969. Belvedere-Tiburon. landmarks society. ils. octavo. orig tan and burgundy printed wrps. stapled. F. R3. $12.50.

TEBBEL, J. *Turning the World Upside Down: Inside American Revolution*. 1993. NY. 1st. maps. 448p. F/F. M4. $25.00.

TEDLOCK, Dennis. *Popol Vuh. The Definitive Edition*. 1986. NY. S&S. b/w photo ils. 380p. G/wrp. F3. $10.00.

TEGNER, Esaias. *Frithiof's Saga*. 1953. Stockholm. LEC. 1st thus. 1/1500. ils/sgn Eric Palmquist. F/case. Q1. $75.00.

TEGNER, Henry. *White Foxes of Gorfenletch*. 1954. Morrow. 1st Am. VG/VG. O3. $35.00.

TEHON, Leo R. *Fieldbook of Native Illinois Shrubs*. 1942. Urbana. gilt decor blk cloth. 307p w/6 color plates & 72p of line drawings. VG. B26. $14.00.

TEILHET & TEILHET. *Skwee-Gee*. 1940. Doubleday Doran. 1st. Ils Hardie Gramatky. 4to. pict cloth. dj. R5. $175.00.

TEISER, Ruth. *Sudden Empire: California*. 1950. SF. Soc CA Pioneers. 76p. decor gr cloth. AN. K7. $35.00.

TEISER, Ruth and Harroun, Catherine. *Winemaking in California. The Account in Words and Pictures of the Golden State's Two Century Long Adventure with Wine*. 1983. NY. McGraw Hill. 1st. ils. quarto. yellow paper covered brds w/ spine stp in red. pict dj. F/F. R3. $40.00.

TEIZERIA DA MOTA, Avelino. *Regimento Da Altura De Leste-Oeste De Rui Faleiro*. 1953. Lisboa. Agencia Geral do ultramar. inscr pres. F/wrp. O7. $20.00.

TEIZERIA DA MOTA, Avelino. *Viagem De Fernao De Magalhaes E A Questao Das Molucas*. 1975. Lisboa. Junta Investigacoes Cientificas Ultramar. 33 maps. F/dj. O7. $175.00.

TELANDER, Rick. *Joe Namath & the Other Guys*. 1976. HRW. 1st. F/VG. P8. $30.00.

TELFAIR, Raymond Clark II. *Cattle Egret: A Texas Focus & World View*. 1983. College Station. maps/figures. 144p. NF/VG. S15. $10.00.

TELLA, Alfred. *Sundered Soul.* 1990. Three Continents. 1st. sgn. F. M2. $27.00.

TELLEN, Maurice. *Draft Horse Primer.* 1977. Rodale. 386p. VG. A10. $20.00.

TELLER, Edward. *Better a Shield Than Sword.* 1987. NY. Free Pr. 3rd. F/dj. K3. $15.00.

TELLER, Edward. *Edward Teller: Giant of the Golden Age of Physics.* 1990. Scribner. 1st. F/dj. K3. $15.00.

TELLER, Edward. *Teller's War.* 1992. S&S. F/wrp. K3. $15.00.

TELLER, Judd L. *Scapegoat of Revolution.* 1954. Scribner. 352p. VG/G. S3. $25.00.

TELLER, Walter. *Five Sea Captains.* 1960. NY. Atheneum. 431p. dj. T7. $30.00.

TEMPLE, Shirley. *Shirley Temple's Favorite Tales of Long Ago.* 1958. Random. 1st prt. 4to. unp. C14. $17.00.

TEMPLE, William. *Martin Magnus on Mars.* 1956. Muller. 1st. VG/dj. P3. $35.00.

TEMPLE, William. *Memoirs of What Past in Christendom, From War Begun 1672.* 1692. London. Chriswell. 8vo. wrp. R12. $125.00.

TEMPLE, William. *Works Of...* 1757. London. 4 vol. VG. A15. $125.00.

TEMPLETON, Charles. *Act of God.* 1978. Boston. Little, Brn. 1st. Two pages have creases near spine due to binding flaw. Jacket has bit of rubbing at extremities. NF/F. H11. $20.00.

TENN, William (Philip J. Klass). *Time in Advance.* 1963. London. Gollancz. 1st hc ed. F/VG. lt soil & chip. T2. $125.00.

TENN & WESTLAKE. *Once Against the Law.* 1968. Macmillan. 1st. VG/dj. P3. $25.00.

TENNANT, Joseph F. *Rough Times 1870 – 1920.* nd. np. Souvenir 50th Anniversary Red River Expedition. 271p. P4. $45.00.

TENNENBAUM, Silvia. *Yesterday's Streets.* 1981. NY. Random House. 1st. sm4to. sgn. partially removed bookplate on endpaper. 528p. AN/F. H1. $18.00.

TENNEY, Merrill. *Galatians: Charter of Christian Liberty.* 1950. Eerdmans. 200p. G/torn. B29. $8.50.

TENNEY, Merrill C. *The Reality of the Resurrection.* 1963. Harper & Row. 1st ed. 221p. VG/VG. B29. $9.50.

TENNEY, Merrill C. *The Word for this Century.* 1960. Oxford. 184p. VG. ex lib. B29. $5.50.

TENNYSON, Alfred. *Poetical Works of Alfred Lord Tennyson Poet Laureate.* 1917. London. Macmillan. ltd. gr cloth. F/F. F6. $12.00.

TENNYSON, Alfred Lord. *Holy Grail.* 1870. London. Strahan. 1st. 12mo. gr brd. fair. M23. $50.00.

TENNYSON, Alfred Lord. *Idylls of the King.* 1952. LEC. 1st thus. 1/1500. ils/sgn Lynd Ward. F/glassine/case. Q1. $150.00.

TENNYSON, Alfred Lord. *Maud.* 1869. London. Strahan. 12mo. gr brd. G. M23. $30.00.

TENNYSON, Alfred Lord. *Princess & Other Poems.* 1890. Stokes. ils CH Johnson. 400p. teg. maroon cloth. T10. $50.00.

TENNYSON, Alfred Lord. *Queen May, a Drama.* 1875. Osgood. 1st. VG. M19. $45.00.

TEONGE, Henry. *Diary of Teonge.* 1825. London. Chas Knight. ils. 327p. marbled brd. rebacked blk morocco. T7. $150.00.

TEPPER, Sheri S. *Gate to Women's Country.* 1988. Doubleday. 1st. F/clip & dtd 1990. A24. $20.00.

TEPPER, Sheri S. *Raising the Stones.* 1990. NY. Doubleday. 1st. F/F w/ one tear. A24. $25.00.

TEPPER, Sheri S. *Shadow's End.* 1994. Bantam. 1st. F/dj. P3. $23.00.

TEPPER, Sheri S. *The Gate to Women's Country.* 1988. NY. Doubleday. 1st. F/F clip. A24. $22.00.

TERENCE. *Afri Comoediae.* 1772. Birmingham. Eng. Baskerville. Latin text. 4to. aeg. A15. $100.00.

TERHUNE, Albert Payson. *Across the Line.* 1945. Dryden. 116p. VG/dj. M20. $15.00.

TERHUNE, Albert Payson. *Buff, A Collie & Other Dog Stories.* (1921). Grosset Dunlap. pre-1963 rpt. 12mo. F/VG+. C8. $27.50.

TERHUNE, Albert Payson. *Further Adventures of Lad.* (1922). Grosset Dunlap. pre-1943 prt. sm 8vo. NF/VG. C8. $22.50.

TERHUNE, Albert Payson. *Lad of Sunnybank.* (1929). Grosset Dunlap. pre-1943 prt. lg 12mo. NF/NF. C8. $25.00.

TERHUNE, Albert Payson. *My Friend the Dog.* (1926). Grosset Dunlap. pre-1963 prt. lg 12mo. F/NF. C8. $27.50.

TERHUNE, Albert Payson. *Story of Damon & Pythias.* 1915. Grosset Dunlap. VG/dj. P3. $35.00.

TERKEL, Studs. *Giants of Jazz.* 1957. NY. Crowell. 2nd printing. author's 1st book. F/chip dj. B2. $25.00.

TERKEL, Studs. *Giants of Jazz.* 1957. NY. 1st. sgn. ils Robert Galster. NF/VG+. A11. $135.00.

TERKEL, Studs. *Race: How Blacks and Whites Think and Feel About the American Obsession.* 1992. np. The New Press. F/F. A28. $10.95.

TERKEL, Studs. *The Good War. An Oral History of World War Two.* 1984. NY. Pantheon. 1st. sgn by author. F/F. B2. $45.00.

TERRACE, Vincent. *Complete Encyclopedia of TV 1947 – 76 Vol 2.* 1976. Barnes. VG/dj. P3. $20.00.

TERRELL, George W., Jr. *Collecting R. S. Prussia.* 1982. Books Americana. 8vo. 221p. VG. H1. $45.00.

TERRELL, John Upton. *War for the Colorado River.* 1965. Arthur H. Clark. 1st. 2 vol. NF/NF. B19. $60.00.

TERRELL, John Upton. *Zebulon Pike; The Life and Times of an Adventurer.* 1968. NY. Weybright and Talley. 1st. octavo. brds. cloth spine. dj. F. R3. $25.00.

TERRY, Bill. *The Watermelon Kid.* 1984. Baton Rouge. LSU. 1st. VF/VF. H11. $40.00.

TERTZ, Abram. *Fantastic Stories.* 1963. Pantheon. 1st. VG/worn. M2. $12.00.

TERWILLIGER, Charles. *Horolovar 400-Day Clock Repair Guide.* 1974. Bronxville. Horolovar. 7th. 4to. 183p. VG/dj. K3. $25.00.

TESNOHLIDER, Rudolf. *Cunning Little Vixen.* 1985. FSG. 1st thus. 4to. 186p. F/F. T5. $40.00.

TESSIER, Thomas. *Finishing Touches.* 1986. NY. Atheneum. 1st. VF/VF. T2. $25.00.

TESSIER, Thomas. *Finishing Touches.* 1986. NY. Atheneum. 1st. VF/VF. T2. $25.00.

TESSIER, Thomas. *Secret Strangers.* 1992. Arlington Heights. Dark Harvest. 1st US ed. VF/VF. T2. $20.00.

TEVIS, Walter. *Hustler*. 1959. Harper. 1st. NF/VG. B4. $750.00.

TEVIS, Walter. *Queen's Gambit*. 1983. Random. 1st. F/F. H11. $35.00.

TEVIS, Walter. *Steps of the Sun*. 1983. Doubleday. 1st. VG/VG. M22. $15.00.

TEY, Josephine. *Brat Farrar*. 1949. London. Peter Davies. 1st. Spine ends faded. Soiled jacket with chips at spine ends and at corners. VG/dj. M15. $250.00.

TEY, Josephine. *The Daughter of Time*. 1951. London. Peter Davies. 1st. Jacket has chips at spine ends, on front cover, and at corners. F/VG. M15. $250.00.

TEY, Josephine. *The Privateer*. 1952. NY. Macmilan. 1st. Jacket has chips on front panel and at spine ends and several closed tears. F/VG. M15. $45.00.

TEY, Josephine. *To Love and be Wise*. 1950. London. Peter Davies. 1st. Jacket has internal tape mends and nicks at spine ends. VG/dj. M15. $200.00.

THACKERAY, William Makepeace. *Newcomes: Memoirs of a Most Respectable Family*. 1954. Cambridge. LEC. 1st thus. 2 vol. 1/1500. ils/sgn Edward Ardizzone. F/case. $1.00.

THAMES, Susan. *As Much as I Know*. 1992. Random. 1st. author's 1st book. F/F. R13. $25.00.

THAMES, Susan. *I'll Be Home Late Tonight*. 1997. NY. Villard. 1st. Author's first novel. Book has abrasion on front board. NF+/VF. H11. $20.00.

THANE, Elswyth. *Dawn's Early Light*. 1943. Duel. Sloan & Pearce. 2nd. 8vo. Some light browning on endpaper. some small edge tears. 317p. F/G. H1. $20.00.

THANE, Elswyth. *Mount Vernon Is Ours*. 1966. Duell. Sloan & Pearce. 1st. 8vo. minor edge tears. top of spine has small chip & wear. 467p. AN/VG. H1. $16.00.

THANE, Elswyth. *Potomac Squire*. 1963. Duell. Sloan & Pearce. 1st. 8vo. some wear. soil & small tears on edges. 432p. F/VG. H1. $18.00.

THANE, Elswyth. *The Family Quarrel*. 1959. Duell. Sloan & Pearce. 1st. 8vo. light rubbing & lightly soiled. 308p. F/dj. H1. $20.00.

THARPE, Sister Rosetta. *Eighteen Original Negro Spirituals*. 1938. NY. Mills Music. 1st. wrps. 32p folio. VG. B2. $60.00.

THATCHER, Margaret. *Downing Street Years*. 1993. NY. 1/350. sgn. F/box. B5. $105.00.

THAYER, Bert Clark. *Thoroughbred*. 1964. DSP. 1st. VG/VG. O3. $25.00.

THAYER, Charles W. *Checkpoint*. 1964. NY. Harper & Row. 1st. Jacket has wear at spine ends. F/NF. H11. $25.00.

THAYER, Helen. *Polar Dream: Heroic Saga of First Sola Journey*. 1993. NY. S&S. 1st. 8vo. 254p. half cloth. F/dj. $4.00.

THAYER, James Stewart. *Pursuit*. 1986. Crown. 1st. VG/dj. P3. $15.00.

THAYER, June. *Pussy Who Went to the Moon*. (1960). NY. Morrow. 1st probable. sm 4to. F/VG. C8. $20.00.

THAYER, Lee. *Hair's Breadth*. 1946. Dodd Mead. 1st. VG/dj. P3. $25.00.

THAYER, Steve. *Saint Mudd*. 1992. NY. Viking. 1st. author's 1st book. remainder mark. F/F. H11. $20.00.

THAYER, Steve. *Silent Snow*. 1999. NY. Viking. 1st. sgn. VF/VF. T2. $25.00.

THAYER, Steve. *St. Mudd*. 1992. Viking. 1st. author's 1st book. F/NF. B3. $60.00.

THAYER, Steve. *St. Mudd*. 1992. NY. Viking. 1st. ARC. F. D10. $10.00.

THAYER, Steve. *The Weatherman*. 1995. NY. Viking. 1st. sgn. VF/VF. T2. $20.00.

THAYER, Theodore. *Pennsylvania Politics & Growth of Democracy 1740 – 1776*. 1953. Harrisburg. PA Hist & Mus Comm. tall 8vo. 234p. dk bl cloth. F. H1. $25.00.

THAYER, Tiffany. *Illustrous Corpse*. 1930. Fiction League. 1st. VG. N4. $22.50.

THE BLACK BOOK COMMITTEE. *The Black Book. The Nazi Crime Against the Jewish People*. 1946. NY. Duell. Sloan & Pearce. 1st. 560p. F/NF. B2. $75.00.

THE NATIONAL BOOK FOUNDATION. *The National Book Awards: Forty-One Years of Literary Excellence*. 1992. The National Book Foundation. F/WRP. M25. $35.00.

THEINER, George. *Let's Go to the Circus*. 1963. London. Bancroft. ils Rudolf Lukes/5 movable pl. unp. T10. $150.00.

THELWELL, Norman. *Leg at Each Corner*. 1963. Dutton. 1st Am. VG/VG. O3. $22.00.

THEODOR, O. *Fauna Palaestina. Insecta I: Diptera Pupipara*. 1975. Jerusalem. 168p. NF. B1. $40.00.

THEODOSAKIS, Jason, MD. *Arthritis Cure, The*. 1997. NY. St. Martin. NF/NF. A28. $11.95.

THEROUX, Alexander. *Master Snickup's Cloak*. 1979. Harper Row. 1st Am. 4to. unp. F/F. T5. $30.00.

THEROUX, Paul. *Black House*. 1974. Houghton Mifflin. 1st. sgn. F/NF. D10. $75.00.

THEROUX, Paul. *Chicago Loop*. 1991. Random House. UP. F in blue gray coated wrp. M25. $45.00.

THEROUX, Paul. *Chicago Loop*. 1990. NY. Random. 1st. VF/VF. H11. $40.00.

THEROUX, Paul. *Chicago Loop*. 1990. Random. 1st. F/F. H11. $30.00.

THEROUX, Paul. *Consul's File*. 1977. Houghton Mifflin. 1st. NF/dj. M25. $25.00.

THEROUX, Paul. *Great Railway Bazaar*. 1975. Hamish Hamilton. 1st. VG/dj. M25. $125.00.

THEROUX, Paul. *Half Moon Street*. 1984. Boston. Houghton. 1st. F/NF. H11. $25.00.

THEROUX, Paul. *Jungle Lovers*. 1971. Houghton Mifflin. true 1st (1/4500). F/dj. A24. $125.00.

THEROUX, Paul. *Kowloon Tong*. 1997. Houghton Mifflin. UP of Am. ed. F in red wrp. M25. $45.00.

THEROUX, Paul. *London Snow*. 1980. Houghton Mifflin. 1st. F/NF. T11. $70.00.

THEROUX, Paul. *Mosquito Coast*. 1981. Hamish Hamilton. 1st. NF/VG clip. B3. $35.00.

THEROUX, Paul. *Mosquito Coast*. (1982). Boston. Houghton Mifflin. 1st. F/NF. some creases and wear at top edge. B3. $20.00.

THEROUX, Paul. *Murder in Mount Holly*. 1969. London. Alan Ross. 1st. sgn. F/NF. B4. $2,500.00.

THEROUX, Paul. *My Other Life*. (1996). NY. Houghton Mifflin. ARC. pict wrp. F. B3. $20.00.

THEROUX, Paul. *My Secret History*. (1989). NY. Putnam. 1st. NF. shows lt wear/F. B3. $20.00.

THEROUX, Paul. *O-Zone.* 1986. Putnam. 1st. F/dj. A20/P3. $20.00.

THEROUX, Paul. *Old Patagonian Express.* 1979. Houghton Mifflin. 1st. F/NF. B3/T11. $50.00.

THEROUX, Paul. *Picture Palace.* 1978. Houghton Mifflin. 1st. VG/dj. P3. $20.00.

THEROUX, Paul. *Riding the Iron Rooster.* 1988. NY. Putnam. 1st. sgn by author. F/F. B2. $45.00.

THEROUX, Paul. *Sailing through China.* (1984). Boston. Houghton Mifflin. 1st. ils Patrick Procktor. F/NF. B3. $35.00.

THEROUX, Paul. *Saint Jack.* 1973. Houghton Mifflin. 1st. NF/dj. M25. $45.00.

THEROUX, Paul. *The Black House.* 1974. Boston. Houghton Mifflin. 1st. sgn. F. D10. $85.00.

THEROUX, Paul. *The Black House.* (1974). London. Hamish Hamilton. 1st British ed. F/NF. price clip w/sticker attached. B3. $40.00.

THEROUX, Paul. *The Happy Isles of Oceania.* (1992). NY. Putnam. 1st. sgn by author. F/NF. lt creasing to spine. B3. $45.00.

THEROUX, Paul. *The Kingdom by the Sea.* 1983. Houghton Mifflin. 1st. sgn. NF. M25. $25.00.

THEROUX, Paul. *The Kingdom by the Sea.* 1983. Houghton Mifflin. UP. VF. wrp. M25. $25.00.

THEROUX, Paul. *The London Embassy.* 1983. Houghton Mifflin. UP of 1st Am ed. VF. wrp. M25. $45.00.

THEROUX, Paul. *The Old Patagonian Express.* 1979. Houghton Mifflin. 1st. NF/torn dj. M25. $25.00.

THEROUX, Paul. *The Old Patagonian Express: By Train through the Americas.* 1979. NY. Houghton Mifflin. 2nd. ep maps. 404p. G/chipped dj. F3. $15.00.

THEROUX, Paul. *To the Ends of the Earth: The Selected Travels.* 1991. Random House. UP. VF. coated wrp. M25. $45.00.

THEROUX, Paul. *Waldo.* 1967. Houghton Mifflin. true 1st. author's 1st book. NF/VG. A24. $185.00.

THEROUX, Paul. *World's End.* 1980. Boston. Houghton. 1st. board edges slightly sunned. Jacket has nick at top of rear flap. F/F. H11. $50.00.

THESIGER, Wilfred. *Arabian Sands.* 1959. NY. Dutton. 1st. 8vo. ils/fld map. 326p. VG. $1.00.

THESIGER, Wilfred. *Marsh Arab.* 1964. NY. 1st. VG/VG. B5. $50.00.

THIAM, Dijibi. *My Sister the Panther.* 1980. NY. Dodd. Mead. 1st. trans from French by Mercer Cook. F/VG. chip rear panel. rpr w/external tape. B2. $25.00.

THIEL, A. W. *Chinese Pottery & Stoneware.* ca 1953. NY. 1st. NF/attached plastic-covered dj. W3. $75.00.

THIEL, Carl William. *The Basic 100: The 100 Most Important Critical Studies and Association Items to the Sherlock Holmes Canon as Suggested by John Bennett Shaw.* 1996. Shelburne. Ontario. battered silicon dispatch box. 1st. VF/pict wrp. T2. $10.00.

THIEL, Rudolf. *And There Was Light.* 1957. Knopf. 1st Am. VG/poor. M2. $12.00.

THIELICKE, Helmut. *Death and Life.* 1970. Fortress. 230p. VG/VG. B29. $10.00.

THIELICKE, Helmut. *Encounter with Spurgeon.* 1963. Fortress. 283p. G/notes in margin. B29. $11.00.

THIELICKE, Helmut. *Ethics of Sex.* 1964. Harper. 1st. 338p. VG/dj. B29. $8.50.

THIELICKE, Helmut. *Silence of God.* 1962. Eerdmans. 92p. G/dj. B29. $7.50.

THIERRY, Georges Paul. *Travers Und Siecle De Notre Yachting De Course A Voile.* 1948. Paris. Soc d'Editions Geographique. 302 photos. 390p. wrp. T7. $60.00.

THIESSEN, Grant. *Science Fiction Collector Vol 1.* 1980. Pandora. 1/140. sgn/#d. F/sans. P3. $45.00.

THOBY-MARCELIN, Philippe. *Beast of the Haitian Hills.* 1946. Rinehart. 1st. VG. P3. $20.00.

THOMAS, Alfred Barnaby. *Forgotten Frontiers: Study of Spanish Indian Policy.* 1969. Norman. OK. 2nd. 3 fld maps. 420p. cloth. dj. $11.00.

THOMAS, Alfred B. *Teodoro De Croix and the Northern Frontier of New Spain.* 1941. Norman. Univ. of Oklahoma Press. 1st. 273p. G. F3. $40.00.

THOMAS, Alfred Barnaby. *Teodoro De Croix & the Northern Frontier of New Spain 1776.* 1968. OK U. ils/map. 273p. F/dj. M4. $20.00.

THOMAS, Antoine Leonard. *Eloge De Maximilien De Bethune.* Duc De Sully. 1763. Paris. Regnard. 8vo. wrp. R12. $125.00.

THOMAS, Arthur. *Gardening in Hot Countries.* 1965. London. VG in dj. B26. $39.00.

THOMAS, B. P. *Life & Times of Lincoln's Secretary of War.* 1962. np. ils. 642p. O8. $21.50.

THOMAS, Benjamin P. *Portrait for Posterity, Lincoln and His Biographers.* 1947. New Brunswick, NJ. Rutgers Univ. Press. 1/1000 copies. ils by Romaine Proctor. octavo. orig gray cloth. stp. gilt. pict dj. F. slight wear. R3. $15.00.

THOMAS, Charles L. *Catalytic Processes & Proven Catalysts.* 1970. Academic Press. 1st. Tall 8vo. 284p. NM/VG. H1. $15.00.

THOMAS, Craig. *Firefox Down.* 1983. Michael Joseph. 1st. VG/dj. P3. $30.00.

THOMAS, Craig. *Jade Tiger.* 1982. Van Nostrand. F/dj. P3. $20.00.

THOMAS, Craig. *Rat Trap.* 1976. London. Michael Joseph. 1st. tiny light spotting on top of page edges. Jacket has slight fading to red lettering on spine. author's first novel. F/dj. M15. $150.00.

THOMAS, Craig. *Sea Leopard.* 1981. Michael Joseph. 1st. F/dj. P3. $25.00.

THOMAS, Craig. *Wildcat.* 1989. Putnam. 1st. F/F. W2. $30.00.

THOMAS, Craig. *Winter Hawk.* 1987. Collins. 1st. F/dj. P3. $20.00.

THOMAS, D. *Nazi Victory.* Crete 1941. 1973. NY. BC. ils. 252p. VG/VG. S16. $16.50.

THOMAS, D. Gourlay. *Gladiolus: For Garden & Exhibition.* 1955. London. ils/photos. 94p. VG. B26. $14.00.

THOMAS, D. M. *Ararat.* 1983. NY. Viking. 1st. F/F. H11. $30.00.

THOMAS, D. M. *White Hotel.* 1981. Viking. ARC. author's 3rd novel. F/F. T11. $40.00.

THOMAS, Dawn C. *Downtown Is.* 1972. McGraw Hill. later prt. NF/dj. M25. $15.00.

THOMAS, Deborah A. *Dickens & the Short Story.* 1982. Phil. 1st. F/dj. A2. $15.00.

THOMAS, Dwight. *Poe Log.* 1987. 919p. O8. $27.50.

THOMAS, Dylan. *Quite Early One Morning.* 1954. NY. New Directions. 1st. F in lightly used dj w/tears. B2. $50.00.

THOMAS, Dylan. *Quite Early One Morning.* 1954. New Directions. 1st. F/NF. B2. $50.00.

THOMAS, Dylan. *Twenty Years a Growing.* 1964. London. Dent. 1st. F/clip dj. B2. $75.00.

THOMAS, Edison Hugh. *John Hunt Morgan and His Raiders.* 1975. Lexington. Univ. of Ky. Press. 1st. orig paper covered bds. 120p. VG. M8. $35.00.

THOMAS, Eleanor. *Becky & Tatters; A Brownie Scout Story.* 1940. Scribner. ils Gertrude Howe. $35.00.

THOMAS, Emory M. *Confederate Nation 1861 – 1865.* 1979. Harper Row. 1st. 384p. AN/dj. H1. $20.00.

THOMAS, Eugene. *Dancing Dead.* 1933. Sears. 1st. G. M2. $10.00.

THOMAS, Frank. *Sherlock Holmes and the Golden Bird.* 1979. LA. Pinnacle Books. 1st. pb orig. VF/pict wrp. T2. $10.00.

THOMAS, Frank. *Sherlock Holmes and the Sacred Sword.* 1980. LA. Pinnacle Books. 1st. pb orig. VF/pict wrp. T2. $10.00.

THOMAS, Frank J. *Myths of California Isle.* 1966. LA. Tenfingers. 1/200. 71x56mm. 2 full-p ils. linen-backed brd. F. $24.00.

THOMAS, Gary M. *Custer.* Scout of April 1867. 1967. Westport. 1st. 25p. M. J2. $25.00.

THOMAS, Geo. C., Jr. *Golf Architecture in America, Its Strategy and Construction.* 1927. Los Angeles. The Times-Mirror Press. 1st. profusely ils w/photographic plates (some in color) and plans (one folding). xxvi. 342p. dk gr cloth stp in red & lt gr. K1. $650.00.

THOMAS, Herbert. *Classical Contributions to Obstetrics & Gynecology.* 1935. ils. VG. M17. $25.00.

THOMAS, Isaiah. *History of Printing in America.* 1810. Worcester. Isaiah Thomas. 1st. 2 vol. 8vo. contemporary bdg. M1. $1750.00.

THOMAS, Isaiah. *Thomas' Almanack for the Year 1784.* 1783. Boston. self pub. A19. $150.00.

THOMAS, J. *Blue Ridge Country.* 1942. NY. 1st. 338p. F/dj. M4. $25.00.

THOMAS, J. C. *Chasin' the Trane.* 1975. Garden City. Doubleday. 1st. F in NF dj. B2. $50.00.

THOMAS, J. J. *Illustrated Annual Register of Rural Affairs.* Vol II. 1860. Albany. Tucker. 1st. cloth. VG. A10. $50.00.

THOMAS, Kathleen. *Gleanie Bird.* 1956. Frederick Warne. 1st. 117p. VG/dj. M20. $25.00.

THOMAS, L. *Lives of a Cell.* 1974. Viking. 5th. 153p. clip dj. B1. $15.00.

THOMAS, Leslie. *Man with the Power.* 1973. Eyre Methuen. VG/dj. P3. $15.00.

THOMAS, Leslie. *Virgin Soldiers.* 1966. Little, Brn. 1st. VG/dj. P3. $20.00.

THOMAS, Louis. *Good Children Don't Kill.* 1968. Dodd Mead. 1st. F/dj. P3. $15.00.

THOMAS, Lowell. *Count Luckner the Sea Devil.* 1927. NY. Doubleday. ne. orig dj repaired & chip. 10 photo ils. autographed by Luckner. 208p. VG. B14. $99.00.

THOMAS, Lowell. *Out of this World.* 1950. Garden City. A19. $15.00.

THOMAS, Lowell. *Out of this World.* 1950. Greystone. inscr. 320p. VG. B11. $25.00.

THOMAS, Lowell. *Pageant of Life.* 1941. NY. Funk. 1st. sgn. 278p. VG. B11. $32.50.

THOMAS, Michael. *Ropespinner Conspiracy.* 1947. Warner. 1st. F/F. T12. $25.00.

THOMAS, Oswald. *Heaven & Earth.* 1930. Norton. 8vo. 231p. VG/dj. K5. $30.00.

THOMAS, Patricia. *Stand Back, Said the Elephant, I'm Going to Sneeze!* 1971. Lee Shepard. 1st. ils Wallace Tripp. VG/VG-. P2. $25.00.

THOMAS, Piri. *Down these Mean Streets.* 1967. Knopf. 1st. F/NF. M23. $100.00.

THOMAS, Piri. *Down these Mean Streets.* 1967. Knopf. 1st. inscr. NF/NF. T11. $125.00.

THOMAS, Rosanne Daryl. *Amazing Grace.* 1999. NY. Picador USA. AP. F in wrps. B2. $25.00.

THOMAS, Ross. *Briarpatch.* 1984. NY. S&S. 1st. Bottom of boards are slightly discolored. Jacket has several short closed tears. NF/NF. H11. $35.00.

THOMAS, Ross. *Briarpatch.* 1984. NY. S&S. 1st. F/dj. M15. $65.00.

THOMAS, Ross. *Briarpatch.* 1984. S&S. 1st. F/dj. from $30 to $40.00.

THOMAS, Ross. *Cast a Yellow Shadow.* 1967. NY. Morrow. 1st. Book has lightly bumped corners and spine ends. Very bright jacket has just a hint of edge wear. F/F. H11. $250.00.

THOMAS, Ross. *Cast a Yellow Shadow.* 1967. NY. Morrow. 1st. Jacket has short crease on inner front flap. F/dj. M15. $200.00.

THOMAS, Ross. *Cast a Yellow Shadow.* 1967. Morrow. 1st. F/dj. M15. $175.00.

THOMAS, Ross. *Chinaman's Chance.* 1978. NY. S&S. 1st. F/F. H11. $95.00.

THOMAS, Ross. *Chinaman's Chance.* 1978. NY. S&S. 1st. F/dj. M15. $125.00.

THOMAS, Ross. *Missionary Stew.* 1983. NY. S&S. 1st. Inscribed on title page. F+/F. H11. $95.00.

THOMAS, Ross. *Missionary Stew.* 1983. S&S. 1st. VG/dj. P3. $35.00.

THOMAS, Ross. *Out on the Rim.* 1987. NY. Mysterious Press. 1st. F/F. T2. $15.00.

THOMAS, Ross. *Out on the Rim.* 1987. NY. Mysterious. 1st. ARC in wraps. sgn. bottom corners a bit soiled. F/. H11. $30.00.

THOMAS, Ross. *Out on the Rim.* 1987. NY. Mysterious. 1st. F/F. H11. $25.00.

THOMAS, Ross. *Out on the Rim.* 1987. NY. Mysterious. 1st. sgn. VF/dj. M15. $65.00.

THOMAS, Ross. *Out on the Rim.* 1987. Mysterious. ARC. sgn. F/wrp. M25. $35.00.

THOMAS, Ross. *Porkchoppers.* 1972. Morrow. 1st. F/F. M15. $125.00.

THOMAS, Ross. *Protocol for a Kidnapping.* 1971. NY. Morrow. 1st. F/dj. M15. $300.00.

THOMAS, Ross. *Seersucker Whipsaw.* 1967. Morrow. 1st. VG/dj. M15. $300.00.

THOMAS, Ross. *Spies, Thumbsuckers, Etc.* 1989. Northridge. Lord John. 1st. one of 300 numbered copies sgn. VF/. M15. $135.00.

HOMAS, Ross. *The Brass Go-Between.* 970. London. Hodder & Stoughton. 1st ng. inscr. Jacket has tiny wear at corners. /dj. M15. $65.00.

HOMAS, Ross. *The Eighth Dwarf.* 1979. ondon. Hamish Hamilton. 1st. sgn. F/dj. 1. $75.00.

HOMAS, Ross. *The Eighth Dwarf.* 1979. &S. 1st. F/NF. B2. $50.00.

HOMAS, Ross. *The Eighth Dwarf.* 1979. VY. S&S. 1st. Signed on title page. remain- er mark. Jacket has minor wear at extremi- es. F/NF. H11. $55.00.

HOMAS, Ross. *The Fools in Town Are on Our Side.* 1971. NY. Morrow. 1st. VF/dj. M15. $250.00.

HOMAS, Ross. *The Fourth Durango.* 1989. VY. Mysterious. 1st. VF/dj. M15. $30.00.

HOMAS, Ross. *The Fourth Durango.* 1989. VY. Mysterious. 1st. sgn. on half-title page. /F. H11. $40.00.

HOMAS, Ross. *The Fourth Durango.* 1989. Mysterious. 1st. F/F. N4. $20.00.

HOMAS, Ross. *The Money Harvest.* 1975. VY. Morrow. 1st. Book has slight spine reases, sunned edges, and a small damp- tain at lower rear corner. Jacket has wear along bottom edges and slightly soiled rear panel. VG/NF. H11. $40.00.

HOMAS, Ross. *The Money Harvest.* 1975. VY. Morrow. 1st. faint spotting on top of page edges. F/dj. M15. $100.00.

HOMAS, Ross. *The Money Harvest.* 1975. Morrow. 1st. NF/dj. P3. $90.00.

HOMAS, Ross. *The Porkchoppers.* 1972. VY. Morrow. 1st. Jacket has a short closed ear. F/dj. M15. $135.00.

HOMAS, Ross. *The Procane Chronicle.* 1972. NY. Morrow. 1st. F/dj. M15. $250.00.

HOMAS, Ross. *Twilight at Mac's Place.* 1990. NY. Mysterious. 1st. one of 26 lettered copies sgn. VF/. M15. $100.00.

HOMAS, Ross. *Twilight at Mac's Place.* 1990. NY. Mysterious Press. 1st. VF/VF. T2. $15.00.

HOMAS, Ross. *Voodoo, Ltd.* 1992. NY. Mysterious. 1st. F/F. H11. $30.00.

HOMAS, Ross. *Voodoo, Ltd.* 1992. NY. Mysterious Press. 1st. sgn. VF in dj. M15. $50.00.

THOMAS, Ross. *Yellow-Dog Contract.* 1977. NY. Morrow. 1st. White jacket Is slightly soiled. VF/F. H11. $125.00.

THOMAS, Ross. *Yellow-Dog Contract.* 1977. NY. Morrow. 1st. VF/dj. M15. $150.00.

THOMAS, Ross. *Yellow-Dog Contract.* 1977. Morrow. 1st. VG/dj. P3. $100.00.

THOMAS, ROSS (as Oliver Bleeck). *No Questions Asked.* 1976. Morrow. 1st. F/dj. M25. $150.00.

THOMAS, Tony. *Cinema of the Sea: Critical Survey & Filmology 1925 – 1986.* 1988. photos. VG. M17. $25.00.

THOMAS & WIGGINS. *Flora of the Alaskan Arctic Slope.* 1962. Toronto. tall 8vo. 425p. VG/dj. A22. $70.00.

THOMAS & WITTS. *Enola Gay.* 1977. 1st. photos. xl. dj. K3. $15.00.

THOMAS & WITTS. *San Francisco Earthquake.* 1971. Stein Day. 316p. F/dj. D8. $15.00.

THOMASON, John W. *Fix Bayonets!* 1926. 2nd. lg 8vo. VG. E6. $30.00.

THOMASON, John W. *Jeb Stuart.* 1934. Scribner. early prt. 512p. VG/dj. M8. $35.00.

THOMPSON, Blanche Jennings. *Silver Pennies.* 1925. NY. Macmillan. 1st. ils by Winifred Bromhall. sm 8vo. bl cloth w/bl decor. 138p. VG. D6. $60.00.

THOMPSON, D'Arcy Wentworth. *On Growth & Form.* 1942. Cambridge. later prt. ils/diagrams. VG/dj. M17. $25.00.

THOMPSON, Edward. *Roetgen Rays & Phenomena of the Anode & Cathode.* 1896. NY. 1st. 190p. recent blk cloth. A13. $500.00.

THOMPSON, Edwin Porter. *History of the First Kentucky Brigade.* 1868. Caxton. 1st. sgn assn. 391p. cloth. expertly recased and rebacked. VG. M8. $350.00.

THOMPSON, Ellery. *Draggerman's Haul.* 1950. Viking. map. 277p. dj. T7. $18.00.

THOMPSON, Eloise R. *Wildflower Portraits.* 1964. Norman. 1st. 100 mc pl. VG+/dj. B26. $75.00.

THOMPSON, Era Bell. *Africa, Land of My Fathers,* 1954. Doubleday. 1st. 281p. VG+/VG. A25. $22.00.

THOMPSON, Gerald. *Edward F. Beale & the American West.* 1983. Albuquerque. 1st. 8vo. VG+. F7. $35.00.

THOMPSON, Homer C. & Wm. C. Kelly. *Vegetable Crops.* 1957. NY. McGraw-Hill. 5th. sm4to. 611p. VG. H1. $20.00.

THOMPSON, Hunter S. *Fear and Loathing in Las Vegas.* 1972. Random House. 1st. NF/worn dj. few stains. M25. $200.00.

THOMPSON, Hunter S. *Fear & Loathing in Las Vegas.* 1971. Random. 1st. ils Ralph Steadman. VG/VG. M17. $125.00.

THOMPSON, Hunter S. *Fear & Loathing in Las Vegas.* 1971. Random. 1st. NF/NF. B2. $225.00.

THOMPSON, Hunter S. *Fear & Loathing on the Campaign Trail '72.* 1973. Straight Arrow. 1st. 506p. VG/dj. $45.00.

THOMPSON, Hunter S. *Generation of Swine.* 1988. Summit. 1st. F/dj. A24. $25.00.

THOMPSON, Hunter S. *Generation of Swine.* 1988. Summit. 1st. 304p. NF/dj. M20. $18.00.

THOMPSON, Hunter S. *Songs of the Doomed.* 1990. Summit. 1st. F/F. B3. $25.00.

THOMPSON, Hunter S. *The Proud Highway.* (1997). NY. Villard. 1st. F/F. B3. $15.00.

THOMPSON, Hunter S. *The Rum Diary.* 1998. NY. S&S. 1st. sgn. bookplate. F/. D10. $50.00.

THOMPSON, Hunter S. *The Rum Diary.* 1998. S&S. UP. F/wrp. M25. $60.00.

THOMPSON, Hunter S. & Ralph Steadman. *The Curse of Lono.* 1983. Bantam. 1st. poi on half title pg. VG to F in decor wrp. one inch tear at foot of spine. M25. $60.00.

THOMPSON, J. Eric. *Maya Archaeologist.* 1963. Norman, OK. 1st. 248p. dj. F3. $35.00.

THOMPSON, J. Eric. *Maya Archaeologist.* 1971. Norman. Univ. of Oklahoma Press. 2nd. wrp. 284p. G. F3. $15.00.

THOMPSON, J. Eric. *Mexico Before Cortez.* 1933. Scribner. 1st. 298p. F3. $45.00.

THOMPSON, J. Eric. *Thomas Gage's Travels in the New World.* 1958. Norman. Univ. of Oklahoma Press. 1st. 379p. G/chipped dj stated 2nd. F3. $35.00.

THOMPSON, J. Eric. *Thomas Gage's Travels in the New World.* 1958. Norman. Univ. of Oklahoma Press. 3rd. 379p. G/wrp. F3. $20.00.

THOMPSON, Jim. *Child of Rage*. 1991. Los Angeles. Blood & Guts. ltd. 1/500. sgn/#d. F/dj/case. M15. $150.00.

THOMPSON, Jim. *Killer Inside Me*. 1989. Los Angeles. Blood & Guts. 1st hc. 1/350. sgn. F/dj. M15. $175.00.

THOMPSON, Jim. *More Hardcore*. 1987. DIF. 1st. NF/dj. P3. $25.00.

THOMPSON, Jim. *Now and on Earth*. 1986. Belen. Dennis McMillan Publications. ltd ed. 1/400 # copies. VF/VF. T2. $125.00.

THOMPSON, Josiah. *Six Seconds in Dallas*. 1967. NY. 1st. VG/VG. B5. $75.00.

THOMPSON, Joyce. *Conscience Place*. 1984. Doubleday. 1st. F/dj. M2. $15.00.

THOMPSON, Kay. *Eloise in Moscow*. 1959. S&S. 1st. ils Hilary Knight. orange cloth. VG/VG. D1. $225.00.

THOMPSON, Kay. *Eloise in Moscow*. 1959. S&S. 4to. VG/G+. M5. $175.00.

THOMPSON, Leonard. *African Societies in Southern Africa*. 1969. NY/WA. Praeger. 1st. 8vo. 336p. NF/dj. W1. $20.00.

THOMPSON, Maurice. *Alice of Old Vincennes*. nd. Grosset Dunlap. 1st. F/dj. M2. $15.00.

THOMPSON, Neil Baird. *Crazy Horse Called Them Walk-A-Heaps*. 1979. North Star. 150p. VG/VG. J2. $55.00.

THOMPSON, Peter. *Thompson's Narrative of the Little Big Horn Campaign 1876*. 1974. Clark. 1st. ils/maps. 339p. VG. J2. $225.00.

THOMPSON, Phyllis. *Artichoke & Other Poems*. 1969. HI U. 1st. inscr. F/dj. V1. $25.00.

THOMPSON, Rupert. *The Insult*. 1996. NY. Knopf. 1st. F/F. M23. $20.00.

THOMPSON, Ruth Plumley. *Speedy in Oz*. (1934). Reilly Lee. 1st. ils J Neill/12 mc pl. blk cloth. VG. D1. $425.00.

THOMPSON, Ruth Plumly. *Captain Salt in Oz*. 1936. Reilly Lee. 1st/1st state. 1st Oz book issued w/o mc pl. 306p. VG. P2. $250.00.

THOMPSON, Ruth Plumly. *Grandpa in Oz*. 1924. Reilly Lee. 1st. ils John Neill. VG+. P2. $325.00.

THOMPSON, Ruth Plumly. *Hungry Tiger of Oz*. nd. Reilly Lee. decor brd. G. P3. $50.00.

THOMPSON, Ruth Plumly. *Hungry Tiger of Oz*. 1926. Reilly Lee. 1st/1st issue. ils John R Neill. olive-drab cloth. R5. $585.00.

THOMPSON, Silvanus P. *Elementary Lessons in Electricity & Magnetism*. 1888. Chicago. Thompson Thomas. 43rd thousand. 456p. cloth. VG. M20. $40.00.

THOMPSON, Silvanus P. *Light Visible & Invisible*. 1897. London. 1st. 294p. xl. bl cloth. VG. B14. $375.00.

THOMPSON, Slason. *Eugene Field, a Study in Heredity and Contradictions, with Portraits, Views and Facsimile Illustrations. 2 Volumes*. 1901. NY. Scribners. ltd ed. #37/262. sm 4to. vellum spines w/gilt rules & lettering. photo ils. 346p/349p. NF. D6. $135.00.

THOMPSON, Thomas. *Celebrity*. 1982. Garden City. Doubleday. 1st. F/NF. H11. $25.00.

THOMPSON, Waddy. *Recollections of Mexico*. 1846. NY & London. np. 1st ed. 4th issue. orig brown cloth. chipped around spine. shelf wear to edges. foxing. tight. 304p. F3. $100.00.

THOMPSON, William. *Reminiscences of a Pioneer*. 1912. SF. private prt. A19. $75.00.

THOMPSON & THOMPSON. *Science Fiction & Fantasy Collectibles Price Guide*. 1989. 482p. F. M13. $30.00.

THOMSON, Basil. *Case of the Dead Diplomat*. 1935. Crime Club. 1st. xl. VG/dj. P3. $20.00.

THOMSON, Christine Campbell. *Not at Night Omnibus*. 1937. London. 1st. G. M2. $35.00.

THOMSON, D. *Pair Trawling & Pair Seining*. 1978. Fishery News. ils/tables. 167p. pict brd. VG+. M12. $15.00.

THOMSON, David. *Shining Mountains*. 1979. Knopf. A19. $25.00.

THOMSON, David. *Showman: Life of David O. Selznick*. 1992. NY. 1st. 793p. F/dj. A17. $15.00.

THOMSON, David. *Suspects*. 1985. NY. Knopf. 1st. F/F. B2. $25.00.

THOMSON, H. Douglas. *Great Book of Thrillers*. 1937. Odhams. G. P3. $20.00.

THOMSON, H. Douglas. *Mystery Book*. 1934. Odhams. VG. P3. $35.00.

THOMSON, J. E. *Grenville Problem: Roya[l] Society of Canada Special Pub 1*. 195[6] Toronto. 119p. cloth. NF. D8. $24.00.

THOMSON, June. *Question of Identity* 1977. Crime Club. 1st. F/dj. P3. $25.00.

THOMSON, Origen. *Crossing the Plains* 1983. Ye Galleon. 1st thus. ils. M/sans. A18 $17.50.

THOMSON, Richard. *Antique America[n] Clocks & Watches*. 1968. NY. Galahad Books ils/photos. 192p. brd. dj. D2. $30.00.

THOMSON, Robert Dundas. *Experimenta[l] Researches on the Food of Animals, and th[e] Fattening of Cattle, with Remarks on the Food o[f] Man. Based Upon Experiments Undertaken b[y] Order of the British Government*. NY. D Apleton & Co. 1846. 12mo. 172p. tables & (34)p publisher's catalogue. blk cloth. 1s[t] Am ed. Foxing. ffep lacking. minor cloth wear. G to VG. L5. $75.00.

THOMSON, Samuel. *New Guide to Health or, Botanic Family Physician*. 1829. Clairsville OH. Horton Howard. 12mo. 115p. contemporary calf. $1.00.

THOMSON, William. *Practical Treatise o[n] Cultivation of Grape Vine*. 1865. London Blackwood. 77p. cloth. VG. A10. $78.00.

THON, Melanie Rae. *First, Body*. (1997). Boston. Houghton Mifflin. 1st. F/F. B3 $30.00.

THON, Melanie Rae. *Girls in the Grass*. (1991). NY. Random House. 1st. 2nd book. F/NF. barely noticeable rpr closed tear. B3. $60.00.

THON, Melanie Rae. *Girls in the Grass*. 1991. Random. 1st Am. author's 2nd short stories book. VG/VG. L1. $30.00.

THON, Melanie Rae. *Girls in the Grass*. 1991. Random. 1st Am. sgn. author's 2nd book. F/F. D10. $75.00.

THON, Melanie Rae. *Girls in the Grass*. 1991. Random. 1st. F/dj. A24. $50.00.

THON, Melanie Rae. *Iona Moon*. (1993). London. Viking. 1st British ed. F/NF. lt rubbing to corners. B3. $35.00.

THON, Melanie Rae. *Iona Moon*. 1993. Poseidon. 1st. sgn. author's 3rd book. F/F. D10. $45.00.

THON, Melanie Rae. *Meteors in August*. 1990. Random. 1st. author's 1st book. F/dj. A24. $60.00.

THON, Melanie Rae. *Meteors in August*. 1990. Random. 1st. sgn. F/F. D10. $75.00.

THONE, Frank E. A. *Trees and Flowers of Yellowstone National Park.* 1923. Saint Paul. decor. emb cover. VG. B26. $12.50.

THORBURN, Archibald. *British Birds.* 1925 - 26. Longman Gr. 4 vol. 192 mc pl. red cloth. djs. T10. $400.00.

THORBURN, Grant. *Forty Years' Residence in America.* 1834. Boston. Russell. 264p. rebound. A10. $28.00.

THOREAU, Henry David. *A Week on the Concord and Merrimack Rivers.* Boston. Ticknor and Fields. 1868. 12mo. 415p. orig blk cloth. 2nd ed. 1st prt. sgn in ink at top of flyleaf: "E. F. Bartlett/July 1873." top and bottom of spine chipped approx. ⅛ inch. other wear minor. G. L5. $350.00.

THOREAU, Henry David. *A Week on the Concord and Merrimack Rivers, Walden, The Maine Woods, Cape Cod.* (1961). NY. Thomas Y. Crowell Co. 8vo. 492p. 440p. 423p. 319pp. decor by Clare Leighton. lt gr cloth. djs. box. 1st prt of the vols in this format. Box sltly worn and split. NF. L5. $135.00.

THOREAU, Henry David. *Consciousness in Concord. The Text of Thoreau's Hitherto "Lost Journal" (1840 – 1841) Together with Notes and a Commentary by Perry Miller.* 1958. Boston. Houghton Mifflin. 8vo. 243p. facsimile. beige cloth. dj. 1st ed. 1st prt. F/VG. L5. $65.00.

THOREAU, Henry David. *Henry David Thoreau.* 1967. Viking. 1st. ils James Daugherty. sm 4to. F/F. P2. $25.00.

THOREAU, Henry David. *Journal Of.* 1984. Salt Lake. GM Smith. 15 vol. F. M12. $125.00.

THOREAU, Henry David. *Katahdin and Chesuncook.* (1909). Boston and NY. Houghton Mifflin Co. 16mo. 93.(4)p. printed wrp. 1st ed of this format (eight ed of these portions of "The Maine Woods"). VG. L5. $60.00.

THOREAU, Henry David. *The Succession of Forest Trees, Wild Apples and Sounds with a Biographical Sketch By Ralph Waldo Emerson.* (1887). Boston. NY. Chicago. Houghton Mifflin Co. 16mo. 103p. printed wrp. 1st ed of this format (2nd ed of these portions of "Excursions"). slt soiling on front wrp. G to VG. L5. $50.00.

THOREAU, Henry David. *Writings Of.* 1906. Houghton Mifflin. 20 vol. 1/600. Bliss Perry's copy. gr buckram/paper spine label. C6. $6,000.00.

THOREK, Max. *Surgical Errors & Safeguards.* 1932. Phil. 1st. ils. 696p. A13. $75.00.

THORNBURG, Newton. *A Man's Game.* 1996. NY. Forge. 1st. VF/VF. H11. $15.00.

THORNBURG, Newton. *Black Angus.* 1978. Little, Brn. 1st. VG/dj. P3. $23.00.

THORNBURG, Newton. *Cutter and Bone.* 1976. Boston. Little, Brn. 1st. white jacket Is slightly soiled. F+/F. H11. $35.00.

THORNBURG, Newton. *Lion at the Door.* 1990. Morrow. 1st. F/VG. P3. $20.00.

THORNBURG, Newton. *To Die in California.* 1973. Boston. Little, Brn. 1st. VF/F. H11. $75.00.

THORNBURY, W. D. *Principles of Geomorphology.* 1969. John Wiley. 2nd. 594p. pict brd. VG. D8. $17.00.

THORNDYKE, Helen Louise. *Honey Bunch: Her First Little Treasure Hunt (#18).* 1937. Grosset Dunlap. 183p. cloth. VG/dj. M20. $30.00.

THORNE, Anthony. *She Takes a Lover.* 1932. Macmillan. 1st Am. F/F. B4. $85.00.

THORNE, Diana. *Diane Thorne's Dogs: Album of Drawings.* 1944. Messner. 1st. sbdg. VG/dj. M20. $75.00.

THORNE, Diana and Albert Payson Terhune. *The Dog Book.* 1932. Akron. Saalfield. 1/4 cloth w/color pict brds. 12 full pg color plates. wear to edges. G. B18. $35.00.

THORNE, Guy. *When it was Dark.* 1904. Putnam. 1st. VG. P3. $25.00.

THORNE, John. *Simple Cooking.* 1987. Viking. 2nd. sgn. 290p. VG/VG. B10. $12.00.

THORNE, Paul. *Murder in the Fog.* 1929. Penn. 1st. VG. P3. $40.00.

THORNE, S. E. *Discourse Upon Exposition & Understandinge of Statuettes.* 1942. San Marino. Huntington Lib. M11. $85.00.

THORNE, S. E. *Essays in English Legal History.* 1985. London. Hambledon. M11. $50.00.

THORNE-THOMSEN, Kathleen. *Why the Cake Won't Rise & the Jelly Won't Set.* 1979. NY. A&W Pub. G/dj. A16. $8.00.

THORNTON, A. G. *Astronomer at Large.* 1924. Putnam. 1st. VG. P3. $25.00.

THORNTON, B. M. *Steelhead: Supreme Trophy Trout.* 1978. Seattle. Hancock. ils/photos. 159p. VG+/VG. M12. $25.00.

THORNTON, Betsy. *The Cowboy Rides Away.* 1996. NY. St. Martin. 1st. sgn. author's 1st novel. VF/VF. T2. $25.00.

THORNTON, J. Quinn. *California Tragedy.* 1945. Biobooks. 1/1500. 4to. F/F. O4. $30.00.

THORNTON, Lawrence. *Ghost Woman.* 1992. Ticknor & Fields. ARC. F in decor wrp. M25. $25.00.

THORNTON, Lawrence. *Imagining Argentina.* 1987. NY. Doubleday. 1st. author's 1st book. F/F. H11. $40.00.

THORNTON, Robert. *The Temple of Flora, Introduction by Ronald King.* 1981. Boston. 1st Am ed. folio. 111p w/32 color plates. 25 halftone ils. F in VG dj. B26. $115.00.

THORP, Raymond. *WF Carver, Spirit Gun of the West.* 1957. Clark. 1st. ils. 266p. VG/dj. J2. $185.00.

THORP, Roderick. *Rainbow Drive.* 1986. Summit. 1st. VG/dj. P3. $25.00.

THORP, W. *Southern Reader.* 1955. VG/VG. M17. $25.00.

THRAPP, Dan L. *Al Sieber, Chief of Scouts.* 1964. Norman, OK. 1st. 432p. VG. J2. $195.00.

THRAPP, Dan L. *Juh: An Incredible Indian.* 1973. TX W Pr. 1st. 44p. F/wrp. B19. $25.00.

THROM, Edward L. *Boy Engineer.* 1959. Golden. 4to. 248p. G. K5. $18.00.

THROWER, Norman J. W. *The Three Voyages of Edmond Halley in the Paramore. 1698 – 1701.* 1981. London. Hakluyt Society. bl cloth 8vo. gilt titles & cover decor. second series. vols 156. 157. 15 ils including maps. 392p. F. P4. $95.00.

THRUM, Thomas G. *Hawaiian Folk Tales.* 1907. Chicago. McClurg. 1st. ils/glossary/ads. 284p. VG. P4. $185.00.

THUCYDIDES, De Bello Peloponnesiaco. *Libri Octo.* 1594. Frankfurt. Heirs of Andraes Wechel. 16mo. 848p. VG. C6. $375.00.

THUNBERG, Carl Peter. *Flora Japonica.* 1975. NY. Oriole. 8vo. 418p. F/VG. A22. $45.00.

THURBER, James. *Further Fables of Our Time.* 1956. S&S. 1st. 174p. brd/cloth spine. NF/NF. B22. $12.00.

THURBER, James. *Further Fables of Our Times.* 1956 (1956). S&S. Special Ed (on Fine paper). 8vo. 174p. wht cloth. VG. H1. $45.00.

THURBER, James. *Lanterns & Lances.* 1961. Harper. 1st. NF/VG. M19. $25.00.

THURBER, James. *Many Moons.* 1943. Harcourt Brace. 1st. ils Louis Slobodkin. Caldecott Medal. NF/G+. P2. $150.00.

THURBER, James. *Thurber Album.* 1952. S&S. 1st. sgn. xl. G. W2. $75.00.

THURBER, James. *White Deer.* 1945. Harcourt Brace. 1st. NF/VG+. C8. $50.00.

THURBER & WHITE. *Is Sex Necessary? or, Why You Feel the Way You Do.* 1944. Garden City. 197p. VG/dj. B14. $75.00.

THURLO, Aimee & David. *Bad Medicine.* 1997. Forge. 1st. F/F. G8. $20.00.

THURLO, Aimee & David. *Blackening Song.* 1995. NY. Forge. 1st. VF/VF. T2. $25.00.

THURLO, Aimee & David. *Enemy Way.* 1998. Forge. 1st. F/F. G8. $17.50.

THURMAN, Howard. *Growing Edge.* 1956. NY. Harper. 1st. 131p. G+/dj. V3. $15.00.

THURMAN, Howard. *Jesus & the Disinherited.* 1949. NY. Abingdon-Cokesbury. 112p. VG/dj. V3. $9.00.

THURMAN, Howard. *Negro Spiritual Speaks of Life & Death.* 1947. Harper. VG/VG. B4. $25.00.

THURMAN, Sue Bailey. *Pioneers of Negro Origin in California.* ca 1952. SF. Acme. 1st. 70p. sbdg. B4. $150.00.

THURMAN, Wallace. *Blacker the Berry.* 1929. Macaulay. 1st. VG/dj. M25. $750.00.

THURSTON, Clara Bell. *The Jingle of a Jap.* 1908. Boston. H. M. Caldwell Co. ils by author. sm 4to. colorful Japanese cloth w/tie where doll was originally attached. paper title label. color ils. 32p. G+. spine darkened. slightly loose. D6. $40.00.

THURSTON, P.C. *Geology of Ontario.* 1991. Toronto. 711p. B1. $85.00.

THURSTON, Robert. *Alicia II.* 1978. Putnam. 1st. F/dj. P3. $20.00.

THWAITE, Mary. *From Primer to Pleasure in Reading: An Introduction.* 1972. Boston. Horn Book. 1st Am. ils. 4to. 350p. F/F. $4.00.

THWING, Eugene. *World's Best 100 Detective Stories 1.* 1929. Funk Wagnalls. VG. P3. $15.00.

TIBBETS, Paul. *Mission: Hiroshima.* 1985. Stein Day. VG/wrp. K3. $15.00.

TICKNER, John. *Tickner's Dogs.* 1988. London. Sportsman's Pr. VG. O3. $18.00.

TIDYMAN, Ernest. *Line of Duty.* 1974. Little, Brn. 1st. VG/dj. P3. $20.00.

TIERNEY, Richard L. *The House of the Toad.* 1993. Minneapolis. Fedogan & Bremer. 1st. VF/VF. T2. $30.00.

TIGER, John; see Wager, Walter.

TILDEN, W.T. *Art of Lawn Tennis.* 1922. Garden City. rpt/enlarged/expanded. G/G. P8. $20.00.

TILGHMAN, Christopher. *In a Father's Place.* 1990. NY. FSG. 1st. sgn. author's 1st book. F/F. M23. $85.00.

TILGHMAN, Christopher. *In a Father's Place.* 1990. NY. FSG. 1st. author's 1st book. sgn. F/F. O11. $45.00.

TILGHMAN, Christopher. *Mason's Retreat.* 1996. NY. Random House. 1st. F/F. M23. $25.00.

TILGHMAN, Christopher. *Mason's Retreat.* 1996. NY. Random House. special preview ed w/different dj than trade ed. sgn. F/F. O11. $35.00.

TILGHMAN, Christopher. *Mason's Retreat.* 1996. NY. Random House. 1st. sgn. F/F. O11. $30.00.

TILLICH, Paul. *History of Christian Thought.* 1956. Tillich. edit Peter John. 309p. G/wrp. B29. $11.00.

TILLICH, Paul. *Systematic Theology.* 1961. Univ. of Chicago. vol. 1. 300p. VG/VG. B29. $9.50.

TILLICH, Paul. *Theology of Paul Tillich.* 1952. Macmillan. edit Kegley/Bretall. 370p. VG/dj. B29. $14.00.

TILLMAN, Barrett. *Hellcat: The F6F in WWII.* 1979. Annapolis. photos/notes/biblio/index. 265p. VG/VG. S16. $21.50.

TILMAN, H. W. *Ice with Everything.* 1974. Sidney. Gray's Pub. 142p. VG/dj. P4. $25.00.

TILMAN, H. W. *Mostly Mischief.* 1967. London. Adventurers Club. later prt. 8vo. 191p. P4. $35.00.

TILNEY, Frederick. *Form & Function of the Nervous System.* 1921. NY. Hoeber. heavy 4to. 1019p. ruled bl cloth. xl. G1. $50.00.

TILTON, Theodore. *True Church, Ils from Designs by Granville Perkins.* 1883. Phil. Claxton. 8vo. gilt pub cloth. F. B24. $125.00.

TIME LIFE BOOKS. *Fresh Ways with Cakes.* 1988. Alexandria, VA. TLB. 1st. 4to. 144p. F. S14. $9.00.

TIME LIFE BOOKS. *Fresh Ways with Desserts.* 1986. Alexandria, VA. TLB. 1st. 4to. 144p. F. S14. $9.00.

TIME LIFE BOOKS. *Recipes: Classic French Cooking.* 1970. NY. TLB. spiral. rev 1972 ed. 152p. VG. no dj. A28. $6.95.

TIME LIFE BOOKS. *The Enchanted World Series, Fairies and Elves.* 1985 (1984). Chicago. TLB. rev ed. 3rd printing. 4to. 144p. G. S14. $8.00.

TIME LIFE BOOKS. *Understanding Computers Series: Computers and the Cosmos.* 1988. Alexandria, VA. TLB. 4to. ex lib in pict bds. color ils. 128p. VG. ffep removed. K5. $10.00.

TIME LIFE BOOKS. *Voyage Through the Universe Series, Stars.* 1988. Alexandria, VA. TLB. 4to. color ils. 144p. VG/pict cloth. K5. $12.00.

TIME-LIFE EDITORS. *Cosmos.* 1988. Alexandria, VA. Path Through Universe Series. 4to. 144p. pict cloth. K5. $12.00.

TIME-LIFE EDITORS. *Spanish West.* 1979. Alexandria, VA. 2nd. leather. A19. $20.00.

TIMLIN, Mark. *Find My Way Home.* 1996. London. Gollancz. 1st. VF/VF. T2. $20.00.

TIMLIN, Mark. *Paint it Black.* 1995. London. Gollancz. 1st. VF/VF. T2. $20.00.

TIMMIS, R. S. *Modern Horse Management.* nd. London. Cassell. 4to. VG. O3. $25.00.

TIMPERLEY, Rosemary. *Child in the Dark.* 1956. Crowell. 1st. VG/dj. P3. $35.00.

TIMPERLEY, Rosemary. *Eighth Ghost Book.* 1972. Barrie Jenkins. 1st. xl. VG/dj. P3. $15.00.

TINGLEY, Katherine. *Wine of Life: Compilation from Extemporaneous Address.* 1925. Point Loma. Woman's Internat. Theosophical League. ils 332p. D11. $50.00.

TINKCOM, Harry Marlin. *Republicans & Federalists in Pennsylvania 1790 – 1801.* 1950. Harrisburg, PA. Hist & Mus Comm. tall 8vo. 354p. gilt cloth. F. H1. $25.00.

TINKER, F.G. *Some Still Live.* 1937. Funk Wagnalls. 1st. VG/dj. M2. $17.00.

TINKHAM, George H. *History of Stockton.* 1880. SF. WM Hinton. A19. $45.00.

INKLE, Lon. *J Frank Dobie, Makings of an ample Mind.* 1968. Encino. 1st. 1/850. sgn. 7p. VG/box. $2.00.

INSLEY, Jim Bob. *He Was Singin' This ong.* 1981. Orlando. inscr. fwd Gene Autry/S Omar Baker. 255p. F/VG. B11. 75.00.

IONGSON, Nicanor G. *Pilipinas Circa 907: Production Score for Piano & Voice.* 1985. Quezon City. Philippine Edu Theater Assn. 66p. F/VG. P1. $15.00.

TIPPETT, James S. *Crickety Cricket!* 1973. Harper Row. 1st. ils Mary Chalmers. 83p. reinforced cloth. F/F. D4. $35.00.

TIPPING, H. *Avray, English Gardens.* 1925. London. Folio. 600 ils/photos. 366p. aeg. B26. $200.00.

TIPPING, H. *Avray, Gardens Old & New: Country House & Its Garden Environment.* 1900. London. Country Life. 295p. folio. A10. $95.00.

TIRONE SMITH, Mary Ann. *An American Killing.* 1998. London. Headline. 1st. sgn. F/VF. T2. $35.00.

TIRRO, Frank. *Jazz, A History.* 1977. NY. Norton. ARC w/slip. F/NF. B2. $45.00.

TITON, Jeff Todd. *Early Downhome Blues.* 1977. Urbana. Univ. of Illinois Press. 1st. contains fine flexible disc containing cuts by Charley Patton. F. owner's name/NF. tear. B2. $100.00.

TITOV, Gherman. *I Am Eagle!* 1962. Bobbs Merrill. 8vo. photos. 212p. Vg/dj. K5. $30.00.

TOBE, John H. *Proven Herbal Remedies.* 1969. Provoker. 304p. VG/VG. M20. $15.00.

TOBIAS, Philip V. *Brain in Hominid Evolution.* 1971. Columbia. tall 8vo. 170p. blk cloth. VG/tattered. G1. $50.00.

TOBIAS, Robert. *Communist Christian Encounter in East Europe.* 1956. School of Religion. 567p. VG/VG. B29. $8.00.

TODD, Barbara. *Earthy Mangold & Worzel Gummidge.* 1954. London. Hollis Carter. 1st. ils JJ Crockford. 200p. NF/VG-. P2. $25.00.

TODD, Charles. *A Test of Wills.* 1996. NY. St. Martin. 1st. VF/dj. M15. $200.00.

TODD, Charles. *Search the Dark.* 1999. NY. St. Martin. 1st. sgn. VF/VF. T2. $25.00.

TODD, Charles. *Search the Dark.* 1999. London. Headline. 1st UK ed. sgn. VF/VF. T2. $38.00.

TODD, Charles. *Search the Dark.* 1999. NY. St. Martin. ARC. sgn by author. wrp. F. B2. $25.00.

TODD, Charles. *Wings of Fire.* 1998. London. Headline. 1st UK ed. sgn. VF/VF. T2. $35.00.

TODD, David. *The Story of the Starry Universe.* 1941. NY. Collier. rev by Donald H. Menzel. color ftspc. b/w photos. 8vo. 368p. G in cloth. stp on ffep. K5. $7.00.

TODD, Edwin. *Neuroanatomy of Leonardo Da Vinci.* 1983. Santa Barbara. 1st. 189p. A13. $75.00.

TODD, Frank Morton. *Eradicating Plague From San Francisco.* 1908. Citizen Health Comm. 1st/only. 313p. maroon cloth. F. K7. $95.00.

TODD, G. Hall. *Culture and the Cross.* 1959. Baker. 111p. G. ex lib. B29. $4.50.

TODD, John M. *Luther: A Life.* 1982. Crossroad. 396p. VG/dj. B29. $10.00.

TODD, Walter E. *Gathered Treasures.* 1912. Washington, DC. Murray. 1st. F. B4. $250.00.

TODD, William B. *Suppressed Commentaries on Wiseian Forgeries.* 1969. Austin. 1st. 1/750. fld pl. 50p. VG. K3. $60.00.

TODER, C.P. *Delaware Canal Journal.* 1972. Bethlehem, PA. 1st. ils/charts. 287p. VG+/dj. B18. $45.00.

TODOROFF, A. *Food Buying Today.* 1934. Grocery Trade Pub. ils. VG. E6. $15.00.

TOEPPERWEIN & TOEPPERWEIN. *Charcoal & Charcoal Burners.* 1950. Boeme, TX. Highland. 1st. sgns. VG/VG. B11. $40.00.

TOEPPERWEIN & TOEPPERWEIN. *Unkle Kris & His Pets.* 1948. Boeme, TX. Highland. 1/200. sgn/#d. VG/VG. B11. $40.00.

TOFFLER, Alvin and Heidi. *War and Anti-War, Survival at the Dawn of the 21st Century.* 1993. Boston. Little, Brn. 1st. F/F. A28. $11.50.

TOGAWA, Masako. *Lady Killer.* 1963. Dodd Mead. 1st Am. F/F. G8. $12.50.

TOGAWA, Masako. *Lady Killer.* 1986. Dodd Mead. 1st Am. F/F. N4. $27.50.

TOKLAS, Alice B. *Alice B. Toklas Cookbook.* 1984 (1954). Harper. 1st thus. 8vo. F/F. C8. $25.00.

TOKLAS, Alice B. *Aromas & Flavors of Past & Present.* 1958. Harper. 1st. F/clip. B35. $70.00.

TOKLAS, Alice B. *What Is Remembered.* 1963. Holt. 1st. F/NF. B2. $45.00.

TOLAND, John. *Battle: Story of the Bulge.* 1959. NY. maps/photos/index. 400p. VG/G. S16. $27.50.

TOLAND, John. *Last 100 Days: Tumultuous & Controversial Story.* 1966. NY. 622p. VG/G. S16. $23.50.

TOLBER, John. *Who's Who in Rock & Roll.* 1991. Mitchell. NF/dj. P3. $20.00.

TOLKIEN, Christopher. *Pictures by JRR Tolkien.* 1992. Houghton Mifflin. 1st. unp. cloth. VG+/dj. M20. $50.00.

TOLKIEN, J. R. R. *Adventures of Tom Bombadil & Other Verses.* 1962. London. Allen Unwin. true 1st. NF/NF. M22. $75.00.

TOLKIEN, J. R. R. *Adventures of Tom Bombadil & Other Verses.* 1962. London. Allen Unwin. 2nd prt. 8vo. NF/NF. C8. $25.00.

TOLKIEN, J. R. R. *Film Book of the Lord of the Rings.* 1978. Methuen. MTI. VG/G. P3. $30.00.

TOLKIEN, J. R. R. *Film Book of Lord of the Rings Part One.* 1978. Ballantine. 1st thus. ils. obl sm 4to. NF/NF. C8. $45.00.

TOLKIEN, J. R. R. *Hobbit.* 1984. 1st thus. 4to. ils Michael Hague. F/F. A4. $45.00.

TOLKIEN, J. R. R. *Letters of JRR Tolkien.* 1981. Houghton Mifflin. 1st. VG/VG. P3. $20.00.

TOLKIEN, J. R. R. *Lord of the Rings.* 1967. Houghton Mifflin. 2nd Am. 3 vol. F/F. B4. $350.00.

TOLKIEN, J. R. R. *Mr. Bliss.* 1982. London. George Allen & Unwin. 1st. pict brds w/ matching dj. NF/NF. mild wear. A24. $65.00.

TOLKIEN, J. R. R. *Return of the Shadow.* 1988. Houghton Mifflin. 1st. VG/dj. P3. $20.00.

TOLKIEN, J. R. R. *Road Goes Ever On.* 1967. Houghton Mifflin. 1st. F/VG. M19. $50.00.

TOLKIEN, J. R. R. *Sir Gawain and the Green Knight, Pearl and Sir Orfeo.* 1975. Boston. Houghton Mifflin. 1st Am ed. F. clip/NF. mild rubbing. A24. $45.00.

TOLKIEN, J. R. R. *Smith of Wootton Major.* 1967. Boston. Houghton Mifflin. 1st Am ed. 16mo. price clip. F/NF. A24. $35.00.

TOLKIEN, J. R. R. *The Silmarillion.* (1977). London. George Allen & Unwin. 1st British ed. F/F. B3. $75.00.

TOLKIEN, J. R. R. *Unfinished Tales.* 1980. BC. F/dj. M2. $10.00.

TOLKIEN, J. R. R. *Unfinished Tales.* 1980. Houghton Mifflin. 1st. VG/dj. P3. $25.00.

TOLKIN, Michael. *The Player.* 1988. NY. Atlantic. 1st. VF/F+. H11. $50.00.

TOLKOWSKY, Samuel. *They Took to the Sea.* 1964. NY. Yoseloff. ils. 316p. dj. T7. $20.00.

TOLLES, Frederick B. *James Logan & the Culture of Provincial America.* 1957. Boston. Little, Brn. 1st. 228p. VG/dj. V3. $15.00.

TOLLES, Frederick B. *Meeting House & Counting House: Quaker Merchants.* 1948. Chapel Hill. 1st. 292p. VG/worn. V3. $18.00.

TOLMAN, Albert W. *Jim Spurling Fisherman, or Making Good.* 1918. Harper & Bros. sm8vo. pages very slightly tanned. small chip at top of spine & small tear on top edge of front cover. 291p. NF/F. H1. $25.00.

TOLMAN, Richard C. *Relativity, Thermodynamics & Cosmology.* 1962. Clarendon. 6th. 8vo. 501p. G. K5. $60.00.

TOLNAY, Tom. *Celluloid Gangs.* 1990. NY. Walker. 1st. author's 1st book. F/VF. H11. $40.00.

TOLNAY, Tom. *The Big House.* 1992. NY. Walker. 1st. VF/VF. H11. $30.00.

TOLSON, Berneita. *Beer Cookbook.* 1968. Hawthorn. G/dj. A16. $15.00.

TOLSON, M. B. *Harlem Gallery.* (1965). Twayne. 1st. VG/dj. M25. $65.00.

TOLSON, M. B. *Libretto for the Republic of Liberia.* 1953. Twayne. 1st. VG/dj. M25. $60.00.

TOLSTOY, Leo. *Letters.* 1978. NY. 1st. 2 vol. VG/VG. T9. $30.00.

TOLSTOY, Nikolai. *The Coming of the King.* 1989. NY. Bantam. 1st. F/F. T2. $8.00.

TOMAN, James A. *Cleveland's Transit Vehicles, Equipment and Technology.* 1996. Kent. Kent State Univ. photos. 271p. F in lightly soiled dj. B18. $25.00.

TOMAN, James A. *Horse Trails to Regional Rails, The Story of Public Transit in Greater Cleveland.* 1996. Kent. Kent State Univ. 1st. ils. 352p. VG in dj. B18. $19.50.

TOMAN, Rolf. *High Middle Ages in Germany.* 1990. Cologne. Benedikt Taschen. 4to. 140p. T10. $45.00.

TOMCHEK, Jeffrey. *Old Angler's Inn Cookbook.* 1997. Columbiana SA. Bogata. 1st. Folio. NF/NF. A28. $24.95.

TOMKINS, William. *Universal Indian Sign Language.* 1929. San Diego. self pub. A19. $30.00.

TOMLINS, Thomas Edlyne. *Law-Dictionary, Examining the Rise, Progress & Present.* 1835. London. contemporary calf. M11. $375.00.

TOMLINSON, Everett T. *Scouting with Daniel Boone.* 1931. np. Appleton. 1st. ils by Norman Rockwell. F/VG dj. M19. $85.00.

TOMLINSON, Everett T. *Washington's Young Aids. A Story of American Revolution.* 1897. Boston. 1st. ils Charles Copeland. 391p. VG. B14. $75.00.

TOMLINSON, H. M. *Out of Soundings.* 1931. NY. Harper & Bros. ltd ed of 110. numbered & sgn. NF. D10. $65.00.

TOMLINSON, P. B. *Anatomy of the Monocotyledons. 2. Palmae.* 1961. London. biblio. index. VG in slightly chipped. faded dj. B26. $95.00.

TOMLINSON, P. B. *Botany of Mangroves.* 1986. Cambridge. Eng. Cambridge Tropical Biology Series. ils. 413p. F/dj. B26. $70.00.

TOMMAY, Pat. *Crunch.* 1975. Norton. 1st. photos. VG+/VG. P8. $25.00.

TOMPKINS, Ptolemy. *Tree Grows Out of Hell.* 1990. NY. Harper. 1st. 189p. dj. F3. $20.00.

TOMPKINS, Stuart Ramsay. *Triumph of Bolshevism — Revolution or Reaction?* 1967. OK U. 1st. xl. VG/dj. V4. $7.50.

TOMPKINS, Walter A. *Little Giant of Signal Hill.* 1964. Englewood Cliffs. 1st. NF/NF. O4. $15.00.

TONEYAMA, Kojin. *Popular Arts of Mexico.* 1974. NY/Tokyo. Weatherhill/Heibonsha. 2nd. 226p. cloth. dj. D2. $185.00.

TONKIN, Peter. *Coffin Ship.* 1990. Crown. 1st. VG/dj. P3. $20.00.

TONNESSEN, J. N.; A. O. Johnsen. *The History of Modern Whaling.* c. 1982. Berkeley. Univ. of California Press. thick 8vo. 11 plates; 7 maps; 71 tables. trans from Norwegian by R.I. Christophersen. 798p. NF in dj. P4. $65.00.

TONNESSEN, Johnsen. *History of Modern Whaling.* 1982. Berkeley. thick 8vo. 798p. NF/dj. P4. $65.00.

TOOKER, Elva. *Nathan Trotter: Philadelphia Merchant. 1787 – 1853.* 1955. Cambridge. 1st. 276p. G/tattered. V3. $16.50.

TOOKER, L. Frank. *Joys & Tribulations of an Editor.* 1924. Century. 1st. VG. M2. $25.00.

TOOLE, John K. *Neon Bible.* 1989. Grove. 1st. F/F. A20. $15.00.

TOOLEY, M. J. & G. M. Sheail, editors. *The Climatic Scene.* 1985. London. George Allen & Unwin. 8vo. text figures. 306p. VG/VG. K5. $20.00.

TOOLEY, R.V. *English Books with Color Plates 1790 to 1860.* 1954. Boston Book & Art Shop. 8vo. 424p. F/dj. B24. $150.00.

TOOLEY, R.V. *Maps & Map-Makers.* 1990. NY. Dorsett. later prt. 140p. M/dj. P4. $40.00.

TOOMER, Jean. *Essentials.* 1931. Chicago. private prt. 1/1000. author's 2nd book. M/dj. B4. $1.500.00.

TOOMER, Jean. *Flavor of Man.* 1949. Phil. Young Friends Movement Phil Yearly Meeting. 12mo. 32p. V3. $250.00.

TOON, Peter. *Meditating as a Christian. Waiting Upon God.* 1991. Collins. 187p. F. B29. $6. 50.

TOOR, Frances. *A Treasury of Mexican Folkways.* 1985. NY. Bonanza Books. 566p. G/G. F3. $15.00.

TOOR, Frances. *Guide to Mexico.* 1940. McBridge. revised/enlarged. 270p. F3. $15.00.

TOPPING, Seymour. *The Peking Letter: A Novel of the Chinese Civil War.* 1999. NY. Public Affairs. 1st. sgn. VF/VF. T2. $27.00.

TOPSELL, Edward. *Fowles of Heaven; or History of Birds.* 1972. Austin. ils. 332p. VG/VG. S15. $30.00.

TORBET, Robert. *Venture of Faith.* 1955. Judson. 1st ed. 634p. VG/torn dj. minor mks. B29. $12.00.

OREY, B. *Field-Days in California.* 1913. Houghton Mifflin. ils/photos/pl. 235p. gilt cloth. VG+. M12. $37.50.

ORGOVNICK, Marianna. *Gone Primitive.* 1990. Chicago. 1st. F/dj. P3. $25.00.

ORIBIO MEDINA, Jose. *La Imprenta En ima. 1584 – 1824.* 1965 (1904). Amsterdam. Nico Israel. 4 vol. ils. cloth. D11. $100.00.

ORME, Mel. *It Wasn't All Velvet.* 1988. Viking. 1st. inscr. F/F. B2. $40.00.

ORME, Mel. *It Wasn't All Velvet.* 1988. Viking. 1st. NF/NF. A20. $20.00.

ORME, Mel. *Wynner.* 1978. Stein Day. 1st. NF/VG+. A20. $25.00.

TORRES, Edwin. *Carlito's Way.* 1975. NY. at rev. 1st. author's 1st book. Jacket has faded spine and light creases on flaps. F/NF+. H11. $60.00.

TORREVILLAS-SUAREZ, Dominic. *Sounds of Silence, Sounds of Fury.* 1988. Quezon City. New Day. essays. 108p. F/VG. P1. $3.00.

TORREY, Julia Whitemore. *Old Sheffield Plate.* 1918. ils. VG. M17. $35.00.

TOSCHES, Nick. *Trinities.* 1994. Doubleday. 1st. sgn. F/dj. w/promo card. O11. $25.00.

TOSCO, Uberto. *The Flowering Wilderness.* 1972. NY. 4to. VG in dj. B26. $14.00.

TOSKI, Bob. *How to Become a Complete Golfer.* 1984. S&S. revised/later prt. inscr. F/NF. B4. $45.00.

TOULOUSE, Betty. *Pueblo Pottery of the New Mexico Indians.* 1977. Mus of NM. 6th. ils/map. 88p. AN. $19.00.

TOULOUSE, Julian Harrison. *Bottle Makers & Their Marks.* 1972. Thos Nelson. 2nd. 900+ older w/300+ modern marks. 624p. F/dj. H1. $95.00.

TOULOUSE, Julian Harrison. *Bottle Makers & Their Marks.* 1971. Thomas Nelson. Inc. 8vo. library stamps on top edge. back of front endpaper. title & copyright pager; back endpaper has withdrawn stamp & damage from removal of library envelope. bottom edge rubbed. 624p. VG/VG. H1. $165.00.

TOULOUSE, Julian Harrison. *Fruit Jars.* 1969. Thomas Nelson/Everybodys. tall 8vo. 542p. F/dj. H1. $65.00.

TOURGEE, Albion W. *Appeal to Caesar.* 1884. NY. 422p. O8. $12.50.

TOURGEE, Albion W. *Bricks without Straw.* 1880. Howard Hulbert. 1st prt. 16mo. 521p. emb brn cloth. G+. O8. $12.50.

TOURGEE, Albion W. *Figs & Thistles.* 1879. Fords. Howard & Hulbert. 1st. 16mo. frontispiece tissue cover partially missing & bad spot on title page. 538p. G. H1. $22.50.

TOURGEE, Albion Winegar. *A Fool's Errand by One of the Fools.* 1880. NY. Fords, Howard & Hubert. 2nd ed. orig cloth. 361p. VG. M8. $45.00.

TOURNEY, Leonard. *Bartholomew Fair Murders.* 1987. London. Quartet. 1st. F/dj. T2. $20.00.

TOURNEY, Leonard. *Familiar Spirits.* 1985. London. Quartet. 1st Eng. F/dj. T2. $20.00.

TOURNEY, Leonard. *Familiar Spirits.* 1985. London. Quartet Books. 1st British ed. VF/VF. T2. $20.00.

TOURNEY, Leonard. *Knaves Templar.* 1991. NY. St. Martin. 1st. VF/VF. T2. $25.00.

TOURNIER, Michel. *Golden Droplet.* 1987. Doubleday. 1st. F/NF. B35. $16.00.

TOURNIER, Paul. *Guilt and Grace.* 1962. Harper. 224p. VG/VG. B29. $9.50.

TOURNIER, Paul. *Reflections on Life's Most Crucial Questions.* 1976. Harper. 177p. VG/VG. B29. $6.50.

TOURNIER, Paul. *The Healing of Persons.* 1965. Harper. 300p. G/G. marks. B29. $8.00.

TOURNIER, Paul. *The Healing of Persons.* 1965. Harper. 300p. VG/VG. B29. $10.50.

TOURNIER, Paul. *The Meaning of Gifts.* 1970. John Knox. 62p. VG/VG. ex lib. B29. $7.50.

TOURNIER, Paul. *The Stong and the Weak.* 1963. Westminster. 254p. VG. B29. $9.50.

TOURNIER, Paul. *To Understand Each Other.* 1976. John Knox. pb. 62p. VG. B29. $2.00.

TOUSEY, Sanford. *Jerry & the Pony Express.* 1936. Doubleday. stated 1st. ils. F/fair. M5. $45.00.

TOUSEY, Sanford. *Northwest Mounted Police.* 1941. Chicago. VG. C8. $17.50.

TOUSEY, Thomas G. *Military History of Carlisle & Carlisle Barracks.* 1939. Richmond, VA. Dietz. 1st. tall 8vo. 447p. VG. $1.00.

TOWERS, Deirdre. *Dance, Film & Video Guide.* 1991. Princeton. 233p. VG/wrp. C5. $12. 50.

TOWLE, M. A. *Ethnobotany of Pre-Columbian Peru.* 1961. NY. photos. 180p. NF/stiff wrp. C12. $50.00.

TOWLE, Mike. *True Champions: The Good Guys in American Sports Speak Out.* 1994. TX. The Summit Group. 1st. foreword by David Robinson. F/F. A28. $11.95.

TOWLE, Tony. *North.* 1970. Columbia. 1st. inscr/dtd 1975. F/NF. L3. $45.00.

TOWN, Harold. *Tom Thomson: Silence & The Storm.* 1977. McClelland Stewart. 1st. F/dj. A26. $100.00.

TOWNE, Morgan. *Treasures in Truck & Trash.* 1949. Doubleday. 205p. xl. H6. $32.00.

TOWNE, Robert D. *Little Johnny & the Teddy Bears.* 1907. Chicago. Reilly Britton. obl 4to. cloth-backed stiff paper wrp. R5. $400.00.

TOWNE, Robert D. *Teddy Bears at the Circus.* 1907. Reilly Britton. 1st thus. ils JR Bray. 12mo. mc pict brd. R5. $150.00.

TOWNE, Robert D. *Teddy Bears Go Fishing.* 1907. Reilly Britton. 1st. ils JR Bray. ils brd. fair. B27. $35.00.

TOWNSEND, C. W. *Along the Labrador Coast.* 1907. Boston. 1st. ils/fld map. 289p. VG. B5. $35.00.

TOWNSEND, G. W. *Memorial Life of William McKinley.* 1901. np. sm 4to. 520p. emb gilt bdg. VG. H1. $28.00.

TOWNSEND, George A. *Rustics in Rebellion.* 1950. 1st/2nd state. 292p. O8. $14.50.

TOWNSEND, John Rowe. *Tom Tiddler's Ground.* 1986. Lippincott. 1st Am. 8vo. 170p. rem mk. NF/NF. T5. $20.00.

TOWNSEND, Sue. *Adrian Mole Diaries.* 1986. Grove. 1st Am. F/clip. D10. $65.00.

TOWNSEND, Virginia F. *Mostly Marjorie Day.* 1892. Lee Shepard. 383p. VG. P12. $7.00.

TOWNSEND, W. H. *Lincoln & His Wife's Hometown.* 1929. Indianapolis. 1st. VG/dj. B5. $50.00.

TOWNSEND. *Written for Children: Outline of English Language.* 1983. 2nd revised/1st prt. ils. 384p. F/F. A4. $35.00.

TOWNSLEY, Gardner H. *Historic Lebanon, Beginning with Beedle's Station in 1795.* 1940. np. Western Star. pict wrp. ils by Egner & Tartt. 48p. VG. paper browned. lt soiling. B18. $22.50.

TOXOPEUS, Klaas. *Flying Storm.* 1954. Dodd Mead. ils. 246p. T7. $20.00.

TOYE, Randall. *The Agatha Christie Who's Who.* 1980. NY. Holt. 1st. F/F. B2. $30.00.

TOYNBEE, Arnold. *Lectures on the Industrial Revolution in England.* 1884. London. Rivington. 1st. 8vo. 256p. gilt gr cloth. VG. $10.00.

TOYNBEE, Arnold J. *Acquaintances.* 1967. OUP. 1st. photos. 312p. NF/VG. M7. $50.00.

TOYNBEE, Philip. *Friends Apart: A Memoir.* 1954. London. 1st. fair dj. T9. $25.00.

TOYNBEE, Philip. *Garden to the Sea.* 1953. London. 1st. inscr. T9. $50.00.

TOZZER, Alfred M. *Maya Grammar with Bibliography & Appraisement of Works.* 1921. Cambridge. 301p. F3. $40.00.

TRACHSEL, Herman H. *Government & Administration of...Wyoming.* 1956. NY. Crowell. A19. $20.00.

TRACHTENBERG, Alexander, Ed. *The American Socialists and the War.* 1917. NY. Rand School. 1st. NF/wrps. B2. $25.00.

TRACHTMAN, Paula. *Disturb Not the Dream.* 1981. NY. Crown. 1st. author's 1st novel. F/F. T2. $6.00.

TRACY, Clarence. *Rape Observed.* 1974. Toronto. 1st. 4to. 101p. gilt red cloth. F/NF. H13. $65.00.

TRACY, Don. *On the Midnight Tide: A Novel.* 1957. NY. Dial. 1st. NF/dj. A14. $25.00.

TRACY, Jack. *Subcutaneously, My Dear Watson: Sherlock Holmes and the Cocaine Habit.* 1978. Bloomington. James A. Rock. 1st. sgn. VF/VF. T2. $50.00.

TRACY, Jack. *Subcutaneously, My Dear Watson: Sherlock Holmes and the Cocaine Habit.* 1978. Bloomington. James A. Rock. 1st. trade pb. VF/pict wrp. T2. $10.00.

TRACY, Jack, editor. *Strange Studies from Life and Other Narratives: The Complete True Crime Writings of Sir Arthur Conan Doyle.* 1988. Bloomington. Gaslight Publications. 1st ed. 2nd printing. VF/VF. T2. $15.00.

TRACY, Louis. *American Emperor.* 1918. Putnam. decor brd. VG. P3. $75.00.

TRACY, Louis. *Black Cat.* 1925. Clode. 1st. VG/G. G8. $25.00.

TRACY, Louis. *Man with the Sixth Sense.* nd. Hodder Stoughton. G/dj. P3. $25.00.

TRACY, Louis. *Pelham Affair.* 1923. Clode. 1st. VG. G8. $17.50.

TRACY, Louis. *Pillar of Light.* 1904. Clode. 1st. VG. M2. $15.00.

TRACY, Marian. *Picnic Book.* 1957. Scribner. G/dj. A16. $7.50.

TRACY, T. H. *Book of the Poodle.* 1958. NY. 4th. ils/photos. 136p. VG/dj. A17. $15.00.

TRAIN, Arthur. *Mr. Tutt Comes Home.* 1941. Scribner. 1st. VG/dj. Q1. $60.00.

TRAIN, Arthur. *Mr. Tutt's Case Book.* 1945. Scribner. VG. P3. $25.00.

TRAIN, Arthur. *Old Man Tutt.* 1938. Scribner. 1st. VG/dj. Q1. $60.00.

TRALINS, Bob. *Green Murder.* 1990. London. MacDonald. 1st. F/dj. M15. $45.00.

TRALL, R. T. *Digestion & Dyspepsia: A Complete Explanation.* 1873. NY. SR Wells. ils. 160p. xl. VG. K3. $20.00.

TRANSEAU, E. N. *Textbook of Botany.* 1953. Harper. revised. xl. G. S5. $15.00.

TRANTER, Nigel. *Drug on the Market.* 1962. Hodder Stoughton. 1st. VG+/clip. A14. $35.00.

TRAUB, Charles. *Beach.* 1978. NY. Horizon. photos. 60p. wrp. D11. $30.00.

TRAUSCH, William. *Grab Bag.* 1939. Pegasus. 1st. 156p. dj. A17. $20.00.

TRAUSELD, W. R. *Wild Flowers of the Natal Drakensberg.* 1969. Cape Town. ep maps. red lettered. gray cloth. minor dust soiling on edges of text. else VG in dj. B26. $59.00.

TRAVEN, B. *General from the Jungle.* 1971. NY. F S G. 1st. F/F. D10. $75.00.

TRAVEN, B. *General from the Jungle.* 1972. NY. Hill and Wang. 1st Am ed. F/F. D10. $60.00.

TRAVEN, B. *Government.* 1971. NY. Hill and Wang. 1st Am ed. NF/NF. D10. $45.00.

TRAVEN, B. *Rebellion of the Hanged.* 1952. Knopf. 1st Am. NF/dj. M25. $200.00.

TRAVEN, B. *The Carreta.* 1970. NY. Hill and Wang. 1st Am ed. F/F. D10. $50.00.

TRAVEN, B. *The Creation of the Sun and the Moon.* 1968. NY. Hill and Wang. 1st Am ed. author's 1st children's book. ils Alberto Beltran. F/F. D10. $75.00.

TRAVEN, B. *The Night Visitor and Other Stories.* 1966. NY. Hill and Wang. 1st Am ed. F/NF. lt fading on spine. D10. $75.00.

TRAVEN, B. *The Rebellion of the Hanged.* (1952). NY. Knopf. 1st Am ed. exceptionally bright copy. F/NF. price clip. minor rub & fading to spine. B3. $175.00.

TRAVEN, B. *The White Rose.* (1979). Westport. Lawrence Hill. 1st. F/NF. minor wear to spine. B3. $30.00.

TRAVEN, B. *The White Rose.* 1979. Westport. Lawrence Hill & Co. 1st Am ed. F/F. D10. $45.00.

TRAVEN, B. *To the Honorable Miss S....and Other Stories.* 1981. Westport. Lawrence Hill & Co. 1st Am ed. trans from German by Peter Silcock. F/NF. lt wear. D10. $40.00.

TRAVEN, B. *Trozas.* 1994. Chicago. Ivan R. Dee. 1st Am ed. review copy. F/F. D10. $35.00.

TRAVER, Robert. *Laughing Whitefish.* 1965. McGraw Hill. 1st. VG/dj. P3. $25.00.

TRAVER, Robert. *Trout Madness.* 1960. NY. 1st. 178p. Quarter Buckram. VG/dj. B18/M20. $35.00.

TRAVER, Robert. *Trout Magic.* 1974. NY. 1st. 216p. F/dj. A17. $50.00.

TRAVERS, Hugh. *Madame Aubry Dines with Death.* 1967. Harper Row. 1st. VG/dj. P3. $10.00.

TRAVERS, Louise A. *Romance of Shells in Nature & Art.* 1962. NY. Barrows. 1/400. sgn. F/F case. B11. $18.00.

TRAVERS, P. L. *Friend Monkey.* 1971. HBJ. 1st. cloth. VG. B27. $55.00.

TRAVERS, P. L. *Friend Monkey.* 1971. HBJ. 1st/2nd prt. inscr. ils Mary Shepard. 122p. VG. T5. $25.00.

TRAVERS, P. L. *Mary Poppins.* 1981. NY. HBJ. revised. G. A28. $3.95.

TRAVERS, P. L. *Mary Poppins & Mary Poppins Comes Back.* 1939 (1937). Reynal Hitchcock. 1st/2nd prt. ils Mary Shepard. VG. B27. $65.00.

TRAVERS, P. L. *Mary Poppins from A – Z.* 1962. Harcourt. stated 1st. 8vo. F/VG. M5. $55.00.

TRAVERS, P. L. *Mary Poppins in Cherry Tree Lane.* 1982. London. Collins. 1st. ils Mary Shepard. VG+. C8. $15.00.

TRAVERS, P. L. *Mary Poppins in the Kitchen.* 1975. HBJ. 1st/B prt. 122p. mauve brd. VG/VG. T5. $45.00.

TRAVERS, P. L. *Mary Poppins in the Park.* 1952. Harcourt Brace. 1st. ils Mary Shepard. VG/dj. M5. $45.00.

TRAVERS, P. L. *Mary Poppins in the Park.* 1952. Harcourt. stated 1st. ils Mary Shepard. VG+/dj. M5. $60.00.

TRAVERS, Robert. *A Funeral for Sabella.* 1952. NY. Harcourt. 1st. F in NF dj w/ tiny chips. B2. $30.00.

TRAVIS, Tristan Jr. *Lamia.* 1982. Dutton. 1st. F/F. H11. $25.00.

TREADWAY, Jessica. *Absent Without Leave & Other Stories.* 1992. NY. Delphinium. 1st. sgn. author's 1st book. F/dj. B4. $45.00.

TREASE, Geoffrey. *So Wild the Heart.* 1959. Vanguard. 1st. VG/fair. P3. $12.00.

TREASE, Geoffrey. *The Condottieri, Soldiers of Fortune.* 1971. Holt, Rinehart & Winston. 1st. tall 8vo. Top & bottom covers have scattered discoloration. light foxing on initial pages. Top of front, spine & back have edge tears. heavy wear. 367p. VG. H1. $30.00.

TREAT, Lawrence. *H as in Hangman.* 1944. Books Inc. VG/dj. P3. $20.00.

TREAT, Mary. *Injurious Insects of the Farm & Garden.* 1887. Orange Judd. 296p. VG. A10. $35.00.

TREAT, Roger. *Walter Johnson.* 1948. Messner. 1st. ils Robert Robison. VG/G. P8. $200.00.

TREATT, Stella Court. *Cape to Cairo, Record of a Historic Motor Journey.* 1927. London. Harrap. 1st. ils. VG. K3. $25.00.

TREDGOLD, Thomas. *Elementary Principles of Carpentry.* 1875. London. 48 pl. B14. $125.00.

TREE, Isabella. *Ruling Passion of John Gould.* 1992. Grove Weidenfeld. 1st Am. 8vo. VG/dj. B11. $20.00.

TREE SOCIETY OF SOUTHERN AFRICA. *Trees and Shrubs of the Witwatersrand, An Illustrated Guide.* 1969 (1964). Johannesburg. 2nd. F in dj. B26. $39.00.

TREECE, Henry. *Amber Princess.* 1963. Random. 1st. NF/dj. P3. $25.00.

TREECE, Henry. *Golden Strangers.* 1956. Random. 1st. F/dj. M2. $38.00.

TREECE, Henry. *Jason.* 1961. Random. 1st. 383p. F/dj. D4. $35.00.

TREECE, Henry. *The Great Captains.* 1956. np. Random House. 1st. VG/VG dj. M19. $25.00.

TREFIL, James S. *Living in Space.* 1981. NY. Scribners. text figures. 8vo. 133p. F/F. K5. $12.00.

TREFOUSSE, H. L. *Andrew Johnson: A Biography.* 1989. NY. 1st. ils. 463p. NF/dj. M4. $25.00.

TREGANOWAN & WEEKS. *Rugs & Carpets of Europe & the Western World.* 1969. Chilton. ils/bibliography/index. cloth. dj. D2. $40.00.

TREGARTHEN, Enys. *White Ring.* 1949. Harcourt Brace. 1st. ils Nora Unwin. sq 8vo. 65p. VG/VG-. P2. $40.00.

TREGASKIS, Richard. *Guadalcanal Diary.* 1943. NY. photos/maps. 263p. VG. S16. $17.50.

TREHERNE, John. *Strange History of Bonnie & Clyde.* 1984. Stein Day. 1st. VG/dj. B5. $15.00.

TREITEL, Jonathan. *Red Cabbage Cafe.* 1990. Pantheon. 1st. author's 1st book. F/F. H11. $25.00.

TRELEASE, William. *Winter Botany.* 1918. Urbana. self pub. 1st. 394p. VG. A10. $24.00.

TREMAINE, Rose. *Restoration.* 1990. NY. Viking. 1st. F/F. D10. $35.00.

TRENHAILE, John. *Mah-Jongg Spies.* 1986. Dutton. 1st. F/NF. H11. $25.00.

TRENHAILE, John. *Nocturne for the General.* 1985. Congdon Weed. 1st. VG/dj. P3. $15.00.

TRENHOLM, Virginia Cole. *Footprints on the Fontier.* 1945. np. 1st. 284p. VG/dj. J2. $385.00.

TRENTO, Joseph J. *Prescription for Disaster.* 1987. NY. Crown. 8vo. 312p. VG/dj. K5. $20.00.

TRENTO, Joseph J. *Prescription for Disaster; From the Glory of Apollo to the Betrayal of the Shuttle.* 1987. NY. Crown. 1st printing. b/w photo ils. 8vo. 312p. VG/VG. K5. $20.00.

TRESSELT, Alvin. *Beaver Pond.* 1970. Lee Shepard. 1st. ils Roger Duvoisin. 4to. VG+/VG. P2. $40.00.

TREUTLEIN, Theodore E. *San Francisco Bay, Discovery & Colonization 1769 – 1776.* 1968. CA Hist Soc. 1st. 4 facsimile maps. quarter bl cloth/gr sides. dj. K7/O4. $25.00.

TREVANIAN. *Shibumi.* 1979. NY. Crown. 1st. F/F. T2. $15.00.

TREVANIAN. *The Eiger Sanction.* 1972. NY. Crown. 1st. author's 1st book. Book has slight slant, lightly bumped corners and owner name on front ffep. Price clipped jacket has light wear and minor chipping at spine ends. NF/NF. H11. $85.00.

TREVANIAN. *The Eiger Sanction.* 1972. NY. Crown. 1st. shelf-wear along bottom front cover edge and erasure on front endpaper. Jacket has scratches on back panel, small open punch-tear on spine, several closed tears and wear at corners. VG/dj. M15. $45.00.

TREVANIAN. *The Loo Sanction.* 1973. NY. Crown. 1st. Front board Is loose. Price clipped jacket has minor chipping at spine ends. NF/NF. H11. $20.00.

TREVANIAN. *The Loo Sanction.* 1972. NY. Crown. 1st. Jacket has a couple of short closed tears. F/dj. M15. $45.00.

TREVANIAN. *The Main.* 1976. NY. HBJ. 1st. F/F. H11. $40.00.

TREVANIAN. *The Summer of Katya.* 1983. NY. Crown. 1st. F/F. H11. $30.00.

TREVANIAN. *The Summer of Katya.* 1983. NY. Crown. 1st. VF/dj. M15. $45.00.

TREVELYAN, Percy, Md. *Mr. Holmes in Cornwall: A Critical Explanation of the Late Dr. Watson's Narrative Entitled "The Devil's Foot."* 1980. Cornwall. Penwith Books. repro of 1927 booklet. VF/plain wrp. printed dj. T2. $15.00.

TREVER, John C. *Scrolls from Qumran Cave I: Great Isaiah Scroll.* 1972. Jerusalem. Allbright Inst Archaeological Research. 163p. VG+. S3. $75.00.

TREVER, John C. *The Untold Story of Oumran.* 1965. Revell. 214p. VG/VG. B29. $11.50.

TREVINO, Lee. *Snake in the Sandtrap.* 1985. HBW. 1st. sgn. F/F. A23. $50.00.

TREVOR, Elleston. *Blaze of Roses.* 1952. Harper. 1st. 249p. VG/dj. M20. $12.00.

TREVOR, William. *Family Sins.* 1990. Toronto. Dennys. 1st Canadian. F/F. B3. $30.00.

TREVOR, William. *Family Sins & Other Stories.* 1990. NY. Viking. 1st. F/F. D10. $40.00.

TREVOR, William. *News from Ireland & Other Stories.* 1986. Viking. 1st Am. F/F. D10. $45.00.

TREVOR, William. *Nights at the Alexandra.* 1987. London. Hutchinson. 1st. ils Paul Hogarth. F/F. A24. $30.00.

TREVOR, William. *Old Boys.* 1964. NY. Viking. 1st. F/NF. L3. $125.00.

TREW, Anthony. *Kleber's Convoy.* 1973. St. Martin. 1st Am. F/NF. T11. $25.00.

TREW, Anthony. *Two Hours to Darkness.* 1963. London. Collins. 1st. F/VG+. T11. $50.00.

TREW, Antony. *Ultimatum.* 1976. St. Martin. 1st. VG/VG. M22. $15.00.

TRIBUTSCH, H. *When the Snakes Awake.* 1982. Cambridge. MIT. 248p. dj. B1. $25.00.

TRICE, James E. *Butter Molds: Identification & Value Guide.* 1980. Collector Books. 1st. 8vo. 176p. VG/glossy wrp. H1. $35.00.

TRIER, Walter. *10 Little Negroes: A New Version.* 1944. London. Sylvan. 1st. obl 8vo. pict brd. R5. $275.00.

TRIGGS, J.H. *History of Cheyenne & North Wyoming Embracing Gold Fields.* 1955. Laramie. WY. Powder River Pub. 2 vol. boxed. A19. $45.00.

TRILLIN, Calvin. *Alice, Let's Eat.* 1978. Random. G/dj. A16. $7.00.

TRILLIN, Calvin. *American Stories.* 1991. Ticknor Fields. 1st. F/dj. R14. $25.00.

TRIMBLE, Allen. *Autobiography…Allen Trimble.* Governor of Ohio. 1909. np. 240p. G/wrp. B18. $25.00.

TRIMBLE, Barbara Margaret. *Fifth Rapunzel.* 1991. Hodder Stoughton. 1st. VG/dj. P3. $20.00.

TRIMBLE, Marshall. *Arizona.* 1977. Garden City. dj. A19. $20.00.

TRIMBLE, Michael R. *Post-Traumatic Neurosis: From Railway Spine to Whiplash.* 1981. Chichester. Eng. Wiley. 3rd. 8vo. 156p. navy cloth. $0.00.

TRIMBLE, Stephen. *Words from the Land.* 1988. Salt Lake City. Smith. 303p. AN/dj. A10. $22.00.

TRIMBLE, Vance H. *Sam Walton.* 1990. Dutton. 1st. F/F. W2. $30.00.

TRIMBLE, William F. *High Frontier: History of Aeronautics in Pennsylvania.* 1982. Pittsburgh. 344p. VG+/wrp. B18. $17.50.

TRIMMER. *National Book Awards for Fiction: An Index.* 1978. 345p. VG. A4. $85.00.

TRIMPEY, Alice. *Story of My Dolls.* 1935. Whitman. 1st. sgn. ils JL Scott. 76p. VG. D4. $65.00.

TRIPLEIT, Frank. *Life. Times & Treacherous Death of Jesse James.* 1970. Chicago. Sage Swallow. 1st. VG/dj. B5. $30.00.

TRIPP, Alonzo. *Crests from the Ocean World.* 1860. Whittemore. Niles Hall. 408p. VG. S17. $10.00.

TRIPP, Miles. *Cords of Vanity.* 1989. St. Martin. 1st Am ed. F/NF. G8. $10.00.

TRIPP, Miles. *Death of a Man-Tamer.* 1987. St. Martin. 1st Am ed. NF/VG+. G8. $10.00.

TRIPP, Miles. *Death of a Man-Tamer.* 1987. St. Martin. 1st. VG/dj. P3. $15.00.

TRIPP, Miles. *Fifth Point of the Compass.* 1967. Macmillan. 1st. VG/dj. P3. $23.00.

TRIPP, Miles. *Video Vengeance.* 1991. St. Martin. 1st Am ed. F/F. G8. $10.00.

TRIPP, Wallace. *Sir Toby Jingle's Beastly Journey.* 1976. CMG. 1st. ils. VG-/G. P2. $20.00.

TRIPTREE, James Jr. *Her Smoke Rose Up Forever.* 1990. Arkham. 1st. VG/dj. M22. $30.00.

TRISTRAM, E. W. *English Medieval Wall Painting.* 1944. Humphrey Milford/OUP. lg 4to. 105 pl/ftspc. 164p. rust buckram. K1. $300.00.

TROCHECK, Kathy Hogan. *Every Crooked Nanny.* 1992. NY. Harper Collins. 1st. author's 1st book. F/F. H11. $190.00.

TROCHECK, Kathy Hogan. *Homemade Sin.* 1994. NY. Harper Collins. 1st. F/F. H11. $25.00.

TROCHECK, Kathy Hogan. *Lickety-Split.* 1996. NY. Crown. 1st. VF/VF. H11. $20.00.

TROCHECK, Kathy Hogan. *Midnight Clear.* 1998. NY. Harper Collins. 1st. VF/VF. T2. $15.00.

TROCHECK, Kathy Hogan. *To Live & Die in Dixie.* 1993. NY. Harper Collins. 1st. sgn. F/F. A24. $40.00.

TROLLEY, Jack. *Balboa Firefly.* 1994. NY. Carroll & Graf. 1st. F/F. H11. $30.00.

TROLLEY, Jack. *Juarez Justice.* 1996. NY. Carroll & Graf. 1st. VF/VF. H11. $15.00.

TROLLEY, Jack. *Manila Time.* 1995. NY. Carroll & Graf. 1st. F/VF. H11. $20.00.

TROLLOPE, Anthony. *Barchester Towers.* 1958. NY. LEC. 1st thus. 1/1500. ils/sgn Fritz Kredel. F/case. Q1. $100.00.

TROLLOPE, Anthony. *Orley Farm.* 1862. London. Chapman Hall. 2 vol. 1st. lg 8vo. bumpus bdg. H13. $495.00.

TROLLOPE, Anthony. *Rachel Ray, A Novel.* 1868. London. Chapman Hall. so-called 10th. tall 8vo. 347p. Victorian bdg. $13.00.

TROLLOPE, Anthony. *Warden.* 1955. NY. LEC. 1st thus. 1/1500. ils/sgn Fritz Kredel. F/glassine/case. Q1. $100.00.

TROLLOPE, Mrs. Frances. *Domestic Manners of the Americans.* 1949. edit D Smalley. VG/VG. M17. $25.00.

TROLLOPE, Thomas Adolphus. *Decade of Italian Women.* 1859. London. Chapman Hall. 2 vol. 1st. 8vo. teg. 3-quarter crushed morocco. $0.00.

TROTZKY, Leon. *The Bolsheviki and World Peace.* 1918. NY. Boni and Liveright. 1st. VG+. B2. $65.00.

TROUT, Kilgore; see Farmer, Philip Jose.

TROW, M. J. *Brigade: Further Adventures of Inspector Lestrade.* 1998. Washington, DC. Regnery Publishing. 1st Am ed. UP. VF/printed wrp. T2. $15.00.

TROW, M. J. *Brigade: Further Adventures of Inspector Lestrade.* 1998. Washington, DC. Regnery Publishing. 1st Am ed. VF/VF. T2. $20.00.

TROW, M. J. *Lestrade and the Brother of Death.* 1999. Washington, DC. Regnery Publishing. 1st Am ed. VF/VF. T2. $20.00.

TROW, M. J. *Lestrade and the Deadly Game.* 1999. Washington, DC. Regnery Publishing. 1st Am ed. VF/VF. T2. $20.00.

TROW, M. J. *Lestrade & the Gift of the Prince.* 1991. London. Constable. 1st. F/dj. T2. $25.00.

TROW, M. J. *Lestrade and the Guardian Angel*. 1990. London. Constable. 1st. F/VF. T2. $5.00.

TROW, M. J. *Lestrade and the Guardian Angel*. 1999. Washington, DC. Regnery Publishing. 1st Am ed. VF/VF. T2. $20.00.

TROW, M. J. *Lestrade and the Hallowed House*. 1999. Washington, DC. Regnery Publishing. 1st Am ed. VF/VF. T2. $20.00.

TROW, M. J. *Lestrade and the Leviathan*. 1999. Washington, DC. Regnery Publishing. 1st Am ed. VF/VF. T2. $20.00.

TROW, M. J. *Lestrade and the Magpie*. 1991. London. Constable. 1st. VF/VF. T2. $25.00.

TROW, M. J. *Lestrade and the Ripper*. 1999. Washington, DC. Regnery Publishing. 1st Am ed. VF/VF. T2. $20.00.

TROW, M. J. *The Adventures of Inspector Lestrade*. 1998. Washington, DC. Regnery Publishing. 1st Am ed. VF/VF. T2. $20.00.

TROWBRIDGE, J. T. *Cudjo's Cave: Story of the Civil War*. nd. NY. AL Burt. 308p. V3. $12.00.

TROWBRIDGE, J. T. *Darius Green & His Flying Machine*. 1910. Houghton Mifflin. 1st. NF. T11. $40.00.

TROWBRIDGE, J. T. *South: A Tour of Its Battle-Fields & Ruined Cities*. 1866. 1st. ils. 590p. O8. $55.00.

TROWBRIDGE, John Townsend. *The Three Scouts*. 1888. Boston. Lee and Shepard. 1st. orig cloth. historical novel. 383p. VG. M8. $22.50.

TROWBRIDGE, Lydia Jones. *Frances Willard of Evanston*. 1938. Chicago. Willett Clark. 1st. pres. photos. 207p. VG. $25.00.

TROWBRIDGE, W.R.H. *Court Beauties of Old Whitehall*. 1906. Scribner. 1st. F. M19. $65.00.

TROY, Judy. *Mourning Doves*. 1993. NY. Scribner. 1st. F/F. H11. $40.00.

TROY, Judy. *Mourning Doves*. 1993. NY. Scribner's. 1st. F/F. M23. $25.00.

TROY, Simon. *Drunkard's End*. 1961. Walker. 1st. VG/dj. P3. $15.00.

TRUAX, Rhoda. *Doctors Warren of Boston: First Family of Surgery*. 1968. Boston. 1st. 369p. A13. $20.00.

TRUAX, Rhoda. *Joseph Lister: Father of Modern Surgery*. 1944. Indianapolis. 1st. 287p. A13. $30.00.

TRUDEAU, Gary. *Doonesbury Deluxe*. 1987. Holt. sc. F. M13. $19.00.

TRUE, Frederick W. *Whalebone Whales of the Western North Atlantic*. 1983. Smithsonian. rpt. 50 pl. 332p. gr cloth. F. P4. $75.00.

TRUEBLOOD, David Elton. *The Incendiary Fellowship*. 1967. Harper. 121p. VG/torn dj. B29. $9.50.

TRUEBLOOD, David Elton. *The Validity of the Christian Mission*. 1972. Harper. 1st ed. 113p. VG/VG. B29. $7.00.

TRUEBLOOD, Elton. *Abraham Lincoln: Theologian of American Anguish*. 1973. NY. Harper Row. 1st. 149p. VG/dj. V3. $16.00.

TRUEBLOOD, Elton. *Company of the Committed*. 1961. Harper. 1st. 113p. VG/dj. V3. $12.00.

TRUEBLOOD, Elton. *Doctor Johnson's Prayers*. 1947. Harper. 1st. 66p. VG/G+. V3. $12.00.

TRUEBLOOD, Elton. *Lord's Prayers*. 1965. Harper Row. 1st. 128p. VG/dj. V3. $12.00.

TRUEBLOOD, Elton. *Signs of Hope in a Century of Despair*. 1950. Harper. 324p. dj. V3. $12.00.

TRUEBLOOD, Elton. *Validity of the Christian Mission*. 1972. Harper Row. 1st. 113p. VG/dj. V3. $12.00.

TRUEBLOOD, Elton. *While it Is Day: An Autobiography*. 1974. Harper Row. sgn. 170p. VG/dj. V3. $17.50.

TRUEBLOOD, Ernest V.; see Faulkner, William.

TRUEMAN, Stuart. *Ghosts*. Pirates & Treasure Trove. 1975. McClelland Stewart. 1st. VG/dj. P3. $15.00.

TRUETT, George. *The Prophet's Mantle*. 1948. Eerdmans. Vol 3. Truett Mem series. 206p. VG. B29. $10.00.

TRUMAN, Margaret. *Murder in Georgetown*. 1986. Arbor. 1st. F/F. B4. $45.00.

TRUMAN, Margaret. *Murder in the White House*. 1980. NY. Arbor House. 1st. author's 1st novel. F/NF. T2. $16.00.

TRUMBALL, Charles G. *Taking Men Alive*. 1915. Assoc. 199p. G. B29. $6.00.

TRUMBO, Dalton. *A Century of the Common Man*. 1943. NY. International Workers Order. 1st. ils Hugo Gellert. 46p. NF/wrps. B2. $30.00.

TRUMBO, Dalton. *Night of the Aurochs*. 1979. Viking. 1st. F/F. A20. $30.00.

TRUMBULL, Clay. *Prayer: Its Nature and Scope*. 1896. Revell. ffep removed. 160p. VG. B29. $12.00.

TRUMBULL, H. Clay. *The Captured Scout of the Army of the James. A Sketch of the Life of Sergeant Henry H. Manning of the Twenty-Fourth Mass. Regiment*. Boston. Nichols and Noyes. 1869. 12mo. 60p. actual albumen photo as ftspc (¾ pose in uniform, standing of Henry Manning). gr cloth. 1sted. ftspc beginnning to loosen at top of gutter. VG.L5. $150.00.

TRUMBULL, Robert. *Nine Who Survived Hiroshima & Nagasaki*. 1965. Dutton. 5th. VG/dj. K3. $25.00.

TRUMP, Donald J. *Art of the Deal*. 1987. Random. 1st. F/dj. W2. $30.00.

TRUMP, Ivana. *For Love Alone*. 1992. Pocket. 1st. F/F. W2. $35.00.

TRUMPS. *American Hoyle/Hoyle's Games*. 1907. NY. 18th. 532p. VG. S1. $15.00.

TRUSS, Lynne. *Making the Cat Laugh: One Woman's Journal*. 1995. London. 1st. sgn. VG/dj. M17. $17.00.

TRUSS, Lynne. *Tennyson's Gift*. 1996. London. 1st. sgn. VG/dj. M17. $17. 50.

TRUSS, Lynne. *Tennyson's Gift*. 1996. London. Hamish Hamilton. 1st. VF/VF. T2. $20.00.

TRUSS, Seldon. *Doctor Was a Dame*. 1953. Crime Club. 1st. VG/dj. P3. $20.00.

TRUSS, Seldon. *Truth About Claire Veryan*. 1957. Crime Club. F/NF. M19. $17. 50.

TRUSSLER, D. J. *Early Commercial Vehicles*. 1968. London. 1st. 10 full-p mc pl. 45p. F. M4. $35.00.

TRYON, R. M. Jr., et al. *The Ferns and Fern Allies of Wisconsin*. 1940. Madison. autographed by Tryon. gr cloth. B26. $22.50.

TRYON, Thomas. *Crowned Heads*. 1976. Knopf. 1st. 8vo. 399p. F/NF. W2. $35.00.

TRYON, Thomas. *Night of the Moonbow*. 1989. Knopf. 1st. F/F. B4. $45.00.

TRYON, Thomas. *Harvest Home*. 1973. Knopf. 1st/3rd prt. 401p. F/dj. W2. $40.00.

TRYON, Thomas. *Harvest Home*. 1973. Knopf. 1st. F/F. H11. $40.00.

TRYON, Thomas. *Harvest Home*. 1973. Knopf. 1st. NF/dj. M2. $30.00.

TRYON, Thomas. *The Night of the Moonbow.* 1989. NY. Knopf. 1st. VF/VF. T2. $8.00.

TRYON, Thomas. *The Other.* 1971. NY. Knopf. 1st. author's 1st novel. F/F. T2. $75.00.

TRYON, Thomas. *Wings of the Morning.* 1990. Franklin Lib. 1st. sgn. full leather. F. Q1. $40.00.

TSCHIRKY, O. *Cook Book by Oscar of the Waldorf.* 1896. 4to. 907p. VG. E6. $95.00.

TSE-TUNG, Mao. *Poems.* 1976. Foreign Language Pr. 1st. F/dj. V1. $25.00.

TSIOLKOVSKY, K. *Will of the Universe: Intellect Unknown.* Mind & Passions. 1992. Memory. 8vo. 30p. VG/wrp. K5. $10.00.

TSUJI, A. *Hornbills: Masters of the Tropical Forests.* 1996. Bangkok. 1st. 154 mc photos. 93p. F. C12. $35.00.

TSUKIYAMA, Gail. *The Samurai's Garden.* (1995). NY. St. Martin. 1st sgn by author. F/F. B3. $35.00.

TSUNA, Masuda. *Kodo Zuroku.* 1983. Norwalk. CT. Burndy Lib. ils. wrp. K3. $25.00.

TU, A. T. *Marine Toxins & Venoms, Handbook, Vol 3.* 1988. NY. Marcel Dekker. $8.00.

TUCHMAN, Barbara. *The Proud Tower: A Portrait of the World Before the War: 1890 – 1914.* 1966. Macmillan. 1st. NF/lightly worn dj. M25. $35.00.

TUCHMAN, Barbara W. *Practicing History: Selected Essays.* 1981. Knopf. 1st. sm 4to. 306p. G/dj. S14. $9.00.

TUCK, Father. *Somebody's Luggage.* nd. London. Raphael Tuck & Sons. Father Tuck's Family Pet series. F. A16. $25.00.

TUCK, Jim. *Pancho Villa & John Reed.* 1984. Tucson. 1st. photo. 252p. dj. F3. $20.00.

TUCK, Lily. *Interviewing Matisse.* 1991. NY. Knopf. 1st. UP. F. D10. $10.00.

TUCKER, Charlotte Maria. *Aloe's Picture Story Book.* 1872. London. Thos Nelson. 1st. 10 full-p ils. G. B27. $300.00.

TUCKER, David M. *Lt. Lee of Beale St.* 1971. Vanderbilt U. VG/dj. B30. $40.00.

TUCKER, E. F. J. *Intruder into Eden.* 1984. Columbia. Camden. M11. $45.00.

TUCKER, G. C. *Taxonomy of Cyperus (Cyperaceae) in Costa Rica & Panama.* 1983. Ann Arbor. 8vo. 85p. stiff wrp. B1. $22.00.

TUCKER, George. *Federal Penal Code in Force Jan. 1, 1910.* 1910. Little, Brn. buckram. M11. $50.00.

TUCKER, George Fox. *Quaker Home.* 1891. Boston. George Reed. 426p. G. V3. $12.00.

TUCKER, Glenn. *High Tide at Gettysburg: Campaign in Pennsylvania.* 1995. Gettysburg. rpt. 462p. VG. S16. $15.00.

TUCKER, Glenn. *Mad Anthony Wayne: Story of Washington's Front-Line General.* 1973. Harrisburg. 1st. F/NF. M4. $40.00.

TUCKER, Glenn. *Zeb Vance: Champion of Personal Freedom.* 1965. Bobbs Merrill. 1st. 564p. VG/torn. S16. $35.00.

TUCKER, James. *Novels of Anthony Powell.* 1976. Columbia U. VG/dj. M17. $25.00.

TUCKER, Kerry. *Cold Feet.* 1992. NY. Harper Collins. 1st. F/F. H11. $25.00.

TUCKER, Kerry. *Death Echo.* 1993. NY. Harper Collins. 1st. F/F. H11. $20.00.

TUCKER, Kerry. *Still Waters.* 1991. NY. Harper Collins. 1st. Inscribed. Jacket Is price clipped. F/F. H11. $45.00.

TUCKER, Louis Leonard. *Clio's Consort: Jeremy Belknap & Founding of MA Hist Soc.* 1990. Boston. ils. VG/dj. M17. $20.00.

TUCKER, Sarah. *Memoirs of Life & Religious Experience.* 1848. Moore Choate. 204p. G. V3. $16.00.

TUCKER, William. *Family Dyer & Scourer...Arts of Dyeing & Cleaning.* 1831. Phil. 2nd. 12mo. woodcut. 123p. cloth/lacks label. M1. $250.00.

TUCKER, Wilson. *Ice & Iron.* 1974. Doubleday. BC. sgn. VG/G. B11. $20.00.

TUCKER, Wilson. *Ice & Iron.* 1974. Doubleday. 1st. NF/dj. M2. $30.00.

TUCKER, Wilson. *Ice & Iron.* 1974. Doubleday. 1st. VG/dj. P3. $25.00.

TUCKER, Wilson. *Procession of the Damned.* 1965. Crime Club. 1st. VG/dj. P3. $25.00.

TUCKERMAN, Edward. *Synopsis of Lichens of New England.* 1848. Cambridge. inscr. 93p. VG. B26. $60.00.

TUCKETT, Christopher. *Nag Hammadi & The Gospel Tradition.* 1986. T&T Clark. 194p. VG/dj. B29. $11.50.

TUCKEY, H.B. *Dwarfed Fruit Trees.* 1964. Macmillan. 8vo. cloth. B1. $50.00.

TUDOR, Tasha. *A Is for Anna Belle.* 1954. Walck. rpt. obl 8vo. VG/G. B17. $65.00.

TUDOR, Tasha. *Advent Calendar from Tasha Tudor.* 1978. NY. 1st. mc ils fld panorama. never opened/F. H3. $100.00.

TUDOR, Tasha. *Alexander the Gander.* (1939). NY. OUP. 4th. 16mo. gilt gr cloth/pict label. dj. R5. $225.00.

TUDOR, Tasha. *All for Love.* 1984. Philomel. 1st. 8vo. F/dj. B17. $65.00.

TUDOR, Tasha. *Amy's Goose.* 1977. Crowell. 2nd. 8vo. VG/dj. B17. $65.00.

TUDOR, Tasha. *Becky's Birthday.* (1960). NY. Viking. 1st. 4to. red lettered yel cloth. mc pict dj. R5. $385.00.

TUDOR, Tasha. *Becky's Birthday.* 1960. Viking. 1st. 4to. xl. VG/dj. M5. $75.00.

TUDOR, Tasha. *Christmas Cat.* 1976. Harper Collins. rpt. sgn. F/dj. B17. $110.00.

TUDOR, Tasha. *Corgiville Fair.* 1971. Crowell. 1st. obl 4to. F/VG. P2. $200.00.

TUDOR, Tasha. *Dolls' Christmas.* 1950. Oxford. 1st. red cloth/wht pl. G. M5. $95.00.

TUDOR, Tasha. *First Delights. A Book About the Five Senses.* 1991. Platt Munk. 8vo. F/dj. B17. $50.00.

TUDOR, Tasha. *First Graces.* 1991. Lutterworth. rpt. 16mo. F/dj. B17. $25.00.

TUDOR, Tasha. *First Poems of Childhood.* 1988. Platt Munk. rpt. 8vo. F/dj. B17. $55.00.

TUDOR, Tasha. *Give Us This Day: The Lord's Prayer.* 1987. Philomel. rpt/lg format. 8vo. F/dj. B17. $25.00.

TUDOR, Tasha. *Lord Is My Shepherd.* 1989. Philomel. rpt of mini ed. less than 16mo. F/dj. B17. $7.00.

TUDOR, Tasha. *Mother Goose.* nd. Random. rpt. sgn. F/dj. B17. $60.00.

TUDOR, Tasha. *Mother Goose.* nd. Walck. rpt. VG/dj. B17. $50.00.

TUDOR, Tasha. *Take Joy! Tasha Tudor Christmas Book.* 1966. World. 1st. obl lg 4to. F/VG. M5. $95.00.

TUDOR, Tasha. *Take Joy! The Tasha Tudor Christmas Book.* 1966. NY. Philomel Books. VG in dj. A16. $40.00.

TUDOR, Tasha. *Tasha Tudor Book of Fairy Tales.* 1961. Platt Munk. early ed. G+. B17. $45.00.

TUDOR, Tasha. *Tasha Tudor Book of Fairy Tales.* 1961. Platt Munk. 1st. sgn. 4to. pict brd. R5. $200.00.

TUDOR, Tasha. *Tasha Tudor Sketchbook.* 1989. Jenny Wren. 1st. obl 4to. VG. B17. $85.00.

TUDOR, Tasha. *Tasha Tudor's Old-Fashioned Gifts.* 1979. McKay. 1st. 8vo. VG+/dj. M5. $65.00.

TUDOR, Tasha. *Thisly B.* 1949. NY. Oxford. 1st. 12mo. red-brn cloth/label/gilt spine. R5. $100.00.

TUDOR, Tasha. *Treasury of First Books.* 1990s. Lutterworth. 4 vol. VG/box. B17. $65.00.

TUDOR, Tasha. *Twenty-Third Psalm.* 1965. Achille J St Onge. mini ed/less than 16mo. aeg. gr polished calf. F/dj. B17. $50.00.

TUDOR, Tasha. *White Goose.* 1943. Oxford. 1st. 12 full-p pl. 12mo. gray cloth. dj. R5. $450.00.

TUDOR, Tasha. *White Goose.* 1943. Oxford. 2nd. VG. M5. $125.00.

TUDOR, Tasha. *Wings from the Wind, An Anthology of Poems.* (1964). Phil. Lippincott. 1st. 4to.

TUDOR, Williams. *Letters on the Eastern States.* 1821. Boston. Wells Lily. 2nd/corrected/revised. inscr. 423p. O1. $200.00.

TUDORAN, Radu. *Schicksak Aus Deiner Hand.* 1968. Germany. Fackelverlag. sm 8vo. 563p. NF. W2. $30.00.

TUER, Andrew W. *History of the Horn Book.* 1979. NY. Arno. rpt. 8vo. cloth. F/NF. O10. $30.00.

TUFTS, Jay Franklin. *Tufts Family History: A True Account & History, 1617 – 1963.* 1963. Cleveland. 280p. G. S5. $65.00.

TUKE, Samuel. *Plea on Behalf of George Fox & the Early Friends.* 1837. London. Darton Harvey. 41p. V3. $20.00.

TUKEY, H. *Pear & Its Culture.* 1928. 1st. photos. xl. VG. E6. $20.00.

TULLETT, Tom. *Strictly Murder: Famous Cases of Scotland Yard's Murder Squad.* 1980. NY. SMP. 1st. F/F. H11. $30.00.

TULLIUS, F.P. *Out of the Death Bag in West Hollywood.* 1971. Macmillan. 1st. F/F. B4. $100.00.

TUNIS, Edwin. *Colonial Living.* 1957. World. dj. A19. $40.00.

TUNIS, John R. *Measure of Independence.* 1964. Atheneum. 1st. VG/dj. P8. $65.00.

TUNIS, John R. *Rookie of the Year.* 1944. Harcourt Brace. 1st. VG/dj. P8. $50.00.

TUNIS, John R. *Schoolboy Johnson.* 1958. Morrow. 1st. G/dj. P8. $30.00.

TUNIS, John R. *This Writing Game: Selections.* 1941. NY. Barnes. 1st. NF/fair. B4. $125.00.

TUNIS, John R. *Two by Tunis.* 1972. Morrow. 1st. G. P8. $20.00.

TUNIS, John R. *World Series.* 1945. Harcourt Brace. 1st. VG/dj. P8. $45.00.

TUPLING, G. H. *South Lancashire in the Reign of Edward II.* 1949. Manchester. gilt bl cloth. M11. $65.00.

TUPPER, Frieda B. *Down in Bull Creek.* 1975. Webster. SD. sgn. A19. $20.00.

TURBEVILLE, Deborah. *Wallflower.* 1978. NY. Congreve. photos. 128p. brd. clip dj. D11. $75.00.

TURBIN, Carole. *Working Women of Collar City: Gender, Class & Community.* 1992. IL U. 1st. F/F. V4. $20.00.

TUREK, Leslie. *Noreascon Proceedings Sept. 3 – 6, 1971.* 1976. NESFA. 1st. F/F. P3. $75.00.

TURK, H.C. *Black Body.* 1989. Villard. 1st. F/dj. M2. $20.00.

TURKLE, Brinton. *Deep in the Forest.* 1976. Dutton. 1st. ils. unp. xl. VG. T5. $25.00.

TURKUS, Burton. *Murder Inc.* 1951. Farrar Straus. 1st. VG/dj. B5. $35.00.

TURLEY, R. E. *Victims: LDS Church & Mark Hoffmann Case.* 1992. IL U. 1st. 519p. F/dj. M4. $20.00.

TURNBAUGH, D.B. *Duncan Grant & the Bloomsbury Group: Illustrated Biography.* 1987. ils. VG/VG. M17. $17.50.

TURNBULL, Archibald Douglas. *Commodore David Porter 1780 – 1843.* 1929. NY. The Century Co. 1st printing. emb bl cloth w/ gilt titles. 8vo. 16 ils. 326p. VG in worn dj. P4. $75.00.

TURNBULL, Archibald Douglas. *Commodore David Porter 1780 – 1843.* 1929. NY. Century. 1st. 8vo. 326p. VG/worn. P4. $75.00.

TURNBULL, Colin M. *Human Cycle, The.* 1983. NY. S&S. BCE. VG/VG. A28. $10.95.

TURNBULL, Colin M. *Mountain People.* 1972. S&S. 1st. ils/maps. 309p. VG/dj. W1. $16.00.

TURNBULL, Colin M. *Wayward Servants: Two Worlds of African Pygmies.* 1976 (1965). Greenwood. rpt. 8vo. 390p. VG. W1. $25.00.

TURNBULL, H.W. *Correspondence of Isaac Newton, Vol. 1, 1661 – 1675.* 1959. Cambridge. fld pl. F/dj. K3. $45.00.

TURNBULL, Ralph. *A Minister's Obstacles.* 1966. Revell. 192p. VG/VG. B29. $4.50.

TURNBULL, Ralph. *Baker's Dictionary of Practical Theology.* 1969. Baker. 469p. VG/VG. B29. $14.00.

TURNBULL, Robert J. *Bibliography of South Carolina 1563 – 1950.* 1999. Mansfield Centre. Conn. Martino Fine books. reprint of rare 5 vol set pub by Univ of Va 1956. 60 sets printed. orig cloth. AN. M8. $225.00.

TURNER, A. E. *Earps Talk.* 1980. College Station, TX. Creative. 1st. sgn. ils/index. $0.00.

TURNER, A. Logan. *Joseph, Baron Lister, Centenary Vol. 1827 – 1927.* 1927. Edinburgh/London. Oliver Boyd. 1st. ils. $182.00.

TURNER, A. Richard. *Vision of Landscape in Renaissance Italy.* 1966. Princeton. 219p. dj. A10. $40.00.

TURNER, Adrian. *Making of David Lean's Lawrence of Arabia.* 1994. Eng. Dragon World Ltd. 1st. 183p. F/clip. M7. $85.00.

TURNER, Ann. *Dakota Dugout.* 1985. Macmillan. 1st. ils Ronald Himler. brd/cloth spine. F/NF. T5. $30.00.

TURNER, Ann. *Grass Songs.* (1993). San Diego. HBJ. 1st. ils & sgn by Barry Moser. NF. very minor wear/F. B3. $45.00.

TURNER, Ann. *Heron Street.* 1989. Harper Row. 1st. inscr. sm 4to. unp. NF/VG+. C14. $20.00.

TURNER. *Boys Will be Boys: Story of Sweeney Todd, Deadwood Dick*. 1957. London. Michael Joseph. New ed. ils. 277p. VG/VG. A4. $65.00.

TURNER, C. C. *Old Flying Days*. 1927. London. photos. 347p. G-. B18. $250.00.

TURNER, Dennis C. *Vampire Bat: A Field Study in Behavior & Ecology*. 1975. Johns Hopkins. 148p. VG/torn. S5. $20.00.

TURNER, Edward. *Elements of Chemistry Including Recent Discoveries*. 1835. DeSilver Thomas. 5th Am from 5th London. 682p. ES. full leather. VG. H1. $185.00.

TURNER, Ethel Duffy. *Revolution in Baja, California: Richardo Flores Magon*. 1981. Detroit, MI. Blaine Ethridge. 1st. NF. O4. $20.00.

TURNER, Frederick. *Double Shadow*. 1978. Berkeley. 1st. NF/dj. S18. $30.00.

TURNER, Frederick. *Remembering Song*. 1982. NY. Viking. 1st. F/F. tiny scrape on rear panel. B2. $25.00.

TURNER, Frederick Jackson. *Frontier in American History*. 1921. Holt. G. A19. $65.00.

TURNER, Frederick Jackson. *Frontier in American History*. 1937. Holt. A19. $35.00.

TURNER, George. *Beloved Son*. 1978. London. Faber. 1st. F/dj. M25. $25.00.

TURNER, George. *Samoa: A Hundred Years Ago & Long Before*. 1884. London. 8vo. 7 full-p ils/3 maps. 395p. red cloth.

TURNER, George. *Yesterday's Men*. 1983. London. Faber. 1st. F/dj. M25. $25.00.

TURNER, J.V. *Below the Clock*. 1936. Appleton Century. 1st Am. VG/dj. M15. $35.00.

TURNER, Joseph. *True Israel*. 1850. Hartford. 8vo. prt yel wrp. R12. $140.00.

TURNER, L. W. *Ninth State: New Hampshire's Formative Years*. 1983. NC U. 1st. 21 maps. 479p. F/dj. M4. $30.00.

TURNER, L. M. *Ethnology of the Ungave District, Hudson Bay Territory*. 1984. BAE 11th Annual Report. new cloth. facsimile title p. F. M4. $25.00.

TURNER, Lana. *Lady, The Legend, the Truth: Lana*. 1982. Dutton. 1st. ils. 311p. VG/clip. $25.00.

TURNER, Mary M. *Forgotten Leading Ladies of the American Theatre*. 1990. McFarland. 170p. VG. C5. $12.50.

TURNER, Nancy Byrd. *Zodiac Town*. 1021. Atlantic Monthly. 1st. ils Winifred Bromhall. gilt bl cloth. VG+/dj. M20. $65.00.

TURNER, Nancy E. *These Is My Words*. 1998. NY. Harper Collins. 1st. VF/pict brds. no dj as issued. T2. $30.00.

TURNER, Ralph V. *English Judiciary in the Age of Glanvill & Bracton*. 1985. Cambridge. M11. $65.00.

TURNER, Robert. *Gunsmoke*. 1958. Whitman. TVTI. VG. P3. $20.00.

TURNER, Tina. *I, Tina*. 1986. Viking. 1st. F/NF. A20. $15.00.

TURNER, W. J. *Duchess of Popocatapetl*. 1939. London. 1st. Vg/dj. M2. $35.00.

TURNER, William. *Fruits & Vegetables Under Glass*. 1912. DeLaMare. tall 8vo. 266p. VG. A22. $35.00.

TURNILL, Reginald. *Observer's Spaceflight Directory*. 1978. London. Warne. 1st. 384p. VG/dj. K5. $50.00.

TUROLLA, Pina. *Beyond the Andes*. 1980. Harper. 1st. 364p. F3. $15.00.

TUROW, Scott. *Burden of Proof*. 1990. FSG. 1st. NF/dj. A23. $32.00.

TUROW, Scott. *Burden of Proof*. 1990. Franklin Lib. 1st. sgn. full leather. F. Q1. $75.00.

TUROW, Scott. *Laws of Our Fathers*. 1996. FSG. 1st trade. F/dj. W2. $45.00.

TUROW, Scott. *One l*. 1988. NY. F S G. reissue. 1st ed thus. author's 1st book. VF/VF. T2. $15.00.

TUROW, Scott. *Pleading Guilty*. 1993. F S g. 1st. F/F. G8. $10.00.

TUROW, Scott. *Presumed Innocent*. 1987. FSG. 1st. NF/F. H11. $40.00.

TUROW, Scott. *Presumed Innocent*. 1987. Farrar Straus Giroux. 1st. G+. s19. $30.00.

TUROW, Scott. *The Laws of Our Fathers*. 1996. Farrar Straus Giroux. 1st trade ed. F/chip dj. s19. $40.00.

TURTLEDOVE, Harry. *Agent of Byzantium*. 1987. 1st. F/F. M19. $35.00.

TURTLEDOVE, Harry. *Different Flesh*. 1988. Congdon Weed. 1st. VG/dj. P3. $17.00.

TUSKA, Jon. *Films of Mae West*. 1973. Citadel. 1st. VG/dj. P3. $20.00.

TUTE, George. *Fleece Press Guide to Art of Wood Engraving*. 1986. Fleece. mini. 1/40 (255 total). w/extra prt. full leather/case. B24. $275.00.

TUTE, Warren. *Tarnham Connection*. 1971. Dent. 1st. NF/dj. P3. $22.00.

TUTEIN, Peter. *The Sealers Translated From The Danish*. NY. G. P. Putnam's Sons. 1938. 8vo. 247p. bl cloth. 1st Am ed. Lacking dj. minor dust soiling. dedication page torn. G. L5. $10.00.

TUTHILL, Franklin. *The History of California*. 1866. San Francisco. H.H. Bancroft & Co. xvi. 658p. orig brown cloth. bit soiled and faded. minor fraying of spine. K1. $100.00.

TUTTLE, Dennis. *Juan Gonzales*. 1995. Chelsea. 1st. sgn Gonzales. F/sans. P8. $85.00.

TUTTLE, Lisa. *Gabriel*. 1987. Severn. 1st. F/dj. P3. $25.00.

TUTTLE, Margaretta. *Feet of Clay*. 1923. Grosset Dunlap. photoplay ed. 368p. VG/dj. M20. $20.00.

TUTTLE, S.B. *Miniature Motors for Space Instruments*. 1966. Pasadena. sbdg. K5. $20.00.

TUTTLE, William M. *Race Riot: Chicago in Red Summer of 1919*. 1970. Bantam. VG/VG. V4. $17.50.

TUTUOLA, Amos. *Palm-Wine Drunkard*. 1953. NY. Grove. 1st. NF/dj. Q1. $100.00.

TWAIN, Mark. *A Double Barrelled Detective Story*. 1902. NY. Harper & Brothers. 1st. spine slightly darkened and small stain on back cover. red cloth-covered boards. F/. M15. $250.00.

TWAIN, Mark. *Adventures of Tom Sawyer*. 1917. NY. Harper & Bros. G. A16. $35.00.

TWAIN, Mark. *The Adventures of Huckleberry Finn*. 1927. NY. Harper & Bros. 1st. orig pub in 1896; this ed ils by Worth Brehm. blk cloth w/ pict label on front panel. 421p. VG+. A24. $30.00.

TWAIN, Mark. *The Adventures of Huckleberry Finn. Illustrated by Norman Rockwell*. (1940). NY. The Heritage Press. sgn by Rockwell. 8 mtd color plates. 346p. orange cloth. K1. $150.00.

TWAIN, Mark; see Clemens, Samuel L.

TWEED, Thomas F. *Destiny's Man*. 1935. Farrar. 1st. VG/dj. M2. $30.00.

TWENHOFEL, W. H. *Principles of Sedimentation*. 1950. McGraw Hill. 2nd. 673p. cloth. VG. D8. $30.00.

TWICHELL, Heath. *Northwest Epic: Buildings of the Alaska Highway*. 1992. NY. St. Martin. 8vo. 368p. map ep. half cloth. P4. $35.00.

TWISSELMAN, Ernest C. *A Flora of Kern County, California*. 1967. San Francisco. glossy paper stock. sgn by author & one photographer. B26. $47.50.

TWOMBLY, Wells. *200 Years of Sports in America*. 1976. McGraw Hill. later prt. ils. VG+/dj. P8. $30.00.

TWOMBLY, Wells. *Blanda: Alive and Kicking*. 1972. NY. Nash. 1st. NF/dj clip. R16. $45.00.

TYCKARE, Tre. *Lore of Ships*. 1963. NY. HRW. ils. 276p. bl cloth. VG/dj. P4. $95.00.

TYLER, Ann. *Celestial Navigations*. 1974. Knopf. 1st. VG/NF. S18. $75.00.

TYLER, Anne. *A Patchwork Planet*. 1998. Knopf. UP ARC. F/WRP. M25. $100.00.

TYLER, Anne. *Breathing Lessons*. 1988. Franklin. 1st. sgn. aeg. emb gr leather. F/swrp. D10. $185.00.

TYLER, Anne. *Breathing Lessons*. 1988. NY. Knopf. 1st. F/F. H11. $30.00.

TYLER, Anne. *Celestial Navigation*. 1974. NY. Knopf. 1st. F/F. D10. $225.00.

TYLER, Anne. *Celestial Navigation*. 1974. Knopf. 1st. F/NF. M25. $150.00.

TYLER, Anne. *Dinner at the Homesick Restaurant*. 1982. NY. Knopf. 1st. crease in spine. very slightly soiled. NF/F. H11. $75.00.

TYLER, Anne. *Dinner at the Homesick Restaurant*. 1982. NY. Knopf. 1st. F/F. D10. $60.00.

TYLER, Anne. *Dinner at the Homesick Restaurant*. 1982. Knopf. ARC. sgn author's 9th novel. F/F. D10. $125.00.

TYLER, Anne. *Dinner at the Homesick Restaurant*. 1982. Knopf. 1st. F/F. T11. $80.00.

TYLER, Anne. *Dinner at the Homesick Restaurant*. 1982. Knopf. 1st. NF/F. H11. $75.00.

TYLER, Anne. *Earthly Possessions*. 1977. Knopf. 1st. NF/NF. T11. $125.00.

TYLER, Anne. *Earthly Possessions*. 1977. Knopf. 1st. sgn. NF/NF. R14. $225.00.

TYLER, Anne. *If Morning Ever Comes*. 1964. Knopf. 1st. 1/4000. author's 1st novel. F/F. L3. $1.850.00.

TYLER, Anne. *Ladder of Years*. 1995. Knopf. 1st trade. sgn. F/dj. R14. $100.00.

TYLER, Anne. *Ladder of Years*. 1995. Knopf. ARC. F in decor wrp. M25. $45.00.

TYLER, Anne. *Ladder of Years*. 1995. NY. Knopf. 1st. F/VF. H11. $20.00.

TYLER, Anne. *Ladder of Years*. 1995. NY. Knopf. 1st. ARC. NF. D10. $10.00.

TYLER, Anne. *Ladder of Years*. 1995. NY. Knopf. 1st. NF/NF. R16. $40.00.

TYLER, Anne. *Ladder of Years*. (1995). NY. Knopf. ARC. pict wrp. F. B3. $40.00.

TYLER, Anne. *Morgan's Passing*. Knopf. 1st. F/clip. M19. $45.00.

TYLER, Anne. *Morgan's Passing*. 1980. Knopf. 1st. F/rubbed dj. M25. $25.00.

TYLER, Anne. *Morgan's Passing*. 1980. NY. Knopf. 1st. F/F. D10. $85.00.

TYLER, Anne. *Morgan's Passing*. 1980. Knopf. 1st. F/clip. M25. $60.00.

TYLER, Anne. *Saint Maybe*. 1991. NY. Knopf. 1st. F/F. H11. $30.00.

TYLER, Anne. *Searching for Caleb*. 1976. Knopf. 1st. F/F. B4. $450.00.

TYLER, Anne. *Slipping-Down Life*. 1983. Severn House. 1st. F/F. T11. $125.00.

TYLER, Anne. *The Accidental Tourist*. (1985). NY. Knopf. 1st. F/NF. very minor edgewear. B3. $20.00.

TYLER, Anne. *The Accidental Tourist*. (1985). NY. Knopf. 1st. F/VG. lt edgewear. B3. $20.00.

TYLER, Anne. *The Accidental Tourist*. 1985. NY. Knopf. 1st. winner of Natl Book Critics Circle award. F/F. D10. $50.00.

TYLER, Anne. *Tin Can Tree*. 1966. Macmillan. 1st Eng. F/F. B4. $750.00.

TYLER, Anne. *Tumble Tower*. 1993. Orchard Books. 1st. unp. F/dj. C14. $25.00.

TYLER, Anne. *Tumble Tower*. 1993. NY. Orchard Books. 1st. ils by author's daughter, Mitra Modarressi. author's 1st children's book. F/F. D10. $35.00.

TYLER, Anne. *Visit with Eudora Welty*. 1980. Chicago. Pressworks. 1st. 1/100. F/wrp. Q1. $250.00.

TYLER, David Budlong. *Bay & River Delaware, A Pictorial History*. 1955. Cornell Maritime. 1st. 344p. F/G. H1. $30.00.

TYLER, David Budlong. *Steam Conquers the Atlantic*. 1939. NY. Appleton Century. 1st. ils. 425p. VG/dj. K3. $35.00.

TYLER, Gus. *Scarcity: A Critique of the American Economy*. 1976. NY. Times. 1st. sgn. VG/dj. S13. $12.00.

TYLER, J. E. A. *New Tolkien Companion*. 1979. St. Martin. 1st. F/dj. M2. $15.00.

TYLER, M. C. *Literary History of the American Revolution*. 1957 (1897). NY. 2 vol. F/dj. M4. $70.00.

TYLER, M. L. *Anne Boleyn, A Tragedy in Six Acts*. 1884. London. Kegan Paul. 12mo. 102p. gilt gr cloth. VG. $10.00.

TYLER, Martin. *Olympics 1984*. 1984. Phillips. 1st. ils. F/VG+. P8. $10.00.

TYLER, Parker. *Classics of the Foreign Film*. 1962. Citadel. 253p. VG. C5. $15.00.

TYLER, Parker. *Three Faces of the Film*. 1960. NY. Yoseloff. 150p. dj. A17. $15.00.

TYLER, Ron. *Alfred Jacob Miller: Artist on the Oregon Trail*. 1982. Ft. Worth, TX. Amon Carter Mus. 1st. 4to. 480p. F/F. $10.00.

TYLER, Sandra. *After Lydia*. 1995. NY. Harcourt Brace. 1st. UP. F. D10. $10.00.

TYMN, Marshall B. *Year's Scholarship in Science Fiction: 1972 – 1975*. 1979. Kent State. VG. P3. $15.00.

TYNAN, Kathleen. *Agatha*. 1978. Ballantine. 1st. VG/dj. P3. $18.00.

TYRE, Peg. *In the Midnight Hour*. 1995. NY. Crown. 1st. F/F. H11. $20.00.

TYRE, Peg. *Strangers in the Night*. 1994. Crown. 1st. NF/NF. G8. $12.50.

TYREE, M. *Housekeeping in Old Virginia*. (1879). rpt. VG. E6. $20.00.

TYRRELL, J.W. *Across the Sub-Arctics of Canada.* (1908). Toronto. Brigs. 3rd revised/enlarged. photos. 280p. cloth. VG. $12.00.

TYSON, Ian. *Ian Tyson: I Never Sold My Saddle.* 1994. Gibbs Smith. dj. A19. $23.00.

TYSON, Martha E. *Bannecker. The African-American Astronomer.* 1884. Phil. Friends Book Assn. 1st. 12mo. 72p. cloth. $0.00.

TYSON, W. A. *Revival.* 1925. Cokesbury. 287p. VG. B29. $8.00.

TYSSOT DE PATOT, Simon. *Voyages Et Avantures De Jacques Masse.* 1710. Bordeaux. L'Aveugle. 8vo. calf. R12. $600.00.

— U —

UCCELLO, Linda. *Death of a Renaissance Man.* 1986. St. Martin. 1st. NF/dj. P3. $18.00.

UDEALL, D. H. *Practice of Veterinary Medicine.* 1954. Ithaca. self pub. VG. O3. $25.00.

UDY, M. J. *Chromium Vol I: Chemistry of Chromium & Its Compounds.* 1956. Reinhold. 433p. cloth. VG. D8. $30.00.

UEBERROTH, Peter. *Made in America.* 1985. Morrow. 1st. NF/VG. W2. $25.00.

UEMATSU & WALKER. *Manual of Echoencephalography.* 1971. Baltimore. 1st. 149p. A13. $125.00.

UGARTE, Michael. *Shifting Ground: Spanish Civil War Exile Literature.* 1989. Duke. 1st. AN/dj. V4. $15.00.

UHNAK, Dorothy. *False Witness.* 1981. S&S. 1st. VG/dj. P3. $10.00.

ULANOV, Ann Belford. *Feminine in Jungian Psychology & Christian Theology.* 1971. Northwestern. 2. 8vo. 347p. cream cloth. F. H1. $25.00.

ULANOV, Barry. *A Handbook of Jazz.* 1957. NY. Viking. ARC w/slip. F. lightly soiled/lightly sunned. barely worn dj. B2. $35.00.

ULANOV, Barry. *Incredible Crosby.* 1948. NY. 1st. 336p. VG/dj. B5. $35.00.

ULANOV, Barry A. *A Handbook of Jazz.* 1957. NY. Viking. 1st. F in NF dj. B2. $30.00.

ULLMAN, James Michael. *Venus Trap.* 1966. S&S. 1st. VG/VG. G8. $12.50.

ULLMANN, Alex. *Afghanistan.* 1991. Ticknor. 1st. author's 1st book. F/F. H11. $20.00.

ULLMANN, Walter. *Medieval Idea of Law as Represented by Lucas de Penna.* 1969. (1946). NY. Barnes Noble. facsimile. M11. $85.00.

ULLOM. *Folklore of the North American Indians.* 1969. ils. 136p. F. A4. $55.00.

ULLYETT, Kennth. *British Clocks & Clockmakers.* 1987. London. Bracken. 8vo. 8 mc pl/24 b&w ils. 48p. NF. K3. $10.00.

ULPH, Owen. *Leather Throne.* 1984. Dream Garden. 1st. sgn. F/F. A18. $50.00.

ULRICH, Paul. *Great Mysteries of Vanished Civilizations.* nd. Pleasant Valley Pr. VG. P3. $25.00.

ULRICK, Peter. *Brief Sketch of Real Lancasterian System of Education.* (1818). Baltimore. prt for Author. 1st. 8vo. 24p. M1. $225.00.

UMLAND & UMLAND. *Use of Arthurian Legend in Hollywood Film.* 1996. Greenwood. F/sans. P3. $55.00.

UNDERBRINK, R. L. *Destination Corregidor.* 1971. MD. ils. 240p. VG/VG. S16. $23.50.

UNDERHILL. J. *Mineral Land Surveying.* 1922. John Wiley. 3rd. 237p. G. D8. $25.00.

UNDERHILL, Harold A. *Jamaica White: Story of the Witch of Rose Hall.* 1968. London. WH Allen. 1st. 256p. NF/NF. B4. $50.00.

UNDERHILL, Harold A. *Masting & Rigging: Clipper Ship & Ocean Carrier.* 1976. Glasgow. Brn. Son & Ferguson. rpt. 300p. gr cloth. NF. P4. $55.00.

UNDERWOOD, John. *Spoiled Sport.* 1984. Little, Brn. 1st. 287p. NF/NF. W2. $20.00.

UNDERWOOD, Kathleen. *Town Building on the Colorado Front.* 1987R. Albuquerque. photos. dj. A19. $30.00.

UNDERWOOD, L. H. *Fifteen Years Among the Top-Knots; or, Life in Korea.* 1904. NY. Am Tract Soc. 1st. 271p. VG. W3. $65.00.

UNDERWOOD, Michael. *A Dangerous Business.* 1991. NY. St. Martin. 1st Am ed. VF/VF. T2. $12.00.

UNDERWOOD, Michael. *Clear Case of Suicide.* 1980. St. Martin. 1st. 190p. red brd. AN/dj. H1. $18.00.

UNDERWOOD, Michael. *Death in Camera.* 1984. NY. St. Martin. 1st Am ed. F/F. T2. $12.00.

UNDERWOOD, Michael. *Double Jeopardy.* 1981. NY. St. Martin. 1st Am ed. VF/F. T2. $12.00.

UNDERWOOD, Michael. *Dual Enigma.* 1988. NY. SMP. 1st. Jacket has minor wear at spine ends. F/F. H11. $15.00.

UNDERWOOD, Michael. *Goddess of Death.* 1982. St. Martin. 1st. VG/dj. P3. $18.00.

UNDERWOOD, Michael. *The Injudicious Judge.* 1987. NY. St. Martin. 1st Am ed. F/F. T2. $12.00.

UNDERWOOD, Peter. *Haunted London.* 1974. Harrap. 2. VG. P3. $15.00.

UNDERWOOD, Peter. *Vampire's Bedside Companion.* 1975. London. 1st. VG/dj. M2. $50.00.

UNDERWOOD, R. S. *Jaunts into Space.* 1935. Boston. Christopher Pub. 8vo. 79p. VG/dj. K5. $20.00.

UNDERWOOD, Tim. *Bare Bones.* 1988. McGraw Hill. 1st. F/dj. P3. $18.00.

UNDSET, Sigrid. *Catherine of Sienna.* 1954. Sheed Ward. 1st. F/VG. M19. $35.00.

UNGER, Douglas. *El Yanqui.* (1986). NY. Harper & Row. 1st. F/F. B3. $15.00.

UNGER, Douglas. *El Yanqui.* 1986. Harper Row. 1st. F/F. A20. $30.00.

UNGER, Douglas. *Leaving the Land.* 1984. Harper Row. 1st. F/F. A20. $35.00.

UNGERER, Tomi. *Hat.* nd (1970). Parents' Magazine. possible 1st. VG+/sans. C14. $10.00.

UNGERER, Tomi. *Mellop's Go Flying.* 1957. Harper. presumed 1st. ils. obl 4to. pict brd. VG+. M5. $40.00.

UNGERER, Tomi. *Orlando the Brave Vulture.* 1966. Harper Row. probable 1st. 4to. 32p. VG/G+. P2. $35.00.

UNGERER, Tomi. *Slow Agony.* 1983. Zurich. Diogenes. Sm Folio. F/F. C8. $75.00.

UNITAS, Johnny. *Improving Health & Performance in the Athlete.* 1979. Prentice Hall. 1st. F/VG. P8. $12.50.

UNITAS, Johnny. *Pro Quarterback: My Own Story.* 1965. S&S. 1st. photos. VG+/G. P8. $30.00.

UNITED STATES EMBASSY. *El Cookbook By the Embassy Women's Group.* np. 1971. Eng/Spanish text. 276p. sbdg. B10. $15.00.

UNSWORTH, Barry. *Mooncranker's Gift.* 1974. Boston. Houghton Mifflin. 1st. F/NF. M23. $45.00.

UNSWORTH, Barry. *Mooncranker's Gift.* 1974. Houghton Mifflin. 1st Am. F/NF. M23. $45.00.

UNSWORTH, Barry. *Sacred Hunger.* 1992. NY. Doubleday. 1st. winner of the Booker Prize. F/F. M23. $40.00.

UNSWORTH, Barry. *The Hide.* 1996. NY. Norton. 1st. F/F. M23. $25.00.

UNTERBRINK, Mary. *Jazz Women at the Keyboard.* 1983. Jefferson, McFarland. 1st. VG+/wrp. B2. $60.00.

UNTERMEYER, Louis. *Tales from the Ballet.* 1967. NY. Golden Press. 1st ed. VG. A16. $17.50.

UNTERMEYER, Louis. *This Singing World. A Collection of Modern Poetry for Young People.* 1926. NY. HBW. ils by Decie Merwin. sm 8vo. blk cloth w/yellow lettering & ils. b/w ils throughout. 375p. VG. D6. $10.00.

UNWIN, Charles W. J. *Gladioli & Dahlias.* 1951. (1949). London. photos. 125p. dj. B26. $14.00.

UPCHURCH, Boyd. *Slave Stealer.* 1968. Weybright Talley. 1st. VG/dj. P3. $20.00.

UPDIKE, John. *Assorted Prose.* (1965). NY. Knopf. 1st. F/VG. soiling. edgewear & sm closed tears. B3. $60.00.

UPDIKE, John. *Assorted Prose.* 1965. Knopf. 1st. sgn. F/NF. B4. $250.00.

UPDIKE, John. *Bech Is Back.* 1982. NY. Knopf. 1st. bottom corners are lightly bumped. F/F. H11. $25.00.

UPDIKE, John. *Bech Is Back.* 1982. Knopf. 1st. NF/VG. B35. $32.00.

UPDIKE, John. *Bech Is Back.* 1982. Knopf. 1st. VG/dj. P3. $20.00.

UPDIKE, John. *Bech Is Back.* 1982. Knopf. 1st. 1/500. sgn. blk cloth. F/dj/case. B24. $150.00.

UPDIKE, John. *Bottom's Dream.* 1969. Knopf. 1st. oblong 4to. ils Warren Chappell. F/F. B4. $200.00.

UPDIKE, John. *Brazil.* 1994. NY. Knopf. 1st. VF/VF. H11. $35.00.

UPDIKE, John. *Carpentered Hen & Other Tame Creatures.* 1958. Harper. 1st. author's 1st book. F/dj. from $750 to $800.00.

UPDIKE, John. *Coup.* 1978. Knopf. 1st. F/F. H11. $45.00.

UPDIKE, John. *Facing Nature.* 1985. NY. Knopf. 1st. VF/VF. H11. $35.00.

UPDIKE, John. *Getting Older.* 1986. Helsinki. Eurographica. 1st. 1/350. sgn. F/stiff wrp/dj. B4. $250.00.

UPDIKE, John. *Hugging the Stone.* 1983. NY. Knopf. 1st. F/dj. Q1. $75.00.

UPDIKE, John. *Magic Flute.* (1962). Knopf. ils Warren Chappell. unp. VG. T5. $18.00.

UPDIKE, John. *Marry Me.* 1976. Knopf. 1st. F/dj. Q1. $40.00.

UPDIKE, John. *Midpoint & Other Poems.* 1969. Knopf. 1st. F/F. B2. $35.00.

UPDIKE, John. *Music School.* 1966. Knopf. 1st/2nd state. F/VG. M19. $100.00.

UPDIKE, John. *Picked-Up Pieces.* 1975. Knopf. 1st. inscr/dtd 1996. VG/VG. A23. $46.00.

UPDIKE, John. *Problems & Other Stories.* 1979. Knopf. 1st. F/F. B35. $30.00.

UPDIKE, John. *Rabbit at Rest.* 1990. Knopf. 1st. F/dj. H11/Q1. $35.00.

UPDIKE, John. *Rabbit Is Rich.* 1981. Knopf. 1st. F/F. B35. $35.00.

UPDIKE, John. *Rabbit Redux.* 1971. NY. Knopf. 1st. F/NF few tiny tears. A24. $30.00.

UPDIKE, John. *Rabbit Redux.* 1971. Knopf. 1st. F/dj. H11/Q1. $40.00.

UPDIKE, John. *Rabbit Run.* 1960. Knopf. true 1st (top edge gr). F/NF. A24. $325.00.

UPDIKE, John. *Rabbit Run.* 1977. Franklin Lib. sgn. F. M19. $75.00.

UPDIKE, John. *Recent Poems 1986 – 1990.* 1990. Helsinki. Eurographica. 1st. 1/350. sgn. F/stiff wrp/dj. B4. $200.00.

UPDIKE, John. *S.* 1988. NY. Knopf. 1st. VG+/VG+. R16. $25.00.

UPDIKE, John. *The Poorhouse Fair.* 1959. (1958). Knopf. 1st. thin 8vo. 185p. quarter orange cloth. F/1st state. H1. $90.00.

UPDIKE, John. *The Poorhouse Fair.* 1959. Knopf. 6th prt. F/chip dj. S19. $35.00.

UPDIKE, John. *Trust Me.* 1987. Knopf. 1st. F/dj. Q1. $35.00.

UPDIKE, John. *Twelve Terrors of Christmas.* 1994. Gotham Book Mart. 1st trade. sgn. ils/sgn Gorey. F/gr-gray wrp. A11. $75.00.

UPDIKE, John. *Witches of Eastwick.* 1984. Franklin Lib. 1st/ltd. sgn. ils Michael Deas. aeg. full leather. F. Q1. $75.00.

UPDIKE, John. *Witches of Eastwick.* 1984. Knopf. 1st. VG/dj. P3. $20.00.

UPDIKE, John & Kenison, Katrina. *The Best American Short Stories of the Century.* 1999. Boston. Houghton Mifflin. 1st. F/F. M23. $35.00.

UPDYKE, James; see Burnett, W. R.

UPFIELD, Arthur W. *Bachelors of Broken Hill.* 1969. Heinemann. VG/dj. P3. $25.00.

UPFIELD, Arthur W. *Battling Prophet.* 1956. London. Heinemann. 1st. sgn. VG/clip. Q1. $200.00.

UPFIELD, Arthur W. *Bony and the Black Virgin.* 1959. London. Heinemann. 1st. telephone # in ink on front flyleaf. photo of author on back panel of dj. NF/lightly worn dj. M25. $100.00.

UPFIELD, Arthur W. *Bony and the Mouse.* 1959. London. Heinemann. 1st. Angus & Robertson sticker on front pastedown. VG/soiled. chipped dj. M25. $80.00.

UPFIELD, Arthur W. *Bony & the Kelly Gang.* 1961. Heinemann. 1st. Jacket has light wear at the head of the spine. NF/dj. M25. $100.00.

UPFIELD, Arthur W. *Gripped by Drought.* 1990. Dennis McMillan. 1st Am. F/F. M15. $45.00.

UPFIELD, Arthur W. *Sinister Stones.* 1954. Doubleday. 1st Am. F/dj. M25. $75.00.

UPFIELD, Arthur W. *The Devil's Steps.* 1965. Sydney. Angus & Robertson. 1st Australian ed. NF/lightly worn. clipped dj. M25. $75.00.

UPFIELD, Arthur W. *The Mountains Have a Secret.* 1948. Doubleday. 1st. lightly rubbed. price clipped jacket. F/dj. M25. $150.00.

UPFIELD, Arthur W. *The Mystery of Swordfish Reef.* 1960. Heinemann. 1st. price clipped jacket worn along the edges. F/dj. M25. $45.00.

UPFIELD, Arthur W. *The Widows of Broome.* 1950. Doubleday. 1st Am. worn jacket that Is internally mended. F/dj. M25. $75.00.

UPFIELD, Arthur W. *The Will of the Tribe.* 1962. NY. Crime Club. 1st. worn jacket. name marked out on the front pastedown; number on the rear panel of the jacket. VG/dj. M25. $60.00.

UPFIELD, Arthur W. *Venom House.* 1952. Doubleday. 1st. VG/G. P3. $25.00.

UPFIELD, Arthur W. *Widows of Broome.* 1950. Doubleday. 1st. VG. P3. $30.00.

UPHAM, Charles W. *Lectures on Witchcraft.* 1831. Boston. Carter. Hendee & Babcock. 1st. foxed. faded. edgewear. 280p. F. B18. $95.00.

UPHAM & WRIGHT. *Greenland: Icefields & Life in the North Atlantic.* 1896. London. Kegan Paul. 1st Eng. ils/5 maps. 407p. P4. $250.00.

UPTON, Bertha. *Adventures of Two Dutch Dolls.* 1898. Longman Gr. 1st. ils F Upton/29 full-p pl. pict brd. VG. D1. $350.00.

UPTON, R. *Bird in the Hand: Celebrated Falconers of the Past.* 1980. London. Debrett. ils/photos. 160p. F/VG. M12. $60.00.

UPTON, Richard. *Ft. Custer on the Big Horn 1877–1898.* 1973. Clark. 1st. ils/maps. 316p. VG/VG. J2. $150.00.

UPTON, Robert. *Killing in Real Estate.* 1990. Dutton. 1st. NF/dj. P3. $18.00.

URE, Stellanie. *Hawk Lady.* 1980. Doubleday. 216p. NF/dj. S15. $12.00.

URIBE, C., Andres. *Brown Gold: The Amazing Story of Coffee.* 1954. NY. 1st. index. decor pict cloth. dj. B26. $26.00.

URIS, Leon. *Armageddon.* 1964. NY. Doubleday. 1st. NF/VG lt edgewear. A24. $20.00.

URIS, Leon. *Battle Cry.* 1953. Putnam. 1st. sgn. author's 1st book. NF/NF. L3. $400.00.

URIS, Leon. *Exodus.* 1958. Garden City. Doubleday. 1st. Book Is a little shaken, has minor shelf wear and light spotting on top-stain. Jacket has 1½" x 1" piece missing at bottom of slightly faded spine, several tape-reinforced closed tears, and rubbing along folds. NF/VG-. H11. $60.00.

URIS, Leon. *The Angry Hills.* 1955. NY. Random House. 1st. Name stamped on front endpaper. Jacket has some rubbing on back panel and nicks at spine ends. F/dj. M15. $100.00.

URIS, Leon. *The Haj.* 1984. Doubleday. 1st. F/G. B35. $14.00.

URIS, Leon. *The Haj.* 1985. Bantam. pb. 525p. VG. F6. $1.30.

URIS, Leon. *Topaz.* 1967. NY. McGraw Hill. 1st. VF/F. T2. $9.00.

URIS, Leon. *Trinity.* 1977. Bantam. 5th prt pb. VG. F6. $1.25.

URIS, Leon. *Trinity.* 1976. Doubleday. 1st. F/NF. M25. $25.00.

UROQUHART, John. *The Wonders of Prophecy.* nd. Christian Alliance. 6th ed. 241p. G. B29. $5.50.

URQUHART, Beryl Leslie. *Rhododendron Vol 1.* 1958. Sharpthorne. Sussex. ils/map ep. NF/dj. B26. $145.00.

URQUHART, Fred. *Seven Ghosts in Search.* 1983. Wm Kimber. 1st. VG/dj. P3. $20.00.

URQUHART, Jane. *The Underpainter.* (1997). Toronto. McClelland & Stewart. 1st Canadian ed. sgn & dated by author. F/F. B3. $70.00.

URQUHART, Jane. *The Whirlpool.* (1989). London. S&S. 1st British ed. precedes Am ed. sgn & dated by author. F/F. B3. $60.00.

URREA, Luis Alberto. *By the Lake of Sleeping Children.* (1996). NY. Anchor. pb orig. sequel to author's 1st book. pict wrp. sgn. F. B3. $30.00.

URREA, Luis Alberto. *Ghost Sickness.* (1997). El Paso. Cinco Puntos Press. pb orig. sgn & dated by author. pict wrp. F. B3. $30.00.

URREA, Luis Alberto. *In Search of Snow.* (1994). NY. Harper Collins. 1st. author's 1st novel. sgn by author. VF/VF. B3. $30.00.

URREA, Luis Alberto. *In Search of Snow.* 1994. NY. Harper Collins. 1st. author's 1s novel. NF/NF. M23. $20.00.

URREA, Luis Alberto. *Nobody's Son.* (1998) Tucson. U of AZ Press. 1st. sgn & dated by author. author's 3rd book in border trilogy F/F. B3. $25.00.

URREA, Luis Alberto. *The Fever of Being.* (1994). NY. West End Press. 1st. pict wrp sgn by author. F. B3. $25.00.

URREA, Luis Alberto. *Wandering Time.* (1999). Tucson. U of AZ Press. 1st. sgn & dated by author. F/F. B3. $30.00.

URRUTIA, Miguel. *Development of the Columbian Labor Movement.* 1969. Bantam. 1st. VG/VG. V4. $17.50.

URSULINE ACADEMY, editors. *Recipes and Reminiscences of New Orleans.* 1971. LA. Parents Club of Ursuline Academy. 11th printing. lt edgewear. spiral bdg. NF. A28. $14.95.

URTON, Gary. *The History of a Myth.* 1990 Norman. Univ of Oklahoma Press. 1st. wrp. 172p. VG. slight cover wear. bottom stp 'damaged.' F3. $20.00.

USHER, James. *Body of Divinitie; or, Summe & Substance of Christianity.* 1645. London. MF for Theo Downes. 1st. 4to. orig bdg. VG T10. $400.00.

USPENSKII, S. M. *Life in High Latitudes: A Study of Bird Life.* 1984. New Delhi. Amerind Pub. 385p. VG/dj. P4. $65.00.

USSHER, Arla. *Magic People: Irishman Appraises the Jews.* 1951. NY. Devin Adair. 177p. VG/G. S3. $27.00.

UTLEY, Robert M. *Frontier Regulars: United States Army & the Indian 1866–91.* 1973. NY. ils. 466p. F/dj. M4. $20.00.

UTLEY, Robert M. *Indian Frontier of the American West 1846–1890.* 1984. Albuquerque. dj. A19. $25.00.

UTLEY, Robert M. *Last Days of the Sioux Nation.* 1963. Yale. 1st. 336p. VG/VG. J2. $85.00.

UTLEY, Robert M. *Billy the Kid: A Short & Violent Life.* 1989. NE U. 1st. 302p. cloth. VG/dj. M20. $35.00.

UTRILLO, Maurice. *Exposition D'Oeuvres Recentes De Maurice Utrillo.* 1938. Fevrier-Mars. ils/photos. D2. $40.00.

UTTER, William T. *Granville, the Story of an Ohio Village.* 1956. Granville, OH. Denison Univ. 1st. 1/4 cloth. ils. 347p. VG/torn dj. B18. $25.00.

UTTLEY, Alison. *Christmas at the Rose & Crown*. 1952. London. Heinemann. 1st. ils Katherine Wigglesworth. 72p. pict brd. R5. $100.00.

UTTLEY, Alison. *Fuzzypeg Goes to School*. 1938. London. Collins. 1st. ils Margaret Tempest. 12mo. 100p. pict brd. R5. $100.00.

UTTLEY, Alison. *Knot Squirrel Tied*. 1937. London. Collins. 1st. ils Margaret Tempest. 12mo. 101p. pict brd. R5. $100.00.

UTTLEY, Alison. *Little Gray Rabbitt's Second Painting Book*. ca. 1950. London. Collins. 4to. ils Tempest/8 full-pc mc pl. mc pict limp brd. R5. $175.00.

UTTLEY, Alison. *Moldy Warp the Mole*. 1940. London. Collins. 1st. ils Margaret Tempest. 87p. pict brd. R5. $75.00.

UTTLEY, Alison. *Sam Pig & the Wind*. 1989. (1940). London. Faber. 1st thus. 12mo. unp. orange brd. VG+. T5. $18.00.

UTTLEY, Alison. *Sam Pig's Trousers*. 1989. (1940). London. Faber. 1st thus. 12mo. unp. bl glossy brd. VG+. T5. $18.00.

UTTLEY, Alison. *Snug & Serna Meet A Queen*. 1950. London. Heinemann. 1st. ils Katherine Wigglesworth. gray-gr pict brd. R5. $100.00.

— V —

VACHE, Warren W., Sr. *Crazy Fingers: Claude Hopkins' Life in Jazz*. 1922. Washington. Smithsonian. ARC w/slip. F/wrps. B2. $25.00.

VACHSS, Andrew. *Blue Belle*. 1988. NY. Knopf. 1st. ARC. VF/pict wpr. T2. $15.00.

VACHSS, Andrew. *Blue Belle*. 1988. NY. Knopf. 1st. NF/F. T2. $15.00.

VACHSS, Andrew. *Blue Belle*. 1988. NY. Knopf. 1st. VF/F. H11. $35.00.

VACHSS, Andrew. *Blue Belle*. 1988. np. Knopf. ARC. F. M19. $17.50.

VACHSS, Andrew. *Born Bad*. 1994. NY. Vintage Crime/Black Lizard. 1st. pb orig. sgn. F in pict wrp. D10. $60.00.

VACHSS, Andrew. *Down in the Zero*. 1994. NY. Knopf. 1st. VF/VF. T2. $18.00.

VACHSS, Andrew. *Down in the Zero*. 1994. Knopf. 1st. NF/NF. G8. $12.50.

VACHSS, Andrew. *False Allegations*. 1996. Knopf. 1st. NF/F. G8. $12.50.

VACHSS, Andrew. *Flood*. 1985. NY. Fine. 1st. author's 1st book. Price clipped. F/F. H11. $50.00.

VACHSS, Andrew. *Footsteps of the Hawk*. 1995. Knopf. 1st. NF/NF. G8. $15.00.

VACHSS, Andrew. *Hard Candy*. 1989. NY. Knopf. 1st. VF/VF. T2. $25.00.

VACHSS, Andrew. *Hard Candy*. (1989). NY. Knopf. 1st. NF. owner's inscr on ffep/F. B3. $30.00.

VACHSS, Andrew. *Hard Looks: Adapted Stories*. 1996. Milwaukee. Dark Horse Comics. 1st. graphic novel format. 20 stories. VF/pict wrp. T2. $15.00.

VACHSS, Andrew. *Shella*. 1993. NY. Knopf. 1st. VF/VF. T2. $15.00.

VACHSS, Andrew. *Strega*. 1987. NY. Knopf. 1st. F/F. H11. $40.00.

VACHSS, Andrew. *Strega*. 1987. NY. Knopf. 1st. F/F. D10. $55.00.

VALDER, Peter. *The Garden Plants of China*. 1999. Portland. 4to. new in dj. B26. $49.95.

VALEE, Rudy with Gil McKean. *My Time Is Your Time, The Story of Rudy Valee*. 1962. NY. Ivan Obolensky. 4th printing. F/lightly used dj. B2. $30.00.

VALENTINETTI, Joseph. *Glint*. 1995. NY. SMP. 1st. author's 1st book. F/F. H11. $20.00.

VALERY, Paul. *The Selected Writings*. 1950. NY. New Directions. 1st. F but w/owner's name. in chip dj. B2. $35.00.

VALIN, JONATHAN. *Final Notice*. 1980. NY. Dodd Mead. 1st. VF/dj. M15. $125.00.

VALIN, Jonathan. *Fire Lake*. 1987. NY. Delacorte. 1st. F/NF. T2. $12.00.

VALIN, Jonathan. *Fire Lake*. 1987. NY. Delacorte. 1st. Inscribed. F/F. H11. $30.00.

VALIN, Jonathan. *Life's Work*. 1986. NY. Delacorte. 1st. VF/VF. T2. $15.00.

VAN ALLSBURG, Chris. *The Sweetest Fig*. (1993). Boston. Houghton Mifflin. 1st. ils by author. children's. F/F. B3. $35.00.

VAN ALLSBURG, Chris. *The Widow's Broom*. (1992). Boston. Houghton Mifflin. 1st. ils & sgn by author. children's. F/F. B3. $60.00.

VAN ALLSBURG, CHRIS. *The Widow's Broom*. (1992). Boston. Houghton Mifflin. 1st. ils by author. children's. F/F. B3. $30.00.

VAN ASH, Cay. *The Fires of Fu Manchu*. 1987. NY. Harper & Row. 1st. F/F. H11. $30.00.

VAN DE WATER, Frederic. *Havoc*. 1931. London. Skeffington. 1st. F/dj. M15. $165.00.

VAN DE WETERING. *Mangrove Mama*. (1995). Tucson. Dennis McMillan. 1st. 1/2000 copies. sgn by author. F/F. B3. $45.00.

VAN DE WETERING, Janwillem. *Afterzen: Experiences of a Zen Student Out on His Ear*. 1999. NY. St. Martin. 1st. sgn. VF/VF. T2. $25.00.

VAN DE WETERING, Janwillem. *Inspector Saito's Small Satori*. 1985. NY. Putnam. 1st. F/F. H11. $25.00.

VAN DE WETERING, Janwillem. *Mangrove Mama and Other Tropical Tales of Horror*. 1995. Tucson. Dennis McMillan. 1st. sgn. VF/VF. T2. $30.00.

VAN DE WETERING, Janwillem. *The Amsterdam Copy: Collected Stories*. 1999. Soho. ARC. F/WRP. M25. $35.00.

VAN DE WETERING, Janwillem. *The Butterfly Hunter*. 1982. Boston. Houghton Mifflin. 1st. sgn. F/F. T2. $35.00.

VAN DE WETERING, Janwillem. *The Butterfly Hunter*. 1982. Boston. Houghton. 1st. Jacket has wear at top of flap folds. F/F-. H11. $30.00.

VAN DE WETERING, Janwillem. *The Butterfly Hunter*. 1982. Boston. Houghton Mifflin. 1st. sgn. F/F. T2. $35.00.

VAN DE WETERING, Janwillem. *The Hollow Eyed Angel*. 1996. Soho. UP. F in red wrp. M25. $35.00.

VAN DE WETERING, Janwillem. *The Hollow Eyed Angel*. 1996. NY. Soho Press. 1st. sgn. VF/VF. T2. $25.00.

VAN DE WETERING, Janwillem. *The Maine Massacre*. 1979. Boston. Houghton. 1st. Book has light shelf wear and lightly soiled page edges. Jacket has short tears and creasing at bottom of front panel. F-/NF. H11. $25.00.

VAN DE WETERING, Janwillem. *The Perfidious Parrot*. 1997. Soho. UP. NF in red wrp. M25. $35.00.

VAN DE WETERING, Janwillem. *The Rattle Rat.* 1985. NY. Pantheon. 1st English language ed. sgn. F/F. T2. $35.00.

VAN DE WETERING, Janwillem. *The Rattle-Rat.* 1985. NY. Pantheon. 1st. F/F. H11. $20.00.

VAN DEN HAAG, Ernest. *The Jewish Mystique.* 1969. Stein & Day. 252p. G. ex lib. B29. $6.00.

VAN DINE, S. S. *The Garden Murder Case.* 1935. NY. Scribners. 1st. Jacket has minor chipping at extremities. Flap folds and rear panel are rubbed. F/NF. H11. $250.00.

VAN DINE, S. S. *The Kennel Murder Case.* 1933. NY. Scribners. 1st. Book has slightly loose front board and bumped corners. Jacket has rubbed front panel. light chipping at spine ends and creases along folds and edges. NF/VG. H11. $225.00.

VAN DOREN, Carl. *Benjamin Franklin's Autobiographical Writings.* 1945. Viking Press. 1st. 8vo. inner flap chipped. frayed edges. 810p. VG/dj. H1. $18.00.

VAN DOREN, Carl. *Mutiny in January.* 1943. Viking Press. 1st. tall 8vo. owner's stamp on endpapers. darkening at folds of both endpapers. Edges worn with minor chips & tears. spine a little darkened. 288p. VG/G. H1. $13.50.

VAN DUYN, Mona. *A Time of Bees.* 1964. Univ. of North Carolina Press. 1st. poet's 2nd book. F/VG. V1. $37.00.

VAN DYKE, Henry. *The White Bees & Other Poems.* 1909. NY. Scribner. 1st. sm8vo. uncut pages. 105p. F. H1. $22.50.

VAN GELDER, Arthur Pine & Hugo Schlatter. *History of the Explosives Industry in America.* 1927. NY. Columbia Univ. 1st. pict ep. ils. edges worn. slightly loosened. 1132p. G. B18. $125.00.

VAN GELDEREN, C. J. & D. M. *Maples for Gardeners, A Color Encyclopedia.* 1999. Portland. 4to. 294p w/683 color photos. 2 color maps. New in dj. B26. $49.95.

VAN GIESON, Judith. *Ditch Rider.* 1998. NY. Harper Collins. 1st. review copy w/promo materials & author's photo. sgn. VF/VF. T2. $25.00.

VAN GIESON, Judith. *Hotshots.* 1996. NY. Harper Collins. 1st. sgn. VF in dj. M15. $40.00.

VAN GIESON, Judith. *Mercury Retrograde.* 1994. Huntington Beach. James Cahill Publishing. 1st. 1/124 # copies. sgn by Van Gieson. Satterthwait. Phil Parks. VF/no dj. in slipcase as issued. T2. $65.00.

VAN GIESON, Judith. *Mercury Retrograde.* 1994. Huntington Beach. James Cahill Publishing. 1st. sgn by Van Gieson & Satterthwait. VF/no dj as issued. T2. $30.00.

VAN GIESON, Judith. *Mercury Retrograde.* 1994. CA. James Cahill. 1st. intro by Walter Satterthwait. glossy pict brds. sgn by both Van Gieson & Satterthwait. F. corners bumped/F. A24. $37.00.

VAN GIESON, Judith. *Parrot Blues.* 1995. Harper Collins. 1st. sgn. VF. dj. M25. $50.00.

VAN GIESON, Judith. *Parrot Blues.* 1995. NY. Harper Collins. 1st. sgn by Van Gieson. VF/VF. T2. $25.00.

VAN GIESON, Judith. *Parrot Blues.* 1995. NY. Harper Collins. 1st. sgn. F/F. A24. $35.00.

VAN GIESON, Judith. *Raptor.* 1990. NY. Harper & Row. 1st. sgn. author's 2nd novel. VF/VF. T2. $125.00.

VAN GIESON, Judith. *Raptor.* 1990. NY. Harper & Row. 1st. book store ink stamp on front fep and page one. F/F. H11. $100.00.

VAN GIESON, Judith. *Raptor.* 1990. NY. Harper & Row. 1st. sgn. F/F. A24. $150.00.

VAN GIESON, Judith. *The Lies that Bind.* 1993. NY. Harper Collins. 1st. VF in dj. M15. $40.00.

VAN GIESON, Judith. *The Lies that Bind.* (1993). NY. Harper Collins. 1st. sgn by author. F/F. B3. $40.00.

VAN GIESON, Judith. *The Other Side of Death.* 1991. NY. Harper Collins. 1st. sgn. F/F. A24. $75.00.

VAN GIESON, Judith. *The Wolf Path.* 1992. NY. Harper Collins. 1st. VF in dj. M15. $45.00.

VAN GIESON, Judith. *The Wolf Path.* 1992. NY. Harper Collins. 1st. rem mk. VG+/VG+. R16. $35.00.

VAN GREENAWAY, Peter. *The Medusa Touch.* 1973. Stein & Day. 1st Am ed. VG+/VG. G8. $10.00.

VAN GREENAWAY, Peter. *The Medusa Touch.* 1973. NY. Stein. 1st. F/F. H11. $45.00.

VAN GULIK, Robert. *The Chinese Bell Murders.* 1958. London. Michael Joseph. 1st Eng. jacket has tiny scrapes at top of spine. F/dj. M15. $250.00.

VAN GULIK, Robert. *The Chinese Lake Murders.* 1960. London. Michael Joseph. 1st Eng. page edges slightly darkened and top corner bumped. jacket has small chips at corners and nicks at top of spine. NF/dj. M15. $150.00.

VAN GULIK, Robert. *The Chinese Maze Murders.* 1962. London. Michael Joseph. 1st Eng. jacket has two inch piece missing from back panel. several closed tears and wear at spine ends and at corners. VG/dj. M15. $50.00.

VAN GULIK, Robert. *The Emperor's Pearl.* 1963. London. Heinemann. 1st Eng. F/dj. M15. $250.00.

VAN GULIK, Robert. *The Given Day.* 1984. San Antonio. Dennis Macmillan. 1st Am. VF/dj. M15. $75.00.

VAN GULIK, Robert. *The Monkey and the Tiger.* 1965. London. Heinemann. 1st Eng. one of the plates has been hand-colored. price clipped jacket. F/dj. M15. $125.00.

VAN GULIK, Robert. *The Red Pavilion.* 1968. NY. Scribners. 1st Am ed. F/F. T2. $35.00.

VAN HORN, Larry. *Communications Satellites.* 1985. Brasstown. NC. Grove Enterprises. edited by Robert B. Grove. b/w photos & diagrams. 4to. 216p. VG in wrp. K5. $20.00.

VAN LOON, Hendrik. *The Story of Mankind.* 1921. Boni & Liveright. 26th. tall 8vo. lightly soiled edge wear. 489p. F/dj. H1. $20.00.

VAN LUSTBADER, Eric. *Jian.* 1986. Fawcett Crest. pb. F. F6. $1.50.

VAN LUSTBADER, Eric. *Sirens.* 1982. Fawcett Crest. pb. G. F6. $1.00.

VAN LUSTBADER, Eric. *The Miko.* 1985. Fawcett Crest. pb. NF. F6. $1.35.

VAN LUSTBADER, Eric. *The Ninja.* 1980. Fawcett Crest. pb. VG. F6. $1.15.

VAN LUSTBADER, Eric. *Zero.* 1988. NY. Random House. 1st. VG/VG. R16. $35.00.

VAN PAASSEN, Pierre. *Earth Could be Fair.* 1946. Dial Press. 1st. 8vo. 509p. F. H1. $8.00.

VAN PELT, Mary & Wanda Huffman. *Animal Kingdom in Treasured Glass.* 1972. self-published. sm4to. 48p. VG. H1. $26.00.

AN ROYEN, P. *The Alpine Flora of New uinea. Vols 1 – 4*. 1979 – 83. F. B26. $475.00.

AN TYNE, Claude Halstead. *The Loyalists the American Revolution*. 1902. NY. 1st. rear p missing. 360p. VG. B18. $27.50.

AN WYK, P. *Trees of the Kruger National ark (2 Vols)*. 1972/74. Cape Town. gr ather w/raised bands and red leather bels on spines. 597p. 808 color photos & aps. F. B26. $375.00.

AN WYK, Piet. *South African Trees, A hotographic Guide*. 1993. London. pocket ze. sc. New. B26. $19.95.

AN-OLLENBACH, Aubrey W. *Planting uide to the Middle East*. 1978. London. ppendices. 154p w/150 line drawings. lew. B26. $29.00.

ANCE, Ethel (Grace Zaring Stone). *scape*. 1939. Brown & Co. 1st. 8vo. uncut ages. 428p. VG+. H1. $8.50.

VANCE, Jack (John Holbrook Vance). *A oom to Die in*. 1987. London. Kinnell. 1st hc d. written as Ellery Queen. VF/VF. T2. 30.00.

ANCE, Jack (John Holbrook Vance). *raminta Station*. 1988. NY. tor. 1st US trade d. VF/VF. T2. $25.00.

ANCOUVER, George. *The Voyage of eorge Vancouver 1791 – 1795*. 1984. London. Iakluyt Society. 4 volumes. second series. o. 163. 164. 165. 166. bl cloth 8vo.; gilt titles cover decor. 46 ils. 10 maps. 1752p num-ered consecutively. F in rubbed dj. P4. 250.00.

ANDENBURGH, Jane. *Failure to Zigzag*. 989. San Francisco. North Point. 1st. VF/F. l11. $35.00.

ANDERHAEGHE, Guy. *Things as They Are?* 1992. Toronto. McClelland & Stewart. st Canadian ed. F/F. B3. $75.00.

ANDERVELDE, Marjorie. *Keep Out of Paradise*. 1966. TN. Broadman Press. 1st. 27p. G. F3. $20.00.

ANDIVER, Frank Everson, editor. *The dea of the South Pursuit of a Central Theme*. 964. Chicago. Univ. of Chicago Press. 1st. rig cloth. one sm rubber lib stp on front fly-eaf. 82p. NF/NF. M8. $45.00.

ANGORDER, W. B. *Catalogue of the Flora f Noble County, Indiana*. 1885. Kendallville. dedication on front wrp. wrp. spine slightly chip. B26. $25.00.

VANKAT, John L. *The Natural Vegetation of North America, An Introduction*. 1992 (1979). reprint. cover edges rubbed. else VG. B26. $24.00.

VANKIRK, Jacques & Parney. *Remarkable Remains of the Ancient Peoples of Guatemala*. 1996. Norman. Univ. of Oklahoma Press. 1st. 4to. b/w photo ils. map. biblio. index. 243p. G/wrp. F3. $25.00.

VANLAWICK-GOODALL, Jane. *In the Shadow of Man*. 1971. BC. picts. F/chip dj. S19. $35.00.

VARGAS LLOSA, Mario. *The Notebooks of Don Rigoberto*. 1997. NY. Farrar. ARC. wrps. F. B2. $30.00.

VARGAS LLOSA, Mario. *The Time of the Hero*. 1966. NY. Grove Press. 1st Am ed. author's 1st novel. F/F. few stains. A24. $60.00.

VACHSS, Andrew. *Born Bad*. 1994. NY. Vintage Crime. 1st. sgn. F. D10. $65.00.

VACHSS, Andrew. *Safe House*. 1998. NY. Knopf. 1st. sgn. F/F. D10. $35.00.

VAUGHAN, Roger. *Fastnet — One Man's Voyage*. 1980. Seaview Books. 1st. F/chip dj. S19. $25.00.

VEA, Alfredo. *Gods Go Begging*. 1999. NY. Dutton. 1st. sgn. VF/VF. T2. $26.00.

VEDDER, Elihu. *Miscellaneous Moods in Verse: One Hundred and One Poems with Illustrations by Elihu Vedder*. 1914. Boston. Porter E. Sargent. 1 of 100. tipped in plates. label. gilt lettered brd. NF. B14. $150.00.

VEIGA, Jose J. *The Misplaced Machine and Other Stories*. 1970. NY. Knopf. 1st. VF/F. H11. $30.00.

VEIGA, Jose J. *The Three Trials of Manirema*. 1970. NY. Knopf. 1st. F in VG dj. B2. $25.00.

VELEY, Charles. *Children of the Dark*. 1979. Garden City. Doubleday. 1st. author's 1st novel. F. rem spray/F. T2. $3.00.

VELIE, Lester. *Countdown in the Holy Land*. 1969. Funk & Wagnalls. 224p. G/torn dj. B29. $4.50.

VERDCOURT, B. & E. C. Trump. *Common Poisonous Plants of East Africa*. 1969. London. VG in dj. B26. $35.00.

VERDELLE, A. J. *All Lined Up and Smiling*. 1995. Chapel Hill. Algonquin. 1st. sgn by author. pict wrp. F. B3. $40.00.

VERDELLE, A. J. *The Good Negress*. 1995. Chapel Hill. Algonquin. 1st. author's 1st book. F/F. D10. $55.00.

VERDELLE, A. J. *The Good Negress*. 1995. Chapel Hill. Algonquin. 1st. author's 1st novel. sgn by author. went into later prt before distribution. F/F. B3. $75.00.

VERDELLE, A. J. *The Good Negress*. 1995. Chapel Hill. Algonquin. ARC. wrps. F. B2. $60.00.

VERISSIMO, Erico. *Mexico*. 1960. NY. Orion Press. 3rd. 341p. G/chipped dj. F3. $15.00.

VERMANDEL, Janet Gregory. *Dine with the Devil*. 1970. NY. Dodd. 1st. name on front pastedown. VF/F. H11. $25.00.

VERMES, Geza. *Discovery in the Judean Desert*. 1956. Desclee. 237p. G. B29. $17.00.

VERONELLI, Luigi. *The Wines of Italy*. nd (circa 1950s). Rome. Canesi Editore. ils 6 color plates. 236p +60p w/84 orig mtd wine labels. bl cloth. soiled dj. K1. $125.00.

VICKERS, Roy. *Hounded Down*. 1923. London. Hodder & Stoughton. 1st. VG/. M15. $45.00.

VICKERS, Roy. *Seven Chose Murder*. 1959. London. Faber & Faber. 1st. F/dj. M15. $100.00.

VICTOR, Daniel D. *The Seventh Bullet: A Holmes and Watson American Adventure*. 1992. NY. St. Martin. 1st. VF. small rem mk/VF. T2. $25.00.

VIDAL, Gore. *A Thirsty Evil*. 1956. NY. Zero Press. 1st. F/NF. D10. $75.00.

VIDAL, Gore. *Empire*. 1987. NY. Random House. 1st. one of unknown # sgn by author on tip in leaf. F/F. B2. $65.00.

VIDAL, Gore. *Messiah*. 1954. NY. Dutton. 1st. this copy from prominent American author w/his sgn on ffep. VG/G. clip. A24. $35.00.

VIDAL, Gore. *Palimpsest*. 1995. NY. Random House. 1st. sgn. pict brds. F/F. D10. $45.00.

VIDAL, Gore. *Screening History*. 1992. Cambridge. Harvard Univ. Press. 1st. sgn. F/F. D10. $50.00.

VILLACORTA, C. J. Antonio. *Mongrafia Del Departmento De Guatemala*. 1926. Guatemala. Tipografia Nacional. 4to. b/w photo ils. foldout maps. tables. 378p. VG/orig dj cover disbound; glued to front & rear stiff paper bds. F3. $30.00.

VILLARD, Oswald Garrison. *John Brown 1800 – 1859 A Biography Fifty Years After.* 1910. Boston. Houghton Mifflin. 1st. third impression. orig cloth. plates. 738p. VG. M8. $125.00.

VILLARD, Oswald Garrison. *John Brown, A Biography 1800 – 1859.* 1910. NY. 1st. ils. 738p. some wear. G. B18. $35.00.

VILLARD, Zella M., ed. *William McKinley, 100Th Anniversary Souvenir, 1843 – 1943.* 1943. Canton, OH. The McKinley Club. ils. photos. pict wrp. 100p. VG. lt soiling. edgewear. B18. $25.00.

VILLEGAS, Liliana & Benjamin. *Artefactos, Columbian Crafts From the Andes to the Amazon.* 1992. NY. Rizzoli. 1st. sq 4to. color photo ils. 2 maps. 240p. F/F. F3. $60.00.

VILLER, Frederick. *The Black Tortoise: Being the Strange Story of Old Frick's Diamond.* 1901. London. Heinemann. 1st Eng. front endpaper replaced. pictorial cloth-covered boards. VG/. M15. $120.00.

VILLIERS-STUART, C. M. *Spanish Gardens: Their History, Types and Features.* 1929. NY. 1st Am ed. decor cloth. slight foxing at prelims. else VG. B26. $85.00.

VINE, Barbara aka Ruth Rendell. *A Dark-Adapted Eye.* 1986. NY. Bantam. 1st. F/F. H11. $40.00.

VINE, Barbara aka Ruth Rendell. *A Dark Adapted Eye.* 1986. NY. Bantam. 1st Am ed. review copy. Rendell's 1st mystery under pseudonym. winner of Edgar award. F/F. D10. $50.00.

VINE, Barbara aka Ruth Rendell. *Gallowglass.* 1990. NY. Harmony. 1st. sgn by author. F/F. B3. $40.00.

VINE, Barbara aka Ruth Rendell. *Gallowglass.* 1990. NY. Harmony Books. 1st Am ed. VF/VF. T2. $15.00.

VINE, Barbara aka Ruth Rendell. *King Solomon's Carpet.* 1991. NY. Harmony. 1st. sgn by author. VF/VF. B3. $40.00.

VINE, Barbara aka Ruth Rendell. *The House of Stairs.* 1988. NY. Harmony Books. 1st Am ed. VF/VF. T2. $15.00.

VINE, Barbara aka Ruth Rendell. *The House of Stairs.* 1989. NY. Harmony. review copy w/promo folder. includes a photo of author. sgn by author. F/NF. lt wear to extremities. B3. $40.00.

VINGE, Vernor. *The Peace War.* 1984. NY. Bluejay Books. 1st. sgn. VF/VF. T2. $30.00.

VIOLA, Herman & Carolyn Margolis, editors. *Seeds of Change, A Quincentennial Commemoration.* 1991. DC. Smithsonian Institution Press. 1st. 4to. photos b/w & color. 278p. G/G. F3. $40.00.

VIOLA, Herman & Carolyn Margolis, editors. *Seeds of Change, A Quincentennial Commemoration.* 1991. DC. Smithsonian Institution Press. 1st. pb. 4to. photos b/w & color. 278p. G. F3. $25.00.

VIRAMONTES, Helena Maria. *The Moths and Other Stories.* 1985. Houston. Arte Publico. pb orig. author's 1st book. pict wrp. NF. corners turned. B3. $50.00.

VIRVILLE, A. D. De. *Histoire De La Botanique En France.* 1954. Paris. orig wrp. index. rear wrp mildly creased. B26. $55.00.

VISSER, Johann. *South African Parasitic Flowering Plants.* 1981. Cape Town. 4to. F in dj. B26. $72.50.

VIVIAN, E. Charles. *Fields of Sleep.* 1980. West Kingston. Donald M. Grant. reissue. 1st thus. sgn by artist Thomas Canty. VF/VF. T2. $20.00.

VODOPYANOV, M. *Moscow, North Pole, Vancouver, Washington.* 1939. Moscow. Foreign Languages Publishing House. sm pamphlet in orig wrp. 5 photos. early Russian Arctic aviation. 40p. G. some soil. rust from staples. P4. $125.00.

VOGUE Magazine. *The Arts of Living.* 1954. NY. S&S. 1st. 8vo. 190p. G. lightly soiled. edgewear. S14. $6.00.

VOIGT, J. O. *Hortus Suburbanus Calcuttensis. A Catalogue of the Plants.* 1984 (1845). Dehra Dun. reprint. new in dj. B26. $25.00.

VOLLMANN, William. *An Afghanistan Picture Show.* 1992. NY. FSG. 1st. review copy. F/F. D10. $50.00.

VOLLMANN, William T. *An Afghanistan Picture Show.* 1992. NY. FSG. 1st Am ed. F/F. mild bump. A24. $25.00.

VOLLMANN, William T. *An Afghanistan Picture Show.* 1992. NY. FSG. 1st. sgn w/drawing by author. F/F. O11. $50.00.

VOLLMANN, William T. *Butterfly Stories.* 1993. NY. Grove Press. 1st Am ed & 1st hc printing. F/F. mild crease to top spine edge. A24. $30.00.

VOLLMANN, William T. *Fathers and Crows.* 1992. London. Andre Deutsch. 1st. British/US eds were pub simultaneously. F/F. O11. $30.00.

VOLLMANN, William. *The Rainbo Stories.* 1989. NY. Atheneum. 1st. F/. D1 $125.00.

VOLLMANN, William. *The Rifles.* 199 NY. Viking. 1st. review copy. sgn. F/F. D1 $50.00.

VOLLMANN, William T. *Thirteen Storie and Thirteen Epitaphs.* 1993. NY. Pantheon 1st Am ed. F/F. A24. $20.00.

VOLLMANN, William T. *Whores for Glori* 1992. NY. Pantheon. 1st. F/F. A24. $30.00.

VOLLMER, Philip. *The Modern Student Life of Christ.* 1917. Revell. 353p. G/G. B2 $5.00.

VON BALTHASAR, Kehl & Loser. *Th Von Balthasar Reader.* 1982. Crossroad. 437p VG/VG. B29. $19.00.

VON BRAUN, Wernher & Frederick I Ordway. *New Worlds; Discoveries from Ou Solar System.* 1979. Garden City. NY. Ancho Press/Doubleday. 1st. photos. some color drawings & diagrams. 284p. VG/chippe dj. K5. $40.00.

VON BREITENBACH, Jutta. *The Wild Fig of Southern Africa.* 1974. Johannesburg. Th Tree Society of Southern Africa. Monograph No. 2. limp card covers. sm4to. F. B26 $15.00.

VON HAGEN, Victor. *F. Catherwood Architect Explorer of Two Worlds.* 1968. MA Barre Pub. 1st. 60p. G/G. F3. $40.00.

VON HAGEN, Victor. *Frederick Catherwoo Archt.* 1950. NY. Oxford Univ. Press. 2nd 177p. G/chipped dj. F3. $30.00.

VON HAGEN, Victor. *Maya Explorer: John Lloyd Stephens & the Lost Cities of Central America & Yucatan.* 1947. Norman. Univ. of Oklahoma Press. 1st. 324p. G. F3. $25.00.

VON HAGEN, Victor. *Maya Explorer: John Lloyd Stephens & the Lost Cities of Central America & Yucatan.* 1947. Norman. Univ. of Oklahoma Press. 1st. 324p. G/scattered foxing ep. lt shelf wear. F3. $20.00.

VON HAGEN, Victor. *Maya Explorer: John Lloyd Stephens & the Lost Cities of Central America & Yucatan.* 1948. Norman. Univ. of Oklahoma Press. 324p. G/chipped dj. F3. $20.00.

VON HAGEN, Victor. *Maya Explorer: John Lloyd Stephens & the Lost Cities of Central America & Yucatan.* 1967. Norman. Univ. of Oklahoma Press. 5th ed. 324p. G/chipped dj. F3. $20.00.

VON HAGEN, Victor. *The Golden Man: A Quest for El Dorado.* 1974. London. Book Club. 1st Am ed. 346p. G/chipped dj. F3. $30.00.

VON HAGEN, Victor Wolfgang. *F. Catherwood, Architect Explorer to Two Worlds.* 1968. Barre, MA. Barre Publishers. octavo. orig brown cloth. pict ep & dj. F. R3. $30.00.

VON HAGEN, Victor Wolfgang. *The Ancient Sun Kingdoms of the Americas.* 1961. Cleveland. World Publishing Company. ils. quarto. decor printed brds. blk cloth spine. rubbing. bkplt. else F. R3. $15.00.

VON HAGEN, Victor Wolfgang. *The Aztec and Maya Papermakers. With an Intro by Dard Hunter.* 1944. NY. J. J. Augustin Publisher. tall 8vo. 120p text + 30 plates. ftspc. gr cloth. printed dj. soiled. K1. $125.00.

VON HOFFMAN, Nicholas. *We are the People Our Parents Warned Us Against.* 1968. Chicago. Quadrangle Books. 1st. octavo. cloth backed brds w/printed spine and cover titles. pict dj. NF. R3. $60.00.

VON HOFFMAN, Nicholas and Garry Trudeau. *The Fireside Watergate.* 1973. NY. Sheed and Ward. ARC w/slip. photos laid in. F in NF dj. B2. $35.00.

VON RAD, Gerhard. *Old Testament Theology.* 1962. Harper & Row. Vol 1. 483p. VG. minor mks. B29. $15.00.

VONNEGUT, Kurt. *Bluebeard.* 1987. NY. Delacorte. 1st. F/VF. H11. $30.00.

VONNEGUT, Kurt. *Bluebeard.* 1987. NY. Delacorte Press. 1st trade ed. sgn. F/F. D10. $95.00.

VONNEGUT, Kurt. *Bluebeard.* 1987. NY. Delacorte. 1st trade ed. corners slightly rubbed. F/F. A24. $20.00.

VONNEGUT, Kurt. *Breakfast of Champions.* 1973. NY. Delacorte. 1st. jacket has minor wear. F/F. H11. $60.00.

VONNEGUT, Kurt. *Breakfast of Champions.* 1973. NY. Delacorte. 1st. F/NF. spine faded. B3. $40.00.

VONNEGUT, Kurt, Jr. *Breakfast of Champions.* 1973. NY. Delacorte. 1st. F in F dj. B2. $25.00.

VONNEGUT, Kurt. *Deadeye Dick.* 1982. NY. Delacorte. 1st. F/F. H11. $30.00.

VONNEGUT, Kurt. *Deadeye Dick.* 1982. NY. Delacorte. 1st. NF. lt sunning/F. very bright. B3. $60.00.

VONNEGUT, Kurt. *Galapagos.* 1985. NY. Delacorte. 1st. blindstamp on title page. F/F. H11. $30.00.

VONNEGUT, Kurt. *Hocus Pocus.* 1990. NY. Putnam. 1st. jacket Is price clipped. F/F. H11. $25.00.

VONNEGUT, Kurt. *Jailbird.* 1979. NY. Delacorte. 1st. F/F. H11. $35.00.

VONNEGUT, Kurt. *Jailbird.* 1979. NY. Delacorte. 1st. F/F. B3. $50.00.

VONNEGUT, Kurt. *Jailbird.* 1979. NY. Delacorte Press. 1st trade ed. sgn. F/F. D10. $140.00.

VONNEGUT, Kurt. *Slapstick or Lonesome No More.* 1976. NY. Delacorte. 1st. F/NF. H11. $35.00.

VONNEGUT, Kurt. *The Sirens of Titan.* 1959. NY. Dell. orig pb 1st ed. color pict wrp. VG+. lt wear. mild creasing. A24. $75.00.

VONNEGUT, Kurt. *Welcome to the Monkey House.* 1968. NY. Delacorte. 1st thus. scarce 2nd ed and 1st hc ed of *Canary in a Cathouse.* F/NF. lt rubbing & wrinkles. B2. $400.00.

VORZIMMER, Peter J. *Charles Darwin: The Years of Controversy, the Origin of Species and Its Critics 1859 – 1882.* 1970. Philadelphia. VG in dj. B26. $29.00.

VOSS, Edward G. *Michigan Flora, Part 1: Gymnosperms & Monocots.* 1972. Bloomfield Hills. F in dj. B26. $12.50.

VOYNICH, E. L. *The Gadfly.* 1897. Henry Holt & Col. 1st. sm8vo. 373p. G. H1. $15.00.

VUILLEUMIER, Beryl S. *The Systematics and Evolution of Perezia Sect. Perezia (Compositae).* 1969. Cambridge, MA. from the Gray Herbarium. VG/wrp. B26. $12.50.

— W —

W. REG ENVIR ED, Council. *Project Wild: Secondary Activity Guide.* 1983. revised ed. ils. notes. glossary. bib. index. 288p. G. B19. $5.00.

WADE, Brent. *Company Man.* 1992. Chapel Hill. Algonquin. 1st. author's 1st book. VF/F. H11. $30.00.

WAGENVOORD, James. *Doubleday Wine Companion, 1983.* 1983. NY. Doubleday. browned brds. sunned. VG. A28. $6.50.

WAGER, Walter. *Blue Leader.* 1979. NY. Arbor House. 1st. 1st novel in the Alison Gordon trilogy. VF/VF. T2. $20.00.

WAGER, Walter. *Blue Leader.* 1979. NY. Arbor. 1st. F/F. H11. $20.00.

WAGER, Walter. *Blue Moon.* 1980. NY. Arbor House. 1st. 3rd 2nd. VF/VF. T2. $20.00.

WAGER, Walter. *Blue Murder.* 1981. NY. Arbor House. 1st. 3rd novel in the Alison Gordon trilogy. VF/VF. T2. $20.00.

WAGER, Walter. *Blue Murder.* 1981. NY. Arbor. 1st. Book has slight slant and rubbing at spine ends. NF+/F+. H11. $15.00.

WAGER, Walter. *Designated Hitter.* 1982. NY. Arbor. 1st. F/F. H11. $20.00.

WAGLEY, Charles. *The Social & Religious Life of a Guatemalan Village.* 1949. Wisconsin. Am. Anthropologist. Vol. 51. No. 4. Pt 2. index. biblio. 3 b/w plates. 150p. G/wrp. F3. $15.00.

WAGNER, E. Glenn. *The Awesome Power of Shared Beliefs.* 1995. Focus on the Family. 193p. VG/VG. B29. $9.50.

WAGNER, Karl Edward. *Exorcisms and Ecstacies.* 1997. Minneapolis. Fedogan & Bremer. 1st. Stephen Jones. editor. VF/VF. T2. $32.00.

WAGNER, Maurice E. *Put it all Together; Developing Inner Security.* 1974. Zondervan. 162p. VG/VG. B29. $5.50.

WAGNER, Maurice E. *The Sensation of Being Somebody; Building An Adequate Self Concept.* 1975. Zondervan. 251p. G/torn dj. B29. $5.00.

WAGNER, Philip M. *A Wine Grower's Guide, An Interesting & Informative Book for the Amateur Viticulturist on the Cultivation & Use of Wine Grapes.* 1969 (1945). NY. 2nd rev ed. F in dj. B26. $29.00.

WAGNER, Warren H. Jr. *The Fern Genus Diellia: Its Structure, Affinities & Taxonomy.* 1952. Berkeley. 212p w/21 plates. 31 text figures. wrp. B26. $22.50.

WAGONER, Don M., ed. *Conditioning to Win.* 1974. Grapevine. Equine Research. VG. O3. $25.00.

WAGONER, Don M., ed. *Feeding to Win.* 1973. Grapevine. Equine Research. VG. O3. $25.00.

WAHLOO, Per. *A Necessary Action.* 1969. NY. Pantheon. 1st Am ed. F/F. T2. $20.00.

WAIN, John. *Wildtrack.* 1965. NY. Viking. UP w/label on ffep. proof marked Macmillan but crossed out w/Viking penciled in. cloth over brds. NF. V1. $35.00.

WAITE, Arthur Edward. *Alchemists Through the Ages*. 1970. Blauvelt. NY. Rudolf Steiner. 8vo. ils. 315p. G/rubbed. chipped dj. clip. K5. $30.00.

WAKEFIELD, Geoffrey R. *Rhododendrons for Every Garden*. 1965. London. marginal marks. generous use of name stp by previous owner. dj. B26. $14.00.

WAKEFIELD, H. R. *Imagine a Man in a Box*. 1997. Ashcroft. BC. Ash Tree Press. reissue. 1st thus. VF/VF. T2. $40.00.

WAKEFIELD, H. R. *Strayers from Sheol*. 1999. Ashcroft. BC. Ash Tree Press. revised & expanded. 1st thus. VF/VF. T2. $40.00.

WAKEFIELD, H. R. *The Clock Strikes Twelve and Other Stories*. 1998. Ashcroft. BC. Ash Tree Press. reissue. 1st thus. VF/VF. T2. $40.00.

WAKELEY, Philip C. *Planting the Southern Pines*. 1954. Washington, DC. Forest Service. USDA. Ag. Monograph No. 18. 4to. B26. $21.00.

WAKOSKI, Diane. *Virtuoso Literature for Two & Four Hands*. 1975. NY. Doubleday. 1st. review copy w/slip. F/NF. V1. $30.00.

WALCOTT, Derek. *Another Life*. 1973. Farrar, Straus and Giroux. ARC. lightly browned jacket. 'With the compliments (of the publisher)' card laid in. F/dj. M25. $100.00.

WALDO, Terry. *This Is Ragtime*. 1976. NY. Hawthorn. ARC w/slip/promo. F/F. B2. $40.00.

WALDRON, Jan L. *In the Country of Men: My Travels*. 1997. NY. Anchor. 1st. VF/VF. H11. $25.00.

WALDROP, Howard. *A Dozen Tough Jobs*. 1989. Willimantic. Mark V. Ziesing. 1st hc ed. VF/VF. T2. $16.00.

WALDROP, Howard. *Them Bones*. 1989. Willimantic. Mark V. Ziesing. 1st hc ed. VF/VF. T2. $20.00.

WALI, Kameshwar C. *Chandra; A Biography of S. Chandrasekhar*. 1992. Chicago. Univ. of Chicago Press. 32 photo ils. 8vo. 341p. VG in pb. K5. $20.00.

WALKER, Abbie Philips. *Sandman's Might Be So Stories*. 1922. NY. Harper & Bros. May 1924 ed. ils by Lang Campbell. 12mo. gray/gr cloth. full color ils on dj by Harold Gaze. sgn 1923. 157p. VG/VG+. D6. $65.00.

WALKER, Alice. *Her Blue Body Everything We Know*. 1991. Harcourt Brace Jovanovich. UP. F/WRP. M25. $100.00.

WALKER, Alice. *Her Blue Body Everything We Know*. 1990. NY. HBJ. 1st. F/F. B3. $30.00.

WALKER, Alice. *Horses Make a Landscape Look More Beautiful*. 1984. NY. HBJ. 1st. brds sunned. F/VG. clip. lt edgewear. A24. $20.00.

WALKER, Alice. *In Search of Our Mothers' Gardens*. 1983. Harcourt Brace Jovanovich. UP. spine very lightly sunned. F/WRP. M25. $150.00.

WALKER, Alice. *Living by the Word: Selected Writings. 1973 – 1987*. 1988. San Diego. HBJ. 1st. sgn. F in F dj. D10. $50.00.

WALKER, Alice. *Possessing the Secret of Joy*. 1992. NY. HBJ. 1st. NF/NF. R16. $35.00.

WALKER, Alice. *Possessing the Secret of Joy*. 1992. Harcourt Brace Jovanovich. UP. F/WRP. M25. $50.00.

WALKER, Alice. *Possessing the Secret of Joy*. 1992. NY. HBJ. 1st. sgn. F in F dj. D10. $50.00.

WALKER, Alice. *The Same River Twice*. 1996. Scribner. 1st. F/F. s19. $35.00.

WALKER, Alice. *The Same River Twice. Honoring the Difficult*. 1996. NY. Scribner. 1st. sgn. F in F dj. D10. $40.00.

WALKER, Alice. *The Temple of My Familiar*. 1989. NY. HBJ. 1st. VG+/NF. R16. $40.00.

WALKER, Alice. *The Temple of My Familiar*. 1989. San Diego. HBJ. 1st. sgn. F in F dj. D10. $60.00.

WALKER, Alice. *You Can't Keep a Good Woman Down*. 1981. NY. HBJ. 1st. front brd & dj mildly bumped. F/F. A24. $235.00.

WALKER, David J. *Half the Truth*. 1996. NY. St. Martin. 1st. sgn. VF/VF. T2. $25.00.

WALKER, Egbert H. *Flora of Okinawa and the Southern Ryukyu Islands*. 1976. Washington, DC. biblio. indexes. ep maps. 4to. AN. B26. $45.00.

WALKER, Gerald. *Cruising*. 1970. NY. Stein. 1st. book has slight slant. two small ink marks on front fep and light rubbing at spine ends. jacket has light rubbing at extremities. NF+/NF+. H11. $35.00.

WALKER, Jan. *The Singular Case of the Duplicate Holmes*. 1994. Romford, Essex. Ian Henry Publications. 1st. VF/VF. T2. $35.00.

WALKER, Margaret. *October Journey*. 1973. Broadside Press. 1st. water discoloration on front cover. F/WRP. M25. $45.00.

WALKER, Mary Willis. *All the Dead Lie Down*. 1998. NY. Doubleday. 1st. VF/F. H11. $20.00.

WALKER, Mary Willis. *All the Dead Lie Down*. 1998. NY. Doubleday. ARC. F/wrp. B2. $35.00.

WALKER, Mary Willis. *The Red Scream*. 1994. NY. Doubleday. 1st. UP. F/pict wrp. T2. $75.00.

WALKER, Mary Willis. *The Red Scream*. 1994. NY. Doubleday. 1st. VF/VF. T2. $85.00.

WALKER, Mary Willis. *The Red Scream*. 1994. NY. Doubleday. 1st. VF/VF. H11. $110.00.

WALKER, Mary Willis. *The Red Scream*. 1994. NY. Doubleday. 1st. F/dj. M15. $85.00.

WALKER, Mary Willis. *The Red Scream*. 1994. NY. Doubleday. 1st. UP. F/pict wrp. T2. $75.00.

WALKER, Mary Willis. *The Red Scream*. 1994. NY. Doubleday. 1st. VF/VF. T2. $85.00.

WALKER, Mary Willis. *The Red Scream*. 1994. NY. Doubleday. 1st. sgn by author. F in F dj. B2. $100.00.

WALKER, Mary Willis. *The Red Scream*. 1994. NY. Doubleday. 1st. sgn by author. Edgar award winner for best novel. mystery. F/F. B3. $125.00.

WALKER, Mary Willis. *The Red Scream*. 1994. NY. Doubleday. UP. author's 2nd novel. NF in pict wrp. M23. $50.00.

WALKER, Mary Willis. *Under the Beetle's Cellar*. 1995. NY. Doubleday. 1st. sgn. VF/VF. T2. $35.00.

WALKER, Mary Willis. *Under the Beetle's Cellar*. 1995. NY. Doubleday. 1st. VF/F. H11. $30.00.

WALKER, Mary Willis. *Under the Beetle's Cellar*. 1995. NY. Doubleday. 1st. sgn. F/F. D10. $40.00.

WALKER, Mary Willis. *Under the Beetle's Cellar*. 1995. NY. Doubleday. 1st. sgn by author. F/F. B3. $40.00.

WALKER, N., ed. *Soil Microbiology*. 1975. NY. Wiley. 262p ils. F in dj. B26. $15.00.

WALKER, Norris. *A History of the Christian Church.* 1985. Scribner's. 756p. VG/VG. B29. $16.00.

WALKER, Walter. *A Dime to Dance By.* 1983. NY. Harper & Row. 1st. author's 1st book. name on front fep. F/F. H11. $50.00.

WALKER, Walter. *Rules of the Knife Fight.* 1986. NY. Harper & Row. 1st. F/NF. H11. $20.00.

WALKER, Walter. *The Two Dude Defense.* 1985. NY. Harper & Row. 1st. book has very slight slant and a book store stamp on rear pastedown. jacket has four ¼" tears on bottom edges. F/NF. H11. $20.00.

WALKER, Wyatt Tee. *Somebody's Calling My Name: Black Sacred Music and Social Change.* 1979. Valley Forge. Judson Press. ex lib copy. VG/VG. B2. $45.00.

WALL, John F. & Frank Jennings. *Judging the Horse.* 1955. NY. Funk. 1st ed. VG/VG. O3. $35.00.

WALLACE, Arthur. *Solute Uptake by Intact Plants.* 1963. Los Angeles. pub by author. VG. B26. $14.00.

WALLACE, Daniel. *Big Fish.* 1998. Chapel Hill. Algonquin. sgn 1st ed. F/F. M23. $35.00.

WALLACE, David Foster. *A Supposedly Fun Thing I'll Never Do Again.* 1997. Boston. Little, Brn. 1st. sgn. F/F. O11. $50.00.

WALLACE, David Foster. *A Supposedly Fun Thing I'll Never Do Again.* 1997. Boston. Little, Brn. 1st. F/F. O11. $25.00.

WALLACE, David Foster. *Brief Interviews With Hideous Men.* 1999. Boston. Little, Brn. 1st. sgn. F in F dj. D10. $40.00.

WALLACE, David Foster. *Girl with Curious Hair.* 1989. NY. Norton. 1st. sgn. F/F. D10. $70.00.

WALLACE, David Foster. *Girl with Curious Hair.* 1989. NY. Norton. 1st. sgn. F in NF dj. D10. $65.00.

WALLACE, David Foster. *Girl with Curious Hair.* 1989. NY. Norton. 1st. F/F. B2. $40.00.

WALLACE, David Foster. *Infinite Jest.* 1996. Boston. Little, Brn. 1st. Signed. ARC. VNF. D10. $85.00.

WALLACE, David Foster. *Infinite Jest.* 1996. Boston. Little, Brn. 1/1000 special galleys. sgn. NF in wrp. D10. $75.00.

WALLACE, David Foster. *Infinite Jest.* 1996. Boston. Little, Brn. 1st. F/F. B3. $75.00.

WALLACE, David Foster. *Infinite Jest.* 1996. Boston. Little, Brn. 1st. sgn. NYTimes Book of the Year 1996. F/F. O11. $125.00.

WALLACE, David Foster. *The Broom of the System.* 1987. NY. Viking. 1st. PBO. sgn. hc & pb eds pub simultaneously. F. O11. $150.00.

WALLACE, David Foster. *The Girl with the Curious Hair.* 1989. NY. Norton. 1st. sgn. F/F. O11. $75.00.

WALLACE, David Foster. *The Girl with the Curious Hair.* 1989. NY. Norton. 1st. F/F. O11. $30.00.

WALLACE, E. R. *The Modern Babes in the Wood Or Summerings in the Wilderness...To Which Is Added a Reliable and Descriptive Guide to the Adirondacks.* Hartford. Columbian Book Company. 1872. 8vo. 444p. ils. reddish-brncloth. 1st ed. lengthy Adirondack guide (approx. 50% of the book). two sgns just beginning to loosen. spine lettering faded. minor wear top & bottom of spine. G to VG. L5. $70.00.

WALLACE, Edgar. *Sanders of the River.* 1930. Garden City. Doubleday. 1st Am. small stain at base of spine. F/VF. M15. $125.00.

WALLACE, Edgar. *The Death Safe.* 1933. NY. Einson Freeman. 1st. puzzle box has some light wear. NF/. M15. $300.00.

WALLACE, Edgar. *The Law of the Three Just Men.* 1931. Garden City. Doubleday. 1st Am. NF/VF. M15. $125.00.

WALLACE, Edgar. *The Ringer Returns.* 1931. Garden City. Doubleday. 1st Am. VG/VF. M15. $125.00.

WALLACE, Edgar. *White Face.* 1931. Garden City. Doubleday. 1st Am. VG/VF. M15. $125.00.

WALLACE, Gary D. *Vascular Plants of the Channel Islands of Southern California and Guadalupe Island, Baja, California, Mexico.* 1985. Los Angeles. 4to. sc. F. B26. $21.00.

WALLACE, Irving. *The Seventh Secret.* 1986. Signet. pb. F. F6. $1.25.

WALLACE, Irving. *The Word.* 1972. NY. S&S. 1st. F/F. H11. $40.00.

WALLACE, John. *Carpetbag Rule in Florida. The Inside Workings of the Reconstruction of Civil Gov't in Florida After the Close of the Civil War.* 1959. Kennesaw, GA. Continental Book Co. reprint of rare 1888 ed. orig cloth. NF. M8. $65.00.

WALLACE, Paul A. W. *Pennsylvania, Seed of a Nation.* 1962. Harper & Row. 1st. 8vo. sgn. 2 tears in middle of spine. 322p. F/G. H1. $15.00.

WALLACE, William. *Tales of Mystery and Crime.* 1948. London. Edmund Ward. 1st. F in dj. M15. $45.00.

WALLER, Fats. *Boogie Woogie with Fats Waller.* 1941. NY. Mills. 1st. wrp. 32p. VG w/ some penciling. B2. $35.00.

WALLER, Fats. *Fats Waller's Boogie Woogie Conceptions of Popular Favorites.* 1943. NY. Mills. 1st. wrp. 24p. VG. B2. $35.00.

WALLER, Fats. *Swing Sessions for Piano.* 1937. NY. Mills. 1st. wrp. 32p. NF. B2. $35.00.

WALLER, Robert James. *Old Songs in a New Cafe.* 1994. Warner Books. inscr 1st ed. F/F. s19. $35.00.

WALLER, Robert James. *Slow Waltz in Cedar Bend.* 1993. Warner Books. 1st. F/F. s19. $50.00.

WALLER, Robert James. *The Bridges of Madison County.* 1992. NY. Warner. 1st. VF/F. H11. $175.00.

WALLER, Robert James. *The Bridges of Madison County.* 1992. NY. Warner. 1st. F/F. D10. $135.00.

WALLER, Robert James. *The Bridges of Madison County.* 1992. NY. Warner Books. 1st ed of author's 1st book. F in F dj. D10. $125.00.

WALLER, Robert James. *The Bridges of Madison County.* 1992. Warner Books. 1st. F/F. s19. $90.00.

WALLER, Robert James. *The Bridges of Madison County.* 1992. NY. Warner. 1st. F/F. B3. $30.00.

WALLING, William English. *Russia's Message. The True World Import of the Revolution.* 1908. NY. Doubleday. 1st. ils w/photos. VG. over repaired front hinge. B2. $40.00.

WALLINGTON, C. E. *Meteorology for Glider Pilots.* 1966. London. John Murray. 2nd. b/w photos & diagrams. 8vo. 302p. VG/rubbed dj. K5. $24.00.

WALLIS, Charles. *Notable Sermons from Protestant Pulpits.* 1958. Abingdon. 206p. G. B29. $7.00.

WALLIS, Ethel Emily. *God Speaks Navajo.* 1968. Harper. 146p. VG. B29. $4.00.

WALSH, J. M. *The White Mask.* 1927. NY. George H. Doran. 1st Am ed. VG in worn dj. M15. $65.00.

WALSH, John Evangelist. *Midnight Dreary: The Mysterious Death of Edgar Allan Poe.* 1998. Brunswick. Rutgers Univ. Press. 1st. sgn. VF/VF. T2. $35.00.

WALSH, Joseph M. *Coffee: Its History, Classification & Description.* 1894. John C. Winston co. 12mo. 300p. G. H1. $95.00.

WALTARI, Mika. *A Stranger Came to the Farm.* 1952. np. 1st. pc. F/F dj. M19. $25.00.

WALTCH, Lilla M. *Fearful Symmetry.* 1988. Dodd, Mead. 1st. NF/NF. G8. $10.00.

WALTCH, Lilla M. *Third Victim.* 1987. Dodd, Mead. 1st. NF/NF. G8. $10.00.

WALTERS, Helen B. *Hermann Oberth; Father of Space Travel.* 1962. NY. Macmillan. 1st printing. b/w photo ils. 8vo. inscr/sgn in ink on ffep. 169p. VG/chipped dj. ink mk on front cover of dj. K5. $45.00.

WALTERS, Minette. *The Dark Room.* 1996. NY. Putnam. 1st Am ed. sgn. VF/VF. T2. $35.00.

WALTERS, Minette. *The Dark Room.* 1995. London. Macmillan. 1st. UPC. One of 1000 numbered copies. Pictorial colored wrappers which are totally different than the dust jacket illustration on the first edition. F/WRP. M15. $125.00.

WALTERS, Minette. *The Dark Room.* 1995. London. Macmillan. 1st. sgn. VF in dj. M15. $75.00.

WALTERS, Minette. *The Dark Room.* (1995). NY. Putnam. 1st. author's 4th book. sgn by author. F/F. B3. $60.00.

WALTERS, Minette. *The Dark Room.* 1996. NY. Putnam. 1st Am ed. F/F. A24. $20.00.

WALTERS, Minette. *The Echo.* 1997. London. Macmillan. 1st. sgn. VF/VF. T2. $45.00.

WALTERS, Minette. *The Echo.* 1997. NY. Putnam. 1st Am ed. UP. sgn. F/pict wrp. T2. $25.00.

WALTERS, Minette. *The Echo.* 1997. London. Macmillan. 1st. sgn. VF in dj. M15. $65.00.

WALTERS, Minette. *The Echo.* 1997. NY. Putnam. 1st Am ed. sgn & dated by author. F/F. B3. $45.00.

WALTERS, Minette. *The Echo.* 1997. NY. Putnam. 1st Am ed. sgn. F/F. A24. $40.00.

WALTERS, Minette. *The Scold's Bride.* 1994. London. Macmillan. 1st. sgn. VF in dj. M15. $85.00.

WALTERS, Minette. *The Scold's Bridle.* 1994. NY. St. Martin. 1st Am ed. sgn. VF/VF. T2. $35.00.

WALTERS, Minette. *The Scold's Bridle.* 1994. London. Macmillan. 1st. sgn. NF/VF. T2. $35.00.

WALTERS, Minette. *The Scold's Bridle.* 1994. Bristol. Scorpion. 1st. one of 75 specially bound numbered copies sgn. VF/WPR. M15. $200.00.

WALTERS, Minette. *The Scold's Bridle.* 1994. London. Macmillan. 1st. sgn. VF/dj. M15. $85.00.

WALTERS, Minette. *The Scold's Bridle.* 1994. NY. St. Martin. 1st Am ed. sgn. VF/VF. T2. $35.00.

WALTERS, Minette. *The Scold's Bridle.* 1994. London. Macmillan. 1st. sgn. NF/VF. T2. $35.00.

WALTERS, Minette. *The Scold's Bridle.* 1994. NY. St. Martin. 1st Am ed. F/F. A24. $25.00.

WALTERS, Minette. *The Scold's Bridle.* 1994. NY. St. Martin. 1st Am ed. sgn. F/F. O11. $35.00.

WALTERS, Minette. *The Sculptress.* 1993. NY. SMP. 1st. F/F. H11. $65.00.

WALTERS, Minette. *The Sculptress.* 1993. NY. St. Martin. 1st Am ed. sgn by author. F/F. B2. $85.00.

WALTERS, Minette. *The Sculptress.* 1993. NY. St. Martin. 1st Am ed. sgn. F/F. O11. $65.00.

WALTERS, Minette. *The Scultpress.* 1993. NY. St. Martin. 1st Am ed. sgn. NF/NF. lt wear. A24. $50.00.

WALTERS, Minette. *The Scultpress.* 1993. NY. St. Martin. 1st Am ed. F/F. A24. $30.00.

WALTON, Clyde C. *Mr. Lincoln Opens His Mail.* 1967. Lincoln, IL. Lincoln College. 1st. Historical Society Pamphlet Series No. 5. orig printed wrp. 31p. NF. M8. $22.50.

WAMBAUGH, Joseph. *Echoes in the Darkness.* 1987. NY. Morrow. 1st. F/NF. H11. $20.00.

WAMBAUGH, Joseph. *Finnegan's Week.* 1993. NY. Morrow. 1st. F/F. H11. $25.00.

WAMBAUGH, Joseph. *The Black Marble.* 1978. NY. Delacorte. 1st. blind stp on ffep. F/F. short tear & crease. A24. $25.00.

WAMBAUGH, Joseph. *The Choirboys.* 1975. Delacorte. 1st. F/NF. H11. $25.00.

WAMBAUGH, Joseph. *The Choirboys.* 1975. NY. Delacorte. 1st. F/NF. H11. $30.00.

WAMBAUGH, Joseph. *The Onion Field.* 1973. NY. Delacorte. 1st. author's 1st nonfiction wk. VG+/VG+. lt edgewear. short tear. A24. $35.00.

WAMPLER, Joseph. *Havasu Canyon: Gem of the Grand Canyon.* 1959. Berkeley. 1st. VG. F7. $22. 50.

WAMSLEY, James S. *Idols, Victims, Pioneers: Virginia's Women from 1607.* 1976. VA Chamber of Commerce. ils. 307p. VG/G. B10. $35.00.

WANDREI, Donald. *Colossus: The Collected Science Fiction of Donald Wandrei.* 1999. Minneapolis. Fedogan & Bremer. 2nd printing. VF/VF. T2. $29.00.

WANDREI, Donald. *Don't Dream: The Collected Horror and Fantasy Fiction of Donald Wandrei.* 1997. Minneapolis. Fedogan & Bremer. 1st. VF/VF. T2. $29.00.

WANDREI, Donald. *Ecstasy and Other Poems.* Athol, MA. published by W. Paul Cook, The Recluse Press. 1928. 8vo. 40p. purple cloth author's 1st book. paper title label. lst ed. glassine dj torn on rear. book F. L5. $475.00.

WANDREI, Howard. *The Last Pin.* 1996. Minneapolis. Fedogan & Bremer. 1st. DH Olson, editor. VF/VF. T2. $29.00.

WANDREI, Howard. *The Last Pin.* 1996. Minneapolis. Fedogan & Bremer. 1st. 1/100 # copies. sgn by Wandrei & DH Olson, editor/artist Gary Gianni. receipt for liquor purchase by Wandrei laid in. short story chapbook # & sgn by Olson Is inserted in slipcase. VF/VF dj & slipcase. T2. $125.00.

WANDREI, Howard. *Time Burial: The Collected Fantasy Tales of Howard Wandrei.* 1995. Minneapolis. Fedogan & Bremer. 1st. D. H. Olson, editor. VF/VF. T2. $35.00.

WANG, Dajun & Shao Jin Shen. *Bamboos of China.* 1987. Portland. 4to. OP. 167p w/68 b&w photos. 64 line drawings. 4 color plates. F in dj. B26. $95.00.

WANGER, E. D. *Arts & Decoration Book of Successful Houses.* 1940. McBride. 112p. cloth. VG. A10. $25.00.

WANTE, Stephen, and Walter De Block. *V Disc Catalogue Vol. 1, Nos. 1 – 500.* nd. Berchem-Antwerp. Van Laerstraat. 1st. 84p. NF/wrp. B2. $35.00.

WAPSHOTT, Nicholas. *Carol Reed: A Biography.* 1994. NY. 1st Am. photos. VG/dj. M17. $17.50.

WARBURG, James P. *It's Up to Us.* 1934. NY. Knopf. inscr/sgn. F. B14. $45.00.

WARD, Geoffrey C. *The Civil War: An Illustrated History.* 1990. NY. Knopf. 5th printing. orig cloth. plates. maps. ils. 425p. NF/NF. M8. $25.00.

WARD, Lynd. *Gods' Man.* 1929. Cape Smith. 1st. ils brd/blk cloth backstrip. VG. C15. $75.00.

WARD, Lynd. *Story of Siegfried.* 1931. NY. Cape Smith. 1st. 4to. dk bl cloth/bstp Vignette. mc dj. R5. $150.00.

WARD, Lynd. *The Biggest Bear.* 1952. Boston. Houghton Mifflin. later printing. juvenile. VG. B2. $25.00.

WARD, Mrs. Humphrey. *Testing of Diana Mallory.* 1908. NY. Harper. ils W Hatherell. 549p. G. G11. $7.00.

WARD, Nanda. *Wellington & the Witch.* 1959. Hastings. 1st. xl. VG/G. P2. $20.00.

WARD, Nathaniel. *Simple Cobbler of Aggawam in America.* 1843. Boston. Monroe. rpt (1657 London). 8vo. 96p. gilt bstp cloth. NF. $1.00.

WARD, Robert. *The Cactus Garden.* 1995. NY. Pocket Books. 1st. VF/VF. T2. $9.00.

WARD, Robert. *The Cactus Garden.* 1995. NY. Pocket Books. ARC. NF/wrp. B2. $25.00.

WARDEN, Carl John. *Animal Motivation: Experimental Studies on Albino Rats.* 1931. Columbia U. 502p. panelled straight-grain bl cloth. NF. G1. $65.00.

WARDEN, Herbert W. *In Praise of Sailors: A Nautical Anthology of Art.* 1978. NY. Abrams. 1st. 4to. 299p. $0.00.

WARDLE, John. *The New Zealand Beeches: Ecology, Utilisation and Management.* 1984. Wellington. N. Z. Forest Service. extensive biblio. subject index. 447p w/map & 107 text figures. VG in dj. B26. $39.00.

WARDWELL, Allen. *Island Ancestors: Oceanic Art from the Masco Collection.* 1994. np. Univ. of Washington Press. 1st printing. burgundy cloth 4to. w/ gilt spine titles & cover decor. decor ep. 282p. new in dj. P4. $60.00.

WARE, Harry S. *The Unforgettables.* 1965. Hertford. Mimram Books. octavo. blk cloth. spine lettered in gilt. pict dj. F. R3. $15.00.

WARE, J. D. *George Gauld: Surveyor & Cartographer of Gulf Coast.* 1982. FL U. 1st. 13 facs charts. F/dj. M4. $30.00.

WARE, Joseph A., compiler. *Post Office Department. The Postal Laws and Regulations. Published by the Authority of the Postmaster General.* 1866. Washington. GPO. orig cloth backed bl printed wrp. 114.90p. K1. $100.00.

WARFIELD, Benjamin B. *The Person and Work of Christ.* 1950. presb. & reformed. 575p. G/broken back/ex lib. B29. $11.00.

WARFIELD, Don. *Roaring Redhead.* 1987. Diamond Comm. 1st. photos. F/dj. P8. $25.00.

WARGA, Wayne. *Fatal Impressions.* 1989. NY. Arbor House. 1st. VF/VF. T2. $30.00.

WARGA, Wayne. *Hardcover.* 1985. Arbor. 1st. NF/F. H11. $30.00.

WARGA, Wayne. *Hardcover.* 1985. NY. Arbor House. 1st. sgn inscr. author's 1st book. VF/VF. T2. $40.00.

WARGA, Wayne. *Hardcover.* 1985. NY. Arbor. 1st. book has a spine crease and one bumped corner. NF/F. H11. $30.00.

WARGA, Wayne. *Hardcover.* 1985. NY. Arbor House. 1st. sgn inscr. author's 1st book. VF/VF. T2. $40.00.

WARHOL, Andy. *America.* 1st. sgn twice. sc. O8. $385.00.

WARHOL, Andy. *Philosophy of Andy Warhol From A to B & Back Again.* 1975. HBJ. 1st. NF/F. T12. $80.00.

WARLICK, Ashley. *The Distance from the Heart of Things.* 1996. Boston/NY. Houghton Mifflin. sgn 1st ed. F/F. M23. $40.00.

WARMAN, Edwin G. *Milk Glass Addenda.* 1959. Uniontown, PA. E. G. Warman Publishing. 2nd. 8vo. wraps. covers scuffed. VG. H1. $97.50.

WARMAN, Edwin G. *Milk Glass Addenda.* 1952. Uniontown, PA. E. G. Warman Publishing. 1st. 8vo. wraps. unpaginated. VG. H1. $45.00.

WARMAN, Edwin G. *Milk Glass Addenda.* 1952. Uniontown, PA. E. G. Warman Publishing. 1st. tall 8vo. wraps. unpaginated. VG. H1. $97.50.

WARNER, Frances Lester. *On a New England Campus.* Boston and NY. Houghton Mifflin Co. 1937. 8vo. (280)p. ils. bl cloth. 1st ed. lacks a dj. VG. L5. $35.00.

WARNER, Oliver. *Chatto & Windus: A Brief Account of Firm's History.* 1973. London. Chatto Windus. 1st. sm 8vo. cloth. dj. O10. $25.00.

WARNER, Sylvia Townsend. *Lolly Willowes & Mr. Fortunes Maggot.* 1966. Viking. 40th Anniversary ed. G/dj. L1. $35.00.

WARNER, Jack. *Bijou Dream.* 1982. NY. Crown. 1st. F/F. H11. $20.00.

WARNER & WHITE. *Chesapeake: Portrait of the Bay Country.* Creative Resource. sgn. VG/G. R8. $100.00.

WARREN, Charles. *The Supreme Court in United States History. New and Revised Ed. In Two Volumes. Vol One 1789 – 1835. (Vol Two 1836 – 1918).* 1926. Boston. Little, Brn. ils 16 plates. orig gr cloth. xviii, 814p. fine set in djs. K1. $75.00.

WARREN, Edward. *Doctor's Experiences on Three Continents.* 1885. Baltimore. Cushings Bailey. 1st. 619p. ES. $8.00.

WARREN, Frank A. *Liberals & Communism: Red Decade Revisited.* 1966. Bloomington, IN. 1st. 8vo. VG/dj. A2. $20.00.

WARREN, H. G. *Paraguay: Informal History.* 1949. OK U. 1st. ils/maps. 393p. F/dj. M4. $20.00.

WARREN, J. Russell. *Murder from Three Angels.* 1939. Lee Furman. 1st Am. VG/dj. M15. $45.00.

WARREN, John C. *Comparative View of Sensoral & Nervous System of Man.* 1822. Boston. Ingraham. 6 engravings. 159p. sugar brd/rb. $7.00.

WARREN, Mary Bowers. *Little Journeys Abroad.* 1895. Boston. Knight. 1st. ils. xl. VG. W1. $22.00.

WARREN, Raymond. *Prairie President.* 1930. Chicago. Reilly Lee. 8vo. 427p. brn cloth. G. S17. $5.00.

WARREN, Robert Penn. *A Place to Come to.* 1977. NY. Random. 1st. remainder mark. F/F. H11. $30.00.

WARREN, Robert Penn. *Promises: Poems 1954 – 1956*. 1957. Random. 1st. 84p. F/dj. H1. $35.00.

WARREN, Robert Penn. *Remember the Alamo!* 1958. Random. 3rd. ils Wm Moyers. 182p. VG/dj. B36. $11.00.

WARREN, Robert Penn. *The Cave*. 1959. NY. Random House. 1st. octavo. orig brown cloth. pict dj. F. slight fading to spine. R3. $22.50.

WARREN, Robert Penn. *Who Speaks for the Negro?* 1965. Random. 1st. NF/VG. Q1. $60.00.

WARREN, S. Edward. *Stereotomy: Problems in Stone Cutting*. 1888. NY. Wiley. 10 fld pl. 126p. fair. H10. $25.00.

WARREN, Samuel. *Ten Thousand a Year*. 1841. Edinburgh. William Blackwood. 3 vols. 1st. bstp cloth. fading & edgewear. G. B18. $125.00.

WARREN, William. *Thai Garden Style*. 1996. Singapore. 10" x 10". 192p w/over 250 color photos by Luca Invernizzi Tettoni. VG in dj. B26. $32.50.

WARREN COMMISSION. *Report of the Warren Commission on the Assassination of President Kennedy*. 1964. NY. McGraw Hill. 1st. Oct 1964. hc. G. no dj. A28. $24.95.

WARSHAWSKY, Abel G. *Paris Unconquered, with a Foreword by Paul Scott Mowrer*. 1957. Sanbornville, NH. Wake-Brook House. presentation copy. sgn. lg 4to. 42 plates. 116p. gray cloth over marbled brds. paper spine label. slipcase w/mtd color ils. K1. $100.00.

WASHBURN, Stan. *Intent to Harm*. 1994. NY. Pocket. 1st. F/F. H11. $20.00.

WASHINGTON, Booker T. *The Future of the American Negro*. 1899. Boston. Small, Maynard. 1st. superior copy. owner's name. dulled spine. F. B2. $300.00.

WASHINGTON, George. *Diary of George Washington September – December 1785*. (Ed by Worthington Chauncey Ford). 1902. Boston. privately printed. 8vo. 75p. orig printed paper wrps (pamphlet). reprinted from "The Publications of the Colonial Society of Massachusetts." ltd to 250 copies. pamphlet pages unopened. wrp dust soiled and beginning to chip at edges. VG. L5. $20.00.

WATANABE, John. *Maya Saints & Souls in a Changing World*. 1992. Austin. Univ. of Texas Press. 1st. 280p. G/wrp. F3. $20.00.

WATERHOUSE, Francis A. *Bun Running Into the Red Sea*. 1930s. London. Sampson Low. 1st? 8vo. 244p. red cloth. G. M7. $40.00.

WATERMAN, Charles F. *Fisherman's World*. 1971. NY. 1st. biblio/index. 250p. F/dj. A17. $18. $50.00.

WATERMAN, Charles F. *Hunter's World*. nd. NY. biblio/index. 250p. F/dj. A17. $17.50.

WATERMAN, Charles F. *Hunter's World*. 1976. Ridge/Random. 1st. ils. NF/dj. B27. $35.00.

WATERMAN, George. *Practical Stock Doctor. 300 Tried & Tested Remedies*. 1912. Detroit. enlarged. $840.00.

WATERMAN, Lucius. *Eras of the Christian Church; The Post Apostolic Age*. 1898. Clark. 505p. VG. B29. $12.50.

WATERMAN, Thomas Tileston. *Mansions of Virginia 1706 – 1776*. 1945. UNC. 7th. photos/plans. 456p. B10. $50.00.

WATERS, Frank. *Brave are My People*. 1993. Santa Fe. Clear Light. 1st. fwd by Vine Deloria Jr. this copy sgn by Deloria and Waters. F/F. B3. $75.00.

WATERS, Frank. *Earp Brothers of Tombstone*. 1962. London. Spearman. F. A19. $35.00.

WATERS, Frank. *Mexico Mystique: Coming 6th World of Consciousness*. 1975. Chicago. Swallow. 2nd. 326p. dj. F3. $20.00.

WATERS, Frank. *To Possess the Land*. 1973. Sage. 1st. F/VG. T11. $45.00.

WATERS, George & Nora Harlow. *Pacific Horticulture Book of Western Gardening*. 1990. Boston. 4to. fully indexed. 300p w/100+ color photos. VG in dj. B26. $39.00.

WATERS, Howard J. *Jack Teagarden's Music, His Career and Recordings*. 1960. Stanhope. Walter C. Allen. 1st. wrps. F/F. B2. $65.00.

WATKINS, Eleanor Preston. *The Builders of San Francisco and Some of Their Early Homes*. 1935. San Francisco. Nat'l. Society of Colonial Dames of America in the State of CA. ils. octavo. brown wrps. lettered in blk. F. R3. $20.00.

WATKINS, Paul. *Archangel*. 1996. Random House. ARC of Am ed. F in decor wrp. M25. $25.00.

WATKINS, Paul. *Archangel*. 1996. NY. Random House. 1st. F/F. B3. $30.00.

WATKINS, Paul. *Calm at Sunset, Calm at Dawn*. 1989. Boston. Houghton. 1st. F/F. H11. $60.00.

WATKINS, Paul. *Calm at Sunset, Calm at Dawn*. 1989. NY. Random House. 1st. author's 2nd book. F/NF. lt edgewear. B3. $40.00.

WATKINS, Paul. *Calm at Sunset, Calm at Dawn*. nd. London. Hutchinson. 1st British ed/true 1st. author's 2nd book. sgn. F/F. A24. $75.00.

WATKINS, Paul. *Calm at Sunset, Calm at Dawn*. 1989. NY. Houghton Mifflin. 1st Am ed. author's 2nd book. F/F mild crinkle at top back corner. A24. $35.00.

WATKINS, Paul. *In the Blue Light of African Dreams*. 1990. Boston. Houghton. 1st. F/F. H11. $45.00.

WATKINS, Paul. *In the Blue Light of African Dreams*. 1990. Boston. Houghton Mifflin. 1st Am ed. author's 3rd book. F/F. A24. $30.00.

WATKINS, Paul. *Night Over Day Over Night*. 1988. Knopf. 1st Am. author's 1st book. sgn. F/dj. Q1. $100.00.

WATKINS, Paul. *Night Over Day Over Night*. 1988. NY. Knopf. 1st. author's 1st book. rem mk. NF/dj. B3. $60.00.

WATKINS, Paul. *Night Over Day Over Night*. 1988. NY. Knopf. 1st. author's 1st book. F/F. H11. $120.00.

WATKINS, Paul. *Night Over Day Over Night*. 1988. NY. Knopf. 1st. author's 1st book. a Booker nominee. F/NF. price clipped. B3. $150.00.

WATKINS, Paul. *Night Over Day Over Night*. 1988. NY. Knopf. 1st. author's 1st novel. F/F. rem mk. M23. $30.00.

WATKINS, Paul. *Night Over Day Over Night*. 1988. NY. Knopf. 1st Am ed/true 1st. author's 1st book. F/F. A24. $85.00.

WATKINS, Paul. *Story of My Disappearance*. 1997. London. Faber. 1st. sgn. F/dj. R14. $75.00.

WATKINS, Paul. *The Archangel*. 1995. London. Faber & Faber. true 1st British ed. F/F. A24. $37.00.

WATKINS, Paul. *The Archangel*. 1995. NY. Random House. 1st Am ed. F/F. A24. $20.00.

WATKINS, Paul. *The Promise of Light*. 1992. NY. Random. 1st. F/F. H11. $30.00.

WATKINS, Paul. *The Promise of Light.* 1992. London. Faber & Faber. true 1st British ed. F/F. lt wear to spine ends. A24. $35.00.

WATKINS, Paul. *The Promise of Light.* 1993. NY. Random House. 1st Am ed. F/F. A24. $25.00.

WATKINS, Ron. *Sinner Takes All.* 1979. London. Hale. 1st. F/dj. M15. $40.00.

WATKINS, S. C. G. *Reminiscences of Montclair.* 1929. NY. Barnes. inscr. G. A19. $60.00.

WATKINS, T. H. *Great Depression: America in the 1930s.* 1993. Boston. 1st. ils. 375p. F/dj. M4. $15.00.

WATKINS, T. H. *On the Shore of the Sundown Sea.* 1972. Sierra Club. 1st. natural linen. F/NF. O4. $20.00.

WATKINS, T. H. *Vanishing Arctic: Alaska's National Wildlife Refuge.* 1988. Aperture. 88p. dj. A17. $17. 50.

WATKINSON, Ray. *William Morris as Designer.* 1990. London. Trefoil. ils/pl. 84p. gilt cream cloth. F/NF. F1. $15.00.

WATSON, Aldren A. *Hand Bookbinding: A Manual of Instruction.* 1986. NY. 1st. VG/dj. T9. $18.00.

WATSON, Colin. *One Man's Meat.* 1977. London. Eyre Methuen. 1st. price clipped jacket. F/dj. M15. $85.00.

WATSON, Colin. *Plaster Sinners.* 1980. London. Eyre Methuen. 1st. F/dj. M15. $45.00.

WATSON, Elizabeth. *Guests of My Life.* 1996. Friends General Conference. 1996. VG/wrp. V3. $9.00.

WATSON, Elmo Scott. *Professor Goes West (JW Powell).* 1954. Bloomington, IL. 1st. 138p. gilt gr cloth. NF. F7. $40.00.

WATSON, G. R. *Roman Soldier.* 1981 (1969). London. rpt. ils. 256p. cloth. VG/dj. $2.00.

WATSON, George William. *The Last Survivor, The Memoirs of Geo. Wm. Watson, A Horse Soldier.* 1993. Washington, WV. Night Hawk Press. 1st. orig stiff decor wrp. 68p. NF. sgn by compiler Brian Stuart Kesterson. M8. $37.50.

WATSON, Ian. *Gardens of Delight.* 1980. London. Gollancz. 1st. AN/dj. M21. $20.00.

WATSON, Ian. *God's World.* 1990. NY. Carroll & Graf. 1st Am ed. F/F. T2. $15.00.

WATSON, Ian. *Lucy's Harvest: First Book of Mana.* 1993. London. Gollancz. 1st. F/dj. G10. $27.50.

WATSON, Ian. *Oracle.* 1997. London. Gollancz. 1st. VF/VF. T2. $30.00.

WATSON, Ian. *Salvage Rites and Other Stories.* 1989. London. Gollancz. 1st. VF/VF. T2. $30.00.

WATSON, Ian. *Stalin's Teardrops and Other Stories.* 1991. London. Gollancz. 1st. VF/VF. T2. $25.00.

WATSON, Ian. *The Book of Ian Watson.* 1985. Willimantic. Mark V. Ziesing. 1st. VF/VF. T2. $20.00.

WATSON, Ian. *The Flies of Memory.* 1990. London. Gollancz. 1st. VF/VF. T2. $25.00.

WATSON, Ian & Michael Bishop. *Under Heaven's Bridge.* 1980. London. Gollancz. 1st. review copy w/pub slip. sgn inscr by Bishop. F/F. T2. $85.00.

WATSON, Larry. *Justice.* 1995. Minn. Milkweed. 1st. sgn. F/F. D10. $45.00.

WATSON, Larry. *Justice.* 1995. Minnesota. Milkweed Editions. 1st. sgn. F in F dj. D10. $50.00.

WATSON, Larry. *Justice.* 1994. Minneapolis. Milkweed. 1st. sgn by author. F/F. B3. $40.00.

WATSON, Larry. *Montana 1948.* 1995. London. Macmillan. 1st British ed. sgn by author. F/F. B3. $60.00.

WATSON, Larry. *White Crosses.* 1997. NY. Pocket Books. 1st. sgn by author. F/F. B3. $40.00.

WATSON, Margaret G. *Silver Theatre. Amusements of the Mining Frontier in Early Nevada. 1850 to 1864.* 1964. Glendale, CA. Arthur H. Clark. 1st. octavo. bl cloth. pict dj. ils. F. R3. $60.00.

WATSON, Peter. *Sotheby's: The Inside Story.* 1997. NY. Random House. 1st Am ed. sgn. VF/VF. T2. $25.00.

WATSON, Sidney. *The Mark of the Beast.* 1945. Loizeaux. 245p. G. B29. $8.00.

WATSON, Thomas. *Story of France.* 1899. Macmillan. 2 vol. G. S17. $12. 50.

WATSON, Virginia. *With Cortes the Conquerer.* 1917. Penn. 1st. ils. F. M5. $75.00.

WATSON, W. C. *Men & Times of the Revolution or Memoirs.* 1856. NY. 1st. 460p. VG. M4. $90.00.

WATSON, W. H. L. *Adventures of a Dispatch Rider.* 1915. Toronto. McClelland. Goodchild. Steward. pict cloth. faded spine. 285p. VG. B18. $25.00.

WATSON, A. Conan. *A Pragmatic Enigma: Being a Chapter from the Failures of Sherlock Holmes.* 1999. NY. Mysterious Bookshop. 1st separate ed. 1/221 copies. a chapbook. VF/pict wrp. T2. $10.00.

WATT, George. *Essay on Dental Surgery for Popular Reading.* 1856. Cincinnati. 72p. new brd/orig label. xl. G7. $145.00.

WATT, Henry Jackson. *Common Sense of Dreams.* 1929. Worcester, MA. Clark U. Internatl. U Series Psychology Vol 6. 212p. G1. $35.00.

WATT, J. M. & M. G. Breyer Brandwijk. *Medicinal and Poisonous Plants of Southern and Eastern Africa.* 1962. Edinburgh. 2nd. printed on glossy paper. thick 8vl. 1457p w/286 plates. drawings & photos+57 tables. upper front corner lightly bumped. B26. $595.00.

WATTERSON, T., photographer. *Palomar Pictorial.* 1965. Pasadena, CA. California Institute of Technology. oblong 4to. photos by Watterson. drawings by R. W. Porter. 60p. VG in pict wrp. K5. $40.00.

WATTS, Alan W. *In My Own Way: An Autobiography.* 1972. Pantheon. 1st. poi on title page. NF/clip dj. some wear along edges. M25. $35.00.

WATTS, Alan W. *The Book: On the Taboo Against Knowing Who You Are.* 1966. Pantheon. 1st. Lightly soiled jacket. F/dj. M25. $50.00.

WATTS, Alan W. *The Two Hands of God: The Myths of Polarity.* 1963. George Braziller. 1st. Lightly soiled. foxed. price clipped jacket. F/dj. M25. $35.00.

WATTS, Gilbert S. *Roadside Marketing.* 1928. NY. Orange Judd Pub Co. Inc. 1st. pict cloth cover. lt foxing. G in soiled dj w/edge tears. B18. $22.50.

WATTS, Mabel. *Story of Zachary Sween.* 1967. Parent's Magazine. 1st? ils Marylin Haffner. VG. M5. $8.00.

WATTS, May Theilgaard. *Reading the Landscape: An Adventure in Ecology.* 1963. Macmillan. 4th. 230p. VG/dj. A10. $30.00.

WATTS, Ralph. *Vegetable Gardening.* 1931. Orange Judd. revised. 511p. cloth. VG. A10. $22.00.

WATTS, Timothy. *Steal Away.* 1996. NY. Soho. 1st. F/dj. A23. $46.00.

WAUGH, Alec. *Fuel for the Flame.* 1960. NY. Farrar. 1st. pages are yellowing. NF/F. H11. $30.00.

WAUGH, Alec. *In Praise of Wine & Certain Noble Spirits.* 1959. Wm. Sloane. 1st. F/G. M19. $17. 50.

WAUGH, Alec. *Most Women.* 1931. Farrar Rinehart. 1st. ils Lynd Ward. VG. S13. $12.00.

WAUGH, Auberon. *Bed of Flowers.* 1972. London. Michael Joseph. 1st. VG/clip. R14. $25.00.

WAUGH, Dorothy. *Emily Dickinson's Beloved. A Surmise.* 1976. NY. Vanguard. 1st. 75p. VG. M10. $20.00.

WAUGH, E A. *American Peach Orchard: A Sketch of Practice.* 1915. NY/London. ils. 236p. brn cloth. VG. H3. $50.00.

WAUGH, Evelyn. *Brideshead Revisited.* 1946. Little, Brn. 1st Am trade (precedes ltd). NF/VG. B4. $200.00.

WAUGH, Evelyn. *Handful of Dust.* 1934. Farrar Rinehart. 1st Am. NF/dj. Q1. $450.00.

WAUGH, Evelyn. *Helena.* 1950. London. Chapman Hall. 1st. inscr. NF/dj. L3. $1. $500.00.

WAUGH, Evelyn. *Helena.* 1950. London. Chapman and Hall. 1st. F in G dj. B2. $85.00.

WAUGH, Evelyn. *Letters.* 1992. NY. 1st. edit Artemis Cooper. VG/dj. M17. $20.00.

WAUGH, Evelyn. *Men at Arms.* 1952. Chapman Hall. 1st. NF/dj. M25. $75.00.

WAUGH, Evelyn. *Officers & Gentlemen.* 1955. Little, Brn. 1st. VG/dj. S13. $18.00.

WAUGH, Evelyn. *The Loved One.* 1948. Little, Brn. 1st Am. Lightly browned jacket Is worn at the spine ends. F/dj. M25. $65.00.

WAUGH, Evelyn. *Tourist in Africa.* 1960. London. 1st. dj. T9. $50.00.

WAUGH, F. A. *Book of Landscape Gardening, Treatise on the General Principles Governing Outdoor Art.* 1928 (1899). NY. 3rd rev ed. eps tanned. foxed. B26. $26.00.

WAUGH, Hillary. *Murder on Safari.* 1987. Dodd, Mead. 1st. NF/NF. G8. $10.00.

WAUGH, Julia. *Silver Cradle.* 1955. Austin. 1st. 160p. dj. F3. $15.00.

WAUGH, T. *Travels of Marco Polo.* 1984. NY. ils. 218p. F/dj. M4. $20.00.

WAUGH & WAUGH. *South Builds: New Architecture in the Old South.* 1960. UNC. photos. 173p. F/G. B10. $25.00.

WAVELL, Archibald P. *Allenby in Egypt.* 1943. London. Harrap. 1st. 156p. VG/dj. M7. $50.00.

WAXELL, Sven. *The American Expedition.* 1952. London. William Hodge & Company Ltd. 1st UK ed. bl/gr cloth 8vo. map ep. foldout ils. 236p. F. some general wear. P4. $55.00.

WEALES, Gerald. *Clifford Odets, Playwright.* 1971. NY. Pegasus. 1st. F/F. B2. $25.00.

WEATHERBY, Harold. *Cardinal Newman in His Age: His Place in English Theology and Literature.* 1973. Nashville. Vanderbilt Univ. 296p. VG/VG. B29. $14.50.

WEATHERFORD, Fred M. *The Cross Interprets Christianity.* 1942. Nazarene. 181p. VG. B29. $6.50.

WEATHERHEAD, Leslie. *The Key Next Door and Other London City Temple Sermons.* 1960. Abingdon. 255p. G/G. B29. $7.00.

WEATHERHEAD, Leslie. *The Significance of Silence and Other Sermons.* 1945. Abingdon Cokesbury. 238p. G/worn dj. B29. $8.00.

WEATHERMAN, Hazel Marie. *Colored Glassware of the Depression Era Book 1.* 1970. self-published. 1st. 8vo. owner's label on front endpaper. price clipped. 239p. AN/VG. H1. $80.00.

WEATHERMAN, Hazel Marie. *Colored Glassware of the Depression Era Book 1.* 1970. self pub. 1st/2nd prt. 8vo. 239p. F/NF. H1. $38.00.

WEATHERMAN, Hazel Marie. *Colored Glassware of the Depression Era Book 2.* 1974. self pub. 1st. 401p. ils brd. VG. H1. $85.00.

WEATHERMAN, Hazel Marie. *Fostoria: Its First 50 Years.* 1972. self pub. 1st. ils. 320p. VG/prt Mylar dj. H1. $150.00.

WEATHERMAN, Hazel Marie. *Fostoria: Its First Fifty Years.* 1985. Springfield, MO. self-published. 2nd. oblong 4to. 320p. VG. H1. $125.00.

WEATHERS, Lee B. *Living Past of Cleveland County: A History.* 1956. Shelby, NC. Star. photos/map ep. 269p. VG. B10. $35.00.

WEATHERSPOON, C. P., et al. *Proceedings of the Workshop on Management of Giant Sequoia.* 1986. Berkeley. 4to. sc. B26. $14.00.

WEAVER, Harriett E. *There Stand the Giants: The Story of the Redwood Trees.* 1963. Menlo Park, CA. Sunset Junior Book. 1st ed. 2nd prt. sturdy bdg. pict pastedown on cover. 70p well ils in color & b&w. VG in dj. B26. $17.50.

WEAVER, Louise Bennett & Helen Cowles Lecron. *A Thousand Ways to Please a Husband with Bettina's Best Recipes.* 1917. A. L. Burt. sm8vo. owner's name on endpaper & title page. back hinge broken. 479p. VG. H1. $22.50.

WEAVER, Warren. *The Library Chronicle of The University of Texas at Austin.* 1970. Austin. Humanities Research Center. New Series Number 2. octavo. orig tan printed wrps. F. R3. $10.00.

WEBB, George Ernest. *Tree Rings and Telescope; The Scientific Career of A. E. Douglass.* 1983. Tucson. Univ. of Arizona Press. 8vo. b/w photo ils. 242p. VG/VG. clip. K5. $40.00.

WEBB, Jack. *Make My Bed Soon.* 1963. HRW. 1st. F/NF. T12. $25.00.

WEBB, Jack. *One for My Dame.* 1961. Holt. Rinehart & Winston. 1st. worn and rubbed jacket; sgn; insc. NF/dj. M25. $60.00.

WEBB, Jack. *The Big Sin.* 1952. Rinehart. 1st. jacket chipped at the spine ends. VG/dj. M25. $45.00.

WEBB, Jack. *The Deadly Sex.* 1959. Rinehart. 1st. worn and rubbed jacket. NF/dj. M25. $45.00.

WEBB, James. *The Emperor's General.* 1999. NY. Broadway. 1st. VF/VF. H11. $15.00.

WEBB, James Josiah. *Adventures in the Santa Fe Trade, 1844 – 1847.* 1931. Arthur H. Clark. 301p. D11. $125.00.

WEBB, Joe. *Care & Training of the Tennesse Walking Horse.* 1962. Searcy, AZ. private prt. 1st. sgn. VG. O3. $45.00.

WEBB, Kenneth. *As Sparks Fly Upward: Rationale of Farm & Wilderness Camp.* 1973. Canaan. Phoenix. sgn. ils. 196p. VG/clip. R11. $20.00.

WEBB, Lance. *Conquering the Seven Deadly Sins.* 1955. Abingdon. 224p. VG. B29. $9. 50.

WEBB, Martha G. *Darling Corey's Dead.* 1984. Walker. 1st. NF/NF. G8. $10.00.

WEBB, Martha G. *Even Cops' Daughters.* 1986. Walker. 1st. sgn. F/F. G8. $15.00.

WEBB, Quilla. *Cyclopedia of Sermon Outlines.* 1923. Harper. 336p. fair/broken hinge. B29. $4.50.

WEBB, Roy. *If We Had a Boat: Green River Explorers.* Adventurers. 1986. U. UT. 8vo. ils. 194p.

WEBB, Sharon. *Half Life.* 1989. NY. Tor. 1st. F/NF. G10. $12.00.

WEBB, Sharon. *The Half Life.* 1989. NY. Tor. 1st. F/F. T2. $7.00.

WEBB, T. W. *Celestial Objects for Common Telescopes.* 1881 (1859). Longman Gr. 4th. ils/pl. 493p. cloth. K5. $150.00.

WEBBER, A. Bernard. *More Illustrations and Quotable Poems.* 1945. Zondervan. 119p. VG. B29. $4.00.

WEBBER, Robert. *Evangelicals on the Canterbury Trail; Why Evangelicals are Attracted to the Liturgical Church.* 1985. Jarrell. 174p. VG/VG. B29. $8.50.

WEBER, Francis J. *California on US Postage Stamps.* 1975. Achille St Onge. 1/150. mini. ils+tipped-in stamp. aeg. B27. $45.00.

WEBER, Francis J. *California on US Postage Stamps.* 1975. Worcester. St Onge. mini. 1/1500+US postage stp. aeg. gilt bl leather. B24. $85.00.

WEBER, Francis J. *Catholica on American Stamps.* 1976. Tilton, NH. Hillside. mini. 1/250. pub/sgn Frank Irwin. gr cloth brd. $0.00.

WEBER, Francis J. *The United States Versus Mexico: The Final Settlement of the Pious Fund.* 1969. Los Angeles. Historical Society of Southern California. 1/330 copies. octavo. gr cloth. spine lettered in gilt. foreword by Earl Warren. F. R3. $45.00.

WEBER, Katharine. *Objects in Mirror are Closer than They Appear.* 1995. NY. Crown. 1st. author's 1st book. VF/F. H11. $35.00.

WEBER, Katherine. *The Music Lesson.* 1999. London. Phoenix House. 1st. VF/VF. T2. $30.00.

WEBER, Stu. *Locking Arms: God's Design for Masculine Friendships.* 1995. Multnomah. 287p. F/F. B29. $8.50.

WEBER, William A. *Colorado Flora: Eastern Slope.* 1990. Niwot. ils. 526p. AN/dj. B26. $37.50.

WEBSTER, A. L. *Improved Housewife; or, Book of Receipts.* 1844 (1843). Hartford. 214p. fair. $6.00.

WEBSTER, Daniel. *On the Powers of Government Assigned to It by Constitution.* 1952. Worcester. St Onge. mini. 1/1000. red cloth brd. B24. $185.00.

WEBSTER, Ernest. *Cossack Hide-Out.* 1981. London. Robert Hale. 1st. F/dj. M15. $45.00.

WEBSTER, John. *Introduction to Fungi.* 1970. Cambridge. 424p. xl. VG. S5. $25.00.

WEBSTER, Noah. *Spanish Maze Game.* 1991. Crime Club. 1st Am ed. NF/NF. G8. $10.00.

WECHSER, Lorainne. *Encyclopedia of Graffiti.* 1974. Galahad. rpt. F/NF. S18. $10.00.

WECHSLER, David. *Measurement & Appraisal of Adult Intelligence.* 1958 (1939). Baltimore. Wms. Wilkins. 4th/1st prt. sgn. 297p. red cloth. G1. $35.00.

WEDDA, John. *Gardens of the American South.* 1971. NY. 4to. 256p w/many color & b&w photos. most full or double pg. rear pastedown scraped. edges of dj damp stained. B26. $15.00.

WEDDLE, A. E. *Techniques of Landscape Architecture.* 1969. Elsevier. 2nd. 226p. VG/dj. A10. $30.00.

WEDDLE, Dennis R. *I Would Have Gave My Life… But I Don't Think My Parents…* 1978. np. ils/photos. unp. VG/dj. R11. $75.00.

WEDEMEYER, Albert C. *Wedemeyer Reports: An Objective, Dispassionate Examination.* 1958. Henry Holt. 1st. 497p. VG/torn. S16. $35.00.

WEEDEN, Robert B. *Alaska: Promises to Keep.* 1978. Boston. Houghton Mifflin. 1st. 8vo. 254p. blk cloth. NF. $4.00.

WEEKS, Delores. *Cape Murders.* 1987. Dodd, Mead. 1st. NF/NF. G8. $10.00.

WEEKS, Stephen b. *A Bibliography of the Historical Literature of North Carolina.* 1895. Cambridge. Mass. Library of Harvard Univ. 1st. Biographical Contributions No. 48. orig printed wrp. slightly soiled & chipped. VG. M8. $45.00.

WEEMS, John Edward. *The Tornado.* 1977. NY. Doubleday. poi stp on edges. photo ils. 8vo. 180p. VG/VG. K5. $25.00.

WEEMS, M. L. *The Life of Benjamin Franklin; With Many Choice Anecdotes and Admirable Sayings of this Great Man, Never Before Published by Any of His Biographers.* Philadelphia. J. B. Lippincott & Co. 1883. 12mo. 239p & (16)p Lippincott catalogue. orange cloth. later ed. front inner hinge beginning to crack. title page foxed. G to VG. L5. $20.00.

WEEVERS, Th. *Fifty Years of Plant Physiology.* 1949. Waltham, MA. Chronica Botanica. intro by F.W.Went. VG. B26. $22.50.

WEGMAN, William. *A B C.* 1994. NY. Hyperion. 1st. children's picture book of dogs. F/F. B3. $20.00.

WEHR, Julian. *Puss in Boots.* 1944. NY. Duenwald. 8vo. 6 tab-activated moveables. pict sbdg. dj. R5. $175.00.

WEIGEL, George. *Tranquillitas Ordinis: Present Failure & Future Promise.* 1987. OUP. 1st. VG/dj. N2. $10.00.

WEIGHT WATCHERS. *Weight Watchers International Cookbook.* SC. Plume. VG. A28. $6.95.

WEIGHT WATCHERS. *Weight Watchers Meals in Minutes.* 1990. NY. NAL. VG/VG. A28. $8.25.

WEIGHTMAN, G. H. *George H. Weightman: Forty Years in Philippine Studies, An Oral History.* 1990. Cal State Fullerton. M. P. Onorato. sm4to. cloth. 44p. F. P1. $30.00.

WEIL, Danielle. *Baseball: The Perfect Game.* 1992. Rizzoli. 1st. photos. VG/dj. P8. $22.50.

WEIL, Ernst. *Collected Catalogs of Dr. Ernst Weil.* Bookseller. 1/300. 237p index. F. A4. $165.00.

WEIMARCK, Henning. *Monograph of the Genus Cliffortia.* 1934. London. 229p w/47 text figures & maps. wrp. cover inscr. B26. $60.00.

WEINBAUM, Stanley G. *The Black Flame.* 1995. San Francisco. Tachyon Publications. restored ed. 1st ed thus. VF/VF. T2. $26.00.

WEINBAUM, Stanley G. *The Black Flame.* 1995. San Francisco. Tachyon Publications. restored ed. 1st ed thus. 1/100 #. leather-bound copies. sgn by introducer Sam Moskowitz. VF/VF. T2. $45.00.

WEINBAUM, Stanley G. *The Black Flame.* 1995. San Francisco. Tachyon Publications. restored ed. 1st ed thus. VF/VF. T2. $26.00.

WEINBAUM, Stanley G. *The Black Flame.* 1995. San Francisco. Tachyon Publications. restored ed. 1st ed thus. 1/100 #. leather-bound copies. sgn by introducer Sam Moskowitz. VF/VF. T2. $45.00.

WEINBERG, Larry. *Star Wars: Making of the Movie.* 1980. Random. 1st. 8vo. 69p. NF. C14. $10.00.

WEINBERG, Robert. *Weird Vampire Tales.* 1992. Gramercy. 1st thus. VG/dj. L1. $45.00.

WEINER, Michael. *Earth Medicine — Earth Food.* 1980. NY. Collier. 230p. VG. A10. $12.00.

WEINTRAUB, Stanley. *Whistler: A Biography.* 1974. Weybright Talley. 1st. inscr. 495p. hospital xl. NF/VG+. C15. $20.00.

WEINTZ, Walter H. *Solid Gold Mailbox.* 1987. Wiley. 1st. NF/clip. P3. $25.00.

WEIR, Ruth Hirsch. *Language in the Crib.* 1962. The Hague. Moulton. Janua Linguarum Series Major XIV. lg 8vo. 216p. cloth. G1. $65.00.

WEIS, G. *Stock Raising in the Northwest 1884. Translated with Historical Note by Herbert O. Brayer.* Evanston, IL. The Branding Iron Press. 1951. 12mo. xii. 24p. ils with a few small cuts. cloth spine & printed brd. 1st ed of this translation. #5/500 copies with sgn and dated presentation inscr by Brayer. VG. L5. $50.00.

WEISEL, Elie. *Legends of Our Time.* 1968. HRW. 1st. inscr. NF/dj. R14. $50.00.

WEISMAN, John. *Evidence.* 1980. NY. Viking. 1st. F/F. H11. $50.00.

WEISS, Gaea and Shandor. *Growing and Using the Healing Herbs.* 1985. PA. Rodale Press. G/G. A28. $9.95.

WEISS, Paul A. *Science of Life.* 1973. Futura. 137p. xl. VG. S5. $7. 50.

WEISS, Peter. *Exile.* 1968. Delacorte. 1st Am. F/dj. B2. $25.00.

WEIZMAN, Ezer. *Battle for Peace.* 1981. Bantam. 1st. photos. VG/clip. S14. $9.00.

WELCH, Denton. *Journals.* 1952. London. 1st. intro Jocelyn Brooke. VG/G. M17. $32. 50.

WELCH, Galbraith. *Unveiling of Timbuctoo: Astounding Adventures of Caillie.* 1939. NY. Morrow. 1st. sm 8vo. ils/map. 351p. xl.

WELCH, James. *Fool's Crow.* 1986. NY. Viking. 1st. NF. lightly bumped at one corner/NF+. sm crease on inside flap. B3. $60.00.

WELCH, James. *Fools Crow.* 1986. Viking. 1st. sgn. F/dj. O11. $115.00.

WELCH, James. *Fools Crow.* 1986. NY. Viking. 1st. Rem. mark. F/F. D10. $40.00.

WELCH, James. *Fools Crow.* 1986. NY. Viking. ARC. wrps. F. B2. $35.00.

WELCH, James. *Indian Lawyer.* 1990. NY. Norton. 1st. sgn. F/F. B3/R14. $60.00.

WELCH, James. *Riding the Earthboy 40.* 1971. NY. World. 1st. author's 1st book. F/dj. L3/O11. $150.00.

WELCH, James. *Riding the Earthboy 40.* 1971. World. 1st. sgn. author's 1st book. F/NF. B3. $275.00.

WELCH, James. *Riding the Earthboy 40.* 1971. NY. World Pub. 1st. F/F. D10. $150.00.

WELCH, James. *Winter in the Blood.* 1974. NY/London. Harper Row. 1st. F/dj. Q1. $125.00.

WELCH, James. *Winter in the Blood.* (1974). NY. Harper & Row. 1st. author's 1st novel. NF. shows lt use/VG. closed tear and lt wear to extremities. B3. $110.00.

WELCH, Robert. *The New Americanism and Other Speeches and Essays.* 1966. Boston. Western Islands. 1st. inscr by author. F in NF dj. B2. $40.00.

WELCH, William C. *Antique Roses for the South.* 1990. Dallas. 201p w/200 color photos. new in dj. B26. $24.00.

WELDON, Fay. *Cloning of Joanna May.* 1990. NY. Viking. 1st Am. F/NF. G10. $14.00.

WELDON, Fay. *Hearts & Lives of Men.* 1988. NY. Viking. 1st. sgn. F/NF. B3. $20.00.

WELDON, Fay. *Life Force.* 1992. London. Harper Collins. 1st. rem mk. F/dj. G10. $18. $50.00.

WELDON, Fay. *Remember Me.* 1976. NY. Random House. 1st. NF. lt shelfwear/F. B3. $20.00.

WELDON, Fay. *The Hearts and Lives of Men.* 1988. NY. Viking. 1st. sgn by author. F/NF. lt creasing to spine. B3. $20.00.

WELK, Lawrence. *Musical Family Album.* 1977. Prentice Hall. unp. G/dj. C5. $12. 50.

WELKER, Mary, Lyle & Lynn. *Cambridge Ohio Glass In Color.* 1969. self-published. 8vo. some pencil notes on title page. VG. H1. $26.00.

WELLARD, James. *Great Sahara.* 1965. Dutton. 1st. ils/map ep. 350p. NF/dj. W1. $16.00.

WELLER, Jac. *Fire & Movement: Bargain-Basement Warfare in Far East.* 1967. NY. Crowell. photos/maps. 268p. VG/dj. R11. $30.00.

WELLS, A. Laurence. *The Microscope Made Easy.* 1969. London. Frederick Warne. 2nd ed reprinted. ex lib in dj. usual lib mks. sm 8vo. 15 plates, 8 in color, and 26 line drawings. 256p. G. K5. $15.00.

WELLS, Carolyn. *A Phenomenal Fauna.* 1902. R. H. Russell. 1st. rubbed corners; ils Oliver Herford. VG. B15. $150.00.

WELLS, Carolyn. *The Ghosts' High Noon.* 1930. Philadelphia. Lippincott. 1st. jacket has internal tape mend. 1½" piece missing from front panel. several tears and chipping at spine ends. VG/dj. M15. $45.00.

WELLS, Edward. *Historic Geography of the New Testament: In Two Parts.* 1708. London. Botham/Knapton. 2 parts in 1. ils/16 copper pl/2 fld maps. K1. $300.00.

WELLS, H. G. *Autocracy of Mr. Parham,* 1930. Doubleday Doran. 1st. 328p. G. G11. $10.00.

WELLS, H. G. *Critical Edition of the War of the Worlds.* 1993. Bloomington. IU. 1st. F/dj. $10.00.

WELLS, H. G. *Experiment in Autobiography.* 1934. Canada. Macmillan. 1st. VG. P3. $35.00.

WELLS, H. G. *Joan & Peter.* 1918. Macmillan. 1st. 594p. G. G11. $12.00.

WELLS, H. G. *Star Begotten.* 1937. Chatto Windus. 1st. VG. A24. $50.00.

WELLS, H. G. *World of William Clissold.* 1926. London. Benn. 3 vol. 1st. 1/198. sgn.

WELLS, Helen. *Cherry Ames, Camp Nurse.* 1957. Grosset Dunlap. lists to title. 182p. VG/dj. B36. $10.00.

WELLS, Helen. *Cherry Ames, Flight Nurse.* 1945. Grosset Dunlap. 1st. VG/dj. R8. $15.00.

WELLS, James S. *Plant Propagation Practices.* 1955. Macmillan. ils/index. 344p. G. H10. $15.00.

WELLS, Rosemary. *My Very First Mother Goose.* 1996. Candlewick. 1st. folio. VG/dj. B17. $17. 50.

WELLS, Rosemary. *Peabody.* 1983. Dial. 1st. ils. F/VG. M5. $24.00.

WELLS, Rosemary. *Shy Charles.* 1988. Dial. Books for Young Readers. ils/inscr. NF/dj. T5. $35.00.

WELLS, Tobias. *Dead by the Light of the Moon.* 1967. Garden City. Doubleday. 1st. book has small stain at top of one page and minor shelf wear. price clipped jacket has tiny chip at top of front flap fold. F-/NF+. H11. $45.00.

WELSH, Irvine. *Trainspotting.* 1996. NY. Norton. 1st Am ed of author's 1st book. pb orig w/2 figures in skull masks on front cover; precedes 1st w/movie wrp. F in wrp. D10. $200.00.

WELTY, Eudora. *Eye of the Story.* 1977. Random. 1st. F/dj. B30. $60.00.

WELTY, Eudora. *Little Store.* 1985. Newton, PA. Tamazunchale. mini. 1/250. aeg. gilt gr leather. $24.00.

WELTY, Eudora. *Losing Battles.* 1970. Random. 1st. NF/F clip. H11. $35.00.

WELTY, Eudora. *Losing Battles.* 1970. NY. Random House. 1st. NF/NF. lt wear. D10. $50.00.

WELTY, Eudora. *One Writer's Beginnings.* 1984. Cambridge. Harvard U Press. UP. wrp but for sunning. B2. $85.00.

WELTY, Eudora. *Photographs.* 1989. Jackson, MS. U MS. 1st. 1/52. sgn. full leather. F/purple silk fld case. B4. $1,000.00.

WELTY, Eudora. *Ponder Heart.* 1954. Harcourt Brace. 1st. inscr. NF/VG. R14. $225.00.

WELTY, Eudora. *Ponder Heart.* 1954. Harcourt Brace. 1st. sgn. VG/dj. B30. $200.00.

WELTY, Eudora. *Robber Bridegroom.* 1942. Doubleday Doran. 1st. author's 2nd book. F/VG. B4. $450.00.

WELTY, Eudora. *Robber Bridegroom.* 1987. Harcourt Brace. 1st. sgn Welty/Moser. VG+/dj. B30. $160.00.

WELTY, Eudora. *The Collected Stories of Eudora Welty.* 1980. NY. HBJ. 1st trade ed. boi inside front brd. F/F. D10. $50.00.

WELTY, Eudora. *The Golden Apples.* 1949. NY. Harcourt Brace. 1st. VG+/VG+. lt fading & rubbing. A24. $200.00.

WELTY, Eudora. *The Optimist's Daughter.* 1972. NY. Random House. 1st. winner of 1973 Pulitzer Prize. NF. lt sunning to edges/NF. soiling and sunning to edges. B3. $40.00.

WELTY, Eudora. *The Optimist's Daughter.* 1972. NY. Random House. 1st. NF/VG+. tiny tears. very slight wear. A24. $60.00.

WENDT, Edmund. *Treatise on Asiatic Cholera.* 1885. NY. 1st. 403p. A13. $65.00.

WENDT, Lloyd. *Wall Street Journal.* 1982. Rand McNally. 1st. photos. 448p. NF/VG. S14. $10.00.

WENGER, M. A. *Studies in Infant Behavior III.* 1936. Geo Stoddard. 206p. cloth. G1. $28.00.

WENKER, Mary Albert. *Art of Serving Food Attractively.* 1951. Doubleday. G/dj. A16. $7.00.

WENTWORTH, Edward Norris. *America's Sheep Trails, History, Personalities.* 1948. Ames. IA State College. 667p. tan cloth. VG/rpr. $4.00.

WENTWORTH, Patricia. *Girl in the Cellar.* 1961. Hodder Stoughton. 1st. F/NF. M15. $45.00.

WENTWORTH, Patricia. *Queen Ann Is Dead.* 1915. London. Andrew Melrose. 1st. red/gilt bl cloth. F. M15. $200.00.

WENTWORTH, Patricia. *Vanishing Point.* 1953. Philadelphia. J.B. Lippincott. 1st. F in dj. M15. $60.00.

WENTZ, Abdel Ross. *The Lutheran Church in American History.* 1933. Lutheran. 465p. VG. B29. $14.00.

WERDWL, Franz. *The Song of Bernadette.* 1943. Viking. ne. trans by Ludwig Lewisohn. yellowing. G. s19. $15.00.

WERNER, Herman. *On the Western Frontier with the U S Cavalry.* 1934. np. 1st. wrp. ftspc. ring on front cover. G+. B18. $50.00.

WERNHAM, Herbert F. *A Monograph of the Genus Sabicea.* 1914. London. British Museum. ex lib (no external marking). 82p plus 12 plates. fold out diagram. VG. B26. $17.50.

WERTHAM, Fredric. *Seduction of the Innocent.* 1954. NY. Rinehart. 2nd state. lacking comic list appendix. F. owner's name/VG. sm chips. B2. $200.00.

WESCOTT, Glenway. *Apple of the Eye.* 1924. NY. MacVeagh/Dial. 1st. NF/dj. Q1. $100.00.

WESLAGER, C. A. *Brandywine Springs, the Rise and Fall of a Delaware Resort.* 1949. Wilmington. Hambleton Co. 1st. inscr. musty. ils. 124p. VG in soiled dj. B18. $75.00.

WESLAGER, C. A. *The Richardsons of Delaware, with the Early History of the Richardson Park Suburban Area.* 1957. Wilmington. Knebels Press. 1st. inscr by author. ltd ed 1/500. pict ep. ils. VG in dj. B18. $45.00.

WESLEY, John. *Primitive Physic or Essay & Natural Method of Curing.* 1858 (1858). 24th. G+. E6. $75.00.

WESLEY, Mary. *Jumping the Queue.* 1983. London. Macmillan. 1st. F/VG. B3. $85.00.

WESLEY, Mary. *Not that Sort of Girl.* 1987. London. Macmillan. 1st. NF/F. B3. $30.00.

WESLEY, Mary. *Second Fiddle.* 1988. Viking. 1st. NF/F. B3. $20.00.

WESLEY, Valerie Wilson. *Devil's Gonna Get Him.* 1995. NY. Putnam. 1st. sgn. VF/VF. T2. $25.00.

WESLEY, Valerie Wilson. *Devil's Gonna Get Him.* 1995. NY. Putnam. 1st. sgn by author. F/F. B3. $30.00.

WESLEY, Valerie Wilson. *When Death Comes Stealing.* 1994. NY. Putnam. 1st. sgn by author. F/F. B3. $35.00.

WESLEY, Valerie Wilson. *Where Evil Sleeps.* 1996. NY. Putnam. 1st. UP. F/printed wrp. T2. $10.00.

WESLEY, Valerie Wilson. *Where Evil Sleeps.* 1996. NY. Putnam. 1st. VF/VF. T2. $25.00.

WESSEL, John. *This Far, No Further.* 1996. NY. S&S. 1st. sgn by author. author's 1st book. F/F. B3. $55.00.

WESSEL, John. *This Far, No Further.* 1996. NY. S&S. 1st. author's 1st book. F/F. B3. $40.00.

WESSON, Marianne. *Render Up the Body.* 1998. NY. Harper Collins. 1st. review copy w/pub letter. author's 1st novel. VF/VF. T2. $20.00.

WESSON, Marianne. *Render Up the Body.* 1997. London. Headline. 1st. VF in dj. M15. $75.00.

WESSON, Marianne. *Render Up the Body.* 1997. London. Headline Book. 1st. F/F. M23. $50.00.

WEST, Charles. *The Tenant.* 1996. Aurora. Write Way Publishing. 1st. author's 1st novel. sgn. VF/VF. T2. $25.00.

WEST, Christopher. *Death of a Blue Lantern.* 1994. London. Harper Collins. 1st. author's 1st novel. VF/VF. T2. $40.00.

WEST, Christopher. *Death on Black Dragon River.* 1995. London. Harper Collins. 1st. VF/VF. T2. $35.00.

WEST, Dorothy. *The Wedding.* 1995. NY. Doubleday. 1st. F/VF. H11. $35.00.

WEST, Dorothy. *The Wedding.* 1995. NY. Doubleday. 1st. F/F. M23. $40.00.

WEST, Jessamyn. *The Massacre at Fall Creek.* 1975. np. HBJ. inscr 1st ed. F/F dj. M19. $25.00.

WEST, Lenon. *Making an Etching.* 1932. NY. Studio. 1st. ils. 79p. VG. B5. $27.00.

WEST, Michael Lee. *American Pie.* 1996. NY. Harper Collins. 1st. VF/VF. H11. $40.00.

WEST, Michael Lee. *Crazy Ladies.* 1990. Atlanta. Longstreet Press. 1st. author's 1st novel. F/F. M23. $55.00.

WEST, Morris L. *Clowns of God.* 1981. NY. 1st. VG/dj. T9. $8.00.

WEST, Morris L. *Vatican Trilogy.* 1993. Wings. 1st. sm 4to. 721p. F/dj. W2. $50.00.

WEST, Nigel. *Faber Book of Espionage.* 1993. London. 1st. dj. T9. $20.00.

WEST, Owen; see Koontz, Dean R.

WEST, Pamela. *Yours Truly, Jack the Ripper.* 1987. NY. St. Martin. 1st. F/F. T2. $25.00.

WEST, Paul. *Lord Byron's Doctor.* 1989. NY. 1st. 277p. A13. $20.00.

WEST, Paul. *Love's Mansion.* 1992. NY. Random House. 1st. F/F. B3. $30.00.

WEST, Paul. *Sheer Fiction.* 1987. New Paltz. McPherson. 1st. F/F. B3. $25.00.

WEST, Paul. *Sheer Fiction.* 1987. New Paltz. McPherson & Company. 1st. F/F. B3. $25.00.

WEST, Paul. *The Snow Leopard.* 1965. NY. HBW. 1st Am ed. review copy w/slip. F/F. V1. $45.00.

WEST, Paul. *Women of Whitechapel & Jack the Ripper.* 1991. Random. 1st. F/dj. R14. $25.00.

WEST, Ray. *Kingdom of the Saints: Story of Brigham Young.* 1957. Viking. 389p. VG/dj. J2. $75.00.

WEST, Richard C. *Tolkien Criticism: An Annotated Checklist.* 1981. Kent. Kent State Univ. Press. revised ed. 1st thus. VF/no dj as issued. T2. $15.00.

WEST, Richard S. *Mr. Lincoln's Navy.* 1957. NY. 1st. 328p. VG/dj. E1. $30.00.

WEST, Thomas Reed. *Flesh & Steel: Literature & Machine in American Culture.* 1967. Vanderbilt. 1st. VG/dj. N2. $10.00.

WESTALL, Robert. *Haunting of Charles McGill.* 1983. Greenwillow. 1st Am. F/NF. T12. $25.00.

WESTBROOK, Robert. *Rich Kids.* 1992. NY. Birch Lane. 1st. NF/F. H11. $15.00.

WESTBROOK, Robert. *Rich Kids.* 1992. Birch Lane. 1st. NF/NF. G8. $10.00.

WESTCOTT, Cynthia. *Anyone Can Grow Roses.* 1952. Van Nostrand. 1st. inscr. 147p. VG/VG. A25. $20.00.

WESTLAKE, Donald & Abby. *High Jinx: A Mohonk Mystery.* 1987. Miami Beach. Dennis Macmillan. 1st. VF/pict wrp. T2. $12.00.

WESTLAKE, Donald as Richard Stark. *The Score.* 1985. Allison & Busby. 1st hc ed. sgn. VF. dj. M25. $25.00.

WESTLAKE, Donald as Tucker Coe. *Wax Apple.* 1970. Random House. 1st. name & address stp on ffep. NF/clipped dj. M25. $45.00.

WESTLAKE, Donald E. *Enough.* 1977. NY. M. Evans. 1st. sgn. F in dj. M15. $50.00.

WESTLAKE, Donald E. *High Adventure.* 1985. Mysterious. 1st. VG/VG. G8. $25.00.

WESTLAKE, Donald E. *Humans.* 1992. NY. Mysterious Press. 1st. VF/VF. T2. $8.00.

WESTLAKE, Donald E. *Nobody's Perfect.* 1977. NY. M. Evans. 1st. F. rem mk/NF. B2. $45.00.

WESTLAKE, Donald E. *Sacred Monster.* 1989. NY. Mysterious Press. 1st. VF/VF. T2. $8.00.

WESTLAKE, Donald E. *The Hot Rock.* 1970. NY. S&S. 1st. book has bumped top corners. remainder stripe. bright white jacket. F-/F. H11. $60.00.

WESTLAKE, Donald E. *Trust Me on This.* 1988. NY. Mysterious Press. 1st. VF/VF. T2. $8.00.

WESTLAKE, Garnett. *The Hidden Portal.* 1946. Garden City. Doubleday Crime Club. 1st. F in dj. M15. $45.00.

WETHERILL, Phyllis Steiss. *Cookie Cutters & Cookie Molds.* 1985. Schiffer Publishing. ltd. Oblong 8vo. 243p. VG. H1. $40.00.

WETMORE, Alexander. *The Birds of the Republic of Panama.* 1981. DC. Smithsonian Institution. Part 1. Tinamidae to Rynchopidae. color frontis. drawings. index. 483p. G/G. F3. $25.00.

WETMORE, Alexander. *The Birds of the Republic of Panama.* 1972. DC. Smithsonian Institution. Part 3: Passeriformes Dendrocolaptiiade to Oxyruncidae. 1st ed. color frontis. drawings. index. 631p. G/G F3. $25.00.

WETMORE, Alexander. *The Birds of the Republic of Panama.* 1984. DC. Smithsonian Institution. Part 4: Passeriformes Hirundinidae to Oxyruncidae. 1st ed. color frontis. drawings. index. 670p. G/G. F3 $25.00.

WETZEL, Charles M. *American Fishing Books. A Bibliography to 1948.* nd. 1/75. ils 235p. F. A4. $55.00.

WEYER, Diane. *Assassin & the Deer.* 1989 Norton. 1st. F/F. H11. $30.00.

WEYER, Edward. *Primitive Peoples Today.* 1958. Doubleday. 4to. 288p. dj. F3. $20.00.

WEYGAND, James Lamar. *Papyrus Weygand.* 1980. Maestro Books. mini 1/about 45. brd. B24. $150.00.

WHALE, J. S. *Christian Doctrine,* 1956. Cambridge. VG/worn. B29. $3.50.

WHALE, J. S. *Protestant Tradition: An Essay in Interpretation.* 1955. Cambridge. 360p. VG B29. $13.50.

WHALE, J. S. *The Protestant Tradition: An Essay in Interpretation.* 1955. Cambridge. 360p. VG. B29. $13.50.

WHALEN, Philip. *Prolegomena to a Study of the Universe.* 1976. Berkeley. Poltroon Press. 1st. 1/290. wrp. F. B2. $60.00.

WHARTON, Edith. *A Son at the Front.* 1923. NY. Scribner's. 1st. red cloth. gilt lettering. VG. lt rubbing. missing dj. A24. $45.00.

WHARTON, Edith. *Artemis to Actaeon.* 1909. London. Macmillan. 1st Eng (from Am sheets). inscr. cloth. VG. B4. $5.00.

WHARTON, Edith. *Certain People.* 1930. NY. Appleton. 1st. NF/VG. B4. $375.00.

WHARTON, Edith. *Descent of Man: and Other Stories.* 1904. Scribner. 1st. teg. VG. Q1. $200.00.

WHARTON, Edith. *Glimpses of the Moon.* 1922. NY. Appleton. 1st/1st prt. 12mo. 364p. gilt bl cloth. VG/dj. $3.00.

WHARTON, Edith. *Henry James and Edith Wharton Letters: 1900 – 1915.* 1990. NY. Scribner's. 1st ed by Lyall H. Powers. F/F. A24. $20.00.

WHARTON, Edith. *Hudson River Bracketed.* 1929. NY. Appleton. 1st. VG+. missing dj. A24. $40.00.

WHARTON, Edith. *In the Custom of the Country.* 1913. Scribner. 1st. F. Q1. $200.00.

WHARTON, Edith. *Marriage Playground.* 1928. Grosset Dunlap. MTI. VG/dj. B4. $200.00.

WHARTON, Edith. *Mother's Recompense.* 1925. Appleton. 1st. 12mo. 342p. gilt maroon cloth. NF/dj. J3. $500.00.

WHARTON, Edith. *Ring of Conspirators: Henry James & His Literary Circle.* 1989. Houghton Mifflin. 1st Am. 283p. gilt bdg. NF/dj. $3.00.

WHARTON, Edith. *The Children.* 1928. NY. Appleton. 1st. red cloth. gilt lettering. NF/VG. all corners of dj are clip as issued. A24. $140.00.

WHARTON, William. *Birdy.* 1978. London. Jonathan Cape. 1st British ed. true 1st. F/NF. price clip. but pub price sticker affixed to dj. B3. $50.00.

WHARTON, William. *Dad.* 1981. NY. Knopf. 1st. book has slight spine roll and bumped bottom corners. NF/F. H11. $30.00.

WHARTON, William. *Ever After.* 1995. NY. Newmarket Press. 1st. sgn by author. F/F. B3. $30.00.

WHARTON, William. *Pride.* 1985. Knopf. 1st. F/F. B3. $30.00.

WHEAT, Carolyn. *Mean Streak.* 1996. NY. Berkley. 1st. sgn. VF/VF. T2. $25.00.

WHEAT, Carolyn. *Troubled Waters.* 1997. NY. Berkley. 1st. UP. sgn. VF/pict wrp. T2. $15.00.

WHEAT, Marvin T. *Travels of the Western Slope of Mexican Cordillera.* 1857. SF. Whitton Towne. 1st. 438p. marbled brd/leather spine. $11.00.

WHEATLEY, Dennis. *Desperate Measures.* 1974. London. Hutchinson. 1st. F/dj. M19. $17. 50.

WHEATON, J. M. *Report on the Birds of Ohio.* 1882. Columbus, OH. 440p. F. C12. $65.00.

WHEELER, Daniel. *Extracts from Letters of Journal of Daniel Wheeler.* 1840. Phil. Joseph Rakestraw. 1st Am. 342p. V3. $140.00.

WHEELER, Daniel. *Memoir of Daniel Wheeler with Account of His Gospel Labours.* 1859. Phil. Assoc. Friends for Diffusion. 24mo. 259p. V3. $40.00.

WHEELER, J. Talboys. *India and the Frontier States of Afghanistan, Nipal, and Burma.* 1899. Collier. Vol. 2. 444p. VG. B29. $13.00.

WHEELER, Kate. *Not Where I Started From.* 1993. Boston. Houghton Mifflin. 1st. author's 1st book. F/F. D10. $50.00.

WHEELER, Kate. *Not Where I Started From.* 1993. NY. Houghton Mifflin. 1st. F/F. B3. $60.00.

WHEELER, Richard. *Children of Darkness.* 1973. Arlington. 189p. VG/dj. B29. $9.50.

WHEELER, Richard. *Lee's Terrible Swift Sword: From Antietam.* 1992. Harper Collins. 1st. F/dj. A14. $25.00.

WHEELER, Richard. *Siege of Vicksburg: Seven-Month Battle.* 1978. NY. Crowell. 1st. NF/dj. A14. $25.00.

WHEELER, W. M. *Demons of the Dust: Study of Insect Behavior.* 1930. NY. 1st. 378p. VG/dj. B5. $45.00.

WHEELHOUSE, M. V. *Holly House & Ridges Row: A Tale of London.* 1908. Chambers. 1st. thick 8vo. ils MV Wheelhouse. aeg. VG+. M5. $70.00.

WHELAN, Michael. *The Art of Michael Whelan.* 1993. NY. Bantam. 1st. sgn. VF/VF. T2. $60.00.

WHELAN, Michael. *Works of Wonder.* 1987. Del Rey/Ballantine. 1st. NF/VG. A28. $30.00.

WHERRY, Edgar T. *Guide to Eastern Ferns.* 1948 (1942). 2nd ed. 2nd prt. 252p. VG in dj. B26. $15.00.

WHIPPLE, A. B. C. *To the Shores of Tripoli.* 1991. Morrow. 1st. 8vo. 357p. VG/dj. $17.00.

WHIPPLE, A. B. C. *To the Shores of Tripoli.* 1991. NY. Morrow. 1st. 357p. F/VG. $7.00.

WHIPPLE, Allen. *Evolution of Surgery in the United States.* 1963. Springfield. 1st. 180p. A13. $75.00.

WHIPPLE, Fred L. *Orbiting the Sun: Planets & Satellites of the Solar System.* 1981. Cambridge. new/enlarged. 338p. VG. K5. $10.00.

WHIPPLE, Guy Montrose. *Manual of Mental & Physical Tests: Part I.* 1914 & 1915. Baltimore. Warwick York. 2 vol. 2nd revised. ils/tables.

WHISHAW, Fred. *The Diamond of Evil.* 1902. London. John Long. 1st. page edges foxed. red cloth-covered boards with gold stamped titles on spine. F/. M15. $175.00.

WHISTLER, W. Arthur. *Coastal Flowers of the Tropical Pacific.* 1980. Lawai. photos. 82p. wrp. VG. B26. $20.00.

WHISTLER, W. Arthur. *Ethnobotany of Tonga: Plants, Their Tongan Names & Uses.* 1991. Honolulu. Bishop Mus. 8vo. checklist. 155p. $0.00.

WHISTLER, W. Arthur. *Polynesian Herbal Medicine,* 1992. Lawai. Kauai. ils/photos. 237p. sc. AN. $263300.00.

WHITAKER & WHITAKER. *Potter's Mexico.* NM U. 1978. 1st. ils. 136p. NF/dj. B19. $35.00.

WHITBOURN, John. *Binscombe Tales: Sinister Saxon Stories.* 1998. Ashcroft, BC. Ash Tree Press. 1st. VF/VF. T2. $50.00.

WHITBOURN, John. *More Binscombe Tales: Sinister Sutangli Stories.* 1999. Ashcroft, BC. Ash Tree Press. 1st. VF/VF. T2. $40.00.

WHITCOMB, Adah F. *Old Mother Goose in a New Dress.* 1932. Chicago. Laidlaw. 1st. obl 4to. yel-orange pict cloth. R5. $125.00.

WHITE, Anne Terry. *First Men in the World.* 1953. Random. 5th. ils Aldren Watson. 178p. VG/dj. B36. $14.00.

WHITE, Bailey. *Mama Makes Up Her Mind.* 1993. NY. Addison Wesley. 1st. author's 1st book. F/F. B3. $75.00.

WHITE, Bailey. *Mama Makes Up Her Mind.* 1993. Reading, MA. Addison Wesley. 1st. author's 1st book. F/F. M23. $40.00.

WHITE, Bailey. *Sleeping at the Starlight Motel.* 1995. NY. Addison Wesley. 1st. sgn by author. F/F. B3. $30.00.

WHITE, Claire Nicolas. *River Boy.* 1988. Typographeum. 1/150. sgn. dj. T9. $30.00.

WHITE, Dale. *John Wesley Powell, Geologist-Explorer.* 1962. Julian Messner. 2nd. 8vo. 192p. VG+. F7. $22.00.

WHITE, E. B. *Charlotte's Web.* 1952. Harper Row. 1st. ils Garth Williams. VG+. D1. $650.00.

WHITE, E. B. *Geese.* 1985. Newton, IA. Tamazunchale. mini. 1/250. 46p.

WHITE, E. B. *Letters of E. B. White.* 1976. Harper. 1st. inscr. NF/VG+. B4. $450.00.

WHITE, E. B. *Poems & Sketches of E. B. White.* 1981. NY. Harper. 1st. NF/dj. L3. $35.00.

WHITE, E. B. *Stuart Little.* 1945. NY. Harper. 1st. ils Garth Williams. tan cloth. pict dj. $5.00.

WHITE, E. B. *Stuart Little.* nd (c 1945). Harper Row. K-N prt. sm 8vo. 131p. VG/dj. C14. $15.00.

WHITE, E. B. *Every Day Is Saturday.* 1934. NY. Harpers. 1st. dj scarce in any condition. VG. foxing. browning. bookplate on front pastedown/G. chip. browning. A24. $150.00.

WHITE, E. B. *The Trumpet of the Swan.* 1970. Harper & Row. ils Edward Frascino. F/VG. B15. $50.00.

WHITE, Edmund. *Caracole.* 1984. NY. Dutton. 1st. sgn. F/F. O11. $45.00.

WHITE, Edmund. *Genet: A Biography.* 1993. NY. Knopf. 1st Am ed. sgn. F/F. O11. $65.00.

WHITE, Edmund. *Skinned Alive.* 1995. Knopf. 1st. sgn. F/dj. B4. $50.00.

WHITE, Edmund. *States of Desire.* 1980. Dutton. 1st. NF/dj. C9. $60.00.

WHITE, Ethel Lina. *Man Who Was Not There.* nd. Grosset Dunlap. rpt. VG/G. G8. $15.00.

WHITE, G. Edward. *Creating the National Pastime.* 1996. Princeton. UP. photos. P8. $12.50.

WHITE, Grace. *Family Circle's What's for Dinner?* 1963. Family Circle. G. A16. $5.00.

WHITE, I. Andrew. *Mr. Whittle Invents the Airplane.* 1938. Lee Shepard. 1st. ils Alexander. VG/G. P2. $25.00.

WHITE, James. *The White Papers.* 1996. Framingham. Nesfa Press. 1st. sgn. VF/VF. T2. $40.00.

WHITE, Jerry. *The Power of Commitment.* 1986. Navpress. The Christian Character Library. 161p/study guide 81p. VG/VG. B29. $12.00.

WHITE, John H. *American Locomotives, An Engineering History 1830 – 1880.* 1968. Baltimore. Johns Hopkins Univ. Press. 1st. oblong 8vo. gilt decor cloth. pict ep. VG+/chip dj. B18. $45.00.

WHITE, Lionel. *Night of the Rape.* 1967. Dutton. 1st. VG+/VG. G8. $10.00.

WHITE, Lionel. *To Find a Killer.* 1954. Dutton. 1st. VG/G. G8. $15.00.

WHITE, Mary Grant. *Pots and Pot Gardens.* 1969. London. inscr by author. 160p w/109 b&w photos. VG in dj. B26. $19.00.

WHITE, Michael. *A Brother's Blood.* 1996. NY. Harper Collins. 1st. F/F. M23. $35.00.

WHITE, Michael C. *A Brother's Blood.* 1996. NY. Harper Collins. 1st. author's 1st novel. sgn. VF/VF. T2. $75.00.

WHITE, Michael C. *A Brother's Blood.* 1996. NY. Harper Collins. 7th prt. author's 1st book. sgn by author. F/F. B3. $10.00.

WHITE, Michael C. *A Brother's Blood.* 1996. NY. Harper Collins. 1st. author's 1st novel. F/F. A24. $75.00.

WHITE, Michael C. *The Blind Side of the Heart.* 1999. NY. Harper Collins. 1st. sgn. VF/VF. T2. $26.00.

WHITE, Michael C. *The Blind Side of the Heart.* 1999. NY. Harper Collins. 1st. UP. sgn. VF/pict wrp. T2. $26.00.

WHITE, Natalie D. & W. B. Garrett. *Water Resources Data, Arizona Water Year 1983.* 1986. USGS. 1st. maps. charts. index. 387p. NF. B19. $3.50.

WHITE, Nelia Gardner. *The Thorn Tree.* 1955. Viking. 1st. G. S19. $20.00.

WHITE, Nelson C. *Abbot H. Thayer Painter and Naturalist.* 1967. Hartford. Ct. Printers. ne. 69 ils in color and b&w. blue buckram. 7 line inscr by N.C. White. scarce. 269p. VF. B14. $200.00.

WHITE, Patrick. *Burnt Ones.* 1964. Viking. 1st Am. VG/dj. A14. $35.00.

WHITE, Patrick. *Cockatoos.* 1974. London. Cape. 1st. F/dj. A14. $52.50.

WHITE, Patrick. *Fringe of Leaves.* 1977. Viking. 1st Am. NF/VG clip. A14. $21.00.

WHITE, Patrick. *The Aunt's Story.* 1948. NY. Viking. 1st Am ed. NF/VG. chips. wear. stain shows through front panel. spine slightly darkened. A24. $200.00.

WHITE, Paul Dudley. *Clues in the Diagnosis & Treatment of Heart Disease.* 1955. Chas. Thomas. 2nd. 190p. F. C14. $15.00.

WHITE, Paul Dudley. *My Life in Medicine: An Autobiographical Memoir.* 1971. Boston. Gambit. 1st. 8vo. 269p. VG. C14. $12.00.

WHITE, Philo. *Philo White's Narrative of a Cruise in the Pacific to South America and California on the Us Sloop of War, " Dale" 1841 – 1843.* 1965. Denver. Old West Publishing Co. 1 of 1000 ltd ed. gr cloth w/ gilt spine titles & wht cover decor. designed & printed by Lawton and Alfred Kennedy of San Francisco. ed by Charles L. Camp. 84p. NF. some wear to edges. P4. $75.00.

WHITE, Ramy Allison. *Sunny Boys at the Seashore.* Barse Hopkins. ils Chas. Wrenn. F/VG. M19. $17.50.

WHITE, Randy Wayne. *Captiva.* 1996. Putnam. UP/1st. F/wrp. M15. $75.00.

WHITE, Randy Wayne. *Captiva.* 1996. Putnam. 1st. rem mk. NF/dj. A14. $17.50.

WHITE, Randy Wayne. *Captiva.* 1996. NY. Putnam. 1st. Jacket has abrasion on verso of rear flap fold. F/F-. H11. $30.00.

WHITE, Randy Wayne. *Captiva.* 1996. NY. Putnam. 1st. sgn. VF/dj. M15. $65.00.

WHITE, Randy Wayne. *Captiva.* 1996. NY. Putnam. 1st. sgn by author. F/F. B3. $65.00.

WHITE, Randy Wayne. *Cuban Death-Lift.* 1981. NY. NAL. 1st. sgn. F/wrp. M15. $85.00.

WHITE, Randy Wayne. *North of Havana.* 1997. NY. Putnam's. 1st. sgn. VF in dj. M15. $45.00.

WHITE, Randy Wayne. *North of Havana.* (1997). NY. Putnam. 1st. sgn by author. F/F. B3. $45.00.

WHITE, Randy Wayne. *Sanibel Flats.* 1990. NY. St. Martin. 2nd prt. sgn by author. F/NF. some creasing & one tiny chip at top of spine. B3. $225.00.

WHITE, Randy Wayne. *Tarpon Tales.* 1990. Sanibel Island. Lost Stories. pb orig. sgn by author. scarce sm prt run. pict wrp. F. B3. $225.00.

WHITE, Randy Wayne. *The Heat Islands.* 1992. NY. St. Martin. 1st. jacket has usual minor edge wear. F/F. H11. $245.00.

WHITE, Randy Wayne. *The Heat Islands.* 1992. NY. St. Martin. 1st. VF/dj. M15. $200.00.

WHITE, Randy Wayne. *The Man Who Invented Florida.* 1993. NY. St. Martin. 1st. Jacket has two ½" tears at bottom of spine and rubbing at extremities. F/NF. H11. $180.00.

WHITE, Randy Wayne. *The Man Who Invented Florida.* 1993. NY. St. Martin. 1st. Jacket has short closed tear. F/dj. M15. $200.00.

WHITE, Randy Wayne. *The Mangrove Coast.* 1998. NY. Putnam. 1st. sgn. F/F. A24. $30.00.

WHITE, Randy Wayne. *The Mangrove Coast.* 1998. NY. Putnam. 1st. sgn. VF/VF. T2. $25.00.

WHITE, Reginald. *Beneath the Cross of Jesus.* 1959. Eerdmans. 159p. G/torn dj. ex lib. B29. $3.50.

WHITE, Stephen. *Manner of Death.* 1999. NY. Dutton. 1st. sgn & dated by author. F/F. B3. $40.00.

WHITE, Stephen. *Manner of Death.* 1999. NY. Dutton. ARC. sgn by author. pict wrp. B3. $45.00.

WHITE, Stephen. *Remote Control.* 1997. NY. Dutton. 1st. sgn by author. F/F. B3. $30.00.

WHITE, Stewart Edward. *Camp & Trail.* 1907. Toronto. Musson. 1st Canadian. 8vo. 2-tone bl cloth. NF. R3. $20.00.

WHITE, Stewart Edward. *Daniel Boone: Wilderness Scout.* 1957. NY. Jr. Deluxe Eds. 254p. VG/clip. V3. $12.00.

WHITE, Stewart Edward. *Daniel Boone: Wilderness Scout.* 1922. NY. Garden City Publishing. G. A16. $25.00.

WHITE, Stewart Edward. *Riverman.* 1909. NY. McClure. 1st. ils NC Wyeth/Clarence F Underwood. 368p. G11. $15.00.

WHITE, Stewart Edward & Samuel H. Adams. *Thy Mystery.* 1907. NY. McClure Phillips. 1st. Name and address on front endpaper. Pictorial boards with gold-stamped titles on spine. NF/. M15. $50.00.

WHITE, T. H. *Letters to a Friend.* 1982. NY. edit/intro Francois Gallix. VG. M17. $17.50.

WHITE, T. H. *Scandal Monger.* 1952. London. Cape. 1st. ils. NF/clip. S9. $100.00.

WHITE, Ted. *Phoenix Time: Quest of the Wolf Vol I.* 1982. VA. Donning Starblaze. 1st thus. ils Tom Yeates. F/wrp. G10. $12.00.

WHITE, Teri. *Max Trueblood and the Jersey Desperado.* 1987. Mysterious. 1st. VG+/NF. S8. $10.00.

WHITE, Theodore H. *Breach of Faith: Fall of Richard Nixon.* 1975. Atheneum. 1st. sgn. VG/dj. B30. $35.00.

WHITE, Tom. *Buffalo Soldiers.* 1996. Tom Doherty. 1st. F/dj. T11. $40.00.

WHITE, W. L. *They Were Expendable,* 1942. BC. 209p. gl cloth. VG/dj. M7. $16. $50.00.

WHITE, W. L. *They Were Expendable.* 1942. NY. Harcourt Brace. cloth. 209p. VG/G. P1. $8.00.

WHITE-MULLIN, Anna Jane. *Judging Hunters and Hunter Seat Equitation.* 1984. NY. Arco. 1st prt. VG/VG. O3. $18.00.

WHITECLOUD, Tom. *Indian Prayer.* 1964. Berkeley. Peacock. mini. 1/600. brn/gr prt. yel prt wrp. B24. $40.00.

WHITECOMB, Ian. *Irving Berlin and Ragtime America.* 1988. NY. Limelight. 1st Am ed. F/F. B2. $25.00.

WHITECOTTON, Joseph. *Zapotecs: Princes, Priests & Peasants.* 1977. Norman. 1st. 338p. F3. $35.00.

WHITEHEAD, Alred North. *The Principle of Relativity with Applications to Physical Science.* 1922. Cambridge. Univ. Press. 1st. xii.190p. orig gilt bl cloth. K1. $250.00.

WHITEHEAD, Colson. *The Intuitionist.* 1999. NY. Anchor Books. 1st. F/F. M23. $30.00.

WHITEHEAD, Don. *FBI Story: A Report to the People.* 1956. Random. inscr. F/dj. A19. $35.00.

WHITEHEAD, George. *Christian Progress of that Ancient Servant & Minister.* 1725. London. Sowle. 1st. 712p. worn leather.

WHITEHEAD, George. *Memoirs of George Whitehead, Being Substance of Account.* 1832. Phil. Kite. $2.00.

WHITEHEAD, J. *Chicago Herald Cooking School: Professional Cook's Book.* 1883 (1882). lg 8vo. ads. G+. E6. $65.00.

WHITEHOUSE, Arch. *Hero without Honor.* 1972. Garden City. Doubleday. 1st. jacket Is price clipped. F/F. H11. $40.00.

WHITFIELD, Theodore M. *Slavery Agitation in Virginia, 1829 – 1832.* 1969 (1930). Negro U. rpt. 162p. VG. B10. $25.00.

WHITFORD, David. *Extra Innings.* 1991. Burlingham. 1st. F/dj. P8. $20.00.

WHITING, F. *Modern Mastoid Operation.* 1905. 4to. 25 halftone pl. half leather. VG. E6. $50.00.

WHITING, John. *Treasury of American Gardening.* 1955. Garden City. Flower Grower/Doubleday. BC. VG/dj. A10. $10.00.

WHITLEY, William T. *Artists & Their Friends in England 1700 – 1799.* 1928. London. Medici Soc. 2 vol. lg 8vo. 23 pl. H13. $185.00.

WHITLOCK, Brand. *Turn of the Balance.* 1907. Bobbs Merrill. ils Jay Hambridge. 622p. G. G11. $10.00.

WHITLOCK, Herbert P. *Story of the Gems.* 1946. Emerson Books. 8vo. 206p. F/dj. H1. $12.00.

WHITMAN, Walt. *Leaves of Grass.* 1946. Modern Library. 8vo. owner's bookplate on endpaper. Minor edge chips. price clipped on inner flap. 423p. VG/F. H1. $18.00.

WHITMAN, Walter. *Franklin Evans or The Inebriate.* NY. Random House. 1929. 12mo. 249p. teg. bluish/gray pattern cloth. 2nd ed. ltd to 700 copies printed by D. B. Updike. The Merrymount Press. ltd ed of Walt Whitman's 1st book. VG. L5. $25.00.

WHITMYER, Margaret & Kenn. *Bedroom & Bathroom Glassware of the Depression Era.* 1990. Paducah. Collector Books. 1st. 4to. 253p. F. H1. $65.00.

WHITMYER, Margaret & Kenn. *Children's Dishes.* 1984. Paducah. Collector Books. 1st. 8vo. Owner's name on back of front cover. 175p. F. H1. $40.00.

WHITNEY, Christine M., ed. *The Bermuda Garden.* 1955. Bermuda. VG. B26. $19.00.

WHITNEY, George H. *Hand-Book of Bible Geography.* 1877. NY. Nelson Phillips. 1st. sm 8vo. 14 mc maps. 495p. VG. $1.00.

WHITNEY, Janet. *Abigail Adams.* 1949. London. Harrap. 1st. ils. 333p. VG/dj. M10. $12.00.

WHITNEY, P. A. *Mystery of the Golden Horn.* 1962. Westminster Pr. ils Helmes. xl. VG. B36. $12. $75.00.

WHITNEY, Polly. *Until Death.* 1994. NY. St. Martin. 1st. author's 1st book. VF/VF. H11. $25.00.

WHITNEY, R. M. *Reds in America,* 1924. Beckwith. 1st. F/worn. B2. $75.00.

WHITTELSEY, Charles B. *Ancestry & Descendants of John Pratt of Hartford, CT.* 1900. Hartford. 204p. bstp cloth. G+. B18. $65.00.

WHITTEMORE, C. P. *General of the American Revolution: John Sullivan.* 1961. Columbia. 1st. ils. 317p. $0.00.

WHITTEN, R. C. & I. G. Poppoff. *Fundamentals of Aeronomy.* 1971. NY. John Wiley & Sons. 8vo. text ils. 446p. VG in cloth. K5. $25.00.

WHITTLE, D. W. *Memoirs of Philip P. Bliss.* 1878. AS Barnes. intro DL Moody. maroon cloth. VG. S17. $15.00.

WHITTLE, Jenny. *Beetle Assembly.* 1985. Lilliput. mini. 1st. 1/250. prt/sgn Armstrong. silk ep/bl morocco. B24. $175.00.

WHITTLE, T. & C. Cook. *Curtis's Flower Garden Displayed.* 1981. Oxford. 1st. sm4to. F in dj. B26. $34.00.

WHITTLESEY, Charles. *Early History of Cleveland, Ohio.* 1867. Cleveland. 1st. ils. 487p. VG. B10. $225.00.

WHITTLESEY, Charles. *Fugitive Essays.* 1852. Hudson, OH. 1st. 397p. G. B18. $225.00.

WHITTMAN, George. *Matter of Intelligence.* 1975. Macmillan. 1st. F/dj. P3. $15.00.

WHITTON, Blair. *Paper Toys of the World.* 1986. Hobby House. obl 8vo. F/dj. B17. $25.00.

WHYTE, Grederic. *William Heinemann, a Memoir.* 1929. Doubleday Doran. 326 p. G. B18. $17.50

WICHT, Hein. *Palms for Gardens in Southern Africa.* 1962. Cape Town. #306 of ed ltd to 500 copies. ep tanned. dj slightly chipped. B26. $50.00.

WICHT, Hein. *The Indigenous Palms of South Africa.* 1969. Cape Town. ltd to 1000 copies. ep maps. VG in dj. B26. $55.00.

WICKENDEN, Leonard. *Make Friends with Your Land.* 1949. NY. Devin-Adair. 132p. cloth. VG. A10. $20.00.

WICKER, Tom. *Time to Die.* 1975. Quadrangle/NY Times. 1st. ils. 342p. VG/dj. S14. $10.00.

WICKERSHAM, James. *Old Yukon Tales.* 1973. St. Paul. 514p. F. A17. $30.00.

WIDDENMER, Margaret. *Unrevised Memories of Golden Friends I Had.* 1964. Doubleday. 1st. 340p. VG/VG. A25. $20.00.

WIDDER, William J. *Fiction of L. Ron Hubbard.* 1994. Bridge. 1st. F. P3. $50.00.

WIDDIFIELD, Hannah. *Widdifield's New Cookbook.* Practical Recipes. 1856. Phil. 410p. VG. E6. $95.00.

WIDEMAN, John Edgar. *Fever.* 1989. NY. Holt. 1st. F+/F. H11. $25.00.

WIDEMAN, John Edgar. *Fever.* 1989. NY. Holt. 1st. F/NF. very lt wear to extremities. B3. $25.00.

WIDEMAN, John Edgar. *Hiding Place.* 1984. London. Allison Busby. 1st/1st hc. sgn. F/dj. O11. $40.00.

WIDEMAN, John Edgar. *Hiding Place.* 1984. London. Allison & Busby. 1st British ed. F/F. B3. $20.00.

WIDEMAN, John Edgar. *Hiding Place.* 1981. London. Allison & Busby. 1st UK ed. 1st hc ed. sgn by author. F/F. B2. $50.00.

WIDEMAN, John Edgar. *Lynchers.* 1973. HBJ. 1st. Nf/dj. A24. $40.00.

WIDEMAN, John Edgar. *Philadelphia Fire.* 1990. NY. Holt. 1st. sgn. F/dj. O11. $30.00.

WIDEMAN, John Edgar. *Philadelphia Fire.* 1990. NY. Henry Holt. 1st. sgn by author. F/F. B2. $60.00.

WIDEMAN, John Edgar. *Reuben.* 1987. NY. Holt. 1st. sgn. F/dj. O11. $25.00.

WIDEMAN, John Edgar. *Reuben.* 1987. NY. Henry Holt. 1st. sgn by author. F/F. B2. $50.00.

WIDEMAN, John Edgar. *Sent for You Yesterday.* 1984. London. Allison Busby. 1st/1st hc. sgn. F/dj. O11. $40.00.

WIDEMAN, John Edgar. *Sent for You Yesterday.* (1984). London. Allison & Busby. 1st British ed. author's 3rd book. winner of PEN/Faulkner award. F/NF. lt wear to top edge. B3. $25.00.

WIDEMAN, John Edgar. *Sent for You Yesterday.* 1984. London. Allison & Busby. 1st UK ed. 1st hc ed. sgn by author. F/F. B2. $50.00.

WIDEMAN, John Edgar. *The Cattle Killing.* 1996. Boston. Houghton Mifflin. 1st. sgn by author. F/F. B2. $45.00.

WIDEMAN, John Edgar. *The Stories of John Edgar Wideman.* 1992. NY. Pantheon. 1st. sgn by author. F/F. B2. $50.00.

WIDEN, Bjorn. *Reproductive Biology in the Helianthemum Oelandicum Complex on Oland, Sweden.* c. 1982. Lund. Sweden. 4to. sc. B26. $9.00.

WIDLENSTEIN, Daniel. *Gauguin.* 1974. Doubleday. 1st. ils. 95p. VG. T11. $20.00.

WIDMANN, Karl. *Paramos Venezolanos.* 1980. Caracas. Fundacion Polar. 1st. VG/d. B26. $30.00.

WIDMER, Jack. *A Practical Guide for Hors Owners.* 1957. NY. Scribner's. 1st ed. VG/F O3. $20.00.

WIDMER, Jack. *American Quarter Horse* 1959. NY. Scribner. VG/fair. O3. $25.00.

WIENER, Herbert & Freda Lipkowitz *Rarities in American Cut Glass.* 1975 Houston. tx. Collectors House of Books. 4to In original. unopened shrink-wrap. 294p AN/AN. H1. $125.00.

WIENERS, John. *Nerves.* 1970. London Caper Goliard. 1st. 1/100 specially bound cloth. numbered & sgn by author. F in F d B2. $85.00.

WIENERS, John. *Selected Poems.* 1972. NY Grossman Publishers. 1st pb ed. F. V1 $17.00.

WIER, Allen. *Place for Outlaws.* 1989 Harper. 1st. F/NF. S18. $15.00.

WIERWILLE, Victor Paul. *Receiving the Holy Spirit Today.* 1972. Am. Christian Press 358p. VG/VG. B29. $6.00.

WIESE, Kurt. *You Can Write Chinese.* 1945 NY. Viking. 1st. 1st. obl 4to. 1946 Caldecott pict dj. $5.00.

WIESEL, Elie. *Beggar in Jerusalem.* 1970 Random. 1st. NF/dj. S13. $10.00.

WIESEL, Elie. *Fifth Son.* 1985. Franklin Lib. 1st. sgn. full leather. F. Q1. $30.00.

WIESEL, ELIE. *Form the Kingdom of Memory* 1990. NY. Summit. 1st. F/F. H11. $25.00.

WIESSE, Carlos. *Historia Del Peru Independiente/La Revolucion.* 1938. Lima. np. 4th ed. maps. pencil notes. 283p. G. F3. $20.00.

WIGGIN, Kate Douglas. *Children's Rights, A Book of Nursery Logic.* 1892. Boston. Houghton Mifflin. 1st. 12mo. deep bl cloth w/blk title & decor. 235p. VG. spine slightly darkened. D6. $40.00.

WIGGIN, Kate Douglas. *My Garden of Memory: An Autobiography.* 1926. Houghton Mifflin. 10th. sm 8vo. 465p. reading copy. C14. $7.00.

WIGGIN, Kate Douglas. *New Chronicles of Rebecca.* 1907. Houghton Mifflin. 1st. 278p. VG. D4. $45.00.

WIGGIN, Kate Douglas. *Rebecca of Sunnybrook Farm.* 1903. Grosset Dunlap. posble 1st. G. A19. $50.00.

WIGGIN, Kate Douglas. *Rose O'the River.* 1905. Houghton Mifflin. 1st. 177p+3 ads. G. 14. $15.00.

WIGGIN, Kate Douglas. *Story of Waitstill Baxter.* 1913. Houghton Mifflin. 1st. ils HM rett. 373p. G. G11. $15.00.

WIGGIN, Kate Douglas. *Summer in a Canon, a California Story.* 1889. Boston. Houghton Mifflin. 1st. ils by F. T. Merrill. in 8vo. brown cloth w/bl & gilt ils. few ips on spine. ils chapter hdgs are only ils. arce. 272p. VG. D6. $75.00.

WIGGIN, Kate Douglas. *Susanna and Sue.* 1909. Boston. Houghton Mifflin. VG. A16. 30.00.

WIGGINS, Walt. *Alfred Morang: A Neglected Master.* 1979. NM. Pintores. AN/dj. A19. 15.00.

WIGHAM, Eliza. *Anti-Slavery Cause in America & Its Martyrs.* 1863. London. ennett. 8vo. bl cloth. R12. $225.00.

WIGHT, Richard. *Story of Goochland.* 1935. ichmond. 1st. inscr/dtd. ils. 51p. VG. B10. 85.00.

WILBUR, Richard. *More Opposites.* 1991. BJ. 1st. inscr/dtd 1996. F/dj. R14. $30.00.

WILBUR, Richard. *Some Atrocities.* 1990. its Press. ltd 1/300. wrp. mild creases. V1. 10.00.

WILBUR, Richard. *The Catabird's Song Prose ieces 1963 – 1995.* 1997. NY. Harcourt Brace. st. US poet Laureate. F/F. B3. $25.00.

WILCHER, Talmage S. *King of Assateague.* 964. Vantage. 1st. photos. 64p. VG. O3. 15.00.

WILCKENS, Ulrich. *Resurrection.* 1978. ohn Knox. 134p. VG/VG. B29. $6.50.

WILCOX, Barbara. *Bunty Brown: Probationer.* 1940. Oxford. 1st. ils. VG/clip. 25. $22.00.

WILCOX, Colin. *Hire a Hangman.* 1991. NY. Iolt. F/F. B3. $20.00.

WILCOX, Colin. *Switchback.* 1993. NY. Holt. /F. B3. $15.00.

WILCOX, James. *North Gladiola.* 1985. Iarper Row. 1st. author's 2nd book. NF/dj. R14. $35.00.

WILCOX, L. A. *Mr. Pepy's Navy.* 1966. Barnes. 1st Am. NF/VG. T11. $35.00.

WILDE, Oscar. *Ballad of Reading Gaol.* 1910. Duffield. 1st thus. 12mo. gilt bl cloth. VG. M5. $75.00.

WILDE, Oscar. *Ballad of Reading Gaol.* 1937. NY. Heritage. NF/case. B9. $20.00.

WILDE, Oscar. *House of Pomegranates.* nd. NY. Brentano. 1st Am. ils Jessie M King/16 mtd pl. 162p. red cloth. VG. $1.00.

WILDE, Oscar. *Salome.* 1911. Portland, ME. Thos Mosher. 1/50 on Japan vellum. sm 4to. F/dj/case. H5. $250.00.

WILDE, Oscar. *Salome: Tragedy in One Act.* 1927. Dutton. 1/500. ils/sgn Beardsley. F/tattered box. B9. $200.00.

WILDE, Oscar. *The Birthday of the Infanta.* 1929. Macmillan. 1st. ils Pamela Bianco. 58p. VG/dj. D1. $85.00.

WILDE, Oscar. *The Birthday of the Infanta.* 1979. NY. Viking Press. 1st. ils by Leonard Lubin. sm 8vo. red cloth w/blk lettering & designs. red dj. 55p. NF/VG. D6. $35.00.

WILDE, Oscar. *The Happy Prince: An Oscar Wilde Fairy Tale Adapted and Directed by Orson Wells.* 1946. np. Decca Records. ils by Walt Disney Studios. 4to. blk cloth spine w/color ils bds. photo of Bing Crosby/Orson Wells/Vic Young reading. contains 2 records. VG. some rubbing at edges. D6. $35.00.

WILDE, Percival. *Moran, Detective.* 1947. NY. Random House. 1st. F/dj. M15. $50.00.

WILDE, Percival. *P. Moran, Operative.* 1947. NY. Random House. 1st. F in dj. M15. $65.00.

WILDER, Laura Ingalls. *By the Shores of Silver Lake.* 1953. Harper. ils Garth Williams. pk/beige cloth. VG. B11. $25.00.

WILDER, Laura Ingalls. *Farmer Boy.* 1953. Harper. newly ils uniform ed. ils Garth Williams. B11. $25.00.

WILDER, Laura Ingalls. *On the Banks of Plum Creek.* 1965. Harper Row. ils Garth Williams. xl. VG. B36. $10.00.

WILDER, Laura Ingalls. *These Happy Golden Years.* 1943. NY. Harper. 1st. ils Helen Sewell/Mildred Boyle. tan pict cloth. R5. $285.00.

WILDER, Louise Beebe. *Adventures in a Suburban Garden.* 1931. NY. index. spine faded. ftspc neatly removed. B26. $12.50.

WILDER, Louise Beebe. *Pleasures & Problems of a Rock Garden.* 1937 (1928). Garden City. 294p. dj. B26. $32. 50.

WILDER, Louise Beebe. *The Garden in Color.* 1937. NY. sm4to. 327p w/320 color plates. cup rings. minor spotting of cloth. B26. $25.00.

WILDER, Lucy. *Mayo Clinic.* 1936. Rochester. 1st. 82p. A13. $30.00.

WILDER, Thornton. *The Eighth Day.* 1967. NY. Harper & Row. 1st. F/F. H11. $45.00.

WILDER, Thornton. *The Merchant of Yonkers.* 1939. NY. Harper & Bros. 1st. NF. cloth edge slightly darkened/VG+. lt wear. short closed tear. A24. $250.00.

WILEY, Bell Irvin. *Life of Johnny Reb: Common Soldier of the Confederacy.* 1952. Bobbs Merrill. 8vo. 444p. VG. B11. $32.00.

WILEY, Richard. *Festival for Three Thousand Maidens.* 1991. NY. Dutton. 1st. UP. F. D10. $10.00.

WILEY, Richard. *Indigo.* 1992. NY. Dutton. 1st. UP. F. D10. $10.00.

WILHELM, Hans. *Tales from Land Under My Table.* 1983. Random. 1st. ils. NF. M5. $20.00.

WILHELM, Kate. *Justice for Some.* 1993. St. Martin. 1st. F/F. G8. $17.50.

WILHELM, Kate. *More Bitter than Death.* 1963. S&S. 1st. xl. G. N4. $35.00.

WILHELM, Kate. *Seven Kinds of Death.* 1992. St. Martin. 1st. F/F. G8. $10.00.

WILHELM, Peter. *Nobel Prize.* 1983. Stockholm. 4to. ils. gilt bl cloth. F/dj. R3. $20.00.

WILKIE, Franc B. *Davenport Past and Present.* 1858. Davenport, IA. Luse. Lane & Co. 1st. ils lithographs. engravings. woodcuts. orig blk emb cloth. 334p. extremeties of spine lightly frayed. minor foxing/staining. K1. $175.00.

WILKIN, Eloise. *Eloise Wilkin Treasury.* 1985. Western. 1st. lg 4to. 70p. G. P2. $20.00.

WILKIN, Eloise. *Singing Every Day.* 1950. Ginn. rpt. 8vo. VG. B17. $15.00.

WILKIN, Eloise, illustrator. *Prayers for Children.* 1974. WI. Western Publishing. A Little Golden Book. cover scuffed. G. no dj as issued. A28. $7.95.

WILKINSON, Doug. *Arctic Fever: Search for the Northwest Passage.* 1971. Toronto. Clarke Irwin. 1st. F/NF. A26. $20.00.

WILKINSON, E. S. *Shanghai Bird Year: Calendar of Bird Life.* 1935. Shanghai. 4 photos. 219p. gilt decor cloth. $0.00.

WILKINSON, Frederick. *Militaria.* 1969. London. Ward Lock. ltd. F. A19. $30.00.

WILKINSON, John. *Jerusalem Pilgrims Before the Crusades.* 1977. Warminster. Avis Phillips. ils/47 maps/map ep. 225p. cloth. VG/dj. Q2. $92.00.

WILKINSON, John. *The Jerusalem Jesus Knew.* 1978. Nelson. 208p. VG. B29. $6.00.

WILKINSON, Norman. *E. I. DuPont: Botanist, Beginning of a Tradition.* 1972. Charlottesville. 139p. VG. A10. $25.00.

WILLAN, Anne. *Entertaining Menus.* 1974. NY. CMG. G/dj. A16. $6.00.

WILLARD, Emma & William Channing Woodbridge. *Universal History in Perspective.* 1853. NY. A. S. Barnes & Co. 12th ed. 8vo. library sheep spine w/gilt lettering. brown bstp cloth bds. 17 full pg maps. charts. tables. 494p. G. leather spine cracked at front. hinges tender. D6. $20.00.

WILLARD, Frances E. *Glimpses of Fifty Years.* 1889. Chicago. Woman's Temperance Pub. ils. emb gr cloth. F. P4. $60.00.

WILLARD, Fred. *Down on Ponce.* 1997. Atlanta. Longstreet Press. 1st. pb orig. author's 1st novel. sgn. VF/pict wrp. T2. $20.00.

WILLARD, Fred. *Down on Ponce.* 1997. Atlanta. Longstreet Press. 1st. pb orig. author's 1st novel. sgn. VF/pict wrp. T2. $20.00.

WILLARD, James F. *Union Colony at Greeley, Colorado.* Vol 1. 1918. Denver, CO. Robinson Prt. G. A19. $60.00.

WILLARD, Nancy. *Childhood of the Magician.* 1973. NY. Liveright. 1st. author's 1st book. short stories. F/NF. 2 sm closed tears. B3. $75.00.

WILLARD, Nancy. *East of the Sun & West of the Moon.* 1989. San Diego. HBJ. 1st. children's. ils Barry Moser. F/F. B3. $30.00.

WILLARD, Nancy. *Night Story.* 1986. San Diego. HBJ. 1st thus. children's. ils Ilse Plume. text copyright 1981. F/F. B3. $15.00.

WILLARD, Nancy. *Things Invisible to See.* 1984. NY. Knopf. 1st. F/F. B3. $35.00.

WILLARD, W. *Leathernecks Come Through.* c 1944. 5th. VG/dj. E6. $13.00.

WILLCOCK, Colin. *Enormous Zoo.* 1965. NY. photos. 210p. VG/dj. S15. $15.00.

WILLEFORD, Charles. *A Guide for the Undehemorrhoided.* 1977. Miami. Charles Willeford. 1st. VF/VF. T2. $125.00.

WILLEFORD, Charles. *Cockfighter.* 1972. NY. Crown. 1st. F/VG. B4. $375.00.

WILLEFORD, Charles. *Cockfighter.* 1962. Chicago. Paperback House. 1st. VG+ in pb. cover Is rubbed. edges of rear worn away. M25. $75.00.

WILLEFORD, Charles. *Cockfighter.* 1972. NY. Crown. 1st. jacket has light wear at corners and a couple of tiny tears. F/dj. M15. $185.00.

WILLEFORD, Charles. *Cockfighter Journal.* 1988. Santa Barbara. Neville. 1st. one of 300 numbered copies sgn. VF/. M15. $100.00.

WILLEFORD, Charles. *Cockfighter Journal: Story of a Shooting.* 1989. Santa Barbara. Neville. 1st. 1/300. sgn/intro James Lee Burke. F/sans. T2. $100.00.

WILLEFORD, Charles. *Everybody's Metamorphosis.* 1988. Missoula. Macmillan. 1st. 1/400. sgn. F/dj. M15. $150.00.

WILLEFORD, Charles. *High Priest of California/Wild Wives.* 1953. Beacon. 2nd appearance of High Priest. 1st appearance of Wild Wives. NF. pb. M25. $200.00.

WILLEFORD, Charles. *Honey Gal.* 1958. Beacon. 1st. VG+. M21. $150.00.

WILLEFORD, Charles. *I Was Looking for a Street.* 1988. Countryman. 1st. NF/dj. M21. $25.00.

WILLEFORD, Charles. *Miami Blues.* 1984. NY. St. Martin. 1st. F/dj. M15. $250.00.

WILLEFORD, Charles. *New Hope for the Dead.* 1985. NY. St. Martin. 1st. VF/dj. M15. $250.00.

WILLEFORD, Charles. *Off the Wall.* 1980. Montclair. Pegasus Rex. 1st. VF/dj. M15. $200.00.

WILLEFORD, Charles. *Sideswipe.* 1987. St. Martin. 1st. F in dj. M25. $35.00.

WILLEFORD, Charles. *Sideswipe.* 1987. NY. St. Martin. 1st. VF/dj. M15. $45.00.

WILLEFORD, Charles. *Sideswipe.* 1987. NY. St. Martin. 1st. F in dj. M15. $50.00.

WILLEFORD, Charles. *Something About Soldier.* 1986. NY. Random House. 1st. VF/VF. T2. $40.00.

WILLEFORD, Charles. *Something About Soldier.* 1986. NY. Random House. 1st. VF/dj. M15. $45.00.

WILLEFORD, Charles. *The Difference.* 1999. Tucson. Dennis McMillan. 1st. VF/VF. T2. $30.00.

WILLEFORD, Charles. *The Difference.* 1999. Tucson. Dennis McMillan. 1st. VF/dj. M15. $35.00.

WILLEFORD, Charles. *The Shark Infested Custard.* 1993. Novato/Lancaster. Underwood Miller. 1st combined ed. VF/VF. T2. $25.00.

WILLEFORD, Charles. *The Shark-Infested Custard.* 1993. Novato. Underwood-Miller. 1st. VF/dj. M15. $45.00.

WILLEFORD, Charles. *The Way We Die Now.* 1988. Random House. UP. F in dj. M25. $100.00.

WILLEFORD, Charles. *The Way We Die Now.* 1988. NY. Random House. 1st. VF in dj. M15. $45.00.

WILLEMS, Emilio. *Buzio's Island.* 1952. Seattle. Univ. of Washington Press. 1st. 116p. lt gr cloth faded. hinges loose. contents VG. F3. $15.00.

WILLEMS, Emilio. *Buzio's Island.* 1966. Seattle. Univ. of Washington Press. 2nd printing. 116p. VG+. F3. $10.00.

WILLER, Thomas F. *Southeast Asian References in the British Parliamentary Papers 1801–1972/73: An Index.* 1973. Athens. Ohio University Center for International Studies. 4to. 88p. F/VG+. P1. $20.00.

WILLETT, John. *Art & Politics in Weimar Period: The New Sobriety 1917–33.* 1978. NY. 1st. ils. VG/dj. M17. $30.00.

WILLEY, Basil. *18th Century Background.* 1941. Columbia. 1st Am. F. H13. $65.00.

WILLIAM, Richard Pardee Jr. *High School History of the Episcopal High School in Va.* 1964. Vincent-Curtis. 225p. VG. B10. $15.00.

WILLIAMS, A. B. *Game Trails in British Columbia.* 1925. NY. Scribner. ils/index 360p. G. B5. $45.00.

WILLIAMS, A. Susan. *Lifted Veil.* 1992. Carroll Graf. 1st Am. F/NF. M21. $30.00.

WILLIAMS, Alan. *The Widow's War.* 1978. NY. Rawson. 1st. F/F. H11. $15.00.

WILLIAMS, C. K. *The Vigil.* 1997. NY. F S G. 1st. F/F. V1. $10.00.

WILLIAMS, Clara Andrews. *The Farm that Glue Made.* 1909. NY. Frederick A. Stokes. covers chip. lib mark on title p. G. A16. $150.00.

WILLIAMS, Daniel Day. *What Present Day Theologians are Thinking.* 1952. Harper. 158p. G/G. B29. $4.50.

WILLIAMS, David. *Advertise for Treasure.* 1984. London. Collins Crime Club. 1st. F/dj. M15. $45.00.

WILLIAMS, David. *Divided Treasure.* 1987. London. Macmillan. 1st. F/dj. M15. $45.00.

WILLIAMS, David. *Treasure in Oxford.* 1988. London. Macmillan. 1st. F/dj. M15. $45.00.

WILLIAMS, David. *Treasure in Roubles.* 1986. London. Macmillan. 1st. F/dj. M15. $45.00.

WILLIAMS, Elizabeth Yahn. *The Music of Poetry.* 1997. San Luis Rey Chorale. 1st. 71p. F. F6. $4.00.

WILLIAMS, Elsie. *Popular Fox Terrier.* 1965. Popular Dogs. 1st. NF/dj. A21. $35.00.

WILLIAMS, Frances Leigh. *They Faced the Future: Sage of Growth.* 1951. Whittet Shepperson. ils. 105p. VG/box. B10. $12.00.

WILLIAMS, Garth. *My Bedtime Book.* 1973. Golden. 4th. unp. VG. C14. $12.00.

WILLIAMS, George C. *Adaptation and Natural Selection. A Critique of Some Current Evolutionary Thought.* 1967 (1966). Princeton. 2nd prt. 307p. F in dj. B26. $14.00.

WILLIAMS, Gladys. *Semolina Silkpaws Comes to Catstown.* 1967. Hart. 1st. ils Ronald Ferns. F/VG+. M5. $20.00.

WILLIAMS, Gordon. *Pomeroy.* 1982. NY. Arbor House. 1st. F/F. B2. $25.00.

WILLIAMS, Hank Jr. *Living Proof.* 1979. NY. 1st. VG/dj. B5. $17. 50.

WILLIAMS, Harold S. *Shades of the Past, or Indiscreet Tales of Japan.* 1959. np. Charles Tuttle. 1st. ils by Jean Williams. pc. F/NF dj. M19. $25.00.

WILLIAMS, J. D. *History of the Name O'Kelly.* 1983. History House. 64p. G. S5. $5.00.

WILLIAMS, J. H. *Great & Shining Road: Epic Story of Transcontinental.* 1988. NY. 1st. 341p. F/dj. $4.00.

WILLIAMS, Jay P. *Alaskan Adventure.* 1952. Harrisburg. Stackpole. ils. 299p. map ep. bl cloth. VG. $4.00.

WILLIAMS, Joan. *County Woman.* 1982. Little, Brn. 1st. inscr. VG/dj. B30. $30.00.

WILLIAMS, Joan. *Pariah & Other Stories.* 1983. Atlantic Monthly. 1st. sgn. VG/dj. B30. $20.00.

WILLIAMS, Jonathan. *Lines About Hills Above Lakes.* 1964. Fort Lauderdale. Roman Books. 1st. sgn by author. sewn wrps. NF. broken thread. B2. $60.00.

WILLIAMS, Jonathan. *Lullabies Twisters Gibbers Drags.* 1963. Highlands. Nantahala Foundation. issued as Jargon 61. F. bit of darkening/wrp. B2. $30.00.

WILLIAMS, Joseph J. *Voodoos & Obeahs: Phases of West India Witchcraft.* 1932. Dial Press. 4th. sm4to. some limited edge chews. 257p. F/VG. H1. $30.00.

WILLIAMS, Martin, Ed. *The Art of Jazz.* 1959. NY. Oxford. 1st. wrps. author's 1st book. F/F. B2. $65.00.

WILLIAMS, Martin, Ed. *The Art of Jazz.* 1959. NY. Oxford. 1st. author's 1st book. F/NF. B2. $65.00.

WILLIAMS, Nigel. *Black Magic.* 1988. London. Hutchinson. 1st. VF/VF. T2. $50.00.

WILLIAMS, Pat & Jill. *Kindling: Daily Devotions for Busy Couples.* 1987. Nelson. 245p. VG/VG. B29. $5.00.

WILLIAMS, R. O. & R. O., Jr. *The Useful and Ornamental Plants in Trinidad and Tobago.* 1951 (1927). Port of Spain. rev 4th ed. no ils. keys. alpha list of plants w/ descriptions. perfect bd in wrp. spine faded. else VG. B26. $34.00.

WILLIAMS, Robert Chadwell. *Klaus Emil Julius Fuchs Atom Spy.* 1987. Harvard. 1st. sm 4to. 267p. F/NF. W2. $30.00.

WILLIAMS, Robert R. *Schleirmacher the Theologian.* 1978. Fortress. 196p. G. B29. $9.00.

WILLIAMS, Roger. *Resurrection Men.* 1985. London. Hale. 1st. F/dj. M15. $40.00.

WILLIAMS, Roger D. *National Foxhunters' Association Studbook 1904 Vol II.* Lexington, KY. F. O3. $65.00.

WILLIAMS, Samuel H. *Voodoo Roads.* 1939. Vienna. Jugen Volk. English text. F/dj. B2. $50.00.

WILLIAMS, Stanley T. *The Life of Washington Irving.* 1935. Oxford U. Press. 1st. 2 vols. uncut pages. edge chipping & tears. 501p & 445p. F/F. H1. $45.00.

WILLIAMS, Stephen. *Invisible Darkness.* 1996. Little, Brn. 1st Canadian. F/dj. T12. $60.00.

WILLIAMS, T. *Harry Hayes of the Twenty-Third, the Civil War Volunteer Officer.* 1965. Knopf. 1st. 324p. VG. H1. $35.00.

WILLIAMS, T. *St. John, Judy O'Grady & the Colonel's Lady.* 1988. London. 1st. ils. $269.00.

WILLIAMS, Tennessee. *Collected Stories.* 1985. NY. New Directions. 1st. intro by Gore Vidal. includes both previously & previously pub stories. 574p. NF/NF. A24. $25.00.

WILLIAMS, Tennessee. *World of Tennessee Williams.* 1978. Putnam. 1/250. sgn. F/case. R14. $325.00.

WILLIAMS, Terry Tempest. *Pieces of White Shell.* 1984. NY. Scribner's. 1st. author's 1st adult book. sgn by author. F/NF. lt edgewear. B3. $400.00.

WILLIAMS, Terry Tempest. *Refuge.* 1991. NY. Pantheon. 1st. sgn. F/F. B3. $80.00.

WILLIAMS, Thomas Harry. *Lincoln and His Generals.* 1952. NY. Knopf. 1st. orig cloth. 363p. VG/VG. M8. $35.00.

WILLIAMS, Valentine. *Clock Ticks On.* 1933. London. Hodder Stoughton. 1st. F/dj. M15. $150.00.

WILLIAMS, Valentine. *The Mysterious Miss Morrisot.* 1930. Boston. Houghton Mifflin. 1st Am. jacket has tiny wear at corners and tiny closed tears. F/dj. M15. $125.00.

WILLIAMS, W. *American Nation.* 1888. Cleveland. Williams. 3 vol. 3-quarter leather. G. S17. $50.00.

WILLIAMS, W. *Chemistry of Cooking.* 1892 (1885). gilt red brd. VG. E6. $40.00.

WILLIAMS, W. K. *American Farmer's Business Guide.* 1902. Columbus. Rural Pub. 101p. VG. A10. $10.00.

WILLIAMS, W. W. *History of the Fire Lands.* 1973. Evansville, IN. Unigraphic. rpt of 1879. 524p. B18. $75.00.

WILLIAMS, Walter Jon. *Angel Station.* 1989. NY. Tor. 1st. sgn. sgn errata sheet. VF/VF. T2. $30.00.

WILLIAMS, Walter Jon. *Aristoi.* 1992. NY. Tor. 1st. sgn. VF/VF. T2. $30.00.

WILLIAMS, Walter Jon. *Facets.* 1990. NY. Tor. 1st. sgn. VF/VF. T2. $25.00.

WILLIAMS, Walter Jon. *Handwired.* 1986. NY. Tor. 1st. sgn. VF/VF. T2. $35.00.

WILLIAMS, Walter Jon. *Handwired.* 1987. London. MacDonald. 1st British ed. sgn. VF/VF. T2. $35.00.

WILLIAMS, Walter Jon. *Metropolitan.* 1995. NY. Harper Prism. 1st. F/dj. M23. $25.00.

WILLIAMS, Walter Jon. *Wall, Stone, Craft.* 1993. Eugene. Axolotl Press. 1st. 1/300 # copies. sgn. VF/VF. T2. $45.00.

WILLIAMS, William. *Journal of Life, Travels & Gospel Labours of.* 1828. Cincinnati. Lodge L'Hommedieu Hammond. 12mo. 272p.

WILLIAMS, William Carlos. *Tempers.* 1913. London. Elkin Mathews. 1st. 1/100. author's 2nd book. gilt lt yel brd. NF. $24.00.

WILLIAMS, William Carlos, and John Sanford. *A Correspondence.* 1984. Santa Barbara. Oyster Press. 1st. wrp. F. B2. $25.00.

WILLIAMS, William Carlos, trans. *Last Nights of Paris by Philippe Soupault.* 1929. NY. Macaulay. 1st. VG. owner's name. B2. $30.00.

WILLIAMS, William W., ed. *Magazine of Western History. Vol 1.* 1884. Ohio. 4 vols. 1/2 leather. ils. lt wear to edges. marbled ep. some browning of paper. VG. B18. $195.00.

WILLIAMS & WILLIAMS. *Treasury of Great American Houses.* Putnam. 1970. 1st. ils. F/NF clip. B9. $20.00.

WILLIAMS & WILLIAMS. *Modernizing Old Houses.* 1948. Doubleday. 269p. VG/dj. M10. $15.00.

WILLIAMSON, Chet. *Ask Wednesday.* 1987. NY. Tor. 1st. inscr by author. F/F. B3. $25.00.

WILLIAMSON, Chet. *McKain's Dilemma.* 1988. Tor. 1st. sgn. AN/dj. S18. $40.00.

WILLIAMSON, Chet. *Reign.* 1990. Arlington Heights. Dark Harvest. 1st. VF/VF. T2. $21.00.

WILLIAMSON, Graham. *The Orchids of South Central Africa.* 1977. NY. 1st Am ed. 4to. F in dj. B26. $65.00.

WILLIAMSON, Harold F. *Winchester: Gun that Won the West.* 1952. Combat Forces. 1st. NF/dj. T11. $125.00.

WILLIAMSON, Henry. *The Sun in the Sands.* 1945. London. Faber & Faber. 1st. octavo. orig red cloth. gilt lettered spine. printed dj. ink inscr on ffep. dj slightly browned. R3. $50.00.

WILLIAMSON, Henry. *The Village Book.* 1930. London. Jonathan Cape. 1st. orig brown cloth. gilt lettered spine. printed dj. F/NF. R3. $60.00.

WILLIAMSON, J. N., editor. *Masques 2: All New Works of Horror and the Supernatural.* 1987. Baltimore. Maclay & Associates. 1st. sgn by contrib Joe Lansdale. VF/VF. T2. $20.00.

WILLIAMSON, J. N. Editor. *Masques: All New Works of Horror and the Supernatural.* 1984. Baltimore. Maclay & Associates. 1st. sgn by contrib Joe Lansdale. VF/VF. T2. $20.00.

WILLIAMSON, Jack. *Darker than You Think.* 1948. Reading. Fantasy Press. 1st. F. slight crease/F. used dj. B2. $100.00.

WILLIAMSON, Jack. *Firechild.* 1986. NY. Bluejay books. 1st. F/F. T2. $9.00.

WILLIAMSON, Jack. *Lifeburst.* 1984. NY. Ballantine/Del Rey. 1st. F/F. T2. $7.00.

WILLIAMSON, James J. *Mosby's Rangers. A Record of the Operations of the 43rd Battalion of Va. Cavalry.* 1909. NY. Sturgis & Walton Co. 2nd & best ed. greatly enlarged. orig cloth. some cover speckling to front bd. plates. ils. 554p. VG. M8. $350.00.

WILLIAMSON, Ray A. *Living the Sky: Cosmos of the American Indian.* 1984. Houghton Mifflin. ils. 366p. VG/dj. K5. $40.00.

WILLINGHAM, Calder. *Providence Island.* 1969. np. Vanguard. 1st. NF/VG dj. M19. $25.00.

WILLIS, Connie. *Lincoln's Dreams.* 1987. NY. Bantam. 1st. F/NF. G10. $70.00.

WILLIS, H. *Charleston (SC): Stage in the 18th Century.* 1924. Columbia. 1st. ils. 483p. VG/dj. B5. $50.00.

WILLIS, J. C. *Dictionary of Flowering Plants & Ferns.* 1982 (1973). Dehra Dun. 8th/rpt. 1245p. AN. B26. $40.00.

WILLIS, Ted. *Man Eater.* 1977. NY. Morrow. 1st. VG+/G+. R16. $20.00.

WILLISON, George F. *Saints and Strangers.* 1945. Reynal & Hitchcock. 513p. VG. B29. $7.50.

WILLIUS, F. A. *Aphorisms of Dr. Charles Horace Mayo & Dr. William J. Mayo.* 1988. Rochester. 109p. A13. $25.00.

WILLKIE, Wendell. *One World.* 1943. S&S. 1st/2nd prt. inscr. VG. B30. $45.00.

WILLMAN, Paul. *Dynasty of Western Outlaws.* 1961. Doubleday. 1st. VG/dj. B5. $30.00.

WILLOCKS, Tim. *Bloodstained Kings.* 1995. NY. Random. 1st. VF/VF. H11. $20.00.

WILLOCKS, Tim. *Green River Rising.* 1994. London. Cape. 1st. F/dj. O11. $35.00.

WILLOCKS, Tim. *Green River Rising.* 1994. NY. Morrow. 1st. author's 1st novel. VF/VF. T2. $25.00.

WILLOCKS, Tim. *Green River Rising.* 1994. NY. Morrow. 1st. ARC. author's 1st novel. F/pict wrp. T2. $15.00.

WILLOCKS, Tim. *Green River Rising.* 1994. NY. Random. 1st. VF/F. H11. $25.00.

WILLS, Garry and Ovid Demaris. *Jack Ruby, The Man Who Killed the Man Who Killed Kennedy.* 1968. NY. NAL. 1st. F in G dj. B2. $50.00.

WILLYS, Rufus Kay. *Pioneer Padre: Life & Times of Eusebio Francisco Kino.* 1935. Dallas. Southwest Pr. 1st. inscr assn to HE Bolton. 230p. cloth. dj. $11.00.

WILMERDING, John. *American Views: Essays on American Art.* 1991. Princeton. ils/29 pl/notes/index. cloth. F/dj. D2. $50.00.

WILMERDING, John. *Important Information Inside: Art of John F. Peto.* 1983. WA. Nat Gallery of Art. 1st. ils. VG/dj. $17.00.

WILSIE, Carroll. *Crop Adaptation & Distribution.* 1962. SF. Freeman. 448p. cloth. VG. A10. $22.00.

WILSON, A. E. *King Planto: Story of Pantomime.* 1935. Dutton. 1st. ils. NF/VG. O4. $30.00.

WILSON, A. N. *Love Unknown.* 1986. London. 1st. dj. T9. $25.00.

WILSON, A. N. *Penfriends from Porlock: Essays & Reviews 1977 – 1986.* 1989. NY. 1st. VG/dj. M17. $15.00.

WILSON, A. N. *Rise & Fall of the House of Windsor.* 1993. NY. 1st. dj. T9. $12.00.

WILSON, Adrian. *Design of Books.* 1967. Reinhold. 1st. 4to. 160p. F/dj. O10. $65.00.

WILSON, Adrian. *Printing for Theater.* 1957. SF. 1/250. author's 1st book. folio. 57p. cloth. F. $24.00.

WILSON, Adrian. *Work & Play of Adrian Wilson.* 1983. Austin. W. Thomas Taylor. 1/325. folio. 160p. w/samples & prospectus. F. $24.00.

WILSON, Andrew. *Modern Physician: Being a Complete Guide.* 1900. London. Caxton. 5 vol. ils. G. $10.00.

WILSON, Angus. *Travel Pieces: Reflections in a Writer's Eye.* 1986. NY. 1st. dj. T9. $14.00.

WILSON, Ann. *Familiar Letters of Ann Wilson.* 1850. Phil. Parrish. 12mo. 270p. G+. V3. $20.00.

WILSON, August. *Seven Guitars.* 1996. Dutton. 1st. sgn. F/dj. O11. $25.00.

WILSON, Barbara. *Noel Streatfield, A Walck Monograph.* 1964. NY. Walck. 1st Am. 61p. F/dj. D4. $25.00.

WILSON, Bill & Betty. *19th Century Medicine in Glass.* 1971. Amador City, CA. 19th Century Hobby & Publishing Co. 4to separate 1971 price guide. 147p. VG. H1. $97.50.

WILSON, Carol Green. *Chinatown Quest: The Life Adventures of Donaldina Cameron.* 1931. Stanford. Stanford Univ. Press. 1st. octavo. stp gr cloth. dj. sgn by Cameron. F. R3. $45.00.

WILSON, Charles. *Middle America.* 1944. Norton. 1st. 317p. F3. $15.00.

WILSON, Colin. *Schoolgirl Murder Case.* 1974. Crown. 1st. VG+/VG+. G8. $17.50.

WILSON, Derek. *The Swarm of Heaven: A Renaissance Mystery.* 1999. London. Constable. 1st. sgnf. VF/VF. T2. $39.00.

WILSON, Edmund. *Travels in Two Democracies.* 1936. NY. Harcourt. 1st. bookplate. NF/lightly used dj. B2. $150.00.

WILSON, Edward O. *Naturalist.* 1994. Washington, DC. Island. NF/dj. B9. $15.00.

WILSON, Ernest. *China: Mother of Gardens.* 1929. Boston. Stratford. 1st. 408p. G+. B5. $150.00.

WILSON, F. Paul. *Keep.* 1981. Morrow. 1st. VG/NF. M21. $30.00.

WILSON, F. Paul. *Black Wind.* 1988. NY. TOR. 1st. VG+/VG. R16. $35.00.

WILSON, Gahan. *Eddy Deco's Last Caper: An Illustrated Mystery.* 1987. NY. Times Books. 1st. F/pict brds w/o dj as issued. T2. $15.00.

WILSON, John. *Reason and Morals.* 1961. Cambridge. 185p. VG. ex lib. B29. $3.50.

WILSON, John Morgan. *Simple Justice.* 1996. NY. Doubleday. 1st. VF/VF. T2. $25.00.

WILSON, John Morgan. *Simple Justice.* 1996. NY. Doubleday. 1st. UP. VF/pict wrp. T2. $25.00.

WILSON, John Morgan. *Simple Justice.* 1996. NY. Doubleday. 1st. VF/dj. M15. $45.00.

WILSON, John S. *The Collector's Jazz: Modern.* 1959. Philadelphia. Lippincott. 1st. wrp. F but for owner's name on inside front cover. B2. $30.00.

WILSON, Joseph M. *The Presbyterian Historical Almanac, and Annual Remembranceer of the Church, for 1858 – 1859.* Philadelphia. Joseph M. Wilson. 1859. 8vo. 316p. ils. & ads. stiff printed wrp & gr cloth spine. 1st ed of this annual. contains 26 very nice lithographs of individuals & churches. minor wear & wrapers soiled. G to VG. L5. $60.00.

WILSON, Mary. *Dream Girl: My Life as a Supreme.* 1986. St. Martin. 1st. G/F. W2. $30.00.

WILSON, Mary. *Supreme Faith: Someday We'll be Together.* 1990. Harper Collins. 1st. sgn. F/dj. O11. $35.00.

WILSON, Mona. *The Life of William Blake.* 1927. London. The Nonesuch Press. ltd ed of 1480 numbered copies. ils 24 plates. vellum-like paper over marbled brds. 4to. (2).xvi.398p. spine soiled. brds rubbed. unopened. K1. $150.00.

WILSON, Pearl Cleveland. *Living Socrates: Man Who Dared to Question.* 1975. Owings Mills, MD. 1st. ils. VG/dj. $17.00.

WILSON, R. L. *Colt, an American Legend.* 1950. NY. Abbeville. 10th printing. oblong quarto. blind stp bl cloth. pict dj. F. R3. $40.00.

WILSON, Robert C. *Icefire.* 1984. Putnam. 1st. F/F. H11. $20.00.

WILSON, Robert Charles. *Gypsies.* 1989. NY. Doubleday. 1st. F/F. M23. $25.00.

WILSON, Robert Charles. *The Divide.* 1990. NY. Doubleday. 1st. F/F. M23. $20.00.

WILSON, Robert Thomas. *History of the British Expedition to Egypt.* 1802. London. C Roworth. 4to. ils/3 tables. 354p.

WILSON, Robley. *Victim's Daughter.* 1991. S&S. 1st. sgn/dtd 1996. NF/F. R14. $30.00.

WILSON, Rufus Rockwell. *Out of the West.* 1933. Pr of Pioneers. 1st. ils. 452p. VG. B19. $75.00.

WILSON, Rufus Rockwell. *Out of the West.* 1933. Pr of Pioneers. 1st. VG/dj. J2. $135.00.

WILSON, Ruth. *Here Is Haiti.* 1957. NY. Philosophical Lib. 1st. inscr. 204p. dj. F3. $20.00.

WILSON, Samuel M. *Year Book of the Society, Sons of the Revolution in the Commonwealth of KY 1894 – 1913 and Catalogue of Military Land Warrants Granted by the Commonwealth of Virginia.* 1913. Lexington, KY. State Land Office. thick octavo. bl & yellow cloth. lettered in gilt. patterned ep. F/covers slightly soiled. browned. R3. $45.00.

WILSON, T. P. Cameron. *Magpies in Picardy.* 1919. London. Poetry Bookshop. 1st. G. Q1. $75.00.

WILSON, T. P. Cameron. *Violent World of Hugh Greene.* 1963. Houghton Mifflin. 1st. VG/dj. Q1. $50.00.

WILSON, Teddy. *Piano Patterns.* 1938. NY. Miller Music. 1st. 48p. NF/wrp. B2. $40.00.

WILSON, Teddy. *Piano Rhythms.* 1937. NY. Leo Feist. 1st. wrp. 48p. VG. B2. $35.00.

WILSON, William P. *The Grace to Grow; The Power of Christian Faith in Emotional Healing.* 1984. Word. 165p. VG/VG. B29. $7.00.

WILTSE, David. *Blown Away.* 1996. NY. Putnam. 1st. UP. VF/printed wrp. T2. $10.00.

WILTSE, David. *Bone Deep.* 1995. Putnam. 1st. F/dj. R8. $12.00.

WILTSE, David. *Close to the Bone.* 1992. Putnam. 1st. NF/dj. G8. $22.50.

WILTSE, David. *Into the Fire.* 1994. NY. Putnam. 1st. F/F. H11. $15.00.

WILTSE, David. *Prayer for the Dead.* 1991. NY. Putnam. 1st. VF/VF. T2. $20.00.

WILTSE, David. *The Fifth Angel.* 1985. NY. Macmillan. 1st. F/F. T2. $20.00.

WILTZ, Chris. *A Diamond Before You Die.* 1987. NY. Mysterious. 1st. VF/dj. M15. $35.00.

WILTZ, Chris. *The Killing Circle.* 1981. NY. Macmillan. 1st. F/dj. M15. $45.00.

WIMBER, John. *Power Evangelism.* 1986. Harper. 201p. VG/torn dj. B29. $9.50.

WIMBER, John. *Power Healing.* 1987. Harper. 293p. VG/torn dj. B29. $9.50.

WIMBERLEY, Darryl. *A Rock and a Hard Place.* 1999. NY. St. Martin. 1st. author's 1st novel. sgn. VF/VF. T2. $25.00.

WIMPRESS, R. N. *Internal Ballistics of Solid-Fuel Rockets.* 1950. McGraw Hill. 1st. 214p. G. $5.00.

WINCHELL, A. *First Biennial Report.* Geological Survey of Michigan. 1861. Lansing. 339p. VG. A17. $75.00.

WINCHESTER, Alice. *Antiques Book.* 1950. NY. AA Wyn. 1st. ils. F/torn. T10. $35.00.

WINCHESTER, Simon. *The Professor and the Madman.* 1998. NY. Harper Collins. 1st. F/F. M23. $45.00.

WINCOR, Richard. *Sherlock Holmes in Tibet.* 1968. NY. Weybright and Talley. 2nd printing. F/F. T2. $20.00.

WIND, Herbert Warren. *World of P.G. Wodehouse.* 1972. Praeger. 1st. NF/dj. G8. $30.00.

WINDSOR, Justin. *Cartier to Frontenac, Geographical Discovery in the Interior of No. America in its Historical Relations, 1534 – 1700.* 1894. London. Sampson Low. 1st British ed. teg. ils. 379p. VG. B18. $225.00.

WINE ADVISORY BOARD. *Adventures in Wine Cookery by California Winemakers.* 1965. CA. Wine Advisory Bd. poi on inside front cover. folio. spiral bd w/hard brds. F. A28. $6.95.

WINFIELD, Arthur M. *Rover Boys on Sunset Trail.* 1925. Grosset Dunlap. 1st/4th format. 304p. brn cloth. VG/dj. H1. $18.00.

WINFIELD, Arthur M. *Rover Boys Shipwrecked.* 1924. Grosset Dunlap. 1st/4th format. 306p. G/dj. H1. $15.00.

WINFIELD, Arthur M. *The Rover Boys at School.* Grosset & Dunlap. sm8vo. shaken. owner's inscriptions on both endpapers. front & back only with edge damage & cello tape repairs or stains on each. 250p. G/dj. H1. $8.00.

WINFIELD, Arthur M. *The Rover Boys in Alaska.* Grosset & Dunlap. sm8vo. shaken. spine has some wear. 2 pages have stains. owner's inscriptions on front endpaper. 285p. G. H1. $12.00.

WINFIELD, Arthur M. *The Rover Boys in the Air.* Grosset & Dunlap. sm8vo. front hinge weak. owner's inscription on front endpaper. spine darkened with some spotting. edges worn. masking tape reinforcement on verso across top & bottom. down both flap folds & down spine edges. thin cello tape strip at bottom of spine. 288p. VG/dj. H1. $18.00.

WINFIELD, Arthur M. *The Rover Boys in the Land of Luck.* 1921. Grosset & Dunlap. 1st. sm8vo. front hinge cracked. shaken. owner's inscriptions on front endpaper. spine darkened with ½" missing at bottom & tears with cello tape repairs at top. edges worn. front flap fold darkened with splits. extreme left corners of front have cello pieces. 310p. G/dj. H1. $18.00.

WINFIELD, Arthur M. *The Rover Boys on a Tour.* Grosset & Dunlap. sm8vo. front hinge broken. owner's inscription on front endpaper. spine darkened with some spotting & ½" d. rub in center. large chips at extremes of spine & all cover corners covered with masking tape. edges worn. masking tape reinforcement on verso across top & bottom. down both flap folds & down spine edges. 3126p. G/dj. H1. $12.00.

WINFIELD, Arthur M. *The Rover Boys on the Plains.* Grosset & Dunlap. sm8vo. covers faded to light green & spine yellowed. owner's inscription on endpaper. 255p. G. H1. $9.00.

WINFIELD, Arthur M. *The Rover Boys Winning a Fortune.* Grosset & Dunlap. 1st. sm8vo. owner's date of acquisition written on front endpaper was June, 1926, the year this last title in the series was published. spine darkened with many cello tape repairs on face. cello tape along front flap fold. cello tape repairs on verso. back flap detached. front Is fair. 306p. H1. $25.00.

WINFIELD, Charles H. *Block-House by Bull's Ferry.* 1904. NY. Wm Abbott. 1/200. ils. 61p. VG. B18. $75.00.

WINFIELD, Dave. *Winfield: A Player's Life.* 1988. Norton. 1st. F/dj. T12. $35.00.

WINFIELD, Dave. *Winfield: A Player's Life.* 1988. NY. Norton. 1st. VG/NF clip. R16. $35.00.

WINGFIELD, R. D. *Frost at Christmas.* 1989. London. Constable. 1st. VF/dj. M15. $200.00.

WINGFIELD, R. D. *Hard Frost.* 1995. London. Constable. 1st. sgn. VF/dj. M15. $135.00.

WINGFIELD, R. D. *Winter Frost.* 1999. London. Constable. 1st. VF/VG. T2. $39.00.

WINGFIELD, R. D. *Winter Frost.* 1999. London. Constable. 1st. sgn. VF/dj. M15. $55.00.

WINGFIELD, R. D. *Winter Frost.* 1999. London. Constable. 1st. VF/VG. T2. $39.00.

WINGROVE, David. *Chung Kuo.* 1990. NY. Delacorte. 1st. jacket has usual rubbing at spine ends. F/F. H11. $35.00.

WINGROVE, David. *The Broken Wheel.* 1991. NY. Delacorte. 1st. F/F. H11. $25.00.

WINGROVE, David. *The White Mountain.* 1992. NY. Delacorte. 1st. closed tear (½") at top of front spine fold. F/F. H11. $25.00.

WINGROVE, David. *White Mountain.* 1992. Delacorte. 1st. F/NF. H11. $25.00.

WINGS, Mary. *She Came by the Book.* 1996. NY. Berkley Pub. 1st. F/dj. C9. $25.00.

WINGS, Mary. *She Came to the Castro.* 1997. Berkeley. 1st. F/F. G8. $17.50.

WINKELMANN, Friedhelm. *Studien Zu Konstantin Dem Grossen Und Zur Byzantinischen.* 1993. Birmingham. 250p. VG. Q2. $24.00.

WINKLER. *Greatest of Greatness: Life & Work of Chas. C. Williamson.* 10 photos. 1992. 370p. F. A4. $30.00.

WINKLER. *History of Books & Printing: A Guide.* 1979. 776 entries. 225p. F. A4. $95.00.

WINKS, Robin W. *Frederick Billings, a Life. The Story of One of the 19th Century's Great Railway Builders and Early American Conservationists.* 1991. NY. Oxford Univ. Press. octavo. cloth. dj. F. R3. $25.00.

WINKS, Robin W. *Modus Operandi.* 1982. Godine. 1st. NF/dj. G8. $25.00.

WINOKUR, Jon. *Fathers.* 1993. Dutton. 1st. author's 9th book. F/dj. T11. $15.00.

WINSHIP, A. E. *Jukes-Edwards: Study in Education & Heredity.* 1900. Harrisburg, RL Myers. 12mo. 88p. prt gr cloth. xl. VG. G1. $65.00

WINSHIP, George Parker. *Journey of Coronado, 1540 – 1542, from City of Mexico.* 1922. Allerton Book Co. 12mo. 251p. $1.00.

WINSHIP, George Parker. *Journey of Coronado, 1540 – 1542.* 1900. Fulcrum. rpt. ils. 233p. F/F. B19. $25.00.

WINSLOW, Don. *A Cool Breeze on the Underground.* 1991. NY. St. Martin. 1st. Sign. VF/dj. M15. $150.00.

WINSLOW, Don. *A Cool Breeze on the Underground.* 1991. NY. St. Martin. 1st. sgn. F/F. D10. $175.00.

WINSLOW, Don. *A Long Walk Up the Water Slide.* 1994. NY. St. Martin. 1st. sgn. VF/VF. T2. $45.00.

WINSLOW, Don. *A Long Walk Up the Water Slide.* 1994. NY. St. Martin. 1st. F/F. B3. $60.00.

WINSLOW, Don. *A Long Walk Up the Waterslide.* 1994. NY. St. Martin. 1st. VF in dj. M15. $65.00.

WINSLOW, Don. *A Long Walk Up the Water Slide.* 1994. St. Martin. 1st. F/dj. M15. $50.00.

WINSLOW, Don. *California Fire and Life.* 1999. NY. Knopf. 1st. sgn. VF/VF. T2. $25.00.

WINSLOW, Don. *Isle of Joy.* 1996. London. Arrow Books. 1st. sgn. VF/pict wrp. T2. $35.00.

WINSLOW, Don. *The Death and Life of Bobby Z.* 1997. Knopf. ARC. F. decor wrp. M25. $25.00.

WINSLOW, Don. *The Death and Life of Bobby Z.* 1997. London. Century. 1st. sgn. VF/pict wrp. T2. $20.00.

WINSLOW, Don. *The Death and Life of Bobby Z.* 1997. NY. Knopf. 1st Am ed. sgn. VF/VF. T2. $30.00.

WINSLOW, Don. *The Death and Life of Bobby Z.* 1997. NY. Knopf. ARC. F. O11. $20.00.

WINSLOW, Don. *The Death & Life of Bobby Z.* 1997. Knopf. 1st. inscr. AN/dj. S18. $35.00.

WINSLOW, Don. *The Death & Life of Bobby Z.* 1997. Knopf. 1st. NF/F. G8. $30.00.

WINSLOW, Don. *The Trail to Buddha's Mirror.* 1992. NY. St. Martin. 1st. sgn. VF/dj. M15. $175.00.

WINSLOW, Don. *Way Down the High Lonely.* (1993). NY. St. Martin. 1st. author's 3rd book. F/F. B3. $75.00.

WINSLOW, Don. *While Drowning in the Desert.* 1996. St. Martin. 1st. sgn. F/dj. G8. $27. 50.

WINSLOW, Don. *While Drowning in the Desert.* 1996. NY. St. Martin. 1st. sgn. F/F. D10. $50.00.

WINSLOW, Don. *While Drowning in the Desert.* 1996. NY. St. Martin. 1st. sgn by author. F/F. B3. $40.00.

WINSLOW, John H. *Darwin's Victorian Malady: Evidence for its Medically Induced Origin.* 1971. Philadelphia. American Philosophical Society. Series: Memoirs. Vol 88. biblio. index. review loosely inserted. 94p. VG in wrp. name on cover. B26. $15.00.

WINSLOW, Margaret C. *International Landscape Design. Architecture of Gardens, Parks, Playgrounds & Open Spaces.* 1991. Glen Cove, NY. foreword by Theodore Osmundson. prt on coated paper. 4to. 239p w/over300 color photos & plans. F in dj. B26. $39.00.

WINSOR, Kathleen. *Forever Amber.* 1945. Macmillan. 11th. 8vo. broken spine & worn covers. jacket complete but edges worn with tears. 652p. H1. $10.00.

WINSOR, Kathleen. *Forever Amber.* 1945. Macmillan. 11th. 8vo. 652p. NVG. H1. $10.00.

WINSWORTH, William. *Works Of.* nd. London. 16 vol. ils Cruikshank. half leather/marbled brd. F. $30.00.

WINTER, Douglas E. *Black Wine.* 1986. Dark Harvest. 1st trade. AN/dj. T12. $40.00.

WINTERICH, John T. *Early American Books & Printing.* 1935. Boston. Houghton Mifflin. 1/300 copies. sgn by author. octavo. red cloth. teg. ils. F. R3. $60.00.

WINTERSON, Jeanette. *Art & Lies.* 1994. London. Jonathan Cape. 1st British ed. true 1st. F/F. B3. $60.00.

WINTERSON, Jeanette. *Art & Lies.* 1994. London. Jonathan Cape. 1st. F/F. A24. $25.00.

WINTERSON, Jeanette. *Art & Lies.* 1995. NY. Knopf. 1st Am ed. sgn. F/F. O11. $50.00.

WINTERSON, Jeanette. *Gut Symmetries.* 1997. NY. Knopf. 1st Am ed. F/F. B3. $15.00.

WINTERSON, Jeanette. *Gut Symmetries.* 1997. London. Jonathan Cape. 1st British ed. true 1st. F/F. B3. $40.00.

WINTERSON, Jeanette. *Gut Symmetries.* 1994. NY. Knopf. 1st Am ed. sgn. F/F. O11. $35.00.

WINTERSON, Jeanette. *Oranges are Not the Only Fruit.* 1985. NY. Atlantic. 1st Am ed. 1st prt (stated) w/$6.95 price on rear wrp. NF. B2. $60.00.

WINTERSON, Jeanette. *Oranges are Not the Only Fruit.* 1985. London. Pandora. 1st British ed. true 1st. author's scarce 1st book. pb orig. NF+. lt edgewear. B3. $400.00.

WINTERSON, Jeanette. *Oranges are Not the Only Fruit.* 1985. London. Pandora Press. true 1st/UK ed. PBO. only 1000 copies printed of 1st ed. author's 1st book. NF in printed wrp. slight reading crease on spine. D10. $425.00.

WINTERSON, Jeanette. *The Passion.* 1988. NY. Atlantic Monthly Press. 1st. author's 2nd book. F/F. B3. $40.00.

WINTERSON, Jeanette. *The Passion.* 1988. NY. Atlantic Monthly Press. 1st Am ed. author's 2nd novel. F/F. D10. $60.00.

WINTERSON, Jeanette. *The World and Other Places.* 1999. NY. Knopf. 1st. UP. F. D10. $10.00.

WINTERSON, Jeanette. *The World and Other Places.* 1999. NY. Knopf. 1st Am ed. special issue. 1/unspecified # copies sgn on tipped in page. F/F. O11. $35.00.

WINTERSON, Jeanette. *The World and Other Stories.* 1999. NY. Knopf. UP. F in wrp. D10. $35.00.

WINTERSON, Jeanette. *Written on the Body.* 1993. NY. Knopf. 1st Am ed. sgn. F/F. O11. $50.00.

WINTHER, Oscar. *Transportation Frontier.* 1964. HRW. VG. A19. $30.00.

WINTHROP, Elizabeth. *Belinda's Hurricane.* 1984. Dutton. 1st. 8vo. 54p. NF. C14. $14.00.

WINTHROP, Robert C. *Life & Letters of John Winthrop.* 1867. Boston. xl. VG. M17. $45.00.

WINTHUR, Oscar Osborn. *Via Western Express & Stagecoach.* 1945. Stanford. Stanford U Press. VG/G. O3. $45.00.

WINTLE, Justin. *Paradise for Hire.* 1984. London. Secker Warburg. 1st. author's 1st book. rem mk. NF/dj. A14. $25.00.

WINTLE, W. J. *Ghost Gleams: Tales of the Uncanny.* 1999. Ashcroft, BC. Ash Tree Press. reissue. 1st thus. VF/VF. T2. $42.00.

WINTON, John. *Fighting Temeraire.* 1971. Coward McCann. 1st. NF/VG. T11. $30.00.

WINTON, John. *Sir Walter Raleigh.* 1975. CMG. 1st. ils. 352p. VG/dj. M10. $28. $50.00.

WINTON, Tim. *Minimum of Two.* 1988. Weidenfeld Nicolson. 1st Eng. sgn. F/dj. R14. $50.00.

WIRTH, Don. *Adventures of Harry 'N' Charlie: 2 Vols.* 1981. Montgomery. Bass. 144/144p. F. A17. $25.00.

WIRTH, Zdenek. *Castles & Mansions (Bohemia & Moravia).* 1955. Prague. Artia. 1st. 272p. 307p. gilt tan cloth. VG/dj. $1.00.

WIRTH, Zdenek. *Prague in Pictures of Five Centuries.* 1954. Prague. Artia Prague. 4to. pict cloth. 56.xiip + 264 plates. some in color. some folding. dj. F in slipcase. K1. $85.00.

WISE, Henry A. *Yesteryears on the Eastern Shore & Some Other Things.* 1968. Eastern Shore News. 1st. 105p. VG/VG. B10. $15.00.

WISE, John. *System of Aeronautics. Comprehending.* 1850. Phil. Joseph Speel. 1st. sgn. $12.00.

WISE, John S. *End of an Era.* 1899. Houghton Mifflin. 18th imp. 474p. VG. B10. $30.00.

WISEMAN, Robert E. *Complete Horseshoeing Guide.* 1973. Norman, OK. 2nd. VG/G. O3. $15.00.

WISER, William. *Disappearances.* 1980. NY. Atheneum. 1st. jacket has minor wear on top edges near rear flap fold. F/F. H11. $35.00.

WISHNIA, K. J. A. *23 Shades of Black.* 1997. East Setauket. Imaginary Press. 1st. pb orig. sgn. VF/pict wrp. T2. $20.00.

WISHNIA, K. J. A. *Soft Money.* 1999. NY. Dutton. 1st. sgn. VF/VF. T2. $25.00.

WISNER, Benjamin B. *History of the Old South Church in Boston.* 1830. Boston. Crocker Brewster. 8vo. lg fld plan. 122p. self wrp. O1. $40.00.

WISSINGER, Joanna. *Best Kit Homes Save Time & Money.* 1987. Emmaus. 1st. ils. VG/dj. M8. $25.00.

WISSLER, Clark. *Indians of the United States.* 1940. Doubleday Doran. G. A19. $45.00.

WISTER, Fammy Kemble. *Owen Wister Out West: His Journals & Letters.* nd. U Chicago. 269p. VG/dj. J2. $50.00.

WISTER, Isaac Jones. *Autobiography Of, 1827 – 1905: Half a Century.* 1937. Phil. Wistar Inst. 4to. 528p. G. V3. $50.00.

WISTER, Owen. *Lady Baltimore.* 1906. NY. Macmillan. 1st. 406p. G. G11. $17.00.

WISTER, Owen. *Journey in Search of Christmas.* 1904. NY. Harper. 1st. 8vo. 92p. teg. VG. H5. $100.00.

WISTER, Owen. *Padre Ignacio; or, Song of Temptation.* 1925. Harper. 8vo. ils Zack Hogg (NC Weyth?). blk cloth. NF. R3. $75.00.

WISTER, OWEN. *The Virginian.* 1929. Grosset & Dunlap. sm8vo. front loose endpaper missing. spine slightly darkened. 506p. G. H1. $15.00.

WISTER, Owen. *Virginian: Horseman on the Plains.* 1902. Macmillan. ils. 504p. worn. B19. $10.00.

WITHAM, G. F. *Shiloh, Shells & Artillery Units.* 1980. Memphis. 1/990. sgn. F. M4. $70.00.

WITHER, George. *Love Song.* 1903. Concord, MA. Sign of the Vine. woodcut title. lt bl brd. F. F1. $65.00.

WITHERINGTON, H. C. *Psychology of Religion: A Christian Interpretation.* 1955. Eerdmans. 344p. VG/VG. B29. $9.50.

WITHERS, E. L. *Diminishing Returns.* 1960. Rinehart. 1st. VG/VG. G8. $15.00.

WITHNER, Carl L. *Orchids: A Scientific Survey.* 1959. Ronald. 648p. xl. VG. S5. $40.00.

WITHROW, Robert B. *Photoperiodism & Related Phonomena in Plants & Animals.* 1959. AAAS. 903p. xl. VG. S5. $25.00.

WITKIN, Joel-Peter. *Masterpieces of Medical Photography.* 1987. Pasadena. Twelvetrees. 1st. 4to. 40 pl. F/NF. S9. $150.00.

WITKIN, Lee. *Ten Year Salute.* 1979. Addison House. 1st. NF/VG. P2. $35.00.

WITT, Lana. *Slow Dancing on Dinosaur Bones.* 1996. NY. Scribner. 1st. F/F. M23. $40.00.

WITTEN, Barbara Yager. *Isle of Fire Murder.* 1987. Walker. 1st. F/dj. N4. $15.00.

WITTIG, Monique. *Opoponax.* 1966. S&S. 1st Am. F/NF. M25. $25.00.

WITTLIN, Thaddeus. *Modigliani: Prince of Montparnasse.* 1964. Bobbs Merrill. 1st. VG/dj. S13. $10.00.

WITTMER, Margaret. *Floreana: Woman's Pilgrimage to Galapagos.* 1990. NY. Moyer Bell. 1st. 240p. wrp. F3. $10.00.

WITTNER, Ruth. *Chirp, a Little Clown in a Big Circus.* 1942. Am Book Co. 1st. inscr. ils Ottlie Foy. VG. M5. $10.00.

WODEHOUSE, P. G. *Divots.* 1927. NY. 1st. VG. B5. $100.00.

WODEHOUSE, P. G. *Fish Preferred.* 1929. Doubleday Doran. 1st. xl. G+. M21. $15.00.

WODEHOUSE, P. G. *Full Moon.* 1947. Doubleday. 1st. VG. M21. $15.00.

WODEHOUSE, P. G. *Girl in Blue.* 1971. S&S. 1st. VG/dj. M21. $35.00.

WODEHOUSE, P. G. *William Tell Told Again.* 1904. London. Blk. 1st. 8vo. 105+2p ads. teg. VG. H5. $1,250.00.

WOFFORD, James C. *Training the Three Day Event Horse and Rider.* 1995. NY. Doubleday. 1st. VG/VG. O3. $35.00.

WOIWODE, Larry. *Born Brothers.* 1988. FSG. 1st. F/NF. R14. $25.00.

WOIWODE, Larry. *Even Tide.* 1977. FSG. 1st trade. F/dj. L3. $35.00.

WOIWODE, Larry. *Poppa John.* 1981. FSG. 1st. sgn/dtd 1996. NF/dj. R14. $45.00.

WOIWODE, Larry. *Poppa John.* 1981. NY. FSG. 1st. F/F. B3. $20.00.

WOJCIECHOWSKI, Susan. *Patty Dillman of Hot Dog Fame.* 1989. NY. Orchard Books. 1st. VG/VG-. A28. $7.50.

WOLCOT, John. *Works of Peter Pindar, Esq.* 1812. London. Walker. 5 vol. new/revised/corrected. tall 8vo. tan polished calf. H13. $395.00.

WOLCOTT, R.H. *Proceedings of the Nebraska Ornithologist's Union Vol 1 – 6. 1900 – 1914.* Neligh/Lincoln. 6 vol. ils. 8vo. 450+p. F. C12. $45.00.

WOLDERING, Irmgard. *Art of Egypt.* 1963. NY. 1st Am. 8vo. 256p. VG. B11. $15.00.

WOLF, Gary K. *Killerbowl.* 1975. Garden City. Doubleday. 1st. F in dj. M15. $65.00.

WOLF, Gary K. *Who Censored Roger Rabbit?* 1981. NY. St. Martin. 1st. F/dj. M15. $100.00.

WOLF, Gary K. *Who P-P-P-Plugged Roger Rabbit?* 1991. NY. Villard. 1st. ARC with slip laid in. VF/dj. M15. $45.00.

WOLF, Gary. *Who P-P-P-Plugged Roger Rabbit?* 1991. NY. Villard. 1st. VF/VF. T2. $20.00.

WOLF, George D. *William Warren Scranton: Pennsylvania Statesman.* 1981. Pa. State University Press. 1st. sm4to. 220p. NM/NM. H1. $22.50.

WOLF, Joan. *The Road to Avalon.* 1988. NY. NAL. 1st. F/F. H11. $50.00.

WOLF, Leonard. *Annotated Dracula.* 1975. Clarkson Potter. 1st. VG/dj. L1. $150.00.

WOLF, Leonard. *Dream of Dracula: In Search of the Living Dead.* 1972. Little, Brn. 1st. VG/G. L1. $75.00.

WOLF & WOLF. *Fungi.* 1947. NY. 2 Vol. Ils. F/Dj. B26. $40.00.

WOLFE, Aaron; see Koontz, Dean R.

WOLFE, Bernard. *The Magic of Their Singing.* 1961. Scribners. 1st. NF/rubbed dj. M25. $35.00.

WOLFE, Gene. *Citadel of the Autarch.* 1983. NY. Tor. 1st. F/NF. M21. $25.00.

WOLFE, Gene. *Claw of the Conciliator.* 1981. NY. Timescape. 1st. F/dj. M21. $65.00.

WOLFE, Gene. *Lake of the Long Sun.* 1994. NY. Tor. 1st. F/NF. G10. $12.00.

WOLFE, Gene. *Pandora by Holly Hollander.* 1990. NY. Tor. 1st. sgn inscr by Wolf. VF/VF. T2. $25.00.

WOLFE, Gene. *Shadow of the Torturer.* 1980. S&S. 1st. F/dj. M21. $120.00.

WOLFE, Gene. *The Castle of the Otter.* 1982. Willimantic, CT. Ziesing Brothers. 1st. 1/100 # copies. sgn by Wolfe & artist Stephen E. Fabian. VF/VF. T2. $400.00.

WOLFE, Gene. *The Castle of the Otter.* 1982. Willimantic, CT. Ziesing Brothers. 1st. 1/100 # copies. sgn by Wolfe & artist Stephen E. Fabian. VF/VF. T2. $400.00.

WOLFE, Gene. *The Urth of the New Sun.* 1990. NY. Tor. 1st. sgn inscr by Wolf. VF/VF. T2. $25.00.

WOLFE, Gene. *There are Doors.* 1988. NY. Tor. 1st. F/dj. A24. $25.00.

WOLFE, Humbert. *Cursory Rhymes.* 1927. London. Ernest Benn. 1st. 124p. VG. M10. $35.00.

WOLFE, Susan. *The Last Billable Hour.* 1989. NY. St. Martin. 1st. price clipped jacket. F/dj. M15. $100.00.

WOLFE, T. *Western Journal.* 1951. Pittsburgh. 1st. VG. B5. $35.00.

WOLFE, Thomas. *Letters to His Mother.* 1943. Scribner. 1st. 368p. xl. G. G11. $35.00.

WOLFE, Thomas. *Of Time & the River.* 1935. Scribner. 1st/1st prt. gilt blk cloth. F/NF. M24. $200.00.

WOLFE, Thomas. *Story of a Novel.* 1936. Scribner. 1st. gilt apricot cloth. F/NF. M24. $150.00.

WOLFE, Tom. *A Man in Full.* 1998. NY. FSG. 1st trade ed. VF/VF. T2. $30.00.

WOLFE, Tom. *A Man in Full.* 1998. NY. FSG. 1st. book has small stain on page fore edges. F/F. H11. $20.00.

WOLFE, Tom. *In Our Time.* 1980. NY. FSG. 1st. sgn. ils by author. F/F. D10. $65.00.

WOLFE, Tom. *Kandy-Kolored Tangerine-Flake Streamline Baby.* 1965. FSG. 1st. author's 1st book. F/F. A4. $250.00.

WOLFE, Tom. *Radical Chic & Mau-Mauing The Flak Catchers.* 1970. np. np. 1st. own. inscr. NF/NF dj. M19. $25.00.

WOLFE, Tom. *The Bonfire of the Vanities.* 1987. NY. FSG. 1st. VF/VF. H11. $65.00.

WOLFE, Tom. *The Bonfire of the Vanities.* 1987. FSG. 1st. sgn; inscr. F/dj. M25. $100.00.

WOLFE, Tom. *The Bonfire of the Vanities.* 1987. NY. FSG. 1st. F/F. M23. $25.00.

WOLFE, Tom. *The Bonfire of the Vanities.* 1987. FSG. 1st. F/F. H11. $40.00.

WOLFE, Tom. *The Bonfire of the Vanities.* 1987. FSG. 1st. sgn. NF/dj. Q1. $125.00.

WOLFE, Tom. *The Right Stuff.* 1979. NY. FSG. 1st. NF/NF. price clip. M23. $25.00.

WOLFE, Tom. *The Right Stuff.* 1979. NY. FSG. 1st. sgn. F/F. D10. $85.00.

WOLFE, Tom. *The Right Stuff.* 1979. NY. Farrar. 1st. F/F. B2. $45.00.

WOLFE, Tom. *The Right Stuff.* 1979. FSG. 1st. VG/G. B30. $30.00.

WOLFENSTINE, Manfred R. *Manual of Brands & Marks.* 1970. Norman, OK. 1st. VG. O3. $65.00.

WOLFERT, Ira. *American Guerrilla in the Philippines.* 1945. NY. S&S. cloth. 301p. F. P1. $4.00.

WOLFF, Geoffrey. *Bad Debts.* 1969. S&S. 1st. sgn. NF/VG. R14. $85.00.

WOLFF, Geoffrey. *Inklings.* 1977. Random. 1st. sgn/dtd 1994. NF/dj. R14. $50.00.

WOLFF, Larry. *Postcards from the End of the World.* 1988. Atheneum. 1st. NF/dj. w/review material. S13. $15.00.

WOLFF, Michael. *White Kids.* 1979. NY. Summit. 1st. F/dj. R11. $20.00.

WOLFF, Perry. *Tour of the White House with Mrs. John F. Kennedy.* 1962. NY. 1st. ils. VG/dj. M17. $17.50.

WOLFF, Perry S. *History of the 334th Infantry, 84th Division.* (1945). Mannheim. 1st. photos/fld map. 230p. VG. B18. $65.00.

WOLFF, Tobias. *Back in the World.* 1985. Boston. Houghton Mifflin. 1st. author's 2nd book. NF. lt sunning to edges. lt ink marks to ffep/NF+. very lt edgewear. B3. $125.00.

WOLFF, Tobias. *Back in the World.* 1986. London. Jonathan Cape. 1st British ed. sgn. F/F. O11. $75.00.

WOLFF, Tobias. *Back in the World.* 1985. Boston. Houghton Mifflin. 1st. sgn. F/F. w/pub postcard. D10. $60.00.

WOLFF, Tobias. *Back in the World.* 1986. London. Cape. 1st. sgn. F/dj. O11. $55.00.

WOLFF, Tobias. *Hunters in the Snow.* 1982. London. Jonathan Cape. 1st British ed. F/F. O11. $125.00.

WOLFF, Tobias. *In Pharaoh's Army.* 1994. NY. Knopf. 1st. F/NF. M23. $25.00.

WOLFF, Tobias. *In Pharaoh's Army.* 1994. London. Bloomsbury. 1st British ed. F/F. O11. $40.00.

WOLFF, Tobias. *In Pharaoh's Army: Memories of the Lost War.* 1994. NY. Knopf. 1st. F/F. H11. $30.00.

WOLFF, Tobias. *In Pharoah's Army: Memories of the Lost War.* 1994. Knopf. 1st. F/F. B4. $45.00.

WOLFF, Tobias. *Night in Question.* 1996. Knopf. 1st. sgn. F/dj. O11. $50.00.

WOLFF, Tobias. *Night in Question.* 1996. Knopf. 1st thus. 1/1500. sgn. F/sealed pict wrp. Q1. $60.00.

WOLFF, Tobias. *The Barracks Thief.* 1987. London. Jonathan Cape. 1st British ed. F/F. O11. $85.00.

WOLFF, Tobias. *The Night in Question.* 1996. Knopf. 1 of 1500 sgn copies. hc chapbook. F/no dj as issued. M25. $50.00.

WOLFF, Tobias. *The Night in Question.* 1996. NY. Knopf. 1st. F/NF. M23. $25.00.

WOLFF, Tobias. *The Night in Question.* 1994. NY. Knopf. 1st. sgn. F/F. O11. $45.00.

WOLFF, Tobias. *This Boy's Life.* 1989. NY. Atlantic Monthly. 1st. NF. fraying/F. B2. $30.00.

WOLFF, Tobias. *This Boy's Life: A Memoir.* 1989. NY. 1st. VG/dj. M17. $40.00.

WOLFF, Tobias. *Two Boys & a Girl.* 1996. London. Bloomsbury. chapbook. sgn. F. R14. $35.00.

WOLFF, Werner. *Island of Death: A New Key to Easter Island's Culture.* 1948. NY. JJ Augustin. 4to. 20 pl. 228p. blk cloth. VG/dj. G1. $65.00.

WOLFF, RICK. *What's a Nice Harvard Boy Like You Doing in Business?* 1975. Prentice Hall. 1st. F/VG. P8. $35.00.

WOLFGANG, Chauncey E. *History of Columbiana, Ohio.* nd. Columbiana. Wolfgang. wrps. ils. paper soiled. browning. 85p. G. B18. $75.00.

WOLLASTON, Nicholas. *Red Rumba.* 1964. London. Readers Union. 192p. dj. F3. $15.00.

WOLLHEIM, Donald A. *Daw Science Fiction Reader.* 1976. Daw. VG/wrp. M20. $15.00.

WOLLHEIM, Donald A. *The Men from Ariel.* 1982. Cambridge. Nesfa Press. 1st. VF/VF. T2. $20.00.

WOLLHEIM, Donald A. *The Men from Ariel.* 1982. Cambridge. Nesfa Press. 1st. VF/VF. T2. $20.00.

WOLLHEIM, Donald A. *Up There and Other Strange Directions.* 1988. Cambridge. Nesfa Press. 1st. 1/250 # copies. sgn. VF/VF dj & slipcase. T2. $50.00.

WOLLMAN-TSAMIR, Pinchas. *The Graphic History of the Jewish Heritage.* 1963. Shengold. ils. 224p. VG. B29. $22.00.

WOLMAN, Benjamin B. *Handbook of Development of Mental Disorders.* 1978. Prentice Hall. heavy 4to. 475p. VG/dj. G1. $65.00.

WOLMAN, Benjamin B. *Psychological Aspects of Obesity: A Handbook.* 1982. Van Nostrand Reinhold. 1st. 8vo. 318p. F/dj. C14. $25.00.

WOLRAB, Johann Jacob. *Military Exercises: 1730.* 1962. Ontario. West Hill. rpt. ils. F. E1. $45.00.

WOLSELEY, Garnet. *American Civil War: An English View.* 1964. U. VA. 1st. 230p. F/VG. B10. $35.00.

WOLTERS, Richard A. *Gun Dog Revolutionary Rapid Training Method.* 1962. NY. E. P. Dutton & Co. 8vo. 150p. ils. salmon cloth. dj. 1st ed. 3rd printing. dj with a few nicks. VG/VG. l5. $20.00.

WOMACK, Bob. *Echo of Hoofbeats.* 1973. Walking Horse. VG/dj. A21. $95.00.

WOMACK, Jack. *Ambient.* 1987. NY. Weidenfeld & Nicolson. 1st. author's 1st novel. sgn. F/F. O11. $65.00.

WOMACK, Jack. *Ambient.* 1987. Weidenfeld Nicolson. 1st. author's 1st novel. NF/dj. N4. $25.00.

WOMACK, Jack. *Ambient.* 1987. Weidenfeld Nicolson. 1st. sgn. author's 1st book. F/dj. O11. $65.00.

WOMACK, Jack. *Elvissey.* 1993. NY. Tor. 1st. sgn. F. O11. $25.00.

WOMACK, Jack. *Heathern.* 1990. NY. Tor. 1st. F/F. D10. $45.00.

WOMACK, Jack. *Random Acts of Senseless Violence.* 1994. NY. Atlantic Monthly. 1st. sgn. F/F. D10. $45.00.

WOMACK, Steven. *Smash Cut.* 1991. NY. St. Martin. 1st. F/VF. H11. $25.00.

WOMEN's DAY, editors. *Women's Day Encyclopedia of Cookery.* 1965. Fawcett. 12 vol. 1st. 4to. VG. H1. $42.00.

WONG, Shawn. *American Knees.* 1995. NY. S&S. 1st. author's 1st novel. sgn by author. F/F. B3. $35.00.

WOOD, Alphonso. *How to Study Plants; or, Introduction to Botany, Being an Illustrated Flora.* 1882 (1879). NY. gr gilt stp cloth. some wear at extremities. B26. $19.00.

WOOD, Bari. *Amy Girl.* 1986. NY. NAL. 1st. F/F. H11. $20.00.

WOOD, Bari & Jack Gleasland. *Twins.* 1977. NY. Putnam. 1st. F/F. T2. $6.00.

WOOD, Charles Erskine Scott. *Earthly Discourse.* 1937. np. Vanguard. 1st. NF/VG dj. M19. $65.00.

WOOD, Dennis W. *Principles of Animal Physiology.* 1974. Am. Elsevier. ils. 342p. NF/VG. S15. $13.00.

WOOD, Dodd, Bevan, etc. *The Kingdom of God and History.* 1938. George Allen. Vol 3. 216p. VG/VG. B29. $8.50.

WOOD, Dodd, Bevan, etc. *The Kingdom of God and History.* 1938. Willett. Clark & Co. Vol 3. 216p. G/worn back. B29. $6.50.

WOOD, Elena. *Compadrazgo En Apas.* 1982. Mexico. 1st. 89p. wrp. F3. $10.00.

WOOD, Frank B. *Photoelectric Astronomy for Amateurs.* 1963. NY. Macmillan. 1st. 8vo. 223p. dj. K5. $30.00.

WOOD, Henry. *New Old Healing.* 1908. Lee Shepard. 304p. teg. gr cloth. VG. S17. $5.00.

WOOD, James. *Interpretation of the Bible.* 1958. Duckworth. 179p. VG/dj. B29. $8.00.

WOOD, James. *The Interpretation of the Bible.* 1958. Duckworth. 179p. VG/VG. underlining. B29. $6.50.

WOOD, James. *The Interpretation of the Bible.* 1958. Duckworth. 179p. VG/VG. B29. $8.00.

WOOD, James. *Voyage into Nowhere.* 1966. NY. Vanguard. 1st. F/VG clip. T11. $20.00.

WOOD, James. *Wisdom Literature: An Introduction.* 1967. Duckworth. 164p. VG/VG. underlining. B29. $5.00.

WOOD, John Sumner. *Virginia Bishop: Yankee Hero of the Confederacy.* 1961. Garret Massie. 187p. VG/dj. B10. $25.00.

WOOD, Kerry. *Birds & Animals in the Rockies.* ca. 1950. Saskatoon. 1st. ils Beebe. VG. A17. $20.00.

WOOD, Lawson. *Lawson Wood Nursery Rhyme Book.* ca. 1920. London. Nelson. lg 4to. cloth backed mc pict brd. R5. $200.00.

WOOD, Lawson. *Lawson Wood's Fun Fair.* 1931. London. Arundel Prts. 4to. cloth backed brd/mc label. R5. $175.00.

WOOD, Lawson. *Marking Time with Gran'Pop.* ca. 1950. St. Paul. Brn, Bigelow. sbdg. R5. $100.00.

WOOD, Morrison. *More Recipes with a Jug of Wine.* 1968. FSG. 11th. 8vo. 400p. NF/dj. W2. $25.00.

WOOD, Morrison. *With a Jug of Wine.* 1949. SC. G/dj. A16. $10.00.

WOOD, N. A. *Birds of Michigan.* 1951. Ann Arbor. 559p. gilt bl cloth. F. C12. $50.00.

WOOD, Nancy. *Taos Pueblo.* 1989. Knopf. 1st. ils. 162p. F/NF. B19. $55.00.

WOOD, Peter H. *The Winged Wheel.* 1995. Toronto. Metropolitan Toronto Reference Library. 1st. VF/VF. T2. $25.00.

WOOD, Peter H. *The Winged Wheel.* 1995. Toronto. Metropolitan Toronto Reference Library. 1st. VF/VF. T2. $25.00.

WOOD, Richard G. *Stephen Harriman Long, 1784 – 1864.* 1966. Glendale. AH Clark. ils. 292p. F. F1. $45.00.

WOOD, Robert. *Day Trips to Archaeological Mexico.* 1991. Hastings. revised/updated. ils. 174p. wrp. F3. $10.00.

WOOD, Robert Lee. *Nineteenth-Century Fiction: A Bibliographical Catalogue. 1981 – 1986.* NY/London. 5 vol. gilt gr cloth. F. F1. $550.00.

WOOD, Robin. *Hitchcock's Films.* 1965. Zwemmer/Barnes. 1st. VG/wrp. C9. $48.00.

WOOD, T. *Natural History of Mammals.* 1886. London/NY. Nister/Dutton. ils. 244p. VG. M12. $37.50.

WOOD, Ted. *Flashback.* 1992. Scribner. 1st Am. NF/dj. G8. $20.00.

WOOD, Tom. *Bright Side of Billy Wilder, Primarily.* 1970. Doubleday. 1st. F/G. T12. $25.00.

WOOD, William P. *Court of Honor.* 1991. NY. Pocket. 1st. VF/VF. H11. $25.00.

WOODARD, L. T., M.D, see Silverberg, Robert.

WOODBERRY, George Edward. *Complete Poetical Works of Percy Bysshe Shelley.* 1892. Cambridge, MA. Riverside. 8vo. lg paper ed. 1/250. VG. S17. $75.00.

WOODBURN, James A. *American Republic & Its Government.* 1916 (1903). Putnam. 2nd. 8vo. VG. A2. $15.00.

WOODBURY, David O. *Around the World in 90 Minutes.* 1958. Harcourt Brace. ils. 248p. dj. K5. $25.00.

WOODBURY, David O. *Colorado Conquest.* 1941. Dodd Mead. 1st. 8vo. tan cloth. VG. F7. $45.00.

WOODCOCK, H. B. D. & W. T. Stearn. *Lilies of the World, Their Cultivation & Classification.* 1950. London/NY. 1st. orig bstp. gilt on russet cloth. F in dj. B26. $75.00.

WOODEN, John. *They Call Me Coach.* 1973. Waco, TX. Word. NF/VG clip. R16. $30.00.

WOODFORD, M. H. *Manual of Falconry.* 1960. London. 1st. NF. C12. $45.00.

WOODHOUSE, Henry. *Textbook of Aerial Laws.* 1920. NY. Frederick Stokes. 1st. ils. 171p. VG edgewear. B18. $125.00.

WOODHOUSE, Henry. *Textbook of Naval Aeronautics.* 1918. NY. 2nd. 288p. cloth. VG. M8. $250.00.

WOODHOUSE, Robert. *Elementary Treatise on Astronomy.* 1812. Cambridge. 8Vo. 471P. VG. K5. $150.00.

WOODING, F.H. *Angler's Book of Canadian Fishes.* 1959. Ontario. 1st. ils. 303p. F/G. A17. $20.00.

WOODLEY, Richard. *Dealer.* 1971. NY. Holt. 1st. F/F. H11. $25.00.

WOODMAN, John. *Journal of Life, Gospel Labours & Christian Experiences.* 1837. Phil. TE Chapman. 12mo. 396p. G+. V3. $60.00.

WOODMAN, Richard. *Baltic Mission.* 1986. NY. Walker. 1st Am. F/NF. T11. $50.00.

WOODMAN, Richard. *Bob Vessel.* 1986. NY. Walker. 1st Am. VG+/dj. A14. $28.00.

WOODMAN, Richard. *Brig of War.* 1983. London. Murray. 1st. NF/dj. A14. $87.50.

WOODMAN, Richard. *Brig of War.* 1983. London. Murray. 1st. VG+/clip. A14. $70.00.

WOODMAN, Richard. *Private Revenge.* 1989. NY. 1st. VG/dj. M17. $22.50.

WOODMAN, Richard. *Private Revenge.* 1989. St. Martin. 1st Am. F/dj. T11. $35.00.

WOODRELL, Daniel. *Give Us a Kiss.* 1996. NY. Henry Holt. 1st. sgn. VF/VF. T2. $30.00.

WOODRELL, Daniel. *Muscle for the Wing.* 1988. NY. Henry Holt. 1st. sgn. VF/VF. T2. $55.00.

WOODRELL, Daniel. *Muscle for the Wing.* 1988. NY. Holt. 1st. Signed on title page. F/VF. H11. $65.00.

WOODRELL, Daniel. *Muscle for the Wing.* 1988. NY. Holt. 1st. author's 3rd book. F/F. B3. $45.00.

WOODRELL, Daniel. *The Ones You Do.* 1992. NY. Holt. 1st. sgn on title page. F/VF. H11. $40.00.

WOODRELL, Daniel. *The Ones You Do.* 1992. NY. Holt. 1st. ARC. F. D10. $10.00.

WOODRELL, Daniel. *The Ones You Do.* 1992. NY. Henry Holt. 1st. author's 4th book. sgn by author. VF/VF. B3. $75.00.

WOODRELL, Daniel. *Tomato Red.* 1998. NY. Henry Holt. 1st. sgn. VF/VF. T2. $25.00.

WOODRELL, Daniel. *Under the Bright Lights.* 1986. NY. Holt. 1st. author's 1st book. VF/VF. H11. $80.00.

WOODRELL, Daniel. *Under the Bright Lights.* 1986. NY. Henry Holt. 1st. author's 1st book; w/ complimentary card laid in. F in F dj. D10. $75.00.

WOODRELL, Daniel. *Under the Bright Lights.* 1986. NY. Henry Holt. 1st. author's 1st novel. F/NF. M23. $50.00.

WOODRELL, Daniel. *Under the Bright Lights.* 1986. Holt. 1st. author's 1st book. F/NF. B3. $75.00.

WOODRELL, Daniel. *Woe to Live On.* 1987. NY. Holt. 1st. book has small damp stain at bottom of spine. NF/F. H11. $55.00.

WOODRESS, James. *Willa Cather: A Literary Life.* 1987. U. NE. VG/dj. P3. $35.00.

WOODRIDGE, C. W. *Perfecting the Earth, a Piece of Possible History.* 1902. Cleveland. Utopia Pub. NF. B2. $125.00.

WOODROW, Mrs. Wilson. *Come Alone!* 1928. Macauley. 1st. VG. G8. $15.00.

WOODS, G. K. *Personal Impressions of the Grand Canyon of Colorado.* 1899. SF. ils. aeg. 164p. red cloth. VG. F7. $395.00.

WOODS, Margaret. *Extracts from Journal of Late Margaret Woods, 1771 – 1821.* 1850. Phil. Longstreth. 3rd. 378p. poor. V3. $35.00.

WOODS, Paul L. *Inner City Blues.* 1999. NY. Norton. 1st. sgn. author's 1st novel. VF/VF. T2. $25.00.

WOODS, Sara. *Knives Have Edges.* 1968. Collins Crime Club. 1st. F/dj. C15. $25.00.

WOODS, Stuart. *Dead Eyes.* 1994. Harper Collins. 1st. 1/150. F/dj. M15. $85.00.

WOODS, Stuart. *Dead in the Water*. 1997. Harper & Row. 1st. VG/VG. G8. $12.50.

WOODS, Stuart. *Deep Lie*. 1986. NY. Norton. 1st. F/F. H11. $45.00.

WOODS, Stuart. *Deep Lie*. 1986. NY. Norton. 1st. F/NF. price clip. lt edgewear. B3. $40.00.

WOODS, Stuart. *Heat*. 1994. NY. Harper Collins. 1st. inscr by author. F/F. B3. $40.00.

WOODS, Stuart. *Imperfect Strangers*. 1995. NY. Harper Collins. 1st. sgn. VF/VF. T2. $25.00.

WOODS, Stuart. *L. A. Times*. 1993. NY. Harper Collins. 1st. sgn. VF/VF. T2. $25.00.

WOODS, Stuart. *New York Dead*. 1991. NY. Harper Collins. 1st. sgn. VF/VF. T2. $25.00.

WOODS, Stuart. *New York Dead*. 1991. NY. Harper Collins. 1st. F/F. H11. $25.00.

WOODS, Stuart. *Palindrome*. 1991. NY. Harper Collins. 1st. sgn. VF/VF. T2. $25.00.

WOODS, Stuart. *Run Before the Wind*. 1983. NY. Norton. 1st. jacket has light wear at spine ends. F/F-. H11. $120.00.

WOODS, Stuart. *Santa Fe Rules*. 1992. NY. Harper Collins. 1st. VF/VF. H11. $25.00.

WOODS, Stuart. *Under the Lake*. 1988. Avon. pb. VG. F6. $1.15.

WOODS, Stuart. *Under the Lake*. 1987. NY. S&S. 1st. F/clip. A14. $21.00.

WOODS, William Crawford. *Killing Zone*. 1970. NY. Harper. 1st. NF/dj. R11. $35.00.

WOODS & WOODWARD. *Urban Disease & Mortality In 19th-Century England*. 1984. NY. 1st. 255p. A13. $25.00.

WOODSON, R. Dodge. *Home Plumbing Repair & Replacement*. 1992. Betterway Books. 1st. 224p. F. W2. $50.00.

WOODSTONE, Norma Sue. *Up Against The War: A Personal Introduction*. 1970. NY. Tower. 187p. NF/wrp. R11. $50.00.

WOODTHORPE, R. C. *Death Wears a Purple Shirt*. 1934. Crime Club. 1st. VG. G8. $20.00.

WOODWARD, Arthur. *Feud on the Colorado*. 1955. Westernlore. 1st. sgn. 8vo. 165p. red cloth. VG/dj. F7. $100.00.

WOODWARD, Bob. *Commanders*. 1991. S&S. 1st. sm 4to. 398p. F/dj. W2. $35.00.

WOODWARD, Edward. *The House of Terro*. 1930. NY. Mystery League. 1st Am ed. F in VF dj. M15. $50.00.

WOODWARD, Edward. *The House of Terror*. 1930. NY. Mystery League. 1st Am. F/VF. M15. $50.00.

WOODWARD, Ian. *Glenda Jackson: Study in Fire & Ice*. 1985. St. Martin. 1st. F/dj. T12. $25.00.

WOODWARD, J. J. *Medical & Surgical History of the War of the Rebellion. 1870 – 1888*. Washington, DC. 6 vol. 4to. mixed issue/bdg/some xl. G7. $1.500.00.

WOODWARD, W. E. *Meet General Grant*. 1928. Garden City. 1st. photos. VG/dj. S13. $12.00.

WOODWARD, Walter C. *Timothy Nicolson, Master Quaker*. 1927. Richmond, IN. Nicholson. 252p. xl. V3. $21.00.

WOODWARD, William E. *Meet General Grant*. 1934. Garden City. NY. Garden City Publishing Co. 2nd ed. top of spine chipped. orig cloth. plates. 524p. VG/quite scarce. but very worn & tape rpr pict dj. M8. $25.00.

WOODWARD & WOODWARD. *Woodward's Country Homes*. 1865. NY. Woodward. 1st. ils. 166p. VG. H10. $95.00.

WOODWORTH, Robert Sessions. *Adjustment & Mastery: Problems in Psychology*. 1933. Wms. Wilkins. 12mo. orange cloth. VG/tattered. G1. $32.50.

WOODWORTH, Robert Sessions. *Contemporary Schools of Psychology*. 1948. Ronald Pr. revised/1st prt. sgn. 8vo. 279p. ruled red cloth. G. G1. $35.00.

WOODWORTH, Robert Sessions. *Experimental Psychology*. 1938. Holt. inscr/sgn. 889p. gray cloth/painted labels. VG/dj. G1. $250.00.

WOODWORTH, Robert Sessions. *Le Mouvement*. 1903. Paris. Octave Doin. 12mo. 421p. prt gray wrp. G1. $75.00.

WOODWORTH, Robert Sessions. *Psychology*. 1929. Holt. 2nd revised. inscr/sgn. 12mo. 590p. panelled thatched gr cloth. G1. $50.00.

WOODWORTH, Steven E. *Jefferson Davis & His Generals*. 1990. BC. ils. VG/dj. M17. $15.00.

WOODWORTH, Steven E. *Jefferson Davis & His Generals: Failure of Confederate*. 1990. Lawrence. KS. 1st. F/dj. A14. $25.00.

WOODY, Allen. *Side Effects*. 1980. Random. 1st. F/dj. O4. $20.00.

WOODY, Robert Henley. *Encyclopedia of Clinical Assessment*. 1980. San Francisco. Jossey-Bass. 2 vol. gr cloth. VG/dj. G1. $65.00.

WOOFTER, T.J. *Landlord & Tenant on the Cotton Plantation*. 1936. WPA. Div. Social Research. ils/charts. 287p. VG. B10. $75.00.

WOOLEN, William Watson. *Inside Passage to Alaska 1793 – 1920*. 1924. Cleveland. AH Clark. 2 vol. 1st. ils/map. gilt gr cloth. B11. $650.00.

WOOLF, Douglas. *The Hypocritic Days*. 1955. np. The Divers Press. 1st. wrps. F. lt soiling to rear wrp. B2. $75.00.

WOOLF, Virginia. *Hours in a Library*. 1957. Harcourt Brace. 1st. 1/1800. F/tissue dj. Q1. $125.00.

WOOLF, Virginia. *Letter to a Young Poet*. 1932. London. Hogarth. Hogarth Letters #8. 28p. NF/wrp. O11. $75.00.

WOOLF, Virginia. *Pargiters*. 1978. London. Hogarth. 1st. F/dj. A24. $60.00.

WOOLF, Virginia. *The Waves*. 1931. NY. Harcourt. 1st Am ed. (lacking the dj). VG. B2. $40.00.

WOOLF, Virginia. *Three Guineas*. 1938. London. Hogarth. 1st. sm Crown 8vo. 329p. lemon-yel brd. VG/dj. J3. $600.00.

WOOLHOUSE, H.W. *Dormancy & Survival*. 1969. Academic. 598p. xl. VG. S5. $30.00.

WOOLLEY, C. Leonard. *Digging Up the Past*. 1931. NY. 1st. photos. VG. M17. $20.00.

WOOLLEY, C. Leonard. *Sumerians*. 1995. Barnes Noble. ils. 198p. NF/dj. W1. $18.00.

WOOLLEY, Sir Leonard. *Excavations at Ur*. 1955. Crowell. 262p. G/worn dj. B29. $18.00.

WOOLMAN, John. *Serious Considerations on Various Subjects of Importance*. 1773. London. Mary Hinde. 12mo. 137p. worn leather. V3. $55.00.

WOOLMAN, John. *Works Of..., in Two Parts*. 1775. Phil. Cruikshank. 2nd. sm 8vo. 432p. worn leather. V3. $150.00.

WOOLNER, Frank. *Grouse & Grouse Hunting*. 1970. NY. 192p. F/dj. A17. $30.00.

WOOLNER, Frank. *Timberdoodle. Woodcock & Woodcock Hunting*. 1974. NY. 168p. F/dj. A17. $25.00.

WOOLRICH, Cornell. *4 by Cornell Woolrich.* 1983. London. Zomba. Omnibus. F/dj. M15. $85.00.

WOOLRICH, Cornell. *After-Dinner Story.* 1944. Lippincott. 1st. VG/dj/clamshell box. L3. $950.00.

WOOLRICH, Cornell. *Best of William Irish.* 1960. Lippincott. Omnibus. F/NF. M15. $175.00.

WOOLRICH, Cornell. *Dead Man Blues.* 1948. Lippincott. 1st. VG/dj. C15. $85.00.

WOOLRICH, Cornell. *Four by Cornell Woolrich.* 1983. London. Zomba. Omnibus. VF in dj. M15. $75.00.

WOOLRICH, Cornell. *Six Nights of Mystery.* 1950. NY. Popular Lib. 1st. F/wrp. M15. $150.00.

WOOLRICH, Cornell. *The Best of William Irish.* 1960. Philadelphia. Lippincott. Omnibus edition. Contains Phantom Lady, After-Dinner Story, and Deadline at Dawn. jacket has tiny wear at corners. F/dj. M15. $175.00.

WOOLRICH, Cornell. *Times Square.* 1929. Liveright. 1st. VG. C15. $100.00.

WOOS, Prince. *Open-Air Poultry Houses for All Climates.* 1912. Chicago. Am. Poultry Journal. 86p. cloth. A10. $28.00.

WOOSTER, Ralph A. *Politicans, Planters & Plain Folk: Courthouse & Statehouse.* 1975. Knoxville, TN. U. TN. 1st. 8vo. F/dj. A2. $15.00.

WOOSTER, Robert. *Nelson A. Miles & The Twilight of the Frontier Army.* 1993. U. NE. ils. VG/dj. M17. $20.00.

WOOTTERS, John. *Hunting Trophy Deer.* 1977. Winchester. index/photos. 251p. F/dj. A17. $15.00.

WORBY, John. *Other Half.* 1937. NY. Lee Furman. 1st. F/NF. B2. $60.00.

WORCESTER, Donald E. *Forked Tongues & Broken Treaties.* 1975. Caldwell. ID. VG/dj. A19. $30.00.

WORDSWORTH, William. *Decade of Years.* 1911. Hammersmith. Doves. 1/200 (212 total). sm 4to. 230p. NF/case. H5. $850.00.

WORKS PROJECTS ADMINISTRA-TION. *Pennsylvania Cavalcade.* 1942. U. Of Pennsylvania Press. 1st. 8vo. owner's stamp on endpapers. several light stain spots on cover. a few edge tears & chips. edges worn & soiled. 462p. VG/G. H1. $28.00.

WORLD's FAIR. *Chicago and World's Columbian Exposition.* 1893. Columbus, OH. Ward Brothers. accordion panoply. 44 photos. G. S14. $40.00.

WORMINGTON, H.S. *Prehistoric Indians of the Southwest.* 1947. Denver. 8vo. 191p. VG/dj. F7. $40.00.

WORMSER, Richard. *Kidnapped Circus.* 1968. Morrow. 1st. VG/G. O3. $22.00.

WORTH, C. Brooke. *Naturalist in Trinidad.* 1967. Lippincott. 1st. ils Don Eckelberry. 291p. F/VG+. S15. $20.00.

WORTLEY, Emmeline Stuart. *Travels in the United States, Etc., During 1849 – 1850.* 1855. NY. Harper. early ed. 8vo. 463p. H7. $35.00.

WORZEL, J. L. *Pendulum Gravity Measurements at Sea 1936 – 1959.* 1965. Wiley. 1st. ils. cloth. VG. B27. $45.00.

WOUK, Herman. *Don't Stop the Carnival.* 1965. Garden City. Doubleday. 1st. top corners are lightly bumped. jacket has minor wear to spine ends. F/F-. H11. $45.00.

WOUK, Herman. *Glory.* 1994. Little, Brn. 1/200. sgn. F/sans/F case. R14. $125.00.

WOUK, Herman. *The Hope.* 1993. Little, Brn. 1st. F/F. s19. $25.00.

WOUK, Herman. *War and Remembrance.* 1978. London. Collins. 1st British ed. NF. one corner bumped/NF. edgewear. B3. $20.00.

WOUK, Herman. *War & Remembrance.* 1978. Boston. 1st. dj. T9. $15.00.

WOZENCRAFT, Kim. *Rush.* 1990. NY. Random. 1st. author's 1st book. name on front pastedown. Jacket has 1¼" closed tear at top of rear flap fold. F/NF. H11. $20.00.

WPA. *Copper Camp, Stories of the World's Greatest Mining Town, Butte, Montana.* 1945. NY. Hastings House. 4th printing. VG+. B2. $25.00.

WPA, Alabama Historical Records Survey. *American Imprints Inventory No. 8 Check List of Alabama Imprints 1807 – 1840.* 1939. Birmingham. Alabama Historical Records Survey. 1st. orig printed wrp. ex lib. scarce. 159p. VG. M8. $75.00.

WPA SURVEY. *Check List of Ohio Imprints, 1796 – 1820.* 1941. Columbus, OH. Ohio Historical Records Survey. ex lib. wrp in metal binder. 202p. VG. some browning. B18. $45.00.

WPA WRITERS PROGRAM. *Alabama Historical Records Survey.* 1939. Birmingham. 1st. 159p. VG/prt wrp. M8. $75.00.

WPA WRITERS PROGRAM. *American Imprints Inventory Number 31, Imprints 1833 – 55.* 1942. SF. 109p. lib buckram w/orig wrp bdg in. D11. $50.00.

WPA WRITERS PROGRAM. *Hands That Built New Hampshire.* 1940. Brattleboro. 1st. 288p. F/dj. M4. $65.00.

WPA WRITERS PROGRAM. *Jefferson's Albermarle: A Guide to Albemarle County.* 1941. Jarman's. ils. 157p. G+. B10. $35.00.

WPA WRITERS PROGRAM. *Kansas.* 1949. Hastings House. 2nd prt. picts. G+. s19. $30.00.

WPA WRITERS PROGRAM. *Mississippi: Guide to the Magnolia State.* 1943. NY. 1st. ils. 545p. VG. B18. $65.00.

WPA WRITERS PROGRAM. *New Orleans City Guide.* 1938. Boston. 1st. ils. 430p. VG. B18. $65.00.

WRANGHAM, Richard. *Demonic Males: Apes & Origins of Human Violence.* 1996. Houghton Mifflin. 1st. 8vo. 350p. F/dj. C14. $18.00.

WREN, Daniel A. *White Collar Hobo: Travels of Whiting Williams.* 1987. IA State. 1st. 8vo. F/dj. A2. $15.00.

WREN, M. K. *A Gift Upon the Shore.* 1990. NY. Ballantine. 1st. F/F. price clip. M23. $25.00.

WREN, M. K. *Seasons of Death.* 1981. Firecrest. 1st British ed. VG/VG. G8. $15.00.

WRIGHT, Anna Rose. *Barefoot Days.* 1937. NY. Grosset & Dunlap/Jr. Lit Gld. cream cloth w/gr design/lettering. gr ils ep/tp vignette & 32 b/w ils. sgn by author. ils by Paul Chapman. 148p. VG. D6. $30.00.

WRIGHT, Anna Rose. *Summer at Buckhorn.* 1943. NY. Viking Press. 1st ed. 8vo. rust cloth w/antler design. bl/orange pict ep. 243p. ex lib. worn at spine ends. o/w VG. D6. $25.00.

WRIGHT, Austin. *First Persons.* 1973. NY. Harper & Row. 1st. NF/. D10. $50.00.

WRIGHT, Austin. *Tony and Susan.* 1993. Dallas. Baskerville. 1st. VF/VF. T2. $10.00.

WRIGHT, Austin. *Tony and Susan.* 1993. Dallas. Baskerville. 1st. F/F. D10. $45.00.

WRIGHT, B. *Road to Tokyo.* Nov 1947. 2nd. sq 4to. 254p. VG. E6. $60.00.

WRIGHT, Bruce. *High Tide & an East Wind: Story of the Black Duck.* 1954. Stackpole. 1st. ils/index. 162p. F/G. A17. $25.00.

WRIGHT, C. D. *Tremble.* 1996. Ecco Press. 1st. F/F. V1. $10.00.

WRIGHT, Charles S. *Silas, The Antarctic Diaries and Memoir of Charles S. Wright.* 1993. Columbus. Ohio State Univ. Press. 1st printing. brown cloth. gilt spine titles. ils Pat F. Wright. 418p. new in dj. P4. $62.00.

WRIGHT, Dare. *Edith & Midnight.* 1978. Doubleday. 1st. folio. xl. VG/dj. B17. $35.00.

WRIGHT, Dare. *Lonely Doll Learns a Lesson.* nd (c 1961). Random. apparent 2nd. 4to. unp. VG. C14. $45.00.

WRIGHT, Denis. *English Amongst the Persians During Qajar Period 1787 – 1921.* 1977. London. Heinemann. ils/dbl-p map. 218p. VG/dj. Q2. $20.00.

WRIGHT, Edmond. *History of the World.* 1985. Bonanza. VG/dj. M20. $20.00.

WRIGHT, Eric. *A Fine Italian Hand.* 1992. NY. Scribners. 1st. VF/VF. H11. $20.00.

WRIGHT, Eric. *Death by Degrees.* 1993. Toronto. Doubleday. 1st. sgn. F/dj. M25. $35.00.

WRIGHT, Frank Lloyd. *Future of Architecture.* 1953. NY. 1st. photos/diagrams. VG/G. M17. $60.00.

WRIGHT, Frank Lloyd. *Living City.* 1958. NY. 1st. photos/diagrams/fld plan for Broadacre City. VG/dj. M17. $120.00.

WRIGHT, Frank Lloyd. *Testament.* 1957. NY. 1st. photos. VG/G. M17. $90.00.

WRIGHT, Gordon. *Learning to Ride, Hunt, and Show.* 1966. Garden City. Doubleday. new & revised ed. obl 4to. VG/VG. O3. $25.00.

WRIGHT, H. *Headaches: Their Causes & Cure.* 1856. 1st. VG. E6. $50.00.

WRIGHT, H. Norman. *How to Have a Creative Crisis.* 1986. Word. 169p. VG/VG. B29. $10.50.

WRIGHT, Harold Bell. *Calling of Dan Matthews.* 1909. Chicago Book Supply. 1st. VG. N2. $15.00.

WRIGHT, Harold Bell. *Eyes of the World.* 1914. Chicago. Book Supply. 1st. 464p. VG. G11. $22.00.

WRIGHT, Harold Bell. *Helen of the Old House.* 1921. NY. Appleton. 1st. 372p. G. G11. $10.00.

WRIGHT, Harold Bell. *Re-Creation of Brian Kent.* 1919. Chicago. Book Supply. 1st. ils J. Allen St. John. G+. G11. $17.50.

WRIGHT, Harold Bell. *The Winning of Barbara Worth.* 1911. The Book Supply Co. 1st. sm8vo. hinge cracked. owner's signature on endpaper. 511p. VG. H1. $5.00.

WRIGHT, Harold Bell. *Their Yesterdays.* 1912. Book Supply. 1st. 310p. F. H1. $12.00.

WRIGHT, Harold Bell. *When a Man's a Man.* 1916. Chicago. Book Supply. 1st (#245223). G+. G11. $15.00.

WRIGHT, Ida Russell and Susan Clark Wright. *Household Stuff, and Some Other Things.* Boston. privately printed. 1866. 8vo. 173. (2)p. aeg. bl cloth. 1st ed. sgn presentation inscr by the copyright holder and one of the authors, Susan Clark Wright. extemities worn. top & bottom of spine chiped ⅛". G. L5. $30.00.

WRIGHT, Irene A. *Spanish Documents Concerning English Voyages To Caribbean.* 1929. London. Hakluyt Soc. 8vo. 2 maps/1 facs. 167p. cloth. F. O1. $55.00.

WRIGHT, J. *Lectures on Diseases of the Rectum.* 1884. Birmingham Medical Lib. 1st. VG. E6. $60.00.

WRIGHT, J. E. *With Rifle and Plow, Stories of the Western PA Frontier.* 1938. Pittsburgh. Univ. of Pittsburgh Press. 1st. map ep. ils in color. drawings by Alexander Ross. lightly soiled. edgewear. 212p. VG. B18. $12.50.

WRIGHT, J. E. & Doris S. Corbett. *Pioneer Life in Western Pennsylvania.* 1940. Pittsburgh. U. of Pittsburgh Press. 2nd. 8vo. 251p. VG. H1. $12.00.

WRIGHT, James. *Secret Field.* 1985. Durango. Logbridge-Rhodes. F/wrp. R14. $25.00.

WRIGHT, Jim. *Saskatchewan: History of a Province.* 1955. McClelland Stewart. 1st/Golden Jubilee. F/VG. A26. $55.00.

WRIGHT, John. *Trout on a Stick: A Mountain Cookbook.* 1991. Minocqua. 1st. 143p. VG/wrp. A17. $10.00.

WRIGHT, L.R. *Love in the Temperate Zone.* 1988. Viking. 1st. F/dj. H11. $20.00.

WRIGHT, L.R. *Touch of Panic.* 1994. Scribner. 1st. sgn. NF/dj. G8. $30.00.

WRIGHT, Laurie. *Mr. Jelly Lord.* 1980. Chigwell. Storyville. 1st. F/issued w/o dj. B2. $125.00.

WRIGHT, Lyle H. *Am. Fiction 1774 – 1850, A Contribution Towards a Bibliography.* San Marino. The Huntington Library. 1969. 8vo. 411p. bl cloth. dj. 2nd revised ed. F. L5. $20.00.

WRIGHT, Lyle H. *American Fiction 1774 – 1900: A Contribution.* 1969. San Marino, CA. Huntington Lib. 3 vol. 2nd revised. F/VG. H7. $75.00.

WRIGHT, Lyle M. *American Fiction 1774 – 1875.* 1948 – 1957. San Marino, CA. 2 vol. revised. cloth. NF/VG. M8. $85.00.

WRIGHT, Mabel Osgood. *Flowers and Ferns in Their Haunts.* 1928 (1901). full pg b&w photos by author & J. Horace McFarland. numerous text drawings. 358p. wear at tips. head & foot of spine. but solid copy. B26. $15.00.

WRIGHT, Marcus J. *Official & Illustrated (Civil) War Record.* 1898. Washington, DC. folio. ils Thos Nast/others. reading copy. H1. $30.00.

WRIGHT, Michael. *Complete Indoor Gardener.* 1980. London. Pan. 4to. 256p. NF. M10. $12.50.

WRIGHT, N. Pelham. *Orquideas De Mexico.* 1958. Mexico. DF. text in English & Spanish. inscr by author. VG/chip dj. B26. $35.00.

WRIGHT, Norman. *Mexican Kaleidoscope.* 1948. London. ils/index. F3. $10.00.

WRIGHT, Richard. *American Hunger.* 1977. Harper & Row. UP. very light wear. F/WRP. M25. $200.00.

WRIGHT, Richard. *Black Boy.* 1945. NY. Harper & Bros. VG-/G. R16. $35.00.

WRIGHT, Richard. *Black Boy.* 1945. NY. Harper. 1st. NF/lightly chip dj. B2. $125.00.

WRIGHT, Richard. *Lawd Today.* 1963. NY. Walker. 1st. NF/NF. M25. $125.00.

WRIGHT, Richard. *Native Son.* 1940. Harper. BCE. NF/lightly worn dj. sunned on spine. M25. $100.00.

WRIGHT, Richard. *Native Son.* 1940. Harper. 1st. 359p. gilt bl cloth. G/fair 2nd state. H1. $12.00.

WRIGHT, Richardson. *Story of Gardening.* 1934. Dodd Mead. 475p. VG. A10. $30.00.

WRIGHT, Ronald Selby. *The Kirk in the Canongate; A Short History From 1128 to the Present Day.* 1956. Edinburgh. Oliver & Boyd. 192p. VG/VG. B29. $22.00.

WRIGHT, Sarah E. *This Child's Gonna Live.* 1969. Delacorte. 1st. F/dj. M25. $60.00.

WRIGHT, Sewell Peaslee. *Half Wolf Wright.* 1951. Phil. Westminster Pr. 253p. VG/dj. B6. $26.00.

WRIGHT, Stephen. *Going Native.* 1994. NY. SG. 1st. VF/VF. H11. $30.00.

WRIGHT, Stephen. *Going Native.* 1995. SG. 1st. F/dj. R14. $25.00.

WRIGHT, Stephen. *M31, A Family Romance.* 1988. NY. Harmony Books. 1st. author's 2nd book. F/F. D10. $40.00.

WRIGHT, Stephen. *Meditations in Green.* 1983. NY. Scribner's. 1st. author's 1st book. F/F. D10. $85.00.

WRIGHT, Thomas. *Caricature History of the Georges.* 1898. Chatto Windus. 8vo. 629p. gilt cloth. VG. H13. $85.00.

WRIGHT, Thomas. *History of Domestic Manners & Sentiments in England.* 1862. London. 1st. sq 8vo. full blk leather. E6. $75.00.

WRIGHT, Thomas. *Some Habits & Customs of the Working Classes.* 1967 (1867). Augustus Kelley. rpt. 276p. VG. S5. $15.00.

WRIGHT, Thomas. *Womankind in Western Europe from Earliest Times to 17th C.* 1869. London. Groombridge. ils. 340p. rb. VG. H10. $125.00.

WRIGHT, W. *Grammar of the Arabic Language. Translated from the German.* 1955. Cambridge. reissue (1896 – 98 3rd ed.). 2 vol. cloth. VG/dj. Q2. $75.00.

WRIGHT, W.J. *Greenhouses: Their Construction & Equipment.* 1917. Orange Judd. revised. 269p. F/G. H1. $18.00.

WRIGHT, Winifred G. *Wild Flowers of Southern Africa.* 1963. Johannesburg. 168p. G/dj. B26. $25.00.

WRIGLEY, John W. & Murray Fagg. *Australian Native Plants, A Manual for Their Propagation, Cultivation, and Use in Landscaping.* 1981 (1979). Sydney. F in dj. B26. $47.50.

WROTH, Lawrence. *Early Cartography of the Pacific.* 1944. Bibliographical Soc. 22 fld pl. 110p. VG. A4. $275.00.

WU, William F. *Hong on the Range.* 1989. NY. Millennium Walker. 1st. F/dj. G10. $14.50.

WUENNELL, Peter. *Prodigal Rake: Memoirs of William Hickey.* 1962. Dutton. 1st/3rd. 452p. VG. W2. $12.00.

WUNDER, John R. *At Home on the Range.* 1985. Greenwood. 213p. AN/dj. A10. $20.00.

WUNDT, Wilhelm Max. *Einleitung in Die Philosophie.* 1901. Leipzig. Wilhelm Engelmann. 466p. bl cloth. G1. $100.00.

WUNDT, Wilhelm Max. *Elements of Folk Psychology: Outlines.* 1994. NY. Classics of Psychiatry & Behavioral Sciences Lib. F. G1. $65.00.

WUNDT, Wilhelm Max. *Ethical Systems. Ethics: An Investigation of Facts.* 1897. Sonnenschein/Macmillan. 1st Eng-language/British issue. brn cloth. G1. $75.00.

WUNDT, Wilhelm Max. *Ethics: An Investigation of Facts of the Moral Life.* 1901. 1902 & 1906. Sonnenschein/Macmillan. 3 vol. 2nd Eng-language. G1. $250.00.

WUNDT, Wilhelm Max. *Grundzuge Der Physiologischen Psychologie.* 1874. Leipzig. Wilhelm Engelmann. 870p. contemporary bdg. F. G1. $2.250.00.

WUNDT, Wilhelm Max. *Handbuch Der Medicinischen Physik.* 1867. Erlangen. Ferdinand Enke in Stuttgart. thick 8vo. 556p. rare. G1. $375.00.

WUNDT, Wilhelm Max. *Untersuchungen Zur Mechanik Der Nerven & Nervencentren.* 1876. Stuttgart. Ferdinand Enke. 71 woodcuts. 144p. prt yel wrp. G1. $375.00.

WURDACK, John J. *Flora of Ecuador, 138 Melastomataceae.* 1980. Stockholm. 406p w/41 text figures. F in wrp. B26. $44.00.

WURDEMANN, Audrey. *Bright Ambush.* 1934. NY. John Day. 1st. author's 1st book. NF/chip. A18. $25.00.

WURLITZER, Rudolph. *Flats.* 1970. Dutton. 1st. author's 2nd book. F/torn. rubbed dj. M25. $35.00.

WURTMAN, Richard. *Pineal.* 1968. NY. Academic. 1st. 8vo. 199p. F/VG. C14. $28.00.

WURTS, Janny. *Way Lies Camelot.* 1994. NY. Harper Prism. 1st Am. F/NF. G10. $13.50.

WYATT, Joan. *Middle Earth Album.* 1979. NY. S&S. 1st. ils. NF/wrp. G10. $18.00.

WYCKOFF, Ralph W.G. *World of the Electron Microscope.* 1958. Yale. 164p. xl. G. S5. $20.00.

WYETH, Betsy James. *Wyeth at Kuerners.* 1976. Houghton Mifflin. 1st. obl folio. pl. F/VG clip. T11. $65.00.

WYETH, John Allan. *Life of General Nathan Bedford Forrest.* 1904 (1899). Harper. ils. 655p. G. B10. $125.00.

WYETH, John Allen. *Life of General Nathan Bedford Forrest.* 1899. NY. Harper & Bros. 1st. later cloth. ex lib. some tape repairs. written by Confederate who served under Forrest. 655p. G. M8. $275.00.

WYETH, N.C. *American Vision: Three Generations of Wyeth Art.* 1987. Boston. 1st. ils. VG/dj. M17. $40.00.

WYETH, N.C. *American Vision: Three Generations of Wyeth Art.* 1987. NYGS. 1st. photos. gilt brn cloth. F/NF. T11. $75.00.

WYETH, N.C. *Pike County Ballads.* 1912. Boston. 1st. VG. B5. $90.00.

WYETH, N.C. *Robin Hood.* 1917. Phil. McKay. 1st. VG. B5. $90.00.

WYKA, Frank. *Wishful Thinking.* 1988. NY. Carroll & Graf. 1st. author's 1st book. F/F. H11. $15.00.

WYKES, Alan. *Circus.* 1977. London. Jupiter. 1st. sm 4to. ils. VG/G. O3. $25.00.

WYLER, Michael. *A Glimpse at the Past.* 1957. np. Jazz Publications/UK. memeo. printed on rectos only. No. 27 of ltd ed. 32p. F/wrp. B2. $50.00.

WYLER, Seymour B. *Book of Old Silver.* 1937. Crown. G/dj. A19. $50.00.

WYLIE, Philip. *The End of the Dream.* 1972. Garden City. Doubleday. 1st. F/F. H11. $45.00.

WYLIE, Phillip. *Disappearance.* 1951. Rinehart. 1st. VG/G. B5. $30.00.

WYMAN, Donald. *Dwarf Shrubs.* 1974. BC. 137p. VG/dj. B26. $12.00.

WYMAN, Leland C. *Blessingway: With Three Versions of the Myth.* 1970. Tucson, AZ. 1st. ils. 660p. NF/VG. B19. $75.00.

WYMAN, Leland C. *Windways of the Navaho.* 1962. Taylor Mus. 1st. ils. VG/wrp. B19. $75.00.

WYMAN, Max. *Royal Winnipeg Ballet: First Forty Years.* 1978. Toronto. Doubleday. 1st. NF/VG. A26. $20.00.

WYNDHAM, Francis. *Other Garden.* 1988. Mt. Kisco, NY. Moyar Bell. UP/1st ed. F/pk wrp/dj. M25. $25.00.

WYNDHAM, John. *Jizzle.* 1954. London. Dennis Dobson. 1st. author's 1st collection short stories. VG/dj. M21. $75.00.

WYNDHAM, Lee. *On Your Toes Susie.* 1958. Scholastic. 4th. ils Jane Miller. 115p. VG. P12. $10.00.

WYNESS, Fenton. *City by the Gray North Sea.* 1972. Aberdeen. Impulse. 2nd. 8vo. 324p. NF. W2. $25.00.

WYNTER, A. *Borderlands of Insanity.* 1875. xl. VG+. E6. $65.00.

WYRICK, E. L. *A Strange and Bitter Crop.* 1994. NY. St. Martin. 1st. F/F. H11. $30.00.

WYSE, Lois. *Grandmothers are to Love.* 1967. Parent's Magazine. probable 1st. 12mo. unp. gr cloth. T5. $20.00.

— Y —

YADIN, Yigael. *Masada.* 1966. NY. Random House. photos. 265p. G/G. B29. $15.00.

YAN, Mo. *Red Sorghum.* 1993. NY. Viking. 1st Am. VG/dj. C9. $25.00.

YANDELL, Elizabeth. *Henry.* 1976. St. Martin. 1st Am. sm 8vo. 136p. NF/VG. C14. $12.00.

YANG, Belle. *Baba: A Return to China Upon My Father's Shoulders.* 1994. Harcourt Brace. stated 1st. sq 4to. 211p. H4. $15.00.

YANG, Y. C. *China's Religious Heritage.* 1943. Abingdon. 196p. VG. ex lib. B29. $9.00.

YAPKO, Michael D. *Brief Therapy Approaches to Treating Anxiety & Depression.* 1989. Brunner/Malzel. 1st. 8vo. 357p. F/VG. C14. $20.00.

YAPP, M. E. *Near East Since the First World War.* 1991. London. Longman. ils/map. 526p. F/wrp. Q2. $20.00.

YARBOROUGH, Tom. *Da Nang Diary: Forward Air Controller's Year of Combat.* 1990. St. Martin. 1st. 8vo. 280p. F/NF. $14.00.

YARBRO, Chelsea Quinn. *Better in the Dark.* Dec 1993. NY. Tor. 1st. sgn. VG/dj. L1. $45.00.

YARBRO, Chelsea Quinn. *Blood Games.* 1979. NY. St. Martin. 1st. book has small crayon mark on front pastedown. jacket has minor edge wear. F-/F-. H11. $30.00.

YARBROUGH, Steve. *Family Men.* 1990. Baton Rouge. LSU Press. 1st. author's 1st book. F/F. M23. $50.00.

YARBROUGH, Steve. *Family Men.* 1990. Baton Rouge. LSU Press. 1st. author's 1st book. F/F. A24. $40.00.

YARBROUGH, Steve. *The Oxygen Man.* 1999. Denver. MacMurray & Beck. sgn 1st ed. F/F. M23. $40.00.

YARBROUGH, Steve. *The Oxygen Man.* 1999. Denver. MacMurray & Beck. 1st ed. F/F. M23. $30.00.

YASTRZEMSKI, Carl. *Batting.* 1972. Viking. 1st. VG/dj. P8. $30.00.

YATES, Dornford. *Red in the Morning.* 1946. Ward Locke. 1st Eng. VG/dj. G8. $40.00.

YATES, Elizabeth. *Amos Fortune, Free Man.* 1950. NY. 2nd. ils Nora S Unwin. VG. M17. $17. $50.00.

YATES, Elizabeth. *Continuing Diary of My Widening World.* 1983. Phil. Westminster. 1st. 192p. VG/dj. $3.00.

YATES, Elizabeth. *Howard Thurman: Portrait of a Practical Dreamer.* 1964. NY. John Day. 8vo. 249p. dj. V3. $12. $50.00.

YATES, Elizabeth. *One Writer's Way: Creative Years.* 1984. Phil. Westminster. 1st. 192p. VG/dj. V3. $12.00.

YATES, Richard. *Easter Parade.* 1978. London. Methuen. 1st Eng. F/dj. Q1. $40.00.

YATES, Richard. *Eleven Kinds of Loneliness.* 1962. Atlantic/Little, Brn. 1st. F/NF. B4. $150.00.

YATES, Richard. *Lie Down in Darkness.* 1985. Ploughshares. 1st. VG/dj. C9. $90.00.

YEAKLEY, Virginia & Loren. *Heisey Glass in Color.* 1973. Newark, OH. self-published. 2nd. 8vo. one comb partially missing. G. H1. $18.00.

YEATS, William Butler. *Collected Poems of WB Yeats.* 1951. Macmillan. 2nd (later poems/1st thus). 8vo. 490p. F/VG. H4. $25.00.

YEATS, William Butler. *Discoveries: A Volume of Essays.* 1907. Dundrum. Dun Emer. 1st. 1/200. 43p. bl brd. NF. $24.00.

YEATS, William Butler. *Essays & Introductions.* 1965. Macmillan. 1st Am. F/G. H4. $25.00.

YEATS, William Butler. *In the Seven Woods Being Poems Chiefly of Irish Heroic Age.* 1903 Macmillan. 1st Am. 12mo. 87p. teg. gilt b cloth. VG. $4.00.

YEATS, William Butler. *Stories of Re Hanrahan.* 1904. Dundrum. Dun Emer. 1st 1/500. F. B24. $400.00.

YEATS, William Butler. *Tables of the Law and Adoration of the Magi.* 1914. Shakespeare Head. 1st. 1/510. VG. L3. $75.00.

YEE, Chiang. *Silent Traveller in Paris.* nd NY. 1st. sgn. ils. VG/dj. M17. $37. $50.00.

YEE, Chiang. *Silent Traveller in San Francisco.* 1964. NY. Norton. 1st. NF/VG O4. $25.00.

YEO, Margaret. *Greates of the Borgias.* 1936 NY. ils. VG/G. M17. $17. 50.

YEOMAN, R. C. *Rural Efficiency Guide. Vo* 2. Engineering. 1918. Cleveland. People's 363p. cloth. VG. A10. $18.00.

YERBY, Frank. *Serpent & the Staff.* 1958. NY Dial. 1st. NF/VG. A24. $30.00.

YERBY, Frank. *Speak Now.* 1969. NY. Dial NF/NF. trace of old price sticker. B2. $40.00

YERBY, Frank. *Tobias & the Angel.* 1975. NY Dial. 1st. NF/dj. A24. $25.00.

YERKES, Robert Mearns. *Almost Human* 1925. NY. Century. 2m 8vo. 63 pl. 278p. pic olive cloth. G1. $75.00.

YERKES, Robert Mearns. *Dancing Mouse Study in Animal Behavior.* 1907. Macmillan sm 8vo. 290p. prt thatched brn cloth. VG G1. $85.00.

YEVTUSHENKO, Yevgeny. *Divided Twins. Alaska & Siberia.* 1988. Viking. 1st Am. 4to VG/F. A2. $22.00.

YEVTUSHENKO, Yevgeny. *From Desire to Desire.* 1976. Doubleday. stated 1st. 8vo 126p. F/dj. H4. $20.00.

YGLESIAS, Jose. *Home Again.* 1987. NY Arbor House. UP. wrp. F. B2. $25.00.

YGLESIAS, Raphael. *Fearless.* 1993. NY Warner. 1st. Red Star (library sale) on bottom edges. F/F. H11. $35.00.

YGLESIAS, Raphael. *Fearless.* 1993. NY Warner. 1st. sgn by author. F/F. B3. $30.00.

YGLESIAS, Raphael. *Dr. Neruda's Cure for Evil.* (1996). NY. Warner. 1st. sgn by author F/F. B3. $20.00.

GLESIAS, Raphael. *The Murderer Next Door.* 1990. NY. Crown. 1st. VF/VF. T2. $8.00.

ODER, Paton. *Traverns & Travelers: Inns of the Early West.* 1969. Bloomington. 1st. 246p. /dj. E1. $30.00.

ODER, Samuel A. *Middle-East Sojourn.* 1951. Scottsdale, PA. Herald. sm 8vo. ils. 10p. VG/tattered. $1.00.

OLEN, Jane. *Dream Weaver.* 1979. Collins. 1st. ils Michael Hague. F/VG+. M5. $42.00.

OLEN, Jane. *How Beastly!* 1980. Honesdale. Wordsong. 1st. children's. ils James Marshall. F/F. B3. $30.00.

OLEN, Jane. *Piggins.* 1987. HBJ. 1st. ils. /G/dj. M20. $25.00.

OLEN, Jane. *Sister Light, Sister Dark.* 1988. NY. Tor. 1st. F/F. B3. $20.00.

OLEN, Jane. *Storyteller.* 1992. Cambridge. Nesfa Press. 1st. VF/VF. T2. $20.00.

OLEN, Jane. *White Jenna.* 1989. NY. Tor. 1st. F/NF. G10. $13. 50.

ONGE, Charlotte. *The Lances of Hollywood.* 1929. np. Macmillan. 1st. ils by Marguerite De Angeli. NF/VG dj. M19. $35.00.

ONGE, Charlotte. *The Little Duke: Richard the Fearless.* 1923. Duffield & Co. 1st. clt letters. corner rubs; ils Beautrice Stevens. VG. B15. $75.00.

YORKE, Margaret. *Speak for the Dead.* 1988. Viking. 1st. rem mk. F/dj. H11. $20.00.

YORKE, Margaret. *The Hand of Death.* 1981. NY. St. Martin. 1st. VF/F. H11. $30.00.

YOSHIMOTO, Banana. *Kitchen.* 1993. NY. Grove. 1st Eng-language. F/dj. C9. $30.00.

YOSHIMOTO, Banana. *Kitchen.* 1993. NY. Grove Press. 1st. F/F. M23. $20.00.

YOUATT, History. *Treatment & Diseases of the Horse.* 1883. Lippincott. rpt. 470p. VG. A10. $45.00.

YOUNG, Al. *Seduction by Light.* 1988. Delta. UP. light spotting on rear panel. VG/WRP. M25. $25.00.

YOUNG, Al. *The Song Turning Back Into Itself.* 1971. Holt. NF/WRP. M25. $25.00.

YOUNG, Andrew. *Easy Burden: Civil Rights Movement & Transformation of Am.* 1996. Harper Collins. 1st. F/dj. B30. $30.00.

YOUNG, Arthur Henry. *Hell Up to Date: Reckless Journey of R. Palasco-Drant.* (1893). Chicago. Schulte. 8vo. 85p. red cloth. VG. H4. $175.00.

YOUNG, Arthur P. *Books for Sammies: American Library Association & WWI.* 1981. Beta Phi Mu. 1st. F/sans. N2. $10.00.

YOUNG, B. A. *Rattigan Version.* 1986. London. Hamish Hamilton. 1st. 8vo. 228p. F/dj. $7.00.

YOUNG, Brigham. *Diary of Brigham Young.* 1857. 1980. UT U. 1st. edit. EL Cooley. ils/index. 106p. F/VG. $19.00.

YOUNG, Charles. *Manual of Astronomy: A Text-Book.* 1902. Boston. Ginn. ils. 611p. cloth. G. K5. $18.00.

YOUNG, Clarence. *Jack Ranger's Gun Club.* 1910. Cupples & Leon. sm8vo. owner's inscriptions in ink on both endpapers. jacket complete but tape repairs on inside to fold along front. tape across outside of spine & large chip in spine. 288p. VG/F. H1. $10.00.

YOUNG, Clarence. *The Motor Boys.* 1906. Cupples & Leon. sm8vo. front hinges cracked. a few scattered wear spots. 246p. G. H1. $7.50.

YOUNG, Clarence. *The Motor Boys Bound for Home.* 1920. Cupples & Leon. 1st. sm8vo. front & back hinges cracked. heavily worn at spine tip. owner's inscriptions on both endpapers. jacket poor with cello tape repairs to spine & both folds on verso. cello tape repairs to edges. spine sections missing. 1" tear & some creases on front. 246p. G/P. H1. $9.50.

YOUNG, Clarence. *The Motor Boys on Road & River.* 1915. Cupples & Leon. 1st. sm8vo. front hinge slightly cracked. slightly faded cover. owner's inscription on front endpaper. 248p. G. H1. $12.00.

YOUNG, Clarence. *The Motor Boys Overland.* 1906. Cupples & Leon. sm8vo. owner's inscriptions on both endpapers. sections off spine missing with several cello tape repairs. back flap detached. front flap attached by cello tape on verso. front has edge damage, but Is all there. 228p. G/dj. H1. $9.50.

YOUNG, Delbert A. *According to Hakluyt: Tales of Adventure & Exploration.* 1973. Toronto. Clarke Irwin. 1st. rem mk. F/dj. A2. $15.00.

YOUNG, Dick. *Roy Campanella.* 1952. Barnes. 1st. photos. VG. P8. $60.00.

YOUNG, Ernie W. D. *Alpha & Omega: Ethics at Frontiers of Life & Death.* 1989. Addison-Wesley. ARC. 8vo. 209p. F/NF. C14. $18.00.

YOUNG, Harry. *Hard Knocks: Life Story of the Vanishing West.* 1915. Portland. Wells. ils. 242p. marbled brd/cloth spine. D11. $50.00.

YOUNG, Harry. *Hard Knocks: Life Story of the Vanishing West.* 1915. Laird Lee. ils. 242p. VG. J2. $125.00.

YOUNG, J. P. *Standard History of Memphis.* 1912. Knoxville. full leather (rpr hinges). G. B30. $300.00.

YOUNG, J. Russell. *Around the World with General Grant.* 1879. NY. Am. News. 2 vol. 1st. VG. H4. $75.00.

YOUNG, Otis. *West of Philip St. George Cooke, 1809 – 1895.* 1955. Arthur Clark. ils/maps. VG. J2. $295.00.

YOUNG, Paul E. *Back Trail of an Old Cowboy.* 1983. NE U. 1st. 229p. F/F. B19. $25.00.

YOUNG, Percy M. *Handel.* 1966. NY. White. 1st. F/VG. T12. $20.00.

YOUNG, Peter. *Bedouin Command with Arab Legion 1953 – 1956.* 1956. London. Wm. Kimber. ils/map/plan of Jerusalem ep. 203p. cloth. VG/dj. Q2. $30.00.

YOUNG, Peter. *Bedouin Command with the Arab Legion 1953 – 1956.* 1956. London. Wm. Kimber. 1st. photos/map ep. 203+5p. VG. H7. $15.00.

YOUNG, Rida Johnson. *Little Old New York.* 1923. Grosset Dunlap. early rpt. ils. VG/G. H7. $17. 50.

YOUNG, Scott. *Gordon Sinclair: A Life and Then Some.* 1987. Macmillan. 1st. F/dj. T12. $20.00.

YOUNG, Scott. *Murder in a Cold Climate.* 1989. NY. Viking. 1st Am. author's 1st mystery novel. F/dj. T2. $25.00.

YOUNG, Scott. *Murder in a Cold Climate.* 1989. NY. Viking. 1st Am ed. author's 1st mystery novel. VF/VF. T2. $25.00.

YOUNG, Scott. *The Shaman's Knife.* 1993. NY. Viking. 1st. VF/VF. T2. $20.00.

YOUNG BEAR, Ray. *Black Eagle Child.* 1992. Iowa City. Iowa Univ. 1st. UP. F. D10. $10.00.

YOUNGDAHL, Reuben. *Turbulent World Tranquil God.* 1958. Revell. 157p. G/G. B29. $3.50.

YOUNGSON, A. J. *Scientific Revolution in Victorian Medicine.* 1979. London. 1st. 237p. dj. A13. $22. $50.00.

YOURCENAR, Marguerite. *Coup De Grace.* 1957. NY. FSC. 1st. trans from French by Grace Frick w/author. F/NF. D10. $60.00.

YOURCENAR, Marguerite. *Memoirs of Hadrian.* 1954. London. Secker Warburg. 1st Eng. 8vo. map ep. 320p. cloth.

YOWELL, Claude Lindsay. *History of Madison County Virginia.* 1974 (1926). VA Book Co. facs. 203p. VG. B10. $35.00.

YUILL, P. B. *Hazel Plays Solomon.* 1974. NY. Walker. 1st. VG/dj. M20. $15.00.

YUNGBLUT, John R. *Gentle Art of Spiritual Guidance.* 1991. Rockport, MA. Element. 12mo. 148p. wrp. V3. $9.00.

YUNGJOHANN, John. *White Gold: Diary of a Rubber Cutter in the Amazon.* 1989. Synergetic. 1st. 103p. wrp. F3. $15.00.

YUNIS, Jorge J. *Human Chromosome Methodology.* 1965. Academic. 258p. xl. VG. S5. $20.00.

YURICK, Sol. *The Warriors.* 1965. NY. HRW. 1st. author's 1st book. F in F dj. D10. $85.00.

— Z —

ZACOUR, N. P. *Impact of Crusades on Near East.* 1985. Madison, WI. U WI. History of Crusades #5. ils/maps. VG+. $2.00.

ZADAN, Craig. *Sondheim & Company.* 1974. Macmillan. 1st. VG/dj. C9. $48.00.

ZAHER, Ameen. *Arabian Horse Breeding & the Arabians of America.* 1961. Cairo. 2nd/revised. VG. O3. $275.00.

ZAHL, Paul. *Coro-Coro: World of the Scarlet Ibis.* 1954. Bobbs Merrill. 1st. 264p. dj. F3. $30.00.

ZAHN, Timothy. *Star Wars: The Last Command.* 1993. NY. Bantam. 1st. sgn. VF/VF. T2. $25.00.

ZAHN, Timothy. *Star Wars: The Last Command.* 1993. NY. Bantam Books. 1st ltd ed. 1/350 numbered & sgn copies. Vol 3 of the book cycle. front panel of trade dj laid in. F in glassine dj & purple slipcase. O11. $100.00.

ZALUAR, A. Emilio. *Peregrinacao Pela Provincia De Sao Paulo.* 1945. Sao Paulo. Edicoes Cultura. 2nd ed. 266p. stiff wrp stamped in gilt. VG/G. rubbed dj. F3. $30.00.

ZAMORANO CLUB. *Zamorano Club: First Half Century. 1928 – 78.* 1978. LA. Zamorano Club. 1/200. 99p. patterned brd. D11. $125.00.

ZANDMAN, Felix. *Never the Last Journey.* 1996. NY. 1st. F/dj. T12. $15.00.

ZANELLI, Leo. *Home Winemaking from A to Z.* 1972. Barnes. 1st. 8vo. F/NF. W2. $20.00.

ZANGER, Jack. *Baseball Spark Plug.* 1963. Doubleday. F/G. P8. $15.00.

ZANGER, Jack. *Brooks Robinson Story.* 1967. Messner. 1st. VG/G. P8. $65.00.

ZANGWILL I. *Dreamers of the Ghetto.* 1899. NY/London. Harper. detached title/lacks ffe. H4. $15.00.

ZANUCK, Darryl F. *Tunis Expedition.* 1943. Random. 1st. 160p. map ep. VG/dj. R11. $20.00.

ZARA, Louis. *Rebel Run, an Adventure Novel.* 1951. NY. Crown. 1st. orig cloth. 272p. VG/chipped dj. M8. $15.00.

ZAREM, Lewis. *New Dimensions of Flight.* 1959. Dutton. sm 4to. photos. 256p. cloth. xl. K5. $12.00.

ZARING, Jane. *Return of the Dragon.* 1981. Houghton Mifflin. 1st. inscr/dtd 1981. NF/VG. M21. $75.00.

ZARIT, Steven H. *Aging & Mental Disorders: Psychological Approaches.* 1980. Free Pr. 1st. 8vo. 454p. F/VG. $14.00.

ZAROULIS, Nancy. *Call the Darkness Light.* 1979. Garden City. Doubleday. 1st. F/NF. H11. $30.00.

ZASLAVSKI, Victor A. *Insect Development.* 1988. Springer-Verlag. trans from Russian. ils. 187p. F. S15. $30.00.

ZATARAIN, Michael. *David Duke: Evolution of a Klansman.* 1990. Pelican. 1st. sm 4to. 304p. xl. VG/dj. S14. $8.00.

ZAVIN, Theodora and Freda Stuart. *Working Wives' Salaried or Otherwise, Cookbook, The.* 1963. NY. Cook Ahead Cookery. red brds. BCE. VG/VG. A28. $6.50.

ZECK & ZECK. *Mississippi Sternwheelers.* Minneapolis. 1982. photos. VG/dj. M17. $15.00.

ZEHMER, John G. *Early Domestic Architecture of Dinwiddie County.* Virginia. 1970. U. VA. Master of Architectural Hist. 213p. VG. B10. $65.00.

ZELAZNY, Roger. *Blood of Amber.* 1986. NY. Arbor. 2nd. 8vo. 215p. F/NF. H4. $15.00.

ZELAZNY, Roger. *Changing Land.* 1981. Underwood Miller. 1st hc. F/dj. T2. $30.00.

ZELAZNY, Roger. *Sign of Chaos.* 1987. NY Arbor. 1st. NF/dj. G10. $13. 50.

ZELAZNY, Roger. *Timescape.* 1982. 1st. sgn rem mk. G/dj. B30. $30.00.

ZELAZNY, Roger. *To Spin Is Miracle Cat* 1981. Underwood Miller. 1st. 1/200 sgn/#d. F/dj. A24. $60.00.

ZELIGS, Meyer A. *Friendship & Fratricide an Analysis.* 1067. Viking. 1st. 8vo. VG/dj A2. $20.00.

ZEMACH, Harve. *Awake & Dreaming.* 1970 FSG. 1st. ils Zemach. bl brd. F/dj. D1/D4 $45.00.

ZEMACH, Margot. *Duffy & the Devil: A Cornish Tale.* 1973. NY. FSG. 1st. lg 4to. 1974 Caldecott. gilt gr cloth. mc pict dj. $5.00.

ZEMACH, Margot. *Jake & Honeybunch Go to Heaven.* 1982. FSG. 1st. 32p. F/dj. D4. $45.00.

ZEMACH & ZEMACH. *Princess & Froggie.* NY. FSG. 1975. 1st. unp. F/NF. D4. $45.00.

ZEMEL, Evelyn & Ada Wilson. *American Glass Animals A to Z.* 1978. North Miami, FL. self-published. 1st. 8vo. 290p. F. H1. $85.00.

ZEMJANIS, R. *Diagnostic Therapeutic Techniques in Animal Reproduction.* 1962. Baltimore. Williams Wilkins. 1st. VG. O3. $20.00.

ZERMATTEN, Maurice. *Une Cloche Pour Ursli.* nd. Fribourg. Office du Livre. VG. A16. $15.00.

ZETA. *Diagnosis of the Acute Abdomen in Rhyme.* 1955. London. 3rd. 96p. A13. $50.00.

ZETTERLING, Mai. *Night Games.* 1966. Coward McCann. 1st. F/dj. C9. $25.00.

ZETTNER, Pat. *Shadow Warrior.* 1990. Atheneum. 1st. author's 1st book. F/F. H11. $20.00.

ZHU LIANGFENG ET AL. *Aromatic Plants and Essential Constituents (Supplement 1).* 1995. Hong Kong. sc. F. B26. $39.00.

ZIADEH, N. A. *Syria & Lebanon.* 1957. London. Benn. 5 maps. 312p. VG/dj. Q2. $30.00.

ZICH, Arthur. *Rising Sun.* 1978. Alexandria. VA. Time Life. 2nd. ils. F. M7. $10.00.

ZIEFERT, Harriet. *Lewis the Firefighter.* 1986. Random. 1st. 8vo. VG+. M5. $12.00.

ZIEGENFUSS, Law. *Medicine & Health Care: A Bibliography.* 1984. 274p. VG. A4. $35.00.

ZIEGLER, Philip. *King Edward VIII.* 1991. Knopf. 1st Am. photos. 552p. VG/dj. P12. $15.00.

ZIEHEN, Theodor. *Die Psycholigie Grosser Heerfuhrer/Der Krieg Gedanken.* 1916. Leipzig. Johann Ambrosius Barth. 94p. VG. G1. $50.00.

ZIGAL, Thomas. *Hardrock Stiff.* 1996. NY. Delacorte. 1st. sgn. VF/VF. T2. $20.00.

ZIGAL, Thomas. *Into Thin Air.* 1995. NY. Delacorte. 1st. sgn. author's 1st novel. VF/VF. T2. $25.00.

ZIGLAR, Zig. *Confessions of a Happy Christian.* 1980. Pelican. 199p. VG. B29. $6.50.

ZIGMAN, Laura. *Animal Husbandry.* 1998. NY. Dial. 1st. ARC. F. D10. $10.00.

ZIGMAN, Laura. *Animal Husbandry.* 1998. NY. Dial Press. 1st. author's 1st book. sgn by author. F/F. B3. $45.00.

ZIGMOND, M. L. *Kawaiisu Ethnobotany.* 1981. U. UT. rto. 102p. F/wrp. B1. $37.00.

ZIGROSSER, Carl. *Guide to the Collecting & Care of Original Prints.* 1966. NY. Crown. later prt. 8vo. 120p. F/dj. O10. $25.00.

ZIGROSSER, Carl. *Misch Kohn.* 1961. NY. Am. Federation Arts. ils. 28p. F/dj. H4. $15.00.

ZIMMER, Norma. *Norma.* 1976. Tyndale. stated 1st. 8vo. 368p. F/F. H4. $8. $50.00.

ZIMMERMAN, Arthur. *Francisco De Toledo: 5th Viceroy of Peru 1569 – 1581.* 1938. Caxton. 1st. 307p. F3. $15.00.

ZIMMERMAN, Bruce. *Blood Under the Bridge.* 1989. NY. Harper & Row. 1st. ARC with slip laid in. VF/dj. M15. $30.00.

ZIMMERMAN, Paul. *Los Angeles Dodgers.* 1960. Coward McCann. 1st. VG/G. P8. $50.00.

ZIMMERMAN, R. D. *Blood Trance.* 1993. NY. Morrow. 1st. sgn on title page. VF/VF. H11. $25.00.

ZIMMERMAN, R. D. *Death Trance.* 1992. NY. Morrow. 1st. F/F. H11. $15.00.

ZIMMERN, Alfred. *Greek Commonwealth.* 1956. Random/Modern Lib. 1st. 12mo. 487p. F/dj. H1. $10.00.

ZINBERG, Israel. *History of Jewish Literature.* 1975. Cincinnati/NY. Hebrew Union College/KTAV. 1st. 8vo. 403p. F/NF. H4. $25.00.

ZINBERG, Len. *What D'Ya Know for Sure.* 1947. Doubleday. 1st. chipped and soiled jacket. VG/dj. M25. $60.00.

ZINDEL, Paul. *Begonia for Miss Applebaum.* 1989. Harper Row. 1st. 8vo. 180p. NF/VG clip. C14. $20.00.

ZINGG, Paul. *Harry Hooper: American Baseball Life.* 1993. U. IL. 1st. photos. F/dj. P8. $25.00.

ZINKIN, N. I. *Mechanisms of Speech.* 1968. The Hague. Mouton. 1st Eng. lg 8vo. 463p. bl cloth.

ZINMAN, David. *50 Classic Motion Pictures: Stuff Dreams are Made Of.* 1971. NY. Crown. 3rd. ils. VG/dj. C9. $36.00.

ZINN, Howard. *The Southern Mystique.* 1964. Knopf. 1st. VF in red cloth bds. missing dj. M25. $25.00.

ZINSSER, William. *Spring Training.* 1989. Harper. 1st. F/dj. C15. $10.00.

ZOCHERT, Donald. *Murder at the Hellfire Club.* 1978. NY. HRW. 1st. F/dj. M15. $30.00.

ZOHN, Harry. *Ich Bin Ein Sohn Der Deutschen Sprache Nur.* 1986. Vienna. Amalthea. inscr by author. F/NF. B2. $45.00.

ZOLOTOW, Charlotte. *My Grandson Lew.* nd (c 1974). NY. Harper Row. 12mo. 32p. xl. VG. C14. $14.00.

ZOLOTOW, Charlotte. *Song.* 1982. Greenwillow. 1st. ils Nancy Tafuri. VG/dj. M20. $25.00.

ZOLOTOW, Maurice. *Marilyn Monroe.* 1960. Harcourt Brace. 1st. ils. VG/dj. C9. $90.00.

ZOLTAN, Anne. *Annie: The Female Experience.* 1973. NY. Julian Press. 1st American ed. octavo. purple cloth lettered in wht on spine. pict dj. F. R3. $15.00.

ZOMLEFER, Wendy B. *Guide to Flowering Plant Families.* 1994. Chapel Hill. 430p. AN. B26. $55.00.

ZONARAS, Johannes. *La Prima (-Terza) Parte Dell'Historie Di Giovanni Zonara.* 1570. Venice. Gabriel Giolito di Ferrarii. 3 parts in 1. 4to. vellum. $1.00.

ZOSS, Joel. *Pictorial History of Baseball.* 1986. Gallery. 1st. photos. F/VG+. P8. $20.00.

ZUBRO, Mark R. *Rust on the Razor.* 1996. St. Martin. 1st. sgn. F/F. G8. $17.50.

ZUBRO, Mark Richard. *Simple Suburban Murder.* 1989. St. Martin. 1st. inscr. F/dj. N4. $40.00.

ZUCKERMAN, George. *Last Flapper.* 1969. Little, Brn. 1st. F/VG+. H11. $25.00.

ZWEIG, Stefan. *Balzac.* 1946. Viking. 1st. intl. trans by William & Dorothy Rose. G+. S19. $15.00.

ZWERGER, Lisbeth. *The Art of Lisbeth Zwerger, Afterword by Suzanne Koppe, Printed in German and in English.* 1993. 1994. NY. North South Books. 1st ed. ils by Zwerger. 4to. acrylic wrapper over blk corrugated paper wrps w/window revealing color ils. NF/NF. D6. $35.00.

ZWINGER, Ann. *John Xantus; The Fort Tejon Letters 1857 – 1859.* 1986. Tucson. U of AZ Press. 1st. sgn by author. F/F. B3. $45.00.

ZWINGER, Ann. *Wind in the Rock.* (1978). NY. Harper & Row. 1st. F/F. B3. $50.00.

ZWIREN, Scott. *God Head.* 1996. Normal, IL. Dalkey Archive Press. PBO. F in pict wrp. M23. $25.00.

Glossary of Terms

4to, 8vo, 12mo, etc. — the number of pages into which a single printed sheet has been folded in the production of a book. Although this is not strictly speaking an indication of size, the fewer the folds, the larger the book is likely to be.

a.e.g. — all edges gilt, gilt applied to top edge, bottom edge & fore edge of the volume.

ABAA — Antiquarian Booksellers Association of America.

ABPC — American Book Prices Current, an annual compilation of book, autograph & manuscript auction records.

ADS — [1]Autograph document signed ads., advts., adverts.
[2]advertisements.

advance copy — a copy of a book usually sent to reviewers prior to publication, may be in a different format and may or may not be bound.

advance sheets — the unbound sheets of a new book, often galleys, distributed prior to publication.

advertisements — many books & pamphlets, especially of the 19th century contained ads, especially ones advertising others books by the same publisher, often located at the back of the volume, following the text pages.

Ahearn — BOOK COLLECTING: A Comprehensive Guide. The most comprehensive guide for identifying and pricing modern Firsts and some older titles, too.

all published — the book or set is complete as is, and any additional parts or volumes were never published.

ALS — autograph letter signed, letter handwritten by the person signing the letter as opposed to LS, which is a manuscript letter written by someone other than the signer.

ANS — autograph note signed.

antiquarian (book) — antiquarian books should refer to an old and rare book, preferably 100 years old or more, similar to an antique, but with common usage the term has come to mean any book that is out of print, old, rare, scarce; virtually any book that is not new or in print.

ARC — advanced reading copy, typically sent out by a publisher to solicit reviews or to promote sales of a book prior to its publication. ARCs are sometimes but not always in the form of bound proofs; a message from the publisher may be laid in or tipped in.

association copy — a copy with extraordinary associations, usually because it demonstrably belonged to a notable person, or has a presentation inscription by its author.

b/w — black & white.

BAL — The Bibliography of American Literature (nine volumes, but now also available on CD-ROM), the standard source for definitive descriptions of the different printings and editions of the works of many leading American authors, and as such, an invaluable tool for the proper.

bc, bce — see book club, below.

bdg. — binding.

binding — the method of holding pages or sheets together; may be simply stapled or sewn, or sewn and enclosed in wrappers, but most often refers to a "hard" binding or covers. This type of binding may be covered with cloth, various leathers, paper over boards, or other more exotic materials. The binding can be done by hand or by machine as in a publisher's "trade binding."

binding copy — a book lacking the original binding or with a binding in poor condition, i.e., a book in need of a new binding.

blindstamp — embossed design or text on binding or pages: "blind" because uncolored.

BM or BMC — British Museum or British Museum Catalog.

boards — the covers of a hardbound book; the boards are the stiff cardboard or paperboard which is usually covered with cloth or leather; and when covered with paper, the covers are properly referred to as "boards." Many pre-1850 books were issued by the publishers bound in boards (paper-covered), allowing for an inexpensive binding which could later be replaced with leather by a hand bookbinder. Early (medieval) manuscript volumes were often bound between two oak boards, hence the probable origin of this term. Often abbreviated "bds."

BOMC — Book-of-the-Month Club.

book club edition, BCE — usually an inexpensive reprint utilizing poor quality paper and binding and sold by subscription to members of a book club; in general, of little interest to book collectors and of low monetary value.

book format — the traditional terms in use for describing book format are derived from early printing methodology and the size of early handmade sheets of paper. When two leaves (four pages when printed on both sides) were printed on a sheet so that it could be folded once, collated with other folded sheets and bound, the size of the volume was a "folio." When four leaves (eight pages) were printed on the same size sheet, which would later be folded twice, the size of the resultant volume was a "quarto" (four leaves). The term "octavo" relates to the sheet having eight leaves printed on it. Today some booksellers are providing the height of a book in inches or centimeters rather than using these early terms which do not relate directly to the sheet size or process used for printing today. There are smaller and larger books, i.e., many miniatures are 64mo, and most hardbound books are either octavo or duodecimo in size.

book jacket — the paper, often with illustrations and information about the book and author, used as a protective covering over the book; usually referred to as a "dust jacket" or "dj," sometimes called a "dust wrapper." Dust jacket art work is used to promote and sell the book.

book sizes — see book format

bookworm — any of a number of moth or fly larvae which tunnel through the pages of books leaving behind small channels, holes in individual leaves. Very early books often have some evidence of bookworm damage.

broadside — a printing, often an official announcement, poem, or music, which occurs on a single sheet of paper and only on one side; the verso (other side) is blank. When printed on both sides, the sheet becomes a "broadsheet."

brodart — plastic cover which protects a book's dust jacket or binding.

buckram — a stiff, coarsely woven, filled cloth used for less expensive, but stronger wearing, cloth bookbinding material; often used for library books.

bumped — dented (usually on edge of boards).

calf — book binding leather from a calf hide or cattle hide; a commonly used material for leather binding.

CBEL — Cambridge Bibliography of English Literature.

chipped — small tears or excisions along the edge of pages or dust jacket.

cl — cloth (covering the boards of a book's binding).

clamshell — hinged box (board covered in paper, cloth or leather, or a combination of these), usually custom-made, to hold a book for its protection. On a shelf, the clamshell box may look like a book, with a title on its spine.

cloth — book binding material woven from cotton, linen, wool or synthetic fibers.

cocked — twisted.

collation — used in descriptive bibliography as the term which describes the non-binding portion of the book, verifying the proper sequence and completeness of pages & their gatherings (signatures).

colophon — a statement occurring at the rear of a volume following the text, relating information about the printing history and physical aspects of the book; often includes name of printer, type of paper, typeface, size of edition, date of printing, etc. Early books often had a colophon instead of a title page imprint and modern private press or other examples of fine printing often use a colophon.

conjugate leaves — leaves which are physically attached, part of the same sheet.

covers — the binding of a book; i.e., cloth, calf, morocco, boards, wrappers, etc.

cut edges — the most common type of book edges, trimmed even with a large binders knife prior to finishing the binding process.

DAB — Dictionary of American Biography, a useful 20 volume reference, especially when collecting manuscripts and autographs and attempting to learn about the authors

damp stain — stain often of a shade of tan or gray resulting from water or other liquid damage to a volume; tolerated by collectors when it is minimal and occurs in very old, scarce volumes; its presence does lower the monetary value.

dec., decor — decorated, often to refer to a binding.

deckle edge — natural or sometimes artificial rough edge of page.

disbound — a book or pamphlet or ephemera which has been removed from its binding.

DNB — (British) Dictionary of National Biography.

duodecimo — see definition under book format.

dust jacket — the paper, often with illustrations and information about the book, used as a protective covering over the book; sometimes called a book jacket (dj) or a dust wrapper (dw). Collectors of literary first editions usually insist on having a fine copy of the original dust jacket with the book.

dust wrapper — see dust jacket.

ed — edition.

edition — the copies of a book or other printed material which originate from the same plates or setting of type.

edition & printing — the copies of a book or other printed material which originate from the same plates or setting of type. If 500 copies of a book are printed on Oct. 5 and 300 copies are printed from the same substantially unchanged plates on Dec. 10, all 800 copies are part of the same edition.

printing — the copies of a book or other printed material which originate from the same press run or from the same plates or setting of type at one time. In the example given for "edition" above, the 500 copies would be the first printing and the 300 copies comprise the second printing. In the 19th century some publishers labelled later printings as if they were later editions, i.e., a second printing would be called a "second edition" on the copyright page.

endpaper — paper, often of coated stock or marbled paper or otherwise "fancy" paper, with one half pasted to the cover; used primarily to give a finished appearance to the binding. Abreviated "ep."

ex-library — legitimately removed (discarded/deaccessioned) from an institutional library, such as a public library, university library, historical society, etc. Often has catalog numbers inked or painted on the spine, library bookplates, embossed or rubber-stamped identification on the title page and plates, library card pockets and often shows considerable wear and/or rebinding in a plain buckram. Referred to as "ex-lib" and of considerably lower monetary value than the respective book which has never been the property of an institutional library.

ex-libris — a Latin phrase meaning "from the books" or to paraphrase, "from the library or collection of;" the phrase is frequently used on bookplates.

exlib, ex-lib — book from a library, usually with library markings.

extra-illustrated — usually a volume made into a unique copy with additional illustrations, autographs, or manuscripts added by carefully glueing or tipping-in this extra material.

f, ff, or fol — folio(s); leaves of a book or a size of a book.

ffee, or ffep — front free endpaper (i.e., the blank that is not pasted down onto the boards).

fine — defining a book's description is not an exact science, but probably all would agree that a book in "fine" condition is a mint copy, in the same condition as when it was sent out by the printer or binder.

first appearances — could be one of three concepts: first time author appears in print, first time a specific writing of an author appears in print, or the first time a specific subject is treated in book form.

first books — the first book appearance by an author (usually refers to a book entirely written by the author, not merely a part of anthology). Frequently these are not widely known, even of well-established authors.

first edition — often, but not always, more valuable than later editions (though of course most books don't get beyond a first edition or even a first printing!).

first thus — first thus indicates the volume in question contains some new feature. It does not indicate that this is the first edition of the title, but rather that it is the first published in this particular format, be it with a new illustrator, publisher, binding, or introduction.

flyleaf — a blank leaf (or leaves) inserted during the binding process between the free endpaper and the beginning or end of the printed pages.

folio — see book format.

foxing — rust colored spots which occur on paper resulting from oxidation processes apparently caused by certain mold fungi; there is no visible evidence of mold, only brown to rusty brown spots on the paper.

frontispiece — an illustration or plate inserted immediately in front of the title page, with the illustration facing the title page, often abbreviated as "frontis."

full binding — volume is entirely encased in leather (calf, sheep, morocco, etc.)

gathering — a folded printed sheet of leaves prior to binding; referred to as a signature after binding.

gilt — indicates the pages of a book have been trimmed and the outside edges covered in gilt, or gold. The abbreviation g.e. or gilt edges is sometimes used.

gutter — the inner margin of the leaves of a bound book; adjacent inner margins of facing pages when book is open.

half binding — the spine and corner leather occupy only approx. one half of top edge.

half-title — page before title page, usually only with the book's title printed on it.

hinge — the inside portion of the flexible area where book cover meets the book spine; often used interchangeably with the term joint, which should be used to designate the outside or exterior portion of the "hinge." A volume which has received heavy or rough use often has cracked or broken hinges.

illum. — (illuminated) usually as in illuminated manuscript, referring to polychromeillustrations.

imprint — when used as a noun refers to the publication data located at the base of a title page, usually includes the city of publication,

name of the publisher (sometimes the printer), and the year of publication. Sometimes this information is located in a colophon at the back of a book. Imprint can also be used to refer to a printed piece from a certain location or period of time, i.e., the university has a collection of 18th century Massachusetts imprints.

incunable — anything printed during the 15th century, the first century of printing with "moveable type"; from the Latin, meaning "from the cradle"; can also be used in a relative sense to refer to other early printings, i.e., incunables from the Pacific islands.

incunabulum — a book published before 1501, while publishing was still "in the cradle." Incunabula fetch high prices even though most of them are indescribably dull theological works.

inscribed — a book, or other printed piece, with a handwritten and signed statement usually written for a specific named person(s) and often located on the endpaper or title page; when "inscribed" is used to describe a book, unless otherwise stated, it is implied that the author has written the inscription. When used to designate the recipients of a book as a gift from the author (or publisher), it is called a "presentation inscription."

issue — a portion of an edition printed or published deliberately by the printer or publisher in a distinct form differing from the rest of the printing relative to paper, binding, format, etc. The distinction between "issue" and "state" is that the former relates to changes done on purpose by the publisher or printer and intentionally treated as a separate unit, i.e., a large paper issue or an issue in publisher's leather.

issue — usually refers to a change within a single printing which occurs after some copies of that printing have already been released from the publisher and are in circulation.

joint — the exterior flexible "hinge" where book cover meets book spine; "hinge" is usually used to designate the equivalent inside or interior flexible area. The joint is often an area that splits or cracks or otherwise shows wear in an older cloth or leather volume.

laid in — sometimes, loosely laid in; a letter or other sheet(s) inserted but not glued into a book.

large paper copy — a special edition printed with the pages reconfigured to result in larger leaves with very wide page margins; the text of the individual pages remaining the same as the normal edition; usually large paper copies are printed in small, limited editions.

leaf (leaves) — refers to the smallest, standard physical unit of paper in a printed piece; in the case of books and pamphlets, usually with a printed page on each side of a leaf; a broadside is printed on a single side of a single leaf.

LOC — Library of Congress.

lp — large-paper edition.

ltd., limited ed. — an edition limited to a specified number of copies.

marbled edges — usually the top, bottom and fore edge of a book with a multi-colored, swirled-design, somewhat resembling the coloration pattern of marble stone.

marbled paper — paper decorated with a multi-colored, swirled-design or pattern; often used for endpapers or for paper-covered boards, especially with ¾ or ½ leather bindings.

mint — unread, or as new.

mo — a suffix as in 12mo, 16mo, etc., used for the size of a book.

morocco — leather binding made from goat hides; usually used in high quality or fine bindings for the interesting texture of the leather; originally tanned with sumac in the country of Morocco.

ms, mss — manuscript, manuscripts.

n.d. — this abbreviation means "no date" provided in the imprint.

n.p. — "no place" of publication provided in the imprint.

nd — no date given for publication.

nf — near-fine condition.

np — no place, publisher or printer.

NUC — National Union Catalogue; when used in antiquarian book descriptions, usually refers to the pre-1956 imprints NUC which lists Library of Congress holdings plus the holdings of all reporting libraries in the U.S. When a catalog desciption states "Not in NUC", the item described is usually rare (in terms of U.S. library holdings).

OCLC — online combined catalog of most large US libraries and in some other countries. Has about 50 million records, most with invaluable bibliographic information. Accessed only by fee-paying subscribers, but can be used by readers in some libraries.

octavo, 8vo — book in which the sheet has been folded to make 8 pages; like other such designations (4to, folio, etc.), this is not strictly speaking an indication of size. Generally, however, the fewer the folds, the larger the book is likely to be.

offsetting — the process which causes a reversed image inadvertently to appear on the page facing the original impression.

orig. — original (as in original cloth binding).

out-of-print — no longer available from the publisher; abreviated o.p. or op.

pastedown — page which is pasted onto the front or inside board of a book.

PBO — paperback original.

pc, or price clipped — usually a small triangle cut from the front inside corner of a dust jacket to remove the indication of a book's price. Dust jackets with clipped prices are generally considered inferior to ones that are intact.

plate — an illustration(s) printed on a separate sheet of paper (usually heavy and better quality than the text pages) and added to the book during the binding process.

poi — previous owner inscription.

ppr — paperback.

presentation copy — a copy of a printed item inscribed and signed by the author (or publisher) and provided as a gift; see "inscribed."

printing — the copies of a book or other printed material which originate from the same press run or from the same plates or setting of type at one time.

pub — publisher or published.

quarter binding — usually lacks leather corners and leather of the spine occupies only approx. ¼ of the top edge.

quarto, 4to — book in which the sheet has been folded to make 4 pages; like other such designations (octavo, folio, etc.), this is not strictly speaking an indication of size. Generally, however, the fewer the folds, the larger the book is likely to be. See our book size chart for precise details.

reading copy — well-worn, usually abused copy of a book, often in need of rebinding; i.e., suitable for reading, but unlikely to be included in a book collection unless rebound; sometimes refers to a copy that can be read, but is not of a quality worth rebinding.

rebacked — the spine or backstrip has been replaced with new material, in some cases the original worn backstrip is saved and glued over the new material.

rebound — copy of a book which has had the original binding removed and a new binding attached; when there is no need to resew or trim the book, the term "recased" is sometimes used to indicate that a new binding and new endpapers have been added.

recto — the front side of a leaf or in the case of an open book the page on the right, with the page on the left being the verso.

rem or rm — remainder. A copy sold by a publisher after withdrawing the book from publication. Often slightly disfigured, either with a rubber stamp or with a black line crudely drawn across one of the edges.

rubbed — indicates that the outer layer of the material used on the binding has been rubbed off.

sc — soft cover (paperback or similar).

self-wrappers — the wrappers of a pamphlet consist of the first leaf of the first signature and the final leaf of the last signature; i.e., no special or distinct paper wrappers have been added; often government pamphlets and almanacs have self-wrappers.

sewn-as-issued — a pamphlet which has been sewn together and exists in its original state relative to binding; normally a pamphlet with self-wrappers.

shaken — indicates that sections (signatures) of a book or pamphlet are becoming quite loose, but remain attached to the binding. Used to speak of a book that is no longer firm in its covers (typically, publisher's cloth) because of deteriorating inner hinges (should not be used of a book that is in but detached from its covers).

sheep — a common leather binding material from sheep hides; used like calf for a less expensive binding than morocco, appears to have been frequently used for textbooks and law books in the 19th century.

shelfback — another term for spine or backstrip.

signature — a group or gathering of leaves printed together on a sheet of paper which is folded, bound with other signatures and trimmed to form a book or pamphlet; i.e., a section or grouping of pages in a book resulting from printing and binding methodology;

also refers to a person's self-hand-written name (autograph signature).

signed — refers to a printed item on which the author (or illustrator or publisher) has written their name, usually on the endpapers, title page, or in the case of pamphlets, on the wrappers.

slipcase — container/box with one open side (made of board covered in paper, cloth or leather, or a combination of these) into which a book may be "slipped" for its protection; Publishers often issue a slipcase with two and three volume sets.

solander case — a box in which a book is stored for protection which has one end (often leather) which resembles the spine or backstrip of a book.

spine — bound outer edge; the back portion of a book's binding which is visible when a book is shelved in a bookcase; the portion which is attached at the joints to the front and rear covers.

started — indicates that one or more signatures of a book are protruding beyond the rest of the fore edge, i.e., beginning to pull away from the binding to which they are still attached; not as loosened as the term "shaken" indicates.

state — usually refers to a change made within a single printing prior to any circulation of copies of the printing.

teg — top edge gilt.

three-quarter binding — volume has leather spine and corners which occupy approx. ¾ of the space along top edge of board (cover). The remainder of the board is covered with marbled paper, plain paper, cloth, different leather, etc.

tipped in — a sheet or sheets which were not part of the original bound book, but are now. Pages are tipped in by dabbing minute amounts of glue onto the edge which is to be inserted into the book.

TLS — typed letter signed, as opposed to ALS, a handwritten letter signed by the writer.

tp — title page.

trade edition — usually, "first trade edition" (as distinct from limited editions, often signed or with special paper or bindings, which appear before the full commercial publication of a book).

ts — typescript.

unbound — indicates that the item has never been bound, i.e., unbound sheets; not the same as disbound which indicates that the binding has been removed

uncut — refers to the edges of a book in an untrimmed state, edges are somewhat uneven, also see "deckle edge."

unopened — a book with signatures which have never been cut as opposed to untrimmed and uneven (see "uncut"); unopened books retain the folds of the original gathering and contain many pages which cannot be read without first opening the pages with a knife. Some collectors prefer an unopened book because it indicates that the book has never been read; other collectors who read their books would rather not have the task of cutting open pages and risking tears and jagged leaf edges.

variants — refers to the differences in bindings or endpapers, such as different colors of stamping.

vellum — true vellum is a thin specially treated untanned "leather" from calf skin, also known as parchment (high quality parchment from calf skin is called vellum; general quality parchment is made from calf, goat or sheep skin); used for documents and for book bindings; many early books (of the sixteenth and seventeenth centuries) have vellum bindings; paper makers have produced parchment and/or vellum papers also used for book bindings.

verso — the reverse or opposite or left-hand side, especially used in reference to a leaf which has a recto and verso side; in a open book the recto is the right hand page and the verso is the left hand page; in the case of a broadside only the recto is printed and the verso is blank.

VG — very good condition.

VG/VG — or some variant (e.g., NF/VG) describes the condition of the binding (sometimes of both the binding and interior) and dust-jacket of a book, respectively.

vol. — volume.

w.a.f. — with all faults; indicates a book or other item which is being offered without careful delineation of its condition or without careful collation; usually indicates a less than "very good" copy, which probably does has faults, often including excessive wear or missing leaves, plates, or maps.

wrappers, wrp — abbreviated as "wraps," wrappers are the paper covers of a pamphlet, often of a paper of heavier weight than the text paper; when you see "wrappers," you know the item is not a hardbound book, but is instead a pamphlet or magazine with paper covers; usually not used to refer to 20th century paperback books which are called "soft bound" (with paper covers).

Psuedonyms

Listed below are pseudonyms of many paperback and hardcover authors. This information was shared with us by some of our many contributors, and we offer it here as a reference for our readers. This section is organized alphabetically by the author's actual name (given in bold) followed by the pseudonyms he or she has been known to use. (It is interesting to note that 'house names' were common with more than one author using the same name for a particular magazine or publishing house.)

If you have additional information (or corrections), please let us hear from you so we can expand this section in future editions.

Edward S. Aarons
Paul Ayres
Edward Ronns

Marvin H. Albert
Albert Conroy
Stuart Jason
Nick Quarry
Anthony Rome

William (Thomas) Ard
Ben Kerr
Jonas Ward (some)
Thomas Willis

Paul Auster
Paul Benjamin

Mike Avallone
Nick Carter (a few)
Troy Conway (a few)
Priscilla Dalton
Stuart Jason
Edwina Noone
Sidney Stuart
Max Walker

W. T. Ballard
D'Allard Hunter
Neil MacNeil
John Shepherd

Bill Ballinger
B.X. Sanborn

Robert Barnard
Bernard Bastable

Julian Barnes
Dan Kavanagh
Basil Seal

Charles Beaumont
Keith Grantland

Robert Beck
Slim Iceberg

H. Bedford-Jones
Paul Feval
Lucien Pemjean
L. Pemjion

Roger Blake
Mark Sade

Lurton Blassingame
Peter Duncan

James Blish
William Atheling

Robert Bloch
Collier Young

Lawrence Block
William Ard
Jill Emerson
Chip Harrison
Sheldon Lord
Benjamin Morse, M.D.
Andrew Shaw

Marion Zimmer Bradley
Lee Chapman
John Dexter (some)
Miriam Gardner
Valerie Graves
Morgan Ives

John Brunner
Keith Woodcott

Kenneth Bulmer
Adam Hardy
Manning Norvil
Dray Prescot

W.R. Burnett
John Monachan
James Updyke

William S. Burroughs
William Lee

Stuart Byrne
John Bloodstone

Paul Cain
George Sims

Ramsey Campbell
Carl Dreadstone
Jay Ramsay

John Dickson Carr
Carter Dickson
Roger Fairbairn

Basil Cooper
Lee Falk

Clarence Cooper
Robert Chestnut

John Creasey
Gordon Ashe
Harry Carmichael
Norman Deane
Robert Caine Frazier
Patrick Gill
Michael Holliday
Brian Hope
Colin Hughes
Kyle Hunt
J.J. Marric
Jeremy York

Michael Crichton
John Lange

David Cross
George B. Chesbro

Norman Daniels
Dorothy Daniels
David Wade

Avram Davidson
Ellery Queen
(about 2 titles only)

August Derleth
Stephen Grendon

Thomas B. Dewey
Tom Brandt
Cord Wainer

Thomas Disch
Thomas Demijohn
Knye Cassandra (both
with John Sladek)

James Duffy
Haughton Murphy

Peter Beresford Ellis
Peter Tremayne

Harlan Ellison
Paul Merchant

Dennis Etchison
Jack Martin

Paul Fairman
F.W. Paul

Lionel Fanthorpe
John E. Muller

Philip Jose Farmer
William Norfolk
Kilgore Trout

Frederick S. Faust
Max Brand
George Owen Baxter

John Russell Fearn
Aston Del Martia

Alan Dean Foster
George Lucas

Gardner F. Fox
Glen Chase
Jefferson Cooper
Jeffrey Gardner
Matt Gardner
James Kendricks Gray
Dean Jennings
Simon Majors
Kevin Matthews
John Medford Morgan
Rod Morgan
Bart Summers

Erle Stanley Gardner
A.A. Fair
Carleton Kendrake
Charles Kinney

Randall Garrett
Walter Bupp
David Gordon
½ of Mark Phillips and
Robert Randall

Richard Geis
Robert Owen
Peggy Swenson

Theodor Seuss Geisel
Dr. Seuss

Walter B. Gibson
Douglas Brown
Maxwell Grant

Ron Goulart
Lee Falk
Josephine Kains
Julian Kearney
Kenneth Robeson
Frank S. Shaw(n)
Joseph Silva

Charles L. Grant
Felicia Andrew
Deborah Lewis

Ben Haas
Richard Meade

Joe Haldeman
Robert Graham

Oakley Hall
O.M. Hall

Brett Halliday
Mike Shayne

Joseph Hansen
Rose Brock
James Colton

Terry Harknett
Joseph Hedges
Thomas H. Stone

Timothy Harris
Harris Hyde

Carolyn G. Heilbrun
Amanda Cross

Eleanor Alice Burford Hibbert
Philippa Carr
Victoria Holt
Jean Plaidy

Jamake Highwater
J. Marks
J. Marks-Highwater

Hochstein, Peter
Jack Short

C. Hodder-Williams
James Brogan

John Robert Holt
Elizabeth Giles
Raymond Giles

Cornell Hoppley-Woolrich
George Hopley
William Irish
Cornell Woolrich

E. Howard Hunt
David St. John

Evan Hunter
Curt Cannon
Hunt Collins
Ezra Hannon
Richard Marsten
Ed McBain

Oliver Jacks
Kenneth R. Gandley

J. Denis Jackson
Julian Moreau

John Jakes
William Ard
Alan Payne
Jay Scotland
J.X. Williams

Will F. Jenkins
Murray Leinster

Frank Kane
Frank Boyd

Henry Kane
Anthony McCall

Hal Kent
Ron Davis

Stephen King
Richard Bachman

Philip K. Klass
William Tenn

Andrew Klavan
Keith Peterson

William Knowles
Clyde Allison
Clyde Ames

Dean R. Koontz
David Axton
Brian Coffey
Deanna Dwyer
K.R. Dwyer
John Hill
Leigh Nichols
Anthony North
Richard Paige
Owen West
Aaron Wolfe

Cyril Kornbluth
Simon Eisner
Jordan Park

Jerzy Kosinski
Joseph Novak
Jane Somers

P. Kubis
Casey Scott

Michael Kurland
Jennifer Plum

Louis L'Amour
Tex Burns
Jim Mayo

Lawrence Lariar
Adam Knight

Keith Laumer
Anthony LeBaron

Milton Lesser
Stephen Marlowe

Doris Lessing
Jane Somers

Alfred Henry Lewis
Dan Quinn

Paul Linebarger
Cordwainer Smith

Frank Belknap Long
Lyda Belknap Long

Peter Lovesey
Peter Lear

Mark Lucas
Drew Palmer

Robert Ludlum
Jonathan Ryder
Michael Shepherd

Richard Lupoff
Adison Steele

Dennis Lynds
Michael Collins
John Crowe
Maxwell Grant (some)
Mark Sadler

Barry Malzberg
Mike Berry
Claudine Dumas
Mel Johnson
M.L. Johnson
Barrett O'Donnell
K.M. O'Donnell

Frederick Manfred
Feike Feikema

Mel Marshall
Zack Tayler

Robert Martin
Lee Roberts

Van Wyck Mason
Geoffrey Coffin

Graham Masterton
Thomas Luke

Richard Matheson
Swanson, Logan

Dudley McGaughy
Dean Owen

Marijane Meaker
Ann Aldrich
Vin Packer

H.L. Menken
Owen Hatteras

Barbara Gross Mertz
Barbara Michael
Elizabeth Peters

Kenneth Millar
Ross MacDonald
John Ross MacDonald

Michael Moorcock
Bill Barclay
Edward P. Bradbury

Brian Moore
Bernard Mara
Bryan Michael

James Morris
Jan Morris (after sex change)

Petroleum Nasby
David R. Locke

Andre Alice Norton
Andrew North
Alice Norton
Andre Norton

Alan E. Nourse
Doctor X

Charles Nuetzel
Albert Jr. Augustus
John Davidson
Charles English
Alec Rivere

Joyce Carol Oates
Rosamond Smith

Andrew Offutt
John Cleve
Baxter Giles
J.X. Williams (some)

Edith Mary Pargeter
Ellis Peter

Henry Patterson
Martin Fallon
James Graham
Jack Higgins
Harry Patterson
Hugh Marlowe

Dennis Phillips
Peter Chambers
Peter Chester

James Atlee Philips
Philip Atlee

Judson Phillips
Hugh Pentecost

Richard Posner
Iris Foster
Beatrice Murray
Paul Todd

Richard Prather
David Knight
Douglas Ring

Bill Pronzini
Jack Foxx

Peter Rabe
J. T. MacCargo

R. L. Radford
Ford, Marcia

Clayton Rawson
Stuart Towne

Ruth Rendell
Barbara Vine

Mack Reynolds
Bob Belmont
Todd Harding
Maxine Reynolds

Anne Rice
Anne Rampling
A.N. Roquelaure

Robert Rosenblum
Robert Maxxe

W.E.D. Ross
Rose Dana
Jan Daniels
Clarissa Ross
Dan Ross
Dana Ross
Marilyn Ross

Jean-Baptiste Rossi
Sebastien Japrisot

John Sandford
John Camp

Sandra Scoppetone
Jack Early

Con Sellers
Della Bannion

Alice Bradley Sheldon
Alice Bradley
Raccoona Sheldon
James Tiptree

Robert Silverberg
Loren Beauchamp
W.R. Burnett (some only)
Walter Drummond
Don Elliott (some)
Hilary Ford
Franklin Hamilton
Calvin Knox
Lt. Woodard, M.D.

George H. Smith
J.M. Deer
Jan Hudson
Jerry Jason
M.E. Knerr
Diana Summers

David Stacton
Bud Clifton

Theodore Sturgeon
Frederick R. Ewing
Ellery Queen (1 book only)

Ross Thomas
Oliver Bleeck

Don Tracy
Roger Fuller

Bob Tralins
Keith Miles
Sean O'Shea

E.C. Tubb
Gregory Kern

Jack Vance
Peter Held
Ellery Queen (some/few)

Luther Vidal
Edgar Box
Cameron Kay
Gore Vidal

Walter Wager
John Tiger
Max Walker

Harold Ward
Zorro

Jack Webb
John Farr

Joe Weiss
Ray Anatole
Claude Dauphine
Ken Mirbeau

Donald E. Westlake
John B. Allan
Curt Clark
Timothy Culver
J. Morgan Cunningham
Samuel Holt
Alan Marshall
Richard Stark
Edwin West

Harry Whittington
Whit Harrison
Shep Shepherd

Gordon Williams
P.B Yuill

Jack Williamson
Will Stewart

Don Wollheim
David Grinnell

George F. Worts
Loring Brent

Bookbuyers

In this section of the book we have listed buyers of books and related material. When you correspond with these dealers, be sure to enclose a self-addressed stamped envelope if you want a reply. Do not send lists of books for appraisal. If you wish to sell your books, quote the price you want or send a list and ask if there are any on the list they might be interested in and the price they would be willing to pay. If you want the list back, be sure to send a SASE large enough for the listing to be returned. When you list your books, do so by author, full title, publisher and place, date, edition, and condition, noting any defects on cover or contents.

Adventure
The Silver Door
P.O. Box 3208
Redondo Beach, CA 90277
310-379-6005

African-American
Children's Book Adoption Agency
P.O. Box 643
Kensington, MD 20895-0643
310-565-2834 or fax 301-585-3091
KIDS_BKS@interloc.com

Fran's Bookhouse
6601 Greene St.
Philadelphia, PA 19119
215-438-2729 or fax 215-438-8997

Monroe Stahr Books
4420 Ventura Canyon, #2
Sherman Oaks, CA 91423
818-501-3419 or fax 818-995-0966
MStahrBks@aol.com

Recollection Books
4519 University Way NE
Seattle, WA 98105
206-548-1346

Alaska
Artis Books
201 N Second Ave.
P.O. Box 822
Alpena, MI 49707
517-354-3401
artis@freeway.net

Albania
W.B. O'Neill-Old & Rare Books
11609 Hunters Green Ct.
Reston, VA 20191
703-860-0782 or fax 703-620-0153
nyc1918@aol.com

Alcoholics Anonymous
The Book Baron
1236 S Magnolia Ave.
Anaheim, CA 92804
714-527-7022 or fax 714-527-5634
bkbaron1@pacbell.net or
bkbaron3@qte.net

American Southwest
Arizona, Northern & New Mexcico
Books West Southwest
W. David Laird
Box 6149, University Station
Irvine, CA 92616-6149
714-509-7670 or fax 714-854-5102
bkswest@ix.netcom.com

Americana
Amaranth Books
P.O. Box 421
Wilmette, IL 60091-0421
708-328-2939

Aplan Antiques & Art
James & Peg Aplan
21424 Clover Pl.
Piedmont, SD 57769-9403
605-347-5016 or fax 605-347-9336
aplanpeg@rapidnet.com

The Bookseller, Inc.
174 W Exchange St.
Akron, OH 44302
330-762-3101 or fax 330-762-4413
booklein@apk.net

The Captain's Bookshelf, Inc.
31 Page Ave.
Asheville, NC 28801
828-253-6631 or fax 828-253-4917
captsbooks@aol.com

Chapel Hill Rare Books
P.O. Box 456
Carrboro, NC 27510
919-929-8351
rarebooks@mindspring.com

Duck Creek Books
Jim & Shirley Richards
P.O. Box 203
Caldwell, OH 43724
614-732-4856 (10 am to 10 pm)

Terry Harper, Bookseller
P.O. Box 312
Vergennes, VT 05491-0312
802-877-9262
bookvend@together.net

Susan Heller, Pages for Sages
22611 Halburton Rd.
Beachwood, OH 44122-3939
216-283-2665
hellersu@cyberdrive.net

Jim Hodgson Books
908 S Manlius St.
Fayetteville, NY 13066
315-637-6264
jimhbooks@aol.com

M & S Rare Books, Inc.
P.O. Box 2594, E Side Sta.
Providence, RI 02906
401-421-1050 or fax 401-272-0831
(attention M & S)
dsiegel@msrarebooks.com

Parmer Books
7644 Forrestal Rd.
San Diego, CA 92120-2203
619-287-0693 or fax 619-287-6135
ParmerBook@aol.com

Randall House
Pia Oliver
835 Laguna St.
Santa Barbara, CA 93101
805-963-1909 or fax 805-963-1650
pia@piasworld.com

Thorn Books
P.O. Box 1244
Moorpark, CA 93020
805-529-3647 or fax 805-529-0022
thornbooks@earthlink.net

Yesterday's Books
229 Riverview Dr.
Parchment, MI 49004
616-345-1011
yesbooks@aol.com

Anarchism
Nutmeg Books
354 New Litchfield St. (Rte. 202)
Torrington, CT 06790
203-482-9696
nutmeg@compsol.net

Angling
Book & Tackle Shop
29 Old Colony Rd.
P.O. Box 114
Chestnut Hill, MA 02467
phone/fax 617-965-0459
bktack@ibm.net

Anthropology
The King's Market Bookshops
P.O. Box 709
Boulder, CO 80306-0709
303-232-3321

Anthologies
Cartoonists from 1890 – 1960
Craig Ehlenberger
Abalone Cove Rare Books
7 Fruit Tree Rd.
Portuguese Bend, CA 90275

Antiquarian
A.B.A.C.U.S.®
Phillip E. Miller
343 S Chesterfield St.
Aiken, SC 29801
803-648-4632

Fine, hard-to-find books
Arnold's of Michigan
218 S Water
Marine City, MI 48039-1688
810-765-1350 or fax 810-765-7914

The Book Baron
1236 S Magnolia Ave.
Anaheim, CA 92804
714-527-7022 or fax 714-527-5634
bkbaron1@pacbell.net or
bkbaron3@qte.net

Children's Book Adoption Agency
P.O. Box 643
Kensington, MD 20895-0643
310-565-2834 or fax 301-585-3091
KIDS_BKS@interloc.com

James Tait Goodrich
Antiquarian Books & Manuscripts
135 Tweed Blvd.
Grandview-on-Hudson, NY 10960
914-359-0242 or fax 914-359-0142
jtg.jamestgoodrich.com

Terry Harper, Bookseller
P.O. Box 312
Vergennes, VT 05491-0312
802-877-9262
bookvend@together.net

Murray Hudson
Antiquarian Books & Maps
109 S. Church St.
P.O. Box 163
Halls, TN 38040
901-836-9057 or 800-748-9946
fax 901-836-9017
mapman@usit.net

The Old Map Gallery
Paul F. Mahoney
1746 Blake St.
Denver, CO 80202
303-296-7725 or fax 303-296-7936
oldmapgallery@denver.net

Jeffrey Lee Pressman, Bookseller
3246 Ettie St.
Oakland, CA 94608
510-652-6232

Robert Mueller Rare Books
8124 W 26th St.
N Riverside, IL 60546
708-447-6441

Scribe Company
Attn: Bonnie Smith
427 Hidden Forest S
Longview, TX 75605
903-663-6873

*Also Agriculture, Biographies, Law, Travel,
Turn-of-the-Century Fiction &
Philosophy*
David R. Smith
30 Nelson Cir.
Jaffrey, NH 03452
603-532-8666
Bookinc@Cheshire.net

Antiques, Collectibles & Reference
Antique & Collectors Reproduction News
Mark Chervenka, Editor
Box 12130-OB
Des Moines, IA 50312-9403
515-270-8994 or fax 515-255-4530

Collector's Companion
Perry Franks
P.O. Box 24333
Richmond, VA 23224

Galerie De Boicourt
251 E Merrill St.
Birmingham, MI 48009
248-723-5680

Henry H. Hain III
Antiques, Collectibles & Books
2623 N Second St.
Harrisburg, PA 17110-1109
717-238-0534
antcolbks@ezonline.com

Appraisals
J. Sampson Antiques & Books
107 S Main
Harrodsburg, KY 40330
606-734-7829

Lee Barnett Temares
50 Heights Rd.
Plandome, NY 11030
516-627-8688/fax 516-627-7822
tembooks@aol.com

Arabian Horses; Arabian Nights
Worldwide Antiquarian
P.O. Box 410391
Cambridge, MA 02141-0004
617-876-6220 or fax 617-876-0839
mbalwan@aol.com

Archaelogy
Flo Silver Books
8442 Oakwood Ct. N
Indianapolis, IN 46260
phone/fax 317-255-5118
Flosilver@aol.com

Architecture
Cover to Cover
Mark Shuman
P.O. Box 687
Chapel Hill, NC 27514
919-967-1032

Arctic
Artis Books
201 N Second Ave.
P.O. Box 822
Alpena, MI 49707
517-354-3401
artis@freeway.net

Parmer Books
7644 Forrestal Rd.
San Diego, CA 92120-2203
619-287-0693 or fax 619-287-6135
ParmerBook@aol.com

Armenia
W.B. O'Neill-Old & Rare Books
11609 Hunters Green Ct.
Reston, VA 20191
703-860-0782 or fax 703-620-0153
nyc1918@aol.com

Art
AL-PAC
Lamar Kelley Antiquarian Books
2625 E Southern Ave., C-120
Tempe, AZ 85282
602-831-3121 or fax 602-831-3193
alpac2625@aol.com

Book & Tackle Shop
29 Old Colony Rd.
P.O. Box 114
Chestnut Hill, MA 02467
phone/fax 617-965-0459
bktack@ibm.net

Books West Southwest
W. David Laird
Box 6149, University Station
Irvine, CA 92616-6149
714-509-7670 or fax 714-854-5102
bkswest@ix.netcom.com

The Captain's Bookshelf, Inc.
31 Page Ave.
Asheville, NC 28801
828-253-6631 or fax 828-253-4917
captsbooks@aol.com

Fine, applied
L. Clarice Davis Art Books
P.O. Box 56054
Sherman Oaks, CA 91413-1054
818-787-1322 or fax 818-780-3281
davislc@earthlink.net

Galerie De Boicourt
251 E Merrill St.
Birmingham, MI 48009
248-723-5680

Edison Hall Books
5 Ventnor Dr.
Edison, NJ 08820
908-548-4455

Heritage Book Shop, Inc.
8540 Melrose Ave.
Los Angeles, CA 90069
310-659-3674 or fax 310-659-4872
HBSINCLA@aol.com

David Holloway, Bookseller
7430 Grace St.
Springfield, VA 22150
703-659-1798

Significant Books
3053 Madison Rd.
P.O. Box 9248
Cincinnati, OH 45209
513-321-7567
signbook@iac.net

Lee Barnett Temares
50 Heights Rd.
Plandome, NY 11030
516-627-8688 or fax 516-627-7822
tembooks@aol.com

Xanadu Records, Ltd.
3242 Irwin Ave.
Kingsbridge, NY 10463
212-549-3655

Arthurian
Camelot Books
Charles E. Wyatt
P.O. Box 2883
Vista, CA 92083
619-940-9472

Astronomy
Knollwood Books
Lee & Peggy Price
P.O. Box 197
Oregon, WI 53575-0197
608-835-8861 or fax 608-835-8421
books@tdsnet.com

Atlases
Murray Hudson
Antiquarian Books & Maps
109 S Church St.
P.O. Box 163
Halls, TN 38040
901-836-9057 or 800-748-9946
fax 901-836-9017
mapman@usit.net

The Old Map Gallery
Paul F. Mahoney
1746 Blake St.
Denver, CO 80202
303-296-7725 or fax 303-296-7936
oldmapgallery@denver.net

Atomic Bomb
Key Books
P.O. Box 58097
St. Petersburg, FL 33715
813-867-2931

Autobiographies
Herb Sauermann
21660 School Rd.
Manton, CA 96059

Warren's Collector Books
For Sale Now
112 Royal Ct.
Friendswood, TX 77546
281-482-7947

Wellerdt's Books
3700 S Osprey Ave. #214
Sarasota, FL 34239
813-365-1318

Autographs
Ads Autographs
P.O. Box 8006
Webster, NY 14580-8006
716-671-2651 or fax 716-671-5727

The American Dust Co.
47 Park Ct.
Staten Island, NY 10301
phone/fax 718-442-8253

Michael Gerlicher
1375 Rest Point Rd.
Orono, MN 55364

Susan Heller, Pages for Sages
22611 Halburton Rd.
Beachwood, OH 44122-3939
216-283-2665
hellersu@cyberdrive.net

Heritage Book Shop, Inc.
8540 Melrose Ave.
Los Angeles, CA 90069
310-659-3674 or fax 310-659-4872
HBSINCLA@aol.com

Key Books
P.O. Box 58097
St. Petersburg, FL 33715
813-867-2931

McGowan Book Co.
P.O. Box 4226
Chapel Hill, NC 27515-4226
919-968-1121 or fax 919-968-1644
mcgowanbooks@mindspring.com
www.mcgowanbooks.com

Randall House
Pia Oliver
835 Laguna St.
Santa Barbara, CA 93101
805-963-1909 or fax 805-963-1650
pia@piasworld.com

Aviation
The Book Corner
Michael Tennaro
728 W Lumsden Rd.
Brandon, FL 33511
813-684-1133
bookcrnr@worldnet.att.net

The Bookseller, Inc.
174 W Exchange St.
Akron, OH 44302
330-762-3101 or fax 330-762-4413
booklein@apk.net

Cover to Cover
Mark Shuman
P.O. Box 687
Chapel Hill, NC 27514
919-967-1032

Baedeker Handbooks
W.B. O'Neill-Old & Rare Books
11609 Hunters Green Ct.
Reston, VA 20191
703-860-0782 or fax 703-620-0153
nyc1918@aol.com

Barbie
Glo's Books & Collectibles
Gloria Stobbes
906 Shadywood
Southlake, TX 76092
817-481-1438

Baseball
The American Dust Co.
47 Park Ct.
Staten Island, NY 10301
phone/fax 718-442-8253

R. Plapinger, Baseball Books
P.O. Box 1062
Ashland, OR 87520
503-488-1200

Rising Stars
Don Carnahan
P.O. Box 2991
Yuma, AZ 85366
Phone/fax 520-329-6054

L. Frank Baum
Alcott Books
Barbara Ruppert
5909 Darnell
Houston, TX 77074-7719
713-774-2202

Beat Generation
Twice Read Books & Comics
42 S Main St.
Chambersburg, PA 17201
717-261-8449

Bibliographies
About Books
6 Sand Hill Ct.
P.O. Box 5717
Parsippany, NJ 07054
973-515-4591

Books West Southwest
W. David Laird
Box 6149, University Sta.
Irvine, CA 92616-6149
714-509-7670 or fax 714-854-5102
bkswest@ix.netcom.com

Oak Knoll Books
310 Delaware St.
New Castle, DE 19720
800-996-2556 or 302-328-7232
fax 302-328-7274
oakknoll@oakknoll.com

Big Little Books
Jay's House of Collectibles
75 Pky. Dr.
Syosset, NY 11791

Biographies

Third Time Around Books
Norman Todd
R.R. #1
Mar., Ontario
Canada N0H 1XO
519-534-1382

Herb Sauermann
21660 School Rd.
Manton, CA 96059

Warren's Collector Books
   For Sale Now
112 Royal Ct.
Friendswood, TX 77546
281-482-7947

Black Americana

Especially Little Black Sambo
Glo's Books & Collectibles
Gloria Stobbes
906 Shadywood
Southlake, TX 76092
817-481-1438

History & literature; general literature
Thomas L. Coffman, Bookseller
TLC Books
9 N College Ave.
Salem, VA 24153
540-389-3555

History & literature
David Holloway, Bookseller
7430 Grace St.
Springfield, VA 22150
703-569-1798

Mason's Bookstore, Rare Books &
   Record Albums East
115 S Main St.
Chambersburg, PA 17201
717-261-0541

Black Fiction & Literature

Almark & Co.-Booksellers
P.O. Box 7
Thornhill, Ontario
Canada L3T 3N1
905-764-2665 or fax 905-764-5771
al@almarkco.com or
mark@almarkco.com

The American Dust Co.
47 Park Ct.
Staten Island, NY 10301
phone/fax 718-442-8253

Black Studies

Recollection Books
4519 University Way NE
Seattle, WA 98105
206-548-1346

Black Hills

James F. Taylor
515 Sixth St.
Rapid City, SD 57701
605-341-3224

Book Search Service

Authors of the West
191 Dogwood Dr.
Dundee, OR 97115
503-538-8132
Lnash@georgefox.edu

Ackley Books & Collectibles
Bryant & Suzanne Pitner
912 Hidden Cove Way
Suisun City, CA 94585-3511
707-421-9032 or fax 978-285-6554
(mail order only)

Avonlea Books
P.O. Box 74, Main Station
White Plains, NY 10602-0074
914-946-5923 or fax 914-761-3119
avonlea@bushkin.com

Bookingham Palace
Rosan Van Wagenen & Eileen Layman
52 North 2500 East
Teton, ID 83451
209-458-4431

Heritage Book Shop, Inc.
8540 Melrose Ave.
Los Angeles, CA 90069
310-659-3674 or fax 310-659-4872
HBSINCL@aol.com

Hilda's Book Search
Hilda Gruskin
199 Rollins Ave.
Rockville, MD 20852
301-948-3181

Lost n' Found Books
Linda Lengerich
3214 Columbine Ct.
Indianapolis, IN 46224
phone/fax 317-298-9077

Passaic Book Center
594 Main Ave.
Passaic, NJ 07055
201-778-6646 or fax 201-778-6738

Recollection Books
4519 University Way NE
Seattle, WA 98105
206-548-1346

The Silver Door
P.O. Box 3208
Redondo Beach, CA 90277
310-379-6005

Especially children's out-of-print books
Treasures from the Castle
Connie Castle
1277 Candlestick Lane
Rochester, MI 48306
248-651-7317
treasure23@juno.com

Book Sets

AL-PAC
Lamar Kelley Antiquarian Books
2625 E Southern Ave., C-120
Tempe, AZ 85282
602-831-3121 or fax 602-831-3193
alpac2625@aol.com

Books About Books

About Books
6 Sand Hill Ct.
P.O. Box 5717
Parsippany, NJ 07054
973-515-4591

Books West Southwest
W. David Laird
Box 6149, University Station
Irvine, CA 92616-6149
714-509-7670 or fax 714-854-5102
bkswest@ix.netcom.com

First Folio
1206 Brentwood
Paris, TN 38242
phone/fax 901-644-9940
firstfol@aeneas.net

Susan Heller, Pages for Sages
22611 Halburton Rd.
Beachwood, OH 44122-3939
216-283-2665
hellersu@cyberdrive.net

Key Books
P.O. Box 58097
St. Petersburg, FL 33715
813-867-2931

Oak Knoll Books
310 Delaware St.
New Castle, DE 19720
800-996-2556 or 302-328-7232
fax 302-328-7274
oakknoll@oakknoll.com

Randall House
Pia Oliver
835 Laguna St.
Santa Barbara, CA 93101
805-963-1909 or fax 805-963-1650
pia@piasworld.com

George H. Tweney
16660 Marine View Dr. SW
Seattle, WA 98166
206-243-8243

Botany

Also gardening, horiticulture, etc.
Agave Books
P.O. Box 31495
Mesa, AZ 85275-1495
602-649-9097

Brooks Books
P.O. Box 91
Clayton, CA 94517
925-672-4566 or fax 925-672-3338
brooksbk@netvista.com

Charles Bukowski
Ed Smith Books
20 Paget Rd.
Madision, WI 53704-5929
608-241-3707 or
fax 608-241-3459
ed@edsbooks.com

Edgar Rice Burroughs
W. J. Leveridge
W & L Trading Company
2301 Carova Rd.
Carova Beach, Corolla, NC 27927
252-453-3408

C.S. Lewis & Friends
Aslan Books
191 Dogwood Dr.
Dundee, OR 97115
503-538-8132
Lnash@georgefox.edu

California
Books West Southwest
W. David Laird
Box 6149, University Station
Irvine, CA 92616-6149
714-509-7670 or fax 714-854-5102
bkswest@ix.netcom.com

Thorn Books
P.O. Box 1244
Moorpark, CA 93020
805-529-3647 or fax 805-529-0022
thornbooks@earthlink.net

Canadiana
David Armstrong, Bookseller
Box 551
Letherbridge, Alberta
Canada T1J 3Z4
403-381-3270
dabooks@telusplanet.net

Third Time Around Books
Norman Todd
R.R. #1
Mar., Ontario
Canada N0H 1XO
519-534-1382

Cartography
Overlee Farm Books
P.O. Box 1155
Stockbridge, MA 01262
413-637-2277

Cartoon Art
Jay's House of Collectibles
75 Pky. Dr.
Syosset, NY 11791

Catalogs
Antiques or other collectibles
Antique & Collectors Reproduction News
Mark Chervenka, Editor
Box 12130-OB
Des Moines, IA 50312-9403
515-270-8994 or fax 515-255-4530

Hillcrest Books
961 Deep Draw Rd.
Crossville, TN 38555-9547
phone/fax 931-484-7680
hillcrst@usit.net

Glass, pottery, furniture, doll, toy, jewelry, general merchandise, fishing tackle
Bill Schroeder
5801 Ky Dam Rd
Paducah, KY 42003

Celtic
Camelot Books
Charles E. Wyatt
P.O. Box 2883
Vista, CA 92083
619-940-9472

Central America
Flo Silver Books
8442 Oakwood Ct. N
Indianapolis, IN 46260
phone/fax 317-255-5118
Flosilver@aol.com

Marc Chagall
Paul Melzer Fine Books
12 E Vine St.
P.O. Box 1143
Redlands, CA 92373
909-792-7299 or fax 909-792-7218
pmbooks@eee.org

Children's Illustrated
Noreen Abbot Books
2666 44th Ave.
San Francisco, CA 94116
415-664-9464

Alcott Books
Barbara Ruppert
5909 Darnell
Houston, TX 77074-7719
713-774-2202

Book & Tackle Shop
29 Old Colony Rd.
P.O. Box 114
Chestnut Hill, MA 02467
phone/fax 617-965-0459
bktack@ibm.net

Books of the Ages
Gary J. Overmann
Maple Ridge Manor
4764 Silverwood Dr.
Batavia, OH 45103-9740
phone/fax 513-732-3456

Including Dick & Jane readers, Little Golden Books, older Weekly Reader
Bookcase Books
P. Gayle Hendrington
R.R. 1 Box 242
Newport, NH 03773
603-863-9517
books@bookcasebooks.com

Bromer Booksellers
607 Boylston St.
Boston, MA 02116
617-247-2818 or fax 617-247-2975
books@bromer.com
www.bromer.com

Non-series or published after 1925
Cattermole
20th-Century Children's Books
9880 Fairmount Rd.
Newbury, OH 44065
440-338-3253 or fax 440-338-1675
books@cattermole.com

19th & 20th Century
Children's Book Adoption Agency
P.O. Box 643
Kensington, MD 20895-0643
301-565-2834 or fax 301-585-3091
KIDS_BKS@interloc.com

Free search service
Steven Cieluch
15 Walbridge St., Suite #10
Allston, MA 02134-3808
617-734-7778
scieluch@channel1.com

Ursula Davidson
Children's & Illustrated Books
134 Linden Ln.
San Rafael, CA 94901
414-454-3939 or fax 415-454-1087
davidson_u@compuserve.com

Drusilla's Books
817 N Howard St.
Baltimore, MD 21201-4696
401-225-0277 or fax 401-321-4955
Tues-Sat: 12 a.m. to 5 p.m.
or by appointment
drusilla@mindspring.com

Edison Hall Books
5 Ventnor Dr.
Edison, NJ 08820
908-548-4455

Circa 1850s through 1970s
Encino Books
Diane Yaspan
5063 Gaviota Ave
Encino, CA 91436
818-905-711 or fax 818-501-7711

First Folio
1206 Brentwood
Paris, TN 38242
phone/fax 901-644-9940
firstfol@aeneas.net

Fran's Bookhouse
6601 Greene St.
Phil., PA 19119
215-438-2729 or fax 215-438-8997

*Madeline, Eloise, Raggedy Ann & Andy,
    Uncle Wiggly, Wizard of Oz*
Glo's Books & Collectibles
Gloria Stobbes
906 Shadywood
Southlake, TX 76092
817-481-1438

Susan Heller, Pages for Sages
22611 Halburton Rd.
Beachwood, OH 44122-3939
216-283-2665
hellersu@cyberdrive.net

Ilene Kayne
1308 S Charles St.
Baltimore, MD 21230-4219
410-347-7570
kayne@clark.net

Bob Lakin Books
P.O. Box 186
Chatfield, TX 75105
972-247-3291

Marvelous Books
P.O. Box 1510
Ballwin, MO 63022
314-458-3301 or fax 314-273-5452
marvbooks@aol.com

Much Ado
Seven Pleasant St.
Marblehead, MA 01945
781-639-0400 or fax 781-639-0840
muchado@shore.net

Nerman's Books
410-63 Albert St.
Winnipeg, Manitoba
Canada R3B 1G4
204-956-1214 or 204-475-1050
fax 204-947-0753
nerman@escape.ca

Page Books
Margaret E. Page
HCR 65, Box 233
Kingston, AR 72742
870-861-5831
pagebook@eritter.net

Jo Ann Reisler, Ltd.
360 Glyndon St., NE
Vienna, VA 22180
703-938-2967 or
fax 703-938-9057
Reisler@Clark.net

Scribe Company
Attn: Bonnie Smith
427 Hidden Forest S
Longview, TX 75605
903-663-6873

Barbara Smith Books
P.O. Box 1185
Northampton, MA 01061
413-586-1453

Treasures from the Castle
Connie Castle
1277 Candlestick Lamp
Rochester, MI 48306
248-651-7317
treasure23@juno.com

Yesterday's Books
229 Riverview Dr.
Parchment, MI 49004
616-345-1011
yesbooks@aol.com

Children's Series
Children's Book Adoption Agency
P.O. Box 643
Kensington, MD 20895-0643
301-565-2834 or fax 301-585-3091
KIDS_BKS@interloc.com

Circa 1900s through 1970s
Encino Books
Diane Yaspan
5063 Gaviota Ave
Encino, CA 91436
818-905-711 or fax 818-501-7711

*Judy Bolton, Nancy Drew, Rick Brant,
    Cherry Ames, etc.; also Dick & Jane*
Glo's Books & Collectibles
Gloria Stobbes
906 Shadywood
Southlake, TX 76092
817-481-1438

Ilene Kayne
1308 S Charles St.
Baltimore, MD 21230-4219
410-347-7570
kayne@clark.net

Bob Lakin Books
P.O. Box 186
Chatfield, TX 75105
972-247-3291

Nerman's Books
410-63 Albert St.
Winnipeg, Manitoba
Canada R3B 1G4
204-956-1214 or 204-475-1050
fax 204-947-0753
nerman@escape.ca

Scribe Company
Attn: Bonnie Smith
427 Hidden Forest S
Longview, TX 75605
903-663-6873

Lee Barnett Temares
50 Heights Rd.
Plandome, NY 11030
516-627-8688 or fax 516-627-7822
tembooks@aol.com

Yesterday's Books
229 Riverview Dr.
Parchment, MI 49004
616-345-1011
yesbooks@aol.com

Christian Faith
Books Now & Then
Dennis & Jan Patrick
P.O. Box 337
Stanley, ND 58784
phone/fax 701-628-2084
bnt@stanley.ndak.net

Christmas
Especially illustrated antiquarian
Drusilla's Books
817 N Howard St.
Baltimore, MD 21201-4696
410-225-0277 or fax 410-321-4955
Tues-Sat: 12a.m. to 5p.m.
or by appointment
drusilla@mindspring.com

Sir W.S. Churchill
Chartwell Booksellers
55 E 52nd St.
New York, NY 10055
212-308-0643

Robert L. Merriam
Rare, Used & Old Books
39 Newhall Rd.
Conway, MA 01341-9709
413-369-4052
rmerriam@valinet.com

Cinema, Theatre & Films
The American Dust Co.
47 Park Ct.
Staten Island, NY 10301
phone/fax 718-442-8253

Cinemage Books
105 W 27th St.
New York, NY 10001
212-243-4919
irajoel@aol.com

Xanadu Records, Ltd.
3242 Irwin Ave.
Kingsbridge, NY 10463
212-549-3655

Civil War
Chapel Hill Rare Books
P.O. Box 456
Carrboro, NC 27510
919-929-8351
rarebooks@mindspring.com

Stan Clark Military Books
915 Fairview Ave.
Gettysburg, PA 17325
717-337-1728 or 717-337-0581

Also the South
Elder's Book Store
2115 Elliston Pl.
Nashville, TN 37203
615-327-1867

Rick Harmon
Military Books & Relics
910 Sullivan Dr.
Belvidere, IL 61008
815-547-7580

Jim Hodgson Books
908 S Manlius St.
Fayetteville, NY 13066
315-637-6264
jimhbooks@aol.com

Mason's Bookstore, Rare Books &
    Record Albums East
115 S Main St.
Chambersburg, PA 17201
717-261-0541

K.C. & Jean Owings
Box 389
Whitman, MA 02382
781-447-7850 or fax 781-447-3435

Irvin S. Cobb
*Always paying $3.00 each plus shipping.
    Send for immediate payment:*
Bill Schroeder
5801 KY Dam Rd.
Paducah, KY 42003

Collectibles, Antiques & Reference
Antique & Collectors Reproduction News
Mark Chervenka, Editor
Box 12130-OB
Des Moines, IA 50312-9403
515-270-8994 or fax 515-255-4530

Galerie De Boicourt
251 E Merrill St.
Birmingham, MI 48009
248-723-5680

Henry H. Hain III
Antiques, Collectibles & Books
2623 N Second St.
Harrisburg, PA 17110-1109
717-238-0534
antcolbks@ezonline.com

Color Plate Books
Drusilla's Books
817 N Howard St.
Baltimore, MD 21201-4696
410-225-0277 or fax 410-321-4955
Tues – Sat: 12 a.m. to 5 p.m.
or by appointment
drusilla@mindspring.com

Worldwide Antiquarian
P.O. Box 410391
Cambridge, MA 02141-0004
617-876-6220 or fax 617-876-0839
mbalwan@aol.com

Comics
Passaic Book Center
594 Main Ave.
Passaic, NJ 07055
201-778-6646 or fax 201-778-6738

Cookery & Cookbooks
Arnold's of Michigan
218 S Water
Marine City, MI 48039-1688
810-765-1350 or fax 810-765-7914

Book & Tackle Shop
29 Old Colony Rd.
P.O. Box 114
Chestnut Hill, MA 02467
phone/fax 617-965-0459
bktack@ibm.net

Book Broker
114 Bollingwood Rd.
Charlottesville, VA 22902
804-296-2194 or fax 804-296-1566
bookbrk@cfw.com
mail order or appointment only

RAC Books
P.O. Box 296 RD 2
Seven Valleys, PA 17360
717-428-3776
racbooks@cyberia.com

Barbara Smith Books
P.O. Box 1185
Northampton, MA 01061
413-586-1453

Warren's Collector Books
    For Sale Now
112 Royal Ct.
Friendswood, TX 77546
281-482-7947

Crime
The Silver Door
P.O. Box 3208
Redondo Beach, CA 90277
310-379-6005

Cuba & Panama
The Book Corner
Mike Tennaro
728 W Lumsden Rd.
Brandon, FL 33511
813-684-1133
bookcrnr@worldnet.att.net

Cyprus
W.B. O'Neill-Old & Rare Books
11609 Hunters Green Ct.
Reston, VA 20191
703-860-0782 or fax 703-620-0153
nyc1918@aol.com

Decorative Arts
Robert L. Merriam
Rare, Used & Old Books
39 Newhall Rd.
Conway, MA 01341-9709
413-369-4052
rmerriam@valinet.com

Detective
First editions
Karl M. Armens
740 Juniper Dr.
Iowa City, IA 52245

Monroe Stahr Books
4420 Ventura Canyon, #2
Sherman Oaks, CA 91423
818-501-3419 or fax 818-995-0966
MStahrBks@aol.com

Mordida Books
P.O. Box 79322
Houston, TX 77279
713-467-4280 or fax 713-467-4182
mordida@swbell.net
www.mordida.com

Thomas Books
P.O. Box 14036
Phoenix, AZ 85063
480-247-9289 or fax 480-945-1023
sales@thomasbooks.com

The Silver Door
P.O. Box 3208
Redondo Beach, CA 90277
310-379-6005

Disney
Cohen Books & Collectibles
Joel J. Cohen
P.O. Box 810310
Boca Raton, FL 33481-0310
561-487-7888

Jay's House of Collectibles
75 Pky. Dr.
Syosset, NY 11791

Documents
McGowan Book Co.
P.O. Box 4226
Chapel Hill, NC 27515-4226
919-968-1121 or fax 919-968-1644
mcgowanbooks@mindspring.com
www.mcgowanbook.com

Dogs
Kathleen Rais & Co.
211 Carolina Ave.
Phoenixville, PA 19460
610-933-1388

Earth Science
Used, out-of-print, rare
Patricia L. Daniel, Bookseller
13 English Ave.
Wichita, KS 62707-1005
316-683-2079 or fax 316-683-5448
pldaniel@Southwind.net

Emily Dickinson
Robert F. Lucas
Antiquarian Books
P.O. Box 63
Blandford, MA 01008
413-848-2061

Robert L. Merriam
Rare, Used & Old Books
39 Newhall Rd.
Conway, MA 01341-9709
413-369-4052
rmerriam@valinet.com

Thomas Edison
Edison Hall Books
5 Ventnor Dr.
Edison, NJ 08820
908-548-4455

Ephemera

Antique valentines
Kingsbury Productions
Katherine & David Kreider
4555 N Pershing Ave., Suite 33-138
Stockton, CA 95207
209-467-8438

The Mulberry Cat
Yvonne Davis
Jan Davis Martel
P.O. Box 3573
Boone, NC 28607
704-963-7693

Equestrine

Books, antiques, art
Artiques, Ltd.
Veronica Jochens
P.O. Box 67
Lonedell, MO 63060
314-629-1374
veronica @nightowl.net

Espionage

The Silver Door
P.O. Box 3208
Redondo Beach, CA 92077
310-379-6005

Estate Libraries

The Book Collector
2347 University Blvd.
Houston, TX 77005
713-661-2665

Exhibition Catalogs

L. Clarice Davis Art Books
P.O. Box 56054
Sherman Oaks, CA 91413-1054
818-787-1322 or fax 818-780-3281
davislc@earthlink.net

Exploration

Western
Terry Harper, Bookseller
P.O. Box 312
Vergennes, VT 05491-0312
802-877-9262
bookvend@together.net

Heritage Book Shop, Inc.
8540 Melrose Ave.
Los Angeles, CA 90069
310-659-3674 or fax 310-659-4872
HBSINCLA@aol.com

Key Books
P.O. Box 58097
St. Petersburg, FL 33715
813-867-2931

Flo Silver Books
8442 Oakwood Ct. N
Indianapolis, IN 46260
phone/fax 317-255-5118
Flosilver@aol.com

Fantasy

The Book Baron
1236 S Magnolia Ave.
Anaheim, CA 92804
714-527-7022 or fax 714-527-5634
bkbaron1@pacbell.net or
bkbaron3@qte.net

Camelot Books
Charles E Wyatt
P.O. Box 2883
Vista, CA 92083
619-940-9472

Science fiction, horror or supernatural
Xanadu Records Ltd.
3242 Irwin Ave.
Kingsbridge, NY 01463
718-549-3655

Farming

First editions
Karl M. Armens
740 Juniper Dr.
Iowa City, IA 52245

Also gardening
Hurley Books/Celtic Cross Books
1753 Rt. 12
Westmoreland, NH 03467-4724
603-399-4342 or fax 603-399-8326
hurleybook@adam.cheshire.net

Henry Lindeman
4769 Bavarian Dr.
Jackson, MI 49201
517-764-5728

Fiction

American, European, detective or crime
The American Dust Co.
47 Park Ct.
Staten Island, NY 10301
phone/fax 718-442-8253

McGee's First Varieties
330 Franklin Rd., Suite 135A
Brentwood, TN 37027
615-373-5318
TMcGee@BellSouth.net

Southern
Alice Robbins, Bookseller
3002 Round Hill Rd.
Greensboro, NC 27408
910-282-1964

Third Time Around Books
Norman Todd
R.R. #1
Mar., Ontario
Canada N0H 1XO
519-534-1382

Warren's Collector Books
For Sale Now
112 Royal Ct.
Friendswood, TX 77546
281-482-7947

American, European, detective or crime
Ace Zerblonski Books
Malcolm McCollum, Proprietor
1419 North Royer
Colorado Springs, CO 80907
719-634-3941

Bob Lakin Books
P.O. Box 186
Chatfield, TX 75105
972-247-3291
19th & 20th-C American

Mason's Bookstore, Rare Books
& Record Albums East
115 S Main St.
Chambersburg, PA 17201
717-261-0541

Financial

Warren's Collector Books
For Sale Now
112 Royal Ct.
Friendswood, TX 77546
281-482-7947

Fine Bindings & Books

The Book Collector
2347 University Blvd.
Houston, TX 77005
713-661-2665

Bromer Booksellers
607 Boylston St.
Boston, MA 02116
617-247-2818 or fax 617-247-2975
books@bromer.com
www.bromer.com

Dad's Old Bookstore
Green Hills Ct.
4004 Hillsboro Rd.
Nashville, TN 37215
615-298-5880

Terry Harper, Bookseller
P.O. Box 312
Vergennes, VT 05491-0312
802-877-9262
bookvend@together.net

Heritage Book Shop, Inc.
8540 Melrose Ave.
Los Angeles, CA 90069
310-659-3674 or fax 310-659-4872
HBSINCL@aol.com

George Robert Kane Fine Books
252 Third Ave.
Santa Cruz, CA 95062
phone/fax 408-426-4133
gkanebks@cruzio.com

Kenneth Karmiole, Bookseller, Inc.
509 Wilshire Blvd.
Santa Monica, CA 94001
310-451-4342 or 310-458-5930
karmbooks@aol.com

Mason's Bookstore, Rare Books &
  Record Albums East
115 S Main St.
Chambersburg, PA 17201
717-261-0541

Paul Melzer Fine Books
12 E Vine St.
P.O. Box 1143
Redlands, CA 92373
909-792-7299 or fax 909-793-7218
pmbooks@eee.org

Also sets
Randall House
Pia Oliver
835 Laguna St.
Santa Barbara, CA 93101
805-963-1909 or fax 805-963-1650
pia@piasworld.com

David R. Smith
30 Nelson Cir.
Jaffrey, NH 03452
603-532-8666
Bookinc@Cheshire.net

Fine Press
Susan Heller, Pages for Sages
22611 Halburton Rd.
Beachwood, OH 44122-3939
216-283-2665
hellersu@cyberdrive.net

Heritage Book Shop, Inc.
8540 Melrose Ave.
Los Angeles, CA 90069
310-659-3674 or fax 310-659-4872
HBSINCL@aol.com

Randall House
Pia Oliver
835 Laguna St.
Santa Barbara, CA 93101
805-963-1909 or fax 805-963-1650
pia@piasworld.com

Firearms
Melvin Marcher, Bookseller
6204 N Vermont
Oklahoma City, OK 73112

First Editions
A Tale of Two Sisters
1401 Emerald Circle
Southlake, TX 76092
817-329-0988
tts.mcc@ix.netcom.com

After 1937
A.B.A.C.U.S.®
Phillip E. Miller
343 S Chesterfield St.
Aiken, SC 29801
803-648-4632

Hyper-modern
Almark & Co.-Booksellers
P.O. Box 7
Thornhill, Ontario
Canada L3T 3N1
905-764-2665 or fax 905-764-5771
al@almarkco.com or
mark@almarkco.com

Modern or signed
AL-PAC
Lamar Kelley Antiquarian Books
2625 E Southern Ave., C-120
Tempe, AZ 85282
602-831-3121 or fax 602-831-3193
alpac2625@aol.com

Modern or signed
Alcott Books
Barbara Ruppert
5909 Darnell
Houston, TX 77074-7719
713-774-2202

Amaranth Books
P.O. Box 421
Wilmette, IL 60091-0421
708-328-2939

Modern or signed
The American Dust Co.
47 Park Ct.
Staten Island, NY 10301
phone/fax 718-442-8253

Karl M. Armens
740 Juniper Dr.
Iowa City, IA 52245

Modern
Bella Luna Books
4697 Stone Canyon Ranch Rd.
Castle Rock, CO 80104
800-497-4717 or fax 303-663-2113
Bellalun@aol.com

Between the Covers
35 W Maple Ave.
Merchantville, NJ 08109
609-665-2284 or fax 609-665-3639
mail@betweenthecovers.com

The Book Baron
1236 S Magnolia Ave.
Anaheim, CA 92804
714-527-7022 or fax 714-527-5634
bkbaron1@pacbell.net or
bkbaron3@qte.net

Modern or signed
Burke's Bookstore
1719 Poplar Ave.
Memphis, TN 38104-6447
901-278-7484 or fax 901-272-2340
burkes@netten.net

Modern
Chapel Hill Rare Books
P.O. Box 456
Carrboro, NC 27510
919-929-8351
rarebooks@mindspring.com

Modern
Tom Davidson, Bookseller
3703 Ave. L
Brooklyn, NY 11210
718-338-8428 or fax 718-338-8430
tdbooks@att.net

Modern
Bernard E. Goodman, Bookseller
7421 SW 147 Ct.
Miami, FL 33193
305-385-8526
BCBooks@bellsouth.net

Modern
The Early West/Whodunit Books
P.O. Box 9292
College Station, TX 77842
409-775-6047 or fax 409-764-7758
EarlyWest@aol.com

Edison Hall Books
5 Ventnor Dr.
Edison, NJ 08820
908-548-4455

Ruth Heindel Associates
First Editions, Rare & Used Books
660 Boas St., Suite 1618
Harrisburg, PA 17110
717-213-9010

Modern
Susan Heller, Pages for Sages
22611 Halburton Rd.
Beachwood, OH 44122-3939
216-283-2665
hellersu@cyberdrive.net

Heritage Book Shop, Inc.
8540 Melrose Ave.
Los Angeles, CA 90069
310-659-3674 or fax 310-659-4872
HBSINCLA@aol.com

Modern
David Holloway, Bookseller
7430 Grace St.
Springfield, VA 22150
703-569-1798

Modern
Ken Lopez, Bookseller
51 Huntington Rd.
Hadley, MA 01035
413-584-4827 or fax 413-584-2045
mail@lopezbooks.com

Modern
McGee's First Varieties
330 Franklin Rd., Suite 135
Brentwood, TN 37027
615-373-5318
TMcGee@BellSouth.net

Monroe Stahr Books
4420 Ventura Canyon, #2
Sherman Oaks, CA 91423
818-501-3419 or fax 818-995-0966
MStahrBks@aol.com

Much Ado
Seven Pleasant St.
Marblehead, MA 01945
781-639-0400 or fax 781-639-0840
muchado@shore.net

Robert Mueller Rare Books
8124 W 26th St.
N Riverside, IL 60546
708-447-6441

Jeffrey Lee Pressman, Bookseller
3246 Ettie St.
Oakland, CA 94608
510-652-6232

American & British
Quill & Brush
1137 Sugarloaf Mtn. Rd.
Dickerson, MD 20842
301-874-3200 or fax 301-874-0824
Firsts@qb.com

Alice Robbins, Bookseller
3002 Round Hill Rd.
Greensboro, NC 27408
910-282-1964

Scribe Company
Attn: Bonnie Smith
427 Hidden Forest S
Longview, TX 75605
903-663-6873

Especially fiction, cookery, children's, business, sports & illustrated
Eileen Serxner
Box 2544
Bala Cynwyd, PA 19004
610-664-7960
serxner@erols.com

Modern
Ed Smith Books
20 Paget Rd.
Madison, WI 53704-5929
608-241-3707 or fax 608-241-3459
ed@edsbooks.com

Spellbound Books
M. Tyree
3818 Vickie Ct. #B
Prescott Valley, AZ 86314
520-759-2625

20th-century authors of nature, natural history, 20th-century Americana, historical & nautical fiction
Town's End Books
John D. & Judy A. Townsend
132 Hemlock Dr.
Deep River, CT 06417
860-526-3896
john@townsendbooks.com

Modern; especially British & European literature
The Typographeum Bookshop
246 Bennington Rd.
Francestown, NH 03043
603-547-2425

Harrison Fisher
Parnassus Books
218 N 9th St.
Boise, ID 83702

Fishing
Artis Books
201 N Second Ave.
P.O. Box 208
Alpena, MI 49707
517-354-3401
artis@freeway.net

Edison Hall Books
5 Ventnor Dr.
Edison, NJ 08820
908-548-4455

Jim Hodgson Books
908 S Manlius St.
Fayetteville, NY 13066
315-637-6264
jimhbooks@aol.com

Melvin Marcher, Bookseller
6204 N Vermont
Oklahoma City, OK 73112

Mason's Bookstore, Rare Books & Record Albums East
115 S Main
Chambersburg, PA 17201
717-261-0541

Yesterday's Books
229 Riverview Dr.
Parchment, MI 49004
616-345-1011
yesbooks@aol.com

Florida
The Book Corner
Michael Tennaro
728 W Lumsden Rd.
Brandon, FL 33511
813-684-1133
bookcrnr@worldnet.att.net

Fore-Edge Painted Books
Susan Heller, Pages for Sages
22611 Halburton Rd.
Beachwood, OH 44122-3939
216-283-2665
hellersu@cyberdrive.net

George Robert Kane Fine Books
252 Third Ave.
Santa Cruz, CA 95062
phone/fax 408-426-4133
gkanebks@cruzio.com

Freemasonry
Mason's Bookstore, Rare Books & Record Albums East
115 S Main St.
Chambersburg, PA 17201
717-261-0541

Gambling & Gaming
Gambler's Book Shop
630 S Eleventh St.
Las Vegas, NV 89101
800-634-6243

Games
Card or board; Whist & Bridge
Bill & Mimi Sachen
927 Grand Ave.
Waukegan, IL 60085
847-662-7204
FutileWill@aol.com

Gardening
The American Botanist Booksellers
1103 W Truitt
Chillicothe, IL 61523
309-274-5254 or fax 309-274-6143
www.amerbot.com

Brooks Books
P.O. Box 91
Clayton, CA 94517
925-672-4566 or fax 925-672-3338
brooksbk@netvista.com

The Captain's Bookshelf, Inc.
31 Page Ave.
Asheville, NC 28801
828-253-6631 or fax 828-253-4917
captsbooks@aol.com

Gazetteers
Murray Hudson
Antiquarian Books & Maps
109 S Church St.
P.O. Box 163
Halls, TN 38040
901-836-9057 or 800-748-9946
fax 901-836-9017
mapman@usit.net

Genealogy
Elder's Book Store
2115 Elliston Pl.
Nashville, TN 37203
615-327-1867

General Out-of-Print
Best-Read Books
122 State St.
Sedro-Wooley, WA 98284
206-855-2179

Bicentennial Book Shop
820 S Westnedge Ave.
Kalamazoo, MI 49008
616-345-5987

The Book Baron
1236 S Magnolia Ave.
Anaheim, CA 92804
714-527-7022 or fax 714-527-5634
bkbaron1@pacbell.net or
bkbaron3@qte.net

Book Den South
2249 First St.
Ft. Myers, FL 33901
813-332-2333

Pulp fiction & modern first editions
Bookcase Books
P. Gayle Hendrington
R.R. 1 Box 242
Newport, NH 03773
603-863-9517
books@bookcasebooks.com

The Bookseller, Inc.
174 W Exchange St.
Akron, OH 44302
330-762-3101 or fax 330-762-4413
booklein@apk.com

Cinemage Books
105 W 27th St.
New York, NY 10001

Antiquarian
Eastside Books & Paper
P.O. Box 1581, Gracie Station
New York, NY 10028-0013
212-759-6299

Edison Hall Books
5 Ventnor Dr.
Edison, NJ 08820
908-548-4455

Fran's Bookhouse
6601 Greene St.
Phil., PA 19119
215-438-2729 or fax 215-438-8997

Grave Matters
P.O. Box 32192
Cincinnati, OH 45232-0192
513-242-7527 or fax 513-242-5115
books@gravematters.com
www.gravematters.com

George Robert Kane Fine Books
252 Third Ave.
Santa Cruz, CA 95062
phone/fax 408-426-4133
gkanebks@cruzio.com

McGowan Book Co.
P.O. Box 4226
Chapel Hill, NC 27515-4226
919-968-1121 or fax 919-968-1644
mcgowanbooks@mindspring.com
www.mcgowanbooks.com

Robert L. Merriam
Rare, Used & Old Books
39 New Hall Rd.
Conway, MA 01341-9709
413-369-4052
rmerriam@valinet.com

The Mulberry Cat
Yvonne Davis
Jan Davis Martel
P.O. Box 3573
Boone, NC 28607
704-963-7693

Passaic Book Center
594 Main Ave.
Passaic, NJ 07055
201-778-6646 or fax 201-778-6738

RAC Books
P.O. Box 296 RD 2
Seven Valleys, PA 17360
717-428-3776
racbooks@cyberia.com

J. Sampson Antiques & Books
107 S Main
Harrodsburg, KY 40330
606-734-7829

Significant Books
3053 Madison Rd.
P.O. Box 9248
Cincinnati, OH 45209
513-321-7567
signbook@iac.net

A.A. Vespa
P.O. Box 637
Park Ridge, IL 60068
708-692-4210

Genetics
The King's Market Bookshops
P.O. Box 709
Boulder, CO 80306-0709
303-232-3321

Geographies
Murray Hudson
Antiquarian Books & Maps
109 S Church St.
P.O. Box 163
Halls, TN 38040
901-836-9057 or 800-748-9946
fax 901-836-9017
mapman@usit.net

The Old Map Gallery
Paul F. Mahoney
1746 Blake St.
Denver, CO 80202
303-296-7725 or fax 303-296-7936
oldmapgallery@denver.net

Overlee Farm Books
P.O. Box 1155
Stockbridge, MA 01262
413-637-2277

Sue Grafton
Glo's Books & Collectibles
Gloria Stobbes
906 Shadywood
Southlake, TX 76092
817-481-1438

Thomas Books
P.O. Box 14036
Phoenix, AZ 85063
623-247-9289 or fax 480-945-1023
sales@thomasbooks.com
www.thomasbooks.com

Grand Canyon & Colorado River
Five Quail Books — West
P.O. Box 9870
Phoenix, AZ 85068-9870
602-861-0548 or fax 602-861-1113
5quail@grandcanyonbooks.com
www.grandcanyonbooks.com

The Great Lakes
Artis Books
201 N Second Ave.
P.O. Box 822
Alpena, MI 49707
517-354-3401
artis@freeway.net

Greece
W.B. O'Neill-Old & Rare Books
11609 Hunters Green Ct.
Reston, VA 20191
703-860-0782 or fax 703-620-0153
nyc1918@aol.com

Zane Grey
British Stamp Exchange
12 Fairlawn Ave.
N Weymouth, MA 02191
871-335-3075

Health
Warren's Collector Books
    For Sale Now
112 Royal Court
Friendship, TX 77546
281-482-7947

Herbals
The American Botanist Booksellers
1103 W Truitt
Chillicothe, IL 61523
309-274-5254 or fax 309-274-6143
www.amerbot.com

Brooks Books
P.O. Box 91
Clayton, CA 94517
925-672-4566 or fax 925-672-3338
brooksbk@netvista.com

Heritage Press
Lee Barnett Temares
50 Heights Rd.
Plandome, NY 11030
516-627-8688 or fax 516-627-7822
tembooks@aol.com

History
American & natural
Ace Zerblonski Books
Malcolm McCollum, Proprietor
1419 North Royer
Colorado Springs, CO 80907
719-634-3941

Science & medicine
Amaranth Books
P.O. Box 421
Wilmette, IL 60091-0421
708-328-2939

*Especially US military, US Marine Corps
   & American Civil War*
Stan Clark Military Books
915 Fairview Ave.
Gettysburg, PA 17325
717-337-1728 or 717-337-0581

Camelot Books
Charles E. Wyatt
P.O. Box 2883
Vista, CA 92083
619-940-9472

Early American & Indian
Duck Creek Books
Jim & Shirley Richards
P.O. Box 203
Caldwell, OH 43724
614-732-4856 (10 am to 10 pm)

Postal & postal artifacts
McGowan Book Co.
P.O. Box 4226
Chapel Hill, NC 27515-4226
919-968-1121 or fax 919-968-1644
mcgowanbooks@mindspring.com
www.mcgowanbooks.com

Local & regional
Significant Books
3053 Madison Rd.
P.O. Box 9248
Cincinnati, OH 45209
513-321-7567
signbook@iac.net

General, Civil & Revolutionary Wars
David R. Smith
30 Nelson Cir.
Jaffrey, NH 03452
603-532-8666
Bookinc@Cheshire.net

Twice Read Books & Comics
42 S Main St.
Chambersburg, PA 17201
717-261-8449

Hollywood
Cinemage Books
105 W 27th St.
New York, NY 10001
212-243-4919
irajoel@aol.com

Horror
The Book Baron
1236 S Magnolia Ave.
Anaheim, CA 92804
714-527-7022 or fax 714-527-5634
bkbaron1@pacbell.net or
bkbaron3@qte.net

Kai Nygaard
19421 Eighth Pl.
Escondido, CA 92029
619-746-9039

Pandora's Books, Ltd.
P.O. Box 54
Neche, ND 58265
204-324-8548 or fax 204-324-1628
jgthiess@MTS.Net

Horse Books
October Farm
2609 Branch Rd.
Raleigh, NC 27610
919-772-0482 or fax 919-779-6265
octoberfarm@bellsouth.net
www.octoberfarm.com

Horticulture
The American Botanist Booksellers
1103 W Truitt
Chillicothe, IL 61523
309-274-5254 or fax 309-274-6143
www.amerbot.com

Ornamental
Brooks Books
P.O. Box 91
Clayton, CA 94517
925-672-4566 or fax 925-672-3338
brooksbk@netvista.com

L. Ron Hubbard
AL-PAC
Lamar Kelley Antiquarian Books
2625 E Southern Ave., C-120
Tempe, AZ 85282
602-831-3121 or fax 602-831-3193
alpac2625@aol.com

Hunting
Artis Books
201 N Second Ave.
P.O. Box 822
Alpena, MI 49707
517-354-3401
artis@freeway.net

Edison Hall Books
5 Ventnor Dr.
Edison, NJ 08820
908-548-4455

Jim Hodgson Books
908 S Manlius St.
Fayetteville, NY 13066
315-637-6264
jimhbooks@aol.com

Melvin Marcher, Bookseller
6204 N Vermont
Oklahoma City, OK 73112

Yesterday's Books
229 Riverview Dr.
Parchment, MI 49004
616-345-1011
yesbooks@aol.com

Idaho
Parnassus Books
218 N 9th St.
Boise, ID 83702

Illustrated
Noreen Abbot Books
2666 44th Ave.
San Francisco, CA 94116
415-664-9464

The American Dust Co.
47 Park Ct.
Staten Island, NY 10301
phone/fax 718-442-8253

Books of the Ages
Gary J. Overmann
Maple Ridge Manor
4764 Silverwood Dr.
Batavia, OH 45103-9740
phone/fax 513-732-3456

Bromer Booksellers
607 Boylston St.
Boston, MA 02116
617-247-2818 or fax 617-247-2975
books@bromer.com
www.bromer.com

George Robert Kane Fine Books
252 Third Ave.
Santa Cruz, CA 95062
phone/fax 408-426-4133
gkanebks@cruzio.com

Randall House
Pia Oliver
835 Laguna St.
Santa Barbara, CA 93101
805-963-1909 or fax 805-963-1650
pia@piasworld.com

Barbara Smith Books
P.O. Box 1185
Northampton, MA 01061
413-586-1453

Gary R. Smith
517 Laurel Ave.
Modesto, CA 95351

Indians
Wars
K.C. & Jean Owings
Box 389
Whitman, MA 02382
781-447-7850 or fax 781-447-3435

Plains, Black Hills, etc.
Flo Silver Books
8442 Oakwood Ct. N.
Indianapolis, IN 46260
phone/fax 317-255-5118
Flosilver@aol.com

Iowa
Karl M. Armens
740 Juniper Dr.
Iowa City, IA 52245

Will James
British Stamp Exchange
12 Fairlawn Ave.
N Weymouth, MA 02191
871-335-3075

Jazz
Chartwell Booksellers
55 E 52nd St.
New York, NY 10055
212-308-0643

John Deere
Henry Lindeman
4769 Bavarian Dr.
Jackson, MI 49201
517-764-5728

Judaica
Stanley Schwartz
1934 Pentuckett Ave.
San Diego, CA 92104-5732
619-232-5888 or fax 619-233-5833
Schwartz@cts.com

Juvenile
Cover to Cover
Mark Shuman
P.O. Box 687
Chapel Hill, NC 27514
919-967-1032

Edison Hall Books
5 Ventnor Dr.
Edison, NJ 08820
908-548-4455

Susan Heller, Pages for Sages
22611 Halburton Rd.
Beachwood, OH 44122-3939
216-283-2665
hellersu@cyberdrive.net

Page Books
Margaret E. Page
HRC 65, Box 233
Kingston, AR 72742
870-861-5831
pagebook@eritter.net

Jo Ann Reisler, Ltd.
360 Glyndon St., NE
Vienna, VA 22180
703-938-2967 or fax 703-938-9057
Reisler@Clark.net

Lee Barnett Temares
50 Heights Rd.
Plandome, NY 11030
516-627-8688 or fax 516-627-7822
tembooks@aol.com

John F. Kennedy
British Stamp Exchange
12 Fairlawn Ave.
N Weymouth, MA 02191
871-335-3075

Kentucky Authors
Bill Schroeder
5801 Ky Dam Rd.
Paducah, KY 42003

Kentucky History
Bill Schroeder
5801 Ky Dam Rd.
Paducah, KY 42003

King Arthur
Also early Britain
Thorn Books
P.O. Box 1244
Moorpark, CA 93020
805-529-3647 or fax 805-529-0022
thornbooks@earthlink.net

Stephen King
Fostoria Trading Post
B. L. Foley
P.O. Box 142
Fostoria, IA 51340
712-262-5936

Labor
A\K\A Fine Used Books
4124 Brooklyn Ave. NE
Seattle, WA 98107

Volume I Books
One Union St.
Hillsdale, MI 49242
517-437-2228 or fax 517-437-7923
volume1Books@dmci.net

Lakeside Classics
Linda Holycross
109 N Sterling Ave.
Veedersburg, IN 47987
fax 765-793-2249

Landscape Architecture
The American Botanist Booksellers
1103 W Truitt
Chillicothe, IL 61523
309-274-5254 or fax 309-274-6143
www.amerbot.com

Brooks Books
P.O. Box 91
Clayton, CA 94517
925-672-4566 or fax 925-672-3338
brooksbk@netvista.com

Latin American Literature
Almark & Co.-Booksellers
P.O. Box 7
Thornhill, Ontario
Canada L3T 3N1
905-764-2665 or fax 905-764-5771
al@almarkco.com or
mark@almarkco.com

Flo Silver Books
8442 Oakwood Ct. N
Indianapolis, IN 46260
phone/fax 317-255-5118
Flosilver@aol.com

Law & Crime
Meyer Boswell Books, Inc.
2141 Mission St.
San Francisco, CA 94110
415-255-6400 or fax 415-255-6499
rarelaw@meyerbos.com

T. E. Lawrence
Denis McDonnell, Bookseller
653 Park St.
Honesdale, PA 18431-1445
570-253-6706 or fax 570-253-6786
dmd@ptd.net

Lawrence of Arabia
Denis McDonnell, Bookseller
653 Park St.
Honesdale, PA 18431-1445
570-253-6706 or fax 570-253-6786
dmd@ptd.net

Lebanon
W. B. O'Neill-Old & Rare Books
11609 Hunters Green Ct.
Reston, VA 20191
703-860-0782 or fax 703-620-0153
nyc1918@aol.com

Lewis & Clark Expedition
George H. Tweney
16660 Marine View Dr. SW
Seattle, WA 98166
206-243-8243

Literature
Amaranth Books
P.O. Box 421
Wilmette, IL 60091-0421
708-328-2939

In translation
Almark & Co.-Booksellers
P.O. Box 7
Thornhill, Ontario
Canada L3T 3N1
905-764-2665 or fax 905-764-5771
al@almarkco.com or
mark@almarkco.com

First editions
Karl M. Armens
740 Juniper Dr.
Iowa City, IA 52245

Bromer Booksellers
607 Boylston St.
Boston, MA 02116
617-247-2818 or fax 617-247-2975
books@bromer.com
www.bromer.com

18th & 19th-C English
The Book Collector
2347 University Blvd.
Houston, TX 77005
713-661-2665

African-American
Between the Covers
35 W Maple Ave.
Merchantville, NJ 08109
609-665-2284 or fax 609-665-3639
mail@betweenthecovers.com

The Captain's Bookshelf, Inc.
31 Page Ave.
Asheville, NC 22801
828-253-6631 or fax 828-253-4917
captsbooks@aol.com

Chapel Hill Rare Books
P.O. Box 456
Carrboro, NC 27510
919-929-8351
rarebooks@mindspring.com

Southern
Elder's Book Store
2115 Elliston Pl.
Nashville, TN 37203
615-327-1867

18th century
Hartfield Rare Books
Ruth Inglehart
117 Dixboro Rd.
Ann Arbor, MI 48105
phone/fax 313-662-6035

Susan Heller, Pages for Sages
22611 Halburton Rd.
Beachwood, OH 44122-3939
216-283-2665
hellersu@cyberdrive.net

Ken Lopez, Bookseller
51 Huntington Rd.
Hadley, MA 01035
413-584-4827 or fax 413-584-2045
mail@lopezbooks.com

Mason's Bookstore, Rare Books
    & Record Albums East
115 S Main St.
Chambersburg, PA 17201
717-261-0541

Much Ado
Seven Pleasant St.
Marblehead, MA 01945
781-639-0400 or fax 781-639-0840
muchado@shore.net

Also records and out-of-print comics
Twice Read Books & Comics
42 S Main St.
Chambersburg, PA 17201
717-261-8449

Magazines
Mystery only
Grave Matters
P.O. Box 32192
Cincinnati, OH 45232-0192
513-242-7527 or fax 513-242-5115
books@gravematters.com
www.gravematters.com

Robert A. Madle
4406 Bestor Dr.
Rockville, MD 20853
301-460-4712

Relating to decorative arts
Mordida Books
P.O. Box 79322
Houston, TX 77279
713-467-4280 or fax 713-467-4182
mordida@swbell.net
www.mordida.com

Passaic Book Center
594 Main Ave.
Passaic, NJ 07055
201-778-6646 or fax 201-778-6738

Manuscripts
Susan Heller, Pages for Sages
P.O. Box 2219
Beachwood, OH 44122-3939
216-283-2665
hellersu@cyberdrive.net

Heritage Book Shop, Inc.
8540 Melrose Ave.
Los Angeles, CA 90069
310-659-3674 or fax 310-659-4872
HBSINCL@aol.com

Key Books
P.O. Box 58097
St. Petersburg, FL 33715
813-867-2931

Asiatic languages
Worldwide Antiquarian
P.O. Box 410391
Cambridge, MA 02141-0004
617-876-6220 or fax 617-876-0839
mbalwan@aol.com

Randall House
Pia Oliver
835 Laguna St.
Santa Barbara, CA 93101
805-963-1909 or fax 805-963-1650
pia@piasworld.com

Maps
State, pocket-type, ca 1800s
The Bookseller, Inc.
174 W Exchange St.
Akron, OH 44302
330-762-3101 or fax 330-762-4413
booklein@apk.com

Elegant Book & Map Company
815 Harrison Ave.
P.O. Box 1302
Cambridge, OH 43725
614-432-4068

Maritime
*Including pirates, treasure, shipwrecks, the
    Caribbean, Cuba & Panama*
The Book Corner
Michael Tennaro
728 W Lumsden Rd.
Brandon, FL 33511
813-684-1133
bookcrnr@worldnet.att.net

Book & Tackle Shop
29 Old Colony Rd.
P.O. Box 114
Chestnut Hill, MA 02467
phone/fax 617-965-0459
bktack@ibm.net

Overlee Farm Books
P.O. Box 1155
Stockbridge, MA 01262
413-637-2277

J. Tuttle Maritime Books
1806 Laurel Crest
Madison, WI 53705
608-238-SAIL (7245)
fax 608-238-7249

Martial Arts
Nutmeg Books
354 New Litchfield St. (Rte. 202)
Torrington, CT 06790
203-482-9696
nutmeg@compsol.net

Masonic History
Mason's Bookstore, Rare Books
    & Record Albums East
115 S Main St.
Chambersburg, PA 17201
717-261-0541

Mathematics
Significant Books
3053 Madison Rd.
P.O. Box 9248
Cincinnati, OH 45209
513-321-7567
signbook@iac.net

Cormac McCarthy
Alice Robbins, Bookseller
3002 Round Hill Rd.
Greensboro, NC 27408
910-282-1964

Medicine
Amaranth Books
P.O. Box 421
Wilmette, IL 60091-0421
708-328-2939

Antiquarian
Book & Tackle
29 Old Colony Rd.
P.O. Box 114
Chestnut Hill, MA 02467
phone/fax 617-965-0459
bktack@ibm.net

W. Bruce Fye
1607 N Wood Ave.
Marshfield, WI 54449-1298
715-384-8128 or fax 715-389-2990
byfe@tznet.com

Procedures before 1915
Ron Gibson, The Bookshop
110 Windsor Cir.
Burlington, IA 52601-1477
319-752-4588

Key Books
P.O. Box 58097
St. Petersburg, FL 33715
813-867-2931

M&S Rare Books, Inc.
P.O. Box 2594, E Side Station
Providence, RI 02906
401-421-1050 or fax 401-272-0831
(attention M & S)
dsiegel@msrarebooks.com

Medieval
Camelot Books
Charles E. Wyatt
P.O. Box 2883
Vista, CA 92083
619-940-9472

Metaphysics
AL-PAC
Lamar Kelley Antiquarian Books
2625 E Southern Ave., C-120
Tempe, AZ 85282
602-831-3121 or fax 602-831-3193
alpac2625@aol.com

Meteorology
Knollwood Books
Lee & Peggy Price
P.O. Box 197
Oregon, WI 53575-0197
608-835-8861 or fax 608-835-8421
books@tdsnet.com

Mexico
Flo Silver Books
8442 Oakwood Ct. N
Indianapolis, IN 46260
phone/fax 317-255-5118
Flosilver@aol.com

Michigan
Artis Books
201 N Second Ave.
P.O. Box 822
Alpena, MI 49707
517-354-3401
artis@freeway.net

Yesterday's Books
229 Riverview Dr.
Parchment, MI 49004
616-345-1011
yesbooks@aol.com

Middle Eastern Countries
Denis McDonnell, Bookseller
653 Park St.
Honesdale, PA 18431-1445
570-253-6706 or fax 570-253-6786
dmd@ptd.net

Levant countries: travel, archaeology, history; Byzantine studies
Quest Books
Peter & Veronica Burridge
Harmer Hill
Millington
York YO42 1TX UK
Quesbks@aol.com

Worldwide Antiquarian
P.O. Box 410391
Cambridge, MA 02141-0004
617-876-6220 or fax 617-876-0839
mbalwan@aol.com

Militaria
The Bookseller, Inc.
174 W Exchange St.
Akron, OH 44302
330-762-3101 or fax 330-762-4413
booklein@apk.com

Edison Hall Books
5 Ventnor Dr.
Edison, NJ 08820
908-548-4455

Rick Harmon
Military Books & Relics
910 Sullivan Dr.
Belvidere, IL 61008
815-547-7580

Robert L. Merriam
Rare, Used & Old Books
39 Newhall Rd.
Conway, MA 01341-9709
413-369-4052
rmerriam@valinet.com

Significant Books
3053 Madison Rd.
P.O Box 9248
Cincinnati, OH 45209
513-321-7567
signbook@iac.net

Histories Before 1900
Tryon County Bookshop
2071 State Hwy. 29
Johnstown, NY 12905
518-762-1060

Volume I Books
One Union St.
Hillsdale, MI 49242
517-437-2228 or fax 517-437-7923
volume1Books@dmci.net

Miniature Books
Bromer Booksellers
607 Boylston St.
Boston, MA 02116
617-247-2818 or fax 617-247-2975
books@bromer.com
www.bromer.com

Foreign atlases
Murray Hudson
Antiquarian Books & Maps
109 S Church St.
P.O. Box 163
Halls, TN 38040
901-836-9057 or 800-748-9946
fax 901-836-9017
mapman@usit.net

Hurley Books/Celtic Cross Books
1753 Rt. 12
Westmoreland, NH 03467-4724
603-399-4342 or fax 603-399-8326
hurleybook@adam.cheshire.net

Gary R. Smith
517 Laurel Ave.
Modesto, CA 95351

Movies
Cinemage Books
105 W 27th St.
New York, NY 10001
212-243-4919
irajoel@aol.com

The American Dust Co.
47 Park Ct.
Staten Island, NY 10301
phone/fax 718-442-8253

Mysteries
Alcott Books
Barbara Ruppert
5909 Darnell
Houston, TX 77074-7719
713-774-2202

The American Dust Co.
47 Park Ct.
Staten Island, NY 10301
phone/fax 718-442-8253

Karl M. Armens
740 Juniper Dr.
Iowa City, IA 52245

First editions
Island Books
P.O. Box 19
Old Westbury, NY 11568
516-759-0233

McGee's First Varieties
330 Franklin Rd., Suite 135
Brentwood, TN 37027
615-373-5318
TMcGee@BellSouth.net

Mordida Books
P.O. Box 79322
Houston, TX 77279
713-467-4280 or fax 713-467-4182
mordida@swbell.net
www.mordida.com

mail order; primarily first editions
Norris Books
2491 San Ramon Vly. Blvd.
Suite #1-201
San Ramon, CA 94583
phone/fax 925-867-1218
norrisbooks@slip.net

Pandora's Books, Ltd.
P.O. Box 54
Neche, ND 48265
204-324-8548 or fax 204-324-1628
jgthiess@MTS.Net

RAC Books
P.O. Box 296 RD 2
Seven Valleys, PA 17360
717-428-3776
racbooks@cyberia.com

The Silver Door
P.O. Box 3208
Redondo Beach, CA 90277
310-379-6005

W.J. Leveridge
W & L Trading Company
2301 Carova Rd.
Carova Beach, Corolla, NC 27927
252-453-3408

Napoleonic Memorabilia
The Book Collector
2347 University Blvd.
Houston, TX 7005
713-661-2665

Narcotics
Nutmeg Books
354 New Litchfield St. (Rte. 202)
Torrington, CT 06790
203-482-9696
nutmeg@compsol.net

Natural History
Agave Books
P.O. Box 31495
Mesa, AZ 85275-1495
602-649-9097

Thomas C. Bayer
85 Reading Ave.
Hillsdale, MI 49242
517-439-4134 or fax 517-439-5661
bayerbooks@dmci.net

Noriko I. Ciochon
Natural History Books
1025 Keokut St.
Iowa City, IA 52240-3303
319-354-9088 or fax 319-354-0844
nathist@avalon.net

Melvin Marcher, Bookseller
6204 N Vermont
Oklahoma City, OK 73112

Snowy Egret Books
1237 Carroll Ave.
St. Paul, MN 55104
612-641-0917
snowy@mr.net

Nautical
Much Ado
Seven Pleasant St.
Marblehead, MA 01945
781-639-0400 or fax 781-639-0840
muchado@shore.net

Overlee Farm Books
P.O. Box 1155
Stockbridge, MA 01262
413-637-2277

Needlework
Galerie De Boicourt
251 E Merrill St.
Birmingham, MI 48009
248-723-5680

Stanley Schwartz
1934 Pentuckett Ave.
San Diego, CA 92104-5732
619-232-5888 or fax 619-233-5833
Schwartz@cts.com

Neuroscience
John Gach Books
10514 Marriottsville Rd.
Randallstown, MD 21133
410-465-9023 or fax 410-465-0649
jgach@clark.net
www.gach.com

New England
Book & Tackle
29 Old Colony Rd.
P.O. Box 114
Chestnut Hill, MA 02467
phone/fax 617-965-0459
bktack@ibm.net

Newspapers & Periodicals
Significant & unusual American
Periodyssey
151 Crescent St.
Northampton, MA 01060
413-527-1900 or fax 413-527-1930

Randall House
Pia Oliver
835 Laguna St.
Santa Barbara, CA 93101
805-963-1909 or fax 805-963-1650
pia@piasworld.com

Thorn Books
P.O. Box 1244
Moorpark, CA 93020
805-529-3647 or fax 805-529-0022
thornbooks@earthlink.net

Wellerdt's Books
3700 S Osprey Ave. #214
Sarasota, FL 34239
813-365-1318

Xanadu Records, Ltd.
3242 Irwin Ave.
Kingsbridge, NY 10463
212-549-3655

Nonfiction
Warren's Collector Books
    For Sale Now
112 Royal Court
Friendship, TX 77546
281-482-7947

Novels
The Silver Door
P.O. Box 3208
Redondo Beach, CA 90277
310-379-6005

Occult & Mystics
AL-PAC
Lamar Kelley Antiquarian Books
2625 E Southern Ave., C-120
Tempe, AZ 85282
602-831-3121 or fax 602-831-3193
alpac2625@aol.com

British Stamp Exchange
12 Fairlawn Ave.
N Weymouth, MA 02191
871-335-3075

Ohio
The Bookseller, Inc.
174 W Exchange St.
Akron, OH 44302
330-762-3101 or fax 330-762-4413
booklein@apk.com

Omar Khayyam
Worldwide Antiquarian
P.O. Box 410391
Cambridge, MA 02141-0004
617-876-6220 or fax 617-876-0839
mbalwan@aol.com

Oriental Books & Art
Ruth Woods Oriental Books
266 Arch Rd.
Englewood, NJ 07631
201-567-0149 or fax 201-567-1419

Original Art
By children's illustrators
Kendra Krienke
230 Central Park West
New York, NY 10024
201-930-9709 or 201-930-9765

Paperbacks
Michael Gerlicher
1375 Rest Point Rd.
Orono, MN 55364

Bernard E. Goodman, Bookseller
7421 SW 147 Ct.
Miami, FL 33193
305-385-8526
BCBooks@bellsouth.net

Vintage
Grave Matters
P.O. Box 32192
Cincinnati, OH 45232-0192
513-242-7527 or fax 513-242-5115
books@gravematters.com
www.gravematters.com

Also pulp magazines
Modern Age Books
P.O. Box 325
E. Lansing, MI 48826
517-487-9313

Originals
Mordida Books
P.O. Box 79322
Houston, TX 77279
713-467-4280 or fax 713-467-4182
mordida@swbell.net
www.mordida.com

Olde Current Books
Daniel P. Shay
356 Putnam Ave.
Ormond Beach, FL 32174
904-672-8998
peakmyster@aol.com

Pandora's Books, Ltd.
P.O. Box 54
Neche, ND 58265
204-324-8548 or fax 204-324-1628
jgthiess@MTS.Net

Also trades; want lists welcomed
Roger Reus
9412 Huron Ave.
Richmond, VA 23294
Mail order only

Tom Rolls
230 S Oakland Ave.
Indianapolis, IN 46201

Andrew Zimmerli
5001 General Branch Ct.
Sharpsburg, MD 21781
301-432-7476

Robert B. Parker
Thomas Books
P.O. Box 14036
Phoenix, AZ 85063
623-247-9289 or fax 480-945-1023
sales@thomasbooks.com
www.thomasbooks.com

Pennsylvania
Mason's Bookstore, Rare Books
    & Record Albums East
115 S Main
Chambersburg, PA 17201
717-261-0541

Philosophy
John Gach Books
10514 Marriottsville Rd.
Randallstown, MD 21133
410-465-9023 or fax 410-465-0649
jgach@clark.net
www.gach.com

Photography
The Captain's Bookshelf, Inc.
31 Page Ave.
Asheville, NC 28801
828-253-6631 or fax 828-253-4917
captsbooks@aol.com

Significant Books
3053 Madison Rd.
P.O. Box 9248
Cincinnati, OH 45209
513-321-7567
signbook@iac.net

19th-C Middle & Far East Countries
Worldwide Antiquarian
P.O. Box 410391
Cambridge, MA 02141-0004
617-876-6220 or fax 617-876-0839
mbalwan@aol.com

Xanadu Records Ltd.
3242 Irwin Ave.
Kingsbridge, NY 10463
718-549-3655

Playing Cards
Bill & Mimi Sachen
927 Grand Ave.
Waukegan, IL 60085
847-662-7204
FutileWill@aol.com

Poetry
The American Dust Co.
47 Park Ct.
Staten Island, NY 10301
phone/fax 718-442-8253

Edison Hall Books
5 Ventnor Dr.
Edison, NJ 08820
908-548-4455

Ed Smith Books
20 Paget Rd.
Madison, WI 53704-5929
608-241-3707 or fax 608-241-3459
ed@edsbooks.com

David R. Smith
30 Nelson Cir.
Jaffrey, NH 03452
603-532-8666
Bookinc@Cheshire.net

VERSEtility Books
P.O. Box 1133
Farmington, CT 06034-1133
860-677-0606
versebks@tiac.net

Polar Explorations & Ephemera
Alaskan Heritage Bookshop
174 S Franklin, P.O. 22165
Juneau, AK 99802

Parmer Books
7644 Forrestal Rd.
San Diego, CA 92120-2203
619-287-0693 or fax 619-287-6135
ParmerBook@aol.com

Political
Realm of Colorado
P.O. Box 24
Parker, CO 80134

Radical
Volume I Books
One Union St.
Hillsdale, MI 49242
517-437-2228 or fax 517-437-7923
volume1Books@dmci.net

Postcards
Book & Tackle Shop
29 Old Colony Rd.
P.O. Box 114
Chestnut Hill, MA 02467
phone/fax 617-965-0459
bktack@ibm.net

Posters
The Mulberry Cat
Yvonne Davis
Jan Davis Martel
P.O. Box 3573
Boone, NC 28607
704-963-7693

Pre-Colombian Art
Flo Silver Books
8442 Oakwood Ct. N.
Indianapolis, IN 46260
phone/fax 317-255-5118
Flosilver@aol.com

Press Books
Heritage Book Shop, Inc.
8540 Melrose Ave.
Los Angeles, CA 90069
310-659-3674 or fax 310-659-4872
HBSINCLA@aol.com

Randall House
Pia Oliver
835 Laguna St.
Santa Barbara, CA 93101
805-963-1909 or fax 805-963-1650
pia@piasworld.com

Prints
The Mulberry Cat
Yvonne Davis
Jan Davis Martel
P.O. Box 3573
Boone, NC 28607
704-963-7693

Private Presses
First Folio
1206 Brentwood
Paris, TN 34842
phone/fax 901-644-9940
firstfol@aeneas.net

Susan Heller, Pages for Sages
22611 Halburton Rd.
Beachwood, OH 44122-3939
216-283-2665
hellersu@cyberdrive.net

**Promoters of Paper, Ephemera &
    Book Fairs**
Kingsbury Productions
Katherine and David Kreider
4555 N Pershing Ave., Suite 33-138
Stockton, CA 95207
209-467-8438

Psychedelia
Nutmeg Books
354 New Litchfield St. (Rte. 202)
Torrington, CT 06790
203-482-9696
nutmeg@compsol.net

Psychiatry

John Gach Books
10514 Marriottsville Rd.
Randallstown, MD 21133
410-465-9023 or fax 410-465-0649
jgach@clark.net
www.gach.com

Psychoanalysis

Also related subjects
John Gach Books
10514 Marriottsville Rd.
Randallstown, MD 21133
410-465-9023 or fax 410-465-0649
jgach@clark.net
www.gach.com

Psychology

John Gach Books
10514 Marriottsville Rd.
Randallstown, MD 21133
410-465-9023 or fax 410-465-0649
jgach@clark.net
www.gach.com

The King's Market Bookshops
P.O. Box 709
Boulder, CO 80306-0709
303-232-3321

Pulps

Science fiction & fantasy before 1945
Robert A. Madle
4406 Bestor Dr.
Rockville, MD 20853
301-460-4712

Quaker

Vintage Books
181 Hayden Rowe St.
Hopkinton, MA 01748
508-435-3499
vintage@gis.net

Also Shakers, Christians & Collectivists
Duck Creek Books
Jim & Shirley Richards
P.O. Box 203
Caldwell, OH 43724
614-732-4856 (10 am to 10 pm)

Quilt Books

Bill Schroeder
5801 Ky Dam Rd.
Paducah, KY 42003

Galerie De Boicourt
251 E Merrill St.
Birmingham, MI 48009
248-723-5680

R.R. Donnelley Christmas Books

Linda Holycross
109 N Sterling Ave.
Veedersburg, IN 47987
fax 765-793-2249

Arthur Rackham

Books of the Ages
Gary J. Overmann
Maple Ridge Manor
4764 Silverwood Dr.
Batavia, OH 45103-9740
phone/fax 513-732-3456

Railroading

Mason's Bookstore, Rare Books
    & Record Albums
115 S Main St.
Chambersburg, PA 17201
717-261-0541

Rare & Unusual Books

Chapel Hill Rare Books
P.O. Box 456
Carrboro, NC 27510
919-929-8351
rarebooks@mindspring.com

First Folio
1206 Brentwood
Paris, TN 38242
phone/fax 901-644-9940
firstfol@aeneas.net

Terry Harper, Bookseller
P.O. Box 312
Vergennes, VT 05491-0312
802-877-9262
bookvend@together.net

Susan Heller, Pages for Sages
22611 Halburton Rd.
Beachwood, OH 44122-3939
216-283-2665
hellersu@cyberdrive.net

Heritage Book Shop, Inc.
8540 Melrose Ave.
Los Angeles, CA 90069
310-659-3674 or fax 310-659-4872
HBSINCLA@aol.com

Kenneth Karmiole, Bookseller, Inc.
509 Wilshire Blvd.
Santa Monica, CA 94001
310-451-4342 or 310-458-5930
karmbooks@aol.com

M & S Rare Books, Inc.
P.O. Box 2594, E Side Station
Providence, RI 02906
401-421-1050 or fax 401-272-0831
(attention M & S)
dsiegel@msrarebooks.com

Paul Melzer Fine Books
12 E Vine St.
P.O. Box 1143
Redlands, CA 92373
909-792-7299 or fax 909-793-7218
pmbooks@eee.org

The Old London Bookshop
Michael & Marlys Schon
P.O. Box 922
Bellingham, WA 98227-0922
360-733-7273 or fax 360-647-8946
OldLondon@aol.com

Richard C. Ramer
Old & Rare Books
225 E 70th St.
New York, NY 10021
212-737-0222 or 212-737-0223
fax 212-288-4169
5222386@mcimail.com

Revere Books
P.O. Box 420
Revere, PA 18953
610-847-2709 or fax 610-847-1910

Leona Rostenberg
    & Madeleine Stern
Rare Books
40 E 88th St.
NY, NY 10128
212-831-6628 or fax 212-831-1961

Thorn Books
P.O. Box 1244
Moorpark, CA 93020
805-529-3647 or fax 805-529-0022
thornbooks@earthlink.net

Reference

About Books
6 Sand Hill Ct.
P.O. Box 5717
Parsippany, NY 07054
973-515-4591

Religion

Books Now & Then
Dennis & Jan Patrick
P.O. Box 337
Stanley, ND 58784
phone/fax 701-628-2084
bnt@stanley.ndak.net

Chimney Sweep Books
419 Cedar St.
Santa Cruz, CA 94060-4304
phone/fax 408-458-1044
chimney@cruzio.com

David R. Smith
30 Nelson Cir.
Jaffrey, NH 03452
603-532-8666
Bookinc@Cheshire.net

Reptiles

Mason's Bookstore, Rare Books
    & Record Albums East
115 S Main St.
Chambersburg, PA 17201
717-261-0541

Revolutionary War

K.C. & Jean Owings
Box 389
Whitman, MA 02382
781-447-7850 or fax 781-447-3435

Science & Technology

Thomas C. Bayer
85 Reading Ave.
Hillsdale, MI 49242
517-439-4134 or fax 517-439-5661
bayerbooks@dmci.net

Book & Tackle Shop
29 Old Colony Rd.
P.O. Box 114
Chestnut Hill, MA 02467
phone/fax 617-965-0459
bktack@ibm.net

Thomas L. Coffman, Bookseller
TLC Books
9 N College Ave.
Salem, VA 24153
540-389-3555

Key Books
P.O. Box 58097
St. Petersburg, FL 33715
813-867-2931

M & S Rare Books, Inc.
P.O. Box 2594, E Side Station
Providence, RI 02906
401-272-0831 or fax 401-272-0831
(attention M & S)
dsiegel@msrarebooks.com

Science Fiction

AL-PAC
Lamar Kelley Antiquarian Books
2625 E Southern Ave., C-120
Tempe, AZ 85282
602-831-3121 or fax 602-831-3193
alpac2625@aol.com

Also Fantasy
Ackley Books & Collectibles
Bryant & Suzanne Pitner
912 Hidden Cove Way
Suisun City, CA 94585-3511
707-421-9032 or fax 979-285-6554
(mail order only)

The American Dust Co.
47 Park Ct.
Staten Island, NY 10301
phone/fax 718-442-8253

Karl M. Armens
740 Juniper Dr.
Iowa City, IA 52245

Bernard E. Goodman, Bookseller
7421 SW 147 Ct.
Miami, FL 33193
305-385-8526
BCBooks@bellsouth.net

First editions
Island Books
P.O. Box 19
Old Westbury, NY 11568
516-759-0233

Horror & Occult
Bob Lakin Books
P.O. Box 186
Chatfield, TX 75105
972-247-3291

Robert A. Madle
4406 Bestor Dr.
Rockville, MD 20853
301-460-4712

McGee's First Varieties
330 Franklin Rd., Suite 135
Brentwood, TN 37027
615-373-5318
TMcGee@BellSouth.net

Also fantasy
Kai Nygaard
19421 Eighth Pl.
Escondido, CA 92029
619-746-9039

Pandora's Books, Ltd.
P.O. Box 54
Neche, ND 58265
204-324-8548 or fax 204-324-1628
jgthiess@MTS.Net

Also fantasy
Xanadu Records, Ltd.
3242 Irwin Ave.
Kingsbridge, NY 10463
212-549-3655

Sciences

Cover to Cover
P.O. Box 687
Chapel Hill, NC 27514

Significant Books
P.O. Box 9248
3053 Madison Rd.
Cincinnati, OH 45209
513-321-7567
signbook@iac.net

Series Books

Glo's Children's Series Books
Gloria Stobbes
906 Shadywood
Southlake, TX 76092
817-481-1438

Set Editions

AL-PAC
Lamar Kelley Antiquarian Books
2625 E Southern Ave., C-120
Tempe, AZ 85282
602-831-3121 or fax 602-831-3193
alpac2625@aol.com

Sherlockiana

The Silver Door
P.O. Box 3208
Redondo Beach, CA 90277
310-379-6005

Ships & Sea

Book & Tackle Shop
29 Old Colony Rd.
P.O. Box 114
Chestnut Hill, MA 02467
phone/fax 617-965-0459
bktack@ibm.net

Parmer Books
7644 Forrestal Rd.
San Diego, CA 92120-2203
619-287-0693 or fax 619-287-6135
ParmerBook@aol.com

J. Tuttle Maritme Books
1806 Laurel Crest
Madison, WI 53705
608-238-SAIL (7245)
fax 608-238-7249

Signed Editions

Chapel Hill Rare Books
P.O. Box 456
Carrboro, NC 27510
919-929-8351
rarebooks@mindspring.com

Dan Simmons

Thomas Books
P.O. Box 14036
Phoenix, AZ 85063
623-247-9289 or fax 480-945-1023
sales@thomasbooks.com
www.thomasbooks.com

Socialism

Volume I Books
One Union St.
Hillsdale, MI 49242
517-437-2228 or fax 517-437-7923
volume1Books@dmci.net

South America

Flo Silver Books
8442 Oakwood Ct. N
Indianapolis, IN 46260
phone/fax 317-255-5118
Flosilver@aol.com

South Dakota
Also any pre-1970 Western-related books
James F. Taylor
515 Sixth St.
Rapid City, SD 57701
605-341-3224

Space Exploration
Knollwood Books
Lee & Peggy Price
P.O. Box 197
Oregon, WI 53575-0197
608-835-8861 or fax 608-835-8421
books@tdsnet.com

Speciality Publishers
Arkham House, Gnome, Fantasy, etc.
Robert A. Madle
4406 Bestor Dr.
Rockville, MD 20853
301-460-4712

Sports
Baseball or boxing
Ace Zerblonski Books
Malcolm McCollum, Proprietor
1419 North Royer
Colorado Springs, CO 80907
719-634-3941

Adelson Sports
13610 N Scottsdale Rd. #10
Scottsdale, AZ 85254
602-596-1913 or fax 602-598-1914

Rising Stars
Don Carnahan
P.O. Box 2991
Yuma, AZ 85366
Phone/fax 520-329-6054

Thomas L. Coffman, Bookseller
TLC Books
9 N College Ave.
Salem, VA 24153
540-389-3555

Rare & out-of-print baseball; general
R. Plapinger, Baseball Books
P.O. Box 1062
Ashland, OR 97520
541-488-1220

Randall House
Pia Oliver
835 Laguna St.
Santa Barbara, CA 93101
805-963-1909 or fax 805-963-1650
pia@piasworld.com

Statue of Liberty
Mike Brooks
7335 Skyline
Oakland, CA 94611

Surveying
Also tools, instruments & ephemera
David & Nancy Garcelon
10 Hastings Ave.
Millbury, MA 01527-4314
508-754-2667

Technology
Thomas C. Bayer
85 Reading Ave.
Hillsdale, MI 49242
517-439-4134 or fax 517-439-5661
bayerbooks@dmci.net

Cover to Cover
P.O. Box 687
Chapel Hill, NC 27514

Significant Books
3053 Madison Rd.
P.O. Box 9248
Cincinnati, OH 45209
513-321-7567
signbook@iac.net

Tennessee History
Elder's Book Store
2115 Elliston Pl.
Nashville, TN 37203
615-327-1867

Texana Fiction & Authors
Alcott Books
Barbara Ruppert
5909 Darnell
Houston, TX 77074-7719
713-774-2202

Bob Lakin Books
P.O. Box 186
Chatfield, TX 75105
972-247-3291

Textiles
Galerie De Boicourt
251 E Merrill St.
Birmingham, MI 48009
248-723-5680

Stanley Schwartz
1934 Pentuckett Ave.
San Diego, CA 92104-5732
619-232-5888 or fax 619-233-5833
Schwartz@cts.com

Theology
Books Now & Then
Dennis & Jan Patrick
P.O. Box 337
Stanley, ND 58784
phone/fax 701-628-2084
bnt@stanley.ndak.net

Chimney Sweep Books
419 Cedar St.
Santa Cruz, CA 94060-4304
phone/fax 408-458-1044
chimney@cruzio.com

Hurley Books/Celtic Cross Books
1753 Rt. 12
Westmoreland, NH 03467-4724
603-399-4342 or fax 603-399-8326
hurleybook@adam.cheshire.net

Trade Catalogs
Eastside Books & Paper
P.O. Box 1581, Gracie Station
New York, NY 10028-0013
212-759-6299

Trades & Crafts
19th Century
Cover to Cover
P.O. Box 687
Chapel Hill, NC 27514

Hillcrest Books
961 Deep Draw Rd.
Crossville, TN 38555-9547
phone/fax 931-484-7680
hillcrst@usit.net

Travel
19th-century travel & adventure
The Book Corner
Michael Tennaro
728 W Lumsden Rd.
Brandon, FL 33511
813-684-1133
bookcrnr@worldnet.att.net

Also exploration
Duck Creek Books
Jim & Shirley Richards
P.O. Box 203
Caldwell, OH 43724
614-732-4856 (10 am to 10 pm)

Terry Harper, Bookseller
P.O. Box 312
Vergennes, VT 05491-0312
802-877-9262
bookvend@together.net

Heritage Book Shop, Inc.
8540 Melrose Ave.
Los Angeles, CA 90069
310-659-3674 or fax 310-659-4872
HBSINCLA@aol.com

Jim Hodgson Books
908 S Manlius St.
Fayetteville, NY 13066
315-637-6264
jimhbooks@aol.com

Flo Silver Books
8442 Oakwood Ct. N
Indianapolis, IN 46260
phone/fax 317-255-5118
Flosilver@aol.com

Tasha Tudor
Books of the Ages
Gary J. Overmann
Maple Ridge Manor
4764 Silverwood Dr.
Batavia, OH 45103-9740
phone/fax 513-732-3456

Turkey
W.B. O'Neill-Old & Rare Books
11609 Hunters Green Ct.
Reston, VA 20191
703-860-0782 or fax 703-620-0153
nyc1918@aol.com

UFO
AL-PAC
Lamar Kelley Antiquarian Books
2625 E Southern Ave., C-120
Tempe, AZ 85282
602-831-3121 or fax 602-831-3193
alpac2625@aol.com

Vargas
Parnassus Books
218 N 9th St.
Boise, ID 83702

Vietnam War
A\K\A Fine Used Books
4124 Brooklyn Ave. NE
Seattle, WA 98107
206-632-5870

Thomas L. Coffman, Bookseller
TLC Books
9 N College Ave.
Salem, VA 24153
540-389-3555

Rick Harmon
Military Books & Relics
910 Sullivan Dr.
Belvidere, IL 61008
815-547-7580

Voyages, Exploration & Travel
Chapel Hill Rare Books
P.O. Box 456
Carrboro, NC 27510
919-929-8351
rarebooks@mindspring.com

Terry Harper, Bookseller
P.O. Box 312
Vergennes, VT 05491-0312
802-877-9262
bookvend@together.net

Heritage Book Shop, Inc.
8540 Melrose Ave.
Los Angeles, CA 90069
310-659-3674 or fax 310-659-4872
HBSINCLA@aol.com

Jim Hodgson Books
908 S Manlius St.
Fayetteville, NY 13066
315-637-6264
jimhbooks@aol.com

Key Books
P.O. Box 58097
St. Petersburg, FL 33715
813-867-2931

Overlee Farm Books
P.O. Box 1155
Stockbridge, MA 01262
413-627-2277

George H. Tweney
16660 Marine View Dr. SW
Seattle, WA 98166
206-243-8243

Weapons
All edged types
Knife Readables
115 Longfellow Blvd.
Lakeland, FL 33810
813-666-1133

Western Americana
Dawson's Book Shop
535 N Larchmont Blvd.
Los Angeles, CA 90004
323-469-2186 or fax 323-469-9553
dawsonbk@ix.netcom.com
www.dawsonbooks.com

Terry Harper, Bookseller
P.O. Box 312
Vergennes, VT 05491-0312
802-877-9262
bookvend@together.net

Rare & historical ephemera
Jordon Book Gallery
1349 Sheridan Ave.
Cody, WY 82414
307-587-6689 or fax 307-527-4944

K.C. & Jean Owings
Box 389
Whitman, MA 02382
781-447-7850 or fax 781-447-3435

Thorn Books
P.O. Box 1244
Moorpark, CA 93020
805-529-3647 or fax 805-529-0022
thornbooks@earthlink.net

George H. Tweney
16660 Marine View Dr. SW
Seattle, WA 98166
206-243-8243

Nonfiction 19th-C outlaws, lawmen, etc.
The Early West/Whodunit Books
P.O. Box 9292
College Sta., TX 77842
409-775-6047 or fax 409-764-7758
EarlyWest@aol.com

Wine
Second Harvest Books
Warren R. Johnson
P.O. Box 3306
Florence, OR 97439-3306
phone/fax 541-902-0215
2harvest@presys.com

Warren's Collector Books
   For Sale Now
112 Royal Ct.
Friendswood, TX 77546
281-482-7947

Women Authors
Alice Robbins, Bookseller
3002 Round Hill Rd.
Greensboro, NC 27408
910-282-1964

Women's History
Also related areas of everyday life
An Uncommon Vision
1425 Greywall Ln.
Wynnewood, PA 19096-3811
610-658-0953 or fax 610-658-0961
Uncommvisn@aol.com

Volume I Books
One Union St.
Hillsdale, MI 49242
517-437-2228 or fax 517-437-7923
volume1Books@dmci.net

World War I
Denis McDonnell, Bookseller
653 Park St.
Honesdale, PA 18431-1445
570-253-6706 or fax 570-253-6786
dmd@ptd.net

World War II
Cover to Cover
P.O. Box 687
Chapel Hill, NC 27514

Booksellers

This section of the book lists names and addresses of used book dealers who have contributed the retail listings contained in this edition of *Huxford's Old Book Value Guide*. The code (A1, S7, etc.) located before the price in our listings refers to the dealer offering that particular book for sale. (When more than one dealer has the same book listing codes are given alphabetically before the price.) Given below are the dealer names and their codes.

Many bookdealers issue printed catalogs, list catalogs on the internet, have open shops, are mail order only, or may be a combination of these forms of business. When seeking a book from a particular dealer, it would be best to first write (enclose SASE), e-mail, or call to see what type of business is operated (open shop or mail order).

A1
A-Book-A-Brac Shop
6760 Collins Ave.
Miami Beach, FL 33141
305-865-0092

A2
Aard Books
31 Russell Ave.
Troy, NH 03465
603-242-3638
aardbooks@cheshire.net

A3
Noreen Abbot Books
2666 44th Ave.
San Francisco, CA 94116-2635
415-664-9464

A4
About Books
6 Sand Hill Ct.
P.O. Box 5717
Parsippany, NJ 07054
973-515-4591

A5
Adelson Sports
13610 N Scottsdale Rd. #10
Scottsdale, AZ 85254
480-596-1913 or fax 480-596-1914
www.adelsonsports.com

A6
Ads Autographs
P.O. Box 8006
Webster, NY 14580-8006
716-671-2651 or fax 716-671-5727

A7
Avonlea Books Search Service
P.O. Box 74, Main Station
White Plains, NY 10602-0074
914-946-5923 or fax 914-761-3119
avonlea@bushkin.com

A8
AL-PAC
Lamar Kelley Antiquarian Books
2625 E Southern Ave., C-120
Tempe, AZ 85282
602-831-3121 or fax 602-831-3193
alpac2625@aol.com

A9
Amaranth Books
P.O. Box 421
Wilmette, IL 60091-0421
708-328-2939

A10
The American Botanist
P.O. Box 532
Chillicothe, IL 61523
309-274-5254 or fax 309-274-6143
www.americanbotanist.com

A11
The American Dust Co.
47 Park Ct.
Staten Island, NY 10301
phone/fax 718-442-8253

A13
Antiquarian Medical Books
W. Bruce Fye
1607 N Wood Ave.
Marshfield, WI 54449-1298
715-384-8128 or fax 715-389-2990
bfye@tznet.com

A14
Almark & Co.-Booksellers
P.O. Box 7
Thornhill, Ontario
Canada L3T 3N1
905-764-2665 or fax 905-764-5771
al@almarkco.com or
mark@almarkco.com

A15
Karl M. Armens
740 Juniper Dr.
Iowa City, IA 52245
319-337-7755

A16
Arnold's of Michigan
Judith A. Herba
218 South Water St.
Marine City, MI 48039 -1688
810-765-1350 / 800-276-3092
fax 810-765-7914
arnoldbk@ees.eesc.com

A17
Artis Books
201 N Second Ave.
P.O. Box 822
Alpena, MI 49707-0822
517-354-3401
artis@freeway.net

A18
Authors of the West
191 Dogwood Dr.
Dundee, OR 97115
503-538-8132
Lnash@georgefox.edu

A19
Aplan Antiques & Art
James & Peg Aplan
21424 Clover Pl.
Piedmont, SD 57769-9403
605-347-5016 or fax 605-347-9336
alpanpeg@rapidnet.com

A20
Ace Zerblonski Books
Malcolm McCollum, Proprietor
1419 North Royer
Colorado Springs, CO 80907
719-634-3941

A21
Artiques Ltd.
Veronica Jochens
P.O. Box 67
Lonedell, MO 60360
phone/fax 314-629-1374
veronica@nightowl.net

A22
Agave Books
P.O. Box 31495
Mesa, AZ 85275-1495
602-649-9097

A23
Alcott Books
5909 Darnell
Houston, TX 77074-7719
713-774-2202

A24

A Tale of Two Sisters
1401 Emerald Circle
Southlake, TX 76092
817-329-0988
tts.mcc@ix.netcom.com

A25

An Uncommon Vision
1425 Greywall Ln.
Wynnewood, PA 19096-3811
610-658-0953 or fax 610-658-0961
Uncommvisn@aol.com

A26

David Armstrong, Bookseller
Box 551
Lethbridge, Alberta
Canada T1J 3Z4
403-381-3270
dabooks@telusplanet.net
www.telusplanet.net/public/dabooks

A27

Aslan Books
191 Dogwood Dr.
Dundee, OR 97115
503-538-8132
Lnash@georgefox.edu

A28

Ackley Books & Collectibles
Bryant & Suzanne Pitner
912 Hidden Cove Way
Suisun City, CA 94585-3511
707-421-9032 or fax 978-285-6554
www.ackleybooks.com
(mail order only)

B1

Thomas C. Bayer
85 Reading Ave.
Hillsdale, MI 49242-1941
517-439-4134 or fax 517-439-5661
bayerbooks@dmci.net

B2

Beasley Books
Paul & Beth Garon
1533 W Oakdale, 2nd Floor
Chicago, IL 60657
773-472-4528 or fax 773-472-7857
beasley@mcs.com

B3

Bella Luna Books
4697 Stone Canyon Ranch Rd
Castle Rock, CO 80104
800-497-4717 or fax 303-663-2113
Bellalun@aol.com

B4

Between the Covers
35 W Maple Ave.
Merchantville, NJ 08109
609-665-2284 or fax 609-665-3639
mail@betweenthecovers.com

B5

Bicentennial Book Shop
820 S Westnedge Ave.
Kalamazoo, MI 49008
616-345-5987

B6

Bibliography of the Dog
The New House
216 Covey Hill Rd.
Havelock, Quebec
Canada J0S 2C0
514-827-2717 or fax 514-827-2091

B7

Best-Read Books
122 State St.
Sedro-Woolley, WA 98284
206-855-2179

B9

The Book Baron
1236 S Magnolia Ave.
Anaheim, CA 92804
714-527-7022 or fax 714-527-5634
bkbaron1@pacbell.net or
bkbaron3@qte.net

B10

Book Broker
114 Bollingwood Rd.
Charlottesville, VA 22902
804-296-2194 or fax 804-296-1566
bookbrk@cfw.com
mail order or appointment only

B11

The Book Corner
Michael Tennaro
728 W Lumsden Rd.
Brandon, FL 33511
813-684-1133
bookcrnr@worldnet.att.net
www.abebooks.com/home/bookcrnr

B14

Book & Tackle Shop
Bernard L. Gordon
29 Old Colony Rd.
P.O. Box 114
Chestnut Hill, MA 02467
phone/fax 617-965-0459 (winter)
bktack@ibm.net

B15

Book Treasures
P.O. Box 121
E Norwich, NY 11732

B16

The Book Den South
Nancy Costello
2249 First St.
Ft. Myers, FL 33901
813-332-2333

B17

Books of the Ages
Gary J. Overmann
Maple Ridge Manor
4764 Silverwood Dr.
Batavia, OH 45103-9740
phone/fax 513-732-3456

B18

The Bookseller, Inc.
174 W Exchange St.
Akron, OH 44302
330-762-3101 or fax 330-762-4413
booklein@apk.net

B19

Books West Southwest
W. David Laird
Box 6149, University Station
Irvine, CA 92616-6149
714-509-7670 or fax 714-854-5102
bkswest@ix.netcom.com

B22

Bridgman Books
906 Roosevelt Ave.
Rome, NY 13440
315-337-7252

B23

British Stamp Exchange
12 Fairlawn Ave.
N Weymouth, MA 02191
871-335-3075

B24

Bromer Booksellers
607 Boylston St.
Boston, MA 02116
617-247-2818 or fax 617-247-2975
books@bromer.com
www.bromer.com

B25

Mike Brooks
7335 Skyline
Oakland, CA 94611

B26

Brooks Books
Phil & Marty Nesty
1343 New Hampshire Dr.
P.O. Box 91
Clayton, CA 94517
925-672-4566 or fax 925-672-3338
brooksbk@netvista.com

B27

The Bookstall
570 Sutter St.
San Francisco, CA 94102
fax 415-362-1503
bstallsf@best.com

B29
Books Now & Then
Dennis & Jan Patrick
P.O. Box 337
Stanley, ND 58784
phone/fax 701-628-2084
bnt@stanley.ndak.net
www.ourchurch.com/member/b/boo
ks-now-then

B30
Burke's Bookstore
1719 Poplar Ave.
Memphis, TN 38104-6447
901-278-7484 or fax 901-272-2340
burkes@netten.net

B35
Brillance Books
Morton Brillant, Bookseller
313 Meeting St. #21
Charleston, SC 29401
803-722-6643
brillbooks@aol.com

B36
Bookcase Books
P. Gayle Hendrington
R.R. 1 Box 242
Newport, NH 03773
603-863-9517
books@bookcasebooks.com

C1
Camelot Books
Charles E. Wyatt
P.O. Box 2883
Vista, CA 92083
619-940-9472

C2
The Captain's Bookshelf, Inc.
Chandler W. Gordon
31 Page Ave.
Asheville, NC 22801
828-253-6631 or fax 828-253-4917
captsbooks@aol.com

C3
Cattermole
20th-C Children's Books
9880 Fairmount Rd.
Newbury, OH 44065
440-338-3253 or fax 440-338-1675
books@cattermole.com

C4
Bev Chaney, Jr. Books
73 Croton Ave.
Ossining, NY 10562
914-941-1002

C5
Chimney Sweep Books
Lillian Smith Kaiser
419 Cedar St.
Santa Cruz, CA 95060-4304
phone/fax 408-458-1044
chimney@cruzio.com

C6
Chapel Hill Rare Books
Douglas & Maureen O'Dell
P.O. Box 456
Carrboro, NC 27510
919-929-8351
rarebooks@mindspring.com

C7
Chartwell Booksellers
55 E 52nd St.
New York, NY 10055
212-308-0643

C8
Children's Book Adoption Agency
P.O. Box 643
Kensington, MD 20895-0643
301-565-2834 or fax 301-585-3091
KIDS_BKS@interloc.com

C9
Cinemage Books
105 W 27th St.
New York, NY 10001
212-243-4919
irajoel@aol.com

C10
Cohen Books & Collectibles
Joel J. Cohen
P.O. Box 810310
Boca Raton, FL 33481-0310
561-487-7888

C11
Cover to Cover
Mark Shuman
P.O. Box 687
Chapel Hill, NC 27514
919-967-1032

C12
Noriko I. Ciochon
Natural History Books
1025 Keokut St.
Iowa City, IA 52240-3303
319-354-9088 or fax 319-354-0844
nathist@avalon.net
www.avalon.net/~nathist

C14
Steven Cieluch
15 Walbridge St. Ste. #10
Allston, MA 02134-3808
617-734-7778
scieluch@channel1.com

C15
Thomas L. Coffman
TLC Books
9 N College Ave.
Salem, VA 24153
540-389-3555

C16
Cover to Cover
Meta Fouts
5499 Belfast Rd.
Batavia, OH 45103
513-625-2628 or fax 513-625-2683
METAFOUTS@aol.com

D1
Ursula Davidson
Children's & Illustrated Books
134 Linden Ln.
San Rafael, CA 94901
415-454-3939 or fax 415-454-1087
davidson_u@compuserve.com
www.abebooks.com/home/uschi

D2
L. Clarice Davis
Fine & Applied Art Books
P.O. Box 56054
Sherman Oaks, CA 91413-1054
818-787-1322 or fax 818-780-3281
davislc@earthlink.net

D4
Carol Docheff, Bookseller
1390 Reliez Valley Rd.
Lafayette, CA 94549
925-935-9595 or fax 925-256-8569
docheffc@inreach.com
www.abebooks.com/home/docheff

D5
Dover Publications
Dept. A 214
E Second St.
Mineola, NY 11501

D6
Drusilla's Books
817 N Howard St.
Baltimore, MD 21201-4696
410-225-0277 or fax 410-321-4955
Tues-Sat: 12 to 5; or by appointment
drusilla@mindspring.com

D7
Duck Creek Books
Jim & Shirley Richards
P.O. Box 203
Caldwell, OH 43724
614-732-4856

D8
Patricia L. Daniel, Bookseller
13 English Ave.
Wichita, KS 62707-1005
316-683-2079 or fax 316-683-5448

D9
Dad's Old Bookstore
Green Hills Ct.
4004 Hillsboro Rd.
Nashville, TN 37215
615-298-5880

D10
Tom Davidson, Bookseller
3703 Ave. L
Brooklyn, NY 11210
718-338-8428 or fax 718-338-8430
tdbooks@att.net

D11
Dawson's Book Shop
535 N Larchmont Blvd.
Los Angeles, CA 90004
323-469-2186 or fax 323-469-9553
dawsonbk@ix.netcom.com
www.dawsonbooks.com

E1
The Early West/Whodunit Books
P.O. Box 9292
College Sta., TX 77842
409-775-6047 or fax 409-764-7758
EarlyWest@aol.com

E2
Edison Hall Books
5 Ventnor Dr.
Edison, NJ 08820
908-548-4455

E4
Elder's Book Store
2115 Elliston Pl.
Nashville, TN 37203
615-327-1867

E5
Elegant Book & Map Company
815 Harrison Ave.
P.O. Box 1302
Cambridge, OH 43725
614-432-4068

E6
Eastside Books & Paper
P.O. Box 1581, Gracie Station
New York, NY 10028-0013
212-759-6299

F1
First Folio
Dennis R. Melhouse
1206 Brentwood
Paris, TN 38242-3804
phone/fax 910-944-9940
firstfol@aeneas.net

F2
Fisher Books & Antiques
345 Pine St.
Williamsport, PA 17701

F3
Flo Silver Books
8442 Oakwood Ct. N
Indianapolis, IN 46260
phone/fax 317-255-5118
Flosilver@aolcom

F5
Fran's Bookhouse
6601 Greene St.
Phil., PA 19119
215-438-2729 or fax 215-438-8997

F6
Fostoria Trading Post
B.L.Foley III
P.O. Box 142
Fostoria, IA 51340
712-262-5936
books@ncn.net
www.ncn.net/~books

F7
Five Quail Books — West
P.O. Box 9870
Phoenix, AZ 85068-9870
602-861-0548 or fax 602-861-1113
5quail@grandcanyonbooks.com
www.grandcanyonbooks.com

G1
John Gach Fine & Rare Books
10514 Marriottsville Rd.
Randallstown, MD 21133
410-465-9023 or fax 410-465-0649
inquiry@gach.com

G2
Galerie De Boicourt
Eva M. Boicourt
251 E Merrill St.
Birmingham, MI 48009
248-723-5680

G3
Gambler's Book Shop
630 S Eleventh St.
Las Vegas, NV 89101
800-634-6243

G4
David & Nancy Garcelon
10 Hastings Ave.
Millbury, MA 01527-4314

G5
Michael Gerlicher
1375 Rest Point Rd.
Orono, MN 55364

G6
Glo's Children's Series Books
Gloria Stobbes
906 Shadywood
Southlake, TX 76092
817-481-1438

G7
James Tait Goodrich
Antiquarian Books & Manuscripts
135 Tweed Blvd.
Grandview-on-Hudson, NY 10960-4913
914-359-0242 or fax 914-359-0142

G8
Grave Matters
P.O. Box 32192
Cincinnati, OH 45232-0192
513-242-7527 or fax 513-242-5115
books@gravematters.com
www.gravematters.com

G10
Bernard E. Goodman, Bookseller
7421 SW 147 Ct.
Miami, FL 33193
305-385-8526

G11
Ron Gibson, The Bookshop
110 Windsor Cir.
Burlington, IA 52601-1477
319-752-4588

H1
Henry F. Hain III
Antiques, Collectibles & Books
2623 N Second St.
Harrisburg, PA 17110-1109
717-238-0534
antcolbks@ezonline.com

H2
Rick Harmon
Military Books & Relics
910 Sullivan Dr.
Belvidere, IL 61008
815-547-7580

H3
Terry Harper, Bookseller
P.O. Box 312
Vergennes, VT 05491-0312
802-877-9262
bookvend@together.net

H4
Susan Heller, Pages for Sages
22611 Halburton Rd.
Beachwood, OH 44122-3939
216-283-2665
hellersu@cyberdrive.net

H5
Heritage Book Shop, Inc.
8540 Melrose Ave.
Los Angeles, CA 90069
310-659-3674 or fax 310-659-4872
HBSINCLA@aol.com

H6
Hillcrest Books
961 Deep Draw Rd.
Crossville, TN 38555-9547
phone/fax 931-484-7680
hillcrst@usit.net
www.oldcatalogues.com

H7
Jim Hodgson Books
908 S Manlius St.
Fayetteville, NY 13066
315-637-6264
jimhbooks@aol.com

H9
Murray Hudson
Antiquarian Books & Maps
109 S Church St.
P.O. Box 163
Halls, TN 38040
901-836-9057 or 800-748-9946
fax 901-836-9017
mapman@usit.net

H10
Hurley Books/Celtic Cross Books
1753 Rt. 12
Westmoreland, NH 03467-4742
603-399-4342 or fax 603-399-8326
hurleybook@adam.cheshire.net

H11
Ken Hebenstreit, Bookseller
813 N Washington Ave.
Royal Oak, MI 48067
phone/fax 248-548-5460
kenhebrenstreit@home.com
www.abebooks.com/home/kenhbooks

H13
Hartfield Rare Books
Ruth Inglehart
117 Dixboro Rd.
Ann Arbor, MI 48105
phone/fax 313-662-6035

H14
Ruth Heindel Associates
First Editions, Rare & Used Books
660 Boas St., Ste. 1618
Harrisburg, PA 17110
717-213-9010

I1
Island Books
P.O. Box 19
Old Westbury, NY 11586
516-759-0233

J1
Jay's House of Collectibles
75 Pky. Dr.
Syosset, NY 11791

J2
Jordan Book Gallery
1349 Sheridan Ave.
Cody, WY 82414
307-587-6689 or fax 307-527-4944
jjordan@trib.com

J3
Pricilla Juvelis, Inc.
1166 Massachusetts Ave.
Cambridge, MA 02138
617-497-7570 or fax 617-497-9343
pjbooks@tiac.com

K1
Kenneth Karmiole, Bookseller, Inc.
509 Wilshire Blvd.
Santa Monica, CA 90401
310-451-4342 or fax 310-458-5930
karmbooks@aol.com

K2
Ilene Kayne
1308 S Charles St.
Baltimore, MD 21230-4219
410-347-7570
kayne@clark.net

K3
Key Books
P.O. Box 58097
St. Petersburg, FL 33715-8097
813-867-2931

K4
The King's Market Bookshop
P.O. Box 709
Boulder, CO 80306-0709
303-232-3321

K5
Knollwood Books
Lee & Peggy Price
P.O. Box 197
Oregon, WI 53575-0197
608-835-8861 or fax 608-835-8421
books@tdsnet.com

K6
Kendra Krienke
230 Central Park West
New York, NY 10024
201-930-9709 or 201-930-9765

K7
George Robert Kane Fine Books
252 Third Ave.
Santa Cruz, CA 95062
phone/fax 408-426-4133

L1
Bob Lakin Books
P.O. Box 186
Chatfield, TX 75105
972-247-3291

L2
Henry Lindeman
4769 Bavarian Dr.
Jackson, MI 49201
517-764-5728

L3
Ken Lopez, Bookseller
51 Huntington Rd.
Hadley, MA 01035
413-584-4827 or fax 413-584-2045
mail@lopezbooks.com

L4
W.J. Leveridge
W & L Trading Company
2301 Carova Rd.
Carova Beach, Corolla, NC 27927
252-453-3408

L5
Robert F. Lucas Antiquarian Books
P.O. Box 63
Blandford, MA 01008
413-848-2061
books@lucasbooks.com
www.lucasbooks.com

M1
M & S Rare Books, Inc.
P.O. Box 2594, E Side Station
Providence, RI 02906
401-421-1050
fax 401-272-0831 (attention M & S)
dsiegel@msrarebooks.com

M2
Robert A. Madle
4406 Bestor Dr.
Rockville, MD 20853
301-460-4712

M4
Melvin Marcher, Bookseller
6204 N Vermont
Oklahoma City, OK 73112
405-946-6270
(12 pm to 7 pm **only**)

M5
Marvelous Books
Dorothy (Dede) Kern
P.O. Box 1510
Ballwin, MO 63022
314-458-3301 or fax 314-273-5452
marvbooks@aol.com

M6
Mason's Bookstore, Rare Books
    & Record Albums East
115 S Main St.
Chambersburg, PA 17201
717-261-0541

M7
Denis McDonnell, Bookseller
653 Park St.
Honesdale, PA 18431-1445
570-253-6706 or fax 570-253-6786
dmd@ptd.net
www.denismcd.com

M8
McGowan Book Co.
P.O. Box 4226
Chapel Hill, NC 27515-4226
919-968-1121 or fax 919-968-1644
800-449-8406
mcgowanbooks@mindspring.com
www.mcgowanbooks.com

M9
Paul Melzer Fine & Rare Books
12 E Vine St.
P.O. Box 1143
Redlands, CA 92373
909-792-7299 or fax 909-792-7218
pmbooks@eee.org

M10
Robert L. Merriam
Rare, Used & Old Books
39 Newhall Rd.
Conway, MA 01341-9709
413-369-4052
rmerriam@valinet.com

M11
Meyer Boswell Books, Inc.
2141 Mission St.
San Francisco, CA 94110
415-255-6400 or fax 415-255-6499
rarelaw@meyerbos.com
www.meyerbos.com

M12
Frank Mikesh
1356 Walden Rd.
Walnut Creek, CA 94596
925-934-9243 or fax 925-947-6113

M13
Ken Mitchell
710 Conacher Dr.
Willowdale, Ontario
Canada M2M 3N6
416-222-5808

M14
Modern Age Books
Jeff Canja
P.O. Box 325
E Lansing, MI 48826
517-487-9313

M15
Mordida Books
P.O. Box 79322
Houston, TX 77279
713-467-4280 or fax 713-467-4182
mordida@swbell.net
www.mordida.com

M16
The Mulberry Cat
Yvonne Davis
Jan Davis Martel
P.O. Box 3573
Boone, NC 28607
704-963-7693

M17
Much Ado
Seven Pleasant St.
Marblehead, MA 01945
781-639-0400 or fax 781-639-0840
muchado@shore.net

M19
My Book Heaven
2212 Broadway
Oakland, CA 94612
510-893-7273 or 510-521-1683
MBHR@ix.netcom.com

M20
My Bookhouse
27 S Sandusky St.
Tiffin, OH 44883
419-447-9842
mybooks@bright.net

M21
Brian McMillan, Books
1429 L Ave.
Traer, IA 50675
319-478-2360
(Mon – Sat: 9 am to 9pm)
Brianbks@netins.net

M22
M/S Books
53 Curtiss Rd.
New Preston, CT 06777
860-868-0627 or fax 860-868-0504

M23
McGee's First Varieties
330 Franklin Rd., Ste. 135A
Brentwood, TN 37027
615-373-5318
TMcGee@BellSouth.net
www.mcgees1st.com

M25
Monroe Stahr Books
4420 Ventura Canyon, #2
Sherman Oaks, CA 91423
818-501-3419 or fax 818-995-0966
MStahrBks@aol.com

N1
Nerman's Books
Gary Nerman
410-63 Albert St.
Winnipeg, Manitoba
Canada R3B 1G4
204-956-1214 or 204-475-1050
fax 204-947-0753
nerman@escape.ca

N2
Nutmeg Books
354 New Litchfield St. (Rte. 202)
Torrington, CT 06790
203-482-9696
nutmeg@compsol.net

N3
Kai Nygaard
19421 Eighth Pl.
Escondido, CA 92029
619-749-9039

N4
Norris Books
Charles Chavdarian, Owner
2491 San Ramon Vly. Blvd.
Suite 1, PMB 201
San Ramon, CA 94583
online at abebooks and bibliofind
phone/fax 925-867-1218
norrisbooks@slip.net

O1
David L. O'Neal, Antiquarian
    Bookseller
234 Clarendon St.
Boston, MA 02116
617-266-5790 or fax 617-266-1089
staff@onealbooks.com

O2
W.B. O'Neill
Old & Rare Books
11609 Hunters Green Ct.
Reston, VA 20191
703-860-0782 or fax 703-620-0153
nyc1918@aol.com

O3
October Farm
2609 Branch Rd.
Raleigh, NC 27610
919-772-0482 or fax 919-779-6265
octoberfarm@bellsouth.net
www.octoberfarm.com

O4
The Old London Bookshop
Michael & Marlys Schon
P.O. Box 922
Bellingham, WA 98227-0922
360-733-7273 or fax 360-647-8946
OldLondon@aol.com

O5
The Old Map Gallery
Paul F. Mahoney
1746 Blake St.
Denver, CO 80202
303-296-7725 or fax 303-296-7936
oldmapgallery@denver.net

O6
Old Paint Lick School Antique Mall
Raymond P. Mixon
11000 Hwy. 52 West
Paint Lick, KY 40461
606-925-3000 or 606-792-3000

O7
Overlee Farm Books
P.O. Box 1155
Stockbridge, MA 01262
413-637-2277

O8
K.C. & Jean C. Owings
Box 389
Whitman, MA 02382
781-447-7850 or fax 781-447-3435

O9

Olde Current Books
Daniel P. Shay
356 Putnam Ave.
Ormond Beach, FL 32174
904-672-8998
peakmyster@aol.com

O10

Oak Knoll Books
310 Delaware St.
New Castle, DE 19720
800-996-2556 or 302-328-7232
fax 302-328-7274
oakknoll@oakknoll.com
www.oakknoll.com

O11

Orpheus Books
Don Stutheit/Barbara Wight
11522 NE 20th St.
Bellevue, WA 98004-3005
425-451-8343
orpheusbooks@earthlink.net

P1

Pacific Rim Books
Michael Onorato
P.O. Box 30575
Bellingham, WA 98228
360-676-0256
pacrimbks@aol.com

P2

Margaret E. Page
Page Books
HCR 65, Box 233
Kingston, AR 72742
870-861-5831

P3

Pandora's Books Ltd.
P.O. Box 54
Neche, ND 58265
204-324-8548 or fax 204-324-1628
jgthiess@MTS.Net

P4

Parmer Books
7644 Forrestal Rd.
San Diego, CA 92120-2203
619-287-0693 or fax 619-287-6135
ParmerBook@aol.com

P5

Parnassus Books
218 N 9th St.
Boise, ID 83702

P6

Passaic Book Center
594 Main Ave.
Passaic, NJ 07055
201-778-6646 or fax 201-778-6738

P7

Pauper's Books
206 N Main St.
Bowling Green, OH 43402-2420
419-352-2163

P8

R. Plapinger, Baseball Books
P.O. Box 1062
Ashland, OR 97520
541-488-1220

P9

Prometheus Books
59 John Glenn Dr.
Buffalo, NY 14228-2197
716-691-0133 or fax 716-691-0137

P11

Pelanor Books
7 Gaskill Ave.
Albany, NY 12203

P12

Popek's Pages Past
Pete & Connie Popek
3870 S Hwy 23
Oneonta, NY 13820
607-432-0836
popeks@magnum.wpe.com

P13

Periodyssey
151 Crescent St.
Northampton, MA 01060
413-527-1900 or fax 413-527-1930

Q1

Quill & Brush
Patricia & Allen Ahearn
1137 Sugarloaf Mtn. Rd.
Dickerson, MD 20842
301-874-3200 or fax 301-874-0824
Firsts@qb.com

Q2

Quest Books
Peter & Veronica Burridge
Harmer Hill
Millington
York YO42 1TX UK
Quesbks@aol.com

R1

Raintree Books
432 N Eustis St.
Eustis, FL 32726
904-357-7145

R2

Kathleen Rais & Co.
Rais Place Cottage
211 Carolina Ave.
Phoenixville, PA 19460
610-933-1388

R3

Randall House
Pia Oliver
835 Laguna St.
Santa Barbara, CA 93101
805-963-1909 or fax 805-963-1650
pia@piasworld.com
www.piasworld.com/randall

R5

Jo Ann Reisler, Ltd.
360 Glyndon St., NE
Vienna, VA 22180
703-938-2967 or fax 703-938-9057
reisler@clark.net
www.clark.net/pub/reisler

R6

Wallace Robinson Books
RD #6, Box 574
Meadville, PA 16335
800-653-3280 or 813-823-3280
814-724-7670 or 814-333-9652

R7

Tom Rolls
230 S Oakland Ave.
Indianapolis, IN 46201

R8

RAC Books
P.O. Box 296 RD 2
Seven Valleys, PA 17360
717-428-3776
racbooks@cyberia.com

R9

Realm of Colorado
P.O. Box 24
Parker, CO 80134

R10

Roger Reus
9412 Huron Ave.
Richmond, VA 23294
(mail order only)

R11

Recollection Books
4519 University Way NE
Seattle, WA 98105
206-548-1346

R12

Leona Rostenberg
    & Madeleine Stern
Rare Books
40 East 88th St.
New York, NY 10128-1176
212-831-6628 or fax 212-831-1961

R13

Alice Robbins, Bookseller
3002 Round Hill Rd.
Greensboro, NC 27408
910-282-1964

R14
Revere Books
P.O. Box 420
Revere, PA 18953-0420
610-847-2709 or fax 610-847-1910

R15
Richard C. Ramer
Old & Rare Books
225 E 70th St.
New York, NY 10021
212-737-0222 or 212-737-0223
fax 212-288-4169
5222386@mcimail.com

R16
Rising Stars
Don Carnahan
P.O. Box 2991
Yuma, AZ 85366
Phone/Fax 520-329-6054

S1
Bill & Mimi Sachen
927 Grand Ave.
Waukegan, IL 60085-3709
847-662-7204
FutileWill@aol.com

S2
J. Sampson Antiques & Books
107 S Main
Harrodsburg, KY 40330
606-734-7829

S3
Stanley Schwartz
1934 Pentuckett Ave.
San Diego, CA 92104-5732
619-232-5888 or fax 619-233-5833
Schwartz@cts.com

S4
Scribe Company
Attn: Bonnie Smith
427 Hidden Forest S
Longview, TX 75605
903-663-6873

S5
Significant Books
3053 Madison Rd.
P.O. Box 9248
Cincinnati, OH 45209
800-750-1153 or 513-321-7567
signbook@iac.net

S6
The Silver Door
P.O. Box 3208
Redondo Beach, CA 90277
310-379-6005

S7
K.B. Slocum Books
P.O. Box 10998 #620
Austin, TX 78766
800-521-4451 or fax 512-258-8041

S8
Barbara Smith Books
P.O. Box 1185
Northampton, MA 01061
413-586-1453

S9
Ed Smith Books
20 Paget Rd.
Madision, WI 53704-5929
608-241-3707 or fax 608-241-3459
ed@edsbooks.com

S12
Sweet Memories
Sharyn Laymon
400 Mulberry St.
Loudon, TN 37774
615-458-5044

S13
Eileen Serxner
Box 2544
Bala Cynwyd, PA 19004
610-664-7960 or fax 610-664-1940
serxner@erols.com
www.abebooks.com/home/serxner-
books/

S14
Second Harvest Books
Warren R. Johnson
P.O. Box 3306
Florence, OR 97439-3306
phone/fax 541-902-0215
2harvest@presys.com

S15
Snowy Egret Books
1237 Carroll Ave.
St. Paul, MN 55104
612-641-0917
snowy@mr.net

S16
Stan Clark Military Books
915 Fairview Ave.
Gettysburg, PA 17325
717-337-0581

S17
David R. Smith
30 Nelson Circle
Jaffrey, NH 03452
603-532-8666
Bookinc@Cheshire.net

S18
Spellbound Books
M. Tyree
3818 Vickie Ct. #B
Prescott Valley, AZ 86314
520-759-2625

S19
Vera L. Scheer
408 S. Main St.
Salem, IA 52649
319-258-7641
beeba@lisco.com

T1
Lee Barnett Temares
50 Heights Rd.
Plandome, NY 11030
516-627-8688 or fax 516-627-7822
tembooks@aol.com

T2
Thomas Books
P.O. Box 14036
Phoenix, AZ 85063
623-247-9289 or fax 480-945-1023
sales@thomasbooks.com
www.thomasbooks.com

T4
Trackside Books
8819 Mobud Dr.
Houston, TX 77036
713-772-8107

T5
Treasures From the Castle
Connie Castle
1277 Candlestick Lane
Rochester, MI 48306
248-651-7317
treasure23@juno.com
www.abebooks.com/home/treasure

T6
H.E. Turlington Books
P.O. Box 190
Carrboro, NC 27510

T7
J. Tuttle Maritime Books
1806 Laurel Crest
Madison, WI 53705
608-238-SAIL (7245)
fax 608-238-7249

T8
George H. Tweney
16660 Marine View Dr. SW
Seattle, WA 98166
206-243-8243

T9
Typographeum Bookshop
246 Bennington Rd.
Francestown, NH 03043
603-547-2425

T10
Thorn Books
P.O. Box 1244
Moorpark, CA 93020
805-529-36647 or fax 805-529-0022
thornbooks@earthlink.net

T11
Town's End Books
John D. & Judy A. Townsend
132 Hemlock Dr.
Deep River, CT 06417
860-526-3896
888-732-2668
john@townsendbooks.com
www.townsendbooks.com

T12
Third Time Around Books
Norman Todd
R.R. #1
Mar., Ontario
Canada N0H 1XO
519-534-1382

T13
Twice Read Books & Comics
42 S Main St.
Chambersburg, PA 17201
717-261-8449

T14
Trade Winds
John Singer
201 W 17th St.
Cheyenne, WY 82001
307-638-3400 or fax 307-638-3400

V1
VERSEtility Books
P.O. Box 1133
Farmington, CT 06034-1133
860-677-0606
versebks@tiac.net

V2
A.A. Vespa
P.O. Box 637
Park Ridge, IL 60068
708-692-4210

V3
Vintage Books
Nancy & David Haines
181 Hayden Rowe St.
Hopkinton, MA 01748
508-435-3499
vintage@gis.net

V4
Volume I Books
One Union St.
Hillsdale, MI 49242
517-437-2228 or fax 517-437-7923
volume1book@dmci.net

W1
Worldwide Antiquarian
P.O. Box 410391
Cambridge, MA 02141-0004
617-876-6220 or fax 617-876-0839
mbalwan@aol.com

W2
Warren's Collector Books
For Sale Now
Warren Gillespie, Jr.
112 Royal Ct.
Friendswood, TX 77546
281-482-7947

W3
Ruth Woods Oriental Books & Art
266 Arch Rd.
Englewood, NJ 07631
201-567-0149 or fax 201-567-1419

W4
Glenn Wiese
5078 Lynwood Ave.
Blasdell, NY 14219
716-821-0972

Y1
Yesterday's Books
229 Riverview Dr.
Parchment, MI 49004
616-345-1011
yesbooks@aol.com

X1
Xanadu Records, Ltd.
3242 Irwin Ave.
Kingsbridge, NY 10463
718-549-3655

Reach **Thousands** with Your
Free Listing in Our Next Edition!

 **Booksellers!** If you publish lists or catalogs of books for sale, take advantage of this free offer. Put us on your mailing list right away so that we can include you in our next edition. We'll not only list you in our Bookbuyers directory under the genre that best represents your special interests (please specify these when you contact us), but each book description we choose to include from your catalog will contain a special dealer code that will identify you as the book dealer to contact in order to buy that book. Please send your information and catalogs or lists right away, since we're working on a first-come, first-served basis. Be sure to include your current address, just as you'd like it to be published. You may also include a fax number or an e-mail address. Our dealers tell us that this service has been very successful for them, both in buying and selling.

Send your listings to:

First Class

Lisa C. Stroup
Huxford's Old Book Value Guide
P.O. Box 9471
Paducah, KY 42002-9471

COLLECTOR BOOKS

I n f o r m i n g   T o d a y ' s   C o l l e c t o r

For over two decades we have been keeping collectors informed on trends and values in all fields of antiques and collectibles.

DOLLS, FIGURES & TEDDY BEARS

4707	A Decade of **Barbie Dolls** & Collectibles, 1981–1991, Summers	$19.95
4631	**Barbie Doll** Boom, 1986–1995, Augustyniak	$18.95
2079	**Barbie Doll** Fashion, Volume I, Eames	$24.95
4846	**Barbie Doll** Fashion, Volume II, Eames	$24.95
3957	**Barbie** Exclusives, Rana	$18.95
4632	**Barbie** Exclusives, Book II, Rana	$18.95
4557	**Barbie**, The First 30 Years, Deutsch	$24.95
5672	The **Barbie Doll** Years, 4th Ed., Olds	$19.95
3810	**Chatty Cathy** Dolls, Lewis	$15.95
5352	Collector's Ency. of **Barbie** Doll Exclusives & More, 2nd Ed.,Augustyniak	$24.95
2211	Collector's Encyclopedia of **Madame Alexander** Dolls, Smith	$24.95
4863	Collector's Encyclopedia of **Vogue Dolls**, Izen/Stover	$29.95
5598	**Doll Values**, Antique to Modern, 4th Ed., Moyer	$12.95
56101	**Madame Alexander** Collector's Dolls Price Guide #25, Crowsey	$9.95
5612	**Modern Collectible Dolls**, Volume IV, Moyer	$24.95
5365	**Peanuts Collectibles**, Podley/Bang	$24.95
5253	Story of **Barbie**, 2nd Ed., Westenhouser	$24.95
5277	**Talking Toys** of the 20th Century, Lewis	$15.95
1513	**Teddy Bears & Steiff** Animals, Mandel	$9.95
1817	**Teddy Bears & Steiff** Animals, 2nd Series, Mandel	$19.95
2084	**Teddy Bears, Annalee's & Steiff** Animals, 3rd Series, Mandel	$19.95
5371	**Teddy Bear** Treasury, Yenke	$19.95
1808	Wonder of **Barbie**, Manos	$9.95
1430	World of **Barbie** Dolls, Manos	$9.95
4880	World of **Raggedy Ann** Collectibles, Avery	$24.95

TOYS, MARBLES & CHRISTMAS COLLECTIBLES

2333	Antique & Collectible **Marbles**, 3rd Ed., Grist	$9.95
5353	**Breyer Animal** Collector's Guide, 2nd Ed., Browell	$19.95
4976	**Christmas Ornaments**, Lights & Decorations, Johnson	$24.95
4737	**Christmas Ornaments**, Lights & Decorations, Vol. II, Johnson	$24.95
4739	**Christmas Ornaments**, Lights & Decorations, Vol. III, Johnson	$24.95
4649	Classic Plastic **Model Kits**, Polizzi	$24.95
4559	Collectible **Action Figures**, 2nd Ed., Manos	$17.95
3874	Collectible **Coca-Cola Toy Trucks**, deCourtivron	$24.95
2338	Collector's Encyclopedia of **Disneyana**, Longest, Stern	$24.95
4958	Collector's Guide to **Battery Toys**, Hultzman	$19.95
5038	Collector's Guide to **Diecast Toys** & Scale Models, 2nd Ed., Johnson	$19.95
4651	Collector's Guide to **Tinker Toys**, Strange	$18.95
4566	Collector's Guide to **Tootsietoys**, 2nd Ed., Richter	$19.95
5169	Collector's Guide to **TV Toys** & Memorabilia, 2nd Ed., Davis/Morgan	$24.95
5360	**Fisher-Price Toys**, Cassity	$19.95
4720	The Golden Age of **Automotive Toys**, 1925–1941, Hutchison/Johnson	$24.95
5593	Grist's Big Book of **Marbles**, 2nd Ed.	$24.95
3970	Grist's Machine-Made & Contemporary **Marbles**, 2nd Ed.	$9.95
5267	**Matchbox Toys**, 1947 to 1998, 3rd Ed., Johnson	$19.95
4871	**McDonald's** Collectibles, Henriques/DuVall	$19.95
1540	Modern **Toys** 1930–1980, Baker	$19.95
3888	**Motorcycle Toys**, Antique & Contemporary, Gentry/Downs	$18.95
5368	**Schroeder's Collectible Toys**, Antique to Modern Price Guide, 6th Ed.	$17.95
2028	**Toys**, Antique & Collectible, Longest	$14.95

FURNITURE

1457	American **Oak** Furniture, McNerney	$9.95
3716	American **Oak** Furniture, Book II, McNerney	$12.95
1118	Antique **Oak** Furniture, Hill	$7.95
2271	Collector's Encyclopedia of **American** Furniture, Vol. II, Swedberg	$24.95
3720	Collector's Encyclopedia of **American** Furniture, Vol. III, Swedberg	$24.95
5359	Early **American** Furniture, Obbard	$12.95
1755	Furniture of the **Depression Era**, Swedberg	$19.95
3906	**Heywood-Wakefield** Modern Furniture, Rouland	$18.95
1885	**Victorian** Furniture, Our American Heritage, McNerney	$9.95

3829	**Victorian** Furniture, Our American Heritage, Book II, McNerney	$9.95

JEWELRY, HATPINS, WATCHES & PURSES

1712	Antique & Collectible **Thimbles** & Accessories, Mathis	$19.95
1748	Antique **Purses**, Revised Second Ed., Holiner	$19.95
1278	Art Nouveau & Art Deco **Jewelry**, Baker	$9.95
4850	Collectible **Costume Jewelry**, Simonds	$24.95
3722	Collector's Ency. of **Compacts**, Carryalls & Face Powder Boxes, Mueller	$24.95
4940	**Costume Jewelry**, A Practical Handbook & Value Guide, Rezazadeh	$24.95
1716	Fifty Years of Collectible **Fashion Jewelry**, 1925–1975, Baker	$19.95
1424	**Hatpins** & Hatpin Holders, Baker	$9.95
1181	100 Years of Collectible **Jewelry**, 1850–1950, Baker	$9.95
4729	**Sewing Tools** & Trinkets, Thompson	$24.95
5620	Unsigned Beauties of **Costume Jewelry**, Brown	$24.95
4878	Vintage & Contemporary **Purse Accessories**, Gerson	$24.95
3830	Vintage **Vanity Bags** & Purses, Gerson	$24.95

INDIANS, GUNS, KNIVES, TOOLS, PRIMITIVES

1868	Antique **Tools**, Our American Heritage, McNerney	$9.95
5616	Big Book of **Pocket Knives**, Stewart	$19.95
4943	Field Guide to Flint **Arrowheads** & Knives of the North American Indian	$9.95
3885	**Indian Artifacts** of the Midwest, Book II, Hothem	$16.95
4870	**Indian Artifacts** of the Midwest, Book III, Hothem	$18.95
5685	**Indian Artifacts** of the Midwest, Book IV, Hothem	$19.95
5687	**Modern Guns**, Identification & Values, 13th Ed., Quertermous	$14.95
2164	**Primitives**, Our American Heritage, McNerney	$9.95
1759	**Primitives**, Our American Heritage, 2nd Series, McNerney	$14.95
4730	Standard **Knife** Collector's Guide, 3rd Ed., Ritchie & Stewart	$12.95

PAPER COLLECTIBLES & BOOKS

4633	**Big Little Books**, Jacobs	$18.95
4710	Collector's Guide to **Children's Books**, 1850 to 1950, Jones	$18.95
5596	Collector's Guide to **Children's Books**, 1950 to 1975, Jones	$19.95
1441	Collector's Guide to **Post Cards**, Wood	$9.95
2081	Guide to Collecting **Cookbooks**, Allen	$14.95
5613	Huxford's **Old Book** Value Guide, 12th Ed.	$19.95
2080	Price Guide to **Cookbooks** & Recipe Leaflets, Dickinson	$9.95
3973	**Sheet Music** Reference & Price Guide, 2nd Ed., Pafik & Guiheen	$19.95
4654	**Victorian Trade Cards**, Historical Reference & Value Guide, Cheadle	$19.95
4733	**Whitman Juvenile Books**, Brown	$17.95

Glassware

5602	Anchor Hocking's **Fire-King** & More, 2nd Ed.	$24.95
4561	Collectible **Drinking Glasses**, Chase & Kelly	$17.95
4642	Collectible **Glass Shoes**, Wheatley	$19.95
5357	Coll. **Glassware** from the 40s, 50s & 60s, 5th Ed., Florence	$19.95
1810	Collector's Encyclopedia of **American Art Glass**, Shuman	$29.95
5358	Collector's Encyclopedia of **Depression Glass**, 14th Ed., Florence	$19.95
1961	Collector's Encyclopedia of **Fry Glassware**, Fry Glass Society	$24.95
1664	Collector's Encyclopedia of **Heisey Glass**, 1925–1938, Bredehoft	$24.95
3905	Collector's Encyclopedia of **Milk Glass**, Newbound	$24.95
4936	Collector's Guide to **Candy Containers**, Dezso/Poirier	$19.95
4564	**Crackle Glass**, Weitman	$19.95
4941	**Crackle Glass**, Book II, Weitman	$19.95
4714	**Czechoslovakian Glass** and Collectibles, Book II, Barta/Rose	$16.95
5528	Early American **Pattern Glass**, Metz	$17.95
5682	**Elegant Glassware** of the Depression Era, 9th Ed., Florence	$19.95
5614	Field Guide to **Pattern Glass**, McCain	$17.95
3981	Evers' Standard **Cut Glass** Value Guide	$12.95
4659	**Fenton** Art Glass, 1907–1939, Whitmyer	$24.95
5615	Florence's **Glassware Pattern Identification** Guide, Vol. II	$19.95
3725	**Fostoria**, Pressed, Blown & Hand Molded Shapes, Kerr	$24.95
4719	**Fostoria**, Etched, Carved & Cut Designs, Vol. II, Kerr	$24.95

COLLECTOR BOOKS
Informing Today's Collector

383	**Fostoria Stemware**, The Crystal for America, Long/Seate	$24.95
261	**Fostoria Tableware**, 1924 – 1943, Long/Seate	$24.95
361	**Fostoria Tableware**, 1944 – 1986, Long/Seate	$24.95
604	**Fostoria**, Useful & Ornamental, Long/Seate	$29.95
644	**Imperial Carnival Glass**, Burns	$18.95
386	**Kitchen Glassware** of the Depression Years, 5th Ed., Florence	$19.95
600	Much More Early American **Pattern Glass**, Metz	$17.95
690	Pocket Guide to **Depression Glass**, 12th Ed., Florence	$9.95
594	Standard Encyclopedia of **Carnival Glass**, 7th Ed., Edwards/Carwile	$29.95
595	Standard **Carnival Glass** Price Guide, 12th Ed., Edwards/Carwile	$9.95
272	Standard Encyclopedia of **Opalescent Glass**, 3rd Ed., Edwards/Carwile	$24.95
617	Standard Encyclopedia of **Pressed Glass**, 2nd Ed., Edwards/Carwile	$29.95
731	**Stemware Identification**, Featuring Cordials with Values, Florence	$24.95
732	**Very Rare Glassware** of the Depression Years, 5th Series, Florence	$24.95
656	**Westmoreland Glass**, Wilson	$24.95

POTTERY

927	**ABC Plates & Mugs**, Lindsay	$24.95
929	**American Art Pottery**, Sigafoose	$24.95
630	**American Limoges**, Limoges	$24.95
312	**Blue & White Stoneware**, McNerney	$9.95
958	So. Potteries **Blue Ridge Dinnerware**, 3rd Ed., Newbound	$14.95
959	**Blue Willow**, 2nd Ed., Gaston	$14.95
851	Collectible **Cups & Saucers**, Harran	$18.95
373	Collector's Encyclopedia of **American Dinnerware**, Cunningham	$24.95
931	Collector's Encyclopedia of **Bauer Pottery**, Chipman	$24.95
932	Collector's Encyclopedia of **Blue Ridge Dinnerware**, Vol. II, Newbound	$24.95
658	Collector's Encyclopedia of **Brush-McCoy Pottery**, Huxford	$24.95
034	Collector's Encyclopedia of **California Pottery**, 2nd Ed., Chipman	$24.95
133	Collector's Encyclopedia of **Cookie Jars**, Roerig	$24.95
723	Collector's Encyclopedia of **Cookie Jars**, Book II, Roerig	$24.95
939	Collector's Encyclopedia of **Cookie Jars**, Book III, Roerig	$24.95
040	Collector's Encyclopedia of **Fiesta**, 8th Ed., Huxford	$19.95
718	Collector's Encyclopedia of **Figural Planters & Vases**, Newbound	$19.95
961	Collector's Encyclopedia of **Early Noritake**, Alden	$24.95
439	Collector's Encyclopedia of **Flow Blue China**, Gaston	$19.95
812	Collector's Encyclopedia of **Flow Blue China**, 2nd Ed., Gaston	$24.95
431	Collector's Encyclopedia of **Homer Laughlin China**, Jasper	$24.95
276	Collector's Encyclopedia of **Hull Pottery**, Roberts	$19.95
962	Collector's Encyclopedia of **Lefton China**, DeLozier	$19.95
855	Collector's Encyclopedia of **Lefton China**, Book II, DeLozier	$19.95
609	Collector's Encyclopedia of **Limoges Porcelain**, 3rd Ed., Gaston	$24.95
334	Collector's Encyclopedia of **Majolica Pottery**, Katz-Marks	$19.95
358	Collector's Encyclopedia of **McCoy Pottery**, Huxford	$19.95
337	Collector's Encyclopedia of **Nippon Porcelain**, Van Patten	$24.95
089	Collector's Ency. of **Nippon Porcelain**, 2nd Series, Van Patten	$24.95
665	Collector's Ency. of **Nippon Porcelain**, 3rd Series, Van Patten	$24.95
712	Collector's Ency. of **Nippon Porcelain**, 4th Series, Van Patten	$24.95
447	Collector's Encyclopedia of **Noritake**, Van Patten	$19.95
037	Collector's Encyclopedia of **Occupied Japan**, 1st Series, Florence	$14.95
038	Collector's Encyclopedia of **Occupied Japan**, 2nd Series, Florence	$14.95
035	Collector's Encyclopedia of **Occupied Japan**, 5th Series, Florence	$14.95
951	Collector's Encyclopedia of **Old Ivory China**, Hillman	$24.95
564	Collector's Encyclopedia of **Pickard China**, Reed	$29.95
877	Collector's Encyclopedia of **R.S. Prussia**, 4th Series, Gaston	$24.95
618	Collector's Encyclopedia of **Rosemeade Pottery**, Dommel	$24.95
034	Collector's Encyclopedia of **Roseville Pottery**, Huxford	$19.95
035	Collector's Encyclopedia of **Roseville Pottery**, 2nd Ed., Huxford	$19.95
856	Collector's Encyclopedia of **Russel Wright**, 2nd Ed., Kerr	$24.95
713	Collector's Encyclopedia of **Salt Glaze Stoneware**, Taylor/Lowrance	$24.95
314	Collector's Encyclopedia of **Van Briggle Art Pottery**, Sasicki	$24.95
563	Collector's Encyclopedia of **Wall Pockets**, Newbound	$19.95
111	Collector's Encyclopedia of **Weller Pottery**, Huxford	$29.95
876	Collector's Guide to **Lu-Ray Pastels**, Meehan	$18.95
814	Collector's Guide to **Made in Japan Ceramics**, White	$18.95

4646	Collector's Guide to **Made in Japan Ceramics**, Book II, White	$18.95
2339	Collector's Guide to **Shawnee Pottery**, Vanderbilt	$19.95
1425	**Cookie Jars**, Westfall	$9.95
3440	**Cookie Jars**, Book II, Westfall	$19.95
4924	Figural & Novelty **Salt & Pepper Shakers**, 2nd Series, Davern	$24.95
2379	Lehner's Ency. of **U.S. Marks** on Pottery, Porcelain & China	$24.95
4722	**McCoy Pottery**, Collector's Reference & Value Guide, Hanson/Nissen	$19.95
1670	**Red Wing Collectibles**, DePasquale	$9.95
1440	**Red Wing Stoneware**, DePasquale	$9.95
1632	**Salt & Pepper Shakers**, Guarnaccia	$9.95
5091	**Salt & Pepper Shakers** II, Guarnaccia	$18.95
2220	**Salt & Pepper Shakers** III, Guarnaccia	$14.95
3443	**Salt & Pepper Shakers** IV, Guarnaccia	$18.95
3738	**Shawnee Pottery**, Mangus	$24.95
4629	Turn of the Century **American Dinnerware**, 1880s–1920s, Jasper	$24.95
3327	**Watt Pottery** – Identification & Value Guide, Morris	$19.95

OTHER COLLECTIBLES

4704	Antique & Collectible **Buttons**, Wisniewski	$19.95
2269	Antique **Brass & Copper** Collectibles, Gaston	$16.95
1880	Antique **Iron**, McNerney	$9.95
3872	Antique **Tins**, Dodge	$24.95
4845	Antique **Typewriters & Office Collectibles**, Rehr	$19.95
5607	Antiquing and Collecting on the **Internet**, Parry	$12.95
1128	**Bottle** Pricing Guide, 3rd Ed., Cleveland	$7.95
4636	**Celluloid** Collectibles, Dunn	$14.95
3718	Collectible **Aluminum**, Grist	$16.95
4560	Collectible **Cats**, An Identification & Value Guide, Book II, Fyke	$19.95
4852	Collectible **Compact Disc** Price Guide 2, Cooper	$17.95
5666	Collector's Encyclopedia of **Granite Ware**, Book 2, Greguire	$29.95
4705	Collector's Guide to **Antique Radios**, 4th Ed., Bunis	$18.95
5608	Collector's Gde. to Buying, Selling, & Trading on the **Internet**, 2nd Ed., Hix	$12.95
3880	Collector's Guide to **Cigarette Lighters**, Flanagan	$17.95
4637	Collector's Guide to **Cigarette Lighters**, Book II, Flanagan	$17.95
4942	Collector's Guide to **Don Winton Designs**, Ellis	$19.95
3966	Collector's Guide to **Inkwells**, Identification & Values, Badders	$18.95
4947	Collector's Guide to **Inkwells**, Book II, Badders	$19.95
5621	Collector's Guide to **Online Auctions**, Hix	$12.95
4862	Collector's Guide to **Toasters** & Accessories, Greguire	$19.95
4652	Collector's Guide to **Transistor Radios**, 2nd Ed., Bunis	$16.95
4864	Collector's Guide to **Wallace Nutting Pictures**, Ivankovich	$18.95
1629	**Doorstops**, Identification & Values, Bertoia	$9.95
4717	Figural **Nodders**, Includes Bobbin' Heads and Swayers, Irtz	$19.95
5683	**Fishing Lure** Collectibles, 2nd Ed., Murphy/Edmisten	$29.95
5259	**Flea Market Trader**, 12th Ed., Huxford	$9.95
4945	**G-Men and FBI Toys** and Collectibles, Whitworth	$18.95
5605	**Garage Sale & Flea Market Annual**, 8th Ed.	$19.95
3819	**General Store** Collectibles, Wilson	$24.95
5159	Huxford's Collectible **Advertising**, 4th Ed.	$24.95
2216	**Kitchen Antiques**, 1790–1940, McNerney	$14.95
4950	The **Lone Ranger**, Collector's Reference & Value Guide, Felbinger	$18.95
2026	**Railroad** Collectibles, 4th Ed., Baker	$14.95
5619	**Roy Rogers and Dale Evans** Toys & Memorabilia, Coyle	$24.95
5367	**Schroeder's Antiques Price Guide**, 18th Ed., Huxford	$12.95
5007	**Silverplated Flatware**, Revised 4th Edition, Hagan	$18.95
1922	Standard **Old Bottle** Price Guide, Sellari	$14.95
5694	Summers' Guide to **Coca-Cola**, 3rd Ed.	$24.95
5356	Summers' Pocket Guide to **Coca-Cola**, 2nd Ed.	$9.95
3892	**Toy & Miniature Sewing Machines**, Thomas	$18.95
4876	**Toy & Miniature Sewing Machines**, Book II, Thomas	$24.95
5144	Value Guide to **Advertising Memorabilia**, 2nd Ed., Summers	$19.95
3977	Value Guide to **Gas Station Memorabilia**, Summers & Priddy	$24.95
4877	Vintage **Bar Ware**, Visakay	$24.95
4935	The W.F. Cody **Buffalo Bill** Collector's Guide with Values	$24.95
5281	**Wanted to Buy**, 7th Edition	$9.95

This is only a partial listing of the books on antiques that are available from Collector Books. All books are well illustrated and contain current values. Most of these books are available from your local bookseller, antique dealer, or public library. If you are unable to locate certain titles in your area, you may order by mail from COLLECTOR BOOKS, P.O. Box 3009, Paducah, KY 42002-3009. Customers with Visa, Discover or MasterCard may phone in orders from 7:00–5:00 CST, Monday–Friday, Toll Free 1-800-626-5420; www.collectorbooks.com. Add $3.00 for postage for the first book ordered and $0.40 for each additional book. Include item number, title, and price when ordering. Allow 14 to 21 days for delivery.